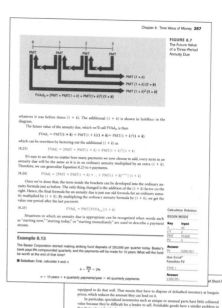

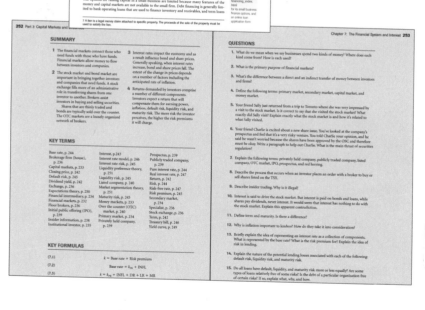

KEY FORMULAS

Key formulas appear in blue type and are numbered so they're easy to identify. A list of key formulas for easy reviewing is provided at the end of each chapter, and Appendix C (page 749) summarizes key formulas at a glance.

INSTRUCTIONS ON USING FINANCIAL CALCULATORS AND EXCEL® FUNCTION BOXES

Calculator manuals are hard to read and easy to forget so instructions on using financial calculators and Excel® function boxes are included where appropriate.

INTERNET NOTES AND PROBLEMS

Internet addresses and notes are included in the margin to direct students to websites that expand on the material being presented.

END-OF-CHAPTER MATERIALS THAT REINFORCE CONCEPTS

A chapter summary, key terms, formula summary, questions, and problems appear at the conclusion of each chapter to support the learning within it.

PRACTICAL FINANCIAL MANAGEMENT

SECOND CANADIAN EDITION

WILLIAM R. LASHER
Nichols College

PEGGY L. HEDGES
Haskayne School of Business
University of Calgary

T. J. (TERRY) FEGARTY
Seneca College of Applied
Arts and Technology

NELSON / EDUCATION

NELSON / EDUCATION

Practical Financial Management,
Second Canadian Edition
by William R. Lasher, Peggy L. Hedges, T. J. (Terry) Fegarty

**Associate Vice President,
Editorial Director:**
Evelyn Veitch

Publisher:
Rod Banister

Marketing Manager:
Shannon White

Senior Developmental Editor:
Elke Price

**Photo Researcher/Permissions
Coordinator:**
Sheila Hall

Production Service:
PrePress PMG

Copy Editor:
Karen Rolfe

Proofreader:
PrePress PMG

Indexer:
PrePress PMG

**Manufacturing Manager—Higher
Education:**
Joanne McNeil

Design Director:
Ken Phipps

Managing Designer:
Katherine Strain

Interior Design:
Peter Papayanakis

Cover Design:
Sharon Lucas

**Cover, Part, and Chapter Opener
Images:**
Cosmo Condina/Getty Images

Compositor:
PrePress PMG

Printer:
RR Donnelley, Inc.
Willard, OH

**Library and Archives Canada
Cataloguing in Publication Data**

Lasher, William

Practical financial management /
William R. Lasher, Peggy L.
Hedges, T.J. (Terry) Fegarty.—2nd
Canadian ed.

Includes bibliographical references
and index.
ISBN 978-0-17-610535-8

1. Business enterprises—Finance—
Textbooks. 2. Corporations—
Finance—Textbooks. I. Hedges,
Peggy L., 1958– II. Fegarty, Terry
J., 1943– III. Title.

HG4026.L38 2008   658.15
C2008-900409-4

ISBN 13: 978-0-17-610535-8
ISBN 10: 0-17-610535-2

Brief Table of Contents

Table of Contents

Chapter 19
Corporate Restructuring

Chapter 20
International Financial Management

Preface

Welcome to the second Canadian edition of *Practical Financial Management*, the latest milestone in a journey in education shared by the authors and our former students. We believe that most finance texts are harder for students to understand than they should be. The issue is relatively unique to this field. No other business discipline seems to have finance's reputation for unfathomable reading material.

We feel that much of the problem lies in the fact that textbook presentations are inconsistent with the background knowledge and abilities of typical business students. That isn't to say that the texts are poorly done. By and large, finance texts are good books. They're logical, well written, and comprehensive. But they're consistently off target in several key areas with respect to the students who read them.

The first problem has to do with background. Texts tend to introduce topics using a voice that assumes students already have some grounding in the area to be studied. Even bright students can be confused and intimidated by this practice, because many know relatively little about the subject area when they start a chapter.

Then there is the thorny issue of quantitative material. A great deal of finance is grounded in math and statistics, so students have to take prerequisite courses in those areas. But most business students aren't really comfortable with quantitative methods, even after they've had the courses. This leads to the biggest pedagogical problem we have. Textbooks assume business students are inherently more skilled in math than they really are, so many readers find it difficult to follow the presentations without an inordinate amount of time and study.

Finally, there is a troubling lack of practicality in much of this literature. For example, texts present financial techniques such as net present value (NPV) and internal rate of return (IRR) in capital budgeting in ways that imply a hair-splitting accuracy that doesn't exist in the real world, where results often depend on biased and uncertain inputs. Textbooks are also silent on the behavioural problems that financial managers deal with every day. For example, the conflict between sales and finance over receivables can threaten to tear a company apart, but it is rarely mentioned in textbooks.

The result of all this has been that finance professors don't get much help from textbooks in teaching introductory courses. We develop classroom approaches that get the ideas across, but spend a great deal of time explaining what the text is trying to say rather than using it to support our teaching.

We, as authors, have served in a variety of corporate finance positions and changed careers, becoming full-time educators in order to pursue our common passion, teaching and writing. One of the results is *Practical Financial Management (PFM)*. *PFM* is unique because of its approach to teaching finance. That approach is the result of a combination of classroom and practical experience. The theme is easy to summarize.

We begin every area of study by presenting the heart of the business problem or issue. We start from scratch, assuming students know nothing about the area. That's critical—to bring readers up from absolute zero so there is no confusion and they know exactly where they are going and why. Look at the beginning of Chapter 11 on portfolio theory for an example (page 387). We begin the chapter by explaining why we study "risk and return" in the first place and define the investor's goals right away in terms that beginning students can understand. After that, key theories are explained clearly and are quickly backed up with practical examples.

Next, wherever math is involved, we explain the physical and business relationships between variables before developing or using equations. We discuss what each aspect of a relationship means as we put it together. That gives the equations substance and provides meaning to students who are less than comfortable in quantitative areas. See the development of IRR in Chapter 12 as an example (pages 440–445).

Then, when we do use math or complex procedures, we carefully explain what we're doing step by step. We assume students have the basic tools of algebra or accounting or statistics, but we don't assume they remember that material well. Because our systematic presentation recognizes that, students don't get lost or stuck. *PFM* is a resource students can use by themselves as well as in class. They can read whole chapters on their own and come to class better prepared than ever before. Look at the first pages in the development of the time value of money in Chapter 8 as an example (pages 259–261). Also see the development of the statement of cash flows in Chapter 2 for the same idea in the context of difficult accounting material rather than math.

Finally, we've drawn on our combined years of business experience to present some insights into how things really work. You'll find these explanations throughout the book, identified by a "From the CFO" icon in the margin. A prime example deals with the problems associated with estimating cash flows for capital budgeting projects, which is found in Chapter 13 (see Example 13.4, page 484; the people who propose capital projects are usually biased toward acceptance).

PFM's end-of-chapter Business Analysis exercises are another important practical feature. They are mini-cases designed to open students' eyes to the realities of applying financial principles in actual business situations. The questions at the end of Chapter 13 (page 488) are good examples.

Throughout, we've tried to write this book in a way that's easy to read, enjoyable, and unintimidating. The word that sums that up is "accessible." We think we've been successful, because reviewers have been unanimous in their praise of the work's conversational style and easy readability.

Thank you for using *Practical Financial Management*. We're absolutely sure you and your students will be pleased with the learning experience they'll have as a result.

New to the Second Canadian Edition

We've made a number of exciting changes in the second Canadian edition that will please both professors and students alike.

Chapter Summaries Tied to Learning Objectives

Chapter summaries are now organized around the numbered learning objectives so that students can use them as a quick check on their achievement of learning goals.

Key Formula Summaries

Each chapter now includes a listing of the important formulas covered in the chapter. The key formula summaries appear at the end of the chapter. The key formulas are also listed in Appendix C and have been provided on tear-out cards for the student's convenience at the back of the book.

Additional Coverage of Executive Ethics and Governance

In the early 2000s the world discovered that an unprecedented fraud had been perpetrated on the investing community by a significant number of corporate executives in the 1990s. Exposure of the wrongdoing resulted in investment losses of staggering proportions. Governments and regulators alike responded with legislation and policies that forever changed the governance of public corporations and the accounting industry. Surprisingly, corporate finance texts have been slow to include discussion of these changes, their roots, or their implications.

We've addressed that omission by discussing these causes and effects, primarily in Chapter 3. We explain how stock-based compensation incentives create a moral hazard for executives that can influence financial reporting. We describe how the financial and auditing systems were supposed to protect investors and how they failed to do so. Only after that foundation is laid, do we get into the regulations, what they are designed to do, and their impact on the business and financial world. The result will be students who understand what went wrong, why it happened, how the regulations are working, and how they have changed the financial world.

Additional End-of-Chapter Problems

A number of problems from the first edition have been improved or updated. In addition, several new problems have been added to the end of every chapter. The emphasis is still on relatively easy exercises that provide a smoother transition into subsequent, more difficult problems.

New INSIGHTS Boxes

PFM's successful series of thought-provoking INSIGHTS boxes have been updated and enhanced with the addition of several new articles. Examples include the *Practical Finance* box on EDI in Chapter 4; the *Real Applications* box on JIT at Dell Computer in Chapter 4, the *Real Applications* box on the Business Development Bank in Chapter 5, and the *Practical Finance* box on dividend policy in Chapter 17. The Ethics series highlights moral or ethical dilemmas faced by financial executives, the Practical Finance series applies chapter concepts to real and hypothetical problems, and Real Applications focuses on well-known companies.

Expanded Coverage of Key Concepts

We know that certain concepts are given only a cursory overview but really important ones need more explanation. Accordingly we have reorganized, expanded, or updated coverage on several topics, including

- Capital cost allowance and other recent tax legislation in Chapters 2 and 13
- Trend analysis and industry ratios in Chapter 3
- Electronic data interchange, credit and collection policy, and credit decision analysis in Chapter 4
- Receivable factoring in Chapter 5
- Crossover rate in Chapter 12
- Foreign direct investment and recent exchange rates in Chapter 20

More Calculator Solutions for Examples Added

It's easy to do basic math and simple time value problems with financial calculators. But more advanced calculations involving uneven cash flow streams can be tedious. Because calculator manuals are hard to read and easy to misplace, we've included instructions on using financial calculators to solve time value of money problems (Chapter 8), to calculate bond prices and yield to maturity (Chapter 9), and to find NPVs and IRRs for projects with uneven cash flows (Chapter 12). In this edition, we have added many more calculator solutions for these and other time value of money applications. Chapters 8 and 12 also reflect increased use of Excel®, and the margin calculator solutions now include which Excel® function box to use.

Coverage of Spreadsheet Applications Expanded

Computer spreadsheets are being used to solve computational problems in virtually all areas of practical finance. However, the more complex functions can be tricky to use. Recognizing this, we've expanded instruction on and/or examples using computer spreadsheets, beginning in Chapter 4.

In this edition we have suggested many more Excel®-based solutions for examples, and specifying the Excel® function to use in each case. Many chapters include Excel®-based problems and solutions, most of which can be completed using Excel® templates available on the text website.

Derivative Securities

Chapter 18 now includes a new appendix exclusively covering the basics of the Black–Scholes Option Pricing Model. This chapter also has added coverage of the moral hazard of stock-based compensation and wealth.

Highlights

A Treatment of Real Options That Is Both Clear and Comprehensive

One of the most exciting new developments in corporate finance is the practice of building options that potentially enhance performance into operating plans. Real options thinking is especially effective in capital budgeting for big-ticket items. In response to heightened interest in academic and business circles, a treatment of real options has been included. The exposition is included as a risk issue in capital budgeting, and is a continuation of the section on decision trees.

Real options is an advanced topic, and contemporary treatments often leave students frustrated and confused. *PFM*'s explanation is detailed and thorough, but is designed to minimize these problems for students.

Capital Budgeting Is Covered in Three Chapters

Capital budgeting is often addressed in one or two chapters. We have found that students need capital budgeting more clearly spelled out; therefore, Chapter 12 covers capital budgeting models, Chapter 13 covers cash flow estimation, and Chapter 14 deals with risk-related topics including real options.

Unique and Important Pedagogical Features

The second Canadian edition continues to make extensive use of pedagogical learning aids to enhance student learning.

Learning Objectives and Summary

Each chapter begins with a set of numbered learning objectives and ends with a numbered summary focusing on key areas covered in the chapter. Chapter summaries are organized around the learning objectives so that students can use them as a quick check on their achievement of learning goals.

Key Formula Summaries

Key formulas presented in the chapter are now listed at the end of each chapter for easy reviewing purposes.

From the CFO

From the CFO

This feature highlights material based on the authors' experiences as financial practitioners. These comments deal with finance in actual practice, and offer tips and insights that are grounded in real-world experience. "From the CFO" material appears throughout the text and is identified by a logo in the page margin and italicized print.

Margin Notes

PFM's summarizing margin notes are particularly complete and thorough. They provide students with a convenient summary/outline of the textual material rather than just a list of keywords.

The finance department *oversees* how other departments spend money.

Key Terms

Definitions of key terms appear in the margins and in the glossary. A list of each chapter's important terms and concepts appears at the end of the chapter, with corresponding page references.

Finance is the art and science of handling money.

Internet Notes

Internet addresses and descriptions are included in the margin material to direct students to websites that expand upon the material being presented.

Insights **PRACTICAL FINANCE**

Insights: Practical Finance
These boxed features provide information, analysis, and commentary on current topics in the real financial world.

Insights **ETHICS**

Insights: Ethics
Our ethics features delve into ethical issues faced by financial managers in their professional lives. The issues are presented alongside relevant subject matter and focus on the ethical problems constantly in today's business news.

Insights **REAL APPLICATIONS**

Insights: Real Applications
We show how chapter materials apply to situations faced by prominent companies and, in several chapters, examine Danier Leather Inc., a national retail chain. We believe that by following one particular company, students will feel more confident in applying the concepts they have learned to other companies in the news.

Supplements

Practical Financial Management comes with a full set of supplements for both students and instructors.

For Students
Study Guide (0–17–647343–2/978–0–17–647343–3). The study guide, prepared by Shelley Meldrum at Nova Scotia Community College, contains learning objectives for each chapter along with chapter summaries, and detailed reviews that encapsulate relevant points and concepts, with important equations highlighted. In addition, each chapter is reinforced with a generous number of self-test questions including true/false, multiple-choice, fill-in, and problems. Answers are provided for all questions.

CENGAGENOW™

CENGAGENOW™ is an **online learning and homework assessment program** created in concert with the text to present a seamless, integrated learning tool. It provides students with a robust set of additional online learning tools, and is available in both Blackboard and WebCT. Here is a tour through some of the study support features found in CENGAGENOW™ for *Practical Financial Management*:

- *Personalized learning path:* Each chapter includes a personalized learning path that allows students to take a pretest to assess their prior knowledge of the material and then, based on the results of that pretest, establishes a learning path that focuses the student's studies on the material where he or she needs the most work. The study materials presented here include the appropriate section of the ebook, video elements, and other multimedia learning objects. A posttest is then available to assess a student's progress after using the personalized learning path.
- *Homework:* CENGAGENOW™ includes end-of-chapter problems that instructors can assign as homework or include in electronically graded quizzes and tests.
- *Test bank:* The complete test bank for this product is also included so that instructors can create tests and exams directly in CENGAGENOW™ and assign them to students for automatic grading and results.

Product Support Website. *Practical Financial Management's* website at **http://www.lasher2e. nelson.com** contains student resources, instructor resources, Internet updates and links, spreadsheet software, slides prepared using Microsoft® PowerPoint® presentation software, online quizzes, and other useful features. Students can go directly to the text website to link to the Internet addresses in the text margins.

Spreadsheet Software. *PFM* contains two types of computer problems in the end-of-the-chapter material. Some problems use spreadsheet templates, while others require students to create their own spreadsheet software. The templates, developed by William Lasher and Terry Fegarty, are available on the text website and through CengageNOW to both students and instructors.

For Instructors

Instructors' Resource CD (0–17–647342–4/978–0–17–647342–6). Managing classroom resources is easier than ever. The comprehensive Instructor's Resource CD contains all key instructor supplements.

Instructor's Manual. The *Instructor's Manual,* by Mary Oxner at St. Francis Xavier University, contains chapter-by-chapter focus statements, pedagogical tips, and teaching objectives. The textbook authors have developed detailed solutions to all of the discussion questions and the problems are fully worked out. The *Instructor's Manual* is also available on the text's website, password-protected for instructors only.

Microsoft® PowerPoint® Slides. PowerPoint® slides, revised for this edition by Terry Fegarty, are available to instructors. These slides are designed for classroom presentation, with summarized illustrative examples, providing a useful lecture tool.

Test Bank. William Lasher and Peggy Hedges have personally edited the test bank, ensuring that all the questions are consistent with the text's style and notation, and that all are clear and appropriate for student's abilities. This edition is revised by Vanessa Oltmann of Malaspina College and contains more than 2,500 insightful questions categorized by topic area. The questions include true/false, multiple-choice, fill-in, and problems.

Computerized Test Bank. The **Examview®** computerized testing program contains all of the questions in the printed test bank. **Examview®** is an easy-to-use test creation software compatible with Microsoft Windows or Macintosh. Instructors can add or edit questions, instructions, and answers, and select questions by previewing them on the screen, selecting them randomly, or selecting them by number. Instructors can also create and administer quizzes online, whether over the Internet, a local-area network (LAN), or a wide-area network (WAN).

JoinIn™ on TurningPoint® This classroom response software tool, prepared by Joe Pidutti at Durham College, gives instructors true integration with Microsoft® PowerPoint® slides. Instructors can author, deliver, show, assess, and grade all in Microsoft® PowerPoint® presentation software without having to toggle back and forth between screens. With **JoinIn™ on TurningPoint®**, instructors can walk about the classroom as they lecture, showing slides and collecting and displaying responses with ease. It is an effective way to turn the lecture hall into a personal, fully interactive experience for the student.

Acknowledgments

We can't say enough in praise of the following reviewers who participated in the reviewing of the first edition and its original proposal. They provided encouragement, criticism, ideas, and enthusiasm, all at the right times.

David E. Allwright	Mount Royal College
Cécile Ashman	Algonquin College

Walt Burton	Okanagan University College
John Cavaliere	Sault College
Nauman Farooqi	Mount Allison University
Jerome Gessaroli	British Columbia Institute of Technology
Marie Madill-Payne	George Brown College
Michael L. McIntyre	Carleton University
Judith I. Palm	Malaspina University College
Traven Reed	Canadore College
Fred Rutman	Humber College
Rod Smith	Cambrian College
J. Terence Zinger	Laurentian University

The following provided commentary and feedback that was invaluable to us in creating the revision for the second Canadian edition:

Colin Kovacs	Algonquin College
Shelley Meldrum	Nova Scotia Community College
Marie Sinnott	College of New Caledonia
Heather Stevens	George Brown College
Peter Wan	Seneca College
Larry Wood	University of Calgary
Zhenyu Wu	University of Saskatchewan
Patricia Zima	Brock University/Mohawk College

We truly appreciate the dedication of the many people responsible for the development and production of *Practical Financial Management*. Completion of our book and its many supplements required the commitment of many editorial, production, and marketing personnel. We would like to thank the team at Nelson Education Ltd. for their enthusiasm, energy, and patience throughout the development of this text. In particular we wish to thank Elke Price, Senior Developmental Editor; Rod Banister, Publisher; Susan Calvert, Director, Content and Media Production; and thanks also to our copy editor, Karen Rolfe; our proofreader, Karen Fraley; and our technical checker, Ann Miciak.

Peggy Hedges would like to thank her colleagues, former clients, and former students. In particular, thank you to Larry A. Wood, who continues to be a mentor and business partner. All have contributed to helping her understand the importance of how to better explain the art and science of finance. Terry Fegarty would like to thank his colleagues and students for their kind words and suggestions, and Anita once more for her encouragement, patience, and technical support. Finally, this book is also dedicated to our students: past, present, and future. We find finance interesting, and sometimes fascinating. We wrote this book for the many students who agree.

We are responsible for the Canadianization of this text, so we invite you to send your comments, suggestions, or questions about the book directly to us.

Peggy L. Hedges
University of Calgary
hedges@haskayne.ucalgary.ca

Terry Fegarty
Seneca College of Applied Arts and Technology
Terry.Fegarty@senecac.on.ca

About the
Authors

William R. Lasher has a unique background spanning both education and practice in finance. Prior to entering full-time academics, he worked for Texas Instruments, Harris Corporation, and the Pacific Telesis organization. He has held positions as a planner, a controller, and a subsidiary CFO. While working in industry he served as an adjunct professor at the University of Dallas, the University of Texas at Dallas, and Golden Gate University in San Francisco. He moved into education full time in 1988 by joining the faculty at Nichols College.

Professor Lasher has a B.S. and an M.B.A from Columbia University, received his Ph.D. from Southern Methodist University, holds a J.D. from New England School of Law, and is a Certified Public Accountant. He has also published books on business planning, franchising, and the strategic management of small firms.

Peggy L. Hedges has a background that includes education and experience in financial services. Before joining the Haskayne School of Business in 1990, Peggy worked for the Canadian Imperial Bank of Commerce (CIBC) as both an administration and commercial lending manager.

Peggy received a B.Sc. and M.B.A. from the University of Calgary. She has a Ph.D. in Environmental Planning from the University of Strathclyde and is a Fellow of the Institute of Canadian Bankers (FICB) and a Fellow of the Canadian Securities Institute (FCSI).

Peggy has developed and taught undergraduate and graduate courses in corporate, personal, investment, financial institutions, and public finance courses for the University of Calgary, University of Northern British Columbia, Athabasca University, and Mount Royal College. Her passion is teaching introductory finance. As well, she is a co-owner of a company specializing in financial education to executives.

T. J. (Terry) Fegarty is a Chartered Accountant (Ontario), and has held several senior financial management positions, both in Canada and abroad, primarily in the retail and computer hardware industries. He is an alumnus of KPMG LLP (Canada) and maintains a practice in accounting and tax services.

Since joining Seneca College in Toronto in 1985, Professor Fegarty has developed and taught many business courses, including distance learning courses, in corporate and international finance, accounting, and taxation. He enjoys teaching financial management. His approach in teaching parallels that of this text: to concentrate on the basics, to keep it simple, and to present the material and design the activities for a business graduate who will need to know how money is managed in small and large businesses.

PART 1

Introduction to Financial Management

Chapter 1

Foundations

Learning Objectives

1 Explain the relationship between financial assets, financial markets, and financial management.

2 Explain the relationship between accounting and finance.

3 Understand the link between financial theory and economics.

4 Describe the goals of management and show how they might cause conflicts with stakeholders.

5 List and describe three forms of business organizations.

Finance is the art and science of handling money. In today's world virtually every organization, public and private, runs on money. That includes families, businesses, governments, and nonprofit enterprises. Money touches everything we do. And finance, the management of money, is behind almost everything we see each day. We don't physically observe the financing behind a building or a new car or a house, but it's there, and without it most of the things we see wouldn't exist. That's because without money to pay for resources and a financial system to make trading possible, no one could organize more than a few people to work together at one time.

Finance is the art and science of handling money.

AN OVERVIEW OF FINANCE

Our study of finance will be broadly divided into two areas: (1) investments and financial markets and (2) the financial management of companies.[1] These are separate but related: a financial system involves flows of money and paper between them.

http

Besides stock quotes and other data and information, the TSX (Toronto Stock Exchange) has a financial glossary at http://www.tsx.com/en/market_activity/glossary.html.

---

1 The banking system, a third sector of the financial world, is generally covered in an economics course on money and banking or financial institutions.

To begin our study of finance, we need a few basic terms and ideas. Let's master these before going any further.

Financial Assets

A **real asset** is an object or thing, such as a car, a house, a factory, or a piece of machinery. Real assets have value because they provide some kind of service, such as transportation, shelter, or the ability to produce something.

Financial assets, on the other hand, are legal documents, pieces of paper. Their value comes from the fact that they give their owners claim to certain future cash flows. Most financial assets are either shares or bonds, and their claim to future income is based on ownership or debt, respectively.

Share ownership means that the holder of a share owns a piece of the company that issued the shares. As a part owner, he or she is entitled to a share of the firm's profits, which may be paid out in dividends or retained to enhance prospects for growth. The shareholder generally expects to sell the share at some time in the future. Thus, the owner of a share certificate can look for two sources of cash in the future: dividends and the eventual selling price of the share. Notice that the terms *stock, shares*, and *shares of stock* are often used interchangeably.

A **bond** signifies a debt relationship. When a person buys a bond, he or she is lending money to the firm issuing the bond. The terminology seems strange—"buying a bond" meaning "lending money." Nevertheless, a bondholder is a lender and as such is entitled to interest on the amount lent and the repayment of principal at the end of the loan period.

Companies issue financial assets to raise money. They generally use that money to buy real assets that are used in running their businesses.

Financial assets are purchased by people or other companies to earn income with funds they don't currently need. Buying such an asset is similar to opening a savings account and receiving interest on the money you've put in the bank. Another name for a financial asset like a share or a bond is *security*, and an all-encompassing term for a security or financial asset is *financial instrument*. A person or organization buying a financial asset is said to be **investing** in that asset, and we generally call that buyer an *investor*.

Investments in financial assets can be made directly by buying securities or indirectly by buying shares or units in a **mutual fund**. A mutual fund pools the contributions of many investors and employs a professional manager to select securities that match a particular set of investment goals.

Financial Markets

Financial assets are issued by companies and purchased by investors in *financial markets*. A **financial market** isn't exactly a place; rather, it's a framework or organization in which people can buy and sell securities in accordance with well-defined rules and regulations. The best known financial market is the **stock market**. After a number of restructurings of the Canadian stock markets, we now have the for-profit TSX Group, which comprises a number of different businesses, including the operation of the Toronto Stock Exchange or TSX (senior capital markets) and the TSX Venture Exchange (junior capital markets). The Montreal Exchange (now the Bourse de Montreal) became responsible for derivatives trading. The New York Stock Exchange (NYSE) is the largest stock exchange in the world, and the TSX is in the top 15.

You don't have to go to an exchange to participate in the market. You simply establish a relationship with a *stockbroker* in your area and communicate with him or her by telephone or the Internet. A **stockbroker** is a person who is licensed to help investors buy and sell securities for a commission. **Brokers** are connected to the various exchanges electronically. The stock market is the entire network of brokers and exchanges connected together. Bond markets for trading in debt securities operate similarly.

A **real asset** is an object that provides a service. A **financial asset** (or *security*) is a document representing a claim to income.

Shares or stock represent an *ownership* interest. **Bonds** represent a *debt* relationship.

Investing involves buying financial assets in the hope of earning *income*.

A **mutual fund** purchases securities with the pooled resources of many investors. Shares in a mutual fund are called *units*.

Securities are traded in **financial markets** like the **stock market**.

A **stockbroker** (or simply **broker**) is licensed to trade securities on behalf of investors.

There are a number of different types of stockbrokers from which to choose. On one side of the spectrum are full-service brokers, who provide a number of services including information and advice. On the other side of the spectrum are discount brokers, who simply execute the orders. The research and administrative overhead for discount brokers is minimal and, as a result, they are able to charge lower fees. Over the past decade, there has been an explosion in the number of Internet-based discount brokers, who have even less overhead and are able to pass on those savings in the form of lower commissions on trades. Many of these online brokers are subsidiaries of the larger securities firms.

In summary, financial markets are "places" where investors buy financial assets from companies that issue them (primary markets). Investors also buy and sell the same financial assets between themselves in the same financial markets (secondary markets). In fact, the vast majority of transactions are between investors; this is because a security is issued by a company only once, but it may be traded among investors many times thereafter (very much like a used car market).

In practice, the term "market" describes the combined actions of investors acting within the marketplace just described. For example, someone might say that the market price for Research In Motion Ltd. (RIM) is $99; this means that the going price among investors buying and selling the shares of RIM within the structure of the stock market is $99.

Figure 1.1 is a schematic representation of the interaction between companies and the market.

The field of investments involves making decisions about buying shares and bonds. Decisions about how to raise money and what to do with it are part of the financial management of a firm. These decisions are made on the two sides of Figure 1.1, which represent the two areas on which our study will focus.

Now let's consider the word "finance" itself. Its use can be a little confusing. It's a noun, as in "the field of finance." It's a verb, as in "to finance something." And it also has an adjective form, as in "financial management." Let's explore these variations in meaning.

Raising Money

To **finance** means to raise money to acquire an asset.

The most common application of the term "**finance**" involves raising money to acquire assets. We've all heard people say they're going to *finance* a car or a house. When they say that, individuals usually mean they're going to borrow money from a bank to buy the item.

The word is used similarly in business. Companies *finance assets* when they raise money to acquire those assets. They do that by borrowing, selling shares, or using money they've earned. To the extent the money is borrowed, we say the company is *debt financed*. To the extent it comes from selling shares, we say the firm is *equity financed*. Equity or **shareholders' equity** implies financing with an owner's own money.

Shareholders' equity is an ownership interest—the portion of a firm's capital representing funds belonging to its shareholders. An equity investment is an investment in shares.

Looking at Figure 1.1, we see that firms in the box on the right are raising money, financing things. They do that by selling shares and bonds to investors in the box on the left. The *field of finance* includes both sides of this money-raising transaction. It relates to the concerns of parties raising money and to those of parties providing it. Further, because the money raised flows through financial markets and institutions, their operation is a part of the field as well.

FIGURE 1.1
Simplified
Financial System

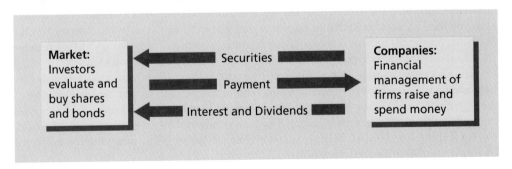

The Changing Focus of Finance

Historically, the field of finance was narrowly limited to activity within financial markets. Today, the perspective has expanded in two directions.

First, in modern finance a great deal of attention is given to the goals and activities of the investor. In the early days, a complete description of a particular security (share or bond) was felt to be all an investor needed to make a decision comfortably. Today we've become concerned with the notion of risk in investing and with how investors put together groups of securities called **portfolios** to minimize that risk. We'll examine these concepts at length in Chapter 11.

A **portfolio** is a collection of securities.

The second direction of expansion involves the role and function of financial management within firms. Historically, financial managers were told how much money their companies needed for particular projects, and they went outside in pursuit of those funds. They had little to do with deciding how much was needed or what was done with the money after it was raised. Today, financial managers are deeply involved in those related decisions.

Financial Management

Financial management means the management and control of money and money-related operations within a business. Companies have finance departments that are responsible for these functions.

The executive in charge of the finance department is the company's **chief financial officer**, abbreviated **CFO**. The title *vice-president of finance* is sometimes used instead of CFO. In either case, the position usually reports to the president of the company.

The corporate executive in charge of finance is called the **chief financial officer (CFO)**.

The term "financial management" refers to the things the CFO and the finance department do. These activities include keeping records, paying employees and suppliers, receiving payments from customers, borrowing money, purchasing assets, selling shares, paying dividends, and a number of other tasks.

It's important to notice that accounting is included in this broad definition of finance and that the accounting function is usually found within the finance department.

http

Wonder what careers in finance are all about? Visit http://www.financejobs.ca.

Business Decisions

Financial management also refers to the financial input that goes into general business decisions. This extremely important concept is best explained by an example.

Suppose a Canadian company is contemplating expanding overseas. That's likely to be a big decision discussed by the firm's key executives over a long period of time. Each executive will have opinions and recommendations related to his or her own area of responsibility, such as marketing or manufacturing. The CFO will similarly have opinions on how to set up the finance function in the new venture, how to do its accounting, and what banks to use. In addition, he or she will probably have to secure funding to support the project, either from a bank or by issuing securities.

Beyond that, however, the CFO must form a judgment about the feasibility of the project in terms of whether it will be profitable enough to justify its own cost. In other words, the bottom line for most projects is money, and the responsibility for assessing that bottom line falls to financial management. (We'll study the techniques used to make this kind of decision in Chapters 12, 13, and 14).

Oversight

Another important aspect of financial management involves the relationship between finance and other departments in the day-to-day management of the firm. It's important to grasp the fact that finance is responsible for its own activities, but has a responsibility for the operation of other departments as well.

The finance department *oversees* how other departments spend money.

Let's look into that idea a little more deeply. Finance is responsible for money, but other departments deal in money too. That's because they have to spend it to do their jobs, and their success is defined in terms of money. For example, manufacturing's task is to produce some quantity of product, but doing the job properly involves keeping costs low and using a reasonable level of inventory.

From the CFO

The finance department generally has an oversight responsibility for the effective management of the money other departments spend. If manufacturing's costs are too high or if it carries too much inventory, finance is responsible for calling attention to those facts and ensuring that corrective action is taken. In other words, part of finance's job involves looking over everyone else's shoulder to make sure they're using money effectively.

The Price of Securities—A Link between the Firm and the Market

The two sides of finance—investments and the financial management of the firm—are connected in that companies sell securities to investors in financial markets.

A fundamental truth, which we'll examine in detail later, is that investors buy securities for the future cash flows that come from owning them. Those cash flows depend on the issuing companies' financial performance. Hence, the prices investors are willing to pay for securities depend on their expectations about how profitable the issuing companies are likely to be in the future in terms of profit. Further, because the future is never guaranteed, the market is also concerned about the risk associated with expected performance. A perception of greater risk tends to lower investor interest and security prices.

Anyone who has watched the financial markets (or the evening news, for that matter) would be aware that market value or price of shares and bonds can fluctuate widely in relatively short periods of time. Why is this so? Part of the answer lies in the fact that prices change as new information arrives, and investors reassess their investments based upon that information. If prices in the marketplace respond quickly and correctly when new information arrives, the market is said to be an *efficient capital market*.

The efficient-market hypothesis contends that well-organized capital markets are efficient, and part of that efficiency is due to competition among investors. If investors can find incorrectly priced shares, they can make money by either buying or selling these shares. Their activity in the market will drive the price of the shares either up to where it should be or down to a price that is reasonable given what is known about the company and its prospects. We will discuss the efficient market hypothesis in Chapter 10.

The link between company management and investments comes from this relationship between price and expected financial results. Everything firms and their managers do is watched by the market and has an impact on investors' perceptions of likely future performance and risk. Those perceptions, in turn, have a direct impact on the prices of shares and bonds.

Insights REAL APPLICATIONS

When Bad News Travels, It Travels Fast ...

Nortel Networks Corp. saw its share price drop nearly 7% shortly after it announced in March 2007 that once again it would be restating its financial results because of calculation errors in its pension and postpension plans and restating of revenue figures. In 2004, Nortel Networks Corp. saw its share price plummet nearly 13% shortly after a report in the *Wall Street Journal* indicated that Nortel had manipulated its books in 2003 in order to show a profit.

Source: Wall Street Journal, June 30, 2004,
http://www.cbc.ca/money/story/2007/03/01/nortelrestate.html.

In other words, the study of investments includes looking at the way companies are managed to estimate future performance. At the same time, the management of companies includes consideration of how business decisions are perceived by investors and the effects those perceptions have on the prices of shares and bonds.

FINANCE AND ACCOUNTING

In many companies, the individuals involved in money-oriented activities are accountants, so people sometimes get the idea that accounting and finance are synonymous. In fact they're not, and it's important to understand how they fit together.

Accounting is a system of recordkeeping designed to portray a firm's operations to the world in a fair and unbiased way. The records are used to produce financial statements that present the company's financial position and results to anyone who reads them.

However, several other financial functions are performed in most companies. These include raising money, analyzing results, and handling relationships with outsiders, such as banks, shareholders, and representatives of the investment community. Most of these functions are performed by the *treasury department*.

The *finance department* normally consists of both the *accounting department* headed by the **controller** and the *treasury department* headed by the **treasurer**. Both of these positions report to the *chief financial officer (CFO)*. The typical organization is depicted in Figure 1.2.

In practice, it has become common to think of accounting as an almost separate field, and to refer to the other financial functions as finance. For the most part, this means that treasury functions are called *finance* and controller functions are called *accounting*.

People tend to have careers in one side of the department or the other, but crossover is possible. It's generally easier for an accountant to move into treasury than the other way around, because of the number of specialized courses required to be a professional accountant. Either controllers or treasurers can become CFOs.

Companies are organized in different ways, and who does what isn't always clear. Many of the activities we'll study in this book are done in the accounting department in one company and in the treasury (finance) department in another. In smaller companies, one person may do both functions (among other things!). Activities such as financial analysis (Chapter 3), financial planning (Chapter 6), and capital budgeting (Chapters 12, 13, and 14) are generally done wherever the resources are available to do the job best.

Finance majors shouldn't be discouraged by the preponderance of accounting jobs in typical industrial companies. The majority of jobs in the investment industry and in financial institutions, such as banks and insurance companies, are in finance rather than accounting.

In most large companies, the **controller** is the executive in charge of the accounting function and the **treasurer** is the executive in charge of external financing. Both positions generally report to the CFO in large companies.

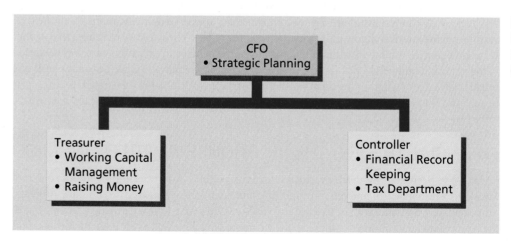

FIGURE 1.2
Finance Department Organization

The Importance of Cash Flow

The relative emphasis placed on cash flow is important in differentiating conceptually between accounting and finance. The accounting system attempts to portray a business's financial results in a way that reflects what is physically going on. In finance, we tend to concentrate on where cash is coming from and going to. In finance, "cash is king"!

In finance, "cash is king"!

This point can be made clear with a simple example. Suppose a firm buys a $1,000 asset to be amortized straight-line over five years at $200 per year. The accounting books show the initial addition of the $1,000 asset followed by yearly amortization entries, each of which has two parts. Every year, amortization expense appears on the income statement to reflect the transfer of $200 from asset to expense. Further, $200 is added to an accumulated amortization account on the balance sheet each year to reflect the wearing out of the item. (We'll review capital asset accounting in more detail in Chapter 2.)

Notice how much information this set of numbers conveys. The asset originally cost $1,000 and results in an expense of $200 each year that reduces profit (this is not actually an out-of-pocket expense, so no cheque was written for the $200, but the expense is deducted to get a lower taxable income figure). At the same time, the balance sheet indicates how worn out the item is by showing the portion of its original value that's left on the books. The accounting representation thus gives us a portrait of the entire life of the asset and its impact on the business in numbers!

From the CFO

When people in the finance department think about the same asset, their orientation is very different. They're interested in only two numbers: the $1,000 cash outflow needed to acquire the asset in the first place, and the annual tax saving generated by the amortization deduction.

The reason for this emphasis is easy to understand. Finance is responsible for raising the initial $1,000, and the future tax saving affects the amount of cash that will have to be raised for other things later on. In fact, a finance person might say that the accounting representation doesn't display the most important piece of financial information about the asset—where the money to buy it came from.

The point behind the illustration is that in finance the emphasis is on cash. That isn't to say accountants are ignorant of the cash requirements associated with the asset in the example. Their emphasis is simply different, involving a broader portrayal of the business. Finance concentrates on cash flow. We'll keep that in mind throughout our study.

The Language of Finance

The practice of finance is closely tied to accounting, because financial transactions are recorded within the structure of accounting systems. It's often said that *accounting is the language of finance*. Because of this connection, all finance professionals need some knowledge of accounting. However, the level of knowledge required varies significantly depending on one's job.

Accounting is the *language of finance.*

A **financial analyst** studies the financial results of businesses and makes recommendations on their values as investments.

A **financial analyst**, who investigates companies and makes recommendations about their investment value, needs to know quite a bit of accounting. That's because analysts have to decipher complex financial statements without missing any of the detailed implications that may be buried in the notes and numbers. Stockbrokers, on the other hand, generally sell securities on the basis of a broad knowledge of what's going on in various industries and expectations generated by the reports of analysts. They can get by without much more than an ability to read basic financial statements.

FINANCIAL THEORY—THE RELATIONSHIP WITH ECONOMICS

So far, we've been examining the practical side of finance and how it fits into the business world. Finance is a field in which millions of people find jobs after they've mastered certain skills. As in any other field, success comes with experience and wisdom after you've learned the basics. In this regard, finance is a lot like accounting—you learn the techniques in school and apply them on the job.

However, there's also a theoretical aspect to finance. Financial theory is a body of thought that is studied and continually developed. In this regard, finance is a lot like economics. Scholars in both fields observe the world of business and government and attempt to model and explain behaviour in abstract terms.

In fact, modern financial theory began as a branch of economics during the 1950s. Since that beginning, finance has grown so much that most people now think of it separately, although the term **financial economics** is still used occasionally. The techniques of advanced financial theory are very similar to those of advanced economic theory.

Financial theory has a big impact on practice in some areas and less influence in others. Where the impact is significant, theory influences the direction and approach that people take in practice. As we go forward, we'll identify and explain theoretical elements that have had a notable influence on the way the world operates. Theory's most significant impact in recent years has been in the area of investments, which we'll cover in Chapter 11.

Financial theory has grown out of economics. **Financial economics** *is a somewhat archaic term for financial theory emphasizing the field's roots in economics.*

THE GOALS OF MANAGEMENT

To run a company, management needs a goal or an objective against which to measure the implications of its decisions. In the study of economics, theorists assume that the goal of the firm is profit maximization. The concept works in theory but is unmanageable in the real world. Truly maximizing profit today (in the short run) is likely to cause serious problems tomorrow (in the long run).

Fortunately, financial markets provide an easy-to-state yet realistic goal for management. Because shareholders own the company and have invested for financial gain, and because management works for those shareholders, the appropriate managerial goal is the *maximization of shareholder wealth*. That's generally taken to be equivalent to *maximizing the price of the company's shares*.

This idea gets around the short-run/long-run problem just described. Remember that stock market investors watch everything the company does and reflect those actions in their expectations about the firm's future performance. Those expectations determine the price of the shares today. Current profits also affect the share price, but only as an indicator of future profit.

Shareholder wealth maximization is a practical goal for corporate management.

For example, the work of most research and development (R&D) departments has little effect on current business, because their efforts are focused on developing products that won't be marketed for years. If a pharmaceutical firm fires its R&D staff, it would increase its current earnings but its share price wouldn't go up. The market would recognize the long-run folly of the move: in two or three years, the firm won't have any new products to sell and will probably be in trouble. Shareholders would sell their shares, anticipating a somewhat bleak future for the firm. From that example, we can deduce that simply maximizing today's profit isn't a very good goal for a real company.

As our study of finance proceeds, we will run into situations in which a management decision has an impact on share price. In such cases, we'll assume that the best decision is the one that results in the highest share price.

Stakeholders and Conflicts of Interest

In any company, several groups of people have special interests in the way the firm is run. These groups include the following:

- shareholders
- employees
- customers
- local community
- management
- creditors
- suppliers

Such interested groups, or *stakeholders* in the company have a vested interest in the way the firm is operated. Various conflicts of interest are possible between stakeholder groups. A conflict of interest occurs when something that benefits one group takes away from another. These conflicts can affect how managers behave and therefore have an impact on share prices.

Conflicts of Interest—An Illustration

Suppose an employee group at a company comes to management with a request: they want the company to build an athletic complex on the factory site so employees can exercise before and after work and during lunch hours. They argue that, although this project will cost money, it will lead to a happier, healthier employee population that will be more effective on the job.

Management agrees that happy, healthy workers are good workers, but also sees a possibility that employees will spend time at the gym at the expense of their jobs or that they will be exhausted on the job after working out. Therefore, the managers aren't sure whether the facility would help or hurt productivity. On balance, management feels the net efficiency effect will be more or less neutral.

It's important to recognize that this situation reflects a conflict of interest between two stakeholder groups: employees and shareholders. If the facility is built, the money will come out of profits that belong to shareholders. Hence, making the employees a little happier entails making shareholders a little poorer and presumably less happy. In this case, management is effectively an arbitrator and has to make a decision in favour of one group or the other.

In this example, the employees' request is something of a luxury, so the decision doesn't generate a lot of emotion when we read about it. But what if working conditions were really terrible, and employees were asking for money to create a clean, safe work environment? The conflict of interest would still be there, but we would be more likely to favour the employees on an emotional or ethical basis.

MANAGEMENT—A PRIVILEGED STAKEHOLDER GROUP

The ownership of a **widely held company** is dispersed so no one has enough control to influence management.

Management often has a special position among stakeholder groups. Although top managers theoretically work for the company's shareholders, they often have little accountability to that group. For example, in a **widely held company**, where ownership is dispersed and no one holds more than 1% or 2% of the company, shareholders have limited influence because no one can muster enough power to force a change in the management team.

In such cases, top managers become entrenched in positions controlling vast company resources and are able to use those resources for their own benefit rather than for the benefit of shareholders.

The Agency Problem

An **agent** is hired by a principal and given *decision-making* authority. The **agency problem** arises when the agent takes advantage of the relationship by diverting corporate resources for his or her own use.

The special position of management in widely held companies leads to a particularly onerous conflict of interest known as the **agency problem**. The term is derived from the legal concept of agency. An **agency** relationship is created when one person hires another and gives him or her decision-making authority over something. For example, if Smith hires Jones to run his business, Jones is the *agent* of Smith, who is called the *principal*. Conversely, if Smith hires Jones to sweep the floor, no agency relationship is created, because no decision-making authority is involved. The agency relationship creates an opportunity for abuse by the agent who has control over the assets of the principal. In general, corporate managers are the agents of the firm's shareholders.

The Abuse of Agency

The most common example of abuse of the agency relationship is the practice in which companies pay top executives excessive compensation (compensation includes salary, bonuses, and special deals on buying the company's shares called stock options). The conflict is with shareholders because the excess pay would otherwise be profit, which belongs to them.

Executive compensation levels in excess of $100 million in a year have recently been recorded. Shareholders have a right to ask whether anyone can be worth that much. Perhaps even more outrageous is the fact that high levels of compensation for top executives aren't necessarily connected to good performance by the company.

Compensation isn't the only way in which managers can feather their own nests. The use of company-owned assets, such as boats, airplanes, and vacation retreats, is common, as are such benefits as expense account meals, chauffeur-driven limousines, and paid country club memberships. These benefits are called **perquisites** ("perks" for short) and have become a way of life among top corporate executives. There are also more insidious agency costs that can creep in. As managers may not have as much at stake as the shareholders (particularly if these shareholders started the company), managers may not work as hard or may choose pet projects. The result is lower profits than if the original owners had continued to run the business. Agency costs such as these are often hard to quantify and hence are given the term **indirect agency costs**.

> Privileges and luxuries provided to executives are called **perquisites** (or "perks").

> Hard-to-quantify costs of management not acting in the best interests of shareholders are called **indirect agency costs**.

Controlling the Agency Problem

Efforts to manage the agency problem generally involve monitoring what the agent is doing. For example, principals can employ auditors to periodically review company books to ensure funds aren't being diverted to questionable uses. Such measures involve costs known as *direct agency costs*.

Another way to manage the agency problem is to pay a good part of managers' compensation in the form of a bonus tied to company profit. This approach reduces the incentive to spend money on company-owned assets that are used by executives. For example, buying a vacation retreat for executive use will reduce profit by the cost of the facility. If the president's bonus goes up or down with the size of profits, he or she will be less inclined to approve the expenditure for the retreat. (But then you might have management overstating profit to get bonuses. See Ethics, Chapter 3).

The government has limited the corporate tax deductibility of certain expenses, such as luxurious meals and club memberships. However, the effect of these efforts has been minimal, and the agency problem remains a major issue in the efficient functioning of the Canadian economy. We will explore governance issues more fully in Chapter 3.

CREDITORS VERSUS SHAREHOLDERS—A FINANCIALLY IMPORTANT CONFLICT OF INTEREST

The conflict of interest between creditors and shareholders is important at this point, because it will begin to develop your concept of risk in finance. Let's explore the idea through an illustration.

Suppose Smith starts a business with $1,000 of his own money and convinces Jones to lend the business another $1,000. The business now has cash of $2,000, which comes from debt of $1,000 and shareholders' equity of $1,000. Smith is the sole owner and decision maker, while Jones is a **creditor**.

> A **creditor** is anyone owed money by a business, including lenders, vendors, employees, or the government.

Now suppose Smith decides to invest the $2,000 in a very risky venture. Imagine that the venture has a high probability of total failure, say 50%, in which case all invested funds would be lost. However, if the venture is successful, it will double invested money in a few months.

It's important to recognize that this is a very unfair deal between Smith and Jones. It is an abuse of the creditor by the shareholder. To see this, consider what happens if the venture fails versus what happens if it is successful.

In the event of failure, both investors lose equally—their entire $1,000 investments. If the venture succeeds, the company will have $4,000 in cash. However, Jones's claim against that sum will still be $1,000, representing the unpaid loan balance (plus a little interest). The remaining $3,000 will belong entirely to Smith.

"Management Fees" at Hollinger International

Conrad Black, CEO of Hollinger International, was forced to resign his position with the company amid accusations that he, along with some close associates, had siphoned millions of dollars in unauthorized payments from the company into his own pockets in the form of "management fees." In some cases, these fees were paid as part of a divestiture, to ensure that Hollinger would not re-enter the market for a period of time. However, it is alleged that some of these fees, which normally would go to the company, were paid directly to Black. In July 2007 Black was found guilty of three counts of fraud and one count of obstruction of justice. He has indicated that he would like a new trial.

Sources: Financial Post (March 3, 2007); CBC News Indepth, http://www.cbc.ca/news/background/black_conrad. Retrieved August 27, 2007; Barbara Shecter, "The Trial of Conrad Black," National Post, March 3, 2007, p. FP 1.

To put it another way, the venture is a gamble. The losses are shared equally between the shareholder and the creditor, but the profits all belong to the shareholder. That's not a very good deal for the creditor.

From the CFO

This situation occurs in practice when companies that have borrowed money take on ventures that are riskier than those they took on before borrowing. To prevent this from happening, lenders generally put covenants or clauses in loan agreements that discourage the borrower from becoming more of a risk taker.

FORMS OF BUSINESS ORGANIZATION AND THEIR FINANCIAL IMPACT

A business can be organized in one of three common ways: a sole proprietorship, partnership, or corporation.

The choice of form is important financially because it can have an impact on taxation, financial liability, and raising money. The issue is relevant only in the context of smaller businesses, because virtually all large companies are organized as corporations.[2]

For financial purposes, a partnership is essentially a sole proprietorship with more than one owner, so in this section we'll concentrate mostly on proprietorships and corporations.[3] We'll explore some of the ideas behind each form through examples that stress its financial advantages and disadvantages.

The Proprietorship Form

A **proprietorship** is a form of business organization in which the business is indistinguishable from the owner; business profit is taxed as personal income to the business owner.

Suppose an entrepreneur wants to open a business, has enough money to get started, and chooses to organize as a sole **proprietorship**.

Getting Started

Starting a proprietorship is very simple. Because the business is indistinguishable from the entrepreneur, all he has to do to get started is obtain a business licence and declare the business open. That's an advantage of the proprietorship form—it's easy to start.

Taxes

Now suppose the entrepreneur operates for a while and makes a profit. That profit will simply be taxed as personal income to the business owner. That's another advantage of the proprietorship

2 The exception to this rule is personal service organizations, such as law or accounting firms, which are generally sole proprietorships, partnerships, or limited partnerships.

3 We will presume the corporate form of a business for the remainder of the book.

form—the business's profits are taxed only once, and that tax is at personal income tax rates. (On page 14, we'll see why this is an advantage.)

Raising Money

Next, suppose the business is successful for six months and the entrepreneur wants to expand but doesn't have enough money to buy the assets required. He therefore looks for outside financing in the form of a loan. Any number of sources are possible, including family, friends, and a bank.

Family and friends might advance some money on the strength of their personal relationship with our entrepreneur (what is often called *love money*), but people who don't know him will always ask two very important questions. First, they'll want to know, "What happens to my money if your business fails?" The honest answer is that the money will be lost. Next, they'll ask, "What happens to me if you're phenomenally successful?" The answer is simply that the lender will get his or her money back with interest.

Now consider the lender's position. Lending to the entrepreneur is a gamble, but not a very good one. The worst possible outcome is a total loss, while the best result imaginable is merely getting back the amount lent with a few dollars of interest. That might be all right if the chance of loss is very small, but in fact the overwhelming majority of small businesses fail. Of course, lenders know this, so the loan isn't very attractive to them.

For this reason it's almost impossible for a new business to get a loan that isn't fully *collateralized*. A collateralized loan is backed by some asset (the **collateral**) that the lender can take and sell in the event the borrower defaults on paying off the loan. Many entrepreneurs use their houses as collateral for start-up loans. In the case we're considering, our business owner's expansion plans would be stopped cold if he didn't have enough collateral to guarantee a loan.

> Assets pledged to guarantee a loan are **collateral**.

This result is a major disadvantage of the sole proprietorship form. The only way a nonowner can advance money to the business is by lending, and that's a very risky proposition. Therefore, raising start-up or expansion money is difficult while the business is new.

Besides the tax and money issues, it can be difficult to transfer ownership of these businesses. Further, these businesses have limited lifespans equal to the lifespan or interest of the owner in the business. Should the owner die or decide he no longer wants to be in business, the business will cease to exist.

> A major financial disadvantage of *proprietorship* is the difficulty encountered in raising money.

The Partnership Form

As mentioned earlier, the **partnership** is much like a proprietorship, but now there are two or more people involved in the business. Partnerships are relatively easy to set up, with the partners usually agreeing to share in the business in terms of money and effort. As well, they agree on how the profits will be distributed. These terms are set out in a *partnership agreement*. Like the proprietorship, they will need to obtain the required business licences.

There are two common types of partnerships: *general* and *limited*. In a general partnership, all partners share in the management and liabilities of the partnership. In a limited partnership, the limited partners provide cash for the partnership to operate, but other partners (the general partners) make the decisions. What do the limited partners get for supplying cash? They get a return on their investment plus some tax advantages they might not have received if they had invested in a corporation.

> In a **partnership**, two or more people agree to share in the business. The two common types of partnerships are general (all partners share in the management and liabilities) and limited (limited partners provide cash for the partnership to operate, but the general partners make the decisions).

With partnerships, the income received flows through to the partners and is taxed as personal income to the partners. Just like the proprietorship, this means income is taxed only once.

In terms of raising money, the partnership has a slight advantage over the proprietorship. As there are more people involved in the business, presumably there is more ability to raise cash. However, if all of the partners are "idea rich" and cash poor, the partnership isn't that much further ahead.

The Corporate Form

Now let's explore what happens when another entrepreneur starts a similar business using the corporate form.

Getting Started

The first thing she'd find is that getting started is somewhat difficult. She must go through the legal process of incorporation either under the federal *Canada Business Corporations Act* or a provincial/territorial act,[4] probably using a lawyer to file the papers. The whole thing would take some work and cost a bit of money.

Taxes

Once set up, the incorporated business operates in much the same way as the sole proprietorship. When the business makes a profit, however, the tax situation is significantly different.

A **corporation** is a separate legal entity subject to *corporate taxes* on whatever it earns. What's left over after the corporate tax is paid (earnings after tax or net income) belongs to the corporation.

That's an important point. Even though the entrepreneur owns the business, she doesn't own its earnings directly. The corporation owns them. To get the earnings into her own pocket, the entrepreneur may declare a dividend that is paid to her as an individual.

However, such a dividend is taxable income to the individual. Hence, our entrepreneur will pay individual taxes on the after-tax (i.e., after corporate tax) earnings of her company.

In other words, the profits of the business will be taxed twice: once at corporate rates and once at individual rates, before the entrepreneur gets to spend any of the business's earnings. This phenomenon is known as the **double taxation of corporate earnings**. It is the main *financial* disadvantage of the corporate form.[5]

To provide some relief for this double taxation, the income tax acts provide for a dividend tax credit on the personal tax paid on dividend income.

Raising Money

Let's assume that our incorporated entrepreneur's business is successful and that she wants to expand but needs money to do it. If she tries to borrow as an incorporated business, she'll run into the same problems that face the sole proprietor. Lending to a new business is risky, and, generally, no one will do it. Whether or not the business is incorporated doesn't make much difference.

However, a corporation has an option that isn't available to a sole proprietor. The incorporated firm can raise money by offering shares to investors. New shareholders will own shares of the business and may have some influence over how it's run. But if less than a 50% interest is sold, effective control can still be maintained by the original owner.

People contemplating buying shares will ask the same two questions that potential lenders ask: "What happens to my investment if the business fails?" and "What happens if it does very well?"

The answer to the first question is the same as it was in the lending case. If the business fails, the shareholder is likely to lose most or all of his or her investment. But the answer to the second question is very different. If the company does extremely well, the share price will go up, perhaps multiplying the value of the original investment many times over. In short, the answer to the second question for a shareholder is "You may get rich!"

Now consider the potential shareholder's position. An investment in the new business is still a gamble in which the worst possible outcome is total loss, but the best result is a very

---

A **corporation** is a form of business organization in which the business is a separate legal entity subject to corporate taxes on whatever it earns.

Double taxation of corporate earnings is the major financial disadvantage of the traditional corporate form.

---

4 The name of the act varies depending on in which province or territory the corporation wishes to incorporate.

5 The owner could pay herself a salary, which wouldn't be taxed twice. The salary would be part of the business's expenses. Only profit is taxed twice.

substantial gain. This is a much more attractive gamble than the loan, because the potential reward justifies the risk.

What this means in practical terms is that although people will almost never make uncollateralized loans to start-ups or new companies, they'll frequently buy shares in such ventures. This leads us to the *most significant financial advantage of the corporate form: the relative ease of raising money.* For larger companies this may be true, but for the small company, raising money whether through debt or a share issue can be expensive, and it may prove difficult to find willing investors.

Ease of raising money by selling shares is the most significant financial advantage of the corporate form.

Transferring Ownership

A further advantage of corporations is the ease of transfer of ownership. To transfer ownership, the present shareholders simply sell their shares to a new interested party. In theory, then, corporations should have an unlimited lifespan as they can outlive their originating owners. Is this true? Absolutely! How old would the original shareholders of the Hudson Bay Co. be if they were still alive? Check your answer by going to the Hudson Bay website and going to the history section.

The Truth about Limited Liability

The most frequently cited advantage of the corporate form is limited liability. In essence this means that a shareholder cannot be held liable for the corporation's debts or for damages it may do to others. That in turn implies that all the shareholder can lose is his or her investment in the shares.

Limited liability means shareholders cannot be held liable for a corporation's debts.

Let's state the matter in another way. Suppose someone has a valid claim against a business that exceeds its assets. For a proprietorship, the claimant can take the owner's personal property after taking the assets of the business. On the other hand, if the business is a corporation, only the assets of the business can be taken, not the personal assets of the shareholders.

The limited liability concept is absolutely true in the context of owning shares in a company that the investor isn't running. But it doesn't usually work when an entrepreneur is operating his or her own incorporated business. Let's explore why.

Companies generally create liabilities that exceed their assets in two ways: by borrowing money they can't repay, and by losing a lawsuit. The first situation is very common. A firm takes out a loan and plans to pay off the debt with the profits from the anticipated business. Trouble arises when the expected sales don't materialize and the firm can't make its loan payments. If things get bad enough, the company goes bankrupt and the value of the unpaid loan along with other debts exceeds the value of its assets.

Theoretically, incorporation protects business owners from having their personal assets seized as a result of such unpaid loans. In practice, however, lenders circumvent this feature of incorporation by demanding personal guarantees from small business owners before making loans to their companies.

Personal guarantees make entrepreneurs liable for loans made to their businesses.

Personal guarantees are side agreements signed along with loan papers that make owners personally responsible for repayment should their businesses fail to meet loan obligations. This device virtually eliminates the value of limited liability where loans to small businesses are concerned.

In the second situation, the entrepreneur or an employee damages some outside party. For example, suppose an auto repair shop fixes a customer's brakes negligently and thereby causes an accident. In such a case, the injured party can sue both the business and the negligent individuals, bypassing the limited liability of the corporate form.

The limited liability feature of corporations is largely a myth for owner-operated small businesses. However, it is real for shareholders who don't participate in the business themselves.

See which companies are on The Globe and Mail 1000 and other lists at http://www. reportonbusiness. com/top1000.

Insights **ETHICS**

Ethics and Ethical Investing

Earlier we said companies sold securities to raise money to finance assets. But suppose the assets are to be used in some business that's unethical or immoral. Doesn't that mean the investor is indirectly participating in the unethical activity? Should investors be concerned about that? Should they refuse to invest in companies whose activities they deem to be unethical?

Let's be precise about what we mean by "unethical." It's important not to get ethics mixed up with legality. Ethics come up when an activity is morally wrong but is technically legal.

Unethical activities generally involve at least two groups of people. One typically has some power over the other and uses its power to gain a benefit at the other's expense. The tobacco industry provides a good example. People smoke by choice, and the production and sale of cigarettes are legal activities. Health Canada estimates that 37,000 Canadians die each year due to tobacco use and that the cost to the economy (medical and lost productivity, among other costs) are in the billions of dollars.[6] Further, media reports allege that tobacco companies have kept sales up by targeting children in advertising and manipulating nicotine levels to promote addiction.

Some people consider the making and selling of tobacco products to be a legal but unethical business activity. Under this view, the groups that benefit are the management and shareholders of tobacco companies who enjoy lucrative jobs and profits. The injured group is smokers who become sick and may die. The power of the benefited groups is seen as coming from advertising and the addictive properties of smoking.

On the other hand, some people feel that smokers are aware of the health risks of tobacco and make their own decisions about using it, and that there's nothing morally wrong with providing the product to those who want it.

The question is whether ethics should keep investors who do morally condemn the industry from buying tobacco shares in pursuit of financial returns. Or should the financial market act as a veil that legally and morally separates investors from what is eventually done with their money?

Ethical, or socially responsible, investing is a growing practice in which people concern themselves with what is done by the companies whose securities they buy. It generally takes the form of avoiding the securities of firms that engage in activities considered questionable by the investor.

Ethical mutual funds exist that avoid the shares of companies that engage in certain activities. For example, "The Ethical Funds Company®" is a Canadian socially responsible mutual fund manager. It provides professional money management while investing in companies that reflect Canadians' commitment to financial, social, and environmental performance.

Ethical issues can be hard to analyze. They're usually charged with emotion and involve costs and benefits that are difficult to see. To keep your thinking clear, go through the following steps when analyzing an ethical problem.

1. Clearly identify the unethical practice. Is it all or part of what the firm is doing? In the tobacco illustration, is it wrong to make cigarettes at all or just wrong to advertise to children?

2. Separate legal and ethical issues. Something may not be okay just because it's legal.

3. Identify the benefited party or group and describe the benefit.

4. Identify the injured party or group and describe the injury or cost.

5. Identify the nature and source of the power of the benefited group. Does the group have the ability to manipulate and preserve its power? How did the power come about? Did the group do something to create it?

6. State any alternatives the injured group has. How difficult are these alternatives to use?

7. State the opposing view. What argument will be made by someone who doesn't feel there's a problem?

As we continue with our study, we'll highlight ethical issues in finance from time to time.

---

6 Health Canada Federal Tobacco Control Strategy. Retrieved September 30, 2007 from http://www.hc-sc.gc.ca/hl-vs/ tobac-tabac/res/news-nouvelles/fs-if/ftcs-sflt_e.html.

SUMMARY

1 Companies raise money to purchase real assets by selling financial assets. Purchasers of financial assets such as shares or bonds are promised claims to future cash flows of the business. Financial management is the management and control of money and money-related operations.

2 Accounting is a system of recordkeeping that is used to produce financial statements needed to make financial decisions. Finance typically deals with raising money, analyzing results, and handling relationships with those outside the company.

3 Financial theory is a body of thought that is continually examined and developed. The impact of this theory can vary from impacting on everyday practices to further developing our understanding of behaviour in abstract terms.

4 As small companies grow, owners must often hire others to help manage the business. There are a number of related decisions that managers must make in order to create value for owners of the company. The goal of creating value for owners might result in managerial actions that are not necessarily value creating. The financial marketplace closely watches the actions taken by management and assesses how these actions will affect future profitability. These actions will have a direct impact on the value of the company's shares.

5 There are various forms of business organization. Depending on what the entrepreneur wants to accomplish, any of the forms might be suitable. The corporation offers limited liability and the potential to raise more capital, but these come at a price to the entrepreneur.

KEY TERMS

Agency, p. 10
Agency problem, p. 10
Bond, p. 3
Broker, p. 3
Chief financial officer (CFO), p. 5
Collateral, p. 13
Controller, p. 7
Corporation, p. 14
Creditor, p. 11
Double taxation of corporate earnings, p. 14

Finance (noun), p. 2
Finance (verb), p. 4
Financial analyst, p. 8
Financial assets, p. 3
Financial economics, p. 9
Financial market, p. 3
Indirect agency costs, p. 11
Investing, p. 3
Limited liability, p. 15
Mutual fund, p. 3
Partnership, p. 13
Perquisites, p. 11

Personal guarantees, p. 15
Portfolio, p. 5
Proprietorship, p. 12
Real asset, p. 3
Shareholders' equity, p. 4
Shares, p. 3
Stockbroker, p. 3
Stock market, p. 3
Treasurer, p. 7
Widely held company, p. 10

QUESTIONS

1. Separate the following list of assets into real assets and financial assets. What are the distinguishing characteristics of each type of asset?

Delivery truck	Corporate bond	Corporate shares	Note receivable
Factory building	Inventory	Land	Computer

2. Discuss the differences, similarities, and ties between finance and accounting.

3. Discuss the relationship between finance and economics.

4. What are the significant financial advantages and disadvantages of the sole proprietorship/partnership form in comparison with the corporate form?

5. Is limited liability a meaningful concept? Why or why not? And if so, for whom?

6. How does the activity of investors in financial markets affect the decisions of executives within the firm?

7. Companies are generally financed with a mix of debt and shareholders' equity. How do you think the riskiness of the company, as perceived by the financial market, changes as the mix shifts from all shareholders' equity to mostly debt? Why? Would changes in perceived risk induced by changes in the debt–equity mix affect the company's share price?

8. What primary factor determines the price of securities? Can you think of another factor that might significantly affect how investors value the first factor? (Think hard: this second factor isn't mentioned in the chapter.)

9. What conflict(s) of interest can you imagine arising between members of the community in which a company operates and some other stakeholders? (*Hint*: Think about pollution.)

10. Is the agency problem an ethical issue or an economic issue?

11. Compare and contrast the terms "shareholder" and "stakeholder."

Business Analysis

1. Diversified companies comprise *divisions* or *segments*, each of which is a separate business. Large companies have divisions spread over the entire country. In such companies, most treasury functions are centralized, whereas most accounting functions are carried out in the individual divisions.
   - The cash management function controls the collection of revenues and the disbursement of funds from various bank accounts. It ensures that the company never runs out of cash by monitoring outflows and having lines of bank credit ready in case temporary shortages occur. Today's banking system is linked electronically so that cash can be transferred around the country immediately.
   - The credit and collection function decides whether a particular customer can be sold to on credit. It is responsible for following up after the sale to ensure that the bill is paid. Customers are often reluctant to pay because of problems and misunderstandings with sales or service departments.

   If you were designing the finance department of a diversified company, would you centralize these functions or locate them in the remote divisions? Why? Address each function separately.

2. The company president is reviewing the performance and budget of the marketing department with the vice-president of marketing. Should that be a one-on-one meeting, or should the CFO be present? Why? If you feel the CFO should be there, what should be his or her role in the meeting?

PROBLEMS

1. Sussman Industries purchased a drilling machine for $50,000 and paid cash. Sussman expects to use the machine for 10 years, after which it will have no value. It will be amortized straight-line over the 10 years. Assume a marginal tax rate of 40%.

   a. What are the cash flows associated with the machine at the time of the purchase?

   b. In each of the following 10 years:

      i. How much amortization expense would there be?

      ii. How much would the company save in taxes each year (assuming it could deduct these amortization payments for tax purposes)?

   c. What is the total after-tax cash cost of the machine over its 10-year life (again, assuming it could deduct these amortization payments for tax purposes)?

Chapter 2

Financial Background: A Review of Accounting, Financial Statements, and Income Taxes

Learning Objectives

1 Explain the accounts commonly used in accounting systems and financial statements.

2 Demonstrate how to prepare the income statement and balance sheet.

3 Demonstrate how to prepare and interpret the statement of cash flows.

4 Explain the main features of Canada's progressive income tax system.

5 Identify the different forms of investment income for individual investors and investigate the different tax treatments applied to this income.

6 Outline the corporate income tax system in Canada.

7 Calculate taxable income and total corporate taxes for various classes of corporations.

8 Determine the effect of corporate taxes on various financing methods.

In the same sense that mathematics is the language of modern physics, accounting can be considered the "language" of financial management. The business's **accounting system** generates the data on costs, earnings, and financial position required for making financial decisions. One of the most significant impacts on earnings is the effect of income taxes.

Some knowledge of accounting is necessary in order to appreciate finance, because financial transactions are recorded in accounting systems and financial performance is stated in accounting terms. In other words, if we want to deal with money in business, we have to deal with the system that keeps track of it, and that's accounting. Some knowledge of taxes is also necessary, because tax considerations influence most financial decisions.

The business's **accounting system** generates the data on costs, earnings, and financial position required for making financial decisions.

Although accounting is generally a prerequisite, finance students have differing levels of knowledge about the subject. Some are quite expert, while others, who may have taken accounting some time ago, don't remember much.

This chapter provides a review of what you need to know about accounting and taxes in a condensed form. If you're not strong in the area, you'll find reading the chapter carefully to be a lot quicker than digging the ideas out of your old accounting text. If you are up to speed, you can skim the material and move on.

We'll conduct our review as painlessly as possible, keeping in mind that while financial people need to know something about accounting, they don't have to be accountants. In fact, we won't even have to use debits and credits!

ACCOUNTING SYSTEMS AND FINANCIAL STATEMENTS

Virtually everything business enterprises do is recorded as a series of money transactions within the structure of an accounting system. That record and the system itself provide the framework most managements use to control their businesses. Accounting systems produce several fairly standard reports (known as financial statements) that reflect business performance.

The Nature of Financial Statements

A business's **financial statements** are numerical representations of what the business is physically doing. Keep that concept firmly in mind as we go forward. The idea behind statements is to give a picture of what's happening within the company and between the company and the rest of the world both physically and financially. This excellent idea creates a problem, however, in that it causes statements to be somewhat counterintuitive. That is, they don't necessarily say what a person untrained in accounting is likely to think they're saying.

> **Financial statements** are numerical representations of a firm's activities for an accounting period.

Is Income "Income"?

Most people think of income as the money they're paid, which, after payroll withholdings, is what they take home. In other words, income means cash in your pocket.

The income statement is one of the traditional financial statements. It starts with the dollar amount the company has sold; deducts costs, expenses, and taxes; and winds up with a figure called net income (also called *earnings after tax* (EAT)). Most people would expect that figure to represent cash in the pocket of the business or its owner, just like a paycheque. However, it doesn't mean that at all. Several accounting concepts get in the way and give accounting net income a character of its own. We'll mention some major differences between accounting net income and changes in the company's cash balance.

Accrual Method

The standard accounting method for reporting revenues and costs in the financial statements is called the **accrual method** of accounting. Using this method, *revenues* are *recognized* as such in the financial statements of the seller when they are *earned*, not necessarily when they are received.

> **Accrual method** is the method of accounting that recognizes revenue when earned and expenses when incurred.

Revenues are normally earned when the seller has delivered goods or has provided services according to the contract with the buyer. *Accounts receivable* reflect a difference between revenue earned and revenue received.

In fact, the firm has less cash than it would have had if it had never made the sale. That's because, although it hasn't collected from the customer, it did supply product or services and to do so it had to pay for labour and materials. Uncollected payments for product or services sold (accounts receivable) can represent a big difference between cash and accounting income. We will return to the topic of accounts receivable on pages 26–27.

Costs are recognized when they are *incurred*, not necessarily when they are paid. Costs are normally incurred when the buyer has received goods or services according to the contract with the seller. *Accounts payable* and *accruals* reflect differences between costs incurred and costs paid. Unpaid amounts for product or services bought can represent another big difference between cash and accounting income. We will return to the topics of accounts payable and accruals on pages 30–31.

Long-Lived Assets

Another example of the difference between cash outflows and accounting expenses is to be found in the way costs of long-lived assets are recognized as expenses. We will cover this topic on page 28 where we discuss the concept of the *matching principle* and the accounting convention called *amortization*.

Clearly, these practices indicate that accounting income is conceptually different from pay-cheque income and that financial statements are concerned with more than just the flow of money in and out of the business. They do tell us about that, but they also tell us about what's going on in other ways.

The Three Financial Statements

Three financial statements are of interest to us at this point: the *income statement*, the *balance sheet*, and the *statement of cash flows*. There is a fourth, the *statement of retained earnings*, but we won't be concerned with it here. The income statement and the balance sheet are the *basic* statements that derive from the books of account. The statement of cash flows is developed from them.

DANIER LEATHER

For an example of published financial statements for Danier Leather Inc., a major Canadian corporation listed on the Toronto Stock Exchange, refer to Chapter 3, Appendix 3A, page 92.

Accounting Periods

In business, time is divided into accounting periods—usually months, quarters, and years—during which the accounting system accumulates and summarizes transactions.

The income statement shows *revenue* earned and *costs and expenses* incurred over the accounting period.

The balance sheet at the end of the accounting period shows the assets that the company owns and the liabilities that the company owes, the difference representing the book value of the *shareholders' interest*.

In business, time is divided into accounting periods—usually months, quarters, and years—during which the accounting system accumulates transactions. At the end of each period, all the transactions that occurred in the period are totalled and the company's books are brought up to date as of the last day of the period. It's important to understand that financial statements are associated with particular accounting periods. A set of statements includes an income statement and statement of cash flows that cover the entire accounting period, and a balance sheet that is associated with the point in time at the end of the period. A fiscal year is a business's year for accounting purposes. Many companies use a *fiscal year* that doesn't coincide with the calendar year.

The income statement shows *revenue* earned and *costs and expenses* incurred over the accounting period. The difference is *net income*. The balance sheet makes a statement as of a moment in time. It says that, at the end of the accounting period, the company owns a particular list of *assets* and owes a particular list of *creditors*, the difference representing the book value of the *shareholders' interest*. The derived statement of cash flows, like the income statement, represents flows over an entire period.

Implications

It's important to keep in mind that last year's financial statements don't say anything about what's going on this year or what will happen next year. They refer only to the past.

Statements can, however, be used as an indication of what is likely to happen in subsequent years. Past financial statements are a little like a person's medical history. If you were sick last year, you're more likely to be sick this year than if you were healthy. However, a sick person can get well, and a healthy person can get sick and die. Similarly, a firm that was financially sound last year can fail this year if it's mismanaged or something dramatic happens to its business.

THE INCOME STATEMENT

An income statement shows how much money a company has earned during the accounting period, commonly a year.

Presentation

Most income statements have a form similar to the one shown in Table 2.1. Let's examine each line individually.

Sales

Sales, also called *revenue*, represent the gross earnings from selling whatever it is the company is in business to sell. In other words, sales are the gross earnings from normal business operations.

This is an important point. If the company earns money from activities outside its usual form of business, that money should be recorded as *other income*, normally shown after operating profit (earnings before interest and taxes), rather than as sales. For example, a retail business might sell the store in which it operates to move to another. That sale of real estate shouldn't be included in the sales line.

Sales may be for cash, such as in a fast food business. However, it is common practice for businesses with *corporate* customers to sell most of their products or services *on credit*, receiving a promise of later payment rather than immediate cash. In addition, businesses such as retailers may provide consumer credit.

Cost of Goods Sold (COGS)

Cost of goods sold is subtracted from sales to arrive at gross margin. Both cost of goods sold and expenses represent costs of doing business, but there's an important distinction between the two.

Cost of goods sold represents costs incurred for items that are closely associated with the production of the product or service being sold. For example, in a retail business COGS is usually just the wholesale cost of product plus incoming freight. In a manufacturing business, however, COGS is much more complex. It includes labour and material directly associated with production as well as any peripheral costs in support of production. These peripheral costs are called *overhead* and can be substantial. They include the cost of such things as factory management, factory operation, and amortization on machinery. An expense is a cost that is not closely related to production.

In a service business, cost of services provided includes the wages of the people who provide the services, amortization of their tools and equipment, travel costs of getting to sites requiring service, and the cost of any facilities housing service operations.

> Cost of goods sold represents costs incurred for items that are closely associated with the production of the product or service being sold.

> Expenses represent costs incurred for items like marketing and sales, accounting, human resources, research, and engineering.

TABLE 2.1
A Conventional Income Statement Format

Sample Corporation

Income Statement

For the Year _____

Sales (Revenue)	$ 1,000
Cost of goods sold	600
Gross margin	400
Expenses	230
Earnings before interest & taxes	170
Interest expense	20
Earnings before tax	150
Tax	50
Net income	$ 100

Gross Margin

Gross margin, sometimes called *gross profit margin*, is simply sales revenue less COGS. It is a fundamental measure of profitability, getting at what it costs to produce the product or service before consideration of the costs of selling, distributing, or accounting for it.

Expenses

Expenses (or *operating expenses*) are subtracted from gross margin to arrive at earnings before interest and taxes. As noted above, expenses represent costs for items that, although necessary, aren't closely related to *product costs*. These include functions like marketing and sales, accounting, human resources, research, and engineering. The costs incurred in those areas tend to be related to the passage of time rather than to the amount produced. Both expenses and COGS may include some amortization.

Earnings Before Interest and Taxes (EBIT)

Most (but not all) income statement presentations give an earnings figure calculated before interest has been paid, then show interest expense separately. **Earnings before interest and taxes** is an important line on the income statement, because it shows the profitability of the firm's operations before consideration of how it is financed. The line is also called *operating income*.

To understand the concept of EBIT, imagine that we want to compare the performance of two businesses that are identical except for their financing. Assume one business is entirely equity financed and the other has a significant amount of debt.

If we try to judge the two companies on the basis of net income, we won't get a true picture of the relative strengths of business operations, because the second firm will have its profit reduced by the interest it pays on borrowed money. But the amount borrowed has nothing to do with how well the product sells, the cost of making it, or how well operations are managed.

The problem arises because interest is shown on the income statement but dividends are not. Therefore, a company with debt financing will always look weaker at the net income line than an otherwise identical firm that's equity financed. To get around this problem, we create the EBIT line. It shows the profitability of business operations *before* results are muddied by the method of financing.

Interest Expense

If the firm has borrowed money, it has to pay interest on those borrowings. It's important to realize that there's a big difference in the amounts of interest various companies pay. If a business is completely financed with the shareholders' money, there's no interest at all. If part of the financing is borrowed, the firm is burdened with debt and the associated interest payments.

Earnings Before Tax

Gross margin less all expenses, including interest, yields earnings before tax. This is conceptually simple: it is what the business produces before the federal and provincial tax departments take their bites.

Tax

The tax line on the income statement refers to income taxes on the amount of earnings before tax. Companies pay other taxes, but those appear as cost or expense items farther up on the income statement.

However, the statutory tax rate applied to earnings before tax doesn't always give the tax shown on the statement. There can be a variety of tax credits and adjustments reflecting differences between accounting principles and tax legislation. The tax figure also doesn't necessarily reflect the tax actually due, because some items are treated differently for tax and reporting purposes.[1] We shall return to this topic when discussing tax amortization on page 43.

Net Income

Net income is calculated by subtracting tax from earnings before tax and is the proverbial "bottom line." As we've already said, it is not equivalent to cash in the firm's pocket. In some cases it may be close to cash flow, but in others it's significantly different. It takes the statement of cash flows to figure out how much the company is earning on a cash basis.

Net income, also called *earnings*, belongs to the company's shareholders. It can be either paid out as dividends or retained in the business. **Retained earnings** become an addition to shareholders' equity on the balance sheet.

Retained earnings are those earnings not paid out as dividends.

Terminology

The terminology used on the income statement is far from uniform among companies. The words "income," "profit," and "earnings" are generally synonyms, so you may see any of them on the various lines instead of the expressions we've used here. "Profit before tax" and "profit after tax," abbreviated PBT and PAT, are particularly common, as are EBT and EAT for "earnings before tax" and "earnings after tax."

THE BALANCE SHEET

The balance sheet lists everything a company owns and everything it owes at a moment in time. Stated another way, it shows where all of the business's money has come from and what it's been used for. The fundamental principle is that all the sources of money and all the uses must be equal.

The firm's money comes from creditors and shareholders (owners). Creditors have lent money in one form or another and thereby have created liabilities for repayment. Shareholders have invested in the company or let past earnings remain in it rather than drawing them out.

A firm uses its money to acquire assets, both tangible and intangible, to increase the profits of the business.

Assets are used to increase the profits of the business. The money for the assets comes from the creditors and the shareholders.

Presentation

A balance sheet has two sides. One lists all of the company's assets, and the other lists all of its liabilities and shareholders' equity.

The balance sheet can be thought of as an equation:

$$\text{Assets} = \text{Liabilities} + \text{Shareholders' equity}$$

On one side we have assets, representing what the company has done with its money. On the other side we have liabilities and shareholders' equity, representing where the money came from. If everything has been accounted for properly, the two sides must be equal, or "balance"— hence the name "balance sheet." The balance sheet is sometimes called the *statement of financial position*.

A typical balance sheet looks like the one shown in Table 2.2. Notice that total assets equal total liabilities plus shareholders' equity. This illustration is somewhat simplified, but it will serve to explain the important features of a balance sheet. We'll start on the asset side and work through the entire statement.

---

1 When the tax due is different from the tax expense on the income statement, most of the difference is usually shown as a *future income tax liability* on the balance sheet. Thus, income tax expenses reported on the income statement can be payable in future years (*deferred*) or previously deferred taxes can be due now. Some complicated accounting is generally involved.

TABLE 2.2
A Conventional
Balance Sheet
Format

Sample Corporation
Balance Sheet
As of _____

Assets		Liabilities and Shareholders' Equity	
Cash	$ 1,000	Accounts payable	$ 1,500
Accounts receivable	3,000	Accruals	500
Inventory	2,000		
Current assets	$ 6,000	Current liabilities	$ 2,000
Capital assets		Long-term debt	$ 5,000
Gross	$ 4,000	Shareholders' equity	$ 2,000
Accumulated Amortization	(1,000)		
Net capital assets	$ 3,000	Total liabilities and	
Total assets	$ 9,000	shareholders' equity	$ 9,000

The ease with which an asset becomes cash is referred to as **liquidity.**

Both assets and liabilities are arranged in decreasing order of liquidity. Liquidity, in this context, means the readiness with which an asset can be turned into cash or a liability will require cash. On the asset side, the most liquid asset is cash itself. Next comes accounts receivable because one expects that in the normal course of business receivables will be collected within a few weeks. Inventory is next because it is normally sold in short order, generating cash or a receivable. Capital assets are low on the list because they would generally have to be sold on the property or used-equipment market to be turned into money. Similar logic applies on the liabilities side.

Assets

In what follows, we'll consider each asset and present the important elements of its financial/accounting treatment.

Cash

Cash is defined as money in bank chequing accounts plus currency on hand. Currency is usually a minor amount. Companies keep cash balances in bank accounts to pay bills and as a precaution against unforeseen emergencies.

Marketable securities are liquid *investments that are held* instead *of cash.*

Larger companies usually hold a *cash equivalent* (or "*near cash*") item called marketable securities as well as cash itself. Marketable securities are short-term investments that pay a modest return and are very secure. They can be sold almost immediately if the need arises. Thus, they fill the precautionary need for cash but earn a little interest at the same time.

Accounts Receivable

Accounts receivable represent credit sales that have not yet been paid. Under normal conditions, these should be paid in cash within a matter of weeks.

Most companies sell on credit terms of approximately 30 days. Customers often *stretch* those terms by taking somewhat longer to pay. That means it isn't unusual for a company to have 45 days of credit sales in receivables.

THE ALLOWANCE FOR DOUBTFUL ACCOUNTS Receivables are usually stated net of an offsetting account called the *allowance for doubtful accounts.* As the name implies, this offset allows for the fact that most businesses make some credit sales that are never paid. These are usually a small percentage of total sales.

WRITING OFF A RECEIVABLE When a receivable is known to be uncollectible (perhaps because the customer is bankrupt), it should be written off. Writing off a receivable means reducing the balance in accounts receivable by the uncollected amount. The other side of the entry normally reduces the allowance for doubtful accounts, which has been provided regularly each month for that purpose.

OVERSTATED RECEIVABLES

Profit reductions caused by uncollectible receivables are distasteful, so managements sometimes postpone writing off bad debts beyond the time when they should be recognized. This causes the receivables balance to include amounts that will never be collected. Such an account is said to be overstated.

From the CFO

Inventory

Inventory is product held for sale in the normal course of business. In a manufacturing company, inventory can be in one of three forms: *raw materials*, *work-in-process* (abbreviated WIP), and *finished goods*. A retailer normally has only finished-goods inventory.

WORK-IN-PROCESS INVENTORIES The nature of raw materials and finished goods is self-explanatory, but WIP needs a little explanation. As raw materials move through the production process, labour is expended to produce product. We think of that labour as being embodied in the inventory. For example, if in a certain production step a piece of wood costing $10 is worked on for one hour by a worker who makes $15 an hour, we would think of the wood as having a value of $25 when it emerges from that process. Thus, work-in-process inventory contains the cost of raw materials and the cost of an increasing amount of labour as it moves toward becoming finished product.

Besides labour, most accounting systems add the cost of factory overhead (for the building, equipment, heat, electricity, supervision, etc.) to the value of inventory as labour is added.

INVENTORY PROBLEMS Inventory on the balance sheet is assumed to be usable but frequently isn't. A number of things can happen to make inventory worth less than the firm paid for it. Items can be damaged, become spoiled, get stolen (called *shrinkage*), become obsolete, or face a fall in market prices.

Inventory is usually stated at *"the lower of cost and market."*

Balance sheet inventories are generally stated net of an *inventory allowance* to provide for a normal amount of problem material. The inventory allowance is conceptually similar to the allowance for doubtful accounts associated with accounts receivable. This allowance is designed to state inventories at "the lower of cost and market."

WRITING OFF BAD INVENTORY If inventory is discovered to be missing, damaged, or obsolete, the balance sheet inventory account must be reduced to reflect the loss.

OVERSTATED INVENTORY

Managements usually try to avoid reducing recorded profits. Therefore, they're prone to accepting any rationalization to the effect that the inventory is holding its original value. This can lead to an overstatement of the inventory balance.

From the CFO

OVERSTATEMENTS

The overstatement of receivables and inventories can be a significant problem to users of financial statements, which purport to reflect the value of a company. To the extent that assets are overstated, the firm's value is less than it is being held out to be. Overstatements can also mean that the company isn't managed effectively. Both of these possibilities are of significant concern in valuing the firm's securities.

Current Assets

The first three assets on our balance sheet are called current assets. The term "current" means that in the normal course of business, these items can be expected to become cash within one year. More complex businesses have a few other current items, but they are of minor importance compared with these.

Current assets become cash within one year.

Capital as a source of financing is long-term debt or shareholders' equity.

The current concept is important in financial analysis, because it relates to a company's ability to meet its obligations in the short run. All of the money the business receives from normal operations flows in through the current asset accounts. In other words, money that isn't in current assets today may be a long time coming in, whereas money now in current assets can be expected to be realized as cash soon.

A **capital asset** is something that has a useful life of at least a year. Capital assets include *property, plant, and equipment.*

Capital Assets

The word "*capital*" can be a little confusing. It simply implies a long-lived asset, normally financed with capital, that is, long-term debt or shareholders' equity. Capital assets include *property, plant, and equipment* (sometimes called *fixed assets*).

A capital asset is something that has a useful life of at least a year. It's important to understand the basics of capital asset accounting and the associated concept of amortization.

Amortization is the proration of an asset's cost over its service life. Evenly prorated amortization is called *straight-line* amortization.

AMORTIZATION Amortization is an artificial accounting device that spreads the cost of an asset over its estimated useful life regardless of how it is acquired or paid for. If the cost is spread evenly over the life of the asset, we say the amortization is *straight-line.* The idea behind amortization is to match the flow of the asset's cost into the income statement with the delivery of its services over time. This matching principle is an important accounting concept.

According to the **matching principle**, recognition of an asset's cost should match its service life.

AMORTIZATION IS A NONCASH EXPENSE Amortization is a financial "fiction"; it doesn't represent a current flow of money even though it's treated as a cost or an expense. It has nothing to do with how an asset is acquired or paid for. It is the primary example of a *noncash charge*, an item of cost of goods sold or expense in the income statement that doesn't require cash.

Accumulated amortization offsets the original cost of a capital asset on the balance sheet.

FINANCIAL STATEMENT PRESENTATION *Amortization expense* appearing on the income statement reflects the portion of the book value of capital assets scheduled for write-off *in that period*. There is a corresponding account on the balance sheet called *accumulated amortization*, which reflects the *cumulative value* of past amortization on existing capital assets. Accumulated amortization is carried as an offset to the value of a capital asset, so at any time the net book value of the asset is the difference between its original cost and its accumulated amortization. An example should make the idea clear.

Suppose a company buys a truck to use in its business, paying $10,000 in cash at the time of purchase. Assume the truck is expected to last four years. How is the cost of the truck recognized as a cost of doing business?

Someone unfamiliar with accounting might think that the cost would be recognized along with the outflow of money that pays for the equipment—that is, a $10,000 cost in the year of purchase. However, accounting theory says that to properly reflect the workings of the business, we have to match the cost of the equipment with the period over which it gives service.

The company will amortize the $10,000 cost over a useful life of four years. If the proration is straight-line (even) over the life of the asset, the income statement will include a $2,500 item for *amortization expense* in each of the asset's four years of life. The *rate of amortization* is said to be 25% straight-line.

From the CFO

Amortization creates a seemingly odd situation in terms of cash in the company's pocket. In the first year, the firm spent $10,000 but could report only $2,500 as an expense of doing business. In other words, it used up a lot more cash than the income statement indicates. In each of the subsequent three years, it didn't spend anything but still reported $2,500 per year in expense. So in those years the income statement indicates that the company used up more money than it actually did.

During the same four-year period, each year's balance sheet will carry three numbers related to the asset: its gross value, its accumulated amortization, and its net value.

Year/Rate	Income Statement		Balance Sheet		
1 (25%)	Amortization expense	$ 2,500	Gross		$ 10,000
			Accumulated amortization		(2,500)
			Net		$7,500
2 (25%)	Amortization expense	$ 2,500	Gross		$ 10,000
			Accumulated amortization		(5,000)
			Net		$ 5,000
3 (25%)	Amortization expense	$ 2,500	Gross		$ 10,000
			Accumulated amortization		(7,500)
			Net		$ 2,500
4 (25%)	Amortization expense	$ 2,500	Gross		$ 10,000
			Accumulated amortization		(10,000)
			Net		$ –0–

TABLE 2.3
Capital Asset Amortization

It's important to understand the pattern of these numbers over time. The accounts will look like those shown in Table 2.3 at the end of each year. Notice that each year's amortization expense is the same. That's because the example is using straight-line amortization.

Also notice that accumulated amortization grows each year by the amount of amortization expense in that year, but the asset's *gross* value stays the same. The asset's accounting value at any point in time is approximated by the net line, which is known as the item's book value or *net book value*, abbreviated NBV.

NET BOOK VALUE IS NOT CURRENT MARKET VALUE Net book value is not meant to reflect current market value. Current market values for used capital assets may be substantially different than their book (accounting) value. In our example, the truck may be saleable on the used-truck market for an amount that's more or less than its NBV at any time.

THE LIFE ESTIMATE Amortization runs over the estimated useful life of an asset. This estimate is normally based on predicted wear and tear and obsolescence factors. However, it's quite common for things to last beyond their estimated lives. Assets still in use beyond their life estimates are said to be fully amortized. Such an asset's gross value remains on the books entirely offset by accumulated amortization. If it is sold after that time, there is zero cost.

ACCELERATED AMORTIZATION In some cases, an argument is made that certain capital assets are subject to more wear and tear or obsolescence in the early years of their life than in the later years. Amortization can be structured to be greater in the early years to reflect that idea. When the amortization schedule is front loaded like that, it's called accelerated amortization.

If accelerated amortization were being used in our example in Table 2.3, the early years would have larger numbers than the later years. The total amortization expense, however, would still be equal to the $10,000 cost of the asset.[2] That's an important idea. Total amortization can never exceed the cost of the asset.

One common method of accelerated amortization is called the declining balance amortization. In this method, the cost of the asset is amortized over its service life, but annual amortization expense (using a higher amortization rate than for straight-line) is based on the net book value rather than the cost of the asset.

Accelerated amortization recognizes more of an asset's cost in the early years of its life.

Declining balance amortization is a method of accelerated amortization where annual amortization expense (using a higher amortization rate than for straight-line) is based on the net book value of the asset.

---

2 We're assuming that at the end of its life the asset will have a zero salvage value. If a positive salvage value is assumed, we would amortize only the difference between the original cost and that value. Otherwise the procedure would be the same.

GAIN ON DISPOSAL OF CAPITAL ASSETS When a business capital asset is sold, the remaining net book value is deducted from the proceeds on sale to calculate the gain or loss on the disposal on the company's books. This gain or loss is reported on the income statement as an adjustment to operating income. Example 2.1 shows how the gain on the disposal of an amortized capital asset is calculated.

Example 2.1

Nguyen Corporation has just sold a computer that it had been using in its business. The company received $3,000 for the machine. The original cost was $5,000 two years ago, and it has been amortized straight-line at 25% per year.

  What is the gain or loss on the disposal?

■ **Solution:**

Proceeds on disposal		$ 3,000
Net book value		
Cost	$ 5,000	
Accumulated amortization*	2,500	2,500
Gain on disposal		$ 500

*Annual amortization is $5,000 × 25% = $1,250

Total Assets

The things we've talked about so far constitute most of the left side of the balance sheet for a majority of companies. Their sum is simply *total assets*.

Liabilities

Liabilities represent what the company owes to outsiders.

Accounts Payable

Accounts payable arise when firms buy from vendors on credit (called **trade credit**). Payables and receivables are opposite sides of the same coin. When a credit sale is made, the seller records a receivable and the buyer records a payable. In most companies, the bulk of accounts payable arises from the purchase of inventory.

TERMS OF SALE The length of time allowed until payment is due on a credit sale is specified in the **terms of sale**. Common terms involve payment within 30 days and include a discount for prompt payment. Terms of two 10, net 30, written 2/10, n.30, mean that a 2% discount is allowed if payment is received within 10 days or the full amount is due in 30 days. Trade credit is generally free in that no interest is charged if the full amount is paid within the allowed time.

  Vendors may become upset if their bills aren't paid in the time specified under the terms of sale. Delaying payment of trade payables is called **stretching payables** or *leaning on the trade*. If a customer abuses a vendor's terms, the credit privilege is likely to be revoked, and the seller will subsequently demand cash in advance before shipping goods.

UNDERSTATED PAYABLES

  When we discussed accounts receivable and inventory, we were concerned about overstatements—conditions in which the balance sheet reports assets the company can't use or doesn't have. On the liabilities side, we're concerned about understatements— conditions in which the firm has liabilities that are not reflected on its balance sheet. For example, it's possible to receive goods from a vendor, use them, and simply not recognize the transaction financially. Eventually, the vendor will demand payment and the issue will be raised, but that may take quite a while.

Vendors extend **trade credit** when they deliver product or services without demanding immediate payment.

Terms of sale specify when payment is expected for sales made on trade credit.

Stretching payables (also called *leaning on the trade*) is delaying payment of trade payables.

From the CFO

Accruals

Accruals are poorly understood by most nonfinancial business people. They are an accounting device used to recognize expenses and liabilities associated with transactions that are not entirely complete.

Accruals represent incomplete transactions.

A PAYROLL ACCRUAL The best way to understand accruals is to consider a simple example involving payroll. Suppose a company pays its employees every Friday afternoon for work through that day. Then suppose the last day of a particular month falls on a Wednesday, and the books are closed as of that afternoon. Figure 2.1 shows this situation graphically.

As of the close of business on Wednesday, the financial statements have to include two things that aren't reflected by paper transactions. These arise from the fact that employees have worked for three days (Monday, Tuesday, and Wednesday) that are in the first month, but won't be paid for those days until Friday, which is in the second month.

The first issue is that, as of the closing date, the firm owes its employees for those days, and the debt (liability) must be reflected on the balance sheet. It's important to realize that the liability will be paid in just two days on the next payday.

The second issue is that the wages were earned in the month just closing and should be reflected in that month's costs and expenses.

OTHER ACCRUALS There are accruals for any number of things. For example, suppose a company is billed in arrears for property tax at the end of a government fiscal year in December. If the firm closes its books at the end of June, it owes the local government for six months of property tax even though it has received no bill and won't until December. A property tax accrual properly reflects this expense in the meantime.

Current Liabilities

Current liabilities are defined as items requiring payment within one year; hence, payables and accruals are classified as current. Other current liabilities include notes payable, short-term loans, and any long-term debt that's within a year of its due date.

Current liabilities require cash within one year.

WORKING CAPITAL Current assets are collectively referred to as *gross working capital*, while the difference between current assets and current liabilities is known as **net working capital**, or just **working capital**.

Conceptually, net working capital represents the amount of money a firm needs to carry on its routine day-to-day activities. Formally,

Net working capital (or just **working capital**) represents the money required to support *day-to-day* activities.

$$\text{Net working capital} = \text{Current assets} - \text{Current liabilities}$$

In practice, people frequently omit the word "net."

Working capital is an important idea to which we'll devote all of Chapters 4 and 5.

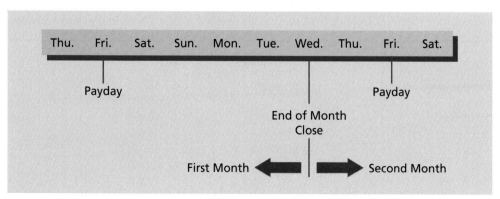

FIGURE 2.1
A Payroll Accrual

Long-Term Debt

Typically, the most significant non-current liability is long-term debt. It is common practice to refer to it simply as *debt*, especially if there isn't much short-term debt. Long-term debt usually consists of bonds and other long-term loans.

LEVERAGE A business that is financed with debt is said to be *leveraged*. The word implies that when things are going well, using borrowed money can enhance the return on an entrepreneur's own investment. It works like this.

Suppose a business is started with a total investment of $100,000 and earns an after-tax profit of $15,000 in the first year. First, imagine that the invested money is entirely from the entrepreneur's own pocket. The return on his or her invested equity is 15% ($15,000/$100,000).

Now suppose the entrepreneur had borrowed half the money, $50,000, at an interest rate that nets to 10% after tax. In that case, profit would be reduced to $10,000 by the $5,000 interest paid on the loan (10% of $50,000), but the entrepreneur's investment would be only half as much, $50,000. Hence, the return on his or her investment would be 20% ($10,000/$50,000). Borrowing money would have *levered* the return up from 15% to 20%. The figures are shown in the table below.

In general, a business is able to produce a higher return to the owner's invested funds by using borrowed money if the return on the total amount of invested money exceeds the interest rate being paid on the loan. Otherwise, the effect is in the opposite direction and the return *is worse* with borrowed money. We will discuss this topic further in Chapters 3 and 16.

FIXED FINANCIAL CHARGES A major concern about borrowed money is the interest charge. It's important to keep in mind that interest charges are *fixed*. That means they must be paid regardless of how the business is doing. You can't go to the bank and say, "Sales are down a little this month, so do you mind if I skip the interest payment?" That can be a real problem in tough times. Many businesses have gone bankrupt because of fixed financial obligations.

Shareholders' Equity

Shareholders' equity represents funds supplied to businesses by their shareholders (owners). These funds are in two forms: direct investment and retained earnings. Direct investment occurs when shares are sold to investors. Retained earnings occur when profits are kept in the business rather than being paid out to the shareholders.

The Representation of Direct Investment by the Shareholders

Direct equity investments are reflected in a shareholders' equity account, entitled *common shares*, representing the money paid for the shares.

Retained Earnings

A company's profit belongs to its shareholders, who can either receive it in the form of *dividends* or leave it in the business. Earnings paid out are said to be *distributed*; those kept in the business are called *retained earnings*. The balance sheet will show retained earnings in a shareholders' equity account separate from the directly invested money shown in the share accounts.

	All Equity	Leveraged
Earnings before interest	$ 15,000	$ 15,000
Interest	–	(5,000)
Net income	$ 15,000	$ 10,000
Debt	–	$ 50,000
Equity	100,000	50,000
Total	$ 100,000	$ 100,000
Return	15%	20%

Long-term debt usually consists of bonds and other long-term loans with maturities longer than one year into the future.

A business financed with *debt* is said to be *leveraged*.

Equity financing is provided by a business's shareholders (owners).

Money retained or "reinvested" in a business is just as much the contribution of its shareholders as directly invested money. That's because they could have taken it out and used it elsewhere if they had wanted to do so.

The retained earnings account is subject to a common misconception. Probably because of the words in the name, people sometimes get the idea that retained earnings represent a reserve of cash on which the firm can draw in times of need. That isn't so. Just like any other invested funds, retained earnings are generally spent on assets shortly after they become available.

The retained earnings account shows all earnings ever retained by the company just as the *share* accounts show all money ever invested directly by shareholders. Neither is generally available as cash at any point in time, because both tend to have been spent on assets to build the business.

Example: Shareholders' Equity Accounts

We'll summarize these ideas with a brief illustration. Suppose a firm is started with the sale of 20,000 common shares at $8 per share and subsequently earns $70,000, of which $15,000 is paid in dividends. The shareholders' equity accounts will then be as follows.

Common shares ($8 × 20,000)	$ 160,000
Retained earnings ($70,000 – $15,000)	55,000
Total shareholders' equity	$ 215,000

Changes in Shareholders' Equity Accounts over the Accounting Period

It is important to understand the how the shareholders' equity accounts may change over the accounting period. If new common shares are issued, the formulation for common share amounts would be

$$\text{Beginning common shares} + \text{New shares} = \text{Ending common shares}$$

If a portion of net income is paid to the shareholders as dividends, the formulation for retained earnings would be

$$\text{Beginning retained earnings} + \text{Net income} - \text{Dividends} = \text{Ending retained earnings}$$

Beginning balance sheet figures, including shareholders' equity accounts, are those of the balance sheet dated at the end of the prior accounting period. For example, the beginning balance sheet for 2008 is the ending balance sheet for 2007. Therefore, 2008's beginning shareholders' equity accounts are 2007's ending shareholders' equity accounts.

Preferred Shares

Preferred shares are securities issued by some firms that are effectively a cross between debt and common shares. They're thought of as a hybrid, because they have some of the characteristics of each of the more traditional securities. Legally, however, they are classified as shareholders' equity and are included in that section of the balance sheet above the common share accounts. Total shareholders' equity then is the sum of common shares, preferred shares, and retained earnings.

Total Capital

The sum of long-term debt and shareholders' equity is sometimes called *total capital*. These funds are generally used to support long-term assets.

Total Liabilities and Shareholders' Equity

The sum of the right side of the balance sheet reflects where all of the company's funds have come from and the obligations it has to creditors and shareholders as a result of those advances. Total liabilities and shareholders' equity must always equal total assets.

THE STATEMENT OF CASH FLOWS

We've made the point that income as reported in the income statement does not equal cash in the pocket of the business or its owner. Accounting income includes things like amortization, which is one of several accounting devices designed to make the income statement a representation of the current financial results of the enterprise. Businesses, however, are run with cold, hard cash on a day-to-day basis. Therefore, another statement is needed to give users information detailing the actual movement of cash in and out of the company. That document is the **statement of cash flows**. It shows a reader where the firm's money came from and what it was spent on during the period covered. Statements of cash flows report inflows and outflows of money. Inflows are usually represented by positive numbers, while outflows are negative; negative numbers are shown in parentheses.

It takes two consecutive balance sheets and an income statement to build a statement of cash flows for an accounting period. The income statement is from the period and the balance sheets are as of its beginning and end. (A beginning balance sheet is the ending balance sheet of the previous period.) For example, consider the three financial statement formats in Figures 2.2 and 2.3.

The statement of cash flows analyzes where money has come from and gone to by doing two things. First, it takes net income for the period from the income statement and adjusts it for some of the items that make it different from the everyday concept of income as cash in one's pocket. Second, it takes the two consecutive balance sheets and analyzes the *changes* in everything the company has in assets, liabilities, and shareholders' equity to determine how those changes have affected the cash balance.

The "come from" and "gone to" are commonly called *inflows* and *outflows of cash*, respectively. A business's net income, adjusted for noncash items, is an *inflow* of cash. An increase in

The **statement of cash flows** details the actual movement of cash in and out of the company during the period covered. It is constructed from the income statement and two consecutive balance sheets. The statement of cash flows presents *operating*, *investing*, and *financing* activities separately.

FIGURE 2.2
Belfry Company Balance Sheet and Income Statement

Belfry Company				**Belfry Company**	
Balance Sheet				Income Statement	
As of 31/12/X2				For the period ended	
	31/12/X1	31/12/X2		31/12/X2	
ASSETS				Sales	$10,000
Cash	$1,000	$1,400		COGS	6,000
Accounts receivable	3,000	2,900		Gross margin	$ 4,000
Inventory	2,000	3,200		Expenses	$ 1,600
CURRENT ASSETS	$6,000	$7,500		Amortization	500
Capital assets				EBIT	$ 1,900
Gross	$4,000	$ 6,000		Interest	400
Accumulated amortization	(1,000)	(1,500)		EBT	$ 1,500
Net	$3,000	$ 4,500		Tax	500
				Net income	$ 1,000
TOTAL ASSETS	$9,000	$12,000			
LIABILITIES AND SHAREHOLDERS' EQUITY					
Accounts payable	$1,500	$2,100			
Accruals	500	400			
CURRENT LIABILITIES	$2,000	$2,500			
Long-term debt	$5,000	$6,200			
Shareholders' Equity	$2,000	$3,300*			
TOTAL LIABILITIES AND SHAREHOLDERS' EQUITY	$9,000	$12,000			

*Assume that the company sold shares for $800 during the year and paid a $500 dividend.

Belfry Company
Statement of Cash Flows
For the period ending 31/12/X2

CASH FROM OPERATING ACTIVITIES
Net income	$1,000
Amortization	500
Net changes in current accounts	(600)
Cash from operating activities	$ 900

CASH FROM INVESTING ACTIVITIES
Purchase of capital assets	($2,000)

CASH FROM FINANCING ACTIVITIES
Increase in long-term debt	$1,200
Sale of shares	800
Dividend paid	(500)
Cash from financing activities	$1,500

NET CASH FLOW	$ 400
Beginning cash balance	$1,000
Net cash flow	400
Ending cash balance	$1,400

FIGURE 2.3
Belfry Company
Statement of Cash
Flows

assets is an *outflow* of cash. When assets are reduced, the reduction is an *inflow* of cash. An increase in liabilities results in an *inflow* of cash. A liability reduction is an *outflow* of cash. Adding inflows and outflows together we get net cash flow. The statement goes on to demonstrate that the beginning balance in the bank plus the net cash flow equals the ending balance in the bank.

Constructing the Statement of Cash Flows

As we have said, constructing a business's statement of cash flows requires balance sheets at the beginning and end of the period under consideration and an income statement for that period.

Cash Flow Rules

All we need to do in order to analyze cash is to remember six simple rules that can be applied to any business's financial statements. The rules are that cash income and changes in balance sheet accounts result in inflows and outflows of cash:

1. Cash income = Inflow
2. Cash loss = Outflow
3. Asset increase = Outflow
4. Asset decrease = Inflow
5. Liability or shareholders' equity increase = Inflow
6. Liability or shareholders' equity decrease = Outflow

Refer to the financial statements for Belfry Company in Figures 2.2 and 2.3.

Standard Presentation

A business's statement of cash flows is organized to show cash flows from three different kinds of activities: operating, investing, and financing.

Operating activities involve the income statement and balance sheet current accounts.

Investing activities typically include purchasing *capital assets*.

Financing activities deal with the *capital* accounts: *long-term debt* and *shareholders' equity*.

Operating activities are the things a company does on a day-to-day basis to conduct its business. Typically they include buying inventory, producing and selling product, paying expenses and taxes, and collecting on credit sales. The focus of these activities is the production of net income.

Investing activities occur when the firm buys (invests in) or sells things such as equipment that enable it to do business. Investing activities also include long-term purchases and sales of financial assets.[3]

Financing activities occur when the company borrows money, pays off loans, sells shares, or pays dividends. They involve raising money and servicing the obligations that come along with it.

We'll develop the statement of cash flows for Belfry one activity at a time.

Operating Activities

We start the cash flow statement with the net income from the income statement.

However, net income includes items that don't represent cash flows in the current period. Our next step is therefore to adjust those out. The result may be called *cash income*.

In Belfry's case, the only adjustment[4] necessary to calculate cash income is to add back amortization, which was subtracted in the calculation of net income.

Net income	$ 1,000
Amortization	500
Cash income	$ 1,500

Next we recognize that the money from operating transactions runs through the current balance sheet accounts. Therefore changes in those accounts are part of operating cash flow. We analyze the balances *other than cash* and classify the changes as inflows or outflows of cash according to the cash flow rules. The cash account is handled separately later.

In Belfry's case, accounts receivable decreased from $3,000 to $2,900, providing a $100 inflow of cash because, according to the fourth rule, an asset decrease is an *inflow*. Similarly, inventory increased from $2,000 to $3,200 for an outflow of $1,200 according to the third rule.

Apply the fifth and sixth rules to the changes in accounts payable and accruals to get the following inflows and outflows.

Account	**Inflow/(Outflow)**
Receivables	$ 100
Inventory	(1,200)
Payables	600
Accruals	(100)
	$ (600)

The sum of the current account changes and cash income is cash from operating activities. The typical presentation is illustrated for Belfry as follows.

---

3 The term "invest" generally means buying something that is expected to return more than its cost in the future. When individuals say "invest" they usually mean buying a financial asset. However, we sometimes use the term with physical things (investing in a house) or even intangibles (investing in an education). When we talk about investment by companies, we generally mean buying the plant and equipment used in doing business, such as machinery, vehicles, and real estate.

4 Other common adjustments include deferred income taxes, restructuring charges, foreign exchange gains or losses, and gains and losses on the sale of long-term assets. This approach to determining cash income is called the *indirect method*. An alternative (and more time-consuming) approach is called the *direct method*, in which every item on the income statement is adjusted from accrual accounting to cash accounting (for example, all sales are adjusted to cash sales).

Net income	$ 1,000
Amortization expense	500
Net changes in current accounts	(600)
Cash from operating activities	$ 900

Investing Activities

Cash from investing activities is simple in this example. The only entry comes from an increase in Belfry's capital assets of $2,000. This is reflected by the increase in gross capital assets from $4,000 to $6,000, which is an *outflow* of cash according to the third rule.

Notice that we use the gross capital assets account for this calculation rather than the net. That's because the net figure includes a reduction for accumulated amortization, the change in which is the other side of the entry that put amortization on the income statement. That amortization is already included in the cash flow statement in the operating section, and we don't want to repeat it here.

Hence, cash from investing activities is

Purchase of capital assets ($2,000)

Financing Activities

There are three financing activities in this example. The first is an increase in long-term debt, an *inflow* according to the fifth rule. The company appears to have taken out another loan. The second is a sale of shares, and the third a dividend payment. The sale of shares results in an increase in shareholders' equity, and is an *inflow* according to the fifth rule. The dividend payment reduces shareholders' equity and is therefore an *outflow* according to the sixth rule.

Cash from financing activities is calculated as follows.

Increase in long-term debt	$ 1,200
Sale of shares	800
Dividend paid	(500)
Cash from financing activities	$ 1,500

The Shareholders' Equity and Cash Accounts

The change in shareholders' equity is the sum of net income and the sale of new shares less the dividend paid. These are as follows for Belfry.

Net income	$ 1,000
Sale of shares	800
Dividend paid	(500)
Total change in shareholders' equity	$ 1,300

The sale of shares and the dividend paid are included under financing activities, while the addition of net income to shareholders' equity shows up under operating activities.

The cash flow total of the three activities we've presented so far must equal the change in the cash account. That's shown as a reconciliation at the end of the statement.

In Belfry's case the sum of operating, investing, and financing activities is a positive $400, so we have the following reconciliation.

Beginning cash balance	$ 1,000
Net cash flow	400
Ending cash balance	$ 1,400

To summarize, the statement of cash flows takes information from the income statement and balance sheets and displays it in a manner that highlights the movement of cash. No new information is created; what is already there is simply rearranged in a way that's more usable in the day-to-day running of the business.

Interpreting the Statement of Cash Flows

The statement of cash flows allows financial managers and analysts to analyze the firm's cash flow. For example, management can determine whether it has sufficient cash resources to pay cash dividends to its shareholders, buy new equipment, or make new investments. Bankers and other creditors can judge the firm's ability to generate sufficient cash inflows to meet its liabilities.

Increases in accounts receivable and inventory may signal credit or inventory problems. Are such increases balanced by increases in accounts payable and short-term bank loans? Normally, temporary or seasonal increases in current assets are financed from these sources.

Are increases in long-term assets balanced by additional long-term debt, share issues, or retained earnings? Normally, such sources of financing are used to support growth in this area.

We shall return to the importance of maintaining a balance between short-term assets and liabilities and long-term assets and long-term financing when we discuss the management of working capital in Chapter 4.

Conclusions

A firm that manages cash poorly can *go out of business* while making an *accounting profit*.

In this case, examination of the statement of cash flows leads to some concern about the Belfry Company. The firm is quite profitable, earning 10% on sales, but still had to borrow substantially during the year. Clearly the capital asset purchase had something to do with the additional funds required. One must ask whether that expenditure was entirely necessary. Another concern is the sudden increase in inventory. Does it mean that some of the existing inventory isn't good? If so, this could portend a big loss.

You should always keep in mind the fact that it's cash that really counts in business, not net income. To drive that point home, let's ask another question about Belfry. Notice that during the year it had to borrow an additional $1,200 from the bank. Would a bank have been likely to extend that additional credit?

From the CFO

In fact, a bank might have been reluctant to advance more money to this company. Notice that the firm's capital (long-term debt plus shareholders' equity) is in the neighbourhood of 70% debt. We'll see later that such a high proportion of debt is beyond the comfort level of most lenders. The bank could have refused further advances, putting the company in a cash bind. If that had caused Belfry to fail to make its payroll, the company could have been out of business overnight.

Yet Belfry is earning great profits in terms of net income, 10% of sales. Take the lesson to heart: A firm can go broke profitably. Small businesses do it all the time, and it happens to big companies with surprising frequency.

Graphic Portrayal

Let's fix these ideas in mind by looking at a graphic representation of cash flows in a business.

Figure 2.4 shows how cash flows in and out of a company. Notice that *operating activities* have to do with the normal course of business and the current accounts of the balance sheet.

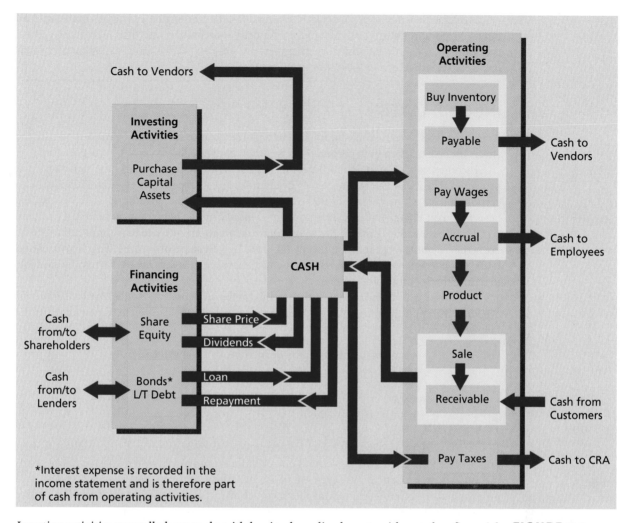

Investing activities generally have to do with buying long-lived assets, either real or financial. *Financing activities* are concerned with debt and shareholders' equity.

FIGURE 2.4
Business Cash Flows

Free Cash Flows

The concept of free cash flow (FCF) has become more prominent in financial analysis. Free cash flow is equal to

> Cash flow from operating activities
> Minus: Capital expenditures
> Minus: Dividends

    Free cash flow refers to whether a firm generates cash beyond its own needs. Under normal conditions, most firms generate positive cash flows from operating activities, but some of those funds have to be used to replace worn-out capital assets, or to satisfy shareholder dividend commitments or expectations. Free cash flow is defined as net cash flow less such requirements.

Cash generated beyond reinvestment and dividend needs is **free cash flow**.

    As we will see in Chapter 17, free cash flow is an important consideration for a corporation considering a share repurchase or a special dividend.

    Free cash flow is also important in *merger analysis* where one company acquires another. The acquiring firm attempts to establish a price for the other company based on cash flows. In addition it needs to know whether its new business will need cash infusions after the acquisition or will generate funds that can be used elsewhere.

Free cash flow has been particularly prominent in the context of *leveraged buyouts*, where a public corporation borrows to buy out its minority shareholders and then takes itself private. Free cash flow helps to determine whether there are sufficient excess funds to pay back the loans involved. We will return to these topics in Chapter 19.

INCOME TAXES

As income taxes have a significant impact on financial decisions, we must be concerned with the effects of these taxes on both corporations and those individuals who invest in corporations.

Income taxes are paid by both people and corporations according to the same basic tax principles. The idea of an **income tax** is straightforward: a taxpayer, whether an individual or a corporation, pays a percentage of net income in a year to the taxing authority. In each case, the tax is levied on a base of *taxable income*, which is *income subject to tax*, less certain *tax deductions*.

Income tax owing is based on *income, tax deductions*, the *tax rates*, and available *tax credits*.

The gross tax due is then calculated using a *tax rate schedule*. The most important income tax is the *federal tax*, because it typically takes the biggest share of income. The provinces and territories also impose income taxes, but their rates are much lower. *Tax credits* may be available to reduce the tax otherwise payable.

The four major components of the tax bill then are *income* or *revenue, tax deductions for expenses*, the applicable *tax rates*, and available *tax credits*. We can relate these factors in the following formulas:

$$\text{(2.1)} \qquad \text{Total income} - \text{Tax deductions} = \text{Taxable income}$$
$$\text{Taxable income} \times \text{Tax rates} = \text{Total tax}$$
$$\text{Total tax} - \text{Tax credits} = \text{Net tax payable}$$

Tax Rates

Tax rates are combined rates levied by the federal and provincial governments on taxable income to determine tax payable. A **progressive tax system** is characterized by higher tax rates on incrementally higher taxable income.

In Canada, at least two sets of **tax rates** are applied to taxable income (income less deductions)—one for federal income tax, and one or more for provincial or territorial taxes, depending on where in Canada we earn our income. The Canadian personal tax system is a **progressive tax system**—higher taxable incomes attract higher rates. As our taxable income grows, we pay more income tax, because our tax base *and* our tax rate increases.

Tax Brackets

Tax rates in progressive systems don't increase smoothly as taxable income goes up. Rather, they remain constant over some range of taxable income and then jump abruptly to a higher level for another range. Ranges of taxable income through which the tax rate is constant are called **tax brackets**.

A **tax bracket** is a range of taxable income in which the tax rate is constant.

In Table 2.4, we illustrate the federal and provincial tax brackets and rates for individuals. This representation of the tax structure is called a *tax table* or a *tax schedule*.

We see that there were four federal *tax brackets* for individuals in 2007. (We have used the 2007 federal tax brackets and tax rates, combined with representative (Ontario) provincial tax

TABLE 2.4
Combined Personal Tax Brackets and Tax Rates, 2007

	First Bracket	Second Bracket	Third Bracket	Fourth Bracket
Taxable income	$0 – $37,178	$37,179 – $74,357	$74,358 – $120,887	$120,888 and over
Federal rates	15.50%	22.00%	26.00%	29.00%
Provincial rates	6.05%	9.15%	11.16%	11.16%
Combined (rounded)	22%	31%	37%	40%

rates, merely for illustration. Tax brackets and tax rates vary among the provinces. Federal and provincial tax brackets are adjusted each year to reflect inflation).

For *each* bracket, both federal and provincial tax rates are applied to any taxable income that we have *in that bracket*. In 2007, the actual federal personal tax system had four brackets and the highest federal tax rate was 29%.

If we earned $30,000 (in the first bracket), we owed about 22% of taxable income in *combined* federal and provincial tax (before any tax credits).

Marginal and Average Tax Rates

Two tax rate concepts are applicable to every taxpayer. The **marginal tax rate** is the rate that will be paid on the *next* dollar of taxable income the person earns. The **average tax rate** is the percentage of total taxable income the person pays in taxes; it is also called the *total effective tax rate (TETR)*.

$$(2.2) \qquad \text{Average tax rate} = \frac{\text{Tax liability}}{\text{Taxable income}}$$

Notice that the marginal rate is almost always the bracket rate. Only at the very top of a bracket is it the rate of the next bracket. The marginal rate is most relevant for investment decisions. It is most useful when considering such questions as, "How much tax do we have to pay on any *additional* taxable income, such as interest income or taxable capital gains?"

If we earned $80,000 and finished up in the third bracket, we would have a *marginal tax rate* of 37%. Our marginal rate is the rate of tax we would pay on our *next* dollar of taxable income. However, our tax bill is determined by our (weighted) *average* tax rate for *all* of our taxable income. We will return to this concept in our discussion of corporate taxes on page 42.

Personal Income Taxes on Investment Income

The federal and provincial governments levy tax on various types of personal taxable income, including employment income, earnings before tax from self-employment, and investment income, whether it is in the form of *interest* from bonds, *dividends* on shares, or *capital gains* from the sale of securities. However, each type of investment income is taxed differently. Interest income is taxed at the highest rate for our level of taxable income. On the other hand, governments levy tax on only 50% of capital gains.

Dividends received from Canadian corporations also receive beneficial tax treatment. Individual investors who receive a dividend are entitled to a **dividend tax credit**, which reduces their effective tax rates on such income. Accordingly, they are left with more *after-tax income* from a dividend than from interest.

Table 2.5 shows how $1,000 for each type of income would be taxed for higher-income individuals. Both dividends (from Canadian companies) and capital gains (on the sale of shares or bonds) receive significant tax breaks, whereas interest is taxed at full marginal rates.

Investors need to consider the different tax treatments (as well as their investment objectives) in making investment decisions. It is *after-tax*, not before-tax, income that counts.[5] Corporations allow for these tax treatments when considering financing methods and distributions to their investors. In Chapter 17, we will return to these concepts when we discuss corporate dividend policy.

We see from Table 2.5 that there was a large difference, $138 ($766 – $628), between the after-tax return from the interest and that from the dividend. This discrepancy happens because the dividend tax credit substantially reduces the tax on the dividend. Because of this tax advantage, companies usually pay lower dividends than the going interest rates on, say, corporate bonds.

The after-tax return for the capital gain was greater than that for the interest by $186 ($814 – $628). This advantage happens because only 50% of the capital gain is taxed.

For the most current *personal* tax rates by province and territory, go to the Canada Revenue Agency at www.cra.gc.ca. Search for "tax rates" or to the KPMG site at http://www.kpmg.ca/en/services/tax/taxrates.html.

The **marginal tax rate** is the rate applied to the *next* dollar of taxable income. The **average tax rate** is applied to *total* taxable income.

For some of the implications of personal taxes on investment strategies, go to the Globe Investor site at http://www.globeinvestor.com/resources/tax.

Dividend tax credits reduce the effective tax rates on dividends received by individual investors.

A **capital gain** arises when an asset that was held for investment is sold for more than what was paid for it.

---

5 When investments are *sheltered* in a Registered Retirement Savings Plan (RRSP) or other registered investment, no return, whether it is interest, dividend, or capital gain, is taxed until withdrawn from the plan.

Capital Gains and Losses

What is a capital gain? A **capital gain** arises when an asset that was held for investment is sold for more than what was paid for it. These assets could be shares, bonds, mutual funds, vacation property, art, antiques, collections, or other types of assets. The most important feature of capital gains for tax purposes is that, at present, only *50%* of a capital gain is subject to tax.

The tax owed on a capital gain from a personal investment can be calculated as follows:

1 Proceeds on sale of the asset $
2 Less the cost of the asset $
3 Less the expenses to sell the asset $_____
4 Equals the capital gain $
5 Less the exempt portion – 50% $_____
6 Equals the taxable capital gain $

Of course, we might also have a capital *loss* if the asset is sold for less than was paid for it. If so, we can offset the allowable capital loss (50% of the actual capital loss) against taxable capital gains, calculated as above, in the same year.

Example

During the last tax year, Helen Zhou sold an investment property for $80,000 that she had purchased three years earlier for $53,000. She also sold some Nortel shares for $4,000 for which she had paid $12,000 two years before. What is her taxable capital gain?

Solution

Gain on investment property	$ 27,000
Loss on shares	(8,000)
Net capital gain	$ 19,000
Taxable capital gain (50%)	$ 9,500

Corporate Taxes

A corporation is a taxpayer separate from its shareholders.

Income taxes on corporations in Canada are in principle similar to taxes on individuals. In fact, a corporation is considered to be a taxpayer separate from its shareholders and is liable for Canadian *corporate taxes* if it was incorporated in Canada, is managed from Canada, or operates in Canada.

Income taxes on corporate profits can significantly reduce a corporation's earnings and cash flow. We need some understanding of how corporations are taxed in Canada to be able to analyze the results of financial decisions.

A corporation is subject to both federal and provincial income taxes.

TABLE 2.5
Taxes on Interest, Dividend, and Capital Gains Income

	Interest	Dividend	Capital Gains[e]
Income received	$ 1,000	$ 1,000	$ 1,000
Net federal tax payable	260[a]	158[c]	130
Net provincial tax payable	112[b]	76[d]	56
Total taxes payable	$ 372	$ 234	$ 186
Effective tax rate (rounded)	37%	23%	19%
After-tax return	$ 628	$ 766	$ 814

We have rounded all dollar amounts to the nearest dollar.

[a] For the 2007 tax year, the federal tax rate on taxable income in the third tax bracket (between $74,358 and $120,887) was 26%. This taxable income range and rate was used in the example.
[b] In 2007, provincial/territorial rates for taxpayers in this range of taxable income were a relatively low 11.16% in Ontario. We have used this rate for this illustration.
[c] When calculating tax owing on a dividend from a Canadian corporation, a *dividend tax credit* is allowed to compensate for the corporation tax already paid. The dividend tax credit reduces the effective amount of tax on the dividend.
[d] As the rates for provincial dividend tax credits are set by reference to provincial *tax rates*, we have used the dividend tax credit for Ontario in 2007.
[e] Only 50% of a capital gain is taxable, so 50% of the capital gain is excluded from income.

Each corporation in Canada is subject to both federal and provincial taxes. However a system of federal tax credits for provincial taxes paid minimizes the effect of dual taxation at the corporate level.

How Much Tax Will a Corporation Pay?

We can answer this question by again looking at three major components of the tax bill: *income*, tax *deductions*, and the *tax rates*. (Corporations may also be eligible for investment or other *tax credits*. We will introduce this feature in Chapter 13.)

INCOME Just like an individual, a corporation is subject to tax on its net income (after expense deductions) from

- operating its business(es)
- investing in debt securities (interest income)
- selling its investments in shares or land (50% of the capital gain)

However, when a building, machinery, or equipment is sold, the transaction is often handled differently on the financial books of the corporation and on the tax returns. On the financial books, the remaining *net book value* rather than the original cost is deducted from the proceeds on sale to calculate the gain or loss on disposal. This item is reported on the income statement as an adjustment to operating expenses. Example 2.1 on page 30 shows how the gain or loss on the disposal of an amortized capital asset is calculated.

On the tax returns, the original cost is deducted from the proceeds on sale to determine the capital gain, if any. The taxable capital gain is 50% of this gain (see Example 2.2 on page 44). The tax rules do not allow a business to deduct a *capital loss* on assets subject to tax amortization.

Another difference between corporation and personal tax involves dividend income. Unlike individuals, corporations are *exempt* from tax on dividend income from other taxable Canadian corporations, to provide relief from double taxation of that income.

DEDUCTIONS Business tax deductions provide tax savings, and include cost of goods sold and operating expenses, interest paid on debt (but *not* dividends paid from shareholders' equity), and *capital cost allowance*, but *not* amortization.

> **Tax deductions** are business expenses that provide tax savings.

TAX AMORTIZATION AND TAX BOOKS The Canadian government and Canada Revenue Agency (CRA) provide many incentives to business through the tax system. One of the most prominent, tax amortization involves *capital cost allowance (CCA)*, which provides a tax-deductible expense for amortization (depreciation). CCA rules generally prescribe the use of declining balance (accelerated) amortization. We will discuss CCA in more detail in Chapter 13.

> **Tax amortization** involves capital cost allowance (CCA), which provides a tax-deductible expense for amortization.

Higher amortization in a given year results in a larger deduction, lower taxable income, and lower tax in that year. That means CCA based on accelerated amortization reduces taxes early in the life of an asset. The savings are given back later in the asset's life when CCA is lower and taxes are higher, but the net effect is to defer taxes when accelerated amortization (declining balance) CCA is used.

> ### From the CFO
>
> **Tax books** refer to the financial records and statements generated by using the tax rules.
>
> **Financial books** refer to the financial records and statements generated by using the accounting rules.

Unfortunately, the lower recorded net income in early years caused by accelerated amortization isn't something management likes to see. It makes the company look less successful in the short run than it would appear if straight-line amortization were used. To get around this conflict, the government allows businesses to use different amortization schedules for tax purposes and for financial reporting purposes. The term **tax books** *is used to mean financial records and statements generated by using the tax rules, and the term* **financial books** *or just "books" is used to mean the regular statements that we have talked about in this chapter. The difference between the two methods can result in accounts called future income taxes on the financial books.*

LOSS CARRYOVERS Both business losses and capital losses may be available as deductions. The tax system allows corporations with a business loss or net capital loss (on shares, land, etc.) in a year to apply these losses to prior years (a *tax loss carryback*) or future years (a *tax loss carryforward*) to recover or reduce taxes. Business losses may be carried back 3 years or forward 20 years. In any particular tax year then, a corporation may be able to deduct a prior-year's loss.

TAX RATES Tax is calculated by applying the appropriate corporate tax rates to taxable income. Table 2.6 illustrates a combined federal and provincial (Ontario) tax rate structure in 2007 for three classes of corporation: small business, manufacturing, and general.[6]

The **Canadian controlled private corporation (CCPC)** is a relatively small, closely held private corporation with fewer than 100 employees and a small market share. In Ontario in 2007, it was subject to tax under two different tax brackets. It was allowed relatively low federal and provincial rates of tax on the first $400,000 of its taxable income. Its combined rate of tax in our illustration was about 19%. Its tax rate on the taxable income *above* $400,000 would be about 23%.

EXAMPLE 2.2

Mustafa Corporation has just sold some vacant land that it had not been using. The company received $200,000 for the property. The original cost was $150,000 two years ago. The corporation tax rate is 35%.

1. What is the capital gain on sale?

Proceeds on sale	$ 200,000
Cost	150,000
Capital gain	$ 50,000

2. What is the taxable capital gain?

Capital gain	$ 50,000
Taxable capital gain (50%)	25,000

3. What is the tax payable?

Taxable capital gain	$ 25,000
Tax: 35% of $25,000 =	8,750

4. What is the cash flow after tax on the sale?

Proceeds on sale	$ 200,000
Tax	8,750
Cash flow after tax	$ 191,250

TABLE 2.6 Combined Corporate Tax Rates on Active Business Income, 2007*

	Private Company (CCPC)		Manufacturing or Processing Company	General Company
Taxable income	$0–$400,000	$400,000 +	All	All
Total federal tax	13.1%	17.12%	22.1%	22.1%
Total provincial tax	5.50%	5.50%	12.0%	14.0%
Total tax	18.6%	22.62%	34.1%	36.1%
Rounded	19%	23%	34%	36%

*Source: KPMG Canada, Combined Federal and Provincial Tax Rates for Income Earned by a Canadian-Controlled Private Corporation, Effective January 1, 2007. http://www.kpmg.ca. Reprinted with permission.

[6] In 2007, there were 11 sets of brackets and rates (federal and provincial), at least two of which would apply to every corporation, depending on where it operates. In addition, federal and provincial tax rates are continually changing, so that the representative rates used here are for illustration only.

A CCPC with a taxable income of $500,000 would be subject to tax as follows:

Taxable Income			Tax
On first	$ 400,000	@19%	$ 76,000
On remaining	$ 100,000	@23%	$ 23,000
Totals	$ 500,000		$ 99,000

The *average* tax rate $= \dfrac{\$99,000}{\$500,000} = 19.8\%$

A *manufacturing or processing* business (but *not* a CCPC) would have paid about 34% in taxes in 2007. Other (*general*) businesses would have paid about 36%. Thus, the tax rates were designed to provide some incentives to small business (the CCPC) and to manufacturing and processing businesses. Examples 2.3, 2.4, and 2.5 illustrate these situations.

EXAMPLE 2.3

Calculate the tax liability for a corporation (CCPC) making EBT of $280,000.

■ **Solution:** Applying the corporate tax table results in the following tax liability.

$$\$280,000 \times 0.19 = \$53,200$$

EXAMPLE 2.4

Calculate the tax liability for a manufacturing corporation making EBT of $500,000.

■ **Solution:** The overall tax rate is 34% for manufacturing businesses.

$$\$500,000 \times 0.34 = \$170,000$$

EXAMPLE 2.5

Calculate the tax liability for a general corporation making EBT of $16 million.

■ **Solution:** The overall tax rate is 36% for general businesses.

$16,000,000 \times 0.36 = \$ 5,760,000$

Taxes and Financing

The Canadian tax system favours *debt* financing of business over equity financing. The reason is that interest payments made to bond investors/creditors are *tax deductible* to the paying company, while dividend payments made to equity investors are not.

To illustrate the point, suppose two companies are identical except that one is financed entirely by debt[7] and one entirely by shareholders' equity. Assume the payments to the debt and equity investors are the same, say $20, that both firms have EBIT of $120, and that the tax rate is a uniform 30% (to make the illustration simple).

---

[7] In reality, some shareholders' equity is always required. We're just imagining total debt financing for the sake of the illustration.

Insights **PRACTICAL FINANCE**

The Other Purpose of the Tax System

The tax system in Canada has two purposes. The first, of course, is to raise money. But the government also uses the system to encourage what it considers to be desirable behaviour. Sometimes these desirable ends are economic and sometimes they're social. Here are a few examples:

• The progressive tax system requires higher taxes from those who have the ability to pay (higher-income individuals).
• Lower taxes on capital gains and dividends make investment more profitable so people buy more shares. That makes more funds available for

business investment, so companies undertake more new projects. That, in turn, creates jobs and expands the economy.
• CCPCs are taxed at favourable rates. That encourages the formation of new companies, which creates jobs and expands the economy.
• Companies get tax credits for employing and training certain types of unskilled, difficult-to-employ people.
• Tax credits or reductions are available for money spent on scientific research, manufacturing, and processing.
• To encourage savings, contributions to registered retirement savings plans (RRSPs) are deductible and tax on plan earnings is deferred.

To see the point, we have to look beyond net income (NI) to the net amount retained by each firm after paying its investors. That is, we have to subtract dividends from NI to arrive at the net addition to retained earnings. The comparison follows.

	Firm Financed by	
	Debt	**Shareholders' Equity**
EBIT	$ 120	$ 120
Interest	20	–
EBT	$ 100	$ 120
Tax @ 30%	30	36
NI	$ 70	$ 84
Dividends	–	20
Net RE addition	$ 70	$ 64

Notice that the firm financed with debt gets to keep $6 more money, about 10% in this case. The difference is in the tax line. The debt-financed firm gets to deduct the payment to its investors before calculating taxes, while the equity-financed business has to pay tax on an amount that is not reduced by the dividend payment.

SUMMARY

1 The accounts commonly used in accounting systems and financial statement include revenue, cost of goods sold, expenses, assets, liabilities, and shareholders' equity.

2 The income statement reports detail on revenue, costs, and expenses so as to measure the firm's profitability over a period. The balance sheet is a snapshot of the firm's financial position at the end of the reporting period. It includes details on assets, liabilities, and shareholders' equity.

3 The statement of cash flows indicates where the firm's money came from and what it was spent on during the period. It groups cash flows under operating, financing and investment activities. It is constructed from the income statement and two successive balance sheets.

4 The Canadian tax system for individuals is progressive, so that those with higher taxable incomes are taxed at higher rates.

5 The federal and provincial governments levy tax on various types of personal income, including investment income such as interest, dividends, and capital gains. Each type of investment income is taxed differently.

6 Each corporation is subject to both federal and provincial income taxes. Corporate tax rates vary by classification of corporation, by province, and by level of taxable income.

7 A corporation is subject to tax on its net income from operating its business, investing in debt securities (interest income), and selling its capital assets. Tax rates are lower for small private corporations.

8 Corporate taxes favour debt over equity financing because interest expense on debt is deductible for tax purposes.

KEY TERMS

Accelerated amortization, p. 29

Accounting periods, p. 22

Accounting system, p. 20

Accrual, p. 31

Accrual method, p. 21

Accumulated amortization, p. 28

Amortization, p. 28

Average tax rate, p. 41

Balance sheet, p. 22

Canadian controlled private corporation (CCPC), p. 44

Capital, p. 28

Capital asset, p. 28

Capital gain, p. 41

Cost of goods sold, p. 23

Current assets, p. 27

Current liabilities, p. 31

Declining balance amortization, p. 29

Dividend tax credit, p. 41

Earnings before interest and taxes (EBIT), p. 24

Expense, p. 23

Financial books, p. 43

Financial statements, p. 21

Financing activities, p. 36

Free cash flow, p. 39

Gross margin, p. 24

Income statement, p. 22

Income tax, p. 40

Investing activities, p. 36

Liquidity, p. 26

Long-term debt, p. 32

Loss carryovers, p. 44

Marginal tax rate, p. 41

Marketable securities, p. 26

Matching principle, p. 28

Net working capital, p. 31

Operating activities, p. 36

Progressive tax system, p. 40

Retained earnings, p. 25

Statement of cash flows, p. 34

Stretching payables, p. 30

Tax amortization, p. 43

Tax books, p. 43

Tax bracket, p. 40

Tax deductions, p. 43

Tax rates, p. 40

Terms of sale, p. 30

Trade credit, p. 30

Working capital, p. 31

KEY FORMULAS

(2.1) $$\text{Total income} - \text{Tax deductions} = \text{Taxable income}$$

(2.2) $$\text{Average tax rate} = \frac{\text{Tax liability}}{\text{Taxable income}}$$

The balance sheet equation: Assets = Liabilities + Shareholders' equity

$$\text{Net working capital} = \text{Current assets} - \text{Current liabilities}$$
$$\text{Beginning common shares} + \text{New shares} = \text{Ending common shares}$$
$$\text{Beginning retained earnings} + \text{Net income} - \text{Dividends} = \text{Ending retained earnings}$$
$$\text{Taxable income} \times \text{Tax rates} = \text{Total tax}$$
$$\text{Total tax} - \text{Tax credits} = \text{Net tax payable}$$

QUESTIONS

1. Why does a financial professional working outside accounting need knowledge of accounting principles and methods?

2. Discuss the purpose of an accounting system and financial statements in terms of the way the system represents the business.

3. Why is EBIT an important line item in the income statement? What does EBIT show us?

4. What is meant by liquidity in financial statements?

5. What are the common misstatements of balance sheet figures, and why do they present a problem?

6. Do the definitions of current assets and current liabilities suggest a quick way of looking at the firm's ability to meet its financial obligations (pay its bills) over the short term? (*Hint:* Think in terms of ratios.)

7. How are capital and working capital different?

8. What is leverage, and how does it work? What is the main concern about using it?

9. If a company's cash account increases from the beginning to the end of the year, there's more cash on hand so that must be an inflow of cash. Yet the cash account is an asset, and the third cash flow rule says that an asset increase is an outflow of cash. Explain this apparent conflict.

10. Why don't we calculate the difference in the shareholders' equity account between the beginning and end of the year and consider that difference as an inflow or outflow of cash? Why do we similarly exclude the cash account?

11. What are free cash flows? Who is likely to be most interested in them? Why?

12. The Canadian tax system for individuals is a progressive system. Explain this in terms of tax brackets and tax rates. Is the tax system for Canadian corporations progressive? Explain.

13. Why is the tax treatment of capital gains and dividends an important financial issue?

14. What are the tax implications of financing with debt versus shareholders' equity? If financing with debt is better, why doesn't everyone finance almost entirely with debt?

Business Analysis

1. The present format for the statement of cash flows is organized according to operating activities, investing activities, and financing activities. That format has been in use only since 1988. The previous format first listed all sources and then all uses of cash, giving a subtotal for each. Cash flow was then the difference between the two subtotals. What advantages or disadvantages do you see of the current format in relation to the old one? Which would you prefer if you had a choice?

PROBLEMS

1. The Johnson Company bought a truck costing $24,000 two and a half years ago. The truck's estimated useful life was four years at the time of purchase. It was accounted for by using straight-line amortization with zero salvage value. The truck was sold yesterday for $19,000. What is the gain or loss on the disposal of the truck to be reported on the income statement?

2. For the Johnson Company of Problem 1, what is the cash flow associated with the sale of the used truck to be reported in the statement of cash flows? In which section would it be reported?

3. Heald and Swenson Inc. purchased a drill press for $810,000 two years ago. The asset has a six-year life and has been amortized on a straight-line basis. The press was just sold for $875,000. The firm's tax rate is 35%. Calculate Heald and Swenson's gain on the disposal, its taxable capital gain, and its cash flow after tax on the sale.

4. Fred Gowen opened Gowen Retail Sales Ltd. and recorded the following transactions during his first month in business:
   i. Purchased $50,000 of capital assets, putting 10% down and borrowing the remainder.
   ii. Sold 1,000 units of product at an average price of $45 each. Half of the sales were on credit, none of which had been collected as of the end of the month.
   iii. Recorded cost of goods sold of $21,000 related to the above sales.
   iv. Purchased $30,000 worth of inventory and paid cash.
   v. Incurred other expenses (including the interest from the loan) of $5,000, all of which were paid in cash.
   vi. The tax rate is 40%. (Taxes will be paid in a subsequent period.)

   a. What will the business report as net income for its first month of business?
   b. List the flows of cash in and out of the business during the month. Show inflows as positives and outflows as negatives (using parentheses). Sum to arrive at a net cash flow figure for the statement of cash flows.
   c. Should Fred pay more attention to net income or cash flow? Why?

5. McFadden Corp. reports the following balances on its December 31, 20X2, balance sheet:

Amounts (in thousands)

Accounts payable	$ 60
Accounts receivable	120
Accumulated amortization	350
Capital assets (net)	900
Inventory	150
Long-term debt	400
Retained earnings	540
Total assets	1,240
Total liabilities	500 (Long-term debt + Current liabilities)

All of the remaining accounts are listed below. Calculate the balance in each.

Accruals	Total current assets
Cash	Total current liabilities
Common shares	Total shareholders' equity
Capital assets (gross)	

6. Using the following information, prepare an income statement (in good form) for 20X1 for Dutree Inc.
   - Sales = $30,000,000
   - Cost of goods sold = 72% of sales
   - Selling and administrative expenses = estimated to be 12% of cost of goods sold
   - Amortization expense = $100,000 per month for January through March, $108,000 per month April through November, and $117,000 in December
   - Interest expense is projected on the basis of the following: 8% on $10,000,000 in long-term loans outstanding throughout the year, and 6% on a three-month bank loan of $2,500,000. There are no other liabilities outstanding.
   - Tax rate = 20 % of earnings before tax

7. On January 1, 20X2, Miller Corp. purchased a milling machine for $400,000. It will be amortized on a straight-line basis over 20 years. On January 1, 20X3, Miller purchased a heavy-duty lathe for $250,000, which will be amortized on a straight-line basis over 40 years.
   a. Compute Miller's amortization expense for 20X2, 20X3, and 20X4.
   b. Prepare the capital asset portion of the balance sheet (for these two capital assets) as of the end of 20X2, 20X3, and 20X4.

8. Becher Industries has three suppliers for its raw materials for manufacturing. The firm purchases $180 million per year from Johnson Corp. and normally takes 30 days to pay these bills. Becher also purchases $150 million per year from Jensen, Inc., and normally pays Jensen in 45 days. Becher's third supplier, Docking Distributors, offers 2/10, n30 terms. Becher takes advantage of the discount on the $90 million per year that it typically purchases from Docking. Calculate Becher's expected accounts payable balance.

9. Belvedere Inc. has an annual payroll of $52 million. The firm pays employees every two weeks on Friday afternoon. Last month, the books were closed on the Tuesday after payday. How much is the payroll accrual at the end of the month?

10. In January 20X3, Elliott Industries recorded the following transactions:
- Paid bills from 20X2 totalling $120,000 and collected $150,000 for sales that were made in 20X2.
- Purchased inventory on credit totalling $500,000, 30% of which remained unpaid at the end of January.
- Sold $400,000 of inventory on credit for $600,000, 20% of which remained uncollected at the end of the month.
- Accruals increased by $10,000 during the month.
- Made additional cash payments for expenses incurred during the month totalling $80,000.

Compute Elliott's change in working capital for the month of January 20X3.

11. Gatwick Ltd. has after-tax profits (net income) of $500,000 and no debt. The shareholders have a $6 million equity investment in the business. Calculate the return on their investment (shareholders' equity).

If they borrow $2 million at 10% and use it to retire shares, how will the return on their investment (equity) change if earnings before interest and taxes remain the same? Assume a flat 40% tax rate and that the loan reduces shareholders' equity dollar for dollar.

(A business owner's return on investment or equity is ROI = ROE = Net income/Shareholders' equity.)

12. Ed Fletcher is planning to start a business in corporate form that requires an investment of $500,000. He has that much money, but he can also borrow virtually the whole amount from a rich relative. (This is very unusual.) Ed feels that, after the business is started, it will be important to retain as much money in the company as possible to fund growth. Nevertheless, he plans to pay the investor, either himself or his relative, a $50,000 return (10% of the amount invested) each year. That's about as much as could be earned elsewhere. Considering cash retention only, should Ed borrow or invest his own money? That is, which option will result in keeping more money in the company available to grow the business? How much more? The company's total combined tax rate will be 22%.

13. Mints Entertainment, Inc. had net income of $170,000 and paid dividends of $0.25 per share on its 100,000 common shares outstanding in 2006. At the end of the year its balance sheet showed retained earnings of $250,000.

What was Mints' retained earnings balance at the end of 2005?

14. Preston Road Inc. was organized last year when its founders contributed $9 million and issued 3 million common shares. The company earned $750,000 in its first year and paid dividends of $325,000. Construct the shareholders' equity section of Preston Road's balance sheet as of the end of that year.

15. The Digital Systems Company was organized two years ago to take advantage of an Internet opportunity. Investors paid $12 a share for 2 million shares. In the next two years, the company had earnings of $2 million and $3 million, respectively. It paid dividends of $1.2 million and $1.3 million, respectively, in those years. At the end of the first year, Digital sold another 500,000 shares at $14 per share. Construct the shareholders' equity section of Digital's balance sheet initially and at the end of its first and second years in business.

16. The Waterford Wax Company had the following current account activity last year.

	Beginning	Ending		Beginning	Ending
Cash	$ 160	$ 333	Accounts payable	$ 722	$ 2,084
Accounts receivable	1,875	3,810	Accruals	217	456
Inventory	438	2,676			
Current assets	$ 2,473	$ 6,819	Current liabilities	$ 939	$ 2,540

a. Calculate and display the current account detail required for the cash from operating activities section of the statement of cash flows.

b. If you also knew that Waterford's revenues had risen by 20% last year, would you be concerned about the firm's financial health? Why or why not? (*Words only.*)

17. Timberline Inc. had the following current accounts last year. (Amounts are in $000.)

	Beginning	Ending		Beginning	Ending
Cash	$ 175	$ 238	Accounts payable	$ 205	$ 182
Accounts receivable	1,456	2,207	Accruals	95	83
Inventory	943	786			
Current assets	$ 2,574	$ 3,231	Current liabilities	$ 300	$ 265

In addition, the company had sales revenues of $9,453 and costs and expenses (including interest and tax) of $7,580. Amortization of $1,462 is included in the cost and expense figures.

Construct a statement showing Timberline's cash from operating activities section, including the detail of changes in balance sheet accounts.

18. Fred Klein started his own business recently. He began by depositing $5,000 of his own money (shareholders' equity) in a business account. Once he'd done that his balance sheet was as follows.

Assets		Liabilities and Shareholders' Equity	
Cash	$ 5,000	Shareholders' equity	$ 5,000
Total	$ 5,000	Total	$ 5,000

During the next month (his first month of business), he completed the following transactions. (All payments were made by cheque out of the bank account.)
- Purchased $2,500 worth of inventory, paying $1,500 down and owing the vendor the remainder.
- Used $500 of the inventory in making product.
- Paid employees' wages of $1,100 on the last day of the month.
- Sold the entire product made in the first month on credit for $3,000.
- Paid rent of $1,200.

a. Construct a balance sheet for Fred's business at the *end* of its first month.

b. Construct Fred's income statement. (Ignore taxes.)

c. Construct Fred's statement of cash flows for the month.

    d. Is Fred's business profitable in an accounting sense? In a cash flow sense? (*Words only.*)

    e. Can the business fail while making a profit? How might that happen in the next month or so? (*Words only.*)

19. The Blandings Home Construction Company purchased a new crane for $350,000 this year. The company sold the old crane for $80,000, well below its original cost; at the time, the crane had a net book value of $20,000. These were the only transactions that affected investing activities this year.

    Construct the cash from investing activities section of the statement of cash flows.

20. Lansing Inc., a profitable food products manufacturer, has undertaken a major expansion that will be financed by new debt and share issues as well as retained earnings. During the last year, the company borrowed $5 million for a term of 30 years to finance a new building to house the expanded operations. It sold 60,000 shares at $51 per share to pay for new equipment. It also paid off short-term loans that support inventory and receivables totalling $700,000, and took out new short-term debt for the same purpose of $850,000, which was outstanding at year-end. Lansing also made a scheduled payment of $500,000 on an old long-term loan with which it had acquired production equipment several years ago. The payment included interest of $425,000. Finally, the firm paid dividends of $2.50 per share on 700,000 shares.

    Calculate and display the cash from financing activities section of Lansing's statement of cash flows.

21. Fitch Inc.'s financial statements are as follows:

Fitch Inc.		
Balance Sheet		
As of 31/12/20X1 ($000)		
ASSETS		
	31/12/20X0	**31/12/20X1**
Cash	$ 2,165	$ 2,647
Accounts receivable	4,832	5,614
Inventory	3,217	2,843
CURRENT ASSETS	10,214	11,104
Capital assets		
Gross	35,183	39,456
Accumulated amortization	(22,640)	(24,852)
Net	12,543	14,604
TOTAL ASSETS	$ 22,757	$ 25,708
LIABILITIES AND SHAREHOLDERS' EQUITY		
Accounts payable	$ 1,642	$ 1,420
Accruals	438	1,228
CURRENT LIABILITIES	2,080	2,648
Long-term debt	1,823	409
Shareholders' equity	18,854	22,651
TOTAL LIABILITIES AND SHAREHOLDERS' EQUITY	$ 22,757	$ 25,708

Fitch Inc.
Income Statement

For the period ended 31/12/20X1 ($000)

Sales	$ 40,506
COGS	14,177
Gross margin	26,329
Expenses	19,487
EBIT	6,842
Interest expense	180
EBT	6,662
Tax	2,265
Net income	$ 4,397

Fitch also sold shares for $2.5 million and paid dividends of $3.1 million. No capital assets were retired during the year. (*Hint*: That implies capital asset purchases and amortization are the only changes in the gross capital assets and accumulated amortization accounts.)
Construct Fitch's statement of cash flows for 20X1.

22. The Seymour Corp attempted to increase sales rapidly in 20X1 by offering a new, low-cost product line designed to appeal to credit customers in relatively poor financial condition. The company sold no new shares during the year but paid dividends of $3,000,000. Amortization for the year was $7,851,000, and no capital assets were retired or sold. The firm had the following financial statements for 20X1.

a. Without preparing a statement of cash flows, examine the changes in each balance sheet account and summarize in rough terms where Seymour got its cash and what it spent the money on. Include the sum of net income and amortization as an inflow of cash.

b. Construct a statement of cash flows for Seymour Corp. How does the information available from the statement compare with the results of your analysis in part (a)?

c. Does it look like Seymour may be headed for financial trouble? Explain the possible implications of the new product and credit strategy on individual accounts. (*Hint*: Consider the implications of two extreme scenarios—the new product is doing very well or very poorly.)

Seymour Corp Balance Sheet 31/12/X1 ($000)			Seymour Corp Income Statement For the period ended 31/12/X1 ($000)	
	31/12/X0	**31/12/X1**		
ASSETS				
Cash	$ 2,745	$ 1,071	Revenue	$ 88,765
Receivables	19,842	24,691	COGS	39,506
Inventory	10,045	15,621	GM	49,259
Current assets	32,632	41,383	Expenses	34,568
Capital assets			EBIT	14,691
Gross	80,128	97,432	Interest	4,312
Accum. amort.	(60,225)	(68,076)	EBT	10,379
Net	19,903	29,356	Tax	4,152
Total assets	$ 52,535	$ 70,739	NI	$ 6,227

LIABILITIES AND SHAREHOLDERS' EQUITY

Accts payable	$ 3,114	$ 6,307
Accruals	768	914
Current liabilities	3,882	7,221
Long-term debt	36,490	48,128
Shareholders' equity	12,163	15,390
Total L&SE	$ 52,535	$ 70,739

23. Slattery Industries reported the following financial information for 20X2 ($ millions).

Revenues	$ 10.0
Costs and expenses (excluding amortization)	8.0
Amortization	0.5
Taxes	0.6
Net income	0.9
Capital assets (gross)	10.0
Working capital	4.0

The firm expects revenues, costs and expenses (excluding amortization), and working capital to grow at 10% per year for the next three years. It also expects to invest $2 million per year in capital assets, which includes replacing worn-out equipment and purchasing enough new equipment to support the projected growth and maintain a competitive position. Assume amortization is 5% of the gross capital asset account, the tax rate is 40%, and that Slattery has no debt and therefore pays no interest.

    a. Make a rough projection of cash flows for 20X3, 20X4, and 20X5 assuming no new debt or shareholders' equity is raised. Simply compute an income statement for each year, add amortization, and subtract increases in working capital and capital asset purchases.

    b. Are your projections free cash flows?

    c. How would you evaluate Slattery's ability to achieve this level of growth (as measured by the increase in capital assets)?

24. Jim Slater had wage earnings of $45,000 this year. He received interest of $2,500 on corporate bonds and $1,500 in taxable dividends. He had a $10,000 capital gain on the sale of securities.

    a. What is his income for income tax purposes?

    b. What is his marginal tax rate? (*Hint*: refer to Table 2.4, page 40.)

25. Joan David's investment income this year includes the following items.

    • She received $2,600 in interest on savings and earned further interest income from two bonds: $1,500 on a 20-year Magna International issue, and $1,600 on a Government of Canada bond.

    • She received a taxable dividend of $1,600 from Manulife Financial.

    • She sold some Canadian Tire shares for $22,000 that had been purchased five years earlier for $10,000. Two years ago, she invested $40,000 in some rural land on the advice of a real estate agent. She sold the property this year for $36,000.

For *each* type of investment income, calculate
a. her combined federal and provincial tax liability
b. her after-tax income

Assume that these and other sources of taxable income place her in the third tax bracket. (*Hint*: refer to Table 2.5, page 42.)

Use Table 2.6 on page 44 in solving the next three problems.

26. Calculate the combined corporate tax if earnings before tax (EBT) is
    a. $47,000 for a corporation qualifying as a CCPC
    b. $248,000 for a (non-CCPC) general company
    c. $610,000 for a CCPC
    d. $1,809,000 for a manufacturing company
    e. $303,000 for a general business company

27. The Tay Corporation had the following income and expense items.

Sales	$ 198,800,000
Cost of goods sold	114,510,000
Expenses	66,550,000
Capital cost allowance	15,410,000

In addition, it received both interest and dividends from The Tiny Corp., a taxable Canadian corporation. The interest received from Tiny was $2,340,000, and the dividends were $2,470,000. Tay is taxed as a manufacturing company on its operating income and as a general company on its investment income.

Calculate its combined tax liability and earnings after tax.

28. McLeod Corporation's sales for the year were $8,600,000, while expenses totalled $6,800,000. The company received $15,000 in dividends from another taxable Canadian corporation. The company also earned a capital gain of $148,600 on the sale of the investment in this other company.

Calculate McLeod's taxable income, combined taxes payable, and average total tax rate under the following conditions:
a. The company qualifies as a CCPC. Its operating income is taxed at CCPC rates. Its capital gain is taxed at the rate for general companies.
b. The company is a general company (not a CCPC).
c. The company is a manufacturing company (not a CCPC). Its operating income is taxed at the rates for manufacturing companies. Its capital gain is taxed at the rate for general companies.

COMPUTER PROBLEMS

29. At the close of 20X3, the financial statements of Northern Manufacturing were as follows.

Northern Manufacturing Balance Sheet

As of 31/12/X3 ($000)

	31/12/X2	31/12/X3
ASSETS		
Cash	$ 500	$ 200
Accounts receivable	6,250	7,300
Inventory	5,180	6,470
CURRENT ASSETS	11,930	13,970
Capital assets		
Gross	7,500	9,000
Accumulated amortization	(2,400)	(3,100)
Net	5,100	5,900
TOTAL ASSETS	$ 17,030	$ 19,870
LIABILITIES AND SHAREHOLDERS' EQUITY		
Accounts payable	$ 1,860	$ 2,210
Accruals	850	220
CURRENT LIABILITIES	2,710	2,430
Long-term debt	11,320	12,335
Shareholders' equity	3,000	5,105
TOTAL LIABILITIES AND SHAREHOLDERS' EQUITY	$ 17,030	$ 19,870

Northern Manufacturing Income Statement

For the period ended 31/12/X3 ($000)

Sales	$ 22,560
COGS	11,506
Gross margin	11,054
Expenses	5,332
Amortization	700
EBIT	5,022
Interest	1,180
EBT	3,842
Tax	1,537
Net income	$ 2,305

In addition, Northern paid dividends of $1.2 million and sold new shares valued at $1.0 million in 20X3. Use the CASHFLO* program to produce Northern's statement of cash flows for 20X3.

*CASHFLO is one of several Microsoft Excel® templates available on the text's support website.

DEVELOPING SOFTWARE

30. Write a program to generate a statement of cash flows yourself. It isn't as hard as you might think.

First, set up the income statement and two balance sheets on the spreadsheet just as they appear in Problem 29. Let the amounts in individual accounts such as cash, A/R, revenue, COGS, interest, and tax be input items, and let the program calculate all the totals and subtotals such as current assets, total assets, gross margin, and net income.

Next, take a different area of the spreadsheet and set up the changes in the current accounts and the statement of cash flows shown below.

Northern Manufacturing
Summary of Changes to Current Accounts

For the period ended 31/12/X3 ($000)

ACCOUNT	INFLOW/OUTFLOW
Receivables	$ xxx
Inventory	xxx
Payables	xxx
Accruals	xxx
	$ XXX

Northern Manufacturing
Statement of Cash Flows

For the period ended 31/12/X3 ($000)

CASH FROM OPERATING ACTIVITIES	
Net income	$ x,xxx
Amortization	xxx
Net changes in current accounts	xxx
Cash from operating activities	$ X,XXX
CASH FROM INVESTING ACTIVITIES	
Purchase of capital assets	$ (x,xxx)
CASH FROM FINANCING ACTIVITIES	
Increase (decrease) in long-term debt	$ x,xxx
Sale of shares	xxx
Dividend paid	(xxx)
Cash from financing activities	$ X,XXX
NET CASH FLOW	$ XXX
RECONCILIATION	
Beginning cash balance	$ x,xxx
Net cash flow	XXX
Ending cash balance	$ X,XXX

Take all of the items shown with lowercase x's (xxx) from the statements in the first part of your spreadsheet. Some will be single items like net income and amortization, but most will be differences between beginning and ending balances like the increase or decrease in long-term debt or the change in receivables. Finally, program the spreadsheet to add up the subtotals where the uppercase Xs (XXXX) appear and display the reconciliation.

The trickiest part is keeping the signs straight in your subtractions for sources and uses. Once you have your program written, test it with the inputs to the CASHFLO* program from Problem 29, and see if you get the same results.

31. You've been hired by the nation of Utopia to computerize its approach to calculating corporation income taxes. Utopia's corporation tax system contains only two brackets. These are as follows.

Taxable Income	Rate
Under $400,000	20%
Over $400,000	35%

No special consideration is given to capital gains or manufacturing operations.

Write a spreadsheet program to compute taxes for a typical Utopian corporation. Test your program with the following cases.

Income	$259,825	$652,590
Deductions	$108,200	$217,541

(*Hint:* Use a single conditional instruction [IF statement] to identify which bracket the corporation is in and make the tax calculation.)

Verify that your program works by calculating the Utopian taxes manually.

Chapter 3

Financial Information and Analysis

Learning Objectives

1 Determine who are the principal users of financial statements and explain their primary interests in using them.

2 Explain the information contained in a public corporation's annual report.

3 Explain the incentives for management to publish misleading financial statements, and how corporate governance has been strengthened to deal with this problem.

4 Explain various techniques of financial analysis.

5 Calculate various financial ratios that measure profitability, market value, liquidity, asset management and debt management.

6 Assess a company's source of profitability using Du Pont equations.

7 Explain some of the problems involved in ratio analysis.

When buying shares, Janet Ozawa researches the company's price-earnings ratio, a statistic that relates the company's earnings per share (another ratio) to its price. In considering this ratio, she is going beyond the published financial statements in an attempt to establish what would be good value to her. The ratio in itself may not be conclusive, but may lead her to further investigation of the company's prospects. Ratios don't usually provide absolute answers (e.g., she should buy the shares), but may lead her to assemble more information, such as the trend in the shares' price, other ratios for the company, or average ratios for the industry in which the company operates.

We'll now turn our attention to financial analysis, a technique designed to get practical information about business operations out of financial statements. Before approaching this topic, however, we need a little background on financial information in general.

FINANCIAL INFORMATION—WHERE DOES IT COME FROM, WHO USES IT, AND WHAT ARE WE LOOKING FOR?

The term **financial information** refers to the results of business operations stated in monetary terms. The idea largely implies the material in financial statements but isn't entirely limited to those documents. Financial information about a company is important because people inside and outside the company use it as a basis for making decisions about the firm and their relationships with it.

Financial information refers to the results of business operations in monetary terms.

Financial information is the responsibility of management. It is created by accountants within the company and reviewed by auditors, but neither accountants nor auditors guarantee its correctness.[1] This creates a conflict of interest, because managements invariably want to portray results as favourably as possible. We'll discuss this idea in further detail later in this chapter.

Once prepared, financial information is published to a variety of audiences, who use it to make decisions about the company. Let's begin our study by looking at these users in a little more detail.

Users of Financial Information

Financial statements are a report on the issuing company's performance. The main user groups are investors, lenders, financial analysts, vendors/creditors, and management itself.

Investors

The most important function of financial statements is to convey information to outside investors. These are people or organizations that have bought or might be interested in buying the company's shares, bonds, or other financial securities.

The primary focus of shareholders is most likely to be the company's prospects for growth. Recent financial results tend to be good predictors of future performance, so investors bid share prices up or down based on the content of published financial statements. The market tends to focus on sales revenue, earnings per share (EPS), and debt as indicators of the future. With respect to revenue and EPS, more is better, and rapid growth is great. In terms of debt, less is safer, and recent increases may not be viewed favourably.

Lenders

Lenders include

- banks, trust companies, and other financial institutions that might provide short- or long-term loans to the company
- investors that might buy the company's bonds or other debt securities

Lenders are concerned with the firm's stability and cash flows.

Financial Analysts

Investors may analyze financial statements themselves, but more often rely on the reports of **financial analysts** who usually work for large brokerage firms or other financial institutions. Their job is to know as much about a particular company and its industry as an outsider can and to use that knowledge to predict the firm's performance. They then make recommendations about its investment value, including whether to buy or sell its shares and whether its debt is safe. Because of their pivotal advisory role, financial analysts can be considered the main audience for investor-oriented information.

A major part of the analyst's job is to carefully study the company's recent financial statements. It's important to realize that published financial statements relate to the past, and the

Go to Globe Investor at http://www. globeinvestor.com. Click on *Research Tools* for a summary of financials and analyst estimates for your company of choice.

Financial analysts interpret information about companies and make recommendations to investors.

---

1 Auditors make certain observations and perform tests that provide a reasonable level of assurance that statements are prepared in the proper manner and that all relevant details are disclosed.

analyst is interested in the future. However, the past factored into current information is usually the best available indicator of the future. In this chapter, we'll have a look at the basic tools used by financial analysts and sophisticated investors.

Vendors/Creditors

Vendors who are asked to do business with the firm on credit are another important group of statement users. Because they're advancing funds in the form of products and services, they tend to be interested in most of the same things that concern lenders. The main issue is whether the firm is likely to have cash available to pay its debts in the immediate future.

Management

The final group of statement users is the firm's own management. Financial results show successes and failures in each of the many facets of running a business. Management can study those results to pinpoint relative strengths and weaknesses in operations. This process shows where to put effort to correct problems and improve performance.

From the CFO

Management should be the most interested user group of all. Managers not only have to worry about the financial health of the firm, but also must be very aware of what these other user groups think about the company's performance.

Sources of Financial Information

A firm's **annual report** *is the primary source of financial information about the company.*

The primary source of financial information about any publicly traded company is its own **annual report.**

The financial statements in an annual report must be audited by an independent accounting firm. That process doesn't guarantee complete accuracy, but it should give a fair level of assurance that the numbers are presented with reasonable objectivity and in accordance with *generally accepted accounting principles (GAAP)*. However, there's a lot more latitude in the nature of the information presented in the *unaudited* accompanying detail.

In fact, there's an inherent problem with annual reports: they tend to portray past performance and future prospects in a very favourable light. That is, they're biased toward reporting that the firm has done as well as could be expected in the past year and that it will do even better in the future. Reports tend to minimize or ignore mistakes and failures, exaggerate successes, and build up future opportunities in unrealistically optimistic terms.

DANIER LEATHER

For a summary of the audited financial statements from the 2006 annual report for Danier Leather Inc., see Appendix 3A, page 92.

Insights PRACTICAL FINANCE

The Annual Report

Some 2,500 companies are listed on one of the two Canadian stock exchanges—the *Toronto Stock Exchange (TSX)* and the *TSX Venture Exchange*.

The *Canada Business Corporations Act*, together with provincial corporations and securities legislation, requires these companies to provide certain financial and other information to their shareholders in an *annual report*.

The annual report typically includes

- The *letter to shareholders*, reviewing the results and events of the past year, and management's strategies and plans for the future;

- The *management discussion and analysis*, analyzing and explaining the financial results for the year;
- *Audited financial statements* for the past year and the previous year, including the income statement, balance sheet, statement of retained earnings, and statement of cash flows;
- *Notes* to the financial statements (audited), (These notes are a "must read" to understand the details behind the summary information in the financial statements.); and
- Other recent and historic financial information.

The annual report is actually a report to shareholders prepared by the company's management. But management works for the shareholders, so the managers are in effect writing their own report cards. Naturally the result may be biased in favour of the people running the firm.

Annual reports tend to be biased in favour of management's performance.

Along these lines, most annual reports have become advertising vehicles and are prepared to be very visually appealing. They're done on glossy paper, in multicoloured inks, and are filled with professional quality photographs. They frequently look more like upscale magazines than business documents.

All this isn't necessarily bad as long as readers understand the biases and don't take everything in reports as strictly true. The truth can be told more or less attractively, and annual reports tend to present things in a rosy glow. More worrisome, as we shall see, there have been instances in recent years of outright lies, fraud, and criminal activity in corporate reporting.

Analyst Reports

Brokerage firms and investment advisory services provide reports on most large companies. These reports are the result of the work of their financial analysts. Brokerage firms provide the information free as a service to clients and prospective clients, while investment advisory services publish it for a fee. One of the best known advisory services is Value Line, which provides information on several thousand U.S. and Canadian company shares. Advisory services provide information to paid subscribers, but it is often available free in libraries.

For recent award-winning annual reports, go to the Canadian Institute of Chartered Accountants at http://www.cica.ca. On the search link, type "annual report awards."

Value Line's March 2007 report on General Motors (GM) is shown in Figure 3.1. Study the layout of the information it contains for a few minutes. The chart at the top shows the share's price performance for the last 12 years. Below that, 16 years of history and 2 years of forecasts are shown for a variety of financial line items. Notice that some items are stated on a per-share basis.

Moving down the page, there's a short summary of the nature of the company's business followed by an analysis of its current situation and prospects for the future. This section is the heart of the report. It tells investors what the analyst thinks is likely to happen to GM's business and, by implication, to the price of its shares.

Company annual reports and other public documents are available at http://www.sedar.com.

At the time this report was written, General Motors was continuing to lose market share, particularly to Toyota, and was considering a possible alliance with Chrysler. The report ended with a comment that an investment in the shares at that time was unlikely to yield big gains because GM's share price had risen substantially in the recent past, leaving little room for further appreciation.

The issues addressed in this descriptive section aren't always purely financial. They can be about any area of business that's crucial—such as markets, products, competition, or mergers. In other words, a lot of "financial information" isn't exactly financial. It might be better described as marketing or strategic information. Keep in mind that financial results are numerical representations of what is physically going on in a business. Thus, deciding whether a firm is a good financial investment begins with a judgment about how it's doing in the market for its products. Notice that Value Line ends the discussion by saying that it has a neutral opinion of the share's investment potential.

Go to Value Line at http://www.valueline.com. Click on *Dow 30 Value Line Reports* to access the most current analyst reports on General Motors and other U.S. shares.

FINANCIAL INFORMATION AND CORPORATE GOVERNANCE

Corporate governance refers to the practices top managements and boards of directors use when running companies. In recent years the concept has focused on ethical issues relating to the personal financial relationships between executives and the corporations they are hired to serve.

The idea is especially important for large, publicly traded corporations in which the bulk of the shares are held by the investing public and lower-level employees whose pension funds are invested in the companies' own shares.

The Agency Problem Revisited

In Chapter 1 we discussed conflicts of interest between groups of stakeholders who have interests in corporations. Such a conflict arises when one group has a power that enables its members to benefit

FIGURE 3.1

Value Line's March 2007 Report on General Motors

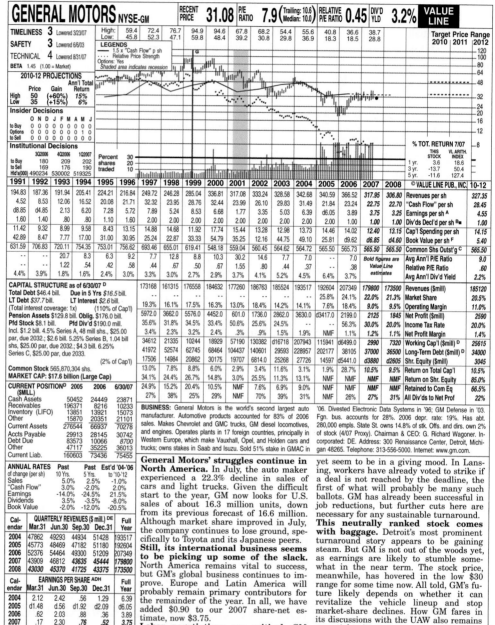

Source: Report on General Motors, Value Line, 2007. Reprinted with permission http://www.valueline.com/dow30/f3822.pdf.

themselves at the expense of another group. Within a corporation there's a major conflict of interest, or agency problem, because executive compensation is tied to share price in ways that may make senior executives enormously wealthy when the price of their company's shares rises rapidly. Huge salaries and bonuses paid to executives are taken from profits otherwise owned by the shareholders.

How to inflate share prices? Let's remember that investors want more revenue and earnings, and rapid growth is great. On the other hand, less debt is better. Share prices can be inflated despite poor performance by issuing financial statements that make results in these areas look better than they really are. Such statements generally *inflate* revenue and earnings and *hide* debt.

Producing Misleading Financial Statements

Financial statements are reputed to be objective representations of business performance. Unfortunately, producing deceptive financial statements isn't especially difficult, as management has a good deal of control over them. Generally accepted accounting principles (GAAP) are filled with grey areas, so there's some latitude in reporting results that can be technically "correct" but still misleading. In other words, management can, to some extent, "engineer" the financial results that are so crucial to investors and the prices they put on shares. Further, it's possible that deceptive entries aren't discovered for years because of the size and complexity of the organization. This can produce a cascading series of misstated reports as executives strive to keep share price up year after year. Top management may get rich by manipulating reported financial performance to drive share price up in the short run. But eventually the fact that results were artificially inflated is discovered, and share prices fall rapidly, with a devastating effect on investors, especially those who bought the shares near their peak price.

Top management is ultimately responsible for producing accurate financial statements and, although there is some oversight by auditors and boards of directors, the bulk content of financial statements is left to people who have a lot to gain from high share prices.

The Events of the 1990s

The calm before the storm. It's important to realize that, in the past, the investing community was aware of these arguably unethical practices but didn't consider them too significant. Most people felt that management might stretch the truth a little, but was basically honest. Investors relied on the audits done by public accounting firms, which had excellent reputations for integrity, to police corporate reporting and keep statements from being misleading. They expected that boards of independent-minded directors drawn from the business elite would control company executives and act as guardians of the investing public's welfare. Finally, they assumed that outside securities (financial) analysts were impartial and would provide unbiased opinions on the quality and safety of corporate securities.

The ethical depths—a major loss of confidence. All that changed in the 1990s and early 2000s when a large number of very substantial companies undertook to pump up their share prices by publishing false or deceptive financial statements. Practices included recording completely bogus transactions to pump up revenue and profit and supporting operations with borrowed money that didn't show up on the balance sheet because the debt was held in shadowy "partnerships" with artificially created businesses. While all this was going on, many of the top executives involved increased their individual wealth by hundreds of millions of dollars. The widespread deceptions were eventually exposed, contributing to a major stock market decline in 2000.

The most widely publicized cases were Enron (a leading player in energy), WorldCom (the telecommunications giant that owned MCI), and Tyco (a firm that participates in a wide variety of businesses). Enron and WorldCom actually went into bankruptcy. Shareholders in all three lost 80% to 100% of their investments. Needless to say, Canada has had its own share of accounting fiascos (see "The Accounting Saga at Nortel" on pages 68 and 69).

The Failure of the Watchdogs

Perhaps the most startling result of the scandals was the role of the public accountants involved. They not only failed to prevent the deceptions allegedly perpetrated by managements, but also were accused in some cases of participating in the deceptions themselves. It seems that because accounting firms are paid by the companies they audit, they have had an interest in staying in the good graces of management. In addition, accounting firms found the consulting side of their business to be much more lucrative than the auditing. As such, it became tempting to bend or even break proper financial reporting rules to please client company executives. In extreme cases the auditors even came up with creative ways to circumvent the intent of the rules without appearing to violate them. These conditions created a conflict of interest with their responsibility to the investing public. Arthur Andersen, Enron's auditor and one of the world's largest and most respected accounting firms, went out of business as a result of its role in the Enron debacle.

Similarly, several well-known and supposedly impartial securities analysts were found to have issued reports biased in favour of companies that did business with the investment side of their brokerage firm employers.

Boards of directors, too, broadly failed to control the agency problem. Too often their members were lax, uninformed, or heavily influenced by company executives.

FINANCIAL ANALYSIS

The Orientation of Financial Analysis

Much of the information in the rest of this chapter may seem similar to material you've studied in accounting. However, our orientation is different here. In accounting, we're concerned with creating financial statements; in finance, we're concerned with using them to evaluate businesses and their prospects for the future.

From the CFO

> *In particular, financial analysis looks for problems, places where things aren't as they seem, or where results indicate the firm may be heading for trouble.*

For example, a statement of cash flows might indicate that a firm borrowed a lot of money last year. Accounting per se stops with the presentation of that fact along with information about the things on which money was spent during the period. The financial analyst, however, must go further and ask why the borrowing occurred and what it implies for the future.

The orientation of the financial analyst is critical and investigative.

Perhaps the borrowing was to finance expansion into an exciting new venture. That might seem great, but the analyst wants to know if the firm will be able to support the interest payments and whether the venture will need more borrowing later before it starts to generate a profit. On the other hand, the borrowing might be because the firm isn't collecting its receivables or is holding significant useless inventory. In that case, the analyst will want to know how the problem will be resolved and what its impact on long-run profitability will be.

Keep this orientation in mind: In finance, our attitude is *critical* and *investigative*.

Techniques of Financial Analysis

Financial ratios are formed from sets of financial statement figures. Ratios *highlight* different aspects of *performance*.

People who make judgments about businesses by reading financial statements have developed some relatively standard methods with which they analyze information. Interrelated techniques include the preparation of comparative financial statements, trend analysis, common size statements and financial ratio analysis.

One general technique is known as *ratio analysis*. Its use is virtually universal among financial professionals, and it is therefore important that you be familiar with the basic technique and a few of the more commonly used ratios. Ratio analysis involves taking sets of numbers out of the financial statements and forming ratios with them. The numbers are chosen so that each ratio has a particular meaning to the operation of the business.

An example will make the idea clear. There is a ratio that gives a quick indication of whether the company will have the means to pay its bills during the next year—it's called the *current ratio* and it is based on the definitions of current assets and current liabilities. Recall from Chapter 2 that the money coming into a firm from normal operations passes through

Strengthening Corporate Governance

The scandals brought on by deceptive financial reporting and share price manipulation led to a major review of financial reporting and auditing procedures by the accounting profession as well as legislation aimed at improving governance and punishing knowing deception by senior executives. All firms listed on the Toronto Stock Exchange are subject to various regulations, some of which have been in place in various forms since the mid-1990s and some of which are in response to the introduction of a strong piece of legislation in the United States called the *Sarbanes-Oxley Act* of 2002 (SOX). We'll briefly discuss how the some of the main regulations have affected public companies and their watchdogs.

Executive Management: Holding CEOs Accountable

When these corporate frauds were exposed, many CEOs attempted to hide behind a veil of ignorance. A number of top executives claimed they knew nothing of the frauds their companies had perpetrated on the investing public and claimed that overzealous subordinates had dreamed up and implemented the convoluted financial schemes that led to their downfalls.

Unfortunately, it's difficult to prove whether someone did or did not know of an activity some time after the fact. It can be especially difficult if the party in question was careful to avoid creating evidence of his or her involvement while the activity was going on.

This has been the case in a number of high-profile cases. Prosecutors have had a hard time making fraud charges stick against CEOs claiming ignorance but there have been successes. An example is the case against Bernard Ebbers, CEO of WorldCom, who was sentenced to a long prison term.

The result of all this is that CEOs and CFOs of public companies must now certify that they have reviewed the financial statements their companies file with the securities commission and that to the best of their knowledge the statements contain no materially false or misleading information. They must also certify that they have reasonable internal controls in place. The scope of certification is to expand substantially over the next few years

Auditors: Maintaining Independence

In 2002, the accounting profession, together with various federal and provincial regulators, set up the Canadian Public Accountability Board (CPAB) to oversee public accounting in the public interest. CPAB is charged with instituting more frequent and rigorous inspections of the auditing services provided to public companies.

Regulations have been introduced that prohibit accounting firms from providing audit clients with certain non-audit services including, among other things, bookkeeping, information technology, appraising, management consulting, and investments. These regulations deal with primarily public companies, so accounting firms may still provide consulting services to audit clients that are privately held. Importantly, tax-related services to audit clients that are public companies have not been prohibited. An immediate consequence of the prohibition of consulting was that many large accounting firms made their consulting operations separate, independent businesses.

Auditors no longer report to senior management of the audited company; instead, they now report directly to the audit committee of the board of directors. In addition, the audit committee comprises exclusively independent directors, all of whom must be financially literate.

The requirement of financial expertise on the audit committee addressed another related issue. Previously, unethical and very complex financial schemes might be approved by board members untrained in finance, because they didn't understand the accounting behind the proposals. Now it's much more likely that the committee will see through such schemes.

Securities Analysts: Disclosing Compensation

Research reports are to disclose whether the research analyst responsible for preparing the report received compensation based upon his or her employer's investment banking revenues in the previous 12 months. In fact the analyst is prohibited from receiving any form of compensation that resulted directly from specific investment banking services that his or her employer provided to a client firm in the previous 12 months.

Life After Increased Regulation

Increased regulation has had tremendous impact on the way companies, the accounting profession, and securities analysts govern themselves. The biggest criticism of the increased regulation is that compliance costs more than the benefits are worth. The expense arises mainly in the area of internal financial control, and appears in the form of both money and management time and attention.

Some people believe that a large number of honest managements are being penalized for the sins of a few dishonest individuals, and, that as it stands now, the cost of compliance isn't worth the benefit it brings to the investing community. No one is suggesting going back to the old ways, but a softening of the rules in the future is a distinct possibility.

Sources: Broshko, E.B and K. Li, 2006, Corporate Governance Requirements in Canada and the United States: A Legal and Empirical Comparison of the Principals-based and Rules-based Approaches, Canadian Investment Review forthcoming; Deloitte & Touche LLP, The Corporate Governance Landscape in Canada, http://www.deloitte.com/dtt/article/0,1002,cid%253D127461,00.html; Department of Finance, Canada, June 8, 2006, Fostering Investor Confidence in Canadian Capital Markets; Investment Dealers Association, Policy No. 11 Research Restrictions and Disclosure Requirements, http://ida.knotia.ca/Knowledge/View/Document.cfm?Ktype=445&linkType=toc&dbID=200703341&tocID=796; Torys LLP, Canada's New Corporate Governance Disclosure Rules: What You Need to Know, No. 2004-26, November 4, 2005; Gilles des Roberts, On the Hot Seat, *CA Magazine*, December, 2003; Ontario Securities Commission, National Instrument 58-101—Disclosure of Corporate Governance Practices (NI 58-101), National Policy 58-201—Corporate Governance Guidelines (NP 58-201), and Multilateral Instrument 52-110—Audit Committees (MI 52-110).

Insights REAL APPLICATIONS

The Accounting Saga at Nortel

On March 12, 2007, the U.S. Securities and Exchange Commission (SEC) filed civil fraud charges against Frank Dunn, former CEO of Nortel Networks Corporation (Nortel), headquartered in Bramalea, Ontario. In addition to Mr. Dunn, three of his top finance officials at Nortel, the former CFO, controller, and VP of Corporate Reporting, were also charged. The SEC alleged that, after the tech bubble burst in 2000, these executives manipulated Nortel's books during the years 2000–03 to meet their previous forecasts, mislead investors, and falsely earn substantial management bonuses. On the same day, the Ontario Securities Commission (OSC) made similar allegations. In particular Dunn and his team of financial executives faced charges in three major areas:

1. *Revenue recognition*: By booking some sales before products were shipped to customers. ("bill and hold accounting"), Nortel increased its reported revenues in 2000 by US$1 billion. The SEC alleged that Dunn and his executives improperly boosted revenue and profits "in complete disregard of U.S. accounting rules" in order to meet their revenue forecasts for 2000.

2. *Reserves*: In 2001 and 2002, Nortel had downsized drastically, writing off huge amounts (nearly US$18 billion) by creating restructuring provisions ("reserves") for the estimated costs and losses. When the Nortel executives discovered US$300 million in excess reserves in 2002, they did not release the reserves as required by generally accepted accounting principles (GAAP), according to the SEC, but falsely set them aside "for future earnings management" (in 2003).

   Instead, the company reversed earlier restructuring provisions to boost 2003 profit by a total of US$498 million. The reported profits were adequate to trigger executive bonuses, including some $10 million in total to three of the executives concerned. The SEC alleged the executives had falsely "orchestrated" Nortel's earnings in 2003 in order to pay themselves the "substantial bonuses."

3. *Restatement of earnings*. Later in 2003, Nortel's external auditor, Deloitte Touche LLP (Deloitte), warned the board of directors about its concerns over accounting for reserves. Nortel issued the first of several "restatements of prior years' earnings." Reported profits for 2003 and prior were reduced by a total of US$984 million. The SEC alleged that the restatement was a "cover-up," that it didn't address the "revenue recognition fraud" from 2000, or all of the manipulations in the reserves, and that the Nortel executives "falsely" attributed this restatement to "internal control mistakes."

In April 2004, Nortel announced that its financial statements for 2001, 2002, and 2003 were not reliable and would be restated for a second time, disclosing US$3.4 billion in misstated revenues. Nortel's board fired its CEO (Dunn), CFO, controller, and seven other finance executives. Nortel's share price fell to about US$4.50 from a high of almost US$12 during the previous 12 months.

Ongoing Problems

In March 2007, criminal investigations by the RCMP and the U.S. Attorney's office were ongoing. Two class-action suits by shareholders were before the U.S. District Court. Nortel proposed to settle them for US$2.4 billion in cash and Nortel shares. Nortel faced another class-action suit by shareholders in Ontario Superior Court seeking $250 million in damages.

Nortel continued to grapple with its accounting. In April 2006, Nortel issued a third restatement reducing 2003–05 revenues by US$12.2 billion. In March 2007, Nortel announced that it would again have to restate results, for the fourth time in four years! This time it would restate its financial results for 2004 to 2006 to correct errors tied to, again, revenue recognition and also pension and postretirement plans.

Nortel shares were then selling for about $33 (after a 10:1 conversion).

The Auditor's Role

The SEC alleged that Deloitte knew about some of the biggest accounting problems at Nortel and had discussed them with Nortel's management as early as October 2000. Even though Deloitte picked up some of the irregularities and reported them to Nortel's board of directors, Deloitte also continued to sign "clean" audit opinions to the shareholders despite the series of four financial statement restatements with adjustments going back to 1999.

Some in the industry asked why, if Deloitte knew about the issues at Nortel, as the SEC alleged, it did not withhold its audit opinion or resign if it felt the problems were material enough. In contrast, the SEC's version of events alleged a "very lax" response from Deloitte. Another observer commented that "auditors' disagreements with management don't get out into the public until the shareholders get wiped out."

Deloitte continued as Nortel's auditor until December 2006, when it was dropped in favour of rival KPMG LLP. Deloitte had been Nortel's auditor for 92 years. It was paid fees of over $80 million from Nortel in 2005, more than from any other client on the Toronto Stock Exchange.

Sources: Duncan Mavin, "Experts Question Deloitte's Role in Nortel Accounting Problems," *National Post* (March 16, 2007), p. FP1; Duncan Mavin, "Charges Tough to Prove," *National Post* (March 13, 2007), p. FP1; Eric Reguly, "Investors Were Misled, SEC Says," *The Globe and Mail* (March 13, 2007), p. B21; Janet Mcfarland, "How Dunn's Misplaced Optimism Snowballed," *The Globe and Mail* (March 13, 2007), p. B6.

current assets. Similarly, the normal outgoing money passes through current liabilities. Further, the definition of "current" is that cash will be generated or required within a year.

It's clear that, to remain solvent, a company must have at least as much money coming in as it has going out. This fact suggests that comparing the sizes of current assets and current liabilities at a point in time will give an indication of whether operating cash flows will be positive or negative in the near future. The current ratio does just that. It's formed by dividing current assets by current liabilities. The current ratio measures *liquidity*, which in this context refers to the company's ability to pay its bills in the short run by converting its current assets into cash in normal business operations. A current ratio of 1.0 would indicate that a firm's current assets are just sufficient to cover its current liabilities.[2] We will examine the current ratio further on page 77.

Numerous ratios have been devised, each having a special significance like the current ratio. We'll cover several of the most commonly used ratios later in this chapter.

Comparisons

Ratios by themselves have some value, but not nearly as much as they have when they're compared with other similar figures. For example, a current ratio of 1.8 in a particular business might seem all right by itself, but it could cause concern if competing firms have current ratios in excess of 3.0. In such a case, we would suspect that some characteristic of the business requires great liquidity, and the firm we are analyzing doesn't have it.

Ratio analysis is usually conducted in the context of one or more of three comparisons with respect to the competition, history, and budget.

The Competition

The performance of other companies in the same field is always a good yardstick for evaluating a firm's performance. If a particular measure is substantially off what others are doing, it's a good idea to find out why. Industry average data are often available through trade associations, government publications, banking publications, and the publications of investment analysts. (See Tables 3.2. and 3.3, pages 87 and 88.)

---

2 The current ratio may need to be quite a bit greater than 1.0. If future inflows and outflows are just equal, timing problems can be expected if the outflows come first.

Industry averages must be treated with caution, however. Because of the differences in the nature of business, ratio averages differ widely *among* industries. *Within* an industry, differences in operating strategies (for instance, owning versus leasing producing assets) may mean that some company ratios are not comparable.

Another popular type of comparison, called benchmarking, involves a company that compares its ratio values to those of a key competitor or group of competitors that it wishes to emulate. By comparing its ratios to those of the benchmark company (or companies), it can identify areas in which it outperforms and others in which it needs to improve.

Benchmarking is a type of analysis in which a company compares its ratio values with those of a key competitor or group of competitors, primarily to identify areas of improvement.

History

Comparison with history means looking at a ratio next to the same figure calculated for the same organization in one or more immediately preceding accounting periods. The idea is to look for trends. If a firm's current ratio is seen to be decreasing steadily over a number of periods, the analyst would ask why.

Trend Analysis

Ratio analysis may compare company results for a particular year to an industry average. However, sales and net income may expand and contract over the course of the business cycle.

Trend analysis of performance over a number of years may present a more complete picture of the health of the firm. Techniques for trend analysis include comparative financial statements for two or more years, comparative financial ratios for a number of years, and growth in sales and net income.

Refer again to the financial statements of Belfry Company, shown in Chapter 2, Figure 2.2, and reproduced below.

FIGURE 3.2
Belfry Company Balance Sheet and Income Statement

Belfry Company
Balance Sheet
As of 31/12/X2

ASSETS	31/12/X1	31/12/X2
Cash	$1,000	$1,400
Accounts receivable	3,000	2,900
Inventory	2,000	3,200
CURRENT ASSETS	$6,000	$7,500
Capital assets		
Gross	$4,000	$ 6,000
Accumulated amortization	(1,000)	(1,500)
Net	$3,000	$ 4,500
TOTAL ASSETS	$9,000	$12,000

LIABILITIES AND SHAREHOLDERS' EQUITY		
Accounts payable	$1,500	$2,100
Accruals	500	400
CURRENT LIABILITIES	$2,000	$2,500
Long-term debt	$5,000	$6,200
Shareholders' equity	$2,000	$3,300
TOTAL LIABILITIES AND SHAREHOLDERS' EQUITY	$9,000	$12,000

Belfry Company
Income Statement
For the period ended 31/12/X2

Sales	$10,000
COGS	6,000
Gross margin	$ 4,000
Expenses	$ 1,600
Amortization	500
EBIT	$ 1,900
Interest	400
EBT	$ 1,500
Tax	500
Net income	$ 1,000

Now let us assume that, for the period ended 31/12/X1, sales were $9,500 and net income was $980. We calculate the growth in sales as

$$\frac{\text{Current year sales } - \text{ Prior year sales}}{\text{Prior year sales}}$$

The growth in sales for X2 is

$$\frac{\$10,000 - \$9,500}{\$9,500} = 5.39\%$$

As a minimum, one would normally expect that sales growth should be greater than an appropriate measure of inflation over the same period.

We calculate the growth in net income as

$$\frac{\text{Current year net income } - \text{ Prior year net income}}{\text{Prior year net income}}$$

The growth in net income for X2 is

$$\frac{\$1,000 - \$980}{\$980} = 2.0\%$$

Where net income is growing at a slower pace than sales, we will want to determine which costs or expenses are growing faster than sales.

For a trend analysis of Danier Leather Inc. see Appendix 3A, page 93.

DANIER LEATHER

Budget

Most businesses of any size develop financial plans for the future. We'll study business planning in Chapter 6. For now, though, it's enough to understand that a plan involves a projected set of financial statements from which ratios can be developed. When financial performance is being evaluated, what the organization really did is always compared with what management said it would do in the plan (budget) for the period. Comparing planned and actual ratios highlights where management needs to put its attention in running the business.

Common Size Statements

The first step in a financial analysis is usually the calculation of a set of ratios known as **common size statements**. The common size income statement is the most frequently used. The idea can best be understood with an example.

A common size income statement presents each line item as a percentage of revenue.

Suppose we're interested in comparing the financial performance of two companies in the same line of business that are substantially different in size. For example, consider the income statements of Alpha and Beta.

	Alpha	Beta
Sales revenue	$ 2,187,460	$ 150,845
COGS	1,203,103	72,406
Gross margin	$ 984,357	$ 78,439
Expenses	505,303	39,974
EBIT	$ 479,054	$ 38,465
Interest	131,248	15,386
EBT	$ 347,806	$ 23,079
Tax	118,254	3,462
Net income	$ 229,552	$ 19,617

It's hard to tell which company is doing a better job of controlling costs and expenses by looking at the dollar figures because Alpha is so much larger than Beta.

The comparison is made much easier by creating a *common size* statement for each company to abstract away from absolute dollars and state things in relative terms. A common size income statement is formed by stating each line as a percentage of revenue. The percentages are usually stated to the first decimal place and displayed next to the dollar figures. Let's look at the comparison of Alpha and Beta with the aid of common size statements.

	Alpha		**Beta**	
	$	%	$	%
Sales revenue	$ 2,187,460	100.0	$ 150,845	100.0
COGS	1,203,103	55.0	72,406	48.0
Gross margin	$ 984,357	45.0	$ 78,439	52.0
Expenses	505,303	23.1	39,974	26.5
EBIT	$ 479,054	21.9	$ 38,465	25.5
Interest	131,248	6.0	15,386	10.2
EBT	$ 347,806	15.9	$ 23,079	15.3
Tax	118,254	5.4	3,462	2.3
Net income	$ 229,552	10.5	$ 19,617	13.0

Each percentage figure below sales is a ratio of that line's dollars to revenue dollars. The ratio of cost of goods sold to sales revenue is generally called the *cost ratio*, while expenses as a percentage of revenue can be called the *expense ratio*. Net income as a percentage of sales has a name of its own, *return on sales*, and is one of the ratios we'll look at later.

Comparing the two columns of ratios in our example, we can immediately see significant differences in the way the two companies are operating. Alpha's cost is 55% of revenues, whereas Beta's is only 48%. This is unusual because one would expect the larger company to have economies of scale in production that would make it more efficient than the smaller firm.

Several explanations are possible. Alpha might have some production problems, Beta might be particularly good at what it does, or there may be a difference in what they're making. In the last situation, Alpha might be producing a simple bottom-of-the-line product that sells at a minimal markup, while Beta might be making a fancy customized version of the same thing that's marked up much higher.

From the CFO

The point is that the common size analysis leads us to ask the right questions. It doesn't give us the answers, but it gets our investigation of problems started in the right direction.

Common size analysis is particularly useful in comparing a firm's performance with its own history. Unfavourable trends in cost or expense ratios from this year to last and the year before are signals to management that should never be overlooked or taken lightly.

A set of common size statements is generally the first thing an analyst prepares when starting an investigation.

DANIER LEATHER

Refer to Appendix 3A, pages 93 and 94 for income statements for Danier Leather Inc. in both dollar and percentage (common size) terms.

Common size balance sheets that state everything as a percentage of total assets can also be constructed. They can be useful in determining whether a firm has relatively too much money tied up in inventory or receivables, or whether it uses more equipment than it should.

Financial Ratios

In the following pages we'll present some of the more commonly used ratios of financial analysis. Each ratio is designed to illuminate some aspect of how the business is doing. In each case we'll illustrate how the ratio is calculated, discuss the rationale behind its use, and explain what it's telling the analyst.

Remember that ratios are most meaningful when used in comparisons. For that reason, it's difficult to make a generalization about what a good or an acceptable value is for any particular figure. For example, one of the ratios we'll be talking about (inventory turnover) measures how effectively the firm uses inventory. With respect to that ratio, a good number for a manufacturing company might be terrible for a retailer.

After we've discussed each ratio, we'll calculate its value for the Belfry Company, using the financial statements for the period X2, shown on page 70.

A Note on Average versus Ending Values

Notice that we have a beginning and an ending balance sheet for the Belfry Company, which brings up a computational question: When a ratio calls for a balance sheet figure, should we use the beginning, the ending, or an average value?

The answer depends on what the ratio is measuring. If it pertains to a position or status at the end of the year, ending values are appropriate. On the other hand, if the ratio measures an activity that goes on during the entire period, average balance sheet figures better reflect performance. Beginning values alone are never appropriate.

The difference between average and ending values isn't very important if the company is relatively stable and account balances aren't changing much. However, it can be significant if the firm is growing or shrinking rapidly.

Professional analysts always use average balances where appropriate. However, in order to keep the computations in our illustrations and problems simple, we will consistently use ending balances. You should just be aware that the issue exists.

Categories of Ratios

Ratios can be categorized according to the kinds of issues they address. The ones we'll discuss fit into five classifications: profitability, market value, liquidity, asset management, and debt management.

Profitability ratios give us several measures by which to assess the success of the whole venture in making money. *Market value* ratios give an indication of how investors feel about the company's financial future. *Asset management* ratios show how the company uses its assets to generate revenue and to minimize cost. *Liquidity* ratios indicate the firm's ability to pay its bills in the short term. *Debt management* ratios show how effectively the firm uses other people's money and whether it's using too much borrowed money.

> Ratios fall into five categories: profitability, market value, liquidity, asset management, and debt management.

Profitability Ratios

The most fundamental measure of a business's success is profit. Without profit there are no dividends, and without dividends or the expectation of them, no one will invest in the shares.

Lenders don't like profitless companies. Firms that are losing money or barely breaking even are perilously close to not being able to repay their loans.

Profitability ratios give us relative measures of the firm's money-making success. That is, they gauge profits per dollar of sales made, assets employed, or shareholders' equity invested. They're generally stated as percentages.

> Profitability ratios measure ability to make money.

Gross Profit Margin (GPM)

Gross profit margin (GPM) focuses on the difference between a firm's revenue and its product costs.

$$\text{GPM} = \frac{\text{Gross margin}}{\text{Sales}}$$

GPM indicates how efficiently a firm buys or manufactures its products, and how well it marks up and maintains its selling prices. Gross profit margin will vary, depending on the industry and product lines involved. For instance, the margin on jewellery typically is much higher than that on most food products.

Belfry's GPM is

$$\text{GPM} = \frac{\$4,000}{\$10,000} = 40\%$$

Operating Margin (OM)

Operating margin (OM) focuses on earnings before interest and taxes (EBIT), the difference between a firm's revenue and its product costs and expenses.

$$\text{OM} = \frac{\text{EBIT}}{\text{Sales}}$$

OM indicates how efficiently a firm buys or manufactures its products, how well it marks up and maintains its selling prices, and how well it controls its operating expenses. Since public corporations are not required to report their cost of goods sold separately, analysts may be limited to the OM ratio.

Belfry's OM is

$$\text{OM} = \frac{\$1,900}{\$10,000} = 19\%$$

Return on Sales (ROS)

Return on sales (ROS) is also called the *profit margin* or *net profit margin*. It is simply net income as a percentage of sales.

Return on sales (ROS) measures control of the income statement: *revenue and all costs and expenses.*

$$\text{ROS} = \frac{\text{Net income}}{\text{Sales}}$$

Notice that this ratio is the bottom line of the common size income statement. It is a fundamental indication of the overall profitability of the business. It gives insight into management's ability to control the income statement items of revenue, product cost, and expenses. A large company, such as Canadian Tire Corporation, may be satisfied with a return on sales less than 5%, because this ratio still would provide hundreds of millions of dollars on the bottom line. Smaller corporations need a higher return on sales to be viable, at least in the long run.

Belfry's ROS is

$$\text{ROS} = \frac{\$1,000}{\$10,000} = 10\%$$

Return on Assets (ROA)

A business uses its assets and the skills of its people to earn a profit. **Return on assets (ROA)** quantifies the success of that effort with respect to assets by stating net income as a percentage of total assets.

Return on Assets (ROA) adds the effectiveness of asset management to ROS.

$$\text{ROA} = \frac{\text{Net income}}{\text{Total assets}}$$

ROA measures the overall ability of the firm to utilize the assets in which it has invested to earn a profit.

Belfry's ROA is

$$\text{ROA} = \frac{\$1,000}{\$12,000} = 8.3\%$$

ROA is often compared to the firm's cost of financing. A firm raises money to acquire assets. Therefore the return after tax on these assets should be higher than the cost (after tax) of the money raised. This is an example of the concept of positive leverage, to which we will return later in this chapter.

From the CFO

Return on Equity (ROE)

Return on equity (ROE) is the most fundamental profitability ratio. It states net income as a percentage of shareholders' equity.

$$\text{ROE} = \frac{\text{Net income}}{\text{Shareholders' equity}}$$

ROE measures the firm's ability to earn a return on the owners' invested capital. It takes the ROA concept one step further by factoring in the effect of borrowed money. If the firm has substantial debt, ROE tends to be higher than ROA in good times and lower in bad times. If there is little or no debt, ROE and ROA are close to the same. We'll talk about the effect of borrowed money, called *leverage*, in detail in Chapter 16.

For Belfry, we have

$$\text{ROE} = \frac{\$1,000}{\$3,300} = 30.3\%$$

Return on equity (ROE) adds the effect of borrowing to ROA.

WHAT IS AN ACCEPTABLE RETURN ON EQUITY? In judging these returns, comparison to the returns for the competition may indicate that the shareholders would be better off investing in these other companies!

More broadly, a shareholder would compare the return on equity in one company against returns available from various other investment opportunities of comparable risk; for instance, companies in other industries.

Note that these profitability ratios are based upon *net income.* Accordingly, the ratios are analyzed individually and *as a group.*

Market Value Ratios

The ratios we've discussed so far all pertain to the internal management of the firm. As such they are all more or less under the control of management. Another set of ratios, the **market value ratios**, compare certain financial statement figures to the value the stock market places on the firm. These ratios are less controllable by management because the perceptions and attitudes of the investing public are imposed on the actions of the company in arriving at market value. Management can influence those perceptions and attitudes, but it doesn't control them.

Market value ratios relate financial data to stock market prices.

The market value of a company is reflected in the price of its shares. Multiplying the per-share price by the number of shares outstanding leads to a value for the company as a whole. However, it is common practice to think in terms of per-share values.

Price/Earnings Ratio

This ratio compares the market price of the share to the *earnings per share* calculated from the latest income statement. Earnings per share is simply net income divided by the number of common shares outstanding. It is usually abbreviated as *EPS*, while the **price/earnings ratio** is referred to as the **P/E ratio**.

$$\text{P/E ratio} = \frac{\text{Share price}}{\text{EPS}}$$

The P/E ratio is an indication of the value the stock market places on a company's earnings.

A firm's P/E is primarily a function of its *expected growth*.

The P/E ratio is very important in the stock market. Notice that it tells us how much investors are willing to pay for a dollar of the firm's earnings. For example, if a company's P/E is 10 and earnings per share are $4.50, the shares are selling for $45. Stock market people would say, "The company is selling for 10 times earnings."

Different companies carry different P/Es. Clearly, the higher the P/E the better for the current shareholders, because a dollar of earnings translates into more shareholder wealth at higher P/Es. The most significant factor leading to a high P/E ratio is a high expected level of growth for the company.

From the CFO

> *A "high" P/E ratio indicates positive expectations for the future of the company, typically based upon its past successes. However, these expectations often take on a speculative or overly optimistic aspect, leading to share prices that are very expensive relative to earnings. At one time before the market crash in technology stocks, shares in Nortel were selling at 100 × earnings, when the average P/E ratio for Canadian shares was closer to 20! A low P/E ratio may indicate conservative or negative expectations for the future of the company, or may suggest that the stock is a better value or buy.*

P/Es must be used with caution. A firm that is losing money doesn't have a meaningful P/E. Further, if profits are very small but the share has some value, the P/E can be enormous. That isn't meaningful either.

To calculate market value ratios for the Belfry Company, we need the number of shares outstanding and the share price. For the sake of illustration we'll assume that there are 300 shares valued at a price of $38 per share. Earnings per share is then

$$EPS = \frac{\$1,000}{300} = \$3.33$$

and the P/E ratio is

$$P/E = \frac{\$38}{\$3.33} = 11.4$$

Market to Book Value Ratio

A company's *book value* is the total value of the shareholders' equity on its balance sheet. That's equal to the value of assets less liabilities to outsiders. Notice that it may be more or less than the amount the firm could actually realize by selling everything and paying off its debts.

A healthy company is usually expected to have a market value in excess of its book value. This is sometimes known as the *going concern value* of the firm. The idea is that the combination of assets and people that creates an enterprise will generate future earnings that are worth more than the assets alone are worth today.

The **market to book value ratio** addresses this idea of excess value. Like P/E, it is generally thought of in per-share terms. Market value per share is just the price of the share, and book value per share is total shareholders' equity divided by the number of shares outstanding. The calculation is

Market to book value ratio relates shareholders' equity to market valuation.

$$\text{Market to book value ratio} = \frac{\text{Share price}}{\text{Book value per share}}$$

The market to book value ratio is a broad indicator of what the market thinks of a particular share. A value below 1.0 indicates grave concern about the company's future. Such a firm is said to be selling *below book*.

Speculative investors sometimes like to gamble on shares whose market to book value ratio is below 1.0. Situations arise in which a share's price is depressed because the market has overreacted to bad news about a fundamentally sound company. In such a case the firm's share price sometimes rebounds quickly, and an investment at the depressed level can be very profitable. Some investors use the market to book value ratio to identify situations in which this *might* be the case.

Inflation and changes in market values over time can distort such comparisons. Inflation can cause the book value of property, in particular, to differ greatly from its current (replacement) value. These distortions typically have a greater impact the older the assets. Companies with older capital assets may appear more overvalued by current share prices than companies with newer capital assets. We have to apply judgment when comparing ratios of older to newer companies, or a company to itself over a long period of time.

Belfry's book value per share is its shareholders' equity divided by the number of shares outstanding.

$$\text{Book value per share} = \frac{\$3,300}{300} = \$11$$

The market to book value ratio is then

$$\text{Market to book value ratio} = \frac{\$38}{\$11} = 3.5$$

For an online ratio calculator, go to the Business Development Bank of Canada at http://www.bdc.ca. Click on *Business Tools*, then *Ratio Calculators*.

Liquidity Ratios

Liquidity ratios are of particular concern to lenders and suppliers who provide products and services to the firm on credit. They want to be sure the company has the ability to pay its debts.

Liquidity ratios measure the ability to meet short-term *financial obligations.*

Current Ratio

The current ratio is the primary measure of a company's liquidity—that is, its ability to meet its financial obligations in the near future. The calculation is

$$\text{Current ratio} = \frac{\text{Current assets}}{\text{Current liabilities}}$$

The reasoning behind the ratio was discussed earlier as an example. If everything coming in the near future is a current asset today, and everything to be paid out in the near future is a current liability today, then current assets should be substantially above current liabilities to ensure solvency. That would mean that the current ratio has to exceed 1.0 or the firm can expect to run short of cash within the next year.

Having said that, we should point out two anomalies that occur with respect to this ratio. If you look at the balance sheets of large, sophisticated companies that are doing well, you'll often see current ratios in the neighbourhood of or even less than 1.0. Does this mean these firms are in danger of insolvency?

The answer is generally no in spite of the low current ratio. The reason is that the firms are being managed very well. Holding current assets like receivables and inventory ties up money that could be used elsewhere. Hence, firms try to operate with as few current assets as possible. Companies that do this well can have relatively low current ratios if they have a line of credit with a bank to cover temporary cash shortages.

It's important to be aware that a high current ratio can be misleading. Inventories and receivables can be overstated, meaning that some items in those accounts are valueless and will never turn into cash. If those items remain on the balance sheet, they can result in an inflated current assets figure and a falsely comforting current ratio.

From the CFO

Belfry's current ratio is

$$\text{Current ratio} = \frac{\$7,500}{\$2,500} = 3.0$$

The current ratio is a pure number and is generally not referred to in units of any kind.

Quick Ratio or Acid Test

The quick ratio is conceptually similar to the current ratio. The calculation is

$$\text{Quick ratio} = \frac{\text{Current assets} - \text{Inventory}}{\text{Current liabilities}}$$

The liquidity measure provided by the current ratio depends on the conversion of inventory to cash in a reasonable time. However, as we described in Chapter 2, inventory is particularly subject to valuation problems and may be overstated. Inventory also takes more time to convert to cash than other current items.

As a result of these problems, analysts look for a liquidity measure that does not depend on inventory. The quick ratio simply takes it out of current assets in the calculation. The quick ratio is also called the *acid test*, which implies a particularly tough, discerning test.

Current assets sometimes contain minor items such as prepaid expenses that never become cash; they, too, should be subtracted when calculating the quick ratio.

In Belfry's case we have

$$\text{Quick ratio} = \frac{\$7,500 - \$3,200}{\$2,500} = 1.7$$

Like the current ratio, the quick ratio isn't stated in any particular units.

Liquidity ratios that are "too high" may indicate that the company has too much money tied up in receivables or inventory. The current ratio and the quick ratio are judged in light of *asset management* ratios for receivables and inventory.

Asset Management Ratios

Asset management ratios address the fundamental efficiency with which a company is run. They help an analyst understand the firm's basic competitiveness. A business can be thought of as using its assets in conjunction with the skills of its employees to generate revenue and profit. These ratios show the relationship between assets and sales. In general, a company that generates more sales with a given level of assets does better than a firm that generates fewer sales with the same assets.

Asset management ratios measure how assets are used to generate sales.

Average Collection Period (ACP)

The **average collection period** (ACP) represents the average number of days the firm takes to collect its receivables. That is, how long does it take to get paid on credit sales? The ACP is also known as the DSO for *days sales outstanding*, or the *receivables cycle*. The ACP is stated in days and is calculated as follows.

The **average collection period (ACP)** measures the time it takes to collect on credit sales.

$$\text{ACP} = \frac{\text{Accounts receivable}}{\text{Average daily sales}}$$

where average daily sales[3] is Sales/365.

$$\text{Alternatively, ACP} = \frac{\text{Accounts receivable}}{\text{Sales}} \times 365$$

Clearly, the longer a firm takes to collect its money, the worse off it is. Although there are significant exceptions, most credit business is done on terms of 30 days. Frequently a discount is offered for faster payment on the invoice, for example, within 10 days.

---

3 Accounts receivable are generated by credit sales, not cash sales. Technically only credit sales should be used in the calculation. If a mix of credit and cash sales (such as a retailer's sales) is used, the resulting ACP is distorted. In our analysis, we will assume that all sales are credit sales.

Customers often stretch credit terms by paying a few days late, and sellers, who are anxious to keep their business, don't complain over minor delays. That means it's not unusual to see ACPs of 35 to 45 days in the normal course of business in some industries. However, if the ACP exceeds the company's terms of sale by more than 50%, there are probably serious credit problems.

From the CFO

Collection problems have several important implications. The most apparent is that the firm may be granting credit to customers that lack either the ability or the intent to pay. Another possibility, however, is that customers are finding something wrong with the company's product. Customer dissatisfaction frequently results in a reluctance to pay the bill.

The proper interpretation of a high ACP is very important. Although the ACP represents an average collection period, a high figure doesn't usually mean that the average customer is paying excessively slowly. It may imply that while most receivables are being collected fairly promptly, a few are very old, as much as six months or a year. These are unlikely ever to be realized in cash.

Remember from our discussion in Chapter 2 that management is sometimes reluctant to write off questionable receivables because doing so reduces profit. The result of that tendency is an overstated receivables account, which means that the firm's balance sheet is worth less than it purports to be.

Old receivables should be written off without delay, or at least provided for through an addition to the allowance for doubtful accounts.

The value of the receivables balance net of the allowance for doubtful accounts should be used in the calculation. For Belfry, we have the following ACP.

$$\text{ACP} = \frac{\$2,900}{\$10,000} \times 365 = 105.9 \text{ days (rounded to 106 days)}$$

This is not a good result. Belfry clearly has a problem collecting money from at least some of its credit customers. When the average collection period is too long, we can suspect the following:

- poor credit management
- inefficient collection procedures
- risk of uncollectible accounts
- risk of cash shortages
- more reliance on bank financing
- more interest expense

Inventory Turnover

The **inventory turnover ratio** is an attempt to measure whether or not the firm has excess funds tied up in inventory. The ratio is calculated as follows.

$$\text{Inventory turnover} = \frac{\text{Cost of goods sold}}{\text{Inventory}}$$

The **inventory turnover ratio** gives an indication of the quality of inventory as well as how effectively it is managed.

Holding inventory costs money. Inventory costs include interest, storage, insurance, and taxes. In addition, the more inventory a company holds, the more it has at risk of spoiling and becoming obsolete.

The inventory turnover measures how many times a year the firm uses up an average stock of goods. A higher turnover is better in that it implies doing business with less tied up in inventory. A higher inventory turnover minimizes the costs and risks of the following:

- unsaleable stock
- damage and shortages
- insurance, storage, and financing costs
- cash shortages

A higher turnover is essential where inventory is perishable (for example, food), fashionable (for example, women's fashions), or low-margin goods (for example, consumer staples).

A low inventory turnover may indicate inefficient ordering methods or other weaknesses in inventory management.

> *A low turnover figure can mean some old inventory is on the books that isn't being used. What is being used may be turning over adequately, but some material can just be dead weight. Such old stock should be disposed of for whatever can be gotten for it.*
>
> *Operating with too little inventory can create problems too. Excessively low inventory levels cause stockouts—running out of raw material in the factory or not having the product a customer wants on hand. The result is work stoppages or lost sales. There is definitely a right amount of inventory somewhere between too much and too little. The inventory turnover ratio helps to find it.*

An alternative formulation of the inventory turnover ratio involves using sales in the numerator rather than cost of goods sold. In practice, we prefer to use cost of goods sold in the formula, since the inventory is also stated at cost. However, many public companies do not disclose cost of goods sold information in their public reports. Either formulation can be used if comparisons are made consistently.

Belfry's inventory turnover using cost of goods sold is

$$\text{Inventory turnover (based on COGS)} = \frac{\$6,000}{\$3,200} = 1.9$$

The alternative formulation with sales in the numerator is

$$\text{Inventory turnover (based on sales)} = \frac{\$10,000}{\$3,200} = 3.1$$

Inventory turnover is usually stated in units of "turns" or "times," which are written as "$\times$". Notice that in this example the results would be considerably different if an average inventory balance were used in the denominator. That's because inventory changed a lot during the year.

Capital Asset Turnover and Total Asset Turnover

Capital asset turnover and total asset turnover (TAT) measure the relationship of the firm's assets to a year's sales.

$$\text{Capital asset turnover} = \frac{\text{Sales}}{\text{Capital assets}}$$

$$\text{Total asset turnover} = \frac{\text{Sales}}{\text{Total assets}}$$

These two ratios allow us to focus on either capital or total assets. The *total assets* turnover ratio tends to be more widely used. The *capital assets* turnover ratio is appropriate in industries where significant plant or equipment is required to do business.

Capital asset turnover ratios (and ratios in general) have to be interpreted with caution. A "high" ratio may indicate full utilization of production capacity; on the other hand, it may reflect old plant and equipment due for upgrading or historic land costs that bear no relation to current market values. A "low" capital ratio may signify unused capacity, or may reflect a temporary downturn in sales, or new capital assets coming on stream.

These ratios are long-term measures of performance, which are of primary interest to equity investors and stock market analysts. Both asset values are stated net of accumulated amortization.

For the Belfry Company, we have the following ratios:

$$\text{Capital asset turnover} = \frac{\$10,000}{\$4,500} = 2.2$$

$$\text{Total asset turnover} = \frac{\$10,000}{\$12,000} = 0.83$$

The units here are generally stated as "times," sometimes with the symbol "×." For example, Belfry's capital asset turnover might be written as 2.2 × for "2.2 times."

Debt Management Ratios

Debt management deals with how the firm uses other people's money to its own advantage. By "*other people's money*" (often called OPM) we mean borrowing as well as trade credit and other liabilities. In financial analysis, we're primarily concerned that a company doesn't use so much of these funds that it assumes excessive risk. This is an important point. The problem with using other people's money is that it requires future cash outflows for interest and/or repayment. If a firm's operations don't supply enough cash for those payments, it can get into big trouble. The **debt management ratios** measure the financial risk the firm has assumed by borrowing.

Debt management ratios measure financial risk from borrowing.

Terminology

The term *debt* in ratio analysis requires a little amplification. In this book, we'll call *total debt* the sum of current liabilities and long-term debt, that is, total debt is any source of money other than shareholders' equity. *Long-term debt* will mean just that, and the word *debt* by itself will mean interest-bearing borrowings (e.g., loans or bonds, both short-term and long-term).

Debt Ratio

The debt ratio uses the *total debt* concept and measures the relationship between total debt and shareholders' equity in supporting the firm's assets. That is, it tells us how much of the firm's assets are supported by other people's money.

Total debt is the sum of current liabilities and long-term debt.

$$\text{Debt ratio} = \frac{\text{Long-term debt} + \text{Current liabilities}}{\text{Total assets}}$$

A high debt ratio is viewed as risky by lenders and investors. Debt management ratios are generally stated as percentages.

Belfry's debt ratio is

$$\text{Debt ratio} = \frac{\$6,200 + \$2,500}{\$12,000} = 72.5\%$$

Debt to Equity Ratio

The debt to equity ratio generally uses just *long-term debt* and is often stated somewhat differently than other ratios.

$$\text{Debt to equity ratio} = \frac{\text{Long-term debt}}{\text{Shareholders' equity}}$$

This ratio is a measure of the mix of long-term debt and shareholders' equity within the firm's total capital. It is an important measure of risk, because a high level of debt can burden the income statement with excessive interest. This makes the firm's profitability fragile in recessionary times. Interest is known as a **fixed financial charge**, and must be paid regardless of whether

Fixed financial charges like interest increase a firm's financial risk.

or not revenues and profits are healthy. Hence, in a business downturn, large interest charges can throw a company into a loss position quickly. The riskiness associated with debt and interest is called *financial risk.*

Generally, a lower debt to equity ratio indicates a reasonable level of risk in financing; that is, the company should be able to repay its debt even if profits decline. A ratio that is too low may indicate that the company has been too conservative in refusing to borrow the money necessary to expand, or perhaps has too much financing from the shareholders, thus reducing their return on equity.

This ratio is unusual in that it is often stated as a proportion rather than as a decimal or a percentage. For example, if capital of $100 includes debt of $33.33, conventional terminology would describe the debt to equity ratio as "one-third–two-thirds," or "33/67." If capital is two-thirds debt, we would say the ratio is "2 to 1 debt to equity."

For Belfry, we have

$$\text{Debt to equity ratio} = \frac{\$6,200}{\$3,300} = 1.9$$

This would be stated as 1.9 or 1.9:1 (1.9 to 1).

Times Interest Earned (TIE)

Times Interest Earned (TIE) focuses on the impact of interest expense on the income statement. It measures the number of times interest can be paid out of earnings before interest and taxes (EBIT).

$$\text{TIE} = \frac{\text{EBIT}}{\text{Interest}}$$

A high level of *interest coverage* implies safety.

TIE is called a *coverage ratio.* For example, if EBIT is $100 and interest is $10, then TIE is 10; we would say that interest is covered 10 times. Clearly, the more times earnings cover existing interest, the safer it is to lend the firm more money.

For the Belfry Company, we have

$$\text{TIE} = \frac{\$1,900}{\$400} = 4.8$$

The appropriate unit is *times.*

A high TIE ratio often means a *low* debt ratio, and a high debt ratio usually indicates a low TIE ratio.

Cash Coverage

There's an obvious problem with the TIE ratio. Interest is a cash payment, but EBIT is not exactly a source of cash. Rather, it's an income statement subtotal that may be considerably different from cash flow. In other words, more or less cash than EBIT may be available in any given year to pay interest. The problem can be partially solved by recognizing that the biggest difference between EBIT and a comparable cash figure is amortization. It is subtracted as part of cost of goods sold and expenses in the calculation of EBIT.

A better approximation of coverage is available if we form another ratio with amortization added back to EBIT (often called *EBITDA*) in the numerator. This ratio is called *cash coverage.*

$$\text{Cash coverage} = \frac{\text{EBIT} + \text{Amortization}}{\text{Interest}}$$

For Belfry,

$$\text{Cash coverage} = \frac{\$1,900 + \$500}{\$400} = 6.0$$

Fixed Charge Coverage

The TIE and cash coverage ratios recognize interest as a *fixed* financing charge. The term "fixed" implies that interest must be paid regardless of business conditions, unlike dividends, which may be reduced if earnings are poor.

In recent years leasing has supplemented debt as a means of acquiring assets. Instead of borrowing to buy equipment, businesses lease the same equipment and make lease instead of interest payments. We'll discuss leasing in Appendix 9A.

If a company's leased equipment is necessary to stay in business, or if the leases are contractually noncancellable, the payments become fixed charges in the sense that they have to be paid regardless of conditions, just like interest.

We can adjust the TIE ratio to recognize this additional fixed charge. Because lease payments have been subtracted along with other costs and expenses to come to EBIT, they must be added back in the numerator to arrive at a cash figure available to pay all fixed charges. The same amounts must also be added to the denominator as fixed charges equivalent to interest. The resulting ratio is known as *fixed charge coverage*.

Lease payments are *fixed* financial charges similar to interest.

$$\text{Fixed charge coverage} = \frac{\text{EBIT} + \text{Lease payments}}{\text{Interest} + \text{Lease payments}}$$

Other fixed charges can be added to the numerator and denominator when appropriate.

We'll assume that the Belfry Company has $700 of lease payments within its expenses figure. Its fixed charge coverage is then

$$\text{Fixed charge coverage} = \frac{\$1,900 + \$700}{\$400 + \$700} = 2.4$$

Debt management ratios are important to both creditors and shareholders. Creditors want to ensure funds are available to pay interest and principal, and are therefore particularly interested in short-run coverage ratios. Shareholders are concerned about the impact of excessive debt and interest on long-term profitability.

Table 3.1 summarizes all of the foregoing ratios.

For the calculation and analysis of the financial ratios of Danier Leather Inc., see Appendix 3A, pages 96–98.

DANIER LEATHER

Du Pont Equations

Each of the ratios we've been talking about measures a particular aspect of running a company. However, the ratio measures aren't entirely independent, and performance on one is sometimes tied to performance on others.

Two insightful relationships between ratios are captured in the **Du Pont equations.**[4] The first is developed from our formula on return on assets.

The **Du Pont equations** express relationships between ratios that give insights into successful operation.

$$\text{ROA} = \frac{\text{Net income}}{\text{Total assets}}$$

We can restate this formula as follows:

4 So called because they were developed at the E.I. Du Pont de Nemours and Company.

TABLE 3.1
Financial Ratios

Profitability Ratios

1. Gross profit margin (%) $= \dfrac{\text{Gross margin}}{\text{Sales}}$

2. Operating margin (%) $= \dfrac{\text{EBIT}}{\text{Sales}}$

3. Return on sales (%) $= \dfrac{\text{Net income}}{\text{Sales}}$

4. Return on assets (%) $= \dfrac{\text{Net income}}{\text{Total assets}^*}$

5. Return on equity (%) $= \dfrac{\text{Net income}}{\text{Shareholders' equity}^*}$

6. Earnings per share ($) $= \dfrac{\text{Net income}}{\text{Number of common shares outstanding}^*}$

Market Value Ratios

7. Price/earnings ratio (%) $= \dfrac{\text{Share price}}{\text{EPS}}$

8. Market to book value ratio ($\times$) $= \dfrac{\text{Share price}}{\text{Book value per share}}$

Liquidity Ratios

9. Current ratio (number) $= \dfrac{\text{Current assets}}{\text{Current liabilities}}$

10. Quick ratio (number) $= \dfrac{\text{Current assets} - \text{Inventory}}{\text{Current liabilities}}$

Asset Management Ratios

11. Average collections (period days) $= \dfrac{\text{Account receivable}^*}{\text{Sales}} \times 365$

12. Inventory turnover ($\times$) $= \dfrac{\text{Cost of goods sold}}{\text{Inventory}^*}$

12. Inventory turnover (sales basis) ($\times$) $= \dfrac{\text{Sales}}{\text{Inventory}^*}$

13. Average holding period (days) $= \dfrac{365}{\text{Inventory turnover}^*}$

14. Capital asset turnover ($\times$) $= \dfrac{\text{Sales}}{\text{Capital assets}^*}$

15. Total asset turnover ($\times$) $= \dfrac{\text{Sales}}{\text{Total assets}^*}$

Debt Management Ratios

16. Debt ratio (%) $= \dfrac{\text{Long-term debt} + \text{current liabilities}}{\text{Total assets}}$

17. Debt to equity (number or proportion) $= \dfrac{\text{Long-term debt}}{\text{Shareholders' equity}}$

18. Times interest earned ($\times$) $= \dfrac{\text{EBIT}}{\text{Interest}}$

19. Cash coverage ($\times$) $= \dfrac{\text{EBIT} + \text{Amortization}}{\text{Interest}}$

20. Fixed charge coverage ($\times$) $= \dfrac{\text{EBIT} + \text{Lease payments}}{\text{Interest} + \text{Lease payments}}$

* Average balance sheet values may be appropriate

$$ROA = \frac{\text{Net income}}{\text{Sales}} \times \frac{\text{Sales}}{\text{Total assets}}$$

Notice that we've formed two ratios, the product of which is ROA. But we've seen the new ratios before; they are *return on sales* and *total asset turnover*. Hence the Du Pont equation is

$$ROA = ROS \times \text{Total asset turnover}$$

The relationship is an important result. ROA is a fundamental measure of performance, indicating how well a company uses its assets to generate profits. But it is the product of two more elementary measures. The first, ROS, measures how well a firm keeps some of its sales dollars in profit. The second, total asset turnover, measures the company's ability to generate sales with the assets it has.

The Du Pont equation tells us that, to run a business well as measured by ROA, we have to manage costs and expenses well and generate a lot of sales per dollar of assets.

The extended Du Pont equation takes the idea one step further by expressing return on equity (ROE) in terms of other ratios. We'll develop it from our formula for return on equity:

$$ROE = \frac{\text{Net income}}{\text{Shareholders' equity}}$$

We can restate this formula as follows:

$$ROE = \frac{\text{Net income}}{\text{Total assests}} \times \frac{\text{Total assets}}{\text{Shareholders' equity}}$$

We have once again formed two ratios, the product of which is ROE.

Again, we've seen the *first* term before. It's the return on assets (ROA) above.

$$ROA = \frac{\text{Net income} \times \text{Sales}}{\text{Sales} \times \text{Total assets}}$$

Therefore,

$$ROE = \frac{\text{Net income}}{\text{Sales}} \times \frac{\text{Sales}}{\text{Total assets}} \times \frac{\text{Total assets}}{\text{Shareholders' equity}}$$

The last term is called the equity *multiplier*. We'll explain it in a minute, but first notice that the ROE expression is the same as the ROA expression with the last term added.

$$ROE = ROS \times \text{Total asset turnover} \times \text{Equity multiplier}$$

$$ROE = ROA \times \text{Equity multiplier}$$

The equity multiplier has to do with the idea of *leverage;* using borrowed money instead of your own to work for you.[5] Hence, the extended Du Pont equation says that, to measure performance in terms of ROE, we add the concept of leverage to performance in terms of ROA.

To understand the equity multiplier, consider the right side of the balance sheet. It lists all of the places from which the firm's money comes: shareholders' equity, long-term debt, and current liabilities. These add to total assets because both sides of the balance sheet sum to that figure. Long-term debt and current liabilities are other people's money, while shareholders' equity is the firm's own money (its owners'). The equity multiplier is related to the proportion of the firm financed by other people's money as opposed to owners' money.

---

5 Conceptually, the equity multiplier is similar to the debt ratio we discussed earlier. In fact, a high debt ratio will be equivalent to a high equity multiplier. As financing must come from either debt or shareholders' equity, a high debt ratio implies a relatively low use of shareholders' equity. Relatively low shareholders' equity in the equity multiplier formula results in a high equity multiplier.

For example, suppose a firm has total assets of $100 and shareholders' equity of $25. That means three-quarters of its assets are financed by long-term debt and/or current liabilities ($75) and one-quarter ($25) is supported by shareholders' equity. The equity multiplier is ($100/$25) = 4, and the extended Du Pont equation says that the firm's ROE will be four times its ROA because of the use of other people's money.

That's very good if the business is making a profit and ROA is a positive number. For example, if ROA is 5%, ROE would be a healthy 20%. However, if times get tough, using other people's money is generally bad news. Suppose the business starts to lose money and ROA is –5%. Unfortunately, the multiplier still works the same way, and ROE will be –20%, a pretty dismal figure.

The extended Du Pont equation says something very important about running a business. The operation of the business itself is reflected in ROA. This means managing customers, people, costs, expenses, and equipment, either to increase sales volume and turnover, or to improve margins, or both. But that result, good or bad, can be multiplied by borrowing. In other words, the way you finance a business can greatly exaggerate the results of nuts and bolts operations.

Write out the Du Pont equations for Belfry to verify the relationships.

In summary, the Du Pont equations emphasize that return on equity (ROE) is affected by three factors:

1. *operating efficiency* (as measured by the return on sales)
2. *asset management efficiency* (as measured by total asset turnover)
3. *financial leverage* (as measured by the equity multiplier) [6]

Weakness in any of the three factors shows up in a lower ROE. If ROE is considered inadequate, the Du Pont equations tell us where to start looking for the reasons. However, a higher ROE does not always signify financial strength. A substantial increase in debt may increase ROE, but also entails greater financial risk.

Using the Du Pont Equations

Comparing the Du Pont equations between a company and an industry average can give some insights into how a firm is doing in relation to its competitors. For example, suppose we have the following data for Samson Inc. and its industry.

	ROS	×TAT	= ROA	×EM	= ROE
Samson Inc.	6%	2×	12%	2×	24%
Industry	5%	3×	15%	1.5×	22.5%

If Samson is trying to figure out why its ROA is below average, this display focuses attention in the right direction. It says that management of the income statement items (like cost and expense) is a little better than average, but the use of assets to generate sales (as measured by total asset turnover) is very poor in comparison to the competition.

The turnover problem is probably in one or both of two areas. Perhaps the company has unnecessary or ineffective assets, such as overstated inventory or inefficient machinery. Or maybe its promotional activities are not on target, so sales are lower than they should be. The job is now to find out what's going on and fix that problem.

On the other hand, Samson's ROE is higher than average, because its use of debt has provided more positive leverage. Of course, this strategy increases the financial risk of the firm.

DANIER LEATHER   For the Du Pont equations as applied to Danier Leather Inc., refer to Appendix 3A, page 98.

---

6 Financial leverage can also be measured by the difference between ROE and return on assets (ROA).

Sources of Comparative Information

One source of comparative information for ratio analysis is an industry average. These averages are widely available, often for a fee, but many colleges and universities subscribe to online data bases that provide ratio information.

Some examples of online and other sources for ratios are found in Table 3.2.

Source	Provides
D&B Canada, at http://www.dnb.ca	Industry norms and business ratios; data on over 800 different lines of business and 1.5 million Canadian corporations (subscription)
Value Line, at http://www.valueline.com	Data and analysis on U.S. companies
Statistics Canada, at http://www.statcan.ca	Financial performance indicators for Canadian business; ratios for major industry groups
Financial Post Datagroup, at http://www.financialpost.com	Online database on Canadian companies (subscription)
Reuters Investor, at http://www.marketguide.com	Ratios for U.S. publicly traded companies (free registration)
Globe Investor, at http://www.globeinvestor.com	Ratios for Canadian publicly traded companies
Strategis Canada, at http://www.strategis.gc.ca *Search* for "Performance Plus"	Online database of comparative data for specific lines of small business

TABLE 3.2
Ratio Sources

Table 3.3 provides selected average ratios for Canadian industries for the seven years ended 2005.

Limitations and Weaknesses of Ratio Analysis

Although ratio analysis is a powerful tool, it has some significant shortcomings. Analysts have to be careful not to apply the techniques blindly to any set of statements they come across. Here are a few of the more significant problems.

Accounting principles allow a great deal of latitude in reporting. That means similar companies might report the same thing differently, making their financial results artificially dissimilar. Amortization is a good example. The choice among methods of amortization is up to the firm, but the method chosen can greatly affect reported amortization in a given period. That in turn can make a big percentage difference in net income between two essentially identical firms.

Pro forma earnings or *"cash earnings"* are an earnings measure different from earnings after tax. This approach ignores certain noncash costs and expenses, but some companies use it to provide a separate set of financial statements. This approach is not recognized by GAAP, but provides more favourable income statements. While the companies may provide both GAAP-based and pro forma reports, users must be aware of which set they are reading and which set management is discussing.

When a company sells or closes a division, its future prospects should be based on continuing operations that represent repeatable performance. Accordingly, the results and closure costs for *discontinued operations* are reported separately on the financial statements. But financial statements may make separating the results of sold units difficult, creating the impression that what's left is better than it is.

Ratio analysis is *not an exact science* and requires judgment and *experienced interpretation.*

TABLE 3.3
Selected Financial
Ratios Averages by
Industry:
1999–2005

Industry	Return on Sales (%)	Return on Equity (%)	Price/ Earnings Ratio (X)	Current Ratio	Total Asset Turnover (X)	Debt to Equity Ratio	Times Interest Earned (X)
Automobile Components	(29.0)	(5.7)	16.2	2.6	1.1	0.17	28.7
Banks	20.7	15.0	13.5	N/A	N/A	0.36	N/A
Metals & Mining	(3.4)	0.2	22.4	4.2	0.5	0.37	18.4
Oil & Gas	(2.3)	6.2	21.0	2.1	0.4	0.32	30.6
Retailing	1.8	8.9	14.1	2.0	2.0	0.22	31.7
Software	(62.6)	(30.9)	28.5	3.6	0.8	0.33	50.4
Telecommunications	(8.9)	5.8	26.1	1.1	0.7	1.10	4.1
Transportation	3.7	2.5	14.8	1.3	1.5	1.01	31.2

* *Source:* Financial Post Industry Reports. Available by subscription at http://www.FPinfomart.ca. Material reprinted with the express permission of: "National Post Company," a CanWest Partnership.

Profits from *activities outside of normal business* should be displayed separately because they usually aren't repeatable. For example, a manufacturing firm's one-time gain on the sale of real estate shouldn't be combined with profits from ongoing operations, because that's likely to mislead investors into overvaluing the firm. Companies may be tempted to lump one-time gains with normal operating income, or to report somewhat normal costs or expenses as *unusual*.

Restructuring means reorganizing to face changed business conditions, usually by getting smaller. It generally involves charges for severance pay and closing facilities. Companies show income before and after restructuring charges, expecting investors to value firms based on the higher income before the charge because restructurings are rare. But many companies restructure every few years. Doing that raises a question as to whether the charges are truly one-time events or just cover-ups for bad management.

Ratios such as the return on assets that use information from both the income statement and the balance sheet can be very misleading, particularly if the company had a major restructuring such as an acquisition during the year. The balance sheet will reflect the full impact, whereas the income statement will include only part-year results for the change.

Diversified companies, large firms with consolidated operations, create what is probably the biggest analysis problem. Such companies often have divisions operating in significantly different industries. The financial information they publish consolidates the results of those different operations into one set of statements. Because the interpretation of ratios is highly dependent on industry norms, this mixing of results from different businesses can greatly reduce the informative value of analysis.

Financial reporting standards set by the accounting profession for diversified businesses require the disclosure of some segment information, but it is generally of limited scope and use.

Window dressing refers to practices at year-end that make balance sheets look better than they otherwise would through improvements that don't last. Here's a simple example. Imagine a firm with a current ratio that's too low whose business is fundamentally sound so it can borrow long term. Suppose this company takes out a long-term loan a few days before the end of the year, holds the proceeds in cash over year-end, and repays the loan a few days later. It thus increases year-end current assets with no impact on current liabilities, thereby improving the reported current ratio.

http

For a good overview of MVA and EVA, including a video on the concepts, go to the Stern Stewart website at http://www.sternstewart.com.

Seasonal differences can distort comparisons between companies or over time. We should compare financial statements at the same point of time during the year to avoid erroneous conclusions resulting from seasonal differences, particularly in industries such as retailing.

Inflation and changes in market values over time can distort results. Inflation can cause the book value of property, in particular, to differ greatly from its current (replacement) value. Additionally, amortization of capital assets based on such book values can significantly affect reported profits. These distortions typically have a greater impact the larger the difference in the ages of the assets being compared. Companies with older capital assets may appear more efficient and profitable than companies with newer capital assets. We have to apply judgment when comparing ratios of older to newer companies, or a company to itself over a long period of time.

Unethical and/or illegal accounting practices can hide overstated assets and unsuspected operating losses from shareholders, regulators, and analysts.

Interpretation of ratios isn't always clear. *Groups of ratios* provide better information to judge performance than just one ratio. For example, a high current ratio may be suspect if the receivable or inventory ratios are weak. In addition, we should consider both the ratios and the underlying numbers in the financial statements for a more complete analysis.

The most important thing to remember with respect to these issues is that ratio analysis doesn't give answers—it helps you ask the right questions.

> **Market value added** is the difference between the book value and market value of a company.

> **Economic value added** is the change in market value added during the year.

Insights PRACTICAL FINANCE

New Ideas in Financial Analysis: MVA and EVA®

In recent years the related ideas of *market value added* (MVA) and *economic value added* (EVA®) have become popular as gauges of business success. The concept behind both measures is the creation of shareholder wealth. We'll consider MVA first.

There are two ways to think about the value of a firm's shareholders' equity. The market value of shareholders' equity is just share price times the number of shares outstanding. At the same time, the equity contributed by shareholders is reflected in the shareholders' equity accounts on the company's books (including retained earnings). If market value is greater than book value, some additional value has been created by the company acting as an ongoing business. This extra is the market value added—it's the cumulative amount that management has made for the shareholders over and above dividends since the inception of the firm.

Notice that MVA can be negative if the shares are selling below their book value. Conceptually MVA is similar to the *market to book value ratio* we discussed earlier. You should be able to see that a negative MVA is equivalent to a market to book ratio of less than 1.0.

The more exciting idea is EVA, economic value added. In theory, it is the amount by which the firm increases or decreases MVA in the current year.

Before defining EVA precisely, it's important to notice something about traditional net income. When we calculate net income, we subtract interest from revenues along with other costs and expenses. You can think of interest as the cost the company pays for the use of its debt capital. We do not, however, subtract a payment to shareholders for the use of equity capital.

That means financial analysis based on net income (EAT) recognizes the cost of debt (interest) but implicitly treats shareholders' equity as a free source of capital. This presents a problem because equity capital does have a cost, basically the return demanded by shareholders on their investments. Ignoring the cost of shareholders' equity makes performance seem better than it is. For example, a company with a small positive net income is profitable in an accounting sense but may be an economic failure because it doesn't provide an adequate return to shareholders on their equity investments.

A better measure of overall performance than accounting net income would be produced if we modified the income statement to subtract the cost of both debt and equity capital instead of just the interest cost of debt. This is exactly what EVA does using a concept called the cost of capital. We'll study the cost of capital in great depth in Chapter 15. For now it's enough to understand that it's a single, average "interest rate" that reflects the rate of return the business pays to the suppliers of its capital, both debt and shareholders' equity. That rate, stated on an after-tax basis, is the "cost" of the capital funds the firm uses.

EVA is defined as follows.

$$EVA = EBIT\,(1 - T) - (Debt + Shareholders'\ equity)\,(Cost\ of\ capital\ \%)$$

where T is the tax rate.

The first term on the right is EBIT adjusted to an after-tax basis by multiplying by $(1 - T)$. This figure is what the firm's after-tax net income would be if there were no charges for the use of capital, either debt or shareholders' equity.

The second term on the right subtracts a charge for the use of capital. Debt plus shareholders' equity is total capital, so the cost of capital percentage times that sum is the dollar amount the firm pays for the use of all of its capital. This term is like the traditional interest charge in the income statement except that it's expanded to include a payment for shareholders' equity. It's an after-tax figure, because the cost of capital percentage is stated after tax.

Hence, EVA is after-tax net income less an after-tax charge for all capital. But the charge for capital is simply the minimum amount shareholders and bondholders demand for investing their money. They could make that amount by putting it in any number of alternative investments. Hence, if EVA is positive, the firm is exceeding its investors' expectations. That is, a positive EVA is an extra, an additional contribution to shareholders' wealth made during the year.

This is a very important idea. If EVA is zero, the firm is earning just what investors expect and demand, nothing more and nothing less. That's adequate performance. On the other hand, if EVA is positive, management is performing above expectations and contributing some additional value to shareholders. A negative EVA, of course, means the firm is losing ground, making an inadequate contribution to shareholder wealth.

EVA began to gain popularity about 15 years ago and is one of the hottest ideas in financial management today. Some Canadian and American companies that have implemented the technique include Domtar, Alcan, AT&T, and Coca-Cola. Several attribute major gains in market value to a management focus on EVA rather than traditional net income. The EVA and MVA concepts were developed by Stern Stewart & Co., a financial consulting firm. Stern Stewart maintains that its clients that use EVA—including Best Buy (consumer electronics), Guidant (medical products), and Noble Drilling (energy)—outperform their peers in the stock market.

Source: New Ideas in Financial Analysis: MVA and EVA® from www.eva.com. Reprinted with permission from Stern and Stewart.

SUMMARY

1 Corporate financial information, primarily from the annual report, is used by investors, analysts, creditors, and management to make decisions about the company.

2 The annual report typically includes the letter to shareholders, the management discussion and analysis, audited financial statements, notes to the financial statements, and other recent and historical financial information.

3 Because management compensation is often tied to share price, corporate executives may publish misleading financial statements that inflate revenue and net income and/or hide debt. As a result, recent legislation has been enacted to strengthen corporate governance.

4 Techniques of financial analysis include comparative financial statements, trend analysis, common size statements and financial ratio analysis.

5 Under ratio analysis, we developed five categories of financial ratios: profitability, market value, liquidity, asset management, and debt management ratios. Using the balance sheet and income statement, we calculated the ratios. These can be compared to historical, budget, and competitors' data.

6 The Du Pont equations break return on equity into three components: return on sales, asset turnover, and debt usage, and can be used to assess the source of company profitability.

7 Some of the problems involved in ratio analysis include varying accounting principles, non-GAAP-based financial statements, difficulty in analyzing diversified companies, discontinued operations and other unusual charges, window dressing at year-end, seasonal effects, inflation and changes in market values over time, unethical and/or illegal accounting practices, and other difficulties in interpretation.

KEY TERMS

KEY FORMULAS

$$\text{Growth in sales}(\%) = \frac{\text{Current year sales} - \text{Prior year sales}}{\text{Prior year sales}}$$

$$\text{Growth in net income }(\%) = \frac{\text{Current year net income} - \text{Prior year net income}}{\text{Prior year net income}}$$

$$\text{Gross profit margin (GPM) }(\%) = \frac{\text{Gross margin}}{\text{Sales}}$$

$$\text{Operating margin (OM) }(\%) = \frac{\text{EBIT}}{\text{Sales}}$$

$$\text{Return on sales (ROS) }(\%) = \frac{\text{Net income}}{\text{Sales}}$$

$$\text{Return on assets (ROA) }(\%) = \frac{\text{Net income}}{\text{Total assets}}$$

$$\text{Return on equity (ROE) }(\%) = \frac{\text{Net income}}{\text{Shareholders' equity}}$$

$$\text{Earnings per share (EPS) (\$)} = \frac{\text{Net income}}{\text{Number of common shares outstanding}^*}$$

$$\text{Price-earnings ratio (P/E ratio) }(\%) = \frac{\text{Share price}}{\text{EPS}}$$

$$\text{Market to book value ratio } (\times) = \frac{\text{Share price}}{\text{Book value per share}}$$

$$\text{Current ratio (number)} = \frac{\text{Current assets}}{\text{Current liabilities}}$$

$$\text{Quick ratio (number)} = \frac{\text{Current assets} - \text{Inventory}}{\text{Current liabilities}}$$

$$\text{Average collection period (days) (ACP)} = \frac{\text{Accounts receivable}^*}{\text{Sales}} \times 365$$

$$\text{Inventory turnover } (\times) = \frac{\text{Cost of goods sold}}{\text{Inventory}^*}$$

$$\text{Inventory turnover (sales basis)} (\times) = \frac{\text{Sales}}{\text{Inventory}^*}$$

$$\text{Average holding period (days)} = \frac{365}{\text{Inventory turnover}^*}$$

$$\text{Capital asset turnover} (\times) = \frac{\text{Sales}}{\text{Capital assets}^*}$$

$$\text{Total asset turnover} (\times) = \frac{\text{Sales}}{\text{Total assets}^*}$$

$$\text{Debt ratio} (\%) = \frac{\text{Long-term debt} + \text{Current liabilities}}{\text{Total assets}}$$

$$\text{Debt to equity (number or proportion)} = \frac{\text{Long-term debt}}{\text{Shareholders' equity}}$$

$$\text{Times interest earned (TIE)} (\times) = \frac{\text{EBIT}}{\text{Interest}}$$

$$\text{Cash coverage} (\times) = \frac{\text{EBIT} + \text{Amortization}}{\text{Interest}}$$

$$\text{Fixed charge coverage} (\times) = \frac{\text{EBIT} + \text{Lease payments}}{\text{Interest} + \text{Lease payments}}$$

$$\text{ROA} = \frac{\text{Net income}}{\text{Sales}} \times \frac{\text{Sales}}{\text{Total assets}}$$

$$\text{ROE} = \frac{\text{Net income}}{\text{Sales}} \times \frac{\text{Sales}}{\text{Total assets}} \times \frac{\text{Total assets}}{\text{Shareholders' equity}}$$

$$\text{ROE} = \text{ROS} \times \text{Total asset turnover} \times \text{Equity multiplier}$$

$$\text{ROE} = \text{ROA} \times \text{Equity multiplier}$$

$$\text{ROA} = \text{ROS} \times \text{Total asset turnover}$$

$$\text{Equity multiplier} = \frac{\text{Total assets}}{\text{Equity}}$$

$$\text{ROS} \times \text{TAT} = \text{ROA} \times \text{EM} = \text{ROE}$$

$$\text{EVA} = \text{EBIT} (1 - T) - (\text{Debt} + \text{Shareholders' equity})(\text{Cost of capital} \%)$$

*Average balance sheet values may be appropriate.

DANIER LEATHER

APPENDIX 3A

Financial Information and Analysis for Danier Leather Inc.

In operation since 1972, Danier Leather is a vertically integrated, publicly traded company that designs, manufactures, and retails leather and suede products. It is Canada's largest leather apparel retailer. The company's clothing and accessories are sold exclusively under the Danier label. In June 2006, Danier operated 95 shopping mall, street-front, and larger format power centre stores across Canada. Danier also sold its merchandise directly to corporate clients through its corporate sales division.[7]

Photo: Permission of Danier Leather Inc.

7 Sales to customers through stores are cash sales and are recognized at the time the transaction is entered into the point-of-sale register net of returns. Sales to corporate customers are normally credit sales and are recognized at the time of shipment.

BACKGROUND

Danier has been scrambling over the last few years amid a waning fashion interest in leather clothing, global warming, and a failed launch in the United States.

Danier has found it tough to sell its goods without having to discount the price. Leather apparel peaked in 2000 and just hasn't had much buzz since. Lower-priced goods such as bomber jackets have been more popular than higher-priced items, such as long coats.

More ominously for Danier, significant numbers of consumers have been opting for denim, micro-fibres, and other materials instead of leather.

Danier's shares were issued in its 1998 IPO at $11.25. They reached their high of $19.50 in 2002. In September 2007 they were selling in the $8.00−$9.00 range.

In 2006 Danier closed two stores, cut 23 head office jobs, and shut down its on-line shopping business as it fought to return to profitability. According to retail consultant David Howell, the latest cutbacks weren't nearly enough, Danier still had too many costly stores and more stores would need to be shut. He said that Danier is specializing in a field that is shrinking in demand. "Leather is strictly a fashion item. The appeal tends to evaporate when you get extreme weather."

Danier Leather Inc.
Trend Analysis

	2006	2005	2004	2003	2002
Number of stores	95	95	98	98	89
Revenue , excluding U.S. operations ($000)	$148,351	$166,350	$175,270	$172,823	$177,704
Same-store sales growth Increase/ (decrease)	(11%)	(6%)	(4%)	(3%)	1%
Net earnings (loss) ($000)	($5,503)	($185)	($7,097)	$5,394	$10,725

Revenue and net earnings peaked at $177.7 million and $10.7 million respectively in 2002. Same-store annual revenue growth had been negative since 2002. Revenue decreased 11% or $18.0 million to $148.4 million in 2006 from $166.4 million in 2005. Revenue decreased 6% in 2005.

According to Danier, major factors in these declines include weak consumer spending on leather outerwear, a more promotional retail environment leading up to Christmas, customer preference for shorter-length jackets and other lower-price-point merchandise, a reduced reliance on price promotions, and unseasonably hot weather.

In the last three years, Danier posted successive losses (including store closing costs, head office reductions, and litigation provisions).

FINANCIAL STATEMENTS

Danier Leather Inc.
Consolidated Statements of Earnings

(Thousands of dollars, except per share amounts)

	For the Year Ended June 24, 2006		For the Year Ended June 25, 2005	
Revenue	$148,351	100.0%	$166,350	100.0%
Cost of sales	76,953	51.9%	82,863	49.8%
Gross profit	71,398	48.1%	83,487	50.2%

Selling, general and administrative expenses	78,796	53.1%	77,215	46.4%
Interest income	(445)	(0.3%)	(340)	(0.2%)
Restructuring costs	1,389	(0.9%)	–	–
Litigation provision and related expenses	–	–	3,098	1.9%
Earnings (loss) before discontinued operations and income taxes	**(8,342)**	**(5.6%)**	**3,514**	**2.1%**
Provision for (recovery of) current and future income taxes	(2,839)	(1.9%)	931	0.5%
Net earnings (loss) before discontinued operations	**(5,503)**	**(3.7%)**	**2,583**	**1.6%**
Loss from discontinued operations, net of income taxes	–	–	(2,768)	1.7%
Net loss	**$(5,503)**	**(3.7%)**	**$(185)**	**(0.1%)**

Consolidated Statements of Retained Earnings

(Thousands of dollars)

	For the Year Ended	
	June 24, 2006	**June 25, 2005**
Retained earnings, beginning of year	$ 32,214	$ 36,902
Net loss	(5,503)	(185)
Dividends	(1,572)	(1,620)
Retained earnings, end of year	**$ 25,139**	**$ 32,214**

Consolidated Balance Sheets

(Thousands of Dollars)

	June 24, 2006	**June 25, 2005**
ASSETS		
Current Assets		
Cash	$ 11,833	$ 21,193
Accounts receivable	402	594
Income taxes recoverable	2,485	939
Inventories	32,348	29,031
Prepaid expenses	1,026	516
Assets of discontinued operations	–	23
Future income tax asset	529	159
Total current assets	48,623	52,455
Other assets		
Property and equipment	27,293	25,314
Goodwill	342	342
Future income tax asset	5,952	5,254
Total assets	$ 82,210	$ 83,365
LIABILITIES		
Current liabilities		

Accounts payable and accrued liabilities	$ 10,708	$ 8,170
Current portion of capital lease obligation	911	–
Future income tax liability	624	–
Total current liabilities	12,243	8,170
Other liabilities		
Capital lease obligation	1,829	–
Accrued litigation provision and related expenses	18,000	18,000
Deferred lease inducements and rent liability	2,125	1,838
Future income tax liability	57	420
Total liabilities	34,254	28,428
SHAREHOLDERS' EQUITY		
Share capital	22,542	22,493
Contributed surplus	275	230
Retained earnings	25,139	32,214
Total shareholders' equity	47,956	54,937
Total liabilities and shareholders' equity	$ 82,210	$ 83,365

Consolidated Statements of Cash Flow

(Thousands of dollars)

	For the Years Ended	
	June 24, 2006	**June 25, 2005**
OPERATING ACTIVITIES		
Net loss	$ (5,503)	$ (185)
Items not affecting cash:		
Amortization	7,055	7,546
Amortization of deferred lease inducements	(399)	(445)
Straight line rent expense	400	–
Stock based compensation	45	11
Accrued litigation provision and related expenses	–	2,550
Future income taxes	(807)	(622)
Net change in non-cash working capital items	(2,643)	(2,205)
Discontinued operations	23	791
Cash flows from (used in) operating activities	(1,829)	7,441
FINANCING ACTIVITIES		
Subordinate voting shares issued	49	27
Subordinate voting shares repurchased	–	(4,583)
Dividends	(1,572)	(1,620)
Proceeds from capital lease obligation	2,902	–
Repayment of obligations under capital lease	(162)	–
Proceeds from lease inducements	286	–
Cash flows from (used in) financing activities	1,503	(6,176)
INVESTING ACTIVITIES		
Acquisition of capital assets	(9,034)	(2,648)
Cash flows used in investing activities	(9,034)	(2,648)
Decrease in cash	(9,360)	(1,383)
Cash, beginning of year	21,193	22,576
Cash, end of year	$ 11,833	$ 21,193

CASH FLOWS

Operating Activities

Cash outflow from operating activities in 2006 amounted to $1.8 million, a decrease of $9.2 million from the inflow of $7.4 million in 2005. Approximately $5.3 million of the decrease resulted from a higher net loss and approximately $3.3 million of the decrease was due to higher year-end inventory balances as Danier began earlier purchases of inventory for 2007.

Financing Activities

Cash inflow from financing activities amounted to $1.5 million in 2006, an increase of $7.7 million from the outflow of $6.2 million in 2005. During 2006, Danier entered 95into a three-year capital lease facility for $2.9 million to fund new point-of-sale hardware and software. Another $4.6 million of the increase related to share repurchases in 2005.

Investing Activities

Capital expenditures were $9.0 million in 2006 compared with $2.6 million during 2005.

Capital expenditures in 2006 included approximately $3.5 million for two new stores, renovations, and store equipment; $5.3 million towards information technology, and $0.2 million for additional production machinery and equipment.

Free Cash Flows

Free cash flows were (thousands of dollars):

	2006	2005
Cash flow from operating activities	$ (1,829)	$ 7,441
Minus: Acquisition of capital assets	9,034	2,648
Minus: Dividends	1,572	1,620
Free cash flow	$ (12,435)	$ 3,173

In fact, Danier Leather had no free cash flow in 2006. Operating cash flows were negative owing to the net loss and larger year-end inventories.

FINANCIAL RATIOS

Danier Leather Inc.
Financial Ratios 2006 ($000 except earnings per share)

1. Gross profit margin $= \dfrac{\text{Gross profit}}{\text{Revenue}} = \dfrac{71,398}{148,351} = 48.1\%$

2. Operating margin $= \dfrac{\text{Loss before income taxes}}{\text{Revenue}} = \dfrac{(8,342)}{148,351} = (5.6\%)$

3. Return on sales $= \dfrac{\text{Net loss}}{\text{Revenue}} = \dfrac{(5,503)}{148,351} = (3.7\%)$

4. Return on assets $= \dfrac{\text{Net loss}}{\text{Total assets}} = \dfrac{(5,503)}{82,210} = (6.7\%)$

5. Return on equity $= \dfrac{\text{Net loss}}{\text{Shareholders' equity}} = \dfrac{(5,503)}{47,956} = (11.5\%)$

6. Earnings per share $= \dfrac{\text{Net loss}}{\text{Number of common shares outstanding}} = \dfrac{(5,503)}{6,547,090} = (\$0.84)$

7. Price-earnings ratio $= \dfrac{\text{Market price per share}}{\text{Loss per share}}$ Not applicable

8. Market to book value ratio $= \dfrac{\text{Market price per share}}{\text{Book value per share}}$ Not available

9. Current ratio $= \dfrac{\text{Current assets}}{\text{Current liabilities}} = \dfrac{48,623}{12,243} = 4.0$

10. Quick ratio $= \dfrac{\text{Current assets} - \text{Inventories}}{\text{Current liabilities}} = \dfrac{16,275}{12,243} = 1.3$

11. Average collection period $= \dfrac{\text{Accounts receivable}}{\text{Revenue}} \times 365 = \dfrac{402}{148,351} \times 365 = 1\text{ day}$

12. Inventory turnover $= \dfrac{\text{Cost of goods sold}}{\text{Inventory}} = \dfrac{148,351}{32,348} = 4.6\times$

12. Inventory turnover (sales basis) $= \dfrac{\text{Revenue}}{\text{Inventory}} = \dfrac{76,953}{32,348} = 2.4\times$

13. Average holding period $= \dfrac{365}{\text{Inventory turnover}} = \dfrac{365}{2.4} = 152\text{ days}$

14. Capital asset turnover $= \dfrac{\text{Revenue}}{\text{Property and equipment}} = \dfrac{148,351}{27,293} = 5.4\times$

15. Total asset turnover $= \dfrac{\text{Revenue}}{\text{Total assets}} = \dfrac{148,351}{82,210} = 1.8\times$

16. Debt ratio $= \dfrac{\text{Total liabilities}}{\text{Total assets}} = \dfrac{34,254}{82,210} = 41.7\%$

17. Debt to equity $= \dfrac{\text{Total liabilities} - \text{Current liabilities}}{\text{Shareholders' equity}} = \dfrac{22,011}{47,956} = 45.9\%$

18. Times interest earned $= \dfrac{\text{Loss before income taxes}}{\text{Interest expense}}$ Not applicable

19. Cash coverage $= \dfrac{\text{Loss before income taxes} + \text{Amortization}}{\text{Interest expense}}$ Not applicable

20. Fixed charge coverage $= \dfrac{\text{Loss before income taxes} + \text{Lease payments}}{\text{Interest expense} + \text{Lease payments}}$ Not available

---

Danier Leather Inc.
Comparative Financial Ratios

		2006	2005	Industry Averages*
1.	Gross profit margin	48.1%	50.2%	Not available
2.	Operating margin	(5.6%)	2.1%	9.7%
3.	Return on sales	(3.7%)	(0.1%)	3.9%
4.	Return on assets	(6.7%)	(0.2%)	9.1%
5.	Return on equity	(11.5%)	(0.3%)	15.2%
6.	Earnings per share	($0.84)	($0.03)	Not applicable
7.	Price-earnings ratio	Not applicable	Not applicable	13.3×
8.	Market to book value ratio $= \dfrac{\text{Market price per share}}{\text{Book value per share}}$ Not available			
9.	Current ratio	4.0	6.4	2.1

10.	Quick ratio	1.3	2.9	0.8
11.	Average collection period	1 day	1 day	5 days
12.	Inventory turnover (cost of goods sold basis)	2.4×	2.9×	Not available
12.	Inventory turnover (sales basis)	4.6×	5.7×	7.1×
13.	Average holding period (cost of goods sold basis)	152 days	126 days	Not available
14.	Capital asset turnover	5.4×	6.6×	12.5×
15.	Total asset turnover	1.8×	2.0×	2.0×
16.	Debt ratio	41.7%	34.1%	Not available
17.	Debt to equity ratio	0.45	0.37	0.16
18.	Times interest earned	Not applicable	Not applicable	34.7×

Source: Financial Post Industry Reports, *Retailing*, 2005. Available by subscription at http://www.FPinfomart.ca.

Danier Leather Inc.
Du Pont Equations (adjusted for rounding)

	ROS	×	TAT	=	ROA	×	EM	=	ROE
2006	(3.7)	×	1.8	=	(6.7)	×	1.7	=	(11.3)
2005	(0.1)	×	2.0	=	(0.2)	×	1.5	=	(0.3)
Industry Average	3.9	×	2.0	=	7.8	×	1.9	=	14.8

Profitability

Losses mounted in 2006 compared with 2005. Net loss for 2006 was $5.5 million compared with $0.2 million in 2005. Consequently, return on sales was negative for both years, worsening from (0.1%) in 2005 to (3.7%) in 2006.

Sales in 2006 decreased by 11% from 2005, reflecting lower consumer demand for Danier's merchandise.

Gross profit margin decreased to 48.1% in 2006 compared with 50.2% in 2005. Sales were stronger in lower-priced goods and weaker in higher-priced items. In addition, more promotional activity and discounts were offered to maximize sales.

Operating margin reflected a loss, (5.6%), in 2006, compared to a positive margin in 2005. Selling, general, and administrative expenses increased by 2% or $1.6 million to $78.8 million in 2006, due primarily to additional brand-related advertising.

The $1.4 million restructuring charge included store closing costs and head office reductions. In 2005, Danier wrote off $2.8 million related to the closure of all three stores in the United States. The litigation provision and related expenses ($3.1 million in 2005) resulted from a class-action suit brought against the company.

In summary, the net loss for 2006 was $5.5 million compared with $0.2 million in 2005. The increased loss was due to an 11% revenue decrease, a 14% decrease in gross profit, a 2% increase in SG&A expense, and a $1.4 million restructuring charge.

Return on assets became more negative (6.7%) in 2006, reflecting the negative return on sales, and lower turnover of inventory and capital assets.

The negative return on equity (11.5%) was magnified by an increased equity multiplier, resulting from increased accounts payable and a new capital lease obligation.

Liquidity

The decline in the current and quick ratios resulted from a decrease in Danier's cash position versus 2005, and an increase in accounts payable and accrued liabilities.

Cash was reduced by $9.4 million, reflecting the 2006 net loss combined with new capital expenditures. Accounts payable and accrued liabilities increased by $2.5 million (31%) due to earlier inventory purchases.

Both current and quick ratios were well above industry averages. Both were inflated by the high cash balance. As well the high inventories balance inflated the current ratio.

Asset Management

Inventories at the end of 2006 were approximately $3.3 million higher than inventories at the end of 2005, due to earlier (spring) purchases of fall outerwear and blazer merchandise, compared with 2005.

As a result of higher inventories and lower sales, inventory turnover dropped from 2.9 times to 2.4 times.

Higher inventories were planned to improve Danier's in-stock position, but may imply additional expenses and risks related to storage, insurance, financing, shrinkage, and unsold merchandise.

Property and equipment was reported at cost and net book value. Annual amortization was provided as follows:

	Net Book Value at June 24, 2006 ($000)	Amortization Method
Land	$1,000	Not applicable
Building	5,515	4% Declining balance
Furniture and equipment	4,199	20% Declining balance
Visual merchandising equipment	Included	Straight-line (2 years)
Computer hardware and software	3,590	30% Declining balance
Computer hardware and software (under capital lease)	2,482	30% Declining balance
Leasehold improvements	10,507	Straight-line (term of lease)
Total property and equipment	$27,293	

Amortization expense totalling $7.1 million was included in cost of sales, selling, general, and administrative expenses, and restructuring costs and included gains and losses on disposals of property and equipment.

Capital expenditures were $9.0 million in 2006 compared with $2.6 million during 2005.

Capital expenditures in 2006 included approximately $3.5 million for two new stores, renovations, and store equipment; $5.3 million toward information technology, and $0.2 million for additional production machinery and equipment. As a result of the new capital expenditures and the 11% decline in sales, capital asset turnover declined from 6.6 times to 5.4 times.

Debt Management

The debt ratio increased from 34.1% in 2005 to 41.7% in 2006. The increase was due to the $2.5 million increase in accounts payable and accrued liabilities related to earlier inventory purchases, and a $2.7 million capital lease obligation to fund new point-of-sale equipment.

The principal liability (accrued litigation provision and related expenses) related to a class-action suit brought against the company. In total the company has provided $18 million in liabilities for potential damages, interest and court costs. The provision was reversed in October 2007, when the Supreme Court of Canada issued judgment in favour of the company.

Real Applications featuring Danier Leather Inc. are found in the following chapters:

Chapter	Pages	Topic
3A	92	Financial Information and Analysis for Danier Leather Inc.
4	122	Working Capital at Danier Leather Inc.
4	144	Inventory at Danier Leather Inc.
5	166	Committed (Revolving) Credit at Danier Leather Inc.
6	189	Planning at Danier Leather Inc.
9A	340	Operating and Capital Leases at Danier Leather Inc.
10	371	Share Capital at Danier Leather Inc.
11	402	Risk Factors at Danier Leather Inc.
12	432	Capital Spending at Danier Leather Inc.
13	472	Capital Investment Plans at Danier Leather Inc.
18	653	Employee Stock Options at Danier Leather Inc.
20	721	Danier Leather International

Sources: Danier Annual Report, 2006; Marina Strauss, "It's Not Always a Straight Line Up," *The Globe and Mail*. (August 27, 2005), p. B4; Marina Strauss, "Danier Axes Staff, Stores, E-commerce," *The Globe and Mail*, (May 31, 2006), p. B19. All Danier Leather, Inc. financial data reprinted with permission.

QUESTIONS

1. List the main user groups of financial information. What are the reasons for their interest?

2. Where do analysts get financial information about companies? What are their concerns about the information?

3. Financial analysts are generally optimists who believe what they're told. Right or wrong? Explain.

4. Outline the thinking behind ratio analysis in brief, general terms (write only a few lines; don't go into each ratio individually).

5. "Financial ratios don't do you much good by themselves." Explain.

6. What is the reasoning behind using the current ratio as a measure of liquidity?

7. Why do we need the quick ratio when we have the current ratio?

8. A company's terms are net 30 and the ACP is 35 days. Is that cause for alarm? Why or why not?

9. Discuss the different definitions of debt in ratio analysis.

10. Why do people view having too much debt as risky? If you were interested in determining whether a company had too much debt, what measure would you use? Why? How much debt do you think would generally be considered too much?

11. It can be argued that the TIE ratio doesn't make much sense. Why? How would you change the measure to be more meaningful? (*Hint*: Think in terms of cash flows.)

12. Can managers affect market value ratios?

Business Analysis

1. A company has been growing rapidly for the last three years. It was profitable before the growth spurt started. Although this year's revenues are almost three times those of three years ago, the firm is now losing money. What's the first thing you would do to try to pinpoint where the problem(s) may be?

2. The term "liquidity" is used in several ways. What does it mean in the context of an asset or liability, such as those on the balance sheet? What does it mean when applied to an operating company? What does the similar term "liquidate" mean when applied to a company?

3. The industry average inventory turnover ratio is 7 and your company's is 15. This could be good or bad news. Explain each possibility. How would you find out whether it is bad news?

4. You invested $10,000 in the shares of HiFly Inc, two years ago. Since then the shares have done very well, more than doubling in value.

   You tried analyze HiFly's financial statements twice in the last two years, but were confused by several of the detailed notes to those statements. You haven't worried about it though, because the statements show a steady growth in revenue and earnings along with an unqualified opinion by the firm's auditors that they were prepared using generally accepted accounting principles (GAAP). While checking your investments in *The Globe and Mail* this morning you were shocked to see that HiFly's price had declined by 30% since you last checked it a week ago. What may have happened?

PROBLEMS

1. PFM Company reported the following data relating to sales and net income (NI) in its most recent annual report.

	Year 5	Year 4	Year 3	Year 2	Year 1
Sales	700,000	675,000	650,000	575,000	500,000
NI	72,000	60,000	52,000	46,000	40,000

   a. Express this data in annual percentage increases.

	Year 5	Year 4	Year 3	Year 2
Sales				
NI				

   b. Comment on any significant information revealed by these trend percentages.

2. Linden Corp. has a 10% market share in its industry. Below are income statements ($ millions) for Linden and for the industry.

	Linden	Industry
Sales	$ 6,000	$ 64,000
Cost of goods sold	3,200	33,650
Gross margin	$ 2,800	$ 30,350
Expenses		
Sales and marketing	430	3,850
Engineering	225	2,650
Finance and administration	650	4,560
Total expenses	1,305	11,060
EBIT	1,495	19,290
Interest expense	230	4,500
EBT	1,265	14,790
Tax	500	5,620
Net income	$ 765	$ 9,170

a. Develop common size income statements for Linden and the industry as a whole.

b. What areas should management focus on to improve performance, and what kind of issues should be examined or looked for in each area?

3. Answer the following questions:

a. The Bubba Corp. had earnings before taxes of $200,000 and sales of $2,000,000. If it is in the 25% tax bracket, what is its return on sales?

b. A firm has total assets of $1,000,000. It has $400,000 in long-term debt. The shareholders' equity is $450,000. What is the debt ratio?

c. A firm has a debt ratio of 75%, $150,000 in debt, and net income of $30,000. What is the return on equity?

d. A firm has operating profit of $120,000 after deducting lease payments of $20,000. Interest expense is $40,000. What is the firm's fixed charge coverage?

e. A firm has current assets of $50,000 and total assets of $250,000. The firm's sales are $600,000. What is the firm's capital asset turnover?

4. Partridge Inc. sells about $45 million a year on credit. Good credit and collections performance results in a 35-day ACP.

a. What is the maximum receivables balance Partridge can tolerate and still receive a good rating with respect to credit and collections?

b. If Partridge is now collecting an average receivable in 40 days, by how much will it have to lower the receivables balance to achieve a good rating?

5. Epsom Co. manufactures furniture and sells about $40 million a year at a gross margin of 45%.

a. What is the maximum inventory level the firm can carry to maintain an inventory turnover (based on COGS) of 8.0?

b. If the inventory contains $1.2 million of obsolete and damaged goods that don't turn over at all, how fast would the active inventory have to turn over to achieve an overall turnover rate of 8.0?

6. The Nelson Sheetmetal Company has current assets of $2.5 million and current liabilities of $1.0 million. The firm needs additional inventory and has an opportunity to borrow money on a short-term basis to buy the needed material. However, a previous financing agreement prohibits the company from operating with a current ratio below 1.8. What is the maximum amount of inventory Nelson can obtain in this manner?

   (*Hint*: The loan payable and the inventory are both current items of equal size on the balance sheet.)

7. The Hardigree Hamburger chain is a private corporation with 400,000 common shares outstanding. The owners would like to take the company public by issuing another 600,000 shares and selling them to the general public in an initial public offering (IPO). (IPOs are discussed in Chapter 7). Benson's Burgers is a similar chain that operates in another part of the country. Its shares are publicly traded at a price-earnings (P/E) ratio of 25. Hardigree had net income of $2,500,000 in 2006. Based upon the IPO:
   a. What is Hardigree's new earnings per share?
   b. What should be the issue (market) price per share?
   c. How much is Hardigree likely to raise with its public offering?
   d. What is the total value of the current owners' interest?

8. Sweet Tooth Cookies, Inc. has the following ratios:

   ```
   ROE          = 15%
   T/A turnover = 1.2×
   ROS          = 10%
   ```

   What percentage of its assets is financed by shareholders' equity?

9. The Paragon Company has sales of $2,000,000 with a cost ratio of 60%, current ratio of 1.5, inventory turnover ratio (based on cost) of 3.0, and average collection period (ACP) of 45 days. Complete the following current section of the firm's balance sheet.

Cash	$ _____	Accounts payable	$ _____
Accounts receivable	_____	Accruals	60,000
Inventory	_____		_____
Current assets	$ _____	Current liabilities	$ 750,000

10. You are given the following selected financial information for The Blatz Corporation.

Income Statement

COGS	$ 750,000
Net income	$ 160,000

Balance Sheet

Cash	$ 250,000
Net capital assets	$ 850,000

Ratios

ROS	10%
Current ratio	2.3
Inventory turnover	6.0×
ACP	45 days
Debt ratio	50%

Calculate accounts receivable, inventory, current assets, current liabilities, long-term debt, shareholders' equity, ROA, and ROE.

11. Companies often use ratios as a basis for planning. The technique is to assume the business being planned will achieve targeted levels of certain ratios and then calculate the financial statement amounts that will result in those ratios. The process always starts with a dollar assumption about sales revenue. Forecast the balance sheet for Lambert Co. using the following projected information ($000). Round all projections to the nearest thousand dollars.

Sales	$ 10,000
Cash	$ 500
Accruals	$ 50
Gross margin	45%
ACP	42 days
Inventory turns	7.0×
Total asset turnover	1.25×
Current ratio	2.0
Debt to equity	1:3

ASSETS

Cash	$ _____
Accounts receivable	_____
Inventory	_____
Current assets	_____
Net capital assets	_____
Total assets	$ _____

LIABILITIES AND SHAREHOLDERS' EQUITY

Accounts payable	$ _____
Accruals	_____
Current liabilities	_____
Long-term debt	_____
Shareholders' equity	_____
Total liabilities & shareholders' equity	$ _____

12. Tribke Enterprises collected the following data from its financial reports for 20X3:

Share price	$ 18.37
Inventory balance	$ 300,000
Expenses (excluding COGS)	$ 1,120,000
Shares outstanding	290,000
Average issue price of shares	$ 5.00
Gross margin	40%
Interest rate	8%
TIE ratio	8×
Inventory turnover	12.0×
Current ratio	1.5
Quick ratio	0.75
Capital asset turnover	1.5×
Tax rate	25%

Complete the following abbreviated financial statements, and calculate per share ratios indicated. (*Hint:* Start by subtracting the formula for the quick ratio from that for the current ratio and equating that to the numerical difference.)

INCOME STATEMENT

Revenue $ _____
COGS _____
GM _____
Expenses _____
EBIT _____
Interest _____
EBT _____
Tax _____
Net income $ _____

BALANCE SHEET

Current assets	$ _____	Current liabilities	$ _____
Capital assets	_____	Long-term debt	$ _____
		Shareholders' equity:	
		Common shares	$ _____
		Retained earnings	_____
		Total shareholders' equity	_____
Total assets	$ _____	Total liabilities & shareholders' equity	$ _____

RATIOS

Book value per share $ _____   Market to book value _____

13. You have been looking for an opportunity to get started in a small business and have heard about FlowThru Distribution. Only now, however, have you received their financial statements. Before looking any further into FlowThru's operations, you need to calculate a number of ratios to give you a better idea of what its performance has been. The financial data are as follows:

FlowThru Distribution
Balance Sheet
As of January 31

Cash	$ 100	Accounts payable	$ 85,700
Accounts receivable	89,200	Short-term loan	53,200
Inventory	82,900	Accrued expenses	5,900
Other current assets	5,400		
Land	18,900	Long-term loan at 9.5%	64,300
Other capital assets net of amortization	100,700	Shareholders' equity	88,100
Total assets	$ 297,200	Total liabilities and shareholders' equity	$ 297,200

FlowThru Distribution
Income Statement

For the Year Ended January 31

Sales		$ 766,500
Cost of goods sold		549,700
Gross margin		216,800
Trucking expenses	$ 34,400	
Sales commissions	34,600	
Wages and salaries	79,200	
Amortization	9,000	
Other operating expenses	39,200	196,400
Earnings before interest		20,400
Interest		6,400
Earnings before tax		14,000
Tax		3,000
Net income		$ 11,000

a. Calculate the following ratios: (1) current ratio, (2) quick ratio, (3) average collection period, (4) inventory turnover (use sales), (5) debt ratio, (6) return on sales, and (7) return on equity.

b. Using the information calculated in part (a), interpret your results in light of the following:
  i. A current ratio of at least 2.50 to 1 is normal in the industry.
  ii. A quick ratio of at least 1.50 to 1 is normal in the industry.
  iii. FlowThru Distribution offers net 30-day credit terms.
  iv. The industry inventory turnover is 12 times.
  v. A normal debt ratio is 0.55.
  vi. Return on sales for the industry is 2.0%.
  vii. Return on equity for the industry is 12.5%.

c. What other information would you like to have before making a decision on whether this is the opportunity you have been waiting for?

14. The following information concerns two competitors, Thomas Ltd. and Jerold Corp.

Balance Sheets

ASSETS	Thomas	Jerold
Cash and marketable securities	$ 79,580	$ 152,594
Accounts receivable	45,477	81,233
Inventory	213,210	47,326
Net capital assets	212,290	222,290
Total assets	$ 550,557	$ 503,443

LIABILITIES AND SHAREHOLDERS' EQUITY

Short-term bank loans	$ 60,146	$ 22,032
Accounts payable	61,276	24,360
Accruals	39,028	20,278
Long-term debt	102,116	143,555
Common shares	201,826	195,408
Retained earnings	86,165	97,810
Total liabilities and shareholders' equity	$ 550,557	$ 503,443
Income Statements		
Sales	$ 771,201	$ 817,666
Cost of goods sold	620,954	671,782
Gross margin	150,247	145,884
Selling and administrative expenses	56,276	66,290
Amortization	27,014	26,632
Miscellaneous expenses	8,919	14,228
EBIT	58,038	38,734
Interest on short-term debt	6,015	2,040
Interest on long-term debt	12,945	14,016
EBT	39,078	22,678
Taxes	8,770	5,632
Net income	$ 30,308	$ 17,046

Calculate the financial ratios for both firms required to answer each of the following questions.
   a. To which firm would you, as a credit manager or short-term lender, be most likely to approve the extension of short-term trade credit or grant a short-term loan?
   b. To which one would you, as a banker, be most likely to extend long-term credit?
   c. In which firm would you, as an investor, be most likely to buy shares?

15. In the fall of 20X3, Maureen Richard (assistant to Janine Beliveau, who was then the chief loan officer of the Imperial National Bank) was reviewing the outstanding line of credit of the Green Manufacturing Company.

   Over the past five years, credit had been extended each spring to meet Green's seasonal requirements. This year, for the first time, the maximum credit line for $300,000 had proven inadequate and an additional $150,000 had been advanced. Furthermore, although borrowings had always been repaid by late July or early August, this time no repayment had yet been made.

   Richard had been asked by Beliveau to file a detailed analysis of the situation along with a recommendation of what should be done. In preparing to do so, Richard first reviewed the management team of Green Manufacturing, headed by Marie Leland, and found them to be an impressive group combining engineering and marketing backgrounds. She also noted that sales and profits had grown fairly steadily over the past several years.

   Richard knew that her report had to be brief and to the point. She also recalled that her superior had a strong preference for presentations that included financial analysis.

   Exhibits 1 and 2 provide comparative income statements and balance sheets for Green Manufacturing.

   Prepare Maureen's report.

Exhibit 1

Green Manufacturing
Income Statements for Years Ended October 31 ($000)

	20X1	20X2	20X3
Net sales	$ 6,000	$ 7,000	$ 9,000
Cost of goods sold*	5,150	6,000	7,750
Gross margin	850	1,000	1,250
Selling, general and administrative	120	170	190
Earnings before interest and taxes	730	830	1,060
Interest expense	30	30	60
Earnings before taxes	700	800	1,000
Taxes at 25%	175	200	250
Net income	$ 525	$ 600	$ 750
Dividends	400	450	400
Addition to retained earnings	$ 125	$ 150	$ 350
*Includes amortization			
on plant	$ 80	$ 90	$ 110
on equipment	$ 35	$ 40	$ 50

Exhibit 2

Green Manufacturing
Balance Sheets as of October 31 (000s)

	20X1	20X2	20X3
ASSETS			
Cash	$ 181	$ 161	$ 81
Marketable securities	210	10	0
Accounts receivable	940	1,060	1,200
Inventories	1,110	1,250	1,450
Total current assets	2,441	2,481	2,731
Plant, net	1,100	1,200	1,800
Equipment, net	900	950	1,010
Total capital assets	2,000	2,150	2,810
Total assets	$ 4,441	$ 4,631	$ 5,541
LIABILITIES AND SHAREHOLDERS' EQUITY			
Accounts payable	$ 870	$ 1,010	$ 1,120
Notes payable	100	0	0
Bank loan	0	0	450
Total current liabilities	970	1,010	1,570
Common shares	801	801	801
Retained earnings	2,670	2,820	3,170
Total liabilities and shareholders' equity	$ 4,441	$ 4,631	$ 5,541

16. Axtel Company has the following financial statements.

Axtel Company
Balance Sheet

As of 31/12/20X1 ($000)

	31/12/20X0	31/12/20X1
ASSETS		
Cash	$ 3,514	$ 2,875
Accts receivable	6,742	5,583
Inventory	2,573	3,220
CURRENT ASSETS	12,829	11,678
Capital assets		
Gross	22,478	24,360
Accumulated amortization	(12,147)	(13,313)
Net	10,331	11,047
TOTAL ASSETS	$ 23,160	$ 22,725
LIABILITIES AND SHAREHOLDERS' EQUITY		
Accounts payable	$ 1,556	$ 1,702
Accruals	268	408
CURRENT LIABILITIES	1,824	2,110
Long-term debt	7,112	6,002
Shareholders' equity	14,224	14,613
TOTAL LIABILITIES AND SHAREHOLDERS' EQUITY	$ 23,160	$ 22,725

Axtel Company
Income Statement

For the period ended 31/12/20X1 ($000)

Sales	$ 36,227
COGS	19,925
Gross margin	16,302
Expenses	10,868
EBIT	5,434
Interest	713
EBT	4,721
Tax	1,605
Net income	$ 3,116

In addition, Axtel retired shares for $1,000,000 and paid a dividend of $1,727,000. Amortization for the year was $1,166,000.

   a. Construct a statement of cash flows for Axtel for 20X1. (*Hint:* Retiring shares means buying shares back from shareholders. Assume the purchase was made at book value, and treat it like a *negative sale* of shares.)

   b. Calculate for Axtel Company all of the ratios discussed in the chapter. Assume Axtel had leasing costs of $7,267 in 20X1 and had 1,268,000 shares outstanding valued at $28.75 per share at year-end.

17. The Protek Company is a large manufacturer and distributor of electronic components. Because of some successful new products marketed to manufacturers of personal computers, the firm has recently undergone a period of explosive growth, more than doubling its revenues during the last two years. However, the growth has been accompanied by a marked decline in profitability and a precipitous drop in the company's share price.

   You are a financial consultant who has been retained to analyze the company's performance and find out what's going wrong. Your investigative plan involves conducting a series of in-depth interviews with management and doing some independent research on the industry. However, before starting, you want to focus your thinking to be sure you can ask the right questions. You'll begin by analyzing the firm's financial statements over the last three years, which are shown below.

Protek Company
Income Statements

For the periods ending 31/12 ($000,000)

	20X1	20X2	20X3
Sales	$ 1,578	$ 2,106	$ 3,265
COGS	631	906	1,502
Gross margin	947	1,200	1,763
Expenses			
Marketing	316	495	882
R&D	158	211	327
Administration	126	179	294
Total expenses	600	885	1,503
EBIT	347	315	260
Interest	63	95	143
EBT	284	220	117
Tax	97	75	40
NI	$ 187	$ 145	$ 77

Protek Company
Balance Sheets

As of 31/12 ($000,000)

	20X1	20X2	20X3
ASSETS			
Cash	$ 30	$ 40	$ 62
Accounts receivable	175	351	590
Inventory	90	151	300
Current assets	295	542	952
Capital assets			
Gross	1,565	2,373	2,718
Accumulated amortization	(610)	(860)	(1,135)
Net	955	1,513	1,583
Total assets	$ 1,250	$ 2,055	$ 2,535

LIABILITIES AND SHAREHOLDERS' EQUITY

Accounts payable	$ 56	$ 81	$ 134
Accruals	15	20	30
Current liabilities	71	101	164
Long-term debt	630	1,260	1,600
Shareholders' equity	549	694	771
Total liabilities & shareholders' equity	$ 1,250	$ 2,055	$ 2,535

The following additional information is provided with the financial statements. Amortization for 20X1, 20X2, and 20X3 was $200, $250, and $275 million, respectively; these amounts were included in COGS and expenses. No shares were sold or repurchased, and, like many fast-growing companies, Protek paid no dividends. Assume the tax rate is 34%, and the firm pays 10% interest on its debt.

a. Construct common size income statements for 20X1, 20X2, and 20X3. Analyze the trend in each line. What appears to be happening? (*Hint:* Think in terms of both dollars and percentages. As the company grows, the absolute dollars of cost and expense spending go up. What does it mean if the percentage of revenue represented by the expenditure increases as well? How much of an increase in spending do you think a department could manage efficiently? Could pricing of Protek's products have any effect?)

b. Construct statements of cash flows for 20X2 and 20X3. Where is the company's money going to and coming from? Make a comment about its free cash flows during the period. Is it likely to have positive or negative free cash flows in the future?

c. Calculate the indicated ratios for all three years. Analyze trends in each ratio and compare each with the industry average. What can you infer from this information? Make specific statements about liquidity, asset management (especially receivables and inventories), debt management, and profitability. Do not simply say that ratios are higher or lower than the average or that they are going up or down. Think about what might be going on in the company and propose reasons why the ratios are acting as they are. Do certain specific problems tend to affect more than one ratio? Which ones?

	Industry Average	20X1	20X2	20X3
Current ratio	4.5			
Quick ratio	3.2			
ACP	42 days			
Inventory turnover	7.5×			
Capital asset turnover	1.6×			
Total asset turnover	1.2×			
Debt ratio	53%			
Debt to equity	1:1			
TIE	4.5×			
ROS	9.0%			
ROA	10.8%			
ROE	22.8%			
Equity multiplier	2.1×			

d. Construct Du Pont equations for both Protek and the industry. What, if anything, do they tell us?

e. One hundred million shares have been outstanding for the entire period. The price of Protek shares in 20X1, 20X2, and 20X3 was $39.27, $26.10, and $11.55, respectively.

Calculate the firm's earnings per share (EPS) and its price/earnings ratio (P/E). What's happening to the P/E? To what things are investors likely to be reacting? How would a slowdown in personal computer sales affect your reasoning?

f. Would you recommend Protek shares as an investment? Why might they be a very bad investment in the near future? Why might they be a very good one?

COMPUTER PROBLEMS

18. Using the data below, complete the income statement and balance sheet for the Silverado Corporation. Prepare a Microsoft Excel® spreadsheet for this purpose, inserting formulas where required. (Alternatively, complete this problem manually.)

Input

Sales	=	$6,000,000
Total asset turnover	=	2×
Gross profit margin	=	25%
Selling & administrative expense	=	10% of sales
Times interest earned	=	10×
Tax rate	=	34%
Current ratio	=	2
Average collection period	=	73 days (all sales are on credit)
Inventory turnover (using sales)	=	6×
Total debt to assets	=	50%
Opening retained earnings	=	$500,000
Silverado paid out		60% of net income in dividends

Output

SILVERADO CORPORATION
Income Statement

For the Year Ended December 31

Sales	FORMULA
Cost of goods sold	FORMULA
Gross margin	FORMULA
Selling & administrative expense	FORMULA
Operating profit (EBIT)	FORMULA
Interest	FORMULA
Earnings before taxes	FORMULA
Tax	FORMULA
Net income	FORMULA

SILVERADO CORPORATION
Balance Sheet
December 31

Assets		Liabilities & Shareholders' Equity	
Cash	$ 200,000	Accounts payable	$ 500,000
Accounts receivable	FORMULA	Notes payable	FORMULA
Inventory	FORMULA	Long-term debt	FORMULA
		Preferred shares	$ 100,000
Gross plant & equipment	FORMULA	Common shares	FORMULA
Less: Accum. amort.	$ 3,000,000	Retained earnings	FORMULA
Net plant & equipment	FORMULA		
Total Assets	FORMULA	Total L & SE	FORMULA

19. Comparative historical financial statements for Northern Manufacturing are as follows.

Northern Manufacturing
Income Statements
For the Years Ended December 31 ($000)

	20X1	20X2	20X3
Sales	$ 17,850	$ 20,510	$ 22,560
COGS	9,100	10,665	11,506
Gross margin	8,750	9,845	11,054
Expenses	5,180	5,702	5,332
Amortization	600	650	700
EBIT	2,970	3,493	5,022
Interest	800	910	1,180
EBT	2,170	2,583	3,842
Tax	868	1,033	1,537
Net income	$ 1,302	$ 1,550	$ 2,305
Lease payments	$ 500	$ 700	$ 800

Northern Manufacturing
Balance Sheets

As of December 31 ($000)

ASSETS	20X1	20X2	20X3
Cash	$ 980	$ 500	$ 200
Accounts receivable	3,570	6,250	7,300
Inventory	3,033	5,180	6,470
CURRENT ASSETS	7,583	11,930	13,970
Capital assets			
Gross	6,650	7,500	9,000
Accumulated amort.	(1,750)	(2,400)	(3,100)
Net	4,900	5,100	5,900
TOTAL ASSETS	$ 12,483	$ 17,030	$ 19,870

LIABILITIES AND SHAREHOLDERS' EQUITY			
Accounts payable	$ 1,650	$ 1,860	$ 2,210
Accruals	742	850	220
CURRENT LIABILITIES	2,392	2,710	2,430
Long-term debt	7,891	11,320	12,335
Shareholders' equity	2,200	3,000	5,105
TOTAL LIABILITIES & SHAREHOLDERS' EQUITY	$ 12,483	$ 17,030	$ 19,870
Dividends paid	$ 650	$ 750	$1,200
Number of shares	300,000	300,000	315,000
Share price	$ 78.12	$ 70.00	$ 65.88

a. Use the ANALYS* program to prepare common size statements and a set of financial ratios for each of the last three years.

b. Analyze the results of ANALYS* for Northern Manufacturing. The firm has been quite successful in terms of revenue and profit growth so far. Do the ratios reveal any disturbing trends that might indicate future problems?

DEVELOPING SOFTWARE

20. Write your own analysis program to calculate a common size income statement and the ratios introduced in this chapter. To keep the exercise reasonably simple, just provide for one year of ratios and one common size statement.

Construct an input area in your spreadsheet in the form of an income statement and a balance sheet. Input the accounts and have the program calculate all totals and subtotals. Define your common size income statement alongside the input income statement by dividing each input line item by revenue. Define your ratios in another area drawing the numerators and denominators from the input statements.

Test your program using the 20X3 statements for Northern Manufacturing from Problem 19. Compare your results with those of the ANALYS* program.

*ANALYS is one of several Microsoft Excel templates available on the text's support website at www.lasher2e.nelson.com.

PART 2

Operating Issues—Working Capital Management

Chapter 4

The Management of Working Capital

Learning Objectives

1 Define working capital as the current assets and liabilities required for routine operations.

2 Explain that the balances in cash, accounts receivable, and inventory require financing, but this need is supplied partly by the accounts payable and accruals that come automatically with the associated inventory and operating activities. Explain that the balance of financing required is typically short-term bank loans.

3 Explain how working capital management involves trade-offs between easier operation and the cost of carrying short-term assets.

4 Identify the cash conversion cycle of the firm.

5 Discuss the seasonal changes in working capital balances.

6 Explain the financing of assets in terms of the maturity matching principle.

7 Discuss the options for financing permanent working capital and temporary working capital. Explain the advantages and disadvantages of short- and long-term financing.

8 Discuss cash management as the control of receipts and disbursements to minimize non-earning bank balances while providing adequate funds to meet the firm's immediate cash needs. Describe techniques to make cash management more efficient.

9 Describe the various marketable securities available for investing temporary surplus cash.

10 Describe accounts receivable as an investment resulting from the firm's credit policies. Outline the considerations in granting credit and determining collection procedures, and evaluate credit decisions that change credit terms to stimulate sales.

11 Explain the benefits and incidental costs of carrying inventory, and apply techniques—such as economic order quantity and just-in-time systems—to reduce these incidental costs.

Many people cannot explain how a profitable operation could possibly go bankrupt. They assume that any profit showing up on the bottom line or in retained earnings must be sitting in the cash account. In some service businesses this may be true, but in many businesses, the funds invested in *working capital* (accounts receivable and inventory) are significant. If there are major problems in selling inventory or collecting accounts, cash flow can dry up quickly!

Working capital consists of certain current balance sheet accounts that arise from the routine operating activities common to most companies. *Working capital management* refers to controlling the balances in the accounts, but more importantly to the way the underlying functions are run. In the remainder of this chapter and in Chapter 5, we'll gain an understanding of the decisions involved in working capital management and the relationships it creates between finance and other departments.

WORKING CAPITAL BASICS

Working capital includes short-term assets and liabilities required to operate a business on a day-to-day basis. The assets include cash, receivables, and inventories, while the liabilities are generally payables and accruals.

It's important to distinguish these accounts from long-term items, such as buildings and equipment on the asset side of the balance sheet and long-term debt and shareholders' equity on the liabilities side. Long-term assets are held for extended periods (at least a year) and tend to be financed or supported with long-term liabilities and/or shareholders' equity that don't have to be paid off for similarly long periods of time, if ever.

Working capital items, on the other hand, are short term. Most turn over continually, meaning that items are held for only a little while. Inventory is a good example. Although firms always have inventory on hand, individual items are purchased and sold relatively quickly. The important point is that normal operating activities create and liquidate the elements of working capital on a regular basis. The word "capital" refers to the idea that funds have to be committed to support these short-term assets, while the word "working" emphasizes the fact that they're associated with the day-to-day operation of the business.

It's important to realize that working capital is an absolute necessity to the operation of virtually all companies. Firms can no more do business without working capital than they can without buildings or equipment.

Working Capital Requires Funds

Providing working capital takes a more or less permanent investment of funds. For example, suppose a company operates with a $10 million inventory. Even though individual inventory items are constantly being bought and sold, approximately $10 million is always required to support the total. In effect, the firm buys an inventory level just as it buys a building or a machine.

The same is true of receivables, although it's a little more difficult to visualize. When product is sold on credit, a receivable is created that won't be realized in cash until the customer pays the bill. In the meantime the receivable represents money the company has recognized from the sale but doesn't have.

Working capital accounts arise from day-to-day operations and include cash, receivables, inventory, payables, and accruals.

The assets and liabilities in working capital accounts turn over regularly.

Maintaining a working capital balance requires a permanent commitment of funds.

Keeping cash in the bank also takes funding. Even though money is constantly flowing in and out of a company's bank account, an average balance has to be maintained to pay bills and conduct business. That money has to come from somewhere and represents a funding requirement just like inventory or receivables. In effect, the company buys a cash balance in its bank account.

Short-Term Liabilities—Spontaneous Financing

Operating activities also create payables and accrued liabilities. When inventory is purchased on credit, the payable represents material that can be used (temporarily) without payment. Similarly, labour that's been received but not yet paid is reflected in an accrual. (Review the coverage of accruals in Chapter 2, page 31, if necessary.)

These liabilities provide an offset to the funding requirements discussed in the last section. It's important to notice that they come automatically with the associated assets and operating activities. In other words, the acts of buying inventory and building product lead directly to the related payables and accruals.

Because of the automatic nature of the liabilities arising from operating activities, they're referred to as **spontaneous financing**: they spontaneously reduce the need for funds to support gross working capital. A *firm's net working capital reflects the net amount of funds required to support routine operations.*

> The *liabilities* created by operations **spontaneously** offset the funding required to support the assets.

Working Capital and the Current Accounts

> In practice, working capital is the net of current assets less current liabilities.

In Chapter 2 (pages 27 and 31) we defined current assets and current liabilities as items that are expected to generate or require cash within a year. The elements of working capital make up the bulk of the current accounts in most companies. For that reason, we have defined working capital on page 31 as follows.

$$\text{Gross working capital} = \text{Current assets}$$

$$\text{Net working capital} = \text{Current assets} - \text{Current liabilities}[1]$$

Common usage isn't particularly consistent in this area. People often use the term "working capital" for "net working capital." In practice it pays to be sure anyone you're talking with is using the same definition you are.

The Objective of Working Capital Management

Good working capital management means running the company effectively with as little money as possible tied up in the current accounts. That involves an important series of cost/benefit trade-offs. The trade-offs arise because it's easier to run a business with more working capital than with less, but it's also more expensive. Let's briefly consider each working capital element to see why.

Inventory: Large inventories keep customers happy because firms always have what customers want right away. Also, production delays due to running out of materials are minimized by carrying big stocks of parts. However, as we saw in Chapter 3, larger inventories cost more to finance, incur bigger losses from obsolescence, breakage, and theft, and take more storage space than smaller inventories.

---

1 There's a minor problem in this definition. Certain items are regularly classified as current that are not related to routine operating activities. For example, when the repayment date for a long-term loan is less than a year away, the loan is normally classified as a current liability. Similarly, a receivable due from the sale of something other than product (like real estate) will be a current asset, but has nothing to do with daily operations. Hence current assets and liabilities don't quite match the working capital concept. Nevertheless, it's common practice to define working capital in terms of the current accounts, ignoring any imprecision implied.

Receivables: A large receivables balance means the firm grants credit to customers easily and is willing to wait a long time to be paid. That makes customers happy and tends to increase sales. However, we saw in Chapter 3 (page 79) that large receivables could also mean relatively large bad debt losses and big interest charges to finance the receivables balance.

Cash: More rather than less cash in the bank makes it easier to conduct business and minimizes the chance of running short, but it also represents excess funds that could be put to better use.

Payables and accruals: On the liabilities side, more net working capital means smaller payables and accruals balances. That comes from paying vendors and employees quickly, which keeps them happy. However, it also reduces spontaneous financing and thus increases the need for costly external funding.

In general, using more working capital increases sales and improves relations with customers and vendors, but costs extra money. There's no magic prescription for setting the right working capital level. The choice is a matter of policy, and involves trade-offs that are often hard to quantify. Therefore, working capital management requires judgment, experience, and an ability to work with others in the organization. To this purpose, we considered certain liquidity ratios (the current and quick ratios) in Chapter 3 (pages 77 and 78) that establish relationships between current assets and current liabilities and help evaluate the firm's ability to pay its short-term liabilities from its current assets.

> Working capital management involves trade-offs between easier operation and the cost of carrying short-term assets.

We'll look into the management of each working capital component in detail later in this chapter and in Chapter 5.

Operations—The Cash Conversion Cycle

In Chapter 2, we constructed and analyzed the statement of cash flows, differentiating among the operating, investing, and financing activities of the firm. In Figure 2.4 (page 39), we showed these business cash flows graphically, looking in particular at the operating activities related to the normal course of business and to the current asset and liability accounts.

Insights PRACTICAL FINANCE

Going Broke Profitably

Can a company that's making a profit and has great prospects for the future fail? That sounds like a trick question, but it isn't. Profitable businesses, especially small ones, fail all the time—through just a few mistakes with working capital.

Here's an example. Suppose an entrepreneur has a great idea for a product she wants to sell to a large company nearby. A unit sells for $1,000, costs $500 to buy, and requires overhead of about $200. That means in the long run every unit makes $300, and the business looks like it will be solidly profitable.

With excitement, our entrepreneur leases space, hires workers, and buys a year's inventory. Then she operates for three months shipping product to a delighted customer who promises to pay in 30 days.

But, at the end of that time, the receivable isn't paid and the business is out of cash. Calling the customer, the entrepreneur gets a long story about minor technical problems with the product, a confusing tale about invoices not matching purchase orders, and an assurance of payment after these problems are worked out.

However, after checking around, she finds that the customer is well known for paying bills slowly and using excuses to delay. It also turns out that the customer is in financial difficulty and has been especially bad about paying bills lately.

Notice that at this point the entrepreneur's income statement says she's doing great, having made $300 on every unit shipped. But the balance sheet tells a different story. She's got a pile of inventory, a big receivable, and no cash. That means she can't pay the rent or her workers in the fourth month of operation. The new business will fail immediately unless a bank bails it out with a loan until it collects some money.

This entrepreneur's failure comes from two mistakes in working capital management: she bought too much inventory, and she didn't do a credit check on the customer. Those seemingly small oversights could cost her everything. We'll learn how to avoid this kind of disaster in this chapter.

Current assets can be thought of as going through a series of transformations as a business operates. In a manufacturing company, cash "becomes" material, labour, and overhead, which combine to become product. In a merchandising company, cash buys finished goods directly. When product is sold on credit, a receivable is created, which in turn becomes cash when collected.

The transformation process is conceptually important. In essence, the firm begins with cash, which it turns into things that eventually turn back into cash. This enables it to make or buy more inventory, which starts the cycle all over again.

Figure 4.1 is usually called the **cash conversion cycle**, but the term *racetrack diagram* is a little more colourful and tends to fix it in mind better. Starting at the left side of the track, a business uses cash to purchase inventory and labour to produce a product. That product is sold (on credit), resulting in a receivable. When the receivable is collected, the firm once again has cash in hand that it uses to buy more inventory and labour to produce more product and so on.

In a sense, the company is running around a racetrack, converting cash to product and product to cash. You can think of the firm continually doing this, equipped with some level of assets.

Given a level of assets, the firm goes around the track faster by making more sales in the period. Clearly, the faster it can go around, the better off it is as long as it doesn't damage something else by going too fast. In other words, it's important to get a lot of sales per dollar of assets employed in the business. That's one of several measures of success.

However, a firm that just ran around the track putting all its money back into inventory wouldn't be doing its owners much good. A successful business has to pull something out each time around to buy new assets for growth and to replace old ones that wear out, to pay taxes, and for profit. Clearly, the larger the slice that can be taken out of cash flow each time around the track, the better off the firm is. This idea is simply profitability and is shown in the lower part of the figure.

Summarizing, the diagram illustrates that a business has to do two things for success: sell a lot for its level of assets and sell at a reasonable profit margin given its costs and expenses.

Product is converted into cash, which is transformed into more product, creating the **cash conversion cycle**.

FIGURE 4.1
The Cash Conversion Cycle—The Racetrack Diagram

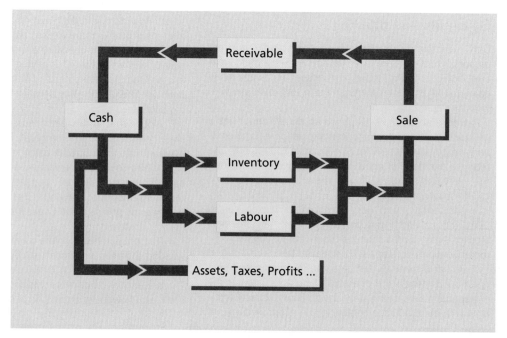

Notice that the two things work against each other. The business can always sell more if it charges less, but then it will have less profit. Conversely, a higher price yields more profit but lower sales.

The Cash Conversion Timeline

Another way to look at the cash conversion cycle is by laying out its elements on a timeline as illustrated in Figure 4.2. In this representation, events occur along the line and processes occupy intervals between the events.

It's important to notice how the two cycles are defined at the bottom of the diagram. A business's **operating cycle** is the period from the acquisition of inventory to the realization of cash from the sale of product. However, the cash conversion cycle is shorter by the period during which the firm holds a payable for the inventory. Cash conversion is the time from the disbursement of cash to pay for materials (or finished goods) to the receipt of cash for product sold.

Therefore:

The **operating cycle** is the time from the *acquisition of inventory* until *cash is collected* from product sales.

	Inventory holding period
plus:	Receivables collection period
equals:	Operating cycle
minus:	Payables payment period
equals:	**Cash conversion cycle**

We have already discussed the (average) receivable collection period and the (average) inventory holding period in Chapter 3.

The average payable payment period may be calculated as follows:

$$\text{Payable payment period} = \text{Accounts payable} \times \frac{365}{\text{Cost of goods sold}}$$

FIGURE 4.2

Timeline Representation of the Cash Conversion Cycle

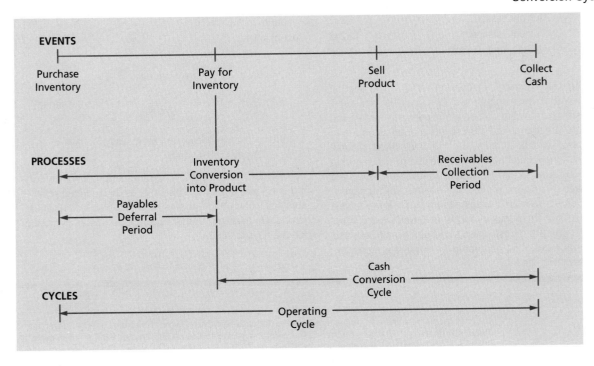

Notice that Figure 4.2 doesn't show labour. In a manufacturing company, production labour is continuously added to inventory during the conversion to product process, and is paid relatively quickly. In a merchandising company, the inventory purchased is usually ready for sale without conversion. Administrative labour is being performed and paid all the time.

The cash conversion concept is important because it contributes to our understanding of just how an ongoing business works. It's particularly enlightening in terms of the relationship between physical things and money.

A longer cash cycle may indicate problems in collecting receivables or excess, unsaleable inventory. The longer the cash cycle, the more financing is required.[2]

From the CFO

However, bankers being conservative may be unwilling to lend money to companies with longer cash cycles than other firms in their industry, particularly if management appears inefficient. An old saying: "Bankers want to lend money only to those who don't need it."

Insights REAL APPLICATIONS

DANIER LEATHER

Working Capital at Danier Leather Inc.

(Refer to the financial statements and other financial information about Danier Leather Inc. in Appendix 3A, page 92.)

From the consolidated balance sheets at June 24, 2006, we see ($000):

Current assets		$ 48,623
Current liabilities		12,243
Thus:	Net working capital =	$ 36,380

The *Management's Discussion and Analysis* section explains that the company's business is seasonal. Generally, a significant portion of the company's sales and earnings are generated during the period October to December, which includes the holiday selling season. Peak working capital needs are expected to occur during the period June to mid-December as inventory levels are increased in advance of the cold-weather selling season from October to March. Sales and inventories are lowest in the spring. The company funds inventory expenditures through operating cash flows and bank credit facilities. Accounts receivable, generated by corporate sales, are relatively insignificant.

The Operating Cycle and Cash Conversion Cycle

Let's calculate these two cycles for Danier Leather Inc. In Chapter 3, page 97, we calculated Danier's *average inventory holding period* for 2006 to have been 152 days. Danier's *average receivable collection period* for 2006 was one day. (It is essentially a cash business.)

Therefore, its *operating cycle* was 152 + 1 = 153 days.

Danier's *average payables payment period* for 2006 can be calculated as follows ($000):

Accounts payable:	$ 10,708
Cost of sales:	$ 76,953

Average payables payment period =

$$\$10,708 \times \frac{365}{\$76,953} = 51 \text{ days (rounded)}$$

Therefore, its cash conversion cycle was 152 days + 1 day − 51 days = 102 days.

Danier's long inventory holding period (low inventory turnover) was somewhat offset by its insignificant receivable collection period and its extended payables payment period. On average, Danier required additional financing for 102 days in 2006.

Source: Danier Leather Annual Report, 2006.

---

2 Increased receivables and inventories that increase the cash conversion cycle also reduce asset turnover, and consequently return on assets and return on equity. With more assets tied up tied up over a longer cash cycle, a company is less efficient and, therefore, less profitable.

Shortening the cash conversion cycle frees up cash to reinvest in the business or to reduce debt and interest. We will discuss strategies to reduce the inventory holding period and the receivables collection period later in this chapter. We will address practices to extend the payment period in Chapter 5.

Permanent and Temporary Working Capital

A firm's need for working capital varies directly with its sales level. The more it produces and sells, the larger its inventories have to be and generally the more receivables and cash it has to carry.

Some businesses operate at relatively even sales levels year-round, and therefore have more or less constant needs for working capital. In *seasonal* businesses such as Danier Leather Inc., sales vary throughout the year, as do working capital needs.

Seasonally variable business gives rise to the ideas of permanent and temporary working capital. **Permanent working capital** supports a constant or *minimum* level of sales. On the other hand, working capital that supports operations above the minimum level doesn't need to be maintained year-round and can be viewed as temporary. Temporary working capital can be thought of as supporting *peak* sales levels. These ideas are portrayed graphically in Figure 4.3.

> **Permanent working capital** refers to the minimum level to operate the business.

> **Temporary working capital** supports *seasonal peaks* in business.

Financing Net Working Capital

The fact that working capital differs from other assets because of its short-term nature leads to the idea that it may be appropriate to support it separately with short-term financing rather than using the firm's general pool of debt and equity capital. The idea arises almost naturally. Let's consider an illustration.

> Working capital tends to be *financed separately* with *short-term debt*.

Suppose a merchant who has a store but no money for inventory approaches a bank for a loan to buy merchandise that he'll sell through his store. He promises to repay the loan with the money from the sale as soon as the goods are sold. Banks are generally reluctant to lend to very small businesses because they're extremely risky. However, this proposal has some attractive features for the bank.

First, the loan is short term because it will be paid off as soon as the merchandise sells. Banks consider short term loans safer than those made for longer periods because they don't allow much time for business conditions to deteriorate before repayment is made.

Second, the bank can see exactly where the money to pay off the loan will come from—the proceeds of the sale of the inventory purchased with the borrowed money. This is an important point. The loan is self-liquidating. The merchant is not at liberty to do anything else with the

> **Self-liquidating debt** is paid off when the *item financed becomes cash* in the borrower's hands.

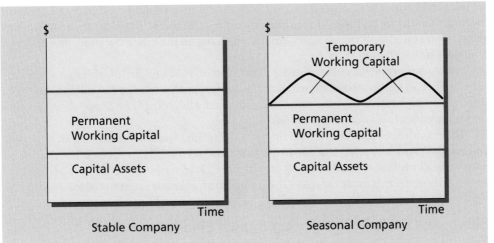

FIGURE 4.3
Working Capital
Needs of Different
Firms

sale proceeds. Such an arrangement is more secure than depending on the business's general profitability for repayment.

Third, the bank can demand that the merchant pledge the inventory itself as security for the loan. Then if payment isn't made, the bank can repossess and sell the inventory, which should be easily marketable. A similar case can be made for a loan based on receivables.

These features enable banks to make working capital loans to businesses that wouldn't qualify for general unsecured loans. The point is that working capital lends itself to short-term financing by offering lenders elements of security that aren't available with loans for other purposes.

The Options Available to Most Companies

Although everyone's situation isn't exactly like the merchant's in our example, most companies have the option of financing at least some of their working capital needs on a short-term basis. In practice, the loans aren't always tied to specific assets, but they're often short term.

On the other hand, firms can just about always use some of their long-term debt/equity capital to finance working capital. Therefore management has a choice between using long-term and short-term funds.

We'll get into the advantages and disadvantages of each option after we review an important financial principle.

The Maturity Matching Principle

Maturity is the date on which the principal of a debt is due, or alternatively, the time from the present until that date. The maturity matching principle says that the maturity date of financing should be roughly matched to the duration of the asset or capital investment being financed. In other words, a loan taken out to finance a capital investment should be repayable at roughly the time of the capital investment's completion. This makes the loan/investment combination a *self-liquidating* proposition.

For example, suppose an investment requires a $1 million investment today and is expected to pay off $1.2 million in six months. Maturity matching implies that a firm should borrow the $1 million for about six months and use the investment's proceeds to pay off the loan. Borrowing for a longer period will leave unused funds incurring interest after the investment's end. Borrowing for a shorter period can result in a default.

To illustrate the danger of borrowing short term, imagine a firm borrows $1 million for just three months with the intention of refinancing for the second three months. But suppose conditions change and the lender refuses to refinance after the first three-month period. The firm won't be able to pay off the loan at that time because the investment will not yet have generated the expected cash. That can lead to default and potential bankruptcy.

Hence, in principle, it's a good idea to match the duration of short- and intermediate-term investments with the maturity of the financing supporting them. Very long-term investments should be financed with shareholders' equity, which has an indefinite duration, or with long-term debt lasting 20 to 40 years.

It's also not a good idea to *overfinance* an investment. For example, imagine that a new venture requires $6 million to get started, but the owner manages to raise $10 million. Investors will expect a high return on the entire $10 million, but will probably be disappointed because earning opportunities are available for only $6 million.

These guidelines shouldn't be interpreted too literally. Modest overfunding in both time and amount provides a safety margin. In our first example, if the $1.2 million is late coming in, borrowing a little longer avoids missing the six-month loan repayment date. In the second example, if the start-up is more expensive than anticipated, a slightly larger initial loan might save the trouble and embarrassment of going back to lenders a second time.

Short- and Long-Term Working Capital Financing

Now let's return to the choice between financing working capital with short- or long-term money. What does the maturity matching principle prescribe in the case of permanent working

The **maturity matching principle** advises that the *term of financing* match the *duration* of the *item supported.*

Permanent working capital can be financed *long or short term,* but *temporary* needs should be supported with *short-term* funds.

capital? Although the inventories and receivables financed are clearly short term, they're continuously replaced so the level of the working capital assets remains constant. In the context of maturity matching, the situation can be interpreted as appropriate for long-term financing. Temporary working capital, on the other hand, is more clearly of limited duration and therefore calls for short-term financing.

Firms clearly have a range of reasonable options other than maturity matching for financing working capital. They can support it very largely with long-term sources using little or no short-term borrowing, or they can use short-term money extensively. Let's look at why a firm might prefer one or the other.

Financing with long-term funds is safe but expensive.[3] It's safe because enough money is raised at the outset to cover anticipated working capital needs for a long time, and the firm is unlikely ever to run short. It's expensive because long-term rates of return are generally higher than short-term rates, and raising long-term money usually involves paying flotation costs.[4]

> Long-term financing is safe but expensive, while short-term money is cheap but risky.

On the other hand, financing with short-term funds is cheap but risky. It's cheap because short rates are generally lower than long rates, and the transaction costs of raising the money are relatively small. But borrowing short-term is risky because every time a new loan is required, the firm has to face a new set of market conditions. For example, if interest rates rise over time, a company borrowing short term will have to pay increasing market rates. These may turn out to be higher than the long-term rate available initially.

There's also a possibility that money can become so tight[5] that financing isn't available at any rate. If that happens, the firm may not be able to finance working capital at all, which can seriously affect its survival.

Alternative Policies

The result of all this is that the degree to which a firm uses short-term financing to support working capital is an issue of policy. Two possible options are illustrated graphically in Figure 4.4 for a firm that has both permanent and temporary working capital.

We say a working capital financing policy is *conservative* if long-term funding is used predominantly, as illustrated in Figure 4.4(a). Notice that short-term funding supports only the peaks of temporary working capital. When temporary working capital is low and the total funding requirement is below the long-term level, the excess funds are invested in short-term marketable securities. This policy is conservative in that there's very little risk of being unable to fund ups and downs in working capital. However, its cost tends to be fairly high.

> The *mix* of short- or long-term working capital financing is a matter of *policy*. Use of *longer-term* funds reflects *conservatism*.

We say a working capital financing policy is *aggressive* if relatively more short-term funding is used, as illustrated in Figure 4.4(b). Here short-term funds support all of temporary and a good part of permanent working capital. The policy is aggressive in the sense that some risk is being taken to reduce cost. The illustration makes it easy to see that a sudden rise in short-term rates will substantially increase the firm's interest costs. Further, a drying up of the availability of short-term funds could make normal business operations very difficult.

Working Capital Policy

Working capital policy refers to the firm's policies on four subissues:

1. How much working capital is used
2. The extent to which working capital is supported by short- versus long-term financing
3. How each component of working capital is managed
4. The nature/source of any short-term financing used

---

3 Long-term funds may include long-term debt, preferred shares, or common equity.
4 We will discuss flotation costs in more detail in Chapters 9 and 15. For now, think of flotation costs as fees that must be paid in order to raise money.
5 "Tight money" means there's little available to borrow, so lenders demand very high rates and may refuse credit to all but the highest-quality borrowers.

FIGURE 4.4
Working Capital
Financing Policies

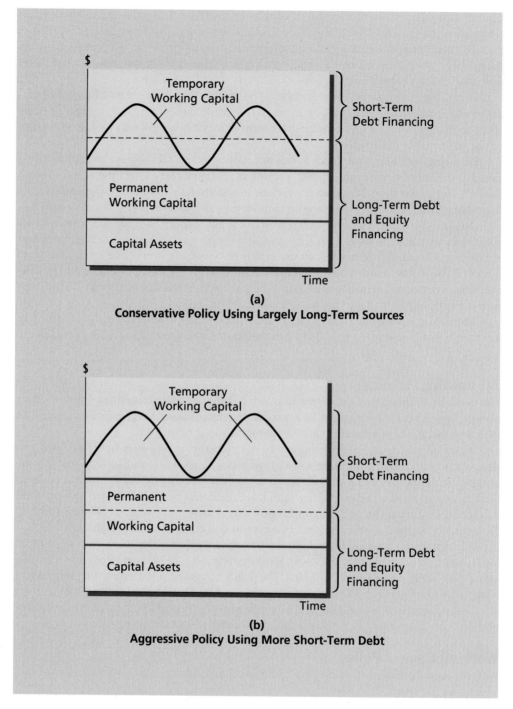

(a)
Conservative Policy Using Largely Long-Term Sources

(b)
Aggressive Policy Using More Short-Term Debt

We've already discussed the first and second of these subissues; we'll consider the third next, and the fourth in Chapter 5.

CASH MANAGEMENT

Although good cash management can improve financial results, it isn't likely to make a weak business strong. Bad cash management, on the other hand, can make a strong company weak to the point of failure. Especially among small firms, it isn't uncommon for companies to be simultaneously profitable and bankrupt. In other words, a firm that doesn't have the cash to pay its bills and meet its payroll goes out of business, regardless of how good its long-term prospects are. For that reason, it pays to understand how cash oils the gears of business and how firms can get the most out of it.

Definitions and Objectives

A firm's *cash* is the money it has on hand in currency and in bank *chequing accounts*.[6] The overwhelming bulk of business cash is in chequing accounts, because very little commercial activity is transacted in currency.

The Motivation for Holding Cash

Firms have to have cash on hand for at least three reasons: *transactions demand*, *precautionary demand*, and *speculative demand*.

Transactions Demand

Firms need money in the bank to pay bills for the goods and services they use. Payments are made to employees, vendors, utility companies, and taxation authorities, to name just a few. Most receipts come in the form of cheques that are deposited in the bank. The constant flow of money in and out of the bank, known as transactions demand, gives rise to an average account balance that we associate with transactions.

If firms had perfect knowledge of when cash would come in and when it should go out, transactions balances could be kept very low. However, we don't generally have such knowledge, especially with respect to receipts. It's therefore necessary to keep the balance high enough to support routine operations. It's especially important to have enough cash on hand to take advantage of prompt payment discounts offered by vendors.

Precautionary Demand

Sometimes emergencies arise with little warning. For example, suppose a shipment intended for a demanding customer is accidentally damaged on the loading dock, and a new shipment has to be produced immediately. That could require extra labour at overtime rates and the quick acquisition of new raw materials. Firms may keep cash on hand to pay for such emergency needs; this is known as precautionary demand.

Speculative Demand

Firms may also keep cash available to take advantage of unexpected opportunities. For example, suppose the price of a particular production material drops suddenly, but is expected to go up again quickly. If cash is available, a bargain can be had; if not, it has to be passed up. Firms may keep money on hand to take advantage of such opportunities; this is known as speculative demand.

The reasons for holding cash aren't entirely additive. Money available for transactions may at times be used for emergencies or unexpected opportunities.

Rather than holding cash per se, many companies use marketable securities or borrowing arrangements for precautionary and speculative purposes. We will address marketable securities later in this chapter. We will discuss borrowing arrangements in Chapter 5.

> Firms hold cash to make **transactions**, as a **precaution**, and for **speculative** opportunities.

---

6 A bank chequing account is known more formally as a demand deposit. The bank pays money out of the account to third parties on the basis of cheques that represent demands of the account owner. In the normal course of business, when buyers and sellers know each other well, cheques are accepted as readily as currency. Therefore, the money available in the economy is defined to include chequing account balances. The financial definition of cash follows the same principle.

The Objective of Cash Management

The problem with cash in the bank is that it doesn't earn a return. Banks don't pay interest on the balances in commercial chequing accounts. That means companies have to devote a certain amount of their financial resources to maintaining cash in the bank, but receive no return on those resources. For this reason, it's desirable to operate with as little cash as possible.

At the same time, it's clearly easier to run a business with more cash than with less. A firm with a substantial bank balance will never be embarrassed by running out of money. This is described as *liquidity*. An adequately liquid firm will always be able to pay its bills on time, take the appropriate discounts, and take emergencies and opportunities in stride.

Cash management involves striking a balance between these conflicting objectives. Good cash management minimizes the amount of cash in the bank, but at the same time assures there's enough available to operate efficiently. We'll see shortly that there are several relatively standard techniques for doing that.

> Good *cash management* implies maintaining adequate *liquidity* with *minimum cash* in the bank.

Marketable Securities

Notice that the precautionary and speculative motives call for having cash on hand that isn't used very often. These demands can be largely satisfied by assets that are only slightly less liquid than cash but do earn a return. This compromise is known as investing in *marketable securities*. It sacrifices a little liquidity for a modest but significant return.

Marketable securities are short-term obligations of very strong organizations, including Treasury bills, short-term government bonds, and commercial paper. The fact that the securities are short term is important: it insulates them from changes in value due to interest rate fluctuations. The word "marketable" implies that the issues can be sold quickly. Marketable securities are also referred to as *near-cash* or *cash equivalents*, and are bought and sold in the "money market."

For example, suppose a firm invests some of its cash in short-term *Treasury bills*,[7] and then has an emergency need for funds. Because there's a ready market for government debt, the securities can be sold within a day and the proceeds used to satisfy the emergency need. In the meantime, the Treasury bills pay a modest return on the funds invested.

Commercial paper and *bankers' acceptances*[8] are normally considered very safe investments because of their short maturity and the strength of the borrowing organizations. They therefore pay a relatively low interest rate, typically about 1% to 2% below the prime interest rate. Rather than bearing interest, the notes are generally sold at a *discounted price*, meaning that the interest is taken out of the price when the notes are sold. For example, a six-month (182-day), $1 million note selling for $970,968 would yield (to the investor) 6% on an annualized basis; that is,

> Marketable securities are liquid investments that can be held instead of cash and earn a modest return.

For current rates on commercial paper and Treasury bills, go to http://www.bankof canada.ca/en/ rates/monmrt.htm.

$$r = \frac{100 - 97.0968}{97.0968} \times \frac{365}{182}$$

$$= 0.0299 \times 2.0055$$

$$= 6.00\%$$

---

7 Treasury bills (or T-bills) are short-term borrowing by the federal government. We will discuss them in more detail in Chapter 7.

8 Commercial paper and bankers' acceptances are instruments for short-term borrowing by financial institutions or other large corporations. We will examine commercial paper and bankers' acceptances in more detail in Chapter 5.

Treasury bills, commercial paper, and bankers' acceptances are all sold on a discount basis.

(4.1)   Annualized yield on a discounted money market security:

$$r = \frac{100 - P}{P} \times \frac{365}{d}$$

where P = Discounted price as a percentage of maturity value

d = Number of days to maturity

r = Annualized yield[9]

Other examples of marketable securities include *money market funds, certificates of deposit (CDs)* from Canadian and U.S. banks, foreign currency (*swapped*) deposits, and Canadian currency deposited in foreign banks (*eurodollar deposits*). We will return to these foreign deposits in Chapter 20.

Investing excess cash in marketable securities is a specialized function carried out by the treasury departments of larger firms working with banks and investment dealers. People who work in the area develop considerable expertise about the pros and cons of the various investment vehicles available. We won't delve into the operating details here, but the concept of marketable securities and the fact that most large companies invest in them regularly is very important.

Cheque Disbursement and the Cheque Clearing Process

The amount of cash companies need is directly related to the method by which the *financial system* gets money from a paying organization (the *payer*) to the receiving party (the *payee*). Understanding the rudiments of this system is key to understanding cash management.

The Basic Procedure for Transferring Cash

Let's look at the routine procedure through which one party pays another with a cheque through the banking system. The *cheque clearing process* is written out below and portrayed graphically in Figure 4.5. In both, typical elapsed time requirements are indicated in parentheses near each step.

1. The payer writes a cheque on his bank and mails it to the payee. (takes two to three days)
2. The payee receives the cheque, records it, and processes it internally for deposit.
3. The payee then deposits the cheque in her own bank. (two days—steps 2 and 3)
4. The payee's bank sends the cheque into the interbank *clearing system*.
5. The clearing system processes the cheque. This transfers money from the payer's account at his bank into the payee's account at her bank. The funds are now available for the payee's use. The cancelled cheque is returned to the payer through his bank. (one day—steps 4 and 5)[10]

---

9 The annualized yield as calculated ignores the effect of interest on interest, that is—compounding. The effective yield that considers compounding is expressed by the formula

$$r = \left(1 + \frac{100 - P}{P}\right)^{\frac{365}{d}} - 1$$

In our example, the annualized yield on a compound interest basis would be

$$r = \left(1 + \frac{100 - 97.0968}{97.0968}\right)^{\frac{365}{182}} - 1$$

$$r = .0609 = 6.09\%.$$

10 Canadians usually have immediate use of the proceeds from cheques deposited even though it takes another day for the cheques to clear.

FIGURE 4.5
The Cheque
Clearing Process

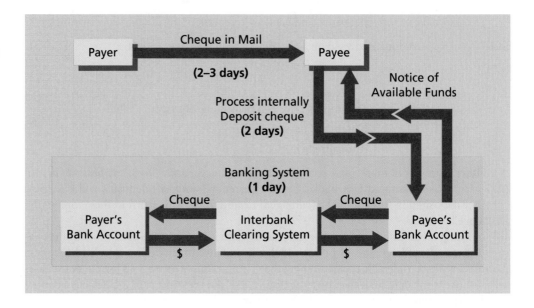

Float is money tied
up in the cheque
clearing process.

It's important to pay particular attention to the length of time taken by each step. Money tied up in the process is called **float**. During the time cheques are in the mail they're part of *mail float,* when they're being processed at the payee's office they're in *processing float*, and when they're in the banking system they're in *transit float*. Collectively the money in the entire process is called *cheque cashing float* or just *float*.

The farther the payer is located from the payee, the longer will be the mail float. We'll return to this point later.

Objectives in Managing Use of the Cheque Clearing Process

Payees are interested
in *speeding* the
cheque clearing
process while *payers*
may want to *slow* it.

The cheque clearing process may take five or six days. During that time, the payee doesn't have the use of the cash even though the payer has written and mailed the cheque. In fact, funds remain in a payer's account balance and are technically usable until the cheque clears through the banking system.

This leads to two important cash management ideas. First, from the perspective of a payee receiving money, speeding the collection of cheques *after they've been mailed* gets the cash in faster. Second, from the perspective of a payer sending money to someone else, withholding cheques until they are due gives a company the maximum use of its cash.

All companies are simultaneously payers and payees, so any firm can use both ideas to reduce the funds that need to be committed to cash balances.

Accelerating Cash Receipts

In this section, we'll take the point of view of the payee, the party receiving money, and examine approaches to accelerating the receipt of cash.

Lock Box Systems

Lock box systems are services provided by banks to accelerate the collection of cash once a cheque has been mailed to a payee. The idea behind the system is very simple.

Notice that in Figure 4.5 the first step of the payment process involves the payer mailing a cheque, which is processed and deposited by the payee in the second step. Together, these steps take four to five days. A lock box system reduces this float period by moving the cheque directly from the payer to the bank, eliminating the stop at the payee's office.

In a **lock box system**, the payee rents a post office box near its customers and its branch bank. It then directs payers to mail their cheques to the post office box rather than to its own headquarters. The bank opens the box several times a day, collects the cheques received, and deposits them in the payee's account. This may cut an average of two or three days out of the whole process. The idea is illustrated in Figure 4.6.

After the bank deposits the cheques, copies are sent to the payee's office. Its internal processing is based on those copies after the deposit has been made and the clearing process has begun.

FINE-TUNING THE LOCK BOX SYSTEM Geographic details can make lock boxes especially effective. Suppose a payer is on the West Coast and the payee and its primary bank are on the East Coast. If mailed to the payee, the payer's cheques have to make a time-consuming trip across the country before they're received.

The payee can accelerate the process by establishing a lock box at a branch bank on the West Coast, thus eliminating much of the mail float. When funds are deposited into the West Coast bank, they're electronically transferred to the payee's primary bank on the East Coast. Big companies that receive payments from all over the country may maintain lock boxes in all the areas in which their customers are concentrated.

Electronic Data Interchange (EDI) refers to the direct, electronic information exchange and direct computer-to-computer transactions between businesses.

Lock boxes are located near customers and *shorten mail and processing float.*

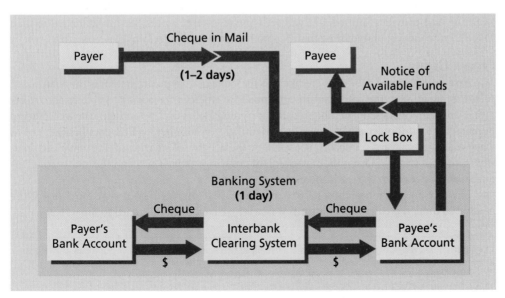

FIGURE 4.6
A Lock Box System in the Cheque Clearing Process

Concentration Banking

Large companies often have a great many *depository*[11] bank accounts spread around the country. This is a result of the multiple lock box systems we described in the last section. It also happens when firms have widespread retail outlets, because each store has to deposit its receipts in a local bank every day.

Holding cash in a number of small accounts tends to be administratively inefficient because of duplicated effort and lack of central control. It also makes it difficult to invest in marketable securities, which tend to be traded in large sums. When cash is separated into a number of small bundles under the control of local divisions, no one has enough to take advantage of short-term investment opportunities.

Concentration banking is a system in which a single *concentration bank* manages the balances in remote accounts to target levels, and sweeps excess cash into its own central location. Special documents called *depository transfer cheques* are used to move funds from one bank to another within a concentration network. Funds can also be moved electronically using an *automated clearing house transfer*, which is a preauthorized electronic withdrawal from payers' accounts.

Once the funds are in the concentration account, the treasurer's department or the bank can make transfers to pay down the firm's bank loans or buy marketable securities.

> **Concentration banks** sweep excess balances in *distant depository accounts* into *central locations* daily.

Electronic Funds Transfer

Newer cash management systems are based upon *electronic funds transfer (EFT)*. EFT is a system in which funds are moved between computers without the use of a cheque. Such systems may reduce or even eliminate float. Examples include *preauthorized payments, debit cards,* and *smart cards.*

Preauthorized Payments

When there's a very good working relationship between a payer and a payee, *preauthorized payments* can eliminate mail float entirely. In this arrangement, the payer (a customer) authorizes the payee (a vendor) in advance to transfer funds from the customer's account to that of the vendor. The transfer occurs when the vendor ships product or provides service to the customer. Clearly this arrangement requires a certain amount of trust on the part of the payer. Preauthorized payments are increasingly used to collect recurring monthly charges such as utility bills and insurance payments.

Debit Cards

> For an overview, statistics, and video on Interac, go to the Interac Association at http://www.interac.org.

Another EFT application is integral to retail point-of-sale systems. Through the use of a debit card and the *Interac* system, a retail purchase is automatically charged against the buyer's bank account. For the customer, it is a efficient and safe way to pay. For the retailer, it avoids cheque handling and provides immediate cash settlement. Interac states that, in 2005, more than 391,000 merchants operated more than 571,000 direct payment terminals.

Smart Cards

The next generation of debit and credit cards for Canada's payments system is the *smart card.* As the name implies, the cards feature an embedded microprocessor that's able to add, store, delete, and manipulate information. Instead of signing a sales draft to authenticate a credit card purchase, the cardholder enters a personal identification number, or PIN on a keypad, just as when making debit card purchases. For vendors, the benefits of smart cards are enhanced security to combat fraud; a faster, more convenient customer experience; and the ability to introduce new services onto the cards themselves.

The card industry has chosen 2010 as a target date by which most—if not all—of the nearly 100 million credit and debit cards we carry will have been upgraded to Smart Cards.[12]

---

11 A large company's working bank accounts are usually of two kinds for administrative purposes. The depository account receives incoming cash, while outgoing cheques are written on the disbursing account.
12 Source: "Smarts Are On The Way," Trevor Marshall, *Backbone*, March/April, 2007, p. 24.

Managing Cash Outflow

When looking at managing outflows from the perspective of the payer, there are two issues: maintaining control of disbursements, and slowing cheques in the clearing process.

Control Issues

A major responsibility of the treasurer is to control disbursements. He or she should try to pay payables on the last day appropriate for the payment terms agreed with the vendor. This may involve mailing a cheque timed to arrive on the due date, or programming the payment in advance for electronic transfer on the future due date. In any case, companies often maintain separate disbursement bank accounts for payments to vendors, payroll, etc.

Corporations routinely make electronic fund transfers from firm payroll accounts for direct deposit into employee accounts.

Most large companies are decentralized, meaning they have operating divisions in locations remote from headquarters. There are benefits to central control of cash, but there are also benefits associated with decentralized control.

In large companies, most agreements with customers and vendors are made at the division level. Because cash payments are a key element in the process of managing such agreements, it makes sense to place disbursing authority in the hands of division management. However, that results in at least one disbursing account at every division, which in turn leads to an undesirable distribution of cash balances around the country.

Zero balance accounts are funded only when cheques are presented for payment.

Zero Balance Accounts (ZBAs)

Zero balance accounts solve this control problem. They are empty disbursement accounts established at the firm's concentration bank for its various divisions. Divisions write cheques on their ZBAs that are automatically funded as they're presented for payment. The funds come out of a master account at the concentration bank. In essence, ZBAs are subdivisions of the master account. Although the ZBA never has a positive balance, it has a number and receives statements that enable the division to use it to manage its business just like any other chequing account.

Cash Information Systems

Coordinating the treasurer's efforts in all areas of cash management is the company's *cash information system*. Chartered banks offer cash information systems that link the manager's computer with the bank's system, providing the cash manager with up-to-date information on transactions, cash balances, and money market rates. The system also allows the manager the option to transfer funds and make money market investments, or to authorize the bank to do so.

http

The Bank of Montreal offers a number of business banking services including lock boxes and electronic funds transfers. Visit http://www.bmo.com and click on *Business Banking*, then *Cash Management* for more information.

Insights ETHICS

Ethical Cash Management

Is remote disbursing ethical? Is it, in general, right to take advantage of mail float to keep cash longer? Isn't the payer who uses the practice essentially stealing a little interest from the recipient on each cheque?

Is the situation more sensitive to ethical issues if the payer is a financial institution with a "fiduciary" duty to the payee client? A fiduciary relationship is one of trust and confidence in which one party relies on the professional integrity of the other. It usually exists between certain professionals

and their clients where money is involved. Banks, brokers, accountants, and lawyers may be fiduciaries.

In other words, is it less appropriate to exploit the other party in a transaction when that party trusts you to look after his or her interests? Most people would say that it is.

U.S. courts have held that remote disbursing is indeed a violation of the trust implied in relationships between parties, like stockbrokers and clients, and have disallowed the practice in that context. Such strategies are becoming less common in Canada as there are significant ethical and legal issues involved.

Remote Disbursing

Payers sometimes *disburse* cheques from *remote* banks to *lengthen* mail float and *slow* cash outflow.

Look back at Figures 4.5 and 4.6 (pages 130 and 131) and take the perspective of the payer. Payers might be tempted to slow the cheque collection processes and expand float as much as possible to prolong the time cash remains in their bank accounts.

Remote disbursing is a way to keep cheques in the cheque clearing process. If a cheque is issued from a distant city, it will take longer to reach the payee. This delay has the effect of increasing mail float, keeping money in the payer's account longer.

Evaluating the Cost of Cash Management Services

To be *effective*, a *cash management* system must lower balances enough to *save more* in interest than it costs.

Cash management, especially acceleration of receipts, can free up the financial resources firms have tied up in their cash accounts. The general implication is that a firm can borrow less money by the amount of the reduction in its cash balance, and pay commensurately less interest. This saving has to be measured against the cost of the cash management system to see if it's worthwhile. The calculations are relatively straightforward.

Cash management systems are subject to significant economies of scale, so larger companies benefit more clearly from having sophisticated systems than do smaller firms.

Example 4.1

Kelso Systems Inc. operates primarily on the East Coast, but has a cluster of customers in British Columbia who remit about 500 cheques a year. The average cheque is for $10,000. West Coast cheques currently take an average of eight days from the time they're mailed by customers to clear into Kelso's East Coast account. A British Columbia bank has offered Kelso a lock box system for $1,000 a year plus $0.20 per cheque. The system can be expected to reduce the clearing time to six days. Is the bank's proposal a good deal for Kelso if it borrows at 8%?

■ **Solution:** The cheques represent revenue of $5 million per year. The average amount of West Coast revenue tied up in the cheque-clearing process is

$$\frac{8}{365} \times \$5,000,000 = \$109,589$$

The proposal will reduce this to

$$\frac{6}{365} \times \$5,000,000 = \$82,192$$

The difference, $27,397, is the amount of cash freed up by the lock box system. If Kelso installs the system, it should be able to *reduce its borrowings* by this much money all the time. The interest saved at 8% is

$$\$27,397 \times 0.08 = \$2,192$$

However, the cost of the system is the annual fee plus the per-cheque charge.

$$\$1,000 + \$0.20(500) = \$1,100$$

The net saving is

$$\$2,192 - \$1,100 = \$1,092$$

Hence, the bank's proposal is worth accepting.

MANAGING ACCOUNTS RECEIVABLE

A firm's accounts receivable represent the obligations of customers for future payments that arise when sales are made on credit. The management of receivables is a relatively unique function in finance in that it involves an interface with customers, something usually reserved for the sales department.

Objectives and Policy

In general, companies like to operate with as little tied up in receivables as possible. There are basically two reasons for that preference. First, carrying fewer receivables minimizes the interest cost of supporting the receivable asset. Second, it minimizes bad debt losses because whenever money is owed, there's a chance that it will never be collected.

There are trade-offs, however. For several reasons we'll point out shortly, a higher level of receivables generally increases sales and leads to better customer relations.

Managing accounts receivable means striking a balance between these effects. Receivables tend to increase as sales go up, which increases net income. At the same time, interest cost and collection losses increase, which decreases net income.

It's important to notice that the focus of the trade-off is at the EBT level. Managing receivables means finding the point at which *profitability* is maximized as a result of the opposing forces, not the point at which sales are maximized.

Receivables policy involves credit standards, terms of sale, and collection procedures.

The things firms do to influence profitability through receivables management are collectively called *receivables policy* or *credit and collections policy*. Three broad issues are involved.

> Higher receivables improve sales and customer relations, but lead to more bad debts and interest expense.

1. *Credit policy:* How financially strong must a customer be for the firm to sell to it on credit?
2. What *terms of sale* (due dates and discounts) should be offered to credit customers?
3. *Collections policy:* How should customers whose bills aren't paid on time be handled?

Who Is Responsible for Receivables Policy?

Although receivables policy is under the control of financial management in most companies, it has a major effect on sales. Therefore most policy decisions are joint efforts between financial and sales/marketing management. As a practical matter, it's not unusual for this shared area of responsibility to create quite a bit of conflict between the two departments. We'll understand why this happens as we go along.

Determinants of the Receivables Balance

The size of a firm's receivables balance is determined primarily by the level of its credit sales. The more it sells for cash, the smaller will be its receivables and the fewer associated problems it will have. It is axiomatic that everyone prefers to sell for cash when possible. However, business-to-business sales are usually on credit.[13]

Credit Policy

Credit policy is the most important decision variable available for influencing the level of receivables. It determines the customers to which a company is willing to make credit sales.

Most larger firms have *credit departments* staffed by credit specialists. When an order is received from a new customer, or an old customer wants to buy more on credit than it has previously, the credit department has the responsibility of approving or denying the request.

> A firm's **credit policy** is a statement of the *minimum customer quality* it will accept for *credit sales*.

To make its decision, the department investigates the creditworthiness of the customer by using a number of information sources. These sources include the customer's payment history with the firm, if applicable, the reports of *credit agencies* (also called *credit bureaus*), the customer's own financial statements, bank references, and the customer's reputation among other vendors.

The primary source of information is usually the report of a **credit agency**, an organization that keeps files on the financial condition and bill-paying records of vast numbers of companies. For a fee, the credit agency will provide a vendor with a report on any customer or potential customer. Depending on the fee structure, the vendor may ask for a detailed credit check on only large and doubtful orders.

> A **credit agency** provides credit reports and credit ratings on companies.

---

13 In consumer markets, retailers usually demand cash at the time of sale, either from the customer or from a credit card company such as Visa™.

For an overview of D&B's credit reporting services and sample reports, go to http://www.dnb.ca and click on *Credit and Risk* Equifax is another credit agency. To obtain a free report on *your* personal credit rating, go to http://www.equifax.ca and click on *Consumer Information Centre.*

D&B (formerly Dun and Bradstreet) Canada publishes the *Reference Book*, listing many thousands of companies and providing information on their lines of business, net worth, and creditworthiness. D&B also provides detailed individualized credit reports on potential corporate customers, including ratings on their credit risk.

A company's credit policy revolves around how good a risk a customer has to be before it will be extended credit. A typical policy might require that a customer:

- be in business at least three years;
- have a net worth of three times the amount of credit requested;
- have a current ratio of 2.5:1 or higher; and
- have no adverse comments on its credit report from other vendors.

If the conditions aren't met, the firm would sell to the customer only on a *cash* basis.

It's important to understand that customers whose credit applications are denied generally do not buy from the firm. They either can't because they don't have the cash, or they can find another vendor with a more liberal policy.

Hence, a *tighter* credit policy, meaning higher quality requirements for credit customers, generally has the effect of reducing sales. On the other hand, a *looser* credit policy accepts lower-quality customers and increases sales. However, some of the incremental customers brought in by a looser policy generally prove unable or unwilling to pay their bills. The result is an uncollectible account (also called a *bad debt loss*) of the value of their receivables. The frequency of bad debt losses tends to increase substantially as credit policy is relaxed.

Clearly, setting credit policy requires striking a balance between these effects. We want to find the policy that maximizes *profit.*

CREDIT SCORING When a company has a small, regular clientele, the credit manager can usually judge credit risk on an order-by-order basis. However when the company is dealing with consumers or a large number of small trade accounts, a scoring system may be used to rate or prescreen credit applications.

Credit scoring refers to the process of calculating a numerical credit rating for a customer based on financial information collected, and granting or refusing credit as a result.

Credit scoring refers to the process of calculating a numerical credit rating for a customer based on financial information collected, and granting or refusing credit as a result. Credit card issuers such as Visa™ and MasterCard™ have developed elaborate statistical models for scoring new credit applications received. This approach has the advantage of being objective as compared to scoring based solely on judgment. Important variables include marital status, length of time in current job, monthly income, home owner or tenant, other debts, etc. Scoring models are also used by chartered banks for small business loan applications. Credit scoring for corporate accounts is based primarily on financial ratios.

There are often *conflicts* between the *sales* and *credit* departments.

THE CONFLICT WITH SALES OVER CREDIT POLICY The job of the sales department is generally to sell as much product as it can. When salespeople's compensation is based on commissions, the task becomes a very personal challenge. The philosophy in most companies is that the salesperson delivers a willing buyer to the credit department, which then approves or disapproves a credit sale.

If the sale is approved, the customer gets product on credit, the salesperson gets his or her commission, and everyone is happy. If the credit sale is disapproved, it is generally lost. That means the salesperson doesn't get a commission and has wasted whatever work has gone into the account. This understandably creates a good deal of resentment on the part of the salesperson toward the credit department, especially if the customer's credit quality was marginal.

But what happens if a credit sale is approved and the customer eventually fails to pay? It's logical to assume that the salesperson in such a case would be charged back his or her commission.

From the CFO

> However, most companies don't operate that way. The credit decision is viewed as strictly the responsibility of the credit department, so the blame for a bad debt loss is laid at its door alone and the salesperson gets to keep the commission.
>
> This practice can create a counterproductive conflict of interest. Salespeople are generally in close contact with customers and may be aware of things no one else knows about. But if those things are negative, the commission system motivates them not to share the information with the credit department. Credit personnel therefore may harbour some resentment toward salespeople when receivables go sour.

In most companies, optimizing collections performance takes a familiarity with the customers and their problems that the finance department simply doesn't have. The best results come only when senior management directs the sales function to actively participate in identifying and correcting problems.

The Terms of Sale

Recall that credit sales are made on terms that specify the number of days after which the net payment is due and a period during which a prompt payment discount may be taken. For example, terms of 2/10, n.30 mean a 2% discount can be taken if payment is made within 10 days; otherwise the entire amount is due in 30 days.

Terms can have an effect on receivables in two ways. First, shortening or extending the net period tends to affect the length of time a nondelinquent customer takes to pay its bill. It would therefore seem that shortening the term would reduce the receivables balance. As a practical matter, however, companies don't have a great deal of latitude in making the net period shorter than whatever is customary in the industry.

The prompt payment discount tends to be a more effective policy variable. A generous discount usually reduces receivables balances (and the average collection period) because customers pay quickly to save money. The vendor thus benefits from the earlier availability of funds, lower collection costs, and reduced bad debt losses. However, discounts are expensive for the firm giving them.[14]

The prompt payment discount is usually an effective tool for managing receivables.

Occasionally, prompt payment discounts don't help to reduce receivables at all. That happens when a firm's customers are too cash poor to take the discount regardless of how attractive it is. That's often the case when the customers are struggling small businesses. In such situations, increasing the discount in an effort to reduce receivables can backfire and cost money because only customers who are already paying promptly take the increased discount.

Collections Policy

A firm's credit department is usually closely connected with its *collections department*. The function of the collections department is to monitor receivables to spot problem accounts, and to follow up on overdue receivables to get delinquent customers to pay their bills.

MONITORING RECEIVABLES The collection department keeps track of the *average collection period* (ACP) over time, watching for unexpected increases in the ACP. Collections staff ask: Are customers in general taking longer to pay? Or are particular accounts seriously overdue? If so, why?

A monthly or weekly aging schedule is another basic tool for monitoring receivables. Table 4.1 provides an example. The schedule classifies and totals accounts by age category, for instance 0–30 days, 31–60 days, 61–90 days, and over 90 days. The older the account, the greater the risk that it will prove to be uncollectible, and the more attention it will receive.

An aging schedule classifies and totals accounts by age category.

There is apparently a high risk of bad debt loss on the Donner Leather account. The analysis for Z-Score Agencies may indicate a dispute with the customer about one or both of the overdue amounts, particularly if Z-Score has paid more recent invoices.

---

14 We will determine the equivalent annual interest rate for a cash discount in Chapter 5, when we discuss trade credit.

TABLE 4.1
An Aging Schedule of Accounts Receivable

Customer	0–30 Days	31–60 Days	61–90 Days	91+ Days	Total Owing
Alpha Chemical	$ 15,000	$ 0	$ 0	$ 0	$ 15,000
Baker Sporting Goods	$ 12,000	$ 2,500	$ 0	$ 0	$ 14,500
Charleston Corp	$ 0	$ 6,000	$ 0	$ 0	$ 6,000
Donner Leather	$ 0	$ 0	$ 0	$ 11,000	$ 11,000
....					
Other accounts (totals)	$ 218,200	$ 53,500	$ 16,500	$ 41,000	$ 329,200
Z-Score Agencies	$ 4,800	$ 0	$ 3,500	$ 0	$ 8,300
Total	$ 250,000	$ 62,000	$ 20,000	$ 52,000	$ 384,000

Dunning is the process of following up on *overdue* receivables.

COLLECTION EFFORTS The process of communicating with delinquent customers to settle overdue accounts is known as **dunning** the debtor. Procedures are set and employees are designated to undertake this critical task. The sequential procedures include timelines for prompt and increasingly aggressive action, if necessary. Table 4.2 provides a sample set of procedures for a 30-day account that has become overdue.

The dunning procedure may begin with mailing a polite reminder that payment is overdue a few days after the net date on the invoice. If payment isn't received, two or three additional *dunning letters* may follow using progressively stronger language. After that, phone calls are often made first to the customer's payables department and then to responsible executives. If a customer is substantially in arrears, further shipments usually are stopped until some payment is received.

In many cases, unpaid bills are the result of some product or administrative problem. For example, if the product purchased doesn't work as expected, many firms don't pay the bill. In such a case, the collections department gets the customer together with the firm's sales and service personnel to try to straighten out the problem.

Another common problem involves mismatches between the firm's invoice and what the customer's records show as having been ordered and received. If these don't match exactly, many organizations don't pay. In such cases, the collections department works to reconcile the paperwork and get the bill paid.

Collection agencies specialize in *pursuing overdue accounts*, and are usually very *aggressive*.

In other cases, customers don't pay because they don't have the cash or are disreputable and just don't pay bills until they're forced to. When that happens, letters and phone calls often don't work and smaller accounts may be turned over to a **collection agency**, a company that specializes in dunning and collecting overdue accounts for a commission ranging up to 50% of the amounts collected. They use the same techniques as the selling firm, but tend to be more persistent, aggressive, and threatening.

TABLE 4.2
Sequential Collection Procedures

Age of Account	Action Required
40 days	Letter to customer's accounts payable department
50 days	Warning letter (mild)
60 days	Warning letter (strong)
75 days	Telephone call to customer's accounts payable department
90 days	Telephone call to customer's management
	Future deliveries on a COD basis only
120 days	Stop further deliveries
	Turn account over to collection agency or start legal proceedings

---

Insights **REAL APPLICATIONS**

How Lafarge's Western Region Controls Receivables—Sharing Responsibility for Collections with Sales

Lafarge Group, a giant French company, is a dominant player in the international construction materials business. The firm, with some 71,000 employees worldwide, generates annual sales of about $26 billion from operations in 71 countries. Lafarge North America, a 54% owned subsidiary, is headquartered in Virginia, and is this continent's largest diversified supplier of construction materials. It operates out of regional offices throughout the United States and Canada.

CFO, The Magazine for Senior Financial Executives, posts the *Working Capital Scoreboard,* which ranks 1,000 public companies on the efficiency of their working capital management. Some years ago, Lafarge North America's Western Region, based in Calgary, Alberta, racked up an impressive 36-place advance in its scoreboard position largely due to shortening its average collection period by 11 days. The region's vice-president and controller listed 12 fundamentals behind this improvement in collections, including the following points.

- Focus all management on collections; it's not just a finance responsibility.

- Assign ownership of customer accounts among the sales staff to prevent passing the buck on delinquent accounts.
- Clearly define Lafarge's responsibilities to customers including terms and conditions of sale.
- Establish monthly collection targets by salesperson.
- Train salespeople to focus on customer profitability (rather than just on sales volume).
- Engage in weekly credit and collections meetings with the sales team, the credit and collections manager, and the general manager.

The message should be clear. Excellence in receivables management depends on making sure the sales department recognizes that it shares the responsibility for collections with finance. At Lafarge, the responsibility is made explicit by holding salespeople accountable for delinquent customer accounts, and engaging in constant management review of overall collections activity.

Sources: Steven L. Mintz, "Dollars in the Details, Winners Sweat the Small Stuff in the Third Annual Analysis of Working Capital," *CFO, The Magazine for Senior Financial Executives* (July 1999): 55. http://www.lafarge.com and http://www.lafargenorthamerica.com.

A lawsuit may be advisable to collect a larger delinquent balance. If the suit is successful, the firm is awarded a judgment, which still may not be collectible if the customer is missing or bankrupt.

A company's collections policy determines how quickly and aggressively it pursues overdue accounts. There's a great deal of difference, for example, between a firm that sends polite letters and calls for several months and one that threatens a lawsuit when a bill is 30 days overdue.

> Collections policy is the *manner* and *aggressiveness* with which a firm *pursues payment* from delinquent customers.

COLLECTIONS AND CUSTOMER RELATIONS Overly aggressive collection efforts can damage customer relations. For example, imagine that a particular shipment has become very confused because of malfunctioning product and mistakes in shipping, receiving, and invoicing. Also suppose the customer and the firm's sales and service departments are working reasonably diligently to straighten out the problems. Now imagine that in the middle of all this the customer is served with a lawsuit initiated by the collections department for payment of the disputed bill.

Clearly, that would create a tendency for the customer to buy from another vendor in the future. It would also upset the sales department, because it wants to continue selling to the customer. On the other hand, it isn't unusual for salespeople to attempt to placate the collections department in order to sell more commissionable product to a customer they know to be a payment risk.

Credit Decision Analysis

In analyzing the effect on profitability of a proposed change to credit and collection policy, there are several related factors to consider.

1. *Effect on sales revenue:* A company grants credit to increase sales, either by increasing the quantity sold or raising prices or both.
2. *Effect on costs:* When a company increases its sales volume, its total cost to produce or buy the product will increase.
3. *Effect on expenses:* When a company increases sales revenue, variable expenses such as commissions will increase.
4. *Effect on bad debts and collection expense:* When a company increases credit sales, bad debts and collection expenses may increase more than proportionately if the additional sales are to higher-risk accounts.
5. *Effect on discount expense:* If the company offers cash discounts, these expenses will likely increase with higher credit sales.
6. *Effect on interest expense:* When a company increases credit sales, it must arrange to finance the resulting increase in accounts receivable. As a result, its cost of short-term borrowing will rise.

We now provide an example of a credit decision that brings together the various factors in accounts receivable management. We will consider a potential change in credit policy, focusing on the effects on a firm's sales, cost of goods sold, operating expenses, receivable levels, and financing costs. By comparing the firm's profitability before and after the potential changes, we can determine whether the profitability will be increased or decreased.

Example 4.2

Consider the following income statement for Brodeur Company

Sales	$ 1,000,000
Cost of goods sold	500,000
Gross margin	500,000
Selling expense	100,000
Bad debt expense	50,000
Collection expense	30,000
EBIT	320,000
Financing expense	7,397
EBT	$ 312,603

All sales are on credit, and the firm collects its receivables in 45 days. Accordingly, its average receivable balance can be calculated as follows:

$$\text{Accounts receivable} = \text{Sales} \times \frac{\text{Average collection period}}{365}$$

$$\text{Accounts receivable} = \$1,000,000 \times \frac{45}{365} = \$123,288$$

There is an opportunity cost on the firm's funds tied up in receivables. If bank financing is used to finance accounts receivable, we can use the interest rate on short-term loans to calculate this cost. If the rate is 6%, the financing cost is $123,288 \times 0.06 = \$7,397$.

Now, assume that management wants to increase its sales volume by selling to a group of new, higher-risk customers. This change would result in a 10% increase in sales. The ratios of cost of goods sold and selling expenses to sales would remain unchanged. Bad debt expense and collection expense would increase to 7% and 5% of sales respectively. The average collection period for all receivables would increase to 50 days.

Consider the resulting changes to the income statement:

	Before	After
Sales	$ 1,000,000	$ 1,100,000
Cost of goods sold	500,000	550,000
Gross margin	500,000	550,000
Selling expense	100,000	110,000
Bad debt expense	50,000	77,000
Collection expense	30,000	55,000
EBIT	320,000	308,000
Financing expense	7,397	9,041
EBT	$ 312,603	$ 298,959

$$\text{Accounts receivable} = \$1,100,000 \times \frac{50}{365} = \$150,685$$

$$\text{Financing cost} = \$150,685 \times .06 = \$9,041$$

Their decision would be to reject the new credit policy as it would reduce EBT by ($298,959 − $312,603 =) $13,644.[15]

Using Excel®

Using an Excel® spreadsheet, the previous example might be formatted as follows.

Microsoft Excel - Book1.xls				
File Edit View Insert Format Tools Data Window Help				
□ ☞ 🗄 🖴 🖻 🖨 ◲ 🖺	↻ ▾ 🌐 Σ ▾ ᄅ↓ 🛍 ?	» Arial	▾ 10	
A2 ▾ ƒx				

	A	B	C	D	E
1		**Before**	**After**	**Change**	
2					
3	Sales	$1,000,000	(=1.10*B3)		
4	Cost of goods sold	500,000	(=B4/B3*C3)		
5	Gross margin	500,000	(=C3−C4)		
6	Selling expense	100,000	(=B6/B3*C3)		
7	Bad debt expense	50,000	(=.07*C3)		
8	Collection expense	30,000	(=.05*C3)		
9					
10	EBIT	320,000	(=C5−C6−C7−C8)		
11	Financing expense	7,397	(=C15*B16)		
12	EBT	312,603	(=C10−C11)	(=C12−B12)	
13					
14	Average collection period	45	50		
15	Accounts receivable	123,288	(=C3*C14/365)		
16	Interest rate	.06			
17					

15 This analysis ignores such factors as possible investments in inventories or plant or equipment that may result from increased sales, and sources of receivable financing, other than bank credit, such as equity funding.

INVENTORY MANAGEMENT

Inventory is product held for sale to customers. Its significance and the complexity of managing it vary tremendously among businesses. For example, in retailing operations inventory management is critically important but may be relatively simple, while in manufacturing it can be as complex as it is crucial. At the other extreme, most service businesses carry only incidental inventories, so the issue is relatively minor.

It's important to realize that in any business in which inventory is significant, its mismanagement has the potential to ruin the company.

Who Is Responsible for Inventories?

Unlike cash and receivables, inventory is virtually never the direct responsibility of the finance department. It is usually managed by a functional area, such as merchandising, manufacturing, or operations. The executives in charge of those areas generally have broad latitude in choosing inventory levels and management methods.

Finance gets involved in an oversight or policing way. If inventory levels become too high, it's the job of financial management to call attention to the fact that things might be run more efficiently. Financial people generally monitor the level of lost or obsolete inventory that has to be written off and ensure that it doesn't become excessive. They also participate in periodic *physical inventories* (counts) that reconcile quantities actually on hand with the firm's records.

In short, although the finance department does not itself manage the typical firm's inventory, it has a responsibility to ensure that those who do manage it act cost effectively.

The Benefits and Costs of Carrying Inventory

As might be expected, for firms to which inventory is important, it's easier to operate with more usable inventory than with less. However, carrying the extra product costs money, so there's a trade-off between cost and benefit. The idea behind inventory management is to find a level that's close to optimal in balancing the pluses against the minuses.

The Benefits of Carrying Adequate Inventory

In manufacturing, inventory separates and smooths the work of different production departments. For example, suppose departments *A* and *B* work on product sequentially. If product moves directly out of department *A* into *B*, everything runs smoothly as long as there are no delays in *A*'s operation. However, if some defect or accident causes a delay in *A*, department *B* will run out of work and be idle until the problem is fixed. Clearly, time and money will be wasted. But if some product is inventoried between the two departments, *B* can avoid idle time by working on it while department *A* is fixing its problem.

In any business, carrying more inventory rather than less reduces *stockouts* and *backorders*. A stockout occurs when something the company doesn't have on hand is needed in production or by a customer. The firm is out of stock on the item and places a *backorder* with its supplier to get it. The term "backorder" implies that the order is remedial in the sense that the item is currently needed, and usually implies a request for expedited handling.

In manufacturing, stockouts disrupt operations and cause idle time and missed schedules, which cost money. At the point of sale, stockouts mean customers don't get what they want right away. That causes dissatisfaction and can drive customers to other suppliers or vendors, which means lost sales. Too many stockouts can drive customers away permanently.

All in all, carrying more active, usable inventory makes operations run more smoothly, improves customer relations, and increases sales.[16]

Finance has an *oversight* responsibility for inventory management.

A stockout occurs when required inventory is not on hand.

---

16 It should be obvious that carrying extra obsolete or damaged inventory doesn't convey these benefits. Hence, we have to look beyond the dollar inventory figure on the balance sheet to see whether the firm has enough or too much.

The Cost of Carrying Inventory

Keeping inventory on hand takes money. The reasons can be separated into traditional costs of the inventory and potential losses in its value. In general, both increase with the amount of inventory carried.

The following traditional inventory carrying costs are associated with holding inventory.

- *Interest:* Firms have to pay a return on the funds used to acquire inventory just as they do on any other asset.

- *Storage and security:* Inventory takes up space and is often subject to pilfering. Storage space has to be provided along with security to prevent theft.

- *Insurance:* Firms generally buy insurance to protect themselves against large inventory losses due to fire, theft, or natural disaster.

- *Taxes:* The provinces may levy a tax on company assets, including inventory.

> Inventory carrying costs are storage, insurance, and other costs of holding inventory.

Several phenomena cause inventory to lose value. In general, the more inventory a firm carries, the more it is exposed to a risk of loss from each of the following causes and the higher is its overall loss.

- *Shrinkage:* In spite of security measures, some inventory inevitably disappears. Such vanishing, presumably due to theft, is known as shrinkage.

- *Spoilage:* Many items have a limited shelf life, after which they lose their value partially or entirely. Even when inventory is monitored carefully, some spoilage of perishable items is expected.

- *Breakage:* Inventory in stock can be run over, stepped on, leaked on or into, or broken in any number of ways.

- *Obsolescence:* New products, for instance new computers, often do jobs better, faster, or more cheaply than their predecessors. When that happens, the old products lose value rapidly because no one wants them unless their prices are heavily discounted.

> More inventory means fewer *lost sales* and production *delays*, but more carrying costs.

These costs and losses together can be called the *carrying cost* of inventory. When storage costs or interest rates are high, inventory levels should be kept low.

Inventory Ordering Costs

The process of ordering and receiving goods generates a different sort of inventory-related expense. The carrying costs we've talked about so far depend on the amount of inventory on hand during a period. Inventory ordering costs reflect the internal[17] expenses of placing orders with suppliers, receiving shipments, and processing materials into inventory. These costs are related to the number of orders placed rather than to the amount of inventory held, and are assumed to be fixed. When ordering costs are high, the number of orders should be reduced and inventory levels increased. Ordering costs and carrying costs tend to vary inversely with one another.

> Inventory ordering costs are costs to order and receive inventory.

Inventory Control and Management

Companies develop elaborate systems for tracking and controlling their inventories. The cost of such systems and the people to run them are additional expenses associated with inventory. This kind of cost doesn't necessarily increase with incremental inventory or orders. Rather, it's tied to the number of different pieces carried and the way they're used.

Inventory management refers to the overall way a company oversees its inventory and uses its control system to manage the benefits of carrying inventory against the cost. You can think of the process as defining an acceptable level of operating efficiency in terms of stockouts, backorders, and production problems, and then trying to achieve that level of efficiency with the minimum inventory cost.

> Inventory management refers to the *overall* way a firm *controls* inventory and its cost.

---

17 In this context, ordering costs do not include payments to suppliers for product.

Insights REAL APPLICATIONS

DANIER LEATHER

Inventory at Danier Leather Inc.

(For the financial statements and other financial information about Danier Leather Inc., refer to Appendix 3A, page 92.)

Danier had the following inventory on hand at its 2006 and 2005 year-ends ($000):

	June 24, 2006	June 25, 2005
Raw materials	$ 1,738	$ 3,456
Work-in-process	1,000	634
Finished goods	29,610	24,941
	$ 32,348	$ 29,031
Inventory turnover	2.4	2.9

Even though Danier's is a seasonal business, it has followed a "year-round purchasing policy" to earn preferred customer status with its suppliers and to ensure access to the best quality materials. Danier would also benefit from attractive prices, but would incur additional carrying costs, including markdowns on older stock.

Danier sources about 75% of its garments (finished goods) from independent foreign contract manufacturers, who produce these items overseas, mainly in China, under Danier's supervision and to Danier's specifications. Likewise, a significant portion of Danier's raw material, principally leather, is also purchased from foreign vendors.

Inventory at the end of 2006 was approximately $3.3 million higher than inventory at the end of 2005. Finished goods inventory increased by approximately $4.7 million. This increase was due to earlier purchases of fall outerwear and blazer merchandise. Raw material and work-in-process inventory decreased by $1.4 million compared with 2005.

Source: Danier Leather Annual Report, 2006.

There's no single, all-encompassing approach to managing inventory. Success is achieved through frequent reviews, attention to detail, and the use of a variety of automated and manual systems. In the rest of this section we'll review some well-known techniques that address portions of the inventory management process.

The Economic Order Quantity (EOQ) Model

We've defined carrying and ordering costs as being related to inventory in different ways. Inventory carrying costs increase with the amount of inventory held. On the other hand, inventory ordering costs increase when the firm holds a small amount of inventory, because more orders are required to replenish depleted stocks. The total cost of having inventory is the sum of the two. The economic order quantity (EOQ) model is an approach to minimizing total inventory cost by recognizing that under certain conditions there's a trade-off between carrying cost and ordering cost.

The **economic order quantity (EOQ) model** minimizes the sum of ordering and carrying cost.

Imagine that an inventory item is used evenly during the year and is periodically reordered in quantity Q. For the moment we'll ignore time lags in ordering and delivery. We'll assume the item is used steadily until none is left, then immediately restocked by a delivery of Q units. Figure 4.7 is a plot of the number of units on hand over time under these assumptions.

Notice that inventory in stock decreases steadily along the diagonal lines until it is replenished. Under these conditions, the average quantity on hand is $\frac{Q}{2}$ units and the number of reorders is the annual usage divided by Q.

The model assumes that carrying costs vary directly with the average inventory balance and that ordering costs are fixed on a per-order basis. If C represents carrying cost per unit per year,[18] total carrying cost can be written as

---

[18] We have used a yearly timeframe in developing our formulas and calculations. However, EOQ techniques are often used with seasonal, quarterly, or monthly timeframes, depending on the pattern of demand for the product.

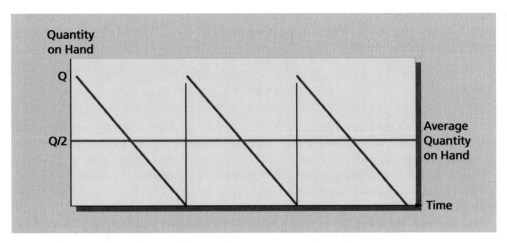

FIGURE 4.7
Inventory on Hand
for a Steadily Used
Item

(4.2)
$$\text{Carrying cost} = C\left(\frac{Q}{2}\right)$$

It's clear from Equation 4.2 and Figure 4.8 that total carrying cost can be reduced by ordering more frequently in smaller quantities. If Q were smaller, Figure 4.7 would have more saw-toothed peaks, but each would be lower and the average quantity on hand $\frac{Q}{2}$ would be lower.

However, ordering more frequently will increase the number of orders placed each year. Because each order costs a fixed amount, this increases total ordering cost. If demand is D *units per year*, the firm places

(4.3)
$$\text{Number of orders} = N = \frac{D}{Q}$$

orders per year. Then if the fixed cost per order is F, total ordering cost will be

(4.4)
$$\text{Ordering cost} = FN = F\left(\frac{D}{Q}\right)$$

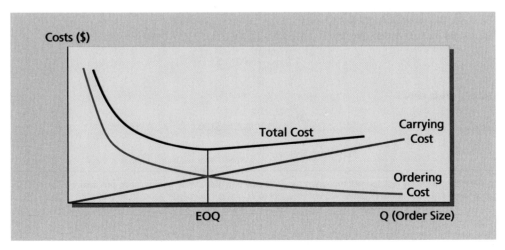

FIGURE 4.8
Inventory Costs
and the EOQ

This expression clearly increases as order size decreases because Q appears in the denominator. Total inventory cost, which we'll call TC, is the sum of carrying cost and ordering cost. Adding Equations 4.2 and 4.4 gives

(4.5)
$$\text{Total inventory cost} = TC = C\left(\frac{Q}{2}\right) + F\left(\frac{D}{Q}\right)$$

These ideas are represented graphically in Figure 4.8. The diagram shows carrying cost increasing and ordering cost decreasing with order size, Q. Notice that the sum of these costs, total cost, first decreases and then increases as Q gets larger. Hence, it's possible to choose an optimal order size that minimizes the cost of inventory. That value of Q is known as the *economic order quantity*, abbreviated EOQ. On the diagram, it is directly below the minimum point on the total cost line.

A technique for finding the minimum value of an expression like Equation 4.5 is available using calculus. We'll accept the following result without getting into the math.[19]

(4.6)
$$EOQ = \left(\frac{2FD}{C}\right)^{\frac{1}{2}}$$

Example 4.3

The Galbraith Corp. buys a part that costs $5. The carrying cost of inventory is approximately 20% of the part's dollar value per year. It costs $50 to place, process, and receive an order. The firm uses 900 of the $5 parts a year. What ordering quantity minimizes inventory costs and how many orders will be placed each year if that order quantity is used? What inventory costs are incurred for the part with this ordering quantity?

■ **Solution:** First note that the unit carrying cost per year is 20% of the part's price, so

$$C = (0.2)(\$5) = \$1$$

Next, write Equation 4.6 and substitute from the information given.

$$EOQ = \left(\frac{2FD}{C}\right)^{\frac{1}{2}}$$
$$= \left(\frac{2(\$45)1,000}{\$1}\right)^{\frac{1}{2}}$$
$$= (90,000)^{\frac{1}{2}}$$
$$= 300$$

The economic order quantity is 300 units.
The annual number of reorders is

$$\frac{900}{300} = 3$$

Carrying costs are

$$\frac{300}{2} \times \$5 \times 0.2 = \$150$$

---

[19] The mathematically inclined will recognize the EOQ as a straightforward minimization problem with respect to the variable Q. Differentiate Equation 4.5 with respect to Q and set the result equal to zero to get

$$0 = \frac{C}{2} - \frac{FD}{Q^2}$$

Then solve for Q to get Equation 4.6.

and ordering costs are

$$\$50 \times 3 = \$150$$

Hence, the total inventory cost of the part is $300.

As an exercise, demonstrate that this is a minimum by calculating the cost at several different ordering quantities around 300 units.

Notice from Figure 4.8 that the minimum total cost is achieved where the two component cost lines cross one another. That means that, at the optimal point, carrying cost and ordering cost are equal.

Safety Stocks, Reorder Points, and Lead Times

Notice that the inventory model represented in Figure 4.7 (page 145) assumes a perfectly even and predictable flow of parts or goods out of inventory until it reaches zero. The company then reorders and receives an instantaneous delivery of new inventory exactly when needed.

In reality, a company reorders *before* its inventory goes to zero because usage or sales rates vary, because there is a time lag between placing the order and delivery of the order, and because orders don't always arrive on time.

Clearly these factors can cause the firm to run out of inventory and suffer the problems associated with stockouts we described earlier. Such outages can be largely avoided by carrying a safety stock of inventory for emergencies—this is simply an additional supply of inventory that is carried all the time to be used when normal working stocks run out.

The EOQ model of Figure 4.7 can be modified conceptually to include safety stocks by placing the saw-toothed lines on top of a safety stock as shown in Figure 4.9.

Safety stock provides a *buffer* against *unexpectedly* rapid use or delayed delivery.

Lead Times and Reorder Points

As a practical matter, a restocking order has to be placed in advance of the time at which it's needed. The advance period, known as an ordering *lead time*, is generally estimated by the item's supplier.

Referring to the leftmost diagonal in Figure 4.9, we see that, as time passes, the quantity on hand diminishes along the diagram's diagonal line until the reorder point (indicated on the

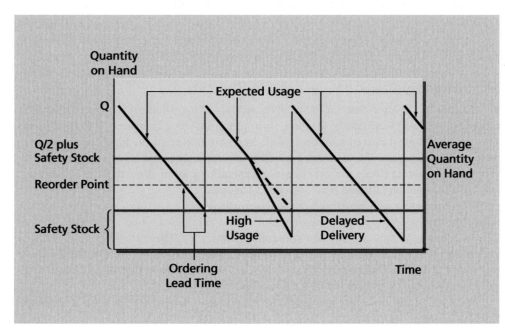

FIGURE 4.9
Pattern of Inventory on Hand Including Safety Stock Showing Reorder Point, Lead Time, and the Effects of High Usage and Delayed Delivery

vertical axis) is reached. At that time, an order for resupply is placed with the supplier. The reorder point is calculated so that the expected usage during the ordering lead time will bring the stock to its lowest planned level just as the new supply is delivered.

However, if the usage rate increases after an order is placed, the stock will diminish faster than planned and the inventory balance will dip into the safety stock range. That situation is depicted along the second diagonal in the diagram. If there were no safety stock, the increased usage would result in a stockout.

It is also easy to see that a delay in delivery after a reorder will cause a dip into safety stock. This situation is depicted along the third diagonal, and would also result in a stockout if there was no safety stock.

SAFETY STOCK AND THE EOQ The inclusion of safety stocks does not change the EOQ. It just increases the total cost of inventory by the carrying cost of the safety stock. In effect, the EOQ model sits on top of a safety stock level as shown in Figure 4.9.

THE RIGHT LEVEL OF SAFETY STOCK Choosing a safety stock level involves another cost trade-off. The extra inventory increases carrying cost but avoids losses from production delays and missed sales. These opposing effects have to be balanced in the choice of an appropriate level of safety inventory. The choice can be difficult because the savings aren't visible. They're the result of problems that didn't happen, so they don't appear anywhere on the financial statements. The carrying cost, on the other hand, is quite visible and measurable.

It's rarely advisable to carry so much safety inventory that stockouts are avoided entirely. Under most conditions, that would require a huge amount of inventory at an excessive cost. It's generally best to tolerate an occasional outage to keep inventory levels reasonable. In some businesses, backorders are filled quickly and outages don't cause a lot of trouble. In such cases, safety stocks can be minimal.

Materials Requirement Planning Systems

A materials requirement planning (MRP) system is a computerized process for ordering and/or scheduling production of the inventories that a manufacturer requires to satisfy customer demand. Once planned sales and finished goods inventory levels are set, the MRP system plans what raw material, component, and work-in-process inventories will be required to produce those finished goods. The system forecasts material requirements by comparing production needs to available inventory balances. On the basis of its estimates of production time and vendor lead time, it will determine when orders should be placed.

Tracking Inventories—the ABC System

The amount of attention that should be given to controlling inventories of particular items varies with the nature and cost of the item. Some pieces are very expensive, and for that reason alone warrant a great deal of attention. Some items are critical to the firm's processes or to those of customers, and therefore are important whether they cost a lot or not. On the other hand, some items are cheap and easy to get, so expending a lot of effort to control them isn't worthwhile. Common nuts and bolts are a good example.

Most companies recognize this fact and use a variant of the ABC system in their inventory control systems where applicable. Items designated *A* are important because of their value or the consequences of running out, and are carefully controlled. They're usually serialized, kept under lock and key, and signed out to a responsible individual when used. *C* items are cheap and plentiful, kept in a bin accessible to anyone, and reordered when the bin gets low. *B* items are between *A*s and *C*s and are handled accordingly.

Recognizing that inventory items differ in importance enables companies to keep control costs low.

Just In Time (JIT) Inventory Systems

In recent years, a manufacturing inventory concept developed by Toyota in Japan has received a lot of publicity. In theory, the just in time (JIT) inventory system virtually eliminates factory inventory. Under JIT, suppliers deliver raw materials, parts, and components to manufacturers just in time (within a few hours) to be used in production. The idea requires a great deal of faith and cooperation between a manufacturer and its suppliers, because a late delivery can stop a factory's entire production line.

JIT eliminates manufacturing inventory by pushing it back on suppliers.

Under JIT, the manufacturer is essentially pushing the task of carrying inventory back onto its suppliers. Conceptually the supplier will push its inventory back onto its suppliers, which do the same to their suppliers. Ultimately the entire production chain works in a coordinated manner, largely eliminating inventories.

An effective JIT system most often uses a materials requirement planning (MRP) system as described above, and an electronic data interchange (EDI) ordering/inventory tracking system (see page 130) connecting the assembly line and supplier production facilities. These systems automatically prepare documents such as purchase orders, invoices, and receiving documents as well as update the inventory and receivable and payable accounts of each business as required. EDI often uses electronic funds transfer (EFT) directly from the bank account of a business to its suppliers.

In a JIT system, suppliers must meet very high ("zero defects") quality standards, as their parts and components are quickly used in the customer's production line. For this reason JIT manufacturers tend to rely on a small number of major suppliers.

JIT reduces carrying cost but increases the number of orders. EDI systems process these orders efficiently, so that order costs are well controlled.

From the CFO

Supply chain management software is a related application. A company and its key suppliers are linked over the web to automate the company's ordinary banking, purchasing, inventory management, and payment processes.

JIT sounds good in theory, and does work under certain conditions, but hasn't proven as successful as its proponents originally hoped. In many situations, it doesn't work at all.

http

For an overview and webcast demonstration of EDI application software, go to http://www.sageac cpac.com/ products/edi.

JIT works best when the manufacturer is very large and powerful with respect to the supplier and buys most of the supplier's output. In such cases, the supplier is willing to do almost anything to keep the manufacturer's business, including orchestrating JIT deliveries. Even then the concept works really well only when the supplier is located near enough to the manufacturer that shipping delays aren't a problem. The automobile industry tends to be organized like that, and has had some success with JIT.

For smaller companies that don't have any particular clout over suppliers that may be located far away, the idea may not be practical. In such cases, suppliers have little incentive to go to the trouble and expense of making the precise and timely deliveries that JIT requires.

Insights **REAL APPLICATIONS**

Just In Time Inventory at Dell Computer Corporation

Dell Computer Corporation (Dell), based in Round Rock, Texas, was founded in 1984 by Michael Dell. The company develops and manufactures personal computers, servers, data storage devices, personal digital assistants (PDAs), and software. In 2006, Dell employed 63,700 people worldwide, the second largest computer company (after Hewlett Packard) in the world.

Dell pioneered the use of JIT inventory in the computer industry. It revolutionized the selling of personal computers, using a direct-business model whose fundamental tenets include taking custom orders directly from customers, producing only to order, and maintaining only minimum levels of parts and components.

Dell's philosophy has been to manufacture only what its customers ask the company to make, and only when the customers ask. This strategy has allowed Dell to keep only five days of inventory on hand, the smallest amount of inventory of any company in the industry.

Dell has operated on the "built to order" model, what Dell calls "pull to order":

- The customer orders a computer.
- Using an Internet-based supply-chain management system, parts are ordered from suppliers and often delivered within 1.5 hours.
- The parts are prepared to meet order needs.
- The computer is manufactured. Special hydraulic tools and conveyor belts and tracks have reduced human intervention by 50%.
- The computer is tested.
- Further customization is undertaken as necessary.
- The product is delivered to the customer.

Dell has achieved a four-hour production cycle time.

This strategy has provided Dell with several significant advantages. In the case of time-to-market, it can get customers the freshest, latest, technology and all associated operating systems much faster than competitors such as Hewlett Packard (HP). In 2006 HP had about 90 days of inventory compared to Dell's 5. The 5-day inventory also minimized customers' ability to change their order before they receive their computer. For example, if a customer tells a manufacturer what he wants today but the manufacturer does not fill the order for 90 days, chances are by that time the customer wants something else!

The minimal amount of inventory (raw materials, work in process, or finished goods) held by Dell has provided major cost savings as well.

- Dell does not have to incur financing costs on large inventories.

- Dell enjoys the benefits of a "negative cash conversion" cycle. Dell receives payment from the customer before it buys the components.
- Factory warehouses are replaced with additional production lines.
- Dell's exposure to the declining value of computer components and manufacturing materials (about 1% per week) is limited.

Dell's use of JIT results in superior customer satisfaction, cost savings, limited waste, and tight working relationships with its suppliers. Dell has estimated that it saved US$150 million in its first three years of operations.

Naturally, this level of manufacturer/supplier integration poses major challenges. The assembly line process is very disciplined. The entire factory must be in sync and Dell can afford few errors in the supply chain. Getting web-based JIT processes up and running is difficult and expensive, but all suppliers must be operating on the same system.

This business model continues to work quite well for Dell's corporate and government customer orders, some 85–90% of its total business. However, rivals such as HP and Apple Inc. have hurt its consumer business by offering more eye-catching designs for similar prices directly from major retailers. To address this fast-growing consumer segment, Dell agreed to sell selected models through Wal-Mart stores Ltd. beginning in June, 2007 and planned to unveil several new consumer products later in that year.

Sources: Chris Sorensen, "Dell Mixes Direct Sales with New Retail Strategy," *Toronto Star,* May 31, 2007, p. B1; Memorial University, "Company Profile: Dell," *Mun. 2007;* Broyles, David et al., "Just-In-Time Inventory Management Strategy & Lean Manufacturing," *Academic Mind,* April 2005.

SUMMARY

1 Working capital accounts arise from day-to-day operations and include cash, receivables, inventory, payables, and accruals. These current assets and liabilities turn over regularly.

2 Maintaining working capital balances in cash, receivables, and inventory requires a permanent commitment of funds. However, the accounts payable and accruals created by operations spontaneously offset some of the funding required to support the assets.

3 Working capital management involves trade-offs between easier operation and the cost of carrying short-term assets. In general, using more working capital increases sales and improves relations with customers and vendors, but costs extra money.

4 The cash conversion cycle of the firm reflects the time period from paying for inventory until collecting cash from its sale.

5 Working capital balances are often subject to large seasonal variations. Permanent working capital refers to the

minimum level to operate the business. Temporary working capital refers to the temporary increases required to support seasonal peaks in the business.

6 According to the maturity matching principle, the maturity date of financing should be roughly matched to the duration of the asset or capital investment being financed. The debt is paid off when the item financed becomes cash in the borrower's hands. This makes the loan/investment combination a self-liquidating proposition. Short-term assets such as inventory and receivables are usually financed with trade credit or other short-term debt, whereas long-term assets are normally financed with long-term debt or shareholders' equity.

7 Permanent working capital can be financed long or short term, but temporary needs are normally supported with short-term funds. A working capital financing policy is conservative if long-term funding is used predominantly, and aggressive if relatively more short-term funding is used. Short-term loans may have lower interest rates than long-term loans, but are riskier.

8 Managing cash involves maintaining cash balances sufficient to meet the operating needs of the business. Management tries to speed deposits and time payments to maximize the cash flow available to the business. Management must analyze the benefits and costs of banking services in accelerating receipts and minimizing unproductive balances.

9 To earn a return at low risk, excess cash can be invested in marketable securities such as Treasury bills, commercial paper, bankers' acceptances, certificates of deposit, and money market funds.

10 As a general rule, businesses must grant credit to their wholesale/commercial customers to facilitate and complete sales. In doing so, they may incur substantial risks and costs; good management of credit administration and collection activities is essential. To evaluate a proposed change in credit policies, management must determine the net effect on company earnings by comparing the change in gross margin earned to the change in expenses incurred.

11 Merchandising and manufacturing companies must plan for and manage significant inventory ordering and carrying costs such as insurance, storage, and losses from damage. To meet sales or production demand while minimizing these inventory costs, inventory decision models are often used. Two well-known models are the economic order quantity (EOQ) and the just in time system (JIT).

KEY TERMS

ABC system, p. 148
Aging schedule, p. 137
Cash conversion cycle, p. 120
Collection agency, p. 138
Collections policy, p. 139
Concentration banking, p. 132
Credit agency, p. 135
Credit policy, p. 135
Credit scoring, p. 136
Dunning, p. 138
Economic order quantity (EOQ) model, p. 144
Electronic Data Interchange (EDI), p. 131

Float, p. 130
Inventory carrying costs, p. 143
Inventory ordering costs, p. 143
Just in time (JIT) inventory system, p. 149
Lock box system, p. 131
Marketable securities, p. 128
Materials Requirement Planning (MRP) system, p. 148
Maturity matching principle, p. 124
Operating cycle, p. 121

Permanent working capital, p. 123
Precautionary demand, p. 127
Reorder point, p. 148
Safety stock, p. 147
Self-liquidating debt, p. 123
Speculative demand, p. 127
Spontaneous financing, p. 118
Stockout, p. 142
Temporary working capital, p. 123
Transactions demand, p. 127
Zero balance accounts, p. 133

KEY FORMULAS

(4.1)   Annualized yield on a discounted money market security:

$$r = \frac{100 - P}{P} \times \frac{365}{d}$$

(4.2) $$\text{Carrying cost} = C\left(\frac{Q}{2}\right)$$

(4.3) $$\text{Number of orders} = N = \frac{D}{Q}$$

(4.4) $$\text{Ordering cost} = FN = F\left(\frac{D}{Q}\right)$$

(4.5) $$\text{Total inventory cost} = TC = C\left(\frac{Q}{2}\right) + F\left(\frac{D}{Q}\right)$$

(4.6) $$EOQ = \left(\frac{2FD}{C}\right)^{\frac{1}{2}}$$

$$\text{Payable payment period} = \text{Accounts payable} \times \frac{365}{\text{Cost of goods sold}}$$

$$\text{Accounts receivable} = \text{Sales} \times \frac{\text{Average collection period}}{365}$$

QUESTIONS

1. Explain the different circumstances under which firms should use short-term or long-term financing.

2. "Because companies always have inventory and accounts receivable, most banks are happy to make long-term loans to support those assets." Either refute or support that statement.

3. Describe the maturity matching principle. What are the risks of not matching maturities? How would you characterize a firm that ignores the principle? Can you think of situations in which it would be advisable for an otherwise prudent firm to deviate from the principle?

4. "Working capital spontaneously finances itself because it's being turned over all the time." Is this statement true, false, or a little of both? Exactly what is meant by "spontaneous financing"? Does working capital require funding? Why or why not?

5. Working capital is generally defined as the difference between current assets and current liabilities. Is this definition precisely correct? Why or why not?

6. Support or challenge each of the following statements individually.
   a. "Because accounts receivable aren't purchased like inventory or capital assets, they don't require financing."
   b. "Cash represents a pool of available money, so it actually reduces financing needs."

7. How does a firm's operating cycle differ from its cash conversion cycle? Explain fully.

8. You work in the finance department of a manufacturing company. Over lunch, a friend in the engineering department said she'd heard that the firm used a lot of temporary working capital. Because temporary equipment is usually of lower quality than permanent equipment, she wonders why the company, which is quite prosperous, doesn't buy the best and store it when it isn't needed.

   What misconceptions does your friend have? Write a brief explanation for someone who knows nothing about finance to improve her understanding.

9. Why does it make sense to finance net working capital separately from capital assets?

10. You work in the finance department of HiTech Inc. The firm's owner and CEO, Charlie Dollars, is very profit oriented. He understands that short-term interest rates are quite low at the moment, and has suggested that the firm finance all of its working capital needs with short-term loans. The CFO has asked you to prepare a memo for his signature outlining why this may not be the best strategy. In your memo, outline the working capital financing options available to most firms and discuss the trade-offs involved in using long-term versus short-term financing.

11. Outline the reasons for holding cash and the big cost associated with it. How do these lead to the objective of cash management? How do marketable securities help or hinder achievement of the objective?

12. The Medco Supply Co. operates out of Calgary, and has a number of customers around Toronto. It seems to take a particularly long time for the Toronto customers' payment cheques to reach Medco. What can the company do to speed payment? Explain how your solution would work.

13. Sally Johnson lives in Halifax and does business with a large, national brokerage firm. When she sends the broker a cheque, she mails it to a local address in Halifax. However, when she receives a cheque from the broker, it comes from Vancouver. Her sister Joan lives in Victoria and uses the same firm. She mails payments to an office a few blocks from her home, but receives cheques from an office in Toronto. What's going on? Should the Johnson sisters be upset?

14. You're the cash manager for Huge Inc., which has factories and stores all over the country. Each operation has several bank accounts to receive deposits and pay vendors, so the company's cash is spread all over the country under the control of divisional CFOs. It's essential that those divisional executives have control of their cash to run their operations effectively. However, the rather substantial cash total isn't earning anything because it's too dispersed to be invested in marketable securities. Suggest a way to fix this problem and explain how it would work.

15. "Every company should take full advantage of the sophisticated cash management services offered by today's banking industry." Is this statement right or wrong? Explain.

16. Outline the costs and benefits involved in the trade-off between a tighter versus a looser receivables policy.

17. "Inventory management is a shared responsibility between finance and manufacturing just as receivables management involves both sales and finance." Is this statement right or wrong? Explain.

18. "Because of the advances in computer technology, inventory management is a precise science, and there's no excuse for not having the optimal quantity on hand at all times." Is that statement true or false? Explain.

19. Does the EOQ model, properly applied, prevent stockouts? Does it address stockouts at all? Do you think the EOQ model solves very many of management's inventory problems?

20. Wildebrant Inc. runs out of inventory all the time, both in the factory and at the point of sale. However, the company is profitable, and no one worries about it much. Is this okay? What's probably going on that management doesn't see? Why don't they see it? What would you suggest to fix the problem? How would it work?

Business Analysis

1. You're a supervisor in the treasury department of Big Corp. Recently there's been increasing concern about the firm's rising interest expense. Fred Eyeshade is an analyst in your group who transferred from the accounting department a short time ago. He has suggested that senior management mandate a 50% across-the-board cut in cash, inventory, and receivables along with a doubling of payables to reduce the firm's financing needs for net working capital. Explain why this might not be a good idea with respect to each of these elements of net working capital (four accounts).

2. "Things tend to run more smoothly and efficiently with more working capital." With respect to each working capital account (cash, receivables, inventory and payables, exclude accruals), explain why this statement isn't absolutely true. In other words, why might a very large inventory or receivables balance not do much good at all?

3. You're the CFO of the Waubuno Window Company, which sells windows to residential builders. The firm's customers tend to be small, thinly capitalized construction companies that are frequently short of cash. Over the past year, there's been a slump in the housing industry and Waubuno's sales have slowed. Several months ago, the marketing department initiated a program to attract new customers to counteract the downward sales trend. The VP of marketing and the president agreed that the firm would have to deal with even smaller, newer builders if it was going to keep up sales. At the time, the president overruled your concerns about the credit quality of such customers. He personally approved a number of accounts brought in by the sales department that ordinarily wouldn't have qualified for credit.

    More recently, receivables have gone up substantially, and collection efforts have been less successful than usual. Collectors have asked for help from sales representatives in chasing down delinquent customers, but the VP of marketing says they don't have time because "reps have to be out on the street selling."

    The president has suddenly become concerned about the receivables increase, and has demanded to know why finance has let it happen.

    a. Prepare a memo explaining the processes behind the creation and management of receivables and explain what's behind the increase. Tactfully explain why the blame should not be placed solely on the finance department. Can you argue that finance is completely without fault in this matter?

    b. Do you think a higher prompt payment discount alongside the new sales program would have kept receivables down? Why?

    c. Speculate on the nature of the relationship between the credit and collections department and the sales department at Waubuno Window.

4. The Philipps Lighting Company manufactures decorative light fixtures. Its revenues are about $100 million a year. It purchases inputs from approximately 20 suppliers, most of which are much larger companies located in various parts of the country. Sam Spade, the VP of manufacturing, is a sophisticated executive who has always been impressed by the latest innovative techniques in management.

Last week, Sam came into a meeting of the executive team with a proposal to cut inventory costs to almost nothing. Just in time (JIT) is the wave of the future, he said, and proposed that Philipps enter into negotiations with all of its suppliers to implement the concept immediately.

You're the CFO and tend to be more skeptical about new methods. Prepare a memo to the team, tactfully outlining the problems and risks involved in Sam's proposal.

5. Refer to the Insights "Inventory at Danier Leather Inc." on page 144. Would a type of JIT be possible or advisable for Danier's imports of finished goods? Argue for and against such a system.

DANIER LEATHER

PROBLEMS

1. Scherbert Industries has the following balance sheet accounts as of 31/12/X3 (not a complete balance sheet):

Calculate gross and net working capital.

Accounts payable	$ 650,000
Accounts receivable	845,000
Accruals	257,500
Cash	137,200
Common shares	1,200,000
Capital assets (net)	8,250,000
Inventory	655,000
Long-term debt	3,500,000

2. Northpost Inc. has an inventory turnover of 5 times, an ACP of 42 days, and turns over its payables once a month. How long are Northpost's operating and cash conversion cycles?

3. The Langley Corporation is in a seasonal business. It requires a permanent base of net working capital of $10 million all year long, but that requirement temporarily increases to $20 million during a four-month period each year. Langley has three financing options for net working capital:
   a. Finance the peak level year-round with shareholders' equity, which costs 20%, and invest temporarily unused funds in marketable securities, which earn 3%.
   b. Finance permanent net working capital with shareholders' equity and temporary net working capital with a short-term loan at 6%.
   c. Finance all net working capital needs with short-term debt at 6.5%.

   Calculate the cost of each option. Which would you choose? Why?

4. Tambourines Inc. collects $12 million per year from customers in a remote location. The average remittance cheque is $1,200. A lock box system would shorten the overall float on these receipts from eight days to seven days, but would cost $2,500 per year plus $0.20 per cheque. The relevant interest rate is 9%. Should Tambourines implement the system?

5. The Rally Motor Company is located in Ontario but has a number of customers in Western Canada. Sales to those customers are $30 million a year paid in cheques that average about $1,500. The cheques take an average of eight days to clear into Rally's Toronto bank account. A bank in Edmonton will operate a lock box system for Rally for $8,000 a year plus $0.50 per cheque. The system can be expected to reduce the clearing time to four days.
   a. Is the lock box system worthwhile if Rally borrows at 7.5%?
   b. What is the minimum number of days of float time the system has to save (to the nearest tenth of a day) to make it worthwhile?

6. Cockburn Ltd. is considering a lock box system. The firm has analyzed its credit receipts and determined the following:
   - Average time cheques are in mail—three days
   - Average internal cheque processing time—three days
   - Average time to clear the banking system—one day
   - Total credit sales—$150 million
   - Average cheque—$6,500

   Cockburn funds its accounts receivable with short-term debt at 8%. First Bank has indicated that its lock box system will reduce mail float by an average of one day and eliminate internal processing time. The cost of the system is $0.50 for each cheque processed, plus 0.05% of the gross revenues processed. Should Cockburn implement the lock box system? If the charge based on gross revenue remains constant, at what per-cheque charge would Cockburn be indifferent to the lock box arrangement?

7. Better Business Machines (BBM) has analyzed the value of implementing a lock box system. The firm anticipates revenues of $630 million with an average invoice of $1,500. BBM borrows at 8% and has made an arrangement with Old Scotia Bank to manage a lock box for $0.24 per cheque and 0.06% of total receipts. BBM has estimated that the lock box will save $130,000 annually. How many days does BBM expect the system will save in the collection process?

8. The Bailey Machine Tool Company thinks it can increase sales by $10 million by loosening its credit standards somewhat. The firm normally experiences bad debts of about 2% of sales, but the marketing department estimates that the incremental business would be from financially weaker customers who would not pay about 5% of the time. Bailey's average collection period on the new business would increase from 30 days to 45 days. The firm's gross margin is 35% (production-related costs are 65% of revenue). The company can obtain financing at a rate of 8%.
   a. Should Bailey lower its credit standards to get the new business?
   b. Would your answer change if taking on the new business also involved incremental collection expenses of $50,000 per year?

9. (Use an Excel® spreadsheet to solve this problem; alternately, solve the problem manually.)

   Over the past few years, the marketing department at Goldston & Co. has convinced the finance department to permit credit sales to increasingly marginal customers. Revenue has risen as a result, but bad debts are now at 6% of sales. Finance has suggested that the credit policy be tightened to reduce bad debt losses. The proposal calls for a more restrictive policy under which sales would fall by 8% but bad debt losses would drop to 2.6% of revenue. Under the current policy, Goldston's revenue forecast is $400 million with a margin before bad debts of 38%. Goldston's average collection period would decrease from 50 days to 40 days. The company can obtain financing at a rate of 6%. Implementing the new credit policy would require an additional $500,000 in annual overhead costs.

   a. Should Goldston implement Finance's new credit policy?

   b. What nonfinancial considerations should be evaluated?

   c. Should the new policy be implemented if bad debts are expected to drop only to 4% of revenues?

10. The Kustomer Kids Klothing Kompany is in the volatile garment business. The firm has annual revenues of $220 million and operates with a 30% gross margin on sales. Bad debt losses average 3% of revenues. Kustomer is contemplating an easing of its credit policy in an attempt to increase sales. The loosening would involve accepting a lower quality of customer for credit sales. It is estimated that sales could be increased by $20 million a year in this manner. However, the collections department estimates that bad debt losses on the new business would run four times the normal level, and that internal collection efforts would cost an additional $1 million a year. Kustomer's average collection period on all sales would increase from 36 days to 45 days. The company can obtain financing at a rate of 7%.

   a. Is the policy change a good idea?

   b. Is it likely that coupling an increased prompt payment discount with the looser guidelines would reduce the bad debt losses?

   c. Is it possible that the idea in part (b) could have a net negative impact? How?

11. Perry Air Conditioning has annual credit sales of $1.6 million. Current collection department cash outflows are $35,000, bad debts are 1.5% of sales, and the average collection period is 30 days. Perry is considering easing its collection efforts so that the collection department outflows will be reduced to $22,000 per year. The change is expected to increase bad debts to 2.5% of sales and to increase the collection period to 45 days. In addition, sales are expected to increase to $1.75 million. If the financing cost is 10% and variable cash outflows are 75% of sales, should Perry make the change?

12. In processing an application for trade credit, Markon & Associates receives the following financial statements of Misty River Corp. for 20X1, 20X2, and 20X3.

MISTY RIVER CORP.
Balance Sheets

ASSETS	20X3	20X2	20X1
Cash	$ 1,000	$ 8,000	$ 20,000
Accounts receivable	36,000	30,000	30,000
Inventories	60,000	54,000	50,000
Total current assets	97,000	92,000	100,000
Net property	50,000	50,000	52,000
Other assets	4,000	4,000	4,000
Total assets	$ 151,000	$ 146,000	$ 156,000

LIABILITIES AND SHAREHOLDERS' EQUITY

	20X3	20X2	20X1
Accounts payable	$ 22,000	$ 20,000	$ 24,000
Notes payable (6%)	16,000	14,000	14,000
Accrued expenses.	6,000	2,000	4,000
Total current liabilities	44,000	36,000	42,000
Long-term debt (8%)	30,000	30,000	30,000
Common shares (25,000 shares)	25,000	25,000	25,000
Retained earnings	52,000	55,000	59,000
Total liabilities and shareholders' equity	$ 151,000	$ 146,000	$ 156,000

MISTY RIVER CORP.
Income Statements

	20X3	20X2	20X1
Sales	$ 240,000	$ 220,000	$ 260,000
Cost of goods sold	192,000	173,000	201,000
Gross margin	48,000	47,000	59,000
Selling and administrative expenses	39,000	38,500	37,500
Operating profit	9,000	8,500	21,500
Interest expense	3,360	3,240	3,240
Net income before taxes	5,640	5,260	18,260
Taxes (20%)	1,128	1,052	3,652
Net income	$ 4,512	$ 4,208	$ 14,608

Fixed charges included in selling and administrative expenses:

Amortization expense:	$ 6,000	$ 5,500	$ 5,000
Lease costs:	$ 3,500	$ 3,200	$ 3,000

a. Markon uses the following model to evaluate customer trade credit:
Credit score   = 5 × (Current ratio)
+ 7 × (Times interest earned)
− 9 × (Debt to equity)

What is Misty River's credit score for each of the three years? Is it getting better or worse?

b. Calculate five other ratios for each year that would be relevant to the credit decision.

c. Should Markon grant credit to this company? Give your reasons.

13. Sharon's Sweater Shop orders 5,000 sweaters per year from a supplier at a wholesale cost of $65 each. Carrying costs are 20% of inventory, and it costs $52 to place and receive an order. How many orders should Sharon place with the supplier each year, and how large should each be?

14. Heart & Soul Hydraulics (HSH) Inc. carries an inventory of plastic heart valves that cost $500 each. The firm's inventory carrying cost is approximately 20% of the value of the inventory. It costs $40 to place, process, and receive an order. The firm sells 2,000 valves a year.

  a. What ordering quantity minimizes the inventory costs associated with the valves?
  b. How many orders will be placed each year if the EOQ is used?
  c. What are the valves' carrying and ordering costs if the EOQ is used?
  d. Now assume that the supplier offers HSH a 1% discount on its annual purchases if HSH will continue to order 2,000 valves per year, but will agree to only 4 deliveries per year. What will be the amount of average inventory? What will be the total cost of ordering and carrying the inventory?
  e. Should HSH accept this arrangement? Show your calculations.

15. Emmons Motors is a distributor of electric motors. The firm projects product demand of 25,000 units next year. It costs $320 to place an order with suppliers. Management has determined that the EOQ is 1,000 units. How much per year does it cost Emmons to carry a unit of inventory?

16. A firm has a demand for 5,600 units per year, the carrying cost per unit is $10, and the ordering cost is $70 per order.
  a. Fill in the blanks in the following table.

Size of Order	Average Inventory	Carrying Cost	Number of Orders per Year	Ordering Cost	Total Cost
80					
160					
280					
400					
700					

  b. What is the EOQ?

17. The Milling Corp. has developed a new type of widget. The local distributor expects to increase his unit sales by 20% over the past year's sales due to this new development. Last year's sales were $50,000 at a selling price of $10 per unit.
    Relevant cost information includes the following:

Warehouse space	$2.30/unit
Material handling expense	$1.50/unit
Insurance premium	$1.00/unit
Total ordering cost	$100.00/per order

  a. What is the economic order quantity?
  b. What is the amount of average inventory?
  c. How many orders will be made per year?
  d. What is the total cost of this inventory?
  e. Now assume that the company decides to carry a safety (minimum) stock of 100 units. What will be the amount of average inventory? What will be the total cost of ordering and carrying the inventory?

18. For several years, Clover Stores has attempted to achieve a target inventory turnover of 15 times a year. Clover Stores carries no safety stock. Clover Stores is open 240 days a year,

and its average sales are five units each working day. The company president, G. Clover, has heard about the economic order quantity and is curious about how an inventory policy based on the economic order quantity would differ from the one the company is currently following. Clover's accountant determines that the cost of carrying one unit in inventory for a year is $2. The cost of placing an order is $12.

    a. With its current policy, how many units does Clover Stores order at a time?

    b. What is Clover's annual cost of placing orders and carrying inventory?

    c. What is Clover's economic order quantity?

    d. If Clover bases its inventory policy on your answer to part (c), what will be its annual cost of placing orders and carrying inventory?

    e. Suppose Clover Stores' average daily demand increases by 44%. By what percentage do the order sizes in parts (a) and (c) increase?

19. ABC Manufacturing projects its material usage as follows:

Month	Projected Usage (in units)
January	1,000
February	1,200
March	1,500
April	1,400

The company pays $5 per unit for material. Current inventory policy is to start a month with material on hand equal to that month's projected usage.

    a. Determine average material inventory in units and in dollars for the first quarter under this policy.

    b. Company management has heard about JIT inventory and believes that such a policy would allow the business to start a month with material on hand equal to 10% of the month's projected usage. Determine average material inventory in units and in dollars for the first quarter if the company adopts this policy.

    c. Compare your answers to parts (a) and (b) to indicate an obvious advantage of a JIT inventory policy.

    d. What is a disadvantage of a JIT inventory policy?

20. EverFit Inc. manufactures commercial-grade fitness equipment used in spas and health clubs. The firm produces complex resistance exercise machines designed to strengthen specific muscles. EverFit's engineering department designs the equipment and then contracts with metal working shops to produce parts to their specifications. The parts are inventoried at EverFit's factory and assembled for shipment to customers. The $250,000 parts inventory is financed with short-term debt at 6% interest. Shrinkage and obsolescence cost about 1%, while taxes and insurance run about $10,000 per year.

    EverFit has discussed a JIT system with its suppliers, all of which are located within 50 miles. The suppliers are small firms that depend on EverFit's business, and are willing to try to deliver parts in accordance with its production schedule.

    However, EverFit's CFO is concerned that although their intentions are good, the suppliers won't be able to manage their operations precisely enough to consistently meet its JIT requirements. Further, he thinks that when a JIT delivery is missed, it will generally be a day and a half before it is finally received. During that time the assembly staff of

25 people will be idle. Each assembly worker earns about $30 per hour and must be paid for eight hours a day whether working or not.

    a. If the measure of the system is saving money, how many JIT failures can the system tolerate and still break even?

    b. Comment on the advisability of the JIT idea based on your answer to part (a).

    c. What qualitative factors might also be concerns?

    d. Suggest a way to test the system before making a final decision.

Chapter 5

Sources of Short-Term Financing

Learning Objectives

1 Describe the purpose and sources of short-term financing.

2 Distinguish between the two leading short-term financing tools available to the financial manager: trade credit and bank loans.

3 Explain the features of trade credit and calculate its cost to the firm if a discount is forgone.

4 Describe short-term bank loans as self-liquidating and as having their interest cost tied to the prime rate.

5 Describe various arrangements for secured financing of receivables.

6 Describe various arrangements for secured financing of inventory.

7 Describe money market alternatives such as commercial paper, bankers' acceptances, and asset-backed securities.

The financial manager must be careful in evaluating the trade terms offered by suppliers. A 2% discount for paying early may at first glance not appear attractive, particularly on a small invoice amount, but further analysis may indicate that the firm should surely pay early to get the discount, even if it has to borrow the money to pay its supplier from its bank! As we will see, missing the discount would likely have a high opportunity cost, so the firm might well arrange a short-term operating loan to be able to take the discount.

Working capital is the major reason most firms seek short-term loans. It's worth noting explicitly that short-term financing is always debt of one form or another. We'll divide the sources of short-term financing into the following four categories and review each in some detail:

1. Spontaneous financing, consisting of accounts payable and accruals
2. Bank operating loans
3. Secured loans for accounts receivable and inventory from banks or other sources
4. Money market instruments

SPONTANEOUS FINANCING

As we saw in Chapter 4, spontaneous financing consists of accounts payable and accruals. We'll consider accruals first.

Accruals

Accruals arise because firms receive services continually, but make payments at fixed intervals. (Review Chapter 2, page 31, if necessary.) Accruals are made for any number of services and obligations, such as payroll, property taxes, insurance, and rents. Effectively, they're interest-free loans from whoever provides the service.

Payables and accruals arise in the normal course of business and represent spontaneous financing.

Accruals, especially payroll accruals, tend to be very short term. In most companies, they're liquidated every week or two. They're also not very controllable. Labour market practices and tax laws dictate when payments have to be made and provide little or no flexibility. In other words, accruals provide a modest financing advantage, but they're not a policy issue.

Accounts Payable—Trade Credit

Over half of short-term financing in Canada is trade credit. Effectively, the selling company *lends* the buyer the purchase price, without interest, from the time the goods are shipped until payment is made. The practice is called extending *trade credit* to the customer. (Review Chapter 2, page 30, if necessary.)

There's typically no security and very little contractual support for trade credit. The contract between the parties is limited to the terms written on the buyer's purchase order and the seller's invoice.

Trade credit is an attractive source of financing because it's free. However, it typically isn't extended for very long periods of time.

The Prompt Payment Discount

If the supplier offers a *cash discount* for early payment and the buyer takes advantage of the cash discount, the buyer, in effect, gives up some of the free financing in return for a reduction in cost.

Passing prompt payment discounts is generally a very expensive source of financing.

The early payment discount is typically a very generous offer on the part of the vendor. We'll illustrate with the 2/10, n.30 term, although any combination of discount period, net period, and discount is possible.

On a purchase of $1,000, the buyer can choose to pay

1. $1,000 after 30 days with no interest
2. $980 after 10 days

Taking the second option, the buyer gives up (30 − 10 =) 20 days of free financing in return for saving $20.

Or, to say it differently, the buyer receives 2% back for paying 20 days early. Two percent for a year might not be much of an incentive to pay early, but 2% for only 20 days is probably attractive.

If the buyer forgoes (misses) the discount, he has suffered an *opportunity cost*; he has lost the opportunity to earn income (save money). Because payment is due in 30 days and the discount can be taken within 10, forgoing the discount buys the buyer an additional 20 days of trade credit. We can think of this as paying 2% interest for 20 days' use of money.

In either case, the discount rate can be converted to an equivalent annual interest rate as follows.

$$\frac{2\%}{98\%} \times \frac{365}{20} = 37.2\%$$

In general

(5.1)
$$\text{Cost of missing discount}$$
$$= \frac{\text{Discount percentage}}{100 - \text{Discount percentage}} \times \frac{365}{\text{Final payment date} - \text{Last discount date}}$$

The implication is that, by not taking the prompt payment discount, the firm is effectively borrowing at 37.2%,[1] clearly a very high rate. It's apparent that when such a discount is offered, early payment should be made and the discount taken.

Most prompt payment discounts, like the illustration, are quite attractive. Therefore many companies have simply ordered their payables departments to take all discounts offered. This has prompted some vendors to offer discounts that aren't such a good deal. As an exercise, calculate the approximate interest cost of 0.25/15, n.30. Is it clearly a good idea to take the discount?

Abuses of Trade Credit Terms

Stretching payables is a common *abuse* of trade credit.

On its face, trade credit is purely an accommodation to customers. In fact, however, the practice has become so ingrained in industry that it's come to be expected. In other words, vendors offer credit because they have to rather than because they want to.

In that context, the trade credit relationship can become somewhat adversarial, with customers abusing credit privileges when they can. Paying late, beyond the net date specified in a vendor's invoice, isn't uncommon at all. As we saw in Chapter 2 (page 30), the practice is called *stretching payables* or *leaning on the trade*. Another common practice involves taking the prompt payment discount after the specified period has elapsed.

From the CFO

Vendors will tolerate a limited amount of abuse because they want to keep the customer's business. But if the practice becomes excessive, the customer is labelled a slow payer and can start to have problems. Slow-paying customers can be cut off from further shipments until debts are caught up or can be refused product unless payment is made in advance.

Slow-paying companies receive poor credit ratings in credit reports issued by credit agencies.

In addition, vendors usually report slow payers to a *credit agency* (also known as a *credit bureau*). Credit agencies prepare credit reports on virtually all companies doing business in the country. When new customers approach vendors asking for trade credit, it's customary to consult an agency about the applicant's record. A bad *credit rating* from a credit agency generally prevents a firm from getting trade credit.

---

1 The money made available by not taking the discount isn't the invoiced amount, but 98% of that amount. The extra 2% is interest. That means the cost of the 20 days' use of the funds is 2% ÷ 0.98 = 2.04%. The remaining part of the calculation shown is a simplification. We should really compound the 20-day rate into a year rather than multiplying it. Because there are (365/20 =) 18.25 20-day periods in a year, the effective compound interest rate implied by not taking the discount is
$$[(1.0204)^{18.25} - 1] = 0.446 = 44.6\%$$
Although this is the more technically correct calculation, most people think in terms of the simple interest approach.

BANK OPERATING LOANS

An operating loan is often negotiated to finance inventory and receivables and is intended to be repaid within months from collections of receivables. Most operating loans are provided by banks and trust companies.[2]

Collateral Security and Covenants

Large corporations with excellent credit ratings may be able to arrange an unsecured operating loan. Operating loans for other business borrowers are *secured*.

A secured loan is backed by a specific asset (collateral). If the borrower defaults, the bank can take the asset, which it can sell to repay the debt.

Collateral security is intended to reduce the lender's risk. The ideal collateral is money market investments such as Treasury bills, which the bank can sell quickly without a loss in value. In most cases, security for short-term loans includes accounts receivable, inventory, or both. Normally, banks will advance no more than 75% of the value (the *lending margin*) of the borrower's current receivables and 50% of the value of the borrower's inventory. In his way, they provide themselves some margin of safety in case the borrower defaults on the loan.

Loan covenants are additional commitments by the borrower and are specified in the loan agreement as conditions for receiving and maintaining the loan. The borrower may promise to do something, such as providing the bank with timely information on accounts receivable and inventory, or to refrain from doing something, such as taking on additional debt from other lenders. Loan covenants are frequently a feature of small business loans.

Operating loans may be arranged for specific transactions, or as a *line of credit*, an arrangement whereby the bank regularly provides financing (to an agreed maximum) for inventory and expenses. The business pays down (reduces) the loan balance outstanding as it collects its accounts receivable.

Revolving Credit and Line of Credit Agreements

Depending on the bank a business deals with, the size of the company, and its financing needs, it may arrange either a *revolving credit agreement*, sometimes called a *committed credit*, or a *line of credit*. From the borrower's standpoint, they are similar, but there are some technical differences.

With a revolving credit agreement, the bank guarantees the availability of funds up to a maximum amount during the specified period, provided that the borrower meets the terms and conditions of the agreement. After the agreement is signed, the bank agrees to deposit money in the borrower's chequing account as needed, in the increments stipulated in the agreement (i.e., $5,000, $10,000, and so on). The agreement also stipulates the nature of supporting collateral, if there is any, and any other terms and conditions that may have been agreed on (for example, the repayment schedule).

The bank's commitment to advance funds up to a maximum is not usually free. The borrower is typically required to pay a commitment fee (or standby fee) on the unborrowed balance of the agreement whether it's used or not[3] (see Chapter 14). These fees are often in the neighbourhood of 0.25% per year. The borrower pays interest only on the amounts actually borrowed.

The typical line of credit is very much like the overdraft protection feature offered on personal chequing accounts. As in the revolving credit, the bank states its intention, but does not necessarily commit, to lend up to some maximum amount during the specified period.

An operating loan provides financing for working capital and expenses.

For extensive facts and statistics on Canadian chartered banks, go to the Canadian Bankers Association at http://www.cba.ca and click on *Resource Centre*.

Collateral security is assets of the borrower that the lender can sell to repay the debt.

Loan covenants are additional commitments by the borrower that further limit lender risk.

Under a revolving credit agreement, a bank guarantees loan funds will be available, provided that the borrower meets the terms and conditions of the agreement.

A commitment fee is a fee charged on the unborrowed balance of a revolving credit agreement.

---

2 Although chartered banks do make longer-term loans, more of their lending activity entails maturities of less than a year.
3 In some cases banks will charge the commitment fee as a percentage of the total committed funds per year.

These types of bank loans are constantly monitored by the bank, and the borrower must abide by all of the terms and conditions agreed to. As well, these loans are reviewed annually and will be renewed or extended only if the borrower continues to meet the lender's criteria.

Interest Rates on Loans

In general, the interest rates on bank loans are variable. They're usually specified relative to the bank's **prime rate**, which is the rate it charges its largest and most creditworthy corporate customers. The banks follow the lead of the Bank of Canada's *overnight rate* in setting their prime rates. The interest rate on an operating loan is usually set equal to the bank's prime lending rate plus an additional percentage. The interest rate on a smaller firm's bank loans is likely to be stated as prime plus 2% or 3%. If prime changes, the firm's borrowing rate will change accordingly, as will its interest charges.

The *premium* charged over prime reflects the banker's assessment of the borrower's *risk*. The interest rate, including the premium, quoted by the bank will depend on such factors as the following.

Prime rate is the bank's lending rate for its largest and most creditworthy customers.

- How strong is financial, marketing, and general management?
- Does the borrower have adequate security?
- Does the borrower have a good credit history and credit rating?
- Does the borrower have an adequate and reliable cash flow?
- What is the term of the loan?
- What is the health of the economy in general and the borrower's industry in particular?
- What is the borrower's past relationship with the bank?

Bankers may prefer to decline risky business loans that would require a premium greater than 3 percent.

The *annual percentage interest rate* (APR) on a loan is calculated on the loan amount, the dollar amount of interest paid, the length of the loan, and the timing of repayment.

The annual interest rate on a loan is calculated on the loan amount, the dollar amount of interest paid, the length of the loan, and the timing of repayment. For instance, $600 interest on a $12,000 loan for a year, and payable at the end of the year, would be an interest rate of 5%. If the same loan were for seven months, the **annual percentage interest rate (APR)** on the loan would be

$$\frac{\$600}{\$12,000} \times \frac{365}{210} = 8.7\%$$

Insights | **REAL APPLICATIONS**

DANIER LEATHER

Committed (Revolving) Credit at Danier Leather Inc.

(For the financial statements and other financial information about Danier, refer to Appendix 3A, page 92.)

Danier had, until June 30, 2007, a committed credit facility available to a maximum amount of $35 million for working capital and for general corporate purposes. This operating facility bore interest at prime plus 0.25%. Standby fees of 0.50% were paid quarterly on any unused portion of the credit facility. Danier was required to comply with covenants regarding financial performance and certain other limitations. The credit facility was secured by all of the working capital and a mortgage over Danier's head office/distribution facility.

Source: Danier Leather Annual Report, 2006.

(5.2)   Annual percentage interest rate on a loan:

$$\text{APR} = \frac{I}{P} \times \frac{365}{d}$$

where APR = Annual percentage rate (simple interest)[4]

   I = Interest paid (dollars)

   P = Principal

   d = Number of days loan is outstanding

When borrowing arrangements entail commitment fees or other costs in addition to interest, such costs are added to interest paid to determine an *effective annual rate* for the cost of financing. (See Example 5.1)

Example 5.1

The Arcturus Company has a $10 million revolving credit agreement with its bank at prime plus 2.5% based on a calendar year. Prior to the month of June, it had borrowed $4 million that was outstanding for the entire month. On June 15, it borrowed another $2 million (assume the funds were available on June 15). Prime is 9.5% and the bank's commitment fee is 0.25% annually. What bank charges will Arcturus incur for the month of June? What is its effective annual rate for the cost of financing?

■ **Solution:** Arcturus's payment will consist of the interest on money actually borrowed and the commitment fee for the unused balance of its revolving credit agreement. Its monthly[5] interest rate is

$$\frac{(\text{Prime} + 2.5\%)}{12} = \frac{(9.5\% + 2.5\%)}{12} = 1\%$$

and the monthly commitment fee is

$$\frac{0.25\%}{12} = 0.0208\%$$

In June, a loan of $4 million was outstanding for the entire month and an additional $2 million was outstanding for 15 days. Hence the interest charge is

$$(\$4,000,000 \times 0.01) + \left(\$2,000,000 \times 0.01 \times \frac{15}{30}\right) = \$50,000$$

The unused balance of the revolving credit was $6 million for 15 days and $4 million for 15 days, for an average of $5 million. The commitment fee is then

$$\$5,000,000 \times 0.000208 = \$1,040$$

Thus, the total interest and commitment fee payment is $51,040.

The loan balance was $4 million for 15 days and $6 million for 15 days, for an average of $5 million. The effective annual rate is

$$\frac{\$51,040}{\$5,000,000} \times \frac{365}{30} = 12.4\%$$

---

4 The annualized interest rate as calculated ignores the effect of interest on interest (compounding). The annual compound interest rate is expressed by the formula

$$\left(1 + \frac{I}{P}\right)^{\frac{365}{d}} - 1$$

In our example, compound annual interest $= \left(1 + \frac{600}{12,000}\right)^{\frac{365}{210}} - 1 = .089 = 8.9\%.$

5 In practice, the lender would calculate interest on a daily basis.

Cleanup Requirements

Theoretically, a firm can maintain a balance of short-term debt all the time by borrowing on a new note to pay off each old one as it comes due. Doing that makes it possible to fund long-term projects with short-term money, refinancing the debt again and again throughout the life of the project.

This procedure is rather risky for two reasons. If short-term rates rise, interest expense can increase quickly, putting a strain on the firm's profitability. Worse, if refinancing funds become unavailable, a default on the short-term notes is likely as they come due.

This kind of risk for a borrowing company is also risk for the bank, because a defaulted customer is likely to mean a lending loss. Therefore, banks try to keep customers from falling into the trap of using short-term funds to support long-term projects.

Banks may require that borrowers **clean up** short-term loans once a year.

Their approach is the cleanup requirement. Banks may simply require that borrowers pay off all unsecured short-term debt periodically and remain out of debt for a specified period. Most cleanup requirements stipulate that borrowers be out of short-term debt for 30 to 45 days once a year. Although the lender may stipulate a cleanup, most are satisfied if the client simply shows good turnover and is not borrowing the full limit for extended periods of time.

SHORT-TERM CREDIT SECURED BY CURRENT ASSETS

Several short-term financing arrangements are available in which the debt is secured by the current asset financed.

The operating loans we have discussed so far may be considered general purpose in nature: funds raised to finance working capital and augment operating cash flows. Several other common loan arrangements enable companies to fund specific current assets using the value of the current assets themselves to guarantee the loan. The assets that are funded and that provide such credit security are accounts receivable and inventories. The funding sources are often banks, but can also be other financial institutions.

Borrowing against receivables and inventories tends to be more popular in some industries than in others. It's especially common in seasonal businesses, such as retail, where temporary working capital needs are substantial.

The commitments, rules, and procedures vary considerably between different arrangements. We'll consider receivables financing first and then inventory financing.

Receivables Financing

Under normal circumstances, accounts receivable represent cash that is to be received in the near future. Lending institutions are generally willing to recognize the value of this about-to-be-received money, and will extend credit backed by that value where they otherwise would not. A key lending issue is the collectibility of the receivables, which relates to the creditworthiness of the firm's customers rather than to its own creditworthiness. Two common receivables arrangements are *pledging* and *factoring*.

Pledging Accounts Receivable

A borrowing firm can **pledge receivables** by agreeing to use the *cash collected* only to *pay off* the loan.

Pledging (assigning) receivables involves using their cash value as collateral for a loan. The borrower signs a binding agreement (a "general assignment of book debts") stating that the lender has the receivables as security.

The distinguishing feature of the arrangement is that the receivables continue to belong to the borrowing firm, which receives the cash directly from its customers as it would in the absence of the pledging agreement. In fact, the company's customers are generally unaware that their obligations have been pledged.

Uncollectible accounts remain the responsibility of the *borrower* if the pledging agreement is with **recourse**.

Under a pledging arrangement, if a particular receivable proves uncollectible, the *borrowing* firm is not relieved of its obligation to the lender. This feature is known as recourse. The lender is said to have *recourse to the borrowing firm* for the value of a defaulted receivable.

Pledging can be accomplished in two ways with respect to the receivables offered as security.

In the first approach, a lender can provide a *general line of credit* tied to the firm's receivables without reviewing individual accounts in detail. In such a case, the lender is unlikely to advance much more than 75% of current receivables because of the risk that some accounts may not pay.

In the second approach, the lender reviews each receivable individually, considering the creditworthiness of the customer owing the money. Then funds are advanced only on the basis of acceptable accounts. In this approach, the lender may advance as much as 90% of the balance of accounts accepted.

Under a straight pledging of receivables, the borrowing company continues to do all of its own credit and collection functions. Hence, the lender is relying on the borrower to a great extent for the quality of the assets securing the loan. Some banks offer billing and collection services that the borrower can use for an additional fee.

Pledging receivables is a relatively expensive form of financing. Financing sources generally charge interest at rates over prime plus an administrative fee.

Example 5.2

The Kilraine Quilt Company has an average receivables balance of $100,000, which turns over once every 50 days. It generally pledges all of its receivables to the Cooperative Finance Company, which advances 75% of the total at 4% over prime plus a 1.5% administrative fee. If prime is 5%, what total financing rate is Kilraine effectively paying for its receivables financing?

■ **Solution:** Because the finance company advances 75% of the receivables balance, the average loan outstanding is $75,000. Traditional interest of (5% + 4% =) 9% is charged on this amount.

The administrative fee is 1.5% of all new receivables. The $100,000 balance turns over every 50 days or (365 ÷ 50 =) 7.3 times a year. That means ($100,000 × 7.3 =) $730,000 in new receivables is pledged each year. The administrative fee is 1.5% of this total, or ($730,000 × 0.015 =) $10,950, which can be stated as a percentage of the average loan balance:

$$\frac{\$10,950}{\$75,000} = 14.6\%$$

Hence, the total financing cost including traditional interest and the administrative fee is (9% + 14.6% =) 23.6%, a high rate indeed.

Factoring Receivables

As an alternative to borrowing on the strength of their accounts receivable, some companies *sell* their receivables to a financial services company (*factor*) and let the factor collect the money. Factoring receivables means *selling them at a discount* to a *factor*. The cash from the sale of the receivables provides financing to the selling company (client).

When a receivable is factored, the factor takes over the receivable and the responsibility for its collection. The factor covers its expenses and makes a profit from the difference (discount) between the face value of the receivable and what it pays the client. This can be anywhere between 4 and 10%, depending on the size of the account, the estimated time and expense to collect, and other services provided.

Factors generally review the credit standing of the customers[6] whose receivables they buy, and don't accept everything offered by the selling firm. Rejected accounts have to be handled by the selling firm on its own.

Factoring means selling receivables to a finance company, which then becomes responsible for collection.

6 The word "customer" can be a little confusing with respect to factoring. The company selling its receivables has customers, and is at the same time the customer of the factor. We'll use the word "customer" to mean the customer of the firm selling the receivable. That's the party actually owing the money that gives the receivable value. We'll call the firm that sells (factors) the receivable the *client* of the factor.

Companies that factor their receivables generally do so continually. That means a routine procedure is set up under which incoming orders are submitted directly to the factor and funded on an ongoing basis.

The procedures just described are the basic factoring function. In practice, factors offer a wide range of services with respect to receivables. They are willing to virtually take over a firm's credit and collection function. However, it isn't necessary to use everything they offer. Firms can select from a menu of services and tailor an arrangement to suit their needs. In general, a factor is willing to do any or all of the following things for the appropriate fees:

1. Perform credit checks on potential customers
2. Advance cash on accounts it accepts or remit cash after collection
3. Collect cash from customers
4. Assume the bad-debt risk when customers don't pay

The companies that use the other services offered by factors do so because they can save them money. It can be cheaper to hire an expert to do a specialized administrative function than to gear up and do it yourself. This is especially true for smaller firms.

The main clients for factors in Canada are small to medium-sized manufacturers in the apparel and other consumer products industries.

Two basic arrangements are common in factoring:

1. maturity factoring, with or without recourse
2. advance factoring

MATURITY FACTORING As accounts are collected, the factor pays the selling company (client) the face amount of the invoice less a 1 to 2% discount. The ultimate responsibility for uncollectible accounts depends upon whether the factoring arrangement is on a recourse basis or a non-recourse basis.

In *recourse factoring*, the factor purchases the invoices from the client, but, in case of customer default, has the right to resell the account back to the client. Thus, the customer credit risk remains with the client. Recourse factoring is attractive to small and medium-sized companies that are unable to borrow from the banks.

In *non-recourse factoring*, the arrangement includes a *credit guarantee* that, if the factor cannot collect a legitimate account receivable within, say 180 days, the factor nevertheless, will pay the client for the receivable. Bad debts are the factor's problem.

Non-recourse factoring appeals to small and medium-sized companies that are anxious to eliminate customer credit risk and outsource their collection function. Obviously, the factor's rates for the non-recourse service will be greater than for recourse arrangements. However, the client will save on bad debt expenses, as well as collection costs.

The factor may also provide credit checking, credit authorization, and customer billing services, allowing the client to also outsource additional administrative functions.

ADVANCE FACTORING To supplement the above arrangements, the factor may agree to advance (lend) to the client 75 to 90% of the face value of the receivables *when they are taken over*. If payment is made when the receivable is taken over, the factor is out the cash until it collects from the customer. Its fee therefore includes interest until the receivable is collected from the customer. Advances usually bear interest at prime plus 2 to 3%. If payment to the client is delayed until cash is received from the customer (maturity factoring), the factor doesn't charge any interest.

Financing *secured by inventory* is difficult to obtain because specialized or perishable items are *hard* to *sell*.

Inventory Financing

Inventory financing uses a firm's inventory as security for a short-term loan. The method is popular, but is subject to a number of problems that can make it expensive and difficult to administer.

A basic problem is the marketability of the inventory in the hands of a lender. Unlike receivables, inventory doesn't turn into cash by itself. It has to be sold, and lenders aren't generally equipped to do that well. That means they have to dispose of defaulted inventory at bargain prices, which reduces the amount they can lend on it.

In particular, specialized inventories such as unique or unusual parts have little collateral value because they're difficult for a lender to sell. Perishable goods have a similar problem in that their value is lost by the time a lender can take possession. Other commodity-type inventories are quite marketable and make good loan collateral. Canned foods are a good example.

If an inventory does have an acceptable collateral value, its availability in the event of a default must somehow be guaranteed to the lender. This is difficult, because the borrowing firm is continuously using and replacing inventory in running its business. Several methods of inventory management are used and involve varying amounts of administrative attention and cost.

Blanket Inventory Lien[7]

A blanket inventory lien gives the lender a lien against all inventories held by the borrower. However, the borrower remains in complete physical control of the inventory, and can draw it down to any level without consulting the lender.

For example, suppose a firm borrows $600,000 collateralized by a blanket lien on an inventory of $1 million verified by a bank representative on the date the loan is disbursed. As long as the lender does not inspect the operating facility, nothing prevents the borrower from suspending inventory purchases while continuing to sell the existing stock until its level has reached, say, $200,000. This can easily put the lender in an unsecured position unless it spends an inordinate amount of time and effort monitoring the borrower's activities.

Trust Receipt or Chattel Mortgage Agreement

Under a trust receipt or *chattel mortgage agreement*, financed inventory is identified by serial number and cannot be sold legally without the lender's permission. When the items are sold, the proceeds must be used to repay the lender. The arrangement is legally binding, but the borrower is still in control of the inventory and might sell it without paying the lender. Guaranteeing that the borrower is in compliance requires inspection by representatives of the lender. This type of inventory financing is used extensively by automobile, household appliance, and heavy equipment dealers.

Warehousing

Under a warehousing arrangement, financed inventory is placed in a warehouse and the borrower's access to it is controlled by a third party. When the borrower draws a piece of inventory, paperwork is created that signals the lender to look for repayment of the money lent to finance that inventory. *Warehousing companies* specialize in administering such arrangements.

There are two kinds of warehousing arrangements. A *field warehouse* is a secured area within the borrower's own facility that's accessible only to employees of the warehousing firm. Field warehousing is used extensively in the food canning industry.

A *public warehouse* is operated by the warehousing firm at a site physically removed from the borrower's facility. This arrangement provides the lender maximum security because the material is completely out of the borrower's control.

Warehousing gives lenders excellent security, but tends to be expensive because of the administrative cost of operating the warehouse and tracking individual inventory items.

Loans for Small Business

The options for raising capital in a small business are limited because many features of the money and capital markets are not available to the small firm. Debt financing is generally limited to bank operating loans that are used to finance inventory and receivables, and term loans

A **blanket inventory lien** gives the lender a general claim against the inventory of the borrower.

A **trust receipt** requires that proceeds from sale of inventory are used to pay the lender.

Warehousing *companies* control secured inventories for the *benefit* of *lenders*.

For an overview of debt and equity financing options, including government assistance programs available to small firms, go to the federal government's Strategis site at http://www.strategis.gc.ca.

Go to the Royal Bank of Canada at http://www.royalbank.com/business/financing_index.html for its small business finance options, and an online loan application form.

---

7 A lien is a legal money claim attached to specific property. The proceeds of the sale of the property must be used to satisfy the lien.

Start-up Financing at Business Development Bank of Canada

The Business Development Bank of Canada (BDC) is a financial institution wholly owned by the Government of Canada. BDC promotes entrepreneurship by providing financing, consulting and venture capital services to Canadians who are creating and growing small and medium-sized enterprises. These services complement those of private sector financial institutions.

In particular, BDC offers *start-up loans* that can be used for

- working capital, to supplement an existing line of credit
- acquiring fixed assets
- marketing and start-up fees
- buying a franchise

Depending on the borrower's situation a BDC start-up loan may feature

- long-term financing
- possibility of deferred capital payments

- a guaranteed term: the loan cannot be recalled without due cause
- an option of floating or fixed interest rates
- an option to accelerate repayment without penalty

BDC start-up financing is for entrepreneurs who

- are in the start-up or early growth phase (first 12 months of sales)
- can demonstrate realistic market and sales potential
- possess experience or expertise in their chosen field
- demonstrate key personal characteristics of a successful entrepreneur
- have assembled a competent management team
- have invested reasonable financial resources in the enterprise
- can provide personal and credit references

Reprinted with permission from the Business Development Bank of Canada, www.bdc.ca.

secured by capital assets. The costs of these loans are often several percentage points above the prime rate unless special government or bank programs are available.

MONEY MARKET INSTRUMENTS

Short-term financing is also available in the money market. Among the short-term debt instruments available to sophisticated borrowers (larger public corporations) are money market instruments that are sold by these borrowers to meet temporary cash needs.

We discuss three money market instruments: commercial paper, bankers' acceptances, and securitization of receivables.

Commercial Paper

Commercial paper is short-term borrowing done by the largest corporations.

We previously introduced commercial paper in Chapter 4 (page 128). Commercial paper refers to notes issued by large, strong companies to borrow money from investors for relatively short periods. The paper itself is simply a promise to repay the money borrowed at a given date. Conceptually, commercial paper is simply a very short-term corporate bond, but there are a number of administrative differences.

Buyers and Sellers
Commercial paper may be unsecured or "asset-backed" (securitized); (see Securitization of Receivables on page 174).

About one-third of commercial paper is *unsecured* debt issued by more than 200 of the nation's largest and strongest companies. Finance companies such as Household Finance Corporation issue commercial paper to raise funds to relend to their corporate and consumer borrowers. Industrial corporations such as Bombardier Inc. use "corporate" paper to provide working capital. It tends to be purchased by other large organizations that have excess funds to invest for short periods. Typically buyers are insurance companies, money market mutual funds, banks, pension funds, and other large corporations. The notes are generally placed with buyers for a fee by an investment dealer (an organization that assists companies in issuing securities and selling them to investors).

Maturity and Terms

Commercial paper is actually a debt security of the issuing corporation. However, it can be sold without Ontario Securities Commission (OSC) registration as long as its maturity is under 270 days and the buyers are "sophisticated" investors. (Security registration will be covered in detail in Chapter 7.) Maturities generally range from one to nine months, averaging five or six.

As we saw in Chapter 4, commercial paper is normally considered a very safe investment. It therefore can be sold (at a discount) to pay a relatively low interest rate, typically about 1% to 2% below the prime interest rate. Rather than bearing interest, the notes are generally sold at a discounted price. For example, a three-month (91-day), $1 million note selling for $985,462 would cost (the issuer) 5.9% on an annualized basis; that is:

$$\text{APR} = \frac{(\$1,000,000 - \$985,462)}{\$985,462} \times \frac{365}{91}$$

$$= 5.9\%$$

(**5.3**)   Annual percentage interest rate on a discounted money market security:

$$\text{APR} = \frac{(M - P)}{P} \times \frac{365}{d}$$

where M = Maturity (face) value of the security
P = Discounted price (net proceeds on issue)[8]
d = Number of days to maturity
APR = Annual interest rate[9]

Commercial paper has one drawback, even for the large, strong companies that issue it. The commercial paper market is very rigid and formal. If a company is a little short of cash when a note is due, there's no flexibility in repayment terms. Banks, on the other hand, are generally willing to bend a little to accommodate business ups and downs.

Bankers' Acceptances

An important source of short-term financing in Canada has been the **bankers' acceptance** (BA). We may think of bankers' acceptances as commercial paper with an additional guarantee. A bankers' acceptance is created when a chartered bank adds its guarantee of payment to the promissory note or draft of a corporate borrower. The borrowing company receives the money from the bank. The bank then sells the bankers' acceptance in the money market to investors looking for a guaranteed return on surplus funds. Bankers' acceptances are more widely used than unsecured commercial paper because the banks enjoy stronger credit ratings than most other corporations. Typically buyers of bankers' acceptances are financial institutions such as insurance companies, money market mutual funds, and other banks. At maturity, the bank repays the face value to the investor and the issuing company repays the bank.

Bankers' acceptances are traded on a discount basis to yield a rate slightly lower than that of commercial paper. The usual terms are 30, 60, and 90 days.

In a **bankers' acceptance,** the borrower's promise to pay is guaranteed by a bank.

For current rates on corporate paper go to the Bank of Canada at http://www.bank-banque-canada.ca/en/rates/monmrt.html.

8 The proceeds on issue may be reduced by transaction (flotation) costs, such as investment dealer fees. We will examine these costs in more depth in Chapter 15.
9 The annualized yield as calculated ignores the effect of interest on interest, that is—compounding. For the approach to calculating the effective yield that considers compounding, see Chapter 4, page 129.

Securitization of Receivables

Securitization of receivables involves the sale of receivables in public offerings.

Securitization of receivables or *structured financing* involves converting an income-producing asset to cash. The cash becomes a source of financing for the company. When used with accounts receivable, this technique involves the sale of receivables by large firms in public offerings arranged by securities dealers. The issuing firm thus receives immediate cash for future cash flows. Unlike the pledging or factoring of accounts receivable, the financing is raised at a relatively low cost, often lower than the prime or commercial paper rate, because the issue is *asset-backed*. Examples include major public offerings by GMAC, Chrysler, CIBC Visa, Sears, and Telus Corporation. Asset-backed commercial paper (about 2/3 of the commercial paper market) is one application of this technique. Investment trusts buy debt obligations such as auto loans, credit card debt, and mortgages from various lenders, package them and use them as security to issue 30- or 60-day commercial paper.[10]

Insights REAL APPLICATIONS

Canadian Tire's Securitization Program

Through its wholly owned subsidiary, Canadian Tire Bank (CTB), retailer Canadian Tire Corporation (CT) manages an extensive financial services business, including its Canadian Tire MasterCard and personal loan operations. In 2005, CTB had over 1.7 million CT MasterCard holders with receivables exceeding $3.1 billion and 35,000 personal loans outstanding, primarily to these card holders. In 2003, CTB implemented a securitization program for its credit card receivables and other consumer financing that provided an alternative source of funding and a strategy to reduce credit risk.

As of December 2005, CTB had sold an interest in 77% of its credit card receivables to an independent credit card trust. The trust then issued asset-backed notes on the financial markets at high credit ratings and therefore low interest cost. As at December 31, 2005, the trust had $2.5 billion of this financing outstanding.

CTB also securitizes its personal loan balances through another independent trust.

Source: Canadian Tire Annual Report, 2005.

SUMMARY

1 Firms need short-term financing to support working capital balances. Available sources of short-term financing include accounts payable and accruals, bank operating loans, secured financing for accounts receivable and inventory, and money market instruments.

2 The two leading short-term financing tools are trade credit from suppliers and operating loans from chartered banks.

3 Trade credit is usually available with no interest, risk, or conditions, and may offer attractive discounts for early payment.

4 Bank financing is usually in the form of a short-term self-liquidating loan, where the amount outstanding increases when goods are paid for and decreases when cash is received from sales. Loans bear an interest cost, often based on the prime rate, and often involve liens or pledges of company assets.

5 Receivable financing arrangements include pledging and factoring. Pledging involves using the cash value of receivables as collateral for a loan. Factoring of accounts receivable is a form of

10 The money market for asset-backed securities faced a severe liquidity shortage beginning in August, 2007 due to the "sub-prime" mortgage crisis in the U.S. Massive defaults on high-risk housing loans there called into question the quality of the home and car loans, credit card debt, industrial leases and similar financial assets used to back money market securities. As a result, many new and refinancing issues of asset-backed commercial paper (ABCP) could not be sold. As well, many corporations and financial institutions that had previously invested in these instruments could not redeem them (or sell them without substantial loss).

short-term financing whereby the company's accounts receivable may be "sold" to a factoring company at a discount.

6 Inventory financing techniques include blanket inventory liens, trust receipts, and warehousing arrangements. A blanket inventory lien gives the lender a claim against the borrower's inventory. Under a trust receipt, inventory can not be sold without the lender's knowledge and permission. Under a warehousing arrangement, the borrower's access to inventory is controlled by an agent of the lender.

7 Other short-term financing alternatives include money market instruments such as commercial paper, bankers' acceptances, and asset-backed securities.

KEY TERMS

Annual percentage interest
  rate (APR), p. 166
Bankers' acceptance (BA),
  p. 173
Blanket inventory lien, p. 171
Cleanup requirement,
  p. 168
Collateral security, p. 165

Commercial paper, p. 172
Commitment fee, p. 165
Factoring receivables, p. 169
Loan covenant, p. 165
Operating loan, p. 165
Pledging receivables, p. 168
Prime rate, p. 166
Recourse, p. 168

Revolving credit agreement
  (committed credit), p. 165
Securitization of receivables,
  p. 174
Trust receipt, p. 171
Uncollectible account, p. 168
Warehousing, p. 171

KEY FORMULAS

(5.1)
$$\text{Cost of missing discount}$$
$$= \frac{\text{Discount percentage}}{100 - \text{Discount percentage}} \times \frac{365}{\text{Final payment date} - \text{Last discount date}}$$

(5.2) Annual percentage interest rate on a loan:
$$\text{APR} = \frac{I}{P} \times \frac{365}{d}$$

(5.3) Annual percentage interest rate on a discounted money market security:
$$\text{APR} = \frac{(M - P)}{P} \times \frac{365}{d}$$

QUESTIONS

1. What are the advantages and disadvantages of stretching payables? If you owned your own business, would you do it? Why or why not?

2. Explain how a line of credit arrangement operates as a self-liquidating loan.

3. What's the difference between a promissory note, a line of credit, and a revolving credit agreement? Are they mutually exclusive? That is, might one be part of another?

4. Factoring may involve interest even though it isn't a loan. How can this come about?

5. What is the biggest problem associated with financing secured by inventory? How is it addressed in practice?

6. Explain the difference between pledging and factoring receivables. Which is likely to be a more expensive source of financing? Is factoring the same kind of financing as pledging?

PROBLEMS

1. What is the cost of not taking the discount on trade credit of 3/10, net 35?

2. Calculate the annual interest rate implied by the following terms of sale.
   a. 2/10, n.30
   b. 1/5, n.15
   c. 0.5/10, n.30
   d. 2.5/10, n.25
   e. 1/5, n. 20

3. The Untied Shoe Company is experiencing a temporary shortage of funds. The treasurer has suggested two ways in which funds could be raised. First, the company could forgo the cash discounts it has been taking and pay its invoices at the end of the credit period. The firm's suppliers offer terms of 2/15, n.60. Second, the company could borrow funds from the local bank at an interest rate of 8%. Which alternative should be chosen?

4. Rocky Inc. can buy its inventory from any of four suppliers, all of which offer essentially the same pricing and quality. Their credit terms, however, vary considerably as follows:
   i.   2/10, n.40
   ii. 3/15, n.50
   iii. 1/10, n.60
   iv. 2/5, n.90
      a. Calculate the implied annual interest rate associated with each policy.
      b. If Rocky buys some material from each vendor, which discounts should it take and which should it forego if it pays 10% for working capital financing? Why?

5. Mr. Jones borrows $1,500 for 90 days and pays $35 interest. What is his annual rate of interest?

6. Thompson Inc. has a $10 million revolving credit agreement with its bank. It pays interest on borrowing at 2% over prime and a 0.25% commitment fee on available but unused funds. Last month, Thompson had borrowings of $5 million for the first half of the month and $10 million for the second half. Calculate its borrowing costs (in $) for the month. The bank's prime rate is 6%.

7. The Conejo Corp. borrows from its bank under an $8 million revolving credit arrangement. It pays an interest rate of 9% on its outstanding loan plus a 0.25% commitment fee on the unused balance. The firm had borrowed $2 million going into April and borrowed an additional $4 million on April 11. No further borrowing or repayment was made during the month. Calculate Conejo's borrowing costs (in $) for April.

8. The Grass Knoll Company has the following current asset accounts.

Cash	$ 1,900,000
Accounts receivable	$ 4,600,000
Inventory	$ 5,500,000

   Its current ratio is 2.5:1. The bank is willing to lend the company enough to finance its working capital needs under a $10 million revolving credit arrangement at an interest rate of 8% with a 3/8% commitment fee on the unused balance. If the current accounts stay relatively constant throughout the year, what will Grass Knoll pay the bank for working capital financing?

9. Bridgeport Inc. has a $30 million revolving credit agreement with its bank at prime plus 3.2% based on a calendar year. Prior to the month of April, it had borrowed $15 million that was outstanding for the entire month. On April 10, it borrowed another $5 million. Prime is 8.2%, and the bank's commitment fee is 0.25% annually. Calculate the charges associated with Bridgeport's revolving credit agreement for the month of April.

10. Regale Card Company borrowed $20,000 for a 60-day period to finance the increased sales and activities around the Christmas holidays. The rate on the bank loan remained at 10% for 20 days, then increased to 12% for 20 days, and then dropped to 8% for the remainder of the lending period. What was the annual percentage interest rate (APR) to Regale?

11. Minnow Industries has decided to borrow against its receivables, which average $80,000 per month. The firm's bank will lend against 80% of the receivables at 12% with a monthly processing fee of 0.5% of the amount borrowed. Alternatively, the receivables can be factored: The factor will accept 80% of the monthly receivables for a factoring fee of 2% per month. If factoring is selected, collection expenses will decrease by $200 per month. What is the effective annual cost (%) of each financing option (assuming 12 equal months)?

12. Good Boy Appliances has cash flow problems and needs to borrow between $50,000 and $60,000 for approximately 60 days. Because the business is small and relatively new, loans are very hard to get and are expensive when they are available. A private lender has offered an unsecured loan at 12%. Climax Inc., a finance company, has offered an alternative loan if receivables are pledged as collateral. Climax will lend 70% of the average receivables balance for 10% plus an administrative fee of $1,200. Good Boy's average receivables balance is $80,000. Assume that the lender is willing to lend the same amount as Climax. Which alternative should Good Boy choose?

13. DeSquam Inc. pledges receivables of $250 million per year to the Sharkskin Finance Company, which advances cash equal to 80% of the face value of the accounts pledged. DeSquam's receivables are usually collected in about 36 days, so 10% of the annual amount advanced is generally outstanding at any time. Sharkskin charges 14% interest plus an administrative fee of 1.6% of the amount pledged. What is DeSquam's cost of receivables financing? State the result in dollar terms and as a rate.

14. The York Company has an average receivables balance of $55,000, which turns over once every 30 days. It offers all of its receivables to its bank as collateral for short-term borrowing (pledging). The bank generally accepts 60% of the accounts offered and advances cash

equal to 85% of those. Interest is 3% over prime and the bank charges a 1% administrative fee on the gross value of all accounts offered. The prime rate is currently 6%. What effective rate is York paying for its receivables financing?

15. Northern Resources factors all of its receivables. The firm does $150 million in business each year and would have an ACP of 36.5 days if it collected its own receivables. The firm's gross margin is 35%. The factor operates without recourse and pays immediately upon taking over the accounts. It discounts the gross amount factored by 10% and pays Northern immediately. Because the factor doesn't collect from customers until they pay, it charges interest at 10% in the interim.
    a. Calculate the gross cost of factoring to Northern if all receivables are collectible.
    b. What financing rate is implied by the arrangement?
    c. Suppose Northern is considering giving up the factoring arrangement and handling its own collections. Should the firm do it if bad debt losses are expected to average 3% of gross sales and running a collections department will cost about $1.5 million per year? Assume the interest cost of carrying the receivable balance is also 10%.

16. Royal Dominion Bank will lend Williams Inc. 60% of the value of its inventory at 6% if Williams will pledge the inventory as collateral for the loan. The bank also insists that Williams employ a warehousing company to monitor and control the inventoried material. Blyth Warehousing will do the job for an annual fee of $150,000 plus 2% of the value of all the inventory it handles. Williams moves inventory valued at about $15 million through its plant each year at a turnover rate of five times. What will be the cost of financing under this proposal? State the result in both dollar and percentage (of amount borrowed) terms.

17. The Shamrock Company has a raw materials inventory of $20 million, which is completely replaced approximately 10 times a year. The Dominion Bank is willing to advance financing of 75% of the value of Shamrock's inventory at an interest rate of 9%. However, it requires a warehousing system to secure its interests. A warehousing company will install and operate the system for $800,000 a year plus 0.5% of the value of materials entering the system. What is the effective cost of this financing in percentage terms to Shamrock?

18. Harbour Import needs $400,000 for the next 91 days. Two alternative sources are available.
    a. The firm's bank has agreed to make a loan secured by accounts receivable. It will lend Harbour 80% of the value of its pledged receivables (which are just large enough to provide the $400,000 loan). The interest rate is 11% per year. In addition, there is a processing fee of 1% (for the 91-day period) of the value of the *total* receivables pledged.
    b. An insurance company has agreed to lend the $400,000 at a rate of 9% per year, using a loan secured by Harbour's inventory. A field warehousing agreement will be used, which costs $2,100 per 30 days.

    By calculating the effective annual rate, determine which financing source should be used.

19. Estate Enterprises is holding, as an investment, a banker's acceptance payable 91 days from today at a face value of $250,000. Wiley Corporation is prepared to pay Estate

Enterprises $241,500 from its excess cash balance if Estate Enterprises endorses over the acceptance to Wiley. If Estate accepts this transaction, what is its equivalent annual interest rate?

20. The Mann Corporation has a need for $300,000 in short-term financing for the next 30 days. Based on the following four options, which source should Mann select to minimize its costs? (Calculate the effective annual financing rate.)
    a. A 30-day line of credit with a bank in the amount of $500,000. There is a 0.1% commitment fee on the unused portion, and the rate of interest on borrowed funds is 8.5% per year.
    b. Forgo cash discounts on $300,000 of payables. The terms are 2/10, n.40.
    c. Issue commercial paper with a 30-day maturity. If the entire $300,000 is borrowed, the maturity value of the issue will be $305,000. The firm incurs $1,000 in additional expenses.
    d. Obtain a 30-day loan against $400,000 worth of receivables. The factor will lend an amount equal to 75% of the receivables. The factoring commission is 0.5%, and the interest rate is 10% per year.

21. When the Twins Corporation buys inventory, it must often rely on short-term bank financing to pay for the goods. Bank financing is usually in the form of a short-term self-liquidating loan, where the amount outstanding increases when goods are paid for and decreases when cash is received from sales. Twins' bank charges interest at prime (7%) plus 1%.
    Consider the following example.

November 1	December 1	January 30	March 15
Buy inventory for $10,000	Pay supplier/ borrow $10,000	Sell goods for $20,000	Collect receivables, $20,000, and repay loan, $10,000

- Twins buys and receives $10,000 worth of inventory on November 1.
- The supplier's invoice is due on December 1.
- Twins expects to sell the goods about January 30, say for $20,000.
- Twins expects to receive the cash about March 15.
- Accordingly, Twins would borrow $10,000 on December 1 in order to pay the supplier. Twins would repay the loan on March 15, when the cash becomes available.

Required:
a. What is the inventory holding period?
b. What is the receivables collection period?
c. What is the operating cycle?
d. What is the payables payment period?
e. What is the cash conversion cycle?
f. Calculate Twins' interest expense in this situation.
g. Suppose the supplier offered terms of 1/10, n.30. Should Twins pay early to take the discount? Show your calculations.
h. Suppose that Twins had negotiated a one-year $100,000 committed line of credit with its bank on July 1. Twins had agreed to pay an annual commitment fee of

0.5% on unused funds and interest at prime (7%) plus 1%. If Twins made no drawings other than the $10,000 over the 12 months until June 30, what is the effective annual cost (%) on the loan?

i. Suggest methods by which the Twins Corporation can reduce its loan period (and interest expense). For instance, what could Twins do to reduce its collection period? Explain your points.

Chapter 6

Financial Planning

Learning Objectives

1 Discuss components of the business planning process and the rationale behind business planning.

2 Explain how financial projections fit into the planning process and the role of internal and external financing.

3 Prepare a financial plan using an iterative approach.

4 Discuss the strengths and weaknesses of simple and comprehensive financial plans.

5 Understand what is meant by sustainable growth and how this relates to debt capacity.

6 List and discuss some practical problems encountered by management when using financial planning models.

There are many examples of companies going broke profitably. Managers scratch their heads trying to understand how, even with strong sales, they lose money. We discussed what might be part of the problem in Chapter 4; that is, many companies forget to take a good look at their working capital management. A second look at these companies might reveal that they had also overlooked some important details on their operations, marketing, and even capital asset management. To be successful, all facets of the business need to be examined. Business planning will not guarantee success, but it will help managers better appreciate the strengths and weaknesses of their companies and provide them with some insight into how to solve (or avoid) problems with minimum impact on the bottom line.

Planning is a big part of corporate life, especially in large companies. Firms plan their futures constantly, addressing everything from cash flow and short-term profitability to long-run strategy.

Generally, the higher up in management people are, the more time they devote to planning. It isn't unusual for top executives to spend 80% of their time thinking about the future. At the same time, some planning functions involve virtually everyone in management. For example, one thing you can be sure you'll do in your first management job is prepare a budget.

This chapter deals primarily with financial planning. Simply put, that means projecting a company's financial statements into the future. However, financial planning is a part of a broader activity known as business planning. To really appreciate financial planning, we have to understand the nature and purpose of business planning, and see how the financial element fits into the broader concept.

BUSINESS PLANNING

A **business plan** is a model of what management expects a business to become in the future expressed in *words* and *financial projections*.

The easiest way to describe business planning is in terms of its result. The process produces a document called a business plan, which can be thought of as a picture or model of what a business unit is expected to become in the future. The business plan generally looks like a magazine (with graphs and diagrams rather than pictures), and consists of a combination of words and numbers that describe the business.

The numbers in a plan are largely projected financial statements. That is, they're estimates of what the firm's statements will look like in the future if the assumptions about the business made by the planners come true. Such statements, based on hypothetical circumstances, are called *pro forma*, meaning they are presented "as if" the planning assumptions are true.

The words in a business plan describe the operation in a realistic yet concise way. They discuss broad strategic issues, detail the handling of short-term tactical questions, and amplify the financial projections.

The overall image conveyed by a good business plan is very comprehensive. It includes information on products, markets, employees, technology, facilities, capital, revenue, profitability, and anything else that might be relevant in describing the organization and its affairs.

Component Parts of a Business Plan

Although the detail within business plans varies a great deal from company to company, most follow a fairly standard overall format. A typical outline follows.

1. Contents
2. Executive Summary
3. Mission and Strategy Statement
4. Market Analysis
5. Operations (of the business)
6. Management and Staffing
7. Financial Projections
8. Contingencies

The first two sections are introductory. The table of contents is just that, and the executive summary is a one-page overview of everything that follows.

The mission and strategy section lays out the basic charter of the business and establishes its long-term direction. The market analysis attempts to demonstrate why the business will succeed against its competitors. The section on operations describes how the firm creates and distributes its product or service. The management and staffing portion details the firm's projected personnel needs and in some cases lays out the credentials of key managers.

A firm's **financial plan** is a projection of its financial statements into the *future*.

The financial section of the business plan projects the company's financial results into the future, and is the firm's financial plan. How that projection is put together will be our main focus in this chapter. The section on contingencies tells what the company will do if things don't go as planned.

The Purpose of Planning and Plan Information

The two major audiences for a firm's business plan and the information it contains are the firm's own management and outside investors.

The Managerial Value of Planning

Business planning has several managerial benefits. One has to do with the process of creating the plan, while the others are related to using the finished product.

THE PLANNING PROCESS The planning process can pull a management team into a cohesive unit with common goals. Creating a plan forces the team to think through everything that has to be done in the coming period, making sure everyone understands what they have to do. In many ways, a business plan functions as a road map for getting an organization to its goal. Comparing the details of operating performance with the plan and investigating deviations is an important management process. When a business goes off course, such a comparison is the best way to understand the firm's problems and come up with solutions. The idea is illustrated in Figure 6.1.

The *planning process* helps to pull the management team together.

A completed plan serves as a *road map* for guiding a business toward the goals stated in the plan.

A STATEMENT OF GOALS A business plan is a projection of the future that generally reflects what management would like to see happen. Accordingly, it can be viewed as a set of goals for the company as a whole and for its individual divisions or departments.

A plan contains revenue targets, departmental expense constraints, and various development goals for products and processes. Different people are responsible for different goals, and performance against them can be measured and evaluated.

It's especially common to tie executive bonuses to the achievement of goals within business plans. We'll have more to say about goals within plans later in the chapter.

PREDICTING FINANCING NEEDS Financial planning is extremely important for companies that rely on outside financing. Only through accurate financial planning can a corporate treasurer predict when he or she will need to turn to financial markets to raise additional money to support operations.

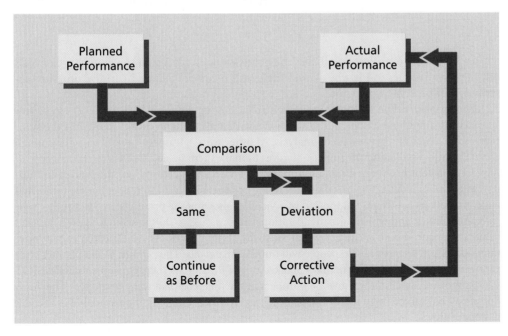

FIGURE 6.1
Using a Plan to Guide Business Performance

Communicating Information to Investors

A business plan is management's statement about what the company is going to be in the future, and can be used to communicate those ideas to investors. A plan predicts the future character of the enterprise. It makes an estimate of profitability and cash flow. The financial information tells equity investors what returns they can expect and creditors where the firm will get the money to repay loans.

Small firms use the business plan document itself in dealing with investors, including creditors. Large companies convey selected plan information to securities analysts who use it and past performance as a basis for recommendations to clients.

Business Planning in Divisions of Large Companies

Large companies are usually organized into decentralized operating divisions that function more or less like independent companies. Most large firms engage in a nearly continuous planning process. Divisions produce their own plans, which are consolidated to create overall corporate plans.

The business planning process is an important vehicle through which divisions communicate with corporate management. A division's final business plan is a statement of its goals that reflects the parent company's expectations as well as its own. Divisional plans are generally approved by corporate management after lengthy reviews, and nearly everything a division does is compared with its plan.

Credibility and Supporting Detail

Predictions of the future may not come true. Everyone knows that, so there's always an issue of believability surrounding business plans. Financial plans are especially subject to skepticism because it's usually hard to tell how the planners developed the numbers in the projected statements. Let's consider a simplified example to illustrate the idea.

Suppose Poorly Inc. has revenue of $100 million and profit of $1 million this year. The board of directors is pressuring management for better performance and has demanded a plan showing an improvement. In response, management submits the following.

**Financial Plan
for Poorly Inc.**

	This Year	Next Year
Revenue	$ 100 million	$ 120 million
NI	$ 1 million	$ 12 million

Technically, this projection satisfies the board's request for a plan showing improvement, but the obvious question is why should the board members believe it? In the situation described, they probably would not.

The problem is that this "plan" as presented lacks supporting detail. A reader doesn't know whether it's something made up just to satisfy the board's demand or if it represents the summarized product of a great deal of analysis. In other words, it doesn't tell the reader enough about the thinking behind the financial figures to make them believable.

A competent plan may display summarized financial projections, but the figures are supported by enough detail to show that they're the product of logical thinking. For example, revenue projections are usually supported by schedules showing the products and quantities to be sold, their prices, and which sales organizations are expected to do the selling. These schedules in turn are backed up by reasoning that tells why certain products are expected to sell more than others and why some salespeople will outsell their rivals. The point is that a planner can't just write down a revenue figure that's plucked out of thin air and expect people to believe it.

Supporting detail shows how the numbers in the financial plan were developed. The detail doesn't all have to be included in the plan document itself, but should be available if a reader has questions.

The business plan is a vehicle for communicating with potential *investors, including creditors.*

A good business plan shows enough *supporting detail* to indicate that it is the product of *careful thinking.*

As we proceed, we'll see that financial plans are constructed with varying levels of supporting detail depending on their use. It's important to match the level of detail to the purpose of the plan.

Four Kinds of Business Plans

There are variations on the basic idea of business planning. Each serves a different purpose and results in a separate document. Large, sophisticated companies tend to do all of these different kinds of planning while small firms usually can do one plan that combines features of the four variations.

The four kinds of planning are (1) strategic, (2) operational, (3) budgeting, and (4) forecasting.[1,2] They differ according to four attributes: the length of the planning period (the **planning horizon**), the kinds of issues addressed, the level of financial detail projected, and the responsibility for results.

Strategic Planning

Strategic, or **long-range, planning** involves broad, conceptual thinking about the nature of a business, whom it serves, and what it does. It's generally a long-term exercise in which senior management tries to predict in rough terms what the business will do and become over a period of several years. As a five-year horizon is the most common, these plans are often called the five-year plans.

Strategic planning begins by questioning the company's very existence. Why is the firm doing what it does? Would it be better off doing something else? What customer need does it serve? How? What opportunities and threats exist in the marketplace? Strategy demands that a company develop a mission and a charter, that it define what it does and why, while stating goals that are achievable.

Once that base is established, strategic planners look forward over several years and consider broad, sweeping issues. At the end of five years, will the firm be in the same lines of business and in the same geographic areas? How large will it have grown? Who will be its competitors and so on.

Strategic planning deals with concepts and ideas expressed mostly with words rather than numbers. They may include projected financial statements, but they're approximate and possibly ideal, and usually not supported by much detail. For example, a firm's strategic plan might establish a goal of being the number-one-rated company in its industry based on sales or market share. Or a firm might set a sales goal of about $500 million a year, stating that revenue figure without a lot of supporting detail.

In a nutshell, systematic strategic thinking says that a business must first analyze itself, its industry, and the competitive situation. Then it must construct an approach to doing business that takes advantage of its strengths and minimizes the vulnerabilities created by its weaknesses. A strategic plan is a vehicle for documenting this kind of thinking.

Operational Planning

Operational planning involves translating business ideas into concrete, shorter-term projections usually encompassing about a year. Projections are a great deal more detailed here than in strategic planning.

Among other things, operational plans specify how much the company will sell, to whom, and at what prices. They also spell out where the firm will get its inputs and equipment, what those things will cost, and what the firm expects to earn.

Planning horizon is the time a business plan covers. Typically between a few months and five years.

The **strategic plan** addresses broad, long-term issues, and contains only summarized, *approximate financial projections.*

The Bayer Group has its mission statement online at http://www.bayer.com/en/Bayer-Mission-Statement.pdfx.

---

1 Planning terminology isn't consistent between companies. In some firms, people talk about an annual operating budget, while others make a long-term forecast. The words "outlook" and "view" are also common. The important distinction is the length of the planning horizon: multi- (usually five-) year—long-term, strategic; one year—intermediate term, operating; three to six months—short-term, budgetary; two weeks to three months—very short-term, forecast.
2 Budgets and forecasts are abbreviated business plans and often don't have all the parts described earlier. They are predominantly financial projections.

The annual **operating plan** projects the business *in detail* over a year, and is the *most important* planning exercise.

The word "operational" or "operating" means having to do with the day-to-day running of the business. Major short-term goals are generally set up in the operating plan. Revenue targets and sales quotas are established along with profit objectives and product development milestones. Managers responsible for meeting these goals are identified. Compensation and bonus systems are also specified. Most companies do an annual plan that is an operational plan.

A typical annual operating plan is conceptually an almost even mix of words and numbers. The document verbally explains what's going on, but backs up the explanation with financial projections containing substantial supporting detail. This detail is often termed a budget.

Budgeting

A **budget** supports the annual operating plan and is sometimes updated when business *conditions change* rapidly.

In many industries, changes in business conditions mean that an operating plan and budget can be badly out of date by the second half of the year it covers. In such cases, the company may prepare a short-term budget or update, typically covering a three-month quarter.

The budgeting process involves trying to predict exactly how much of which products will be sold and at what cost. Along with that it attempts to estimate precisely how many dollars will be spent in each department, on exactly what items: salary, material, travel, and so on. In short, the budget attempts to pin down exactly how much money, material, and labour will flow through the organization and fix responsibility on specific people for making it happen.

It's important to realize that the budgetary time frame is too short to make major conceptual changes in the businesses. Policy issues and long-term direction aren't usually discussed, so budgets have relatively fewer words and more financial detail than annual plans. Clearly, a budget can also be considered an operating plan because it details the day-to-day operation of the business.

Forecasting

A **forecast** is a *very short-term* projection of *profit* and *cash flow*.

A forecast is a projection of where the financial momentum of a business will carry it over a short period. Forecasts usually consist almost entirely of numbers with very little supporting verbiage.

Forecasts are generally made either to estimate cash flows or when management gets worried about how the company will close out a period in terms of profits.

Short-term forecasting is especially important with respect to cash requirements. If a company is to pay its bills and make its payroll, it has to have an accurate picture of the cash ins and outs that can be expected over the next few weeks and months. If a temporary shortage is predicted, bank borrowing has to be arranged to keep the firm running until collections catch up with disbursements.

Cash forecast (budget). A forecast of cash flows, based on expected receipts and disbursements rather than on projections of income statement and balance sheet accounts.

A cash forecast's sole purpose is to predict short-term cash needs. Most large firms do monthly cash forecasts.[3]

The Business Planning Spectrum

It helps one's understanding of planning to imagine the different kinds of plans arrayed along a spectrum. The broad, conceptual thinking of long-term strategic planning is on one end, while the numerical detail of short-term forecasting is on the other. The idea is illustrated in Figure 6.2. As we move from left to right, the planning horizon (time covered) gets shorter and the documents progress from qualitative to quantitative, that is, from being mostly words to being mostly numbers.

Ideally, companies practise the whole spectrum of planning. That's the way most large companies operate, producing all the different documents. In such an environment, the strategic

---

3 The words "plan" and "forecast" have slightly different implications when used as nouns and verbs. A *forecast* (noun) tends to mean a short-term projection. A *plan* (noun) has a longer-term implication. The verbs are used more generally and don't tend to be tied to the length of the planning horizon. Hence, we routinely talk about forecasting the numbers within a plan or planning the numbers within a forecast.

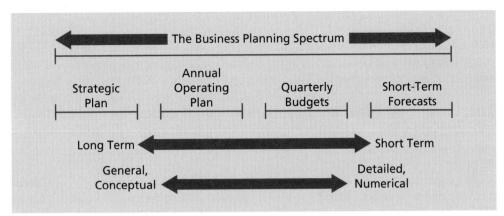

FIGURE 6.2
The Business
Planning Spectrum

plan and the annual operating plan are each produced once a year about six months apart.[4] In addition, there are usually four quarterly budgets and any number of forecasts.[5]

Relating Planning Processes of Small and Large Businesses

The planning spectrum for small businesses is usually compressed into one document known simply as the company's "business plan." It tends to be produced when the firm is getting started and updated later when money is needed from a bank or another outside source.

The business plan produced by small companies can be related to the full planning spectrum found in larger firms. The idea is illustrated in Figure 6.3. The (small) business plan overlaps three of the exercises along the spectrum. It includes everything we normally think of as operational (annual) planning, as well as elements of both strategic planning and budgeting.

The entrepreneur's plan must do everything the big corporation's annual operating plan does. It has to provide a thorough rationale for the concrete actions planned in the next year and make some fairly detailed projections of quantities, staffing, and dollars over that period. For a start-up business the plan must project at least the first year in budget-like detail. Investors generally demand at least this much precision from entrepreneurs.[6]

When in need of funding, *small businesses* tend to do a single *business plan* that contains both strategic and operating elements.

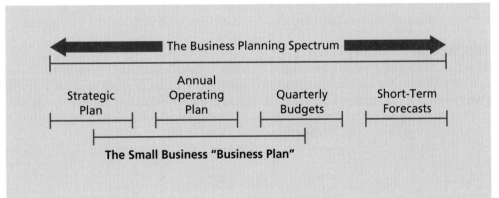

FIGURE 6.3
Relating Business
Planning in Large
and Small
Companies

4 It's important to notice that even though the strategic plan may cover five or more years, it is revised annually.
5 Companies in very stable businesses may omit the budget segment of the spectrum. Producers of basic foods and certain regulated utilities are good examples. Their revenues don't change much from year to year so revisiting budgets quarterly may not be necessary. High-tech industries represent the opposite extreme. Technology and the markets for it change rapidly, and the companies constantly engage in revising plans.
6 For a comprehensive treatment of business planning in the context of small business, see *The Perfect Business Plan Made Simple* by William Lasher (New York: Random House, 2005).

The *financial plan* is an integral part of the overall *business plan*.

Most financial planning involves forecasting changes in ongoing businesses based on *planning assumptions*.

With respect to strategy, however, the small business plan doesn't need to cover the broadest issues. For example, it doesn't have to discuss why the entrepreneur chose this business over others because that decision has already been made. The plan does have to establish that a market clearly exists and that it can be served by the business. The small business plan must also make longer-term strategic projections of what the business will be three to five years in the future.

The Financial Plan as a Component of a Business Plan

A financial plan is simply the financial portion of any of the business plans we've been talking about. It is a set of pro forma financial statements projected over the time period covered by the plan.[7]

It's important to appreciate the role of the financial plan in each of the four planning documents we discussed earlier. No business plan is complete without a financial projection, but it's of secondary importance in the strategic plan. On the other hand, the financial projection is the centrepiece of the annual plan. In operational terms, a company's financial plan is its business plan. There are usually a great many words in an annual plan, but they tend to be explanations of how the operating figures are to be achieved rather than discussions that stand by themselves.

Budgets, and especially forecasts, are almost entirely financial planning exercises.

MAKING FINANCIAL PROJECTIONS

Projecting financial statements involves translating planned physical and economic activity into dollars. That generally means making a sales forecast first, and then developing what the rest of the company needs to do to support those sales. Those physical projections lead to the dollar figures in the financial statements.

Planning for New and Existing Businesses

Financial plans are constructed for both new and ongoing businesses. The processes are conceptually similar, but as a practical matter it's a good deal harder to plan for an operation that's either very new or has yet to be started.

It's difficult to forecast how much a new business will sell or how much support it will need, because there's no history on which to base projections. That means everything has to be developed from the ground up. Forecasting for an established business is much easier, because recent results and the existing base of assets and liabilities can be used as points of departure for the projection.

The Typical Planning Task

Most financial planning is done for existing businesses. Basically, it involves forecasting changes to what's happened in the past. The changes are generally referred to as *planning assumptions*. (We'll expand on this definition shortly.) Anything about which an explicit assumption isn't made is implicitly assumed to remain unchanged from the previous year. (For a new business, everything has to be explicitly assumed.)

For example, an existing business might plan next year's operations assuming the following changes:

- a 10% growth in unit sales
- a 3% reduction in product price
- a $2 per unit increase in the cost of materials
- overall labour cost increases of 4%

---

7 The terms "financial plan" and "financial planner" have a common meaning that shouldn't be confused with their use in this chapter. Advisers who set up investment programs (financial plans) for clients are known as *financial planners*. The field has nothing to do with business planning or projecting financial statements.

- an improvement in inventory turnover from 5 times to 6 times
- an improvement in the ACP from 45 to 40 days
- an increase in interest rates from 9% to 11%
- and so on

Insights REAL APPLICATIONS

DANIER LEATHER

Planning at Danier Leather Inc.

(For the financial statements and other financial information about Danier Leather Inc., refer to Appendix 3A, page 92.)

Planning Assumptions for 2007

After five years of declining sales and two years of losses, Danier planned to take further measures to return to profitability and to improve its financial position. Danier's planning assumptions for 2007 included actions to:

- Focus on its core baby boomer customer by widening the merchandising appeal to them.
- Raise average prices by aggressively promoting higher-priced merchandise
- Improve merchandise planning processes and purchase fall merchandise earlier so that sufficient quantities and sizes of merchandise are in-stock when the customer comes to the store
- Strengthen the management of the company's supply chain
- Spend $3.6 million for renovations and equipment in the retail division, $1.1 million for new information technology and $0.3 million for manufacturing equipment and building improvements
- Reduce advertising expense (by $2.5 million) by placing a greater emphasis in favour of newspaper flyer inserts, and less transit shelter, billboard and magazine advertising
- Save personnel costs ($1 million) from head office staff reductions in 2006
- Discontinue on-line sales through the Danier website, saving $300,000
- Suspend the dividend, saving $1.6 million annually, and only resume dividends "when financial conditions permit"
- Close the flagship store on Bloor Street West in Toronto and three underperforming power centre locations. Danier did not plan to open any new stores in 2007.

Long-Run Growth Strategy

Over the next several years Danier indicated that its growth strategy would focus on the following:

1. ITS CORE BUSINESS OF LEATHER GARMENTS
   Danier would continue to focus on being the dominant destination for better leather outerwear and sportswear. Outerwear represented approximately 60% of Danier's total sales and sportswear represented another 20% of Danier's total sales.

2. CONTINUED GROWTH OF ACCESSORIES
   Leather accessory sales represented 20% of total company revenue during 2006. Danier's long-term objective was to continue to grow this less seasonally sensitive line of business.

3. SELECTIVELY OPEN NEW STORE LOCATIONS
   In 2006, Danier operated 55 shopping mall and street-front stores and 40 power centre locations (large format stores). Locations would be selectively added where sales, store profit and return on investment criteria were met.

4. CORPORATE SALES
   Sales of Danier products to corporations and other organizations for use as incentives and premiums for employees, suppliers and customers offered an incremental sales opportunity. Corporate sales represented about 2% of total company revenue during 2006.

5. INTERNATIONAL
   Licensing opportunities for countries outside of North America would be explored.

Contingency Planning

Danier has provided $18 million in liabilities (Accrued litigation provision and related expenses) for potential damages, interest, and court costs related to a class action suit brought against the company. The provision will remain until the Supreme Court of Canada makes a final determination, probably in 2008. If the court issues judgment against the company, current assets may not be available to pay the award. On the other hand, if the court finds for the company, a reversal of the provision would significantly improve the profitability and debt position of the company.

Source: Danier Leather Annual Report, 2006.

The financial planner's task is to put together a plan, benchmarking from last year's performance, that reflects these changes in the projected financial statements.

The General Approach to Planning

In this section, we'll outline how any financial planning problem is tackled, and consider the peculiar problem of forecasting debt and interest. We'll begin by establishing exactly what we're trying to forecast and exactly what we have to start with.

What We Have and What We Need to Project

Every financial planning problem involves forecasting future financial statements beginning with the next period, given the results of the last period.[8, 9] Only the income statement and balance sheet have to be forecast. The statement of cash flows is developed from those two without any additional projections.

Figure 6.4 shows the planner's task conceptually. The current (this) year's income statement is available, as is the ending balance sheet (which is next year's beginning balance sheet). These items are indicated by $XX in the figure. Using those as references, next year's income statement and ending balance sheet must be forecast incorporating the physical and economic assumptions made in the plan. If the plan is for a new business, the $XX values are simply all zeros.

Planning Assumptions

We introduced the idea of a planning assumption briefly in the last section. At this point we'll define the concept more precisely and illustrate how it works.

A **planning assumption** is some physical or economic condition that is expected to exist during the planning period. Assumptions can reflect any of the forces that influence a firm's financial results. Some things originate outside the company, like interest rates and taxes. Others come from planned management actions, like pricing or cost control. Still others come from customer behaviour, like the volume response to a price change.

> A **planning assumption** is an *expected condition* that dictates the size of one or more *financial statement items*.

FIGURE 6.4
The Planning Task

Income Statements	This Year	Next Year	Balance Sheets	Next Year Beginning	Ending
Revenue	$ XX	?	Assets		
COGS	XX	?	Current	$ XX	?
Gross margin	$ XX	?	Capital	XX	?
Expenses	XX	?	Total assets	$ XXX	?
EBIT	$ XX	?	Liabilities and Shareholders' equity		
Interest	XX	?	Current liabilities	$ XX	?
EBT	$ XX	?	Long-term debt	XX	?
Tax	XX	?	Shareholders' equity	XX	?
NI	$ XX	?	Total L&SE	$ XXX	?

---

8 For discussion purposes, we'll assume yearly time periods.
9 Most of the time, planning for a particular year is done toward the end of the preceding (current) year. That means planners don't have actual financial results for the current year with which to work. However, because year-end is close, they generally have relatively good estimates of the year's actual results.

In general, each line on a projected set of financial statements is forecast on the basis of one or more assumptions about the business. Here's a simplified example to illustrate the idea.

Example 6.1

This year, Crumb Baking Corp. sold 1 million coffee cakes per month to grocery distributors at $1 each for a total of $12 million. The firm had year-end receivables equal to two months of sales or $2 million. Crumb's operating assumptions with respect to sales and receivables for next year are as follows.

1. The price will be decreased by 10% in order to sell more product.
2. As a result of the price decrease, unit sales volume will increase to 15 million coffee cakes.
3. Collection efforts will be increased so that the average collection period will be 30 days.

Forecast next year's revenue and ending receivables balance on the basis of these assumptions. Assume sales are evenly distributed over the year.

■ **Solution:** There are three interrelated planning assumptions in this example. The first reflects a management action with respect to pricing, and the second defines the expected customer response to that action. Together, they establish the revenue forecast: Next year, 15 million coffee cakes will be sold at $0.90 each, so total revenue will be

$$\text{Revenue} = 15,000,000 \times \$0.90 = \$13,500,000$$

The third assumption is that the company's credit and collection activities will be more effective next year. This will be reflected by a decrease from two to one in the number of months of revenue that remain uncollected in accounts receivable at year-end.

$$\text{A/R} = \frac{\$13,500,00}{12} = \$1,125,000$$

Notice that the receivables calculation depends on all three assumptions, because it uses the revenue projection developed from the first two as well as the third assumption about the effectiveness of credit and collections.

The Procedural Approach

Financial plans are built by attacking line items one at a time starting with revenue, doing the kind of thing illustrated in Example 6.1.

The substance of financial planning is the logical translation of assumptions into the forecast figures they imply. It's important to realize that the calculations required for that translation differ, depending on the line item and the nature of the assumption. Some are very simple while others can become involved. We'll go through some more examples shortly.

The procedure moves down the income statement through cost of goods sold and expenses, stopping just *before* the interest expense line. Then the balance sheet projections are addressed. All the asset and liability accounts other than long-term debt and shareholders' equity are forecast. At that point, the planning procedure encounters a problem.

The Debt/Interest Planning Problem

The next items needed to complete the financial statements are interest expense on the income statement and debt on the balance sheet. The problem is that each depends on the other, so a straightforward forecast is impossible.

It's important to understand the reason for this difficulty, but the explanation can be a little hard to follow. The problem is described in the following paragraphs and illustrated in Figure 6.5. Read the explanation carefully, referring to the illustration at the same time.

Start by examining Figure 6.5. $XX values imply that dollar forecasts have already been made and question marks (?) indicate that they haven't. Notice that on the income statement we lack a forecast of interest expense and everything below it, including earnings after tax

The *debt/interest* dilemma: Planned debt is required to forecast interest, but interest affects net income and shareholders' equity (retained earnings), which is required to forecast debt.

FIGURE 6.5
The Debt/Interest
Planning Problem

Income Statement	This Year	Balance Sheets	Next Year Beginning	Ending
Revenue	$ XX	Assets		
COGS	XX	Current	$ XX	$ XX
Gross margin	$ XX	Capital	XX	XX
Expenses	XX	Total assets	$ XXX	$ XXX
EBIT	$ XX	Liabilities and Shareholders' equity		
Interest	?	Current liabilities	$ XX	$ XX
EBT	??	Long-term debt	XX	?
Tax	?	Shareholders' equity	XX	?
NI	?	Total L&SE	$ XXX	$ XXX

NI (less dividends) is added to
beginning equity to arrive at ending equity,
which is required to compute ending debt.

Ending debt is averaged with beginning debt
and multiplied by the interest rate to calculate
interest expense.

or net income (EAT or NI). On the balance sheet we have forecasts for all the asset and liability accounts other than debt and shareholders' equity. Notice that we do have the total liabilities and shareholders' equity figure, because it's equal to total assets.

To complete the income statement, we need a forecast of interest expense. But interest is calculated by applying the interest rate to the average projected debt balance during the coming year. (As a simplifying assumption, we assume that there is no interest-bearing debt in current liabilities, and use the terms *debt* and *long-term debt* interchangeably.) We know the beginning debt balance, but we have to forecast the ending figure to get an average.

Forecasting ending debt requires that we complete the ending balance sheet, which requires that we forecast ending shareholders' equity. Ending shareholders' equity is computed by adding the year's NI from the income statement, less any dividends to be paid, to beginning shareholders' equity.

But we don't have a forecast for NI because we weren't able to complete the income statement without interest expense, which we don't have because we don't have a forecast for ending debt.

In other words, the problem is circular. We need debt to calculate interest, but we have to have interest to calculate debt (through NI and shareholders' equity).

All of this means that we can't make a direct forecast of either debt or interest expense. Therefore we can't complete the financial plan with the direct line-by-line approach we've been using so far. Every financial plan runs into this technical impasse, unless simplifying assumptions are made about interest expense.

An Iterative Numerical Approach

The problem may be solved using a numerical technique that begins with a guess at the solution. The guess is usually wrong, but it gives us a starting point from which we can work toward the correct answer.

The procedure works as follows.

1. Interest: Guess a value of interest expense.
2. NI: Complete the income statement.

3. Ending shareholders' equity: Calculate ending shareholders' equity as beginning shareholders' equity plus NI (less dividends plus new shares to be sold if either of these exists).
4. Ending debt: Calculate ending debt as total L&SE (= total assets) less current liabilities less ending shareholders' equity.
5. Interest: Average beginning and ending debt. Calculate interest by multiplying average debt by the interest rate.
6. Test results: Compare the calculated interest from step 5 to the original guess in step 1.
   a. If the two are significantly different, return to step 1, replacing the guess at interest with the value just calculated and repeat steps 2 through 6.
   b. If the calculated value of interest is close to the guess, stop.

Procedures like this one that find solutions to problems though a repetitive series of calculations are known as numerical methods or **iterative techniques.** Each pass through the procedure is an iteration. It rarely takes more than two or three iterations to arrive at an acceptable solution regardless of the initial guess. We will see the same approach used to calculate a bond's yield to maturity in Chapter 9 and a capital project's internal rate of return in Chapter 12. An example will illustrate how the iterative approach is used in this situation.

*An **iterative** numerical approach solves the debt/interest problem.*

Example 6.2

The following partial financial forecast has been done for Graybarr Inc. Complete the financial plan, assuming that Graybarr pays interest at 10% and has a combined federal and provincial tax rate of 40%. Also assume no dividends are to be paid and no new shareholders' equity is to be sold.

Financial Plan for Graybarr Inc. ($000)

Income Statement		Balance Sheets		
			Next Year	
	Next Year		**Beginning**	**Ending**
Revenue	$ 10,000	Assets		
Cost/Expenses	9,000	Total assets	$ 1,000	$ 3,000
EBIT	$ 1,000			
Interest	?	Liabilities and Shareholders' equity		
EBT	?	Current liabilities	$ 300	$ 700
Tax	?	Long-term debt	100	?
NI	?	Shareholders' equity	600	?
		Total L&SE	$ 1,000	$ 3,000

■ **Solution:** First, notice that we're assuming a rather large growth rate in this illustration. Graybarr's assets are forecast to triple in one year. That's possible, but unusual. In this case, it will cause the company's debt to increase rather dramatically in the coming year.

We'll complete the forecast using the procedure outlined above, considering each step in turn.

1. Guess at interest: In most practical situations, the interest paid last year makes a good starting guess for next year's interest. Since we don't have that here, we'll make an arbitrary guess of $200,000.

The forecast is completed in the next three steps. We'll display the result now, and then show the details of steps 2 through 4. The bottom of the income statement and the liabilities and shareholders' equity portion of the balance sheet based on our interest guess are as follows.

First Iteration ($000)

		Liabilities and shareholders' equity		
EBIT	$ 1,000			
Interest	200	Current liabilities	$ 300	$ 700
EBT	$ 800	Long-term debt	100	1,220
Tax	320	Shareholders' equity	600	1,080
NI	$ 480	Total L&SE	$ 1,000	$ 3,000

The following steps get us to this result.

2. Compute NI: Assuming interest expense of $200,000, NI is $480,000 calculated as follows.

EBIT	$ 1,000,000
Interest	200,000
EBT	$ 800,000
Tax (@ 40%)	320,000
NI	$ 480,000

3. Ending shareholders' equity: Ending shareholders' equity is beginning shareholders' equity plus NI less dividends, which in this case are zero.

Beginning shareholders' equity	$ 600,000
NI	480,000
Ending shareholders' equity	$ 1,080,000

4. Ending debt: Ending long-term debt is total L&SE less ending shareholders' equity less ending current liabilities.

Total L&SE	$ 3,000,000
Ending shareholders' equity	(1,080,000)
Current liabilities	(700,000)
Ending long-term debt	$ 1,220,000

At this point we have a set of financial statements based on our guess at interest expense. Next we test to see whether the calculated long-term debt and the implied interest are consistent with that guess.

5. Interest: The interest implied by our calculated long-term debt is the product of average long-term debt and the interest rate.

$$\text{Average long-term debt} \times \text{Interest rate} = \frac{\$100,000 + \$1,220,00}{2} \times 0.10 = \$66,000$$

6. Test results: Our next step is to test the calculated interest from step 5 against the original guess. As is usually the case, the two aren't very close. The original guess of $200,000 is much higher than the calculated interest of $66,000.

We begin the next iteration of the procedure by using the calculated interest figure ($66,000) in place of the guess. Verify that steps 2 through 4 result in the following figures (rounded to the nearest thousand dollars).

Second Iteration ($000)

		Liabilities and shareholders' equity		
EBIT	$ 1,000			
Interest	66	Current liabilities	$ 300	$ 700
EBT	$ 934	Long-term debt	100	1,140
Tax	374	Shareholders' equity	600	1,160
NI	$ 560	Total L&SE	$ 1,000	$ 3,000

Given these results, average long-term debt is

$$\frac{\$100,000 + \$1,140,000}{2} = \$620,000$$

and interest is

$$\$620,000 \times 0.10 = \$62,000$$

Thus, the second guess and the calculated result are off by only $4,000 out of $62,000.

As an exercise, demonstrate that one more iteration gives a result that's accurate to within a thousand dollars with interest of $62,000 and ending debt of $1,137,000.[10]

Plans with Simple Assumptions

Financial plans can be constructed roughly or with great precision. The difference lies in the amount of thought and detail put into the assumptions on which the plans are based. A rough plan is based on just a few assumptions about the future, while a detailed plan can involve a great many. In this section we'll look into creating a financial plan for an existing business in simple, rough terms.

The Quick Estimate Based on Sales Growth

The percentage of sales method is a simple, approximate approach to forecasting financial statements for an existing business. The method involves estimating the company's sales growth rate, and assuming that all income statement and balance sheet line items grow at the same rate. The technique implicitly assumes that the firm's efficiency and all of its operating ratios (Chapter 3) stay the same through the growth period.

The assumption that everything varies proportionately with (grows at the same rate as) sales is an oversimplification that's of theoretical interest, but isn't usually applicable in practice. Most of the time, the method is modified to assume that most, but not all, things vary directly with sales. We'll call such an approach the modified percentage of sales method. Here's an example.

Percentage of sales methods assume most financial statement line items *vary directly with revenues.*

From the CFO

Example 6.3

The Overland Manufacturing Company expects next year's revenues to increase by 15% over this year's. The firm has some excess factory capacity, so no new capital assets beyond normal replacements will be needed to support the growth. This year's income statement and ending balance sheet are estimated as follows.

---

10 If you find the iterative approach tedious, we can develop an equation that captures the link between the balance sheet and the income statement. In essence, we want the balance sheet to balance, so we need to remember that Assets = Debt + Shareholders' equity. As shareholders' equity will grow by next year's net income, less any dividends, we can derive the following:

(6.1) Forecast total assets = Forecast current liabilities + Forecast debt + Last year's shareholders' equity
− Forecast dividends + (1 − T)[EBIT − Int% (0.5)(Last year's debt + Forecast debt)

The last variable in this equation links the interest to be paid on the debt with the amount that will be added to retained earnings. Rearranging and simplifying we get

(6.2) Forecast total assets − Forecast current liabilities − Last year's shareholders' equity + Forecast
dividends = Forecast debt + (1 − T)[EBIT − Int%(0.5)(Last year's debt + Forecast debt)]

So, for this example:

$$\$3,000 - \$700 - \$600 + \$0 = \text{Forecast debt} + (1 - 0.4)[1,000 - 0.1(0.5)(100 + \text{Forecast debt})]$$
$$\$1,700 = \text{Forecast debt} + 600 - 3 - 0.03(\text{Forecast debt})$$
$$\$1,103 = 0.97(\text{Forecast debt})$$
$$\text{Forecast debt} = \$1,137,000$$

Once you have determined debt you have the information required to finish both the balance sheet and income statement.

Overland Manufacturing Company This Year ($000)

INCOME STATEMENT		BALANCE SHEET	
Revenue	$ 13,580	ASSETS	
COGS	7,470	Cash	$ 348
Gross margin	$ 6,110	Accounts receivable	1,698
Expenses*	3,395	Inventory	1,494
EBIT	$ 2,715	Current assets	$ 3,540
Interest	150	Net capital assets	2,460
EBT	$ 2,565	Total assets	$ 6,000
Tax	1,077	LIABILITIES &	
NI	$ 1,488	SHAREHOLDERS' EQUITY	
* includes marketing,		Accounts payable	$ 125
engineering,		Accruals	45
and administration		Current liabilities	$ 170
		Long-term debt	1,330
		Shareholders' equity	4,500
		Total L&SE	$ 6,000

Assume the firm pays a combined tax rate of 42%, borrows at 12% interest, and expects to pay no dividends.

Project next year's income statement and balance sheet by using the modified percentage of sales method.

■ **Solution:** In this problem, we'll grow everything except net capital assets by 15%. That means we'll multiply the following items by 1.15: revenue, COGS, expense, all current assets, and all current liabilities. Then we'll hold net capital assets constant because of the assumption that the firm has excess capacity, and will just replace equipment that wears out. The result is reflected in the following incomplete statements.

Incomplete Statements for Next Year ($000)

INCOME STATEMENT		BALANCE SHEET	
Revenue	$ 15,617	ASSETS	
COGS	8,591	Cash	$ 400
Gross margin	$ 7,026	Accounts receivable	1,953
Expenses*	3,904	Inventory	1,718
EBIT	$ 3,122	Current assets	$ 4,071
Interest	–	Net capital assets	2,460
EBT	$ –	Total assets	$ 6,531
Tax	–	LIABILITIES &	
NI	$ –	SHAREHOLDERS'	
* includes marketing,		EQUITY	
engineering,		Accounts payable	$ 144
and administration		Accruals	52
		Current liabilities	$ 196
		Long-term debt	–
		Shareholders' equity	–
		Total L&SE	$ 6,531

At this point, we're at the debt/interest impasse. To complete the projection, we can guess at interest and work through the procedure illustrated in the last section, use the algebraic approach or use a spreadsheet. We will begin by using the algebraic approach (Equation 6.2), and then use a spreadsheet.

(6.2) Forecast total assets − Forecast current liabilities − Last year's shareholders' equity + Forecast dividends = Forecast debt + (1 − T)[EBIT − Int%(0.5) (Last year's debt + Forecast debt)]

So, for this example:

$6,531 − $196 − $4,500 + 0 = Forecast debt + (1 − 0.42)[3,122 − 0.12(0.5) ($1330 + Forecast debt)]

$1,835 = Forecast debt + $1,810.76 − $46.284 − 0.0348 (Forecast debt)

$70.524 = 0.9652(Forecast debt)

Forecast debt = $73.07

Once you have determined debt, you have the information required to finish both the balance sheet and income statement. That is:

$$\text{Interest cost} = 0.12 \times \frac{(\$1,330 + \$73)}{2}$$
$$= 84$$

so the income statement can be finished. With the net income figure, we can determine that the shareholders' equity will be $4,500 + $1,762 = $6,262. Plugging this figure into the balance sheet along with the debt figure of $73, we are finished.[11]

---

11 Using a spreadsheet like Excel®, we need to set up the equations for the bottom section of the income statement as well as the liability and shareholders' equity sections of the balance sheet. Once that is complete, we can use a function in Excel® called Goal Seek, which basically is an iterative solver function. Before using Goal Seek, we need to decide what it is we want to solve for. In this example, we are solving for long-term debt. We can see from the spreadsheet below that we guessed long-term debt to be $700 (this is wrong, and with Goal Seek, the worse the guess, the better!).

To use Goal Seek, go to Tools and click on Goal Seek. For "Set cell" we need to decide what cell we want to equal some number. For this example, we want L&SE to equal $6,531 (the value for total assets). So in the "Set cell," enter E16, and for the "To value" type 6531 (note that Goal Seek would not allow us to put in cell address E9, as it needs a value). Lastly, we need to tell Goal Seek which cell we want to solve for. In this example, we want to know the maximum long-term debt, so type in E14 and then click OK. Goal Seek will then solve for the long-term debt. The income statement and balance sheet that results will be identical to the one we calculated using the iterative process or the algebraic equation.

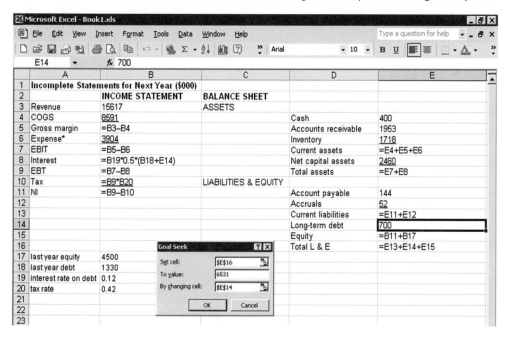

Overland Manufacturing Company Next Year ($000)

INCOME STATEMENT		BALANCE SHEET	
Revenue	$ 15,617	ASSETS	
COGS	8,591	Cash	$ 400
Gross margin	$ 7,026	Accounts receivable	1,953
Expenses*	3,904	Inventory	1,718
EBIT	$ 3,122	Current assets	$ 4,071
Interest	84	Net capital assets	2,460
EBT	$ 3,038	Total assets	$ 6,531
Tax	1,276	LIABILITIES & SHAREHOLDERS' EQUITY	
NI	$ 1,762	Accounts payable	$ 144
* includes marketing,		Accruals	52
engineering,		Current liabilities	$ 196
and administration		Long-term debt	73
		Shareholders' equity	6,262
		Total L&SE	$ 6,531

Forecasting Cash Needs

Recall that a key reason for doing financial projections is to forecast the firm's external financing needs. We can observe that need quickly in the preceding example by comparing Overland's beginning and ending debt balances for the forecast year. If the balance increases, the plan implies that the firm will need more cash than it is generating through operations, and will have to borrow more. A decrease in debt implies that cash will be generated beyond the firm's immediate needs, so debt can be paid down.[12] In this example, Overland is planning to generate $1,257,000 in cash, enough to pay down its debt from $1,330,000 to $73,000.

When a plan shows increasing debt, the implication is that additional external financing will be needed during the forecast year. Of course, the funds could be acquired by selling additional common shares rather than borrowing. That would be reflected as an increase in the ending shareholders' equity account beyond the addition of NI to retained earnings, which in turn would reduce the amount of ending debt required to balance the balance sheet.

The Percentage of Sales Method—A Formula Approach

In Example 6.3 (page 195), we used a modified percentage of sales method to create a financial projection based on an assumed growth in revenue and a separate assumption about capital assets. If we're willing to assume that net capital assets also grows proportionally with revenue, the percentage of sales method can be condensed into a single formula for the purpose of estimating external funding requirements. We'll call the formula the EFR relationship for *external funding requirement*.

The idea behind the EFR relationship is very simple: A growing firm must have enough money on hand to purchase the new assets it needs to support its growth. However, that funding requirement is reduced by two automatic sources: (1) the amount by which current liabilities grow,[13] and (2) the amount the firm earns during the year but doesn't pay out in dividends.[14] In other words, for the year being planned (next year):

(**6.3**)

$$\begin{aligned} &\text{Growth in assets}\\ -\ &\text{Growth in current liabilities}\\ \underline{-\ &\text{Earnings retained}}\\ =\ &\text{External funding requirement} \end{aligned}$$

12 A negative figure for ending debt is possible and implies that cash will be generated beyond the firm's beginning debt level.
13 Recall that current liabilities are known as spontaneous financing because they reflect the acquisition of assets that don't have to be paid for immediately. See Chapter 4.
14 In the unmodified percentage of sales method, we shortcut the iterative debt/interest procedure by assuming NI grows at the same rate as sales. This is equivalent to assuming that the return on sales ratio (ROS) stays constant.

Equation 6.3 is true for any financial projection, but can be written in simple terms when sales, earnings, assets, and current liabilities are all assumed to grow at the same rate, which we'll call g.

We generally define g in terms of sales growth. That is,

$$g = \frac{\text{Increase in sales}}{\text{Sales}_{\text{this year}}}$$

For example, if this year's sales are \$100,000 and next year's are projected to be \$115,000, $g = 0.15$ or 15%.

In terms of Equation 6.3, the assumption that assets and current liabilities grow at rate g means

(6.4) $$\text{Growth in assets} = g \times \text{Assets}_{\text{this year}}$$

and

(6.5) $$\text{Growth in current liabilities} = g \times \text{Current liabilities}_{\text{this year}}$$

The EFR relationship provides an estimate of funding needs assuming all financial items vary directly with sales.

(The following derivation of the EFR can be skipped without loss of continuity. Just resume reading at Equation 6.8 below).

To develop an expression for current earnings retained in terms of profits, begin by recalling the expression for return on sales (ROS) (see Chapter 3, page 74).

$$\text{ROS} = \frac{\text{NI}}{\text{Sales}}$$

Solve for NI in terms of ROS and sales.

$$\text{NI} = \text{ROS} \times \text{Sales}$$

Notice that since we're assuming both NI and sales grow at the same rate, ROS will remain constant from year to year. Then next year's NI can be written as the constant ROS times next year's sales, which are just $(1 + g)$ times this year's sales. So

(6.6) $$\text{NI}_{\text{next year}} = \text{ROS} \times (1 + g)\text{Sales}_{\text{this year}}$$

Next, write the dividend payout ratio, which is defined as the ratio of dividends paid to NI.

$$d = \frac{\text{Dividends}}{\text{NI}}$$

From that definition, earnings (NI) are split between those paid out as dividends, $d(\text{NI})$, and those retained, $(1 - d)\text{NI}$. We can call $(1 - d)$ the *earnings retention ratio* or *plowback ratio*.

Then, for next year,

$$\text{Earnings retained} = (1 - d)\text{NI}_{\text{next year}}$$

Substituting for $\text{NI}_{\text{next year}}$ from Equation 6.6 yields

(6.7) $$\text{Earnings retained} = (1 - d)\text{ROS} \times (1 + g)\text{Sales}_{\text{this year}}$$

Now, to get the EFR relation, rewrite Equation 6.3, substituting from Equations 6.4, 6.5, and 6.7:

$$\begin{aligned} \text{EFR} = {} & g\,(\text{Assets}_{\text{this year}}) \\ & - g\,(\text{Current liabilities}_{\text{this year}}) \\ & - [(1 - d)\text{ROS}][(1 + g)\text{Sales}_{\text{this year}}] \end{aligned}$$

Simplifying further, we get:

(6.8) $$\text{EFR} = g[\text{Assets}_{\text{this year}} - \text{Current liabilities}_{\text{this year}} - \text{NI}(1 - d)] - \text{NI}(1 - d)$$

Although Equation 6.8 looks messy, it's easy to use because everything on the right side comes from this year's financial statements and the growth rate assumption.

Example 6.4

Reforecast the external financing requirements of the Overland Manufacturing Company of Example 6.3, assuming net capital assets and NI grow at the same 15% rate as sales. However, also assume the firm plans to pay a dividend equal to 25% of earnings next year.

■ **Solution:** First, note Overland's sales, assets, and current liabilities for this year (from Example 6.3, on page 195) as well as its payout ratio. Then calculate its return on sales. (Omit $000 as before.)

$$\text{Sales}_{\text{this year}} = \$13,580$$
$$\text{Assets}_{\text{this year}} = \$6,000$$
$$\text{Current liabilities}_{\text{this year}} = \$170$$
$$d = 25.0\%$$

$$\begin{aligned} \text{ROS} &= \frac{\text{NI}}{\text{Sales}} \\ &= \frac{\$1,488}{\$13,580} \\ &= 10.96\% \end{aligned}$$

Next, write Equation 6.8 and substitute.

$$\text{EFR} = g[\text{Assets}_{\text{this year}} - \text{Current liabilities}_{\text{this year}} - \text{NI}(1 - d)] - \text{NI}(1 - d)$$
$$\text{EFR} = 0.15[\$6,000 - 170 - \$1,488(1 - 0.25)] - \$1,488(1 - 0.25)$$
$$\text{EFR} = -\$408.90$$

This result says that Overland will generate enough funds during the projected year to reduce its debt by about $409,000.

It's important to keep in mind that the EFR approach and the related unmodified percentage of sales method are of limited value because of the general impracticality of the assumption that everything varies directly with sales. To see that, notice that the $409,000 net cash flow in Example 6.4 is substantially lower than the forecast in Example 6.3 (page 195) of $1,257,000 (see Forecasting Cash Needs on page 198 immediately following the example). About half of the $848,000 difference comes from the fact that we assumed a dividend in Example 6.4 that wasn't in Example 6.3. The other half, however, comes from the fact that the percentage of sales method forces an assumption of a 15% growth in net capital assets, which in this case is probably unrealistic.

The Sustainable Growth Rate

A firm can grow at its **sustainable growth rate** without selling new shares if its financial ratios remain constant.

A firm's **sustainable growth rate** is a theoretical measure of its strength. It is the rate at which the firm can grow if none of its financial ratios changes and if it doesn't raise any new shareholders' equity by selling shares. These conditions are equivalent to the assumptions of the unmodified percentage of sales method.

Sustainable growth is simply the growth in shareholders' equity created by profits. We can develop an expression for the rate by noticing that business operations create new shareholders' equity equal to the amount of current earnings retained. In the last section we showed that to be equal to

$$(1 - d)\text{NI}$$

where d is the dividend payout ratio.

This implies a sustainable growth rate in shareholders' equity, g_s, equal to the amount of new shareholders' equity created divided by shareholders' equity itself.

(6.9a)
$$g_s = \frac{\text{NI}(1 - d)}{\text{Shareholders' equity}}$$

from which

(6.9b)
$$g_s = \text{ROE}(1 - d)$$

because
$$\text{ROE} = \frac{\text{NI}}{\text{Shareholders' equity}}$$

Notice that although the idea of sustainable growth implies that no new shareholders' equity is raised through the sale of shares, it does require new borrowing to keep the debt/equity ratio constant as shareholders' equity grows through retaining earnings.

The value of the sustainable growth concept is largely theoretical. It gives an indication of the determinants of a firm's inherent growth capability. Recall from our study of Du Pont equations (Chapter 3, page 85) that ROE can be written as

$$\text{ROE} = \text{ROS} \times \text{Total asset turnover} \times \text{Equity multiplier}$$

Substituting this expression for ROE into Equation 6.9b, we have

$$g_s = (1 - d)[\text{ROS} \times \text{Total asset turnover} \times \text{Equity multiplier}]$$

which can be written more explicitly as

(6.10)
$$g_s = (1 - d) \times \frac{\text{NI}}{\text{Sales}} \times \frac{\text{Sales}}{\text{Assets}} \times \frac{\text{Assets}}{\text{Equity}}$$

Equation 6.10 says that a firm's ability to grow depends on four fundamentals:

1. its ability to earn profits on sales as measured by its ROS (NI/Sales)
2. its talent at using assets to generate sales as measured by its total asset turnover (Sales/Assets)
3. its use of leverage (borrowed money) as measured by the equity multiplier (Assets/Equity)
4. the percentage of earnings it retains as measured by $(1 - d)$, the earnings retention ratio

These ideas can be used to analyze why a particular firm's growth has been good or bad in relation to that of other firms. For example, after having lower than average growth, Slowly Inc. might compare its sustainable growth rate with an industry average as follows.

	g_s	=	$(1 - d)$	×	ROS	×	Total asset turnover	×	Equity multiplier
Industry	13.5%		0.75		6%		1.2		2.5
Slowly Inc.	4.8%		0.40		8%		1.0		1.5

Notice that Slowly's sustainable growth rate is much lower than the average. The question is why. The comparison immediately shows that profitability is not the problem, as Slowly's ROS is better than average. It's also apparent that total asset turnover is a bit low, but not enough to make much difference.

Slowly's growth problem seems to be associated with its modest use of leverage. The firm's equity multiplier is substantially lower than average, meaning it is financed with proportionately less debt and more shareholders' equity than other firms. Its *earnings retention ratio*, $(1 - d)$, is also lower than average.

These things may explain why the firm isn't growing rapidly. It's paying most of its earnings out in dividends rather than reinvesting them in growth opportunities. At the same time, it's chosen a low-risk strategy of not using much debt. These combined strategies don't lead to rapid growth.

Plans with More Complicated Assumptions

The percentage of sales methods (modified and unmodified) are appropriate for quick estimates, but aren't generally used in formal plans because they gloss over too much detail.

Real plans generally incorporate *complex assumptions* about important financial items.

It's usually possible to make intelligent estimates of a large number of individual items within a financial plan. Putting those separate pieces of intelligence into the projections clearly makes sense. That's done by incorporating a series of detailed assumptions into the process. Each assumption is worked into the plan in a manner that depends on the way the related item is managed and on its accounting treatment. As an illustration, let's take a closer look at the treatment of capital assets for the Overland Manufacturing Company of Example 6.3 (page 195).

In that example we made the assumption that the firm had excess factory capacity, which implied that a certain amount of growth could be accommodated in the plant without adding new assets. Hence, net capital assets could be expected to remain roughly constant. That assumption is reasonable but somewhat simplistic. It would rarely be used in a serious operating plan.

Acquiring capital assets calls for the commitment of large amounts of money, and tends to be analyzed very carefully. That means a great deal of information about capital assets is usually available.

In fact, the business planning process generally includes a capital plan, a list of the assets and projects on which the firm intends to spend money during the coming period. The items on the list are selected through the process of capital rationing that we will discuss in Chapter 12 (page 454).

For Danier Leather's Capital Investment Plans for 2007, see Chapter 13, page 472.

In the next example, we'll assume a capital plan has been done for Overland and show how some of the information it contains can be worked into the financial plan.

Example 6.5

Assume the following for the Overland Manufacturing Company of Example 6.3.

1. The ending balance sheet for the current year contains the following capital asset accounts.

Gross	$ 5,600,000
Accumulated amortization	(3,140,000)
Net	$ 2,460,000

2. Next year's amortization on the assets owned at the end of this year is $450,000, and there are no plans to dispose of old assets.
3. The capital plan indicates that assets will be acquired at the beginning of next year at an estimated total cost of $1.2 million.
4. The average life of the new equipment is 10 years. Straight-line amortization will be used.

    Notice that items 1 and 2 are not planning assumptions. They're financial facts available from the company's accounting records. Items 3 and 4 are planning assumptions summarizing the information contained in Overland's capital plan.

    Forecast Overland's capital asset accounts for next year.

■ **Solution:** Gross capital assets will grow by the amount of new capital expenditures:

Beginning gross capital assets	$ 5,600,000
Planned additions	1,200,000
Ending gross capital assets	$ 6,800,000

Amortization during the year will come from two sources: the old assets already on board at the beginning of the year, and the new additions. We've already established that the amortization on the old equipment will be $450,000. Amortization on the new equipment would be

$$\frac{\$1,200,000}{10} = \$120,000$$

Then total amortization next year is as follows:

Old assets	$ 450,000
New assets	120,000
Total	$ 570,000

With this information, the balance sheet capital asset accounts at year-end are forecast as follows. (Review the accounting for capital assets in Chapter 2, page 28, if necessary.)

	Actual Beginning	Planned Additions	Planned Ending
Gross	$ 5,600,000	$ 1,200,000	$ 6,800,000
Accumulated amortization	(3,140,000)	(570,000)	(3,710,000)
Net	$ 2,460,000	$ 630,000	$ 3,090,000

It's important to notice that this approach produces the following capital asset-related items for the projected financial statements:

1. the year-end balance sheet account detail
2. an estimate of the use of cash for capital spending for the cash flow statement
3. an estimate of total amortization for the income statement and the cash flow statement

The approach in Example 6.3, on the other hand, gave us no information beyond the net capital asset figure, which was not very accurate.

Capital assets are forecast by projecting the *gross* account using the *capital plan* and handling *amortization* separately.

Two Kinds of Planning Assumptions—Direct and Indirect—Management by Ratios

A financial planning assumption can be made directly about the financial item to which it's related or indirectly about a derivative of the item, usually a ratio. In Example 6.5 we made direct assumptions about capital expenditures to forecast items related to capital assets.

An indirect planning assumption is usually based on the use of financial ratios. Instead of forecasting a particular item, we forecast a related ratio. Accounts receivable is a good example. Managers generally think of receivables in terms of the average time it takes to collect cash from customers rather than in terms of the magnitude of the receivables account on the balance sheet. In other words, receivables are managed through the average collection period (ACP) ratio. (See Chapters 3, 4, and 5, pages 78, 137, and 178.) This means that financial planning assumptions about receivables tend to be made in terms of the ACP. Projected statements are then put together using receivables balances calculated from those assumptions.

Indirect planning assumptions are made about financial *ratios*, which in turn lead to line-item values.

Accounts receivable are generally forecast by making an assumption about the *ACP* and calculating the implied balance.

Example 6.6

The Mylar Corporation currently has receivables of $1.2 million on revenues of $7.2 million for an ACP of 61 days calculated as follows.

$$ACP = \frac{A/R}{\text{Average daily (credit) sales}}$$

$$= \frac{A/R}{\text{Sales}} \times 365 = \frac{\$1.2 \text{ million}}{\$7.2 \text{ million}} \times 365 = 61 \text{ days}$$

A review of the receivables has revealed that there are no very old or plainly uncollectible accounts.

Management feels that a 61-day ACP represents unacceptably slow payment by customers, and plans to tighten credit and collection policy enough to reduce it to 40 days in the coming year. Next year's revenue projection reflects a growth of approximately 10% to $7.9 million after consideration of the credit and collections policy change.

What balance sheet figure for receivables should be included in the financial plan to reflect this assumption about ACP?

■ **Solution:** The indirect planning assumption is that the ACP will be 40 days next year. To put together a financial plan consistent with that assumption, we calculate the year-end receivables balance that results in a 40-day ACP. Begin by rewriting the ACP formula.

$$ACP = \frac{A/R}{Sales} \times 365$$

Then substitute next year's figures, treating A/R as an unknown.

$$40 \text{ days} = \frac{A/R}{\$7,900,000} \times 365$$

Solve this expression for the A/R balance implied by the ACP assumption.

$$A/R = \$865,753 \text{[15]}$$

A Comprehensive Example—A Complex Plan for an Existing Business

In this section, we'll take an ongoing business and make a projection for next year based on a fairly broad set of assumptions. Notice that most of the assumptions are based on changes from last year.

Example 6.7

The Macadam Company is developing its annual plan for next year. The company expects to finish this year with the following financial results.

Macadam Company Income Statement
This Year ($000)

	$	%
Revenue	$ 14,200	100.0
COGS	7,810	55.0
Gross margin	$ 6,390	45.0
Expenses		
Marketing	$ 2,556	18.0
Engineering	525	3.7
Finance & administrative	1,349	9.5
Amortization	540	3.8
Total expenses	$ 4,970	35.0
EBIT	$ 1,420	10.0
Interest	568	4.0
EBT	$ 852	6.0
Income tax	341	2.4
NI	$ 511	3.6

---

15 In practice, the calculation would usually be somewhat more complicated. Most people calculate ACPs on the basis of an average A/R balance over the year using the following formula.

$$ACP = \frac{(\text{Beginning A/R} + \text{Ending A/R}) \div 2}{Sales} \times 365$$

Next year's beginning A/R balance is this year's ending balance, $1.2 million in this case. Substituting yields

$$40 \text{ days} = \frac{(\$1,200,000 + \text{Ending A/R}) \div 2}{\$7,900,000} \times 365$$

From which

$$\text{ending A/R} = \$531,507$$

Notice that this figure is unrealistically low because of the inclusion of the high ending balance from last year. If the ACP calculation is based on average A/R balances, the target ACP should be raised in a transitional year to reflect that fact. In this case, a 50-day target over the entire year would be appropriate to get the firm operating at a 40-day level by year-end.

Macadam Company Balance Sheet

This Year ($000)

ASSETS			LIABILITIES & SHAREHOLDERS' EQUITY		
Cash	$	1,560	Accounts Payable	$	716
Accounts receivable		3,550	Accruals		230
Inventory		2,603	Current liabilities	$	946
Current assets	$	7,713			
			Long-term debt	$	4,000
Capital assets			Shareholders' equity		
Gross	$	12,560	Common shares	$	6,000
Accumulated amortization		(3,620)	Retained earnings		5,707
Net	$	8,940	Total shareholders' equity	$	11,707
Total assets	$	16,653	Total L & SE	$	16,653

(The income statement is presented with a common size statement, because certain planning assumptions are commonly based on projected percentages of revenue. See Chapter 3, page 71.)

The current values of Macadam's ACP and inventory turnover ratios can be calculated from the statements. (We'll use ending balances only.)

The ACP is

$$ACP = \frac{A/R}{Sales} \times 365 = \frac{\$3,550}{\$14,200} \times 365 = 91.25 \text{ days}$$

and the inventory turnover based on COGS is

$$\text{Inventory turnover} = \frac{COGS}{Inventory} = \frac{\$7,810}{\$2,603} = 3.0$$

The following facts (not assumptions) are also available about the firm's operations.

Facts

- Virtually all payables are due to inventory purchases, and the COGS is approximately 60% purchased material.
- Assets currently on the firm's books will generate amortization of $510,000 next year.
- The only balance sheet accrual represents unpaid wages. Preliminary estimates indicate that next year's payroll will be about $6.1 million. Next year's closing balance sheet date will be nine working days after a payday.
- The combined provincial and federal income tax rate is 40%.
- Interest on current and future borrowing will be at a rate of 10%.

The management team has met and agreed upon the following assumptions under which the plan will be developed.

Planning Assumptions
Income, Cost of Goods Sold, and Expenses

1. During the coming year, the firm will mount a major program to expand sales. The expected result is a 20% growth in revenue. Pricing and product mix will remain unchanged.
2. The revenue growth will be accomplished by increasing efforts in the marketing/sales department. It is anticipated that the marketing department expenses will increase to 19% of the expanded revenue rather than the current 18%.
3. A major cost-reduction effort is under way in the manufacturing department, which is expected to reduce the cost ratio (COGS/Revenue) to 53% from its current level of 55%.
4. The engineering department will be cutting back due to improvements in technology. Its dollar expenses are estimated to be 80% of last year's level.

5. Finance and administrative expenses will need to expand to support the higher volume, but because of scale economies the expansion will be at a lower rate than the growth in sales. A target growth of 5% is planned for those expenses.

Assets and Liabilities

6. A new cash management system will reduce the cash balance by 20%.
7. The current 91.25-day collection period (ACP) is considered unacceptable. Increased attention to credit and collections is expected to bring the ACP down to 65 days.
8. Top management feels that the firm is operating with more inventory than it needs. Manufacturing management has been challenged to increase the inventory turnover ratio (based on COGS) to 5.0 from its present level of 3.0.
9. The capital plan has been put together in preliminary form, and indicates capital spending of $5 million. The average life of the asset being acquired is 20 years. Straight-line amortization will be used.
10. Vendors are complaining because the firm pays its bills in 55 days even though most terms call for payment within 30 days. Fearing that deliveries of inventory and supplies will be cut off, management has decided to shorten the payment cycle to 45 days.
11. No dividends will be paid next year, and no new common shares will be sold.

Construct a financial plan for next year for Macadam based on last year's statements and these assumptions. To keep the computation simple, we'll assume that all balance sheet ratios are calculated by using ending balances (not averages).

■ **Solution:** We'll begin Macadam's plan by projecting each operating line of the income statement and balance sheet. Then we'll complete those statements by iterating for debt and interest. Finally, we'll construct a projected statement of cash flows from the completed income statement and balance sheet.

Notice as we go along that each line item is handled differently. Some are very simple, while others take some calculation. We'll omit the $000 and round all results to the nearest thousand dollars for convenience.

Revenue: Our revenue forecast is based on the direct assumption of a 20% growth rate on last year's figure.

$$\text{Revenue} = \$14,200 \times 1.20 = \$17,040$$

Cost of goods sold (COGS): The forecast of COGS is based on an assumed improvement in manufacturing efficiency, which is reflected in an improvement (lowering) in the *cost ratio* from last year's 55% to 53% next year. The cost ratio is the ratio of COGS to revenue and appears on the COGS line of the common size income statement. Because we know next year's cost ratio as well as its revenue, we can multiply to project COGS.

$$\text{COGS} = \$17,040 \times 0.53 = \$9,031$$

Marketing expense: Departmental expenses are frequently managed in common size terms. This implies comparing those expenses as percentages of revenue to industry averages to keep them in reasonable ranges. In this case, Macadam's top management is planning for an increase in spending in marketing from 18% to 19% of sales to allow for an expanded effort in sales. The figure is easily forecast as 19% of next year's sales.

$$\text{Marketing expense} = \$17,040 \times 0.19 = \$3,238$$

Notice that this represents a very substantial growth (27%) over last year's spending *in dollar terms.*
Engineering expense: Engineering is a long-term development function that isn't directly related to the current year's sales. Hence there's no reason to assume it has to grow a great deal to support the marketing expansion and in fact, in this case the firm is able to reduce these costs.

$$\text{Engineering expense} = \$525 \times 0.8 = \$420$$

Finance and administrative expense: Finance and administrative expenses pay for things like account-ing, personnel, and executive management. These functions grow with revenue, but economies of scale tend to make them more efficient as size increases, implying that they should grow less rapidly than sales. In this case, management has assumed a growth of 5%.

$$\text{Finance and administrative expense} = \$1{,}349 \times 1.05 = \$1{,}416$$

The next line on the income statement is interest, which we can't address until we've completed the balance sheet down to debt. Therefore we'll move on to current assets at this point.

Cash: A cash management system is forecast to improve Macadam's cash management, resulting in a 20% decrease in the balance from its current level. This assumption is quite aggressive in the face of an increase in business.

$$\text{Cash} = \$1{,}560 \times (1 - 0.20) = \$1{,}248$$

Accounts receivable: Macadam manages its receivables indirectly by addressing the ACP, which it has forecast at 65 days for next year.

$$\text{ACP} = \frac{\text{A/R}}{\text{Sales}} \times 365$$

from which

$$\text{A/R} = \frac{\text{Sales}}{365} \times \text{ACP}$$

and

$$\text{A/R} = \frac{\$17{,}040}{365} \times 65$$

$$\text{A/R} = \$3{,}035$$

Notice that this forecast represents a decrease in A/R in spite of the planned increase in revenue, which would normally be expected to raise receivables. That's because the improvement in collections is forecast to have a bigger effect than the growth in revenue. This too is a very aggressive assumption.

Inventory: Management has assumed an improvement in inventory utilization, which is reflected by an increase in the inventory turnover ratio to 5.0 from its current level of 3.0. This (indirectly) implies an inventory level through the equation defining the turnover ratio.

Inventory is generally forecast *indirectly* through the *inventory turnover* ratio.

$$\text{Inventory turnover} = \frac{\text{COGS}}{\text{Inventory}}$$

from which

$$\text{Inventory} = \frac{\text{COGS}}{\text{Inventory turnover}}$$
$$= \frac{\$9{,}031}{5.0}$$
$$= \$1{,}806$$

Here again it's important to notice the aggressiveness of management's planning assumption. A 20% volume increase would normally lead to larger inventories, but this forecast is for a substantial decline due to the projected efficiency improvement.

Capital assets: The capital asset forecast is handled exactly as illustrated in Example 6.5. Additions and amortization are as follows.

Gross capital asset additions =	$ 5,000
Amortization	
New equipment = $5,000/20 =	250
Old equipment =	510
	$ 760

From these and the beginning balances in the capital asset accounts, the ending balances are forecast as follows:

	Beginning	Additions	Ending
Gross	$ 12,560	$ 5,000	$ 17,560
Accumulated amortization	(3,620)	(760)	(4,380)
Net	$ 8,940	$ 4,240	$ 13,180

Accounts payable: The slow paying of vendors could lead to production problems if suppliers hold up delivery. The plan to pay in 45 days is still a violation of most 30-day terms, but it's less flagrant and more likely to be tolerated by vendors over the long run. Our problem is to calculate the payables balance implied by the policy.

Payables are generated almost entirely by inventory purchases, which are 60% of product cost. Hence the total amount passing through the payables account in a year is 60% of COGS. If bills are paid in 45 days, the unpaid amount at any time is 45/365 of that annual total. This thinking leads to the following calculation.

$$\text{Accounts payable} = \text{Purchases} \times \frac{45}{365}$$

$$= 0.60 \times \text{COGS} \times \frac{45}{365}$$

$$= 0.60 \times \$9,031 \times \frac{45}{365}$$

$$= \$668$$

(As an exercise, demonstrate that this year's payables balance represents a 55-day payment policy.)

Accruals: Macadam's only accrual reflects unpaid wages. Recall that the amount of such an accrual represents wages earned between the year's last payday and its closing date. (See Chapter 2, page 31.) The amount can be estimated by examining a calendar to determine the ending date of the year being planned and the date of the immediately preceding payday. The period between the two dates represents the time for which wages have to be accrued. In this case there are nine working days between the two dates, which represent 1.8 (= 9/5) normal five-day workweeks. Hence the accrual must be for 1.8/52 of the total amount paid to employees in a year. Next year's annual payroll is estimated at $6,100, so the amount that will be accrued is

$$\text{Accruals} = \frac{\$6,100 \times 1.8}{52} = \$211^{[16]}$$

This completes the forecast of the operating items in Macadam's income statement and balance sheet. To complete those statements we can go through any of the processes we have discussed previously to determine debt and interest. The figures that come from the iterative procedure are shown in bold.

Notice the side-by-side (comparative) format in which the statements are presented. This year and next year are shown together for both statements, and a common size presentation is included for the income statement. This format is highly recommended for planning work because it makes it easy to work with the year-to-year changes that are the essence of most planning exercises.

[16] In practice, accrual calculations tend to be more complex than this. Firms often have different payrolls for different types of employees, and everyone isn't always fully paid off as of payday. In addition, a number of things besides wages are generally accrued.

Macadam Company

Projected Income Statement ($000)

	This Year		Next Year	
	$	%	$	%
Revenue	$ 14,200	100.0	$ 17,040	100.0
COGS	7,810	55.0	9,031	53.0
Gross margin	$ 6,390	45.0	$ 8,009	47.0
Expenses				
Marketing	$ 2,556	18.0	$ 3,238	19.0
Engineering	525	3.7	420	2.5
Finance & administrative	1,349	9.5	1,416	8.3
Amortization	540	3.8	760	4.5
Total expenses	$ 4,970	35.0	$ 5,834	34.2
EBIT	$ 1,420	10.0	$ 2,175	12.8
Interest	568	4.0	**483**	**2.8**
EBT	$ 852	6.0	$ **1,692**	**10.0**
Income tax	341	2.4	**677**	**4.0**
NI	$ 511	3.6	$ **1,015**	**6.0**

Macadam's financial plan is completed by constructing a projected statement of cash flows. That is readily done by using the procedures we studied in Chapter 2. No new projecting is required because the cash flow statement comes entirely from the income statement and balance sheet, which have already been forecast. The comparative format we're using makes constructing a cash statement particularly convenient. We begin with a summary of the planned changes in working capital items.

Macadam Company

Projected Balance Sheet ($000)

ASSETS	This Year	Next Year	LIABILITIES & SHAREHOLDERS' EQUITY	This Year	Next Year
Cash	$ 1,560	$ 1,248	Accounts payable	$ 716	$ 668
Accounts receivable	3,550	3,035	Accruals	230	211
Inventory	2,603	1,806	Current liabilities	$ 946	$ 879
Current assets	$ 7,713	$ 6,089	Long-term debt	$ 4,000	$ 5,668
Capital assets			Shareholders' equity		
Gross	$ 12,560	$ 17,560	Common shares	$ 6,000	$ 6,000
Accumulated amortization	(3,620)	(4,380)	Retained earnings	5,707	6,722
Net	$ 8,940	$ 13,180	Total shareholders' equity	$ 11,707	$ 12,722
Total assets	$ 16,653	$ 19,269	Total L&SE	$ 16,653	$ 19,269

Macadam Company

Projected Changes in Working Capital ($000)

	Beginning	Ending	Change
Accounts receivable	$ 3,550	$ 3,035	$ 515
Inventory	2,603	1,806	797
Accounts payable	716	668	(48)
Accruals	230	211	(19)
Decrease/(increase) in working capital	$ 5,207	$ 3,962	$ 1,245

The projected statement of cash flows follows immediately.

Macadam Company

Projected Statement of Cash Flows ($000)

OPERATING ACTIVITIES	
NI	$ 1,015
Amortization	760
Decrease in working capital	1,245
Cash from operating activities	$ 3,020
INVESTING ACTIVITIES	
Increase in gross capital assets	$ (5,000)
Cash from investing activities	$ (5,000)
FINANCING ACTIVITIES	
Increase in debt	$ 1,668
Cash from financing activities	$ 1,668
NET CASH FLOW	$ (312)
RECONCILIATION	
Beginning cash	$ 1,560
Net cash flow	(312)
Ending cash	$ 1,248

The Cash Budget

Forecasting cash is an especially important part of financial planning. Companies need to be able to predict cash balances accurately, because running out can be a complete disaster. For example, even if everything else is going well, a firm without the cash to meet its payroll is likely to fail quickly. Hence, well-managed companies pay a lot of attention to cash.

There are two ways to forecast cash. We've already looked at the first, which involves forecasting the income statement and balance sheet and deriving a projected statement of cash flows from those documents.

The *cash budget* is a detailed projection of *receipts and disbursements* of cash.

The second approach, known as *cash budgeting*, is more detailed. It involves forecasting cash receipts and disbursements on the dates they're likely to occur. Then the ins and outs are summed in each planning period, usually months, to get net cash flows.

Receipts generally come from cash sales, collecting receivables, borrowing, and selling new shares. Disbursements include paying for purchases, wages, taxes, and other expenses such as rent, utilities, supplies, and outside services.

Receivables and Payables—Forecasting with Time Lags

Forecasting the collection of receivables is difficult, because it's hard to know exactly when customers will pay their bills. Some pay within the terms of sale, usually 30 days, but others stretch the terms ("lean on the trade") and don't pay for 50 or 60 days. A few never pay at all.

However, firms generally have historical information on the percentage of revenues that tend to be collected in each month following credit sales. For example, on the average a firm's collections may behave according to the following time lagged pattern.

Months after Sale	1	2	3
Percentage collected	60%	30%	8%

Notice that the total collected is 98%, which recognizes that on the average 2% of sales turn out to be bad debts.

Applying the pattern to each month's forecast of sales revenue lets us build up a projection of collections. Here's an illustration showing how sales might be collected.

	Jan	**Feb**	**Mar**	**Apr**	**May**	**Jun**
Sales	$ 500	$ 600	$ 700	$ 600	$ 500	$ 500
Collections from sales made in						
Jan		$ 300	$ 150	$ 40		
Feb			360	180	$ 48	
Mar				420	210	$ 56
Apr					360	180
May						300
Total collections				$ 640	$ 618	$ 536

There's an added complication if a prompt payment discount is offered. In that case, first-month collections are reduced to reflect some customers' taking the discount.

Payables are handled similarly but with more precision, because the firm knows its own payment policy. For example, if a company pays its bills 30 days after receipt of product, it simply lags forecast inventory receipts by one month to predict disbursements. If the policy is to pay in 45 days, split the payment evenly between the first and second months after receipt.

Let's assume that the company orders its materials one month prior to their sale and then pays for the goods two months later. If the cost of materials was, say, 40% of the sales, then the disbursement schedule for materials would be as follows:

	Jan	**Feb**	**Mar**	**Apr**	**May**	**Jun**	**Jul**
Sales	$500	$600	$700	$600	$500	$500	$500
Order placed for upcoming month	$240	$280	$240	$200	$200	$200	
Payment due on orders			$240	$280	$240	$200	$200

Forecasting most other items is fairly straightforward. Payroll dates are known, so wages are easy to forecast. The payment dates for interest and repayment on long-term debt are also generally easy to predict, as are big disbursements for things like taxes and capital spending.

To finish this problem, we need to estimate other outflows to get a complete disbursement schedule. Ultimately, we want to figure out how much the company will need to borrow or how much it will have on hand at the end of each month. As we have most of the detail for April, May, and June, we will finish these columns.

	Apr	**May**	**Jun**	**Jul**
Cash paid for inventory (from above)	$ 280	$ 240	$ 200	$ 200
Wages	$ 180	$ 180	$ 180	
Rent/utilities	$ 40	$ 40	$ 40	
Quarterly tax payment			$ 12	
Purchase of capital asset	$ 150		$ 60	
Quarterly dividend			$ 50	
Total cash disbursements	$ 650	$ 460	$ 542	

Debt and Interest

Forecasting short-term debt and interest can be a little tricky if a company is funding current cash needs directly by borrowing, which, as we have seen in Chapter 5, isn't unusual. Under that arrangement, the current month's interest payment may be based on the loan balance at the end of the last month. But that balance changes depending on whether the month's cash flow is positive or negative. That means we have to work our way through a forecast, month by month, to calculate the interest payments.

Continuing with our example, we'll assume that interest is charged at 1% per month and that, at the end of March, the company owes $600. Interest is charged on cumulative negative cash flow (this is debt when negative). Typically we assume that the borrowing occurs at the beginning of the month with the interest due on the loan being paid at the end of the month. To keep the calculations somewhat straightforward, we will calculate interest owed and pay it in the following month. In some cases, companies find that they are not in a borrowing position, but rather they have cash balances. Unless the amount is substantial, these surpluses rarely have interest earned on them. For simplicity, we will assume that credit balances do not receive any interest.

	Mar	**Apr**	**May**	**Jun**
Cash flow before interest (Total collections − Total cash disbursements)		$ (10)	$ 158	$ (6)
Interest		$ (6)	$ (6.16)	$ (4.64)
Net cash flow		$ (16)	151.84	$ (10.64)
Cumulative cash flow at month end	$ (600)	$ (616)	$ (464.16)	$ (474.8)

Working from left to right, the first payment in April is made on the $600 debt at the end of March. Interest of $6 is charged on that balance in April. That adds to the month's negative cash flow, making the cumulative debt $616. That generates $6.16 in interest expense in May, which is then subtracted from the inflow of $158, leaving a cumulative cash flow deficit of $464.16, and so on.

Example 6.8

The Pulmeri Company's revenues tend to go through a quarterly cycle. It's now mid-March and management expects the first quarter's pattern to be repeated in the second quarter. The six-month period is as follows ($000):

	Jan	Feb	Mar	Apr	May	Jun
Revenue	$5,000	$8,000	$9,000	$5,000	$8,000	$9,000

Historically, Pulmeri collects its receivables according to the following pattern:

Months after Sale	1	2	3
Percentage collected	65%	25%	10%

No prompt payment discount is offered, and there are virtually no bad debts. The firm purchases and receives inventory one month in advance of sales. Materials cost about half of sales revenue. Invoices for inventory purchases are paid 45 days after receipt of material.

Payroll runs a constant $2.5 million per month, and other expenses (such as rent, utilities, and supplies) are a fairly steady $1.5 million per month. A $0.5 million tax payment is scheduled for mid-April. Pulmeri has a short-term loan outstanding that is expected to stand at $5 million at the end of March. Monthly interest is 1% of the previous month-end balance. Pulmeri does not require any balance in its cash account.

Prepare Pulmeri's cash budget for the second quarter.

■ **Solution:** First, layout revenue and collections according to one historical pattern.

	Jan	Feb	Mar	Apr	May	Jun
Revenue	$ 5,000	$ 8,000	$ 9,000	$ 5,000	$ 8,000	$ 9,000
Collections from sales made in						
Jan		$ 3,250	$ 1,250	$ 500		
Feb			5,200	2,000	$ 800	
Mar				5,850	2,250	$ 900
Apr					3,250	1,250
May						5,200
Second-quarter collections				$ 8,350	$ 6,300	$ 7,350

Next, make inventory purchases (half of sales dollars) one month prior to the date of sale and then make the payments for purchases two months forward in two equal parts.

	Jan	Feb	Mar	Apr	May	Jun
Purchases		$ 4,500	$ 2,500	$ 4,000	$ 4,500	
Payment						
Feb			$ 2,250	$ 2,250		
Mar				1,250	$ 1,250	
Apr					2,000	$ 2,000
May						2,250
Payment for materials				$ 3,500	$ 3,250	$ 4,250

Next, summarize these results along with payroll and other disbursements and work through the interest charges. Interest is 1% per month on the loan balance at the end of the previous month. As well, we will assume that the company does not have any minimum monthly payments of principal on this loan.

Pulmeri Company

Cash Budget

Second Quarter 20X1 ($000)

	Jan	Feb	Mar	Apr	May	Jun
Revenue	$ 5,000	$ 8,000	$ 9,000	$ 5,000	$ 8,000	$ 9,000
Collections				$ 8,350	$ 6,300	$ 7,350
Disbursements						
Materials purchases				$ 3,500	$ 3,250	$ 4,250
Payroll				$ 2,500	$ 2,500	$ 2,500
General expenses				$ 1,500	$ 1,500	$ 1,500
Tax payment				$ 500		
Disbursements before interest				$ 8,000	$ 7,250	$ 8,250
Cash flow before interest				$ 350	$ (950)	$ (900)
Interest				(50)	(47)	(57)
Net cash flow				$ 300	$ (997)	$ (957)
Beginning cash balance						
Additional borrowing					$ 997	$ 957
Loan repayments				(300)		
Ending cash balance[17]						
Loan balance			$ 5,000	$ 4,700	$ 5,697	$ 6,654

---

17 Some firms maintain a minimum cash balance (greater than zero) for unexpected emergencies, unforeseen opportunities, or just to pay bills. (See Chapter 4, page 128.) To maintain this balance, a firm might need to increase borrowings or reduce loan repayments.

MANAGEMENT ISSUES IN FINANCIAL PLANNING

Financial plans and their use in business create a number of potential managerial problems. It's a good idea to be aware of these problems before you run into them at work.

The Financial Plan as a Set of Goals

The Macadam Company of Example 6.7 can be used to illustrate an important practical use of a financial plan. Look back at the way the ACP and the inventory turnover ratio have been used to construct next year's financial statements, and notice the large size of the forecast improvements. In essence, the ratios and the associated balance sheet accounts are set up as targets to be achieved by the responsible managers.

In most companies, executive pay is part salary and part bonus. In well-managed companies, executive bonuses are tied to the achievement of measurable goals like the ACP and inventory turnover in this example. In the Macadam Company, it's quite likely that the CFO's bonus will be in some part dependent on lowering the ACP to the planned level, and that the VP of manufacturing's bonus will depend on increasing the inventory turnover ratio.

Seen in this context, the financial plan becomes a tool with which to manage the company and motivate desirable performance. It's easy to identify several bonusable features and the responsible departments in the Macadam plan:

- 20% growth in revenue—marketing/sales
- Inventory turnover—manufacturing
- 53% cost ratio—manufacturing
- ACP—finance and marketing/sales
- Reduction in vendor complaints—finance
- Control cash balance—finance
- Overall profitability and cash flow—general manager and staff VPs
- Operating departments within planned expense levels—all departments

Inherent Conflicts

Stretch goals can lead to confusion. Is the plan a reliable prediction or an unreachable goal?

Financial plans are used as management goals all the time. A problem sometimes arises, however, when top management puts in what may be described as *stretch goals*. A stretch goal serves as a target toward which the organization strives, but isn't likely to be achieved.

In the Macadam example, inventory turnover is probably a stretch goal. Notice that the plan calls for a 67% improvement, from 3 times to 5 times. In most factories, that would be a Herculean achievement in one year. Top management probably wants the organization to work hard on turnover, but doesn't really expect it to achieve the goal in a year.

From the CFO

> A stretch goal can sometimes backfire in terms of motivation. Instead of stretching toward the goal, people may give up on it if they consider it impossible.
> Another problem arises if someone else uses the plan and assumes it's an accurate estimate of what's going to happen in the future.

To understand this issue, let's evaluate the cash flow implication of the assumption that inventory turnover will increase to 5.0. Notice that, in the statement of changes in working capital, the source of cash resulting from the decrease in inventory is $797,000. However, that's after a 20% volume increase. If there were no improvement in turnover, instead of shrinking, inventory would actually grow by $407,000 [($9,031/3) − $2,603]. That means the cash flow effect of the turnover assumption is a source of roughly $1.2 million.

Now suppose Macadam uses the plan's cash flow projection as a basis for arranging next year's bank borrowing. If the turnover assumption doesn't come true, the firm will have understated its borrowing requirements by up to $1.2 million. That means the arrangement it makes with the bank is unlikely to provide enough cash to get it through the year.

Obviously, the CFO should take a modified plan to the bank, or the original plan should be achievable.

Risk in Financial Planning in General

Let's pursue this idea a little further. We'll begin by re-examining Macadam's overall plan with an eye toward judging whether or not it's likely to come true. In doing that, it's important to keep in mind that what a plan says about a business's future flows directly from the assumptions made by the planners. Therefore, the impression conveyed may or may not be realistic.

Look back at Macadam's list of assumptions. Everything is marvellously positive: revenue is going to grow by a whopping 20%, the cost of production will decrease by 2% (that's a lot in an established factory), and asset management will be terrifically successful. We have to ask ourselves if all of these positive things are likely to come true without any offsetting negatives. The answer is generally no.

> The situation depicted for Macadam is typical of corporate business plans. Every-thing is routinely forecast to improve in the future, regardless of whether recent perfor-mance has been good or bad. The positive assumptions made by managements tend to be a combination of stretch planning and what might be called aggressive optimism. This is a condition in which people allow what they want to happen to overshadow their forecast of what's likely to happen.

For example, suppose a business operation is planning for next year after having had sales of $100 million and profits of $6 million last year. The chances are that the performance of the organization's top management is measured primarily by growth in revenue and profit. An "A" report card might be revenue of $120 million and profit of $8 million next year. In such a situa-tion, it is very common for top management to define its expectations about next year's perfor-mance in terms of the "A" report card. It is then likely to force the organization into a plan that shows those goals being met even if market conditions are such that the goals are unrealistic.

The practice is called **top-down planning** because top executives force a plan on the rest of the organization. Middle and lower-level managers often feel that such plans are unrealistic. The risk in financial planning is that a great many plans overstate achievable performance be-cause of the top-down phenomenon.

Excessive optimism in business planning can be a major problem because important oper-ating and investment decisions are based on the information in plans. If an optimistic future is projected, resources tend to be committed in ways that will take advantage of that success. If it doesn't materialize, there is generally considerable loss.

The issue can be stated another way. It's never quite clear whether a company's plan (for periods of a year or longer) is a candid statement of what's likely to happen in the future or rather a set of desirable goals. All plans are ultimately a little of each, but which idea predomi-nates and the extent of the diversion between the two is generally a bit of a mystery.

Underforecasting—The Other Extreme

The opposite phenomenon can also occur when people know their performance is going to be graded relative to a plan. Underforecasting sets up a goal that's easy to meet and ensures success in the future. The practice is especially common when department managers submit their ex-pense requirements as inputs to the planning process. The philosophy is "ask for more than you need, because you won't get everything you ask for." This is especially true in operational plan-ning where targets are set that are tied to compensation.

Bottom-up planning puts together the requests and forecasts of lower and middle man-agement without judgment by top-level executives. Bottom-up plans have a tendency to under-state achievable performance.

Stretch planning and *aggressive optimism* can lead to *unrealistic plans* that have little chance of coming true.

From the CFO

Top-down plans are forced on the organi-zation by manage-ment and are often *unrealistically optimistic.*

Bottom-up plans are consolidated from lower management's inputs, and tend to understate what the firm can do.

Underforecasting is a less serious problem in that it results in plans that are beaten by actual performance. That's a pleasant problem in comparison to significantly underperforming a widely published estimate.

The Ideal Process

Planning ideally combines top-down and bottom-up processes.

Ideally, the financial planning process is a combination of top-down and bottom-up elements. Healthy planning begins with a completely bottom-up pass at a plan to which top management applies its judgment in a give-and-take process. The end result is a realistic compromise that stretches the organization's abilities, but can be achieved.

In well-run companies, it's common for financial management to assume an important role in addressing the problem of unrealistic forecasting in either direction. Led by the CFO, the finance staff acts as a voice of reason in reviewing planning assumptions. Unrealistic assumptions should be challenged and sent back to the responsible departments for justification or revision.

Scenario Analysis—"What If-ing"

Scenario analysis. A business planning technique in which the implications of variations in planning assumptions are explored. Also known as "what if-ing."

Many companies address the risk issue through scenario analysis—producing a number of plans reflecting different scenarios, each of which is a variation on the assumptions underlying the plan. The term "what if-ing" means the same thing, analyzing what would happen if an assumption takes on one value rather than another.

In scenario analysis, assumptions can be varied singly or several can be changed at a time. In Example 6.7, Macadam's management might be concerned that the assumption of a

Insights ETHICS

Judgment Calls and Ethics in Business Planning

It's common for the planning system to put financial executives in uncomfortable ethical positions. Plans are vehicles for communications to outsiders and they are usually put together by the finance department. But outside communications are ultimately the responsibility of the chief executive officer (CEO). That means if the CEO doesn't like what a plan says, he can apply his "judgment" and tell outsiders something else.

Problems arise when CEOs use judgment to further their personal ends or just refuse to accept unpleasant realities. Chief financial officers (CFOs) get caught in the middle, they're supposed to have an overriding responsibility for truth and fairness in financial representations but they also have to stand up next to the CEO when the message is delivered and at least act as if they support every word.

Here's an illustration. Suppose the planning process at a division of a large corporation reveals that it's likely to lose market share and a great deal of money in the future. The parent company executives are expecting an updated plan at an upcoming meeting and, if given this information they'll likely replace the division's general manager if they think his strategy is responsible for the poor performance. On the other hand, if a falsely optimistic plan is presented, the current general manager and his policies will continue in place, but the eventual loss is likely to be much larger.

The general manager plans to present the optimistic version of the plan. The division CFO feels this constitutes

misleading corporate management. What is her ethical responsibility?

To appreciate this dilemma, it's important to understand that plans are, to some extent, matters of opinion. No one can say with certainty that the executive is proposing to lie. He's just supporting a planning position that most people would find very unrealistic if they knew all the details. The fact that it serves his own personal ends makes him suspect, but it doesn't prove he doesn't believe in the better plan. Optimistic people frequently believe what they want to in spite of overwhelming evidence to the contrary!

If the CFO insists on presenting the more likely plan herself, she'll be setting up a confrontation with her boss in front of senior management. That will probably destroy her relationship with the general manager forever. And she may not win. Remember that the head office put the general manager in charge because they valued his judgment and they may still do that in spite of strong evidence that he's wrong. The fact that the CFO may eventually be proven right doesn't help, because the damage will be done, and she'll be long gone by then.

On the other hand, if the CFO doesn't state her opinion, there's no doubt the optimistic plan will be accepted. That will probably mean deeper losses for the company, which might lead to closing the division and laying off its employees. At that time head office will probably want to know why the division's management team didn't see the problem coming.

What are the CFO's options? What would you do?

20% growth in revenue is too aggressive. It would then be appropriate to construct another plan based on the assumption of only 10% growth.[18]

On the other hand, there might be concern about several issues. Then a scenario could be constructed varying all of the questionable assumptions at once. For example, the implication of lower revenue growth coupled with a less significant improvement in asset management could be investigated. This might be achieved by constructing a plan based on a 15% revenue growth, an ACP of 75 days, and an inventory turnover ratio of 4.0.

Scenario analysis gives planners a feel for the impact of their assumptions not coming true. It produces a range of values within which the important results of a plan can be expected to occur.

We will talk about scenario analysis in the context of estimating cash flows for capital budgeting projects in Chapter 14 (page 511). The idea here is essentially the same, but the result is a complete financial plan rather than a single cash flow estimate.

Communication

Perhaps the biggest problem related to risk in planning is communication. A business unit is expected to have a financial plan that management is confident it will achieve. Holding more than a brief discussion with outsiders about how likely the plan is to come true casts doubt on management's confidence in its own ability to steer the company. As a result, a single plan tends to be published with the attendant risks we've been discussing.

Financial Planning and Computers

Today, virtually all financial planning is done with the aid of computers. It's important to understand what computers do for planning and what they don't do.

Computers help us create plans once we've made judgments about the underlying business assumptions, but they don't help us with those judgments. It's very important to realize that the heart and substance of financial planning lies in making assumptions, not in cranking out numbers. Hence computers have made us quicker, but not necessarily better planners.

What if-ing. See Scenario analysis.

Some companies plan for several *scenarios* representing *variations* in their *assumptions* about the future.

Computers make planning *quicker* and more thorough, but *don't improve the judgments* at the heart of the process.

SUMMARY

1 Financial planning is a critical part of the business planning process, whether formal or informal. Planning can consume enormous amounts of managerial time and attention. Managers need to recognize this and use plans to assist them in reaching the operating and strategic goals of the company. Planning helps identify potential problems before they occur.

Depending on the size of the firm, the business plan can comprise four basic documents: strategic, operational, budget, and forecasts, or all four can be combined into one working document.

2 Financial plans usually start with projecting sales and forecasting what the company needs to do to support those sales, as well as whether to finance them with internal or external financing.

3 All financial plans run into the debt/interest planning problem. To complete the income statement, we need the interest figure; however, in order to determine the interest, we need to know the level of debt.

4 The percentage of sales approach assumes financial statement items vary directly with sales while complicated plans also incorporate capital plans, operational changes, and the like.

---

[18] It's important to realize that many assumptions are interrelated, so changing one implies some change in others. This is especially true of revenue, which tends to drive the whole plan. For example, the assumption of an improved cost ratio in the Macadam example is probably partially dependent on spreading overhead over the larger production volume implied by the revenue growth assumption. Therefore, changing the revenue assumption is likely to require modifying the cost ratio improvement assumption to a less aggressive figure.

5 Sustainable growth is the growth in equity resulting from profits retained by the company. If the company wants to keep its debt/equity ratio constant, it will have to borrow as equity increases through retained earnings.

6 The financial plan is often used as a set of goals; however, setting the goals too high or too low can cause conflicts between upper and lower-level management. As the plans are often used to judge performance, managers may be tempted to downplay certain components of the plan or be overly optimistic about other components that may result in poor decisions being made.

KEY TERMS

KEY FORMULAS

(6.1)
$$\text{Forecast total assets} = \text{Forecast current liabilities} + \text{Forecast debt} + \text{Last year's shareholders' equity} - \text{Forecast dividends} + (1-T)[\text{EBIT} - \text{Int\%}(0.5)(\text{Last year's debt} + \text{Forecast debt})]$$

(6.2)
$$\text{Forecast total assets} - \text{Forecast current liabilities} - \text{Last year's shareholders' equity} + \text{Forecast dividends} = \text{Forecast debt} + (1-T)[\text{EBIT} - \text{Int\%}(0.5)(\text{Last year's debt} + \text{Forecast debt})]$$

(6.3)
$$\text{External funding requirement} = \text{Growth in assets} - \text{Growth in current liabilities} - \text{Earnings retained}$$

(6.4)
$$\text{Growth in assets} = g \times \text{Assets}_{\text{this year}}$$

(6.5)
$$\text{Growth in current liabilities} = g \times \text{Current liabilities}_{\text{this year}}$$

(6.6)
$$\text{NI}_{\text{next year}} = \text{ROS} \times (1+g)\text{Sales}_{\text{this year}}$$

(6.7)
$$\text{Earnings retained} = (1-d)\text{ROS} \times (1+g)\text{Sales}_{\text{this year}}$$

(6.8)
$$\text{EFR} = g[\text{Assets}_{\text{this year}} - \text{Current liabilities}_{\text{this year}} - \text{NI}(1-d)] - \text{NI}(1-d)$$

(6.9a)
$$g_s = \frac{\text{NI}(1-d)}{\text{Shareholders' equity}}$$

(6.9b)
$$g_s = \text{ROE}(1-d)$$

(6.10)
$$g_s = (1-d) \times \frac{\text{NI}}{\text{Sales}} \times \frac{\text{Sales}}{\text{Assets}} \times \frac{\text{Assets}}{\text{Equity}}$$

QUESTIONS

1. "A financial plan has to be either a prediction about the future or a statement of goals; it can't be both." Explain this statement and comment on its validity.

2. Why is it important that physical assumptions precede financial results in the planning process? For example, what's wrong with assuming you want a business that sells $50 million a year earning a profit of $5 million, and then building a revenue and cost plan to fit those goals?

3. Why is planning for a new business harder than planning for an established operation? In which do you have to make more assumptions? Why? What implicit assumption provides a shortcut in one situation?

4. How are planning assumptions reflected in projected financial statements? Is there a standard computational procedure for incorporating assumptions into planned numbers? What's the difference between simple, estimated plans and more complex, precise plans? Can a plan be precise, complex, and inaccurate at the same time? How?

5. Briefly describe the debt/interest planning problem and the approach that leads to its solution. (Use a few brief sentences. Don't list the procedural steps or give a numerical example.)

6. "Financial planning is no longer a problem in business because of the advent of personal computers. Armed with a PC and the appropriate software, anyone can do a plan for even the largest and most complicated company." Evaluate this statement.

7. You're a new member of the planning staff within the finance department at Bertram Enterprises, a large manufacturer of household goods. The firm creates an annual operating plan and a long-range plan every year. You've just received a note from the CFO asking you to help him prepare for a meeting with the firm's investment dealers to discuss issuing new securities in the future. The note asks you to prepare an estimate of the company's funding needs and suggests that you "start with" the most recent annual and long-range plans. You're confused by the term "start with," since the plans clearly indicate future funding needs. What might the CFO be getting at, and how would you approach the assignment?

8. Comment on the value of the formula (EFR) approach to estimating funding requirements. Could it create more problems than it solves?

9. The following issues are related to the accuracy and reliability of financial plans. Explain the process/issues related to each.
   - Top-down versus bottom-up planning
   - Plans as statements of goals versus plans as predictions of what's going to happen
   - Planning assumptions
   - Aggressive optimism versus underforecasting
   - Scenario analysis

10. Contrast planning cash requirements, especially borrowing, using the statement of cash flows derived from forecast financial statements with a cash budget. Which is likely to be more useful in running a finance department?

11. You are developing next year's financial plan for Ajax Inc., a medium-sized manufacturing company that's currently operating at 80% of factory's capacity. The firm is launching a sales promotion that's expected to generate a sudden 20% increase in revenues starting at the beginning of the new year. Unlike current sales, which are virtually all on credit, approximately 50% of the new business will be paid in cash. No changes are planned in the company's operations other than acquiring the resources necessary to support the

sales growth. Develop some reasonable planning assumptions for the following balance sheet line items and explain your reasoning for each. (*Hint*: Which balance sheet items will be affected by an increase in sales proportionately or less than proportionately? Assume any additional cash needed is borrowed.)

- Cash
- Accounts receivable
- Inventory
- Gross capital assets
- Shareholders' equity
- Accounts payable
- Accruals (wage)
- Debt
- Accumulated amortization

Business Analysis

1. Ed Olachuk has always wanted to run his own restaurant. He worked part-time in the food service business during high school and college and has worked for a large restaurant chain since graduating from college four years ago. He's now ready to open a franchised family-style restaurant. However, a large investment is required to get started. Ed has saved some money but will also have to secure a substantial loan.

   Fortunately, Ed's old college roommate, Joe Dixon, is now a loan officer with the local bank. Besides being a good friend, Joe knows that Ed is a stable, hard-working businessman and an excellent credit risk.

   Ed is now meeting with Joe to apply for the loan. After exchanging pleasantries, Joe asks to see Ed's business plan. In response, Ed tells him all about the idea and shows him the written information from the franchisor, which Joe glances at briefly.

   Joe listens politely, leans back in his chair, and says, "Ed, I've known you for years. I'm sure this is a great idea, and that you'll make a terrific restaurateur, but we can't even begin to consider a loan until we see a fully developed business plan that looks at least five years into the future."

   a. Why is Joe (the bank) insisting that Ed prepare a business plan?
      i. What will it show the bank?
      ii. List some specific concerns the bank might have that a plan would answer outside the financial section.
      iii. List several concerns that the financial plan might answer for the bank.
      iv. Why is the bank insisting on such a long planning horizon? Does that imply the bank is looking for a strategic plan?

   b. What will preparing a business plan do for Ed?
      i. Before he gets started?
      ii. After he gets started?
      iii. What will he learn by doing the financial plan?

   c. What kind of thinking is the bank looking for in Ed's plan? That is, should the plan be strategic or operational or short term?

2. You're the CFO of the Ramkin Company, which makes and sells electronic equipment. The firm was originally an independent business, but was acquired by the larger BigTech Inc. 10 years ago and is now operated as a division. BigTech has an elaborate planning system requiring all divisions to produce a strategic plan and an annual operating plan once a year, a budget each quarter, monthly cash forecasts, and several quick forecasts near the end of each quarter.

   The forecasts are done primarily by the finance department and don't require much of anyone else's time. However, the strategic plan takes a good deal of executive effort, while budgets and the annual operating plan demand a great deal of management effort at all levels.

It's 8:00 a.m. on a day in mid-October, and the executive team is about to start a meeting to kick off the preparation of the annual operating plan for the next calendar year. As the meeting convenes, Charlie Gogetter, the VP of marketing, is clearly upset. He takes the floor and makes the following statement.

I'm tired of spending all this time on these silly plans! We just finished a strategic plan in June that must've taken a month of my time while the Western sales region got itself into big trouble. We also did a third-quarter budget in June, and a fourth-quarter budget in September. Now we're starting another plan that will probably tie up half of my sales managers' time until Christmas.

On top of that it seems whenever we're not planning, we're putting together reviews comparing actual performance to plan. Before we were acquired by BigTech, we hardly ever planned and we did just fine! It's true we're a lot larger and more complex now, but I don't think we can spend this much time planning rather than doing!

I suggest that the CFO [he gestures toward you] be assigned to throw together something we can submit to BigTech, and that the rest of us get on with our work.

Other members of the group to some extent share Charlie's feelings, and his comments have created some unrest among the executive team about the company's management style. Prepare a response to his statement and proposal. Don't rule out the possibility that BigTech is overdoing planning.

3. You've just been hired as CFO of the Gatsby Corp., a new company in the high-tech computer business. Shortly after your arrival you were amazed to find that the firm does virtually no planning. An extensive business plan was put together when it was started with venture capital eight years ago, and revised when another round of funding was needed four years later. Other than on those occasions, no planning seems to have been done at all.

The firm was founded by its entrepreneur president, Harvey Gatsby, based on a new technical product he'd invented. Initial demand for the gadget was overwhelming and the firm grew rapidly, if chaotically, until about a year ago, when competitive devices started to affect its business. The following conditions exist today:
   - Sales of the original product are beginning to decline.
   - The organization seems to have a number of people and departments whose function and value aren't clear.
   - The engineering department is pursuing several new developments that have commercial possibilities, but progress has been haphazard and no one seems to have thought through how any money will be made from the ideas.
   - Additional funding is required to get any new products that might be developed to market. Harvey has suggested that you dust off the old business plan for another run at investors.

You feel that the company is in real danger, and that the source of the problem is that management hasn't done any real forward planning in years. In your opinion, the first step toward recovery is to install a competent planning system. Write a memo to Harvey outlining your concerns and suggestions. Include the following:
   a. The problem—why the happy chaos of the past may be about to come to an end, and what that may mean.
   b. How management's approach has to change if the firm is to survive (i.e., it will have to do a good deal of forward thinking and structured planning).
   c. A statement of how planning systems differ between small and larger companies.
   d. The benefits Gatsby can expect to realize by planning in a careful, structured way.
   e. The need for a well-defined financial plan.

PROBLEMS

1. The Libris Publishing Company had revenues of $200 million this year and expects a 50% growth to $300 million next year. Costs and expenses other than interest are forecast at $250 million. The firm currently has assets of $280 million and current liabilities of $40 million. Its interest-bearing debt to equity ratio is 3:1. (That is capital, ignoring current liabilities, is 75% long-term debt and 25% shareholders' equity.) It pays 12% interest on its debt, and is subject to federal and provincial income taxes at a total effective rate of 39%.

   Libris expects assets and current liabilities to grow at 40%, 10% less than the revenue growth rate. The company plans to pay dividends of $10 million next year.
   a. What is the planned interest-bearing debt to equity ratio at the end of next year?
   b. Do these results indicate a problem?

2. The Winthrop Company is constructing a five-year plan. The firm's ACP is currently 90 days, while its inventory turnover ratio is 3 times based on COGS. The company has forecast aggressive revenue growth along with efficiency improvements in manufacturing and credit and collections as follows. (Year 0 is the current year.)

Year	0	1	2	3	4	5
Revenue ($000)	$50.0	$57.5	$66.0	$76.0	$87.5	$100.0
Cost ratio	60%	59%	58%	57%	56%	55%
ACP (days)	90	70	60	50	45	40
Inventory turnover	3×	4×	5×	6×	6.5×	7×

   For each planned year:
   a. Calculate the COGS.
   b. Calculate the A/R balance at year-end.
   c. Calculate the inventory balance at year-end.

3. The Eagle Feather Fabric Company expects to complete the current year with the following financial results ($000).

INCOME STATEMENT		BALANCE SHEET	
Revenue	$ 36,100	ASSETS	
COGS	14,440	Cash	$ 1,000
GM	$ 21,660	Accounts receivable	5,000
Expenses	12,635	Inventory	2,888
EBIT	$ 9,025	Current assets	$ 8,888
Interest (11%)	625	Net capital assets	7,250
EBT	$ 8,400	Total assets	$ 16,138
Tax (42%)	3,528	LIABILITIES & SHAREHOLDERS' EQUITY	
NI	$ 4,872	Accounts payable	$ 1,550
		Accruals	530
		Current liabilities	$ 2,080
		Long-term debt	5,598
		Shareholders' equity	8,460
		TOTAL L&SE	$ 16,138

   Forecast next year using a modified percentage of sales method assuming no dividends are paid and no new shares are sold, along with the following:

a. A 20% growth in sales and a 40% growth in net capital assets.

b. A 15% growth in sales and COGS with a 10% growth in expenses and a 20% growth in net capital assets. (Negative debt means the business will generate more cash than is currently owed.)

4. Assume we're at the end of "this year" planning "next year's" financial statements. Calculate the following using indirect planning assumptions as indicated.

a. Sales are forecast to be $58,400,000. Management wants to plan for a 45-day ACP next year. What ending receivables balance should be planned for next year?

b. What ending inventory should be planned if revenue is expected to be $457,000 and the cost ratio is 53% (cost of goods sold as a percentage of revenue) and management wants to forecast an inventory turnover of 5 times?

c. Normal credit terms from suppliers request payment within 30 days. In an effort to conserve cash, management has decided to pay in 50 days. Nearly all payables come from purchases of inventory. Materials make up 60% of the cost of goods sold. Next year's revenue is forecast to be $378 million. The firm's cost ratio is expected to be 56%. What figure should be included in next year's ending balance sheet for accounts payable?

5. Lap Dogs Inc. is planning for next year and has the following summarized results so far ($000):

Income Statement		Balance Sheet		
			This Year	**Next Year**
EBIT	236	Assets	582	745
Interest	?	Current Liabilities	63	80
EBT	?	Debt	275	?
Income Tax	?	Shareholders' equity	244	?
NI	?	Total Liab & Equity	582	745

The firm pays interest of 12% on all borrowing and is subject to an overall tax rate of 38%. It paid interest of $20,000 this year and plans a $75,000 dividend next year. Complete Lap Dog's forecast of next year's financial statements. Round all calculations to the nearest $1,000.

6. Fleming, Inc. had a dividend payout ratio of 25% this year, which resulted in a payout of $80,000 in dividends. Return on sales (ROS) was 8% this year and is expected to increase to 9% next year. If Fleming expects to have $305,100 available from next year's retained earnings, what percentage increase is it forecasting in revenues?

7. The Dalmation Corporation expects the following summarized financial results this year ($000).

INCOME STATEMENT		BALANCE SHEET	
Revenue	$10,500	ASSETS	
Cost/expenses	9,100	Current assets	$ 5,500
Tax	560	Net capital assets	6,900
NI	840	Total assets	$ 12,400
Dividends	420	LIABILITIES & SHAREHOLDERS' EQUITY	
		Current	$ 320
		Long-term debt	5,080
		Shareholders' equity	7,000
		Total L&SE	$ 12,400

Use the EFR relation to estimate Dalmation's external funding requirements under the following conditions.
   a. Sales growth of 15%
   b. Sales growth of 20% and a reduction in the dividend payout ratio to 25%
   c. Sales growth of 25%, elimination of dividends, and a 4% improvement in ROS to 12%

8. Lytle Trucking projects a $3.2 million EBIT next year. The firm's marginal tax rate is 40%, and it currently has $8 million in long-term debt with an interest rate of 8%. Management is projecting a requirement for additional assets costing $1.5 million and no change in current liabilities, and plans to maintain a 30% dividend payout ratio. Any additional borrowing required to fund next year's asset growth will carry a 7% interest rate. Lytle does not plan on issuing additional shares next year. Using the EFR concept rather than the EFR equation, develop an algebraic formula of your own to compute the additional debt needed to support an asset growth of $1.5 million. (*Hint*: Start with the idea that Additional debt = New assets − Internally generated funds. Then write an algebraic expression for internally generated funds based on the income statement from EBIT to NI and the dividend payout ratio.)

9. The Bubar Building Co. has the following current financial results ($000).

Revenue	$ 45,000	Assets	$ 37,500
NI	$ 3,600	Shareholders' equity	$ 28,580
Dividends	$ 1,800		

On the average, other building companies pay about one-quarter of their earnings in dividends, earn about six cents on the sales dollar, carry assets worth about six months of sales, and finance one-third of their assets with debt.

Use the sustainable growth rate concept to analyze Bubar's inherent ability to grow without selling new shareholders' equity versus that of an average building company. Identify weak areas and suggest further analyses.

10. Broxholme Industries has sales of $40 million, shareholders' equity totalling $27.5 million, and an ROS of 12%. The sustainable growth rate has been calculated at 10.9%.
   a. What is the company's net income?
   b. What dividend payout ratio was assumed in this calculation?

11. The Cambridge Cartage Company has partially completed its forecast of next year's financial statements as follows.

Cambridge Cartage Company
Financial Plan ($000)

Income Statement		Balance Sheet		
				Next Year
	Next Year		**Beginning**	**Ending**
Revenue	$ 17,220	ASSETS		
Cost/Expenses	14,120	Total Assets	$ 12,540	$ 18,330
EBIT	$ 3,100	LIABILITIES & SHAREHOLDERS' EQUITY		
Interest	?	Current liabilities	$ 410	$ 680
EBIT	?	Long-term debt	5,630	?
Tax	?	Shareholders' equity	6,500	?
NI	?	Total L&SE	$ 12,540	$ 18,330

The firm pays interest at 10% on all borrowings and pays a combined provincial and federal tax rate of 40%. Complete the forecast income statement and balance sheet. Begin by guessing at interest expense as 10% of beginning debt.

12. Larime Corp. is forecasting 20X5 near the end of 20X4. The estimated year-end financial statements and a worksheet for the forecast are shown below.

Larime Corp. Projected Income Statement ($000)

	20X4		20X5	
	$	%	$	%
Revenue	$ 245,622	100.0		100.0
COGS	142,461	58.0	___	___
Gross margin	$ 103,161	42.0		
Expenses	$ 49,124	20.0	___	___
EBIT	$ 54,037	22.0		
Interest (12%)	9,642	3.9	___	___
EBT	$ 44,395	18.1		
Income tax (43%)	19,090	7.8	___	___
NI	$ 25,305	10.3		

Larime Corp. Projected Balance Sheet ($000)

ASSETS	20X4	20X5	LIABILITIES & SHAREHOLDERS' EQUITY	20X4	20X5
Current assets	$ 178,106		Current liabilities	$ 85,700	
Capital assets	142,128	___	Long-term debt	78,178	
Total	$ 320,234		Shareholders' equity	156,356	___
			Total	$ 320,234	

Management expects the following next year:
- An 8% increase in revenue.
- Price cutting will cause the cost ratio (COGS/Sales) to increase by 1% (of sales) from its current level.
- Expenses will increase at a rate that is three-quarters of that of sales.
- The current accounts will increase proportionately with sales.
- Net capital assets will increase by $5 million.
- All interest will be paid at 12%.
- Federal and provincial income taxes will be paid at a combined rate of 43%.

Make a forecast of Larime's complete income statement and balance sheet. Work to the nearest thousand dollars.

13. The Owl Corporation is planning for 20X2. The firm expects to have the following financial results in 20X1 ($000).

Income Statement

	$	%
Revenue	37,483	100.0
COGS	14,807	39.5
Gross margin	22,676	60.5
Expenses	17,721	47.3
EBIT	4,955	13.2
Interest	1,380	3.7
EBT	3,575	9.5
Income tax	1,430	3.8
NI	2,145	5.7

Balance Sheet

Assets		Liabilities and Shareholder' Equity	
Cash	1,571	Accts pay	1,388
Accts rec	6,247	Accruals	985
Inventory	2,468	Curr liab	2,373
Curr assets	10,286		
Capital assets		Capital	
Gross	25,608	Long-term debt	12,390
Acc amort	(14,936)	Sh. equity	6,195
	10,672		18,585
Total Assets	20,958	Total L&SE	20,958

Management has made the following planning assumptions:

Income Statement
- Revenue will grow by 10%.
- The cost ratio will improve to 37% of revenues.
- Expenses will be held to 44% of revenues.

Balance Sheet
- The year-end cash balance will be $1.5 million.
- The ACP will improve to 40 days from the current 60.
- Inventory turnover will improve to 7 times from 6 times.
- Trade payables will continue to be paid in 45 days.
- New capital spending will be $5 million.
- Newly purchased assets will be amortized over 10 years using the straight-line method, taking a full year's amortization in the first year.
- The company's payroll will be $13.7 million at the end of 20X2.
- No dividends or new common share sales are planned.

The following facts are also available:
- The firm pays 10% interest on all of its debt.
- The combined income tax rate is 40%.
- The only significant payables come from inventory purchases, and product cost is 75% purchased materials.
- Existing assets will be depreciated by $1,727,000 next year.

- The only significant accrual is payroll. The last day of 20X2 will be one week after a payday.

Forecast Owl's income statement and balance sheet for 20X2. Round all calculations to the nearest $1,000 and use a 365-day year.

14. The Haverly Company expects to finish the current year with the following financial results, and is developing its annual plan for next year.

Haverly Company Income Statement This Year ($000)		
	$	**%**
Revenue	$ 73,820	100.0
COGS	31,743	43.0
Gross margin	$ 42,077	57.0
Expenses		
Marketing	$ 17,422	23.6
Engineering	7,087	9.6
Finance & administrative	7,603	10.3
Total expenses	$ 32,112	43.5
EBIT	$ 9,965	13.5
Interest	2,805	3.8
EBT	$ 7,160	9.7
Income tax	3,007	4.1
NI	$ 4,153	5.6

Haverly Company Balance Sheet This Year ($000)			
ASSETS		**LIABILITIES AND SHAREHOLDERS' EQUITY**	
Cash	$ 8,940	Accounts payable	$ 1,984
Accounts receivable	12,303	Accruals	860
Inventory	7,054	Current liabilities	$ 2,844
Current assets	$ 28,297	Long-term debt	$ 22,630
Capital assets		Shareholders' equity	
Gross	$ 65,223	Common shares	18,500
Accumulated		Retained earnings	25,559
amortization	(23,987)	Total Shareholders' equity	$ 44,059
Net	$ 41,236	Total L&SE	$ 69,533
Total assets	$ 69,533		

Facts
- Payables are almost entirely due to inventory purchases and can be estimated through COGS, which is approximately 45% purchased material.
- Currently owned assets will amortize an additional $1,840,000 next year.
- There are two balance sheet accruals. The first is for unpaid wages. The current payroll of $32 million is expected to grow by 12% next year. The closing date of the year will be six working days after a payday. The second accrual is an estimate of the cost of purchased items that have arrived in inventory, but for which vendor invoices have not yet been received. This materials accrual is generally about 10% of the payables balance at year-end.
- The combined provincial and federal income tax rate is 42%.
- Interest on current and future borrowing will be at a rate of 12%.

Planning Assumptions
Income Statement Items

1. Revenue will grow by 13% with no change in product mix. Competitive pressure, however, is expected to force some reductions in pricing.
2. The pressure on prices will result in a 1.5% increase in the next year's cost ratio.
3. Spending in the marketing department is considered excessive and will be held to 21% of revenue next year.
4. Because of a major development project, expenses in the engineering department will increase by 20%.
5. Finance and administration expenses will increase by 6%.
   Assets and Liabilities
6. An enhanced cash management system will reduce cash balances by 10%.
7. The ACP will be reduced by 15 days. (Calculate the current value to arrive at the target.)
8. The inventory turnover ratio (COGS/inventory) will decrease by 0.5 times.
9. Capital spending is expected to be $7 million. The average life of the assets acquired is 10 years. The firm uses straight-line amortization.
10. Bills are currently paid in 50 days. Plans are to shorten that to 40 days.
11. A dividend totalling $1.5 million will be paid next year. No new shares will be sold.

Develop next year's financial plan for Haverly on the basis of these assumptions and last year's financial statements. Include a projected income statement, balance sheet, and statement of cash flows.

15. Blue & Noble is a small law firm that does all of its business through billings (no cash sales). Historically, the firm has collected 40% of its revenue in the month of billing, 50% during the first month after billing, and 8% during the second month after billing; 2% typically remains uncollectible. Revenue projections for the coming year are $47,500 for January and $50,000 for February. Cash receipts of $50,600 are expected in March. What revenues are projected for March?

16. Crabby Cats Inc. has been asked by its banker to provide a cash budget for the upcoming quarter in support of a loan application. Crabby Cats has forecast, based on its performance last year and the best estimates for this year, that its revenues will be as follows ($000):

	Oct	Nov	Dec	Jan	Feb	Mar	Apr
Sales	$700	$840	$900	$400	$500	$400	$500

The results for October through December are actual, January through April are estimates.

Historically Crabby collects its receivables according to the following pattern:

Months after Sale	1	2	3
Percentage collected	60%	30%	10%

Crabby orders inventory one month in advance of sales. Materials costs are 55% of sales. Invoices are paid 30 days after receipt of materials (so for this problem, the payments are made the month after ordering).

The firm uses a dedicated labour pool to meet its production needs so payroll and many employees take unpaid leaves during January to March. The company estimates its payroll costs for these three months will be $180 per month. Other expenses, such as rent, insurance, and utilities are estimated to be a constant $70 per month. Crabby makes a contribution to the employees' pension fund every February. Management estimates that this year the company will need to make a contribution of $110. The last installment payment on a new addition to the plant is due at the end of March in the amount of $150.

At the end of December, Crabby had a short-term loan of $528 outstanding. Monthly interest is 0.75% of the previous month-end balance.

a. Prepare Crabby's cash budget for January, February, and March.

b. Assume that at December 31 the balance for accounts receivable was $1,306, for inventory was $220, and for accounts payable was $220.

Calculate the balances that would be recorded on the March 31 balance sheet for each of these accounts.

17. Lapps Inc. makes a gift product that sells best during the holiday season. Retailers stock up in the fall so Lapps's sales are largest in October and November and drop dramatically in December. The firm expects the following revenue pattern for the second half of this year ($000). The third-quarter figures are actual results while the fourth quarter is a projection.

	Jul	Aug	Sep	Oct	Nov	Dec
Revenue	$5,500	$6,000	$7,500	$8,000	$9,500	$4,000

Historically Lapps collects its receivables according to the following pattern:

Months after Sale	1	2	3
Percentage collected	60%	30%	9%

The firm offers a 2% prompt payment discount, which is taken by about half of the customers that pay in the first month.

Lapps receives inventory one month in advance of sales. The cost of material is 40% of revenue. Invoices are paid 45 days after receipt of material.

The firm uses temporary labour to meet its seasonal production needs so payroll can be estimated at 35% of the current month's sales. Other expenses are a constant $1,800 per month. A $700 tax payment is scheduled for November and an expansion project will require cash of $500 in October and $800 in December. Lapps has a $6,000 short-term loan outstanding at the end of September. Monthly interest is 1% of the previous month-end balance.

a. Prepare Lapps's cash budget for the fourth quarter.

b. Assume that at September 30 the balance for accounts receivable was $10,450, for inventory was $3,200, and for accounts payable was $4,700.

Calculate the balances that would be recorded on the December 31 balance sheet for each of these accounts, assuming that Lapps orders $3,000 worth of inventory in December.

PART 3

Capital Markets and Securities

Chapter 7

The Financial System and Interest

Learning Objectives

1 Explain the relationship between saving and investing.

2 Discuss the role of brokers, exchanges, and over-the-counter (OTC) markets.

3 Explain the relationship between interest and the stock market.

4 Describe the components of interest rates.

For many investors, placing an order online is routine. However, it wasn't long ago that all orders were executed by open outcry on a trading floor (or pit). It might sound romantic, but was it really efficient?

What about the bigger question of investing in debt or equity—how are investors and borrowers brought together in such a large marketplace and what effect do changes in the economy have on this market?

THE FINANCIAL SYSTEM

Financial markets are where buyers and sellers of financial assets meet. Firms that need money issue securities, usually shares or bonds, which are sold to individuals. Consumers buy the securities with their savings, and firms use the proceeds to do their projects.

Consumers are said to *invest* in the securities, which are expected to generate a *return* on (as well as the return of) the money invested in their purchase. That return comes in the form of interest on bonds or dividends on shares along with any price appreciation on these investments.

Financial markets provide a conduit for the transfer of savings from the consumption sector (consumer households) to the production sector (firms producing goods and services).

Financial markets connect buyers and sellers of financial assets.

When the production sector uses this money it is said to be *investing* in projects, enterprises, and assets. Hence, economists say that *savings equals investment* in the economy.[1]

Financial markets are extremely important to the health of an economy. Their role and function will be a major focus of our study in this book.

Raising and Spending Money in Business

We can think of a firm as spending two kinds of money. One kind is the day-to-day funds that come from normal profits and are used to support routine activities. The other kind is the large sums occasionally needed to support major projects and get businesses started. These funds are typically raised by selling financial assets, not from operating funds. Firms more frequently raise that money as needed through financial markets.

If the money for a project is raised by borrowing, we say that the project is *debt financed*. When the money comes from the sale of common shares or from the firm's earnings, we say that the project is *equity financed*.

Term

The word "term" refers to the length of time between the present and the end or *term*ination of something. Both financial investments and physical projects have terms. A long-term project is one that will take a long time to complete. A long-term loan is one that doesn't have to be repaid in full for several years. The word "maturity" is also used to indicate the term of a loan. Debt *matures* on the day it is to be repaid.

Debt financing may be either long or short term depending on the length of time allowed until it has to be paid back. *Short term* generally means less than a year, *intermediate term* is one to five years, and *long term* is more than five years. People frequently leave out the intermediate-term concept and just think of long- and short-term debt as being more or less than one year.

Shares have an indefinite term in that they have no specified repayment date. Therefore, they're thought of as very long-term financing.

The projects we talked about in the Raising and Spending Money in Business section tend to be long term, like getting businesses started or buying capital assets. It's common practice to match the term of a project or asset with the term of the financing that pays for it. For example, funding for a project expected to take 10 years shouldn't need to be repaid in much less than 10 years. The practice is called *maturity matching*, which we introduced in Chapter 4 (page 124).

Maturity matching: A project's duration should match the term of financing that supports it.

Financial Markets

Financial markets are classified in several ways. We'll discuss classifications with respect to term and purpose.

Capital Markets

Money acquired for long periods is referred to as *capital*, and the financial markets that deal with it are known as capital markets. They trade in shares and in debt securities having terms longer than one year.

Capital markets deal in long-term debt and shares.

Money Markets

Markets in which short-term debt is traded are called money markets. They play an important role in setting interest rates for the rest of the economy, which we'll get into later in the chapter.

Money markets deal in short-term debt.

---

1 Notice that the term "invest" seems to have two slightly different meanings. Individuals are said to invest in financial assets, while firms invest in production facilities and equipment. What economists actually mean when they say savings equals investment is that investment by consumers in financial assets (savings) equals investment by companies in the means of production.

In business, most of the money that supports day-to-day operations is generated by sales. However, firms do borrow short term to cover temporary operating shortages. Most of the time, short-term corporate borrowing is done from banks, but there are financial markets that deal in short-term debt instruments[2] known as *notes, bills,* and *commercial paper.*

The federal government is active in issuing short-term debt, such as Treasury bills.

Primary and Secondary Markets

The basic purpose of financial markets is to facilitate the flow of funds from the saving public to the production sector for investment in business projects. However, most of what goes on in the largest and best known markets has little to do with that original transfer.

Funds are actually transferred from individual investors to companies only when securities are issued and purchased for the first time. Immediately after that first sale, securities belong to individual investors who may or may not choose to retain them permanently. In most cases, investors hold onto securities for a while but eventually sell them to others. Security sales subsequent to the first one are *between investors* and don't involve the issuing firm at all.

The initial sale of a security is a **primary market** transaction. Subsequent sales between investors are in the **secondary market**.

The first sale of a security, in which the money proceeds go to the issuing company, is called a **primary market** transaction. Subsequent sales of the security, between investors, are called **secondary market** transactions. The vast majority of transactions in traditional financial markets like the stock market are secondary. Without secondary markets companies would not be able to find willing buyers for their securities.

From the CFO

> *Corporate financial managers are concerned about secondary stock market transactions even though there's no immediate cash impact on their companies. The secondary market sets the level of a share's price and therefore influences how much can be raised in future issues. In addition, senior managers' compensation is usually tied to the company's share price, and that tends to generate an intense interest in the secondary market.*

Direct and Indirect Transfers, Financial Intermediaries

Primary market transactions, which transfer money from individual investors to companies, can occur directly or indirectly through a financial intermediary. These transfers of funds are illustrated in Figure 7.1. Let's consider the direct method first.

In a direct transfer, an investor simply buys the security of a company. That kind of transfer is shown in Figure 7.1a, but it's a rare occurrence. Firms don't usually market new securities to the public by themselves. Rather, they use the services of an investment dealer, an organization that helps market new securities.

An investment dealer helps companies market their securities.

The investment dealer typically lines up investors interested in buying a new issue beforehand, and functions as a broker bringing buyers and sellers together. A direct transfer through such an organization is illustrated in Figure 7.1b. The transfer is direct because, even though the investment dealer may take temporary possession of the securities, it actually just passes them through to the buyer.

A **financial intermediary** sells shares in itself and invests the funds collected on behalf of its investors.

The indirect transfer is illustrated in Figure 7.1c. Although the diagram looks similar to 7.1b, something very different is taking place. In an indirect transfer, a financial intermediary collects money from many individuals, pools it, and then makes investments with it. The securities purchased are not passed through to the individual investors. Instead, the financial intermediary holds on to those securities and gives the individual investors a *security of its own.* That is, it gives them some kind of claim upon itself.

A *mutual fund* is a good example. It takes money from many individual investors and uses it to buy a portfolio of shares and bonds. (A portfolio is a collection of financial assets.) Each investor receives a number of *shares or units in the fund* proportionate to the size of his or her investment, but none of the individual shares and bonds from the portfolio.

---

2 The term "financial instrument" is another expression for a security or a document evidencing a debt.

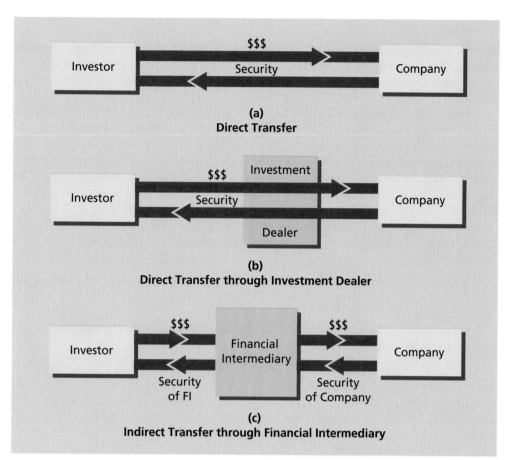

FIGURE 7.1
Transfer of Funds
from Investors to
Businesses

The important point is that the portfolio is owned *collectively* by individuals who have invested in the fund, but no one can identify any particular share or bond as his or her own. An important result of this arrangement is that the fund's management controls the pooled resources of many people, which often amounts to a vast sum of money. As a result, funds have a great deal of influence in financial markets.

Mutual funds and similar financial intermediaries are called institutional investors and play a major role in today's financial markets. They own more than one-quarter of the shares listed on the major exchanges but make about three-quarters of the trades. That makes them very influential in setting prices and trends in the secondary market.

Here are some other kinds of financial intermediaries.

Pension funds receive the retirement contributions of workers and employers, and invest the money in shares, bonds, and real estate. Employees own pension accounts representing their proportionate share of the fund assets.

Insurance companies collect premiums from customers and invest the money to provide a pool of assets from which to pay claims.

Banks receive deposits from individuals and make loans to clients. The bank's portfolio of financial assets is its loan portfolio, while depositors' accounts represent claims on those assets.

Institutional investor. A business organization that buys and sells securities. Generally a fund of some kind, such as a mutual fund or a pension fund that invests the pooled money of its clients.

A detailed history of the TSX can be found at http://www.tsx.com/en/pdf/TSXHistory.pdf.

THE STOCK MARKET AND STOCK EXCHANGES

We briefly described the stock market in Chapter 1. In this section, we'll amplify that description and develop an understanding of the market's workings.

Overview

The stock market is a financial system or organization embedded within the larger economic system of the nation. It isn't a single place where people go to buy and sell shares, although many people associate it with the Toronto Stock Exchange (TSX) or New York Stock Exchange (NYSE).

Rather, the stock market is a network of *exchanges* and *brokers*. A stock exchange (or simply an exchange) is actually a company that provides a physical marketplace and the administrative capability of transferring shares from one owner to another. A brokerage firm (house) is also a company. It employs individuals (the *brokers*) who are licensed by the government to assist people in buying and selling securities. Both the exchanges and the brokers earn a living from commissions and fees charged on transactions made by people who buy and sell securities.

In Canada, provincial and territorial governments grant exchanges the basic right to make a market in securities. Beginning in 1999, five Canadian exchanges consolidated to form two exchanges:

1. the Toronto Stock Exchange (TSX), which has two main roles—the TSX is responsible for senior equity issues and the TSX Venture Exchange focuses on the junior capital market
2. the Montreal Exchange or Bourse de Montreal (ME), which is responsible for derivatives and derivative instruments

Historically, brokers were *members* of stock exchanges, each exchange had a limited number of *seats* that were purchased by brokerage firms, and by owning a seat the broker (now called a member) was given the right to do business on the exchange. This still applies in the United States but not in Canada after the realignment of responsibilities along with the *demutualization* of the TSX. In 2002, the TSX became a public company, known as the *TSX Group Inc.* (its trading or ticker symbol is X). As a result of this change, the TSX was no longer owned by "member" brokers but rather by the public at large. It was felt that by separating the exchange's ownership from its members there would be more accountability and responsiveness to the ever-changing markets. The TSX Group Inc. controls both the TSX and the TSX Venture Exchange.

Trading—The Role of Brokers

Whether buying or selling shares online or on the telephone, an individual investor must have an account with a broker. The investor is said to be the broker's customer or client. When customers want to trade in shares, they place orders with their brokers to buy or sell. Major brokerage houses have offices located throughout the country, and people usually deal with individual brokers who might be located in a nearby office or in a call centre.[3]

Under the old system (old for Canada but still used in many exchanges worldwide, including the New York Stock Exchange), brokerage firms also had representatives at the exchange. Upon receiving orders from customers, local brokers called the orders to representatives known as floor brokers on the trading floor of the exchange. Figure 7.2 shows the trading floor of the New York Stock Exchange.

Each share was traded in a particular spot on the exchange floor in an auction-like process, supervised by an individual called a specialist in that share. Specialists were responsible for conducting an orderly market in the shares they were assigned.

Stock exchange. A physical place in which stocks are traded by brokers on behalf of their investor clients.

Brokerage firm (house). A company of stockbrokers generally having the right to trade on an exchange.

The TSX contains a wealth of information. To find out which companies have recently issued new shares or monthly statistics, go to http://www.tsx.com/en/news_events/media_kit.html and http://www.tsx.com/en/news_events/news_archives/toronto_stock_exchange_archives/new_listings.html.

For information about the differences between listing on the TSX and TSX Venture Exchange, go to http://www.tsx.com/en/listings/index.html.

Floor brokers trade on the floor of the exchange.

Specialists make markets in designated securities.

---

3 You might find, upon calling to make a trade, that you are transferred to a different broker than the one who originally picked up the telephone. This is likely due to the first broker not being licensed to buy or sell securities in the province that you are living in. It sounds rather complex, but remember that in Canada securities regulation is a provincial and territorial responsibility.

FIGURE 7.2
The Trading Floor
of the New York
Stock Exchange
Source: © Getty Images.

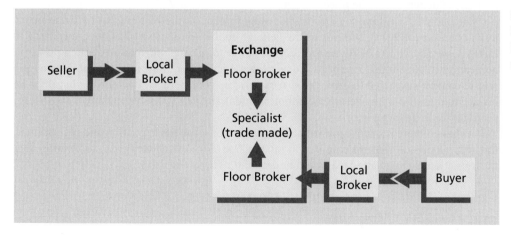

FIGURE 7.3
Schematic
Representation
of a Stock Market

Floor brokers would take the phoned-in orders to the spots where representatives of buyers and sellers met and executed transactions. Once trades were made, confirmations were passed back to the local brokers and their clients. Actual settlement for the sale and transfer of the shares would happen a few days later. Figure 7.3 is a representation of the process.

Notice that people in Figure 7.2 are doing business while standing in groups at various places around the floor. Trading between floor brokers and specialists goes on in such groups continually while the exchange is open.

Since 1997, all trades on the Toronto Stock Exchange have been conducted electronically. With the emergence of the new Montreal Exchange (ME) and the TSX and the TSX Venture Exchanges, floor traders were no longer required. The exchanges still assign a specialist role to exchange participants, however, to ensure that there is an orderly market for listed securities. Looking again at Figure 7.3, in Canada, there is no floor broker at the exchange; rather the buy and sell orders are matched electronically by the exchange's computerized system. The specialist will trade in the shares if there are unusual circumstances, such as a temporary disparity between demand and supply.

The Market

All the activity we've just described and more make up the *stock market*. Although the exchange represents a physical centre for much of what goes on, the term "market" refers to the entire interconnected set of places, organizations, and processes, which is exactly what we have in Canada.

Regulation

Securities markets are regulated primarily under provincial and territorial legislation. Although each jurisdiction has its own requirements, most companies that want to list on the TSX follow the regulations set in place by Ontario and the Ontario Securities Commission. Depending on the province or territory, the securities regulations are set out in securities acts or consumer affairs legislation. All jurisdictions require companies to disclose certain information to potential investors when issuing new securities in the primary market and extend the disclosure requirements to existing shares. Further, all jurisdications establish securities commissions or their equivalent to oversee financial market activities.

The legislation and regulations are aimed primarily at disclosure and the prevention of certain kinds of manipulative and deceptive behaviour. *Disclosure* means that investors must be given full and accurate information about the companies and people behind shares that are offered for sale. *Manipulation* means exploiting an official or privileged position to make profits on fluctuations in the prices of securities.

For example, it's illegal to profit from **insider information**, which is information available to an executive of a firm but not to the general public.[4] Suppose a drug company, such as MethylGene Inc. (ticker MYG on the TSX), is about to release information about a powerful new cancer treatment that is expected to be a big money maker in the future. That information release could be expected to drive the share's price up considerably. It would be illegal for an insider to buy shares just before the announcement and sell just after, making a short-term profit on the price increase.

Although there is a move toward harmonization of securities legislation and regulation in Canada, the process remains complex, to say the least. For now, all we need is to be aware that the legislation and regulation exists and understand its basic direction.

Private, Public, and Listed Companies, and the OTC Market

Suppose you notice a small company in your neighbourhood that seems to be doing well and decide to buy some of its shares. Could you do this as easily as you could buy shares of the Royal Bank or Canadian Tire, by simply contacting your broker?

If a company is small, buying its shares might not be easy and you might not be able to get any at all. That's because not all firms are traded on exchanges, and many aren't for sale to the public. Let's trace the life of a typical business enterprise to see how and when its shares become available for investment.

Suppose an entrepreneur starts a small unincorporated business. Because the firm isn't a corporation, it has no shares for outsiders to buy, and ownership is entirely vested in the entrepreneur. If the business is successful and the owner wants to raise money for expansion, he can incorporate in order to sell shares to others. We'll assume he does that.

The sale of securities is regulated provincially.

Securities law is primarily aimed at *disclosure*.

Insider information is information about companies that can influence share price which is available to insiders but not to the general public. It is illegal to profit from insider information.

For up-to-date information on the reform of the Canadian Securities System go to http://www.securitiescanada.org.

4 People like accountants and lawyers who have access to privileged information but are not employees are also considered insiders.

Privately Held Companies

At this point, the firm is said to be a privately held company (or a *closely held company*). The shares of privately held companies can be sold to other people, but those sales are severely restricted by provincial regulations. Generally there can't be a large number of shareholders, and sales solicitations can't be made across provincial and territorial borders. These regulations are aimed at limiting fraudulent investment schemes in which confidence artists offer bogus securities to unwary and unsophisticated investors.

Suppose our entrepreneur raises money by selling shares to a few people he knows and continues to expand the company. We'll assume that things continue to go well and, after some time, more and bigger growth opportunities present themselves. Taking advantage of such opportunities requires a lot more funding, but the business owner has run out of friends and relatives. To sell a substantial amount of shares, he has to make an offering to a large number of people.

> Privately held companies can't sell securities to the general public.

> Privately held companies aren't necessarily small. Canada boasts many large, privately held companies like McCain Foods Ltd., Cirque du Soleil, and James Richardson & Sons.

Public Companies

Offering securities for sale to the general public requires the approval of the provincial securities commission and the registration of each security offered with the commission. A firm that has received such approval is known as a *public company* or a publicly traded company. The process of obtaining approval and registration is known as *going public*.

Going public requires the assistance of an investment dealer. The dealer determines whether a market can be expected for the company's shares and the likely price at which the shares can be sold. If the estimated price is acceptable to the firm's owners, the registration procedure begins with the preparation of a document known as a *prospectus*.

The prospectus gives detailed information about the firm's business, its financing, and the background of its principal officers. When securities are eventually offered for sale, a copy of the prospectus must be provided to potential investors. However, the prospectus must be submitted to the appropriate provincial securities commission and approved before anything can be sold.

The purpose of the prospectus is *disclosure*. That is, the document must truly and accurately inform potential investors of the nature of the business and the risks involved. If the president was recently in jail for securities fraud, for example, that fact must be disclosed. Similarly, if the company is depending on the success of some new technological process or the granting of a patent, those facts must be revealed.

There are severe penalties for fraud on the part of *anyone* involved in the preparation of a prospectus—not only owners and officers of the firm but also accountants, lawyers, and dealers who might have been hired to assist in the process.

While the securities commission is reviewing a prospectus, the firm may not offer its securities for sale to the public. However, it may circulate the prospectus stamped with the word "PRELIMINARY" in red letters. Such a document is known as a *red herring*, indicating that it does not yet represent an actual offering.

It's important to understand that approval of a prospectus by a securities commission doesn't represent an endorsement of the security as a good investment opportunity. That is, a firm could be in an absolutely terrible business, one almost guaranteed to fail (like selling saltwater at the beach!) and still receive securities commission approval because all the appropriate information was disclosed. In fact, securities commission approval doesn't even guarantee that everything relevant is disclosed, because the commission doesn't have the resources to check much of the information that's submitted.

> A publicly traded company can sell securities broadly after a *prospectus* is approved by the appropriate securities commission.

> Prospectus. A document disclosing the details of a security and the underlying business to prospective investors.

> A preliminary prospectus is called a *red herring*.

The IPO

When a prospectus is approved by a securities commission, the securities described may be sold to the public. This initial sale is called an initial public offering (IPO).

IPOs constitute a subdivision of the general stock market and are considered quite risky. The prices of newly traded companies sometimes advance very rapidly after their IPOs, but can drop dramatically as well.

> Initial public offerings (IPOs) are shares in a new company offered to the public for the first time. The market for IPOs is very volatile and risky.

See which companies have IPOs at http://ipo. investcom.com.

Investment dealers generally line up buyers for IPOs before the securities are actually released. In some cases, the general public doesn't get involved right away, especially if institutional investors, such as mutual funds, are interested in buying the issue (called a *bought deal*).

Notice that the IPO is a primary market transaction. Once the securities are placed with investors, further trading will involve secondary market transactions.

If our entrepreneur went through all this, he would probably have retained a good proportion of the firm's shares for himself. The IPO would have placed a value on the shares that were sold and thereby would have implicitly valued the shares still held by the entrepreneur. In a successful IPO, that value is far in excess of book value and the entrepreneur can become a millionaire overnight, at least on paper!

The Over-the-Counter (OTC) Market

Notice that we haven't as yet said anything about a stock exchange in this scenario. Also recall that stock exchanges trade only in certain shares that are *listed* on those exchanges. In other words, our firm's securities aren't listed on an exchange, so investors can't buy or sell shares there. A vast number of companies fit this description. They're public and therefore available to be generally traded, but they're not listed on an exchange.

Small public companies are traded on the **over-the-counter (OTC) market**.

Such unlisted securities can be bought and sold by the general public in what is known as the **over-the-counter (OTC) market**, which consists of a loosely organized network of brokers who contact one another to find buyers and sellers for the securities of smaller companies. The OTC market is computerized on a nationwide system. In the United States, the OTC market is called *NASDAQ*, which stands for the National Association of Securities Dealers Automated Quotation system. Although most of the shares traded over the counter are issued by relatively small firms, a few very large companies are traded in this market (particularly NASDAQ). In Canada, the OTC market was originally rolled into Tier 3 of the TSX Venture Exchange.

In general, it is more expensive to trade in the smaller firms handled in the OTC market than in shares listed on exchanges. This is because fewer investors are interested in any particular small company and, as a result, brokers have to work hard to match up buyers and sellers. For that service they receive higher commissions and fees than those paid for trades in shares listed on exchanges where there is an active market all the time.

Find information on small companies that have graduated to the TSX at http://www.tsx. com/en/listings/ venture_issuer_ resources/ graduation_to_tsx/ index.html.

Listing on an Exchange

Now suppose the company we've been talking about continues to grow and becomes popular among investors. It's in the company's interest to make it easy for those investors to trade in the secondary market for the firm's shares even though no money from those trades goes to the company itself. That's because a smoothly operating secondary market in the shares will make further new issues of the firm's securities easier to sell in the future.

Companies **list** themselves on an exchange to make trading their securities easier.

So, if the trading volume warrants, the company can *list* its shares on an exchange. This is a relatively easy process if the exchange's requirements for size and length of time in business are met. After that the firm is a **listed company**, being traded on an organized exchange.

Reading Stock Quotations

Select a company from the TSX list at http://www.tsx.com. Select *Listed Company Directory*, then check on its stock quotes, market data, and charts.

Share prices are reported every day in a variety of newspapers. Both the *Financial Post* and the *Globe and Mail* provide comprehensive coverage of the Canadian and U.S. markets. Quotations summarize the trading activity of the previous business day on the various exchanges.

The format in which stock market information is presented requires a little explanation. We'll illustrate with the listing for CIBC shown in Figure 7.4. This listing is from Wednesday, April 4, 2007, so the information reflects trading on Tuesday, April 3, 2007.

Let's look at each of the columns, starting with the third (the column numbers don't appear in the newspaper). The third column, labelled "Stock," gives the abbreviated name of the company followed by the firm's tickertape or ticker symbol (fourth column). This latter is an even shorter abbreviation used in displaying and transmitting trading information from the exchange floor.

FIGURE 7.4
Stock Market
Quotation for
CIBC, Tuesday,
April 3, 2007

1	2	3	4	5	6	7	8	9	10	11	12
365 day											
High	Low	Stock	Sym	Div	High	Low	Close	Chg	Vol 100s	Yld	P/E ratio
104.63	73.25	CIBC	CM	3.08	101.93	101.05	101.21	+0.12	8132	3.0	12.7

Source: *The Globe and Mail*, Wednesday, April 4, 2007, page B18.

Columns 1 and 2 show the highest and lowest prices at which the share was traded during the past year. Notice how big the swing in value was, roughly between $105 and $73. The highest price was more than 40% above the lowest price in the period, and this is a well-known and relatively stable company.

Column 5 gives the last dividend paid by the company on an annualized basis. Because dividends are usually paid quarterly, this figure is generally the latest dividend multiplied by 4. Column 11 shows the *dividend yield*, also known as the *current yield*,[5] which is simply the dividend in column 5 divided by the share's current price, expressed as a percentage.

Insights REAL APPLICATIONS

It's All in the Timing—IPOs Are a Risky Business

The first time a company sells its shares to the general public, the sale is called an *initial public offering*, an *IPO* in the jargon of the financial world. IPOs represent one of the most volatile and risky segments of the investment industry. The prices of IPO shares frequently skyrocket shortly after the shares are issued and, just as frequently, drop precipitously. Hence, early investors in brand new shares can make or lose a great deal of money quickly.

The reason behind the volatility is that it's hard to judge just how much the investing community will pay for a new share. If the firm, its investment dealers, and the initial buyers underestimate the price investors are generally willing to pay, the shares increase in value rapidly after they are issued, and the lucky buyers do very well. However, the reverse is also possible. When the initial price is too high, the share's price drops quickly, and early buyers suffer big losses.

It's also common for the prices of recent IPOs to increase rapidly for a relatively short time and then to come tumbling down just as rapidly. The people who really get hurt then are those who bought shortly after the initial sale when the price was near its peak.

One reason for all this volatility is that investors tend to anticipate IPOs in certain "hot" industries and from particular companies. IPOs in those fields are met with a frenzy of buying activity when they first come out. But that enthusiasm often cools rapidly.

In the late 1990s, the most prominent IPO darlings were Internet shares, but investors' love affair with these dot-com shares ran its course and died. In 2003 the technology IPO market again surged and, although investors were receptive, they were also very cautious.

For example, Sandvine Corporation completed an IPO on the TSX in October 2006. The issue was well received, with the price quickly rising to just over $3.60 within the first three months of trading (from the issuing price of $1.90). Some other technology IPOs were equally lucky, with their share prices gaining. However, not all were so fortunate.

Sources: http://www.google.com, search *Industry Canada* and *IPO*. Also http://money.cnn.com, search *IPO*.

5 "Yield" is another word for return, which is similar to interest rate. We'll discuss this in detail in later chapters.

The **dividend yield** gives an indication of the current income an investor can expect.

The **closing price** records the last trade of the day.

The **dividend yield** gives an immediate indication of how much an investor can expect to make on his or her investment without depending on price increases. It's important because it shows how much cash or current income can be expected while the shares are held.

Column 6 reports the highest price paid that day, while column 7 indicates the lowest price paid that day. Column 8 records the price of the day's last or final trade, also known as the **closing price**. The net change up or down from the previous day's closing price is shown in column 9.

Column 10 shows the day's trading volume in lots of 100 shares. We see that 813,200 CIBC shares changed hands on April 3. Finally, column 12 gives the P/E ratio we described in Chapter 3 (page 75). On this date CIBC was selling for 12.7 times earnings.

Serious investors check the financial press (or web listings) several times a week for the progress of shares they've purchased. Local newspapers often carry some stock market information, but the format isn't necessarily the same as that of *The Globe and Mail.*

INTEREST

Return The payment to an investor for the use of funds. Usually expressed as a percent of the investment.

Interest rate info in a nutshell is available at http://www.money.canoe.ca, click on *Rates.*

A debt's **term** or *maturity* is the time until it must be repaid.

Investing in a security implies entrusting money to the organization that issued the security. The issuer uses the money and pays the investor for the use. The payment is called the **return** on the investment, and is usually stated in terms of a percentage of the money invested.

The term "interest" is reserved for the return on a debt investment, meaning the investor lends money to the issuer of the security. The primary vehicle for making debt investments is the *bond.* An investor in a bond is making a loan to the issuing company even though we say he or she buys the bond. Every bond has an associated interest rate that is paid to the investor who holds it.

People often talk about "the" interest rate as though there were only one. In fact, there are many rates, depending on the nature of the debt and on the characteristics of the borrowers and lenders. The various interest rates tend to move up and down more or less together. A statement like "the interest rate is moving up" is a reference to an approximate, average level rather than to anything specific.

As discussed earlier in the chapter, debt investments are loans and have a *term.* The **term** of a loan or a bond is the time measured from the present until the obligation must be repaid. The word "maturity" can be synonymous with "term." That is, a bond with a 10-year term can also be said to have a maturity of 10 years.

It's important to notice that bonds are *non-amortized* debt. An amortized debt is one in which the principal is paid back regularly along with interest over the life of the loan. Most consumer credit, including home mortgages and car loans, is amortized. Most business and government debt is non-amortized. Borrowers issuing bonds pay interest only (usually semi-annually) until the maturity date, and then must repay the entire principal at once.

The Relationship between Interest and the Stock Market

Shares (equity) and *bonds* (debt) compete for investors' dollars. Shares offer higher returns but have more risk.

Returns on equity (share) investments and interest rates on debt are related. Investors always have a choice between investing in debt instruments like bonds or savings accounts or in equity securities like shares. In other words, shares (equity) and bonds (debt) compete for investors' dollars.

Debt investments are generally safer than shares, so people prefer them if the expected return on the shares and the interest on the debt are nearly equal. As a result, shares have to offer higher returns (usually in the form of dividends and/or price appreciation) than debt to entice people to invest in equity. As interest rates on debt move up and down over time, the return on share investments moves up and down as well, usually remaining somewhat above the interest rate on debt.

This movement has a significant effect on the stock market because of the relationship between the return on an investment in shares and the price of a share. *A higher return is associated with a lower price.* This should be clear if you think in terms of bargains. Suppose a particular share is expected to produce a barely acceptable return over the next year. You're thinking of buying some, but you aren't quite sure if it's a good deal. Then imagine that the price is suddenly cut in half, while nothing else changes. That makes the share a much better deal, a bargain. The return it now offers as a percentage of the lower invested price is much higher.

In general, the market changes the return on a share by changing its price, so if share prices move up, returns move down, and if prices move down, returns move up. We'll understand this idea much better when we study the material in Chapters 9 and 10. For now, the basic principle is what's important: *Share prices and returns move in opposite directions.*

Interest rates and security prices move in opposite directions.

But remember what we just said about returns and interest rates. Changes in the overall level of share returns are driven by changes in interest rates on debt investments. That means the general price level of the stock market is driven up and down by changes in interest rates on debt. As interest rates go up, share prices go down, and as rates go down, prices go up.

That's a very good reason for us to be familiar with the inner workings of interest rates! Interest isn't the only thing that affects the general price level of shares, but it's very important and more predictable than other influences.

Interest and the Economy

The interest rate has a significant effect on the economy in general. High interest rates tend to stifle economic activity, whereas low rates tend to promote it. That's because both in business and in our personal lives a lot is done on credit.

When interest rates are low, people buy more houses, cars, refrigerators, and just about everything else. Because someone has to manufacture those products, more sales lead to more jobs and a healthier economy.

Lower interest rates stimulate business and economic activity.

The same idea applies to business. Companies often use borrowed money to buy new equipment and undertake new projects. When interest rates are high, borrowing is expensive, and not many projects look good because they don't earn enough to cover their interest cost. When rates are low, more projects are viable and are undertaken. The increased activity in turn leads to a healthier economy.

All of this causes the financial community to be very interested in interest rates, and gives us good reason to examine exactly what's in an interest rate and how rates are determined.

Debt Markets

Interest rates are set by the forces of supply and demand in debt markets. In the market for debt, people are borrowing and lending money. The price of borrowing is **interest**. Think of borrowing as renting a lender's money for a period of time, and interest as the rent payment. The price of borrowing is expressed as a percentage of principal. That's simply the annual interest rate with which we're all familiar.

Interest is the *price of money* in a debt market.

Borrowers are companies and the government. They sell bonds. They will borrow more (sell more bonds) if interest rates are low. Lenders are individuals and organizations that *buy* bonds. They are willing to lend more (buy more bonds) when interest rates are high.

Borrowers *sell* bonds. Lenders *buy* bonds.

The Determinants of Supply and Demand

The demand for borrowed funds depends on the opportunities available to use those funds and the attitudes of people and businesses about doing things on credit. If people feel good about the economy and their futures, they'll be willing to buy houses, cars, vacations, and other things with borrowed money. Similarly, businesses will borrow for expansion and new projects if demand for their products is strong and they have confidence in the future. If these conditions aren't met, they'll borrow only for what they have to.

The supply of loanable funds ultimately depends on the willingness of consumers to invest their savings. Changes in the economy affect consumers' willingness to save or spend and, as a result, the market interest rate moves up or down most of the time.

For most of the 20th century, movement was modest. The rates stayed at relatively low levels, about 3% to 6% until the early 1970s when the fluctuation became much more dramatic. In the early 1980s, some rates exceeded 20%. In the 1990s and early 2000s, rates have again been low and stable. The ability to forecast interest rates would clearly be very valuable, but as yet no one has been able to do it with any consistency.

THE COMPONENTS OF AN INTEREST RATE

Interest rates include base rates and risk premiums.

Any interest rate can be broken into two pieces, each of which can be further subdivided into components. Let's look at the two major pieces first.

All rates can be thought of as the sum of a base rate and a premium for risk borne by the lender. We'll represent the interest rate by the letter k, so we can write

(7.1) $$k = \text{Base rate} + \text{Risk premium}$$

Components of the Base Rate

*The **base rate** is pure interest plus expected inflation.*

The **base rate** is the rate at which people lend money when there's no risk involved in the loan. It has two components: the pure interest rate (also known as the earning power of money), and the expected rate of inflation over the life of the loan. We'll use the symbols k_{PR} to denote the pure interest rate and INFL to represent the expected inflation rate. Then we can write

(7.2) $$\text{Base rate} = k_{PR} + \text{INFL}$$

The Pure Interest Rate

*The **pure interest rate** is the earning power of money.*

The **pure interest rate** is more of an abstract concept than anything observable in the real world—it's the rate that would exist in a perfect economy in which (1) there was no inflation, (2) securities could always be sold quickly for their full value, and (3) people always lived up to their promises to repay their loans as agreed.

The pure rate can be thought of as compensation to lenders for the loss of the productive power of their money. It's generally taken to be between 2% and 4%.

The Inflation Adjustment

Inflation refers to a general increase in prices. We usually assume that the increase is uniform over all prices and wages, although in reality some things inflate faster than others.

Interest rates include estimates of average annual inflation over loan periods.

The key notion behind the idea of inflation is the cost of a particular bundle of goods. If the bundle costs $100 at the beginning of a year and prices inflate by 5% during the year, the same bundle will cost $105 at year-end. In other words, money will have lost some of its value.

Now imagine that you lent someone $100 at 5% interest during a year in which the inflation rate was also 5%. Assume the loan is successfully paid off with interest so you have $105 at year-end. Are you any better off than you were at the beginning of the year? The answer, of course, is no, because your year-end $105 won't buy any more than $100 bought before you made the loan. To come out ahead, you have to charge an interest rate that *exceeds* the inflation rate.

In fact, that's exactly what lenders do. Interest rates always include the anticipated inflation rate over the loan period as an add-on to the pure rate. That addition is reflected in the formulation of Equation 7.2. INFL in the equation can be thought of as an inflation adjustment equal to the *average* inflation rate anticipated over the life of the loan.

Risk (in finance) The probability that the return on an investment will be more or less than expected; the variability of the return on a particular investment; or the variance of the probability distribution of return.

Risk Premiums

Most lenders are willing to make loans that involve **risk** (the probability that the return on an investment will be more or less than expected). However, they always demand compensation for bearing higher levels of risk. That simply means they want to be paid more for making a risky loan than for making a safe one. Because the payment lenders receive is interest, they demand more of it in the form of higher rates when making riskier loans.

The difference between the interest rate charged on a given loan and the rate charged on a zero-risk loan is called the loan's **risk premium**. This idea is expressed in Equation 7.1 where the base rate is implied to have zero risk.

Different Kinds of Lending Risk

We'll think of business loans as typically being made through bond issues. In that context, lenders face risks that come from several sources. The simplest to understand is **default risk**, which occurs when a borrower doesn't repay the obligation, repays late, or has a high probability of not being able to pay. If any of these possibilities are present, a lender will be hesitant to lend money, or will make the loan only if it can be priced high enough to compensate the lender for a likely loss. The size of the *default risk premium* demanded by lenders depends on their perception of the creditworthiness of the borrowing company.

Other risks are associated with bond prices. When people lend by buying bonds, they generally terminate their investments long before the bonds mature by selling them to other investors. This involves risk because the price at the time of sale may be different from the amount the investor paid for the bond. If the price is lower, selling will cause a loss. The situation is especially difficult if the lender has an immediate need for funds and has to get out of the investment quickly at whatever price is available. In such cases, the lender may need to drop the price in order to get the money.

In such cases, the lender may be faced with a liquidity issue, a maturity problem, or both. For example, if the lender is dealing with a company that is small or not widely known, there is a chance that the lender will be unable to sell the bonds to another investor; this is known as a **liquidity risk**. The liquidity risk premium is extra interest demanded by lenders as compensation for bearing it.

Even if the borrower is well known, the lender may still have problems finding another investor to buy the bond due to changes in the prevailing interest rates in the debt market. If interest rates increase after an investor purchases a bond, the bond's price will decline and the investor will take a loss if he or she has to get out of the investment quickly. If the bond's term is short, the loss is small and can almost be ignored. But if the security has a long maturity, the loss can be significant.[6]

This means that longer-term bonds are riskier for investors than shorter-term bonds. We call this idea **maturity risk** because it varies with the term or maturity of the bond. Investors demand a *maturity risk premium*, which ranges from virtually nothing for short-term instruments to 2% or more for longer-term issues. Slight variations on this idea are called *price risk* and **interest rate risk**.

It's important to notice that the loss we're talking about here doesn't occur if the investor holds the bond to maturity. It happens only if he or she has to sell early at a depressed price.

The sum of these premiums will be the overall risk premium in Equation 7.1. The three sources of risk then are *default*, *liquidity*, and *maturity* risk.

Putting the Pieces Together

We can now rewrite Equation 7.1, substituting the elements we've discussed for the base rate and the risk premium.

---

6 Bond prices and interest rates move in opposite directions. We made a similar statement about shares earlier, but the relation is more precise and predictable for bonds than for shares. At this point in our study we haven't developed enough knowledge to understand why this relationship between prices and interest rates occurs and exactly how it works. We'll gain a full understanding of the phenomenon when we study Chapter 9. For now, we have to accept two things. The first is what we've already said, that prices and rates move against each other. The second is that the price change associated with a given interest rate change is larger for bonds with a longer maturity (time to go until they are due to be repaid) than for bonds with a shorter maturity.

(7.3)
$$k = k_{PR} + INFL + DR + LR + MR$$

where k_{PR} = Pure interest rate

INFL = Inflation adjustment (the average expected inflation rate over the life of the loan)

DR = Default risk premium

LR = Liquidity risk premium

MR = Maturity risk premium

This important equation says that an interest rate generally consists of the pure earning power of money, plus an allowance for inflation, plus an adjustment for each of three identifiable sources of risk.

We'll call Equation 7.3 the **interest rate model**, meaning that it's an abstract portrayal of how interest rates work.

People often refer to k on the left side of the equation as the *nominal* or *quoted* interest rate. It's the market rate that we've been talking about all along.

The **interest rate model** is an abstract portrayal of how interest rates work.

Setting Interest Rates

It's important to understand that Equation 7.3 represents a theoretical construct. People don't actually sit around thinking about how much each of the elements should be and then add them to come up with a rate to charge on a loan. Rates are set by the forces of supply and demand. If a particular lender doesn't feel the going rate is high enough, he or she simply doesn't invest.

The equation is an economic model of reality, an *explanation* of what generally has to be behind the interest rate given the needs of investors. However, like most economic models, it occasionally doesn't seem to be consistent with reality.

For example, at times a reasonable estimate of the pure rate plus the current inflation rate equals or exceeds the prevailing interest rate in some markets. That means the risk premiums in those markets must be zero or negative, which doesn't make a lot of sense.

For information on government securities, see http://www.fin. gc.ca/invest/ instru-e.html.

Securities—Risk-Free and Real Rates

The interest rate model represented by Equation 7.3 enables us to understand three special situations that are important in practical finance. We'll consider each in turn.

Government Securities

Governmental bodies at all levels issue debt securities that are similar to those issued by companies. Cities, provinces, and the federal government issue long-term bonds, but the Government of Canada also issues a great many short-term securities. **Treasury bills** have terms from 90 days to a year, while bonds mature in one to ten years.[7] The interest rate model, Equation 7.3, can be applied to government debt as well as to corporate debt securities.

Government of Canada **Treasury bills** are default and liquidity risk–free.

However, the Government of Canada debt has an important characteristic that isn't shared by anyone else's: there is no default risk associated with it. Therefore, the default risk premium in Equation 7.3 is zero when the model is applied to Treasury bills.

It's tempting to think that the reason behind this confidence on the part of the investors is a belief that there will always be a federal government. (If there isn't, we won't be worried about money and interest rates anyway!) But the reason is more subtle. For example, as long as there's a Government of Canada, we'd expect provincial and territorial governments to exist. Yet provincial default risks and the associated premiums are definitely not zero. Think about this

---

7 Treasury bills and Government of Canada bonds are sold by the Bank of Canada in order to raise short- and long-term funds for the government.

for a moment before reading on. Can you figure out why the federal government can never default on a loan?

The answer lies in a power that the Government of Canada keeps to itself: it can print money! No one else can. The federal government could pay off all of its debt simply by printing huge stacks of money. It doesn't do so because such an action would create a massive inflation that would disrupt the economy, but the capability is always there. As a result, there's no chance of federal default.

As a practical matter, liquidity risk is also zero for Government of Canada debt. That's because there's always an active market in the federal government's obligations. The chance of being unable to sell Government of Canada debt at the going price is very small. That statement definitely cannot be made for the securities of lower governmental units. In fact, a major problem with the obligations of local governments (cities, municipalities, etc.) is that they are often illiquid.

Maturity risk is not zero for government securities, however; it's the same as it is for any other borrower.

The Risk-Free Rate

The foregoing ideas give rise to the notion of a **risk-free rate**, which includes the pure interest rate and an allowance for inflation, but nothing for any of the risks we've been talking about.

Noting that government debt has no default or liquidity risk, and that maturity risk is insignificantly small for short-term debt, we can surmise that short-term Treasury securities are essentially risk-free. In fact, people generally take the 90-day Treasury bill rate to be the current risk-free rate.

Notice that the risk-free rate is the same as the base rate we used to introduce the idea of the components of interest (see Equations 7.1 and 7.2). All interest rates are essentially the risk-free rate plus premiums for various risks.

The risk-free rate is an important idea in financial theory. It provides an alternative place for investors to put their money that's always available. In other words, if investors don't like the general opportunities available in debt markets, they can always park their money in short-term government securities until something more attractive comes along. It can also be viewed as a conceptual floor for the structure of interest rates. If investors can always get the risk-free rate without bearing risk, no investment that does have risk can offer the same or a lower rate. When we encounter the risk-free rate, we'll denote it as k_{RF}.

> The **risk-free rate** is approximately the yield on short-term Treasury bills.

The Real Rate of Interest

In economics, the term *real* refers to figures and statistics that are adjusted to remove the effects of inflation. The **real interest rate** is the rate that currently exists less the inflation adjustment. In terms of Equation 7.3, INFL is zero.

The real interest rate tells investors if they're actually getting ahead. Suppose, for example, that you invest some money in a long-term security at 8% interest. Several years later, you discover that the inflation rate has risen to 10%, and you're actually losing purchasing power on your investment at a rate of 2% per year.

This situation hasn't been unusual in the last 30 years. For that reason, people have become reluctant to make long-term commitments at lower market rates. The solution has often been to make long-term contracts at variable interest rates that move up and down as the inflation rate and the nominal interest rate change.

There are also occasional periods in which the real interest rate is negative on most investment opportunities. That can happen because we don't really know what the rate of inflation is at a point in time until the government statistics come out several months later. If inflation rises rapidly while supply and demand forces push interest rates down, the actual interest rate can wind up below the inflation rate for some period. Obviously, when that happens, the model expressed in Equation 7.3 isn't working very well.

> **Real interest rates** have no adjustment for inflation.

The Real Risk-Free Rate

Putting the last two concepts together results in the idea of a real risk-free rate, a term that is sometimes used in financial circles. "Real" implies that the inflation adjustment is zero, and "risk-free" implies that all the risk premiums are also zero.

Looking at the interest rate model, we can immediately see that the real risk-free rate is conceptually identical to the pure interest rate, k_{PR}.

Example 7.1

You're a junior analyst in the treasury department of the Bullwork Company. The treasurer is contemplating raising money for a new plant expansion by issuing debt securities, but is unsure of the interest rates the firm might have to pay. He has asked you to estimate the interest cost of issues with maturities ranging from one to ten years.

You are aware that rates are actually set by supply and demand forces in the debt market, but feel that the interest rate model (Equation 7.3 on page 246) will provide some reasonable estimates under normal conditions. The following assumptions seem to provide a reasonable starting point:

a. The pure rate of interest is 3%.
b. Inflation is expected to rise in the near future and then subside. Your favourite economist projects the following pattern.

Year	Inflation Rate
1	4%
2	6
3	8
4	6
5–10	5

c. The default risk premium will be zero for one-year debt, but it will increase 0.2% for each additional year of term to a maximum of 1%.
d. The liquidity premium is zero for one- and two-year debt and 0.5% for longer issues.
e. The maturity risk premium is zero for a one-year term and increases by 0.3% for each additional year of term to a maximum of 2.5%.

Prepare a table showing the projected interest rate for loans of various terms and the components of each rate.

■ **Solution:** First, we'll calculate the inflation adjustment for securities having terms from one to ten years. That involves taking the average inflation rate over the entire projected term.

Year	Inflation Rate	Inflation Adjustment
1	4.0%	4.0%
2	6.0	5.0
3	8.0	6.0
4	6.0	6.0
5	5.0	5.8
6	5.0	5.7
7	5.0	5.6
8	5.0	5.5
9	5.0	5.4
10	5.0	5.4

Next, we'll create a table with a column for each of the elements of the model and fill in each column according to the assumed behaviour of the factor. The estimated interest rate is simply the sum of each row across the columns.

Term	k_{PR}	+ INFL	+ DR	+ LR	+ MR	= k
1	3.0	4.0	0.0	0.0	0.0	7.0%
2	3.0	5.0	0.2	0.0	0.3	8.5
3	3.0	6.0	0.4	0.5	0.6	10.5
4	3.0	6.0	0.6	0.5	0.9	11.0
5	3.0	5.8	0.8	0.5	1.2	11.3
6	3.0	5.7	1.0	0.5	1.5	11.7
7	3.0	5.6	1.0	0.5	1.8	11.9
8	3.0	5.5	1.0	0.5	2.1	12.1
9	3.0	5.4	1.0	0.5	2.4	12.3
10	3.0	5.4	1.0	0.5	2.5	12.4

Notice that the interest rate is higher for longer-term loans. That's the normal state of affairs, although sometimes the reverse is true. In this case, the rising rate can be traced to the action of the risk factors; each increases with increasing term for its own reason. The inflation factor has an unusual impact in this instance: it first rises and then falls away as the projected annual rates of inflation rise and then subside to a constant level.

Yield Curves—The Term Structure of Interest Rates

As the example in the last section illustrates, interest rates generally vary with the term of the debt. The relationship is known as the *term structure of interest rates*.

A graphic portrayal of the term structure is known as a **yield curve**. *Yield* is simply another term for return or interest. Figure 7.5 shows two yield curves of different shapes.

Most of the time, short-term rates are lower than long-term rates and the yield curve is upward sloping to the right. This is called a *normal* yield curve because it is the most common. Sometimes, however, long rates are lower than short rates and the curve slopes downward. That's called an *inverted* yield curve.

A great deal of thought has gone into trying to explain the forces that drive the yield curve to take a particular shape. That is, why should long and short rates differ in either direction? Three explanations have emerged, all of which have some appeal.

The **yield curve** plots interest against term for otherwise similar loans. The *normal curve* slopes upward, reflecting higher rates on longer loans.

FIGURE 7.5
Yield Curves

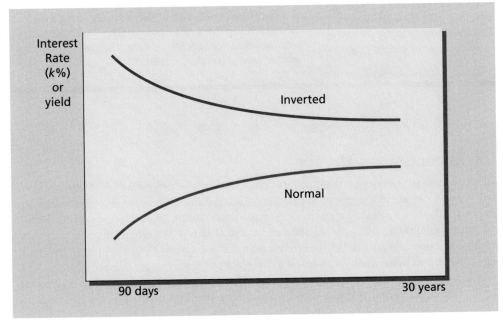

The Implications of an Inverted Yield Curve

The yield curve inverts only rarely, but when it does it's usually a signal that an economic slowdown is ahead. Economists agree that an inverted yield curve isn't a perfect predictor of a weakening economy, but history indicates that it's a fairly good one. There have been eight inversions in the last fifty years and six were followed by downturns, the last occurring in 1998.

The reasoning behind the link between the shape of the yield curve and the future of the economy is based on expectations about interest rates. If bond investors think rates are going down, they'll try to lock in the higher rates available before the decline by buying long-term bonds. If enough investors do that, the prices of long-term bonds are driven up (therefore lowering their yields).

But lower interest rates are associated with economic downturns because in such times the Bank of Canada puts downward pressure on rates to stimulate the economy. Hence an expectation of lower rates due to government pressure is associated with the end of a boom and the beginning of a slowdown.

The economy began to flirt with a mildly inverted yield curve in 2005 and early 2006. There was, however, little else to indicate a slowdown was around the corner. In fact, at that time, the economy was enjoying an unusually long period of sustained, stable growth. Numerous articles appeared in the financial press wondering if some fundamental economic change had stripped the yield curve of its predictive power, or if some other phenomenon was behind the boom-time inversion.

By late 2007, at this writing, some parts of the economy had slowed a little while the yield curve had flattened. But neither movement was significant enough to draw any conclusions about the yield curve as a modern-day economic predictor.

Students reading this page in 2008 and beyond will know the answer. Did the economy slow significantly after the inverted yield curve appeared? Or did the predictor miss its mark a third time?

The Inverted Yield Curve and Banks

An inverted yield curve's effect on banks and bank shares is far more certain. Banks' primary source of income comes from borrowing at low rates and lending the borrowed money at higher rates. That generally means borrowing short term by taking in savings deposits and term deposits. (These are short-term loans to banks because savings deposits can be withdrawn on demand, and term deposits typically have terms that vary from a couple of months to a few years.) Banks then make long-term loans to individuals and businesses.

This works fine under a normal yield curve when short rates are substantially below longer rates. But when the yield curve inverts and short rates are higher than long rates, this basic source of banking income evaporates, and industry earnings take a dive. That, of course, drives investors away and bank share prices fall. At the time of writing, bank shares had not appeared to be affected by any weakening in the economy. Profits for 2006 were up 50% from 2005; however, there was some weakness in the third quarter 2007 results due to market fears over credit quality.

Sources: Mark Whitehouse, "Economists Ask If Bonds Have Lost Their Predictive Power," *The Wall Street Journal* (December 29, 2005); Clint Riley, "Investors Puzzle: Banks and Flat Yield Curve," *The Wall Street Journal* (January 30, 2006); David Roberts and Tobias Moeschen, "Inverted U.S. Yield Curve Points Toward Increased Recession Risk in 2007," Dominion Bond Rating Service (November 29, 2006) http://cache.dbrs.com/pdf/20989008270461.pdf?transactionID=347306; Michael Kane, "Canadian Banks' Profits up 50%," *National Post* (April 4, 2007), FP9.

The Expectations Theory

Expectations theory says that today's rates rise or fall with term as future rates are expected to rise or fall.

The **expectations theory** says that the curve slopes upward or downward on the basis of people's expectations about the general level of future interest rates. For example, suppose that on a given day all interest rates are a uniform 5% regardless of term, and everyone expects them to stay there indefinitely. That means the yield curve is flat at 5%. Then imagine something happens to cause everyone to believe interest rates will increase to 10%, but only after remaining at 5% for two more years. Put yourself in the place of a lender under these conditions. You'd be willing to make a loan of up to two years at 5%, because that would be the prevailing rate during that entire period. But would you make a three-year loan at 5%? Clearly you wouldn't, because in the third year you'd be stuck earning 5% on your money while everyone else was making 10%.

However, you might be willing to make the loan at a rate that reflects an average of two years at 5% and one year at 10%, [(5 + 5 + 10)/3 =] 6.67%. That way, your overall yield would be the same as it would have been if you had made three one-year loans.

What if someone wanted to borrow for four years? You'd want a rate that averaged two 5% years and two 10% years for 7.5%. Notice that the average rate is increasing as the term of the loan increases and we get more 10% years into the calculation. That increase is the essence of an upward sloping normal yield curve.

A variation on the expectations theory says that the shape of the curve depends on people's expectations about inflation. But because the inflation rate is a large part of the interest rate (see Equation 7.3), expectations of increasing inflation are essentially equivalent to expectations of an increasing interest rate.

The Liquidity Preference Theory

The **liquidity preference theory** says that the yield curve should be upward sloping because lenders generally prefer short-term loans. They're more liquid, making it easier to get invested cash back if you have to. As a result of that preference, there has to be an additional interest inducement to lend long term. Hence, long rates will usually be higher, and the normal yield curve slopes upward.

This argument involves two of the ideas we discussed in the development of the interest rate model of Equation 7.3. One is the liquidity risk concept, that short-term loans are better for lenders because people can wait for maturity rather than sell their bonds. The second is the maturity risk idea, that short bonds are better for bondholders (lenders) because they are less subject to price variation due to interest rate movement. That makes them less risky and perhaps easier to sell.

In a nutshell, liquidity preference means that investors like short-term securities because they're easier to get out of in a hurry. Therefore, longer-term securities have to offer higher rates to attract buyers (lenders).

The Market Segmentation Theory

The **market segmentation theory** goes back to the forces of supply and demand in the market for debt. It says that the debt market isn't represented by a single set of supply and demand curves, but by many sets, each representing a separate market for money of a specific term.

When people are interested in borrowing money, they have a definite term in mind that is based on the use they intend to make of the funds. For example, a company interested in building a factory wouldn't want to fund it by borrowing for 90 days; it would be in the market for a very long-term loan. If it couldn't get that, it wouldn't want any loan at all.

Lenders operate similarly. They want to commit their funds for a definite period of time at a known yield. If they have long-term money available, they don't want short-term borrowers.

This results in a debt market that's *segmented* by term. Each segment has its own supply and demand picture with an independent set of forces pushing the curves back and forth. That means the market interest rate in each segment is independently determined, and not related to the market rate in other segments.

This independence leads to a pattern of rates that just happens. Most of the time market forces are such that short rates are lower than long rates and the yield curve takes its normal upward-sloping shape. However, at times independent market forces push short rates higher and the yield curve slopes down.

To learn more about interest rates and yield curves go to http://www. smartmoney.com/ tools and click on Economy and bonds.

Liquidity preference theory: Investors prefer shorter-term securities and must be induced to make longer loans.

Market segmentation theory suggests that loan terms define independent segments of the debt market, which set separate rates.

SUMMARY

1 The financial markets connect those who need funds with those who have funds. Financial markets allow money to flow between investors and companies.

2 The stock market and bond market are important in bringing together investors and companies that need funds. A stock exchange fills more of an administrative role in transferring shares from one investor to another. Brokers assist investors in buying and selling securities.

Shares that are thinly traded and bonds are typically sold over the counter. The OTC markets are a loosely organized network of brokers.

3 Interest rates impact the economy and as a result influence bond and share prices. Generally speaking, when interest rates increase, bond and share prices fall. The extent of the change in prices depends on a number of factors including the anticipated rate of inflation.

4 Returns demanded by investors comprise a number of different components. Investors expect a return that will compensate them for earning power, inflation, default risk, liquidity risk, and maturity risk. The more risk the investor perceives, the higher the risk premiums it will charge.

KEY TERMS

Base rate, p. 244
Brokerage firm (house), p. 236
Capital markets, p. 233
Closing price, p. 242
Default risk, p. 245
Dividend yield, p. 242
Exchange, p. 236
Expectations theory, p. 250
Financial intermediary, p. 234
Financial markets, p. 232
Floor brokers, p. 236
Initial public offering (IPO), p. 239
Insider information, p. 238
Institutional investor, p. 235

Interest, p.243
Interest rate model, p. 246
Interest rate risk, p. 245
Liquidity preference theory, p. 251
Liquidity risk, p. 245
Listed company, p. 240
Market segmentation theory, p. 251
Maturity risk, p. 245
Money markets, p. 233
Over the counter (OTC) market, p. 240
Primary market, p. 234
Privately held company, p. 239

Prospectus, p. 239
Publicly traded company, p. 239
Pure interest rate, p. 244
Real interest rate, p. 247
Return, p. 242
Risk, p. 244
Risk-free rate, p. 247
Risk premium, p. 245
Secondary market, p. 234
Specialist, p. 236
Stock exchange, p. 236
Term, p. 242
Treasury bill, p. 246
Yield curve, p. 249

KEY FORMULAS

(7.1) $$k = \text{Base rate} + \text{Risk premium}$$

(7.2) $$\text{Base rate} = k_{PR} + INFL$$

(7.3) $$k = k_{PR} + INFL + DR + LR + MR$$

QUESTIONS

1. What do we mean when we say businesses spend two kinds of money? Where does each kind come from? How is each used?

2. What is the primary purpose of financial markets?

3. What's the difference between a direct and an indirect transfer of money between investors and firms?

4. Define the following terms: primary market, secondary market, capital market, and money market.

5. Your friend Sally just returned from a trip to Toronto where she was very impressed by a visit to the stock market. Is it correct to say that she visited the stock market? What exactly did Sally visit? Explain exactly what the stock market is and how it's related to what Sally visited.

6. Your friend Charlie is excited about a new share issue. You've looked at the company's prospectus and feel that it's a very risky venture. You told Charlie your opinion, and he said he wasn't worried because the shares have been approved by the OSC and therefore must be okay. Write a paragraph to help out Charlie. What is the main thrust of securities regulation?

7. Explain the following terms: privately held company, publicly traded company, listed company, OTC market, IPO, prospectus, and red herring.

8. Describe the process that occurs when an investor places an order with a broker to buy or sell shares listed on the TSX.

9. Describe insider trading. Why is it illegal?

10. Interest is said to drive the stock market. But interest is paid on bonds and loans, while shares pay dividends, never interest. It would seem that interest has nothing to do with the stock market. Explain this apparent contradiction.

11. Define term and maturity. Is there a difference?

12. Why is inflation important to lenders? How do they take it into consideration?

13. Briefly explain the idea of representing an interest rate as a collection of components. What is represented by the base rate? What is the risk premium for? Explain the idea of risk in lending.

14. Explain the nature of the potential lending losses associated with each of the following: default risk, liquidity risk, and maturity risk.

15. Do all loans have default, liquidity, and maturity risk more or less equally? Are some types of loans relatively free of some risks? Is the debt of a particular organization free of certain risks? If so, explain what, why, and how.

16. Explain the ideas of a risk-free rate and the real rate of interest. Is either approximated by anything that exists in the real world?

17. What is a yield curve? Briefly outline three theories that purport to explain its shape. How does the yield curve influence the behaviour of lenders?

Business Analysis

1. "Brokers and mutual funds do the same thing: invest your money for you." Is that statement true or false? Explain. What kind of financial institution is a mutual fund? What is its distinguishing feature? Describe how savings banks and insurance companies are similar to mutual funds.

2. Does the so-called risk-free rate actually have some risk? (This is a tough question that isn't discussed in the chapter. Think about what makes up the risk-free rate and what among those pieces is an estimate of the future.)

3. Your Aunt Olga has a large portfolio of corporate bonds of different maturities. She has asked your advice on whether to buy more or get rid of some. You anticipate an increase in interest rates in the near future. How would you advise her? Would your advice depend on the maturity of individual bonds?

PROBLEMS

1. Refer to the CIBC stock quotation in Figure 7.4 on page 241.
   a. Demonstrate that CIBC's dividend yield shown is correct using other information in the listing.
   b. Estimate earnings per share from the information in the listing.

2. Economists have forecast the following yearly inflation rates over the next 10 years:

Year	Inflation Rate
1	3.0%
2	2.5
3–6	4.0
7–10	3.0

   Calculate the inflation components of interest rates on new bonds issued today with terms varying from one to ten years.

3. Nu-Mode Fashions Inc. manufactures quality women's wear and needs to borrow money to get through a brief cash shortage. Unfortunately, sales are down, and lenders consider the firm risky. The CFO has asked you to estimate the interest rate Nu-Mode should expect to pay on a one-year loan. She's told you to assume a 3% default risk premium, even though the loan is relatively short, and to assume the liquidity and maturity risk premiums are each 0.5%. Inflation is expected to be 4% over the next 12 months. Economists believe the pure interest rate is currently about 3.5%.

4. Calculate the rate that Nu-Mode in the last problem should expect to pay on a two-year loan. Assume a 4% default risk premium, and liquidity and maturity risk premiums of 0.75% due to the longer term. Inflation is expected to be 5% in the loan's second year.

5. Keena is saving money so she can start a two-year graduate school program two years from now. She doesn't want to take any chances going to grad school, so she's planning to invest her savings in the lowest-risk securities available, short-term Government of Canada bonds. She will need the first year's tuition in two years and the second year's in three. Use the interest rate model to estimate the returns she can expect on two- and three-year bonds. The inflation rate is expected to be 4% next year, 5% in the following year, and 6% in the year after that. Maturity risk generally adds 0.1% to yields on shorter-term bonds like these for each year of term. Assume the pure rate is 1.5%.

6. Adams Inc. recently borrowed money for one year at 9%. The pure rate is 3%, and Adams's financial condition warrants a default risk premium of 2% and a liquidity risk premium of 1%. There is little or no maturity risk in one-year loans. What inflation rate do lenders expect next year?

7. The Habender Company just issued a two-year bond at 9%. Inflation is expected to be 3% next year and 4% the year after. Habender estimates its default risk premium at about 1.5% and its maturity risk premium at about 0.5%. Because it's a relatively small and unknown firm, its liquidity risk premium is about 2% even on relatively short debt like this.
    a. What is the average inflation rate over the two years?
    b. What pure interest rate is implied by these assumptions?

8. Charles Jackson, the founder and president of the Jackson Company, is concerned about his firm's image in the financial community. The concern arose when he went to the bank for a one-year loan and was quoted a rate of 10%, which was considerably more than the firm had been paying recently. He has asked you, the treasurer, for an analysis that could shed some light on what might be causing the bank to ask for such a high rate.

    Your research indicates the following. The economy is stable with a 3% inflation rate that isn't expected to change in the near future. The local banking community consistently considers the pure interest rate to be about 4%. Liquidity risk for firms of Jackson's size and reputation is generally not more than 1%, and maturity risk is virtually zero for one-year loans. In the past, Jackson's reputation has warranted a low default risk premium of 1%. The firm's financial condition has been stable for some time. Two months ago, Jackson had a major dispute with one of its suppliers; Charles refused to pay for a large shipment due to poor quality. The vendor did not agree and claimed that Jackson was just using the quality issue to avoid paying its bills. Prepare the analysis.

9. Mountain Sports Inc. borrowed money last week for two years at 9%. The pure rate is 2%, and Mountain's financial condition warrants a default risk premium of 2% and a liquidity risk premium of 2%. The maturity risk premium for two-year loans is 1%. Inflation is expected to be 3% next year.
    a. What is the inflation adjustment using the assumptions given?
    b. What does the interest rate model imply that the lender expects the inflation rate to be in the following year?

10. Use the interest rate model to solve the following problem. One-year Government of Canada bonds are yielding 6% and two-year bonds yield 7%. The maturity risk premium is zero for one-year debt and 1% for two-year debt. The real risk-free rate is 3%. What are

the expected rates of inflation for the next two years? (*Hint:* Set up a separate model for each term with the yearly inflation rates as unknowns.)

11. Inflation is expected to be 3% next year and a steady 4% each year thereafter. Maturity risk premiums are zero for one-year debt but have an increasing value for longer debt. One-year government debt yields 7%, whereas two-year debt yields 9%.
    a. What is the real risk-free rate and the maturity risk premium for two-year debt?
    b. Forecast the nominal yield on one- and two-year government debt issued at the beginning of the second year.

12. The interest rate outlook for Montrose Inc., a large, financially sound company, is reflected in the following information:
    - The pure rate of interest is 4%.
    - Inflation is expected to increase in the future from its current low level of 2%. Predicted annual inflation rates follow:

Year	Inflation Rate
1	2%
2	3
3	4
4	5
5–20	6

    - The default risk premium will be 0.1% for one-year debt, but will increase by 0.1% for each additional year of term to a maximum of 1%.
    - The liquidity premium is zero for one- and two-year debt, 0.5% for three-, four-, and five-year terms, and 1% for longer issues.
    - The maturity risk premium is zero for a one-year term and increases by 0.2% for each additional year of term to a maximum of 2%.
    a. Use the interest rate model to estimate market rates on the firm's debt securities of the following terms: 1 to 5 years, 10 years, and 20 years.
    b. Plot a yield curve for the firm's debt.
    c. Using different colours on the same graph, sketch yield curves for
        i. Government of Canada debt
        ii. Shaky Inc., a firm currently in financial difficulty.
    d. Explain the pattern of deviation from Montrose's yield curve for each of the others.

13. Atkins Company has just issued a series of bonds with five- through ten-year maturities. The company's default risk is 0.5% on five-year bonds, and grows by 0.2% for each year that's added to the bond's term. Atkins' liquidity risk is 1.0% on five-year bonds, and grows by 0.1% for each additional year of term. Maturity risk on all bonds is 0.2% on one-year bonds, and grows by 0.1% for each additional year of term. What is the difference between the interest rates on the Atkins bonds and those of the Government of Canada bonds of like terms?

14. Assume that interest rates on Government of Canada bonds are as follows:

1 year	6.5%
2 year	6.3%
3 year	6.0%
4 year	5.8%
5 year	5.5%
10 year	5.2%
15 year	5.0%
20 year	5.0%

    a. Do the theories of the shape of the yield curve offer any insights into this rate pattern?

    b. Discuss the expectations, liquidity preference, and market segmentation theories separately.

15. The real risk-free rate is 2.5%. The maturity risk premium is 0.1% for one-year maturities, growing by 0.2% per year up to a maximum of 1.0%. The interest rate on four-year Government of Canada bonds is 6.2%, 7.5% on eight-year, and 8.0% on ten-year Government of Canada bonds. What conclusions can be drawn about expected inflation rates over the ten-year period?

Chapter 8

Time Value of Money

Learning Objectives

1 Explain the basic concept behind time value of money.

2 Calculate the present value and future value of single amounts.

3 Calculate the present value and future value of advance and arrears perpetuities and annuities.

4 Determine values for other terms such as payment, interest rate, time, or number of payments.

5 Understand how to manipulate these principles when dealing with uneven cash flows and differing compounding and payment frequencies.

Intuitively, most of us are aware that money never seems to go as far as it once did—that is, we seem to pay more and get less. Some would say it is clever marketing, others would say that it is a finance phenomenon. Perhaps it is both. Nevertheless, what about trying to decide whether to buy now or buy later? We know that a dollar today will likely buy more than it would in the future. Why? Because of the effects of inflation, uncertainty, and, of course, other options and how they affect our limited resources.

The time value of money is based on the idea that a sum of money in your hand today is worth more than the same sum promised at some time in the future, even if you're absolutely certain to receive the future cash.

The idea is pretty easy to grasp if you think in terms of having a bank account and being promised an amount of money a year from now. Money in the bank earns interest, so it grows over time. The value today of the sum promised in one year is an amount that will grow into that sum if deposited in the bank now. In other words, a sum promised in a year is worth only as much as you'd have to put in the bank today to have that sum in a year.

That value obviously depends on the interest rate that the bank is paying. The higher the interest rate, the faster money grows, so the less you'd have to deposit today to get a given amount next year.

Let's look at an example using a future amount of $1,000. How much would a promise of $1,000 in one year be worth today if the bank paid 5% interest? That question is equivalent to asking how much money will grow into $1,000 in one year at 5% interest. The answer is $952.38; we'll worry about how we got it a little later. The important thing to understand now is that if we deposit $952.38 for one year, we'll earn interest of 5% of that amount,

$$\$952.38 \times 0.05 = \$47.62$$

which, when added to the original deposit, yields $1,000.

$$\$952.38 + \$47.62 = \$1,000.00$$

Therefore, a guaranteed promise of $1,000 in a year is worth $952.38 today *if* the interest rate is 5%.

We say that $952.38 is the **present value** of $1,000 in one year at 5%. Alternatively, we say that $1,000 is the **future value** of $952.38 after one year at 5%.

If the interest rate were 7%, the present value of $1,000.00 in one year would be $934.58, a smaller number:

$$\$934.58 \times 0.07 = \$65.42$$

and

$$\$934.58 + \$65.42 = \$1,000.00$$

In other words, a higher rate of interest makes the present value of a future amount smaller. This makes sense; the bank deposit is earning faster, so you don't have to put as much in to get to the desired amount at the end of the year.

The **time value of money** is one of the most important principles in finance. It's based on the simple ideas we've just stated, but the applications can get quite complicated as we'll see later in this chapter.

The subject can also be called **discounted cash flow** (DCF). Using that terminology in our first example, we would say that $952.38 is the *discounted* value of the $1,000.

Here's another way of looking at the same thing. Suppose that you have a firm, written contract promising to pay you $1,000 in one year's time, but you need as much cash as you can get today. You could take the contract (called a **note**) to a bank, which would **discount** it for you at whatever interest rate it charges. If the bank's interest rate was 5%, it would give you $952.38 for the note. If the rate was 7%, the bank would be willing to give you only $934.58.

OUTLINE OF APPROACH

Our study of time value will involve learning to deal with *amounts* and *annuities*. An amount problem is similar to what we've already been talking about, involving a single amount of money that grows at interest over time into a larger sum. An annuity problem deals with a stream of equal payments, each of which is invested at interest and grows over time. We'll further divide each of these categories into two more. Within each, we'll look at situations dealing with present values and those dealing with future values. In all, we'll be looking at four types of problems:

- amount—present value
- amount—future value
- annuity—present value
- annuity—future value

The **present value** of a sum at a future time is the amount that must be deposited at interest today to have the sum at that time. The **future value** is the amount a present sum will grow into at a specified interest rate over a specified period of time.

The **time value of money** involves calculating the present and future values of money under the action of compound interest. It is also called **discounted cash flow**.

A **note** is a security reflecting an intermediate-term debt relationship between the issuer and the holder.

The **discounted** value of a sum is its present value.

After we've mastered these, we'll put the techniques together and work with some relatively complicated problems.

MATHEMATICS As we approach each of the four categories, we'll develop a formula suited to doing that type of problem. The algebra needed to develop the formula may look a little intimidating, but don't be alarmed. The math required to do the financial problems, once you accept the formula, is quite simple. Developing the formulas is background that's good to know, but you don't have to remember it to do the practical work.

A *timeline* is a graphic portrayal of a time value problem.

TIMELINES Students sometimes find time value problems confusing. A *timeline* is a graphic device that helps keep things straight. Time is divided into periods and portrayed along a horizontal line. Time zero is the present, and we count periods to the right.

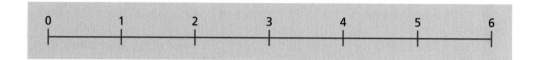

Time 1 is the *end* of the first period, time 2 the end of the second, and so on. We can make notations above and below the timeline to keep track of various pieces of the problem we're working on, such as interest rates and amounts. For example, a timeline for the illustration we talked about before would look like this:

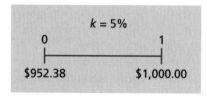

Most people don't need timelines for simple situations like this one, but timelines can help a lot in more complicated problems. We'll use them where appropriate as we go forward. We'll begin with yearly periods, but later we will introduce shorter spans.

A NOTE ABOUT THE EXAMPLES Several of the examples in this chapter are used to teach important financial practices as well as to illustrate computational techniques. You should be sure to learn and understand the business situations described in each of these illustrations. For instance, Example 8.2 on page 262 describes the equivalence of deferred payment terms and a cash discount.

AMOUNT PROBLEMS

Amount problems involve a single or lump sum of money that can be thought of as moving back and forth through time under the influence of interest. As it moves into the future, the sum gets larger as it earns interest. Conversely, as it moves back in time, the sum gets smaller. We'll begin with future value-oriented situations.

The Future Value of an Amount

To find the future value of an amount, we need a convenient way to calculate into how much a sum of money placed at interest will grow in some period of time. Let's start with a simple situation. Suppose we invest a sum of money in the bank at interest rate k. How much will it be worth at the end of one year?

Call the sum today PV for present value, and the amount we'll have at the end of the year FV_1 for future value in one year, and call the decimal equivalent of the interest rate k (0.05 for 5%).

At the end of a year we'll have the amount originally invested, PV, plus the interest on that amount, kPV. So we can write

$$FV_1 = PV + kPV$$

Factor PV out of the right side, and we have

(**8.1**) $$FV_1 = PV(1 + k)$$

Now suppose we leave FV_1 in the bank for another year, and we want to know how much we'll have at the end of that second year. We'll call that FV_2. The second year's calculation will be the same as the one we just did, but we'll use FV_1 instead of PV:

$$FV_2 = FV_1 + kFV_1$$

Factor out FV_1.

$$FV_2 = FV_1(1 + k)$$

Now substitute for FV_1 from Equation 8.1 to get

$$FV_2 = PV(1 + k)(1 + k)$$

(**8.2**) $$FV_2 = PV(1 + k)^2$$

Notice the similarity between Equations 8.1 and 8.2. FV_1 is equal to PV times $(1 + k)$ to the *first* power, while FV_2 is PV times $(1 + k)$ to the *second* power. It's easy to see that if we performed the same calculation for a third year, FV_3 would be equal to PV times $(1 + k)$ to the *third* power, and so on for as many years into the future as we'd care to go.

We can *generalize* the relationship and write:

(**8.3**) $$FV_n = PV(1 + k)^n$$

for any value of n. This expression gives us a very convenient way to calculate the future value of any present amount given that we know the interest rate, k, and the number of years the money is invested, n.

For example, if we deposited $438 at 6% interest for five years, how much would we have? Using Equation 8.3 gives:

$$FV_5 = \$438(1.06)^5$$

Raising 1.06 to the fifth power on a calculator gives 1.3382, so

$$FV_5 = \$438(1.3382)$$
$$= \$586.13$$

The only messy part of the calculation is raising 1.06 to the fifth power. Looking at Equation 8.3, we can see that calculating $(1 + k)^n$ will always be tedious, especially for larger values of n.

However, notice that the value of $(1 + k)^n$ depends only on the sizes of k and n, and that in business situations these variables take on a relatively limited number of values. Therefore, it's feasible to make up a table that contains the value of $(1 + k)^n$ for common combinations of k and n. We'll call $(1 + k)^n$ the *future value factor for k and n*, and write it as $FVF_{k,n}$. Table 8.1 is a partial table of values for this factor. A more extensive version is given in Appendix A–1 for use in solving problems.

We can now rewrite Equation 8.3 in a more convenient form by referring to the table.

The *future value factor* for k and n is the calculated value of $(1 + k)^n$.

(**8.4**) $$FV_n = PV[FVF_{k,n}]$$

TABLE 8.1
The Future Value
Factor for k and n
$\text{FVF}_{k,n} = (1 + k)^n$

k / n	1%	2%	3%	4%	5%	6%	...
1	1.0100	1.0200	1.0300	1.0400	1.0500	1.0600	...
2	1.0201	1.0404	1.0609	1.0816	1.1025	1.1236	...
3	1.0303	1.0612	1.0927	1.1249	1.1576	1.1910	...
4	1.0406	1.0824	1.1255	1.1699	1.2155	1.2625	...
5	1.0510	1.1041	1.1593	1.2167	1.2763	1.3382	...
6	1.0615	1.1262	1.1941	1.2653	1.3401	1.4185	...

Example 8.1

How much will $850 be worth if deposited for three years at 5% interest?

■ **Solution:** To solve the problem, write Equation 8.4 and substitute the amounts given.

$$FV_n = PV[FVF_{k,n}]$$
$$FV_3 = \$850[FVF_{5,3}]$$

Look up $FVF_{5,3}$ in the three-year row under the 5% column of Table 8.1, getting 1.1576, and substitute.

$$FV_3 = \$850[1.1576]$$
$$= \$983.96$$

Problem-Solving Techniques

In time value problems, *three* of four variables are *given*, and *we solve for the fourth.*

Equation 8.4 is the first of four formulas that you will use to solve a variety of time value problems. Each equation contains four variables. In this case, the variables are PV, FV_n, k, and n. Every problem will give you three of the variables and ask you to find the fourth.

If you're asked to find PV or FV_n, the solution is very easy. Simply look up the factor for the given k,n combination in the table, and substitute it into the equation along with the given PV or FV_n. The last example gave us PV and asked for FV_n. Here's one that gives us the future value and requires us to find the present value.

Example 8.2

Ed Lowe sold four hectares of land to Harriet Smith for $25,000. The terms of the agreement called for Harriet to pay $15,000 down and $5,000 a year for two years. What was the real purchase price if the interest rate available to Ed on invested money is 6%?

■ **Solution:** What Ed is getting today is $15,000 plus the present value of two $5,000 payments, each to be received at different times in the future. The problem is to compute these present values and add them to the $15,000.

The present value of the payment due at the end of the first year is calculated by writing Equation 8.4 and substituting the known elements.

$$FV_n = PV[FVF_{k,n}]$$
$$\$5,000 = PV[FVF_{6,1}]$$

Table 8.1 or Appendix A–1 gives $FVF_{6,1} = 1.0600$. Substitute and solve for PV.

$$\$5,000 = PV[1.0600]$$
$$PV = \$4,716.98$$

The second calculation is the same, but the payment is two years away so we use $FVF_{6,2} = 1.1236$. That gives a present value of $4,449.98.

In a present value sense, the actual sale amount is the sum of these two present values and the down payment:

$$\$15,000.00 + \$4,716.98 + \$4,449.98 = \$24,166.96$$

That's $833.04 less than the $25,000 price quoted.

In real estate finance we would say that the *terms of sale* resulted in an effective price reduction of $833.04 even though the real estate records would indicate a transaction price of $25,000. The seller's willingness to accept part of the price later is worth a specific amount of money. In other words, it is the equivalent of a cash discount.

The Opportunity Cost Rate

Notice that in the last example we calculated the present values using the interest rate available to the seller, 6%, even though nothing was actually invested at that or any other rate. We used the 6% rate because if the seller had received the full price at the time of sale, he would have been able to invest the deferred payments at that rate. Therefore, in a sense, he lost the income from that investment by giving the deferred payment terms.

We say that the lost interest income is the *opportunity cost* of giving the discount. In this case, because the seller's alternative is stated as a rate of interest at which he could have invested, we call it the *opportunity cost rate*.

The opportunity cost concept is a bit slippery. For example, you could argue that Ed Lowe might not have been able to sell the property to anyone without giving the deferred terms or an equivalent discount, and, therefore, there wasn't really any cost to the deferred terms at all. Nevertheless, we still say that the opportunity cost rate from Lowe's viewpoint is 6%.

The opportunity cost rate frequently isn't the same to different parties in the same transaction. In Example 8.2, Ed Lowe's opportunity cost rate is 6%, because that's the rate at which he can invest. But suppose that Harriet Smith has to borrow to pay for the land and she must do so at a rate of 10%. Her opportunity cost rate is then 10%, not 6%. To her, the deferred payment terms are worth a discount of $1,322.32, quite a bit more than what they implicitly cost Ed Lowe. (Verify this by calculating the effective price at 10% as we did in the example at 6%.)

In this example the deferred terms are a pretty good deal. They're worth more to the recipient than to the donor!

In general, the opportunity cost of using a resource in some way is the amount it could earn in the next best use.

> The *opportunity cost* of a resource is the benefit that would have been available from its next best use.

Financial Calculators and Spreadsheets

Financial calculators and spreadsheets take most of the drudgery out of time value problems. They work directly with mathematical relationships like Equation 8.3 rather than with tables.

There's a temptation to skip the mathematical work we've been doing here and go directly to using a calculator or spreadsheet without mastering the algebraic approach. That's a big mistake. If you go straight to the calculator or spreadsheet, you'll never truly understand what's behind time value or be comfortable with it. Certainly in practice we use calculators or computers almost exclusively, but it's very important to know what's behind the numbers that flash on the display.

In the rest of this chapter, we'll concentrate on the approach we've been developing that uses formulas and financial tables, but we'll also show calculator and Excel® solutions in the page margins.

How to Use a Typical Financial Calculator in Time Value

Recall that there are four variables in any time value problem. Values for three are given, and the fourth is unknown. Financial calculators have a key for each variable. To use a calculator, enter the three known variables, pressing the appropriate key after each input. Then press a compute key, followed by the key for the unknown variable. The calculator responds by displaying the answer.

There are actually five time value keys, because annuities require one that isn't used in the amount problems we've looked at so far. When we solve a problem, we use four keys and zero, or ignore the fifth. The keys selected tell the calculator which kind of problem is being done. The time value keys and their meanings are as follows.

n	Number of time periods or number of payments
I/Y	Interest rate (other labels: %i, I/YR, I% YR)
PV	Present value
FV	Future value
PMT	Payment

The last key is the periodic payment associated with an annuity. We'll talk about it later when we get to annuities. For now it should be ignored (if you clear the time value registers before starting) or set to zero.

The compute key is usually labelled either CPT or 2nd. On some calculators there isn't a compute key; the calculator just knows the last key hit is the unknown.

Before trying a problem, take a look at your calculator's instruction manual. You may have to get into a particular mode of operation and clear the time value registers before starting. Some calculators also have a feature regarding the interest rate that needs to be set to one compounding period per year. We'll get into non-annual compounding periods later. For now, set the calculator for one period per year.

Now solve Example 8.1 on page 262, using your calculator. Here's how.

Some websites have present/future value calculators, such as the ones at http://www.dinkytown.net and http://www.fiscalagents.com/toolbox/index.shtml.

1. The problem runs for three years. Enter 3 and then press n.
2. The interest rate is 5%. Enter 5 and then press I/Y.
3. The present value is $850. Enter 850 and then press PV.
4. Press 2nd or CPT (if necessary) and then press FV.
5. The calculator displays 983.98 or −983.98.

Some calculators use a sign convention intended to reflect inflows as positive numbers and outflows as negatives. For example, if PV is entered as a positive, FV shows up as a negative. The idea is that PV is a deposit and FV is a withdrawal.

Notice that a calculator solution may be a little off a table solution because the table carries only four decimal places; the calculator carries many more. Also notice that the interest rate is generally entered as a whole number even though the equations work with the decimal form.

In the remainder of this chapter, we'll show abbreviated calculator solutions for examples in the margins. Here's an illustration showing the first $5,000 payment in Example 8.2. (although the acronym for the table factor does give you the key strokes i.e., for Example 8.2 we had $FV_6 = PV[FVF_{k,n}]$ or $5,000 = PV[FVF_{6,1}]$ so put 6 in as I/Y, 1 n, 5,000 FV, 0 PMT then solve for PV).

Key	Input
n	1
I/Y	6
FV	5,000
PMT	0
	Answer
PV	4,716.98

How to Use a Typical Spreadsheet in Time Value

Just as financial calculators have a key for each variable, spreadsheets such as Excel® do too. You can set up a timeline and then insert values in the dialogue box, or you can simply enter the values you want in the dialogue box.

To use the financial functions in Excel®, click on the *fx* button and select for the category "Financial." So you can follow the previous example, once in the insert function box, select PV. You will see in bold **PV(rate, nper, pmt, fv, type)**. Press OK and a dialogue box comes up with those categories. Simply fill in the following (making sure your interest rate is entered as a percentage, not just 6) and enter OK.

You'll notice that the inputs on the dialog box are similar to the ones used in the financial calculator so in the margin calculator solutions we'll indicate which dialog box to use).

The Expression for the Present Value of an Amount

Notice that we are able to use Equation 8.4 to solve problems asking for *either* the present value or the future value. However, the expression is set up to make the future value calculation a little easier, because FV_n is isolated on the left side.

For convenience, we can develop another equation that's oriented toward solving the present value problem. We'll begin with Equation 8.3,

$$FV_n = PV(1 + k)^n$$

Now simply solve for PV by dividing through by $(1 + k)^n$ and switching the terms to opposite sides.

(8.5) $$PV = FV_n \times \frac{1}{(1 + k)^n}$$

Slightly more sophisticated mathematical notation enables us to write the same thing with a negative exponent.

(8.6) $$PV = FV_n(1 + k)^{-n}$$

The term $(1 + k)^{-n}$ can be thought of as a factor depending only on k and n that can be tabulated. We'll call that factor the *present value factor for k and n* and write it as $PVF_{k,n}$. The values of $PVF_{k,n}$ are given in Appendix A–2. We can now rewrite Equation 8.6 by using this factor and reference to the table.

(8.7) $$PV = FV_n[PVF_{k,n}]$$

We use this expression and the associated table just like we used Equation 8.4. It too can be used to solve for either present or future values, but it is more conveniently formulated for present values. Do Example 8.2 on your own using Equation 8.7.

The Relation between the Future and Present Value Factors

The future and present value factors are *reciprocals. Either* amount equation can be used to solve any amount problem.

It's important to notice that Equations 8.4 and 8.7 really express the same relationship, as they both come from Equation 8.3. It's also important to realize that the present and future value factors are reciprocals of one another. That is,

$$(8.8) \qquad \text{FVF}_{k,n} = \frac{1}{\text{PVF}_{k,n}}$$

More on Problem-Solving Techniques

So far we've looked at problems that ask us to solve for FV_n or PV. When the unknown element in the equation is k or n, the approach is a little different. Notice that in both Equations 8.4 and 8.7, k and n appear as subscripts on the factors referring to table values. Although traditional algebraic methods to solve for an unknown k or n can be used with the equations, we will focus on calculating k and n using either financial calculators or Excel®.

Solving for k or n involves searching a table.

We'll change Example 8.1 a little to illustrate what we mean. In that problem, we asked how much $850 would grow into in three years at 5% interest, and got an answer of $983.96.

Example 8.3

Suppose instead we were asked what interest rate would grow $850 into $983.96 in three years. In this case, we have FV_3, PV, and n, but we don't have k.

Calculator Solution[1]

Key	Input
n	3
PV	850.00
FV	983.96
PMT	0

Answer

I/Y	5.0

Use Excel® Function Rate

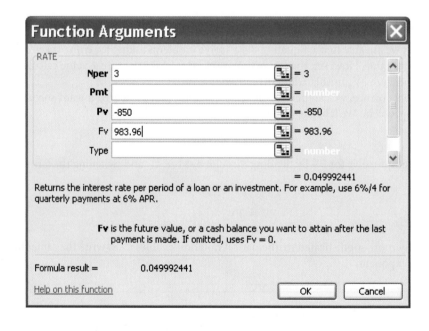

Function Arguments

RATE

Nper	3		= 3
Pmt			= number
Pv	-850		= -850
Fv	983.96|		= 983.96
Type			= number

= 0.049992441

Returns the interest rate per period of a loan or an investment. For example, use 6%/4 for quarterly payments at 6% APR.

Fv is the future value, or a cash balance you want to attain after the last payment is made. If omitted, uses Fv = 0.

Formula result = 0.049992441

Help on this function

OK   Cancel

---

1 Using Excel®, this time we are solving for RATE. Simply fill in the numbers on the dialogue box directly and notice that the solution is .05 or 5%.

■ **Solution:** We'll use Equation 8.7 this time, just for variety. The general approach is to write the equation

$$PV = FV_n[PVF_{k,n}]$$

and substitute what's known,

$$\$850.00 = \$983.96[PVF_{k,3}]$$

With some manipulation this equation can be solved algebraically for k, however, it is easier to solve for the whole factor, $PVF_{k,3}$, and then find its value in the table. Once we've done that, we can read off the unknown value for k from the column heading. Solving for the factor gives

$$PVF_{k,3} = \$850.00/\$983.96 = 0.8639$$

We have to find 0.8639 in Appendix A–2. We know that in this problem $n = 3$, so we can confine our search to the row that contains the three-year values. Looking along that row, we don't find 0.8639 exactly, but we do find 0.8638. That's close enough to assume that the difference is due to rounding error. Looking up to the top of the column, we read 5% as the solution to the problem.

Solutions between Columns and Rows

Most of the time, solutions for k and n don't come out exactly on numbers in the table. That is, the calculated factor is somewhere between the columns or rows. The appropriate approach when that happens depends on the accuracy needed in the solution. For some purposes it's enough to round the answer to the closest tabulated row or column. If a more accurate answer is necessary and you're using tables like the ones provided here, you have to estimate between columns and rows.

In practice, financial calculators or spreadsheets are used to solve time value problems. They give exact results without using tables. Before financial calculators were invented, people used enormously detailed tables that filled entire volumes.

Example 8.4

How long does it take money invested at 14% to double?

■ **Solution:** Don't be confused by the fact that we're not given a present and future value in this case. What we are given is a relation between the two. If the money is to double in value, the future value must be twice the present value. Alternatively, we could ask how long it would take $1 to double into $2. We'll use Equation 8.4 in this case.

$$FV_n = PV[FVF_{k,n}]$$

Solving for the factor and substituting yields

$$FVF_{14,n} = \frac{FV_n}{PV} = 2.0000$$

Next we look for 2.0000 in Appendix A–1, confining our search to the column for $k = 14\%$. We find that the table value is between five and six years.

n	14%
5	1.9254
6	2.1950

Clearly, 2.0000 is closer to 1.9254 than it is to 2.1950; therefore, the nearest whole integer number of years is 5. Notice that the calculator and spreadsheet solution gives an exact answer of 5.29 years.

Calculator Solution[2]

Key	Input
I/Y	14
FV	2
PV	1
PMT	0

Answer

n	5.29

Use Excel® Function
NPER

---

2 Now we need to solve for the number of periods, or NPER, using Excel®. Like many of the financial calculators, Excel® needs one of the cash variables, either PV or FV, to be entered as a negative number.

Function Arguments

NPER

Rate	14%	= 0.14
Pmt		= number
Pv	-1	= -1
Fv	2	= 2
Type		= number

= 5.290058556

Returns the number of periods for an investment based on periodic, constant payments and a constant interest rate.

Fv is the future value, or a cash balance you want to attain after the last payment is made. If omitted, zero is used.

Formula result =   5.290058556

Help on this function   [OK]   [Cancel]

ANNUITY PROBLEMS

The second major class of time value problems involves streams of payments called *annuities.* These are generally more complex than amount problems and harder to visualize, so using timelines can be important.

Annuities

An **annuity** is a finite series of equal payments separated by equal time intervals.

An **annuity** is a stream of equal payments, made or received, separated by equal intervals of time. Hence $5 a month for a year is an annuity. Other examples include monthly lease, pension, and car loan payments. A stream of monthly payments that alternates from $5 to $10 is not an annuity, nor is a stream of $5 payments that skips an occasional month. Both the amount and the time interval must be constant to have an annuity.

When payments occur at the end of the time periods, we have what's called an *ordinary annuity.* This is the usual situation. If the payments occur at the beginning of each period, we call the stream an *annuity due.* Figures 8.1 and 8.2 show timelines for both cases for a stream of four $1,000 payments.

Annuities have definite beginning and end points in time; they don't go on forever. A stream of equal payments at regular time intervals that does go on forever is called a *perpetuity.* It has to be handled by its own rules, which we'll study later in the chapter.

The Time Value of Annuities

Annuities are common in business and have important time value implications. For example, suppose a long-term contract calls for payments of $5,000 a year for 10 years. A question that arises immediately concerns the value of the agreement today. That is, if the recipient wants to discount all the payments for immediate cash, how much will they be worth in total?

FIGURE 8.1
Ordinary Annuity

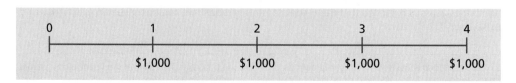

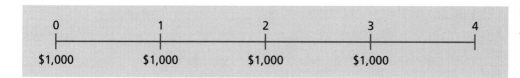

FIGURE 8.2
Annuity Due

A similar question asks for the future value of the entire annuity if all 10 payments are put in the bank when received and left there until the end of the contract.

Either of these questions can be answered by taking the present or future value of each payment separately and adding the results. That is a tedious process, however, involving 10 separate calculations. It's much more convenient to develop expressions that enable us to calculate the present or future value of the entire annuity at once.

We'll begin with the future value problem.

The Future Value of an Annuity—Developing a Formula

We can develop an expression for the future value of an annuity that's similar to the formulas we studied for single or lump-sum amounts. We'll approach the task by examining the future value of a three-year ordinary annuity, using the tools we acquired in dealing with amounts.

We'll portray the annuity along a timeline and represent the yearly cash payment as a variable called PMT as shown in Figure 8.3.

The Future Value Problem

Precisely stated, the assumption behind the future value of an annuity is that each amount, PMT, earns interest at some rate, k, from the time it appears on the timeline until the end of the last period. The future value of the annuity is simply the sum of all the payments and all the interest. This is the same as taking the future value of each PMT treated as an amount and adding them.

For example, imagine that someone gives you $100 a year for three years, and that you put each payment in the bank as soon as you get it. The future value of an annuity problem is to calculate how much you have at the end of the third year. It's clearly more than $300 because of interest earned.

> The *future value of an annuity* is the sum, at its end, of all payments and all interest if each payment is deposited when received.

The Future Values of the Individual Payments

We'll develop an expression for the future value of an annuity by projecting the future value of each payment to the end of the stream individually. The approach is illustrated in Figure 8.4. We'll call the end of the third year time 3, the end of the second year time 2, and so on.

First, consider the third payment. It occurs at the end of the annuity, so it spends no time earning interest at all. Therefore, its value at time 3 is simply PMT.

The second payment occurs at time 2, one year before the end of the annuity, and spends one year earning interest. Its value at time 3 is PMT$(1 + k)$. Think of this as the future value of the present amount PMT for one year at interest rate k. This comes from Equation 8.1 with PMT substituted for PV.

Now consider the first payment. It occurs at the end of the first year and spends two years earning interest. Its value by the end of the annuity is PMT$(1 + k)^2$.

FIGURE 8.3
Timeline Portrayal of an Ordinary Annuity

FIGURE 8.4

Future Value of a
Three-Year
Ordinary Annuity

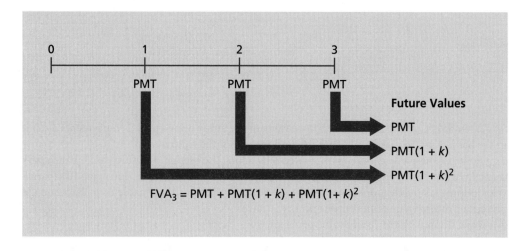

$$\text{FVA}_3 = \text{PMT} + \text{PMT}(1 + k) + \text{PMT}(1+ k)^2$$

All of this is portrayed graphically in Figure 8.4, along with the sum of the future values of the three payments, which we're calling FVA_3 for future value of an annuity of three payments.

The Three-Payment Formula

Let's rewrite the expression for FVA_3 from Figure 8.4 with two changes and then examine what we have. The first change will be to explicitly recognize the exponent of 1 on $(1 + k)$ in the middle term on the right. That is, $(1 + k) = (1 + k)^1$. It's simply common practice not to write an exponent of 1 even though it's there. The second change involves recognizing that anything raised to a zero exponent equals 1. That is, $x^0 = 1$ for any value of x. In this case, we're going to multiply the first term on the right by $(1 + k)^0$. This gives

(**8.9**) $$\text{FVA} = \text{PMT}(1 + k)^0 + \text{PMT}(1 + k)^1 + \text{PMT}(1 + k)^2$$

Notice the regular progression of the terms on the right side of Equation 8.9. Each contains PMT multiplied by an increasing power of $(1 + k)$ starting from zero. Notice also for this three-payment case that there are three terms and that the exponents start with zero and increase to 2, one less than the number of years.

Generalizing the Expression

Now imagine that we have a four-year annuity, and we want to develop a similar expression for it. How would that expression differ from what we've written here for the three-year case?

In a four-year model, the first payment would earn interest for three years, so its future value would be $\text{PMT}(1 + k)^3$. The second payment would earn interest for two years, and the third for one year; the fourth would earn no interest at all. These latter payments would be just like the ones in the three-year case, so the only thing different in the four-year model is the addition of the new term: $\text{PMT}(1 + k)^3$. That addition fits our progression perfectly. It adds one more term with the next higher exponent.

This could be done for any number of additional years. Each will add one more term with the next higher exponent of $(1 + k)$. Further, the highest exponent will always be one less than the number of years. Hence we can *generalize* Equation 8.9 for any number of years, n.

(**8.10**) $$\text{FVA}_n = \text{PMT}(1 + k)^0 + \text{PMT}(1 + k)^1 + \text{PMT}(1 + k)^2 + \ldots + \text{PMT}(1 + k)^{n-1}$$

Equation 8.10 can be written more conveniently by using the mathematical symbol, which implies summation over the values of some index.

(**8.11**) $$\text{FVA}_n = \sum_{i=1}^{n} \text{PMT}(1 + k)^{n-i}$$

As i ranges from 1 to n, each of the terms of Equation 8.10 is formed in reverse order. For example, when $i = 1$, $n - i = n - 1$, and we get the last term. When $i = 2$, we get the next to last term, and so on until $i = n$ and $n - i = 0$, which gives us the first term.

Because PMT appears identically in every term, we can factor it outside of the summation.

(8.12)
$$\text{FVA}_n = \text{PMT} \sum_{i=1}^{n} (1 + k)^{n - i}$$

The Future Value Factor for an Annuity

Now look at the entire summation term. It depends only on the values of n and k. For example, for $n = 3$ years the summation is

$$(1 + k)^0 + (1 + k)^1 + (1 + k)^2$$

which is equivalent to

$$1 + (1 + k) + (1 + k)^2$$

In general, the summation term for n years is

$$1 + (1 + k) + (1 + k)^2 + \ldots + (1 + k)^{n - 1}$$

This expression can be calculated for pairs of values of n and k and placed in a table. The idea is identical to what we did in developing the future value factor for an amount [$\text{FVF}_{k,n} = (1 + k)^n$], only this expression is more complex.[3]

It is worth noting that, when dealing with annuities, n is the number of payments to be made or received, not the number of years. This is particularly important to keep in mind when the annuity payment does not start one period from now. We will deal with this somewhat more complex issue later in the chapter.

We'll call the summation in Equation 8.12 the *future value factor for an annuity* and write it as $\text{FVFA}_{k,n}$. Values for ranges of k and n are given in Appendix A–3.

The Final Formulation

The future value factor for an annuity can replace the summation in Equation 8.12 like this.

$$\text{FVA}_n = \text{PMT} \boxed{\sum_{i=1}^{n} (1 + k)^{n - i}}$$

$$\longrightarrow = \text{FVFA}_{k,n}$$

Rewriting 8.12 using the factor, we get

(8.14)
$$\text{FVA}_n = \text{PMT}[\text{FVFA}_{k,n}]$$

The Future Value of an Annuity—Solving Problems

We'll use Equations 8.13 and 8.14 to solve future value problems that involve annuities. Notice that there are four variables in this equation: FVA_n (the future value itself), PMT (the payment), k (the interest rate), and n (the number of payments). Problems will generally give three of them and ask for the fourth. The first step in problem solution is always writing down the equation and substituting the known elements. Once this is done, the solution procedure is very similar to that used for amount problems.

---

3 The mathematical derivation of the algebraic formula is not important to furthering our understanding of the future value concept. However, the algebraic formula is important if a spreadsheet or financial calculator are unavailable. The future value of an annuity at the end of the nth payment is:

(8.13)
$$\text{FVA}_n = \frac{\text{PMT}(1 + k)^n - 1}{k}$$

Example 8.5

The Brock Corporation owns the patent to an industrial process and receives licence fees of $100,000 a year on a 10-year contract for its use. Management plans to invest each payment until the end of the contract to provide a fund for development of a new process at that time. If the invested money is expected to earn 7%, how much will Brock have after the last payment is received?

■ **Solution:** The timeline for this straightforward problem looks like this.[5]

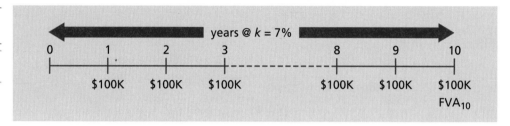

First, write Equation 8.14:

$$FVA_n = PMT[FVFA_{k,n}]$$

and substitute the given information:

$$FVA_{10} = \$100,000[FVFA_{7,10}]$$

Next, look up $FVFA_{7,10}$ in Appendix A–3, getting 13.8164. Substitute and solve for the future value.

$$FVA_{10} = \$100,000[13.8164]$$
$$= \$1,381,640$$

Notice that the actual money received is only $1,000,000; the rest is interest.

Calculator and Spreadsheet Solutions for Annuities

Annuity problems are similar to amount problems in that they have four variables, of which three are given and one is unknown. However, the variables are somewhat different.

All amount problems involve both the present and future values of the amount. Annuity problems involve a payment (PMT) and *either* the future value *or* the present value of the annuity. Hence, in an annuity problem we use the PMT key, and we zero either PV or FV, depending on the nature of the problem.

Example 8.5 is a future value of an annuity problem, so we use the FV key or FV function, and use zero for the PV. That, along with putting in a value for PMT, tells the calculator what kind of a problem it's doing (if using Excel® you've already indicated what kind of problem it is by choosing the function). Notice that although we write the future and present values of

4 Using Excel®, we are now solving for FV. If you are using the spreadsheet functions, you might have noticed by now that we generally can choose one function (say PF or FV) and then solve for any of the other values. As the functions are similar in so many ways to the calculator inputs, we will not include any further Excel® examples.

You'll also likely notice that there is a slight rounding difference when we compare the Excel® and financial calculator solutions to the tables. Although the differences are not significant amounts, it can be frustrating when first learning the material. Since the table acronyms provide us with a convenient way of expressing the equation as well as providing us with a guideline for calculator and spreadsheet, we will continue to use them in setting up the problem. The exact answers will be shown in the margins along with the proper keystrokes.
5 A capital K is frequently used to denote thousands of dollars, replacing a comma and three zeros. M can be used to denote millions (replacing two commas and six zeros).

annuities as FVA and PVA, we just use the FV and PV buttons on the calculator and FV and PV functions on Excel®. As we discussed on page 264, the FVA and PVA acronyms can be used to help you input the proper keystrokes. For example, FVA indicates that you have a stream of *n* payments for which you want to know the future value, using some *k*.

Again, note that *n* is the number of payments when we are dealing with annuity-type problems!

The Sinking Fund Problem

In Chapter 7, we learned that companies borrow money by issuing bonds for periods as long as 30 or 40 years. Bonds are non-amortizing debt, meaning that borrowers make no repayment of principal during bonds' lives. Borrowers pay only interest until maturity, and then they must repay the entire principal in a lump sum. This means that, on the maturity date, a bond-issuing company must either have a great deal of money on hand or must reborrow to pay off the old bonds coming due.

> *Lenders can become quite concerned about this practice. They may feel that a borrowing company can generally earn enough to pay annual interest, but it won't have enough cash on hand at maturity to pay off principal. If the borrower's financial position deteriorates or if financial markets become tight, it may not be able to reborrow either. This can spell bankruptcy for the bond-issuing company and a big loss for the investor/lender.*

From the CFO

The solution to the problem can be a sinking fund. A **sinking fund** is a series of payments made into an account that's dedicated to paying off a bond's principal at maturity. Deposits are planned so that the amount in the bank on the date the bonds mature will just equal the principal due.

A **sinking fund** provides cash to pay off a bond's principal at maturity.

If lenders require a sinking fund for security, it's included as a provision in the bond agreement. The sinking fund problem is to determine the periodic deposit that must be made to ensure that the appropriate amount is available at the bond's maturity. This is a future value of an annuity problem in which the payment is unknown.

Example 8.6

The Greenville Company issued bonds totalling $15 million for 30 years. The bond agreement specifies that a sinking fund must be maintained after 10 years, which will retire the bonds at maturity. Although no one can accurately predict interest rates, Greenville's bank has estimated that a yield of 6% on deposited funds is realistic for long-term planning. How much should Greenville plan to deposit each year to be able to retire the bonds with the money put aside?

■ **Solution:** First, recognize that the time period of the annuity is the last 20 years of the bond issue's life, because the bond agreement states that the sinking fund must be maintained only after 10 years. In other words, time zero isn't today but the beginning of the eleventh year in the bond's life.

The problem's timeline looks like this.

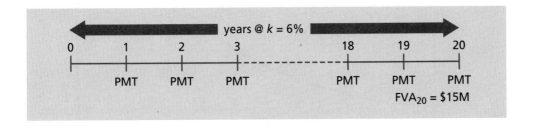

First, write the future value of an annuity formula, Equation 8.14.

$$FVA_n = PMT[FVFA_{k,n}]$$

In this case, the future value itself is known: it's the principal amount of the bond issue that will have to be repaid, $15 million. Also, k is 6% and n is 20 payments (over 20 years), the duration of the sinking fund according to the contract. Substitute these values.

$$\$15,000,000 = PMT[FVFA_{6,20}]$$

Next, look up $FVFA_{6,20}$ in Appendix A–3, getting 36.7856, and substitute.

$$\$15,000,000 = PMT[36.7856]$$

Finally, solve for PMT.

$$PMT = \$407,768.26$$

Greenville will have to deposit just under $408,000 per year starting in the eleventh year of the bond issue's life to ensure that the bonds will be retired on schedule without a problem.

At this point, we're going to digress from time value problems themselves to study a little more detail about the workings of interest rates.

Compound Interest and Non-Annual Compounding

Until now we've been working with annually compounded interest. Although interest rates are always quoted in annual terms, they're usually not compounded annually, and that varies the actual amount of interest paid. Before going any further, let's be sure we know exactly what the term "compound interest" means.

Compound Interest

Compounding refers to the idea of earning interest on previously earned interest. Imagine putting $100 in the bank at 10%. We would earn $10 in the first year and have a balance of $110 at year-end. In the second year, we would earn $11 for a balance of $121, in the third year $12.10, and so on. The interest is larger each year because it's calculated on a balance that increases with the accumulation of all prior interest.

Compound interest refers to earning interest on interest.

Under **compound interest** the balance in the bank grows at an exponential rate. Graphically, an amount placed at compound interest grows as shown in Figure 8.5. The increasing steepness of the curve as time progresses is characteristic of exponential growth.

FIGURE 8.5
The Effect of
Compound Interest

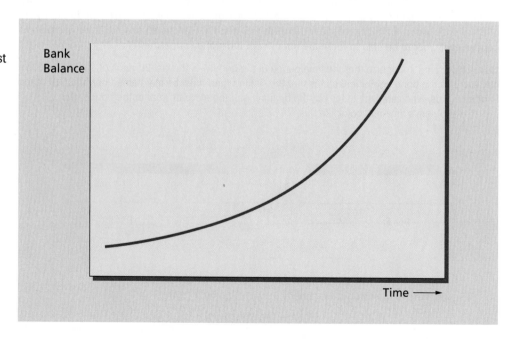

Compounding Periods

The **compounding period** associated with an interest rate refers to the frequency with which interest is credited into the recipient's account for the purpose of calculating future interest. Commonly used periods are annual, semiannual, quarterly, and monthly. When none is mentioned, an annual period is implied. The shorter the period, the more frequently interest is credited and the more interest is earned *on interest.*

An example will make the idea clear. If a bank pays 12% interest compounded annually, someone depositing $100 is credited with $12 at the end of a year, and the basis for the second year's interest calculation is $112. A timeline portrayal of the year would look like this.

The **compounding period** is the time after which interest is credited to the depositor's account to compute subsequent interest. Interest is usually compounded annually, semiannually, quarterly, or monthly.

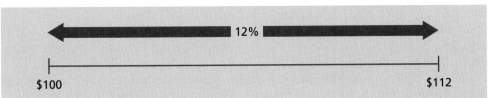

If the 12% is compounded semiannually, the year is divided into two halves and 6% interest is paid in each. However, the first half-year's interest is credited to the depositor at midyear and earns additional interest in the second half. The additional interest is 6% of $6 or $0.36. The timeline portrayal looks like this.

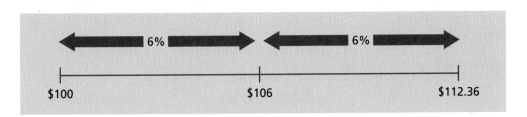

Compounding 12% quarterly involves dividing the year into four quarters, each paying (12%/4 =) 3%. Each quarter's interest is credited at the end of the quarter. The timeline looks like this.

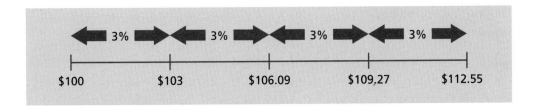

It's easy to get each successive quarter's ending balance by multiplying the previous balance by (1 plus the *quarterly* interest rate in decimal form). That's 1.03 in this case. This is just the (1 + *k*) idea we've been working with, but *k* is stated for a quarterly compounding period.

Compounding 12% monthly involves dividing the year into 12 monthly periods, each bearing a 1% interest rate. If $100 is initially deposited, the year-end balance will be $112.68.

It's common practice to quote an annual rate and state the compounding period immediately afterward. The quarterly case in our 12% example would be quoted as "12% compounded quarterly." Those words literally mean 3% interest paid on quarterly periods.

Interest rates are quoted by stating the **nominal interest rate** followed by the *compounding period.*

The quoted rate, 12% in this case, is called the **nominal interest rate.** We'll write it as k_{nom}. The term "nominal" simply means the stated rate.

It's possible to pay interest compounded on any time period; however, the periods we've mentioned are the most common in business. Daily compounding is rare.

The theoretical limit as periods become shorter is continuous compounding in which interest is instantaneously credited as earned. Continuous compounding takes some special math that we'll discuss later.

The Effective Annual Rate

Notice in the 12% example above that the final bank balance increases with more frequent compounding. Let's summarize those calculations. For an initial deposit of $100 and a nominal rate of 12%, Table 8.2 shows the amounts in the bank at the end of one year.

These differences in a depositor's balance mean that although all four rates are quoted as 12%, different amounts of interest are actually being paid. As we've explained, the difference is due to the frequency of compounding.

It's important to quantify the effect of different compounding methods to avoid confusion in financial dealings. That is, people need to know just how much more monthly or quarterly compounding pays than annual compounding at any nominal rate. This need for clarification has led to the idea of an **effective annual rate,** referred to as **EAR (or sometimes EFF)**. It's the rate of annually compounded interest that is just equivalent to the nominal rate compounded more frequently. Stated another way, it's the annually compounded rate that gets the depositor the same account balance after one year that he or she would get under more frequent compounding.

The **effective annual rate (EAR)** is the annually compounded rate that pays the same interest as a lower rate compounded more frequently.

Let's consider 12% compounded monthly as an example. What annually compounded interest rate will get a depositor the same interest? Table 8.2 shows that monthly compounding results in an ending balance of $112.68 on an initial deposit of $100; hence, the total interest paid is $12.68.

The annually compounded rate that pays this much interest is calculated by dividing the interest paid by the principal invested.

$$\frac{\$12.68}{\$100.00} = 12.68\%$$

Hence, 12.68% compounded annually is *effectively* equal to 12% compounded monthly. What are the EARs for semiannual and quarterly compounding at 12%?

Provinces and territories have regulations imposing controls on advertising the cost of borrowing. Most of these regulations require that an annual percentage rate be quoted, according to some prescribed mathematical formula. Watch for it the next time you see an advertisement for a bank.

In general, the EAR can be calculated for any compounding period by using the following formula.

(8.15)
$$EAR = \left(1 + \frac{k_{nom}}{m}\right)^m - 1$$

where m is the number of compounding periods per year (12 for monthly, 4 for quarterly, and 2 for semiannually).

TABLE 8.2
Year-End Balances at Various Compounding Periods for $100 Initial Deposit and $k_{nom} = 12\%$

Compounding	Final Balance
Annual	$ 112.00
Semiannual	112.36
Quarterly	112.55
Monthly	112.68

The effect of more frequent compounding is greater at higher interest rates. Table 8.3 illustrates this point. At a nominal rate of 6%, the effective increase in interest due to monthly rather than annual compounding is only 0.17%, which represents a 2.8% increase in the rate actually paid (0.17%/6.00% = 0.028 = 2.8%). At 18%, however, the effective increase is 1.56%, which represents an 8.7% increase in what's actually paid.

The APR and the EAR

Credit card companies charge monthly interest on unpaid balances at rates in the neighbourhood of 1.5%. This represents a monthly compounding of interest on the cardholder's debt. The companies advertise that the **annual percentage rate**, known as the APR, is 18%, 12 times the monthly rate.

Don't confuse the APR with the EAR. The APR is actually the nominal rate. Table 8.3 shows that, at a nominal rate of 18%, the EAR for monthly compounding is 19.56%, somewhat more than 18%.[6]

> The **annual percentage rate (APR)** associated with credit cards is actually the nominal rate and is less than the *EAR*.

Example 8.7

In 2007 you could get a typical, no-fee bank credit card that quoted an annual interest rate of 18.5% with a 19-day grace period. Assuming you don't pay the balance of your credit card off for a whole year (not exactly good financial management), what interest rate would you actually pay?

■ **Solution:** To answer this we need to convert the quoted APR to an EAR. The card has 365/19 = 19.21 compound periods per year. The EAR is $(1+.185/19.21)^{19.21} - 1 = 0.2022$ or 20.12%. It doesn't seem much of a difference but many consumers pay just the minimum payment on their credit card purchases. Even a small difference in interest rates can result in hundreds of dollars of additional interest charges.

Compounding Periods and the Time Value Formulas

Each of the time value formulas contains an interest rate, k, and a number of time periods or payments, n. In using the formulas, the time periods must be compounding periods, and the interest rate must be the rate for a single compounding period.

The problems we've dealt with so far have all involved annual compounding. In that case, the compounding period is a year, and the appropriate interest rate is the nominal rate itself. Things are a little more complicated with non-annual compounding periods. Let's consider quarters as an example.

Suppose we have a time value problem that runs for five years and has an interest rate of 12%. If compounding is annual, k and n are simply 12 and 5, respectively. However, if compounding is quarterly, the appropriate period is one quarter and the rate for that period is (12%/4=) 3%. Further, the time dimension of the problem needs to be stated as 20 quarters

Nominal Rate	EAR for Monthly Compounding	Effective Increase	Increase as % of k_{nom}
6%	6.17%	0.17%	2.8%
12	12.68	0.68	5.7
18	19.56	1.56	8.7

TABLE 8.3
Changes in the Effect of Compounding at Different Rates

---

6 For those students who worked through Chapter 5, this discussion might sound familiar. On page 163 we discussed the cost of forgoing an early payment discount. The APR was 37.2% and the EAR was 44.6%.

rather than five years (5 years $\times$ 4 quarters/year = 20 quarters). Hence k and n for the problem should be 3 and 20, respectively.

Whenever we run into a problem with non-annual compounding, we have to calculate the appropriate k and n for use in the formulas from the nominal rate and time given in the problem. Some simple rules make that relatively easy to do.

If a problem gives a nominal rate and states time in years, compute k and n for use in the formulas as follows.

Semiannual: $\qquad k = \dfrac{k_{nom}}{2} \qquad\qquad n = \text{Years} \times 2$

Quarterly: $\qquad k = \dfrac{k_{nom}}{4} \qquad\qquad n = \text{Years} \times 4$

Monthly: $\qquad k = \dfrac{k_{nom}}{12} \qquad\qquad n = \text{Years} \times 12$

Recall that some calculators will automatically divide the interest input by a number of compounding periods for you. That feature is convenient if you're working with the same kind of compounding all the time. But because we're switching from one to another, it's better to leave the setting at 1 and input the interest rate for the compounding period.

Let's try two problems involving the future value of an annuity to get used to these ideas (Examples 8.8 and 8.9).

Example 8.8

You want to buy a car costing $15,000 in 2 1/2 years. You plan to save the money by making equal monthly deposits in your bank account, which pays 12% compounded monthly. How much must you deposit each month?

Calculator Solution

Key	Solution
n	30
I/Y	1
FV	15,000
PV	0

Answer

PMT	431.22

Use Excel® Function PMT

■ **Solution:** In this situation the future value of a series of payments must accumulate to a known amount, indicating a future value of an annuity problem.

First calculate the correct k and n. Because compounding is monthly,

$$k = \frac{k_{nom}}{12} = \frac{12\%}{12} = 1\% = 1\%$$

and

$$n = 2.5 \text{ years} \times 12 \text{ monthly payments/year} = 30 \text{ monthly payments.}$$

Next write the future value of an annuity expression and substitute.

$$FVA_n = PMT[FVFA_{k,n}]$$
$$\$15,000 = PMT[FVFA_{1,30}]$$

Use Appendix A–3 to find $FVFA_{1,30} = 34.7849$ and substitute.

$$\$15,000 = PMT[34.7849]$$

Finally, solve for PMT.

$$PMT = \$431.22$$

Example 8.9

Tuong and Susan Nguyen have a daughter, Molly, just entering high school, and they've started to think about sending her to college. They expect to need about $50,000 in cash when she starts. Although the Nguyens have a good income, they live extravagantly and have little or no savings. Susan analyzed the family budget and decided they could realistically put away $750 a month or $2,250 per quarter toward Molly's schooling. They're now searching for an investment vehicle that will provide a return sufficient to grow these savings into $50,000 in four years. If quarterly compounding is assumed, how large a return (interest rate) do the Nguyens have to get to achieve their goal? Is it realistic?

■ **Solution:** Once again we recognize this as a future value of an annuity problem because of the stream of payments involved and the fact that the Nguyens are saving for a known future amount.

Because the problem runs for four years and the compounding along with the payments is quarterly, n is calculated as

$$n = 4 \text{ years} \times 4 \text{ quarterly payments/year} = 16 \text{ quarterly payments}$$

Equation 8.14 gives the future value of an annuity expression.

$$FVA_n = PMT[FVFA_{k,n}]$$

Substituting values from the problems, we have

$$\$50,000 = \$2,250[FVFA_{k,16}]$$

Solving for the factor yields

$$FVFA_{k,16} = 22.2222$$

In Appendix A–3 we search for this value along the row for 16 payments and find that it lies between 4% and 4.5%. In this case it's fairly easy to estimate that the factor is about half of the way between 4% and 4.5%.

Hence, the approximate solution is 4.2%; however, that's a quarterly rate. The appropriate nominal rate is

$$4.2\% \times 4 = 16.8\%$$

This is a high rate of return to expect on invested money. Is it reasonable to expect such a rate to be sustained over four years?

There's no definite answer to that question. There have been times when that expectation would have been reasonable, but such a high rate can always be expected to involve substantial risk. Because they probably don't want to risk not being able to send Molly to college, the Nguyens should probably try to save a little more and opt for a more conservative investment.

Calculator Solution	
Key	**Input**
n	16
PMT	2,250
FV	50,000
PV	0

Answer	
I/Y	4.2

**Use Excel®
Function Rate**

Dealing with Differences in Compounding and Payment Frequencies

Converting n and k to like terms works well when the interest compounding occurs with the same frequency as the payments. However, in some cases these frequencies do not correspond; that is, the compounding occurs more or less often than the payments. In such cases, we must calculate an appropriate k—one that matches the payment cycle.

Using our Example 8.9, let's assume that the Nguyens wanted to save $750 per month over the next four years but the investment vehicle they are considering pays 6% per annum and compounds the interest semiannually. How much will the Nguyens have accumulated at the end of four years?

SOLUTION Now we have payments occurring monthly and interest compounded semiannually. The interest and payment cycle must be in like terms, and it is the payment frequency that dictates how k will be handled! So to get the proper k, we must make a few adjustments to our Equation 8.15.

$$(8.15) \qquad EAR = \left(1 + \frac{k_{nom}}{m}\right)^m - 1$$

We will call the appropriate k (that is, the one that matches our payment cycle) k^*. With a little algebra, Equation 8.15 becomes:

$$(8.16) \qquad k^* = \left(1 + \frac{k_{nom}}{m}\right)^{\frac{m}{n}} - 1$$

where m is the number of times during the period that interest is compounded and n is the number of payments to be made during that period.

So for our problem k^* is

$$k^* = \left(1 + \frac{0.06}{2}\right)^{\frac{2}{12}} - 1$$

$$= (1 + 0.03)^{\frac{1}{6}} - 1$$

$$= 0.004939 \text{ or } 0.4939\% \text{ per month}$$

And n, the number of payments to be made, is $4 \times 12 = 48$. As the interest rate is not on the tables, we need to use Equation 8.13 on page 271 to solve the problem.

$$FVA_n = \frac{750\left[(1 + 0.004939)^{48} - 1\right]}{0.004939}$$

$$= \$40,513$$

Let's look at another situation with the Nguyens. Say they decided to make quarterly payments of \$2,250, but the investment vehicle paid 6% per annum, compounded monthly. How much would they have saved by the end of the fourth year?

SOLUTION Again, the payments occur less frequently than the interest is compounded. To get the proper k, we use our Equation 8.16, where m is the number of times during the period that interest is compounded and n is the number of payments to be made during that period.

So for our problem k^* is:

$$k^* = \left(1 + \frac{k_{nom}}{m}\right)^{\frac{m}{n}} - 1$$

$$= \left(1 + \frac{0.06}{12}\right)^{\frac{12}{4}} - 1$$

$$= (1 + 0.005)^3 - 1$$

$$= 0.01508 \text{ or } 1.508\% \text{ per quarter}$$

And n, the number of payments to be made, is $4 \times 4 = 16$. As the interest rate is not on the tables, we need to use Equation 8.13 on page 271 to solve the problem.

$$FVA_n = \frac{2,250\left[(1 + 0.01508)^{16} - 1\right]}{0.01508}$$

$$= \$40,373$$

You'll notice that when using a financial calculator or Excel® we have adjusted k and n to like terms. Some financial calculators will allow you to change the payment and compounding frequencies so that you do not have to adjust k and n. This is a handy feature and the owner's manual for your calculator gives step–by-step instructions for changing the frequencies.

The Present Value of an Annuity—Developing a Formula

The present value of an annuity is simply the sum of the present values of all of the annuity's payments. We could always calculate these individually, but it's much easier to develop a formula to do all the calculations in one step as we did with the future value. The method we'll use is similar to that used in developing the future value formula, but we'll proceed more quickly because we've used the approach before.

We begin with a timeline portrayal of a three-payment annuity and write down the present value of each payment in terms of the interest rate, k. In this case, we divide by powers of $(1 + k)$ instead of multiplying as in the future value case. Review Equations 8.5 and 8.6 on page 265 to see that this gives the present value of an amount. Figure 8.6 is the timeline portrayal.

Calculator Solution

Key	Input
n	48
PMT	750
PV	0
I/Y	.4939

Answer

FV	40,513

Use Excel®
Function FV

Calculator Solution

Key	Input
n	16
PMT	2,250
I/Y	1.508
PV	0

Answer

FV	40,373

Use Excel®
Function FV

http

Stone Street Capital will buy your winning lottery ticket by paying you its present value. See the website at http://www. stonestreet.com.

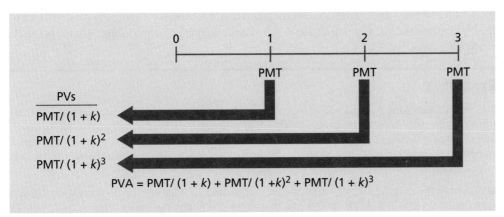

FIGURE 8.6
Present Value of a
Three-Payment
Ordinary Annuity

The present value is formed for the first payment by dividing the payment amount by $(1 + k)$, for the second payment by dividing by $(1 + k)^2$, and so forth. Notice that this is equivalent to multiplying by present value factors, because $1/(1 + k)$ is the present value factor for k and one period, $PVF_{k,1}$; $1/(1 + k)^2$ is the present value factor for k and two periods; and so on.

The present value of the three-payment annuity is

(**8.17**) $$PVA = \frac{PMT}{(1 + k)} + \frac{PMT}{(1 + k)^2} + \frac{PMT}{(1 + k)^3}$$

which can also be written as

(**8.17**) $$PVA = PMT(1 + k)^{-1} + PMT(1 + k)^{-2} + PMT(1 + k)^{-3}$$

with negative exponents to indicate 1 over the powers of $(1 + k)$.

Notice how regular the expression is. Every payment produces a term involving PMT divided by $(1 + k)$ to a successively larger power beginning with 1.

Examining Figure 8.6, we can easily see that adding more payments to the annuity would just add more terms to the equation. For example, a fourth payment would produce a term $PMT(1 + k)^{-4}$, and so on.

Thus we can generalize Equation 8.17 for any number of payments, n, as follows.

(**8.18**) $$PVA = PMT(1 + k)^{-1} + PMT(1 + k)^{-2} + \ldots + PMT(1 + k)^{-n}$$

Next, we can factor PMT out of the right side of Equation 8.18 and use summation notation to represent the terms involving negative powers of $(1 + k)$.

(**8.19**) $$PVA = PMT \sum_{i=1}^{n} (1 + k)^{-i}$$

Once again, we notice that the expression in the brackets is a function of only k and n, and can be tabulated for likely values of those variables. This is the present value factor for an annuity and is written as $PVFA_{k,n}$.

(**8.20**) $$PVFA_{k,n} = \sum_{i=1}^{n} (1 + k)^{-i}$$

Values of the present value factor for an annuity are tabulated in Appendix A–4.

Finally, we can rewrite Equation 8.19 by substituting from Equation 8.20. The resulting expression is convenient for use in solving problems when used in conjunction with Appendix A–4.

(**8.21**) $$PVA = PMT[PVFA_{k,n}]$$

The Present Value of an Annuity—Solving Problems

Equation 8.21 for the present value of an annuity works just like Equation 8.14 does for the future value of an annuity. There are four variables: PVA (the present value itself), PMT (the payment),

k (the interest rate), and n (the number of payments). Problems will generally present three of them as known and ask you to find the fourth. The general approach is similar to what we've already been doing.[7]

Example 8.10

The Shipson Company has just sold a large machine to Halifax on an installment contract. The contract calls for Halifax to make payments of $5,000 every six months (semiannually) for 10 years. Shipson would like its cash now and asks its bank to discount the contract and pay it the present (discounted) value. Halifax is a good credit risk, so the bank is willing to discount the contract at 14% compounded semiannually. How much will Shipson receive?

Calculator Solution

Key	Input
n	20
I/Y	7
PMT	5,000
FV	0

Answer

PV	52,970.07

**Use Excel®
Function PV**

■ **Solution:** The contract represents an annuity with payments of $5,000. The bank is willing to buy it for its present value at a relatively high rate of interest. The higher the rate of interest, the lower the price the bank is willing to pay for the contract.

First, calculate the appropriate k and n for semiannual compounding.

$$k = \frac{k_{nom}}{2} = \frac{14\%}{2} = 7\%$$

$n = 10$ years $\times$ 2 payments/year $= 20$ semiannual payments

The timeline looks like this.

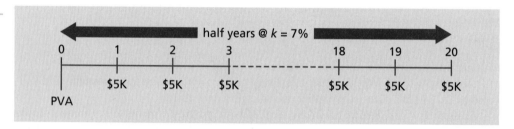

Write Equation 8.21 and substitute the known information.

$$PVA = PMT[PVFA_{k,n}]$$

$$PVA = \$5,000[PVFA_{7,20}]$$

Appendix A–4 gives $PVFA_{7,20} = 10.5940$. Substituting and solving for PVA yields

$$PVA = \$52,970$$

If we look at the algebraic formula in Equation 8.22 (a or b) and how it was derived, you might notice that the formula gives you the value of the annuity one period *before* the first payment is received. Congratulations if you did notice it and not to worry if you did not. What you need to remember, though, is that the formula (tables, financial calculator or Excel®) will give you the value of the annuity one period before the first payment. Why? Because the

---

7 As in the case of future value, the mathematical derivation of the algebraic formula is not important to furthering our understanding of present value but it is important if financial tables or a financial calculator are unavailable. The present value of an annuity is

(8.22)   a) $PVA = FVA_n \times PVF_{k,n}$

$$= \frac{PMT[(1 + k)^n - 1]}{k} \times \frac{1}{(1 + k)^n}$$

Simplifies to

b) $PVA = \dfrac{PMT}{k}\left(1 - \dfrac{1}{(1 + k)^n}\right)$

first payment is received one period from now and we are trying to find out how much it is worth in today's dollars!

As well, although we have mentioned this before, when dealing with annuities n is often described as periods when in fact you should be thinking about the number of payments to be received. You will soon see why we are taking the time now to make the distinction.

Amortized Loans

The most common application of the present value of an annuity concept is in dealing with amortized debt. Debt is said to be amortized when the principal is paid off gradually during its life. Car loans, home mortgages, and many business loans are amortized.

An amortized loan is generally structured so that a *constant* payment is made periodically, usually monthly, over the loan's term. Each payment contains one month's interest and an amount to reduce principal. Interest is charged on the outstanding loan balance at the beginning of each month, so as the loan's principal is reduced, successive interest charges become smaller. Because the monthly payments are equal, successive payments contain larger proportions of principal repayment and smaller proportions of interest.

In applying the present value of an annuity formula to a loan, the amount borrowed is always the present value of the annuity, PVA, and the loan payment is always PMT.

> An amortized loan's principal is paid off regularly over its life.

Example 8.11

Suppose you borrow $10,000 over four years at 18% compounded monthly repayable in monthly installments. How much is your loan payment?

■ **Solution:** First, notice that for monthly compounding k and n are

$$k = \frac{k_{nom}}{12} = \frac{18\%}{12} = 1.5\%$$

$$n = 4 \text{ years} \times 12 \text{ monthly payments/year} = 48 \text{ monthly payments}$$

Then write Equation 8.21 and substitute.

$$PVA = PMT[PVFA_{k,n}]$$

$$\$10,000 = PMT[PVFA_{1.5,48}]$$

Appendix A–4 gives $PVFA_{1.5,48} = 34.0426$, and

$$PMT = \$293.75$$

Calculator Solution

Key	Input
n	48
I/Y	1.5
PV	10,000
FV	0

Answer

PMT	293.75

**Use Excel®
Function PMT**

Insights **PRACTICAL FINANCE**

The Lottery: Congratulations, You're Rich—But Not as Rich as You Thought

Various lottery jackpots are enormous sums of money, but some are not really as big as they're made out to be. That's because of the time value of money and the way the prizes are paid. Large lottery prizes are often paid over 25 years, but lottery authorities state the winnings as the sum of the payments without consideration of time value. For example, a $25 million prize could be a $1 million per year for 25 years, or an annuity.

What the winner really has today is the present value of that annuity. If a lucky player wants her money immediately, she has to accept the discounted value of the stream of payments. For example, the Western Canada Lottery Corporation recently offered a "Millionaire Life" lottery. If you won, you could choose between receiving $1 million per year for 25 years or $17 million immediately. Assuming the first million came one year after the draw date, the implied interest rate you'd receive from accepting the $17 million prize now would be 3.22%. That's nothing to sneeze at, but it is a far cry from $25 million.

Example 8.12

Suppose you want to buy a car and can afford to make payments of $500 a month. The bank makes three-year car loans at 12% compounded monthly. How much can you borrow toward a new car?

■ **Solution:** For monthly compounding,

$$k = \frac{k_{nom}}{12} = \frac{12\%}{12} = 1\%$$

n = 3 years × 12 monthly payments/year = 36 monthly payments.

Write Equation 8.21 and substitute.

$$PVA = PMT[PVFA_{k,n}]$$
$$PVA = \$500[PVFA_{1,36}]$$

Appendix A–4 gives $PVFA_{1,36}$ = 30.1075, and

$$PVA = \$15,053.75$$

That is, the bank would lend you $15,053.75.

Loan Amortization Schedules

Loan amortization schedules detail the interest and principal in each loan payment.

A loan amortization schedule lists every payment and shows how much of it goes to pay interest and how much reduces principal. It also shows the beginning and ending balances of unpaid principal for each period.

To construct an amortization schedule, we have to know the loan amount, the payment, and the periodic interest rate. That's PVA, PMT, and k. Let's use the loan in the last example as an illustration. Table 8.4 shows the completed computation for the first two lines. Follow the explanation in the next paragraph for the first line, then verify the second, third, and fourth lines yourself.

The loan amount is $15,053.75. This is the beginning balance for the first monthly period. The payment is a constant $500; that amount is entered on every row in the payment column. Although the nominal interest rate in this case is 12%, the monthly interest rate is 1% because compounding is monthly. Therefore the monthly interest charge is calculated as 1% of the month's beginning loan balance.

$$\$15,053.75 \times 0.01 = \$150.54$$

As the payment is $500 and $150.54 goes to interest, the remaining ($500 − $150.54 =) $349.46 reduces principal. The ending loan balance is the beginning balance less the principal reduction, ($15,053.75 − $349.46 =) $14,704.29. This amount becomes the beginning balance for the next period, and the process is repeated.

TABLE 8.4
A Partial Amortization Schedule

Period	Beginning Balance	Payment	Interest @ 1%	Principal Reduction	Ending Balance
1	$ 15,053.75	$ 500.00	$ 150.54	$ 349.46	$ 14,704.29
2	14,704.29	500.00	147.04	352.96	14,351.33
3	14,351.33	500.00	143.51	356.49	13,994.84
4	13,994.84	500.00	139.95	360.05	13,634.79
⋮	⋮	⋮	⋮	⋮	⋮

This procedure carried out for 36 monthly periods will bring the ending balance to zero at the end of the last period. It's important to notice what happens to the composition of the payment as the loan is paid down. The interest charge declines, and the portion devoted to principal reduction increases, while the total payment remains constant.

Mortgage Loans

Loans used to buy real estate are called mortgage loans or just *mortgages*. A home mortgage is often the largest single financial transaction in an average person's life. A typical mortgage is an amortized loan with semiannual compounding and payments that run for 25 years; that's 300 payments.[8]

In the beginning of a mortgage's life, most of the payment goes to pay interest. To demonstrate how much interest is paid on a mortgage, we will begin with a simplified example.

For example, consider that a 25-year mortgage at 6% (compounded monthly) for $100,000 has a monthly payment of $644.30 (verify this by using Equation 8.19 and Appendix A–4). The first month's interest on such a loan is 0.5% of $100,000 or $500. Hence, only $144.30 is applied to principal. The first payment is 77.6% interest!

This situation reverses toward the end of the mortgage when most of the payment is principal. In other words, during the early years of a mortgage, the principal is paid down slowly, but near the end it's amortized quickly.

The second implication of the mortgage payment pattern is that halfway through a mortgage's life, the homeowner hasn't paid off half the loan. To see that in the loan we've been talking about, let's calculate the present value of the second half of the payment stream as of the end of 12.5 years. That will be the amount one could borrow making 150 payments of $644.30. Because this is what's left after 12.5 years, it must represent the remaining loan balance. We'll use the same expression for the present value of an annuity.

$$PVA = PMT[PVFA_{k,n}]$$
$$= \$644.30[PVFA_{0.5,150}]$$
$$= \$644.30[105.350]$$
$$= \$67,877.00$$

Thus, halfway through the life of this $100,000 mortgage, roughly $68,000 is still outstanding. In other words, only about 32% of the original loan has been paid off.

Another interesting feature of a long-term amortized loan like a mortgage is the total amount of interest paid over the entire term. At 6%, the homeowner pays almost the amount of the loan in interest.

Total payments ($644.30 × 300)	$ 193,290
Less original loan	100,000
Total interest	$ 93,290

Of course, this effect varies dramatically with the interest rate. Over the last 25 years, rates have varied between 5% and 16%. In the early 2000s, they've been on the low end of that range.[9]

Now that we have looked at the simplified mortgage, let's examine what would happen to the payments and amount left owing after 12.5 years if the 6% interest were compounded *semiannually*. The payments would be $639.83 per month and, after paying 150 payments, you

A **mortgage loan** is a loan secured by real estate. Early mortgage payments are *almost all interest.*

Calculator Solution

Key	Input
n	300
I/Y	0.5
PV	100,000
FV	0

Answer

PMT	644.30

Use Excel® Function PMT

Calculator Solution

Key	Input
n	150
I/Y	0.5
PMT	644.30
FV	0

Answer

PV	67,876.99

Use Excel® Function PV

8 Canadian banks governed under federal statutes are required under Section 6 of the *Interest Act* to compound interest no more frequently than semiannually even though the payments are made monthly (or more frequently). Banks governed by provincial or territorial statutes are not limited to semiannual compounding on their standard fixed rate mortgages.
9 At 12%, a typical mortgage rate in the late 1980s, the first mortgage payment is 95% interest and the net interest cost over 25 years is almost twice the amount.

would still owe $67,678.29 (verify this by using Equation 8.16 to get $k^* = 0.004939$ or 0.4939% and then Equation 8.22 (a or b), first to find the payment amount and second to verify the balance owing with 150 payments remaining).

When we compare the payments and balance remaining under the two different compounding scenarios, we see that the semiannual compounding results in lower monthly payments and less principal owing at some point in time. This is due to the fact that interest is not allowed to compound on itself as often! Which mortgage would you rather have? (*Hint:* Calculate the EAR of each.)

AMORTIZED LOANS AND TAX PLANNING Because interest payments on business and investment loans are tax deductible, we're sometimes interested in projecting the total interest and principal payments to be made during a particular future year of a loan's life. If we don't want to write out the entire amortization schedule, we can solve the problem by calculating the loan balance at the beginning and end of the year.

To illustrate, let's calculate the principal and interest payments in the third year of the simplified $100,000 loan with which we've been working. Remember, on this loan we were using 6%, compounded monthly. The loan balance at the beginning of the third year will be the amount left after 24 payments have been made and there are 276 left to go. We find it by using Equation 8.19.

$$PVA = PMT[PVFA_{k,n}]$$
$$= \$644.30[PVFA_{0.5,276}]$$
$$= \$644.30[149.511]$$
$$= \$96,329.94$$

Similarly, 264 payments will be left after three years.

$$PVA = \$644.30[PFVA_{0.5,264}]$$
$$= \$644.30[146.397]$$
$$= \$94,323.54$$

The difference between these balances, $2,006.35, is the amount paid against principal during the year. There are 12 payments totalling ($644.30 × 12 =) $7,731.60, so the interest portion is this amount less the contribution to equity. Assuming a business had this mortgage, its tax-deductible interest would be:

Total payments	$ 7,731.60
Principal reduction	(2,006.35)
Deductible interest	$ 5,725.25

Calculator Solution

Key	Input
n	276
I/Y	0.5
PMT	644.30
FV	0

Answer
PV	96,329.94

Use Excel® Function PV

Calculator Solution

Key	Input
n	264
I/Y	0.5
PMT	644.30
FV	0
Answer	
PV	94,323.59

Use Excel® Function PV

The Annuity Due

So far we've dealt only with ordinary annuities in which payments occur at the end of time periods. When payments occur at the *beginning* of time periods, such as monthly rent in advance, we have an **annuity due**, and our formulas need to be modified somewhat.

*In an **annuity due**, payments occur at the beginning of each period.*

The Future Value of an Annuity Due

First consider the future value of an annuity formula as developed in Figure 8.4. Review that figure on page 270 now. Because the end of one period is the beginning of the next, we can create the annuity due by simply shifting each payment back one period in time. This is shown schematically in Figure 8.7. There is now a payment at time 0, but none at time 3.

Because each payment is received one period earlier, it spends one period longer in the bank earning interest. Therefore, each payment's future value at the end of the annuity will be

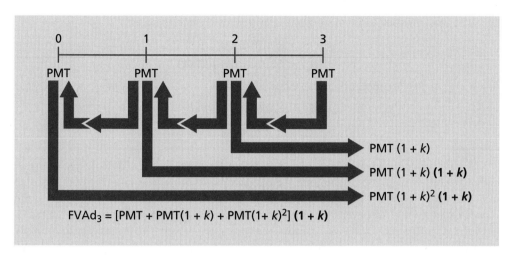

FIGURE 8.7
The Future Value
of a Three-Period
Annuity Due

whatever it was before times $(1 + k)$. The additional $(1 + k)$ is shown in boldface in the diagram.

The future value of the annuity due, which we'll call FVAd$_3$, is then

$$FVAd_3 = PMT(\mathbf{1 + k}) + PMT(1 + k)(\mathbf{1 + k}) + PMT(1 + k)^2(\mathbf{1 + k})$$

which can be rewritten by factoring out the additional $(1 + k)$ as

(**8.23**) $\qquad FVAd_3 = [PMT + PMT(1 + k) + PMT(1 + k)^2](1 + k)$

It's easy to see that no matter how many payments we now choose to add, every term in an annuity due will be the same as it is in an ordinary annuity multiplied by an extra $(1 + k)$. Therefore, we can generalize Equation 8.23 to n payments.

(**8.24**) $\qquad FVAd_3 = [PMT + PMT(1 + k) + ... + PMT(1 + k)^{n-1}] (1 + k)$

Once we've done that, the term inside the brackets can be developed into the ordinary annuity formula just as before. The only thing changed is the addition of the $(1 + k)$ factor on the right. Hence, the final formula for an annuity due is just our old formula for an ordinary annuity multiplied by $(1 + k)$. By multiplying the ordinary annuity formula by $(1 + k)$, we get the value one period after the last payment.

(**8.25**) $\qquad FVAd_n = PMT[FVFA_{k,n}](1 + k)$

Situations in which an annuity due is appropriate can be recognized when words such as "starting now," "starting today," or "starting immediately" are used to describe a payment stream.

Example 8.13

The Baxter Corporation started making sinking fund deposits of $50,000 per quarter today. Baxter's bank pays 8% compounded quarterly, and the payments will be made for 10 years. What will the fund be worth at the end of that time?

■ **Solution:** First, calculate k and n.

$$k = \frac{8\%}{4} = 2\%$$

$$n = 10 \text{ years} \times 4 \text{ quarterly payments/year} = 40 \text{ quarterly payments}$$

Calculator Solution

BEGIN MODE

Key	Input
n	40
I/Y	2
PMT	50,000
PV	0

Answer

FV	3,080,501

**Use Excel®
Function FV**

TYPE 1

Answer

3,080,501

Next, write Equation 8.25 and substitute known values from the problem.

$$FVAd_n = PMT[FVFA_{k,n}](1 + k)$$
$$FVAd_{40} = \$50,000[FVFA_{2,40}](1.02)$$

Get $FVFA_{2,40} = 60.4020$ from Appendix A–3 and substitute.

$$FVAd_{40} = \$50,000[60.4020](1.02)$$
$$= \$3,080,502$$

Financial calculators and Excel® let you set annuity payments at either the beginning or end of periods. If set in the begin mode, the calculator and spreadsheet take care of the $(1 + k)$ multiplication automatically. But remember, n is still the number of payments. So for the Baxter example $n = 40$, even if using the begin mode (or on Excel® put 1 in for type). However, if you're only doing an occasional annuity due problem, it's just as easy to multiply manually.

The Present Value of an Annuity Due

Applying very similar logic to the derivation of the present value of an annuity expression developed in Figure 8.6 (page 281) yields a formula for the present value of an annuity due, which we'll call PVAd.

(**8.26**) $$PVAd = PMT[PVFA_{k,n}](1 + k)$$

This expression is used in the same way as Equation 8.25.

As an exercise, work your way through the development of Equation 8.26 by using Figure 8.7 and the approach we've just gone through in developing Equation 8.25.

Recognizing Types of Annuity Problems

The most common error in working annuity problems results from confusion over whether to use the present or future value technique. Here's a little guidance on how to keep the two straight.

First, an annuity problem is always recognized by the presence of a *stream* of *equal* payments. Whether the value of the payments is known or unknown, a series of them means an annuity.

There are a number of investment and loan calculators at http://www.fiscalagents.com/toolbox/index.shtml.

Annuity problems always involve some kind of a transaction at one end of the stream of payments or the other. If the transaction is at the end of the stream, you have a future value problem. If the transaction is in the beginning, you have a present value problem. Here's a graphic representation of this idea.

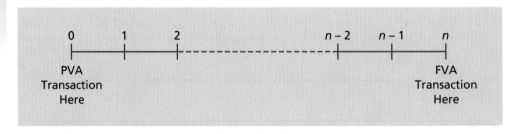

A loan is always a present value of an annuity problem. The annuity itself is the stream of loan payments. The transaction is the transfer of the amount borrowed from the lender to the borrower. That always occurs at the beginning of the payment stream.

Putting aside money to pay for something in the future (saving up) is always a future value of an annuity problem. For example, suppose we're saving up to buy a car by depositing equal sums in the bank each month. The deposits are the payments, and the car purchase is the transaction at the end of the payment stream.

Perpetuities

A series of equal payments that occur at equal intervals and go on forever (kind of like this chapter) is called a perpetuity. You can think of a perpetuity as an infinite annuity although it's not really an annuity. The concept of future value clearly doesn't make sense for perpetuities, because there's no end point in time to which future values can be projected. The present value of a perpetuity, however, does make sense.

A perpetuity is a stream of regular payments that goes on forever.

The present value of a perpetuity, like that of an annuity, is the sum of the present values of all the individual payments. At first that doesn't seem to make sense either, because you'd think the sum of the present values of an infinite number of payments would be an infinite number itself.

However, the *present value* of each payment in an infinite stream is a diminishing series of numbers. Each payment's PV contribution to the sum is smaller than that of the one before because of the fact that it's farther out into the future. Mathematically, the sum of such a diminishing series of numbers turns out to be finite. Further, the computation of that finite value turns out to be rather simple.

The present value of a perpetuity of payments of amount PMT, at interest rate k, which we'll call PV_p, is just

(8.27)
$$PV_p = \frac{PMT}{k}$$

where k is the interest rate for the period on which the payment is made. For example, if the payment is made quarterly and interest is compounded quarterly, k is the interest rate for quarterly compounding, $k_{nom}/4$.

Notice that the present value of a perpetuity at a given interest rate is a sum, which, if deposited at that rate, will just earn the amount of the payment each period without compounding.

Example 8.14

The Longhorn Corporation issues a security that promises to pay its holder $5 per quarter indefinitely. Money markets are such that investors can earn about 8% compounded quarterly on their money. For how much can Longhorn sell this special security?

■ **Solution:** Longhorn's security represents a perpetuity paid on a quarterly basis. The security is worth the present value of the payments promised at the going interest rate.

$$PV_p = \frac{PMT}{k} = \frac{\$5.00}{0.02} = \$250$$

Preferred shares are securities that offer a deal like this. We'll study these in some detail in Chapter 10.

Preferred share dividends are a perpetuity.

Calculator Solution[10]

Key	Input
n	999
I/Y	2
PMT	5
FV	0

Answer

PV	250

**Use Excel®
Function PV**

Bursaries and Scholarships

If you're the recipient of a bursary or scholarship, the funds likely came from an endowment. These funds are donated for a specific purpose and only the income from these funds can be spent. Many charities have management guidelines for these funds and a good example of how an endowment fund is administered can be found at the University of Calgary's website http://www.fp.ucalgary.ca/financial/treasury/endowment_admin%202005_04.pdf.

10 For most calculators, the largest number that can be entered for a present value calculation is 999. As you can see by the answer given, there is no problem with rounding forever down to 999 payments.

Example 8.15

Ebertek is a privately held corporation that is currently being offered for sale. Big Corp. is considering buying the firm. Ebertek's revenues and earnings after tax have averaged $40 million and $2.5 million, respectively, for the last five years without much variation around those averages. Interest rates are about 10%. What is a realistic starting point for price negotiations?

A steady stream of *earnings* is *capitalized* at its present value as a perpetuity.

■ **Solution:** If the parties agree that Ebertek's earnings stream is stable, a fair price for the company is the present value of those earnings in perpetuity. In other words, the fair price is the present value of a perpetuity of annual payments equal in size to the annual earnings. In this case the company should be worth approximately

$$PV_p = \frac{PMT}{k} = \frac{\$2,500,000}{0.10} = \$25,00,000$$

This valuation process is called the *capitalization of earnings,* at the relevant interest rate, which is 10% in this case. In essence, we equate the stream of payments to an amount of capital (money) that would earn an equivalent series of payments at the current interest rate.

In this situation, negotiations would move up or down from this starting point depending on whether future earnings prospects look better or worse than the earnings record of the recent past.

Calculator Solution

Key	Input
n	999
I/Y	10
PMT	2,500,000
FV	0

Answer

PV	25,000,000

Use Excel® Function PV

Continuous Compounding

In the section on compound interest earlier in this chapter, we discussed compounding periods of less than a year. We specifically addressed annual, semiannual, quarterly, and monthly periods.

Compounding periods can theoretically be even shorter than a day. Hours, minutes, or seconds are indeed possible. In the limit, as time periods become infinitesimally short, we have the idea of *continuous compounding in which* interest is instantaneously credited to the recipient's account as it is earned.

The development of formulas for continuous compounding is more mathematically advanced than we want to deal with in this text. Therefore we'll just present an expression for amount problems without derivation.

$$(8.28) \qquad\qquad FV_n = PV(e^{kn})$$

where k is the nominal rate *in decimal form*, and n is the number of years in the problem.

The letter e represents a special number in mathematics whose decimal value is 2.71828 .... Financial and scientific calculators have an e^x key for calculating exponential values of e. Notice that you can use Equation 8.28 to solve for either the present or future value of an amount. Fractional values for k and/or n can be used directly in this equation.

Example 8.16

The First National Bank of Cardston is offering continuously compounded interest on savings deposits. Such an offering is generally more of a promotional feature than anything else.

    a.   If you deposit $5,000 at 6.5% compounded continuously and leave it in the bank for 3.5 years, how much will you have?

    b.   What is the equivalent annual rate (EAR) of 12% compounded continuously?

■ **Solution:** To solve part (a), write Equation 8.28 and substitute from the problem.

$$FV_n = PV(e^{kn})$$
$$FV_{3.5} = \$5,000(e^{(0.065)(3.5)})$$
$$= \$5,000(e^{0.2275})$$

Use a financial calculator to calculate $e^{0.2275} = 1.255457$, then multiply.

$$FV_{3.5} = \$6,277.29$$

For part (b), calculate the interest earned on a $100 deposit at 12% compounded continuously. Use 1 for n.

$$FV_n = PV(e^{kn})$$
$$FV_1 = \$100(e^{(0.12)(1)})$$
$$= \$100(e^{0.12})$$
$$= \$100(1.1275)$$
$$= \$112.75$$

Because the initial deposit was $100, the interest earned is $12.75, and the EAR is $12.75/$100 = 12.75%.

Compare this result to the year-end balances and resulting EARs for other compounding periods at 12% shown in Table 8.2 on page 276 and the related discussion.

Multipart Problems

Real situations often demand putting two or more time value problems together to get a final solution. In such cases, a timeline portrayal can be critical to keeping things straight. Here are two examples.

Example 8.17

Exeter Inc. has $75,000 invested in securities that earn a return of 16% compounded quarterly. The company is developing a new product that it plans to launch in two years at a cost of $500,000. Exeter's cash flow is good now but may not be later, so management would like to bank money from now until the launch to be sure of having the $500,000 in hand at that time. The money currently invested in securities can be used to provide part of the launch fund. Exeter's bank has offered an account that will pay 12% compounded monthly. How much should Exeter deposit with the bank each month to have enough reserved for the product launch?

■ **Solution:** Two things are happening at once in this problem. Exeter is saving up money by making monthly deposits (an annuity), and the money invested in securities (an amount) is growing independently at interest.

To figure out how much the firm has to deposit each month, we need to know how much those deposits have to accumulate into by the end of two years. That's not given, but it can be calculated. The stream of deposits must provide an amount equal to $500,000 less whatever the securities investment will grow into.

Thus, we have two problems that must be handled sequentially. First, we have an amount problem to find the future value of $75,000. Once we have that figure, we'll subtract it from $500,000 to get the contribution required from the annuity. Then we'll solve a future value of an annuity problem for the payment required to get that amount.

It's important to notice that k and n aren't the same for the two parts of the problem. For the amount problem, we have quarterly compounding over two years at 16%, so $k = 4\%$ and $n = 8$ quarters. In the annuity problem, we have monthly compounding of 12% for two years, so $k = 1\%$ and $n = 24$ monthly payments. The two-part timeline follows.

Calculator Solution

Key	Input
n	8
I/Y	4
PV	75,000
PMT	0

Answer

FV	102,643

**Use Excel®
Function FV**

Find the future value of $75,000 by using Equation 8.4.

$$FV_n = PV[FVF_{k,n}]$$
$$FV_8 = \$75,000[FVF_{4,8}]$$
$$= \$75,000[1.3686]$$
$$= \$102,645$$

Then the savings annuity must provide

$$\$500,000 - \$102,645 = \$397,355$$

In other words, the future value of the annuity of the savings deposits is $397,355. Use Equation 8.14 to solve for the required payment.

$$FVA_n = PMT[FVFA_{k,n}]$$
$$\$397,355 = PMT[FVFA_{1,24}]$$
$$\$397,355 = PMT[26.9735]$$
$$PMT = \$14,731$$

Example 8.18

The Atwal family plans to buy a new house three years from now for $200,000. They'll take out a traditional 25-year mortgage at the time of purchase. Mortgage lenders generally base the amount they'll lend on the borrower's gross family income, allowing roughly 25% of income to be applied to the mortgage payment. The Atwals anticipate that their family income will be about $48,000 at the time they'll purchase the house. The mortgage interest rate is expected to be about 9.16% at that time.

The mortgage alone won't provide enough cash to buy the house, and the family will need to have a down payment saved to make up the difference. They have a bank account that pays 6% compounded quarterly in which they've already saved $10,000. They plan to make quarterly deposits from now until the time of purchase to save the rest. How much must each deposit be?

■ **Solution:** We need three timelines to visualize this problem: one for the $10,000 already in the bank, one for the loan, and one for the savings to be made over the next three years. A timeline diagram is very helpful in problems like this one.

Notice that the problem is focused around the date of purchase of the house. The amount problem and the annuity of the savings end at that time, but that's when the loan begins. That is, time 0 for the loan isn't the present but a time three years in the future. Nevertheless, we'll refer to the loan amount as the present value of the annuity of the payments.

The problem asks us to calculate how much the Atwals need to save each quarter. To do that we have to know how much they need to save up in total. That's the future value of the annuity of their savings, FVA_{12} in the diagram on page 293. That sum is going to be $200,000 less the amount that can be borrowed, less the amount that the money already in savings will have grown into. Those amounts are PVA and FV_{12}, respectively, in the diagram.

First calculate the amount that can be borrowed by using the present value of an annuity formula (Equation 8.21). A 25-year mortgage at 9% implies $k = 0.75\%$ (actually, using Equation 8.16, $(1 + 0.0916/2)^{0.1667} - 1 = 0.007492$ or 0.7492% and $n = 300$). The Atwals' annual income is $48,000 or $4,000 a month; 25% of that amount, $1,000, can be used for a mortgage payment.

$$PVA = PMT[PVFA_{k,n}]$$
$$= \$1,000[PVFA_{0.7492,300}]$$
$$= \$1,000[119.255]$$
$$= \$119,255$$

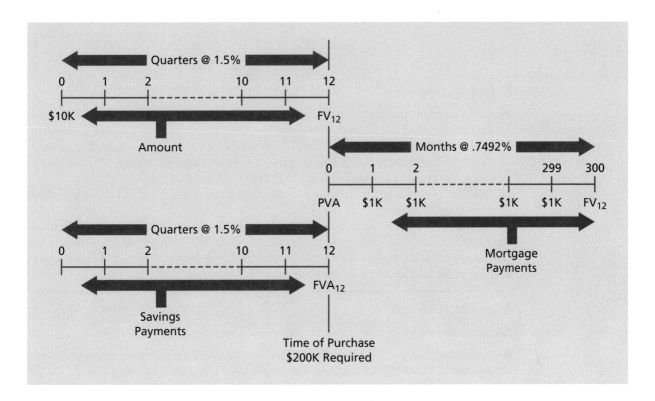

Next calculate the future value of the $10,000 already in the bank by using Equation 8.4. Interest at 6% compounded quarterly for three years implies $k = 1.5\%$ and $n = 12$.

$$FV_{12} = \$10,000[FVF_{1.5,12}]$$
$$= \$10,000[1.1956]$$
$$= \$11,956$$

The savings requirement is $200,000 less these amounts, that's $68,789. This sum is the future value of the annuity of the savings deposits. We can solve for the required deposit by using the future value of an annuity formula (Equation 8.14). Because this money is going into the same bank account as the previous $10,000, k and n are the same.

$$FVA_n = PMT[FVFA_{k,n}]$$
$$\$68,789 = PMT[FVFA_{1.5,12}]$$
$$\$68,789 = PMT[13.0412]$$
$$PMT = \$5,275$$

Calculator Solution	
Key	**Input**
n	12
I/Y	1.5
PV	10,000
PMT	0

Answer

FV	11,956

Use Excel® Function FV

Calculator Solution	
Key	**Input**
n	12
I/Y	1.5
FV	68,789
PV	0

Answer

PMT	5,275

Use Excel® Function PMT

Don't be confused by the fact that the savings deposits and the $10,000 already saved are in the same account. For purposes of calculation, they can be treated as though they're in identical but separate accounts.

Our figures show that the Atwals would have to deposit almost $5,300 a quarter, which is about $1,750 a month. That's probably a bit too much to be realistic at their income level.

Uneven Streams and Embedded Annuities

Many real-world problems involve streams of payments that aren't even. When that occurs, we can't use the annuity formulas to calculate present and future values, and generally we must

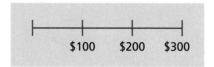

treat each payment as an independent amount problem. For example, consider the payment stream represented by the following timeline.[11]

The only way to deal with this stream is to handle each payment as an individual amount. That's not too hard if we're looking for the present or future value, but it's quite difficult if we're looking for an interest rate that yields a particular present or future value.

For example, we might be asked to find the interest rate at which the PVs of the individual amounts just add up to $500.

The correct approach to that question is iterative. That means we guess at an interest rate and calculate the PV of the stream. If the calculated PV isn't $500, we make another, better guess and recalculate. As we'll see shortly, there's a way of making sure the second guess moves us closer to the solution. We'll do this problem as an illustration.

Example 8.19

Calculate the interest rate at which the present value of the stream of payments shown above is $500.

■ **Solution:** We'll use the present value of an amount formula for each successive payment and start off by guessing at an interest rate of 12%. The present value of the entire stream is then

$$PV = FV_1[PVF_{k,1}] + FV_2[PVF_{k,2}] + FV_3[PVF_{k,3}]$$
$$= \$100[PVF_{12,1}] + \$200[PVF_{12,2}] + \$300[PVF_{12,3}]$$
$$= \$100(0.8929) + \$200(0.7972) + \$300(0.7118)$$
$$= \$462.27$$

This figure is lower than the $500 we're looking for, so our guess was wrong. Because our guess discounted the figures by too much, and higher interest rates discount amounts more, we conclude that the next guess should be lower.

Using 11% gives $471.77, which is closer but still not high enough. Try a few more iterations to show that the answer is between 8% and 9%.

Calculator and Spreadsheet Solutions for Uneven Streams

Financial calculators and Excel® have the ability to handle uneven streams with a limited number of payments. Your calculator' operating manual includes instructions on how to input uneven cash flows and produce these results. The general key strokes for Example 8.19, once in the cash flow register would be:

C0 = −500
C1 = 100, N = 1
C2 = 200, N = 1
C3 = 300, N = 1
CPT I

---

11 Although we haven't shown one here, you should recognize that one or more payments in a stream like this can be negative. A negative payment simply means that money is going the other way. For example, if a series of payments represents projected profits from a business, a negative number would just reflect a loss in some period. It would make a negative contribution to the present or future value calculation.

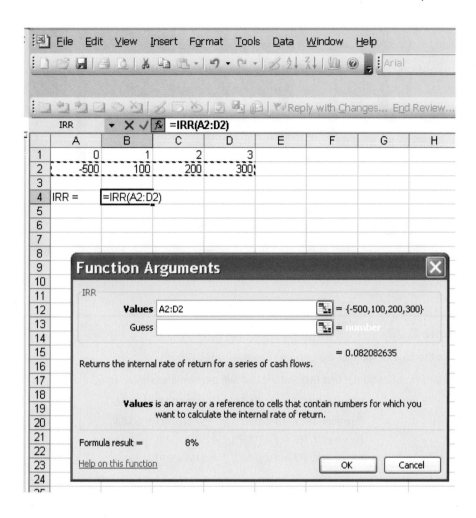

Using Excel®, set up the timeline and this time use the IRR (Internal Rate of Return) function. Although we'll get to a full explanation of IRR in Chapter 12, we can use it here. In essence, IRR tells us what return we are getting on our investment over time.

Embedded Annuities

Sometimes uneven streams have regular sections, called embedded annuities. An embedded annuity is a series of regular payments within an uneven stream of payments. The *"present value"* of an embedded annuity is moved back in time *as an amount*. We can use the annuity formula to reduce the number of calculations required to compute the present or future values.

Consider calculating the present value of the following uneven stream in which the third through sixth payments represent four $3 annuity payments.

Instead of calculating the present value of each term, we can recognize the annuity and use the PVA formula for that part. However, we have to remember that the annuity formula gives the present value at the beginning of the annuity. In this case that's at time 2, not at time 0. Hence, we have to bring the "present" value of the annuity forward another two periods as an amount to get its "present" value as of time 0 as indicated schematically in the diagram.

An **embedded annuity** is a series of regular payments within an uneven stream of payments.

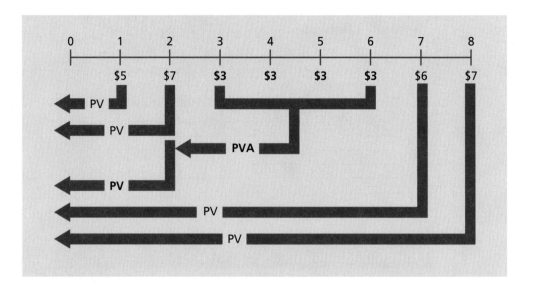

Example 8.20

Calculate the present value of the uneven stream above at 12%.

■ **Solution:** First handle the first two and the last two payments as simple amount problems.

$$Payment\ 1: PV = FV_1[PVF_{12,1}] = \$5(0.8929) = \$4.46$$
$$Payment\ 2: PV = FV_2[PVF_{12,2}] = \$7(0.7972) = \$5.58$$
$$Payment\ 7: PV = FV_7[PVF_{12,7}] = \$6(0.4523) = \$2.71$$
$$Payment\ 8: PV = FV_8[PVF_{12,8}] = \$7(0.4039) = \$2.83$$

Next find PVA for the annuity at the beginning of period 3 (end of period 2), and bring it forward two years as an amount.

$$PVA = PMT[PVFA_{12,4}] = \$3(3.0373) = \$9.11$$

and

$$PV = FV_2[PVF_{12,2}] = PVA(0.7972) = \$9.11(0.7972) = \$7.26$$

Now add up all the PVs to get the final answer of $22.84

SUMMARY

1 Time value of money is based on the idea that cash today is worth more than the same sum at some future time. In order to forego spending today, we must be compensated. In finance terms that means we need to add interest onto our money. The result of this added interest plus our original amount is called future value.

2 In many cases, we know what the cash flows are that we will receive in the future but want to know what they are worth today. We flipped the future value concept around to figure out how much a future sum of money was worth today, again at some desired interest rate.

3 The cash we forecast may be individual sums (lump sums) or a stream of payments (annuity). In whatever form, time value looks at when do we receive the cash, what rate of interest rate do we want, and how much is it worth—either now or in the future. With close examination, we see that all of the other calculations we did in this chapter—future value of annuity and present value of an annuity and a perpetuity, uneven cash flows and the like—are simply those two earlier calculations cleverly disguised.

4 When dealing with time value questions we must also make sure that the com-

pounding periods and payment period match. To do this, carefully determine when the payments are to be received (monthly, quarterly, semiannually) and then adjust the nominal interest rate to an effective rate that matches that payment cycle.

5 The interest rate on an investment or loan is called the nominal rate or APR. If the loan or investment interest compounds annually, this APR equals the EAR. If the interest is compounded more frequently than annually, the EAR will be higher than the APR.

KEY TERMS

Amortized debt, p. 283
Annual percentage rate (APR), p. 277
Annuity, p. 268
Annuity due, p. 286
Compounding period, p. 275
Compound interest, p. 274

Discount, p. 259
Discounted cash flow, p. 259
Effective annual rate (EAR), p. 276
Embedded annuity, p. 295
Future value, p. 259
Mortgage loan, p. 285

Nominal interest rate, p. 276
Note, p. 259
Perpetuity, p. 289
Present value, p. 259
Sinking fund, p. 273
Time value of money, p. 259

KEY FORMULAS

Equation Number	Formula	Appendix	Calculator (solving for) and Excel® function
	Amounts		
8.3 and 8.4	$FV_n = PV(1 + k)^n$ $FV_n = PV[FVF_{k,n}]$	A-1	FV, set PMT 0
8.5	$PV = FV_n \times \dfrac{1}{(1 + k)^n}$	A-2	PV, set PMT 0
8.7	$PV = FV_n[PVF_{k,n}]$		
	Ordinary Annuities		
8.13	$FVA_n = \dfrac{PMT(1 + k)^n - 1}{k}$	A-3	FV, set PV 0
8.14	$FVA_n = PMT[FVFA_{k,n}]$		

| 8.21 | $PVA = PMT[PVFA_{k,n}]$ | A–4 | PV, set FV 0 |
| 8.22b | $PVA = \dfrac{PMT}{k}\left(1 - \dfrac{1}{(1+k)^n}\right)$ | | |

Annuities Due

| 8.25 | $FVAd_n = PMT[FVFA_{k,n}](1+k)$ | | FV, set PV 0, Calculator Begin or Excel® Type 1 for the value one period after the last payment |
| 8.26 | $PVAd = PMT[PVFA_{k,n}](1+k)$ | | PV, set FV 0, Calculator Begin or Excel® Type 1 |

Perpetuity

| 8.27 | $PV_P = \dfrac{PMT}{k}$ | | PV, set FV 0, use 999 n |

Equivalent Annual Rate

| 8.15 | $EAR = \left(1 + \dfrac{k_{nom}}{m}\right)^m - 1$ | | |

Continuous Compounding

| 8.28 | $FV_n = PV(e^{kn})$ | | |

A Note on The Similarity of the Equations

Either of the two amount equations can be used to solve any amount problem, because both come from Equation 8.3. The four variables are the same, and the time value factors are reciprocals of one another.

The two annuity expressions appear to have the same symmetry, but they don't. The annuity equations are not interchangeable, and each is suited only to its own type of problem. Further, there isn't a reciprocal relationship between the factors. You therefore must choose the correct annuity formula before starting a problem.

QUESTIONS

1. Calculate the present value of one dollar 30 years in the future at 10% interest. What does the result tell you about very long-term contracts?

2. What's an opportunity cost interest rate?

3. Why are time value concepts important in ordinary business dealings, especially those involving contracts?

4. In a retail store, a discount is a price reduction. What's a discount in finance? Are the two ideas related?

5. "Deferred payment terms are equivalent to a cash discount." Discuss and explain this idea.

6. "The amount formulas share a closer relationship than the annuity formulas." Explain and interpret this statement.

7. Write a brief verbal description of the logic behind the development of the time value formulas for annuities.

8. Why are time value concepts crucial in determining what a bond or a share should be worth?

9. Discuss the idea of capitalizing a stream of earnings in perpetuity. Where is this idea useful? Is there a financial asset that makes use of this idea?

10. Discuss the idea of a sinking fund. How is it related to time value?

11. Discuss mortgage loans in terms of the time value of money and loan amortization. What important points should every homeowner know about how mortgages work?

12. What information is contained in a loan amortization schedule?

13. Describe the underlying meaning of compounding and compounding periods. How does it relate to time value? Include the idea of an effective annual rate (EAR). What is the annual percentage rate (APR)? Is the APR related to the EAR?

14. When an annuity begins several time periods into the future, how do we calculate its present value today? Describe the procedure in a few words.

Business Analysis

1. A business can be valued by capitalizing its earnings stream (see Example 8.15, page 290). How might you use the same idea to value securities, especially the shares of large publicly held companies? Is there a way to calculate a value that could be compared to the shares' market price to tell an investor whether it is a good buy? (If the market price is lower than the calculated value, the shares are a bargain.) What financial figures associated with shares might be used in the calculation? Consider the per share figures and ratios discussed in Chapter 3 (including EPS, dividends, book value per share, etc.). Does one measure make more sense than the others? What factors would make a share worth more or less than your calculated value?

PROBLEMS

Amount Problems

The solutions shown in Appendix B are based on using either a financial calculator or Excel®. Slight rounding differences will occur if using financial tables.

1. The Prince Rupert Property Development Company has a $10,000 note receivable from a customer due in three years. How much is the note worth today if the interest rate is
   a. 9%?
   b. 12% compounded monthly?
   c. 8% compounded quarterly?
   d. 18% compounded monthly?
   e. 7% compounded continuously?

2. What will a deposit of $4,500 left in the bank be worth under the following conditions?
   a. Left for nine years at 7% interest
   b. Left for six years at 10% compounded semiannually
   c. Left for five years at 8% compounded quarterly
   d. Left for 10 years at 12% compounded monthly

3. What interest rates are implied by the following lending arrangements?
   a. You borrow $500 and repay $555 in one year
   b. You lend $1,850 and are repaid $2,078.66 in two years
   c. You lend $750 and are repaid $1,114.46 in five years with quarterly compounding
   d. You borrow $12,500 and repay $21,364.24 in three years under monthly compounding
      (*Note:* In parts (c) and (d), be sure to give your answer as the annual nominal rate.)
   e. For parts (c) and (d), what is the effective annual rate?

4. How long does it take for the following to happen?
   a. $856 grows into $1,122 at 7%
   b. $450 grows into $725.50 at 12% compounded monthly
   c. $5,000 grows into $6,724.44 at 10% compounded quarterly
   d. What is the effective annual rate for parts (b) and (c)?

5. Given the following effective annual rates, what is the annual percentage rate that was quoted?
   a. 10.25% EAR, compounded semiannually
   b. 8.36% EAR, compounded quarterly
   c. 10% EAR, compounded monthly
   d. 18.25% EAR, compounded daily (use a 365-day year)

6. Alli Guthrie is looking for an investment vehicle that will double her money in five years.
   a. What interest rate, to the nearest whole percentage, does she have to receive?
   b. At that rate, how long will it take the money to triple?
   c. If she can't find anything that pays more than 11%, approximately how long will it take to double her investment?
   d. What kinds of financial instruments do you think Alli is looking at? Are they risky? What could happen to Alli's investment?

7. Per owes Abu $8,000 on a note that is due in five years with accumulated interest at 6%. Abu has an investment opportunity now that he thinks will earn 18%. There's a chance, however, that it will earn as little as 4%. A bank has offered to discount the note at 14% and give Abu cash that he can invest today.
   a. How much will Per's note be worth in five years?
   b. How much will Abu receive today, if the bank discounts the note at 14%?
   c. How much ahead will Abu be if he takes the bank's offer and the investment does turn out to yield 18%?
   d. How much behind will he be if the investment turns out to yield only 4%?

8. John Cleaver's grandfather died recently and left him a trunk that had been locked in his attic for years. At the bottom of the trunk John found a packet of 50 World War I U.S.

"liberty bonds" that had never been cashed in. The bonds were purchased for $11.50 each in 1918 and pay 3% interest as long as they're held. (These U.S. Government savings bonds accumulate and compound their interest, unlike corporate bonds, which regularly pay out interest to bondholders.)

    a. How much were the bonds worth in 2007?

    b. How much would they have been worth if they paid interest at a rate more like that paid in recent years, say 7%?

    c. Comment on the difference between the answers to parts (a) and (b).

9. Branson Inc. has sold product to the Brandywine Company, a major customer, for $20,000. As a courtesy to Brandywine, Branson has agreed to take a note due in two years for half of the amount due.

    a. What is the effective price of the transaction to Branson if the interest rate is (1) 6%, (2) 8%, (3) 10%, (4) 12%?

    b. Under what conditions might the effective price be even less as viewed by Brandywine?

10. Paladin Enterprises manufactures printing presses for small-town newspapers that are often short of cash. To accommodate these customers, Paladin offers the following payment terms: one-third on delivery, one-third after six months, and one-third after 18 months.

    The Nipawin *Sentinel* is a typically cash-poor newspaper considering one of Paladin's presses.

    a. What discount is implied by the terms from Paladin's point of view if it can invest excess funds at 8% compounded quarterly?

    b. The *Sentinel* can borrow limited amounts of money at 12% compounded monthly. What discount do the payment terms imply to the *Sentinel*?

    c. Reconcile these different views of the same thing in terms of opportunity cost.

11. Ralph Renner just borrowed $30,000 to pay for a new sports car. He took out a 60-month loan and his car payments are $761.80 per month.

    a. What is the effective annual interest rate (EAR) on Ralph's loan?

    b. What is the annual nominal rate?

    c. Which rate means more to Ralph? Why?

Annuity Problems

12. How much will $650 per year be worth in eight years at interest rates of

    a. 12%?

    b. 8%?

    c. 6%?

13. The Poons are planning ahead for their son's education. He's eight years old now and will start university in 10 years. How much will they have to set aside each year to have $65,000 when he starts if the interest rate is 7%?

14. What interest rate would you need to get to have an annuity of $7,500 per year accumulate to $279,600 in 15 years?

15. How many years will it take for $850 per year to amount to $20,000 if the interest rate is 8%?

16. What would you pay for an annuity of $2,000 paid every six months for 12 years if you could invest your money elsewhere at 10% per annum, compounded semiannually?

17. Construct an amortization schedule for a four-year, $10,000 loan at 6% interest compounded annually.

18. A $10,000 car loan has payments of $361.52 per month for three years. What is the annual percentage rate quoted on the loan? What is the effective annual rate on the loan? Assume monthly compounding.

19. Calculate the payments for the following $200,000 loan:
    a. 8% compounded quarterly, paid monthly, 5-year term
    b. 10% compounded monthly, paid semiannually, 5-year term
    c. 6% compounded annually, paid bi-annually (every two years), 6-year term
    d. 8% compounded weekly, paid monthly, 5-year term

20. Joe Ferro's uncle is going to give him $250 a month for the next two years starting today. If Joe banks every payment in an account paying 6% per annum, compounded monthly, how much will he have at the end of *three* years?

21. How long will it take a payment of $500 per quarter to amortize a loan of $8,000 at 16% per annum, compounded quarterly?
    a. Approximate your answer in terms of years and months.
    b. How much less time will it take if loan payments are made at the beginning of each quarter rather than at the end?
    c. What is the effective annual rate on this loan?

22. What are the monthly mortgage payments on a 25-year loan for $150,000 at 12% per annum, compounded semiannually? What is the effective annual rate (EAR)? Construct an amortization table for the first six months of the loan.

23. Construct an amortization schedule for the last six months of the loan in the previous problem. (*Hint:* What is the unpaid balance at the end of 24.5 years?)

24. If the borrower in Problem 22 made a single additional payment of $17,936.29 to reduce principal at the end of the fifth year:
    a. How soon would she pay off the loan, if she kept the annual payment the same?
    b. Assuming the borrower wanted to keep the amortization period the same (so 20 more years), what would her new monthly payment be?

25. What are the payments to interest and principal during the 25th year of the loan in Problem 22?

26. Juan and Marie Sanchez just purchased their first home with a traditional (monthly payments, compounded semiannually) 6% 30-year mortgage loan of $178,000.
    a. How much is their monthly payment?
    b. How much interest will they pay the first month?
    c. If they make all their payments on time over the 30-year period, how much interest will they have paid?
    d. If Juan and Marie decide to move after 7 years what will the balance of their loan be at that time?
    e. If they finance their home over 15 rather than 30 years at the same interest rate, how much less interest will they pay over the life of the loan?

27. Adam Hiro just purchased a home and took out a $250,000 mortgage for 25 years at 8% per annum, compounded semiannually, paid monthly.
    a. How much is Adam's monthly mortgage payment?
    b. How much sooner would Adam pay off his mortgage if he made an additional $100 payment each month?
    c. Assume Adam makes his normal mortgage payments and at the end of five years, he refinances the balance of his loan at 6% per annum, compounded semiannually. If he continues to make the same mortgage payments, how soon after the first five years will he pay off his mortgage?
    d. How much interest will Adam pay in the tenth year of the loan:
       i. If he does not refinance?
       ii. If he does refinance?

28. Shali's uncle died recently and left her some money in a trust that will pay her $500 per month for five years starting on her 25th birthday (the first payment will occur one month after her 25th birthday). Shali is getting married soon, and she would like to use this money as a down payment on a house now. If the trust allows her to assign its future payments to a bank, and her bank is willing to discount them at 9% per annum, compounded monthly, how much will she have toward her down payment? (Shali just turned 23.)

29. Lee Childs is negotiating a contract to do some work for Haas Corp. over the next five years. Haas proposes to pay Lee $10,000 at the end of each of the third, fourth, and fifth years. No payments will be received prior to that time. If Lee discounts these payments at 8%, what is the contract worth to him today?

30. Referring to the previous problem, Lee wants to receive the payments for his work sooner than Haas proposes to make them. He has counterproposed that the payments be made at the beginning of the third, fourth, and fifth years rather than at the end. What will the contract be worth to Lee if Haas accepts his counterproposal?

31. The Orion Corp. is evaluating a proposal for a new project. It will cost $50,000 to get the undertaking started. The project will then generate cash inflows of $20,000 in its first year and $16,000 per year in the next five years, after which it will end. Orion uses an interest rate of 15% compounded annually for such evaluations.
    a. Calculate the net present value (NPV) of the project by treating the initial cost as a cash outflow (a negative) in the present, and adding the present values of the subsequent cash inflows as positives.
    b. What is the implication of a positive NPV? (Use words only.)
    c. Suppose the inflows were somewhat lower, and the NPV turned out to be negative. What would be the implication of that result? (Use words only.)

    (This problem is a preview of a technique called capital budgeting, which we'll study in detail in Chapters 12, 13, and 14.)

Multipart Problems

32. The Verdugo family wants to make a home improvement that is expected to cost $60,000. They want to fund as much of the cost as possible with a home equity loan but can afford payments of only $600 per month. Their bank offers equity loans at 12% per annum, compounded monthly for a maximum term of 10 years.
    a. How much cash do they need as a down payment?
    b. Their bank account pays 8% per annum, compounded quarterly.

If they delay starting the project for two years, how much would they have to save each quarter to make the required down payment if the loan rate and estimated cost remain the same?

33. The Stein family wants to buy a small vacation house in a year and a half. They expect it to cost $75,000 at that time. They have the following sources of money.
    a. They have $10,000 currently in a bank account that pays 6% per annum, compounded monthly.
    b. Uncle Murray has promised to give them $1,000 a month for 18 months starting today. These payments will be deposited in the account indicated above.
    c. At the time of purchase, they'll take out a mortgage. They anticipate being able to make payments of about $300 a month on a 15-year, 12% mortgage. The mortgage terms specify that interest will be compounded semiannually.

    In addition, they plan to make quarterly deposits to an investment account to cover any shortfall in the amount required. How much must those additions be if the investment account pays 8% per annum, compounded quarterly?

34. Clyde Yamagishi wants to buy a car when he graduates from college in two years. He has the following sources of money.
    a. He has $5,000 now in the bank in an account paying 8% per annum, compounded quarterly.
    b. He will receive $2,000 in one year from a trust. This payment will be deposited into the bank account indicated above.
    c. He'll take out a car loan at the time of purchase on which he'll make four years of monthly payments of $500 at 18% per annum, compounded monthly.
    d. Clyde's uncle is going to give him $1,500 a quarter starting today *for one year*. These payments will also be deposited in the bank account indicated above.

    In addition, Clyde will save up money in a credit union through monthly payroll deductions at his part-time job. The credit union pays 12% per annum, compounded monthly. If the car is expected to cost $40,000 (Clyde has expensive tastes!), how much must he save each month?

35. Joe Osayande expects to retire in 15 years and has suddenly realized that he hasn't saved anything toward that goal. After giving the matter some thought, he has decided that he would like to retire with enough money in savings to withdraw $85,000 per year for 25 years after he retires. Assume a 6% return on investment before and after retirement and that all payments into and withdrawals from savings are at year end.
    a. How much does Joe have to save in each year for the next 15 years to reach this goal?
    b. How much would Joe have needed to save each year if he had started when retirement was 25 years away?
    c. Comment on the difference between the results of parts a and b.

36. Janet Elliott just turned 20 and received a gift of $20,000 from her rich uncle. Janet plans ahead and would like to retire on her 55th birthday. She thinks she'll need to have about $2 million saved by that time in order to maintain her lavish lifestyle. She wants to make a payment at the end of each year until she's 50 into an account that she'll open with her uncle's gift. After that she'd like to stop making payments and let the money grow with

interest until it reaches $2 million when she turns 55. Assume she can invest at 7% compounded annually. Ignore the effect of taxes.
  a. How much will she have to invest each year in order to achieve her objective?
  b. What percent of the $2 million will have been contributed by Janet (including the $20,000 she got from her uncle)?

37. Merritt Manufacturing needs to accumulate $20 million to retire a bond issue that matures in 13 years. The firm's manufacturing division can contribute $100,000 per quarter to an account that will pay 8% per annum, compounded quarterly. How much will the remaining divisions have to contribute every month to a second account that pays 6% per annum, compounded monthly, in order to reach the $20 million goal?

38. Carol Pasca just had her fifth birthday. As a birthday present, her uncle promised to contribute $300 per month to her education fund until she turns 18 and starts university. Carol's parents estimate that university will cost $2,500 per month for four years, but don't think they'll be able to save anything toward it for eight years. How much will Carol's parents need to contribute to the fund each month starting on her 13th birthday to pay for her education? Assume the fund earns 6% per annum, compounded monthly.

39. Joan Diao is approaching retirement and plans to purchase a condominium in Fernie in three years. She now has $40,000 saved toward the purchase in a bank account that pays 8% compounded quarterly. She also has five $1,000 face value corporate bonds that mature in two years. She plans to deposit the bonds' principal repayments in the same account when they're paid. Joan's son also gives her $1,200 per month, which will continue for two more years until he marries (24 cheques including one that arrived today). She's decided to put her remaining money from her son toward her condo, depositing it as received in a credit union account that pays 8% compounded monthly. She'll make the first deposit today with the cheque she already has. Joan anticipates buying a $200,000 property. What will her monthly payment be on a 15-year mortgage at 6%, compounded semiannually? What would the payment be on a 30-year loan at the same interest rate?

COMPUTER PROBLEMS

40. At any particular time, home mortgage rates are determined by market forces, and individual borrowers can't do much about them. The length of time required to pay off a mortgage loan, however, varies a great deal with the size of the monthly payment made, which is under the borrower's control.

    You're a junior loan officer for a large Canadian bank. The head of the mortgage department is concerned that customers don't fully appreciate that a relatively small increase in the size of mortgage payments can make a big difference in how long the payments have to be made. She feels homeowners may be passing up an opportunity to make their lives better in the long run by not choosing shorter-term mortgages that they can readily afford.

    To explain the phenomenon to customers, she's asked you to put together a chart that displays the variation in payment size with term at typical interest rates. The starting point for the charts should be the term for a typical 25-year (300-month) loan. Use the TIMEVAL program to construct the following chart. Remember, interest is compounded semiannually and paid monthly. TIMEVAL is one of the several Excel© templates available on the text's support website.

Mortgage Payments per $100,000 Borrowed as Term Decreases
Mortgage Term in Years

		25	20	15
Rate	6%			
	8%			
	10%			
	12%			

Write a paragraph using the chart to explain the point. What happens to the effect as interest rates rise? Why?

41. Amitron Inc. is considering an engineering project that requires an investment of $250,000 and is expected to generate the following stream of payments (income) in the future. Use the TIMEVAL program to determine if the project is a good idea in a present value sense. That is, does the present value of expected cash inflows exceed the value of the investment that has to be made today?

Year	Payment
1	$63,000
2	$69,500
3	$32,700
4	$79,750
5	$62,400
6	$38,250

a. Answer the question if the relevant interest rate for taking present values is 9%, 10%, 11%, and 12%. In the program, notice that period zero represents a cash flow made at the present time, which isn't discounted. The program will do the entire calculation for you if you input the initial investment as a negative number in this cell.

b. Use trial and error in the program to find the interest rate (to the nearest hundredth of a percent) at which Amitron would be just indifferent to the project.

This problem is a preview of an important method of evaluating projects known as *capital budgeting*. We'll study the topic in detail in Chapters 12 and 13. In part (a) of this problem, we find the *net present value (NPV)* of the project's cash flows at various interest rates and reason intuitively that the project is a good idea if that figure is positive. In part (b), we find the return inherent in the project itself, which is called the *internal rate of return (IRR)*. We'll learn how to use that in Chapter 12.

42. The Centurion Corp. is putting together a financial plan for the company covering the next three years, and it needs to forecast its interest expense and the related tax savings. The firm's most significant liability is a fully amortized mortgage loan on its real estate. The loan was made exactly 10.5 years ago for $3.2 million at 11% per annum, compounded monthly for a term of 25 years. Use the AMORTIZ program to predict the interest expense associated with the real estate mortgage over the next three years. (*Hint:* Run AMORTIZ from the loan's beginning and add up the months in each of

the next three years.) AMORTIZ is one of the several Excel© templates available on the text's support website.

DEVELOPING SOFTWARE

43. Write your own program to amortize a 10-year, $20,000 loan at 10% compounded annually. Input the loan amount, the payment, and the interest rate. Set up your spreadsheet just like Table 8.4, and write your program to duplicate the calculation procedure described.

Chapter 9

The Valuation and Characteristics of Bonds

Learning Objectives

1 Define various terminology for bonds.

2 Calculate the price of a bond.

3 Differentiate the main features of junk bonds and investment grade bonds.

4 Discuss what is meant by yield to maturity.

5 Calculate yield to maturity.

6 Describe and discuss various bond covenants.

7 Understand the concept of interest rate risk.

8 Discuss the use of a lease in financing.

9 Differentiate between capital and operating leases

10 Discuss the relative advantages and disadvantages of leasing from the perspective of the lessor and the lessee

11 Calculate the value of leasing and contrast it with purchasing.

We often hear investment advisors extolling the virtues of using fixed income investments, particularly for those investors who are risk averse. Those investors usually want worry-free investments with modest but stable returns. That may be what they are looking for, but from the early 1980s to the end of the 1990s, interest rates were extremely volatile. Did this increase in volatility affect these risk-averse investors? For some, such volatility resulted in significant realized capital gains and losses.

Valuation is a systematic process through which we establish the price at which a security *should* sell. We can call that price the security's *intrinsic* value.

THE BASIS OF VALUE

Securities are pieces of paper, and unlike real assets have no utility of their own. Real assets, such as houses and cars, have worth because they provide services like shelter and transportation. Paper assets must rely on something else to make them valuable: that something is the expectation of future income that goes along with owning securities. This is an important point. *Every* financial asset depends for its value on the future cash flows that come with it.

Since money expected in the future is worth its present (discounted) value today, *a security's value is equal to the present value of its expected future cash flows.* Further, the security should sell in financial markets for a price very close to that value.

There are often differences of opinion about what the price of a security should be. They arise because people make different assumptions about what the security's cash flows will turn out to be and about the appropriate interest rate to use for discounting. The most arguable cash flows are associated with shares, because future dividends are never guaranteed and the eventual selling price of a share is always speculative.

The idea of valuation is bound closely to the concept of return on investment. Because of the precise nature of the work we're about to undertake, we need to be very exact in our understanding of what the terms "investment" and "return" mean.

INVESTING

Investing means using a resource in a way that generates future benefits rather than in a way that results in immediate satisfaction. We say an investor foregoes current consumption in order to improve his or her position in the future. In everyday language that means a person buys securities or puts money in the bank rather than spending it on a new car or going out to dinner.

In finance, investing means putting money to work to earn more money, generally by entrusting it to a person or an organization that uses it and pays the owner for its use. The two most common methods of entrusting money are lending (debt) and buying an ownership interest (equity) in a business. The vehicle for a debt investment is generally a bond, while for an equity investment it's shares.

Return

Returns on One-Year Investments

Return is what an investor receives for making an investment. It can be expressed as a dollar amount or as an annual rate. For investments held for one year, the *rate of return is what the investor receives during the year divided by what he or she invests.*

For debt, that's simply the interest received divided by the amount lent, which is the interest rate we've been calling k. Let's look at the idea a little more deeply in terms of the time value of money.

An amount PV loaned for one year at interest rate k earns interest of kPV. If the lender receives the principal plus the interest at the end of the year, these are the future cash flows that come from making the original investment of PV. Call these future cash flows FV_1 and write

$$FV_1 = PV + kPV$$

$$FV_1 = PV(1 + k)$$

We recognize this as Equation 8.1 from our study of the time value of money (page 261).

Valuation is a systematic process to determine the price at which a security should sell in financial markets.

Securities are worth the *present value of the future cash income* associated with owning them.

Investing means using a resource to benefit the future rather than for current satisfaction.

Now solve for the original investment.

$$PV = \frac{FV_1}{(1 + k)}$$

The rate of return on a security is the interest rate that *equates the present value of its expected future cash flows with its current price.*

Again we recognize this expression from our study of time value. It's the present value of a future amount due in one year, Equation 8.5 (page 265), with $n = 1$.

In the context of valuing a security that represents a loan (usually a bond), think of PV as the *price* of the security that returns cash flows FV_1. Then the rate of return, k, can be thought of as the *interest rate that makes the present value of the future cash flows equal to the price.* This is a fundamental definition that applies to any investment held for any length of time.

The details are a bit more involved for equity investments than for debt, because the future cash flows are more complicated. Nevertheless, the basic rule is the same. We'll discuss the returns to equity investments in Chapter 10.

Returns on Longer-Term Investments

When the holding period is longer and there are a number of cash flows at different times, the concept remains the same. The return is still the discount rate that makes the present value of the future cash flows equal to the price.

For example, suppose someone offers to sell you an investment today for $363 that will pay $200 one year from now and $250 two years from now. If you accept the offer, the return on your investment will be the interest rate at which the present value of the two payments just equals the $363 "price" of the investment today. A timeline for the arrangement looks like this.

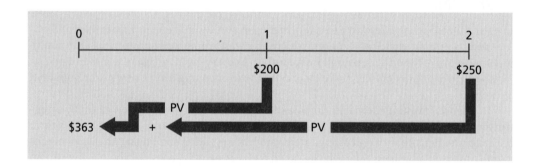

As an exercise, show that the return on this hypothetical investment would be very close to 15%.

The terms *yield, return,* and *interest rate* mean essentially the same thing.

The term "yield" is synonymous with "rate of return." Its use is especially common with debt securities and traditional loans.

In the remainder of this chapter we'll look closely at the valuation of bonds and then at their institutional[1] characteristics. We'll turn our attention to valuing shares in Chapter 10.

BOND VALUATION

Bonds represent a debt relationship in which the issuing company borrows and the buyer lends. Remember from Chapter 7 that bonds enable firms to raise large amounts by spreading a loan among a number of lenders. For example, suppose a large firm wants to borrow $10 million, but can't find anyone willing to lend that much. Many people might be willing to lend smaller amounts, however, if the firm's credit reputation is good. If the company issues

---

1 The term "institutional" refers to the rules and practices according to which things are done in an organized society.

10,000 bonds at $1,000 each, as many as 10,000 people could participate in the loan by buying one bond apiece.

Before we get into the valuation of bonds, we need to learn a little about terminology and practice. We've introduced some of these ideas before, but will repeat them here for convenience.

Bond Terminology and Practice

A bond represents a loan made by the buyer to the issuer for a period known as the *term*. The bond itself is a *promissory note* that serves as legal evidence of the debt. Bonds are said to *mature* on the last day of their term. Every bond issued has a **par** or **face value**, which is printed on the face of the document. This is the amount the issuing company intends to borrow; in effect, it's the principal of the loan.

Bonds are *non-amortized* debt. That means no repayment of principal is made during the term. Rather, the face value is repaid in a lump sum on the maturity date. (However, some bond issues have a sinking fund provision, which we'll examine on page 331.) This repayment at the maturity date is often called a balloon payment. Interest is paid regularly during the term, however, usually semiannually.

Lenders extend *credit* to borrowers. Therefore, bondholders are called *creditors* of the company issuing the bonds. The term "creditor" also applies to banks that make loans to companies and vendors that sell products without receiving immediate payment.

As one might expect, newly issued bonds are called *new issues,* while older bonds are commonly called **seasoned issues**.

The Coupon Rate

Most bonds pay interest at rates set at the time of issue called **coupon rates**. The coupon rate applied to the face value of a bond yields the dollar amount of interest paid, called the **coupon payment** or simply *coupon*.[2] Coupon rates and payments are generally fixed throughout the life of a bond regardless of what happens to interest rates in financial markets.

Coupons are rarely used today. Interest payments are now mailed directly to bondholders whose names and addresses are *registered* with the issuing company or its agent. Nevertheless, the term "coupon" is still associated with bond interest.

Bond Valuation—Basic Ideas

Now we have enough background to begin studying bond valuation. Keep in mind that valuation simply means determining the price a security should command in the financial market in which it is traded.

Adjusting to Interest Rate Changes

Let's put several facts from our earlier work together with what we've just learned about bonds. First recall from Chapter 7 that securities including bonds are sold in both primary and secondary markets. A primary market transaction refers to the original sale of the bond by the issuing company, and secondary market transactions are subsequent trades among investors. Second, recall from our discussion of financial markets in Chapter 7 that interest rates change all the time. Finally, we've just learned that most bonds pay interest at coupon rates that are fixed throughout their lives.

All this raises a question: how can a bond that pays a fixed rate be sold in the secondary market if interest rates have changed since it was originally issued? An example will make the idea clear.

A *bond issue* allows an organization to borrow from many lenders at one time under a single agreement.

The face value is the amount of principal to be repaid by the borrower. Also called *par value*.

A bond's *term* or *maturity* is the time from the present until the principal is to be returned.

A **seasoned issue** is an older bond.

The **coupon rate** is the interest rate paid by a bond on its face value. The **coupon payment** is the dollar amount of the interest payment, which is usually made semiannually.

2 The term "coupon" is outdated, but is still in common use. Years ago, bonds were issued with a number of coupons attached that looked something like a sheet of postage stamps. When an interest payment was due, a bond owner would clip off a coupon and send it to the issuing company, which would return a cheque for the interest. Hence the term "coupon" became associated with bond interest.

Suppose Paul Singh, a typical investor, buys a newly issued 10-year bond directly from the Groton Company for its face value of $1,000. The bond pays interest at a coupon rate of 10%, which is the market rate for bonds of comparable risk at the time. From the discussion we've already had about valuation, we know that Paul has actually purchased a stream of future income. He'll receive interest payments of $100 a year (10% of $1,000) for 10 years and a payment of $1,000 returning principal along with the last interest payment.

Now imagine that, a few days after Paul's purchase, interest rates rise to 12%. Also assume that coincidentally something occurs in Paul's financial situation and he needs the cash he used to buy the bond for something else.

Paul can't go back to Groton, the issuing company, and ask for a refund. The company borrowed the funds expecting to keep them for 10 years, and would be unwilling to give up those terms. So to get his money back, Paul has to sell the bond to another investor in a secondary market transaction.

Let's suppose Paul approaches Sandra Forget, a friend who he knows is in the market for an investment, and asks if she'd like to buy his Groton Company bond. She says she might be interested and asks how much he wants. Paul answers that he bought it only a few days ago for $1,000 and would like to get about that much. What would Sandra's reaction be to Paul's asking price?

Unfortunately for Paul, Sandra wouldn't be willing to pay $1,000, because the increase in interest rates has given her better options. New bonds now being issued offer 12%, which means they'll pay $120 a year for 10 years plus the final $1,000. Sandra, as a rational investor, would have to refuse Paul's offer.

But suppose Paul is desperate, and really has to sell his bond. What is he to do? Clearly the only way he'll interest a buyer is to lower the price. In fact, he'll have to lower the price until the return to the new buyer on his or her investment is just 12%. It turns out that he'd have to lower the price to exactly $887.02. We'll see how that figure is calculated later in the chapter. For now, the important thing to understand is that the price of a bond on the secondary market *drops* in response to an increase in interest rates.

What would have happened if interest rates had fallen rather than having gone up? In that case, new issues would have offered less interest than Paul's bond, and he could have sold it for *more* than $1,000. In general, bond prices *rise* in response to a *drop* in interest rates.

Summarizing, we see that *bond prices and interest rates move in opposite directions*. This phenomenon is a fundamental and critically important law of finance and economics. When interest rates decline, the prices of debt securities go up; when rates increase, prices go down. The price changes are just enough to keep the yields (returns) on investments in seasoned issues equal to the yields on new issues of comparable risk and maturity. In other words, *bonds adjust to changing yields by changing their prices.*

> Bond *prices* respond to *changes* in the market rate of *interest* by moving in a direction *opposite* to the change.

As a result of all this, bonds don't generally sell for their face values until they are close to maturity. They trade for more or less, depending on where the current interest rate is in relation to their coupon rates. The terminology associated with this phenomenon is important. Bonds selling above their face values are said to be trading at a *premium*, while those selling below face value are said to trade at a *discount*. If at a point in time the market interest rate returns to a bond's coupon rate, the bond sells for its face value at that time. At such a time, we say the bond is trading at *par value*.

Determining the Price of a Bond

We made the point earlier that the value and hence the price of any security should be equal to the present value of the expected future cash flows associated with owning that security. In the case of bonds, those future cash flows are quite predictable, because they're specified by the bond agreement.

Bondholders receive interest payments periodically and a lump sum return of principal at the bond's maturity. Yearly interest is determined by applying the coupon rate to the face value of the bond, and the principal is simply the face value itself.

Let's illustrate the pattern of these payments by setting up a timeline to display the cash flows coming from Paul's bond. Most bonds pay interest semiannually, but for illustrative purposes we'll assume this one pays annually. The timeline of cash flows is illustrated in Figure 9.1.

Notice that the amount received in the tenth year is the sum of the last interest payment and the return of principal. Also notice that the interest payments are all the same and occur regularly in time.

It's important to realize that it doesn't matter whether or not the bond is new at time zero. The picture shown would be valid for a new 10-year bond, a 20-year bond that's currently 10 years old, or any other 10% $1,000 bond that has 10 years to go until maturity. Time zero is now, and the only thing that matters in today's valuation is *future* cash flows. Past cash flows are gone and irrelevant to today's buyer.

Having used Figure 9.1 to visualize bond cash flows in a simple numerical case, let's generalize the idea by showing a time to maturity of *n* periods, an interest payment represented as PMT, and a face value of FV. Recognize that each of these elements varies with different bonds. The general case is represented by the timeline at the top of Figure 9.2.

In practice, most bonds pay interest semiannually. That means the periods represented along the timeline in Figure 9.2 are usually half-years. Under those conditions, the interest payment, PMT, is calculated by applying the coupon rate to the face value and dividing by 2. For example, if the bond in Figure 9.2 had 10 years to go until maturity, had a face value of $1,000, and paid 10% interest semiannually, the timeline would contain 20 periods, and each PMT would be $50.

The Bond Valuation Formula

As we've been saying, a security's price should be equal to the present value of all the cash flows expected to come from owning it. In the case of a bond, the expected cash flows consist of a series of interest payments and a single payment returning principal at maturity. Hence the price of a bond, which we'll write as P_B, is the present value of the stream of interest payments plus the present value of the principal repayment.

(9.1) $P_B = PV(\text{Interest payments}) + PV(\text{Principal repayment})$

Because the interest payments are made regularly and are constant in amount, they can be treated as an annuity and we can calculate their present value by using Equation 8.21, the present value of an annuity formula. We'll rewrite that formula here for convenience.

(8.21) $PVA = PMT[PVFA_{k,n}]$

Applying this formula directly to the bond's interest, we can write

(9.2) $PV(\text{Interest payments}) = PMT[PVFA_{k,n}]$

where PMT is the bond's regular interest payment, *n* is the number of interest payments remaining in the bond's life, and *k* is the current market interest rate for comparable bonds for the interest-paying period.

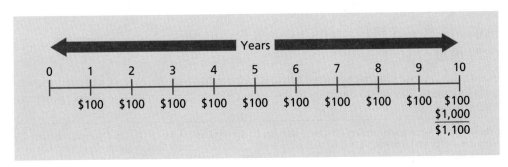

FIGURE 9.1
Cash Flow Timeline for a Bond

FIGURE 9.2
Bond Cash Flow
and Valuation
Concepts

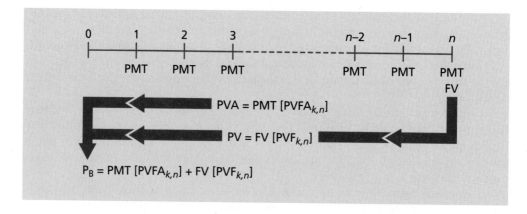

A bond's principal is always equal to its face value, so the return of principal is an expected payment of that amount n periods in the future. Its present value can be calculated by using Equation 8.7, the present value of an amount formula, which we'll repeat here.

$$(8.7) \qquad PV = FV_n[PVF_{k,n}]$$

We'll drop the subscript on FV_n and think of FV as face value rather than future value in this application. Then we can write

$$(9.3) \qquad PV(\text{Principal repayment}) = FV[PVF_{k,n}]$$

Substituting Equations 9.2 and 9.3 in 9.1, we get a convenient expression for calculating the price of a bond based on its future cash flows using our familiar time value techniques.

$$(9.4)^3 \qquad P_B = PMT[PVFA_{k,n}] + FV[PVF_{k,n}]$$

The approach is illustrated graphically in Figure 9.2. In essence, pricing a bond involves doing an annuity problem and an amount problem together, and summing the results.

> A bond's value is the sum of the present value of the *annuity of its interest payments* plus the present value of the *return of principal*, both taken at the current *market rate* of interest.

> **Yield to maturity** refers to the average annual rate of return required by investors over the remaining term of a bond; it is affected by market interest rates, the time remaining to maturity, and the bond's coupon.

> **Current yield** refers to a bond's annual interest payment divided by its market price.

Two Interest Rates and One More

It's important to notice that two interest rates are associated with pricing a bond. The first is the coupon rate, which, when applied to the face value, determines the size of the interest payments made to bondholders. The second is k, the market yield on comparable bonds at the time the price is being calculated. Don't confuse the two. The rate at which the present value of cash flows is taken is k. The only thing you do with the coupon rate is calculate the interest payment.

The return or yield on the bond investment to the bondholder is k. It is the interest rate that makes the present value of all the payments represented in Figure 9.2 equal to the price of the bond. Because this return considers all payments until the bond's maturity, it's called the yield to maturity (YTM). When people refer to a bond's yield, they generally mean the YTM.

The third yield associated with a bond is called the current yield. This is a summary piece of information used in financial quotations, and is not associated with the pricing process. The current yield is the annual interest payment divided by the bond's current price.

Solving Bond Problems with a Financial Calculator or Excel®

In Chapter 8, we noted that financial calculators have five time value keys and the function boxes in Excel® allow you to put in up to four values. When doing amount or annuity problems

---

3 Remember from our discussions in Chapter 8 that you do not need to use the tables. The factor abbreviations make it easier to set up the equation and they do give us a guide to the keystrokes or spreadsheet functions needed. With bonds, P_B is PV.

on the calculator, we used four of the five keys and zeroed the fifth. In Excel® we simply left one of the amount boxes blank.

In bond problems we use all five keys or fill in all five boxes. The calculator and Excel® are programmed to recognize the five inputs as two problems and add the results together. In a bond problem, the keys have the following meanings.

n or *nper*	Number of periods until maturity (this also equals the number of coupon payments)
I/Y or RATE	Market interest rate or YTM
PV	Price of the bond, i.e., the present value of all the cash flows
FV	Face value of the bond (normally $1,000)
PMT	Coupon interest payment per period

Although the unknown could be any of the five variables, the unknown is usually the price of the bond (PV) or the market interest rate (I/Y or RATE). Remember, the market interest rate is equal to the bond's yield to an investor buying at the current price. Using the calculator to solve a problem, we enter the four known variables first, press the compute key, and then the key for the unknown variable. For Excel®, you must determine what you want to solve for and use that function box.

Remember, most financial calculators and Excel® use a sign convention, cash flows to and from the bondholder must be of opposite signs. That means PMT and FV, flows to the bondholder, will be of one sign (positive), while PV, the price coming from the bondholder, will be the other sign (negative).[4]

http

Yield to maturity is easily calculated using the "calculator" provided at http://moneychimp.com.

Example 9.1

Looking back at the bond issued by Groton Company, let's see how we come up with the value of $887.02. Remember that at the time of issue it sold for its par (face) value of $1,000. Interest rates changed shortly after Paul bought it and comparable bonds now yield 12%. What must Groton's bond sell for in today's market to yield 12% (YTM) to the buyer? Assume the bond pays interest annually. Also calculate the bond's current yield.

■ **Solution:** This is the typical bond problem. We're given a bond's face value, coupon rate, and remaining term, and are asked to find the price at which it must sell to achieve a particular return. Since the return is the market interest rate, we're being asked to find the market price of the bond. The question is equivalent to asking for the present value of the bond's expected cash flows at today's interest rate.

To solve the problem, we first write Equation 9.4, the bond valuation formula.

$$P_B = PMT[PVFA_{k,n}] + FV[PFV_{k,n}]$$

If we substitute the numbers calculated earlier into the equation (PMT or coupon = $100, Face Value or FV = $1,000, *n* = 10, and Sandra's required return or YTM = 12%) then

$$P_B = \$100[PVFA_{12,10}] + \$1,000[PVF_{12,10}]$$

and use Appendix A for the factors. Appendix A-4 gives

$$PVFA_{12,10} = 5.6502$$

while Appendix A-2 yields

$$PVF_{12,10} = 0.3220$$

---

4 Some of the more sophisticated calculators have a bond mode or bond register that allows exact pricing for bonds sold between coupon payments and bonds with unusual provisions. The time value keys we have been using are sufficient for our purposes since our goal is to gain a broad understanding of bond pricing.

Substituting, we get

$$P_B = \$100[5.6502] + \$1,000[0.3220]$$
$$= \$565.02 + \$322.00$$
$$= \$887.02$$

Now, what would happen to the process if the bond paid interest semiannually? The interest payment is found by applying the coupon rate to the face value and dividing by 2, because payments are semiannual.

$$PMT = \frac{\text{Coupon rate} \times \text{Face value}}{2}$$
$$= \frac{0.10 \times \$1,000}{2}$$
$$= \$50.00$$

Next, we need n, the number of interest-paying periods from now until the end of the bond's term. This bond, like most, pays interest semiannually, so we multiply the number of years until maturity by 2 to get n. Notice that n represents the time from now until maturity. It doesn't matter how long the bond has been in existence previously. In this case,

$$n = 10 \text{ years} \times 2 = 20$$

Next we need k, the current market interest rate. Recall that when using time value formulas for non-annual compounding, we have to state n and k consistently for the compounding period. Here, n represents a number of semiannual periods, so k must be stated for semiannual compounding. That just means dividing the nominal rate by 2,

$$k = \frac{12\%}{2} = 6\%$$

Finally, the face value is given directly as $1,000, so

$$FV = \$1,000$$

Substitute these values into the bond equation,

$$P_B = \$50[PVFA_{6,20}] + \$1,000[PVF_{6,20}]$$

and use Appendix A for the factors. Appendix A–4 gives

$$PVFA_{6,20} = 11.4699$$

while Appendix A–2 yields

$$PVF_{6,20} = 0.3118$$

Substituting, we get

$$P_B = \$50[11.4699] + \$1,000[0.3118]$$
$$= \$573.50 + \$311.80$$
$$= \$885.30$$

This is the price at which the Groton bond must sell to yield 12%. It won't be competitive with other bonds at any higher price. Notice that it's selling at a discount, a price below its face value, because the current interest rate is above the coupon rate.

The bond's current yield is calculated as follows.

$$\text{Current yield} = \frac{\text{Annual Interest}}{\text{Price}} = \frac{\$100}{885.30} = 11.30\%$$

Although using the bond valuation formula is easy once you get used to it, students often have trouble knowing where to put what first. We have included a self-test example at the end of the chapter using the method we've just illustrated.

Estimating the Answer First

If we think of the bond as having been issued at a time when the market rate was equal to the coupon rate, we can make a rough estimate of the current price before starting the problem. That provides a good check on how reasonable our solution is. We base the estimate on the fact that bond prices and interest rates move in opposite directions.

In Example 9.1, we knew that the current price of the bond had to be below the face value of $1,000. That's because the market interest rate had risen from 10% at the time of the bond's issue to its current value of 12%. Further, the increase was fairly substantial, so we were looking for a significant drop in price, which is what we found.

It doesn't matter whether the interest rate fluctuated up and down past 10% after the bond was issued or moved directly to 12%. The only rates that count for today's price are the original coupon rate and the current rate.[5]

Before starting a bond problem, you should always decide whether the new price will represent a premium or a discount from the face value.

In general, price changes due to a given interest rate change will be larger the more time there is remaining until maturity. We'll see that more clearly in the next section.

Maturity Risk Revisited

In Chapter 7, we developed an interest rate model in which rates generally consist of a base rate plus premiums for various risks borne by lenders. In particular, the model recognizes *maturity risk*, which is related to the term of the debt. We're now in a position to fully understand this important idea.

The risk arises from the fact that bond prices vary (inversely) with interest rates. When an investor buys a bond, the only way to recover the invested cash before maturity is to sell it to someone else. If interest rates rise and prices fall while the investor is holding the bond, the sale to someone else will be at a loss. (Review page 312 if necessary.)

This is exactly what happened to Paul Singh in our illustration of price adjustments to interest rate changes. The possibility of such a loss viewed at the time of purchase is the risk we're talking about.

Maturity risk has two other names: *price risk* and *interest rate risk*. These terms reflect the fact that bond prices move up and down with changes in interest rates (page 315).

The expression of maturity risk emphasizes the fact that the degree of risk is related to the maturity (term) of the bond. The longer the term (time until maturity), the greater the maturity (price, interest rate) risk. The reason for this is that the prices of longer-term bonds change more in response to interest rate movements than do the prices of shorter-term bonds.

Maturity risk exists because the prices of *longer-term* bonds *fluctuate more* in response to *interest rate changes* than the prices of shorter-term bonds.

To see that, let's look again at the bond with semiannual payments in Example 9.1. It was issued at 10% and had 10 years to go until maturity. Interest rates rose to 12%, and the price dropped to $885.30. Let's calculate what the price would have become under varying assumptions about the remaining term to maturity without changing anything else in the problem.

Table 9.1 gives the bond's price and the price drop from $1,000 at terms of 2, 5, 7, and 10 years. You might want to verify that these figures are correct as an exercise. Each of the price changes

---

5 Bonds aren't always issued at coupon rates equal to the current market interest rate, but it helps to understand the pricing process if we imagine that they are. In practice, coupon rates are usually targeted at or near the current market rate. However, the mechanics of printing and issuing cause a delay between the time the rate is chosen and the time the bond actually hits the market. As a result there's usually a slight difference between coupon rates and current market rates. Bonds issued above or below market rates simply sell at premiums or discounts, respectively, when offered on the primary market. Because market rates change constantly some discount or premium is almost always associated with a new issue.

TABLE 9.1
Price Changes at Different Terms Due to an Interest Rate Increase from 10% to 12%

Time to Maturity	Price	Drop from $1,000
2 years	$ 965.35	$ 34.65
5	926.40	73.60
7	907.05	92.95
10	885.30	114.70

in Table 9.1 is the result of the same increase in interest rates, from 10% to 12%. Notice how much larger the price drop becomes as the term of the bond increases. This is the essence of maturity risk. The possible loss on debt investments due to interest rate-induced price changes increases with the term of the debt.

Realizing this fact, investors demand a premium to compensate for the additional risk they bear with longer issues. This is the *maturity risk premium*.

As Time Goes By

Let's consider the original (semiannual) Groton Company bond in Example 9.1 again. Recall that the interest rate rose from 10% to 12%, and the price fell from $1,000 to $885.30 with 10 years of term to go.

Let's imagine a very unlikely event just to enhance our understanding of the processes involved in bond pricing.

What would happen to the price of the Groton bond as time goes by *if interest rates didn't change again* for the remainder of the bond's life (a practical impossibility)? Would the price remain at $885.30, or move to something else? Test your understanding by answering the question before reading on.

In fact, the bond's price would slowly rise to $1,000 as maturity approached. If you have trouble seeing that, think of what it would be worth on the day before maturity. Someone buying at that time would be getting virtually no interest, because the last interest payment would be prorated almost entirely to the person who owned the bond during most of the last period. A buyer on the day before maturity would be buying a payment of $1,000 to be made the next day. That would be worth very nearly $1,000. This logic tells us that as we get closer to maturity, the price has to approach the bond's face value of $1,000.

We've already calculated what the price would be at two points along the way to maturity in our hypothetical example. Table 9.1 tells us that with five years to go the price will be $926.40 and when just two years remain it will be $965.35. Graphically, the progression in prices is shown in Figure 9.3.

Finding the Yield at a Given Price

Basically, only two questions are asked about the dollars and cents of bonds. We've just explored the first, finding the price at which a bond achieves a specified yield (YTM). The second question is the reverse of the first. It asks for the yield on a bond investment if the security sells at a particular price. In the bond valuation formula, Equation 9.4, this question asks us to find the market interest rate, k, given a value for P_B.

Let's rewrite Equation 9.4 for convenient reference.

(9.4) $$P_B = PMT[PVFA_{k,n}] + FV[PVF_{k,n}]$$

Recall that finding P_B when the market yield is known simply involves doing two time value problems and adding the results together. We do a present value of an annuity problem for the interest payments and a present value of an amount problem for the return of the face value. Finding k when P_B is known is conceptually the same but much more difficult.

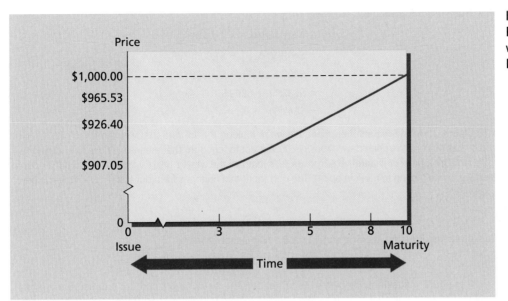

FIGURE 9.3
Price Progression
with Constant
Interest Rate

Recall the time value problems we studied in Chapter 8. In both amount and annuity problems we were able to solve for an unknown k quite easily. We did so by solving one of the time value formulas for a factor, and then finding the factor in the table.

Even though the bond formula utilizes present value factors and the same tables we used in Chapter 8, this approach doesn't work. It fails because Equation 9.4 uses two time value factors at the same time. As we have only one equation, we can't solve for both, and therefore can't find the right column and row in each table simultaneously.

This mathematically unfortunate state of affairs means we could resort to a rather tedious approach to solving the problem, trial and error. We begin by guessing at a solution for k. Then we value the bond at that return by using Equation 9.4 and whatever other information we have. That process results in a price we can compare with the price given by the problem. If they're significantly different, we have to guess at the return again and re-evaluate for another price. We keep doing that until we get a price that's very close to the one we're looking for.

The trial and error approach isn't as haphazard as it may seem. By applying a little logic, we can usually get close to the answer in a few tries. An example will make the process clear.

Example 9.2

The Benson Steel Company issued a 30-year bond 14 years ago with a face value of $1,000 and a coupon rate of 8%. The bond is currently selling for $718. What is the yield to an investor who buys it today at that price? (Assume semiannual interest.)

■ **Solution:** First we make an educated guess at the answer on the basis of our knowledge that interest rates and bond prices move in opposite directions. In this case the $718 price is substantially below the face value of $1,000, so we know the bond's yield must be quite a bit above the coupon rate. Let's make a first guess at 10%. Evaluating at 10%, we have the following variables.

$$\text{PMT} = \frac{0.08 \times \$1,000}{2} = \$40$$

$$n = 16 \times 2 = 32$$

$$k = \frac{10\%}{2} = 5\%$$

$$\text{FV} = \$1,000$$

Calculator Solution

Key	Input
n	32
PV	718.00
FV	1,000
PMT	40

Answer

I/Y	$6 \times 2 = 12.0$

Use Excel® Function Rate

Then, using Equation 9.4, we have

$$P_B = PMT[PVFA_{k,n}] + FV[PVF_{k,n}]$$
$$= \$40[PVFA_{5,32}] + \$1,000[PVF_{5,32}]$$
$$= \$40(15.8027) + \$1,000(0.2099)$$
$$= \$632.11 + \$209.90$$
$$= \$842.01$$

Clearly 10% isn't the solution, because we're looking for the rate that yields a price of $718. Our choice has brought the price down from $1,000, but not far enough. That means we have to bring the rate up quite a bit more. For illustrative purposes, let's jump all the way to 14% (we probably wouldn't go that far if we weren't trying to make a point). The only input that changes from our last try is k, which is now

$$k = \frac{14\%}{2} = 7\%$$

Substitute into Equation 9.4 and verify that the calculation leads to

$$P_B = \$620.56$$

This figure is substantially *below* the target of $718, so we've pushed our interest rate too high. Now we know the answer has to be between 10% and 14%. Let's try a figure right in the middle. Evaluate the bond at 12% to verify that the resulting price is

$$P_B = \$718.36$$

This is just a shade higher than the actual selling price, so the true yield is just below 12%. For most purposes, declaring 12% the solution would be close enough.[6]

Financial calculators and Excel® are programmed to solve bond problems, including finding yields. The internal workings of such calculators do exactly what we've just done: they find the solution by trial and error.

Reading Bond Quotations

As with shares, bond prices are reported daily in a variety of newspapers and various websites. The format in which bond market information is presented requires a little explanation. We'll illustrate with the web listing for Molson Coors Capital Finance ULC shown in Figure 9.4. This listing is from Tuesday, April 17, 2007, so the information reflects trading that occurred on Monday, April 16, 2007.

Let's look at each of the columns starting with the first (again, the column numbers don't appear in the web site listing). The first column gives the abbreviated name of the company.

---

6 **An Approximate Yield Formula**—With the advent of financial calculators and spreadsheets, determining YTM is relatively straightforward. However, those students who prefer to do interpolation might find the following approximation formula useful in determining a rate to begin in the trial and error process to find an exact YTM.

$$\text{Approximate YTM} = \frac{\text{Annual interest payment} + \dfrac{(\text{Principal payment} - \text{Price of bond})}{\text{Number of years to maturity}}}{0.6(\text{Price of the bond}) + 0.4(\text{Principal payment})}$$

In our example:

$$\text{YTM} = \frac{40 + \dfrac{(1000 - 718)}{32}}{0.6(718.00) + 0.4(1000.00)}$$
$$= \frac{40 + \dfrac{282}{32}}{430.80 + 400.00}$$
$$= \frac{48.8125}{830.80} = 5.875 \text{ semiannualy}$$

Annual YTM $= 5.875 \times 2 = 11.75\%$

1	2	3	4	5
Issuer	Coupon	Maturity Date	Bid $	Yield%
MolsonC	5.000	Sep 22/15	98.43	5.23

FIGURE 9.4
Bond Quotation for Molson Coors Capital Finance ULC, Monday April 16, 2007

Source: http://www.canada.com/nationalpost/financialpost/fpmarketdata/bond_trading_summary.html, April 17, 2007.

Column 2 lists the coupon on an annualized basis. Interest is usually paid semiannually, so this figure is generally the semiannual interest payment multiplied by 2. Column 3 is the maturity date for the bond, when the last interest payment and principal (face) will be repaid.

Column 4 is the bid price. For this particular bond, the bid price was 98.43. This price is quoted as a percent, so for each $1,000 face, an investor would pay $984.30. The last column is the Yield to Maturity that an investor would get if she bought this bond today. That is, if she spent $984.30 today and held the bond until it matured, her overall return on the investment would be 5.23%.

We can apply what we have learned so far to see if we can come up with the same price. These bonds typically pay interest semiannually, so the semiannual coupon for a $1000 bond would be $25.00, the number of semiannual periods would be 17 (assuming the next coupon was due September 22, 2007) and k would be 2.615%. Plugging these numbers into the formula or calculator, we would get a present value of $984.38. Although not exact (we did not make any adjustments for the fact that the first coupon payment September 22, 2007 was just over five months away) we are quite close.

Call Provisions

Circumstances sometimes arise in which bond issuers want to pay off their indebtedness early. This commonly occurs when interest rates drop a great deal after bonds are issued.

http

Check on current rates for government bonds on the Bank of Canada website http://www.bank-banque-canada.ca/en/rates/bonds.html.

A **zero coupon bond** pays no interest during its life, but imputed interest is still taxable.

Insights | PRACTICAL FINANCE

Can a Bond Be a Bond Without Paying Interest?

The answer to that mysterious question is yes; they're called **zero coupon bonds**.

To understand the idea, think about a bond issued at a very low coupon rate, say, half the market rate. It would sell at a deep discount because the interest payments would be less than investors could get elsewhere. But, offsetting the low interest payments, investors would receive the bond's face value at maturity, which would be more than they paid for it. In other words, investors who chose the bond would be trading some current income for a "capital gain" later on. But that capital gain would be unusual in that it wouldn't come from changing market values. It would actually be interest earned on the debt all along but not paid until maturity.

If we take this idea to the extreme, making the coupon interest smaller and smaller until it's gone, we've got a **zero coupon bond**. Essentially it's just a promise to pay a face amount in the future that sells for the present value of

that amount today. In that sense, the zero coupon bond is quite comparable to short-term T-bills, commercial paper, and bankers' acceptances, which are also bought at a discount. We discussed these instruments in Chapter 4.

The April 17, 2007, *Globe and Mail* (page B23) showed a quote for a Province of Manitoba bond that matured March 5, 2014, and yielded 4.35%. Using our bond value concepts, we would enter 1,000 as FV, 7 as N, 4.35% as I/Y and compute for PV. The answer, $742.25 is quote close to the quote of $744.00 (74.4).

The "zero" has some interesting tax implications. You'd think the investor would pay no tax until maturity because no money is received until then. But that isn't the case. CRA imputes interest during the bond's life and demands tax on the phantom income. Imputed interest simply means that once the investor has bought the bond (and knows the yield), the difference between the value of the bond at the beginning of the year and the value at the end of the year is considered interest. Although the investor has not physically received an interest cheque in this amount, it is considered taxable income for that year.

For example, suppose a company issues a 30-year bond with a 15% coupon rate when interest rates are at about that level. Some years later, suppose rates drop to 7%. The firm will be stuck paying above-market rates on the bond's principal until maturity unless it can somehow get out of the loan arrangement with the bondholders.

Companies that issue bonds anticipate this sort of thing, and like to include *call provisions* in bond agreements to protect themselves. A **call provision** is a clause that gives the issuing organization the right to pay off the bond prior to maturity. In our illustration, the company would like to borrow money at the new lower interest rate of 7%, and use it to retire the old bond that pays 15%. The process is called *refunding* the debt.

Investors who buy bonds don't like call provisions, because they feel the clauses give firms the opportunity to renege on interest rate obligations. In the example we've just described, the bondholders were getting a 15% return on funds in a market that currently offered only 7%. If the bond is paid off early, they'll lose that 15% and will have to reinvest at 7%.

These conflicting interests are reconciled with a two- or three-part compromise. First, call provisions are generally written to include a *call premium* that must be paid to bondholders if the feature is exercised. This means that if the company chooses to pay a bond off early, it must pay bondholders some extra money as compensation for their loss of the original deal. The premium is usually stated in terms of extra interest at the coupon rate, and diminishes as the bond's maturity approaches.

Second, issuers usually agree that the bond won't be called for a certain number of years at the beginning of its life. This initial time is the period of *call protection.*

Finally, to attract buyers, a bond with a call provision may require a somewhat higher interest rate than similar bonds without call provisions.

Call provisions are also sometimes exercised to free companies of restrictions imposed by certain agreements associated with bond contracts called *indentures*. We'll discuss indentures later in the chapter.

Figure 9.5 portrays a declining call premium starting at one year's interest on a 10%, $1,000 bond with a term of 10 years and a call-protected period of five years.

The call premium is also known as a *call penalty*. This apparent conflict is easily explained by point of view. The payment is a premium to the investor who receives it but a penalty to the company that pays it. Call provisions are also called *call features*.

The Effect of a Call Provision on Price

A special situation arises when a bond with a call provision is in its protected period but appears certain to be called as soon as that period is over. In such a case, the traditional bond valuation procedure doesn't work because it includes cash flows projected to occur after the protected period. These cash flows aren't likely to be forthcoming because the bond will probably be paid off exactly at the end of the protected period. In such cases, bondholders will actually

Call provisions allow bond issuers to *retire* bonds *before maturity* by paying a premium (penalty) to bondholders.

FIGURE 9.5
The Call-Protected Period and a Declining Call Premium

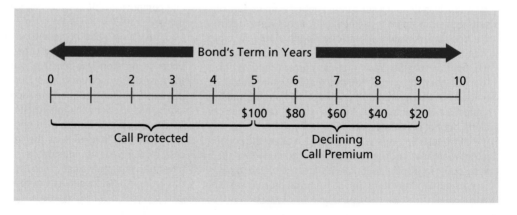

receive their usual interest payments up until call, at which time they'll receive the bond's face value plus the call premium. The situation is illustrated graphically in Figure 9.6.

Examine the diagram carefully. It shows the entire life of a bond that was originally intended to pay interest for 10 semiannual periods. This would normally be a five-year bond. The first three years are call protected in this example. We're assuming the first year has passed, so the present is indicated by "Now" at the end of period 2.

We assume the interest rate has dropped substantially, so the bond is very likely to be called at the end of the third year, period 6. Cash flows planned after that time probably won't happen. These are shown in italics.

We'd normally value this bond by taking the present value of all the payments from "Now" until maturity, including the return of the face value at maturity. This would mean that in the bond valuation formula we would use $n = 8$ and substitute the face value for FV.

What's actually going to happen, however, is a shorter series of interest payments ending with the sixth, and a final payment equal to FV *plus* the call premium.

Valuing the Sure-to-Be-Called Bond

We can value this bond with the same formula we've used up until now by making two simple modifications to our inputs. All we have to do to realistically represent what is likely to happen is to let n equal the time to call instead of the time to maturity, and add the call premium to the face value when we portray the final payment. The sum of the face value and the call premium is known as the *call price*.

We can express these ideas in a modification of the bond formula as follows:

(**9.5**) $$P_B(\text{Call}) = \text{PMT}[\text{PVFA}_{k,m}] + \text{CP}[\text{PVF}_{k,m}]$$

where

$$m = \text{Number of periods to call}$$
$$\text{CP} = \text{Call price} = \text{Face value} + \text{Call premium}$$

PMT and k are computationally the same as in the problem *without* a call. However, k is known as the **yield to call (YTC)**, because it's used in taking the present value of cash flows only until the call is likely to occur.

> **Yield to call** refers to bond pricing calculations that assume the bond will be called at the end of the protected period.

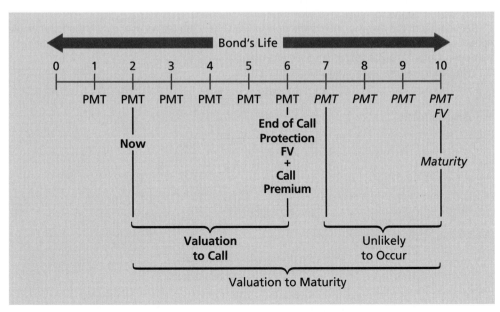

FIGURE 9.6
Valuation of a Bond Subject to Call

Example 9.3

The Northern Timber Co. issued a $1,000, 25-year bond five years ago. The bond has a call provision that allows it to be retired any time after the first 10 years with the payment of an additional year's interest at the coupon rate. Interest rates were especially high when the bond was issued, and its coupon rate is 18%. Interest rates on bonds of comparable risk are now 8%. What is the bond worth today? What would it be worth if it didn't have the call feature? Assume interest payments are semiannual.

■ **Solution:** This problem asks us to evaluate the price of the bond, first assuming the call feature will be exercised (which is very likely) and then in the normal way. The basic assumption is that the bond must yield the current rate of interest in either case. That is, even if the bond is going to be called, the price will adjust to bring the yield to the market rate of 8%. A graphic depiction of the problem follows (the interest payments are omitted).

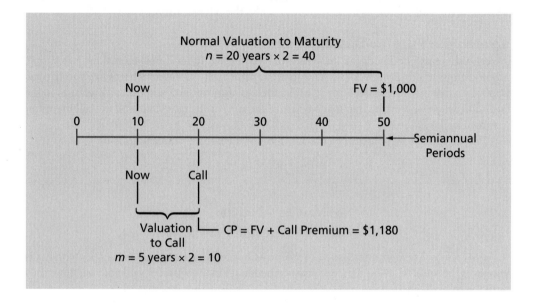

Notice that the timeline shows semiannual periods rather than years. The call premium is 18% of $1,000 or $180, so the call price is ($1,000 + $180 =) $1,180.

At the top of the diagram, above the timeline, we show the period over which the bond would normally be evaluated and the face value to be returned of $1,000. At the bottom we show the relevant period for a likely call and a call price of $1,180.

First we'll evaluate to maturity using Equation 9.4.

$$P_B = PMT[PVFA_{k,n}] + FV[PVF_{k,n}]$$

The variables follow.

$$PMT = \frac{0.18 \times \$1,000}{2} = \$90$$

$$n = 20 \times 2 = 40$$

$$k = \frac{8\%}{2} = 4\%$$

$$FV = \$1,000$$

Calculator Solution

Key	Input
n	40
I/Y	4
FV	1,000
PMT	90

Answer

PV	1,989.64

**Use Excel®
Function PV**

Substituting, we have

$$P_B = \$90[PVFA_{4,40}] + \$1,000[PVF_{4,40}]$$
$$= \$90[19.7928] + \$1,000[0.2083]$$
$$= \$1,781.35 + \$208.30$$
$$= \$1,989.65$$

Notice how much the price has risen, almost doubling the original $1,000. That's because the drop in the interest rate was very substantial and the bond has a long time to go until maturity. This price represents the present value of Northern Timber's (the bond issuer's) cash flow commitment if the bond isn't called.

Next we'll evaluate to call using Equation 9.5.

$$P_B(\text{Call}) = \text{PMT}[\text{PVFA}_{k,m}] + \text{CP}[\text{PVF}_{k,m}]$$

The variables follow.

$$\text{PMT} = \frac{0.18 \times \$1,000}{2} = \$90$$

$$m = 5 \times 2 = 10$$

$$k = \frac{8\%}{2} = 4\%$$

$$\text{CP} = \$1,000 + 0.18(\$1,000) = \$1,180$$

Substituting,

$$P_B(\text{Call}) = \$90[\text{PVFA}_{4,10}] + \$1,180[\text{PVF}_{4,10}]$$

$$= \$90[8.1109] + \$1,180[0.6756]$$

$$= \$729.98 + \$797.21$$

$$= \$1,527.19$$

Calculator Solution

Key	Input
n	10
I/Y	4
FV	1,180
PMT	90

Answer

PV	1,527.15

**Use Excel®
Function PV**

Notice that the price is substantially above $1,000, but is much less than the price without a call. From the point of view of a bond buyer, the only relevant price is $1,527.19, because the likelihood of call is very high. This price represents the value of Northern Timber's cash flow commitment if the bond is called. Notice how much Northern will save if it calls the bond.

The Refunding Decision

Whenever the current interest rate is substantially below a bond's coupon rate and the issue has a call feature, the issuing company has to decide whether or not to exercise the call. The company will compare the interest savings from calling the bond with the cost of making the call and issuing a new bond to raise the money required to pay the old one off.

The difference in bond prices in the last example shows the interest savings associated with a call and includes a major cost item, the call premium. However, the figure does not include administrative expenses or the cost of issuing a new bond.

The costs incurred in issuing new bonds are known as **flotation costs** and can be rather substantial. They're primarily brokerage fees paid to investment dealers, but they also include administrative expenses and the costs of printing and engraving.

As a result of these costs, interest rates have to drop a lot before it's advisable for a company to refund by calling in one bond issue and floating another.

Flotation costs refer to the administrative cost of issuing new securities.

Dangerous Bonds with Surprising Calls

Bonds can occasionally have obscure call features buried in their contract terms that can cause unwary investors real grief. These generally take the form of a clause that says if some particular event occurs the bond will be called at face value.

From the CFO

The most common of these clauses involve sinking fund provisions. Recall that in Chapter 8 we described a sinking fund as a way lenders guarantee that borrowers will have enough money put aside to pay off a bond's principal when it comes due. (Review page 273 if necessary.) There we said that borrowing firms can make deposits in a separate account whose future value will be the amount of the bond's principal.

Another way to provide for an orderly payoff of principal is to require that the individual bonds of an issue be called in and paid off over a series of years rather than all at once. For example, suppose a company borrowed $1 million for 25 years by issuing 1,000 25-year bonds, each with a face value of $1,000. Repayment could be made a lot more secure if, instead of paying off all the bonds at the maturity date, the company called and retired a few each year during the last five years of the issue's life.

Sinking fund provisions often require companies to do just that—call in and retire a fixed percentage of the issue each year toward the end of the term. Since this procedure is for the benefit of the bondholders (to increase their security), the agreements don't generally include a call premium. The bonds called are usually determined by a lottery, so no one knows which bonds will be called early and which will continue to maturity.

Now, suppose a particular bond that's subject to sinking fund provisions like these happens to be selling at a premium because of interest rate changes. An unlucky investor might buy a $1,000 face value bond for, say, $1,100, and in short order receive a call at $1,000 that results in an immediate loss of $100! This does happen, even though bond investments are supposed to be relatively safe.

Here's another example. Government agencies, such as Canada Mortgage and Housing Corporation, and financial institutions issue bonds called mortgage-backed securities or mortgage-backed bonds. The repayment of principal and interest are guaranteed by the Government of Canada under the *National Housing Act*. If the mortgages underlying the bonds are held to maturity, the bonds pay interest until maturity. But if the mortgages are paid off early, the funds are used to retire the bonds at face value. Because no one knows how quickly people will pay off their home mortgages, you can never be sure the mortgage-backed bonds won't be called early.

Needless to say, it's wise to check the details of bond agreements before investing.

Risky Issues

Sometimes bonds sell for prices *far below* those indicated by the valuation techniques we've described so far in this chapter. For example, suppose we applied Equation 9.4 to a particular $1,000 face value bond and came up with a value of $950. However, suppose we checked the financial pages of a newspaper and found the bond to be trading at $500.

From the CFO

> *This would usually mean the company that issued the bond is in financial trouble, and there is some question about its ability to honour the obligations of the bond agreement. In other words, analysts feel it might default on the payment of interest and/or principal. Obviously such a risk will cause investors to lower their estimates of what any security is worth.*

Financial purists argue that in such a situation Equation 9.4 still gives the right answer if we properly select the interest rate, *k*. The argument is that the increased risk should be reflected in a higher expected return to the investor. Using a higher *k* results in a lower calculated price. In other words, the bond has slipped into a lower quality class, which should be reflected by the requirement of a higher yield to compensate for the chance that the investor may lose everything if things go poorly for the company.

However you look at it, a major deterioration in a bond-issuing company's financial performance will substantially depress the price of its securities, including bonds.

We will look at bond ratings on page 328.

INSTITUTIONAL CHARACTERISTICS OF BONDS

In the remainder of this chapter, we'll describe some of the more important features of bonds and bond agreements that aren't directly related to pricing. Keep the fundamental definition of a bond in mind as we go forward: a bond is a device that enables an organization (generally a corporation or a government unit) to borrow from a large number of people at the same time under one agreement.

Registration, Transfer Agents, and Owners of Record

A **bearer bond** is an unregistered bond, owned by the "bearer," the person in possession. Contrast with a registered bond.

Bonds are classified as either bearer bonds or registered bonds. Bearer bonds belong to whoever possesses them, a convention that makes them dangerously subject to loss and theft. Bearer bonds have coupons attached for the payment of interest as described earlier.

The owners of registered bonds are recorded with a transfer agent. This organization, usually a trust company, keeps track of the owners of shares and bonds for issuing companies. When one investor sells a security to another, the agent transfers ownership in its records as of the date of the sale. On any given date, there is a particular owner of record on the transfer agent's books for every bond (and share) outstanding. Interest payments are sent directly to the owners of record of registered bonds as of the date the interest is paid.

> Registered bond or security in which the issuer or a transfer agent keeps a list of the names of owners. Dividends or interest payments are made to owners of record as of specified dates.

Kinds of Bonds

Several distinguishing features divide bonds into different categories. We'll briefly discuss a few of the more important distinctions.

Secured Bonds and Mortgage Bonds

Secured bonds are backed by the value of specific assets owned by the issuing company. If the firm defaults, the secured bondholders can take possession of the assets and sell them to recover their claims on the company. The essence of the secured arrangement is that the assets tied to specific debt aren't available to other creditors until that debt is satisfied. When the securing assets are real estate, the bond is called a mortgage bond.

> A mortgage bond is a bond secured by real estate.

Debentures

Debentures are unsecured bonds. They rely on the general creditworthiness of the issuing company rather than the value of specific assets. Debentures are clearly more risky than the secured debt of the same company. Therefore, they must usually be issued to yield higher returns to investors.

> A debenture is an unsecured bond.

Subordinated Debentures and Senior Debt

The term "subordinated" means lower in rank or priority. In terms of debt, it means that subordinated debt has lower priority than other debt for repayment in the event the issuing company fails. Debentures can be subordinated to specific issues or to all other debentures in general. The debt having priority over a *subordinated debenture* is known as senior debt.

> Subordinated debt is *lower in priority* for payment of principal and interest than senior debt.

Conceptually, subordination arises with the senior debt. For example, suppose a lender is considering making a loan but fears the borrower will take on more debt from other lenders in the future. If that happened, if the borrower failed, whatever assets were available to satisfy unpaid loans would have to be shared among a large number of creditors. Some security is afforded to the first lender by writing a clause into the loan agreement requiring the subordination of all future debt.

Because subordinated debt is riskier than senior or unsubordinated debt, it generally requires a higher yield than those issues.

Convertible Bonds

A convertible bond can be converted into a specified number of shares at the option of the owner. Bondholders generally *exercise the conversion privilege* if the share's price rises enough to make the converted shares worth more than the bond.

> Convertible bonds can be exchanged for specified amounts of shares.

Recall that an important distinction between shares and bonds is that shares have a potential for significant price appreciation if the issuing company does very well, but bonds do not. Convertible features are designed to share a limited amount of that appreciation potential with bondholders. Hence, they're sweeteners that make bonds more attractive.

For example, a $1,000 bond might be convertible into 50 shares, implying a conversion price of $20 per share. The bond is issued when the share price is substantially below $20. Then suppose the share's price rises to $25. The bondholder converts, effectively paying $20 for shares with a market value of $25, making a gain of

$$\$5 \times 50 \text{ shares} = \$250$$

Of course, if the share's price never exceeds $20, the conversion feature is never exercised and turns out to have no value.

Convertibles can generally be issued at somewhat lower interest rates than regular bonds. Such a rate reduction reflects the value placed on the conversion potential by the market. Further, companies can occasionally borrow using convertibles when traditional debt would be impossible to market because of risk.

We will discuss convertible bonds further in Chapter 18.

Perpetual Bonds

Perpetual bonds have no maturity date.

There have been occasions when borrowers have issued perpetual debt—that is, debt that does not have a maturity date. Although they are not common (other than in the minds of finance professors!), **perpetual bonds** do indeed exist. One example is from Canadian Pacific Railway. If you look in the notes that accompany the company's financial statements, you will find a listing (under long-term debt) for Perpetual 4% Consolidated Debenture Stock. Although listed as stock (shares), when you investigate further you will find this "stock" (created by an Act of Parliament in 1889) has a first charge, with some exceptions, over all the undertakings of the company including its main assets. You can call it stock, but it is a bond!

Junk Bonds

Junk bonds are issued by risky companies and pay high interest rates.

Junk bonds are issued by companies that are not in particularly sound financial condition, or are considered risky for some other reason. They generally pay interest rates that are as much as 5% higher than the rates paid by the strongest companies. Hence, they're also called *high-yield* securities.

Before the mid-1970s it was virtually impossible for risky firms—especially new, small companies—to borrow by issuing unsecured bonds. Investors were simply unwilling to accept the risks associated with such firms at any promised rate of return. At that time, however, a concept of pooling risky bonds arose, and seemed to make high-risk, high-yield issues viable in the sense of being reasonably safe investments.

In the late 1980s and early 1990s, the safety perceived in the pooling technique evaporated when the economy went into a sustained recession. As a result, the junk bond vehicle lost most of its popularity. We'll discuss junk bonds again in the next section and again in Chapter 19.

Bond Ratings—Assessing Default Risk

Recall that in Chapter 7 we discussed several risks associated with bonds, including the risk of default (page 245). In practice, investors and the financial community go to great lengths to assess and control exposure to default risk in bonds.

Bond ratings gauge the probability that issuers will fail to meet their obligations.

Bonds are assigned quality ratings that reflect the probability of their going into default. Higher ratings mean lower default probabilities. The **bond ratings** are developed by *rating agencies* that make a business of staying on top of the things that make bonds and the underlying firms more or less risky. The two Canadian bond rating agencies are the Dominion Bond Rating Service (DBRS), and Standard & Poor's Ratings Direct Canada (formerly the Canadian Bond Rating Service). In the United States, the best known rating agencies are Moody's Corporation (known as Moody's) and Standard & Poor's Corporation (generally called S&P).

The agencies rate bonds by examining the financial and market condition of the issuing companies and the contractual provisions supporting individual bonds. It's important to realize that the analysis has these two parts. A bond's strength is fundamentally dependent on that of the issuing corporation, but some things can make one bond safer than another issued by the same company. For example, a mortgage bond backed by real estate will always be stronger than an unsecured debenture issued by the same company. Similarly, senior debt is always superior to subordinated debt.

The process of rating a bond begins with a financial (ratio) analysis of the issuing firm using the kinds of tools we developed in Chapter 3. To that the agencies add any knowledge they have about the company, its markets, and its other dealings. For example, suppose a firm has good financial results and a prosperous market outlook but is threatened by a major lawsuit. If the lawsuit is very serious, it can lower the rating of the firm's bonds.

Bond ratings are not precise in the sense of being the result of a mathematical formula. Although they do rely heavily on standard numerical (ratio) analyses, they also include qualitative judgments made by the rating agencies.

Rating Symbols and Grades

DBRS and S&P use similar scales to describe the bonds they rate. It's important to be generally familiar with the meaning of the terms. Table 9.2 summarizes the symbols used by the two firms and their meanings. The distinction between bonds above and below the BBB grade is especially significant. Bonds at or above that level are said to be **investment grade bonds**, while those below are considered substandard. The latter can be called junk bonds.

Why Ratings Are Important

Throughout our study, we've stressed the fact that risk and return are related, and that investors *require* higher returns on riskier investments. Ratings are the primary measure of the default risk associated with bonds. Therefore, they're an important determinant of the interest rates investors demand on the bonds of different companies.

In effect, the rating associated with a firm's bonds determines the rate at which the firm can borrow. A lower rating implies that the company has to pay higher interest rates, which generally means that it's more difficult for the company to do business and earn a profit, because it's burdened with a higher cost of debt financing. This idea is laid out in Figure 9.7.

All bond yields (interest rates) move up and down over time, but there's always a *differential* between the rates required on high- and low-quality issues. The lower curve associated with high-quality bonds means that the issuing companies can borrow at lower rates (more cheaply) than those associated with risky, low-quality bonds. The safest, highest-quality bond is a Government of Canada bond, which has no default risk (Chapter 7, page 247). Its yield plotted on a graph like Figure 9.7 would be lower than that of any other bond.

A bond's rating affects the size of the differential between the rate it must pay to borrow and the rate demanded of high-quality issues. It does not affect the overall up and down motion of the rate structure. Clearly, the differential reflects the risk of default perceived to exist with lower-quality bonds. This is the default risk premium we discussed in Chapter 7.

THE DIFFERENTIAL OVER TIME Notice that the quality differential tends to be larger when interest rates are generally high than when they're low. This is an important fact, and makes logical sense. High rates tend to be associated with recessions and tough economic times. It's during those periods that marginal companies are prone to fail. In other words, the risk of default associated with weak companies is greater in bad times than in good

> **Investment grade bonds** are above a certain quality rating. (DBRS: BBB; S&P: BBB)

> **http**
> BondsOnline provides information about investing in bonds at http://www.bondsonline.com.

> The *differential* between the yields on high- and low-quality bonds is an indicator of the health of the company.

DBRS	S&P	Implications
AAA	AAA	Highest quality
AA	AA	Extremely safe
A	A	Good quality, satisfactory
BBB	BBB	"Investment grade," adequate
BB	BB	Poor quality
B	B	Risky, highly speculative
CCC	CCC	Low quality
CC	CC	Very risky
C	C	Senior debt in lower categories or in bankruptcy
D	D	In default, repayment questionable

TABLE 9.2
DBRS and S&P Bond Ratings

FIGURE 9.7

The Yield Differential between High- and Low-Quality Bonds

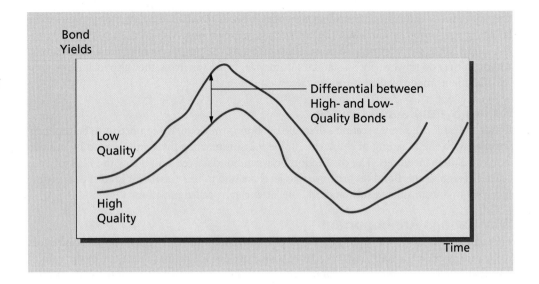

times. Because it expresses the level of risk, the differential tends to be larger in recessionary periods.

In fact, this phenomenon is strong enough to be considered an *economic indicator*. That means a high differential is taken as a signal that harder times are on the way.

THE SIGNIFICANCE OF THE INVESTMENT GRADE RATING Most bonds are purchased by institutional investors rather than by individuals. These investors include mutual funds, banks, insurance companies, and pension funds. Many such institutions are required by law to make only relatively safe, conservative investments. Therefore they can deal only in investment grade bonds or higher. This requirement severely limits the market for the debt of companies whose bonds aren't considered at least investment grade.

Bond Indentures—Controlling Default Risk

In Chapter 1, we discussed a conflict of interest between creditors and shareholders (page 11). Virtually all business operations involve some risk. However, higher levels of risk are usually associated with higher rewards. The conflict of interest arises because the rewards of successful risk taking accrue largely to shareholders, while the penalties for failure can be shared between shareholders and creditors.

Insights **ETHICS**

Ethical Debt Management

Suppose a firm borrows through a bond issue with a relatively weak indenture that doesn't say anything about additional future debt. Then suppose it wants to borrow more later on, but the new lender is concerned about safety, and insists that its debt be made senior to existing debt. If the firm agrees, it will damage the investors who hold the old bonds.

It's fairly obvious that the original bondholders will suffer if the firm fails, because they'll stand behind the new creditors in being paid out of any assets that survive

the failure. But they may be hurt even if the firm does well. That's because the old bond's rating is likely to be lowered because of its new subordinate status. That means the market will perceive the issue as having more risk, and is likely to lower its price immediately. Hence, old bondholders will take a loss if they sell.

Is it ethical for a firm to do that without in some way compensating the old bondholders? What if management argues that the firm desperately needs the new money and will be in big trouble without it. What would you do if you were CFO?

Indeed, bondholders can be hurt even if failure doesn't occur. If a company is perceived to become more risky, the return investors require on its debt increases immediately, which in turn drives down the market price of its bonds. When that happens, bondholders suffer an immediate loss.

Investors contemplating lending to a company by buying its bonds look at the current level of risk associated with the business. If they're comfortable with that level, they purchase bonds, but remain concerned that future operations could become more risky. That might happen if the firm takes on riskier projects, encounters financial problems, or is managed unwisely.

To ensure that bond-issuing companies maintain an even level of risk, lenders usually insist that bond agreements contain restrictions on the borrower's activities until the bonds are paid off. The contractual document containing such restrictive covenants is called the bond indenture. Typical indenture provisions preclude entering certain high-risk businesses and limit borrowing more money from other sources. Indentures may also require that certain financial ratios be held above minimum levels. For example, an indenture might require that times interest earned (TIE) be maintained above a particular figure, say, seven.

Every bond issue has a *trustee* whose job is to administer and enforce the terms of the indenture on behalf of the bondholders. Trustees are usually trust companies, many of which are now wholly owned subsidiaries of Canadian banks.

> **Restrictive covenants** are contractual agreements associated with *loans* that limit the activities of borrowing companies. **Bond indentures** are the same but apply to *bonds*. Both attempt to prevent firms from becoming riskier after the bonds are purchased.

Sinking Funds

Recall that bonds are non-amortized debt, meaning that the borrowed principal is not repaid until maturity. This creates a risk for bondholders in that borrowing firms may not have the funds to make large principal repayments.

> *Sinking funds* provide money for the repayment of bond principal.

Considerable safety is provided by a *sinking fund* that spreads the repayment of principal over time. We've already discussed two sinking fund arrangements. The first calls for periodic deposits such that the amount available at maturity is equal to the principal to be repaid. We illustrated that approach as a future value of an amount problem in Example 8.6 on page 273. A second arrangement involves randomly calling in some bonds for retirement prior to maturity. We discussed that approach starting on page 321 of this chapter.

Still another approach is to issue serial bonds, splitting the total amount borrowed into several separate issues with different maturities, usually about a year apart.

SUMMARY

1 The principal amount or face of the bond represents a loan for a specified time period. Periodic interest payments, or the coupon, are made on the bond over its term.

2 To calculate the price of a bond, sum the present value of the periodic coupon payments (an annuity) and the present value of the face (a lump sum). The interest rate used to value the coupons and face should be the prevailing market rate of interest for that risk and term bond.

3 Bond ratings can affect the prices and yields on various issues. Companies that are having problems making debt repayment schedules or that have recently had poor financial results would likely find their bonds being perceived as higher risk, or junk bonds. Firms with strong financial results and good capacity for debt repayment would be considered investment grade. To the issuers of these bonds (and the buyers), the difference in risk is reflected in their respective yields.

The high risk bond would have a higher yield and lower price while the opposite would be true for the investment grade bond.

4 A number of factors affect the prevailing interest rates including changes in the economy and perceived company risk. As the bond agreement defines the coupon rate, time remaining to maturity, and principal amount, the prevailing price of the bond will change when interest rates in the market place change. The yield to maturity of a bond is the average annual return offered by the bond, based on the coupon rate, current market price, and time remaining to maturity.

5 Yield to maturity is calculated by setting the price of the bond equal to the present value of periodic coupon payments (and annuity) plus the present value of the face and then solving for the interest rate.

6 Bonds may be issued with certain features. A number of features were discussed including callable bonds (can be made shorter term at the option of the issuer), sinking funds (the issuer must repay some of the principal over time), zero coupons, and collateral requirements. Investors perceive different features as benefits or risks, and price these features accordingly.

7 Purchasing fixed income securities such as bonds or debentures exposes investors to interest rate risk or the possibility that interest rate changes will have a negative effect on the bond price.

KEY TERMS

Bearer bond, p. 326
Bond indenture, p. 331
Bond rating, p. 328
Call provision, p. 322
Convertible bond, p. 327
Coupon payment, p. 311
Coupon rate, p. 311
Current yield, p. 314
Debenture, p. 327
Face value, p.311

Flotation costs, p. 325
Investment grade bonds, p. 329
Junk bonds, p. 328
Mortgage bond, p. 327
Perpetual bonds, p. 328
Registered bond or security, p. 327
Restrictive covenants, p. 331

Seasoned issue, p. 311
Senior debt, p. 327
Subordinated debt, p. 327
Transfer agent, p. 327
Valuation, p. 309
Yield to call (YTC), p. 323
Yield to maturity (YTM), p. 314
Zero coupon bond, p. 321

KEY FORMULAS

(9.1) $P_B = PV(\text{Interest payments}) + PV(\text{Principal repayment})$

(9.2) $PV(\text{Interest payments}) = PMT[PVFA_{k,n}]$

(9.3) $PV(\text{Principal repayment}) = FV[PVF_{k,n}]$

(9.4) $P_B = PMT[PVFA_{k,n}] + FV[PVF_{k,n}]$

(9.5) $P_B(\text{Call}) = PMT[PVFA_{k,m}] + CP[PVF_{k,m}]$

Self-Test

Carstairs Inc. issued a $1,000, 25-year bond five years ago at 11% interest. Comparable bonds yield 8% today. What should Carstairs' bond sell for now? What is the current yield of this bond?

It will help your understanding a great deal if you work the problem yourself *before* looking at the solution.

■ **Solution:** The variables are as follows (as usual, assume semiannual interest). Then, using Equation 9.4,

$$PMT = \frac{0.11 \times \$1,000}{2} = \$55$$

$$n = 20 \times 2 = 40$$

$$k = \frac{8\%}{2} = 4\%$$

$$FV = \$1,000$$

Then, using Equation 9.4,

$$P_B = PMT[PVFA_{k,n}] + FV[PVF_{k,n}]$$

$$= \$55[PVFA_{4,40}] + \$1,000[PVF_{4,40}]$$

$$= \$55(19.7928) + \$1,000(0.2083)$$

$$= \$1,088.60 + \$208.30$$

$$= \$1,296.90$$

The current yield is

$$Current\ yield = \frac{\$110}{\$1,296.90} = 8.48\%$$

Calculator Solution

Key	Input
n	40
I/Y	4
FV	1,000
PMT	55

Answer

PV	1,296.89

**Use Excel®
Function PV**

QUESTIONS

1. What is valuation, and why are we interested in the results?

2. Contrast real assets and financial (paper) assets. What is the basis for the value of each?

3. Why do bonds have indentures?

4. How can two knowledgeable people come to different conclusions about the value of the same security? Can this happen if they have access to the same information?

5. Describe the nature of a bond. Include at least the following ideas:
   • term/maturity
   • debt versus equity
   • non-amortized
   • risk
   • face value
   • "buying" a bond
   • one borrower/many lenders
   • conflict with shareholders

6. Describe bond pricing as two time value of money problems.

7. Two interest rates are associated with pricing a bond. Name and describe each. How are they used? Describe a third rate not used in pricing.

8. If bonds pay fixed interest rates, how can they be sold year after year on the secondary market? Include the idea of how yields adjust to changing market interest rates.

9. What is the relationship between bond prices and interest rates? Verbally describe how this relationship comes about. How can we use this relationship to estimate the value of a bond?

10. What is interest rate or price risk? Why is it sometimes called maturity risk? Explain fully.

11. What causes maturity risk? In other words, why do long-term bonds respond differently to interest rate changes than short-term bonds? (*Hint:* Think about how the present value formulas work.)

12. Using words only, describe the process of finding a bond's yield at a given selling price.

13. What is a call provision? Why do companies put them in bonds? Define "call-protected period" and "call premium/penalty."

14. Under what conditions is a bond almost certain to be called at a particular date in the future? How does this condition affect its price?

15. How and why do sinking funds enhance the safety of lenders?

Business Analysis

1. You're an analyst in the finance department of Flyover Corp., a new firm in a profitable but risky high-tech business. Several growth opportunities have come along recently, but the company doesn't have enough capital to undertake them. Share prices are down, so it doesn't make sense to try to raise new capital through the sale of common shares. The company's bank won't lend it any more money than it already has, and investment dealers have said that debentures are out of the question. The treasurer has asked you to do some research and suggest a few ways in which bonds might be made attractive enough to allow Flyover to borrow. Write a brief memo summarizing your ideas.

2. The Everglo Corp., a manufacturer of cosmetics, is financed with a 50−50 mix of debt and common shares. The debt is in the form of debentures that have a relatively weak indenture. Susan Moremoney, the firm's president and principal shareholder, has proposed doubling the firm's debt by issuing new bonds secured by the company's existing assets, and using the money raised to attack the lucrative but very risky European market. You're Everglo's treasurer, and have been directed by Ms. Moremoney to implement the new financing plan. Is there an ethical problem with the president's proposal? Why? Who is likely to gain at whose expense? (*Hint:* How are the ratings of the existing debentures likely to change?) What would you do if you really found yourself in a position like this?

3. You're the CFO of Nildorf Inc., a maker of luxury consumer goods, which, because of its product, is especially sensitive to economic ups and downs (people cut back drastically on luxury items during recessionary times). In an executive staff meeting this morning, Charlie Suave, the president, proposed a major expansion. You felt the expansion would be feasible if the immediate future looked good, but were concerned that spreading resources too thin in a recessionary period could wreck the company. When you expressed your concern, Charlie said he wasn't worried about the economy because the spread between AAA and B bonds is relatively small, and that's a good sign. You observed, however, that rates seem to have bottomed out recently and are rising along with the differential between strong and weak companies. After some general discussion, the proposal was tabled pending further research. Later in the day, Ed Sliderule, the chief engineer, came into your office and asked,

"What in the world were you guys talking about this morning?" Prepare a brief written explanation for Ed.

PROBLEMS

The solutions in Appendix B are based on using either a financial calculator or Excel®. Slight rounding differences will occur if using financial tables.

Assume all bonds pay interest semiannually.

1. Longly Trucking is issuing a 20-year bond with a $2,000 face value tomorrow. The issue is to pay an 8% coupon rate, because that was the interest rate while it was being planned. However, rates increased suddenly and are expected to be 9% when the bond is marketed. What will Longly receive for each bond tomorrow?

2. Smithson Co.'s Class A bonds have 10 years to go until maturity. They have a $1,000 face value and carry coupon rates of 8%. Calculate the yield to maturity at the following prices.
   a. $770
   b. $1,150
   c. $1,000

3. Calculate the market price of a $1,000 face value bond under the following conditions.

	Coupon Rate	Time Until Maturity	Current Market Rate
a.	12%	15 years	10%
b.	7	5	12
c.	9	25	6
d.	14	30	9
e.	5	6	8

4. What is the current yield on each of the bonds in the previous problem?

5. The Sampson Company issued a $1,000 bond five years ago with an initial term of 25 years and a coupon rate of 6%. Today's interest rate is 10%.
   a. What is the bond's current price if interest is paid semiannually as it is on most bonds?
   b. What is the price if the bond's interest is paid annually? Comment on the difference between parts (a) and (b).
   c. What would the price be if interest was paid semiannually and the bond was issued at a face value of $1,500?

6. The Churchill Company issued a 25-year bond five years ago with a face value of $1,000. The bond pays interest semiannually at a 10% annual rate.
   a. What is the bond's price today if the interest rate on comparable new issues is 12%?
   b. What is the price today if the interest rate is 8%?
   c. Explain the results of parts (a) and (b) in terms of opportunities available to investors.
   d. What is the price today if the interest rate is 10%?
   e. Comment on the answer to part (d).

7. Fix-It Inc. recently issued 10-year, $1,000 par value bonds at an 8% coupon rate.
   a. Two years later, similar bonds are yielding investors 6%. At what price are Fix-Its bonds selling?
   b. What would the bonds be selling for if yields had risen to 12%?
   c. Assume the conditions in part (a). Further assume interest rates remain at 6% for the next 8 years. What would happen to the price of the Fix-It bonds over that time?

8. Pam Smith just inherited a $1,000 face value K-S Inc. bond from her grandmother. The bond clearly indicates a 12% coupon rate, but the maturity date has been smudged and can't be read. Pam called a broker and determined that similar bonds are currently returning about 8% and that her bond is selling for $1,326.58. How many more interest payments can Pam expect to receive on her inherited bond?

9. Hoste Corp. issued a $1,000 face value 20-year bond seven years ago with a 12% coupon rate. The bond is currently selling for $1,143.75. What is its yield to maturity (YTM)?

10. The Mariposa Co. has two bonds outstanding. One was issued 25 years ago at a coupon rate of 9%. The other was issued five years ago at a coupon rate of 9%. Both bonds were originally issued with terms of 30 years and face values of $1,000. The going interest rate is 14% today.
    a. What are the prices of the two bonds at this time?
    b. Discuss the result of part (a) in terms of risk in investing in bonds.

11. Tutak Industries issued a $1,000 face value bond a number of years ago that will mature in eight years. Similar bonds are yielding 8%, and the Tutak bond is currently selling for $1,291.31. Compute the coupon rate on this bond. (In practice we generally aren't asked to find coupon rates.)

12. John Wilson is a conservative investor who has asked your advice about two bonds he is considering. One is a seasoned issue of the Capri Fashion Company that was first sold 22 years ago at a face value of $1,000, with a 25-year term, paying 6%. The other is a new 30-year issue of the Gantry Elevator Company that is coming out now at a face value of $1,000. Interest rates are now 6%, so both bonds will pay the same coupon rate.
    a. What is each bond worth today? (No calculations should be necessary.)
    b. If interest rates were to rise to 12% today, estimate without making any calculations what each bond would be worth. Review page 320 on estimating if necessary.
    c. Calculate the prices in part (b) to check your estimating ability. If interest rates are expected to rise, which bond is the better investment?
    d. If interest rates are expected to fall, which bond is better? Are long-term rates likely to fall much lower than 6%? Why or why not? (*Hint:* Think about the interest rate model of Chapter 7 and its components.)

13. Ernie Griffin just purchased a five-year zero coupon corporate bond for $680.60 and plans to hold it until maturity. Assume Ernie has a marginal tax rate of 25%.
    a. Calculate Ernie's after-tax cash flows from the bond for the first two years. Assume annual compounding.

b. Describe in words the difference in cash flows between owning Ernie's bond and a five-year Canada bond for the same amount.

(*Hint:* See the Insights box on page 321 for this problem.)

14. Daubert, Inc., planned to issue and sell at par 10-year, $1,000 face value bonds totalling $400 million next month. The bonds were printed with a 6% coupon rate. Since that printing, however, DBRS has downgraded Daubert's bond rating from AAA to AA. This means the bonds will have to be offered to yield buyers 7%. How much less than it expected will Daubert collect when the bonds are issued? Ignore administrative costs and commissions.

Problems 15 through 17 refer to the bonds of the Apollo Corporation, all of which have a call feature. The call feature allows Apollo to pay off bonds any time after the first 15 years, but requires that bondholders be compensated with an extra year's interest at the coupon rate if such a payoff is exercised.

15. Apollo's Alpha bond was issued 10 years ago for 30 years with a face value of $1,000. Interest rates were very high at the time, and the bond's coupon rate is 20%. The interest rate is now 10%.
   a. At what price should an Alpha bond sell?
   b. At what price would it sell without the call feature?

16. Apollo's Alpha-1 bond was issued at a time when interest rates were even higher. It has a coupon rate of 22%, a $1,000 face value, an initial term of 30 years, and is now 13 years old. Calculate its price if interest rates are now 12%, compare it with the price that would exist if there were no call feature, and comment on the difference.

17. Apollo's Beta bond has just reached the end of its period of call protection, has 10 years to go until maturity, and has a face value of $1,000. Its coupon rate is 16% and the interest rate is currently 10%. Should Apollo refund this issue if refunding costs a total of 8% of the value of the debt refunded plus the call penalty?

18. Snyder Mfg. issued a $1,000 face value 30-year bond five years ago with an 8% coupon. The bond is subject to call after 10 years, and the current interest rate is 7%. What call premium will make a bondholder indifferent to the call? (*Hint:* Equate the formulas for the bond's price with and without the call.)

19. Your friend Marvin is excited because he believes he's found an investment bargain. A broker at QuickCash Investments has offered him an opportunity to buy a bond issued by Galveston Galleries Inc. at a very attractive price. The 30-year bond was issued 10 years ago at a face value of $1,000, paying a coupon rate of 8%. Interest rates have risen recently, driving bond prices down, but most economists think they'll fall again soon, driving prices back up. That makes Marvin and his broker think this bond may be a real money maker if he buys now, holds for a year or two, and then sells. The bonds of companies that were similar to Galveston at the time its bond was issued are now yielding 12%. Galveston's bond is selling at $300, which the broker claims is a fantastic bargain. Marvin knows you're a finance major and has asked your opinion of the opportunity. How would you advise him?

Computer Problems

20. You are a securities salesperson whose clients are mainly elderly people who want very secure investments. They remember the days when interest rates were very stable (before the 1970s) and bond prices hardly fluctuated at all regardless of their terms. You've had a hard time convincing some of them that bonds, especially those with longer terms, can be risky during times when interest rates move rapidly.

Use the BONDVAL program to make up a chart to help illustrate your point during discussions with your clients. BONDVAL is one of the several Excel® templates available on the text's support website.

The Value of a $1,000 Par, 12% Coupon Bond as a Function of Term as Interest Rates Change

Bond Term in Years

	1	5	10	25
6%				
8%				
10%				
12%				

Market Rates

Write out a brief paragraph outlining your warning about bond price volatility to an elderly customer. Refer to your chart.

21. Use BONDVAL to find the YTM of the following $1,000 par value bonds.

	1	**2**	**3**
Market price	$752.57	$1,067.92	$915.05
Coupon rate	6.5%	7.24%	12.5%
Term	15.5 yrs	8.5 yrs	2.5 yrs

APPENDIX 9.A

Lease Financing

*A **lease** is an agreement for the use of an asset in return for payments over a specified period.*

A **lease** is a contract that gives one party the right to use an asset owned by the other in return for a periodic payment. The owner of the property is called the lessor and the user is the lessee. Leasing is a method of financing assets that is similar to term or installment debt.

Most of us are familiar with leases in the context of houses and apartments where the lessor is the landlord and the lessee is the tenant.[7] In recent years, leasing automobiles has also become common practice. In business, companies lease equipment of all kinds as well as real estate.

THE DEVELOPMENT OF LEASING IN BUSINESS

Prior to the 1950s, leasing was almost entirely limited to real estate (i.e., leasing office or factory space). Since then, the technique has spread to equipment to the extent that today approximately 30% of all equipment (including vehicles) acquired by businesses is leased.

The risk in debt comes from the fact that payments are obligatory charges that, if missed, can cause the firm to fail. Essentially the same is true of lease payments when leases are noncancellable. Noncancellability means that if the lessee returns the equipment during the lease term, the remaining payments are still a legal obligation, much the same as an unpaid loan. Since long-term leases on major equipment are virtually always noncancellable, they are effectively debt with all of its problems and risks.

---

7 It's important to distinguish between a lease and a rental. Renting implies paying for the temporary use of an asset, but without a longer-term commitment. However, the term "rent" is often used loosely to refer to lease payments as well as rental payments.

By the early 1970s, the accounting profession expressed concern over distortions in reported financial results due to leasing. In particular, there was no requirement to disclose long-term leases on the balance sheet, understating the true degree of financing leverage and overstating the strength of the balance sheet. The result was a change in accounting rules that would require disclosing long-term leases as the equivalent of debt.

THE CANADIAN INSTITUTE OF CHARTERED ACCOUNTANTS AND LEASING

The task of reporting leasing fairly in financial results fell to the Canadian Institute of Chartered Accountants (CICA), a professional accounting organization that promulgates rules governing how financial statements are put together. The Institute issued new accounting rules (CICA Section 3065 or CICA 3065 for short) for leases in 1978. The rules for the financial reporting of leases are based primarily on economic effects rather than legal technicalities.

CICA rules redefine ownership in an *economic* sense.

Prior to CICA 3065, ownership for financial reporting purposes was defined legally. An asset was owned by whoever held its title (usually a bill of sale). It didn't matter that someone else (a lessee) was using the asset. CICA 3065 said that this concept of ownership didn't reflect economic reality. It maintained that the real owner of an asset is whoever enjoys its benefits and is burdened with its risks and responsibilities.

Specifically CICA says that if a lease transfers those benefits and burdens to a lessee for most of an asset's life, then that lessee is the owner for financial reporting purposes, and must account for the asset on its balance sheet.[8]

CICA also addressed leases that include provisions that pass legal ownership to lessees at their end or provide that lessees can purchase the assets at prices below *fair market value* (called *bargain purchase options*). According to CICA, those leases are just disguised installment sales contracts, and must be accounted for as sales by the lessor. That is, the lessor is really just lending the purchase price to the lessee, and subsequent lease payments are actually loan payments.

Operating and Capital Leases

CICA said that there are essentially two kinds of leases: operating, and capital. Capital leases effectively transfer economic ownership to the lessee, while operating leases do not.

Under CICA 3065, lessees must *capitalize* capital leases. That means they must make accounting entries that put the values of leased assets and the associated liabilities on their balance sheets. The value of a leased asset is usually its fair market value and the associated liability reflects the obligation to make lease payments in the future. The resulting balance sheet accounts are similar to those that would appear if the lessee purchased the asset with borrowed money.

In other words, after CICA 3065, operating leases need not be reported on the balance sheet, but capital leases must. Naturally lessees strive to interpret leases as operating whenever they can. The Institute made it easier to determine the nature of a lease by promulgating three rules. If any one rule applies at the start of the lease contract, the lease is considered to be capital in nature.

In a **capital lease**, the lessee effectively acquires ownership of the leased asset. It must be *capitalized* on the balance sheet. In an **operating lease**, the lessee does not effectively acquire ownership of the leased asset.

1. The lease will transfer legal ownership to the lessee at its end, either automatically or after making payment of a bargain purchase option at the end of the lease.
2. The lease term is at least 75% of the asset's estimated economic life.[9]
3. The present value of the lease payments is at least 90% of the asset's fair market value at the beginning of the lease.[10]

---

8 According to CICA, benefits include potential residual value/capital gain. Burdens include risks of idle capacity, obsolescence, and changing economic conditions.
9 An asset's economic life is the period over which it will be used. That is generally longer than the period over which it is amortized.
10 The interest rate used to take this present value is the rate the lessee would pay if it borrowed new money at the time the lease is signed.

The first rule excludes disguised installment sales contracts from treatment as operating leases. The second says that if the attributes of ownership are transferred for most of the asset's life, it no longer truly belongs to the lessor and the lease must be treated as a capital lease. The third addresses whether the lessor is really selling the equipment through the lease. If the present value of the committed lease payments is close to the asset's value, then the transaction is probably a sale, and ownership should effectively pass to the lessee.

If one or more of the criteria is met, the lease is a capital lease; all other leases are operating leases for accounting purposes. As a practical matter it's fairly easy to identify operating leases: (1) They're usually relatively short, say one to three years; (2) the lease payments usually include a charge for equipment maintenance; and (3) lessors generally pay for insurance and property taxes (because these things are included, operating leases are sometimes called *service leases*); and (4) operating leases are also generally cancellable on short notice (usually 30 days), although a cancellation penalty may be required. Capital leases, on the other hand, are *noncancellable*.

Insights REAL APPLICATIONS

DANIER LEATHER

Operating and Capital Leases at Danier Leather Inc.

(For the financial statements and other financial information about Danier Leather Inc., refer to Appendix 3A, page 92.)

By the end of its 2006 fiscal year, Danier had signed both operating leases for its stores and other facilities, and capital leases for new information technology. Annual commitments over the remaining terms of the leases are summarized below ($000):

	Operating Leases	Capital Leases	Total
2007	$11,615	$1,061	$12,676
2008	10,263	1,061	11,324
2009	8,675	884	9,559
2010	6,469		6,469
2011	5,253		5,253
Thereafter	8,084		8,084
Total	50,359	3,006	53,365

OPERATING LEASES

These were *minimum* rentals, excluding that portion of variable store rentals based upon revenue. Offsetting these expenses were *lease inducements* representing cash benefits received from landlords pursuant to store lease agreements. On the books, these lease inducements were amortized against rent expense over the term of the lease, not exceeding 10.5 years. The unamortized amount at June 24, 2006, was $2,125.

CAPITAL LEASES

The capital leases expire in 2009. Payments total $3,006 including interest of $266 (at a weighted average annual rate of 6.2%). The current portion of the lease liability equalled $911, and the long-term portion amounted to $1,829. Review the balance sheet on pages 93–95 to see how Danier disclosed its capital lease assets and obligations.

Source: Danier Leather Annual Report, 2006.

FINANCIAL STATEMENT PRESENTATION OF LEASES BY LESSEES

The financial statement presentation and accounting for operating leases is very different from that for capital leases. Operating leases are simple, while capital leases are complex. We'll discuss both, presenting only the highlights of the capital lease treatment.

Operating Leases

The financial statement treatment of operating leases is straightforward. There are no balance sheet entries, and lease payments are simply treated as an expense on the income statement. There is, however, a requirement that the details of all leases be disclosed in footnotes to the financial statements.

Capital Leases

At the beginning of a capital lease, the lessee must record an asset on its balance sheet reflecting the leased equipment's value. It must also record an offsetting liability related to its obligation to make lease payments. Both of these amounts are usually taken to be equal to the present value of the stream of committed lease payments, a sum that is usually about equal to the fair market value of the equipment. The liability appears in the debt section of the balance sheet and is normally called "lease obligation." The interest rate for the present value calculation is the rate the lessee would have to pay if it was borrowing new money at the time the lease begins.

- Capital leases are usually capitalized at the present value of committed lease payments.
- Leased assets are amortized as capital assets. Lease obligations are amortized as loans.

Once these accounts are set up, they are amortized[11] independently. The asset is simply amortized. The lease obligation liability is treated like a loan. An effective interest rate is assumed,[12] and lease payments are divided between interest and principal reduction as if they were loan payments. The technique is identical to the one we studied in Chapter 8 under Loan Amortization Schedules (see page 284). The only difference is that these lease payments occur at the beginning of the period; that is, they are an *annuity due*.

Example 9A.1

Emeral Inc. is a moderately sized construction company. Last year it leased a crane from GD Credit Corp for a term of 15 years at an annual rental of $20,000. The crane is expected to be completely worn out and valueless at the end of the lease. Before the lease agreement was made, other financing sources were willing to lend to Emeral at 5%. Emeral will amortize the crane using the straight-line method over the 15-year life of the lease.

Just before the lease was signed, Emeral's balance sheet was as follows:

Emeral Inc.
Balance Sheet
($000)

Current assets	$ 20	Current liabilities	$ 10
Capital assets	180	Long-term debt	90
Total assets	$ 200	Shareholders' equity	100
		Total debt and Shareholders' equity	$ 200

The lease is treated as a capital lease.
a. Construct Emeral's balance sheet after the lease is signed, showing the leased asset and lease obligation separately. (We'll work in whole dollars, but present balance sheet accounts rounded to the nearest $1,000.)
b. Calculate the firm's debt ratio before and after the lease takes effect, and comment on the difference.
c. (Optional) Reconstruct the balance sheet after the first annual lease payment is made, assuming all other accounts are unchanged.

---

11 Amortizing balance sheet accounts means writing them down to zero over time. The cost of a capital asset is amortized over its estimated useful life while liabilities (think in terms of a loan) are amortized as they are paid off.
12 Usually the same rate is used to take the present value of the lease payments.

■ **Solution:**

a. Emeral will capitalize the lease at an amount equal to the present value of the annuity due formed by the contracted lease payments. That amount is calculated using the present value of an annuity due formula, Equation 8.26 (see page 288).

$$PVAd = PMT[PVFA_{k,n}][1 + k]$$
$$= \$20,000[PVFA_{5,15}][1 + k]$$
$$= \$20,000(10.3797)(1.05)$$
$$= \$217,973$$

Hence the balance sheet immediately after the lease is signed is as follows (the first year of lease payments would normally be included in Current liabilities, with the rest in Long-term debt but to keep the example straightforward, we'll deal with the total lease obligation as Long-term debt).

Emeral Inc.
Balance Sheet
($000)

Current assets	$ 20	Current liabilities	$ 10
Capital assets		Lease obligation	218
Leased crane	218	Long-term debt	90
Other capital assets	180	Total long-term debt	308
Total capital assets	398	Shareholders' equity	100
Total assets	$ 418	Total debt and Shareholders' equity	$ 418

b. Emeral's debt ratio before the lease is (in thousands)

$$\text{Debt ratio} = \frac{\text{Current liabilities} + \text{Long-term dept}}{\text{Total assets}}$$
$$= \frac{\$10 + \$90}{200}$$
$$= \frac{\$100}{200}$$
$$= 50\%$$

After the lease is signed, the lease obligation is included as debt in calculating the debt ratio, which increases substantially.

$$\text{Debt ratio} = \frac{\text{Current liabilities} + \text{Lease obligation} + \text{Long-term dept}}{\text{Total assets}}$$
$$= \frac{\$10 + \$218 + \$90}{\$418}$$
$$= \frac{\$318}{\$418}$$
$$= 76\%$$

Comment: The lease creates a major deterioration in Emeral's debt ratio that could jeopardize its viability. It would certainly lessen the firm's ability to borrow from other sources.

c. To construct the new balance sheet, we must calculate the first year's amortization of the Leased Crane and Lease Obligation accounts. Each of those is then subtracted from the respective beginning account balances. The value of the asset is amortized on a straight-line basis while the liability is amortized as if it were a loan at 5%.

First consider the Leased Crane account. After the first year, it is reduced by one year's amortization.

$$\text{Amortization expense} = \frac{\$217,973}{15} = \$14,532$$

Calculator Solution

BEGIN MODE

Key	Input
n	5
I/Y	15
FV	0
PMT	20,000

Answer

PV	217,973

Use Excel®
Function PV

Type 1

Leased Crane:

$$\text{Ending balance} = \text{Beginning balance} - \text{Amortization expense}$$
$$= \$217,973 - \$14,532$$
$$= \$203,441$$

Next, consider the Lease Obligation account. It's treated as a loan bearing 5% interest. We'll calculate the first year's ending balance just as we would if we were constructing a loan amortization schedule (see page 284).

Interest in the first year is 5% of the beginning obligation (loan).

$$\text{Interest} = \$217,973 \times 0.05 = \$10,899$$

Subtract this from the lease payment to calculate the portion of the payment that reduces the lease obligation (loan principal).

$$\text{Obligation reduction} = \text{Lease payment} - \text{Interest}$$
$$= \$20,000 - \$10,899$$
$$= \$9,101$$

Subtract the reduction from the beginning obligation (loan) balance to get the first year's ending balance.

$$\text{New lease obligation} = \text{Beginning balance} - \text{Obligation reduction}$$
$$= \$217,973 - \$9,101$$
$$= \$208,872$$

Finally, put the new asset and obligation balances into the balance sheet rounded to the nearest $1,000.

Emeral Inc.
Balance Sheet
($000)

Current assets	$ 20	Current liabilities	$ 10
Capital assets		Lease obligation	209
Leased crane	203	Long-term debt	90
Other capital assets	180	Total long-term debt	299
Total capital assets	383	Shareholders' equity	94
Total assets	$ 403	Total debt and Shareholders' equity	$ 403

Notice that, because the Leased Crane and the Lease Obligation accounts are amortized using different methods, there's no reason that their balances should be equal until the end of the lease when both will be amortized to zero. We've shown the difference as a reduction in Shareholders' equity (Retained earnings).

Leased assets and obligations are amortized independently and usually have unequal balances.

LEASING FROM THE PERSPECTIVE OF THE LESSOR

Being a lessor is an investment alternative to lending. It's usually done by financial institutions like banks, finance companies, and insurance companies rather than by individuals. Instead of lending money to a customer company to buy equipment, the finance company buys the equipment and leases it to the customer firm. CICA 3065 calls this a "direct financing" lease, and differentiates it from a "sales-type" lease used by a dealer to effect the sale of its products. Both are types of capital leases. In addition, the lessor can have operating leases.

Recall from our work on the time value of money in Chapter 8 that the mathematics of lending is governed by the formula for the present value of an annuity, which we presented as

Equation 8.21 (see page 281 for the equation and page 283 for its application to lending). We'll renumber that expression and repeat it here for convenience.

(9A.1)
$$PVA = PMT[PVFA_{k,n}]$$

When this expression is applied to loans, PVA is the amount borrowed, PMT is the loan payment (including interest and a return of principal), k is the loan's interest rate, and n is its term. $PVFA_{k,n}$ is, of course, a table factor. Keep in mind that the interest rate is the lender's return on its investment in the loan.

If any three of these variables are known, Equation 9A.1 can be solved for the fourth. Specifically, if a lender wants to earn a particular return on an invested amount over some period, the formula lets us calculate the payment it must ask of the borrower.

Basic leases and loans use identical mathematics.

Basic capital leases work the same way. Instead of giving a company money to buy equipment, a lessor buys the equipment, and delivers it along with a lease contract. Then it collects lease payments instead of loan payments. The lease payments required to provide the lessor with a given return are calculated in exactly the same way as the payments would be on a loan of equal term and amount. In the leasing arrangement, the interest rate is referred to either as the lessor's return or the *rate implicit in the lease*. Remember though, it is a lease, and therefore the payments will occur at the beginning of the period, so we will need to use the annuity due formula.

The lessor's return is the rate implicit in the lease.

(9A.2)
$$PVAd = PMT[PVFA_{k,n}][1 + k]$$

Leasing can be a safe way to invest if the leased assets have a continuing market value. The lessor holds legal title, so if the lessee defaults, it's relatively easy to repossess the assets and recover the lessor's investment by selling or leasing those assets again. Lessors also get better treatment than lenders if the lessee/borrower enters bankruptcy. (We'll discuss bankruptcy in Chapter 19.)

Example 9A.2

Suppose Desjardins Group General Insurance is looking for a safe, long-term investment that will earn 6%. Further assume that the Canadian Wheat Board wants to acquire a number of special-purpose railroad cars to transport grain. The Wheat Board wants to lease railroad cars valued at a total of $50 million and expects them to last 20 years, after which they will be essentially worthless. Desjardins considers the investment relatively safe because there's an active market for used railroad cars. It is therefore willing to buy the cars and lease them to the Wheat Board.

a. What annual lease payment should Desjardins ask of the Wheat Board to achieve its targeted 6% return on a 20-year lease?

b. Suppose the Wheat Board wants to take the lease, but is unwilling to pay more than $4 million per year. What will be Desjardins's return if it agrees to the Wheat Board terms?

■ **Solution:**

a. The required lease payment is calculated using Equation 9A.2, the present value of an annuity due formula.

$$PVAd = PMT[PVFA_{k,n}][1 + k]$$
$$\$50,000,000 = PMT[PVFA_{6,20}][1 + 0.06]$$
$$\$50,000,000 = PMT(11.4699)(1.06)$$
$$PMT = \$4,112,487$$

---

13 As in chapter 8, you'll notice that there is a slight rounding difference when we compare the Excel® and financial calculator solutions to the tables. Remember, the table acronym is convenient for expressing the equation and guiding us to the proper key strokes for calculator and spreadsheets.

b. Here, we're asked to solve an annuity problem for the interest rate rather than for the payment. The technique should be familiar from our work in Chapter 8. (Example 8.3 on page 226 is similar.)

$$PVAd = PMT[PVFA_{k,n}][1 + k]$$
$$\$50,000,000 = \$4,000,000 \, [PVFA_{k,20}][1 + k]$$
$$PVFA_{k,20}[1 + k] = \frac{\$50,000,000}{\$4,000,000}$$
$$1 + PVFA_{k,19} = 12.5000$$
$$PVFA_{k,19} = 11.500$$

Examination of Appendix A–4 shows the return at this payment level to be just under 6%. A financial calculator gives an exact answer of $k = 5.62\%$.

Residual Values

In the examples we've considered so far, the equipment was assumed to have no value at the end of the lease. That means the assets' economic lives were estimated to be just equal to the lease terms. In many cases, equipment is expected to have a positive *residual value* at the end of the lease. This makes pricing and return calculations slightly more complex.

A residual value means the lessor can expect an additional cash flow at the end of the lease. The cash can come from one of three sources: the lessee may buy the equipment, the lessor may sell it to someone else, or the equipment may be re-leased to the original or another lessee.

The last alternative is usually associated with operating leases that have relatively short terms. In such cases, lessors may need to lease equipment several times to recover their investments and earn a reasonable return. We'll concentrate on situations in which a relatively small residual is expected at the end of a long-term lease.

Example 9A.3

Reconsider Example 9A.2(a) assuming Desjardins estimates that the railroad cars will be worth $3 million at the end of the 20-year lease. Calculate the lease payment that will bring Desjardins a 6% return on its investment.

■ **Solution:** Even though Desjardins will have to spend $50 million to acquire the railroad cars, it doesn't have to recover quite that much from the lease payments. In a present value sense, Desjardins's investment is $50 million reduced by the present value of the expected residual.

First calculate the present value of the $3 million residual over 20 years at 6% using Equation 8.7 for the present value of an amount. (See page 265.)

$$PV = FV_n[PVF_{k,n}]$$
$$= \$3,000,000[PVF_{6,20}]$$
$$= \$3,000,000(0.3118)$$
$$= \$935,400$$

Now subtract that amount from the $50 million purchase price of the railroad cars.

$$\$50,000,000 - \$935,400 = \$49,064,600$$

Sidebar calculator solutions:

Calculator Solution[14]
BEGIN MODE

Key	Input
n	20
PV	50,000,000
PMT	4,000,000
FV	0

Answer
| I/Y | 5.617% |

Use Excel® Function Rate

Type 1

The leased asset's estimated *value* at the end of the lease is the residual value.

The *present value* of the *residual* is *subtracted* from the lessor's *investment* in payment and return *calculations*.

Calculator Solution

Key	Input
n	20
I/Y	6
PMT	0
FV	3,000,000

Answer
| PV | 935,414 |

Use Excel® Function PV

Calculator Solution
BEGIN MODE

Key	Input
n	20
I/Y	6
FV	0
PV	49,064,586

Answer
| PMT | 4,035,542 |

Use Excel® Function PMT

Type 1

Finally, calculate the required lease payment based on this smaller investment and notice that it is slightly reduced.

$$PVAd = PMT[PVFA_{k,n}][1 + k]$$
$$\$49,064,600 = PMT[PVFA_{6,20}][1 + 0.06]$$
$$\$49,064,600 = PMT(11.4699)(1.06)$$
$$PMT = \$4,035,550$$

It's important to understand that the residual is a very *soft* number. That means it's an inaccurate estimate, largely because it's so far in the future. The actual value of the equipment at the end of 20 years will depend on its condition *and* the market for used railroad cars at that time, both of which are difficult to predict. The residual could turn out to be anything from zero to two or three times the amount estimated.

Residuals are soft numbers.

Residuals in General

A higher residual means a *lower payment* so residuals are important in *negotiations*.

Residual values are included in most leases, and are often important in negotiations between lessors and lessees. A higher residual means lower payments so lessees argue that the equipment will hold its value over a long time. Lessors want higher payments so their investments will be returned quickly and argue the opposite.

Since the actual residual value of equipment at the end of a lease depends in large part on its condition, lessors often insist on a penalty if residual values turn out to be lower than planned. In theory, such a clause simply asks the lessee to pay for abusing the equipment during the lease. But it can be a trap for lessees, because a weak market for used equipment can depress the value of items coming off lease regardless of condition.

Automobile dealers are notorious for manipulating payments and residuals. Lower lease payments can often be negotiated if the lessee accepts a higher residual. That sounds good when the lease is signed. However, the residual is usually the price the customer will pay if he wants to keep the car when the lease is over. If he doesn't, there can be a penalty if the residual in the contract exceeds the used-car value of the vehicle at the end of the lease. So what may seem like a good deal in terms of car payments can lead to a big charge in the longer run.

LEASE VERSUS BUY—THE LESSEE'S PERSPECTIVE

Companies rarely have enough cash on hand to purchase major pieces of equipment or real estate. That means the decision to acquire an asset is usually accompanied by a decision about financing. There are three broad financing possibilities, equity,[15] debt, and leasing. For purposes of this discussion, we'll assume the company doesn't want to use common shares, so the choice is between debt (borrowing to buy) and leasing.

Both lenders and lessors are easy to find if the company needing equipment is a reasonably good credit risk. Firms can borrow through bonds or directly from banks, while lease financing is available from *leasing companies* (lessors), which may be banks or finance companies. Lessors often work through brokers, which match them with equipment users, handle negotiations, and take care of contractual paperwork.

A lease–buy analysis demonstrates whether it's *cheaper* to *lease* or to *borrow* to buy equipment.

It's always appropriate to conduct a *lease–buy analysis* to compare the costs of the two approaches when new assets are being acquired. The analysis involves laying out the cash flows associated with the two financing methods, and calculating the present value of each series. The approach with the lowest cost in a present value sense is the best choice.

15 Money from retained earnings or the sale of new shares.

The interest rate used in taking both present values is the rate the firm is currently paying on new debt adjusted for taxes. The debt rate is used because leasing and borrowing have similar risks, and it is easily ascertained.

The tax adjustment states the debt rate after taxes. The idea is that interest is a tax-deductible expense so every dollar spent on it saves taxes of ($1 $\times$ T), where T is the tax rate. In general an after-tax rate is just the pretax rate times $(1 - T)$. For example, if the interest rate is 10% and the tax rate is 40%, the after-tax debt rate is

$$10\%(1 - T) = 10\%(1 - 0.4) = 10\%(0.6) = 6\%$$

We'll discuss after-tax rates at length in Chapter 15.

Lease–buy analysis is straightforward, but care must be exercised so that amortization, taxes, and residual values are treated properly. The best way to understand the technique is through an example.

Example 9A.4

Halidane Transfer Inc. is an armoured car service that transfers cash between customer locations and various banks. The firm has 22 armoured vehicles, which are fully utilized serving existing customers. Management recently accepted a new business opportunity that requires two additional vehicles, each of which costs $150,000. Halidane expects to use the new cars for 10 years, but will amortize them over five years for tax purposes. Therefore, the allowable amortization in each year for the first five years of the vehicles' life is 20% of original cost.[16]

Halidane can acquire the cars with $300,000 borrowed from its bank at 10% repayable over five years.

Alternatively, it can lease both cars for five years from BNI Leasing Inc. for an annual payment of $70,000 with an option to purchase at fair market value at the end of the lease. BNI and Halidane agree that the cars will probably be worth about $30,000 each at that time.

The terms of the lease specify that Halidane will bear the cost of maintenance, property taxes, and insurance on the vehicles. The firm's marginal tax rate is 40%. Should Halidane lease or buy the new armoured cars?

■ **Solution:** To answer this question, we'll lay out the annual cash flows implied by the alternatives and calculate the present value of net outflows associated with each. The alternative with the lower present value of net outflows is then preferred.

Since all of the cash flows we'll calculate are *after tax*, it's appropriate to take present values with an after-tax interest rate. We're using Halidane's 10% cost of debt, so our discount rate for present value calculations is

A lease–buy analysis compares the present values of cash outflows for leasing versus buying equipment.

$$10\%(1 - T) = 10\%(1 - 0.4) = 6\%$$

Notice that Halidane pays for maintenance, taxes, and insurance in both options, so these costs need not be considered in the analysis. Also recall that brackets mean negative cash flows (i.e., outflows).

We'll start with borrowing to purchase the assets. The following worksheet develops the appropriate cash flows, which are discussed in the subsequent paragraph.

PURCHASE ($000)

	0	1	2	3	4	5
				Year		
(1) Purchase cars	$ (300)					
(2) Allowable amortization %		20%	20%	20%	20%	20%
(3) Tax amortization [(2) × $300]		$ 60	$ 60	$ 60	$ 60	$ 60
(4) Tax savings [(3) × 40%]		24	24	24	24	24
(5) Net cash flow [(1) + (4)]	$ (300)	$ 24	$ 24	$ 24	$ 24	$ 24

16 We're using a simplified amortization schedule to keep the example straightforward. In Chapter 13, we'll discuss and use the capital cost allowance system required for tax purposes.

Line (1) reflects the present (time 0) purchase of the cars with borrowed money.[17] The next three lines calculate the cash flow associated with amortization. Notice that amortization is not itself a cash expense, but has a cash impact because it is deductible and reduces taxes as shown in line (4). Line (5) reflects net cash flow, the sum of the purchase price and tax savings from amortization.

For years 1–5, Halidane will have an annual cash flow from tax savings on the amortization of the $300,000 purchase cost. The annual tax savings from amortization can be treated as an annuity.

The present value of the purchase approach is just the present value of line (5), which is an annuity. (See Chapter 8, page 281.)

$$PV = -\$300,000 + PMT[PVFA_{6,5}]$$
$$= -\$300,000 + \$24,000(4.2124)$$
$$= -\$300,000 + \$101,098$$
$$= -\$198,902$$

The *lease* alternative involves tax-deductible lease payments for five years that result in a constant after-tax cash outflow. However, at the end of the lease, Halidane won't own the vehicles. Since the plan is to use them for 10 years, it will have to exercise the purchase option at the end of year 5 for an estimated $60,000. For years 6–10, it will have another annual cash flow from tax savings on the amortization of the $60,000 purchase option.[18]

Both the annual after-tax lease payments and the annual tax savings from amortization can be treated as annuities.

LEASE ($000)

| | Year | | | | |
	0	1	2	3	4	5
(1) Lease payments	$(70)	$(70)	$(70)	$(70)	$(70)	
(2) Tax savings [(1) × 0.40]	28	28	28	28	28	
(3) After-tax lease payment [(1) – (2)]	$(42)	$(42)	$(42)	$(42)	$(42)	
(4) Purchase option						(60)
(5) Net cash flow [(3) + (4)]	$(42)	$(42)	$(42)	$(42)	$(42)	$(60)

FUTURE PURCHASE OPTION ($000)

| | Year | | | | |
	6	7	8	9	10
(1) Purchase option $60					
(2) Allowable amortization %	20%	20%	20%	20%	20%
(3) Tax amortization [(2) × $60]	$12.0	$12.0	$12.0	$12.0	$12.0
(4) Tax savings [(3) × 40%]	$ 4.8	$ 4.8	$ 4.8	$ 4.8	$ 4.8
(5) Net cash flow [(4)]	$ 4.8	$ 4.8	$ 4.8	$ 4.8	$ 4.8

The easiest way to calculate the present value of the leasing with buyout option is to treat the alternatives separately. The present value of the cash outflows associated with leasing is

$$PVAd = -42,000[PVFA_{6,5}][1 + k]$$
$$= -\$42,000(4.2124)(1.06)$$
$$= -\$187,536$$

Calculator Solution

Key	Input
n	5
I/Y	6
FV	0
PMT	24000

Answer

PV   101,096.73

Minus 300,000 =

198,903.27

Use Excel®
Function PV

Calculator Solution

BEGIN MODE

Key	Input
n	5
I/Y	6
FV	60,000
PMT	42,000

Answer

PV   232,370

Use Excel®
Function PV

Type 1

---

17 There's no reason to show the loan as an inflow and the payments as outflows because their present values will just cancel one another.

18 Some practitioners prefer to assume the lease payments occur at the beginning of the year while the tax savings occur at the end of the year. For this example, the lease payments would begin at year 0 (beginning of year 1) and continue to year 4 but the tax savings would occur at the end of years 1 through 4. This would change the present value of cash outflows associated with leasing to −$194,610 and the final present value of cash outflows associated with the leasing purchase to −$224,338.

And the present value of the purchase option is

$$PV = FV_5[PVF_{6,5}] = -\$60{,}000(0.7473) = -\$44{,}838$$

Summing the cash outflows and the cost of the purchase option, we get a total cost of $232,374 (=187,536 + 44,838) before taking into account the future benefits Halidane will receive from its eventual purchase of the cars.

Lastly, the value of the year 6–10 after-tax annuity *at the end of year 5* is (remember, the arrears annuity formula gives you the value one period before the first payment):

$$PVA = PMT[PVFA_{6,5}] = \$4{,}800(4.2124) = \$20{,}220$$

The present value of the year 6–10 after-tax annuity *at year 0* is

$$PV = FV_5[PVF_{6,5}] = \$20{,}220(0.7473) = \$15{,}110$$

Hence the present value of cash outflows associated with leasing and purchase is

$$PV = -\$232{,}374 + \$15{,}110 = -\$217{,}264[19]$$

Comparing the two alternatives, we see that the leasing plan in this example is about 10% more costly. Further, the lease has a small element of risk in that purchasing the cars at its end may turn out to cost more than $60,000.

Calculator Solution

Key	Input
n	5
I/Y	6
FV	0
PMT	4,800

Answer

PV	20,219.34

Then input this value as FV

PMT	0

Answer

PV	15,109

Use Excel® Function PV and complete both steps

The result shown in the preceding example, that lease financing is more expensive than borrowing, is the usual situation. It exists because lessors generally demand higher returns than lenders do. Given that, and the fact that the CICA rules require full disclosure of financial leases, it's fair to ask why leasing is as popular as it is. We'll look into that in the next two sections.

THE ADVANTAGES OF LEASING

Leasing often offers several advantages that can make it worth its possible extra cost. We'll discuss a few issues in this section and a major tax advantage in the next.

No Money Down

Lenders typically won't finance the entire cost of an asset. They require that the borrower put some of its own money into the deal. We're all familiar with this idea in the context of buying

---

19 This problem is well suited to a spreadsheet. Notice that to determine the present value of the lease and purchase option, we have used the NPV function. You will learn about NPV in Chapter 12. For now, you need to understand that the NPV function is the easiest means of determining the present value of an unequal set of future cash flows.

	A	B	C	D	E	F	G	H	I	J	K	L
1	Halidane lease with purchase											
2	Year	0	1	2	3	4	5	6	7	8	9	10
3	Lease payments	-70	-70	-70	-70	-70						
4	Tax savings	28	28	28	28	28						
5	After tax lease payment	-42	-42	-42	-42	-42						
6	Purchase option						-60					
7	Net cash flow including purchase	-42	-42	-42	-42	-42	-60					
8	Allowable amortization							20%	20%	20%	20%	20%
9	Tax amortization							12	12	12	12	12
10	Tax savings							4.8	4.8	4.8	4.8	4.8
11												
12	Total cash flow	-42	-42	-42	-42	-42	-60	4.8	4.8	4.8	4.8	4.8
13	Present value of cash flows from lease and purchase	($217.26)										
14												

Leasing is usually *more expensive* than borrowing to buy, because lessors demand higher returns than lenders do.

Leasing offers several *advantages* that may *justify extra cost.*

cars and houses, where we call the purchaser's contribution a *down payment.* Lessors don't usually require a down payment; they essentially offer 100% financing. This can be very attractive to firms that have good prospects, but are cash poor. Typically small businesses are in that position.

Restrictions

Lenders usually put restrictions on the activities of borrowers, such as restricting the dividends and maintaining certain ratios, to ensure they will be able to pay off their debt. Lessors' restrictions are usually much less stringent or are nonexistent.

Easier Credit with Manufacturer/Lessors

Equipment manufacturers sometimes lease their own products. In an effort to place their equipment, they will often lease to marginally creditworthy customers. This may be the only way some financially weak companies can acquire equipment.

Avoiding the Risk of Obsolescence

Certain equipment tends to become obsolete very rapidly. In this context, obsolescence means that newer equipment does a job so much better or so much more cheaply that a company using older equipment is at a competitive disadvantage. In certain high-tech businesses, that can happen in a year or two.

Short leases have the effect of transferring that risk to lessors, because lessees can walk away from the obsolete equipment when leases are over. This can be attractive to lessees even though they're paying for the privilege through a higher cost of financing.

Tax Deducting the Cost of Land

Land is not amortized for either tax or financial reporting purposes. Hence if a company owns real estate, the portion of the cost representing land can never be recognized as an expense to be subtracted from income and reduce taxes.

However, if real estate is leased, the entire lease payment can be deducted by a lessee regardless of the fact that some of it represents a recovery of the cost of land purchased by the lessor. Hence leasing effectively allows lessees to amortize land for tax purposes. On the other hand, as the lessee does not own the land, it loses any potential capital gain on the land from price appreciation.

Increasing Liquidity—The Sale and Leaseback

Firms sometimes find themselves short of cash while owning substantial assets that are not encumbered by debt.[20] In that situation, it isn't unusual to sell the asset to a financial institution to generate liquid cash, and then lease the asset back from the same institution over a long period of time. The technique is called a *sale and leaseback,* and is usually used to free up cash invested in real estate.

Tax Advantages for Marginally Profitable Companies

Under certain conditions, for tax reasons, it doesn't make financial sense to own assets when leasing is available. This usually occurs when companies expect to lose money or be marginally profitable for several years. The technique is called leveraged leasing and is described in the next section.

---

20 The asset is not serving as collateral for a loan.

LEVERAGED LEASES

A benefit of owning assets is the ability to deduct amortization from income in the calculation of taxes. This effectively reduces the cost of those assets in the long run. For example, suppose a piece of equipment costs $100 million and the owner's marginal tax rate is 40%. Then for each dollar of cost that flows into amortization, the firm saves $0.40 in taxes, and over the asset's life the owner pays $40 million less tax. In essence, the government subsidizes the cost of ownership. If assets are acquired with borrowed money, interest provides a similar benefit because it is also tax deductible.

> The *government* subsidizes the *cost of ownership* through *lower taxes* from *amortization deductions.*

But if a company isn't making a profit, it doesn't pay any tax, and amortization and interest deductions don't save any money. Situations like that are fairly common; the airline industry provides a good example. The combination of a unionized workforce, federal regulation, and price competition has kept many airlines at or below breakeven profitability for years.

But unprofitable companies still need to acquire new assets. Airlines, for example, must continually acquire new planes to replace old equipment that becomes obsolete. If they don't, they lose the ability to compete.

Leveraged leases (also called *tax leases*) can provide a solution to this problem. In a leveraged lease, a profitable lessor purchases equipment with a combination of its own and borrowed money, and enters into a capital lease with a lessee. The lessor generally contributes 20% to 40% of the asset's cost and borrows the rest. The term *leveraged* refers to the use of debt in a transaction. The higher the proportion of debt, the higher is the degree of leverage. A leveraged lease is illustrated in Figure 9A.1.

> In a **leveraged lease** the *lessor acquires* the equipment with a combination of its own and *borrowed* money.

The lessee treats the transaction as it would any capital lease, but there's a difference in the lessor's treatment on its own books and for tax purposes. Ordinarily, lessors account for capital leases as if they were loans. That means they're not allowed to amortize the assets, and don't get the tax benefits of ownership. But the rules change when assets are purchased with a substantial proportion of borrowed money. Then, lessors are permitted to amortize leased assets and gain the associated tax benefits. For tax purposes they can also deduct the interest on the borrowed money.

> *Leveraged leases* allow *unprofitable lessees* to enjoy some of the *tax benefits* of *ownership* indirectly.

Internalizing the tax benefits of ownership makes the overall transaction more profitable to the lessor, which shares that extra profit with the lessee through reduced lease payments. Thus an unprofitable lessee indirectly gains some of the benefits of ownership through the lower lease payments offered in a leveraged lease.[21]

FIGURE 9A.1
Leveraged Lease

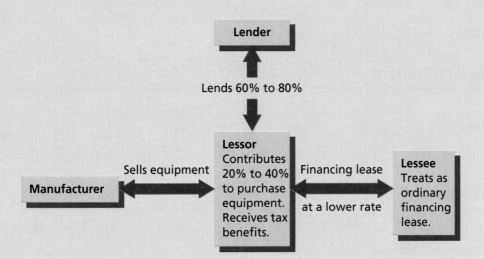

21 The lessee can deduct lease payments for tax purposes only if the lease is qualified by the Canada Revenue Agency. The CRA will disallow tax deductions for lease payments if the lease is really a conditional sales contract.

SUMMARY

8 Leasing can be an attractive alternative for companies looking to expand their business without the hassles of selling new common shares or arranging for debt financing. The advantages of low down payment, fewer restrictions, and the ability to upgrade frequently can justify the increased expense of leases when compared to borrowing to buy.

9 Operating leases are usually short term in nature while capital leases often appear to be long-term financing. If one or more of the criteria is met, the lease is a capital lease: the lease transfers legal ownership to the lessee at the end of the lease automatically or for a bargain price, the lease has a term that is at least 75% of the asset's economic life, or the present value of the lease payments is at least 90% of the asset's fair market value at the beginning of the lease. All other leases are operating leases for accounting purposes.

10 Lessees often find leasing an attractive source of financing. Depending on their circumstances and the type of asset they are financing, the lease may offer little or no down payment, have fewer restrictions on dividends and various ratios, and better flexibility in updating of equipment. The main disadvantage of leasing is that it can be substantially more expensive than borrowing to buy.

Lessors look at offering a lease as an investment opportunity. The lessor buys the asset and then leases it to the lessee. By retaining title to the asset the lessor can repossess the asset if the lessee is unable meet lease payments. As well, the lessor can typically charge a much higher rate on the lease than it could if it simply lent money to the lessee.

11 When comparing leasing versus borrowing to buy, we need to examine the advantages of each. When borrowing to buy, we consider the cost of the asset and the amortization expenses, after tax. In the case of leasing, we must recognize the value of the after-tax lease payments. For both, we discount the relevant cash flows at the after-tax cost of debt and then compare to see which is the least costly alternative.

KEY TERMS

Capital lease, p. 339
Lease, p. 338

Leveraged lease, p. 351
Operating lease, p. 339

Residual value, p. 345

KEY FORMULAS

(9A.1) $$PVA = PMT[PVFA_{k,n}]$$

(9A.2) $$PVAd = PMT[PVFA_{k,n}][1 + k]$$

$$\text{After-tax cost of debt} = k(1 - T)$$

QUESTIONS

1. There's a fundamental difference between rules one and three for identifying the nature of the lease (i.e., is it an operating lease), and rule two (see page 339). What is it?

2. Just what is placed on the balance sheet in a capital lease?

3. In leases with no residuals, lessors calculate the lease payments they must charge as if the lease were a loan. How does the presence of a residual change the calculation?

4. Why are residuals important in negotiations between lessees and lessors?

5. Amortization is a noncash charge. Why then is it important in lease–buy analysis? (Give a very short answer.)

6. Leasing is generally more expensive than borrowing to buy, and the CICA rules have required full disclosure of capital leases. Why then is leasing popular?

7. Leveraged leases offer tax advantages to unprofitable companies.
   a. Why are they called leveraged?
   b. Briefly, how do they work?

Business Analysis

1. You've just joined SeaCraft Inc., a manufacturer of fibreglass boats, as its CFO. When you took the job you knew that the company was not in the best of financial condition. Profits are adequate, but the firm is carrying substantial debt. To make matters worse, the company's largest fibreglass moulding machine is almost completely worn out and needs to be replaced. SeaCraft can't pay for a new machine out of operating profit, and the owner, Sam Alston, doesn't want to sell any new shares (which would dilute his interest).

You've looked into borrowing money to acquire the machine, and can get a deal with practically no down payment and a favourable interest rate through some banking contacts. But Sam is concerned about taking on more debt. He would like to sell the company and retire, but he's afraid that a heavier debt load will depress the price he might get. You agree that his concern is well founded.

Sam rushed into your office this morning with what he described as a great idea. He'd read an article that said just about anything could be leased, and knew that SeaCraft already leased a number of copying machines. On his way to see you, he stopped in at the accounting department and found that neither the copying equipment nor any associated liability was on SeaCraft's balance sheet.

Storming into your office, he declared, "Leasing the moulding machine is going to solve my debt problems! You're supposed to be the financial expert, why didn't you think of it? Why do I have to think of everything? Get on this quick! I want to see a lease deal on my desk by the end of the week." Before you could answer, he rushed out for a meeting with the marketing department.

Prepare a tactful memo to Sam explaining a little more about leasing and why it may not be as wonderful for SeaCraft as he thinks. Write the memo for a reader who is not a financial person (i.e., avoid using technical jargon like "CICA," "CRA," "capitalize," "equity," "annuity," and "present value"; talking about financing, balance sheets, assets, and debt is okay).

PROBLEMS

1. Caruthers Inc is a small manufacturing firm and has the following summarized balance sheet:

Caruthers Inc. Balance Sheet (000)			
Current assets	$ 20	Current liabilities	$ 15
Capital assets	130	Long-term debt	65
Total assets	$ 150	Shareholders' equity	70
		Total debt and Shareholders' equity	$ 150

The firm is interested in acquiring a fleet of 10 company cars for its sales staff. The cars have an economic life of seven years, but Caruthers plans to keep them for only three because it doesn't want its salespeople driving around in old vehicles. The cars cost $20,000 each, and Caruthers is considering borrowing to purchase them.
   a. Restate Caruthers' balance sheet after the loan is made.
   b. Calculate the firm's debt ratio now and immediately after the loan is made.
   c. Comment on the change in part (b). (Use words only.)
   d. Suggest an alternate strategy and explain why it will qualify for accounting treatment that will avoid the problem highlighted in part (b). (Use words only.)

2. Henderson Engineering Ltd. just leased a computer-assisted design system for five years with annual payments of $12,000 payable at the end of each year. The lease contains a provision that allows Henderson to purchase the machine at its fair market value as used equipment when the lease expires. Industry data indicate that systems like these normally last for about eight years. Henderson could have purchased the machine for $50,000 with money borrowed at 9%.
   Does Henderson have to capitalize the lease on its balance sheet? Why?

3. Togo Manufacturing Inc. is a machine shop that recently leased a drill press for a 20-year term at payments of $9,000 per year payable at the beginning of the year. No residual value was assumed in the lease, which is clearly a capital lease. Togo can borrow at 8%, and will amortize the press straight-line over 20 years.
   Shortly before the lease became effective, Togo's balance sheet was as follows:

Togo Manufacturing Inc. Balance Sheet (000)			
Current assets	$ 35	Current liabilities	$ 25
Capital assets	315	Long-term debt	95
Total assets	$ 350	Shareholders' equity	230
		Total debt and Shareholders' equity	$ 350

Answer the following questions working in whole dollars, but present balance sheet accounts rounded to the nearest $1,000.

a. Construct Togo's balance sheet showing the capitalized lease and the related lease obligation.

b. Calculate the firm's debt ratio before and after the lease, and comment on the difference.

c. (Optional) Reconstruct the balance sheet at the end of the first year assuming the other accounts remain the same.

4. Wings Inc. is a commuter airline that serves the Yellowknife area. Wings plans to lease a new plane through Cambridge Bay Capital Inc. (CBC). The lease term is 15 years, and no residual value is expected at its end.

a. What *monthly* lease payment must CBC charge to earn a 12% return on its investment if the plane Wings wants costs $1.5 million?

b. What would CBC's return be if it agreed to accept *annual* payments of $200,000?

5. Suppose Wings and CBC of the last problem agree to assume a $300,000 residual value for the plane at the end of the lease. How much will Wings have to pay *monthly* to give CBC its 12% return?

6. Paxton Sheet Metal Works Inc. is about to acquire a new stamping press that costs $400,000. It is considering purchasing the asset with money it can borrow at 10% repayable in annual, year-end installments over six years. It has also been offered an opportunity to lease the machine for payments of $86,500 per year payable at year-end, also over six years. Although the company anticipates using the press over 10 years the machine will be amortized on a straight-line basis over six years if purchased.

The lease contains a purchase option at its end at fair market value, which is estimated to be $100,000. Paxton will exercise this option and amortize this value for four years. The lease also stipulates that Paxton will be responsible for paying for maintenance, taxes, and insurance. Paxton's marginal tax rate is 30%. Conduct a lease–buy analysis to determine which option is preferable from a purely financial point of view.

Chapter 10

The Valuation and Characteristics of Shares

Learning Objectives

1 Explain how share returns affect value.

2 Calculate the value of a share using various models.

3 Describe and contrast characteristics of common and preferred shares.

4 Explain what is meant by the efficient market hypothesis and how it relates to share prices.

Many people think of the stock market as a mysterious and often intimidating place where share prices often seem to have a mind of their own. In this chapter, we'll be concerned with determining the value of equity securities, including common and preferred shares. We'll use many of the techniques employed by professional analysts. Although we will find that share prices do not have a mind of their own, we will find that valuing them is far less precise than valuing bonds because of the nature of equity cash flows.

COMMON SHARES

Corporations are owned by the holders of their common shares. Shareholders vote for directors, who in turn appoint managers to run the company. In theory this means that shareholders have a voice in running the company through the board of directors, the shareholder-elected governing body of the corporation.

However, most large companies are *widely held*, meaning that share ownership is spread among a large number of people with no individuals or groups controlling more than a few percent. Under those conditions, shareholders have little power to influence corporate decisions, and share ownership is simply an investment.

In other words, we don't tend to think of having any role as owners when we buy common shares. We're just interested in the future cash flows that come from owning shares. In that

Common shares are the security representing ownership of a corporation.

Most *equity* investors aren't interested in a role as *owners*.

sense, *equity* (share) investments are just like *debt* (bond) investments; the only thing we're interested in is money.

The Return on an Investment in Common Shares

In a share investment, receipts come in two forms: investors receive dividends, and they realize a gain or loss on the difference between the price they pay for shares and the price at which they eventually sell them. This difference is called a *capital gain* or *loss*.

It pays to be precise about this idea and write it as an equation. Suppose we buy a share, hold it for one year, and then sell it. Call the price we pay today P_0 and the price at the end of one year P_1. If we receive a dividend during the year, call that D_1. Then our receipts are the dividend, D_1, plus the difference in prices, $(P_1 - P_0)$, and our investment is the original price, P_0. The return, k, can be written as

> The *future cash flow* associated with share ownership consists of *dividends* and the eventual *selling price* of the shares.

(10.1) $$k = \frac{D_1 + (P_1 - P_0)}{P_0}$$

Notice that the return on a share investment can be a negative number if the share's price decreases while the investor holds it. In the equation, this means $P_1 < P_0$.

Next we'll solve Equation 10.1 for P_0, the share's price today. To do that, multiply through by P_0,

$$kP_0 = D_1 + (P_1 - P_0)$$

add it to each side, and factor it out on the left.

$$P_0 + kP_0 = D_1 + P_1$$
$$(1 + k)P_0 = D_1 + P_1$$

Finally, divide through by $(1 + k)$ to get

(10.2) $$P_0 = \frac{D_1 + P_1}{(1 + k)}$$

Notice that D_1 and P_1 are the future cash flows that come from buying the share today at price P_0. Further notice that division by $(1 + k)$ is equivalent to multiplying by the present value factor for interest rate k and one year.

Therefore, Equation 10.2 says that the return on our investment in shares is the interest rate that equates the present value of the investment's expected future cash flows to the amount invested today, the price P_0.

This result is fundamental. The return on any investment in shares and in bonds is the rate that makes the present value of future cash flows equal to the price paid for the investment today. This principle also holds for investments held for more than one year.

Dividend and Capital Gain Yields

The return on an investment in shares can be broken into two parts related to the two sources of income associated with share ownership. Rewrite Equation 10.1 as two fractions.

(10.3) $$k = \frac{D_1}{P_0} + \frac{(P_1 - P_0)}{P_0}$$

The first part, D_1/P_0, is known as the dividend yield, and the second part, $(P_1 - P_0)/P_0$, is called the **capital gain yield** (defined as the capital gain on a share divided by the price at which it was purchased).

> **Capital gain yield** is the capital gain on a share divided by the price at which it was purchased.

The Nature of Cash Flows from Common Share Ownership

As we've said, an investor who buys shares can expect two forms of future cash flow: a stream of dividends, and the proceeds of the eventual sale of the shares.

The *return* on an investment in shares comes from *dividends* and *capital gains*.

Figure 10.1 is a timeline reflecting these ideas for an investment made today and held for n years. In our work with share valuation, we'll use annual time periods[1] and indicate payments in a particular year by subscripting the symbol for the payment with the number of the year.

For example, D_1 and D_2 will mean the dividends paid in the first and second years, respectively, and P_n will mean the price of the share at the end of the nth year. We'll indicate the present with a zero subscript, so P_0 means the price today and D_0 means today's dividend or the most recent one paid.

We'll assume an investor buying today pays P_0, but does not receive D_0, which went to the last owner.

Comparison of Cash Flows from Shares and Bonds

Notice that the cash flow pattern for shares appears similar to the one associated with bonds. In both cases a series of regular payments is followed by a single larger payment that can be thought of as the return of the original investment. That is, dividends seem analogous to interest payments, while the final sale of shares appears to be like the return of a bond's principal.

In fact, however, the similarity is rather superficial because of the differing natures of the cash flows in the two cases. It's worthwhile to explore those differences rather carefully. We'll begin by comparing interest and dividends.

A bond's interest payments are guaranteed by the borrower, and are therefore fairly certain to be received. Companies have to be very close to failure before they default on bond interest. Dividends, on the other hand, carry no such guarantee. This is an important point. There's no agreement associated with common shares that makes any representation about the payment of dividends. Investors depend on them for value, but nothing is committed, promised, or guaranteed by the company. Indeed, a firm with a long history of paying dividends can stop at any time, especially if business turns bad.

Next, recall that the interest payments associated with a bond are constant in amount. That makes it easy to develop a formula to value bonds, because interest can be represented as an annuity. Dividends, on the other hand, are rarely constant. In fact, people generally expect dividends to increase over time as the company grows.

Things are equally imprecise with respect to the final payments received by shareholders versus bondholders. With a bond, the payment is the contractually promised loan principal equal to the bond's face value. A shareholder, on the other hand, has to sell his or her shares at the prevailing market price to realize a final payment. This price can be higher or lower than the price originally paid.

Let's emphasize that last point even further. There's no provision in a common share investment for the repurchase of shares or for any return of the investor's capital by the company. That means the money for the final payment comes from another investor rather than from the issuing company as it does with a bond, assuming that the bond is sold before maturity.[2]

FIGURE 10.1
Cash Flow Timeline for Share Valuation

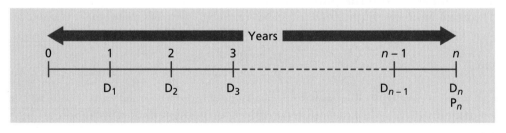

---

1 Dividends are generally paid quarterly, but for valuation purposes things are simplified by working in annual terms.
2 If a bond isn't held until maturity, it too must be sold to another investor, but the bondholder always has the option of holding until maturity and receiving the face value.

In summary, the cash flows associated with share ownership are dividends and the proceeds of the eventual sale of the shares. Both are distinctly imprecise and difficult to forecast.

The Basis of Value

In spite of the imprecision of forecast dividends and prices, the value of a share depends on the present value of those future cash flows. In terms of the portrayal in Figure 10.1, the share's value is the sum of the present value of the n dividend payments and the present value of the selling price in the nth period. Keep in mind that the successive dividends generally have different values, so we have to distinguish between them by carrying the subscripts in D_1, D_2, through D_n.

Valuing a share involves making some *assumptions* about what its future dividends and its eventual selling price will be. Once this has been done, we take the present value of the assumed (projected) cash flows at an appropriate interest rate to estimate the share's current price. Contrast this with bond valuation. There we had no need to make any assumptions about the future cash flows because they were spelled out by the bond contract.

We can write a generalized share valuation formula from these ideas by treating the dividends and the selling price as a series of independent amounts to be received at various times in the future.

Equation 8.7 on page 265 gave us an expression for the present value of an amount to be received n periods in the future at interest rate k. We'll repeat that expression here for convenience.

> The *basis for share value* is the *present value* of expected *cash inflows* even though dividends and share prices are difficult to forecast.

$$(8.7) \qquad PV = FV_n[PVF_{k,n}]$$

Now think of each dividend and the eventual selling price shown in Figure 10.1 as an FV_n where n is the number of periods into the future until that particular amount is received. The present value of the first dividend can be written as $D_1[PVF_{k,1}]$. The second is $D_2[PVF_{k,2}]$, and so on through the nth dividend and the price in the nth period.

P_0, the value of the share today, is the sum of all these amounts, and can be written as follows.

$$(10.4) \qquad P_0 = D_1[PVF_{k,1}] + D_2[PVF_{k,2}] + \ldots + D_n[PVF_{k,n}] + P_n[PVF_{k,n}]$$

Example 10.1

Jose Velis is interested in the shares of Teltex Corp. He feels it is going to have two very good years because of a government contract, but may not do well after that. Jose thinks the shares will pay a dividend of $2 next year and $3.50 the year after. By then he believes they will be selling for $75 a share, at which price he'll sell anything he buys now. People who have invested in the shares of companies like Teltex are currently earning returns of 12%. What is the most Jose should be willing to pay for a share of Teltex?

■ **Solution:** Jose shouldn't pay any more than the present value of the cash flows he expects. Those are $2 at the end of one year and $3.50 plus $75 at the end of two years. Writing Equation 10.4 for two years, we have

$$P_0 = D_1[PVF_{k,1}] + D_2[PVF_{k,2}] + P_2[PVF_{k,2}]$$
$$= \$2.00[PVF_{12,1}] + \$3.50[PVF_{12,2}] + \$75.00[PVF_{12,2}]$$
$$= \$2.00[0.8929] + \$3.50[0.7972] + \$75.00[0.7972]$$
$$= \$64.37$$

If the market price of Teltex is below about $64, Jose should buy; if not, he shouldn't invest.

The Intrinsic (Calculated) Value and Market Price

Example 10.1 illustrates a basic principle of securities analysis. Jose's research led him to forecast the future dividends and price given in the example. According to his analysis, the present value of those cash flows is fundamentally what the share is worth. We call that the share's intrinsic value (according to Jose).

However, if other investors don't agree with Jose's dividend and price estimates, their ideas of Teltex's intrinsic value will differ from his. The firm's market price is generally thought to be a consensus of the intrinsic values calculated by everyone watching the shares. If Jose's value is higher than the consensus, and if he's right, he'll be getting a bargain if he buys.

The process of developing intrinsic values and comparing them with market prices is known as fundamental analysis. We'll come back to the idea later in the chapter.

GROWTH MODELS OF COMMON SHARE VALUATION

Equation 10.4 is a convenient way to look at share valuation when we have a relatively short planning horizon and some reason to make specific assumptions about future prices and dividends. Generally, however, we can't forecast the future in that much detail. We're more likely to look at a company and simply forecast a *growth rate* of earnings and dividends into the future starting from wherever they are now.

For example, suppose a company has grown at an average rate of 5% per year over the last three or four years, and we expect its condition to improve slightly in the short run. The future being as uncertain as it is, it's difficult to make the detailed forecast of dividends and future prices needed to use Equation 10.4. However, most of us would be comfortable in saying that the company and its dividends are likely to grow at 6% into the indefinite future.

Because that's often the best we can do in predicting the future, we'll find it useful to develop expressions that value shares on the basis of only their present positions and assumptions about growth rates.

Developing Growth-Based Models

Notice that Equation 10.4 treats the share's dividends and eventual selling price as separate amounts in the present valuing process. Each is multiplied by the present value factor for the appropriate interest rate and time, which is represented in the equation as $\text{PVF}_{k,i}$ where i takes values from 1 to n.

In Chapter 8, we developed the formulation of any $\text{PVF}_{k,n}$, which we'll repeat here for convenience.

$$(8.5) \qquad \text{PVF}_{k,n} = \frac{1}{(1+k)^n}$$

Remember, multiplying by $\text{PVF}_{k,n}$ is equivalent to dividing by $(1+k)^n$.

In what follows, we'll find it convenient to represent present values of amounts by dividing by $(1+k)^n$ instead of multiplying by the factor of $\text{PVF}_{k,n}$. Rewriting Equation 10.4 to reflect this change in notation, we have

$$(10.5) \qquad P_0 = \frac{D_1}{(1+k)} + \frac{D_2}{(1+k)^2} + \dots + \frac{D_n}{(1+k)^n} + \frac{P_n}{(1+k)^n}$$

An Infinite Stream of Dividends

Notice again that our share valuation formula, now represented by Equation 10.5, involves a stream of dividends followed by a final selling price. This portrayal fits well with our concept of share ownership: buy, hold for awhile, and then sell. However, it's not convenient to work with in terms of valuation.

Think about P_n, the price at the end of the holding period. At that time, the nth period, it will represent the price just as P_0 represents the current price today. Therefore, its value then will involve a stream of dividends that starts in period $n+1$ and a selling price at some point further into the future, say period m. In other words, the person who buys the share in period n will hold it until period m and then sell it. That person's valuation model will look like this.

$$P_n = \frac{D_{n+1}}{(1+k)} + ... + \frac{D_m}{(1+k)^{m-n}} + \frac{P_m}{(1+k)^{m-n}}$$

Conceptually we can replace P_n in Equation 10.5 with this expression, and wind up with a revised expression containing a longer stream of dividends and a final price further away in time.

We can conceptually do the same thing again at period m. That is, we can think about the next sale, and replace P_m with another series of dividends followed by a price in the still more distant future. We can do that as many times as we like and push the eventual selling price as far into the future as we like. Indeed, we can conceptually push the final P infinitely far into the future!

However, the present value of any amount that is infinitely far away in time is clearly zero, so Equation 10.5 becomes the present value of an infinitely long stream of dividends and nothing else.

In short, we've replaced the final selling price with the rest of the dividends forever. This more useful valuation expression is written as follows by using summation notation.

(10.6)
$$P_0 = \sum_{n=1}^{\infty} \frac{D_i}{(1+k)^n}$$

A MARKET-BASED ARGUMENT If shifting from Equation 10.5 to Equation 10.6 seems strange, here's another way to convince yourself that it makes sense.

Imagine that we're pricing a primary market transaction, one in which the firm is initially offering its shares to the investing public. Think of the investment community as a whole setting the shares' price. In other words, ignore the fact that individual investors will subsequently trade the shares back and forth among themselves, and think of them as one unified body setting a price for the shares when they are issued. In fact, that's exactly what the market process does.

This price, set by the market acting collectively, must be based on the present value of future cash flows moving from the company to the investing community. But there's only one kind of payment that moves from the company to investors, and that's dividends. So the only basis for valuation by the community as a whole is the entire future stream of dividends; there's nothing else available. This leads directly to Equation 10.6.

> Conceptually, it's possible to *replace* the final selling *price* with an *infinite series of dividends.*

Working with Growth Rates

Growth rates work just like interest rates. If we're told that something's value is $100 today and will grow at 6% next year, the amount of the growth is

$$\$100 \times 0.06 = \$6$$

and the new size of the variable is

$$\$100 \times 1.06 = \$106$$

We usually represent growth rates with the letter g, which takes the decimal value of the percentage rate. For example, a 6% growth rate implies $g = 0.06$.

Growth rates are usually used to predict future values of variables whose values are known today. For example, if today's dividend is D_0 and we want to forecast year 1's dividend, D_1, assuming growth rate g, we can write

$$D_1 = D_0 + gD_0$$
$$= D_0(1+g)$$

Year 2's dividend is just year 1's multiplied by $(1 + g)$ again.

$$D_2 = D_1(1 + g)$$

Noticing the expression for D_1 just above, we can substitute and write

$$D_2 = D_0(1 + g)^2$$

D_3 is this expression multiplied by $(1 + g)$ again, and so on for as many subsequent D-values as we need. In general the nth dividend is

(10.7) $$D_n = D_0(1 + g)^n$$

When successive values of a growing dividend are needed, we just multiply by $(1 + g)$ repeatedly.

Example 10.2

Apex Corp. paid a dividend of \$3.50 this year. What are its next three dividends if it is expected to grow at 7%?

■ **Solution:** In this case, D_0 = \$3.50 and g = 0.07, so $(1 + g)$ = 1.07

$$D_1 = D_0(1 + g) = \$3.50(1.07) = \$3.75$$
$$D_2 = D_1(1 + g) = \$3.75(1.07) = \$4.01$$
$$D_3 = D_2(1 + g) = \$4.01(1.07) = \$4.29$$

The Constant Growth Model

Equation 10.6 says that the value of a share is the present value of an infinite stream of dividends, but makes no statement about what those dividends are. In other words, the $D_1, D_2, ...$, D_n can have any values, randomly chosen or a regular progression of numbers.

When we know D_0, the last dividend paid, and assume dividends will grow at some constant rate in the future, Equation 10.7 gives us a convenient way to forecast any particular dividend.

We can put these two ideas together by substituting Equation 10.7 into Equation 10.6 and rewriting as follows.

(10.8) $$P_0 = \sum_{n=1}^{\infty} \frac{D_0(1 + g)^n}{(1 + k)^n}$$

This expression is the basis of the constant growth model. It represents the sum of an infinite series of fractions as follows.

$$P_0 = \frac{D_0(1 + g)}{(1 + k)} + \frac{D_0(1 + g)^2}{(1 + k)^2} + \frac{D_0(1 + g)^3}{(1 + k)^3} + ... \infty$$

Notice that the numerators represent a series of dividends, each of which is larger than the last because of multiplication by the factor $(1 + g)$. The denominators reflect the present value factors for successive years into the future. These too get successively larger because of multiplication by $(1 + k)$.

Because D_0 appears in each term of the series, it can be factored out.

(10.9) $$P_0 = D_0\left[\frac{(1 + g)}{(1 + k)} + \frac{(1 + g)^2}{(1 + k)^2} + \frac{(1 + g)^3}{(1 + k)^3} + ... \infty\right]$$

Now, **if k is larger than g**, the fractions in the brackets get smaller as the exponents get larger. Both the numerators and denominators become larger numbers as the exponents grow, but if k is bigger than g, the denominators get large faster. Any fraction whose denominator is much larger than its numerator is a very small number. In this case the successive fractions approach zero as the exponents get big.

As a result, the entire expression in brackets is a finite number when k is larger than g. This leads to a finite value for P_0 even though we're summing an infinite stream of numbers to get it.

When k is larger than g, we say we're forecasting **normal growth**. When g is greater than k, we say we have *super normal growth*. Super normal growth can occur in business, but lasts for limited periods. We'll consider it in detail later. For now we'll concentrate on normal growth situations.

In share valuation, normal growth occurs when $k > g$.

Constant Normal Growth—The Gordon Model

Equations 10.8 and 10.9 look pretty intimidating, but can be reduced to something simple with a little mathematics that we needn't worry about here. We'll just accept the result.

The simplified form of Equation 10.8 is

$$(10.10) \qquad P_0 = \frac{D_0(1 + g)}{k - g} = \frac{D_1}{k - g}$$

This expression is known as the constant growth model, because it assumes that the share's dividends are going to grow at the constant rate, g, into the indefinite future. It is also called the **Gordon model** after Myron J. Gordon, a scholar who was behind its development and popularization.

*The **Gordon model** is a simple expression for forecasting the price of a share that's expected to grow at a constant, normal rate.*

Notice that the equation makes sense only if growth is normal, that is, if $k > g$. Otherwise the denominator is negative (or zero), leading to a negative (or undefined) price, which isn't meaningful.

Also notice that the numerator can be expressed either as $D_0(1 + g)$ or as D_1. Keep in mind that D_0 is the most recent dividend paid to the share's former owner. D_1 is the next dividend. It is the first one that will be received by someone who buys the share today. Think of D_1 as the *first dividend into the period of normal growth*.

The constant growth model is easy to use. Here's a straightforward example.

Example 10.3

Atlas Motors is expected to grow at a constant rate of 6% a year into the indefinite future. It recently paid a dividend of $2.25 a share. The rate of return on shares similar to Atlas is about 11%. What should a share of Atlas Motors sell for today?

■ **Solution:** Write Equation 10.10 and substitute D_0 = $2.25, k = 0.11, and g = 0.06.

$$P_0 = \frac{D_0(1 + g)}{k - g} = \frac{\$2.25(1.06)}{0.11 - 0.06} = \$47.70$$

This price includes the value of all dividends to be paid after time zero, but does not include D_0, which has already been paid to the share's current owner.

The Zero Growth Rate Case—A Constant Dividend

What about valuing a share that's expected to pay a constant, never-changing dividend? In that case we don't need a subscript on the variable representing the dividends because they're all the same. We'll call each dividend D.

A zero growth share is a perpetuity to the investor.

This case can be represented by Equation 10.10 if we let g equal zero; then $D_0 = D_1 = D$ and Equation 10.10 becomes

$$(10.11) \qquad P_0 = \frac{D}{k}$$

You should recognize Equation 10.11 as the expression for the present value of a perpetuity from our work in Chapter 8 (see page 289). A perpetuity is an unchanging payment made regularly for an indefinite period of time. That's exactly what we're describing in the constant dividend model.

Example 10.4

Lillooet Corp. is in a stagnant market, and analysts foresee a long period of zero growth for the firm. It's been paying a yearly dividend of $5 for some time, which is expected to continue indefinitely. The yield on the share of similar firms is 8%. What should Lillooet's shares sell for?

■ **Solution:** Write Equation 10.11 and substitute.

$$P_0 = \frac{D}{k} = \frac{\$5}{0.08} = \$62.50$$

People don't usually assume that common shares will pay the same dividend forever. It's more usual to assume some positive growth rate. However, it is not unusual for preferred shares to pay the same dividend year after year with no expectation of increase or decrease. We'll study them later in the chapter.

The Expected Return

The Gordon model can be recast to focus on the return on the investment implied by the constant growth assumption. This is easily done by solving Equation 10.10 for k. In this formulation, k represents an expected return, and is often written as k_e.

(**10.12**)
$$k_e = \frac{D_1}{P_0} + g$$

The expected return reflects investors' knowledge of a company. It is input to the Gordon model through the growth rate assumption.

The concept of expected return will be important in the next chapter. In this case, it says that if an investor's knowledge and predictions about a company's shares are rolled up into a forecast growth rate, the return implied by the forecast is given by Equation 10.12.

If we take $D_1 = D_0(1 + g)$ and assume that D_0 and P_0 are actual values of the latest dividend and the current price, the equation gives an estimate of the return to be had by investing in the shares at price P_0.

It's worthwhile to compare Equation 10.12 with Equation 10.3, which we'll repeat here for convenience.

(**10.3**)
$$k = \frac{D_1}{P_0} + \frac{(P_1 - P_0)}{P_0}$$

Recall that the two terms on the right side of Equation 10.3 are the dividend yield and the capital gains yield. Compare Equation 10.12 with Equation 10.3 and notice that they're identical in all but the second term on the right. This implies that those terms have the same meaning in both equations. In other words, the capital gains yield in the Gordon model is nothing but the growth rate. That makes intuitive sense because the whole company, including dividends and share prices, is assumed to be growing at rate g.

Two-Stage Growth

Situations sometimes arise in which a firm's future growth isn't expected to be constant. Specifically, we often know something about the near-term future that can be expected to have a temporary effect on the firm's prospects. For example, the release of a new product might create a period of rapidly expanding demand after which further growth slows to normal.

The usual two-stage forecast involves a rapid, super normal growth rate for one, two, or even three years and a normal rate thereafter. Recall that super normal means a rate in excess of k, the return on the share. Our task is to use the tools we've developed thus far to value a share that's expected to behave in this way.

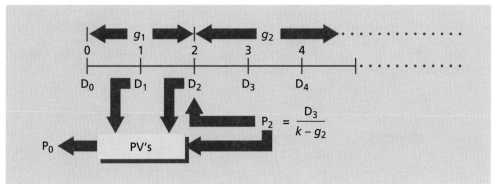

FIGURE 10.2
Two-Stage Growth
Model

First let's look at a timeline picture of such an investment opportunity. The top of Figure 10.2 shows a general case in which the firm grows at rate g_1, the super normal rate, for two years and then grows indefinitely at rate g_2, the slower normal rate.

We can value this share by using the constant growth model, but we have to apply it carefully. The model gives us a value for a share *at the beginning of an infinite period of constant, normal growth*.

In Figure 10.2 we have constant, normal growth, but it doesn't start at time zero. It starts at the end of the second year. Therefore, we have to apply the Gordon model at that point in time.

When we do that, the result is a price for the share at the end of the second year, or equivalently at the beginning of the third. We'll call that price P_2. It includes the value of all dividends to be paid subsequent to year 2, but not the dividend of year 2 itself, D_2. In other words, it takes into account D_3, D_4, D_5, and so on.

Using the Gordon model at the end of the second year requires a modification of the notation we used before. Look back at Equation 10.10. Notice that the numerator in that expression is D_1, which is *the first dividend into the period of normal growth*. In the model we're working with now, that's D_3, because the growth rate changes at the end of year 2.

In addition, the denominator of Equation 10.10 contains the normal growth rate, g. In this case we have two growth rates, but the normal one that continues indefinitely is g_2, so that's the one we must use. The correct way to formulate the constant growth model in this application is

$$P_2 = \frac{D_3}{k - g_2}$$

This expression is portrayed in Figure 10.2 along with its position along the timeline.

A person buying this share today gets three things in the future: D_1, D_2, and P_2. The two dividends are clearly cash flows forecast at the ends of years 1 and 2. P_2, on the other hand, is an actual cash flow only if the purchaser sells the share at the end of the second year. Nevertheless, we'll treat P_2 just as though it was a cash flow expected two years in the future.

The value of a security today is the present value of future cash that comes from owning it, so the value of the share represented in Figure 10.2 is the sum of the present values of D_1, D_2, and P_2. This is indicated schematically in the diagram.

The two-stage growth model allows us to value a share that's expected to grow at an unusual rate for a *limited time.*

Example 10.5

Zylon Corporation's shares are selling for $48 a share according to *The Globe and Mail*. We've heard a rumour that the firm will make an exciting new product announcement next week. By studying the industry, we've concluded that this new product will support an overall company growth rate of 20% for about two years. After that, we feel growth will slow rapidly and level off at about 6%. The firm currently pays an annual dividend of $2.00, which can be expected to grow with the company. The rate of return on shares like Zylon is approximately 10%. Is Zylon a good buy at $48?

■ **Solution:** To determine whether or not Zylon is a good buy, we'll estimate what it *should* be worth on the basis of the present value of future cash flows, and compare that result with the listed price. If our valuation is higher, we might conclude that the shares are a bargain and buy them.

Drawing a diagram similar to Figure 10.2 generally helps in problems like this. The following timeline shows the growth rates and dividends.

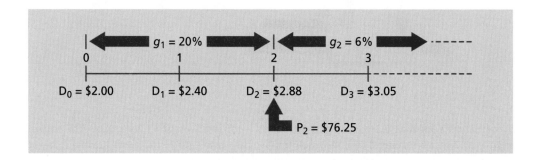

The dividend paid recently, D_0, is given as $2.00. The first future dividend is forecast by growing $2.00 at the first year's growth rate. That's accomplished by multiplying by 1 plus the growth rate in that year.

$$D_1 = D_0(1 + g_1) = \$2.00(1.20) = \$2.40$$

To get the second year's dividend, we multiply by $(1 + g_1)$ again.

$$D_2 = D_1(1 + g_1) = \$2.40(1.20) = \$2.88$$

We do *nearly* the same thing for D_3. The firm is now growing at rate g_2, which is 6% in this example.

$$D_3 = D_2(1 + g_2) = \$2.88(1.06) = \$3.05$$

Next we use the Gordon model at the point in time where the growth rate changes and constant growth begins. That's year 2 in this case, so

$$P_2 = \frac{D_3}{k - g_2} = \frac{\$3.05}{0.10 - 0.06} = \$76.25$$

This result is also indicated in the diagram.

All that remains in calculating a price is to take the present value of each of the elements to which a buyer at time zero is entitled and add them up; these are D_1, D_2, and P_2.

$$P_0 = D_1[PVF_{k,1}] + D_2[PVF_{k,2}] + P_2[PVF_{k,2}]$$
$$P_0 = \$2.40[PVF_{10,1}] + \$2.88[PVF_{10,2}] + \$76.25[PVF_{10,2}]$$
$$P_0 = \$2.40[0.9091] + \$2.88[0.8264] + \$76.25[0.8264]$$
$$P_0 = \$67.57$$

Now we compare $67.57 with the listed price of $48.00. Clearly our valuation is larger. If our assumptions are correct, the share should be worth almost $20 more than its current market price. If we're right, the price will rise substantially in a relatively short time, so we would be wise to buy.

Practical Limitations of Pricing Models

From the CFO

It's important to remember that the growth rate models we've been studying are abstractions of reality. They're simplified representations of the real world that at best can give us only approximations of what's likely to occur in the future. We have to be careful not to view them as being accurate to the penny even though our calculations result in figures like the $67.57 in the last example.

> *It's especially important to understand that our results can never be any more accu-*
> *rate than the inputs that go into the model. In this case those inputs are the projected*
> *growth rates and the interest rate.*

Growth rate estimates are guesses that can be off by quite a bit. For example, in the case we've just illustrated, the predicted 20% growth rate could actually turn out to be anything, positive or negative. Rates of 15% or 25% would make a big difference in the figure we finally get for P_0.

The exact interest rate isn't always known either. The rates of return that people require to invest in shares vary according to the risk they perceive in any particular company. Different investors have different perceptions, so our 10% rate might easily be 9% or 11%.

Another big source of inaccuracy comes from the denominator of the Gordon model. Notice that it's the difference between two of our inputs, the interest rate and a growth rate. If those numbers are estimated to be close together, their difference is small and the calculated price blows up because a small denominator makes the value of a fraction large.

Look at the calculation of P_2 in Example 10.5. The denominator of the fraction, $k - g_2$, is $(0.10 - 0.06 =) 0.04$. But suppose our estimates of k and g_2 were a little off, and k should have been 9% and g_2 more like 7%. Then the denominator would have been $(0.09 - 0.07 =) 0.02$ and P_2 would have been $154.08. [The numerator would also change to ($2.88 \times 1.07 =$) $3.08.] This would have made P_0 $134.31 rather than $67.57. That's a 99% difference in the estimated value of the share coming from input errors that are relatively much smaller (10% for k and 17% for g_2)!

The point is that when it comes to estimating share prices, finance is not exact science! Our numbers just aren't all that accurate. Keep that in mind when using the results the way we did in the last example. The estimated value of the share turned out to be $67.57, which looked very good in comparison with the $48 market price. But suppose the share had been selling for $62 instead of the example's $48. Could we have concluded that it was still a bargain, although not as big a bargain? In other words, could we expect to make $5.57 on the purchase of a share?

The answer to that question is probably no. The difference of about $5 out of $67 isn't large enough to overcome the margin for error inherent in the estimating process. At a market price of $48 we'd be pretty sure we had something, but at $62 we really can't say much at all. Basically, the result would be saying that the share is worth something in the neighbourhood of $65 or $70. Estimates any finer than that are meaningless.

Comparison with Bond Valuation

The comments about inaccuracy in the last section refer only to share valuation; bonds are a completely different story. The bond pricing model gives a precise valuation for the security, because the future cash flows are contractually guaranteed in amount and time. Unless a borrowing company defaults on its obligation, which is rare among higher-grade issues, we can predict the exact pattern of future interest and principal payments. Having that, we can determine the price exactly for any yield (YTM). Yields in turn are established quite accurately by market forces influenced by the stability of the issuing company and the term of the debt.

Share valuation models give *approximate* results because the inputs are approximations of reality. *Bond* valuation is *precise* because the inputs are exact.

Shares That Don't Pay Dividends

Some companies pay no dividends even when their profits are high. Further, many openly state their intention never to pay dividends. Nevertheless, the shares of such firms can have substantial value.

The growth models we've been working with base share values solely on the present value of a dividend stream. How can such a model be valid if there are shares with value that pay no dividends?

The answer to this puzzling question lies in understanding when and why firms pay no dividends to shareholders. Firms that don't pay dividends even when their earnings are good are usually in an early period of their development and growing rapidly. Growth requires cash,

Insights **REAL APPLICATIONS**

Royal Bank of Canada

Let's use what we have learned so far on a real example. All of the following information was taken from the Royal Bank of Canada's annual report for the year ending October 31, 2006. As at its year-end, the Royal Bank had basic EPS = $3.65, dividends of $1.44, and shares selling for $49.80. Using the information provided, we calculated that the company experienced an average ROE of 19.7% over the previous 10 years while the growth in dividends over the same period had been roughly 15.5%.

Based on these numbers, we can estimate the share price:

First calculate the dividend yield.

$$\text{Dividend yield} = \frac{Div_1}{P_0} = \frac{\$1.44(1.155)}{\$49.80} = 0.0334 \text{ or } 3.34\%$$

Investors in the Royal Bank could then expect to receive a return of 15.5% + 3.34% = 18.84%.

Putting this information into Equation 10.10, we get

$$P_0 = \frac{\$1.66}{(0.1884 - 0.155)} = \$49.70$$

Amazingly, we came up with almost the same price using this easily available information. In this example, we were able to come up with a fairly close estimation because the growth rate and profitability for the company had been relatively steady and stable for a number of years.

and managements feel that it's futile to pay out dividends only to turn around and borrow or issue more shares to raise money to support that growth. Shareholders agree because they hope to own a piece of a much larger company if growth continues.

However, most people understand that rapid growth doesn't go on forever. When growth in the industry and firm slows, even the most vocal non-dividend payers eventually begin paying. In other words, shares that don't pay dividends today are expected to pay large dividends at some time in the future. It's those distant dividends that impart value.

If a company truly never paid a dividend, there would be no way for the investing community as a whole to ever get a return on its investment (other than if the value of the share goes up and the investor can sell at a gain). And that doesn't make much sense.

For an example of a firm that "finally" paid a dividend, see "Microsoft to Pay $32bn Dividend" July 21, 2004 at http://news.bbc.co.uk/2/hi/business/3912159.stm.

There is an alternative, somewhat comical, explanation known as the *greater fool theory of investing*. It goes like this. People buy non-dividend-paying shares for price appreciation—that is, with the intention of selling to other investors at higher prices than those at which they bought. But only a fool would buy an investment with no payback, so a buyer is depending on finding a *greater fool* later to buy at a higher price. A dramatic example is provided by Nortel Networks, whose share price during the technology "bubble" climbed to over $120 per share while dividends were nonexistent and reported earnings per share never exceeded $1.00.

There's no doubt that investors sometimes behave as though they were operating under the greater fool theory, but in general we prefer the explanation involving the eventual payment of dividends.

Shares that don't pay dividends have value, because there's a general expectation that someday they will.

http

Current stock market information, data and a share investment calculator can be found at http://canwest.stock group.com/ markets.asp?ticker =sweb.

SOME INSTITUTIONAL CHARACTERISTICS OF COMMON SHARES

Common shares represent an investment in equity (ownership) that theoretically implies control of the company. That is, it's logical to assume that an ownership interest means a shareholder has some influence on the way the company is run.

As a practical matter, however, influence depends on how many shares are held by any one person or group. Because most management issues are decided by a majority vote, shareholders owning minority interests have little power when someone else has a clear majority or when no one owns a substantial percentage of the firm. To understand how all of this works, we have to look at how companies are run.

Corporate Organization and Control

A corporation is controlled by a board of directors whose members are elected by shareholders. The board appoints the firm's senior management, which in turn appoints middle and lower management and runs the company on a day-to-day basis. Major strategic decisions are considered by the board, and a few really big issues, like mergers, must be voted on by the shareholders.

Corporate boards generally comprise the company's top managers and a number of outside directors. Board members may be major shareholders, but they don't have to be.

Companies are said to be widely held when share ownership is distributed among a large number of people and no single party has a significantly large number of shares. When that happens, it is very difficult to make a change in the board, because it's hard to organize voting shareholders against the incumbent members. In such situations, members of top management on the board have effective control of the company with little accountability to shareholders.

The outside directors are supposed to act as a restraint on this autonomy of management, but generally don't do much along those lines.[3] Of course, when a substantial percentage of

> A **board of directors** is the governing body of a corporation, elected by common shareholders.

> Top *management* effectively *controls widely held companies*, because no shareholder group has enough power to remove the top managers.

Insights PRACTICAL FINANCE

Reconciling Valuation Theory and Practice

People who work with share investing day in and day out aren't likely to think of valuation in terms of present value models. Brokers and frequent investors are more likely to work with earnings per share and price/earnings ratios to predict short-term price movements. The EPS model is expressed by the following relation.

$$\text{(a)} \quad P_0 = EPS \times \frac{P}{E}$$

where P_0 is the share's price, EPS is earnings per share, and P/E is the price/earnings ratio.

According to this view, to the extent that companies have different P/E ratios, the market values their earnings differently. For example, if two firms each earn $1 per share, and their P/Es are 10 and 20, their shares will sell for $10 and $20 regardless of the fact that their earnings per share are the same. In other words the market puts a different value on a dollar of earnings depending on who makes it. The price/earnings ratio is influenced by the expected earnings and sales growth of the firm, the expected dividend, the debt–equity structure of the firm, the volatility in the price of the share, the quality of management, and a number of other factors.

This doesn't seem consistent with the valuation models we've been studying, which say that price is based on the present value of dollar earnings only.

Things get more confusing if you look at the relationship expressed in Equation (a) closely. Mathematically, it's just an identity because P/E is just price over EPS. Hence it reduces to

$$P_0 = EPS \times \frac{P_0}{EPS}$$

or

$$P_0 = P_0$$

which doesn't have much value for anything.

But in fact there's more to it than that. The stock market tends to fix short-run P/E ratios within ranges by industry. And within industries, better performers get higher P/Es than poor performers. In other words, certain favoured industries and certain favoured companies are rewarded with higher than normal P/Es. That is, in the short run, the P/E ratio is relatively stable, so price changes depend mainly on changes in recent earnings, EPS.

That still doesn't seem to reconcile well with the models that value shares according to the present value of future cash flows until you realize two things. First, recent earnings are predictors of future earnings, so a higher EPS today means more earnings and dividends in the future. Second, countless studies have shown that the primary determinant of which company gets what P/E is expected growth. The higher a company's expected growth, the higher its P/E.

That means Equation (a) works like a crude Gordon model in which higher growth rates and higher current earnings both imply a higher current share price. In other words the seat-of-the-pants approach used by rough–and–tumble practitioners is very consistent with sophisticated valuation theory. In Chapter 11, we will consider some of the factors that affect stock markets in general and we will examine the relationship between the volatility of the market and the volatility of individual share prices.

---

3 There have been a few notable exceptions in recent years in which CEOs have been removed by groups led by outside directors.

shares are under the control of a single group, that group has effective control of the company because it can elect board members. In widely held companies, 15% to 25% is generally enough for effective control if no one else has more than a few percent.

The Role of the Equity Investor

As we said early in the chapter, most of the investors who buy shares in sizable companies don't look for a role in running the company. They're simply interested in the cash flows that come from share ownership.

Preemptive Rights

Preemptive rights are a shareholder's right to maintain his or her proportionate ownership in a corporation.

Preemptive rights allow shareholders to maintain their proportionate ownership of corporations. When new shares are issued, common shareholders have the right to purchase a portion of the new issue equal to the percentage of the outstanding shares they already own. Existing shareholders must be offered this option before the new shares can be sold to anyone else.

Voting Rights and Issues

Each common share has one vote in the election of directors, which is usually cast by **proxy** (the right to act for another on a specific issue).

Most common shares come with voting rights. That means each share gets an equal vote in the election of directors and on major issues. Voting issues are usually limited to changes in the company's charter, which broadly defines what it does, and questions about mergers.

Shareholders vote on directors and other items at an *annual shareholders' meeting* that corporations are required by law to hold. Most shareholders don't attend, however, and vote by **proxy** if at all. Proxies give the authority to vote shares to a designated party. Generally, the current board members solicit shareholders by mail for their proxies. If the firm's performance has been reasonably good, the proxies are given and the board is re-elected.

A *proxy fight* occurs if parties with conflicting interests solicit proxies at the same time. This usually happens when a shareholder group is unhappy with management and tries to take over the board. We'll talk more about proxy fights in Chapter 19.

Majority and Cumulative Voting

Suppose a company's shares are held by two groups of shareholders with differing interests. Also assume that one group has a clear majority of the shares outstanding. Traditional majority voting gives the larger group control of the company to the virtual exclusion of the minority group. This is because each director is chosen in a separate election, so the majority group can win every seat.

Cumulative voting is a method of electing boards of directors. Shareholders can cast all of their votes for a single seat. It gives minority interests a chance at representation on the board.

Cumulative voting is a way to get some minority representation on the board. Under the cumulative method, each share gets one vote for every seat being elected. Minority shareholders can then cast all their votes for one seat or split them up among several candidates. This means the minority interest can concentrate its votes on one or two seats and be likely to win, thereby getting some representation on the board.

Shares with Different Voting Rights

It's possible to issue more than one class of share with different rights associated with each class. Along these lines, a practice that affects control involves issuing a class of share with limited voting rights or with no votes at all. If such an issue receives the same dividends as traditional voting shares, it may be attractive to the typical investor who has no interest in control anyway. However, there can be problems with such arrangements should the voting shareholders make decisions that the nonvoting shareholders do not agree with.

In Canada, nonvoting or restricted voting shares are quite common (Telus, Bombardier, and Canadian Tire Corp. are a few notable examples) and can make up a significant component of the equity position of a company. However, this has not been the case in the United States. Since the 1930s there has been a general resistance to different voting classes from the U.S. government, its stock exchanges, and American investors. Nevertheless, the idea has re-emerged recently in association with mergers and acquisitions.

In other companies, including Danier, senior management is given multiple voting shares, which in essence can give management an impregnable position.

Shareholders' Claims on Income and Assets

Shareholders have a residual claim on both income and assets. That means they are the last in line among all the claimants on the firm's resources.

With respect to income, shareholders own what's left after all operating costs and expenses are paid, after bondholders receive their interest and any principal due, and after preferred shareholders get their dividends. That doesn't sound like a very good deal, but it often is.

When business is bad, shareholders are in the worst position of all, because the company's money is more likely to run out when other claimants are paid before shareholders are paid. That's why shares are considered the riskiest investment.

When business is good, however, the residual after everyone else is paid can be enormous, and it all belongs to the shareholders. Essentially, the "upside" potential in share ownership is limitless.

The residual income belonging to shareholders is essentially earnings (NI). It is either paid out to them in dividends or retained and reinvested in the business. Both options are clearly beneficial to shareholders. Dividends are immediate money in their pockets, while retained earnings contribute to growth that makes the shares more valuable.

With respect to assets, the residual position means that if the corporation fails and is liquidated, shareholders don't get anything until everyone else is paid. That often means they don't get anything at all.

> A **residual claim** is a shareholder's claim to income and assets after all other claims are satisfied.

> Common shareholders are *last in line* to receive income or assets, and so bear *more risk* than other investors. But their *residual* interest is large when the firm does well.

Insights **REAL APPLICATIONS**

DANIER LEATHER

Share Capital at Danier Leather Inc.

(For the financial statements and other financial information about Danier Leather Inc., refer to Appendix 3A, page 92.)

At June 24, 2006, Danier reported the following information regarding its share capital.

(a) Authorized

1,224,329 Multiple Voting Shares
Unlimited Subordinate Voting Shares
Unlimited Class A and Class B Preference Shares

The *multiple voting shares* entitled the shareholder to 10 votes per share and the *subordinate voting shares* entitled the shareholder to one vote per share.

(b) Issued

Multiple Voting Shares
Balance June 24, 2006

Number	Consideration
1,224,329	Nominal

Senior management of the company owned or controlled all of the multiple voting shares.

Subordinate Voting Shares
Balance June 26, 2004

	Number	Consideration
	5,720,225	$ 24,166,000
Shares repurchased	(402,400)	(1,700,000)
Shares issued upon exercising of stock options	4,000	27,000
Balance June 25, 2005	5,321,825	$ 22,493,000
Shares issued upon exercising of stock options	7,100	49,000
Balance June 24, 2006	5,328,925	$ 22,542,000

(For more information on Danier's stock option plan, see Chapter 18, page 653.)

(c) Loss per share

Basic	($0.84)
Diluted	($0.84)

Weighted average number of shares outstanding (Multiple Voting and Subordinate Voting Shares)

Basic	6,547,090
Diluted	6,583,540

For more information on Danier's financial performance, see Appendix 3A, page 92.

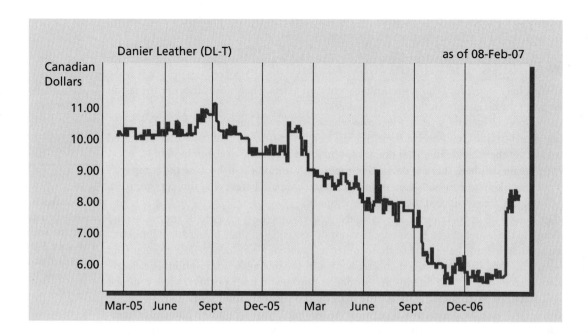

(d) Share prices

The chart below shows the changes in Danier's share price over a two-year period ending February 8, 2007.

From the earlier discussion and analysis of Danier (see Appendix 3A, page 92) you can see that the marketplace wasn't pleased with the company's performance from August to December 2006. The share price began to recover in January 2007 on news that the company's efforts to focus sales and reduce costs had resulted in improved profitability in the first half of its fiscal year.

Sources: Danier Leather Annual Report, 2006; management information circular, filed at http://www.sedar.com, September 11, 2006; www.Globeinvestor.com; Danier Leather Inc. Second quarter results, January 16, 2007 available at http://www.ccnmatthews.com/danier/pdf/Q207FS.pdf.

PREFERRED SHARES

> **Preferred shares** are securities that pay a constant dividend "forever." They are a hybrid between debt and common equity.

Preferred shares are a security that has some of the characteristics of common shares and some of those of bonds. They are often referred to as a hybrid of the two, that is, a cross between common shares and bonds. Preferred shares pay a constant dividend indefinitely. When a share is initially issued, two things are specified: the initial selling price (in the primary market), and the dividend. The ratio between the two reflects the current return on investments of similar risk, the market interest rate or dividend yield.

For example, if the dividend yield is 10% and a company wants to issue preferred shares at $100 each, it would offer a dividend of $10. This would be referred to as a $10 preferred issue rather than a 10% preferred issue.

You can think of the 10% rate as being similar to the coupon rate on a bond. The preferred's initial selling price (issue price) is conceptually similar to a bond's face value.

It's important to notice that typical preferred shares carry no provision for the return of capital to the investor. That is, the issuing company never has to pay back the initial selling price.

Valuation of Preferred Shares

> Preferred shares are valued as a perpetuity.

An investor who purchases a preferred share receives a constant dividend forever. Because all securities are worth the present value of their future cash flows, a preferred share is worth the present value of that infinitely long stream of dividend payments.

Corporate Governance in Large Companies: The Role of Boards of Directors

Do shareholders really control the companies they own through the election of boards of directors? The answer is definitely yes in smaller companies. Owners typically elect themselves or close associates to the board and control their businesses more or less directly. But in large, "widely held" corporations, that answer has traditionally been no. When share ownership is so dispersed that no one owns more than a small fraction of the enterprise, it has been virtually impossible for dissatisfied shareholders to influence management. They simply can't get enough votes together to influence the board, which can alter corporate policy or change top management.

This condition has led to a serious problem that we alluded to in Chapter 3 (see Financial Information and Corporate Governance, page 67). Top executives of some major corporations had been able to act essentially without accountability and boards of directors of these companies had failed to protect the interests of shareholders.

New regulations and the threat of shareholder lawsuits, which can attack directors personally, have served as a wake-up call to board members. Most have gotten the message that being a director isn't the gravy train it used to be. Changes are taking place as a result. Directors who routinely awarded huge pay contracts to managements are now balking instead of rubber-stamping requests. Conflicts of interest between board members and management are now disqualifying some candidates. And there's a trend toward serving on fewer boards so directors can more effectively focus their attention where they do serve.

Generally speaking, boards are reforming. Directors include fewer insiders, director training seminars are popular, and the role of independent board members is becoming stronger. All this means more security for investors, a change that's been needed for decades.

Sources: "The Best & Worst Boards. How the Corporate Scandals Are Sparking a Revolution in Governance," *BusinessWeek* (October 7, 2002) at http://www.businessweek.com/magazine/content/02_40/b3802001.htm; "Corporate Canada Opens Up," reportonbusiness.com, Janet McFarland and Elizabeth Church (October 23, 2006).

Earlier in this chapter, we discussed valuing a share with a constant dividend using a perpetuity formula, which we will repeat here for convenience.

$$(10.11) \qquad P_0 = \frac{D}{k}$$

We'll use this basic equation for preferred shares, but will change the variable names to more appropriately reflect the application. We'll call the preferred dividend D_p. The present value of the perpetuity (PV_p) must equal the security's price, which we'll call P_p. The preferred dividend yield will be k_p. Then the expression for the price of a preferred share is

$$(10.13) \qquad P_p = \frac{D_p}{k_p}$$

Notice that valuation of a preferred share is conceptually identical to that of a zero growth common share, discussed on page 363 of this chapter.

Like bonds, preferred shares are issued to yield approximately the current dividend yield. When dividend yields change, preferred shares have to offer competitive yields to new secondary market buyers. This is accomplished through price changes.

Prices of preferred shares, like those of bonds, move inversely with dividend yields. However, calculating new preferred prices is much easier than calculating bond prices. We simply insert the new dividend yield into Equation 10.13 and solve for P_p.

Example 10.6

Roman Industries's $6 preferred originally sold for $50. Dividend yields on similar issues are now 9%. What should Roman's preferred sell for today?

■ **Solution:** Just substitute the new market dividend yield into Equation 10.13 for today's price.

$$P_p = \frac{D_p}{k_p} = \frac{\$6.00}{0.09} = \$66.67$$

Notice that the original yield on the issue was ($6/$50 =) 12%. Because the dividend yield dropped from 12% to 9%, we know the price has to be above its original value of $50. This gives a reasonableness check on our answer.

Characteristics of Preferred Shares

As a security, preferred shares have some unique characteristics relative to traditional debt and equity. We'll summarize a few issues.

The Cumulative Feature

The **cumulative feature** of preferred shares is a provision to enhance their safety. Common dividends can't be paid unless the dividends on *cumulative preferred* are current.

Nearly all preferred shares come with a **cumulative feature** designed to enhance their safety for investors. The cumulative feature generally states that if preferred dividends are passed (not paid) in any year or series of years, no common dividends can be paid until the preferred dividends in arrears are caught up.

For example, if a firm gets into financial trouble and doesn't pay dividends on a $5 preferred for three years, no common dividends can be paid until each preferred shareholder has received the cumulative total of $15 per share.

Comparing Preferred Shares with Common Shares and Bonds

The features of *preferred shares* allow them to be characterized as a *cross between common shares and bonds.*

Some of the features of preferred shares are like those of bonds, while some are more like those of common shares. Some are in between. Let's consider a few specifics.

PAYMENTS TO INVESTORS The fact that preferred dividends are constant and don't increase even if the company grows makes them similar to the constant interest payments of a bond. They're unlike the dividends on common shares, which are usually expected to grow with the firm.[4]

MATURITY AND RETURN OF PRINCIPAL A bond has a maturity date on which the principal is returned. Preferred shares have no maturity, and never return principal. In that respect they are like common equity, which never returns principal either.

ASSURANCE OF PAYMENT Interest must be paid or bondholders can force a company into bankruptcy. Common share dividends can be passed indefinitely. Preferred dividends can be passed, but are subject to a cumulative feature. In this respect they are somewhere between bonds and common shares. Passing of preferred dividends is not as serious as missing an interest payment on debt; however, there are many good reasons that companies try not to miss any dividends. This includes maintaining a reputation with both equity investors and creditors.

PRIORITY IN BANKRUPTCY In the event of bankruptcy, bondholders have a claim on the company's assets to the extent of the unpaid principal of the bonds. Common shareholders are entitled only to what's left after all other claimants have been paid. Preferred shareholders are again in between. They have a claim in the amount of the original selling price of the shares, but it is

---

4 Having said that, there are a few examples of *participating preferred*. These preferred shareholders enjoy increased dividends in particular instances, typically if the firm has had a windfall profit. The preferred shareholders then are entitled to "share" in the windfall. See the terms of Power Corporation of Canada's Participating preferreds at http://www.powercorporation.com/index.php?lang=eng&comp=powercorp&page=powpre.

subordinate to the claims of all bondholders. That is, it comes before the interests of common shareholders but after those of bondholders.

VOTING RIGHTS Common shareholders have voting rights, while preferred shareholders do not. In that respect preferred shares are like bonds.

TAX DEDUCTIBILITY OF PAYMENTS TO INVESTORS Interest is tax-deductible to the paying company whereas dividends, common or preferred, are not. In this respect, preferred shares are very much equity.

Preferred shares are legally equity, but from what we've just said they're clearly more like debt in many ways. For that reason, they're generally treated separately in financial analysis.

The Order of Risk

The features we've been talking about create an ordering of risk associated with the three securities. Bonds are the safest, common equity is the most risky, and preferred is in the middle. The compensation for the risk in common shares is that the return—through dividend increases and price appreciation—can be very high if the company does exceptionally well. That possibility doesn't exist with either of the other two.

The name "preferred" shares comes from the idea that of the two types of equity, you'd rather have preferred shares if the firm does poorly or fails, because your investment has a prior claim on company assets over the investment of a common shareholder.

Taxes and Preferred Share Investors

The *Income Tax Act* treats preferred dividends just like common dividends in that they're not tax-deductible to the company paying them. That makes preferred shares a relatively expensive source of financing.

Like common dividends, preferred dividends received by another taxable Canadian corporation are exempt from taxation. (See Chapter 2, page 43.) This tax exemption, coupled with preferred shares' relatively low risk, makes them especially attractive to some institutional investors. Hence, those corporate investors may bid up preferred prices until they're not attractive to individual investors who don't have the tax exemption (although they do have the dividend tax credit).

SECURITIES ANALYSIS

Valuation is part of a broader process first introduced in Chapter 3; known as **securities analysis**, it is aimed at selecting investments. The term is applied to both shares and bonds, but most of the activity relates to selecting shares. There are two basic approaches to analysis; we'll briefly describe each.

Securities analysis is the art and science of selecting investments.

Insights REAL APPLICATIONS

Income Trusts

Another category of securities, *income trusts*, has become popular in the past few years. Generally, income trusts have been formed from stable companies with sizable, predictable cash flows. In essence, the company sells some of its stable cash flowing assets to the income trust. The income trust gets the money to buy these assets by issuing trust units (like shares) to interested investors. The cash flows received by the trust are then distributed primarily to investors (usually on a monthly or quarterly basis), rather than being reinvested within the company. No tax is paid by the trust (at least for now) and therefore it can distribute more to the unit holders. As a result the yields on income trusts tend to be higher than on comparable shares. For more information about income trusts, go to http://www.caif.ca/background or see A Special Information Supplement on Income Trusts, The Globe and Mail, March 28, 2005, pp. G1–G6. Additional information on the mechanics behind an income trust and basic valuation can be found at http://www.investmentreview.com/archives/2004/spring/income_trusts.pdf.

Fundamental Analysis

Fundamental analysis involves doing research to discover everything possible about a firm, its business, and its industry. Once analysts become expert in a company's field, they forecast its sales and expenses over the coming years. From that they project earnings and then a stream of dividends based on the firm's stated or implied dividend policy. The forecast dividend stream is used as input to the valuation models we've been discussing.

In short, fundamental analysis involves learning the fundamentals of a business and applying that knowledge to forecasting its future cash flows.

> **Fundamental analysis** looks at a company and its business to forecast value.

Technical Analysis

Technical analysts take a different approach. Technicians believe that market forces dictate prices and, more importantly, price movements. They also believe that movement patterns tend to repeat themselves over time. By studying past price changes, technicians believe they can recognize patterns that precede major up or down movements in the prices of individual shares.

Technicians prepare elaborate charts displaying the prices and volumes[5] of virtually all shares traded. These are examined in an effort to discern patterns that precede major moves. Because of this technique, technical analysts are also called *chartists*.[6]

Technicians feel that one doesn't have to know why a firm's share has value in terms of underlying cash flows. Rather, they believe it's enough to accept that it does have value, and rely on predictable market phenomena to make investment decisions.

> **Technical analysis** bases value on the pattern of past prices and volumes.

> Morningstar at http://morningstar.ca offers access to a wealth of share and fund data.

Fundamentalists versus Technicians

The two schools of thought are rather vocally opposed to one another, although many people use ideas from both camps. Scholars are almost universally fundamentalists. Nevertheless, the technical school of thought has a significant following.

A number of statistical studies have been done in attempts to prove or disprove the validity of technical analysis once and for all. To date no one has definitively proven anything to the satisfaction of the other side.

The Efficient Market Hypothesis (EMH)

The efficient market hypothesis (EMH) pertains to information flows within well-organized financial markets. It says that financial markets are efficient in that new information is disseminated with lightning speed.

The theory asserts that information moves so fast around the thousands of analysts, brokers, and investors who make up the stock market that prices adjust to new information virtually immediately. In other words, when some new knowledge about a share becomes available, it is analyzed and disseminated so quickly that the market price adjusts to reflect the information in a matter of hours or less.

For example, suppose a pharmaceutical company announced that it had discovered a cure for cancer. That would certainly raise the price of the firm's shares. The EMH says that the price rise will happen immediately, because analysts will be on the phone right away telling client investors the news, and they'll bid the price up as fast as they can.

The implication is that, at any time, all available information is already reflected in share prices (called *semistrong form efficient*), and studying historical patterns (called *weak form efficient*) of price movement can't consistently do an investor any good. Hence the EMH is diametrically opposed to the tenets of technical analysis.

> The **efficient market hypothesis** says information moves so rapidly in financial markets that price changes occur immediately, so it's impossible to consistently beat the market to bargains.

---

5 Volume refers to the number of shares traded in a period. A price change at a low volume of trading isn't generally as significant as the same change accompanied by a higher volume.
6 Go to http://finance.yahoo.com and enter the symbol CP (Canadian Pacific Railway Limited). Click on the technical analysis and look at the chart. Experiment with the chart by clicking on range, moving average, and overlays.

However, the EMH implies that we won't find many bargains by using fundamental analysis and the valuation models either. That's because an army of professionals is doing fundamental analysis all the time, and they will have already discovered and disseminated anything an individual can figure out. As well, we have no idea how many *insiders* use private company information for their own gain. Insiders know that it is illegal to use this information, yet some do. If these insiders use this information to buy or sell the company shares, that information becomes incorporated in the price (strong form efficient).

The validity of the EMH is subject to dispute. It will probably never be proven to be either right or wrong. At this point in your study, you should just be aware of its existence, and have a basic grasp of what it says.

SUMMARY

1 Investors purchasing shares expect to get a return on their investment. The return on shares typically comes from dividend and capital gains. Company earnings can fluctuate year to year and that affects the value of the company's shares.

2 The share valuation models we reviewed require investors to estimate the dividend stream that they might expect and a future selling price. These values are then discounted at some desired interest rate, very much like we did in Chapter 8, to estimate the share's current price. The models reviewed were suitable for valuing shares with no growth, constant growth, and two-stage growth in the dividend stream. Although useful, it should be remembered that these models provide only an estimate of value as future dividends, and selling prices vary with changes in the marketplace and investor preferences.

3 Common shares are the true equity capital of the company. Common shareholders elect the board of directors and have a residual claim on any income or assets of the company. Preferred shares are classified as equity capital, but these shares typically offer a dividend (paid only if and when a board of directors has declared them) and holders of preferred shares usually have no right to vote.

4 The efficient market hypothesis says that financial markets are efficient if new information is quickly disseminated. This means that at any time, all available information is reflected in share prices. This information is quickly reflected in share prices as professionals are constantly monitoring the marketplace, and when they discover any new information about a company or industry they act on it by buying or selling shares. That information is soon reflected in share price.

KEY TERMS

Board of directors, p. 369
Capital gain yield, p. 357
Common share, p. 356
Cumulative feature, p. 374
Cumulative voting, p. 370
Efficient market hypothesis (EMH), p. 376

Fundamental analysis, p. 376
Gordon model, p. 363
Intrinsic value, p. 360
Normal growth, p. 363
Preemptive rights, p. 370
Preferred share, p. 373
Proxy, p. 370

Residual claim, p. 371
Securities analysis, p. 375
Technical analysis, p. 376

KEY FORMULAS

(10.1)
$$k = \frac{D_1 + (P_1 - P_0)}{P_0}$$

(10.2)
$$P_0 = \frac{D_1 + P_1}{(1 + k)}$$

(10.3)
$$k = \frac{D_1}{P_0} + \frac{(P_1 - P_0)}{P_0}$$

(10.4)
$$P_0 = D_1[PVF_{k,1}] + D_2[PVF_{k,2}] + \ldots + D_n[PVF_{k,n}] + P_n[PVF_{k,n}]$$

(10.5)
$$P_0 = \frac{D_1}{(1+k)} + \frac{D_2}{(1+k)^2} + \ldots + \frac{D_n}{(1+k)^n} + \frac{P_n}{(1+k)^n}$$

(10.6)
$$P_0 = \sum_{n=1}^{\infty} \frac{D_i}{(1+k)^n}$$

(10.7)
$$D_n = D_0(1+g)^n$$

(10.10)
$$P_0 = \frac{D_0(1+g)}{k-g} = \frac{D_1}{k-g}$$

(10.11)
$$P_0 = \frac{D}{k}$$

(10.12)
$$k_e = \frac{D_1}{P_0} + g$$

(10.13)
$$P_p = \frac{D_p}{k_p}$$

QUESTIONS

1. Discuss the nature of shares as an investment. Do most shareholders play large roles in the management of the firms in which they invest? Why or why not?

2. Compare and contrast the nature of cash flows stemming from an investment in shares with those coming from bonds.

3. Rationalize the validity of a share valuation model that doesn't contain a selling price as a source of cash flow to the investor. Give two independent arguments.

4. Why are growth rate models practical and convenient ways to look at share valuation?

5. What is meant by normal growth? Contrast normal and super normal growth. How long can each last? Why?

6. Describe the approach to valuing a share that is expected to grow at more than one rate in the future. Can there be more than two rates? What two things have to be true of the last rate?

7. Discuss the accuracy of share valuation, and compare it with that of bond valuation.

8. Do shares that don't pay dividends have value? Why?

9. Preferred shares are said to be a hybrid of common shares and bonds. Explain fully. Describe the cash flows associated with preferred shares and their valuation.

10. Discuss the relative riskiness of investment in bonds, common shares, and preferred shares.

11. Compare fundamental analysis and technical analysis. Which makes more sense to you?

12. What does the efficient market hypothesis say? What is its implication for share analysis?

Business Analysis

1. Your cousin Charlie came into a large inheritance last year and invested the entire amount in the common shares of IBD Inc., a large computer company. Subsequently, he's been very interested in the company and watches it closely. Recently the newspaper carried a story about major strategic changes at IBD including massive layoffs and business realignments. Charlie was devastated. He doesn't understand how the firm could have made such changes without the knowledge or approval of its shareholders. Write a brief letter to Charlie explaining how things really work.

PROBLEMS

The solutions in Appendix B are based on using either a financial calculator or Excel®. Slight rounding differences will occur if using financial tables.

1. Paul Dargis has analyzed five shares and estimated the dividends they will pay next year as well as their prices at the end of the year. His projections are shown below.

Share	Current Price	Projected Dividend	Projected Price
A	$37.50	$1.45	$43.00
B	24.50	0.90	26.50
C	57.80	2.10	63.50
D	74.35	None	81.00
E	64.80	3.15	63.00

Compute the dividend yield, capital gain yield, and total one-year return implied by Paul's estimates for each share.

2. Blackstone Corporation's $7 preferred was issued five years ago. The risk-appropriate yield for the issue is currently 11%. What is this preferred selling for today?

3. Fox Woodworking Inc. issued preferred shares at a face value of $50 to yield 9% 10 years ago. The shares are currently selling at $60. What return are they earning for investors who buy them today?

4. The following preferred shares are returning 8.5% to their owners who purchased the shares when they were issued:

Share	Dividend (%)	Current Price
A	5	$ 14.71
B	7	41.18
C	11	129.41

Calculate the prices at which they were issued.

5. Mitech Corp. shares sold for $8.50 per share 20 years ago and are currently selling for $82.00. Based on past growth rate performance, what would you expect the shares' price to be in five years?

6. The Spinnaker Company has paid an annual dividend of $2 per share for some time. Recently, however, the board of directors voted to grow the dividend by 6% per year from now on. What is the most you would be willing to pay for a share of Spinnaker if you expect a 10% return on your share investments?

7. Pine Point Corporation recently paid a $3 dividend, and is expected to grow at 5% indefinitely. Investors generally require an expected return of at least 9% before they'll buy shares similar to Pine Point.
   a. What is Pine Point's intrinsic value?
   b. Is it a bargain if it's selling at $76 a share?

8. The Anderson Pipe Co. just paid an annual dividend of $3.75 and is expected to grow at 8% for the foreseeable future. Harley Bevins generally demands a return of 9% when he invests in companies similar to Anderson.
   a. What is the most Harley should be willing to pay for a share of Anderson?
   b. Is your answer reasonable? What's going on here? What should Harley do with this result?

9. Sudsy Inc. recently paid an annual dividend of $1.00 per share. Analysts expect that amount to be paid for three years after which dividends will grow at a constant 5% per year indefinitely. The shares are currently trading at $20, and investors require a 15% return on similar issues. Has the stock market properly priced Sudsy's shares?

10. Tyler Inc's most recent annual dividend was $3.55 a share. The firm has been growing at a consistent 4% rate for several years, but analysts generally believe better times are ahead and future growth will be in the neighbourhood of 5%. The shares are currently selling for $75. Shares similar to Tyler's earn returns ranging from 8% to 10%.
    a. Calculate values for a share of Tyler at yields of 8%, 9%, and 10%.
    b. Do you think Tyler is a good investment for the long run (that is, for someone planning to hold onto it for 10 or more years)?
    c. Do you think it's a good investment for the short term? That is, should you buy it with the expectation of selling in a relatively short period, say a year or less?
    d. Repeat the calculations in part (a) assuming that, instead of rising, Tyler's growth rate (1) remains at 4% or (2) declines to 3%.
    e. Comment on the range of prices that you've calculated in parts (a) and (d).

11. The shares of Sedly Inc. are expected to pay the following dividends.

Year	1	2	3	4
Dividend	$2.25	$3.50	$1.75	$2.00

At the end of the fourth year the share value is expected to be $37.50. What should Sedly sell for today if the return on shares of similar risk is 12%?

12. Fred Tibbits has made a detailed study of the denim clothing industry. He's particularly interested in a company called Denhart Fashions that makes stylish denim apparel for

children and teenagers. Fred has done a forecast of Denhart's earnings and looked at its dividend payment record. He's come to the conclusion that the firm will pay a dividend of $5.00 for the next two years followed by a year at $6.50. Fred's investment plan is to buy Denhart now, hold it for three years, and then sell. He thinks the price will be about $75 when he sells. What is the most Fred should be willing to pay for a share of Denhart if he can earn 10% on investments of similar risk?

13. Cavanaugh Construction specializes in designing and building custom homes. Business has been excellent, and Cavanaugh projects a 10% growth rate for the foreseeable future. The company just paid a $3.75 dividend. Comparable shares are returning 11%.
   a. What is the intrinsic value of Cavanaugh shares?
   b. Does this seem reasonable? Why or why not?
   c. If Cavanaugh's growth rate is only 8.5% and comparable shares are really returning 12%, what is Cavanaugh's intrinsic value?
   d. Do these relatively small changes in assumptions justify the change in the intrinsic value? Why or why not?

14. The Miller Milk Company has just come up with a new lactose-free dessert product for people who can't consume ordinary dairy products. Management expects the new product to fuel sales growth at 30% for about two years. After that competitors will copy the idea and produce similar products, and growth will return to about 3%, which is normal for the dairy industry in the area. Miller recently paid an annual dividend of $2.60, which will grow with the company. The return on shares similar to Miller's is typically around 10%. What is the most you would pay for a share of Miller?

15. Garrett Corp. has been going through a difficult financial period. Over the past three years, its share price has dropped from $50 to $18 per share. Throughout this downturn, Garrett has managed to pay a $1 dividend each year. Management feels that the worst is over but intends to maintain the $1 dividend for three more years, after which it plans to increase the dividend by 6% per year indefinitely. Comparable shares are returning 11%.
   a. If these projections are accurate, are Garrett shares a good buy at $18?
   b. How do you think the market feels about Garrett's management?

16. Koski and Hass Inc. (K&H) just paid a $2 dividend, which is expected to grow at 5% indefinitely. The return on comparable shares is 9%. What percent of the intrinsic value of K&H shares is attributable to dividends paid more than 20 years in the future?

Problems 17 through 19 refer to Softek Inc., a leader in the computer software field. Softek has two potentially big-selling products under development. Alpha, the first new product, seems very likely to catch on and is expected to drive the firm's growth rate to 25% for the next two years. However, software products have short lives, and growth can be expected to return to a more normal rate of 6% after that period if something new isn't launched immediately. Beta, the second product, is a logical follow-on, but management isn't as confident about its success as it is about Alpha's. Softek's most recent yearly dividend was $4.00, and firms in the industry typically return 14% on shareholder investments.

17. You are an investment analyst for a brokerage firm and have been asked to develop a recommendation about Softek for the firm's clients. You've studied the fundamentals of the industry and the firm, and are now ready to determine what the share should sell for based on the present value of future cash flows.

  a. Calculate a value for Softek's shares, assuming product Alpha is successful but Beta isn't. In other words, assume two years of growth at 25% followed by 6% growth lasting indefinitely.

  b. Calculate a price assuming Beta is also successful and holds Softek's growth rate at 25% for two additional years.

18. Calculate a price for Softek shares assuming Alpha is successful and Beta is successful but doesn't do quite as well as Alpha. Assume Softek grows at 25% for two years and then at 18% for two more. After that it continues to grow at 6%. (*Hint:* Don't be confused by the fact that there are now three growth periods. Just calculate successive dividends, multiplying by 1 plus the growth rate in effect until you get the first dividend into the period of normal growth. Then apply the Gordon model. A timeline is a must for this problem.)

19. How would you advise clients about Softek shares as an investment under the following conditions? Give reasons for your advice. (No calculations.)

  a. Softek is currently selling at a price very near that calculated in part (a) of Problem 17.

  b. It is selling near the price calculated in Problem 18.

  c. It is selling at a price slightly above that calculated in part (b) of Problem 17.

20. It's late in 2007 and Governor Motor Corporation has been going through some tough times lately. It's been losing a great deal of money, and its annual dividend has been cut to $1. The company's strategy is to restructure by getting smaller while working on labour and product line problems at the same time. Once that's done management feels the firm will return to profitability and begin a long period of growth at about 3% per year. Analysts generally feel the firm needs to shrink by a little less than 30%, but won't be able to downsize at a rate of more than 10% per year because of fixed costs and union contracts. GM's share price has been declining steadily for some time and is now selling in the neighbourhood of $20 per share, which is the lowest it's been for many years.

  You're an analyst for Barnstead and Heath, a small brokerage firm that employs a number of financial consultants who advise clients on investments. Some of the consultants feel that GM's management is on the right track and that its strategy will work as planned. Given that assumption, should they tell their clients that this is a good time to buy GM shares? How would you advise them? Investors require a 10% return.

Computer Problems

21. The Rollins Metal Company is engaged in a long-term planning process and is trying to choose among several strategic options that imply different future growth rates for the company. Management believes that the main benefit of higher growth is that it enhances the firm's current share price. However, high-growth strategies have a cost in that they generally involve considerable risk. Higher risk means that investors demand higher returns, which tends to depress current share price.

  Management is having a hard time evaluating this cost–benefit trade-off because growth and risk are conceptual abstractions. In other words, it's hard to visualize how growth and risk interact with each other as well as with other things to determine share prices. Management can, however, intuitively associate each strategy option with a growth rate and a required rate of return implied by risk.

You are a financial consultant who's been hired to help make some sense out of the situation. You feel your best approach is to develop a systematic relationship between return, growth, and share price that you can show to management visually.

Use the STCKVAL program to develop the following chart, assuming the strategic options result in different constant growth rates that start immediately. The firm's last dividend was $2.35 per share. STCKVAL is one of several Excel® templates available on the text's support website.

The Price of Rollins Shares as a Function of Growth Rate and the Return Required by Investors

Growth Rates (g)

		6%	8%	10%	12%
Required Returns (k)	7%				
	9%				
	11%				
	13%				

Can you make any general comments about the risk–return trade-off based on your chart?

22. Suppose that the strategic options available to the Rollins Company in the previous problem result in temporarily enhanced growth. Each option can be associated with a super normal growth rate that lasts for some period, after which growth returns to the firm's normal 5%. Further suppose that the duration of the super normal growth is a variable that can also be affected by strategic policy. Use the STCKVAL program for two-stage growth to develop the following chart assuming a required return of 10%.

The Price of Rollins Shares as a Function of Temporary Growth Rate and Duration at a Required Return Rate of 10%

Super Normal Growth Rates (g_1)

		12%	14%	16%	18%
Duration of g_1 in Years (n)	2				
	4				
	6				
	8				

Can you use your chart to make any general comments about the risk–return trade-off under this assumption about the nature of the strategic options?

Developing Software

23. Program your own two-stage growth model for two years of super normal growth (g_1) followed by normal growth (g_2) lasting indefinitely. Treat both growth rates, the last dividend (D_0), and the required rate of return (k) as inputs. Here's how to do it. (Refer to Figure 10.2 and Example 10.5 on pages 365 and 366. You'll be programming exactly that procedure.)

   a. Lay out four cells horizontally in your spreadsheet (to represent a timeline starting with time zero).

   b. Put D_0 in the first cell.

    c. Form the next two cells by multiplying the one before by $(1 + g_1)$.

    d. Form the fourth cell by multiplying the third by $(1 + g_2)$.

    e. Calculate P_2 in another cell using the Gordon model with the fourth cell in the numerator and $(k - g_2)$ in the denominator.

    f. Form P_0 as the sum of the present values of the middle two cells in the timeline and the present value of the cell carrying P_2.

24. Program a model for three years of super normal growth.

PART 4

Business Investment Decisions—Risk and Capital Budgeting

Chapter 11

Risk and Return

Learning Objectives

1 Discuss the general relationship between risk and return.

2 Calculate expected return for a single investment and a portfolio of investments.

3 Discuss and calculate variance and standard deviation of a share's return.

4 Evaluate the impact of diversification on the risk of a portfolio.

5 Define what is meant by systematic and unsystematic risk.

6 Define and discuss what is meant by beta and how it is used.

7 Calculate beta.

8 Discuss and use the SML for single shares and portfolios.

Throughout our life experiences, we have learned that risk and return are connected. That is, the higher the risk, the higher the reward should be. By the same token, the lower the rewards, the lower the risk should be. The problem is that we often forget this valuable lesson when we invest. This chapter explores the relationship between risk and return inherent in investing in securities, especially company shares. In what follows, we'll define risk and return precisely, investigate the nature of their relationship, and find that there are ways to limit exposure to investment risk.

The body of thought we'll be working with is known as *portfolio theory*. The ideas behind the theory were motivated by observations of the returns on various investments over many years. We'll begin by reviewing those observations.

WHY STUDY RISK AND RETURN?

As we've said before, there are fundamentally two ways to invest: debt and equity. Debt involves lending by buying bonds or putting money into savings accounts. Equity means buying company shares. In this chapter, when we refer to equity investments, we are referring to common shares.

People are constantly looking at the relative returns on these two investment vehicles. It has always been apparent that average returns on equity investments are normally much higher than those available on debt. Indeed, over the last half of the 20th century, equity returns averaged more than 10% while debt returns averaged between 6% and 7%. At the same time inflation averaged about 4.5% so debt investors didn't get ahead by much![1]

But average returns aren't the whole story. Although equity returns tend to be much higher than debt returns in the long run, they are subject to huge swings during shorter periods. In a given one or two-year period, for example, the annual return on common equity investments can be as high as 30% or as low as −30%. The high side of this range is great news, but the low side is a disaster to most investors.

The short-term variability of equity returns was a very important observation, because few people invest for 50 years. Almost everyone has a much shorter time horizon of 2, 10, or perhaps 20 years, but rarely 50. The variability means that if you invest in shares today with a goal of putting a child through university in five years, there's a good chance that you'll lose money instead of making it. That's a frightening possibility to most people.

As a result of these observations, people began to wonder if there wasn't some way to invest in equities (shares) that would take advantage of their high average rate of return but minimize their risk at the same time.

Thinking about that question resulted in the development of some techniques that enable investors to control and manage the risk to which they subject themselves while searching for high returns. These techniques involve investing in combinations of company shares called *portfolios*.

In the rest of this chapter we'll gain a better understanding of the concept of risk and see how it fits into the portfolio idea. Keep in mind throughout that the reason we do this is to capture the high average returns of equity investing while limiting the associated risk as much as possible.

The return on common equity (share) investments has historically been much higher than the return on debt investments.

Equity (common shares) has historically been much riskier than debt.

Portfolios are collections of financial assets held by investors.

The General Relationship between Risk and Return

People usually use the word "risk" when referring to the probability that something bad will happen. For example, we often talk about the risk of having an accident or of losing a job.

In financial dealings, risk tends to be thought of as the probability of losing some or all of the money we put into a deal. For example, we talked about the risk of default on a loan in Chapter 7, page 245, meaning the probability that the loan wouldn't be paid back and the lender would lose his or her investment. Similarly, an investment in shares results in a loss if the price drops before an investor sells. The probability of that happening is what most people think of as risk in equity investments.

In general, investment opportunities that offer higher returns also entail higher risks. Let's consider a hypothetical example to illustrate this central idea.

Suppose you could invest in shares that will do one of two things: they will either return 15% on your investment or become valueless, resulting in a total loss of your money. Imagine for the sake of illustration that there's no middle ground; you either make 15% or lose everything. Suppose the chance of total loss is 1% and the chance of a 15% return is 99%. The risk associated with investing in these shares can be thought of as a 1% chance of total loss.

Let's further assume that all company shares behave in this peculiar way and offer only two possible outcomes, some positive return or a total loss. However, the level of positive return and the probability of total loss can be different for each company's shares.

---

1 Fidelity Investments provides a good overview of investment returns from 1960 to 2006. Check its website at http://www.fidelity.ca/fidelity/media/downloads/brochures_ii/eng/inv4suc_focbigpict_0307.pdf.

It's important to visualize this *hypothetical* world. Every share has a positive level of return that's quite likely to occur. *Investors more or less expect to receive that return*, yet they realize that every share investment also carries some risk, the probability that they'll lose their entire investment instead.

Now, suppose you're not happy with the 15% return offered by the shares we started with, and look around for an issue that offers a higher rate. *As a general rule, you'd find that shares offering higher likely returns also come with higher probabilities of total loss.* For example, an issue offering a 20% return might entail a 3% chance of total loss, while something offering a 25% return might have a 10% chance of loss, and so on.

This relationship is the financial expression of a simple fact of business life. Higher-profit business opportunities are generally untried ventures that have a good chance of doing poorly or failing altogether. As a result, higher likely return goes hand in hand with higher risk.

Of course, in the real world there aren't just two possible outcomes associated with each investment opportunity. The actual return on an investment can be more or less than the most likely value by any amount. The illustration's total loss is in fact a worst-case situation. The real definition of risk therefore has to be more complex than the one in the illustration. Nevertheless, the general rule remains the same: Higher financial rewards (returns) come with higher risks.

Unfortunately, it isn't easy to understand how the real risk/return relationship works—that is, to predict just how much risk is associated with a given level of return. Understanding the real risk/return relationship involves two things. First we have to define risk in a measurable way, and then we have to relate that measurement to return according to some formula that can be written down.

It's important to realize that the true definition of risk isn't simple and easily measurable the way it was in the illustration. There we had only one bad outcome, total loss, so risk was just the probability of that outcome. In reality there are any number of outcomes that are less favourable than we'd like, and each has a probability of happening. Some outcomes are very bad, like losing everything, while others are just mildly unpleasant, like earning a return that's a little less than we expected. Somehow we have to define risk to include all of these possibilities.

Portfolio Theory—Modern Thinking about Risk and Return

Recent thinking in theoretical finance, known as **portfolio theory**, grapples with this issue. The theory defines investment risk in a way that can be measured, and then relates the measurable risk in any investment to the level of return that can be expected from that investment in a predictable way.

Portfolio theory has had a major impact on the practical activities of the real world. The theory has important implications for how the securities industry functions every day, and its terminology is in use by practitioners all the time. Because of the central role played by this piece of thinking, it's important to develop a working familiarity with its principles and terminology. We'll develop that knowledge in this chapter.

The Return on an Investment

We developed the idea of a return on an investment rather carefully in the last two chapters. Recall that investments could be made in securities that represent either debt or equity, and that the return was the discount (interest) rate that equated the present value of the future cash flows coming from an investment to its current price.

In effect, the rate of return ties all of an investment's future cash flows into a neat bundle, which can then be compared with the return on other investments.

Shares with higher likely returns generally also have higher risks of loss.

Investors can look at investment return and estimate risk, and potentially improve the performance of an investment portfolio with online risk management at http://www.riskgrades.com.

Portfolio theory is a body of thought aimed at forming investment portfolios that minimize risk for a given return.

Two Internet sources of up-to-date rates of return are CANNEX at http://www.cannex.com and Pacific Exchange Rate Service at http://fx.sauder.ubc.ca.

One-Year Investments

In what follows, we'll use the idea of returns on investments held for just one year to illustrate points, so it's a good idea to remember those definitions in formula form. We developed the expressions in Chapters 9 and 10, but will repeat them here for convenience.

A debt investment is a loan, and the return is just the loan's interest rate. This is simply the ratio of the interest paid to the loan principal.

$$(11.1) \qquad k = \frac{\text{Interest paid}}{\text{Loan amount}}$$

This formulation leads to the convenient idea that a return is what the investor receives divided by what he or she invests. An equity investment involves the receipt of dividends and a capital gain (loss). If an equity investment is held for one year, the return can be written as

$$(11.2) \qquad k = \frac{D_1 + (P_1 - P_0)}{P_0}$$

Here P_0 is the price today, while P_1 and D_1 are respectively the price and dividend at the end of the year. This is Equation 10.3, which we developed on page 357.

Returns, Expected and Required

Whenever people make an investment, we'll assume they have some expectation of what the rate of return will be. In the case of a bank account, that's simply the interest rate quoted by the bank. In the case of an investment in shares, the return we expect depends on the dividends we think the company is going to pay and what we think the future price of the share will be. This anticipated return is simply called the **expected return**. It's based on whatever information the investor has available about the nature of the security at the time he or she buys it. In other words, the expected return is based on Equation 11.2 with *projected* values inserted for P_1 and D_1.

The **expected return** on a share is the return investors feel is most likely to occur based on currently available information.

It's important to realize that *no rational person makes any investment without some expectation of return*. People understand that in share investments the actual return probably won't turn out to be exactly what they expected when they made the investment, because future prices and dividends are uncertain. Nevertheless, they have some expectation of what the return is most likely to be.

At the same time, investors have a notion about what return they must receive in order to make particular investments. We call this concept the **required return**.

The required return is related to the perceived risk of the investment. People have different ideas about the safety of investments in different shares. If there's a good chance that a company will get into trouble, causing a low return or a loss on an investment in its shares, people will require a higher expected return to make the investment.

The **required return** on a share is the minimum rate at which investors will purchase or hold a share based on their perceptions of its risk.

A person might say, "I won't put money into Telus Corp. unless the expected return is at least 9%." That percentage is the person's required return for an investment in Telus Corp. Each individual will have a different required return for every share offered. Exactly how people formulate required returns is a central subject of this chapter. The important point is that substantial investment will take place in a particular share only if the generally expected return exceeds most people's required return for that share. In other words, people won't buy an issue unless they think it will return at least as much as they require.

Risk—A Preliminary Definition

We talked about risk earlier and alluded to the fact that its definition in finance is somewhat complicated. The definition we'll eventually work with is a little different from the way we normally use the word. We'll need to develop the idea slowly, so we'll begin with a simple definition that we'll modify and add to as we progress.

A *preliminary* defini-
tion of investment
risk *is the probability
that return will be less
than expected.*

For now, risk for an investor is the chance (probability) that the return on an investment will turn out to be less than he or she expected when the investment was made. Notice that this definition includes more than just losing money. If someone makes an investment expecting a return of 10%, risk includes the probability that the return will turn out to be 9%, even though that's a positive return. Let's look at this definition of risk in the context of two different kinds of investment.

First consider investing in a bank account. What's the chance that a depositor will receive less interest than the bank promised when the account was opened? Today, that chance is very small, because most bank accounts are insured either by the Canada Deposit Insurance Corporation (for member banks, trust companies, and loan companies) or, for provincially regulated credit unions and caisses populaires, there is usually some sort of provincial insurance scheme in place.

Even if the bank goes out of business, depositors get their money (in most cases up to $100,000 per depositor), so we're virtually guaranteed the promised return. A bank account has virtually zero risk because there's little or no chance that the investor won't get the expected return.

Now consider an investment in shares. Looking at Equation 11.2, we can see that the return is determined by the future price of the shares and their future dividends. Because there are no guarantees about what those future amounts will be, the return on an investment in shares may turn out to be different from what was expected at the time the shares were purchased. It may be more than what was anticipated or it may be less. Risk is just the probability that it's anything less.

Feelings about Risk

Most people have negative feelings about bearing risk in their investment activities. For example, if investors are offered a choice between a bank account that pays 4% and an equity investment with an expected return of 4%, almost everyone would choose the bank account because it has less risk. People prefer lower risk if the expected return is the same. We call this characteristic **risk aversion**, meaning that most of us don't like bearing risk.

Risk aversion means
investors prefer lower
risk when *expected
returns are equal.*

At the same time, most people see a trade-off between risk and return. If offered a choice between the 4% bank account and shares whose expected return is 10%, some will still choose the bank account, but many will now choose the shares.

It's important to understand that risk aversion doesn't mean that risk is to be avoided at all costs. It is simply a negative that can be offset with more anticipated money—in other words, with a higher expected return.

We're now armed with sufficient background material to attempt an excursion into portfolio theory.

PORTFOLIO THEORY

Portfolio theory is a statistical model of the investment world. We'll develop the ideas using some statistical terms and concepts, but will avoid most of the advanced mathematics. We'll begin with a brief review of a few statistical concepts.

Review of the Concept of a Random Variable

A *random variable* is
the outcome of a
chance process and
has a probability
distribution.

In statistics, a random variable is the outcome of a chance process. Such variables can be either *discrete* or *continuous*. Discrete variables can take only specific values whereas continuous variables can take any value within a specified range.

Suppose you toss a coin four times, count the number of heads, and call the result X. Then X, the number of heads, is a random variable that can take any of five values: zero, one, two, three, or four. For any series of four tosses, there's a probability of getting each value of X [written $P(X)$] as follows.[2]

X	$P(X)$
0	0.0625
1	0.2500
2	0.3750
3	0.2500
4	0.0625
	1.0000

Such a representation of all the possible outcomes along with the probability of each is called the *probability distribution for the random variable X*. Notice that the probabilities of all the possible outcomes have to sum to 1.0. The probability distribution can be shown in tabular form like this or graphically as in Figure 11.1.

The number of heads in a series of coin tosses is a *discrete* random variable because it can take on only a limited number of discrete values, each of which has a distinct probability. In our example, the only outcomes possible are 0, 1, 2, 3, and 4. There can't be more than four heads or fewer than zero, nor can there be a fractional number of heads.

The Mean or Expected Value

The value that the random variable is most likely to take is an important statistical concept. In symmetrical probability distributions with only one peak like the one in Figure 11.1, it's at the centre of the distribution under its highest point. We call this most likely outcome the mean or the expected value of the distribution, and write it by placing a bar over the variable. In the coin-toss illustration, the mean is written as

$$\overline{X} = 2$$

The *mean* or *expected value* of a distribution is the most likely outcome for the random variable.

Thinking of the mean as the value of the random variable at the highest point of the distribution makes intuitive sense, but the statistical definition is more precise. The mean is actually

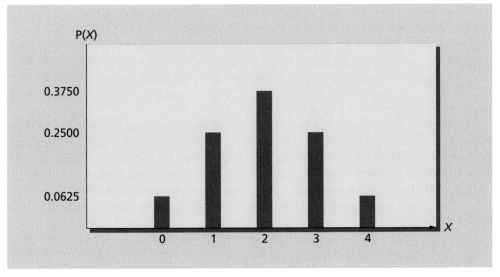

FIGURE 11.1
Discrete
Probability
Distribution

---

2 The probabilities can be calculated by enumerating all of the 16 possible heads–tails sequences in four coin tosses and counting the number of heads in each. Each sequence has an equal one-sixteenth probability (0.0625) of happening. The probability of any number of heads is one-sixteenth times the number of sequences containing that number of heads.

the weighted average of all possible outcomes where each outcome is weighted by its probability. This is written as

$$\overline{X} = \sum_{i=1}^{n} X_i P(X_i)$$

where X_i is the value of each outcome and $P(X_i)$ is its probability. The summation sign means that we add this figure for each of the n possible outcomes.

Calculating the mean for discrete distributions is relatively easy. For the coin-toss illustration, we just list each possible outcome along with its probability, multiply, and sum.

X	P(X)	X × P(X)
0	0.0625	0
1	0.2500	0.25
2	0.3750	0.75
3	0.2500	0.75
4	0.0625	0.25
	1.0000	$\overline{X}$ = 2.00

The mean is simply the mathematical expression of the everyday idea of an average. That is, if we repeat the series of coin tosses a number of times, the average outcome will be 2. Notice that the process of multiplying something related to an outcome (in this case, the outcome itself) by the probability of the outcome and summing gives an average value.

The Variance and Standard Deviation

A second important characteristic of a random variable is its variability. The idea gets at how far a typical observation of the variable is likely to deviate from the mean. Here's an example.

Suppose we define a random variable by estimating the heights of randomly selected buildings in a city. Allow four metres per storey. The results might range from four metres for one-storey structures to more than 300 metres for skyscrapers. Suppose the average height turned out to be 30 storeys or 120 metres. It's easy to see that any building could have a height that's very different from that average. Some office buildings would be hundreds of metres higher while all private homes would be hundreds shorter.

Now, suppose we did the same thing for telephone poles, measuring to the nearest metre, and got an average height of 10 metres. Unlike buildings, we'd find that telephone poles don't vary much around 10 metres. Some might be 10.3 metres and some 9.7 metres, but not very many of them would be far out of that range.

The point is that there's a great deal of difference in *variability around the mean* in different distributions. Telephone pole heights are closely clustered around their average, while building heights are widely dispersed around theirs.

In statistics, this notion of how far a typical observation is likely to be from the mean is described by the standard deviation of the distribution, usually written as the Greek letter sigma σ. You can think of the standard deviation as the average (standard) distance (deviation) between an outcome and the mean. For example, in our building illustration, the "average" (typical) building might be 20 storeys different in height than the mean height of all buildings. As we'll explain shortly, that interpretation isn't quite right because of the way standard deviations are calculated, but it's a good way to visualize the concept.

The *standard deviation* gives an indication of how far from the mean a typical observation is likely to fall.

The standard deviation idea intuitively begins as an average distance from the mean. One would think that could be calculated in the same way as the mean itself. That is, by taking the distance of each possible outcome from the mean, multiplying it by the probability of the outcome, and summing over all outcomes. Mathematically that would look like this:

$$\sum_{i=1}^{n} (X_i - \overline{X}) P(X_i)$$

The problem with this formulation is that the deviations [the $(X_i - \overline{X})$ values] are of different signs depending on the side of the mean on which each outcome (X_i) is located. Hence they cancel each other when summed. Statisticians avoid the problem by squaring the deviations before multiplying by the probabilities and summing. This leads to a statistic called the variance, which is written as

$$\text{Var } X = \sigma_x^2 = \sum_{i=1}^{n}\left[(X_i - \overline{X})^2\right]P(X_i)$$

In words, the variance is the average *squared* deviation from the mean. The *standard deviation* is the square root of the variance.

Intuitively, taking the square root of the variance reverses the effect of the earlier squaring to get rid of the sign differences. Unfortunately, it doesn't quite work. The square root of the sum of squares isn't equal to the sum of the original amounts. Hence the standard deviation isn't an average distance from the mean, but it's *conceptually* close. This is why we use the term *standard* deviation instead of average deviation. In any event, standard deviation and variance are the traditional measures of variability in probability distributions and are used extensively in financial theory.

For a discrete distribution like our coin toss, we calculate the variance and then the standard deviation by (1) measuring each possible outcome's distance from the mean, (2) squaring it, (3) multiplying by the probability of the outcome, (4) summing the result over all possible outcomes for the variance, and then (5) taking the square root for the standard deviation. Of course, the mean has to be calculated first. The computations are laid out in the following table.[3]

X_i	$(X_i - \overline{X})$	$(X_i - \overline{X})^2$	$P(X_i)$	$(X_i - \overline{X})^2 \times P(X_i)$
0	-2	4	0.0625	0.25
1	-1	1	0.2500	0.25
2	0	0	0.3750	0.00
3	1	1	0.2500	0.25
4	2	4	0.0625	0.25

$$\text{Var } X = \sigma_x^2 = 1.00$$
$$\text{Std Dev} = \sqrt{\text{Var } X} = \sigma_x = 1.00$$

This example is unusual in that the variance is exactly 1, so the standard deviation turns out to be the same number.

Keep in mind that the terms "variance" and "standard deviation" are both used to characterize variability around the mean.

The Coefficient of Variation

The *coefficient of variation*, CV, is a *relative* measure of variation. It is the ratio of the standard deviation of a distribution to its mean.

$$\text{CV} = \frac{\sigma_x}{\overline{X}}$$

It is essentially *variability* as a fraction of the average value of the variable. In our coin-toss example, the mean outcome is two heads in a series of four tosses. The standard deviation is one head, meaning a typical series will vary by 1 from the mean of 2. The coefficient of variation is then (1/2 =) 0.5, meaning the typical variation is one-half the size of the mean.

---

3 Most financial calculators and Excel® have variance and standard deviation functions; however, these functions cannot be used if the probability of each outcome is different. In such cases, the table approach must be used (unless you know how to build a macro in Excel®).

Continuous Random Variables

Other random variables are continuous, meaning they can take any numerical value within some range. For example, if we choose people at random and measure their height, that measurement could be considered a random variable called H. A graphic representation of the probability distribution of H is shown in Figure 11.2. In this graph, probability is represented by the area under the curve and above the horizontal axis. That entire area is taken to be 1.0.

When the random variable is continuous, we talk about the probability of an actual outcome being *within a range* of values rather than turning out to be an exact amount. For example, it isn't meaningful to state the probability of finding a person whose height is *exactly 160 cm*, because the chance of doing that is virtually zero. However, it is meaningful to state a probability of finding a person whose height is between 155 cm and 165 cm. In the distribution, that probability is represented by the area under the curve directly above and between those values on the horizontal axis.

Calculating the mean and variance of a continuous distribution is mathematically more complex than in the discrete case, but the idea is the same. The mean is the average of all possible outcomes, each weighted by its probability. When the distribution is symmetrical and has only one peak, the mean is found under that peak.

The Return on an Equity Investment as a Random Variable

In financial theory, the *return on an equity investment* is considered a random variable.

In portfolio theory, the return on an investment in shares is considered a random variable. This makes sense because return is influenced by a significant number of uncertainties. Consider Equation 11.2. In that expression, the value of the return depends on the future market price of the shares, P_1, and a future dividend, D_1. Both of these amounts are influenced by the multitude of events that make up the business environment in which the company that issued the shares operates. The price is further affected by all the forces that influence financial markets. In other words, there's an element of uncertainty or randomness in both the future price and the future dividend. It follows that there's an uncertainty or randomness to the value of k, and we can consider it a random variable.

Return is a continuous random variable whose values are generally expressed as percentages. Equation 11.2 calculates the decimal form of those percentages (e.g., 0.10 for 10%). With investing, the lowest return possible is -100%, a total loss of invested money, but there's technically no limit to the amount of positive return that's possible.

FIGURE 11.2
Probability Distribution for a Continuous Random Variable

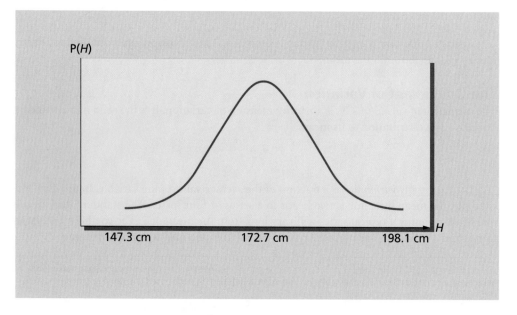

Like any random variable, the return on an equity investment has an associated probability distribution. Figure 11.3 is a graphic depiction of a probability distribution for the return on shares we'll call X. The return on X is k_X. The values the return can take appear along the horizontal axis, and the probabilities of those values appear on the vertical axis. The shape of the distribution depicts the likelihood of all possible actual values of k_X according to areas under the curve.

The total area under the curve is 1.0, and the proportionate area under any section represents the probability that an actual return will fall along the horizontal axis in that area. For example, the shaded area in the diagram represents the probability that in any particular year the actual return on an investment in shares of X will turn out to be between 8.0% and 8.5%. If that area is 0.1 or 10% of the total area under the curve, the probability of the actual return being between 8.0% and 8.5% in any year would be 10%.

The mean or expected value (the most likely outcome) is usually found under the highest point of the curve. It's indicated as $\bar{k}_X$ in the diagram.

The mean is the statistical representation of the average investor's expected return that we talked about earlier. This is an important point. Portfolio theory assumes that all of the knowledge the investment community has about the future performance of a share is reflected in the probability distribution of returns perceived by the investors. In particular, the mean of that perceived distribution is the expected return investors plan on receiving when they buy.

The mean of the distribution of returns is the share's expected return.

The variance and standard deviation of the distribution show how likely it is that an actual return will be some distance away from the expected value. A distribution with a large variance is more likely to produce actual outcomes that are substantially away from the expected value than one with a small variance.

Figure 11.3 shows the variance conceptually as the width of the distribution. We'll use $\sigma_x{}^2$ to indicate that we're talking about the distribution of returns for share X. Similarly, σ_x will be the standard deviation for share X. A large variance implies a wide distribution with gently sloping sides and a low peak. A narrow distribution with steeply sloping sides and a high peak

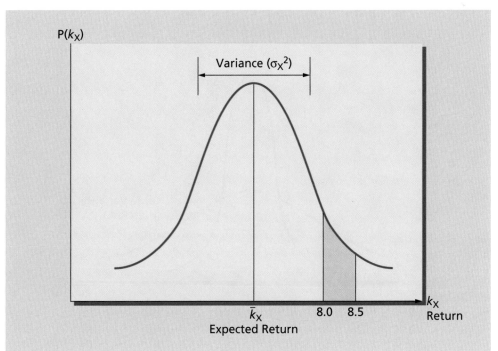

FIGURE 11.3
The Probability Distribution of the Return on an Investment in Share X

has a small variance and standard deviation. Figure 11.4 shows distributions with large and small variances.

Notice that the large variance distribution has more area under the curve farther away from the mean than the small variance distribution. This means that returns will tend to be more variable from year to year when the variance is large. When the variance is small, actual returns in successive years are more likely to cluster closely around the mean or expected value.

Risk Redefined as Variability

In financial theory, *risk* is defined as *variability* in return.

The meaning of risk in portfolio theory differs from the definition we gave earlier. Before, we said that risk is the probability that the return will be less than expected. In portfolio theory, risk is variability. That is, a share whose return is likely to be significantly different from one year to the next is risky, while one whose returns are likely to cluster tightly is less risky. Stated another way, a risky share has a high probability of producing a return that's substantially away from the mean of the distribution of returns, while a low-risk share is unlikely to produce a return that differs from the expected return by very much.

But this is exactly the idea of variance and standard deviation that we've been talking about, so in portfolio theory, a share investment's risk is defined as the standard deviation of the probability distribution of its return. A large standard deviation implies high risk and a small one means low risk. In practical terms, high risk implies variability in return, meaning that returns in successive years are likely to be considerably different from one another.

Figure 11.4 can be interpreted as showing a high-risk share and a low-risk share with the same expected return. The difference is in the variances, which can be visually observed as the widths of the distributions.

This definition is somewhat inconsistent with the earlier version in which we said that risk was the probability that the return would be *less than* what was expected. One would think that a more appropriate definition in statistical terms would equate risk with only the left side of the probability distribution, because in that area return is less than expected. Defining risk as the entire standard deviation includes the probability that the return will turn out to be more than expected, and we're certainly not concerned if that happens.

FIGURE 11.4
Probability Distributions with Large and Small Variances

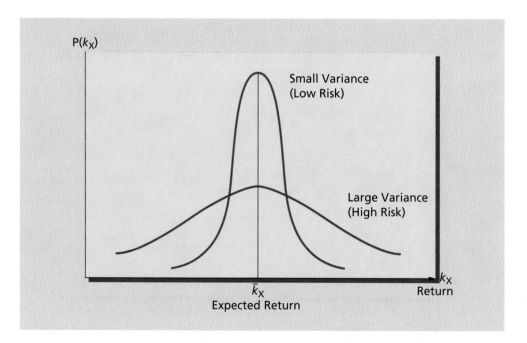

Indeed, a left-side-only definition would make more intuitive sense. However, it would be very difficult to work with mathematically. Theorists solved the problem by noticing that return distributions are usually relatively symmetrical. This means that a large left side always implies a large right side as well. Why not therefore define risk for mathematical convenience as total variability, understanding that we're really only concerned with the probability of lower than expected returns (i.e., those on the left)? Indeed this is what was done. The resulting technical definition of risk is a little strange in that it includes good news as well as bad news, but that doesn't bother us if we keep the reason in mind.

So we actually have two definitions of risk that are both correct. In practical terms, risk is the probability that the return will be less than expected. In financial theory, risk is the variability of the probability distribution of returns.

Terminology isn't entirely consistent. When talking conceptually about risk, people are likely to use the terms "variance" or "variability." But when a precise value is needed to represent risk in a mathematical equation, it's more common to use σ, the standard deviation.

Notice also that defining risk as the probability that the return will be less than expected doesn't tell us much. For more or less symmetrical distributions of returns, that probability will always be about 50%. But for some investments the return is never below the expected value by very much, while for others it can be below by a lot. The variance definition gets right at this distinction. If the distribution has a large variance, the return can be below the expected value by a substantial amount, and an investor can be hurt badly.

An Alternative View

There's another way to visualize risk that many students find helpful. Imagine plotting the historical values of return on a particular share over time. When we do that, we get an up and down graph like one of those shown in Figure 11.5. Over time the share's return is seen to oscillate around its average value, $\bar{k}_x$. The more the share's return moves up and down over time, the more risky we say it is as an investment. That is, the greater the amplitude of the swings, the riskier the investment. This view is simply a graphic result of the variance of the distribution. In the diagram, share A is relatively high risk and share B is relatively low risk. We will use this representation again shortly.

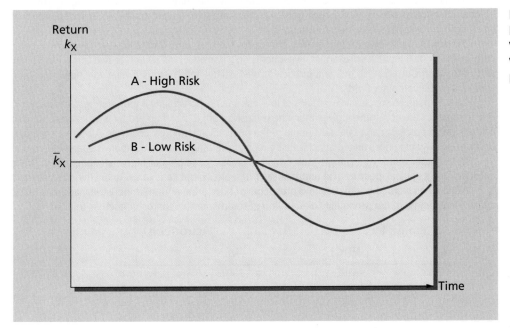

FIGURE 11.5
Investment Risk Viewed as Variability of Return over Time

FIGURE 11.6

Risk Aversion

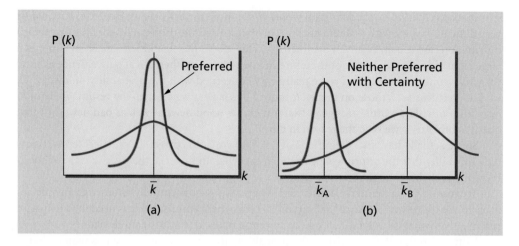

Risk Aversion

Now we're in a position to define risk aversion more precisely. The axiom simply states that people prefer investments with less risk to those with more risk if the expected returns are equal. Figure 11.6(a) illustrates the idea with probability distributions. The narrower distribution has less risk and will be preferred to the wider, riskier distribution.

It's important to understand that this preference is assumed to hold universally only in cases where the expected returns are exactly equal. When the choice is as illustrated in Figure 11.6(b), the principle of risk aversion tells us nothing. There, investment A is preferred on the basis of risk, while investment B is preferred on the basis of expected return. Which will be chosen depends on the individual investor's tolerance for risk.

Example 11.1

Evaluating Stand-Alone Risk

The notions of risk we've just developed are associated with owning a single share by itself. That can be characterized as **stand-alone risk**, because the share's variability stands alone, independent of anything happening in the owner's portfolio.

Michael Okafor is considering buying shares for the first time, and is looking for a single company in which he'll make a substantial investment. He's narrowed his search to two firms, Emera Inc. and Astro Tech Corp. Emera Inc. is a publicly traded utility, and Astro is a relatively new high-tech company in the computer field.

Utility companies are classic examples of low-risk shares, particularly if they are *regulated monopolies.* That means the government gives them the exclusive right to sell their products in an area, but also controls pricing so they can't take advantage of the public by charging excessively. A *utility commission* or *board* usually sets prices aimed at achieving a reasonable return for the company's shareholders.

On the other hand, young high-tech firms are classic examples of high-risk companies. That's because new technical ideas can be enormously profitable, complete failures, or anything in between.

Michael has studied the history and prospects of both firms and their industries, and has made a discrete estimate of the probability distribution of returns for the shares of each as follows.

Emera Inc.		Astro Tech	
k_E	$P(k_E)$	k_A	$P(k_A)$
6%	0.05	−100%	0.15
8	0.15	0	0.20
10	0.60	15	0.30
12	0.15	30	0.20
14	0.05	130	0.15

Stand-alone risk is the risk associated with investing in a share that's held by itself, outside a portfolio.

Evaluate Michael's options in terms of statistical concepts of risk and return.

■ **Solution:** First, calculate the expected return for each company. That's the mean of each distribution.

Emera Inc.			**Astro Tech**		
k_E	$P(k_E)$	$k_E \times P(k_E)$	(k_A)	$P(k_A)$	$k_A \times P(k_A)$
6%	0.05	0.3%	−100%	0.15	−15.0%
8	0.15	1.2	0	0.20	0.0
10	0.60	6.0	15	0.30	4.5
12	0.15	1.8	30	0.20	6.0
14	0.05	0.7	130	0.15	19.5
		$\overline{k_E} = 10.0\%$			$\overline{k_A} = 15.0\%$

Next, calculate the variance and standard deviation of the return on each of the company's shares.

Emera Inc.

k_E	$k_E - \overline{k_E}$	$(k_E - \overline{k_E})^2$	$P(k_E)$	$(k_E - \overline{k_E})^2 \times P(k_E)$
6%	−4%	16	0.05	0.8
8	−2	4	0.15	0.6
10	0	0	0.60	0.0
12	2	4	0.15	0.6
14	4	16	0.05	0.8

$$\text{Variance } \sigma_E^2 = 2.8$$
$$\text{Standard Deviation: } \sigma_E = 1.7\%$$

Astro Tech

k_A	$k_A - \overline{k_A}$	$(k_A - \overline{k_A})^2$	$P(k_A)$	$(k_A - \overline{k_A})^2 \times P(k_A)$
−100%	−115%	13,225	0.15	1,984
0	−15	225	0.20	45
15	0	0	0.30	0
30	15	225	0.20	45
130	115	13,225	0.15	1,984

$$\text{Variance: } \sigma_A^2 = 4,058$$
$$\text{Standard Deviation: } \sigma_A = 63.7\%$$

Finally, calculate the coefficient of variation for each company's return.

$$CV_E = \frac{\sigma_E}{\overline{k_E}} = \frac{1.7}{10.0} = 0.17 \quad CV_A = \frac{\sigma_A}{\overline{k_A}} = \frac{63.7}{15} = 4.25$$

Discussion:

If Michael considers only the expected returns on his investment options, he'll certainly choose Astro. Its most likely return is half again as high as Emera Inc.'s. But a glance at the distributions reveals that's not the whole story. With Emera Inc., Michael's investment is relatively safe, because the worst he's likely to do is a return of 6% rather than the expected 10%.

Investing in Astro is a completely different story. While Michael's most likely return there is 15%, a substantial chance (15%) exists that he'll lose everything. There's also a 20% chance that he'll earn a zero return. Possibilities like these cause people to be concerned about investing in this kind of share.

It's also important to appreciate the high side of the two distributions. With Emera Inc., Michael isn't likely to do much better than the expected return, because the highest yield available is only 14%. The utility commission's pricing regulations guarantee that. But with Astro there's a chance of more than doubling invested money in a relatively short time. That's reflected in the 15% chance of a 130% return. That tends to offset the depressing loss possibilities in the minds of some investors.

It should be clear that on a stand-alone basis, Astro is a relatively risky share while Emera Inc. is relatively safe. Astro's risk and Emera Inc.'s lack of it come from the variation in the distributions of their returns, which we just observed by examining the distributions in detail. But the idea is also available in summarized form from the standard deviations and coefficients of variation.

First, notice that Astro's standard deviation is 63.7%. That means a "typical" return has a good chance of being about 64% above or below the expected return of 15%. That's an enormous range for return, from −49% to 79%. On the other hand, Emera Inc.'s standard deviation is only 1.7%, meaning a typical return will probably be less than two percentage points off the expected return.

It's tempting to compare the two companies by saying that Astro's risk is (63.7/1.7 =) 37 times that of Emera Inc. But that's not quite fair because Astro has a higher expected return. It makes more sense to compare the coefficients of variation, which state the standard deviations in units of their respective means. Emera Inc.'s CV is 0.17 while Astro's is 4.25, so it's more reasonable to say that Astro is (4.25/0.17 =) 25 times as risky as Emera Inc.

A picture is even more telling. Continuous approximations of the two distributions are plotted below.

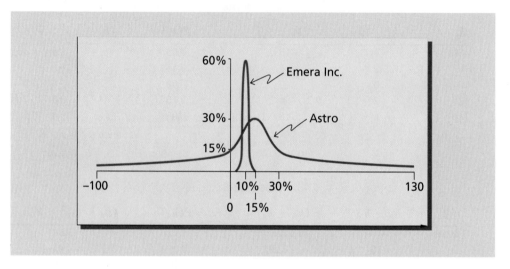

So, after having said all that, which company's shares should Michael choose? Although our analysis has laid out the solution clearly, no one but Michael can answer that question, because his choice depends on his degree of *risk aversion*. Emera Inc. is the better choice with respect to risk, but Astro is better with respect to expected return. Which dominates is a personal choice that only the investor can make.

Decomposing Risk—Systematic (Market) and Unsystematic (Business-Specific) Risk

A fundamental truth of the investment world is that the returns offered on various securities tend to move up and down together. They don't move exactly together, or even proportionately, but for the most part shares tend to go up and down at the same times.

Events and Conditions Causing Movement in Returns

The *returns* on securities tend to *move* up and down *together*.

Returns on equity investments move up and down in response to various events and conditions that affect the environment. Some things influence all company shares, while others affect only specific companies. News of politics, inflation, interest rates, war, and economic events tend to move most shares in the same direction at the same time. A labour dispute in a particular industry, on the other hand, tends to affect only the shares of firms in that industry.

Although certain events affect the returns of all shares, some returns tend to respond more than others to particular things. Suppose news of an impending recession hits the market. The return on most shares can be expected to decline, but not by the same amount. The return on a utility, such as an electric company, isn't likely to change much, because people's demand for electricity doesn't change much in hard times, and if the utility is a regulated monopoly its profitability is more or less guaranteed by the government. On the other hand, the return on the equity of a luxury goods manufacturer may drop sharply, because recession signals a drying up of demand for the company's product.

In short, there's a general but disproportionate movement together, upon which is superimposed a fair amount of individual movement.

Movement in Return as Risk

Remember that one way to look at a share's risk is to consider the up and down movement of its return over time as equivalent to that risk (Figure 11.5 on page 397). Think of that total movement as the total risk inherent in the share.

Separating Movement/Risk into Two Parts

It's conceptually possible to separate the total up and down movement of a share's return into two parts. The first part is the movement that occurs along with that of all other shares in response to events affecting them all. That movement is known as **market risk** or systematic risk. It systematically affects everyone.

The second part is whatever movement is left over after the first part has been removed. This movement is a result of events that are specific to particular companies and industries. Strikes, good or bad weather, good or bad management, and demand conditions are examples of things that affect particular firms. This remaining movement is called **business-specific risk** or unsystematic risk. It affects specific companies.

> A share's risk can be separated into **market risk** (systematic risk) and **business-specific risk** (unsystematic risk).

Portfolios

Most equity investors hold shares in a number of companies rather than putting all of their funds in one firm's securities. We refer to an investor's total share holding as his or her portfolio.

Risk and Return for a Portfolio

Each share in a portfolio has its own expected return and its own risk. These are the mean and standard deviation of the probability distribution of the share's return. As might be expected, the total portfolio also has its own risk and return.

The return (actual or expected) on a portfolio is simply the average of the returns of the shares in it, where the average is weighted by the proportionate dollars invested in each share. For example, suppose we have the following three-share portfolio.

> Portfolios have *their own* risks and returns.

Share	Investment	Return
A	$ 6,000	5%
B	9,000	9
C	15,000	11
	$ 30,000	

The return on the portfolio, expected or actual, is $k_p = w_A k_A + w_B k_B + w_C k_C$, where k_p is the portfolio's return and the terms involving w are the fractions of its total value invested in each asset. The weighted average calculation is as follows.

$$k_p = \frac{\$6K}{\$30K}(5\%) + \frac{\$9K}{\$30K}(9\%) + \frac{\$15K}{\$30K}(11\%)$$
$$= (0.2)(0.05) + (0.3)(0.09) + (0.5)(0.11)$$
$$= 9.2\%$$

The risk of a portfolio is the variance or standard deviation of the probability distribution of the portfolio's return. That depends on the variances (risks) of the returns on the shares in

---

DANIER LEATHER

Risk Factors at Danier Leather Inc.

(For the financial statements and other financial information about Danier Leather Inc., refer to Appendix 3A, page 92.)

Danier was subject to certain risks and uncertainties, some of which were *market* risks, and some of which were *business-specific*. Some of the risks it reported include:

- Fashion and apparel and leather industry changes that can reduce demand for Danier's products, resulting in significant excess inventories and additional markdowns or promotions
- Change in consumer shopping patterns away from shopping malls and power centres
- Unseasonably warm weather or severe weather that reduces consumer demand or prevents customers from going to Danier's stores

- War and acts of terrorism, or if either is threatened, that negatively impact Danier's ability to source leather and import merchandise or that lead to lower customer traffic and spending in shopping malls and power centres
- Existing and potential class action legal proceedings, particularly if the Supreme Court of Canada rules against Danier, resulting in damages, costs and interest in excess of those provided for on the books of the Company
- Higher prices and/or reduced availability for leather
- Foreign currency fluctuations, particularly between the Canadian and U.S. dollars, which result in increased costs of imported raw materials and finished goods
- Other risks associated with foreign sourcing and manufacturing

(For further information on Danier's risks from its international transactions, see "Danier Leather International," Chapter 20, page 721)

Sources: Danier Leather Annual Report, 2006.

---

the portfolio, but not in a simple way. We'll understand more about this relationship of portfolio risk to share risk as we move on.

The Goal of the Investor/Portfolio Owner

As we said earlier, the goal of investors is to capture the high average returns of equities while avoiding as much of their risk as possible. *That's generally done by constructing diversified portfolios to minimize portfolio risk for a given return.*

Investment theory is based on the *premise* that portfolio owners care only about the financial performance of their whole portfolios and not about the stand-alone characteristics of the individual shares in the portfolios.

In other words, an investor evaluates the risk and return characteristics of a new share only in terms of how that share will affect the performance of his or her portfolio and not on the stand-alone merits of the investment. How a share's characteristics can be different in and out of a portfolio will become clear shortly.

> Investors are concerned with how shares *impact portfolio performance* and not with their stand-alone characteristics.

Diversification—How Portfolio Risk Is Affected When Shares Are Added

Our basic goal in investing, to capture a high portfolio return while avoiding as much risk as possible, is accomplished through diversification. Diversification means adding different, or diverse, shares to a portfolio. It's the investor's most basic tool for managing risk. Properly employed, diversification can reduce but not eliminate risk (variation in return) in a portfolio. To achieve the goal, however, we have to be careful about how we go about diversifying. We'll need to address unsystematic (business-specific) risk and systematic (market) risk separately.

> Diversification is selecting a portfolio of different (diverse) investments to limit the overall risk borne by the investor.

Business-Specific Risk and Diversification

If we diversify by forming a portfolio of the shares of a fairly large number of different companies, we can imagine business-specific risk as a series of essentially random events that push the returns on individual shares up or down. The stimuli that affect individual companies are separate events that occur across the country. Some are good and some are bad.

Because events causing business-specific risk are random from the investor's point of view, their effects simply cancel when added together over a substantial number of shares. Therefore, we say that business-specific risk can be "diversified away" in a portfolio of any size. In other words, the good events offset the bad ones, and if there are enough events the net result tends to be about zero.

However, a word of caution is in order. For this idea to work, the shares in the portfolio have to be from companies in fundamentally different industries. For example, if all the companies in a portfolio were agricultural, the effect of a drought wouldn't be random. It would hit all of the shares. Therefore, the business-specific risk wouldn't be diversified away.

Business-specific risk is essentially random and can be diversified away.

This is an easy but powerful concept. For investors who hold numerous shares, business-specific risk simply doesn't exist at the aggregate level because it's "washed out" statistically. Individual shares still have it, but not portfolios, and the portfolio is all the investor cares about.

Systematic (Market) Risk and Diversification

Reducing market risk in a portfolio calls for more complicated thinking than does handling business-specific risk. It should be intuitively clear that if the returns of all shares move up and down more or less together, we're unlikely to be able to eliminate all of the movement in a portfolio's return by adding more shares. In fact, systematic or market risk in a portfolio can be reduced but never entirely eliminated through diversification. However, even the reduction of market risk requires careful attention to the risk characteristics of the shares added to the portfolio.

THE PORTFOLIO To appreciate the issue, imagine we have a portfolio of shares that has an expected return ($\bar{k}_p$). In what follows, we'll assume for simplicity that all the shares have the same expected return. It's all right to make this unrealistic assumption for illustrative purposes, because the points we're getting at involve the interplay of risk among shares and not of returns.

Our portfolio will have its own risk or variation in return, which is determined by the shares in it. We'll assume the portfolio has been put together to mirror exactly the makeup of the overall stock market. That is, if the prices of the shares in the overall market are such that EnCana Corporation makes up 2% of the market's value, we'll spend 2% of our money on EnCana Corporation shares, and so on through all the shares listed on the market. If the portfolio is constituted in this way, its return will move up and down just as the market's return does. In other words, the portfolio's risk will just equal the market's risk. The behaviour of the portfolio's return over time is illustrated in Figure 11.7 by the black line labelled P.

THE IMPACT ON PORTFOLIO RISK OF ADDING NEW SHARES We now want to consider the impact on the portfolio's risk of adding a little of *either* of two new shares to it. We'll call these shares A and B. The special behaviour of the return on each is shown in Figure 11.7. Notice that we're not talking about adding both shares A and B at the same time. Rather the idea is to assess the impact on the risk of the resulting portfolio of adding a little of A or a little of B to the original portfolio.

First consider share A. What happens to the risk of the portfolio if we add a few shares of A? Notice that A's return achieves its highs and lows at exactly the same times as the portfolio's return does, and that its peaks and troughs are higher and lower, respectively, than the portfolio's. It should be clear that the inclusion of a little A will tend to heighten the portfolio's peak returns and depress its lowest returns. In other words, it will make the swings in the portfolio's return larger. That means it will add risk to the portfolio.

In statistical terms, A's return is said to be perfectly positively correlated with the portfolio's return. That means the two returns move up and down at exactly the same times. Such shares will generally add risk to a diversified portfolio.

Now consider the pattern of returns on share B over time. Its peaks occur with the portfolio's valleys and its valleys coincide with the portfolio's peaks. The return on share B is always moving up or down in a direction opposite the movement of the return on the portfolio.

FIGURE 11.7

Risk In and Out of a Portfolio

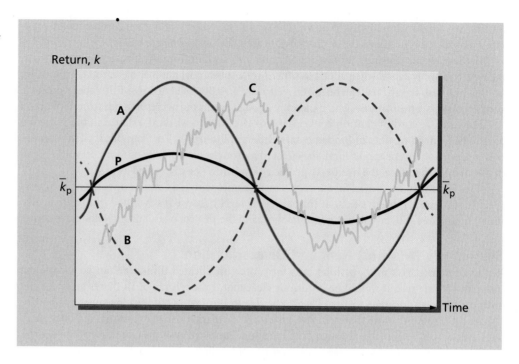

What will happen to the pattern of returns of the portfolio if we add a few shares of B? Clearly, the peaks will be lower and the valleys will be higher; that is, the swings won't be as wide. According to our definitions, that means the risk will be lowered by adding some B. In statistical terms, B's return is said to be perfectly negatively correlated with the portfolio's return. Such shares will always lower the portfolio's risk.

In short, A adds risk to a portfolio while B reduces the portfolio's risk.

THE RISK OF THE NEW ADDITIONS BY THEMSELVES AND IN PORTFOLIOS Now consider the relative riskiness of shares A and B without reference to a portfolio. That is, how risky is each one standing alone? Figure 11.7 shows that A's and B's returns have about the same level of variation. That is, their peaks and troughs are about the same height. Therefore their stand-alone risks as individual investments are about the same.

However, in a portfolio sense, A is risky and B is safe in that A adds and B subtracts risk. This is a central and critically important concept. *Although A and B are equally risky on a stand-alone basis, they have completely opposite risk impacts on a portfolio.*

Shares with *equal stand-alone risk* can have *opposite risk impacts on a portfolio* because of the timing of the variations in their returns.

The portfolio definition of a share's risk is related to the timing of the variability of the share's return rather than to the magnitude of the variation. It has to do with the way the new share's return changes when the portfolio's return changes. Or, if the portfolio is constituted like the market as we've assumed, it has to do with the way the share's return changes with the return on the market.

However, the degree to which a share's return moves with the market is what we've called market risk. Hence we can say that *a share's risk in a portfolio sense is its market risk.*

CHOOSING INVESTMENTS TO DIVERSIFY FOR MARKET RISK How do we diversify to reduce market risk in a portfolio? Figure 11.7 might imply that it's easy: Just add investments like B until the movement of the portfolio is virtually dampened out. Unfortunately, investments like B that move countercyclically with the market are few and far between.

The classic example of such an investment is shares in a gold mining company, such as Barrick Gold, listed on the TSX. When returns on most shares are down, people flee from paper investments and put money in tangible assets, notably gold. That drives the price of gold up. A higher price for gold means a gold mining company becomes more profitable, which elevates the return on its shares. Hence, when the return on most shares is down, the return on gold mining shares tends to be up. The reverse happens when share returns are generally high.

Although people do diversify with gold mining shares to stabilize portfolios, there aren't enough of them to do the job thoroughly. There simply aren't many shares around that are negatively correlated with the market.

However, a great number of shares are available whose returns behave in a manner somewhere between those of A and B in the diagram. In terms of the behaviour of return, that kind of share can be thought of as a combination of A and B. Such an investment is illustrated by line C in Figure 11.7. Shares like C are said to be not perfectly positively correlated with the portfolio.

Adding some C to the portfolio will generally reduce its risk somewhat. If we think of C as a hybrid between A and B, its addition is a way to get a little B into the portfolio indirectly. An intuitive way to put it is to say that C contains a little of the "personality" of B.

In summary, market risk generally can be reduced but not eliminated by diversifying with shares like C that are not perfectly positively correlated with the portfolio.

Of course, while proper diversification will reduce risk, it will also reduce potential *return* (by limiting the range of returns possible).

The Importance of Market Risk

Let's return to shares A and B in Figure 11.7 for a moment. The illustration is constructed to point out two different concepts of risk. Considered individually the shares are equally risky, yet in a portfolio one is risky and the other is not. Which interpretation is appropriate and when?

The relative risk attributes of the two shares are entirely changed if we assume that investors focus on portfolios rather than on individual shares. Modern portfolio theory is based on that assumption. *What matters is how shares affect portfolios rather than how they behave when considered alone. And how they affect portfolios depends only on market risk.*

This is a fundamental result of portfolio theory. According to the theory, what matters in the investment world is market risk alone. It is also a dangerous result. Business-specific risk is truly diversified away only in the context of large portfolios (we will call this a well-diversified portfolio). For the small investor with a limited portfolio, that effect simply doesn't occur. An individual business reversal can devastate an investment program if the share represents a significant portion of a small portfolio. Hence, while the thinking behind portfolio theory may be appropriate for running a mutual fund, it should not be applied blindly to managing one's personal assets.[4]

Market Return

If the investor has gone to the effort of creating a well-diversified portfolio, he or she will want to know what return to expect from this portfolio. This leads us to the idea of return on the market. When we talk about the return on the market or the market portfolio, we really mean the return you would get if you owned *all* the assets in an economy. That is the straightforward part. Practically speaking, we could never own all the assets, but we could, at least in theory, hold all of the shares trading in the marketplace, such as the Toronto Stock Exchange or New York Stock Exchange. This too seems a bit unrealistic, but we can own a piece of these. In Canada, if you wanted to own the S&P/TSX Composite Index, you would not have to buy the entire index—you would buy an Exchange Traded Fund (or EFT for short).[5] What are these? In essence, these are similar to mutual funds except that you purchase them from the stock exchange, rather than from a mutual fund company. These EFTs are sold by trusts whose assets are the shares held by

Market risk in a portfolio can be reduced but not eliminated by diversifying with shares that are not perfectly positively correlated with the portfolio.

Caution: The concepts of risk associated with portfolio theory *may not be appropriate for individual investors.*

A well-diversified portfolio has most of the business-specific risk diversified away.

---

4 A small investor can, with a little effort, hold a portfolio with most of the business-specific risk diversified away. To do this, the investor needs to have carefully chosen shares (many practitioners feel that somewhere between 12 and 50 well-chosen shares are needed) or hold mutual funds that mirror the broad market. These mutual funds are discussed next.
5 These are also called index participation units, or IPUs.

the particular index you are interested in. The shares held by the trust are in the exact same proportion as the index itself. The trust pays dividends based on dividends it may have received along with any other distributions.[6] For example, you could purchase an i60 on the TSX (ticker XIU). What you purchased was a share of a fund comprising the 60 firms that make up the S&P/TSX 60 Index. Each unit is worth roughly 10% of the value of the S&P/TSX 60 Index. Check the latest stock listings to see how the i60s are doing as compared to the S&P/TSX 60.

Measuring Market Risk—The Concept of Beta

Because market risk is of such central importance to investing, it's appropriate to look for a way to measure it for individual shares.

*A share's **beta** measures its market risk.*

A statistic known as a share's beta coefficient has been developed that is commonly considered to be the measure of a share's market risk. Essentially, beta captures the variation in a share's return that accompanies variation in the return on the market.

Developing Beta

A share's beta coefficient is developed by plotting the historical relationship between the return on the share and the return on the market.[7] Figure 11.8 shows such a plot. Each point represents

---

Insights PRACTICAL FINANCE

Is It Investing or Gambling?

Investing is putting money at risk in the hope of earning more money, a return. But isn't that also a definition of gambling? Certainly it is, so what's the difference between investing and gambling, and why do we have such different moral and ethical attitudes about them?

Investing has economic value to the society that gambling doesn't (although gambling does provide considerable employment and tax revenues). But, aside from that, from an individual's perspective it's fair to ask about the distinction between playing the stock market and taking a trip to Las Vegas.

Viewing both processes in terms of the probability distributions of their returns provides some insight. Investing tends to be characterized by probability distributions with positive expected values (means) and relatively small probabilities of very large gains or losses. Gambling, on the other hand, generally has a zero or negative expected value and offers a good chance of losing everything placed at risk. The attraction of gambling is that there's also an apparent chance of winning many times the amount risked along with its entertainment value. Think of playing roulette in a Las Vegas casino. It's no secret that the odds are stacked slightly in favour of the house, and that many visitors leave town with empty pockets. But there are also a few well-publicized examples of people who hit the jackpot. Graphically the distributions might look something like this.

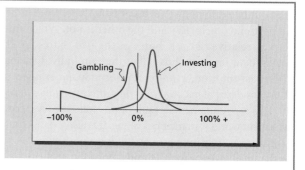

This view leads to another logical question. Are there activities that people normally call investing that are more like gambling? The answer is a resounding yes. Buying the shares of a high-risk new venture might be an example. There are also some financial markets that are risky to the point of bordering on gambling (e.g., commodities and futures markets, which are beyond the scope of this book).

In fact, the whole idea of portfolio theory is to move the investor's exposure toward the investment profile we've just described and away from the gambling profile.

The important thing to take away from this discussion is that something isn't "investing" just because it happens through the financial industry. Brokers like to characterize all their offerings as investing because it has a nobler image. But, in fact, some financial "investments" are really more like gambles.

---

6 Other distributions may be sold by the trust and then paid out to the trust unitholders.
7 The return on the market is estimated by calculating the return on a market index, such as the S&P/TSX Composite Index.

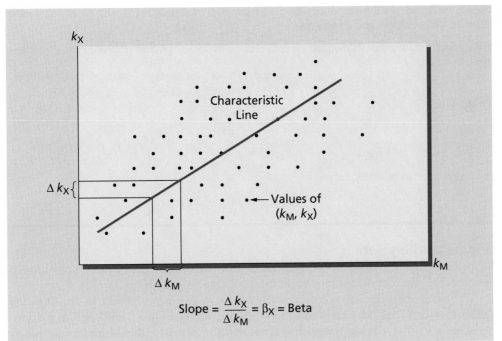

FIGURE 11.8
The Determination
of Beta

a past time period for which we plot the share's return, k_X, on the vertical axis and the market's return, k_M, on the horizontal axis. Doing this for a number of past periods results in a "scatter diagram" of historical observations. A regression line fitted to these data points is known as the *characteristic line* for the share.

The characteristic line represents the average relationship between the share's return and the market's return. Its slope is particularly rich in information. The slope tells us on average how much of a change in k_X has come about with a given change in k_M. This is exactly what we're looking for in terms of measuring market risk. The slope is an indication of how much variation in the return on the share goes along with variation in the return on the market.

To see this, notice that as we move along the characteristic line, a change in k_M, Δk_M, comes with a change in k_X, Δk_X. The relationship between these changes is reflected in the slope of the line. The return of the market is estimated by calculating the return on a market index, such as the S&P/TSX Composite Index (formerly the TSE 300).

> A share's *characteristic line* reflects the average relationship between its return and the market's. *Beta is the slope of the characteristic line.*

$$(11.3) \qquad \text{slope} = \frac{\text{Rise}}{\text{Run}} = \frac{\Delta k_x}{\Delta k_M} = \beta_x = \text{Beta}$$

Market risk is defined as the degree to which the return on the share moves with the return on the market. That idea is summarized perfectly by the slope of the characteristic line. The slope can therefore be defined as the measure of market risk for the share. This measure is called the beta coefficient, or simply beta, for the share.

Projecting Returns with Beta

Knowing a share's beta enables us to estimate changes in its return given changes in the market's return.

Example 11.2

Conroy Corp. has a beta of 1.8 and is currently earning its owners a return of 14%. The stock market in general is reacting negatively to a new crisis in the Middle East that threatens world oil supplies. Experts estimate that the average return on the stock market will drop from 12% to 8% because of investor concerns over the economic impact of a potential oil shortage. Estimate the change in the return on Conroy shares and its new return.

■ **Solution:** Beta represents the past average change in Conroy's return relative to changes in the market's return.

$$\beta_{Conroy} = \frac{k_{Conroy}}{k_M}$$

Substituting,

$$1.8 = \frac{k_{Conroy}}{4\%}$$

$$\Delta k_{Conroy} = 7.2\%$$

The new return can be estimated as

$$k_{Conroy} = 14\% - 7.2\% = 6.8\%$$

Understanding Beta

It's important to understand that beta represents an average relationship based on past history. To appreciate this, consider the movement from one data point to the next in Figure 11.8.

The change between any two successive values of k_X represents movement caused by the combination of market risk forces and business-specific risk forces. In other words, such a change is part of the share's total risk. By regressing k_X versus k_M, we're making the assumption that movement along the line representing an average relationship between the variables reflects only market-related changes. In this view, movement from one data point to the next has two components: movement to and from the line, and movement along the line. Movement to and from the line represents business-specific risk, while movement along the line represents market risk.

Forecasting with beta, as in the last example, uses only the average relationship between the returns, which is assumed to be market related. It says nothing about business-specific risk factors.

Example 11.3

Suppose Conroy Corp. in Example 11.2 makes sophisticated solar panels. Would the estimate of return done in that example be valid? What if Conroy were in the orange juice business?

■ **Solution:** It's unlikely that the estimate would be much good if Conroy were producing solar panels. The threat of an oil shortage could be expected to have a positive impact on the company. In other words, such a threat is likely to have a major business-specific risk impact on the firm's return that would act in a direction opposite the market-related decline.

If Conroy made orange juice, we wouldn't expect a business-specific risk change due to the Middle East crisis, so the market-related estimate would be more realistic.

Betas are developed from *historical data* and *may not be accurate* if a *fundamental change* in the business environment occurs.

BETA OVER TIME Any firm's beta is derived from observation of the behaviour of its return in the past. Use of the statistic implicitly assumes that the return is going to remain constant over time. In other words, using beta assumes the share's return will behave in the same way in the future that it did in the past relative to the market's return. This assumption is usually reasonable, but at times it may not be.

Example 11.4

Let's consider the Conroy Corp. of the last two examples once more. In the early 1990s commodity prices for oil and gas were quite low and there was little incentive for spending large amounts of money on research and development of alternative energy sources. Further, this type of solar technology was still in its infancy. Would a projection using beta have been valid at that time?

■ **Solution:** This situation would make the future of Conroy's beta somewhat uncertain. The data from which the firm's characteristic line was developed would have been from earlier periods when research and development spending was low. The substantial increase in commodity prices in the mid- to late 1990s and improvements in the technology would make Conroy look much more viable, even though it was still quite a risky venture. Therefore the future beta is likely to have been different from the past value at that time.

Volatility

Beta measures volatility in relation to market changes. In other words, it tells us whether the share's return moves around more or less than the return of an average share.

A beta of 1.0 means the share's return moves on average just as much as the market's return. Beta > 1.0 implies that the share moves more than the market. Beta < 1.0 means that the share tends to move with the market but less. Beta < 0 means that the share tends to move against the market, that is, in the opposite direction. Such shares are rare. Share B of Figure 11.7 (page 404) is a negative beta share. Gold mining companies are the primary real-world example of such an investment.

The idea of beta immediately suggests an investment strategy. When the market is moving up, hold high-beta shares because they move up more. When the market is moving down, switch to low-beta shares because they move down less!

Small investors should remember that *beta doesn't measure total risk.*

Beta for a Portfolio

Because beta measures market risk, the degree to which a share moves with the market, it makes sense to think about market risk and beta for an entire portfolio. In fact, the concept is rather simple. Beta for a portfolio of shares is just the weighted average of the betas of the individual shares where the weights are the dollar amounts invested in each share.

For example, suppose a two-share portfolio is made up like this.

Share	Beta	Current Dollar Value	Portion of Value
A	0.7	800	0.8
B	1.1	200	0.2
		1,000	1.0

There are many websites that provide a listing of betas. Look up the beta for a company such as the Royal Bank of Canada or Alcan Inc. On MSN Money Central, click *Company Report* then enter the symbol (RY or AL) http://moneycentral. msn.com/investor/ research/welcome. asp. On Yahoo http://www.ca. finance.yahoo.com enter the symbol and click on *Key Statistics.*

Then the portfolio's beta, written β_B, is calculated as follows.

$$\beta_P = 0.8\beta_A + 0.2\beta_B = 0.8(0.7) + 0.2(1.1) = 0.78$$

A NOTE ON DECIMAL ACCURACY Notice that the portfolio beta we just calculated is expressed to two decimal places. You'll sometimes see betas calculated to three decimal places. However, if you think about the nature of beta and the way it's derived for individual shares, it's apparent that such accuracy is meaningless. Rounding off to one decimal place is generally sufficient.

Using Beta—The Capital Asset Pricing Model (CAPM)

The things we've been discussing in this chapter are inputs to a sophisticated mathematical model of the financial world called the **capital asset pricing model (CAPM)**. The terminology can be a little confusing. A "capital asset" is a share, and "pricing model" implies an attempt to explain how share prices are set in the market.

The CAPM has been around for some time. It was developed during the 1950s and 1960s by economists Harry Markowitz and William F. Sharpe, who shared the 1990 Nobel Prize in economics for their work.

The **CAPM** attempts to explain *share prices* by explaining how investors' *required returns* are determined.

The CAPM's Approach

The model's approach to determining how prices are set is to explain how the required rate of return on a share comes about. Recall that the required rate of return is the return that just holds investors in the share. It's the amount an individual has to expect to get in order to be willing to put his or her money in a particular issue. It's related to the riskiness of the issue as perceived by the investor. (Review page 389 if necessary.) People won't invest unless the expected return is at least equal to their required return.

Price Depends on Return

In general, once a required rate of return is specified, price follows. For example, consider Equation 11.2, our definition of the return on an investment in shares (page 389). If we solve that equation for the current price, P_0, we get

$$P_0 = \frac{D_1 + P_1}{1 + k}$$

where we can think of k as the required rate of return. If we make assumptions about the future price and dividend, P_1 and D_1, the current price of the share, P_0, depends on knowing k.

Another approach involves the Gordon model, Equation 10.10 from Chapter 10, on share valuation. We'll repeat that expression here for convenience, considering k a required rate of return.

(10.10) $$P_0 = \frac{D_0(1 + g)}{k - g}$$

Notice that if the last dividend, D_0, is known and an assumption is made about the growth rate, g, the current price again depends on knowing k. We'll use this relationship in some problems shortly.

All this says that if we understand how required returns are set, we'll understand a great deal about how prices are established.

Rates of Return, The Risk-Free Rate, and Risk Premiums

At this time, we have to make a few points about rates of return in general. First, interest is the rate of return on debt, and is conceptually identical to the rate of return on an equity investment. Therefore we can mix the two ideas as we like. Specifically, we can have both interest rates and rates of return on equity investments within the same equation.

Next we need to recall the concept of a risk-free rate of return from Chapter 7. (Review page 247 if necessary.) A risk-free investment is one in which there is no possibility of receiving less than the expected return. The current rate of interest paid on three-month Treasury bills is generally taken to be the prevailing risk-free rate, written as k_{RF}.

The rate of return on any other investment involves some allowance for bearing risk added to the risk-free rate. The allowance is known as the risk premium for the investment. If we call some investment Y, we can write the return on Y as

$$k_Y = k_{RF} + k_{RPY}$$

where k_{RPY} is the risk premium on investment Y. Solving for the risk premium, we have

$$k_{RPY} = k_Y - k_{RF}$$

The *CAPM* purports to explain how the *risk premiums* in required rates of return are formed.

That is, Y's risk premium is the difference between the return on Y and the risk-free rate.

The required rate of return on an investment in a share is then the risk-free rate plus some premium for bearing the risk associated with that share. The mystery is to try to explain just what that risk premium depends on. This is what the capital asset pricing model purports to do.

Putting the Pieces Together

Each of the concepts we've talked about so far—including return as a random variable, risk defined as variance, risk aversion, all the portfolio ideas, and beta—are necessary assumptions undergirding the CAPM.

All of these ideas can be stated in mathematical terms. When they are, some advanced math can be used to derive a single, simple equation that defines the required return on a share in terms of its risk. That equation, called the **security market line (SML)**, is the heart of the CAPM.

The beauty of the model and probably the reason for its wide acceptance is the simplicity of this result.

The Security Market Line (SML)

The security market line proposes that required rates of return are determined by the following equation.

The **security market line (SML)** is the heart of the CAPM. It purports to explain how the market sets the required return on a share.

(11.4)

$$k_X = k_{RF} + \overbrace{(k_M - k_{RF})}^{\text{Market Risk Premium}}\beta_X$$

Share X's Risk Premium

where k_X is the required return on share X

k_{RF} is the risk-free rate

k_M is the return on the market

β_X is share X's beta coefficient

First notice that the right side of the equation is in two parts: the risk-free rate, and a risk premium for share X. This is consistent with the ideas we expressed earlier about rates of return in general.

Next we'll consider the risk premium in detail. It's made up of two parts, the expression in parentheses and beta. Beta, of course, is our measure of market risk for share X. The expression in parentheses is the difference between the return on the market and the risk-free rate.

THE MARKET RISK PREMIUM In the section before last we said that the difference between the return on an investment and the risk-free rate is the risk premium for that investment. Therefore, the term in parentheses is the risk premium for an investment in the market as a whole. That can be interpreted as an investment in an "average" share or in a portfolio constituted to mirror the market.

The market risk premium reflects the average tolerance for risk of all investors at a point in time. In other words, it's indicative of the degree of *risk aversion* felt by the investing community.

The *market risk premium*, $(k_M - k_{RF})$, is a reflection of the investment community's level of *risk aversion*.

THE RISK PREMIUM FOR SHARE X The risk premium for share X is just the market, or "average," risk premium multiplied by share X's own beta, the measure of its market risk.

What the SML is saying is simple and yet profound. It alleges that a share's risk premium is determined only by the market risk premium factored by the share's beta.

Notice that the only thing in the equation that relates specifically to company X is β_X, the measure of X's market risk! So if management wants to influence share price, an important way to try to do so is by changing the volatility of the firm's return and thereby its beta.

The important implication of the SML is that only market risk counts. Business-specific risk doesn't enter the equation; market risk does through beta. Put another way, investors are rewarded with extra return only for bearing market risk, not for bearing business-specific risk. This makes sense because we've assumed that business-specific risk is diversified away for portfolio investors.

The SML holds for the specific share of any company. That's why we've used the generic "X" to represent the company's name. The model says that any firm's required rate of return, as generally perceived by most investors, can be found by just putting that company's beta into Equation 11.4.

The SML as a Portrayal of the Securities Market

The SML can be thought of as representing the entire securities market, most notably the stock market. To show this, we'll plot the line in risk−return space. That simply means the graph will have return on the vertical axis and risk along the horizontal axis. The variable representing risk will be beta. The SML is portrayed graphically in Figure 11.9, where it's seen as a straight line.

Recall the standard formulation for plotting a straight line from algebra.

$$(11.5) \qquad\qquad y = mx + b$$

Here y is traditionally the vertical axis variable and x is the horizontal axis variable. When the equation of a straight line is in this form, m is the slope of the line and b is its y-intercept.

In our graph of the SML, the variable on the vertical axis is k_X and the variable on the horizontal axis is β_X. We can write Equation 11.4 in the same form as Equation 11.5 and compare the two.

$$k_X = \underbrace{(k_M - k_{RF})}_{} \underbrace{\beta_X}_{} + \underbrace{k_{RF}}_{}$$
$$y = \quad m \qquad x \ + \ b$$

> The *slope of the SML* plotted in *risk−return space* reflects the general level of *risk aversion*.

Don't confuse the x-values in the two equations. In the first, X represents the generic name of any company. In the second, x just refers to the horizontal axis variable. The comparison shows that the slope of the SML is the market risk premium $(k_M - k_{RF})$. Thus the slope of the SML is a reflection of the risk tolerance or level of risk aversion felt by investors in general. If investors become more risk averse, the spread between k_M and k_{RF} will increase because people will demand a larger premium for bearing any level of risk. When that happens, the SML will get steeper. Conversely, if people become less concerned about risk, the market risk premium will shrink and the SML will become flatter.

It's important to understand that attitudes about risk do change over time, and that the changes are indeed reflected in real differences between k_M and k_{RF}.

Next consider the intercept of the SML with the vertical axis. This is the y-intercept in the traditional equation. The value of k_X at the intercept point is clearly k_{RF}. This makes sense because risk, represented by beta, is zero at the left side of the graph. The intercept point is simply saying that an investor always has the option of putting his or her money into government securities earning k_{RF} with no risk.

FIGURE 11.9
The Security Market Line

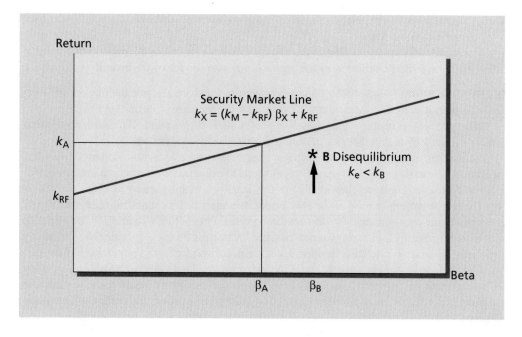

The SML portrays the market in terms of risk and return in that any share can be thought of as occupying a point along the line determined by its level of risk. For instance, share A is shown in Figure 11.9, as A's beta, β_A, we can find A's required return by moving up to the line and then over to the vertical axis at k_A.

The SML as a Line of Market Equilibrium

A system is said to be in equilibrium if it tends to remain in a constant state over time. The equilibrium condition is said to be stable if, when the system is displaced, forces are created that tend to push it back into the equilibrium position.

The SML represents an equilibrium situation if, for every share along the line, the expected rate of return is equal to the required rate of return. In that case investors holding shares are happy because their expected and required rates of return are at least equal. There is no excess of either buyers or sellers, and in theory the market remains where it is.

The *vertical intercept* of the SML represents investment in short-term government securities.

Now suppose conditions change in such a way that the expected return on some share becomes less than its required return. This situation is represented by point B in the diagram where the expected return, shown as k_e, is less than the required return for share B, which is on the SML above β_B.

In this case, people who own the shares will be inclined to sell because the anticipated return no longer meets their needs. That is, it is below their required return, which is on the SML. However, potential buyers will not be interested in purchasing the shares because the expected return is also lower than their required returns. In other words, we have would-be sellers but no interested buyers. When that happens in the market for anything, there's only one solution if trading is to take place—sellers must lower their asking prices. In other words, the market price falls.

Now examine Equation 11.2 once again (page 389). Notice that the current market price is represented as P_0. If P_0 falls while D_1 and P_1 remain unchanged, the value of k on the left side of the equation increases. That means that the expected return becomes higher as new investors have to spend less for the same future cash flows.

In Figure 11.9, this means that market forces drive the expected return back up toward the equilibrium line of the SML. Hence, the stock market equilibrium is stable, because when some external occurrence displaces a return away from the equilibrium line, forces are created to push it back.

The SML represents a condition of *stable equilibrium*.

In reality the market is never quietly in equilibrium, because things are always happening that move share prices and returns around. The important point of the theory is that market forces are constantly being created that tend to push things back toward an equilibrium position with respect to risk and return.

Valuation Using Risk–Return Concepts

We can use the ideas of the capital asset pricing model in another approach to share valuation. The method assumes that the marginal investor buys and sells the shares at the return determined by the SML, and that those sales determine market price.

Given that assumption, we can calculate the price in two steps. First we use the SML to calculate a required rate of return. Then we use that return in the Gordon model to arrive at a price.

Example 11.5

The Kelvin Company paid an annual dividend of $1.50 recently, and is expected to grow at 7% into the indefinite future. Short-term Treasury bills are currently yielding 4%, and the S&P/TSX Composite Index is yielding 10%.[8] Kelvin shares are relatively volatile. Their return tends to move in response to political and economic changes about twice as much as does the return on the average share. What should Kelvin sell for today?

---

8 As of June 2007 91-day T-bills were yielding around 4.3% and the TSX had a one-year yield of 22.73%, and a 20-year average yield of 9.49%. Source: http://www.bankofcanada.ca/en/rates/tbill.html and http://www.globefund.com/servlet/Page/document/v5/data/fund?style=na_eq&id=56816&gf_uid=globeandmail.gf.02224205664.

The SML and the Gordon model provide a two-step *approach to valuation*.

■ **Solution:** First, write the SML for Kelvin from Equation 11.4.

$$k_{Kelvin} = k_{RF} + (k_M - k_{RF})\beta_{Kelvin}$$

Next, notice that the inputs to the SML have been specified in the problem description without being named. The return on short-term Treasury bills reflects the current risk-free rate, k_{RF}, and the return on the S&P/TSX Composite Index is equivalent to the return on the market, k_M. Finally, recognize that we've been given beta in rather cryptic terms. Political and economic changes are things that tend to affect all shares and the response to them relates to market risk. Therefore, saying Kelvin's return responds twice as much as the average to those things implies that Kelvin's beta is 2.0.

Substituting for Kelvin's required return we have

$$k_{Kelvin} = 4 + (10 - 4)2.0 = 16\%$$

Next, write the Gordon model and substitute using k_{Kelvin} for k in the denominator.

$$P_0 = \frac{D_0(1 + g)}{k - g}$$

$$= \frac{\$1.50(1.07)}{0.16 - 0.07}$$

$$P_0 = \$17.83$$

The Impact of Management Decisions on Share Prices

The fact that management decisions can affect both beta and likely future growth rates makes the SML approach to valuation relevant for policy decisions.

Example 11.6

The Kelvin Company described in the last example has an exciting new opportunity. The firm has identified a new field into which it can expand using technology it already possesses. The venture promises to increase the firm's growth rate to 9% from the current 7%. However, the project is new and unproven, so there's a chance it will fail and cause a considerable loss. As a result, there's some concern that the stock market won't react favourably to the additional risk. Management estimates that undertaking the venture will raise the firm's beta to 2.3 from its current level of 2.0. Should Kelvin undertake the new project?

■ **Solution:** A strategic decision such as this should be based on the primary objective of the firm's management: maximizing shareholder wealth. That's equivalent to maximizing the price of the company's shares.

An increased growth rate will have a positive effect on share price. Convince yourself of this by examining how the growth rate, g, influences the value of P_0 in the Gordon model in the last example. A bigger g makes the numerator larger and the denominator smaller, both of which contribute to an increase in P_0. (Remember that g must remain less than k.)

On the other hand, examining the SML of Equation 11.4, we see that a larger beta results in a larger risk premium and therefore a larger required rate of return. That in turn goes into the denominator of the Gordon model as k, and a larger k in the Gordon denominator results in a smaller price unless the required return does not increase enough to offset the increase in growth.

Hence, taking on the new project involves two things that tend to move the share's price in opposite directions: faster growth will increase share price, while higher risk will decrease it. The question is which effect will dominate. We can find out by calculating an estimated price assuming the project is undertaken.

First, recalculate the required rate of return.

$$k_{Kelvin} = 4 + (10 - 4)2.3 = 17.8\%$$

Then recalculate the price using the Gordon model with the new return and the new estimated growth rate.

$$P_0 = \frac{D_0(1 + g)}{k - g} = \frac{\$1.50(1.09)}{0.178 - .09} = \$18.58$$

The resulting price of $18.58 is higher than the $17.83 price before the project, indicating that the positive effect of the increased growth rate outweighs the negative effect of increased risk. Therefore, the venture looks like a good idea.

In actual practice it would be difficult to make accurate estimates of the effect of a project like this on a firm's growth rate and beta. Such estimates would be subjective guesses at best. The impact on beta would be particularly vague. Nevertheless, an exercise like this would give management a valuable insight into the potential effects of its actions on share price.

From the CFO

Adjustments to Changing Market Conditions

As the securities market changes over time, the equilibrium of the SML accommodates to the altered conditions by shifting its position. We'll consider two such movements.

THE RESPONSE TO A CHANGE IN THE RISK-FREE RATE When the risk-free rate changes, all other things held equal, the SML simply shifts up or down parallel to itself. The new equilibrium position is determined by the new rate at the vertical axis intercept. The idea is illustrated in Figure 11.10 for an increase in the risk-free rate from k_{RF} to k_{RF}^1.

The SML shifts *parallel* to itself in response to changes in the *risk-free rate*.

The shift illustrated in Figure 11.10 contains a subtlety. The parallel shift of the SML implies that its slope remains the same. Recall that the slope of the SML is the market risk premium $(k_M - k_{RF})$, which reflects the general degree of investors' risk aversion.

If the slope of the SML doesn't change when k_{RF} changes, k_M must also increase or decrease by the amount of the change in k_{RF}. This makes sense because the market rate, like any other rate, consists of the risk-free rate plus a risk premium.

THE RESPONSE TO A CHANGE IN RISK AVERSION A change in the general sensitivity of investors to risk will be reflected in a change in the market risk premium, represented as $(k_M - k_{RF})$ and as the slope of the SML in the diagram. We'll assume that k_M changes with no accompanying change in k_{RF}.

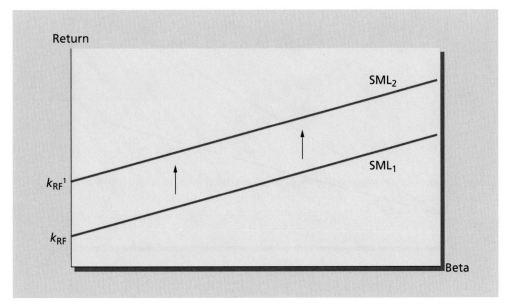

FIGURE 11.10
A Shift in the Security Market Line to Accommodate an Increase in the Risk-Free Rate

Changes in *attitudes toward risk* are reflected by *rotations of the SML* around its vertical intercept.

A change in slope alone is reflected by a rotation of the SML around the constant vertical intercept point at k_{RF}. The idea is illustrated in Figure 11.11 below.

In the illustration, SML_1 rotates to SML_2 in response to an increase in risk aversion. In other words, the average investor demands a higher risk premium on any investment to compensate for his or her increased aversion to risk. The higher premium is reflected in a steeper slope for the resulting SML.

Example 11.7

The Sidel Company has a beta of 1.25. The risk-free rate is currently 4% and the market is returning 10%. According to the SML, Sidel's required rate of return is

$$k_S = k_{RF} + (k_M - k_{RF})\beta_S = 4 + (10 - 4)1.25 = 11.5$$

a. Calculate Sidel's new required rate of return if the risk-free rate increases to 6% and investors' risk aversion remains unchanged.
b. Calculate the new required rate if the return on the market increases to 11% with the risk-free rate remaining at the original 4%.

■ **Solution:**
a. If the risk-free rate changes with no change in risk aversion, the market return has to change with it so the difference between the two remains constant. Substituting into the SML, we have

$$k_S = k_{RF} + (k_M - k_{RF})\beta_S = 6 + (12 - 6)1.25 = 13.5\%$$

In this case, interest rates in general will rise by the increase in the risk-free rate.
b. If the market return changes by itself, simply substitute the new value into the SML as follows.

$$k_S = k_{RF} + (k_M - k_{RF})\beta_S = 4 + (11 - 4)1.25 = 12.75\%$$

Here the increase in the market return reflects a higher risk premium, meaning people are more concerned about bearing risk. As a result, the rate on all risky investments will rise.
In both cases, the price of Sidel shares will fall.

FIGURE 11.11
A Rotation of the Security Market Line to Accommodate a Change in Risk Aversion

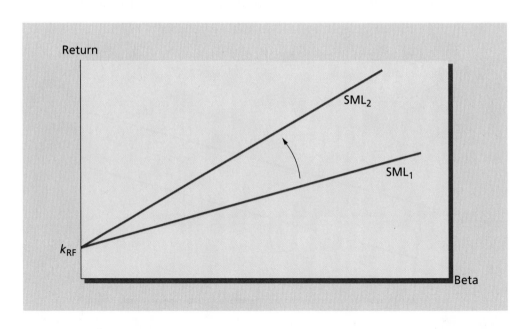

The Validity and Acceptance of the CAPM and Its SML

The capital asset pricing model is like the other models we've discussed in that it is an abstraction of reality. It's a simplification of the complex securities world, designed to help in making predictions about what share prices and returns will do. Such predictions can then be used to make various investment decisions.

The main reason for CAPM's popularity is probably its simplicity. The model's operative equation, the SML, is short and easy to understand.

In addition, CAPM provides something that's very relevant in finance, an explicit statement of the relationship between risk and return. Everyone intuitively feels there's a relation between the two, and that higher risk goes along with higher return. But until CAPM came along, no one had a usable handle on the idea. In other words, there wasn't anything that said *this* much risk is appropriate for *that* much return, and therefore I'll invest, but otherwise I won't.

Unfortunately, because models that simplify the real world have to leave a lot out, they don't always work. CAPM is no exception to that general rule. Scholars are deeply divided on its validity and usefulness. Many question whether there is any real predictive value in the SML at all, while others feel that the equation is sound but people tend to apply it incorrectly. Staunch proponents maintain that the model is entirely valid and works under most conditions.

The most important attack on the CAPM has come from the work of two well-known scholars, Eugene Fama and Kenneth French. They found no historical relationship between the returns on shares and their betas.[9] The CAPM, of course, assumes that a relationship does exist as expressed by the SML. If Fama and French are right, the CAPM isn't worth much. Other researchers, however, have challenged their work on both empirical and theoretical grounds. A lively controversy continues in the scholarly literature that is as yet inconclusive.

For our purposes, you should understand the ideas and assumptions leading up to the SML and appreciate what the equation is saying in terms of the relation between risk and return. We'll assume that it's a pretty good representation of reality most of the time.

It is important, however, to keep one limitation in mind. The model's risk as measured by beta is market risk only, and not a share's total risk. As we said earlier, that limits the concept substantially.

> The CAPM is *not universally accepted*, and a continuing debate exists as to its relevance and usefulness.

Explore a number of the business valuation techniques at http://strategis.ic.gc.ca/sc_mangb/stepstogrowth/eng-doc/download/step3.PDF.

Insights PRACTICAL FINANCE

Beta in Practice

The concept of beta as a measurement of risk is probably the most widely used piece of stock market theory today. Investment advisory services publish betas for all heavily traded shares, and people in the securities industry talk about beta all the time.

However, it's quite likely that many of the people who use the term aren't aware of exactly what it means. Beta measures risk, and risk means volatility of return, both up and down. Most people are aware of that much. But beta measures market-related volatility, not total volatility. That's what the average person forgets.

Beta means market risk only, and that's the relevant measure only if you're dealing with a large, well-diversified portfolio. If you're a moderate or small investor, beta tells only part of the story, and you can get hurt pretty badly by the part it doesn't tell.

---

9 Eugene Fama and Kenneth French, "The Cross-Section of Expected Stock Returns," *Journal of Finance,* 47, No. 2 (June 1992): pp. 427−465.

SUMMARY

1 Risk is essentially fluctuations in an investment's rate of return. The greater the fluctuations, the greater the risk and hence the higher the return demanded.

2 The one-year return on an investment can be calculated by simply taking the profit received over a period (cash flow plus any gain or loss in price) divided by the purchase price. Calculating the returns over a number of periods uses the concepts we learned in Chapters 9 and 10. For portfolios, once we know the returns on the individual investments and the proportions that those investments comprise, we can weight and sum the returns to find the return on the portfolio.

3 One measure of risk often used in analyzing investments is the dispersion about an expected value or variance. This is calculated by squaring the deviation of each outcome from the mean, weighting these by multiplying by the probability of occurrence, and then summing the results. Standard deviation is simply the square root of the outcome.

4 We found that the benefit an investor can derive from adding shares into his portfolio is very much dependent upon the relationship between these shares and the portfolio. That is, if the investor chooses shares that are similar, diversification does not work. He needs to choose shares that do not move exactly together or whose share price changes are imperfectly correlated.

5 Portfolios are used to reduce the unsystematic or business risk that the shares bring with them; once we have a well-diversified portfolio, further diversification does not reduce risk.

6 With well-diversified portfolios, systematic or market risk remains. It is this risk that the investor wants to be rewarded for taking. This risk is measured using beta.

7 Beta can be calculated by measuring the sensitivity of a share's (or portfolio's) rate of return to movement in market rates of return. When these are plotted on a graph, the slope of the resulting line is the beta of that investment.

8 The SML is used to calculate what rate of return should be earned on a share or portfolio, assuming that the markets are efficient. The model in essence says that a portfolio can be created with a beta of more than or less than 1 either by investing in shares with low or high betas, or by altering the portion of the portfolio that is invested in various assets.

KEY TERMS

Beta, p. 406
Business-specific risk, p. 401
Capital asset pricing model
   (CAPM), p. 409
Diversification, p. 402

Expected return, p. 389
Market risk, p. 401
Portfolio theory, p. 388
Required return, p. 389
Risk aversion, p. 390

Security market line (SML),
   p. 411
Stand-alone risk, p. 398

KEY FORMULAS

(11.1)

$$k = \frac{\text{Interest paid}}{\text{Loan amount}}$$

(11.2)
$$k = \frac{D_1 + (P_1 - P_0)}{P_0}$$

(11.3)
$$\text{slope} = \frac{\text{Rise}}{\text{Run}} = \frac{\Delta k_x}{\Delta k_M} = \beta_x = \text{Beta}$$

(11.4)
$$k_X = k_{RF} + (k_M - k_{RF})\beta_X$$

QUESTIONS

1. What is the general relationship between risk and return (in words)?

2. Define and discuss (words only, no equations) the concepts of expected return and required return.

3. Give a verbal definition of risk that's consistent with the way we use the word in everyday life. Discuss the weaknesses of that definition for financial theory.

4. Define risk aversion in words without reference to probability distributions. If people are risk averse, why are lotteries so popular? Why are trips to Las Vegas popular? (*Hint:* Think in terms of the size of the amount risked and entertainment value.)

5. The following definition applies to both investing and gambling: it is putting money at risk in the hope of earning more money. In spite of this similarity, society has very different moral views of the two activities.
   a. Develop an argument reconciling the differences and similarities between the two concepts. That is, why do people generally feel good about investing and bad about gambling? (*Hint:* Think of where the money goes and what part of a person's income is used.)
   b. Discuss the difference between investing and gambling by referring to the probability distributions shown on page 406. Identify the representations of a total loss, a big win, and likely outcomes.

6. Why does it make sense to think of the return on a share investment as a random variable? Does it make sense to think of the return on a bond investment that way? How about an investment in a savings account?

7. In everyday language, risk means the probability of something bad happening. Risk in finance, however, is defined as the standard deviation of the probability distribution of returns.
   a. Why do these definitions seem contradictory?
   b. Reconcile the two ideas.

8. Analyze the shape of the probability distribution for a high-risk share versus that of a low-risk share. (*Hint:* Think in terms of where the area under the curve lies.)

9. Describe risk in finance as up and down movement of return. Does this idea make sense in terms of the variance definition?

10. Define and discuss the idea of separating risk into two parts. Describe each part carefully.

11. What is the fundamental motivation behind portfolio theory? That is, what are people trying to achieve by investing in portfolios of shares rather than in a few individual shares or in debt? What observations prompted this view?

12. Describe the goal of a portfolio owner in terms of risk and return. How does he or she evaluate the risk characteristics of shares being considered for addition to the portfolio?

13. Discuss lowering portfolio risk through diversification. Consider
    a. Unsystematic (business-specific) risk.
    b. Systematic (market) risk.

14. Describe the concept of beta. Include what it measures and how it's developed.

15. Describe the SML in words. What is it saying about how investors form required rates of return? Thoroughly evaluate the implications of the SML's message.

16. How does the SML determine the price of a security?

17. How is risk aversion reflected in the SML?

18. The CAPM purports to explain how management decisions about risk can influence the well-being of shareholders. Describe in words the mechanism through which this works.

19. Is the CAPM a true and accurate representation of the securities world?

DANIER LEATHER

20. Refer to "Risk Factors at Danier Leather Inc." on page 402 and "Danier Leather International," Chapter 20, page 721. Which of the various factors mentioned are *market* risks? Which are *business-specific* risks?

Business Analysis

1. You've just begun work at the brokerage firm of Dewey, Cheatam, and Howe as a stock analyst. This morning you read an article in the paper that said a large-scale reduction in defence spending is imminent. Fred Fastbuck, a broker at the firm, has several clients who are elderly retirees. You recently learned that he's actively putting those clients into several defence industry shares he describes as low risk. Fred has told you that he feels the shares are low risk because they have betas of 1.0 or less. How would you advise Fred? Consider the real meaning of beta and its constancy over time.

PROBLEMS

1. The Duncan Company's shares are currently selling for $15. People generally expect the price to rise to $18 by the end of next year. They also expect that the shares will pay a dividend of $0.50 per share during the year.
    a. What is the expected return on an investment in Duncan's shares?
    b. Recalculate the expected return if next year's price is forecast to be only $17 and the dividend $0.25.

c. Calculate the actual return on Duncan if at the end of the year the price turns out to be $13 and the dividend actually paid was just $0.10.

2. The Rapscallion Company's shares are selling for $43.75. Dave Jones has done some research on the firm and its industry, and he thinks it will pay dividends of $5 next year and $7 the following year. After those two years Dave thinks its market price will peak at $50. His strategy is to buy now, hold for the two years, and then sell at the peak price. Dave is confident about his financial projections but requires a return of 25% before investing in shares like Rapscallion. Should he invest in this opportunity? (*Hint:* The return on a multiyear investment is the discount (interest) rate that makes the present value of the future cash flows equal to the price. See page 310 at the beginning of Chapter 9.)

3. Wayne Merritt drives from Saskatoon to Calgary frequently and has noticed that traffic and weather make a big difference in the time it takes to make the trip. As a result, he has a hard time planning activities around his arrival time. To better plan his business, Wayne wants to calculate his average driving time as well as measure how much an actual trip is likely to vary from that average. To do that, he clocked 10 trips with the following results:

Driving Time	Number of Trips
6 h, 0 min	1
6 h, 15 min	1
6 h, 30 min	2
6 h, 45 min	3
7 h, 0 min	1
7 h, 30 min	1
9 h, 20 min	1

a. Calculate the mean, standard deviation, and coefficient of variation of Wayne's driving time to Calgary.
b. Calculate the average variation in driving time. Compare the standard and average variations. Is the difference significant? Which is more meaningful to Wayne?

4. Suppose dice had four sides instead of six, so rolling a single die would produce equally likely numbers from 1 to 4, and rolling two dice would produce numbers from 2 to 8.
a. Compute the probability distribution of outcomes from rolling two dice.
b. Calculate the mean, standard deviation, and coefficient of variation of the distribution.

5. Conestoga Ltd. has the following estimated probability distribution of returns.

Return	Probability
4%	0.20
12	0.50
14	0.30

Calculate Conestoga's expected return, the variance and standard deviation of its expected return, and the return's coefficient of variation.

6. The probability distribution of the return on an investment in Omega Inc.'s common shares is as follows.

Return	Probability
5%	0.05
8	0.25
10	0.40
12	0.25
15	0.05

   Graph the probability distribution. Calculate the expected return, the standard deviation of the return, and the coefficient of variation. (Notice that to make the calculations manageable, we've made the unrealistic assumption that the probability distribution of returns is discrete.)

7. Calculate the expected return on an investment in Delta Inc.'s shares if the probability distribution of returns is as follows.

Return	Probability
−5%	0.10
5	0.25
10	0.30
15	0.25
25	0.10

   Plot the distribution on the axis with Omega Inc. in the previous problem. Looking at the graph, which company has the lower risk/variance? If offered the choice between making an investment in Delta or in Omega Inc., which would most investors choose? Why?

8. The Creston Company's shares are currently selling for $23. It has the following prospects for next year.

Share Price	Next Year's Dividend	Probability
$25	$1.00	0.25
30	1.50	0.50
35	2.00	0.25

   Calculate Creston's expected return for a one-year holding period.

9. Imagine making choices in the following situation to test your degree of risk aversion. Someone offers you the choice between the following:
   The game: A coin is tossed. If it turns up heads, you get a million dollars. If tails, you get nothing.
   The sure thing: You're given $500,000.
   a. What is the expected value of each option?
   b. Which option would you choose?
   c. Viewing the options as probability distributions, which has the larger variance? What is the variance of the sure thing? (No calculations.)

d. Suppose the game is changed to offer a payoff of $1.2 million for heads but still offers nothing for tails. The sure thing remains $500,000. What is the expected value of each option now? Would your choice of option change now?

e. Most people will have chosen the sure thing in part (d). Assuming you did too, how much would the game's payoff have to increase before you would choose it over the sure thing?

f. Relate this exercise to Figure 11.6 on page 398.

10. A portfolio consists of the following four shares.

Share	Current Market Value	Expected Return
A	$ 180,000	8%
B	145,000	10
C	452,000	12
D	223,000	5
	$ 1,000,000	

What is the expected return of the portfolio?

11. Laurel Wilson has a portfolio of five shares. The shares' actual investment performance last year is given below along with an estimate of this year's performance.

Share	Last Year Investment	Return	This Year Investment	Return
A	$ 50,000	8.0%	$ 55,000	8.5%
B	40,000	6.0	40,000	7.0
C	80,000	4.0	60,000	4.5
D	20,000	12.0	45,000	9.0
E	60,000	3.0	50,000	5.0

Compute the actual return on Laurel's overall portfolio last year and its expected return this year.

12. The shares in the previous problem have the following betas:

Share	Beta
A	1.1
B	0.6
C	1.0
D	1.6
E	0.8

Calculate Laurel's portfolio beta for last year and for this year. Assume that the changes in investment (value) come from changing share prices rather than buying and selling shares. What has happened to the riskiness of Laurel's portfolio? Should she be concerned?

13. Charming Co. manufactures decorating products. Treasury bills currently yield 5.4% and the market is returning 8.1%.

a. Calculate Charming Co.'s beta from its characteristic line as depicted below.

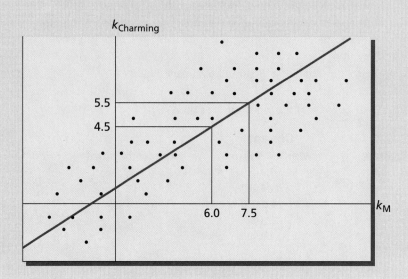

b. What expected return would an average investor require to buy shares of Charming?

c. Would the answer to part (b) be "a 'fair' return"? Why?

14. A four-share portfolio is made up as follows.

Share	Current Value	Beta
A	$ 4,500	0.8
B	2,900	0.6
C	6,800	1.3
D	1,200	1.8

Calculate the portfolio's beta.

15. The return on Holland—Wilson Inc. (HWI) shares over the last three years is shown below along with the market's return for the same period.

Year	HWI	Market
1	4.0%	3.0%
2	9.0	6.0
3	12.0	10.0

Plot HWI's return against that of the market in each of the three years. Make three estimates of HWI's beta by drawing characteristic lines between pairs of data points (1 and 2; 1 and 3; 2 and 3). What does this range of betas imply about the shares' risk relative to an average share?

16. You have recently purchased shares in Topical Inc. which has returned between 7% and 9% over the last three years. Your friend, Bob, has criticized your purchase and insists that you should have invested in Combs Inc., as he did, because it's been returning between 10% and 12% in the last three years. Bob knows nothing about financial theory. Topical's beta is 0.7 and Comb's is 1.2. Treasury bills are currently yielding the risk-free rate of 4.2%, while the stock market is returning an average rate of 9.4%.

    a. What return should you expect from Topical? What return should Bob expect from Combs?

    b. Write a few words explaining to Bob why these expected returns aren't the whole story.

17. Erin Behlen has a three share portfolio and is interested in estimating its overall return next year. She has $25,000 invested in Forms Corp., which has a beta of 1.3, $75,000 in Crete Corp. with a beta of 0.8 and $20,000 in Stalls Corp, which has a beta of 1.45. The stock market is currently returning 10.2% and Treasury bills are yielding 4.6%. What return should Erin anticipate on her portfolio?

18. The CFO of Ramekin Pottery Inc. is concerned about holding up the price of the company's shares. He's asked you to do an analysis starting with an estimate of the return investors are likely to require before they will invest in the firm. The overall stock market is currently returning 16%, 90-day Treasury bills yield 4%, and the return on Ramekin's shares typically responds to changes in the political and economic environment only about 60% as vigorously as does that of the average share.

    a. Prepare an estimate of the firm's required return using the CAPM.

    b. Is a higher or lower required return good for the company? Why?

    c. Suppose the CFO asks you what management can do to improve the required return. How will you respond?

    d. What will you tell him if he wants it done within the next three months?

19. You are a junior treasury analyst at the Pipestone Corporation. The treasurer believes the CAPM gives a good estimate of the company's return to equity investors at any time, and has asked you to prepare an estimate of that return by using the SML. Treasury bills currently yield 4.5%, but may go up or down by 1%. The S&P/TSX Composite Index shows a return of 10% but may vary from that figure up to 12%. Pipestone's beta is 0.8. Construct a table showing all possible values of $k_{Pipestone}$ for 1% increments of k_{RF} and k_M (nine entries). For this problem treat k_M and k_{RF} separately. That is, do not assume an increase in k_M when k_{RF} changes.

20. The Framingham Company expects to grow at 4% indefinitely. Economists are currently asserting that investment opportunities in Treasury bills are readily available at a risk-free rate of 5%. The stock market is returning an average rate of 9%. Framingham's beta has recently been calculated at 1.4. The firm recently paid an annual dividend of $1.68 per share. At what price should Framingham shares be selling?

21. Whole Foods Inc. paid a quarterly dividend of $0.47 recently. Treasury bills are yielding 4%, and the average share is returning about 11%. Whole Foods is a stable company. The return on its shares responds to changes in the political and economic environment only about 70% as vigorously as that of the average share.

    Analysts expect the firm to grow at an annual rate of 3.5% into the indefinite future. Calculate a reasonable price that investors should be willing to pay for Whole Foods shares.

22. Strathclyde Software Inc. recently paid an annual dividend of $1.95 per share and is expected to grow at a 15% rate indefinitely. Government of Canada Treasury bills are paying 4%, while an average share is earning its owner 11%. Strathclyde is a very volatile share, responding to the economic climate two and a half times as violently as an average share. This is, however, typical of the software industry.

    a. How much should a share of Strathclyde be worth?

    b. Do you see any problems with this estimate? Change one assumption to something more reasonable and compare the results.

23. The Aldridge Co. is expected to grow at 6% into the indefinite future. Its latest annual dividend was $2.50. Treasury bills currently earn 5% and the S&P/TSX Composite Index yields 11%.

    a. What price should Aldridge shares command in the market if its beta is 1.3?

    b. Evaluate the sensitivity of Aldridge's price to changes in expected growth and risk by recalculating the price while varying the growth rate between 5% and 7% (increments of 1%) and varying beta between 1.2 and 1.4 (increments of 0.1).

24. Bergman Corp. has experienced zero growth over the last seven years, paying an annual dividend of $2.00 per share. Investors generally expect this performance to continue. Bergman shares are currently selling for $24.39. The risk-free rate is 3.0%, and Bergman's beta is 1.3.

    a. Calculate the return investors require on Bergman's shares.

    b. Calculate the market return.

    c. Suppose you think Bergman is about to announce plans to grow at 3.0% into the foreseeable future. You also believe investors will accept that prediction and continue to require the same return on its shares. How much should you be willing to pay for a Bergman share?

25. Weisman Electronics just paid a $1.00 dividend, the market yield is yielding 10%, the risk-free rate is 4%, and Weisman's beta is 1.5. How fast do investors expect the company to grow in the future if its shares are selling for $27.25?

26. Weisman Electronics from the previous problem is considering acquiring an unrelated business. Management thinks the move could change the firm's share price by moving its beta up or down and decreasing its growth rate. A consultant has estimated that Weisman's beta after the acquisition could be anywhere between 1.3 and 1.7 while the growth rate could remain at 9% or decline to as little as 8%. Calculate a range of intrinsic values for Weisman's shares based on best- and worst-case scenarios. (*Hint:* Consider combinations of the highest and lowest beta and growth rate, but don't make four sets of calculations. Think through which way a change in each variable moves share price and evaluate only two scenarios.)

27. Broken Wing Airlines just paid a $2 dividend and has a beta of 1.3 and a growth rate of 6% for the foreseeable future. The current return on the market is 10%, and Treasury bills earn 4%. If the rate on Treasury bills drops by 0.5% and the market risk premium $(k_M - k_{RF})$ increases by 1.0%, what growth rate would keep Broken Wing's share price constant?

28. Lipson Ltd. expects a constant growth rate of 5% in the future. Treasury bills yield 4% and the market is returning 13% on an average issue. Lipson's last annual dividend was $1.35. The company's beta has historically been 0.9. The introduction of a new line of business would increase the expected growth rate to 7% while increasing its risk substantially. Management estimates the firm's beta would increase to 1.2 if the new line were undertaken. Should Lipson undertake the new line of business?

29. The Picante Corp.'s beta is 0.7. Treasury bills yield 5% and an average share yields 10%.
   a. Write and sketch the SML and locate Picante on it. Calculate Picante's required rate of return and show it on the graph.
   b. Assume the yield on Treasury bills suddenly increases to 7% with no other changes in the financial environment. Write and sketch the new SML, calculate Picante's new required rate, and show it on the new line.
   c. Now assume that besides the change in part (b), investors' risk aversion increases so that the market risk premium is 7%. Write and sketch the resulting SML, calculate Picante's required return, and show it on the last line.

Computer Problems

30. Problem 21 in Chapter 10 concerned the Rollins Metal Company, which is engaged in long-term planning. The firm is trying to choose among several strategic options that imply different future growth rates and risk levels. Reread that problem on page 382 now.

The CAPM gives some additional insight into the relation between risk and required return. We can now define risk as beta, and evaluate its effect on share price by constructing a chart similar to the one called for in Problem 21 of Chapter 10, replacing k on the left side with beta (β).

Rollins's beta calculated from historical data is 0.8. However the risky strategies being considered could influence that figure significantly. Management believes beta could rise to as much as 2.0 under certain strategic options. Treasury bills currently yield 3% while the S&P/TSX Composite Index is showing a return of 8%. Recall that Rollins's last dividend was $2.35.
   a. Use the CAPMVAL program to construct the following chart.

The Price of Rollins Shares as a Function of Growth Rate and Beta

		Growth Rates (*g*)			
		6%	8%	10%	12%
Beta (*β*)	0.8				
	1.2				
	1.6				
	2.0				

CAPMVAL is one of the several Excel® templates available on the text's support website.

b. The effect of beta on required return and price is influenced by the general level of risk aversion, which in the CAPM is represented by $(k_M - k_{RF})$, the market risk premium (also the slope of the SML). In part (a) of this problem, the market risk premium is $(8\% - 3\% =) 5\%$. Economists, however, predict a recession, which could sharply increase risk aversion. Reconstruct the chart above assuming the market risk premium increases to 7% (k_M rises to 10% with no change in k_{RF}).

c. Do your charts give any new insights into the risk-return-growth relationship? (That is, how does the reward for bearing more risk in terms of share price change in recessionary times?) Write the implied required return on your charts next to the values of beta. Then compare the charts with the one from Problem 21 of Chapter 10.

d. Does the inclusion of beta and the CAPM really make management's planning job any less intuitive? In other words, is it any easier to associate a strategy's risk level with a beta than directly with a required return?

Developing Software

31. Write a spreadsheet program to calculate the expected return and beta for a portfolio of 10 shares given the expected returns and betas of the shares in the portfolio and their dollar values.

The calculation involves taking a weighted average of the individual shares' expected returns and betas where the weights are based on the dollar values invested in each share.

Set up your spreadsheet like this:

	Share	Value	Weight	Beta	Factor	k_e	Factor
1.	ABC	$ 5,530	0.0645	.93	0.0600	8.0%	0.5160
2.	EFG	2,745	0.0320	1.25	0.0400	12.2%	0.3904
		•	•	•	•	•	•
		•	•	•	•	•	•
		•	•	•	•	•	•
10.	XYZ	9,046	1.1055	1.12	0.1182	11.5%	1.2133
		$ 85,715	1.0000		XXX		XXX

Sum columns for: Portfolio beta
Portfolio k_e

The computational procedure is as follows.
1. Input the names of the shares, their dollar values, their betas, and their k_e's values.
2. Sum the value column.
3. Calculate the weight column by dividing each row's value cell by the cell carrying the sum of the values.
4. Calculate the beta and k_e factors by multiplying the individual beta and k_e cells by the cells in the weight column on the same row.
5. Sum the two factor columns for the results indicated.

Is your program general in that it will handle a portfolio of up to 10 shares, or will it only work for exactly 10? If it is general, what do you have to be careful about with respect to inputs?

Extra: Assume you have $1 million to invest in shares. Look up several shares' betas at **http://fpdata.finpost.com/suite/autologanalyzer.asp** and estimate k_e for each. Look up the current price of each share in *The Financial Post* and form a hypothetical portfolio by allocating your money among the shares. Find your portfolio's expected return and beta using your program.

Chapter 12

Capital Budgeting

Learning Objectives

1 Define capital budgeting as the financial plans and analysis required to justify large expenditures on long-run investments in capital assets.

2 Explain that an investment project may involve a replacement, expansion, or new venture, and that risk varies with the type of project.

3 Describe the difference between stand-alone projects and mutually exclusive projects.

4 Explain the cash flows that result from such investment decisions.

5 Discuss the use of cost of capital as the discount rate in capital budgeting analysis.

6 Perform analysis using payback period, net present value, internal rate of return, and profitability index to assist in decision making.

7 Use the equivalent annual annuity method to compare competing projects with unequal lives.

8 Explain the concept of capital rationing.

Assume that management is considering a new computer system. In deciding whether or not to spend the money for this capital asset, what factors might be considered? Well, is the investment optional, or is it required to stay in business? If it is optional, will the business get back more than it invested? How long will it take the business to break even on the investment? Does it have the funds or can it raise the money required? Could it invest the money in something else and earn a better return?

We use *capital budgeting* techniques to assist companies in the decision-making process for capital asset investments.

The money companies spend in the normal course of business can be divided into two categories. Funds are used on an everyday basis to buy inventory, pay expenses, and compensate employees. These expenditures can be thought of as short term in that they support daily activity.

In addition to such short-term expenditures, firms spend large sums on special projects from time to time. For example, machines normally wear out and need to be replaced every few years. The replacement expenditures tend to be relatively large, but are infrequent. New business ventures provide a second example because they generally require initial spending to get started. Start-up amounts are usually large, but the opportunities don't come along often. Spending on things like these is long term because the projects involved tend to last for long periods. As a general rule, money spent on long-term projects is called *capital*.

The field known as capital budgeting involves planning and justifying how capital dollars are spent on long-term projects. It provides methods through which projects are evaluated to decide whether or not they make sense for a particular business at a point in time. Capital budgeting also provides a basis for choosing between projects when more than one is under consideration at the same time.

> *All departments in the organization may be involved in the capital budgeting process. For instance, the marketing department may propose new products, the operations department may request additional production facilities, and the financial function may set limits on the amount of financing available.*

Capital budgeting techniques analyze money spent on long-term assets and projects.

From the CFO

CHARACTERISTICS OF BUSINESS PROJECTS

Project Types and Risk

Projects fit into three general categories: replacement, expansion, and new venture. We've already mentioned the first and last of these project types above. Expansion simply involves doing something the firm already does on a larger scale. It usually requires investing money in additional resources and equipment similar to those already on hand.

A risk is associated with investing money in any project. For now, we'll define that risk simply as the chance of making less on the project than management expects when the decision to go ahead is made.

Broadly speaking, risk varies with project type, increasing as we move from replacement to expansion to new venture. A replacement is the safest endeavour because we're doing something that's already being done. Expansion projects are riskier because they are based on a forecast increase in demand for the company's product that may not materialize. Finally, the riskiest project is a new venture, something the company hasn't done before. No one ever knows whether they'll be successful at something they haven't tried.

Capital projects have *increasing risk* according to whether they are *replacements, expansions,* or *new ventures.*

Stand-Alone and Mutually Exclusive Projects

Projects can be evaluated in either of two contexts. The first involves a proposal without a competing alternative. For example, suppose an old machine is wearing out and there's only one replacement product on the market. The choice is simply whether to buy the new machine (the project) or to do nothing.

This single-project situation is known as a stand-alone project. We need to decide on a project's viability by itself, standing alone. Is it a good deal for the company or not? Another way to think of it is to say that no other project is currently competing for the resources required to do this one.

A **stand-alone project** has no competing alternatives, whereas **mutually exclusive projects** exclude one another.

DANIER LEATHER

Capital Spending at Danier Leather Inc.

Refer to the financial statements and other financial information for Danier Leather Inc. in Appendix 3A, page 92.

The statement of cash flows reports that Danier spent some $9,700,000 during 2006 to acquire new capital assets. The *management's discussion and analysis* section provided details:

$3,500,000	Opening one new power centre outlet and one new shopping mall store, renovations in six stores, visual display equipment and other store expenditures
$5,300,000	Implementation of a new point-of-sale hardware, software and customer relationship management system, other information technology
$200,000	Production machinery and equipment

Shopping mall and power centre locations were opened where planned sales, store profit and return on investment criteria were met. Two underperforming shopping mall stores whose leases expired were closed.

Source: Danier Leather Annual Report, 2006.

The second situation involves choosing between projects. It occurs either when there's more than one way to do something, or two different things are proposed but there's only enough money to do one of them. As an example of the first circumstance, assume the worn-out machine can be replaced by either of two new ones. Suppose the first option is relatively cheap to buy, but is expensive to operate and produces low-quality output. The second costs more initially, but runs less expensively and produces better product. Which should the firm choose? Notice that it must choose one or the other, because only one replacement is required. In this context, the alternatives are said to be **mutually exclusive projects**, as choosing either excludes the other.

Sometimes projects can be mutually exclusive even if they're totally different physically. That occurs when a firm has only enough resources to do one project at a time. For example, suppose an electronics firm has new venture opportunities in computer technology and radio transmission, but has only enough money to undertake one new idea. The projects are mutually exclusive because doing one precludes doing the other, even though from business and technical viewpoints they're entirely separate. Further, the limiting resource doesn't have to be money. It might be trained personnel, plant capacity, or management's time.

Project Cash Flows

The first step in the capital budgeting process requires that any project under consideration be represented in a series of cash flows[1] that is incremental to the business.

> The first and usually most difficult step in capital budgeting is *quantifying projects in a series of cash flows.*

This requirement is easiest to picture in the context of a new venture. Imagine that such a new business will take an initial investment of $50,000, will lose $10,000 in the first year, and is expected to generate $15,000 in cash each year for the next five years before being shut down. For capital budgeting purposes, the project can be summarized as just that series of yearly cash outflows and inflows. If we call the cash flow in the first year C_1, in the second year C_2, etc. and let C_0 be the initial investment at the beginning of year 1, we can

---

1 For capital budgeting purposes, we will use the *incremental cash flows, after tax*, which result from the investment in the project. We will discuss these concepts further in Chapter 13.

represent the project as follows, where the numbers in parentheses are negative and represent outflows.

C_0	$(50,000)
C_1	(10,000)
C_2	15,000
C_3	15,000
C_4	15,000
C_5	15,000
C_6	15,000

It's important to notice the pattern of cash flows shown here. Projects nearly always involve an initial outflow of funds followed by inflows at later dates. C_0 is virtually always negative because it represents the initial outlay necessary to get a project started. The remaining figures tend to be positive, although they may include some negatives, as in the example.

> Business projects involve *early cash outflows* and later inflows. The *initial outlay* is required to get started.

The initial investment is $50,000 for the proposed project. This is the cash outflow required now, at time zero (C_0). It may include expenditures for new or increased assets or expenses.

The cash flows (C_1 to C_6) represent the net changes to cash flows, after tax, that result from using the project during its life. These inflows are the reason the initial investment is made: they may involve differences in revenues, costs, or working capital levels.

Sometimes there is an additional cash *inflow* received at the end of the project (the *salvage value*). The salvage value, usually received at the end of the final year, may result from sale or salvage of the remains of the investment.

> The **salvage value** is the estimated proceeds on disposal of an asset at the end of its useful life.

It's conceptually easy to identify incremental cash flows for a new venture. The representation can be more difficult to see when we're talking about a replacement project. Then incremental cash flows are things like savings on fuel and maintenance or improved profitability due to higher-quality product. That kind of incremental cash flow can be hard to quantify.

In fact, the most difficult and inaccurate part of capital budgeting is estimating project cash flows. For the time being we'll proceed by assuming the estimates are given for the projects we'll be talking about. In the next chapter, we'll return to the issue and consider cash flow estimation in more detail.

The Cost of Capital

Capital budgeting theory is based on the time value of money and the idea of return on investment. A central concept in the theory is the idea of a firm's cost of capital. This is the rate of return the firm pays to its long-term investors or creditors for the use of their money.

> A firm's **cost of capital** is the *average rate it pays its investors* or creditors for the use of their money.

The purpose of the concept is intuitively obvious: An investment makes sense only if it earns more than the cost of funds put into it.

For example, suppose you want to start a business in which you expect to earn a return of 15% on invested money. Further suppose you have no money of your own, but can borrow from a relative who demands 18% interest. Does it make sense to start the business? Of course not; you'd be losing money from the outset because you'd have to pay more for your funds than you could earn using them. It would make sense to begin the business only if you could borrow the start-up money at *less than* 15%. In this illustration, the cost of capital is the rate at which you can borrow to undertake the venture.

In general, firms have two sources of capital, equity and debt, and pay different rates of return to the investors and creditors who supply each. In practice, the cost of capital is a single rate that reflects the average of the rates for those two sources.

Here's a simple example. Suppose the total dollar amount of a firm's capital is 75% equity and 25% debt. Assume the shareholders are receiving a 10% return on equity, while the creditors are getting 8% interest on debt. The cost of capital is the *weighted average* of the two returns where the weights are the proportionate amounts of money invested in each of the two kinds of capital. The calculation follows.

	Portion		Return	
Equity	0.75	×	10%	= 7.5%
Debt	0.25	×	8%	= 2.0%
Weighted average cost of capital				= 9.5%

In other words, the cost of capital is a blending of the rates the company pays for its funds. The idea seems simple enough, but can get very complicated in practice.[2]

It's an important concept, and we'll devote an entire chapter (Chapter 15) to it later in the book. For now we'll assume that every firm knows what its cost of capital is, and measures opportunities against it.

CAPITAL BUDGETING TECHNIQUES

In what follows, we'll look at four capital budgeting techniques. Each consists of a series of calculations and a set of decision rules. Using any technique involves calculating a number that the technique associates with a project and then applying the decision rules to that number. Each technique has slightly different decision rules for stand-alone and mutually exclusive situations.

Payback Period

The **payback period** is the time it takes to recover early cash outflows. *Shorter* paybacks are preferred.

The simplest capital budgeting technique is the **payback period**. In it we calculate the amount of time it takes for a project's planned cash flows to "pay back" the initial outlay. In other words, we measure the time it takes for the project to break even. This time period is the parameter used for making comparisons. Payback is most meaningful when there's just one cash outflow at the beginning of the project, and is most easily understood through a numerical illustration.

In the following table, an initial outlay of $200,000 is followed by four inflows of $60,000. The payback period is easily visualized by displaying the cumulative cash flow below the yearly cash flows.

	Year				
	0	**1**	**2**	**3**	**4**
Cash flow (C_n)	$(200,000)	$ 60,000	$ 60,000	$ 60,000	$60,000
Cumulative cash flow	$(200,000)	$(140,000)	$(80,000)	$(20,000)	$40,000

Notice that the cumulative cash flow is negative by $20,000 after three years and positive by $40,000 after four years. If cash is assumed to flow evenly throughout the year, breakeven occurs after (3 + 20,000/60,000 =) 3.33 years, that is, after three years and four months. This length of time is the payback period for the project.

---

2 We've oversimplified for the sake of this preliminary illustration. As we'll see in Chapter 15, the cost of debt must take into account the tax deductibility of interest.

Payback Decision Rules

STAND-ALONE PROJECTS Clearly, decision rules in the payback technique are based on the idea that it's better to recover invested money sooner rather than later. Companies that use the technique generally have stated policies for the maximum time allowable for capital recovery. The stand-alone decision rule is simply that an acceptable project's payback period must be less than that policy maximum. We can state that rule conveniently as follows.

$$\text{NPV} > 0 \rightarrow \text{Accept}$$
$$\text{NPV} < 0 \rightarrow \text{Reject}$$

MUTUALLY EXCLUSIVE PROJECTS By the same reasoning, we generally prefer a project that pays back sooner to one that pays back later. Therefore the mutually exclusive decision rule for payback is simply *shorter is better*. If P/B_A and P/B_B represent the payback periods for projects A and B, respectively, we can write the decision rule like this.

$$P/B_A < P/B_B \rightarrow \text{Choose project A over project B}$$

Weaknesses of the Payback Method

Payback is a generally unsophisticated approach to capital budgeting that is criticized for two major shortcomings. First, it ignores the time value of money. Thus future dollars are weighted equally with current dollars in the calculations. This is clearly a distortion of values. Second, it ignores cash flows after the payback period. This deficiency can lead to a poor decision even in simple cases.

Example 12.1

Use the payback period technique to choose between mutually exclusive projects A and B.

	Project A	Project B
C_0	$ (1,200)	$ (1,200)
C_1	400	400
C_2	400	400
C_3	400	350
C_4	200	800
C_5	200	800

■ **Solution:** Project A's payback period is clearly three years, because its initial $1,200 investment is entirely recovered in that time. Project B is identical to A for the first two years and only slightly different in the third year, when the cash inflow is just $50 lower. However, that slightly lower payment in year 3 means that B's payback isn't complete until sometime in the fourth year. In other words, the payback period is a little longer for project B than for project A. The payback decision rule therefore chooses A over B. But B is clearly the better project because of what goes on after year 3 when B receives much larger cash inflows. The differences in years 4 and 5 overwhelm the minor difference in year 3, but are ignored by the method.

Go to the Business Owner's Toolkit http://www.toolkit. cch.com for more on how to complete a cost–benefit analysis using financial analysis tools. Click on Managing Your Business Finances, Major Projects and Purchases, and How can you make an objective decision to learn how to tell if a project makes sense over the long haul.

Why Use the Payback Method?

It's reasonable to ask why anyone uses the payback method given these weaknesses. The answer is that the method is quick and easy to apply, and serves as a rough screening device.

If a project flunks payback, it's likely to be dismissed without further consideration. If it passes, one of the more sophisticated methods will be applied in further analysis. As well, choosing a shorter payback may be important for some companies, particularly if they are concerned about liquidity.

The Present Value Payback Method

A variation on the method attempts to correct one of its deficiencies, the fact that it ignores time value. In this approach the payback calculation is made after taking the *present value* of all the cash flows at an appropriate discount rate.

This approach makes logical sense, but still ignores cash flows after the payback period while losing the method's "quick and dirty" simplicity. As a result, it's rarely used.

Net Present Value (NPV)

A project's **NPV** is the sum of the present values of its cash inflows and outflows at the *cost of capital*.

A fundamental principle of finance and economics is that the present value of future cash flows is what counts when making decisions based on value. The **net present value (NPV)** technique applies this idea to the analysis of projects.

In the net present value technique, we calculate the present value of each of a project's cash flows and add them together. The result is the net present value of the *project*, usually referred to as the NPV. The word "net" implies an offsetting of pluses against minuses, which reflects the fact that some flows are positive (inflows) and others are negative (outflows). Decisions about which projects to undertake are then based on project NPVs.

The present value calculations are made using the firm's *cost of capital* (k), an interest rate. This is an important point; the appropriate discount rate for most NPV calculations is the firm's cost of capital as described earlier in this chapter.

We can represent a project's NPV with the following equation.

$$(12.1) \qquad NPV = -C_0 + \frac{C_1}{(1+k)} + \frac{C_2}{(1+k)^2} + \dots + \frac{C_n}{(1+k)^n}$$

where C_1 represents the project's cash flow in the first year, etc., and C_0 reflects the initial outlay (hence the negative sign). Notice that we're representing the present value calculation as division by powers of $(1+k)$. Also notice that C_0 isn't divided by anything. That's because the initial cash flow is assumed to occur immediately, in the present.

It's important to think about the signs of the C-values in Equation 12.1, remembering that negatives are cash outflows and positives are inflows. As we said earlier, the negatives tend to occur first, followed by the positives. Equation 12.1 says that the NPV is the difference between the present values of all the positives and all the negatives. If the present value of the inflows (positives) is greater, NPV is a positive number. NPV is negative if the present value of the outflows is larger.

NPV and Shareholder Wealth

An insightful way to look at capital spending projects involves their impact on shareholder wealth. A project's net present value is the net effect that its undertaking is expected to have on the value of the firm. If a positive NPV project is taken on and successfully completed, the economic value of the firm should be increased by exactly the amount of the project's NPV. Conversely, a negative NPV project will decrease the value of the firm by the amount of the negative NPV.

Therefore, a capital spending program that maximizes the NPV of projects undertaken will contribute to maximizing shareholder wealth, the ideal goal of management. This direct link to shareholder wealth maximization makes NPV the most theoretically correct capital budgeting technique.

So far we've been discussing NPVs for projects to be undertaken in the future. It's important to realize that cash flows may not actually turn out as expected. So a project that has a high *planned* NPV may turn out to have a very different impact on shareholder wealth after it's completed. Nevertheless, before the fact, the planned NPV is our best estimate of the future outcome. We'll talk a lot more about the differences between planned and actual numbers in the next chapter.

Decision Rules

STAND-ALONE PROJECTS Clearly, a project in which the present value of planned cash inflows exceeds the present value of outflows is desirable.[3] Conversely, one in which the outflows are larger is undesirable. These situations correspond to projects with positive and negative NPVs, respectively. This logic leads to the *stand-alone decision rule*.

$$NPV > 0 \rightarrow \text{Accept}$$
$$NPV < 0 \rightarrow \text{Reject}$$

In a broader context, a positive NPV means that the project is "financially supported." A final "accept" or "reject" decision depends on all the qualitative and quantitative information available, including the financial analysis. For instance, the project may have an acceptable NPV, but the firm may not have the financial or managerial resources to make the investment!

A *positive NPV* implies an acceptable project on a *stand-alone* basis.

From the CFO

NPV Solutions Using Financial Calculators

Some financial calculators are programmed to find the NPV for a general set of cash flows. The financial calculator will find a project's NPV quickly once the associated cash flows are entered. The input process varies among different models of calculators and can be a little tricky, so you'll probably have to refer to its user manual. We'll outline how to solve problems using a **Texas Instruments BAII PLUS**™ calculator.

To enter cash flows on the BAII PLUS, begin by pressing the **CF** button to enter the cash flow mode, and then clear the working memory by pressing **2nd** and then **CLR Work.**

The calculator is programmed to prompt the user for the cash flows one at a time, starting with the initial outlay that it calls **CF$_0$**(we've called this figure C$_0$). Type in the value, make it negative (an outflow) by hitting the $+/-$ key, and then press **ENTER.** (After entering a number, press the $\downarrow$ key to move to the prompt for the next input item.)

The machine then prompts for up to 24 *different* cash flows, referred to as **C01, C02, ..., C24.** However, after each of these cash flows is entered, the machine prompts for a "frequency" displayed as **F01, F02, ..., F24.** The frequency allows you to repeat the last cash flow entered up to 9,999 times before moving on to the next *different* cash flow. If you don't enter a frequency, the machine assumes 1. For example, the series

$$-500 \quad 100 \quad 200 \quad 200 \quad 200 \quad 800$$

can be entered with the following inputs.

Key	Input
CF$_0$	−500
C01	100
F01	
C02	200
F02	3
C03	800

You can move back and forth through the cash flow and frequency figures you've entered using the $\downarrow\uparrow$ keys. Cash flows can also be inserted, deleted, or changed using procedures outlined in the user's manual.

3 What about a zero NPV? Although we do not mention it in the rule, it too is acceptable. Why? Because a zero NPV means you received exactly the return you demanded. That is, you got a fair deal.

Once a project's cash flows are in the calculator, calculating NPV is easy. To find the NPV, begin by pressing the **NPV** button. The machine will prompt for **I**, the interest rate at which you want to do the present value calculation (this is generally the cost of capital we've called k). Type the interest rate as a whole number (e.g., 12 for 12%) and press **ENTER**. Now press ↓ and then **CPT** (for compute). The project's NPV will appear on the screen.

Example 12.2

Project Alpha has the following cash flows.

C_0	C_1	C_2	C_3
$(5,000)	$1,000	$2,000	$3,000

If the firm considering Alpha has a cost of capital of 12%, should the project be undertaken?

Calculator Solution

Key	Input
CF_0	−5,000
C01	1,000
C02	2,000
C03	3,000
I	12.0

Answer

NPV	$(377.41)^4$

■ **Solution:** Project Alpha's NPV is found by summing the present values of all of the cash flows at the firm's cost of capital. Using Table A-2, page xxx, we'll calculate the present values by multiplying each cash flow by the present value factor for 12% and one, two, or three years, respectively. This is equivalent to dividing by powers of $(1 + k)$ as shown in Equation 12.1; that is:

$$NPV = \$(5,000) + \frac{\$1,00}{1.12} + \frac{\$2,000}{(1.12)^2} + \frac{\$3,000}{(1.12)^3}$$

Remember that C_0 isn't factored because it's a present cash flow.

Year	Cash Flow	PV Factor	PV of Cash Flow
0	$(5,000)	1.0000	$ (5,000.00)
1	1,000	0.8929	892.90
2	2,000	0.7972	1,594.40
3	3,000	0.7118	2,135.40
		NPV = $	$(377.30)^4$

Project Alpha's NPV is negative at the firm's cost of capital, so it should not be undertaken.

It's important to notice that even though a project's total inflows exceed its outflows, it can still have a negative NPV. The reason is that the inflows are generally farther in the future, so the present valuing process diminishes their value more than it does that of the outflows. In the example, the undiscounted value of the inflows adds to $6,000 while the single outflow is only $5,000. Nevertheless, on a present value basis, the inflows are less than the outflows.

MUTUALLY EXCLUSIVE PROJECTS The more the present value of cash inflows exceeds outflows, the larger is a project's NPV and the more it can be expected to contribute to shareholder wealth. In other words, *a bigger NPV is better than a smaller NPV.* This leads to the *mutually exclusive decision rule.*

$$NPV_A > NPV_B \rightarrow \text{Choose project A over B}$$

where NPV_A and NPV_B are the net present values of projects A and B, respectively.

The idea is straightforward on its face: Choose the project with the largest NPV. However, several questions come up in actual practice. The following example provides another drill on calculating NPVs and applying the decision rules; at the same time it raises some issues related to the practical application of the method.

---

4 As in earlier chapters, you'll notice that there is a slight rounding difference when we compare the Excel® and financial calculator solutions to those derived from financial tables.

Example 12.3

The Xavier Motor Company makes outdoor power equipment including lawn mowers and garden tractors, and is considering two diversification ventures. The first involves manufacturing a larger, more powerful tractor than the firm has made up until now. Market research indicates a substantial demand for more powerful equipment, and some competitors are already moving in that direction. The second opportunity involves building snow blowers. The manufacturing and engineering technology required for making snow blowers is essentially the same as that for building garden equipment, but Xavier has never made snow blowers before.

Management wants to make a decision based on only five years of projected cash flows, because it feels that the future beyond that time is too vague to form a basis for current decisions. In other words, if a project isn't expected to earn enough to justify itself in five years, management considers it too risky.

Working with representatives from the marketing, engineering, and manufacturing departments, a financial analyst has put together a set of projected incremental cash flows for each project. Xavier's cost of capital is 9%.

Xavier Motor Company Project Estimates ($000)

Year	Tractor	Snow Blower
0	$(3,000)	$(3,500)
1	(250)	(700)
2	500	800
3	1,000	1,200
4	1,500	2,000
5	1,500	2,000

A financial analysis of the project situation should provide answers to the following questions.

a. If these projects were being considered on a stand-alone basis, would either or both be acceptable?

b. If Xavier can raise no more than $5 million for new projects, which of these projects should be chosen?

c. If Xavier's management were willing to consider two more years of projected cash flow, and the contributions continued at the level of the last two years, which project would be chosen?

d. Are any risk considerations relevant beyond the numbers in this situation?

■ **Solution:** We begin by calculating the NPV for each project. We'll show these calculations in tabular form, multiplying the yearly cash flows by the present value factor for 9% and the appropriate year ($PVF_{9,n}$) rather than dividing by powers of $(1 + k)$.

Xavier Motor Company NPV Project Analysis ($000)

Year	Factor	Cash Flows Tractor	Cash Flows Snow Blower	PV of Cash Flows Tractor	PV of Cash Flows Snow Blower
0	1.0000	$(3,000)	$(3,500)	$ (3,000)	$ (3,500)
1	0.9174	(250)	(700)	(229)	(642)
2	0.8417	500	800	421	673
3	0.7722	1,000	1,200	772	927
4	0.7084	1,500	2,000	1,063	1,417
5	0.6499	1,500	2,000	975	1,300
			NPV =	$ 2	$ 175

We can answer the first two questions immediately from the foregoing calculations.

a. Both projects have a positive NPV and are therefore acceptable on a stand-alone basis. However, neither is positive by very much in relation to the size of the investments involved.

The tractor project is especially marginal. This result is bound to raise some questions about the advisability of the projects. For now we'll just note that the projects are acceptable in accordance with the NPV method, and return to the issue of accuracy later.

b. The projects are mutually exclusive, because their initial outlays total $6.5 million and the company has only $5.0 million available for capital projects. In the mutually exclusive situation, the snow blower appears to have the edge, but not by much.

The next two questions require a few calculations and a lot more judgment.

c. The distant future is always hard to pin down. It's easy to forecast great sales and profitability six or more years in the future. Exuberant sales and marketing people do it all the time. The question is, how much of those forecasts should a reasonably prudent financial manager accept when making decisions about the commitment of substantial amounts of money? Let's calculate the impact of another two years on the NPV analysis.

Xavier Motor Company NPV Project Analysis ($000)

		Cash Flows		PV of Cash Flows	
Year	Factor	Tractor	Snow Blower	Tractor	Snow Blower
6	0.5963	$ 1,500	$ 2,000	$ 894	$ 1,193
7	0.5470	1,500	2,000	821	1,094
			Addition to NPVs	1,715	2,287
			Previous NPVs	2	175
			New NPVs	$ 1,717	$ 2,462

Notice how the entire complexion of the problem has changed. Both projects now clearly appear favourable on a stand-alone basis. That is, the NPVs are substantially positive relative to the size of the early investments. Further, the snow blower now seems to be an obvious choice with a substantial NPV advantage. It's possible to make virtually any project look good by forecasting positive cash flows in the distant future.

d. This question raises another big issue: Are the forecasts for the two projects equally reliable? There's a strong argument that they are not. Snow blowers are a new business for Xavier, whereas the tractor is an extension of something Xavier is already doing. The implication is that the snow blower project may be much riskier than the tractor project. If that's the case, is a simple comparison of the NPVs valid?

For now you should concentrate on being sure you understand the mechanics of the NPV method, that is, how to calculate NPVs and how to apply the decision rules. However, keep the concerns brought up by Example 12.3 in mind. We'll return to them in the next chapter.

Internal Rate of Return (IRR)

A project's **IRR** is the return it generates on the *investment* of its cash outflows.

Instead of comparing present value dollar amounts, the **internal rate of return (IRR)** technique focuses on rates of return. The IRR concept can be defined in two ways. In fundamental terms, a project's IRR is just the return it earns on invested funds. However, the concept can also be defined in terms of the NPV equation, Equation 12.1. We'll have a close look at both approaches.

The Project as an Investment

In the IRR method we view a project as an investment of the company's money, which in principle is similar to the purchase of a financial asset. In this view, the cash outlay at the beginning of a project is like an investor paying cash to purchase a share or a bond. Subsequent cash inflows from the project are similar to dividend or interest payments received by the investor.

The analogy is easy to visualize when a project has only one cash outflow occurring at its beginning, time zero. Consider the project in Example 12.2 (page 438); we'll repeat those cash flows here for convenience.

C_0	C_1	C_2	C_3
$(5,000)	$1,000	$2,000	$3,000

Notice that the project calls for one outflow, or payment, of cash followed by three inflows. The initial $5,000 outlay can be thought of as the "price" of receiving the subsequent inflows. In other words, accepting the project financially amounts to putting up the initial $5,000 in return for which the investing company receives the later inflows.

Recall that in Chapters 9 and 10 we defined the return on an investment as the interest rate at which the discounted value of the future cash flows just equals the price of the investment. The same idea applies here. The IRR is the interest rate at which the present value of the future inflows just equals the $5,000 outflow (price).

In this view, the IRR is analogous to the yield on a bond. Recall that purchasing a bond entitles the owner to a series of interest payments and a repayment of principal. These are cash inflows for which the investor pays the bond's price. The interest rate that equates the present value of the investor's inflows to the price of the bond (outflow) is the bond's yield. Similarly, the rate that equates the present value of a project's inflows to the initial outlay is the IRR.

The idea is a little harder to see when there's more than one outflow; for example, if there are two negative cash flows before the inflows start. In such a case, the IRR is the interest rate that equates the present value of all inflows with the present value of all outflows. That is, by definition, the IRR is just the return on the investment of the outflows.

Defining IRR through the NPV Equation

We can gain additional insight by relating the IRR concept to the NPV method. The two approaches are closely related in that both NPV and IRR can be defined by essentially the same equation.

In the last section we defined a project's NPV with Equation 12.1. Referring to that expression, IRR is simply the value of the interest rate, k, at which NPV equals zero. This occurs when the present value of all the inflows is just equal to the present value of all the outflows, and they offset one another. This means IRR is the solution to the NPV equation with the interest rate treated as the unknown and NPV set to zero. This is the same as saying that *the IRR is the interest rate at which a project's NPV equals zero*.

Rewriting Equation 12.1 (page 436) with NPV = 0 and using IRR in place of k yields the expression that defines IRR.

The *IRR* is the interest rate that *makes a project's NPV zero*.

$$(12.2) \qquad 0 = -C_0 + \frac{C_1}{(1 + \text{IRR})} + \frac{C_2}{(1 + \text{IRR})^2} + ... + \frac{C_n}{(1 + \text{IRR})^n}$$

When the C_n are given for a particular project, Equation 12.2 is one equation in one unknown, IRR. The solution is the IRR for the project. Every project of practical interest has an IRR, just as every project has an NPV.

Decision Rules

IRR decision rules follow directly from thinking in terms of a return on an investment.

STAND-ALONE PROJECTS In the stand-alone case, we're asking whether or not investment in a project is a good use of the company's money. The answer depends on the rate the firm pays to use that money. We described that rate as the company's *cost of capital* earlier in this chapter (page 433), where we provided an illustration that involved starting a business with borrowed money. We can generalize by saying that no one should invest in anything unless the return on the investment is expected to exceed the rate paid for the use of the money invested.

Because a project's IRR is the return on funds invested in the project, and the cost of capital reflects the average rate the company pays for the use of long-term money, the stand-alone

A project is acceptable on a stand-alone basis if its *IRR exceeds the cost of capital.*

decision rule follows from this generalization: *Invest in a project only if its IRR exceeds the firm's cost of capital.*[5] Or,

$$\text{IRR} > k \rightarrow \text{Accept}$$
$$\text{IRR} < k \rightarrow \text{Reject}$$

where k is the firm's cost of capital.

In a mutually exclusive context, projects with larger IRRs are preferred.

MUTUALLY EXCLUSIVE PROJECTS The decision rule for mutually exclusive projects also follows from the definition of IRR as a return on an investment. We prefer investments with higher rates of return to those with lower rates. Hence, *a bigger IRR is better.* Or, if IRR_A and IRR_B related to projects A and B, respectively,

$$\text{IRR}_A > \text{IRR}_B \rightarrow \text{Choose project A over project B}[6]$$

Calculating IRRs

Examination of Equation 12.2 (page 441) shows that using equations to calculate internal rates of return for a general series of cash flows isn't easy.[7] We could use an iterative, numerical approach to solve the equation.

To solve for IRR, we guess at the project's IRR and calculate an NPV using the guess as the interest rate. If the NPV doesn't come out to be zero, the first guess was incorrect and we guess again. However, the result of the first calculation contains information that indicates the direction in which the second guess should be made.

Notice that this technique is similar to the iterative approach we used in Chapter 9 to find the yield on a bond given its price (page 318). Fortunately, financial calculators are programmed to calculate IRR, as is the IRR function in Excel® (see page 447). Internally such machines are going through the iterative process we've just described.

Once a project's cash flows are in the calculator (see page 437), calculating IRR is easy.

To get IRR, just press **IRR** and then **CPT** (for compute). Financial calculators and spreadsheets are especially convenient when we need to find an IRR.

Example 12.4

Using different interest rates, find the corresponding NPVs for the series of cash flows in Example 12.2. Graph your results. What is the IRR?

C_0	C_1	C_2	C_3
$(5,000)	$1,000	$2,000	$3,000

If the firm's cost of capital is 8%, is the project a good idea? What if the cost of capital is 10%?

■ **Solution:** We'll start by guessing that the IRR is 12% and calculating the project's NPV at that rate. As it happens, we've already done that calculation in Example 12.2. Review that calculation on page 438 now and see that the resulting NPV is $(377.30).

Clearly, the project's NPV at 12% is not zero, so we have to make another guess. To focus that guess, look at the problem's pattern of cash flows shown above. The positive numbers are in the future, displayed on the right. These positives are affected by the discounting process when we take

5 Just as with NPV, what happens if the IRR equals the cost of capital? That means the project or investment is a fair deal (i.e., an NPV of zero) and is providing the minimum return required.
6 We'll see (on page 445) that the IRR decision rule can occasionally lead to the wrong choice in mutually exclusive situations.
7 A project's IRR is the solution to that equation when a fixed set of numbers has been substituted for the C_n. Notice that the equation is a polynomial of order n in the variable IRR. Further, it's a very messy polynomial, because the powers of the unknown appear in the denominators of the fractions on the right. In general, such an equation can't be solved algebraically for values of n greater than 2.

present values. In effect, they're shrunk by their respective present value factors before being combined with the negative $5,000 to form the NPV. *Notice that a larger interest rate shrinks the positive numbers more than a smaller rate, but doesn't affect the initial outlay at all, because it isn't discounted.*

Our first guess of 12% shrunk the positive numbers too much, so that they became less than the negative outlay of $5,000 by $377.30. We'd like our next guess to shrink the positive cash flows less, so we'll choose a *smaller* interest rate.

We can summarize this thinking by saying that the magnitude of a project's NPV moves inversely with the interest rate used in its calculation. This relationship is portrayed graphically in Figure 12.1.

The graph depicted is known as a **net present value profile**, or NPV profile. Every project with a defined set of cash flows (the C_n) has an NPV profile that appears as a line on the graph. The lines will generally be down sloping to the right, and cross the horizontal axis at some point. The IRR is the point at which the project's NPV is zero. That occurs where the NPV profile crosses the *k*-axis as shown in the graph.

It's important to realize that the NPV profiles of capital budgeting projects slope downward to the right, because the pattern of cash flows generally involves outflows first (negative numbers) and inflows later (positive numbers). A higher discount rate therefore affects the positives more than the negatives, and has the net effect of shrinking the NPV.

Finding a project's IRR is equivalent to locating the crossover point of the NPV profile and the horizontal axis by testing points on either side. In the current problem, our first guess has taken us to the right of the crossover. Our next guess must be a lower interest rate to move the NPV up and get closer to the IRR.

We'll keep track of our calculations by setting up a two-column table to portray each interest rate choice and the NPV calculated to go along with it. Use the calculation method shown in Example 12.2 to verify that the entries shown below are correct. NPVs are shown rounded to the nearest whole dollar.

Interest Rate Guess	Calculated NPV
12%	$ (377)
10	(184)
9	(83)
8	22
7	130

*A project's **NPV profile** is a graph of its NPV versus the cost of capital. It crosses the horizontal axis at the IRR.*

Calculator Solution

Key	Input
CF₀	−5,000
C01	1,000
C02	2,000
C03	3,000

Answer

IRR	8.21%

The calculated NPV changes sign between 9% and 8%, which means that the IRR is between those interest rates. Using a financial calculator, the IRR = 8.21%.

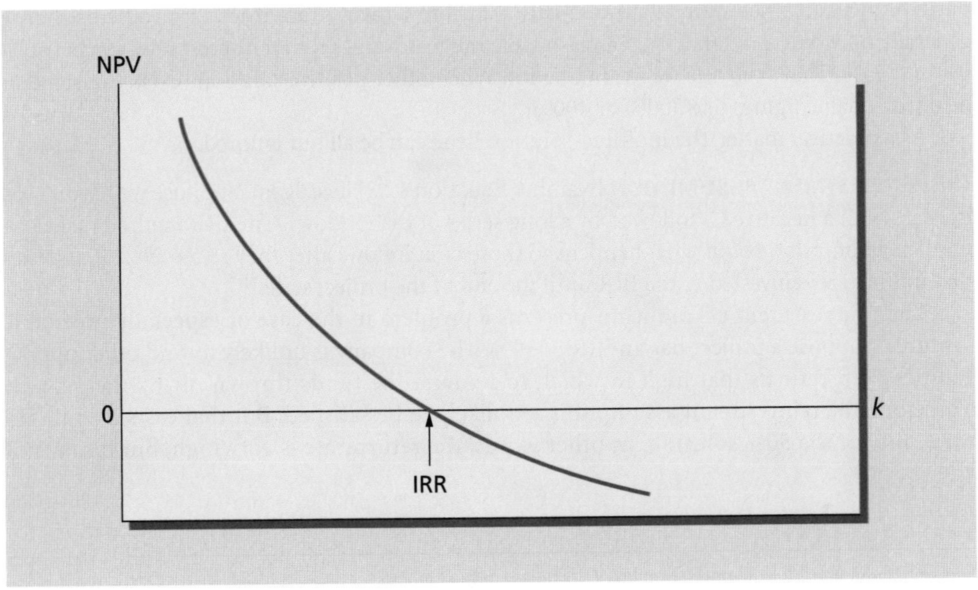

FIGURE 12.1
NPV Profile

If the firm's cost of capital is 8%, the project is marginally favourable. If the cost is 10%, it's clearly unfavourable.

Technical Problems with Internal Rate of Return

In this section, we will introduce two technical problems associated with the IRR method: multiple solutions and the reinvestment assumption. They rarely present practical difficulties, but anyone using the technique should be aware that they exist. In the following section we will examine another situation in which the IRR can mislead in ranking projects.

MULTIPLE SOLUTIONS Recall Equation (12.2):

$$(12.2) \qquad 0 = -C_0 + \frac{C_1}{(1 + \text{IRR})} + \frac{C_2}{(1 + \text{IRR})^2} + ... + \frac{C_n}{(1 + \text{IRR})^n}$$

The IRR for a project is defined as the solution to Equation 12.2 with the project's cash flows substituted for the C_n and the IRR treated as the unknown. The expression comes from the NPV equation operating at the point where NPV equals zero.

A problem arises because Equation 12.2 is an nth-order equation in the variable IRR, where n is the number of years that the project lasts. That means it can have as many as n solutions. How do we know which one is correct? At first glance, this seems like a fatal problem for the IRR method, but it isn't.

Unusual projects can have more than one IRR, but they rarely present practical difficulties.

Solutions to the equation can be either positive, negative, or what mathematicians call imaginary.[8] Negative and imaginary solutions aren't practically meaningful, so we needn't be concerned about them. We worry only when there's more than one *positive* solution.

It turns out that the number of positive solutions to Equation 12.2 depends on the pattern of the project's cash flows. There can be more than one positive solution if there is more than one sign reversal in the cash flow stream. A sign reversal occurs when the C_n values change from negative to positive or from positive to negative.

The normal pattern of project cash flows involves only one sign change. There's almost always a negative initial outlay, C_0, followed by a series of periods with positive cash flows. C_0 is sometimes followed immediately by a few negative flows before the inflows start, but even then there's only one sign change from negative to positive. That means there's only one positive solution for IRR, which is the correct one.

In the occasional project with one or two negative cash flow years interspersed among the positives, there can be more than one IRR solution. However, in practical problems there's generally only one solution within a reasonable range of values for an interest rate, say, between 0% and 50%. That's the one we're looking for. When other positive solutions exist, they tend to be unreasonable figures like 300% or 400%.

As a practical matter, the multiple-solution issue can be all but ignored.

In capital budgeting, the reinvestment assumption is the rate of compound interest at which future cash flows are assumed to be reinvested. In NPV analysis, this rate is the cost of capital used. In IRR analysis, this rate is the internal rate of return.

THE REINVESTMENT ASSUMPTION Examine Equation 12.2 once again. Suppose we have a typical case with a negative C_0 followed by a long series of cash inflows. The IRR method makes an implicit assumption about what happens to those cash inflows after they're received. It assumes that inflows are reinvested at the IRR until the end of the project's life.

The **reinvestment assumption** presents a problem in the case of especially profitable ventures. Suppose a project has an IRR of 50%. The company is unlikely to find other opportunities with returns that high in which to reinvest the funds thrown off by the project. Therefore, the reinvestment assumption is unlikely to be satisfied. But that casts a doubt on the reality of the 50% solution. In other words, the return rate is very high, but it may not truly be 50%.

---

8 Imaginary numbers are an entire branch of advanced mathematics.

Contrast IRR with the NPV method in such a situation. A project with a very high IRR would also have a high NPV, but the reinvestment assumption in the NPV method requires only that cash flows be reinvested at the cost of capital. That's because the discount rate in the NPV technique is just k, the cost of capital, as shown in Equation 12.1. Such investments are virtually always available.

The reinvestment problem is also somewhat academic, that is, not a practical concern. When returns on projects are in the 50% neighbourhood, people don't worry about *exactly* how high they are. In other words, if a project computes to a 50% IRR, people don't argue about whether it's 50% or only 40%. In either case, if the projected cash flows are correct, they indicate a very good opportunity.

Conflicting Results between IRR and NPV

The internal rate of return and the net present value methods are the two major approaches to evaluating capital budgeting projects. It's logical to ask whether or not they always give the same solutions to problems. Surprisingly, the answer to that question is no. Let's explore why with the aid of the NPV profile that we introduced on page 443.

The NPV profile for a project is a graphic representation of the relationship between a project's NPV and the interest rate at which it's calculated. It is simply the graph of Equation 12.1 for a particular set of cash flows (the C_n).

The NPV and IRR methods can occasionally give conflicting results in mutually exclusive decisions.

Look back at the NPV profile in Figure 12.1. The related discussion demonstrated that the line of the profile slopes downward to the right for projects that involve early cash outflows and later cash inflows. That is normally the case for business projects. However, profile shapes aren't identical, and they cross the horizontal axis at different points.

Now, consider the cash flows from the following competing projects, A and B.

Year	A	B
0	−1,275	−1,275
1	1,000	100
2	500	600
3	200	1,200
IRR	21.4%	16.9%

A appears better because it has the higher IRR.

We now calculate the NPV of these projects at different costs of capital.

Cost of Capital	NPV (A)	NPV (B)
0%	$425.00	$625.00
5	303.66	401.06
7	259.56	322.08
10	197.58	213.35
14	121.92	84.37
20	21.30	−80.56

Which project has the higher NPV depends on the cost of capital. B has a higher NPV at lower costs of capital, whereas A has a higher NPV at higher cost rates.

We can use the NPV profiles depicted in Figure 12.2 to show graphically how the NPV and IRR methods can give conflicting directions when we are choosing among mutually exclusive projects. Notice that, in this example, the profiles of the two projects cross one another.

To determine graphically any project's NPV at a particular cost of capital, we find k on the horizontal axis and move vertically to the project's NPV profile. From there we move left to the vertical axis and read the value of NPV.

FIGURE 12.2
Projects for Which
IRR and NPV Can
Give Different
Solutions

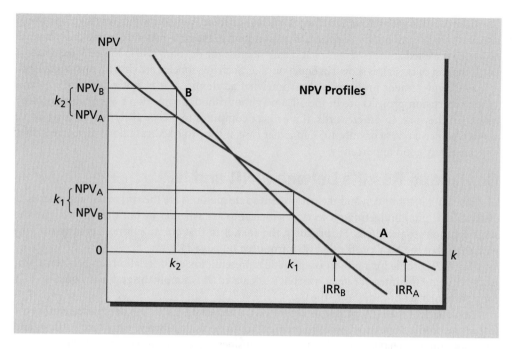

Calculator Solution

(Inputs are the *differ-ences* in annual cash flows between projects)

CF_0	0
C01	900
C02	−100
C03	−1,000

Answer
IRR 11.11%

Calculator Solution

	A	B
CF_0	−1,275	−1,275
C01	1,000	100
C02	500	600
C03	200	1,200
I	11.11	11.11

Answer

NPV	175.80	175.80

Project A's profile crosses the k-axis to the right of project B's. That's because the IRR for project A (21.4%) is higher than the IRR for project B (16.9%). Therefore the IRR method chooses project A over project B. Does the NPV method also choose project A? It depends on the cost of capital.

If the cost of capital is 14% (k_1), the NPV for project A (NPV_A) is $ $121.82 and the NPV for project B (NPV_B) is $84.37, indicating that the NPV method chooses project A just as the IRR method does.

If the cost of capital is 7% (k_2), which is to the left of the point at which the two profiles cross, NPV_A is $259.56 and NPV_B is $322.08. The result is reversed. This time the NPV method chooses project B over A, a result opposite that of the IRR method.

Note that at any discount rate less than about 11%, the NPV for B is higher, although B's IRR is lower. At any greater rate, A has the higher NPV and the higher IRR.

Calculating the Crossover Rate

In Figure 12.2 the NPV profiles cross at about 11%. This **crossover rate** is the discount rate that makes the NPVs of the two projects equal. Therefore, at the crossover rate, we are *indifferent* between the two projects. (The NPV of the *difference* in their cash flows is zero).

We can calculate the crossover rate by calculating the difference in the cash flows each year and calculating the IRR using these differences. The IRR is 11.11%.

At this rate the NPV of each project is $175.80

A high IRR is not an end in itself. We want projects that increase the value of the firm. Projects offering high IRRs but only for short periods may have lower NPVs than those that will earn a somewhat lower rate of return but for a long time.

In general, if two or more investment projects are mutually exclusive:

- The best project is the one with the largest NPV.
- If the discount rate is higher than the crossover rate, the high NPV project will also have the highest IRR.
- If the discount rate is lower than the crossover rate, the high NPV project will not have the highest IRR.

From the CFO

The **crossover rate** is the discount rate that makes the NPVs of two mutually exclu-sive projects equal. Therefore, at the crossover rate, we are *indifferent* between the two projects.

- IRR can mistakenly favour the project with a shorter life, but lower cash inflows (or a project with the same life, but a smaller outlay).
- Mutually exclusive projects should be ranked based upon their relative NPVs.

NPV and IRR Solutions Using Spreadsheets

Spreadsheet software and *financial calculators* can take most of the drudgery out of calculating NPVs and IRRs.

Spreadsheet solutions for NPV and IRR are very easy to do. We simply arrange the project's cash flows in a series of consecutive cells along a row or column and use the spreadsheet software's *NPV* and *IRR functions*. Here's an example using Excel® and the cash flows from Example 12.2.

```
Microsoft Excel - Book1.xls
 File  Edit  View  Insert  Format  Tools  Data  Window  Help                Arial
 D4                fx
        A          B          C          D          E          F          G
 1  Project Cash Flows:
 2              -$5,000   $1,000    $2,000    $3,000
 3
 4  Cost of Capital: k =   0.12   [        ]
 5
 6  NPV =      ($377.41)
 7
 8  IRR =        8.2%
 9
 10
```

The formula in cell B6 is

$$= B2 + NPV(C4,C2:E2)$$

The formula in cell B8 is

$$= IRR(B2:E2,C4)$$

Let's first focus on the NPV function. Its first *argument* (variable) is an interest rate—the cost of capital in this case—which we've put in cell C4. Notice that we input interest rates (cell C4) in decimal form in spreadsheets. The other argument is the range of cells containing the project's *future* cash flows, C2 to E2. Notice that the NPV function calculates the present value of the *future* cash flows only. That means we have to add the initial outlay separately, which we do by including B2 in the formula.

The IRR function, on the other hand, takes the whole series of cash flows including the initial outlay, B2:E2, and includes a guess at the IRR, using the cost of capital in C4.

Projects with a Single Outflow and Regular Inflows

Some projects are characterized by a single initial cash outflow followed by a finite number of equal inflows coming at regular time intervals. Examples include long-term loans (for lenders) and capital leases (for lessors). As an illustration, take the project in our last example and shift $1,000 from the third year to the first.

Annuity formulas can be used to calculate NPV and IRR when projects have *single outlays and regular inflows*.

C_0	C_1	C_2	C_3
$(5,000)	$2,000	$2,000	$2,000

This pattern is much easier to work with because the inflows can be treated as an *annuity*. In such cases we can rewrite the equations, defining NPV and IRR by using the present value of an annuity formula.[9]

Equation 12.1 defining NPV becomes

$$(12.3) \qquad NPV = -C_0 + C[PVFA_{k,n}]$$

where C is the constant annual inflow, k is the cost of capital, n is the project's life in years, and C_0 is the initial outlay. Remember that C_0 is a negative number. The second term on the right is the present value of the annuity formed by the project's positive cash flows over a period of n years at interest rate k.

Similarly, Equation 12.2 defining IRR becomes

$$(12.4) \qquad 0 = -C_0 + C[PVFA_{IRR,n}]$$

Equation 12.4 is especially convenient, because it lets us avoid the iterative procedure otherwise used to find IRRs.

http

Go to http://www. studyfinance.com. For a review of present value concepts, click on Time Value of Money. For an overview of capital budgeting techniques, click on Capital Budgeting.

Calculator Solution

Key	Input
CF_0	−5,000
C01	2,000
C02	2,000
C03	2,000
I	12.0

Answer

NPV	(196.34)

Use Excel® Function NPV. Add result to initial outlay.

Example 12.5

Find the NPV and IRR for the project used as an illustration immediately above. Assume the cost of capital is 12%.

■ **Solution:** To calculate NPV, write Equation 12.3 and substitute from the cash flow pattern.

$$NPV = -C_0 + C[PVFA_{k,n}]$$
$$NPV = -\$5,000 + \$2,000[PVFA_{12,3}]$$

Find the present value factor for an annuity in Appendix A−4 and substitute

$$NPV = -\$5,000 + \$2,000(2.4018)$$
$$NPV = -\$196.40$$

Microsoft Excel - Book1.xls

File Edit View Insert Format Tools Data Window Help — Arial

D4 — fx

	A	B	C	D	E	F	G
1	Project Cash Flows:						
2		−$5,000	$2,000	$2,000	$2,000		
3							
4	Cost of Capital: k =		0.12				
5							
6	NPV =	($196.34)					
7							
8	IRR =	9.7%					
9							
10							

[9] We're using the present value of an annuity from Chapter 8 (page 280), but replacing PMT with C to be consistent with our present notation, which represents cash flows as C values.

To calculate the IRR, write Equation 12.4 and substitute

$$0 = -C_0 + C[PVFA_{IRR,n}]$$

$$0 = -\$5,000 + \$2,000[PVFA_{IRR,3}]$$

Solve for the factor.

$$PVFA_{IRR,3} = \frac{\$5,000}{\$2,000}$$

$$= 2.5000$$

Now search for 2.5000 in Appendix A−4 along the row for three periods. The solution is between 9% and 10%.

Compare these results for NPV and IRR with those we calculated in Examples 12.2 and 12.4. Did shifting the $1,000 forward by two years make a big difference?

Here's the same example using Excel®.

The formula in cell B6 is

$$= B2 + NPV(C4,C2:E2)$$

The formula in cell B8 is

$$= IRR(B2:E2,C4)$$

Calculator Solution

Key	Input
CF_0	−5,000
C01	2,000
C02	2,000
C03	2,000

Answer

IRR	9.70

**Use Excel®
Function IRR**

Profitability Index (PI)

IRR and NPV are the most widely used capital budgeting techniques. Payback is used frequently, but generally as a preliminary screening device before one or both of the other methods. Although new approaches are proposed from time to time, none has caught on in a big way. One approach, however, is used enough to make it worth mentioning briefly. The **profitability index (PI)** is essentially a variation on the NPV method. We'll define it by referring to Equation 12.1.

The PI compares the present value of a project's future cash flows with the initial outlay required to get the project started, making the comparison in the form of a ratio.

Recall that the initial outlay is C_0. Hence, PI is defined as the sum of all the terms to the right of C_0 in Equation 12.1 divided by C_0.

The **profitability index (PI)** is the ratio of the present value of inflows to the initial outlay. Projects are acceptable if PI > 1. Larger PIs are preferred.

(12.5)
$$PI = \frac{\dfrac{C_1}{(1+k)} + \dfrac{C_2}{(1+k)^2} + \dots + \dfrac{C_n}{(1+k)^n}}{C_0}$$

The PI is also known as the *benefit/cost ratio*, reflecting the idea that the positive cash flows expected in the future are benefits while the initial outlay is a cost.

The concept is poorly defined if some of the early C-values after C_0 are negative. In such a case it isn't clear whether those should be considered costs and added to the denominator or negative benefits and subtracted from the numerator. The idea works best when the initial outlay, C_0, is the only negative cash flow, which is a fairly common situation.

Essentially, the PI is the ratio

$$\frac{\text{Present value of inflows}}{\text{Present value of outflows}}$$

NPV, by way of contrast, is the *difference* between the present value of inflows and the present value of outflows.

When the present value of inflows exceeds the present value of outflows, the PI will be greater than 1. This condition is equivalent to a positive NPV. Further, a larger PI is preferable to a smaller PI, because it implies more inflows relative to outflows in a present value sense. This is equivalent to preferring a larger to a smaller NPV.

Decision Rules

All this leads to the decision rules for the profitability index.

STAND-ALONE PROJECTS

$$PI > 1.0 \rightarrow \text{Accept}$$
$$PI < 1.0 \rightarrow \text{Reject}$$

Mutually Exclusive Projects

$$PI_A > PI_B \text{ Choose project A over project B}$$

where PI_A and PI_B are the profitability indices for projects A and B, respectively.

Insights | **PRACTICAL FINANCE**

Which Methods Do Businesses Prefer?

Big Companies

Most large companies do capital budgeting using sophisticated, time value–based methods. However, although NPV is theoretically the best technique, companies use IRR more frequently. That's probably because people are more comfortable with rates than with sums of present valued dollars. We learn about returns on investments early in our adult lives, and businesspeople talk about returns on sales, assets, and equities all the time. The payback method is also common; it is most frequently used in conjunction with the IRR and NPV methods.

Small Companies

Smaller companies tend to use payback more frequently and IRR and NPV less frequently than large companies. Small firms may not have the financial resources to hire employees educated in finance. In addition, the small firm focus is just about always on very short-term cash flow, so that many entrepreneurs naturally focus on payback.

Industry Differences

Time value–based methods of capital budgeting are more often used in some industries than in others. Firms that are better able to estimate cash flows precisely are more likely to use IRR and NPV. Energy-related firms and public utilities were among the first to use these tools. On the other hand, they are less useful in the motion picture business, where movie grosses are very hard to predict.

Strategic and Risk Considerations

In other situations, strategic and risk considerations may outweigh the results of capital budgeting analysis. A case in point is the huge investment in information technology

(IT) required in many companies. For many companies today NPV/IRR is neither the most important nor the most practical tool for making or maintaining investments in information technology. A 2005 study of mid-market companies (revenue of less than $500 million) by the Info-Tech Research Group found that only 37% used a formal IRR/NPV program for IT investments. For smaller firms that figure was even lower.

Even among companies that do use it, IRR/NPV isn't the only metric of importance. In fact one of the most consistent challenges cited by IT executives today is the concept of *business-IT alignment*, building a solid business case for an IT project that directly supports the business' goals or needs.

Another key tool may be called a *portfolio management* approach, based on studies out of the MIT Sloan School of Management. It professes that IT initiatives should be balanced across four key areas: infrastructure ("keeping the lights on"), strategic projects, information projects, and efficiency projects.

Another important consideration is *risk*. What are the operational risks involved in the project? What are the ramifications on other business processes? What's the risk of not doing it? What are the risks of picking the wrong technology? Externally, what's the risk that customers or end users won't like or adopt the new technology? What if the project runs over time and over budget? If IRR is significantly worse than the projections, what is Plan B? We will return to the topic of risk in capital budgeting in Chapter 14.

Sources: Peter Thompson, "The Cost of IT," *Technology Quarterly*, Spring 2007, Volume 2, No. 1, pp. 19–20; V.M. Jog and A. Srivastava, "Capital Budgeting Practices in Corporate Canada," *Financial Practice and Education* 5, (Fall/Winter 1995), pp. 37–43; L.R. Runyon, "Capital Budgeting Decision Making in Small Firms," *Journal of Business Research* 11 (September 1983), pp. 389–397.

COMPARISON WITH NPV The comparison with NPV decision rules is not exact. In the stand-alone case, a PI > 1.0 always coincides with NPV > 0. However, the two methods may compute the relative desirability of projects differently and may not make the same choices among options.[10]

Example 12.6

Compute the profitability index for a project with the following cash flows if the cost of capital is 9%. Is the project acceptable on a stand-alone basis?

C_0	C_1	C_2	C_3
$(4,500)	$1,500	$2,000	$1,600

■ **Solution:** The present value of future cash flows is computed as follows:

Year (n)	C_n	$PVF_{9,n}$	PV
1	$1,500	0.9174	$1,376
2	2,000	0.8417	1,683
3	1,600	0.7722	1,236
			$4,295

Then, from Equation 12.5, the PI is

$$PI = \frac{\$4,295}{\$4,500} = 0.95$$

Because the profitability index is less than 1, the project is not acceptable.

Calculator Solution

Key	Input
CF_0	0
C01	1,500
C02	2,000
C03	1,600
I	9.0

Answer

NPV	4,295

Use Excel® Function NPV. Divide result by initial outlay.

Comparing Projects with Unequal Lives

Mutually exclusive decisions are sometimes complicated by the fact that the competing projects don't extend over the same period of time. When the disparity is significant, it can make a direct comparison of the projects meaningless.

For example, suppose a manufacturing company is replacing a production machine and must choose between two new models that have different lives. Assume both new machines save $750 per year in cost, but the longer-lived model is expected to last six years while the other will be good for only three years. Of course, the more durable replacement will be more expensive. Assume the costs are $2,600 and $1,500, respectively. The comparison is shown in Figure 12.3 (page 452) for an assumed 8% cost of capital.

Notice that the shorter-lived project has a better IRR, but the longer-lived has a superior NPV. This conflict is due to the disparity in the projects' lives.

The problem arises mainly with the NPV method. To visualize the difficulty, think of a replacement machine as having an annual benefit to the firm during its entire life. In broad terms, that just means it will produce income every year in excess of its cost on a present value basis.

The problem here is that the NPV method adds up six years of benefits for one project and only three years for the other. Therefore, the longer-lived machine just about always winds up with a higher NPV.

Putting it another way, the fact that one machine has a six-year life forces us to look at a six-year time horizon for analysis, and the shorter-lived project is implicitly assumed to have nothing going on in the second three years.

Projects with substantially unequal lives aren't directly comparable.

*The **equivalent annual annuity method** is a method for dealing with projects with unequal lives. It replaces each project's NPV with an equivalent annual amount.*

The Equivalent Annual Annuity (EAA) Method

Although a number of methods are available for dealing with unequal lives, here we present the most effective technique, the **equivalent annual annuity (EAA) method.**

---

10 A PI = 1 indicates an NPV of zero.

Turning each project's NPV into an equivalent annual annuity (EAA) is the easiest way to solve the time disparity problem. The EAA method converts the net present value of each project into an equivalent annual amount (in NPV terms). This amount can then be used to select the better project.

To summarize:

1. We calculate the NPV of each project.
2. We replace each NPV with an annuity for the life of the project that has the same NPV.[11]
3. The project with the larger EAA is better if comparing benefits. If comparing costs, the project with the smallest EAA is better (that is, the project that is least negative).

A numerical example will help make the idea clear.

The shorter-lived project we've been working with has a life of three years and an NPV of $432.82 (Figure 12.3). The equivalent three-year annuity is found by substituting that amount into the present value of an annuity formula along with three years and the appropriate interest rate as follows.

$$PVA = PMT[PVFA_{k,n}]$$
$$\$432.82 = PMT[PVFA_{8,3}]$$

Now find the factor in Appendix A–4, substitute, and solve for the annuity payment, which is the EAA.

$$\$432.82 = PMT(2.5771)$$
$$PMT = \$167.95$$
$$= EAA$$

This approach is illustrated in Figure 12.4 for the three-year and six-year projects shown in Figure 12.3. As the diagram indicates, we make two conceptual steps. First, we calculate the NPV of the project. For the three-year project, the NPV is $432.82, as shown in Figure 12.3. Then we replace the NPV with an annuity ($167.95) for the life of the project (3 years), which

Calculator Solution

Key	Input
n	3
PV	432.82
I/Y	8.0

Answer

PMT	167.95

**Use Excel®
Function PMT**

FIGURE 12.3
Comparing Projects with Different Lives

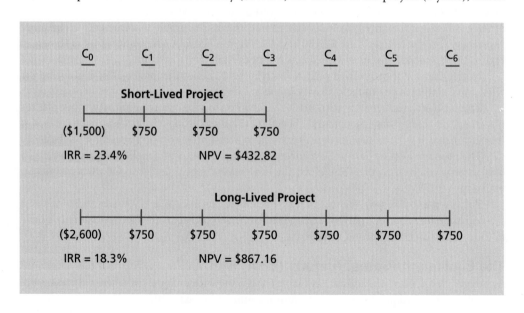

---

11 The underlying assumption is that future cash flows for each project will remain constant.

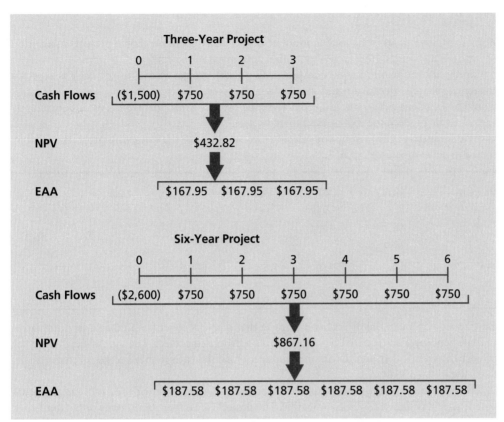

FIGURE 12.4
Replacing a
Project's NPV with
Its EAA

has the same NPV. In this way, we replace the NPV with an indefinitely long stream of equal payments (the EAA). It's important to realize that this is true even though the EAA calculation is based on the number of years in the life of the original project.

Further, we can calculate an EAA for *any* project regardless of its life. And because all EAAs are infinite annuities, we can choose among projects by comparing their annuity payments.

The longer-lived project in our illustration has an NPV of $867.16 and a life of six years. Its EAA is calculated as follows.

$$PVA = PMT[PVFA_{k,n}]$$
$$\$867.16 = PMT[PVFA_{8,6}]$$
$$\$867.16 = PMT(4.6229)$$
$$PMT = \$187.58$$
$$= EAA$$

This is larger than the shorter project's EAA of $167.95, so we again conclude that the longer project is better.

Notice that we can also compare EAAs on the basis of their present values by using the *present value of a perpetuity* formula. This simply amounts to dividing the EAA by the decimal value of the relevant interest rate. Because the cost of capital is the same for both projects, this will result in the same choice.

Decision Rule

When comparing projects with different lives, select the project that has the highest equivalent annual benefit or the lowest equivalent annual cost.

Calculator Solution

Key	Input
n	6
PV	867.16
I/Y	8.0

Answer

PMT	187.58

Use Excel®
Function PMT

Capital Rationing

A firm's *capital budget* is the total amount of money to be spent on capital projects in a period of time, usually a year. How large should that amount of money be?

In theory, the answer to that question is easy. Every project with a positive NPV is expected to increase shareholder wealth and should be undertaken. Therefore, the optimal capital budget would be large enough to undertake all available projects with positive NPVs or equivalently with IRRs that exceed the cost of capital.

We'll illustrate the idea by considering a company with the following projects available, sorted in decreasing order of IRR.

Project	IRR	C0
A	16%	$8M
B	14	5M
C	12	6M
D	11	3M
E	8	6M
F	6	7M

Figure 12.5 plots the projects on a graph that displays cost of capital against cumulative capital spending. Each lettered block represents a proposed project. The blocks' heights are the project IRRs while their widths are the amounts of capital each requires to get started. Usually that's the initial outlay, C_0.

Notice again that the projects are arranged in decreasing order of IRR, and that the firm's cost of capital is shown as a horizontal line. The projects are either stand-alone opportunities or the best choice among mutually exclusive options.

This portrayal makes it easy to see which projects have IRRs that exceed the cost of capital and therefore should be done. In this case, if there is no funds limitation, the firm will

FIGURE 12.5
Capital Rationing

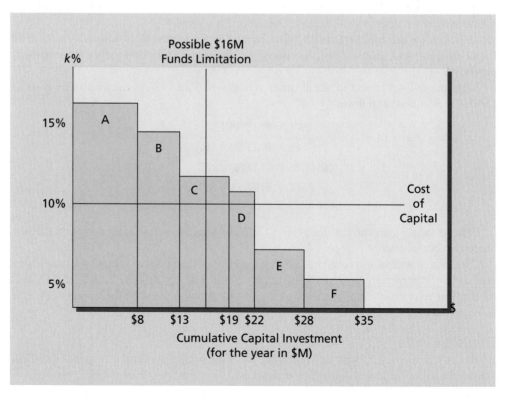

maximize shareholder wealth by undertaking projects A, B, C, and D, while foregoing projects E and F.

In practice, however, there is rarely enough money available to do all proposed projects that appear to have positive NPVs. Some capital constraint is likely to be imposed, such as the one shown in the diagram at $16M. When such a constraint is imposed, we have **capital rationing** in that available capital dollars have to be rationed among projects.

Capital rationing creates a problem because projects are generally not divisible. In this case, we can't do part of project C, so we can't do it at all. That leaves some unused money within the budget between the end of project B and the constraint. The rationing problem is to choose the best set of projects that fits into the capital constraint. By "best" we mean the set that maximizes NPV. In the illustration, the choice appears to be easy because D, the next best project, just fits into the space available. In some cases, however, the choice isn't so obvious. It's possible that the selection of projects that maximizes NPV could omit one of the higher-rated projects in favour of one or more lower-rated projects that fit better within the constraint.

Finding the best possible solution to a capital rationing problem involves using techniques from a field of mathematics known as constrained maximization. The subject is quite complex and beyond the scope of this book, but you should be aware of its existence.

Using sophisticated mathematics to find a precise solution to capital rationing problems implies attributing a great deal of accuracy to the NPV and IRR estimates of the projects being considered. In the next chapter, we'll learn that such accuracy frequently isn't possible.

> *In practice, financial managers ration capital intuitively, choosing among projects for a variety of reasons, not all of which may be strictly financial. In that way they make choices that are usually close to the best, but not exactly optimal.*

Capital rationing involves selecting projects subject to a funding limitation.

From the CFO

SUMMARY

1 Capital budgeting involves planning and justifying how capital dollars are spent on long-term projects.

2 A project may be classified as a replacement, an expansion, or a new venture. Any investment entails a risk of making less on the project than management expects when the decision to go ahead is made. This risk varies with project type, increasing as we move from replacement to expansion to new venture.

3 A project with no competing alternatives is called a stand-alone project. When the firm must choose one project from competing alternatives, the projects are said to be mutually exclusive.

4 Capital budgeting decisions involve the forecasting of cash flows (expenditures and receipts). Business projects usually involve an initial outlay and future inflows.

5 The firm's cost of capital is the rate of return it pays for its capital funds. The firm will measure the profitability of projects against its cost of capital.

6 The payback period method calculates the amount of time, in years, for the investment to produce cumulative cash inflows to equal the initial cost of the investment. The shorter the payback period, the better. It may be used as a rough screening device for proposed investments.

The net present value method uses the company's cost of capital to discount future cash flows and then nets the resulting present values against the initial outlay. A positive result indicates an investment that would increase the wealth of the company and its shareholders.

The internal rate of return method produces an annual return on investment, before interest, which can be compared to the company's cost of capital. A rate of return higher than the cost of capital indicates an attractive investment for the company.

The profitability index is the ratio of the present value of inflows to the initial outlay. Projects are acceptable if the profitability index is greater than 1.

7 Mutually exclusive projects with unequal lives can be compared using the equivalent annual annuity method.

8 Where there is a shortage of funds available for investment, capital may have to be rationed among a selection of acceptable projects.

KEY TERMS

Capital budgeting, p. 431
Capital rationing, p. 455
Cost of capital, p. 433
Crossover rate, p. 446
Equivalent annual annuity (EAA) method, p. 451
Internal rate of return (IRR), p. 440

Mutually exclusive projects, p. 431
Net present value (NPV), p. 436
Net present value profile, p. 443
Payback period, p. 434

Profitability index (PI), p. 449
Reinvestment assumption, p. 444
Salvage value, p. 433
Stand-alone project, p. 431

KEY FORMULAS

(12.1) Net present value of a project

$$= NPV = -C_0 + \frac{C_1}{(1+k)} + \frac{C_2}{(1+k)^2} + \cdots + \frac{C_n}{(1+k)^n}$$

(12.2) Internal rate of return defined

$$0 = -C_0 + \frac{C_1}{(1+IRR)} + \frac{C_2}{(1+IRR)^2} + \cdots + \frac{C_n}{(1+IRR)^n}$$

(12.3) Net present value of a project with constant annual inflows
$$NPV = -C_0 + C[PVFA_{k,n}]$$

(12.4) Internal rate of return defined for a project with constant annual inflows
$$0 = -C_0 + C[PVFA_{IRR,n}]$$

(12.5) Profitability Index $= PI = \dfrac{\frac{C_1}{(1+k)} + \frac{C_2}{(1+k)^2} + \cdots + \frac{C_n}{(1+k)^n}}{C_0}$

QUESTIONS

1. Define mutual exclusivity and describe ways in which projects can be mutually exclusive.

2. Capital budgeting is based on the idea of identifying incremental cash flows, so overheads aren't generally included. Does this practice create a problem for a firm that, over a long period of time, takes on a large number of projects that are just barely acceptable under capital budgeting rules?

3. Relate the idea of cost of capital to the opportunity cost concept (page 263). Is the cost of capital the opportunity cost of project money?

4. The payback technique is criticized for not using discounted cash flows. Under what conditions will this matter most? That is, under what patterns of cash flow will payback and NPV or IRR be likely to give different answers?

5. Explain the rationale behind the NPV method in your own words. Why is a higher NPV conceptually better than a lower one?

6. Projects A and B have approximately the same NPVs. Their initial outlays are similar in size. Project A has early positive cash flows, and little or nothing is expected to come in later on. Project B has much larger positive cash flows than B, but they're further in the future. Can you make any general statement about which project might be better?

7. Suppose the present value of cash inflows and outflows is very close to balanced for a project to build a new $50 million factory, so that the NPV is $25,000. The same company is thinking about buying a new trailer truck for $150,000. The NPV of projected cash flows associated with the truck is also about $25,000. Does this mean that the two projects are comparable? Is one more desirable than the other? If the cash flows have similar risks, are the projects equally risky? (*Hint:* Think in terms of the size of the investment placed at risk in relation to the financial rewards expected.)

8. Think about the cash flows associated with putting $100,000 in the bank for five years, assuming you draw out the interest each year and then close the account. Now think about a set of hypothetical cash flows associated with putting the same money in a business, operating for five years, and then selling out. Write an explanation of why the IRR on the business project is like the bank's interest rate. How are the investments different?

9. What is it about the cash flows associated with business projects that makes the NPV profile slope downward to the right? Would the NPV profile of any randomly selected set of positive and negative flows necessarily slope one way or the other? Why?

10. The following set of cash flows changes sign twice and has two IRR solutions. Identify the sign changes. Demonstrate mathematically that 25% and 400% are both solutions to the IRR equation.

C_0	C_1	C_2
$(320)	$2,000	$(2,000)

On the basis of this example, why would you expect multiple solutions to be an unusual problem in practice?

11. Under what conditions will the IRR and NPV methods give conflicting results for mutually exclusive decisions? Will they ever give conflicting results for stand-alone decisions? Why?

12. Why is the profitability index more appropriately described as a variation on the NPV technique than as a variation on the IRR technique?

13. Show that the profitability index (PI), the initial outlay ($-C_0$), and the net present value (NPV) of a project are related by the following equation:

$$NPV = -C_0(1 - PI)$$

(*Hint:* State both the NPV and the PI in terms of $-C_0$ and the sum of all other cash flows.)

Business Analysis

1. You are a financial analyst for the Ajax Company, which uses about $1 million of inventory per month. The purchasing manager has come to you for help with a buying decision. He can get a big discount on $15 million of inventory by buying it all at once. However, there is some risk of obsolescence when buying that far in advance. He understands that large purchases are frequently analyzed by means of capital budgeting techniques, and asks for your help in deciding whether or not to buy the specially priced inventory. How would you advise him? Is capital budgeting appropriate?

2. Risk in capital projects is the probability that a project will earn less than expected. Make up and describe one hypothetical project in each of the replacement, expansion, and new venture categories. List a few ways in which each might go wrong and cause the cash flows to be less favourable than expected. Can you think of situations in which projects could result in losses? Could the losses exceed the initial investment (C_0)?

3. Charlie Brown is thinking about starting Wing-It Airlines to fly a commuter route in and out of a major city. Four planes are on the market that will do the job, but each has different flight, load, and operating characteristics. Charlie is unsure of the demand for his service, and feels that it may depend to some extent on the type of plane chosen. Whether or not the business is feasible may depend on which airplane is used in conjunction with the demand estimate assumed. Are capital budgeting techniques appropriate for analysis of this problem? If so, is the issue a stand-alone or mutually exclusive decision?

4. The Budwell & Son Oil Company is looking at two drilling proposals. One project lasts for three years, costs $20 million to start, pays back quickly, and has an NPV of $15 million. The other project also costs about $20 million to start, but has an expected life of seven years, takes much longer to pay back, and has an NPV of $17 million. Mr. Budwell, the company's founder, favours the shorter project because of the quick investment recovery. His son Billy, however, has taken finance in university and insists that the only way to judge projects is on NPV. He therefore favours the longer project. They've engaged you as their financial advisor to settle the issue. How would you advise them?

5. Webley Corp. has a capital budget limited to $20 million. Five relatively high-IRR projects are available that have initial investments totalling $15 million. They are all roughly the same size. A sixth project has an IRR only slightly lower than those of the first five, but requires an $8 million investment. Several other smaller projects are available with IRRs quite a bit lower than the sixth. The president has stated that it's too bad the firm has to pass up the sixth project, but it just doesn't fit into the budget. How would you advise him?

PROBLEMS

1. Gander, Inc. is considering two projects with the following cash flows.

Year	Project X	Project Y
0	($100,000)	($100,000)
1	40,000	50,000
2	40,000	0
3	40,000	0
4	40,000	0
5	40,000	250,000

Gander uses the payback period method of capital budgeting and accepts only projects with payback periods of three years or less.

  a. If the projects are presented as stand-alone opportunities, which one(s) would Gander accept? If they were mutually exclusive and Gander disregarded its three-year rule, which project would be chosen?

  b. Is there a flaw in the thinking behind the correct answers to part (a)?

2. A project has the following cash flows.

C_0	C_1	C_2	C_3
$(700)	$200	$500	$244

  a. What is the project's payback period?

  b. Calculate the project's NPV at 12%.

  c. Calculate the project's PI at 12%.

3. Calculate an IRR for the project in Problem 2 using the iterative technique. (*Hint:* start by guessing 15%.)

4. Clancy Inc. is considering a project with the following cash flows.

C_0	C_1	C_2	C_3
$(7,800)	$2,300	$3,500	$4,153

  a. Clancy has a policy of rejecting all projects that don't pay back within three years outright and analyzing more carefully with time value–based methods those that do. Does this project warrant further consideration?

  b. Should Clancy accept the project based on its NPV if the company's cost of capital is 8%?

  c. What conclusion will the firm reach based on PI?

5. Should the project being considered in Problem 4 be accepted or rejected based on IRR? (*Hint:* Using the iterative technique, start by guessing 11% for IRR.)

6. Hamstring Inc. is considering a project with the following cash flows.

C_0	C_1	C_2	C_3	C_4
$(25,000)	$10,000	$12,000	$5,000	$8,000

The company is reluctant to consider projects with paybacks of more than three years. If projects pass the payback screen, they are considered further by means of the NPV and IRR methods. The firm's cost of capital is 9%.

  a. What is the project's payback period? Should the project be considered further?

  b. What is the project's NPV? Does NPV indicate acceptance on a stand-alone basis?

  c. Calculate the project's IRR by using an iterative approach. Start by using the cost of capital and the NPV calculation from part (a). Does IRR indicate acceptance on a stand-alone basis?

  d. What is the project's PI? Does PI indicate acceptance on a stand-alone basis?

7. Project Alpha requires an initial outlay of $35,000 and results in a single cash inflow of $56,367.50 after five years.

    a. If the cost of capital is 8%, what are Alpha's NPV and PI? Is the project acceptable under each of these techniques?

    b. What is project Alpha's IRR? Is it acceptable under IRR?

    c. What are Alpha's NPV and PI if the cost of capital is 12%? Is the project acceptable under that condition?

    d. What is Alpha's payback period? Does payback make much sense for a project like Alpha? Why or why not?

8. The Sampson Company is considering a project that requires an initial outlay of $75,000 and produces cash inflows of $20,806 each year for five years. Sampson's cost of capital is 10%.

    a. Calculate the project's payback period by making a single division rather than accumulating cash inflows. Why is this possible in this case?

    b. Calculate the project's IRR, recognizing the fact that the cash inflows are an annuity. Is the project acceptable? Did your calculation in this part result in any number(s) that were also calculated in part (a)? What is it about this problem that creates this similarity? Will this always happen in such cases?

    c. What is the project's NPV? Is the project acceptable according to NPV rules?

9. Calculate the IRR, NPV, and PI for projects with the following cash flows. Do each NPV and PI calculation at costs of capital of 8% and 12%. Calculate IRRs to the nearest whole percent.

    a. An initial outlay of $5,000 and inflows of $1,050 for seven years.

    b. An initial outlay of $43,500 and inflows of $14,100 for four years.

    c. An investment of $78,000 followed by 12 years of income of $11,500.

    d. An outlay of $36,423 followed by receipts of $8,900 for six years.

10. Prayerful Airlines Inc. needs to replace a short-haul commuter plane on one of its busier routes. Two aircraft on the market satisfy the general requirements of the route. One is more expensive than the other but has better fuel efficiency and load-bearing characteristics, which result in better long-term profitability. The useful life of both planes is expected to be about seven years, after which time both are assumed to have no value. Cash flow projections for the two aircraft follow.

	Low Cost	High Cost
Initial cost	$775,000	$950,000
Cash inflows, years 1 through 7	$154,000	$176,275

    a. Calculate the payback period for each plane and select the best choice.

    b. Calculate the IRR for each plane and select the best option. Use the fact that all the inflows can be represented by an annuity.

    c. Compare the results of parts (a) and (b). Both should select the same option, but does one method result in a clearer choice than the other based on the relative sizes of the two payback periods versus the relative sizes of the two IRRs?

    d. Calculate the NPV and PI of each project assuming a cost of capital of 6%. Use annuity methods. Which plane is selected by NPV? By PI?

e. Calculate the NPV and PI of each project, assuming the following costs of capital: 2%, 4%, 6%, 8%, and 10%. Use annuity methods. Is the same plane selected by NPV and PI at every level of cost of capital? Investigate the relative attractiveness of the two planes under each method.

f. Use the results of parts (b) and (e) to sketch the NPV profiles of the two proposed planes on the same set of axes. Show the IRRs on the graph. Would NPV and IRR ever give conflicting results? Why?

11. Calculate the NPV for the following projects.

a. An outflow of $7,000 followed by inflows of $3,000, $2,500, and $3,500 at one-year intervals at a cost of capital of 7%.

b. An initial outlay of $35,400 followed by inflows of $6,500 for three years and then a single inflow in the fourth year of $18,000 at a cost of capital of 9%. (Recognize the first three inflows as an annuity in your calculations.)

c. An initial outlay of $27,500 followed by an inflow of $3,000 followed by five years of inflows of $5,500 at a cost of capital of 10%. (Recognize the last five inflows as an annuity, but notice that it requires a treatment different from the annuity in part (b).)

12. Calculate the IRR for the following projects.

a. An initial outflow of $15,220 followed by inflows of $5,000, $6,000, and $6,500.

b. An initial outflow of $47,104 followed by inflows of $16,000, $17,000, and $18,000.

13. Calculate the NPV at 9% and the IRR for the following projects.

a. An initial outlay of $69,724 and an inflow of $15,000 followed by four consecutive inflows of $17,000.

b. An initial outlay of $25,424 followed by two zero-cash years and then four years of inflows at $10,500.

c. An outlay of $10,672 followed by another outlay of $5,000 followed by five inflows of $5,000.

14. Calculate the NPV at 12% and the IRR for the following projects. Find IRRs to the nearest whole percent.

a. An initial outflow of $5,000 followed by three inflows of $2,000.

b. An initial outflow of $5,000 followed by inflows of $1,000, $2,000, and $3,000.

c. An initial outflow of $5,000 followed by inflows of $3,000, $2,000, and $1,000.

d. Notice that in parts (a), (b), and (c) a total of $6,000 is received over three years. Compare the NPVs and IRRs to see the impact of shifting $1,000 between years.

15. Grand Banks Mining Inc. plans a project to strip-mine a wilderness area. Setting up operations and initial digging will cost $5 million. The first year's operations are expected to be slow and to net a positive cash flow of only $500,000. Then there will be four years of $2 million cash flows after which the ore will run out. Closing the mine and restoring the environment in the sixth year will cost $1 million.

a. Calculate the project's NPV at a cost of capital of 12%.

b. Calculate the project's IRR to the nearest whole percent.

16. Bagel Pantry Inc. is considering two mutually exclusive projects with widely differing lives. The company's cost of capital is 12%. The project cash flows are summarized as follows.

	Project A	Project B
C_0	$(25,000)	$(23,000)
C_1	14,742	6,641
C_2	14,742	6,641
C_3	14,742	6,641
C_4		6,641
C_5		6,641
C_6		6,641
C_7		6,641
C_8		6,641
C_9		6,641

   a. Compare the projects by using payback.
   b. Compare the projects by using NPV.
   c. Compare the projects by using IRR.
   d. Compare the projects by using the EAA method.
   e. Choose a project and justify your choice.

Calculator Problems

Problems 17–27 should be solved using a financial calculator (or spreadsheet). For assistance in using a financial calculator, see page 437.

17. Callaway Associates, Inc. is considering the following mutually exclusive projects. Callaway's Cost of capital is 12%.

Year	Project A	Project B
0	($80,000)	($80,000)
1	$44,000	$65,000
2	$34,000	$30,000
3	$14,000	$ 0
4	$14,000	$ 5,000

   a. Calculate each project's NPV and IRR.
   b. Which project should be undertaken? Why?

18. Tutak Industries is considering a project requiring an initial investment of $200,000 followed by annual cash inflows of $45,000 for the next six years. A second six-year project has an initial outlay of $325,000.
   a. How much would the second project have to generate in annual cash flows to have the same IRR as the first?
   b. If Tutak's cost of capital is 8%, how much would the second project have to generate in annual cash flows to have the same NPV as the first project?

19. Provide the missing information for the following projects.

Project	Initial Investment	Length (in years)	Annual Cash Flow	Cost of Capital	NPV
A	$100,000	5	$35,000	8%	?
B	200,000	4	?	13%	$35,000
C	300,000	7	50,000	?	15,000
D	400,000	?	56,098	9%	20,000
E	?	6	75,000	10%	25,000

20. Calculate IRRs for the projects in the previous problem.

21. Huron Valley Homes is considering a project requiring a $1 million initial investment. Expected cash inflows will be $25,000 in the first year, $100,000 in the second year, and $200,000 per year for the next six years.
   a. Calculate the project's IRR and the NPV assuming an 8% cost of capital.
   b. How much would each of the last six payments have to be to make the project's NPV $100,000?

22. Consider two mutually exclusive projects, A and B. Project A requires an initial cash outlay of $100,000 followed by five years of $30,000 cash inflows. Project B requires an initial cash outlay of $240,000 with cash inflows of $40,000 in the first two years, $80,000 in the next two years, and $100,000 in the fifth year.
   a. Compute the IRR for each project.
   b. Compute the NPV for each project for each of the following costs of capital: 0%, 4%, 8%, 12%, and 16%, and record your results in a table.
   c. For which costs of capital do the IRR and NPV methods select the same project?
   d. Examine the table created in part (b) and determine the costs of capital between which the methods begin to select different projects. Is your answer consistent with the result of part (a)? Explain your answer in terms of NPV profiles.

23. Haley Motors is considering a maintenance contract for its heavy equipment. One firm has offered Haley a four-year contract for $100,000. Another firm has offered an eight-year contract for $165,000. Haley will be able to save $34,000 per year under either contract because its employees will no longer have to do the work themselves.
   a. If Haley's cost of capital is 10%, which project should be selected? Use the equivalent annual annuity (EAA) method to justify your answer.
   b. If Haley's cost of capital is 12%, does it change the decision? What about 14%?

24. Cassidy and Sons is reviewing a project with an initial cash outflow of $250,000. An additional $100,000 will have to be invested at the end of the first year, followed by an additional investment of $50,000 at the end of the second year. Beginning at the end of year 3, the project is expected to generate cash flows of $90,000 per year for the next eight years.
   a. Calculate the project's payback period, IRR, and its NPV and PI at a cost of capital of 8%.
   b. What concerns might Cassidy have regarding this project beyond the financial calculations from part (a)?

25. Zuker Distributors handles the warehousing of perishable foods and is considering replacing one of its primary cold storage units. One supplier has offered a unit for $250,000 with an expected life of 10 years. The unit is projected to reduce electricity costs by $50,000 per year. However, it requires a $20,000 refurbishing every two years, beginning two years after purchase. Another supplier has offered a cold storage unit with similar capabilities for $300,000. It will produce the same savings in electricity costs, but requires refurbishing every five years at a cost of $40,000. Zuker's cost of capital is 8.5%. Use NPV to determine which cold storage unit Zuker should select.

26. Griffin-Kornberg is reviewing the following projects for next year's capital program.

Project	Initial Investment	Length in Years	Annual Cash Flow
A	$ 3.0 million	6	$ 719,374
B	3.5 million	5	970,934
C	4.0 million	7	904,443
D	5.0 million	4	1,716,024
E	6.0 million	6	1,500,919
F	7.0 million	5	1,941,868
G	8.0 million	7	1,725,240

Projects A and B are mutually exclusive and so are Projects D and E. Griffin-Kornberg has a 9% cost of capital and a maximum of $14 million to spend on capital projects next year. Use capital rationing to determine which projects should be included in Griffin-Kornberg's capital program.

27. Kneelson and Botes Inc. (K&B) is a construction company that does road and bridge work for the provincial highway authority. The provincial government solicits bids on construction projects from private contractors. The winning contractor is chosen based on its bid price as well as its perceived ability to do the work.

Sophisticated contractors develop bids using capital budgeting techniques because most projects require cash outlays for hiring, equipment, and materials before getting started (C_0). After that the province makes progress payments to cover costs and profits until the job is finished ($C_1 \ldots C_n$).

Contractors know that even after they've won a bid, realizing the planned profits and cash flows isn't assured, in part because government budgets can change while construction progresses. If funding is up, officials tend to add to the work originally ordered, leading to increased profits and cash flows. But if funding is down, officials start to nitpick the contract looking for cost savings, which generally leads to lower cash inflows. Provincial budget projections are fairly good for a year or two, but tend to be inaccurate over longer periods.

K&B has been offered two 4-year contracts, but doesn't have enough cash or management depth to take on both (mutually exclusive because of resource limitations). One project involves road repair, most of which will be done and paid quickly. The other requires working on a new bridge. The bulk of the cash inflows on bridge projects generally occur near completion.

K&B's estimating department has put together the following projections of the two projects' cash flows:

	($000)	
	Road Repair	Bridge Work
C_0	($3,000)	($4,500)
C_1	3,000	100
C_2	2,000	2,000
C_3	1,000	3,000
C_4	100	4,500

K&B doesn't know its exact cost of capital, but feels it's between 10% and 15%. This is not uncommon in smaller companies. (In Chapter 15 we'll learn that estimating the cost of capital can be difficult and less than precise for firms of any size.)

The company has hired you as a financial consultant to make a recommendation as to which project to accept.

a. Calculate the payback period for both projects. Which does payback choose?

b. Calculate the IRR for both projects. Which does the IRR method choose? Is the choice clear or is it a close decision? Is the choice consistent with the result of the payback method?

c. Calculate NPVs for both projects for costs of capital from 10% to 15% in 1% increments. Then plot both projects' NPV profiles on a graph similar to that shown in Figure 12.2 on page 446. Does the NPV method give a meaningful result? If so is it consistent with the results of the payback and IRR methods? Which method is theoretically the best? Does that help in this situation?

d. You must make a recommendation to K&B's management regardless of any technical difficulties you've encountered. Provide another, less quantitative argument that tends to support one project over the other. (*Hint:* See question 6 on page 457 and Business Analysis 4 on page 458.)

e. What is your recommendation and why?

Developing Software

28. Write a spreadsheet program to calculate the NPV of a project with an irregular pattern of cash flows for up to 10 periods without using the spreadsheet software's NPV function. Essentially, the task is to program Equation 12.1 with $n = 10$.

First, input the interest rate (k) in a single cell.

Next, set up three horizontal rows of 11 cells (including C_0). The top row will receive the cash flows as inputs.

Program the present value factor for each period into the second row of cells using the interest rate you input earlier as follows.

Period	0	1	2	...	10
Factor	1	$\dfrac{1}{1 + k}$	$\dfrac{1}{(1 + k)^2}$	...	$\dfrac{1}{(1 + k)^{10}}$

Note that we're calling the interest rate k, but it will appear as a cell name in your program.

Next, form the third row by multiplying the top two cells in each column together. This makes the third row the present value of each cash flow.

Finally, sum the values along the third row in another cell to form the project's NPV.

Notice that your program will handle a project of fewer than 10 periods if you simply input zero (or leave blank) the cash flow cells from $n + 1$ to 10.

Also notice that you can easily extend your program to any reasonable number of periods by extending the horizontal rows and the programming logic. Test your program on the data in Example 12.3 (page 439) to make sure it works correctly.

29. The Ontario Motor Company is thinking of automating one of its production facilities. The equipment required will cost a total of $10.0 million and is expected to last 10 years. The company's cost of capital is 9%. The project's benefits include labour savings, and a quality improvement that will lower warranty costs. Savings are estimated as follows.

Year	Cost Savings ($000)
1	$ 574
2	864
3	1,246
4	2,748
5	3,367
6	2,437
7	2,276
8	1,839
9	1,264
10	623

a. Use the program developed in Problem 28 to find the project's NPV. Is the project acceptable?

b. Use the program to develop the data for an NPV profile. Evaluate the NPV for interest rates (costs of capital) from 6 to 14%.

c. Use the program to iteratively find the project's IRR to one hundredth of a percent.

Chapter 13

Cash Flow Estimation

Learning Objectives

1 Identify the incremental cash flows after tax that would result from capital investment decisions.

2 Explain how opportunity costs are relevant to capital budgeting decisions, but that sunk costs are not.

3 Explain that interest expense is not considered when estimating cash flows, as it is accounted for in the discounting process.

4 Calculate the tax shield benefits of capital cost allowance (amortization).

You are looking to sell your old car, so you look up your original purchase contract and set your selling price based upon your original purchase cost. You quickly find that there are no takers at this price because the (*sunk*) cost of the car to you is *irrelevant* to any potential buyers. Their only concern is to get a good deal based upon the current *market value* of the car.

Early in the last chapter we said that any project to be analyzed by capital budgeting techniques must be represented as a series of estimated cash flows. We portrayed the flows for a typical project as $C_0, C_1, ..., C_n$, and assumed that they were readily available. In this chapter we'll consider exactly how such cash flow estimates are developed. In Chapter 14 we'll look into some modern developments in capital budgeting that deal with incorporating risk into the analysis.

CASH FLOW ESTIMATION

We'll begin by placing cash flow estimation within the overall capital budgeting process and making some important observations about people's perceptions.

Capital Budgeting Processes

Capital budgeting consists of two distinct processes. The first is estimation of the cash flows associated with projects. The second is evaluation of the estimates using techniques like NPV and

IRR. There is a tendency to take the forecast cash flows for granted and to overlook the difficulties involved in their estimation. Further, once a set of projections is made, people tend to treat it as a concrete fact not subject to error.

The same tendency leads to associating the capital budgeting concept solely with the evaluation techniques, especially NPV and IRR, and becoming caught up in an incorrect perception of the accuracy and precision of the whole process. Indeed, the techniques we studied in the last chapter seem like "financial engineering" in their direct and unambiguous approach to the task of choosing among projects. Problem solutions come out to what seems like hair-splitting accuracy, and it's easy to get a feeling of comfort and security in the correctness of the method.

However, this secure feeling of great accuracy is misplaced. The results of an NPV or IRR analysis are only as accurate as the cash flow estimates used as inputs. And those estimates are forecasts of the *future*, which are always difficult to make and subject to considerable error.

Estimating project *cash flows* is the *most difficult* and error-prone part of capital budgeting.

In practice, forecasting accurate project cash flows is the more difficult and arbitrary of the two capital budgeting processes. In a sense it's the more important, because it's where error and bias can creep into the analysis. Applying NPV and/or IRR is a straightforward task that isn't likely to result in error or misinterpretation. The calculation may be complicated, but it's easy in the sense that we don't have to make any judgments about what we're doing. Making cash flow estimates, on the other hand, requires the exercise of a good deal of judgment about what to include, what to leave out, and how heavily to weight things in relation to one another. As a result, a particular set of estimated flows may be very good or very bad depending on the nature of the project and who's doing the estimating.

This is an important point that's often overlooked. Anyone can make the right capital budgeting decisions with NPV and IRR *given* a set of cash flows. It's developing the right set of cash flows that's tough.

In this chapter we'll take a close look at what goes into estimating cash flows. We'll be especially concerned with the practical matter of ambiguities and uncertainties in the process.

PROJECT CASH FLOWS—AN OVERVIEW AND SOME SPECIFICS

First we'll sketch a broad approach to the estimating process, then we'll consider a few issues that require special treatment, and finally we'll look into some detailed examples.

The General Approach to Cash Flow Estimation

Cash flow estimation can be a messy calculation, but it's conceptually quite simple. We just think through all the events a project is expected to bring about, and write down the financial implications of each event in the future time period in which we expect it to occur. Then we add up everything in each time period.

Cash flow estimates are often done on *spreadsheets*. Each major factor that impacts cash flow is forecast over the life of the project.

We generally use a spreadsheet format for our estimations. The sheet's columns are time periods starting with the present and extending into the future over the project's life. The rows are financial items that will either generate or require cash.

For example, a sales forecast leads to an estimate of cash inflows from customers, while an expense projection leads to a pattern of outflows to employees and vendors. When everything is itemized, we add up each column to arrive at a forecast of each future period.

It will help your perspective if you look ahead at Table 13.1 on page 475 to get an idea of what the finished product looks like.

Forecasts for new ventures tend to be the most complex, so we'll consider them before talking briefly about expansion and replacement projects. For those projects we generally just leave out some of the issues considered for new ventures. It helps to organize our thinking if we consider things in several separate categories. A general outline for estimating new venture cash flows follows.

Pre-Start-Up: The Initial Outlay

Enumerate everything that has to be spent before the project is truly started. Include expenses and assets that have to be purchased. Also include the tax impact of expense items. The sum of these things is C_0, the *initial outlay.*

The Sales Forecast: Units and Revenues

The incremental business expected from the project is laid out in spreadsheet form (on paper or in a computer application) over future time periods. It's best to forecast in terms of units, if feasible, and then multiply by projected prices to arrive at sales dollars.

Cost of Goods Sold and Expenses

Plan for costs directly related to the new sales forecast as well as expenses necessary for indirect support of the increased activity level. To do that, assume relationships between sales and cost of goods sold and between sales and expense based on the nature of the business being analyzed.

Assets

New assets to be acquired with cash are planned over the project's life whenever they're expected to be acquired. Most are needed during the initial, pre-start-up period. It's important not to neglect working capital, which requires cash like any other asset.

Amortization

When planning for capital assets, it's important to forecast amortization even though it's a non-cash expense because it affects taxes.

Taxes and Earnings

Summarizing the tax-deductible items in each period lets us calculate the project's impact on taxes and earnings. Calculate incremental taxes and treat them like any other cash flow item.

Summarize and Combine

Adjust earnings for amortization and combine the result with the balance sheet items to arrive at a cash flow estimate in each forecast period.

Expansion projects tend to require the same elements as new ventures, but generally require less new equipment and facilities.

Replacement projects are generally expected to save costs without generating new revenue, so the estimating process tends to be somewhat less elaborate. The expected dollar savings are planned over future periods along with the assets required to realize those savings. Amortization and tax calculations are necessary in most cases.

We'll look at some examples after the next section.

Insights | REAL APPLICATIONS

Pelican Media

Pelican Media (Pelican) of Saskatoon is a small graphics design company that makes signs and banners for trade shows. In 2006, Pelican upgraded its 16 computers to Microsoft's new Vista® operating system. Pelican made the move to Vista mainly to clean up a hodge-podge of operating systems the company was using. Its PCs were running three different versions of Windows® as well as Linux® and Unix® software.

Upgrades to the standard and premium versions of Vista sell for $250* and $300 respectively, but the cost of technicians' time, employee training, and upgrades to hardware and software applications must be added to that.

A 2006 survey of 472 North American organizations by Toronto-based Softchoice Corporation concluded that half of business PCs in use today can't run Vista at all and 94% can't support the premium configuration. In most cases the problem is memory, processor power, and/or video card capabilities.

Pelican paid anywhere from $305 to $730 to upgrade each of its computers.

	Vista Standard	Vista Premium
Software licenses	$ 250	$ 300
Upgrade memory to 1 gigabyte		$ 200
Upgrade video card		$ 130
Labour for upgrades	$ 25	$ 60
Vendor training	$ 30	$ 40
Total	$ 305	$ 730

At this point many companies might prefer to buy new computers rather than upgrade older models. Brand-name computers with the standard version Vista® start at less than $900. However, whether they upgrade or buy new, factors such as internal training, support, upgrades to applications software, and revisions to customized software need to be considered.

These costs could easily add another $300 to the costs to upgrade each machine.

If Pelican converted 5 machines to Vista premium® and the remaining 11 machines to Vista standard®, its initial outlay would be

$$
\begin{array}{rcl}
5 \times \$730 & = \$ & 3{,}650 \\
11 \times \$305 & = & 3{,}355 \\
16 \times \$300 & = & \underline{4{,}800} \\
& & \$ 11{,}805
\end{array}
$$

A study commissioned by Microsoft claimed that the relatively certain annual benefits in U.S. dollars per machine of using Vista® included

- $ 35 per year on support and maintenance
- $140 per year of maintenance time
- $ 59 per person per year in increased user productivity, or

US$234 (approximately CDN$246 per year at an exchange rate of US$1 = CDN$1.05). For 16 machines, these annual benefits would total (16 × $246 =) $3,936.

Assuming a five-year service life, use Excel® or your financial calculator to confirm that, based upon Microsoft's claims, Pelican's IRR would be 19.9%!

In any case, what choice did Pelican have? To "keep the lights on" (remain competitive) and support its business goals, was not the upgrade to Vista® a "no-brainer"?

* All financial data ignore the cash flow effect of income and sales taxes.

Source: Adapted from Grant Buckler, "Paying for the WOW Factor," *Technology Quarterly*, Spring 2007, Volume 2, No.1, pp. 22–24. Reprinted with the permission of the author.

A Few Specific Issues

It helps to keep a few specific items in mind when making cash flow estimates. We'll consider several before moving on to more examples.

The Typical Pattern

Most cash *outflows* occur *early*; *inflows* happen *later*.

Nearly all projects require an *initial outlay* of funds before getting started. Subsequently, flows tend to be positive (inflows) with some notable exceptions. The typical pattern is characterized by early outflows followed by later inflows.

A replacement project is generally fairly simple in this respect. The initial outlay is the cost of the new equipment less any salvage value available for the old. Future cash flows are the savings or benefits of using the new, more efficient machinery. They start immediately and are generally relatively stable.

Other kinds of projects can have several negative cash flow periods. New ventures, for example, typically lose money for the first few years after an initial outlay, so there are several negative periods at the outset. More complex projects can require infusions of cash at different times, so it's possible to have negative flows at any time. For example, a cleanup requirement at the end can make the last flow of a project negative.

Cash versus Accounting Results

It's important to keep the distinction between earnings and cash flows in mind when doing project projections. Capital budgeting deals only with cash flows, so in theory we hardly need mention accounting net income at all. However, business managers invariably want to know the *net income impact* of projects as well as the results of the capital budgeting analysis. It's therefore important to keep both available although separate.

Project Cash Flows Are Incremental

The most fundamental concept about project cash flows is that they are incremental to the company's normal business. Incremental means *in addition to,* and at least conceptually *separate from.* In other words, we must answer the following question: What cash flows will occur if we undertake this project that wouldn't occur if we left it undone and continued business as before?

> Only **incremental cash flows** count. They are the cash flows, after tax, that result from making a business decision, such as a capital investment.

Sunk Costs

Some expenditures associated with a project should not be included in capital budgeting cash flows. Sunk costs are monies that have already been spent at the time of the analysis. The fact that sunk money is gone cannot be changed by decisions about the project.

For example, suppose a company spends money to study a new area of business and later conducts an analysis to decide whether or not to enter the field. The cost of the study should *not* be included in the project's cash flow stream for capital budgeting analysis, because at the time of the analysis the money has already been spent.

The analysis of a decision must include only *future* costs that are dependent on the decision. The study money is gone and won't be recovered whether or not the new field is entered, so it's irrelevant to the decision.

> **Sunk costs** have already been spent and are ignored.

Impacts on Other Parts of the Company

Projects sometimes have impacts on other parts of the company that have to be considered. Suppose a company sells a family model product and is considering introducing a luxury model. Some customers who buy the family model will probably switch to the luxury line. The result will be a loss of income in the family line that should be reflected as a negative cash flow in the analysis of the new proposal.

Overhead Levels

Basic overheads are usually considered fixed and left out of project analysis. There are times, however, when overhead changes have to be considered.

For example, suppose a company has a central human resources department that is considered overhead by operating departments. Most capital budgeting projects involve the addition of only a few new people, so the workload of the human resources department isn't increased significantly by the larger staff. But suppose a particular project calls for so many new employees that an additional human resources administrator is required for their support. In such a case the increase in cost in the human resources department must be reflected as a cost of the project. In other words, the project has an *incremental overhead effect* that should be reflected in its projected cash flows.

Taxes

Capital projects are generally expected to improve profitability, but more profit usually means more taxes. It's important to calculate incremental cash flows net of any additional taxes caused by the project.

To do that we have to calculate the incremental impact of the project on earnings before tax, then calculate the extra tax and include it as a cash outflow. In other words, we deal with *after-tax cash flows* in capital budgeting.

> All capital budgeting cash flows are stated after tax.

Opportunity Cost

Resources aren't free even though they sometimes seem to be. Suppose a firm has an idle production facility and is evaluating a project that requires a similar resource. The idle factory will be used if the project is undertaken, and won't require a cash outlay. Does that mean the facility is a zero cost item in the project's capital budgeting analysis?

> The *opportunity cost* of a resource is its value in its best alternative use and is included in capital budgeting analyses.

It's tempting to say yes, especially if there are no other plans for the building. However, that's not the right way to look at the problem. The appropriate cost of any resource is whatever has to be *given up* to use it, in other words, its value in the next best use.

In this example, suppose the firm has no other production use for the idle factory, but can sell it for $1 million (the next most lucrative use). In such a case we'd say $1 million (less applicable taxes) is the *opportunity cost* of the factory and use that amount as a cash outflow in the analysis. In effect, the company is foregoing a cash inflow by using the facility in the project. The factory would be free only if it had no market value and no other use by the company.

Working Capital

Projects that involve increased sales normally also require increases in receivables and inventories (partially offset by payables). In other words, higher revenue demands more working capital, which builds up during the project's early years along with revenue. It's important to recognize that increases in working capital have to be funded with cash outflows just like the acquisition of any other asset, and that these flows have to be included in the project's forecast.

On the other hand, as a project winds down, inventories are sold, receivables are collected, and payables are paid. The net working capital invested is freed up and therefore recovered.

Ignore Financing Costs

When project cash flows are projected, we do *not* include the interest expense of carrying a cumulative outflow over time. This is the most significant difference between cash flow estimation and the financial forecasting associated with business planning (see Chapter 6). Cash flow estimation is concerned with the value of projects irrespective of how they're financed, so we look only at operating cash flows.

This is not to say that the capital budgeting concept ignores interest expenses or the time value of money. The time cost of money is explicitly accounted for in the evaluation process

Projects generally require new working capital, which requires cash.

Ignore interest expense when estimating incremental cash flows.

1 All expenditure numbers were approximate.

when the NPV and/or IRR techniques are applied. Because it's taken into account there, we don't need to consider it when estimating cash flows.

Old Equipment

Some projects, especially replacements, involve getting rid of old capital equipment. Such material generally can be sold on a secondhand market, providing a cash inflow (salvage value) that to some extent offsets the cost of the new equipment.

It's important to consider this source of funds in cash flow estimation. It's also important to recognize that the proceeds from the sale of old equipment may be reduced by taxes if a capital gain results.

ESTIMATING NEW VENTURE CASH FLOWS

New venture projects tend to be larger and more elaborate than expansions or replacements. However, incremental cash flows can be easier to isolate with new ventures, because the whole project is easily seen as distinct and separate from the rest of the company.

Example 13.1

The Wilmont Bicycle Company manufactures a line of traditional multispeed road bicycles. Management is considering a new business proposal to produce a line of off-road mountain bikes. The proposal has been studied carefully and the following information is forecast.

Cost of new production equipment and machinery including		
freight and set-up		$200,000
Expense of hiring and training new employees		125,000
Pre-start-up advertising and other miscellaneous expenses		20,000
Additional selling and administrative expense		
per year after start-up		120,000
Unit sales forecast		
Year 1	200	
Year 2	600	
Year 3	1,200	
Year 4 and beyond	1,500	
Unit price		600
Unit cost to manufacture (60% of revenue)		360

Last year, anticipating an interest in off-road bicycles, the company bought the rights to a new gearshift design for $50,000.

Wilmont's production facilities are currently being utilized to capacity, so a new shop has to be acquired for incremental production. The company owns a lot near the present facility on which a new building can be constructed for $60,000. The land was purchased 10 years ago for $30,700, and would otherwise be sold. It now has an estimated market value of $150,000.

If Wilmont produces off-road bicycles, it expects to lose some of its current sales to the new product—3% of the new unit forecast is expected to come out of sales that would have been made in the old line. Prices and direct costs are about the same in the old line as in the new.

Wilmont's general overhead includes human resources, finance, and executive functions, and runs about 5% of revenue. Small one-time increments in business don't affect overhead spending, but a major continuing increase in volume would require additional support. Management estimates that additional spending in overhead areas will amount to about 2% of the new project's revenues.

New revenues are expected to be collected in 30 days. Incremental inventories are estimated at $12,000 at start-up and for the first year. After that an inventory turnover of 12 times based on cost of goods sold is expected. Incremental payables are estimated to be 25% of inventories.

Wilmont's current business is profitable, so losses in the new line will result in tax savings. The company's marginal tax rate is 34%.

■ **Solution: The Initial Outlay.** First we'll consider cash flows required before start-up, which comprise the initial outlay, C_0. We'll work in thousands of dollars and carry one decimal place. That amounts to forecasting to the nearest $100, which provides more than enough detail for estimating purposes.

Expenses of an operating nature can be expected to be tax-deductible against other income in the period before start-up. These include the costs of hiring, training, advertising, and other miscellaneous items ($000).

Hiring and training	$ 125.0
Advertising and miscellaneous	20.0
Deductible expense	$ 145.0
Tax saving @ 34%	49.3
Net after-tax expenses	$ 95.7

Next add the cash needed for physical assets necessary to get started. As these costs are assets rather than expenses, they are not deductible for tax purposes.

Equipment	$ 200.0
New construction	60.0
Initial inventory	12.0
Assets subtotal	$ 272.0

Add the operating items and the physical assets to get the total, actual pre-start-up outlay.

Net after-tax expenses	$ 95.7
Assets subtotal	272.0
Actual pre-start-up outlay	$ 367.7

Next we have to recognize the opportunity cost of the land. The property has a market value of $150,000, but if it's sold for that amount, income tax will be due on the increase in value over its original cost. Only 50% of the capital gain is taxable.

Sale price ($000)	$ 150.0
Cost	30.7
Capital gain	$ 119.3
Taxable capital gain (50%)	$ 59.6
Tax @ 34%	$ 20.3
Cash foregone (Price − Tax)	$ 129.7

Summarizing, we obtain a figure for C_0.

Actual pre-start-up cash outlay	$ 367.7
Opportunity cost of land	129.7
C_0 (initial outlay for analysis)	$ 497.4

Cash Flows after Start-Up. Incremental sales forecasts often begin small, grow for a few years, and then level off. Other forecast elements commonly do the same thing; they change for a few years and then remain constant. When that happens, we have to forecast out in time only until the numbers stop changing from year to year. Subsequent years are then repetitive.

It's generally best to forecast revenue with *unit and price* detail, where feasible.

In this case, sales are forecast to grow for four years before levelling off. However, a change in amortization[2] after the fifth year affects taxes. Hence, the annual cash flow estimate changes each year until the sixth year and then remains constant. We'll therefore estimate only the first six years, understanding that for a longer forecast we just need to repeat the last year as many times as we like. The calculations are laid out in Table 13.1 on page 475 and discussed in the following paragraphs. Follow Table 13.1 as you continue to read this example.

The revenue forecast at the top of the table is developed by laying out the unit sales projection and multiplying by the projected price of $600. It's important, where feasible, to forecast both physical units and future prices rather than just total revenue. Maintaining unit-price detail makes it easier to alter the forecast to reflect different assumptions as well as to check the reasonability of the entire estimate.

---

2 In this example, we will assume that amortization for tax purposes is based upon straight-line methods.

TABLE 13.1
Cash Flow
Estimation

Wilmont Bicycle Company

Estimated Cash Flows

Mountain Bike Project ($000)

	Year					
	1	**2**	**3**	**4**	**5**	**6+**
Revenue and Gross Margin						
Units	200	600	1200	1500	1500	1500
Revenue	$ 120.0	$ 360.0	$ 720.0	$ 900.0	$ 900.0	$ 900.0
Cost of sales	72.0	216.0	432.0	540.0	540.0	540.0
Gross margin	$ 48.0	$ 144.0	$ 288.0	$ 360.0	$ 360.0	$ 360.0
Tax-Deductible Expenses						
SG&A expense	$ 120.0	$ 120.0	$ 120.0	$ 120.0	$ 120.0	$ 120.0
Amortization	41.5	41.5	41.5	41.5	41.5	1.5
General overhead	2.4	7.2	14.4	18.0	18.0	18.0
Loss old line	1.4	4.3	8.6	10.8	10.8	10.8
Total	$ 165.3	$ 173.0	$ 184.5	$ 190.3	$ 190.3	$ 150.3
Profit Impact and Tax						
EBT impact	$ (117.3)	$ (29.0)	$ 103.5	$ 169.7	$ 169.7	$ 209.7
Tax	(39.9)	(9.9)	35.2	57.7	57.7	71.3
NI impact	$ (77.4)	$ (19.1)	$ 68.3	$ 112.0	$ 112.0	$ 138.4
Add Amortization	41.5	41.5	41.5	41.5	41.5	1.5
Subtotal	$ (35.9)	$ 22.4	$ 109.8	$ 153.5	$ 153.5	$ 139.9
Working Capital						
Accounts receivable	$ 10.0	$ 30.0	$ 60.0	$ 75.0	$ 75.0	$ 75.0
Inventory	12.0	18.0	36.0	45.0	45.0	45.0
Payables	(3.0)	(4.5)	(9.0)	(11.3)	(11.3)	(11.3)
Working capital	$ 19.0	$ 43.5	$ 87.0	$ 108.7	$ 108.7	$ 108.7
Change in working capital	$ (7.0)	$ (24.5)	$ (43.5)	$ (21.7)	–	–
Net Cash Flow						
Net cash	$ (42.9)	$ (2.1)	$ 66.3	$ 131.8	$ 153.5	$ 139.9

Production cost can be built up from components or forecast as a percentage of revenue consistent with previous experience in the same or similar businesses. In this case Wilmont is experienced in making bicycles, and feels that a *cost ratio* of 60% will be appropriate for the new line. Applying this ratio to the revenue figures yields the projected cost of sales line. Gross margin follows by subtracting cost from revenue.

Next we calculate items that affect pretax income, beginning with selling, general, and administrative (SG&A) expense estimated at $120,000 per year.

Deductible amortization is in two separate pieces because equipment and buildings are amortized over different lives. Assume that equipment will be written off over five years for amortization purposes, while the building will be amortized over 39 years. We'll assume straight-line amortization for both and ignore partial-year conventions for convenience. Then the annual amortization is as follows.

Equipment ($200,000/5)	$ 40,000
Building ($60,000/39)	1,538
Amortization, first five years	$ 41,538
Thereafter	$ 1,538

The next line represents the expected increase in general overhead calculated at 2% of incremental revenues. Following that is an allowance for the lost business expected in the old product line. It was estimated that 3% of the unit forecast would come from the old line. Assuming the cost and price relationships are about the same in the old line as in the new, we can estimate the profit impact of this loss as 3% of the new gross margin forecast.

Add these items and subtract from gross margin for the impact on earnings before tax (EBT). The tax calculation is 34% of EBT, which leads to the impact of the project on net income (NI).

Although earnings after tax or net income isn't relevant for capital budgeting purposes, it's invariably important to operating managers and should therefore be calculated and displayed as part of the analysis.

The cash impact of these operating items is calculated by adding back amortization, the only noncash charge in this example.

Finally, we calculate the cash required to build up the working capital necessary to support the project. This means estimating the year-end balances for accounts receivable, inventories, and accounts payable.

We're assuming that receivables are collected in 30 days, meaning there's one month of uncollected revenue in accounts receivable (A/R) all the time. The average level during each year is therefore one-twelfth of that year's revenue.

Inventory is estimated as one month's cost of sales, so take the annual cost figure divided by 12 except in the first year where a $12,000 level has been assumed. Finally, payables are 25% of inventory.

Summarize these items and calculate the year-to-year *change* in working capital, which reflects the cash required to fund it over the project's life. In the first year the change in working capital is $7,000 rather than $19,000, because an initial inventory of $12,000 is assumed to have been acquired before start-up.

The after-tax cash flow estimates for years 1 through 6 are calculated by adding the working capital requirements to the subtotal just above the working capital section. These figures along with the initial outlay calculated earlier represent the cash flows for the off-road bike project ($000).

C_0	C_1	C_2	C_3	C_4	C_5	C_6
$ (497.4)	$ (42.9)	$ (2.1)	$ 66.3	$ 131.8	$ 153.5	$ 139.9

Notice that the cash forecasts for subsequent years will be repetitions of the sixth year if sales remain at a steady 1,500 units. Therefore, in this case, we can extend the forecast by just adding more inflows of $139,900.

Assume that

- Cash flows will continue at $139.9 per year for years 7–10.
- The project will have no further value after year 10.
- Wilmont's applicable cost of capital is 8%.

Then the net present value (NPV) may be calculated as follows ($000):

$$ NPV = -497.4 + \frac{-42.9}{1.08} + \frac{-2.1}{(1.08)^2} + \frac{66.3}{(1.08)^3} + \frac{131.8}{(1.08)^4} + \frac{153.5}{(1.08)^5} + \frac{139.9}{(1.08)^6} + \dots + \frac{139.9}{(1.08)^{10}} $$

$$ = \$95.2 $$

It's important to notice two things that are *not* in the calculations above. First, there is no provision for the $50,000 already spent for the new gearshift design. That money is gone whether the mountain bike project is accepted or not and is therefore irrelevant. Only *future* flows that depend on the decision to go ahead should be considered in the project's analysis. Past or *sunk* costs that can't be changed or recovered aren't considered even though they're related to the project.

Second, there's no allowance for interest in accumulated cash flows as a cost or income of the project. The cost of funds is explicitly included in capital budgeting when the NPV and IRR techniques are applied. Therefore, it doesn't need to be considered in the estimation of project cash flows.

Net present value would be $95.2, and the mountain bike project would be acceptable, as it would increase the value of the company and the wealth of its shareholders by that amount.

Using Excel®. Using an Excel® spreadsheet (to illustrate the estimates for the first three years only) this example might be formatted as follows.

Microsoft Excel - Book1.xls

File Edit View Insert Format Tools Data Window Help Adobe PDF

Arial · 10 · **B** *I* U | ≡ ≡ ≡ | $ % , ... | ... ... | ... · ... · **A** · .

A1 ▾ *fx* Table 13.1

	A	B	C	D	E	F
1	Table 13.1	Cash Flow Estimation				
2		Wilmont Bicycle Company				
3		Estimated Cash Flows				
4		Mountain Bike Project ($000s)				
5						
6		Year				
7						
8		1	2	3		
9	Revenue and Gross Margin					
10	Units	200	600	1200		
11	Revenue	$120.0 (=$60*B10)	$360.0 (=$60*C10)	$720.0 (=$60*D10)		
12	Cost of Sales	72.0 (=0.60*B11)	216.0 (=0.60*C11)	432.0 (=0.60*D11)		
13	Gross margin	$48.0 (=B11–B12)	$144.0 (=C11–C12)	$288.0 (=D11–D12)		
14						
15	Tax-Deductible Expenses					
16	SG&A expense	$120.0	$120.0	$120.0		
17	Amortization	41.5	41.5	41.5		
18	General overhead	2.4 (=.02*B11)	7.2 (=.02*C11)	14.4 (=.02*D11)		
19	Loss old line	1.4 (=.03*B13)	4.3 (=.03*C13)	8.6 (=.03*D13)		
20	Total	$165.3 (=Sum(B16:B19))	$173.0 (=Sum(C16:C19))	$184.5 (=Sum(D16:D19))		
21						
22	Profit Impact and Tax					
23	EBT Impact	($117.3) (=B13–B20)	($29.0) (=C13–C20)	$103.5 (=D13–D20)		
24	Tax	(39.9) (=0.34*B23)	(9.9) (=0.34*C23)	35.2 (=0.34*D23)		
25	NI Impact	($77.4) (=B23–B24)	($19.1) (=C23–C24)	$68.3 (=D23–D24)		
26	Add Amortization	41.5 (=B17)	41.5 (=C17)	41.5 (=D17)		
27	Subtotal	($35.9) (=B25+B26)	$22.4 (=C25+C26)	$109.8 (=D25+D26)		
28						
29	Working Capital					
30	Accounts receivable	$10.0 (=B11/12)	$30.0 (=C11/12)	$60.0 (=D11/12)		
31	Inventory	12.0	18.0 (=C12/12)	36.0 (=D12/12)		
32	Payables	(3.0) (=–0.25*B31)	(4.5) (=–0.25*C31)	(9.0) (=–0.25*D31)		
33	Working Capital	$19.0 (=Sum(B30:B32))	$43.5 (=Sum(C30:C32))	$87.0 (=Sum(D30:D32))		
34	Change in working capital	($7.0) ($(7.0))	($24.5) (=C33–B33)	($43.5) (=D33–C33)		
35						
36	Net Cash Flow					
37	Net Cash Flow	($42.9) (=B27+B34)	($2.1) (=C27+C34)	$66.3 (=D27+D34)		
38						
39	Summary					
40	Discount rate:	0.08				
41	Cash Flow					
42	C0 (The following values would be copied from row 37)	$(497.4)				
43	C1	(42.9)				
44	C2	(2.1)				
45	C3	66.3				
46	C4	131.8				
47	C5	153.5				
48	C6	139.9				
49	C7	139.9				
50	C8	139.9				
51	C9	139.9				
52	C10	139.9				
53						
54	NPV	95.2 (=NPV(B40,B43:B52)+B42)				
55						
56						

The NPV *function* in Excel® requires a discount rate (8%), the series of future cash flows, beginning with C_1, and the initial outlay (negative).

Terminal Values

It's possible to assume that the incremental cash flows associated with a project go on forever. The assumption is especially common with respect to new ventures that are expected to continue as businesses indefinitely. For example, in the Wilmont Bicycle Company problem we've

Cash flows forecast to continue forever are compressed into finite terminal values using perpetuity formulas.

just completed, it's not unreasonable to assume that the year 6 cash flow of approximately $140,000 continues into the indefinite future, instead of ending after 10 years.

There's a convenient way to reflect this assumption in the cash flow stream that Wilmont will use in capital budgeting. The repetitive cash flow starting in period 7 is a perpetuity whose "present" value at the beginning of period 7 (end of period 6) is $\frac{C_7}{k}$, where k is the cost of capital. This amount, known as the project's *terminal value*, is added to the period 6 cash flow to reflect the continuation of the project. If Wilmont's cost of capital is 8%, the project's terminal value would be

$$\frac{\$140,000}{0.08} = \$1,750,000$$

It's also possible to assume a perpetual cash flow that grows at some rate, g. In that case the terminal value is calculated by dividing the first ongoing cash flow by $k - g$ instead of k. Suppose Wilmont forecasts a 3% growth in the mountain bike project's cash flows starting with $140,000 in period 7. The project's terminal value would then be

$$\frac{\$140,000}{0.08 - 0.03} = \$2,800,000$$

Notice how large the terminal value cash flow is relative to the project's earlier flows. Indeed the terminal value assumption overwhelms everything else in the projection. Also notice that the magnitude of the terminal value is very sensitive to the growth rate assumed.

From the CFO

This is a big problem with respect to the accuracy of capital budgeting analyses. An optimistic long-run forecast can make a project look good on an NPV or IRR basis even if the short-run projections are poor. Since the terminal period doesn't start for some time, it's hard to disprove the assumptions behind it. Hence people who propose projects tend to portray them as growing rapidly into the indefinite future. It's generally up to the finance department to keep such projections reasonable and conservative.

There's a strong argument that infinite projections shouldn't be used at all because of the uncertainty of the distant future. This position maintains that if a project can't be justified in a reasonably long time, say, 10 years, it shouldn't be undertaken. In this example, we have not used any cash flow forecasts beyond 10 years.[3]

Accuracy and Estimates

Now that we've had a look at the estimating process we need to revisit the important point about precision that we discussed briefly at the beginning of the chapter.

Capital budgeting results are *no more accurate* than the *projections of the future* used as inputs.

The NPV and IRR techniques give the impression of great accuracy, as NPVs and IRRs are easily calculated to several decimal places. Such precision isn't real, however. Although IRR and NPV calculations are very exact, they're based on the cash flows input to the capital budgeting model. Those flows are *estimates* of the future and, like all estimates, are subject to error and bias.

In Example 13.1, Wilmont's cash flow estimates were built on the unit sales forecast. But for a new product, that forecast could easily be off by 20%. Such variability implies that it usually doesn't pay to expend a great deal of effort to make other elements of the estimate precise. For example, an estimator might spend a lot of time determining whether the appropriate cost ratio for the mountain bike project is 60% or 61%. That would be a waste of time given the inaccuracy of the underlying sales forecast. Notice that we worked in tenths of thousands of dollars in Table 13.1, and could easily have rounded to thousands without loss of substance.

From the CFO

Estimating inaccuracies come from any number of sources, but unintentional biases are probably the biggest problem in capital budgeting. Projects are usually proposed by people who have an interest in their approval, and it's generally those same individuals

3 In addition, we have not forecast any recovery of working capital or salvage values for the land, building, or equipment in year 10. In simplifying the example, we have understated NPV.

who provide the technical input for the estimated cash flows used in capital budgeting. This creates an inherent conflict of interest.

For example, suppose a company's manufacturing department has proposed buying a new, state-of-the-art production machine to replace an old machine that's beginning to wear out. If the new machine is purchased, product quality will be consistently higher, and there will be fewer equipment breakdowns that cause production stoppages. Such problems create the most stress in manufacturing managers' lives and significantly affect their performance ratings. Therefore, manufacturing managers are likely to perceive the new machine as a means of making their lives easier and better.

It is true that the manufacturing department will be charged with the cost of the new machine, but if that cost is included in the department's budget, it won't create an overrun that requires explaining. All things considered, manufacturing executives are likely to perceive the machine in an entirely positive light.

Representing the new machine as a series of cash flows requires putting a dollar value on the improved quality of output and on the machine's higher reliability. The implication is that the increased quality will result in higher customer satisfaction and fewer complaints. The better reliability will presumably result in less lost time on the production floor.

Projects are generally proposed by people who want to see them approved, leading to favourable biases.

Making financial estimates of effects like these is a very subjective affair. We can generally say that the new machine will have a positive effect, but exactly how large it will be is hard to pin down. The results are difficult to identify even after the project is implemented. The effects of happier customers and fewer breakdowns rarely show up clearly on a financial statement. If they happen at all, they're just rolled into the normal financial results of operations.

As a result of all this, estimating the financial impact of such a project often turns out to be little more than educated guesswork that can never be proven right or wrong. But the people making the guesses are probably going to be members of the manufacturing team who proposed the project in the first place and feel that it's a terrific idea. Therefore, their tendency will be to overestimate the benefits and underestimate the costs. We'll consider some of these issues in an example shortly.

CCA—A Note on Amortization for Tax Purposes

The Canada Revenue Agency and other Canadian income tax authorities prescribe certain methods to calculate amortization for tax purposes. Firms must follow the *capital cost allowance (CCA)* rules, first introduced in Chapter 2, which generally provide for *accelerated amortization* when computing income for tax purposes. Under an accelerated method amortization is shifted forward in an asset's life, so more is taken in the early years and less later on. This means taxable income and taxes due are lower in the early years and higher later on. In essence the scheme *defers* taxes.

This is an advantage because of the time value of money. To understand that, think of taking a dollar of deferred tax and putting it in the bank until it has to be paid several years later, and keeping the interest earned in the meantime.

Accelerated amortization creates a problem, however, because companies don't like to show lower profits in the short run even if they'll be made up later on. As a result, companies generally don't use accelerated amortization to calculate the earnings shown to shareholders and the public. It's important to understand that it's perfectly legitimate to use two sets of accounting rules like this, one for *tax* purposes and one for *financial reporting* purposes (see Chapter 2, page 43).

Recall that amortization is a noncash expense item. It represents an accounting allocation of cost over time intended to make financial results match physical activity. It doesn't represent actual spending. Also recall that in capital budgeting we're interested in *cash flow*, not accounting results. Hence the only reason we include amortization in capital budgeting calculations is because of its effect on taxes, which are real cash flow items.

Therefore, when a firm uses accelerated amortization (capital cost allowance) for tax purposes, it should use that amortization in capital budgeting calculations. We haven't shown this detail in our examples as yet, to keep things simple for illustrative purposes, but you should be aware of how this feature of the tax system works.

Capital cost allowance (CCA) is the tax version of amortization, usually on a *declining balance* basis.

Undepreciated capital cost is the undepreciated value of assets that is the basis for the amount of CCA claimed.

The *half-year rule*: When assets are purchased during the year, UCC is increased by only *50% of the additions (less disposals)* for that year.

For further information on current CCA rates, go to the Canada Revenue Agency website at http://www.cra-arc.gc.ca/tax/business/topics/solepartner/reporting/capital/classes-e.html.

CCA rates are set by the Canada Revenue Agency (CRA) for use in calculating CCA on the balance in an asset class.

Capital Cost Allowance System

To forecast cash flows under an investment proposal, we have to consider how amortization that is *allowable for tax purposes* will affect these cash flows.

The *Income Tax Act* lays out an accelerated amortization system, called **capital cost allowance (CCA)**, that reduces taxes for profitable firms. We say that capital cost allowance creates tax savings *or tax shields,* for profitable firms.

For tax purposes, capital assets are divided into a number of *classes,* each of which is assigned a *CCA rate.* Most of the classes call for *declining balance* CCA.

The classification rules are fairly extensive, as are the tables. A sampling of CCA classes, their CCA rates, and some typical items that might be assigned to a particular class are included in Table 13.2.

When an asset is *purchased*, its purchase price is added to the appropriate class for that type of asset. Any net increases in a class (as a result of purchases, for instance) are usually eligible for only *half* of the normal CCA in the year they are added (*the half-year rule*). This rule assumes that the assets are placed in service in the *middle of the year* in which they're acquired.

Once a capital asset has been added to a CCA class, capital cost allowance is calculated on the **undepreciated capital cost (UCC)** of the pool of assets, rather than on a single individual asset.

After year 1, we have created a steadily *declining balance* as long as there are assets in the class.

Disposals of Assets

When an asset is *sold*, the *lower of the sale price or its original cost* is deducted from the pool. If an asset is sold for more than its original cost, the difference is treated as a *capital gain* for tax purposes. Only 50% of the capital gain is added to taxable income for the year.

If the sale of the asset leaves no assets in the class, the resulting *positive* balance, if any, is called a *terminal loss,* and is deductible for tax purposes.

Any *negative* balance in the class at the end of the year is called *recapture* and is taxed as income.

Example 13.2

Table 13.3 on page 481 provides an example of the capital cost allowance calculations on a new capital asset—a vehicle added to Class 10 (30%). Assume the tax rate is 39%. The tax shield represents the first four years' tax savings that result from claiming capital cost allowance for tax purposes. Provided that the firm owns and continues to use other assets in the class, CCA may be claimed in future years on the remaining positive balance in the class.

CCA Tax Shield

For capital budgeting purposes, we need to calculate the *present value* of the tax savings resulting from the yearly capital cost allowance (the **CCA tax shield**).

TABLE 13.2
Some Capital Cost Allowance Classes

Class	Rate	Typical Assets
Class 1	4% on declining balance	Buildings
Class 8	20% on declining balance	Furniture, equipment
Class 10	30% on declining balance	Automobiles
Class 12	100% on declining balance	Computer applications software
Class 13	Straight-line basis	Leasehold improvements
Class 14	Straight-line basis	Patents, licenses, franchises
Class 43	30% on declining balance	Manufacturing and processing machinery, equipment
Class 45	45% on declining balance	Computer hardware and systems software

TABLE 13.3
Capital Cost
Allowance and
Tax Shield

	Year 1	Tax Shield @39%
Original cost	$ 30,000	
Less: Capital cost allowance $\frac{1}{2}$ ($30,000 × 0.30)	4,500	$ 1,755
Undepreciated capital cost	$ 25,500	
Year 2		
Less: Capital cost allowance ($25,500 × 0.30)	7,650	2984
Undepreciated capital cost	$ 17,850	
Year 3		
Less: Capital cost allowance ($17,850 × 0.30)	5,355	2,088
Undepreciated capital cost	$ 12,495	
Year 4		
Less: Proceeds on sale	4,000	
	$ 8,495	
Less: Capital cost allowance ($8,495 × 0.30)*	2,548	994
Undepreciated capital cost	$ 5,947	

*Assuming there are other assets remaining in the class.

The general formula[4] to account for the present value of the CCA tax shield is

CCA tax shield is the tax savings that the firm will experience from being able to claim CCA on its capital assets.

(13.1)
$$PV = (C - S_{pv})\left(\frac{dT}{k + d}\right) + \left(\frac{1 + 0.5k}{1 + k}\right)$$

where

C = Cost of the new asset (less any proceeds on disposal of assets replaced)

d = CCA rate for the asset class

T = Tax rate

k = Discount rate (cost of capital)

S_{pv} = Present value of the terminal (salvage) value of the new asset

$$= \frac{S}{(1 + k)^n}$$

n = Number of years until we sell the asset.

Let's return to Table 13.3. Here we purchase a truck for $30,000.

- We will trade it in four years for $4,000.
- The CCA rate is 30%.
- Our tax rate is 39%.
- Assume that our cost of capital is 12%.

The present value of the salvage in 4 years is $4,000[PVF_{12,4}] = $2,542.

4 This formula assumes that
a. in the year the new asset is sold, another asset (of the same class) will be purchased;
b. the half-year rule will apply to the net difference (purchase cost − salvage value);
c. the asset class will continue after the sale.

The present value of the CCA tax shield is

$$PV = (\$30,000 - \$2,542)\left(\frac{0.30 \times 0.39}{0.12 + 0.30}\right)\left(\frac{1 + .5(.12)}{1.12}\right)$$

$$= \$7,239$$

Alternatively, some practitioners prefer not to apply the half-year rule to the CCA effect from future salvage value, particularly if it appears that the asset will not be replaced in the same year. The formula for the present value of the CCA tax shield is adjusted for the full tax shield lost due to the future salvage value.

The formula becomes

(13.2)
$$PV = C\left(\frac{dT}{k + d}\right)\left(\frac{1 + 0.5k}{1 + k}\right) - S_{pv}\left(\frac{dT}{k + d}\right)$$

$$= 30,000\left(\frac{0.30 \times 0.39}{0.12 + 0.30}\right)\left(\frac{1 + .5(.12)}{1.12}\right) - 2,542\left(\frac{0.30 \times 0.39}{0.12 + 0.30}\right)$$

$$= \$7,201$$

In any case, the future salvage value rarely has a material effect on the present value of the CCA tax shield. In a capital budgeting analysis, the present value of the CCA tax shield would be added to the net present value of all other cash flows generated by the investment in the asset.

Example 13.3

Let's return to the mountain bike project summarized in Table 13.1 on page 475.

We will now use our CCA tax shield (rather than accounting amortization) to calculate the net present value (NPV) of the project. We will use Excel® to restate our estimated cash flows to eliminate the effect of the amortization ($000). Assuming again a project life of 10 years and a cost of capital of 8%, the NPV of the cash flows is $37.5.

Calculator Solution

Key	Input
CF$_0$	−497.4
C01	−57.0
C02	−16.3
C03	52.2
C04	117.7
C05	139.4
C06	139.4
C07	139.4
C08	139.4
C09	139.4
C10	139.4
I	8.0

Answer

NPV	37.5

Microsoft Excel - Wilmont

	0	1	2	3	4	Year 5	6	7	8	9	10
Initial Outlay	−$ 497.4										
Revenue and Gross Margin											
Units		200	600	1200	1500	1500	1500	1500	1500	1500	1500
Revenue		$120.0	$360.0	$720.0	$900.0	$900.0	$900.0	$900.0	$900.0	$900.0	$900.0
Cost of sales		72.0	216.0	432.0	540.0	540.0	540.0	540.0	540.0	540.0	540.0
Gross margin		$48.0	$144.0	$288.0	$360.0	$360.0	$360.0	$360.0	$360.0	$360.0	$360.0
Tax Deductible Expenses											
SG&A expense		$120.0	$120.0	$120.0	$120.0	$120.0	$120.0	$120.0	$120.0	$120.0	$120.0
Amortization											
General overhead		2.4	7.2	14.4	18.0	18.0	18.0	18.0	18.0	18.0	18.0
Loss old line		1.4	4.3	8.6	10.8	10.8	10.8	10.8	10.8	10.8	10.8
Total		$123.8	$131.5	$143.0	$148.8	$148.8	$148.8	$148.8	$148.8	$148.8	$148.8
Profit Impact and Tax											
EBT impact		−$75.8	$12.5	$145.0	$211.2	$211.2	$211.2	$211.2	$211.2	$211.2	$211.2
Tax @ 34%		−25.8	4.3	49.3	71.8	71.8	71.8	71.8	71.8	71.8	71.8
NI impact		−$50.0	$8.3	$95.7	$139.4	$139.4	$139.4	$139.4	$139.4	$139.4	$139.4
Working Capital											
Accounts receivable		$10.0	$30.0	$60.0	$75.0	$75.0	$75.0	$75.0	$75.0	$75.0	$75.0
Inventory		12.0	18.0	36.0	45.0	45.0	45.0	45.0	45.0	45.0	45.0
Payables		−3.0	−4.5	−9.0	−11.3	−11.3	−11.3	−11.3	−11.3	−11.3	−11.3
Working capital		$19.0	$43.5	$87.0	$108.7	$108.7	$108.7	$108.7	$108.7	$108.7	$108.7
Change in working capital		−$7.0	−$24.5	−$43.5	−$21.7	$0.0	$0.0	$0.0	$0.0	$0.0	$0.0
Net Cash Flow	−$497.4	−$57.0	−$16.3	$52.2	$117.7	$139.4	$139.4	$139.4	$139.4	$139.4	$139.4
NPV	$37.5 (=NPV(0.08,E34:N34)+D34)										

We now add the present value of the CCA tax shields for the equipment ($200.0) using 20% CCA, and the new construction ($60.0), using 4% CCA:

$$NPV = -497.4 + \frac{-57.0}{1.08} + \frac{-16.3}{(1.08)^2} + \frac{52.2}{(1.08)^3} + \frac{117.7}{(1.08)^4} + \frac{139.4}{(1.08)^5} + \cdots + \frac{139.4}{(1.08)^{10}}$$

$$= \$34.7$$

$$= \$200.0 \left(\frac{0.20 \times 0.34}{0.08 + 0.20}\right)\left(\frac{1 + 0.5(0.08)}{1 + 0.08}\right)$$

$$+ \$60.0 \left(\frac{0.04 \times 0.34}{0.08 + 0.04}\right)\left(\frac{1 + 0.5(0.08)}{1 + 0.08}\right)$$

$$= 46.8 + 6.5$$

$$= \$53.3$$

To get the total NPV:

Take PV of CCA tax shields	$ 53.3
Add: Net present value of cash flows	37.5
Total NPV	$ 90.8

The project is acceptable, and its IRR is greater than its cost of capital.

Investment Tax Credits and Other Government Incentives

For further information on current ITC rules and other government incentives, go to the Canada Revenue Agency website at http://www.cra-arc.gc.ca/E/pub/tg/t4012/t4012-10-e.html#P3523_266365.

The federal and provincial governments may offer *investment tax credits* (ITCs) as incentives for corporations to invest in certain types of businesses or in certain geographical areas of Canada. Qualified scientific research expenditures and manufacturing and processing activities have been eligible for these credits.

A specified percentage of such expenditures can be offset against taxes otherwise payable.

In capital budgeting analysis, any such investment tax credits (ITCs) represent a positive cash flow and a *reduction in the undepreciated capital cost (UCC)* of the class in the year they are received.

Other government incentives may include cash grants, wage and rent subsidies, interest rate subsidies, and reductions in taxes.

ESTIMATING CASH FLOWS FOR REPLACEMENT PROJECTS

Replacement projects generally have fewer elements to consider than new ventures, but identifying what is incremental can be trickier. It can be especially hard to specify what will happen if we

Insights PRACTICAL FINANCE

A Capital Budgeting Checklist

Include in/Exclude from Cash Flows?
Initial Outlay

New property and equipment	Include
Less: Salvage value of assets replaced	Include
Receipts after tax foregone from continuing use of assets (opportunity costs)	Include
Incidental start-up expenses, after tax	Include
Increase in working capital	Include
Net book value of old assets (sunk costs)	Exclude
Past expenditures	Exclude

Future Cash Flows

Change in revenues	Include
Change in costs and expenses	Include
Change in income taxes	Include
Adjustments for amortization and other noncash expenses	Include
Changes in working capital	Include
Opportunity costs	Include
Revenues, costs, and expenses unchanged	Exclude
Sunk costs	Exclude
Interest expense	Exclude

End of Planning Period

Terminal Value	Include
Salvage value of new assets, less tax	Include
Working capital released	Include

don't do the project. For example, suppose a production machine is getting old and needs to be replaced. Do we compare the performance of the new machine with the current performance of the old one, or assume that the old one will continue to deteriorate? If the latter, how much additional cost will the deterioration bring about? Tax effects are also complicated in replacement projects.

Example 13.4

Harrington Metals Inc. purchased a large stamping machine five years ago for $80,000. To keep the example simple, we'll assume that the tax laws at the time permitted straight-line amortization over eight years and that machinery purchased today can be amortized straight-line over five years (assume no terminal value in either case). The old machine has not performed well, and management is considering replacing it with a new one that will cost $150,000. If the new machine is purchased, it is estimated that the old one can be sold for $40,000. The quoted costs include all freight, installation, and set-up.

The old machine requires three part-time operators, each of whom earns $25,000 a year including all benefits and payroll costs. The new machine is more efficiently designed and will require only two operators, each earning the same amount.

The old machine has the following history of high maintenance cost and significant downtime.

	Year				
	1	**2**	**3**	**4**	**5**
Hours down	40	60	100	130	128
Maintenance expense	Under warranty	$10,000	$35,000	$42,000	$45,000

Downtime on the machine is a major inconvenience, but it doesn't usually stop production unless it lasts for an extended period. This is because the company maintains an emergency inventory of stamped pieces and has been able to temporarily reroute production without much notice. Manufacturing managers estimate that every hour of downtime costs the company $500, but have no hard data backing up that figure.

The makers of the replacement machine have said that Harrington will spend about $15,000 a year maintaining their product and that an average of only 30 hours of downtime a year should be expected. However, they're not willing to guarantee those estimates after the one-year warranty runs out.

The new machine is expected to produce higher-quality output than the old one. The result is expected to be better customer satisfaction and possibly more sales in the future. Management would like to include some benefit for this effect in the analysis, but is unsure of how to quantify it.

Estimate the incremental cash flows over the next five years associated with buying the new machine. Assume Harrington's marginal tax rate is 34% and that the company is currently profitable, so that changes in taxable income result in tax changes at 34% whether positive or negative. Ignore any potential tax consequences of the sale of the old machine.

■ **Solution:** There are two kinds of cash flow items in this problem: those that can be estimated fairly objectively, and those that require some degree of subjective guesswork. Let's consider the objective items first.

The initial outlay is a relatively straightforward matter. The new machine will cost $150,000 less whatever proceeds come from the sale of the old one. The old machine has a market value of $40,000.

The project's initial outlay is ($000).

Cost of new machine	$150.0
Less proceeds from sale of old machine	40.0
Initial outlay	$110.0

Now we'll consider incremental cash flows during the five-year planning period. The straightforward items are the tax implications of a new amortization pattern and the labour savings due to requiring one less operator.

Purchasing the new machine will alter the amortization tax shield as follows ($000).

	Year				
	1	2	3	4	5
New amortization	$ 30.0	$ 30.0	$ 30.0	$ 30.0	$ 30.0
Old amortization	$ 10.0	$ 10.0	$ 10.0	–	–
Net increase in amortization	$ 20.0	$ 20.0	$ 20.0	$ 30.0	$ 30.0
Cash tax savings @ 34%	$ 6.8	$6.8	$6.8	$ 10.2	$ 10.2

The labour savings are just the cost of one employee ($000).

	Year				
	1	2	3	4	5
Labour savings	$25.0	$25.0	$25.0	$25.0	$25.0

Now we have to deal with the subjective items in the estimate. Three effects have to be considered. These are the differences between the new machine and the old in maintenance expense, downtime, and product quality. Each clearly has a value, but it's hard to say how much.

It is at this stage of the analysis that the role of the financial analyst is most crucial. The people putting together the proposal to buy the new machine are likely to be very optimistic about the subjective benefits. It's the job of the finance department to be the voice of reason in the decision-making process, and to ensure that only realistic estimates of subjective benefits are included.

Let's consider the issues in this example one at a time. The most concrete is the maintenance cost. We have to forecast the *difference* in the cost of maintenance on the new machine if we buy it and maintenance on the old one if it is kept. Looking at the record, we can see that the old machine's cost increased steadily for several years, but has recently levelled off at about $45,000. The question is whether to assume it will stay there or resume its increase as the machine gets older. The new machine offers a one-year warranty and promises a cost of $15,000 a year thereafter. However, that figure is not guaranteed. The issue is whether to believe the $15,000 or assume a higher number. We'll lay out a set of maintenance cost figures that reflects maintenance on the old machine continuing at $45,000 and the new machine performing as promised ($000).

	Year				
	1	2	3	4	5
Old machine	$ 45.0	$ 45.0	$ 45.0	$ 45.0	$ 45.0
New machine	Under warranty	$ 15.0	$ 15.0	$ 15.0	$ 15.0
Savings	$ 45.0	$ 30.0	$ 30.0	$ 30.0	$ 30.0

The difference between the two maintenance estimates represents the cash savings due to replacing the machine. Notice that it's possible to manipulate the analysis by varying the assumptions about either or both estimates. If we want to make the project look good, we can assume the old machine's costs will get worse and the new one's will hold at $15,000. If we assume the new machine will cost more while the old one holds at $45,000, the project looks worse.

The point is that there's a great deal of latitude in the forecast, and reasonable estimates of the maintenance cost savings can vary by quite a bit. For purposes of the example, we'll use the one shown here.

Next, let's look at the downtime estimate. Here, two variables are considered: how much downtime will actually be saved by the new machine, and how much each hour is worth. The questions involved in estimating the hours saved are similar to those in dealing with the maintenance cost. The old machine has been having about 130 hours of downtime a year while the new one promises 30 hours, for a saving of 100 hours. However, good arguments can be made for raising or lowering that figure by quite a bit. The confounding question, however, is how much an hour of saved downtime is worth. It clearly should have some value, but it's difficult to say how much. This is a very common problem. We know there's a cost or benefit to something, but we're not able to estimate its value with any precision.

Manufacturing management's subjective estimate of $500 per hour is likely to be on the high side because of the biases we discussed earlier.

A conservative approach, on the other hand, might be to refuse to include anything in the analysis for the saved downtime because its value can't be documented. Anything in between is also possible.

From the CFO

In situations like this, most people favour a middle-of-the-road approach. That implies giving some value to the saved downtime, but choosing a value substantially lower than that recommended by manufacturing.

In this case, $200 per hour is probably reasonable. Combining that figure with the saved time estimate of 100 hours yields an estimated cash flow savings of $20,000 per year.

Next we'll examine the most subjective claim in favour of the new machine: increased quality of output. Once again, this issue is very common when people are trying to justify a project. The issue isn't whether or not the output actually will be of higher quality. That should be ascertainable as a matter of fact by testing the output of a demo machine against the output of the old one. The question is whether or not an increase in the quality of certain component parts will significantly increase customer satisfaction, and whether that will translate into more future sales.

Several scenarios are possible. If customers or service technicians have been actively complaining about the parts from the old machine, it's easier to argue that higher quality will have a future sales impact than if the old parts weren't a problem. But even then, the impact is likely to be very difficult to estimate. As a general rule, when the connection between a project and the claimed cash flow impact is this tenuous, financial people tend to want to leave it out of the analysis. That's what we'll do in this case.

Using Excel®, we summarize the cash flows resulting from installation of the new machine ($000). If the cost of capital (the discount rate) is 10%, the net present value is $116.9.

Excel spreadsheet (Harrington):

	0	1	2	3	4	5
Initial outlay	-$110.0					
Labour savings		$25.0	$25.0	$25.0	$25.0	$25.0
Maintenance savings		45.0	30.0	30.0	30.0	30.0
Downtime savings		20.0	20.0	20.0	20.0	20.0
Total		90.0	75.0	75.0	75.0	75.0
Tax		30.6	25.5	25.5	25.5	25.5
Net after tax		59.4	49.5	49.5	49.5	49.5
Tax savings on amortization		6.8	6.8	6.8	10.2	10.2
Cash flow	-$110.0	$66.2	$56.3	$56.3	$59.7	$59.7
Net present value	$116.9 (=NPV(0.10,D15:H15)+C15)					

Incremental CCA

If we apply CCA rules to this situation, accounting amortization is *not* relevant.

We add the cost of the old and new machines to Class 43 (CCA rate: 30%) and we deduct the sales proceeds of the old machine from Class 8.

Our cash flows before CCA ($000):

Year	0	1	2	3	4	5
	$ (110.0)	$ 59.4	$ 49.5	$ 49.5	$ 49.5	$ 49.5

If the discount rate is 10%,

$$NPV = \$(110.0) + \$54.0 + \$40.9 + \$37.2 + \$33.8 + \$30.7$$
$$= \$86.6$$

The present value of the new CCA tax shield is

$$PV = (C - S_{pv}) \left(\frac{dT}{k + d} \right) \left(\frac{1 + 0.5k}{1 + k} \right)$$

where C = *Change* in capital cost class

$$= \$150.0 - \$40.0$$
$$= \$110.0$$

and where S_{pv} = Present value of salvage on new machine in 5 years (assume 0)

$$PV = 110.0 \left(\frac{0.30 \times 0.34}{0.10 + 0.30} \right) \left(\frac{1 + 0.5(0.10)}{1 + 0.10} \right)$$

$$PV = \$26.8 \ (\$000)$$

Combining this with the net present value of the cash flows, the overall NPV is

$$NPV = \$86.6 + 26.8$$
$$= \$113.4$$

The project would be acceptable as it increases the wealth of the shareholders by this amount.

Insights **ETHICS**

Ethics in Cash Flow Estimation

We've just seen that strong departmental interests can affect capital budgeting decisions, and that wide ranges of inputs can be accepted in making those decisions. It's also true that people stretch the truth to get what they want. What are the ethical issues of knowingly providing biased information to a decision-making process to get an outcome that's favourable to your own department?

In answering, recall that in ethical situations one group often has power over another (page 16). Is information power? Who benefits and who gets hurt if the company buys the new machine in Example 13.4 based on

manufacturing's claims if those claims are exaggerated beyond truth?

Here's another interesting situation. Imagine that an executive puts together a proposal for a new venture. It's common for the person proposing something like that to get to run the start-up. Then, if it's successful, he or she moves up the management ladder rapidly and makes a lot of money. Do you see a motivation for the executive to overstate the project's benefits and understate its negatives? Is the executive's gamble one-sided in that he or she has a lot to gain and little to lose? Who loses if the project is undertaken and fails?

SUMMARY

1 Capital budgeting decisions involve the forecasting of expenditures and receipts, both immediate and future, for long-run investments in capital assets. As money has a time value (an inherent rate of interest), both the amount and timing of the cash flows must be considered. Only the initial outlay and the changes to future cash flows are relevant for capital budgeting purposes. Cash flow estimates

include the future salvage value, after tax, of the new assets to be acquired. The initial outlay includes all costs to buy, build, or assemble the investment and prepare it for use, including new property and equipment, training costs, and increases in working capital. Any salvage or trade-in value received for assets replaced would be deducted from the initial outlay.

2 Opportunity costs are relevant to capital budgeting decisions as they represent cash inflows foregone. Sunk costs cannot be changed and are not relevant.

3 Interest costs are excluded from cash flow estimation as they are recognized

when net present value and internal rate of return are calculated.

4 Changes to future cash flows include the impact of amortization and income taxes; rules for capital cost allowance are used in practice to determine the tax shield available from amortization.

KEY TERMS

Capital cost allowance (CCA), p. 480
CCA tax shield, p. 480

Incremental cash flows, p. 471
Sunk costs, p. 471

Undepreciated capital costs (UCC), p. 480

KEY FORMULAS

(13.1)
$$PV = (C - S_{pv})\left(\frac{dT}{k + d}\right) + \left(\frac{1 + 0.5k}{1 + k}\right)$$

(13.2)
$$PV = C\left(\frac{dT}{k + d}\right)\left(\frac{1 + 0.5k}{1 + k}\right) - S_{pv}\left(\frac{dT}{k + d}\right)$$

QUESTION

1. The typical cash flow pattern for business projects involves cash outflows first, then inflows. However, it's possible to imagine a project in which the pattern is reversed. For example, we might receive inflows now in return for guaranteeing to make payments later. Would the payback, NPV, and IRR methods work for such a project? What would the NPV profile look like? Could the NPV and IRR methods give conflicting results?

Business Analysis

1. You are a new financial analyst at Belvedere Corp., a large manufacturing firm that is currently looking into diversification opportunities. The vice-president of marketing is particularly interested in a venture that is only marginally connected with what the firm does now. Other managers have suggested enterprises in more closely related fields. The proponents of the various ideas have all provided you with business forecasts from which you have developed financial projections including project cash flows. You have also calculated each project's IRR with the following results.

Project	IRR	Comments
A	19.67%	Marketing's project, an almost totally new field
B	19.25%	Proposed by manufacturing, also a very different field
C	18.05%	Proposed by engineering, a familiar field

You are now in a meeting with senior managers to discuss the options. You have just presented your analysis, ending your talk with the information above.

After your presentation, the vice-president of marketing stands, congratulates you on a fine job, and states that the figures clearly show that project A is the best option. He also says that your financial analysis shows that project A has the full backing of the finance department. All eyes, including the CFO's, turn to you. How do you respond?

2. Most top executives are graded primarily on their results in terms of net income rather than net cash flow. Why, then, is capital budgeting done with incremental cash flows rather than with incremental net income?

3. Creighton Inc. is preparing a bid to sell a large telephone communications system to a major business customer. It is characteristic of the telephone business that the vendor selling a system gets substantial follow-on business in later years by making changes and alterations to that system. The marketing department wants to take an *incremental* approach to the bid, basically treating it as a capital budgeting project. They propose selling the system at or below its direct cost in labour and materials (the incremental cost) to ensure getting the follow-on business. They've projected the value of that business by treating future sales less direct costs as cash inflows.

   They maintain that the initial outlay is the direct cost to install the system, which is almost immediately paid back by the price. Future cash flows are then the net inflows from the follow-on sales. These calculations have led to an enormous NPV and IRR for the sale viewed as a project.

   Both support and criticize this approach. (*Hint*: What would happen if Creighton did most of its business this way?)

4. Webley Motors, a manufacturer of small gas engines, has been working on a new design for several years. It's now considering going into the market with the new product, and has projected future sales and cash flows. The marketing and finance departments are putting together a joint presentation for the board of directors that they hope will gain approval for the new venture. Part of the presentation is a capital budgeting analysis of the project that includes only estimated future costs and revenues. Dan Eyeshade, the head of investor relations, insists that calculations shown to the board include the money spent on research in the past several years. He says that to ignore or omit those costs would be deceiving the board about the true cost of the project, which would be both unethical and legally dangerous. Comment on Dan's position. If you disagree, prepare an argument that will convince him to change his mind, and suggest an alternative presentation that will satisfy you both.

5. The Capricorn Company is launching a new venture in a field related to but separate from its present business. Management is proposing that financing for the new enterprise be supplied by a local bank, which it has approached for a loan. Capricorn's finance department has done a capital budgeting analysis of the venture, projecting reasonable cash flows and calculating an NPV and an IRR that both look very favourable.

   The bank's loan officer, however, isn't satisfied with the analysis. She insists on seeing a financial projection that calculates interest on cumulative cash flows, incorporates that interest as a cost of the project, and shows the buildup and decline of the debt necessary to accomplish the proposal. She essentially wants a business plan complete with projected financial statements.

   Reconcile the bank officer's position with capital budgeting theory.

6. Wilson Petroleum is a local distributor of home heating oil. The firm also installs and services furnaces and heating systems in homes and small commercial buildings. The customer service department maintains sales and service records on current customers, who number about 400. Detailed customer records are kept manually in file cabinets, and a small computer system holds all customer names and addresses for mailing and billing purposes. One full-time clerk maintains all the records and handles all billing and

customer inquiries. Customers occasionally complain if delivery or service is late, but only one or two mild complaints are received each month. Delays are primarily a result of problems in the field rather than problems in assigning calls in the service department.

A consultant has proposed a new computer system that will completely automate the customer service function. It will provide online billing and immediate access to all customer records. The cost of the proposed system is $50,000 initially plus about $7,000 a year for maintenance and support. It will still take a person to run it. The consultant says the new system will provide faster service and superior insight into the needs of the customer base, which will result in better customer relations and more sales in the long run.

Discuss the pros and cons of the consultant's proposal. What further justification should management demand before buying? Could the consultant have made the proposal for reasons that aren't in Wilson's best interest? Could the consultant be well meaning yet biased? Explain.

PROBLEMS

1. A project that is expected to last six years will generate a profit and cash flow contribution before taxes and amortization of $23,000 per year. It requires the initial purchase of equipment costing $60,000, which will be amortized over four years. The relevant tax rate is 25%. Calculate the project's cash flows. Round all figures within your computations to the nearest thousand dollars.

2. Auburn Concrete Inc. is considering the purchase of a new concrete mixer to replace an inefficient older model. If purchased, the new machine will cost $90,000 and is expected to generate savings of $40,000 per year for five years at the end of which it will be sold for $20,000. The mixer will be amortized to a zero salvage value over three years using the straight line method. Develop a five-year cash flow estimate for the proposal. Auburn's marginal tax rate is 30%. Work to the nearest thousand dollars.

3. Flextech Inc. is considering a project that will require new equipment costing $150,000. It will replace old equipment with an original cost of $35,000 that can be sold on the secondhand market for $75,000. Assume that 50% of the capital gain is taxable, and that the company's tax rate is 35%. Calculate the project's initial outlay.

4. Tomatoes Inc. is planning a project that involves machinery purchases of $100,000. It will replace old machinery that will be sold for an estimated $36,000 and has an original cost of $22,000. The project will also require hiring and training 10 new people at a cost of about $12,000 each. All of this must happen before the project is actually started. Assume that 50% of the capital gain is taxable, and that the firm's tax rate is 40%. Calculate CF_0, the project's initial cash outlay.

5. The Olson Company plans to replace an old machine with a new one costing $85,000. The old machine originally cost $55,000 and has six years of its expected 11-year life remaining. It has been amortized straight-line assuming zero salvage value and has a current market value of $24,000. Olson's effective tax rate is 36%.
   a. Calculate the book gain or loss on the disposal of the old machine.
   b. Calculate the initial outlay associated with selling the old machine and acquiring the new one.

6. A four-year project has cash flows before taxes and amortization of $12,000 per year. The project requires the purchase of a $50,000 asset that will be amortized over five years straight-line. At the end of the fourth year the asset will be sold for $18,000. The firm's marginal tax rate is 35%. Calculate the cash flows associated with the project. (There is no tax on the sale of the asset.)

7. Voxland Industries purchased a computer for $10,000, which it will amortize straight-line over five years to a $1,000 salvage value. The computer will then be sold at that price. The company's marginal tax rate is 40%. Calculate the cash flows associated with the computer from its purchase to its eventual sale including the years in between. (*Hint*: Amortize the difference between the cost of the computer and the salvage value. At the end of the amortization term, a net book value remains that is equal to the salvage value.)

Problem 8 below is based upon the concepts of capital cost allowance.

8. Resolve the previous problem assuming Voxland uses capital cost allowance to amortize the computer. Continue to assume that the machine is sold at the end of year 5 for $1,000. The CCA rate is 45%.

9. Harry and Flo Simone are planning to start a restaurant. Stoves, refrigerators, other kitchen equipment, and furniture are expected to cost $50,000, all of which will be amortized straight-line over five years. Construction and other costs of getting started will be $30,000. The Simones expect the following revenue stream ($000).

Year	1	2	3	4	5	6	7
Sales	$60	$90	$140	$160	$180	$200	$200

Food costs are expected to be 35% of revenues, while other variable expenses are forecast at 25% of revenues. Fixed overhead will be $40,000 per year. All operating expenses will be paid in cash, revenues will be collected immediately, and inventory is negligible, so working capital need not be considered. Assume the combined federal and provincial tax rate is 25%. Do not assume a tax credit in loss years, and ignore tax loss carry-forwards. (Taxes are simply zero when EBT is a loss.) Develop a cash flow forecast for the Simones' restaurant.

10. (An Excel® spreadsheet is helpful to complete parts (a), (b), and (d) of this problem. Alternatively, complete the problem manually.)

The Leventhal Baking Company is thinking of expanding its operations into a new line of pastries. The firm expects to sell $350,000 of the new product in the first year and $500,000 each year thereafter. Direct costs, including labour and materials, will be 60% of sales. Indirect incremental costs are estimated at $40,000 a year. The project will require several new ovens that will cost a total of $500,000 and be amortized straight-line over five years. The current plant is underutilized, so space is available that cannot be otherwise sold or rented. The firm's marginal tax rate is 35% and its cost of capital is 12%. Assume revenue is collected immediately and inventory is bought and paid for every day, so no additional working capital is required.
   a. Prepare a statement showing the incremental cash flows for this project over an eight-year period.
   b. Calculate the payback period, NPV, and PI.
   c. Recommend either acceptance or rejection.
   d. If the space to be used could otherwise be rented out for $30,000 a year, how would you put that fact into the calculation? Would the project be acceptable in that case?

11. Harrington Inc. is introducing a new product in its line of household appliances. Household products generally have 10-year life cycles and are viewed as capital budgeting projects over that period. Harrington's working capital forecast for the project is as follows:
    - $1.0 million will be invested in inventory before the project begins.
    - Inventory will increase by $100,000 in each of the first six years.
    - Accounts receivable will increase by $150,000 in each of the first four years and by $100,000 in each of the next two years.
    - Accounts payable will increase by $110,000 in each of the first six years.
    - During the last four years, the balance in each of these accounts will return to zero in four equal increments.
    - Accruals are negligible.

    Calculate the cash flows associated with working capital from the initial outlay to the end of the project's life.

12. Meade Metals Inc. plans to start doing its own deliveries instead of using an outside service for which it has been paying $150,000 per year. To make the change, Meade will purchase a $200,000 truck that it will amortize straight-line over 10 years to a $40,000 salvage value. Annual operating expenses are estimated at $80,000, including insurance, fuel, and maintenance on the truck, as well as the cost of a driver. Management plans to sell the truck after five years for $100,000. Meade's tax rate is 40%. Develop the project's five-year cash flows.

13. Assume that Meade Metals Inc. of the previous problem is replacing an old truck with a new one instead of replacing an outside delivery service. The old truck was purchased eight years ago for $120,000. It has been amortized straight-line based on a 10-year life and a $20,000 salvage value. The old truck's annual operating expenses are $110,000, and it has a market value of $40,000. Again, Meade's tax rate is 40%. Develop a five-year cash flow projection for this replacement project.

14. Shelton Pharmaceuticals Inc. is introducing a new drug for pain relief. Management expects to sell 3 million units in the first year at $8.50 each and anticipates 10% growth in sales per year thereafter. Operating costs are estimated at 70% of revenues. Shelton invested $20 million in equipment to develop and produce this product. The equipment will be amortized straight-line over 15 years to a salvage value of $2.0 million. Shelton's marginal tax rate is 40%. Calculate the project's operating cash flows in its third year.

15. Olson-Jackson Corp. (OJC) is considering replacing a machine that was purchased only two years ago because of dramatic improvements in new models. The old machine has been amortized straight-line anticipating a 10-year life based on a cost of $240,000 and an expected salvage value of $20,000. It currently has a market value of $180,000. If the old machine is kept five more years, it would have a market value of $60,000 at the end of that time. A new machine would cost $350,000 and would be amortized straight-line over five years to a salvage value of $50,000, at which time it would be sold at that price. Develop a cash flow projection showing the difference between keeping the old machine and acquiring the new one. Assume OJC's tax rate is 40%. (*Note*: A complete cash flow projection for the project would include the financial benefits of the better performance of the new machine as well as a comparison of the operating costs of the two models. In this problem we're just focusing on the cost of the equipment.)

16. The Catseye Marble Co. is thinking of replacing a manual production process with a machine. The manual process requires three relatively unskilled workers and a supervisor. Each worker makes $17,500 a year and the supervisor earns $24,500. The new machine

can be run with only one skilled operator who will earn $41,000. Payroll taxes and benefits are an additional third of all wages and salaries.

The machine costs $150,000 and has a tax amortization life of five years. Catseye uses straight-line amortization for tax purposes. A service contract covers all maintenance for $5,000 a year. The machine is expected to last six years, at which time it will have no salvage value. The machine's output will be virtually indistinguishable from that of the manual process in both quality and quantity. There are no other operating differences between the manual and the machine processes. Catseye's marginal tax rate is 35% and its cost of capital is 10%.

a. Calculate the incremental cash flows associated with the project to acquire the machine.

b. Calculate the project's payback and NPV. Would you accept or reject the project?

c. Suppose that there is no alternative but to lay off the displaced employees, and the cost of severance is about three months' wages and benefits. How would you factor this information into the analysis? Does it change the project's acceptability?

d. How would you characterize this project's risk?

17. Blackstone Inc. manufactures Western boots and saddles. The company is considering replacing an outmoded leather-processing machine with a new, more efficient model. The old machine was purchased for $48,000 six years ago and was expected to have an eight-year life. It has been amortized on a straight-line basis. The used machine has an estimated market value of $15,000. The new machine will cost $60,000 and will be amortized straight-line over five years. All amortization assumes zero salvage.

The new machine is expected to last eight years (its economic life), and then will have to be replaced. Assume it has no actual salvage value at that time.

Assume Blackstone's marginal tax rate is 35% (losses will generate tax savings). Operating cost savings are summarized as follows.

	Old	New
Annual maintenance cost	$2,000 increasing $200 in each future year	None for two years, $1,500 thereafter
Cost of fixing production defects	$3,000	$1,000
Operators	2 @ $20,000	1.5 @ $24,000

The shop foreman feels that the new machine will produce a higher-quality output and thus affect customer satisfaction and repeat sales. He thinks that benefit should be worth at least $5,000 a year, but doesn't have a way to document the figure.

a. Calculate the relatively certain incremental cash flows associated with the new machine over its projected economic life of eight years. (Losses will generate annual tax recoveries.)

b. Calculate the NPV at a cost of capital of 12%. (Round to whole $.)

c. Calculate the payback period.

d. Suppose the foreman's $5,000 quality improvement estimate were to be included. How big an impact would it have in relation to the NPV? Comment.

18. The Field of Dreams Corp. manufactures baseball gloves. Charlie Botz, the company's top salesman, has recommended expanding into the baseball bat business. He has put together a project proposal including the following information in support of his idea.

- New production equipment will cost $75,000 and will be amortized straight-line over five years.
- Overhead and expenses associated with the project are estimated at $20,000 per year during the first two years and $40,000 per year thereafter.

- There is enough unused space in the factory for the bat project. The space has no alternative use or value.
- Setting up production and establishing distribution channels before getting started will cost $300,000 (tax deductible).
- Aluminum and wood bats will be produced and sold to sporting goods retailers. Wholesale prices and incremental costs per unit (direct labour and materials) are as follows.

	Aluminum	**Wood**
Price	$ 18	$ 12
Cost of sales	11	9
Gross margin	$ 7	$ 3

- Charlie provides the following unit sales forecast (000).

	Year					
	1	**2**	**3**	**4**	**5**	**6**
Aluminum	6	9	15	18	20	22
Wood	8	12	14	20	22	24

The sixth-year sales level is expected to hold indefinitely.
- Receivables will be collected in 30 days, inventories will be the cost of one month's production, and payables are expected to be half of inventories. Assume no additional cash in the bank or accruals are necessary. (Use 1/12 of the current year's revenue and cost for receivables and inventories.)
- Field's marginal tax rate is 35% and its cost of capital is 12%.

a. Develop a six-year cash flow estimate for Charlie's proposal. (Ignore any salvage value or working capital recovery). Work to the nearest $1,000.

b. Calculate the payback period for the project.

c. Calculate the project's NPV assuming a six-year life. Is the project acceptable?

d. Is the cost of capital an appropriate discount rate for the project considering its likely risk relative to that of the rest of the business? Why?

e. What is the project's NPV if the planning horizon is extended to eight years? (Add the incremental PV from two more years at year 6's cash flow.)

f. What is the NPV if management is willing to look at an indefinitely long time horizon? (*Hint:* Think of the cash flows in year 6 and beyond as a perpetuity.)

g. Comment on the results of parts (e) and (f).

Problems 19 to 23 are based upon the concepts of capital cost allowance.

19. Argo Company just purchased a Class 45 asset at a cost of $175,000. Argo's tax rate is 22%.
  a. Calculate the amount of CCA Argo could claim for the first four years of the asset's life.
  b. How much tax shield would the company receive each year?

20. Eastern Manufacturing is considering whether or not to replace one of its machines. The existing machine can be sold now for $485,000. It is two years old, cost $900,000 new, has a $600,000 book value now, and a remaining useful life of five years. After another five years, it would have no salvage value.

The new machine costs $1.8 million and requires additional installation costs of $100,000 (deductible for tax purposes). An immediate increase in net working capital of $35,000 will be needed if the new machine is acquired.

Over its five-year life, the new machine should reduce operating costs by $550,000 per year. The new machine can be sold for $200,000 at the end of five years. The CCA rate on the machines is 30%. The firm has an 8% cost of capital and a 40% tax rate.

a. Calculate the changes in cash flows involved (ignore the CCA tax shield at this point).

b. Determine the net present value (NPV) of the proposal, including the CCA tax shield.

c. Would you accept or reject the replacement proposal? Justify your answer.

d. What is the highest cost of capital the firm could have and still accept the proposal? Explain in words only.

21. Massassauga Developments is considering an investment project that will require an immediate capital expenditure of $1.5 million for required equipment. Additional inventory required on installation of this new equipment will be $30,000.

Massassauga will install the new equipment and inventory in a building the company currently owns, but is not using. The unused building will require $50,000 in new fixtures (capitalized) in order for the equipment to be put into operation. Massassauga has no other intended use for the building, but the company has been renting it out for $60,000 a year. Massassauga will also use equipment that was purchased a year ago for $540,000, but which has yet to be used. If Massassauga were to sell the equipment, the most it would receive is $250,000. As the company has been losing money, no CCA has yet been claimed against the original purchase price.

The incremental operating income for the project is expected to be $455,000 a year for the first four years, and $475,000 a year for another three years. At the end of seven years, all of the equipment can be sold for $155,000. The CCA rate on the fixtures and equipment is 30%. Massassauga's tax rate is 40% and its cost of capital is 12%.

Should Massassauga proceed with the new project? Explain.

22. Hoodoo Corporation is deciding whether or not to purchase a new high-speed network server to replace its existing server. The existing server was purchased two years ago for $260,000. It is expected to have a useful life of five more years, at which time it will be worthless; it can currently be sold for $90,000. Removal and cleanup costs will total $12,000 (deductible for tax purposes) whenever it is replaced.

The new server costs $350,000 and requires another $15,000 in installation costs (also deductible for tax purposes); it has a five-year useful life. To support the increased business resulting from the purchase of the new server, accounts receivable would increase now by $140,000 and spare parts inventory by $30,000. The new server would be sold after five years to net $129,000 and the working capital would be recovered.

For CCA purposes, servers are considered a Class 45 asset with a CCA rate of 45%. Hoodoo's tax rate is 40% and its cost of capital is 10%. The estimated operating income for both the new and existing server are shown in the following table.

Operating Income Before Taxes

Year	New Server	Existing Server
1	$83,000	$36,000
2	96,000	34,000
3	110,000	32,000
4	98,000	30,000
5	88,000	28,000

Should Hoodoo replace the existing server? Explain.

23. Sam Dozier, a very bright computer scientist, has come up with an idea for a new product. He plans to form a corporation to develop the idea and market the resulting product. He has estimated that it will take him and one employee about a year to develop a prototype and another year to bring a working model to market. There will be no income during those years. After that he expects sales to grow rapidly, estimating revenues of $700,000, $1,500,000, and $5,000,000 in the third, fourth, and fifth years respectively.

    Manufacturing the product will require manufacturing equipment in the third year costing about $500,000. For CCA purposes, this equipment will be considered a Class 43 asset with a CCA rate of 30%.

    Sam thinks he can fund the development work including supporting himself and paying an employee with about $400,000 in tax deductible expenses to get going and another $200,000 per year in years one and two. Once sales begin in the third year, direct costs will be 40% of revenues and indirect costs, including salaries for Sam and all employees, will be $300,000, $500,000, and $1,800,000 in the third, fourth, and fifth years respectively.

    The nature of the business is such that working capital requirements are minimal. A net investment of $200,000 in the third year is expected to suffice. Sam has $1,500,000 saved, which he thinks is enough to launch and operate the business until it begins to generate income.

    Sam plans to sell the business at the end of the fifth year. At that time, he thinks it will be worth $2,500,000 including the machinery and working capital. His accountant estimates that his personal tax on the sale will be $250,000.

    a. Develop a yearly cash flow estimate for Sam's business. The business will pay corporate income taxes at an average rate of 34%. (Assume that taxes are simply zero when EBT is a loss.) A loss for any year will be carried forward to be deducted from the net income of future years. (For assistance on loss carry-forwards, see Chapter 2, page 44.)

    b. Does Sam have enough cash to fund this venture without contributions from outside investors?

    c. Calculate the project's NPV and IRR (a financial calculator is recommended). Assume the cost of capital is 12%. Is the venture a good investment of Sam's time and money?

24. Segwick Corp. manufactures men's shoes, which it sells through its own chain of retail stores. The firm is considering adding a line of women's shoes. Management considers the project a new venture because there are substantial differences in marketing and manufacturing processes between men's and women's footwear.

    The project will involve setting up a manufacturing facility as well as expanding or modifying the retail stores to carry two products. The stores are leased, so modification will involve leasing larger spaces and installing new fixtures and equipment. The expected costs are summarized as follows.

Manufacturing Assets

New manufacturing equipment, (CCA rate, 30%)	$ 750,000
Acquisition of a facility for design and manufacturing	
Land (no CCA)	$ 480,000
Building (CCA rate: 4%)	630,000
	$ 1,860,000

Leased Retail Space

Net new lease expense, per year	$ 40,000
New fixtures and equipment (CCA rate: 20%)	200,000

Expense Items

Cost of hiring and training new people	$ 150,000
Initial advertising and promotion	200,000
Yearly advertising and promotion	50,000
Yearly sales salaries	900,000
Additional corporate overhead ($000/yr)	$ 20, $ 42, $ 60, $ 80, $ 80, $ 80

Revenue and Cost

The unit sales forecast is as follows in thousands.

Year	Units	Average Price
1	30	$65
2	40	68
3	50	70
4 and on	60	75

Direct cost excluding amortization is 40% of sales.

Working Capital

Sales are to retail customers who pay with cheques or credit cards. It takes about 10 days to clear both of these and actually receive cash. Inventories are estimated to be approximately the direct cost of two months' sales. Payables are estimated as one-quarter of inventories. Estimate the current accounts based on the current year's sales and cost levels. Assume incremental cash is required equal to 2% of revenues. Accruals are insignificant.
There will be no working capital at start-up.

Estimated Salvage Values at the End of Year 6

Manufacturing equipment	$ 100,000
Land	$ 1,000,000
Building	$ 500,000
Store fixtures and equipment	0
Working capital released	$ 200,000

Assume that the company will retain positive balances in all CCA classes after these assets are salvaged. 50% of capital gains are taxable.

Other Items

Management expects a few of the company's current male customers to be lost because they won't want to shop in a store that doesn't exclusively sell men's shoes. The gross margin impact of these lost sales is estimated to be $60,000 per year.

The company has already purchased designs for certain styles of ladies' shoes for $60,000. Segwick's cost of capital is 10%. Its marginal tax rate is 35%.

a. Complete the following tables to calculate the annual tax shield from claiming CCA for the first six years of the project's life. (Ignore salvage values.)

Annual CCA Tax Shield: Manufacturing Equipment

Year	Calculation	UCC	CCA (30%)	Tax Saving (35%)
1	750,000 × 50%	$375,000	$112,500	$39,375
2	750,000 − 112,500	637,500	_____	_____
3	_____	_____	_____	_____
4	_____	_____	_____	_____
5	_____	_____	_____	_____

Annual CCA Tax Shield: Building

Year	Calculation	UCC	CCA (4%)	Tax Saving (35%)
1				
2				
3				
4				
5				
6				

Annual CCA Tax Shield: Fixtures and Equipment

Year	Calculation	UCC	CCA (20%)	Tax Saving (35%)
1				
2				
3				
4				
5				
6				

Annual CCA Tax Shield: Summary

Year	Manufacturing Equipment	Building	Fixtures and Equipment	Total
1				
2				
3				
4				
5				
6				

b. Develop a six-year forecast of all after-tax cash flows for Segwick, including CCA tax shield.

c. Calculate the project's payback period, NPV, and PI, and make a recommendation about acceptance.

d. Assume you are told that the men's shoe industry is very stable, being served by the same manufacturers year after year. However, firms enter and leave the ladies' shoe business regularly.

  i. Would this knowledge make you more or less comfortable with the analysis you've done of this project? Why?

  ii. How and why does the information affect the appropriateness of using the cost of capital in the analysis?

  iii. Suppose you know of a company that makes only ladies' shoes and its beta is 2.0. If Treasury bills are paying 6% and an average share investment earns 10%, what rate might be more appropriate than the cost of capital for the analysis of this problem?

Computer Problem

25. The Paxton Homes Co. is a successful builder of moderate to high-priced houses. The firm is currently considering an expansion into light commercial construction in which it would build shopping centres and small office buildings. Management considers the idea a new venture because of the major differences between commercial and residential construction.

Getting into the new line of business will require an investment of $12.5 million in equipment and $3 million in expenses. The equipment will be amortized over five years. Part of the start-up money will come from the sale of some old trucks and cranes that are being replaced. These have a total market value of $1.8 million. Selling the equipment will result in an amortization reduction of $200,000 per year for three years.

Revenue from the commercial line is expected to be $6 million in the first year, and to grow by $2 million in each succeeding year until it reaches $20 million (in the eighth year). After that, growth is uncertain and may be anywhere from 0% to 6% per year. Costs and expenses, including incremental overhead, will be 110% of revenues in the first year, 85% in the next two years, and 70% thereafter. Economies of scale in materials purchasing are expected to save the residential business about $250,000 per year but not until the fourth year. Net working capital requirements are estimated at 10% of revenue. The combined federal and provincial tax rate on the incremental business will be 40%. Losses can be offset against other profits and can therefore be viewed as earning a tax recovery at the same rate. Paxton's cost of capital is 12%.

You are a financial analyst assigned to evaluate the commercial construction proposal. Use an Excel® spreadsheet or the CAPBUD* program to analyze the project and prepare a presentation in which you will make a recommendation either favouring or opposing its undertaking. Here are some ideas for approaches to your presentation:

a. Establish a base case using the information given. Forecast into the future until the numbers stop changing (eight years). Assume a terminal value based on a continuation of the eighth year's cash flows with no further growth. Is the project acceptable based on NPV and IRR given these assumptions?

b. Test the sensitivity of the base case analysis to the terminal value assumption by varying the growth rate to 3% and 6%.

   i. Comment on the difference the terminal growth rate assumption makes.

   ii. Construction is a cyclical industry in that it is very subject to the ups and downs of the economy. In good times growth is enormous, but in bad times the industry and the firms in it shrink rapidly. Given that fact, how do you feel about the terminal value assumption?

c. Evaluate the project's NPV and IRR assuming a 10-year planning horizon; that is, assuming cash flows in the ninth and tenth years are equal to the eighth year and cash flows after the tenth year are zero (Ignore any release of working capital). Does this approach make more or less sense to you than the terminal value assumptions used in part (a)?

d. Test the sensitivity of the analysis to changes in revenue growth. For example, in part (a), suppose that revenue grows by only $1 million per year instead of $2 million until the eighth year. Is the project a good idea then? What if cost/expense is a higher percentage of revenue than anticipated?

*CAPBUD is one of several Excel® templates available on the text's support website.

Chapter 14

Risk Topics and Real Options in Capital Budgeting

Learning Objectives

1 Describe risk in capital budgeting as the probability that future cash flows will turn out differently than forecast.

2 Explain why the net present value and internal rate of return of any project are random variables with expected values and variances that reflect risk.

3 Explain how the uncertainty of future cash flows can lead to incorrect decisions.

4 Explain why, in choosing among projects with similar NPVs, management would prefer the project with the lowest risk.

5 Utilize various financial techniques for dealing with risk in capital budgeting analysis, including scenario analysis, sensitivity analysis, simulation, and decision trees.

6 Relate the concept of real options to capital budgeting analysis.

7 Discuss how a project's risk may be considered using risk-adjusted discount rates.

In Chapters 12 and 13, we analyzed proposed capital investments in terms of potential *returns*. However, a capital budgeting analysis is not complete without some consideration of the *risk* inherent in the investment.

A winning bet at a casino will provide a minimum return of 100% (double your money!). This is an attractive potential return. Of course, you *risk* losing your total bet (the probability is almost always greater that you will lose at a casino than that you will win).

What is risk as it relates to capital budgeting? Risk means *uncertainty* about a future outcome, such as a sales forecast or a return from an investment. In financial terms, risk does *not* denote loss. Risk denotes uncertainty as to whether and by how much actual events will vary from what we expect. Capital investments are risky because future revenues and costs will likely vary from forecasts.

In our casino example, our bet is risky because we don't know whether we will win or lose. If we were certain of winning, there would be no risk. Correspondingly, if we were certain of *losing*, there would be no risk!

RISK IN CAPITAL BUDGETING—GENERAL CONSIDERATIONS

In our discussions in Chapter 13, we emphasized the idea that cash flow estimates are subject to a good deal of error. Different people will make different estimates of the same thing, and actual flows are apt to vary substantially from anybody's estimates. A more concise way to put the same thing is just to say that cash flow estimates are *risky*.

In recent years, the subject of risk has been given great attention in financial theory, especially in the area of portfolio theory (Chapter 11). In this section we'll take a look at some attempts that have been made to incorporate risk into capital budgeting, including one approach that applies portfolio theory methods to capital budgeting problems.

Cash Flows as Random Variables

In everyday usage the term "risk" is associated with the probability that something bad will happen. In financial theory, however, we associate risk with random variables and their probability distributions. Risk is the chance that a random variable will take a value significantly different from the one we expect, regardless of whether the deviation is favourable or unfavourable. In terms of a probability distribution, the value we expect is the mean (*expected value*), and the chance that an observation will be significantly different from the mean is related to the *variance*.

Recall that in portfolio theory (Chapter 11) the return on an investment is viewed as a random variable with an associated probability distribution, and risk is defined as the variance or *standard deviation* of that distribution. The risk inherent in estimated cash flows can be defined in a similar way. Each future cash flow can be thought of as a separate random variable with its own probability distribution. In each case, the risk associated with the flow is related to the variance of the distribution. The idea is illustrated in Figure 14.1.

In capital budgeting, the *estimate* of each future period's *cash flow* is a *random variable*.

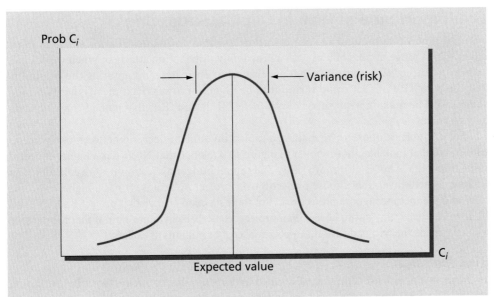

FIGURE 14.1
The Probability Distribution of a Future Cash Flow as a Random Variable

FIGURE 14.2
Risk in Estimated
Cash Flows

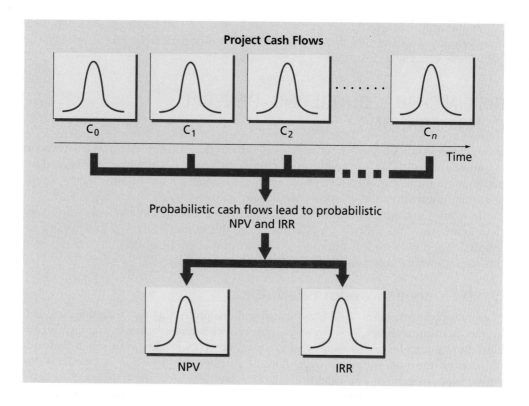

The *NPV* and *IRR*
of any project are
random variables
with expected values
and variances that
reflect *risk*.

When cash flows are viewed like this, the NPVs and IRRs of projects are also random variables with their own probability distributions. That's because they're calculated as functions of the various cash flows, which are random variables themselves. The idea is conceptually illustrated in Figure 14.2.

This view makes explicit the idea that estimated cash flows as well as the resulting NPVs and IRRs have most likely (expected, mean) values, but will probably turn out to be somewhat different from those values. The amount by which the actual value is likely to differ from the expected value is related to the distribution's variance or standard deviation, which can be visualized intuitively as the width of the bell-shaped curve.

The Importance of Risk in Capital Budgeting

Up until now we've thought of each cash flow as a *point estimate*. That's a single number rather than a range of possibilities with a probability distribution attached. When we do that, we're computing NPVs and IRRs that are also point estimates, and ignoring the possibility that the true NPV or IRR could turn out to be higher or lower. That means there's a good chance we'll be making *wrong decisions* by using NPVs and IRRs that come from risky cash flow estimates.

For example, suppose we're making a capital investment decision between two projects with NPVs that look like those shown in Figure 14.3. Notice that NPV_B has a higher expected value than NPV_A, but is also more risky. The capital budgeting techniques we considered in Chapter 12 will invariably choose project B over project A, because it has a higher expected NPV and the methods ignore project risk. But there's a good chance that project B's NPV (and IRR) will actually turn out to be less than project A's, perhaps by quite a bit. If that happens we will have made the wrong decision at a potential cost of millions of dollars.

Risk Aversion

The principle of risk aversion that we studied in portfolio theory applies to capital budgeting equally. All other things being equal, we prefer *less risky* capital projects to those with more risk.

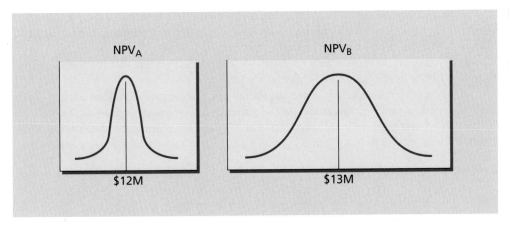

FIGURE 14.3
Project NPVs
Reflecting Risky
Cash Flows

To make the point plainer, imagine that projects A and B have exactly the same expected NPV. The NPV technique would be indifferent between them, yet any rational manager would prefer the one with the lower risk.

Changing the Nature of the Company

Another dimension to the risk issue goes beyond individual projects and relates to the fundamental nature of the firm as an investment. Companies are characterized by investors largely in terms of risk. That was the point of our study of portfolio theory in Chapter 11. When people buy stocks and bonds, expected returns matter, but risk matters just as much.

In capital budgeting we think of projects as incremental to the normal business of the firm. We view them as sort of *stuck onto* the larger body of what goes on every day. Yet every project affects the totality of the company just as every share added to a portfolio changes the nature of that portfolio. In the long run, a company is no more than a collection of all the projects it has undertaken that are still going on. In a very real sense, *a company is a portfolio of projects.*

Hence, if a firm takes on new projects without regard for risk, it's in danger of changing its fundamental nature as perceived by investors. A firm that starts to adopt riskier projects than it has in the past will slowly become a riskier company. The higher risk will be reflected in a more volatile movement of the firm's return, which in turn will result in a higher beta. And that higher beta can generally be expected to have a negative impact on the price of the company's shares.

We can conclude that some consideration of risk *should* be included in project analysis. If it is not, the full impact of projects simply isn't understood at the time they're chosen and implemented.

Ignoring risk in capital budgeting can lead to *incorrect decisions* and *change the risk character of the firm.*

INCORPORATING RISK INTO CAPITAL BUDGETING— SCENARIO/SENSITIVITY ANALYSIS AND SIMULATION

Once the idea that risk *should* be incorporated in the capital budgeting process is accepted, the question of *how* to do it has to be addressed. Considering the capital budgeting techniques we studied in the last chapter, it's not at all obvious how we ought to go about factoring in risk-related ideas.

Quite a bit of thought has been given to the subject and several approaches have been developed. We'll look at a numerical method and then examine a more theoretical approach.

Scenario/Sensitivity Analysis

The fundamental idea behind risk in capital budgeting is that cash flows aren't likely to turn out exactly as estimated. Therefore, actual NPVs and IRRs are likely to be different from those based on estimated cash flows. The management question is just *how much* an NPV or an IRR will change given some deviation in cash flows. A good idea of the relationship between the two changes can be gotten by using a procedure called *scenario analysis*.

In the following discussion we'll refer only to NPV, understanding that the comments apply also to IRR or to any capital budgeting technique.

Suppose a project is represented by a number of estimated future cash flows, each of which can actually take a range of values around the estimate. Also suppose we have an idea of what the best, worst, and most likely values of each cash flow are. Graphically the idea involves a picture like this for *each* cash flow.

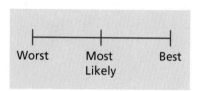

The most likely value of each cash flow is the estimate we've been working with up until now, sometimes called a *point estimate*.

If we calculate the project's NPV using the most likely value of each cash flow, we generally get the most likely NPV for the project. If we do the calculation with the worst possible value of each C_n, we'll get the worst possible NPV. Similarly, we'll get the best NPV if we use all the best cash flows. Notice that we can calculate an NPV with *any* combination of cash flows. That is, we could pick a worst case for C_1, a best case for C_2, something in between for C_3, and so on. All we have to do to calculate an NPV is to choose one value for each cash flow.

Every time we choose a value for each of the project's cash flows, we define what is called a *scenario,* one of the many possible outcomes of the project. When we calculate the NPV of several scenarios we're performing a *scenario analysis*.

This procedure results in a range of values for NPV along with a good estimate of the most likely value. But it doesn't give a very good notion of the probability of various values within the range. We can choose as many scenarios as we like, however, by selecting any number of different sets of outcomes for the cash flows. Evaluating a number of scenarios gives a subjective feel for the variability of the NPV to changes in our assumptions about what the cash flows will turn out to be.

Example 14.1

Project A has an initial outflow of $1,400 and three variable cash inflows defined as follows ($000).

	C_1	C_2	C_3
Worst case	$450	$400	$700
Most likely	550	450	800
Best case	650	500	900

Analyze project A's NPV.

■ **Solution:** The worst possible NPV will result if the three lowest cash inflows all occur. Assume the cost of capital is 9%. Then the worst NPV is:

---

1 As in earlier chapters, you'll notice that there is a slight rounding difference when we compare the Excel® and financial calculator solutions to those derived from financial tables.
2 Remember that only future cash flows are discounted, and then netted against the initial outlay.

$$NPV = -\$1,400 + \$450[PVF_{9,1}] + \$400[PVF_{9,2}] + \$700[PVF_{9,3}]$$
$$= -\$1,400 + \$450[0.9174] + \$400[0.8417] + \$700[0.7722]$$
$$= -\$109.95$$

Similar calculations lead to a best-case scenario with an NPV of $312.14, and an NPV of $101.10 for the scenario involving the most likely cash flow for every C_n, which is the project's traditional NPV.

Now suppose management feels pretty good about the estimates in the first two years, but is uncomfortable with the high cash flow numbers forecast for year 3. The managers essentially want to know what will happen to the traditional NPV if year 3 turns out badly.

To answer that question, we form a scenario including the most likely flows from years 1 and 2 and the worst case from year 3. Verify that the NPV from that scenario is $23.88. Notice that management's concern is well founded, as a worst case in the third year alone yields a marginally positive NPV.

Another name for essentially the same process is *sensitivity analysis*. That is, we investigate the *sensitivity* of the traditionally calculated NPV to changes in the C_n. In the last part of the last example we saw that a change of $100 in the year 3 cash flow led to a change of ($101.10 − $23.88 =) $77.22 in the project's NPV. In other words, the NPV changed by about 77% of the change in the year 3 cash flow. A look at the present value of an amount table on page 695 will confirm that in this simple example the present value factor for 9% and three years is very close to 0.77.

Scenario/sensitivity analysis selects worst, middle, and best outcomes for each cash flow and computes NPV for a variety of combinations.

Computer (Monte Carlo) Simulation

The power of the computer can help to incorporate risk into capital budgeting through a technique called **Monte Carlo**[3] **simulation**, an approach that involves the use of numbers drawn randomly from probability distributions.

Figure 14.2 intuitively suggests the approach. Reexamine that illustration on page 502. Notice that each cash flow is itself a random variable with a probability distribution, and that they combine to create the probability distributions of the project's NPV (and IRR).

Monte Carlo simulation involves making assumptions that specify the shapes of the probability distributions for *each* future cash flow in a capital budgeting project. These assumed distributions are put into a computer model so that random observations[4] can be drawn from each.[5]

Once all the probability distributions are specified, the computer simulates the project by drawing one observation from the distribution of each cash flow. Having those, it calculates the project's NPV and records the resulting value. Then it draws a new set of random observations for each of the cash flows, discards the old set, and calculates and records another value for NPV. Notice that the second NPV will probably be different from the first because it is based on a different set of randomly drawn cash flows.

The computer goes through this process many times, generating a thousand or more values (observations) for NPV. The calculated values are sorted into ranges and displayed as histograms reflecting the number of observations in each range. Figure 14.4 is an example of the resulting display, where the numbers along the horizontal axis represent the centres of ranges of values for the calculated NPVs. For example, the value of 600 over the NPV value of $100 means that 600 simulation calculations resulted in NPVs between $50 and $150.

If the height of each column is restated as a percentage of the total number of observations, the histogram becomes a good approximation of the probability distribution of the project's NPV *given the assumptions made about the distributions of the individual cash flows*.

Monte Carlo simulation is a capital budgeting technique for incorporating risk into capital budgeting.

Simulation models cash flows as random variables and repeatedly calculates NPV, building its distribution.

---

3 Monte Carlo is the site of a famous gambling casino in Monaco.

4 In this context, the term "observation" refers to a number drawn from a probability distribution or to the result of calculations made from such numbers.

5 In more detailed models, a probability distribution can be assumed for *each* of the elements that *go into* the periodic cash flow estimates. For example, if period cash flows are the difference between revenue and cost, one might specify distributions for both, and calculate cash flow as the difference between an observation on revenue and one on cost.

FIGURE 14.4
Results of Monte Carlo Simulation for NPV

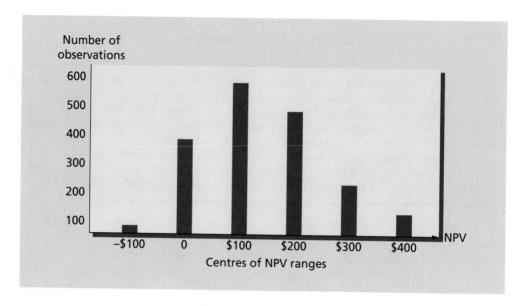

Armed with this risk-related information, managers can make better choices among projects. For example, look back at Figure 14.3 on page 503. Simulation would give us approximations of the shapes of the distributions shown, as well as the most likely values of NPV. In the case illustrated, decision makers might well choose project A over project B in spite of B's NPV advantage, because of A's lower risk.

Using the simulation approach has a few drawbacks. An obvious problem is that the probability distributions of the cash flows have to be estimated subjectively. This can be difficult. However, it's always easier to estimate a distribution for a simple element of a problem, like a single cash flow, than for a more complex element, like the final NPV or IRR.

A related issue is that the distributions of the individual cash flows generally aren't independent. Project cash flows tend to be positively *correlated* so that if early flows are low, later flows are also likely to be low. Unfortunately, it's hard to estimate the extent of that correlation.

Another problem is the interpretation of the simulated probability distributions. There aren't any decision rules for choosing among projects with respect to risk. Just how much risk is too much or how much variance is needed to overcome a certain NPV advantage isn't written down anywhere. Such judgments are subjective, and depend on the wisdom and experience of the decision makers.

In spite of these problems, simulation can be a relatively practical approach to incorporating risk into capital budgeting analyses.

Decision Tree Analysis

We made the point earlier (page 504) that scenario analysis gives us a feel for the possible variation in NPV (and IRR) in a capital budgeting project, but doesn't tell us much about the probability distribution of the NPV outcome. Decision tree analysis lets us approximate the NPV distribution if we can estimate the probability of certain events within the project. A **decision tree** is essentially an expanded time line that "branches" into alternative paths wherever an event can turn out in more than one way.

A **decision tree** is a graphic representation of a business project in which events have multiple outcomes, each of which is assigned a probability.

For example, suppose a capital budgeting project involves some engineering work with an uncertain outcome that won't be completed until the project has been under way for a year. If the engineering turns out well, subsequent cash flows will be higher than if it doesn't. The situation is captured in the decision tree diagram shown in Figure 14.5.

The project starts with initial outlay C_0 followed by cash flow C_1, but after that there are two possibilities depending on the success of the engineering work. Each of the two possible

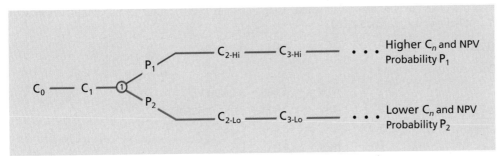

FIGURE 14.5
A Simple Decision
Tree

outcomes is represented by a *branch* of the decision tree. The place at which the branches separate is called a *node,* and is commonly shown as a small numbered circle to help keep track of complex projects.

The estimated probability that a branch will occur is indicated (P_1, P_2) just after the node at which it starts. In this case, the upper branch represents an engineering success, which results in high cash flows indicated by C_{2-Hi}, C_{3-Hi} .... The lower branch represents less success and lower cash flows C_{2-Lo}, C_{3-Lo} ....

Any number of branches can emanate from a node, but their probabilities must sum to 1.0, indicating that one of the branches *must* be taken.

A *path* through the tree starts on the left at C_0 and progresses through node 1 along one branch or the other. There are obviously just two possible paths in Figure 14.5. An overall NPV outcome is associated with each path. In this case, the more favourable outcome is along the upper path and has cash flows C_0, C_1, C_{2-Hi}, C_{3-Hi} ..., while the less favourable lower path has cash flows C_0, C_1, C_{2-Lo}, C_{3-Lo} ....

Evaluating a project involves calculating NPVs along all possible paths and associating each with a probability. From that a probability distribution for NPV can be developed. The technique is best understood through an example. (We're working with NPV, but everything we say is equally applicable to IRR. Read the following example carefully; we will build on it throughout the rest of this section and the next.)

A *probability distribution* of a project's *NPV* can be developed using *decision tree* analysis.

Example 14.2

The Wing Foot Shoe Company is considering a three-year project to market a running shoe based on new technology. Success depends on how well consumers accept the new idea and demand the product. Demand can vary from great to terrible, but for planning purposes management has collapsed that variation into just two possibilities: good and poor. A market study indicates a 60% probability that demand will be good and a 40% chance that it will be poor.

It will cost $5 million to bring the new shoe to market. Cash flow estimates indicate inflows of $3 million per year for three years *at full manufacturing capacity* if demand is good, but just $1.5 million per year if it's poor. Wing Foot's cost of capital is 10%. Analyze the project and develop a rough probability distribution for NPV.

■ **Solution:** First draw a decision tree diagram for the project ($000).

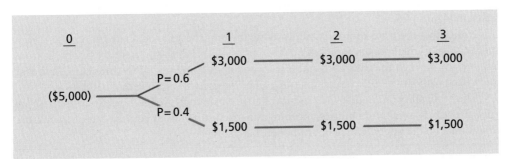

Calculator Solution

Key	Input
CF_0	−5,000
C01	3,000
C02	3,000
C03	3,000
I	10

Answer

NPV	2,461

Use Excel®
Function NPV

Next calculate the NPV along each path, using Equation 12.3 (Chapter 12, page 448), which we'll repeat here for convenience ($000).

(12.3)
$$NPV = -C_0 + C[PVFA_{k,n}]$$

Good consumer demand:

$$NPV = -\$5,000 + \$3,000[PVFA_{10,3}]$$
$$NPV = -\$5,000 + \$3,000(2.4869)$$
$$NPV = -\$5,000 + \$7,461$$
$$NPV = \$2,461$$

Poor consumer demand:

$$NPV = -\$5,000 + \$1,500(2.4869)$$
$$NPV = -\$5,000 + \$3,730$$
$$NPV = -\$1,270$$

Calculator Solution

Key	Input
CF_0	−5,000
C01	1,500
C02	1,500
C03	1,500
I	10

Answer

NPV	−1,270

Use Excel®
Function NPV

Notice that we now have the elements of a probability distribution for the project's NPV. We know there's a 60% chance of an NPV of $2,461,000 along the upper path and a 40% chance of an NPV of −$1,270,000 along the lower path.

The expected NPV (the mean or expected value of the probability distribution of values for NPV) is calculated by multiplying every possible NPV by its probability and summing the results ($000). (See the review of statistics at the beginning of Chapter 11 if necessary.)

Demand	NPV	Probability	Product
Good	$ 2,461	0.60	$ 1,477
Poor	(1,270)	0.40	(508)
		Expected NPV =	$ 969

Summarizing, we can say that the project's most likely NPV outcome is approximately $1.0 million, and that there's a good chance (60%) of making about $2.5 million, *but* there's also a substantial chance (40%) of losing about $1.3 million.

Notice that Wing Foot's management gets a much better idea of the new running shoe project's risk from this analysis than it would from a projection of a single value of $1.0 million for NPV. The decision tree result explicitly calls out the fact that a big loss is quite possible. That information is important because a loss of that size could ruin a small company. It could also damage the reputation of whoever is recommending the project.

The analysis also shows that if things turn out well, the reward for bearing the risk will probably be about half the size of the initial investment. That's also an important observation, because people are less likely to take substantial risks for modest returns than for outcomes that multiply their investment many times over.

The end result of the analysis in this case might well be a rejection of the project on the basis of risk even though the expected NPV is positive.

More Complex Decision Trees and Conditional Probabilities

Most processes represented by decision trees involve more than one uncertain event that can be characterized by probabilities. Each such event is represented by a node from which two or more new branches emerge, and the tree widens quickly toward the right. A typical tree is illustrated in Figure 14.6.

The probabilities emerging from any decision tree node must sum to 1.0.

Notice that there are additional nodes along the branches that emanate from node 1, each splitting the original branch into two or three more. In this diagram there are five paths from left to right through the tree. Each starts at C_0 and ends along one of the branches on the far right. Each path has an NPV calculated using all of the cash flows along that path.

The probability of a path is the product of all of the branch probabilities along it. These are known as *conditional* probabilities, meaning that the probabilities coming out of node 2 are conditional on the upper branch out of node 1 happening.[6]

---

6 The probability of a path is also called *the joint* probability of the individual branches along that path.

FIGURE 14.6
A More Complex
Decision Tree

Keep in mind that the probabilities out of each node must sum to 1.0. For example, $P_1 + P_2 = 1.0$ and $P_3 + P_4 + P_5 = 1.0$.

A number of risk and decision analysis programs can be found at the Palisade site: http://www. palisade.com.

Example 14.3

The Wing Foot Shoe Company of Example 14.2 (page 507) has refined its market study and has some additional information about potential customer acceptance of the new product. Management now believes that there are two possibilities along the upper branch. Consumer response can be good, or it may be excellent. The study indicates that if demand is good during the first year, there's a 30% chance it will grow and be excellent in the second and third years. Of course, this also means there's a 70% chance that demand in years 2 and 3 won't change.

If consumer response to the product turns out to be excellent, an additional investment of $1 million in a factory expansion will allow the firm to make and sell enough product to generate cash inflows of $5 million rather than $3 million in both years 2 and 3. Hence the net cash inflows for the project will be ($5 million − $1 million =) $4 million in year 2 and $5 million in year 3. (The expansion is necessary to achieve the better financial results because Example 14.2 stated that the factory was at capacity along the upper path.) A decision tree for the project with this additional possibility is as follows ($000).

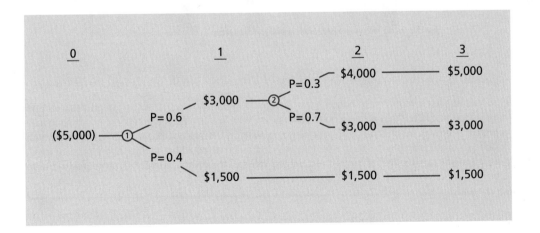

The probabilities coming out of node 2 are conditional probabilities, meaning that they exist only along the good demand path. In other words, they are *conditional upon* good demand happening out of node 1, which itself has a probability of 0.6. The probability of arriving at the end of any path through the decision tree is calculated by multiplying all of the probabilities along the path. Hence the probability of the upper path is (0.6 × 0.3 =) 0.18, the middle path is (0.6 × 0.7 =) 0.42, and the lower path is just 0.40 as it was before. It's important to notice that these probabilities sum to 1.0, indicating that all possible outcomes are achieved by routes through the tree.

Probabilities out of later nodes are *conditional* upon the outcome of earlier nodes along the same path.

The NPV along each path is calculated in the traditional manner using all of the cash flows along the path. The middle and lower paths have the same cash flows as the paths in Example 14.2, so we've already calculated those NPVs. The NPV for the new upper path is just a series of three present value calculations added to the initial outlay ($000).

$$NPV = -\$5,000 + \$3,000[PVF_{10,1}] + \$4,000[PVF_{10,2}] + \$5,000[PVF_{10,3}]$$
$$= -\$5,000 + \$3,000(0.9091) + \$4,000(0.8264) + \$5,000(0.7513)$$
$$= -\$5,000 + \$2,727 + \$3,306 + \$3,757$$
$$= \$4,790$$

Then the probability distribution for the project and the calculation of the expected return are as follows.

Acceptance	NPV	Probability	Product
Excellent	$ 4,790	0.18	$ 862
Good	2,461	0.42	1,034
Poor	(1,270)	0.40	(508)
		Expected NPV =	$ 1,388

The distribution is shown graphically as follows.

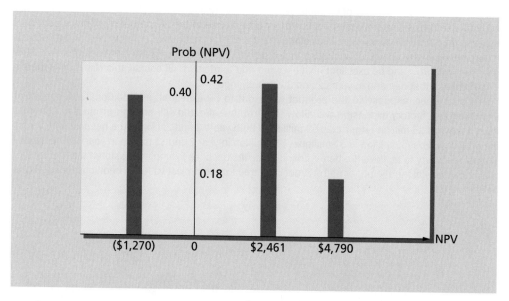

Once again it's important to notice how much more information is available through decision tree analysis than would be from a single point estimate of NPV. In this case the additional information tells us there's a fairly good chance (18%) of doing very well on the project. But there's still a substantial chance (40%) of losing money. As in Example 14.2 that outcome could be ruinous, and a prudent management might avoid it even though the expected value of the NPV is somewhat more positive than before.

REAL OPTIONS

A **real option** is a
course of action that
can be made available,
usually at a cost, which
*improves financial
results* under certain
conditions.

A **real option** is the right or ability to take a certain course of action, which in business situations generally leads to a financially favourable result.

Here's an example. Suppose a business sells sports apparel in a shopping mall, and specializes in jackets and sweatshirts bearing the insignia of professional hockey teams. Also suppose the business depends on bank credit to support routine operations, meaning it generally needs to have a loan outstanding just to keep going.[7] Assume its typical loan is $1 million. Now suppose the local pro hockey team has a chance at the Stanley Cup this year. If they make it, the demand for hockey jackets will double, and the business will need $2 million in bank credit. But if the extra credit isn't available, the additional sales will be lost.

The situation puts the business owner in a dilemma. He doesn't want to borrow the extra $1 million and pay interest on it all year, because he isn't sure the additional sales will materialize. But he also knows that if he goes to the bank for an incremental loan at the last minute, he may not get it, because the bank may be short of funds at that time.

The solution may be an arrangement with the bank in which it makes a *commitment*[8] to lend the extra money in return for a *commitment fee,* which is usually about 0.25% per year of the committed but unborrowed amount. If the business does borrow the money, the bank just charges its normal interest rate while the loan is outstanding. If it doesn't, it just pays the commitment fee, ($1 million $\times$ 0.0025 =) $2,500 in this case.

The arrangement gives the business owner the ability to take advantage of the potential increase in demand for hockey apparel in that he has the *option* of borrowing the extra money to support the increased sales. We call that ability a real option. The word *real* means the option exists in a real, physical business sense. It's inserted to distinguish real options from financial options.[9]

Notice that the real option has a value to the business owner. It's worth at least as much as the commitment fee he pays the bank, and it may be worth a lot more depending on the probability of the local team getting into the Stanley Cup finals and the profit he'd make on the additional sales if that happened.

Real Options in Capital Budgeting

Real options frequently occur in capital budgeting projects. Their impact is best seen when the project is analyzed using a probabilistic approach such as decision tree analysis. A real option's presence generally increases the expected NPV of a project. That increase is often a good estimate of the option's value.

> The *value* of a real option can be estimated as the *increase in project NPV* that its inclusion brings about.

Example 14.4

Consider the Wing Foot Shoe Company's situation after the possibility of excellent demand is introduced as described in Example 14.3 (page 509).

    a.   Is a real option present?

    b.   Suppose space at Wing Foot's plant is scarce, but room for an expansion is available at a cost of $0.5 million at the project's outset. This is in addition to the $1 million the expansion will cost in year 2, if it's done. In other words, the project's initial outlay will increase by $0.5 million if the expansion option is included. If demand isn't excellent, that money will be wasted. Should the expansion space be purchased under the conditions presented in Example 14.3?

■ **Solution:**

    a.   Notice that in Example 14.2 (page 507). Wing Foot's factory is at full capacity at a sales level consistent with good consumer acceptance of the new product. This is shown along the top branch of the decision tree. If capacity expansion isn't possible, there's nothing management can do to take advantage of higher than expected demand. The situation differs in

---

7 That in itself doesn't mean that the business is weak or in danger of failing. We learned about this kind of financing in Chapter 5 when we studied short-term financing.

8 See Chapter 5, page 165.

9 The most common financial option is the right to purchase shares at a fixed price for a specified period. That right is known as a *call option* and is for sale at an *option price.* If the market price of the share rises above the fixed price during the period, the option holder buys the share and immediately sells it for a profit. If the market price doesn't exceed the fixed price during the period, the option expires, and the investor loses what she paid for it. Stock options are covered in more detail in Chapter 18. At this point you should simply be aware of what they are to avoid confusion with real options.

Example 14.3 because the firm has the option of investing an additional $1 million in an expansion if larger demand is experienced. Then the project could generate more sales and increased cash flows that might more than offset the cost of the new capacity.

The opportunity to respond to the realization that consumer acceptance is excellent by expanding the plant is a real option. In other words, management has the *option* of expanding capacity at an incremental cost to meet higher than expected demand. There's no cost associated with this real option as described so far. We'll consider the implications of a real option with a cost in part b.

b. Having the extra space from the beginning of the running shoe project gives management the real option to expand. Without it management doesn't have that choice. Hence in order to decide whether it's wise to purchase extra space, we have to place a value on the ability to expand capacity. We'll then compare that value with the cost of maintaining the option, which is $0.5 million.

It's relatively easy to make a first approximation of the value of the real option in this case. It's just the difference in the *expected values* of the project's NPV calculated with and without the option. That makes sense because expected NPV is the basic measure of the project's value to the firm.

We calculated the expected NPV without the option in Example 14.2 and with the option in Example 14.3. The option was the only difference in those situations. From those examples we have the following ($000).

Expected NPV with option	$ 1,388
Expected NPV without option	969
Real option value	$ 419[10]

Since the value of the real option is less than its $0.5 million cost, it seems that management shouldn't buy the space for the potential expansion ahead of time. However, we'll see shortly that there may be another reason to consider keeping the expansion option alive.

The Abandonment Option

Look at the decision tree in Example 14.3 (page 509) once again. Notice that the lower path representing poor demand has a negative NPV of $(1,270), indicating that the project will be a money-losing failure if customers are reluctant to buy the new design. Once management realizes demand is poor, say, after the first year, does it make sense to continue producing the running shoes in years 2 and 3, earning inflows of just $1,500? It does if there are no alternative uses for the resources involved in making the shoes, since a positive cash contribution of $1,500 per year is better than nothing.

But suppose the facilities and equipment used to make the new shoe can be redeployed into something else. Under those conditions it may make sense to abandon the project altogether.

Example 14.5

The ability to *abandon* a project that is performing poorly is a common *real option* that is often inexpensive.

Wing Foot has other lines of shoes in which most of the equipment purchased for the running shoe project can be used if the new idea is abandoned. Management estimates that after the first year the equipment's value in those other uses will be $4.5 million. How does this information impact the analysis of the running shoe project?

■ **Solution:** If the project is abandoned and the equipment is redeployed after the first year, cash flows along the bottom path of the decision tree in Example 14.3 would be $1,500 in the first year,

---

10 It's important not to confuse the value of the option in an expected value sense with what it's worth if the expansion actually happens. Look at the calculation of the expected value of the project's NPV in Example 14.3. If demand is excellent and the expansion happens, NPV is $4,790 ($000) along the top path. If demand is just good, NPV is $2,461 along the middle path. The difference between those figures is $ 2,329. That's the amount the expansion capability contributes *if* demand actually turns out to be excellent. However, at the beginning of the project, when we're doing capital budgeting, we don't know whether that will happen. At that time we just know that there's an 18% chance of excellent demand. Recognizing this, the expected value calculation adds 18% of $2,329 to the project's expected NPV, which, within rounding error, is ($2,329 × 0.18 =) $419.

$4,500 in year 2, and zero in year 3 ($000). The NPV along the bottom path would then be as follows.

$$NPV = -\$5,000 + \$1,500[PVF_{10,1}] + \$4,500[PVF_{10,2}]$$
$$= -\$5,000 + \$1,500(0.9091) + \$4,500(0.8264)$$
$$= -\$5,000 + \$1,364 + \$3,719$$
$$= \$83$$

Recalculate the project's expected NPV, assuming the bottom path is replaced by abandonment. To do that, repeat the calculation in Example 14.3 replacing the NPV of $(1,270) along the bottom path with $83.

Acceptance	NPV	Probability	Product
Excellent	$ 4,790	0.18	$ 862
Good	2,461	0.42	1,034
Poor	83	0.40	33
		Expected NPV =	$ 1,929

Notice that the expected NPV has increased from $1,463 to $1,929.

It's very important to appreciate two things about the calculations we've just done. First, abandonment is a course of action available to management that improves the project's expected NPV. Therefore if abandonment is possible, it's a real option.

Second, the existence of the abandonment option lowers the project's risk substantially. We can see that by looking at the diagram in Example 14.3 that graphically displays the probability distribution of the project's NPV (page 510). Notice that the project as originally presented has a 40% probability of a negative NPV of $(1,270). This is essentially a loss of that amount. We commented earlier that such a loss could ruin a small firm and might be a reason to avoid the project altogether.

But if the abandonment option exists as we've described it, that outcome is pushed to the right and becomes a 40% probability of a small gain of $83. That makes the project taken as a whole a lot less risky. Indeed, if this abandonment option exists it's unlikely that a firm would need to avoid the project because the risk of ruin is negligible.

Valuing Real Options

In Example 14.4 (page 511) we calculated the value of a real option as the increase it created in the NPV of the project in which it is embedded. That's a good starting point for valuation, but it doesn't capture the whole story because of the risk reduction we've just described.

In fact, real options are generally worth more than their expected NPV impact because of the effect they have on risk. Recall that individuals and managers are *risk averse,* meaning they prefer less risky undertakings when expected returns or NPVs are equal. That preference generally means that people are willing to pay something for risk reduction over and above the amount by which a real option increases expected NPV. Hence the value of a real option is often *more than* the amount by which it increases NPV. Unfortunately it's difficult to say just how much more, because neither a precise measure of risk nor a relationship between risk and value exists in the capital budgeting context. In other words, we know the value of real options may be enhanced by their effect on risk, but we can't say by how much.

The *value* of a real option is *at least* the increase in NPV it brings about.

A real option may be worth more than the increase it causes in NPV, because it also reduces project risk.

Designing Real Options into Projects

It makes sense to design projects so that they contain beneficial real options whenever possible. We've already seen two examples in which thinking about real options at the beginning of a project might make a big difference later on.

The *abandonment option* discussed in Example 14.5 increased expected NPV and lowered risk at the same time. Hence the example illustrates that it's a good idea to design the ability to quit into projects. Unfortunately that isn't always easy. Contractual obligations, for example, can make abandonment tough. In our illustration, suppose Wing Foot guaranteed retailers the new shoes for three years, signed a lease for factory space, and entered long-term purchasing contracts with suppliers. Stopping after one year would require breaking the contracts, which could be difficult and costly. Prudent managers should always try to avoid entanglements that make exit hard.

Expansion options like the one illustrated in Example 14.4 (page 511) are very common. When the ability to expand costs extra money early in the project's life, a careful financial analysis is necessary, as we've indicated. However, the option frequently requires little or no early commitment and should be planned in whenever possible.

Investment timing options also come up frequently. Here's an example. Suppose a company is looking at a project to build a new factory, and has identified an unusually good site, but it can't make a final decision for six months. The managers don't want to buy the property now, because there's a chance they won't build the factory. But they don't want to lose out to another buyer because if they do decide to build later on, they'd then have to start looking for a site all over again.

The solution can be a *land option contract* in which the landowner grants the company the right to buy the site at any time in the next six months at a fixed price in return for a nonrefundable fee called the **option price**.

The option is a purchase contract between a buyer and a seller that's suspended at the discretion of the buyer for a limited time. If the buyer doesn't *exercise* the option by the end of that time, it just expires. The land option lets the firm delay its investment in the land until it's sure about other relevant issues and problems.

> An **option price** is the price an option holder pays for a contract. It is also known as the option premium in financial options.

Insights REAL APPLICATIONS

Real Options = Real Value

Today, most companies' supply chains are increasingly complex. For instance, many now rely on over-ocean shipping, which now accounts for more than 90 percent of worldwide trade. While manufacturers may cut costs by producing goods in offshore facilities, they can suffer when it comes to shipping these items. The tangle of containers, ports, carriers, customs, and border security checkpoints significantly reduces the simplicity and transparency of the supply chain.

Improved visibility, having as much information as possible about replenishment, would improve supply chain efficiency—reducing inventories, lead time, and stock outs, and preventing the loss of containers and their contents. How are manufacturers and importers acquiring information about their products being shipped?

One solution to the visibility problem is the *Radio Frequency Identification (RFID)* tag. Each tag contains a unique digital identification code on a microchip that can be scanned by a reader. An RFID chip attached to any size logistic unit (case, pallet, container, etc.) can be read at key checkpoints—distribution centres, seaports, truck terminals—to beam information into a global computer network based on the Internet.

The network software will thus reflect the location and state of both a container and its contents, providing shippers and their customers with much more visibility. By linking the tag number to the shipper's manifest, they can always know the contents and location of that shipment.

For example, if a reader at the port of discharge indicates that a set of parts has just arrived and has been loaded onto a truck, the inventory manager can release those parts, knowing they are about to be replenished. He doesn't have to wait for the truck to arrive to see what's in it. The visibility into additional information allows him to reduce inventory levels. The reliability and timeliness of this information also allows companies to reduce out-of-stocks, minimize lead-time variance and increase manufacturing uptime.

In addition to timeliness and accuracy, the technology can provide an unprecedented audit trail of each shipment's journey. Where do dwell times, delays, or damages take place? With specific data, you have a history that helps you better understand and improve upon these patterns.

By 2006, Wal-Mart Stores Inc. (U.S.) required its top 100 suppliers to use radio frequency identification (RFID) tags on their cases and pallets. One of these suppliers, a global consumer goods manufacturer was evaluating ways to respond to Wal-Mart's RFID directive.

The manufacturer initially used a net present value (NPV) analysis to model its response to the RFID requirement, developing three scenarios.

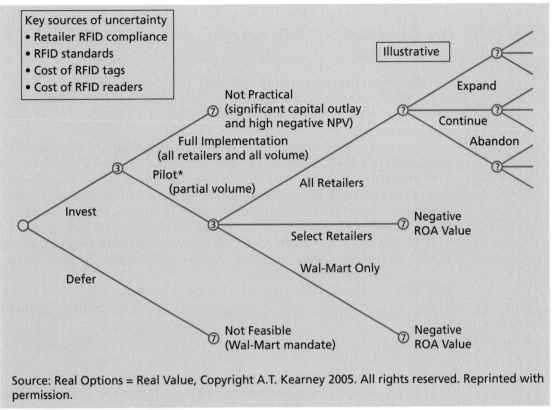

Key sources of uncertainty
• Retailer RFID compliance
• RFID standards
• Cost of RFID tags
• Cost of RFID readers

Illustrative

Expand

Continue

Abandon

Not Practical
(significant capital outlay
and high negative NPV)

Full Implementation
(all retailers and all volume)

Pilot*
(partial volume)

All Retailers

Invest

Negative
ROA Value

Select Retailers

Wal-Mart Only

Defer

Not Feasible
(Wal-Mart mandate)

Negative
ROA Value

* In the first scenario, all shipments for distribution center delivery were RFID tagged, with no assumption of retailers' capability to track pallets and cases.

* In the second scenario, only goods destined for Wal-Mart's distribution centres were tagged, with Wal-Mart providing some of the technology required to give the manufacturer visibility of its goods in Wal-Mart's supply chain.

* In the third scenario, all shipments were tagged for all supply chain routes. In this scenario it was assumed that all retailers would be RFID compliant, thus giving the manufacturer visibility into the downstream supply chain to see out-of-stocks, finished goods inventory, and unsaleable goods.

All three scenarios returned negative NPVs, and the model provided little guidance about how to address Wal-Mart's directive.

Skeptical of the NPV outcomes, the manufacturer turned to real options analysis (ROA). Wal-Mart's RFID directive was well suited to ROA. There was a great deal of uncertainty (RFID technology standards had not been defined), there was a steep learning curve with probable course corrections along the way, and the value of the investment was based on future growth opportunities rather than current cash flow.

Using a decision-tree approach, company executives soon discovered hidden sources of value in the RFID project, which they would not have found using the NPV technique. The benefits included the option to expand more aggressively to realize benefits from reductions in unsaleable goods, out-of-stocks, labour, and inventory holding costs. Indeed, the analysis confirmed what the manufacturer suspected—that the net option value of pursuing an investment in RFID technology was positive and a pilot should move forward.

Although the reasoning behind real options has been around for more than 25 years, it's just starting to catch on in a big way today. It's especially popular in capital-intensive industries. Enthusiastic supporters of the technique include large, well-known firms like Honda, and France's Airbus Industrie.

Flexibility options let companies respond more easily to changes in business conditions. For example, suppose a firm buys the same part from two suppliers for $1 per unit. If it gives all of its business to one supplier, the price would be $0.90 per unit. But if that single supplier fails, the firm's business will suffer while it's unable to get the part. Hence the flexibility of having both suppliers available may be worth the extra $0.10 per unit.

Go to the
Decisioneering site at
http://www.
crystalball.com
for an overview of
risk, Monte Carlo
simulations, and real
options. Case stud-
ies, demos, and arti-
cles explain how risk
analysis software is
applied.

INCORPORATING RISK INTO CAPITAL BUDGETING—THE THEORETICAL APPROACH AND RISK-ADJUSTED RATES OF RETURN

The theoretical approach to incorporating risk into capital budgeting focuses on rates of return. Recall that an *interest rate* plays a central role in both the NPV and IRR methods. Until now we've taken that key rate to be the firm's cost of capital. Let's briefly review how it is used in both techniques.

In the NPV method, we calculate the present value of cash flows using the cost of capital as the discount rate. A higher discount rate produces a lower NPV, which reduces the chances of project acceptance. In the IRR method, the decision rule involves comparing a project's return on invested funds with the cost of capital. A higher cost of capital means a higher IRR is required for acceptance, which also lowers the chance of the project being qualified.

In summary, the acceptance or rejection of projects depends on this key interest rate in both methods, with higher rates implying less likely acceptance. In what follows we'll investigate the implications of doing the calculations with an interest rate other than the cost of capital.

> The *cost of capital* plays a *key role* in both NPV and IRR.

Riskier Projects Should Be Less Acceptable

The idea behind incorporating risk into capital budgeting is to make particularly risky projects less acceptable than others with similar *expected* cash flows. Notice that this is exactly what happens under capital budgeting rules if projects are evaluated using higher interest rates. A higher discount rate lowers the calculated NPV for any given set of cash flows, while a higher threshold rate means calculated IRRs have to be larger to qualify projects.

> Using a higher, risk-adjusted rate for risky projects lowers their chance of acceptance.

Therefore, a logical way to incorporate risk into capital budgeting is to devise an approach that uses the NPV and IRR methods, but analyzes riskier projects by using higher interest rates in place of the cost of capital. Logically, the higher the risk, the higher the interest rate that should be used. This approach will automatically create a bias against accepting higher-risk projects. Higher rates used to compensate for riskiness in financial analysis are called **risk-adjusted rates**.

The Starting Point for Risk-Adjusted Rates

Earlier in this section we said that in the long run a company can be viewed as a collection of projects, and that adopting a large number of relatively risky endeavours can change its fundamental nature to that of a more risky enterprise.

> A **risk-adjusted rate** refers to a higher rate used in place of the cost of capital to reflect especially risky projects.

It makes sense to take the current status of a firm as the starting point for risk measurement and to let the cost of capital be the interest rate representing that point. Then it's logical to analyze projects that are consistent with the current riskiness of the company using the cost of capital and to use higher rates for riskier projects.

Relating Interest Rates to Risk

These ideas are consistent with the interest rate fundamentals we studied in Chapter 7. Recall that every interest rate comprises two parts: a base rate and a premium for risk. The idea was expressed as an equation that we'll repeat here for convenience.

(7.1) $$k = \text{Base rate} + \text{Risk premium}$$

> Projects with risk consistent with *current* operations should be evaluated using the *cost of capital*.

This equation says that investors demand a higher risk premium and consequently a higher interest rate if they are to bear increased risk of losing money. In capital budgeting, the company is investing in the project being analyzed, and the interest rate used in the analysis is analogous to the rate of return demanded by an investor from a security.

If the project's risk is about the same as the company's overall risk, using the firm's cost of capital is appropriate. If the project's risk is higher, a rate with a higher risk premium is needed.

Choosing the Risk-Adjusted Rate for Various Projects

The ideas we've described in this section make logical sense, but run into practical problems when they're implemented. The stumbling block is the arbitrariness of choosing the appropriate risk-adjusted rate for a particular project.

Projects are generally presented with point estimates of future cash flows. Assessing the riskiness or variability of those cash flows is usually a subjective affair, so there's little on which to base the choice of a risk-adjusted rate. However, some logical thinking can help.

Recall that projects fit into three categories of generally increasing risk: replacement, expansion, and new venture. Replacements are usually a continuation of what was being before, but with new equipment. Because the function is already part of the business, its risk will be consistent with that of the present business. Therefore, the cost of capital is nearly always the appropriate discount rate for analyzing replacement projects.

Expansion projects involve doing more of the same thing in some business area. They're more risky than the current level, but usually not very much more. In such cases adding one to three percentage points to the cost of capital is usually appropriate.[11]

New venture projects are the big problem. They usually involve a great deal more risk than current operations, but it's hard to quantify exactly how much. So choosing a risk-adjusted rate is difficult and arbitrary. However, *sometimes* we can get help from portfolio theory.

Estimating Risk-Adjusted Rates Using CAPM

Portfolio theory and the capital asset pricing model (Chapter 11) deal with assigning risk to investments. Under certain circumstances, the techniques developed there can be used to generate risk-adjusted rates for capital budgeting.

The Project as a Diversification

When a company undertakes a new venture, the project can be viewed as a diversification similar to adding a new share to a portfolio. We can look at this idea in two ways.

The first involves seeing the firm as a collection of projects. A new venture simply adds another enterprise to the company's project portfolio, which then becomes more diversified. In the second view, the project diversifies the investment portfolios of the firm's shareholders into the new line of business.

This second idea is important and profound; let's explore it more deeply. Suppose a firm is in the food processing business. Shareholders have chosen to invest in the company because they're comfortable with the risks and rewards of that business. Now suppose the firm takes on a venture in electronics. To the extent of the new project, shareholders are now subject to the risks and rewards of the electronics business. They could have accomplished the same thing by selling off some of their food processing company shares and buying shares in an electronics firm. In essence the company has done that for them, probably without their permission.

A new venture diversifies the company and its shareholders.

Diversifiable and Nondiversifiable Risk for Projects

In Chapter 11 we separated investment risk into *systematic (market)* and *unsystematic (business-specific)* components. Unsystematic risk is specific to individual firms or industries and can be diversified away by having a wide variety of stocks in a portfolio. Systematic risk, on the other hand, is related to movement with the entire market and can't be entirely eliminated through diversification.

Projects viewed as investments have two levels of diversifiable risk because they're effectively in two portfolios at the same time. Some risk is diversified away within the firm's portfolio of projects, and some is diversified away by the shareholders' investment portfolios.

These ideas lead to an additional, intermediate concept of risk, the *undiversified risk* added to a company by the addition of a project. The idea is illustrated in Figure 14.7.

---

11 If the expansion is very large, a bigger adjustment may be necessary.

FIGURE 14.7
Components of
Project Risk

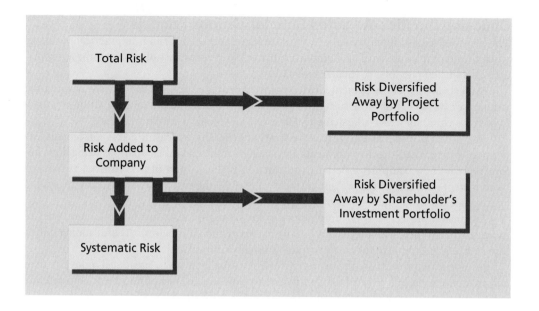

Notice that the risk left over after the two kinds of diversifiable risk are removed is systematic (market) risk. This is the same concept of systematic risk used in portfolio theory, but here it's associated with a project rather than a company.

Estimating the Risk-Adjusted Rate through Beta

The capital asset pricing model that we studied in Chapter 11 gives us an approach to measuring *systematic risk* for *companies* by using the security market line (SML). The SML (Equation 11.4) defines the firm's required rate of return in terms of a base rate and a risk premium. We'll repeat it here for convenience.

(11.4)
$$k_X = k_{RF} + (k_M - k_{RF})\beta_X$$

where k_X is the required rate of return for company X, k_{RF} is the risk-free rate, k_M is the return on the market, and β_X is company X's beta.

The term

$$(k_M - k_{RF})\,\beta_X$$

Under certain conditions the *SML* can be used to determine a *risk-adjusted rate* for a *new venture project.*

is the risk premium for company X's shares, which is a function of β_X, the company's beta. Beta in turn measures only systematic risk. But the bottom block in Figure 14.7 also represents systematic risk. In other words, the SML gives us a *risk-adjusted interest rate* related to a particular kind of risk for the shares of a company, and we find that same kind of risk in the analysis of projects.

If a capital budgeting project is viewed as a business in a particular field, it may make sense to use a beta common to that field in the SML to estimate a risk-adjusted rate for analysis of the project.

Recall, for example, the food processing company that takes on a venture in electronics. It might be appropriate to use a beta typical of electronics companies in the SML to arrive at a risk-adjusted rate to analyze the project. This line of thinking is especially appropriate when an independent, publicly traded company can be found that is in the same business as the venture and whose beta is known. The approach is known as the pure play method of establishing a risk-adjusted rate. The **pure play company** has to be solely in the business of the venture; otherwise its beta won't be truly appropriate.

A **pure play company** is a firm in a single line of business, as opposed to a firm with divisions in several businesses.

Example 14.6

Orion Inc. is a successful manufacturer of citizens' band (CB) radios. Management is considering producing a sophisticated tactical radio for sale to the Canadian Forces, but is concerned because the military market is known to be quite risky.

The military radio market is dominated by Milrad Inc., which holds a 60% market share. Antex Radio Corp. is another established competitor with a 20% share. Both Milrad and Antex make only military radios. Milrad's beta is 1.4 and Antex's is 2.0. Orion's beta is 1.1. The return on an average publicly traded share (k_M) is about 10%. The yield on short-term Treasury bills (k_{RF}) is currently 5%. Orion's cost of capital is 8%.

The military radio project is expected to require an initial outlay of $10 million. Subsequent cash inflows are expected to be $3 million per year over a five-year contract.

On the basis of a five-year evaluation, should Orion undertake the project?

■ **Solution:** The military business is clearly riskier than the CB business judging by the relative betas of Orion and its potential rivals. Therefore a CAPM-based risk-adjusted rate is appropriate for the analysis. Milrad and Antex are both pure play companies, but the fact that Milrad is the market leader probably reduces its risk. If Orion enters the field it will be in a position similar to Antex's, so a risk-adjusted rate based on that firm's beta is most appropriate.

First, we calculate the risk-adjusted rate using the SML and Antex's beta.

$$k = k_{RF} + (k_M - k_{RF})\, \beta_{Antex}$$
$$= 5\% + (10\% - 5\%)2.0$$
$$= 15.0\%$$

Notice that this rate is considerably higher than Orion's cost of capital (8%).
Next, calculate the proposed project's NPV using the risk-adjusted rate ($000).

$$k = -C_0 + C[PVFA_{k,n}]$$
$$= -\$10,000 + \$3,000[PVFA_{15,5}]$$
$$= -\$10,000 + \$3,000(3.3522)$$
$$= \$56.6$$

Notice that the risk-adjusted NPV is barely positive, indicating that the project is marginal.

If Orion's 8% cost of capital had been used in the analysis, the result would have been as follows.

$$NPV = -\$10,000 + \$3,000[PVFA_{8,5}]$$
$$= -\$10,000 + \$3,000(3.9927)$$
$$= -\$10,000 + \$11,978.1$$
$$= \$1,978.1$$

Compare these two results. The capital budgeting rule unadjusted for risk would clearly have accepted the project, but consideration of risk has shown it to be a very marginal undertaking. This can be a crucial managerial insight! However, in the next section we'll see that there are more questions lurking about.

Calculator Solution

Key	Input
CF_0	−10,000
C01	3,000
C02	3,000
C03	3,000
C04	3,000
C05	3,000
I	15

Answer

NPV	56.5

Use Excel®
Function NPV

Calculator Solution

Key	Input
CF_0	−10,000
C01	3,000
C02	3,000
C03	3,000
C04	3,000
C05	3,000
I	8

Answer

NPV	1,978.1

Use Excel®
Function NPV

Problems with the Theoretical Approach—Finding the Right Beta and Concerns about the Appropriate Risk Definition

Using the CAPM to estimate risk-adjusted rates as illustrated in the last section appears straightforward and unambiguous. However, it would be rather unusual for the technique to fit into the real world as neatly as it did in the example. Generally, the biggest problem is finding a pure play company from which to get an appropriate beta. For example, if Milrad and Antex were divisions of larger companies, their separate betas wouldn't be available, and the betas of their parent companies would be influenced by the operations of divisions in other fields. As a result, we're usually reduced to estimating betas based on those of firms in similar rather than exactly the same businesses. This reduces the credibility of the technique by quite a bit.

However, there's another, more basic problem. Look back at Figure 14.7 (page 518). Notice that three levels of risk are attached to projects, and that the CAPM technique uses the last level, systematic risk. But systematic risk is a concept that's really relevant only in the context of a well-diversified portfolio of financial assets. It excludes all unsystematic risks that may be associated with the project itself or with the company. In the context of a firm making day-to-day business decisions, disregarding unsystematic risk may not be appropriate.

For example, suppose the military radio project in Example 14.6 fails because Orion's management doesn't know how to deal with the government.[12] That risk isn't included in systematic risk because it's related specifically to Orion. But shouldn't Orion be concerned about risks like that when considering the project? Most people would agree that it should.

This reasoning suggests that total risk as pictured in Figure 14.7 is the more appropriate measure for capital budgeting. But CAPM doesn't give us an estimate of that. All we can say is that total risk is higher than systematic risk.

Let's look at Example 14.6 again in that light. The military radio project is marginal at a risk-adjusted rate reflecting only systematic risk. If a broader definition of risk is appropriate, the risk-adjusted rate should be even higher, which would lower NPV and make the project undesirable.

Projects in Divisions—The Accounting Beta Method

Sometimes a large company has divisions in different businesses, each of which has substantially different risk characteristics. In such cases, the cost of capital for the entire firm can't be associated with any particular division, so some kind of a proxy rate has to be found for capital budgeting within divisions.

The pure play method just described might be used if pure play companies can be found in the right businesses, but that's often not possible. If an appropriate surrogate can't be found, and a division has separate accounting records, an approximate approach can be used. The approximation involves developing a beta for the division from its accounting records rather than from stock market performance. This is accomplished by regressing historical values of the division's return on equity against the return on a major stock market index like the S&P/TSX Composite Index. The slope of the regression line is then the division's approximate beta and the SML can be used to estimate a risk-adjusted rate. This approach is called the *accounting beta method*.

A Final Comment on Risk in Capital Budgeting

Adjusting capital budgeting procedures to recognize risk makes a great deal of sense. However, the methods available to implement the concept are less than precise. As a result, risk-adjusted capital budgeting remains more in the province of the theorist than of the financial manager.

From the CFO

To put it another way, virtually everyone uses capital budgeting techniques, but only a few overtly try to incorporate risk. Business managers do recognize risk, but they do it through judgments overlaid on the results of analysis when decisions are finally made.

Nevertheless, it's important that students understand the risk issue, because it's a very real part of decision making. Recognizing risk is a major step toward bringing theory into line with the real world. Even though we can't precisely incorporate into our analysis the idea that cash flows are subject to probability distributions, we'll make better decisions for having thought about it.

---

12 This is a very real problem. Government and commercial markets are entirely different worlds.

SUMMARY

1 Proposed capital investments are analyzed in terms of potential returns. However, a capital budgeting analysis is not complete without some consideration of the risk inherent in the investment. Risk as it relates to capital budgeting means uncertainty as to whether and by how much future revenues and costs resulting from capital investments will likely vary from forecasts. The less predictable the outcome, the greater is the risk.

2 The estimate of each future period's cash flow is a random variable with its own probability distribution. In each case, the risk associated with the flow is related to the variance of the distribution. The resulting NPVs and IRRs of projects are also random variables with expected values and variances.

3 Ignoring risk in capital budgeting can lead to incorrect decisions and change the risk character of the firm. A firm that starts to adopt riskier projects than it has in the past will slowly become a riskier company.

4 The principle of risk aversion applies to capital budgeting. All other things being equal, we prefer less risky capital projects to those with more risk.

 Common methods for dealing with risk in capital investments include conducting a scenario or sensitivity analysis, simulation techniques, and decision trees.

5 A scenario or sensitivity analysis is designed to show how much NPV and IRR will change given a change in forecasted cash flows. In a Monte Carlo simulation, assumptions are made about the probability distribution for each future cash flow. A computer model draws random observations from each distribution and calculates the resulting NPV (and IRR) for the project. The program repeats the process many times to provide a probability distribution of the project's NPV.

 A decision tree represents graphically possible project NPVs, each of which is assigned a probability.

6 A real option is a course of action that can be made available, usually at a cost, which improves financial results under certain conditions. Types of real options include abandonment options, expansion options, investment timing options, and flexibility options. The value of a real option can be estimated as the increase in project NPV that its inclusion brings about, but a real option may be worth more than the increase it causes in NPV, because it also reduces project risk.

7 Using a higher, risk-adjusted rate in place of the cost of capital for risky projects lowers their chance of acceptance. Under certain circumstances, the techniques developed in portfolio theory and the capital asset pricing model can be used to determine a risk-adjusted rate for a new venture project.

KEY TERMS

Decision tree, p. 506
Monte Carlo simulation,
 p. 505

Option price, p. 514
Pure play company,
 p. 518

Real option, p. 510
Risk-adjusted rates, p. 516

QUESTIONS

1. In 1983 the U.S. Bell telephone system, which operated as AT&T, was broken up, resulting in the creation of seven regional telephone companies. AT&T shareholders received shares of the new companies and the continuing AT&T, which handled long-distance

services. Prior to the breakup, telephone service was a regulated public utility. That meant that AT&T had a monopoly on the sale of its services, but couldn't charge excessive prices due to government regulation. Regulated utilities are classic examples of low-risk modest-return companies. After the breakup, the "Baby Bells," as they were called, were freed from many of the regulatory constraints under which the Bell system had operated, and at the same time had a great deal of money. The managements of these young giants were determined to make them more than the staid old-line telephone companies they'd been in the past. They were quite vocal in declaring their intentions to undertake ventures in any number of new fields, despite the fact that virtually all of their experience was in the regulated environment of the old telephone system. Many shareholders were alarmed and concerned by these statements. Comment on what their concerns may have been.

2. A random variable is defined as the outcome of one or more chance processes. Imagine that you're forecasting the cash flows associated with a new business venture. List some of the things that come together to produce cash flows in future periods. Describe how they might be considered to be outcomes of chance processes and therefore random variables. In Chapter 12, cash flow forecasts for a project are used in Equations 12.1 (page 436) and 12.2 (page 441) to calculate the project's NPV and IRR. That makes NPV and IRR random variables as well. Is their variability likely to be greater or less than the variability of the individual cash flows they comprise?

3. One of the problems of using simulations to incorporate risk in capital budgeting is related to the idea that the probability distributions of successive cash flows usually are not independent. If the first period's cash flow is at the high end of its range, for example, flows in subsequent periods are more likely to be high than low. Why do you think this is generally the case? Describe an approach through which the computer might adjust for this phenomenon to portray risk better.

4. Why is it desirable to construct capital budgeting rules so that higher-risk projects become less acceptable than lower-risk projects?

5. Rationalize the appropriateness of using the cost of capital to analyze normally risky projects and higher rates for those with more risk.

6. Evaluate the conceptual merits of applying CAPM theory to the problem of determining risk-adjusted interest rates for capital budgeting purposes. Form your own opinion based on your study of CAPM (Chapter 11) and the knowledge you're now developing of capital budgeting. The issue is concisely summarized by Figure 14.7 (page 518). Is the special concept of risk developed in portfolio theory applicable here? Don't be intimidated into thinking that because the idea is presented in textbooks, it's necessarily correct. Many scholars and practitioners believe this application stretches theory too far. On the other hand, others feel it has a great deal of merit. What do you think and why?

Business Analysis

1. Ed Draycutt is the engineering manager of Airway Technologies, a firm that makes computer systems for air traffic control installations at airports. He has proposed a new device whose success depends on two separate events. First, Navigation Canada (Navcan) must adopt a recent proposal for a new procedural approach to handling in-flight calls from planes experiencing emergencies. Everyone thinks that the probability of Navcan accepting the new method is at least 98%, but it will take a year to happen. If the new

approach is adopted, radio makers will have to respond within another year with one of two possible changes in their technology. These can simply be called A and B. The A response is far more likely, also having a probability of about 98%. Ed's device works with the A system and is a stroke of engineering genius. If the A system becomes the industry standard and Airway has Ed's product, it will make a fortune before anyone else can market a similar device. On the other hand, if the A system isn't adopted, Airway will lose whatever it's put into the new device's development.

Developing Ed's device will cost about $20 million, which is a very substantial investment for a small company like Airway. In fact, a loss of $20 million would put the firm in danger of failing.

Ed just presented his idea to the executive committee as a capital budgeting project with a $20 million investment and a huge NPV and IRR reflecting the adoption of the A system. Everyone on the committee is very excited. You're the CFO and are a lot less excited. You asked Ed how he reflected the admittedly remote possibility that the A system would never be put in place. Ed, obviously proud of his business sophistication, said he'd taken care of that with a statistical calculation. He said adoption of the A system required the occurrence of two events, each of which has a 98% probability. The probability of both happening is (0.98 × 0.98 = 0.96 =) 96%. He therefore reduced all of his cash inflow estimates by 4%. He maintains this correctly accounts for risk in the project.

Does Ed have the right expected NPV? What's wrong with his analysis? Suggest an approach that will give a more insightful result. Why might the firm consider passing on the proposal in spite of the tremendous NPV and IRR Ed has calculated?

2. Might Ed's case in Question 1 be helped by a real option? If so, what kind? How would it help?

3. Charlie Henderson, a senior manager in the Bartok Company, is known for taking risks. He recently proposed that the company expand its operations into a new and untried field. He put together a set of cash flow projections and calculated an IRR of 25% for the project. The firm's cost of capital is about 10%. Charlie maintains that the favourability of the calculated IRR relative to the cost of capital makes the project an easy choice for acceptance, and urges management to move forward immediately.

Several knowledgeable people have looked at the proposal and believe that Charlie's projections represent an optimistic scenario that has about one chance in three of happening. They think that the project also has about one chance in three of failing miserably. An important consideration is that the project is large enough to bankrupt the company if it fails really badly.

Charlie doesn't want to talk about these issues, claiming the others are being "negative" and that he has a history of success with risky ventures like this. When challenged, he falls back on the 25% IRR versus the 10% cost of capital as justification for his idea.

The company president has asked you for your comments on the situation. Specifically address the issue of the 25% IRR versus the 10% cost of capital. Should this project be evaluated by using different standards? How does the possibility of bankruptcy as a result of the project affect the analysis? Are capital budgeting rules still appropriate? How should Charlie's successful record be factored into the president's thinking?

4. In evaluating the situation presented in the last problem, you've found a pure play company in the proposed industry whose beta is 2.5. The rate of return on short-term Treasury bills is currently 8% and a typical investment in shares returns 14%. Explain how this information might affect the acceptability of Charlie's proposal. What practical concerns would you overlay on top of the theory you've just described? Do they make the project more or less acceptable? Does the fact that Bartok has never done this kind of

business before matter? How would you adjust for that inexperience? Is the risk of bankruptcy still important? What would you advise doing about that? All things considered, would you advise the president to take on the project or not?

PROBLEMS

1. The Glendale Corp. is considering a real estate development project that will cost $5 million to undertake and is expected to produce annual inflows between $1 million and $4 million for two years. Management believes that if the project turns out really well the inflows will be $3 million in the first year and $4 million in the second. If things go very poorly, on the other hand, inflows of $1 million followed by $2.5 million are more likely. Develop a range of NPVs for the project if Glendale's cost of capital is 12%.

2. If Glendale's management in the last problem attaches a probability of 0.7 to the better outcome, what is the project's most likely (expected) NPV?

3. Keener Clothiers Inc. is considering investing $2 million in an automatic sewing machine to produce a newly designed line of dresses. The dresses will be priced at $200, and management expects to sell 12,000 per year for six years. There is, however, some uncertainty about production costs associated with the new machine. The production department has estimated operating costs at 70% of revenues, but senior management realizes that this figure could turn out to be as low as 65% or as high as 75%. The new machine will be amortized at a rate of $200,000 per year (straight-line, zero salvage). Keener's cost of capital is 14%, and its marginal tax rate is 35%. Calculate a point estimate along with best- and worst-case scenarios for the project's NPV.

4. Assume that Keener Clothiers of the previous problem assigns the following probabilities to production cost as a percent of revenue.

Percent of Revenue	Probability
65%	0.30
70	0.50
75	0.20

   Sketch a probability distribution (histogram) for the project's NPV, and compute its expected NPV.

5. The Blazingame Corporation is considering a three-year project that has an initial cash outflow (C_0) of $175,000 and three cash inflows that are defined by the independent probability distributions shown below. All dollar figures are in thousands. Blazingame's cost of capital is 10%.

C_1	C_2	C_3	Probability
$50	$40	$75	0.25
60	80	80	0.50
70	120	85	0.25

   a. Estimate the project's worst possible, most likely, and best possible NPVs by using a point estimate of each cash flow. What are their probabilities?
   b. Choose a few outcomes at random, calculate their NPVs and the associated probabilities, and sketch the probability distribution of the project's NPV.
   (*Hint:* The project has 27 possible cash flow patterns [3 × 3 × 3], each of which is obtained by selecting one cash flow from each column and combining with the initial

outflow.) The probability of any pattern is the product of the probabilities of its three uncertain cash flows. For example, a particular pattern might be as follows.

	C_0	C_1	C_2	C_3
C_n	$(175)	$50	$120	$80
Probability	1.0	0.25	0.25	0.50

The probability of this pattern would be $0.25 \times 0.25 \times 0.50 = 0.03125$.

6. Sanville Quarries is considering acquiring a new drilling machine that is expected to be more efficient than the current machine. The project is to be evaluated over four years. The initial outlay required to get the new machine operating is $675,000. Incremental cash flows associated with the machine are uncertain, so management developed the following probabilistic forecast of cash flows by year ($000). Sanville's cost of capital is 10%.

Year 1	Prob.	Year 2	Prob.	Year 3	Prob.	Year 4	Prob.
$ 150	0.30	$ 200	0.35	$ 350	0.30	$ 300	0.25
175	0.40	210	0.45	370	0.25	360	0.35
300	0.30	250	0.20	400	0.45	375	0.40

Calculate the project's best and worst NPVs and their probabilities. What is the value of the most likely NPV outcome?

7. Using the information from the previous problem, randomly select four NPV outcomes from the data. (Select one cash flow from each year and compute the project NPV and the probability of that NPV implied by those selections.) Plot the results on your distribution. Do your selections give a sense of where NPV outcomes are likely to cluster?

8. Work Station Inc. manufactures office furniture. The firm is interested in ergonomic products that are designed to be easier on the bodies of office workers who suffer from ailments, such as back and neck pain due to sitting for long periods. Unfortunately, customer acceptance of ergonomic furniture tends to be unpredictable, so a wide range of market response is possible. Management has made the following two-year probabilistic estimate of the cash flows associated with the project arranged in decision tree format ($000).

Work Station is a relatively small company, and would be seriously damaged by any project that lost more than $1.5 million. The firm's cost of capital is 14%.

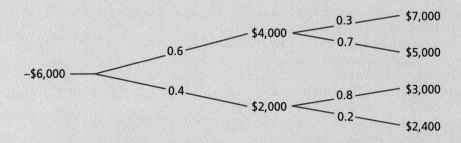

a. Develop a probability distribution for NPV based on the forecast. In other words, calculate the project's NPV along each path of the decision tree and the associated probability.

b. Calculate the project's expected NPV.

c. Analyze your results, and make a recommendation about the project's advisability considering both expected NPV and risk.

9. Resolve the last problem assuming Work Station Inc. has an abandonment option at the end of the first year under which it will recover $5 million of the initial investment in year 2. What is the value of the ability to abandon the project? How does your overall recommendation change?

10. Vaughn Video is considering refurbishing its store at a cost of $1.4 million. Management is concerned about the economy and whether a competitor, Viola Video, will open a store in the neighbourhood. Vaughn estimates that there is a 60% chance that Viola will open a store nearby next year. The state of the economy probably won't affect Vaughn until the second year of the plan. Management thinks that there is a 40% chance of a strong economy and a 60% chance of a downturn in the second year. Incremental cash flows are as follows:

Year 1:
Viola opens a store—$700,000
Viola doesn't open a store—$900,000

Year 2:
Viola opens a store, strong economy—$850,000
Viola opens a store, weak economy—$700,000
Viola doesn't open a store, strong economy—$1,500,000
Viola doesn't open a store, weak economy—$1,200,000

Perform a decision tree analysis of the refurbishment project. Draw the decision tree diagram, and calculate the probabilities and NPVs along each of its four paths. Then calculate the overall expected NPV. Assume that Vaughn's cost of capital is 10%.

11. Vaughn Video of the previous problem has a real option possibility. Carlson Flooring has expressed an interest in trading buildings with Vaughn after Vaughn is refurbished. Carlson has offered to reimburse Vaughn for 70% of its refurbishment costs at the end of the first year if they make the trade. Vaughn would then forego all incremental cash flows for the second year. Carlson is willing to keep the option open for one year in return for a nonrefundable payment of $150,000 now. Should Vaughn pay the $150,000 to keep the option available?

12. Spitfire Aviation Inc. manufactures small, private aircraft. Management is evaluating a proposal to introduce a new high-performance plane. High-performance aviation is an expensive sport undertaken largely by people who are both young and wealthy. Spitfire sees its target market as affluent professionals under 35 who have made a lot of money in the stock market in recent years.

Share prices have been rising rapidly for some time, so investment profits have been very handsome, but lately there are serious concerns about a market downturn. If the market remains strong, Spitfire estimates it will sell 50 of the new planes a year for five years, each of which will result in a net cash flow contribution of $200,000. If the market turns down, however, only about 20 units a year will be sold. Economists think that there's about a 40% chance the market will turn down in the near future.

There are also some concerns about the design of the new plane. Not everyone is convinced it will perform as well as the engineering department thinks. Indeed, the engineers have sometimes been too optimistic about their projects in the past. If performance is below the engineering estimate, word-of-mouth communication among fliers will erode the product's reputation, and unit sales *after the first year* will be 50% of the preceding forecasts. Management thinks there's a 30% chance the plane won't perform as well as the engineers think it will. The cost to bring the plane through design and into production is estimated at $15 million. Spitfire's cost of capital is 12%.

    a. Draw and fully label the decision tree diagram for the project.

    b. Calculate the NPV and probability along each path.

    c. Calculate the project's expected NPV.

    d. Sketch a probability distribution for NPV.

    e. Describe the risk situation in words compared to a point estimate of NPV.

13. In problem 12, if Spitfire elects to do the project, what is an abandonment option at year 1 worth if Spitfire can recover $8 million of the initial investment into other uses at that time? If the recovery is $13 million?

14. The Nova Scotia Brewing Company produces a super premium beer using a recipe that's been in the owner's family since colonial times. Surprisingly, the firm doesn't own its own brewing facilities, but rents time on the equipment of large brewers who have excess capacity. Other small brewers have been doing the same thing lately, so capacity has become difficult to find, and must be contracted for several years in advance.

Nova Scotia's sales have been increasing steadily, and marketing consultants think there's a possibility that demand will really take off soon. Last year's sales generated net cash flows after all costs and taxes of $5 million. The consultants predict that sales will probably be at a level that will produce net cash flows of $6 million per year for the next three years, but they also see a 20% probability that sales could be high enough to generate net cash inflows of $8 million per year.

Meeting such an increase in demand presents a problem because of the advance contracting requirements for brewing capacity. Unless Nova Scotia arranges for extra facilities now, there's a 70% chance that it won't be available if the increased demand materializes. An option arrangement is available with one of the large brewers under which it will hold capacity for Nova Scotia until the last minute for an immediate, nonrefundable payment of $1 million. Nova Scotia's cost of capital is 9%.

    a. Draw a decision tree reflecting Nova Scotia's cash flows for the next three years without the option, and calculate the expected NPV of operating cash flows. (Note that there's no need to include an initial outlay because we're dealing with ongoing operations.)

    b. Redraw the decision tree to include the capacity option as a real option in your calculations. What is its value? Should it be purchased?

    c. Does the real option reduce Nova Scotia's risk in any way?

15. Hudson Furniture specializes in office furniture for self-employed individuals who work at home. Hudson's furniture emphasizes style rather than utility and has been quite successful. The firm is now considering entering the more competitive industrial furniture market where volumes are higher but pricing is more competitive. A $10 million investment is required to enter the new market. Management anticipates positive cash flows of $1.7 million annually for eight years if Hudson enters the field. An average share currently earns 8%, and the return on Treasury bills is 4%. Hudson's beta is 0.5, while that of an important competitor that operates solely in the industrial market is 1.5. Should Hudson consider entering the industrial furniture market?

16. Crest Concrete Inc. has been building basements and slab foundations for new homes in Lac Dubonnet, Manitoba, for more than 20 years. However, new home sales there have slowed recently and residential construction work is hard to get. As a result, management is considering a venture into commercial construction. Although Crest would still be pouring concrete, almost everything else about the commercial building business differs substantially from homebuilding, which is all the firm has done until now.

The local commercial concrete business is dominated by two firms. Readi-Mix Inc. and Toddy Concrete Inc. Readi-Mix has been in business for 50 years, has a market share of 70%, and a beta of 1.3. Toddy has been in the area for only five years and has a beta of 2.4. Crest's own beta is 0.9 and its cost of capital is 9.3%. Both of these were developed during a long period in which the housing market was prosperous and growing steadily. The stock market is currently returning 11% and Treasury bills are yielding 4.2%.

Crest will have to spend $950,000 to get started in the commercial field, and expects net cash inflows of $250,000 in the first year, $400,000 in the second year and $700,000 in the third.

Should Crest give commercial construction a try?

17. Markham Fabrics Inc. makes upholstery that's used in high-quality furniture, largely chairs and sofas. Markham has traditionally sold its fabric to manufacturers who use it to cover furniture frames they produce. These manufacturers then wholesale the finished product to furniture stores. Management has analyzed the finished chairs and sofas of several manufacturers and found that the highest value element they contain is the Markham fabric. Management further found that generally the frames were shoddily produced.

Markham's VP of Manufacturing, Harrison Flatley, has proposed starting a new business called Markham Furniture, which will produce and market the end product using the fabric the firm already manufactures. Harrison has put together a proposal to start such a venture, which results in a steady stream of net cash income of $5 million per year after an initial investment of $25 million to be spent on manufacturing facilities and the development of a sales relationship with retailers. The analysis comes up with the following NPV for the project assuming the income stream is a perpetuity and taking its present value at Markham's 10% cost of capital.

NPV = −$25 million + $5 million / .10 = −$25 million + $50 million = $25 million

Top management likes the idea but is concerned about risk in two areas. First, furniture manufacturing seems to be a riskier business than making fabric as manufacturing firms are always entering and leaving the industry. The average beta of the publicly traded end-product manufacturers is a relatively high 1.9. By contrast, Markham's beta is 0.9.

Second, management fears that an economic downturn would impact a new business more seriously than it would the existing competitors. Management fears that there's a 40% chance of a downturn in the near future, which would reduce Harrison's income projections by 20%.

Re-analyze Harrison's proposal and make a recommendation to management. Treasury bills are yielding 4% and the S&P/TSX Composite index is yielding 10%.

PART 5

Financing Issues

INDICE

&P/TSX CMP   CUR
&P/TSX 60   ↑   947
W JONES   ↑   52
5DAQ   ↑   1038
               ↑   196
               ↑

Chapter 15

Cost of Capital

Learning Objectives

1 Explain that the cost of capital represents the average rate paid for the use of capital funds, and that the cost of capital provides a benchmark against which to measure the firm's investment opportunities.

2 Determine the components of a firm's capital structure: bonds, preferred shares, common shares, and retained earnings. Explain that management may have a target capital structure in mind, and may try to maintain it as money is raised

3 Explain that the differences in cost of the component securities reflect their different risks and returns.

4 Show that the weighted average cost of capital (WACC) reflects the weighted average of component costs where the weights reflect the amount of each component used.

5 Show that capital components and costs stated at current market values are most relevant for calculating WACC.

6 Calculate the current market values of the components of capital structure, and determine the current market costs of these components, based upon current market yields, flotation costs, and income tax effects.

7 Explain the concept of marginal cost of capital (MCC).

8 Explain that projects with dedicated funding should also be evaluated using the weighted average cost of capital.

An old adage talks about "getting rich on other people's money." Many investors borrow, particularly when interest rates are low, to buy shares in the hope that, at least in the long run, the return on their investments will more than compensate for their cost of borrowing. For investors *and for business firms*, the cost of financing (*cost of capital*) is a key element in their investment strategy.

We introduced the cost of capital briefly in Chapter 12 because we needed some appreciation of the concept to grasp the rationale behind capital budgeting. In this chapter, we'll explore the idea in more detail and learn how to calculate a firm's cost of capital.

THE PURPOSE OF THE COST OF CAPITAL

A company's *cost of capital* is the average rate it pays for the use of its capital funds. That rate provides a benchmark against which to measure investment opportunities in the context of capital budgeting.

The idea is very straightforward. No one should invest in any project that will return less than the cost of invested funds. Because a firm's cost of capital is the best estimate of the cost of any money it invests, it should never take on a project that doesn't return at least that rate.

This is equivalent to saying that, to be accepted, a project must either have an IRR that exceeds the cost of capital or an NPV that is positive when computed at that rate. These ideas were developed in Chapter 12 (see pages 433–434) where we used the symbol k to represent the cost of capital.

It's quite important to the effective management of a company that its cost of capital be estimated accurately. Otherwise the firm is likely to make incorrect investment decisions that can jeopardize its profitability and long-run survival.

The cost of capital concept is similar to an idea we've already studied, an individual investor's required return for a particular investment. In Chapter 11 (page 389), we said that an investor wouldn't buy a share unless its expected return was higher than his or her required return for that company. Further, we said that people base required returns on risk.

A company's cost of capital can be thought of as its required return for all capital budgeting projects that have risk levels approximately equal to its own risk. A project's expected return is its IRR. Hence the firm won't invest in a project unless its IRR (expected return) exceeds the firm's cost of capital (required return).

> The *cost of capital* is the average rate paid for the *use of capital funds*. It is used *primarily* in *capital budgeting*.

COST OF CAPITAL CONCEPTS

Capital refers to money acquired for use over long periods of time. The **funds** are generally used for getting businesses started, acquiring long-lived assets, and otherwise doing the kinds of projects we studied in Chapters 12 and 13 under the topic of capital budgeting. On a firm's financial statements, capital appears on the lower right side of the balance sheet as explained below.

> **Funds** is another term for cash.

Capital Components

Capital can be divided into **components** according to the way the money was raised. The two basic classifications are debt and common equity. Debt is borrowed money raised through *capital* (long-term) loans from banks, insurance companies, etc., or the sale of bonds to financial institutions or other large corporate investors (*private placements*). Common equity indicates an ownership interest, and comes from the sale of common shares or from retaining earnings.

A third kind of capital comes from the sale of preferred shares. Preferred can be thought of as a cross between debt and common equity, because it has some of the characteristics of each. Legally it's a kind of equity, but for many financial purposes it behaves more like debt. Because of this hybrid nature, preferred is sometimes combined with one of the other components for purposes of analysis.

> The **capital components** are debt, common equity, and preferred shares.

However, preferred shares offer investors a return that is generally different from that of either debt or common equity. Therefore, in the context of the cost of capital, it's handled separately as a third component.[1]

In the rest of this chapter we'll refer to common equity at times simply as "common" and preferred equity as "preferred shares" or just "preferred."

Capital Structure

Capital structure is the mix of the three capital components.

The mix of capital components in use by a company at a point in time is known as its **capital structure**. We generally describe capital structure in percentage terms referring to the relative sizes of the components. For example, a firm that has the following capital components can be described as 30% debt, 10% preferred shares, and 60% common equity.

Capital Component	Value	Weight
Debt	$ 30,000,000	30%
Preferred shares	10,000,000	10
Common	60,000,000	60
Total capital	$ 100,000,000	100%

The Target Capital Structure

A great deal of importance is sometimes placed on operating with the "right" capital structure. However, the determination of what's right is the subject of some debate. We'll address this issue in Chapter 16. In the meantime, we'll assume that the management of a firm may have a particular mix of capital components that it considers more desirable than any other. We'll call that mix the firm's **target capital structure**, and assume that management strives to maintain it as money is raised.

*A firm's **target capital structure** is a mix of capital components that management considers optimal and strives to maintain.*

Where a target capital structure has been designated, we'll see that it can be used in place of the actual capital structure for certain calculations.

Raising Money in the Proportions of the Capital Structure

As a practical matter, an exact capital structure can't be maintained continuously, because money tends to be acquired in finite amounts by issuing securities of one kind or another, one at a time.

For example, suppose a firm had the capital structure illustrated just above and that mix was also its target. Further suppose the company needed to raise an additional $1 million. To do that it would generally issue and sell $1 million of either debt, preferred shares, or

---

Insights **PRACTICAL FINANCE**

The Cost of Capital—Intuitively

Suppose an entrepreneur plans to open a business that will earn 12% on invested money. If he has no money of his own, but can borrow at 15%, does it make sense to start the business?

Clearly it doesn't. The enterprise is certain to lose money, because it will pay more for funds than it will earn using them. The business makes sense only if the entrepreneur can borrow at a rate below 12%.

This is the idea behind the cost of capital. We shouldn't pay more for a resource than it earns. In this simple case, the cost of capital is just the rate at which borrowed funds are available. In reality, firms have more than one kind of capital and each has a different cost. The cost of capital is a single rate that represents an average of those costs.

---

1 For more information on bonds, refer back to Chapter 9. For more information on common and preferred shares, see Chapter 10.

common shares. Trying to sell some of each security in the proportion of 30–10–60 wouldn't be practical.

Issuing one security for the additional money would throw the proportions in the capital structure off target. Then, the next time it raised capital, the company could try to move back toward the target mix.

In spite of this practical difficulty, cost of capital calculations are generally based on the assumption that money is raised in the exact proportions of some capital structure. In this case, we would assume the firm raised its $1 million by selling $300,000 in new bonds and $100,000 in new preferred shares, along with $600,000 of new common shares. The assumption isn't very realistic, but the distortion it produces is generally small.

> Cost of capital *calculations* assume that capital is *raised in the exact proportions* of some capital structure.

Returns on Investments and the Costs of Capital Components

Investors provide capital to companies by purchasing their securities. The investors' returns are paid out by the companies, so those returns are costs to the firms in which the investments are made. This is a fundamental point. The return received by an investor on a particular type of security (debt, preferred, or common) and the cost to the company of the funds raised through that security are opposite sides of the same coin.

For a particular company, investments in the securities underlying the three capital components tend to offer returns of different magnitudes, because each type of security has different risk characteristics. Thus, each capital component has a distinct cost that's related to the return earned by the investors who provide that component. And because the returns are different, so are the costs.

> The *return earned* by investors on the security underlying a capital component is its *unadjusted cost.*

Generally the return on common shares is higher than the return on debt or preferred because the risk is higher. Hence, the firm's cost of common capital is higher than its cost of debt or preferred shares. The return/cost of debt tends to be the lowest of the three, because debt is the least risky investment. The cost of preferred is usually between the cost of debt and that of common.

Although the cost paid out by the company is the investor's return, there are some adjustments that keep the *effective* cost and return from being exactly the same. Hence we say that cost and return are related rather than equal. We'll describe the adjustments later.

For now, the important point is that there are separate component costs of capital for debt, preferred shares, and common equity. And each component cost is related to the return earned by investors owning the security underlying that component.

The Weighted Average Cost of Capital (WACC)

Calculating the cost of capital is conceptually quite simple. Firms raise capital from several sources, each of which has its own cost. A firm's overall cost of capital is just the average of the costs of its separate sources weighted by the proportion of each source used. The separate sources are the capital components we've been talking about, and the proportions are the percentages of each component in the firm's capital structure.

The procedure has led to the term **weighted average cost of capital** (WACC). The expression has exactly the same meaning as the simpler "cost of capital" we've been using until now. It's customary to use the expression WACC in discussions of the subject, because it avoids confusion with the cost of capital for an individual component.

> The WACC is a *weighted average* of component costs where the weights reflect the amount of each component used.

Computing the WACC—An Example

To compute a WACC, we need two things: the mix of the capital components in use and the cost of each component. We'll get into how we arrive at each shortly, but first let's preview what we'll do once we have them. An example is the easiest way to understand the procedure.

Example 15.1

Calculate the WACC for the Zodiac Company given the following information about its capital structure.

Capital Component	Value	Cost
Debt	$ 60,000	6%
Preferred shares	50,000	4
Common	90,000	10
	$ 200,000	

■ **Solution:** First, we compute the capital structure weights on the basis of the dollar values given. This involves adding up the dollar amounts and stating each as a percentage of the total. That calculation results in the first two numerical columns below. The weight of the debt component, for example, is

$$\frac{\$60,000}{\$200,000} = 0.30 = 30\%$$

Notice that the weights have to add up to 1.00 or 100% and that they are the decimal equivalents of the percentages in the firm's capital structure.

Next, multiply the cost of each component by its weight and sum the results as shown. The result is the WACC.

Capital Component	Value	Weight		Cost		Factor
Debt	$ 60,000	0.30	×	6%	=	1.8%
Preferred shares	50,000	0.25	×	4	=	1.0
Common	90,000	0.45	×	10	=	4.5
	$ 200,000	1.00		WACC	=	7.3%

From the CFO

Because of the dividend tax credit for dividends from taxable Canadian corporations, the dividend rate on preferreds is often lower than the "coupon" rate on bonds. After tax, the net return for investors would be greater for preferreds than for bonds.

Capital Structure and Cost—Book versus Market Value

A major source of confusion about the WACC stems from the fact that both capital structure and component costs can be viewed in terms of either the book or market value of the underlying capital. We'll talk about structure first and then about component costs.

Capital Structure—Book versus Market

The book values of a firm's capital accounts reflect the prices at which the securities that raised its capital were originally sold, and are embodied in the capital section of its balance sheet. Market values reflect the current market prices of those same securities. The firm's capital structure can be based on either.[2] We'll illustrate the difference with a case in which there's only debt and common equity capital (no preferred shares).

Assume that the Diplomat Corporation, a new firm, raises $100,000 by selling 10,000 common shares at $10 each. It also borrows $100,000 by selling 100 bonds at a par value of $1,000. Immediately after those transactions, Diplomat has the capital structure shown in Table 15.1, which reflects both book and market values.

Now imagine that Diplomat's share price increases to $12, while interest rates climb and drive the price of its bonds down to $850. These market adjustments do not change the capital

2 Note that in the Brookfield example on page 535, book values of the capital accounts were used.

Cost of Capital at Brookfield Asset Management Inc.

Brookfield Asset Management Inc. (formerly Brascan Corporation) is a major North American corporation with significant holdings in commercial real estate, residential property and homebuilding, and power generation. In 2006, it had direct investments of $41 billion, including 66 commercial office properties and 140 power-generating plants. Brookfield reported its consolidated capitalization and related cost of capital (before tax) for 2006 as follows.

	Book Value (US$ millions)	Cost of Capital
Term debt	$ 1,507	7%
Mortgages	17,148	7
Subsidiary borrowings	4,153	7
Accounts payable, other liabilities	6,497	9
Preferred shares	689	6
Convertible preferred shares	1,585	6
Equity of minority interests	3,734	19
Common equity	5,395	20*
Total capitalization/ weighted average cost of capital	$ 40,708	9.5%

*required return.

Source: Brookfield Asset Management Inc., *Annual Report,* 2006. Courtesy of Brookfield Asset Management Inc.

entries on the company's books. Therefore, the book value–based structure remains as shown in Table 15.1.

However, the market value–based structure does change significantly. The result is shown in Table 15.2.

Capital structures based on book and market values are generally different because the market values of securities change all the time and those changes are not reflected on company books. Our question is: which basis for capital structure is appropriate for calculating the WACC?

Component Returns/Costs—Book versus Market

Investors' returns and the related component costs of capital can also be thought of in either book or market terms. We'll illustrate with a bond.

Suppose a firm sells a 10% coupon rate bond at its face value. Initially an investor buying the bond earns a 10% return, and the company pays the same 10% interest on the borrowed money. Suppose the market interest rate later falls to 8%.

After the market rate change, two returns can be associated with the bond. The original investor is still receiving 10% on his or her investment, and the company is still paying 10% on the original amount borrowed. However, a new investor buying the bond will have to pay a higher price and will therefore earn a return of only 8%. Hence either an 8% market rate or a 10% book rate can be associated with the debt.

Once again, our question is: which should be reflected in the component cost of debt in the WACC calculation?

Capital Component					Value	Weight
Common equity	10,000 shares	×	$ 10	=	$ 100,000	50.0%
Debt	100 bonds	×	$ 1,000	=	100,000	50.0
			Total		$ 200,000	100.0%

TABLE 15.1
The Diplomat Corporation's Initial Capital Structure— Book and Market Values Equal

TABLE 15.2
The Diplomatic Corporation's Market Value–Based Capital Structure

Capital Component					Value	Weight
Common equity	10,000 shares	×	$ 12	=	$ 120,000	58.5%
Debt	100 bonds	×	$ 850	=	85,000	41.5
			Total		$ 205,000	100.0%

The Appropriate Perspective for the WACC Calculation

Which view, book or market, is more appropriate for calculating the WACC? To answer that question we have to understand exactly what the use of each implies in the context of capital budgeting.

Book values relate to capital the company already has. It was raised in the past to support past projects. Using those values to calculate the WACC results in a figure that reflects the composite cost of existing capital that's already committed.

Market values relate to the current state of capital markets. Using market values to calculate the WACC gives a figure that reflects an average of what capital would cost if it were raised today.

We use the WACC in techniques like IRR and NPV to evaluate newly proposed projects. Old capital isn't available to fund these undertakings because it's already been spent. Hence, firms generally have to fund projects with new capital they have yet to raise. It therefore makes sense to evaluate those new projects against the likely cost of the new capital that will support them.

That means it's appropriate that the WACC reflect current market conditions, because those conditions are the best estimate of what capital will cost during the coming period. Hence, we should use market values throughout the WACC calculation.

Book values reflect the cost of capital *already spent. Market values* estimate the cost of capital to be raised in the *near future.*

Market values are appropriate because new projects are generally funded with *newly raised money.*

The Customary Approach

The customary approach is to assume that, in the future, the firm will either maintain its present capital structure based on market prices or will strive to achieve some target structure also based on market prices. Either of these capital structures is combined with market-based component costs of capital to develop the WACC.

People are generally less concerned with the precision of the capital structure in the calculation than with the accuracy of the component costs of capital. In practice, it turns out that calculating the present structure at market prices is somewhat tedious. Further, the market-based structure is constantly changing. A reasonable target structure is often used for simplicity as much as for any other reason. The error implied is generally very small.

CALCULATING THE WACC

Calculating a real WACC involves three distinct steps. First we develop a market value–based capital structure. Then we *adjust* the market returns on the securities underlying the capital components to reflect the company's true component costs of capital. Finally, we put these together to calculate a WACC.

Developing Market Value–Based Capital Structures

A market value–based capital structure uses the *current* prices of the firm's outstanding securities.

Developing a capital structure involves stating the dollar amounts of the capital components in use by the firm, adding them up, and then restating each as a percentage of the total. A book value structure is easy to calculate because the book values of debt, preferred shares, and common equity are readily available on the balance sheet. Developing a market value–based structure is more difficult. It requires that we compute the current market value of all the securities underlying each category of balance sheet capital, and then develop a structure from those values. The best way to understand the procedure is through an example.

Example 15.2

The Waubuno Corporation has the following capital situation.

Debt: 2,000 bonds were issued five years ago at a coupon rate of 12%. They had 30-year terms and $1,000 face values. They are now selling to yield 10%.

Preferred shares: 4,000 preferred shares are outstanding, each of which pays an annual dividend of $7.50. They originally sold to yield 15% of their $50 face value. They're now selling to yield 13%.

Common shares: Waubuno has 200,000 common shares outstanding, currently selling at $15 per share.

Develop Waubuno's market value–based capital structure.

■ **Solution:** The market value of each capital component is the market price of the underlying security multiplied by the number of those securities outstanding. We can use the valuation concepts from Chapters 9 and 10 to arrive at prices for the bonds and preferred shares. The price of the common shares is given.

Debt: The price of Waubuno's bonds is calculated by using the bond formula developed in Chapter 9, Equation 9.4. (See page 314.) In this case, $k = 5\%$, $n = 50$, PMT $= \$60$, and FV $= \$1,000$.

$$P_b = PMT[PVFA_{k,n}] + FV[PVF_{k,n}]$$
$$= \$60[PVFA_{5,50}] + \$1,000[PVF_{5,50}]$$
$$= \$60(18.2559) + \$1,000(0.0872)$$
$$= \$1,182.55$$

Because there are 2,000 bonds outstanding, the market value of the debt is

$$\$1,182.55 \times 2,000 = \$2,365,100$$

Preferred shares: The preferred shares pay a $7.50 dividend and currently yield 13%. Each preferred share is valued as follows (see Chapter 10, Equation 10.13, page 373).

$$P_p = \frac{D_p}{k} = \frac{\$7.50}{0.13} = \$57.69$$

Because there are 4,000 preferred shares outstanding, their total market value is

$$\$57.69 \times 4,000 = \$230,760$$

Common shares: The market value of Waubuno's common shares is just the market price times the number of shares outstanding.

$$\$15.00 \times 200,000 = \$3,000,000$$

Market value–based weights: Next we summarize and compute the capital component weights based on market values.

Capital Component	Value	Weight
Debt	$ 2,365,100	42.3%
Preferred	230,760	4.1
Common	3,000,000	53.6
	$ 5,595,860	100.0%

Calculator Solution

Key	Input
n	50
I/Y	5
FV	1,000
PMT	60

Answer

PV	1,182.56[3]

Use Excel®
Function PV

Calculating Component Costs of Capital

In this section we'll look into procedures for calculating the component costs of capital for debt, preferred shares, and common equity. In each case, we'll start by considering the market return currently received by *new* investors on the securities underlying the component. Then

---

3 As in earlier chapters, you'll notice that there is a slight rounding difference when we compare the financial calculator solution to that derived from the formula.

we'll make certain adjustments to those returns that are necessary to reflect practical reality. We'll describe the adjustments before getting into the individual component costs.

Adjustments—The Effect of Financial Markets and Taxes

The returns paid to new investors are *adjusted* to arrive at *effective* costs to the company.

Although the returns received by investors and the costs paid out by companies are the same money, the amounts *effectively* paid and received can be different because of taxes and certain transaction costs associated with doing business in financial markets.

TAXES The tax effect applies only to debt. We saw in Chapter 2 (page 45) that this stems from the fact that interest payments are tax-deductible to the paying firm. That effectively makes debt cheaper than it would be if it weren't deductible.

For example, if the firm's tax rate is 40%, the payment of $1 in interest reduces taxable income by $1, and the firm pays $0.40 less tax even though the investor gets the full dollar of interest. By way of contrast, a dollar paid as a dividend is not deductible and results in no tax savings.

The dollar cost of paying an amount of interest, I, is

$$I(1-T)$$

Interest on debt is relatively low due to the low risk for the investor. The *tax deduction* for interest makes debt even *cheaper* as a source of capital.

where T is the tax rate. The same rule applies when interest is expressed as a rate of return. If the firm pays interest at a rate k_d, the effective after-tax cost of paying that rate is

(15.1)
$$k_d(1-T)$$

For example, if the interest rate is 10% and the tax rate is 40%, the cost of debt adjusted for taxes would be

$$k_d(1-T) = 10\%(1-0.4) = 6\%$$

Recall that the return paid to investors on debt (interest) is the lowest return of the three capital components because debt is the least risky investment. The tax effect reduces the cost of debt even further in relation to the cost of the other components, making it a real bargain, particularly when the interest rate is relatively low.

Flotation costs lower the amount received when a security is issued, *increasing the cost* of the capital raised.

FLOTATION COSTS *Flotation costs* are administrative fees and expenses incurred in the process of issuing and selling (floating) securities. They include commissions paid to investment dealers for services performed in raising capital, printing and advertising expenses, and registration costs.

If flotation costs are $f\%$ of the proceeds of a security issue that raises an amount P paid by investors, the amount received by the issuing company is

$$P - fP = P(1-f)$$

where f is in decimal form in the equation.

Clearly, flotation costs lower the amount of money a firm receives when it sells securities. They have the effect of making the cost of the issue higher than the return received by investors. In general we can write

$$\text{Component cost of capital} = \frac{\text{Investor's return}}{(1-f)} = \frac{k}{(1-f)}$$

In words, the component cost of capital is higher than the investor's return by the ratio of $1/(1-f)$.[4]

For example, if the return on a particular security is 10% and flotation costs are 20%, the component cost of capital is

$$\text{Component cost of capital} = \frac{k}{(1-f)} = \frac{10\%}{(1-0.20)} = 12.5\%$$

---

4 This relationship is strictly true only when the investment is assumed to generate an infinite stream of cash flows. If the stream is finite, as in a bond investment, it is an approximation.

The Cost of Debt

In Chapter 9, we studied bond yields, including the *yield to maturity*, the return required by investors buying the bond. To calculate the component cost of debt based on market returns, we take the return received by investors currently purchasing the firm's bonds and adjust it for the effects of taxes. Most bonds aren't sold initially to the general public, but are *privately placed* with large investors. Therefore flotation costs are minimal, and we needn't adjust for them. Similarly, long-term loans from banks and other financial institutions usually do not involve significant flotation costs.

The *cost of debt* is the investor's return adjusted for the *tax-deductibility of interest* payments.

The market return on business debt is generally well known for the firm's own bonds or for issues of similar risk. In Equation 15.1, we called that return k_d. To repeat that formula, the cost of debt is

(15.1) $$\text{Cost of debt} = k_d(1 - T)$$

where $(1 - T)$ adjusts for the fact that interest is tax-deductible to the paying firm.

Example 15.3

Blackstone Inc. has 12% coupon rate bonds outstanding that yield 8% to investors buying them now. Blackstone's marginal tax rate including federal and provincial taxes is 37%. What is Blackstone's cost of debt?

■ **Solution:** First, notice that k_d is the current market yield of 8%, not the coupon rate. To calculate the cost of debt we simply write Equation 15.1 and substitute from the information given.

$$\text{Cost of debt} = k_d(1 - T)$$
$$= 0.08(1 - 0.37)$$
$$= 5.04\%$$

The Cost of Preferred Shares

Preferred shares provide an investor with a constant dividend as long as the share remains outstanding. Recall from our work in Chapters 8 and 10 that such an arrangement is known as a *perpetuity.*

The price of a preferred share is the present value of the perpetuity of the dividend stream, and is given by the expression

(15.2) $$P_p = \frac{D_p}{k_p}$$

where P_p is the current price of a share, D_p is the preferred dividend, and k_p is the return on the investment in preferred shares. (See Chapter 8, page 289 and Chapter 10, page 363.)

Solving Equation 15.2 for the investor's return yields

(15.3) $$k_p = \frac{D_p}{P_p}$$

Preferred dividends are not tax-deductible to the issuing firm, so no tax adjustment needs to be made. However, flotation costs must be incorporated by multiplying Equation 15.3 by $1/(1 - f)$. Rewriting, we have

The *cost of preferred shares* is the investor's return adjusted for *flotation costs.*

(15.4) $$\text{Cost of preferred shares} = \frac{D_p}{(1 - f)P_p} = \frac{k_p}{(1 - f)}$$

Example 15.4

The preferred shares of the Francis Corporation were issued several years ago with each share paying a dividend of 6% of a $100 par value. Flotation costs on new preferred are expected to average 11% of the funds raised.

    a.   What is Francis's cost of preferred capital if the annual dividend yield on similar preferred shares is 9% today?

    b.   Calculate Francis's cost of preferred if the shares are selling at $75 per share today.

■ **Solution:** Notice that parts (a) and (b) of this problem pose the same question with slightly different given information. In part (a), we have the market return directly and in part (b) we have the information needed to calculate it.

    a.   Write Equation 15.4 using only the last term on the right, and adjust the market return for flotation costs directly.

$$\text{Cost of preferred shares} = \frac{k_p}{(1-f)} = \frac{9\%}{(1-0.11)} = 10.1\%$$

    b.   In this case, instead of having the yield, we're told that the shares are currently selling for $75. We also know they pay an annual dividend of 6% of $100 or $6. Write Equation 15.4 using the middle term and substitute.

$$\text{Cost of preferred shares} = \frac{D_p}{(1-f)P_p} = \frac{\$6}{(1-0.11)\$75} = 9.0\%$$

The Cost of Common Equity

The cost of common equity is imprecise because of the uncertainty of future cash flows.

The market return available on common equity isn't as easy to come up with as the market return on debt or preferred shares. Those securities give an investor known streams of future payments in return for the prices paid, so calculating the return is easy. An investment in common shares, on the other hand, depends for its return on *estimates* of future dividends and prices, which are much less certain than interest payments and preferred dividends.

As a result of this uncertainty, the market return on a common equity investment has to be estimated. To do that we can use some of the ideas we've developed in earlier chapters. We'll look at two approaches involving the CAPM and the Gordon model.

Common equity comes from two sources, sales of common shares and retained earnings, which have different costs.

Another complication arises from the fact that common equity comes from two sources, retained earnings and the sale of new common shares. These have to be treated separately because they turn out to have different costs. We'll look at each in turn, beginning with retained earnings.

The Cost of Retained Earnings

The cost of retained earnings is equal to the unadjusted return earned by new buyers of the firm's common shares.

It's tempting to think of retained earnings as free to the company, because they come from its own internal operations. However, all earnings belong to the firm's shareholders whether they're paid out as dividends or retained. To the extent that management retains earnings, it reinvests shareholders' money in the company for them.

The cost of common equity can be estimated using the CAPM or the dividend growth (Gordon) model.

In other words, retained earnings represent money shareholders could have spent if it had been paid out in dividends. Therefore, those shareholders deserve a return on the funds just as though the money had been paid out and reinvested through the purchase of new shares. By this logic, the market return on new shares is the appropriate starting point for estimating the cost of retained earnings.

NO ADJUSTMENTS BETWEEN RETURN AND COST FOR RETAINED EARNINGS It's important to notice that retained earnings are the only *internally generated* capital source. They aren't raised through financial markets, so they don't incur flotation costs. They're also not tax-deductible. Hence, no adjustments are necessary to convert return to cost.

THE CAPM APPROACH–THE REQUIRED RATE OF RETURN We studied the capital asset pricing model (CAPM) in Chapter 11. The model is a theory purporting to explain how investors set required rates of return for particular shares. Recall that the required rate is the return that just entices investors to purchase a share, and is generally assumed to be a function of the share's risk. The expected rate of return, on the other hand, is the return investors expect in the future given the knowledge currently available about a particular share.

Under normal market conditions share prices are more or less *in equilibrium,* meaning that expected and required rates of return are about equal. Hence, the market return on a particular share can be approximated by estimating either the required return or the expected return. The CAPM allows us to estimate the required return; we'll look at estimating with the expected return in the next section.

The CAPM's expression for the required rate of return is the security market line (SML). It was presented in Chapter 11 as Equation 11.4. We'll relabel the expression and repeat it here for convenience.

(15.5)
$$k_X = k_{RF} + (k_M - k_{RF})\beta_X$$

where k_X is the required return on share X

k_{RF} is the risk-free rate, usually taken to be the current return on three-month Treasury bills

k_M is the return on the market or on an "average" share, usually estimated through a market index like the S&P/TSX Composite Index

β_X is share X's beta coefficient, the measure of company X's market risk

Equation 15.5 provides a direct estimate of the current market return available to investors in the common equity of company X. It is therefore also a direct estimate of the cost of common acquired through retained earnings, because no tax or market adjustments are necessary.

Example 15.5

The return on the Strand Corporation's shares is relatively volatile as reflected by the company's beta of 1.8. The return on the S&P/TSX Composite Index is currently 12% and is expected to remain at that level. Treasury bills are yielding 6.5%. Estimate Strand's cost of retained earnings.

■ **Solution:** Write Equation 15.5 and substitute directly, using the return on the S&P/TSX Composite Index as k_M and the Treasury bill yield as k_{RF}.

$$\text{Cost of retained earnings} = k_X = k_{RF} + (k_M - k_{RF})\,\beta_X$$
$$= 6.5\% + (12\% - 6.5\%)1.8$$
$$= 16.4\%$$

THE DIVIDEND GROWTH APPROACH–THE EXPECTED RATE OF RETURN In Chapter 10 we developed an expression for pricing a share that is expected to grow at a constant rate into the indefinite future. The model is alternatively called the *dividend growth model* or the *Gordon model* after the scholar who developed it. The expression was presented as Equation 10.10. We'll relabel and repeat it here with one minor change in notation. We'll replace k in the denominator with k_e to emphasize the idea that the rate is the expected return on an investment in the shares.

(15.6)
$$P_0 = \frac{D_0(1-g)}{k_e - g}$$

where P_0 is the current price of the shares

D_0 is the most recent annual dividend paid by the company

k_e is the expected return on an investment in the shares

g is the anticipated, constant growth rate of the company and its dividend stream

Solving Equation 15.6 for k_e gives a direct estimate of the cost of equity capital obtained through retained earnings. The result is Equation 15.7.[5]

(15.7) $$\text{Cost of retained earnings} = k_e = \frac{D_0(1 + g)}{P_0} + g$$

Example 15.6

Periwinkle Inc. paid a dividend of $1.65 last year and its shares are currently selling for $33.60 a share. The company is expected to grow at 7.5% indefinitely. Estimate the firm's cost of retained earnings.

■ **Solution:** Write Equation 15.7 and substitute for Periwinkle's expected return and the cost of retained earnings.

$$\text{Cost of retained earnings} = k_e = \frac{D_0(1 + g)}{P_0} + g$$

$$= \frac{\$1.65(1.075)}{\$33.60} + 0.075$$

$$= 0.053 + 0.075 = 12.8\%$$

The Cost of New Common Shares

The cost of *new common shares* includes an adjustment for *flotation* costs.

So far, we've been talking about common equity capital from retained earnings. Firms often need to raise more common capital than is available from retained earnings, and do so by selling new common shares.

Common equity from new shares is just like equity from retained earnings, with the exception that raising it involves incurring flotation costs. Therefore, the expressions we've used so far to estimate the cost of equity have to be adjusted to reflect those costs. This is easiest to do in Equation 15.7, the dividend growth model, because the price of the shares appears explicitly in that expression. The adjustment simply involves substituting $(1-f)\,P_0$ for P_0 where f represents the fraction of the price going to flotation cost. The result is as follows.

(15.8) $$\text{Cost of new common shares} = k_e = \frac{D_0(1 + g)}{(1 - f)P_0} + g$$

Example 15.7

Suppose Periwinkle Inc. of Example 15.6 had to raise capital beyond that available from retained earnings. What would be its cost of equity from new common shares if flotation costs were 12% of money raised?

■ **Solution:** Write Equation 15.8 and substitute from Example 15.6, including a 12% flotation cost.

$$\text{Cost of new common shares} = k_e = \frac{D_0(1 + g)}{(1 - f)P_0} + g$$

$$= \frac{\$1.65(1.075)}{(0.88)\$33.60} + 0.075$$

$$= 0.06 + 0.075 = 13.5\%$$

---

5 Recall that in the Gordon model the *next* dividend is $D_1 = D_0(1 + g)$. Hence Equations 15.6 and 15.7 can also be written with D_1 in the numerators of the fractions.

Putting the Weights and Costs Together

Once we've calculated a market value–based capital structure and a series of component costs based on market returns, the weighted average calculation for the WACC is a simple matter. The procedure is identical to the one we illustrated in Example 15.1 (page 534) using the appropriate weights and costs. We'll forego presenting the same computation here.

A comprehensive example presented after the next section includes the weighted average calculation in its proper sequence.

THE MARGINAL COST OF CAPITAL (MCC)

A firm's WACC is not independent of the amount of capital raised. In fact, it tends to increase abruptly from time to time as funding requirements are increased. Marginal cost of capital (MCC) means the cost of the next dollar of capital to be raised. Changes in the WACC are reflected in the marginal cost of capital (MCC) schedule, a graph showing how the WACC changes as a firm raises more capital during a planning period, usually a year. Glance ahead to Figure 15.1 on page 544 to see the idea expressed graphically.

The WACC/MCC terminology is a little confusing. The MCC schedule is a graph showing the values the WACC goes through as larger amounts of money are raised. We could just as easily call it a graph of the WACC.

Notice that the WACC starts out at one level and jumps to a higher level as the total amount of capital raised passes a certain point. If still more capital was to be raised, the MCC would have more step-function jumps like the one shown. The first jump or break is of particular interest.

> Marginal cost of capital (MCC) is the cost of the next dollar of capital to be raised. The MCC schedule is a graph of the *WACC* showing *abrupt increases* as larger amounts of capital are raised in a planning period.

The Break in MCC When Retained Earnings Run Out

The first increase in the MCC usually occurs when the firm runs out of retained earnings and starts raising external equity by selling common shares. The WACC increases at that point because the cost of common equity increases. We can see this phenomenon clearly by comparing two of the examples in the last section.

Examples 15.6 and 15.7 both involve the cost of common equity for Periwinkle Inc. In the first example we calculated the cost of retained earnings, and in the second we dealt with the cost of equity from new common shares. Notice that the 13.5% cost of new common shares is higher than the 12.8% cost of retained earnings. The difference is due to the flotation costs associated with selling the new shares.

> The MCC *breaks* when *retained earnings are exhausted*, and the cost of common equity increases due to *flotation* costs.

We generally assume that firms use all the money available from retained earnings before selling new shares. So the cost of common capital increases abruptly as the firm moves into externally raised money. But if the cost of common increases at some point, the WACC must also increase at the same point because common is an element in the weighted average calculation. A numerical illustration will make these ideas clear.

We'll use the information shown in Table 15.3 about the Brighton Company to develop its MCC schedule. We'll calculate the WACC, first using the cost of retained earnings and then using the cost of new common shares. These are the WACCs before and after the retained

Capital Component	Weight	Cost
Debt	40%	8%
Common equity	60%	From RE 10%
		From new shares 12%
Expected retained earnings		$ 3 million
Total capital requirement		$10 million

TABLE 15.3
The Brighton Company's Capital Structure, Component Costs, and Requirements

TABLE 15.4
The Brighton Company's WACC Calculations

Capital Component	Weight		Cost		Factor
With equity from RE					
Debt	0.4	×	8%	=	3.2%
Common equity	0.6	×	10%	=	6.0%
Total	1.0			WACC =	9.2%
With equity from new shares					
Debt	0.4	×	8%	=	3.2%
Common equity	0.6	×	12%	=	7.2%
Total	1.0			WACC =	10.4%

earnings breakpoint. The two computations are shown in Table 15.4. Notice that the only difference between them is the cost of common equity.

Table 15.4 shows that Brighton's WACC will increase by 1.2% as the firm uses up retained earnings and moves into new shares.

Locating the Break

The next question involves locating the break in terms of total funding. In other words, how much capital will have been raised when the WACC increases?

This turns out to be a simple matter. Recall that we assumed capital will be raised in the proportions of some capital structure. In this case the structure is 60% common equity, so every dollar raised will be 60% common equity. We also expect to have $3 million of retained earnings to use up before turning to new shares. Hence our question is equivalent to asking for the total funding level when 60% of that total is $3 million, or, $3 million is 60% of what number?

The calculation answering that question is division by 0.60. Brighton will have raised a total of

$$\frac{\$3 \text{ million}}{0.60} = \$5 \text{ million}$$

when it runs out of retained earnings. Therefore, the WACC *breaks* at $5 million.

This is an important calculation. The first breakpoint of the WACC is always found by dividing the amount of retained earnings available by the fractional proportion of common equity in the capital structure.

The MCC Schedule

Brighton's results are shown graphically in Figure 15.1. The graph shows the WACC at various funding levels. As we said earlier, the overall portrayal is referred to as the marginal cost of

FIGURE 15.1
The Brighton Company's Marginal Cost of Capital (MCC) Schedule

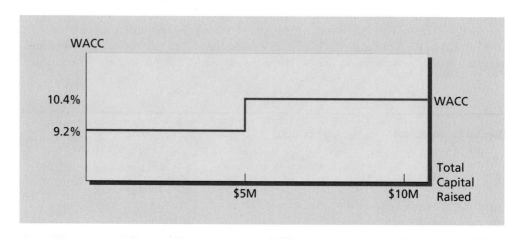

capital (MCC) schedule. Notice how the schedule makes a definitive break at the point where retained earnings are exhausted. Also notice that the break occurs at the level of total capital that has been raised when retained earnings run out ($5 million), not at the level of available retained earnings, $3 million in this case.

Other Breaks in the MCC Schedule

For most companies, the WACC is reasonably constant, aside from the break into external equity, as long as moderate levels of capital are raised. However, low-cost funds cannot be raised at or near the initial WACC without limit. The internal workings of capital markets tend to put restrictions on the amount of new money available to companies in any time period.

For example, suppose Brighton attempted to raise $20 million instead of $10 million. Perceiving such a large capital program as risky, investors would be likely to demand higher returns for further investments in both debt and equity. That means Brighton would have to pay higher interest rates to borrow more and accept a lower price to sell additional shares. Effectively, the MCC would have more upward steps to the right on the graph between $10 million and $20 million.[6]

Combining the MCC and the IOS

A firm's available capital budgeting projects can be sorted into descending order of IRR and displayed on the same set of axes as the MCC. The idea is shown in Figure 15.2 for the Brighton Company. Each block represents a project. The heights and widths of the blocks are, respectively, the projects' IRRs and the amounts of capital they require. The pattern traced by the upper rightward boundary of the projects is known as the **investment opportunity schedule** (IOS). The horizontal segments of the IOS are the IRRs of the respective projects.

This portrayal makes clear which projects should be undertaken and which should not. Brighton should accept projects as long as the IOS (IRR) is above the MCC. Figure 15.2 shows that projects A, B, and C should be undertaken, but projects D and E should not. Notice that the first break in the MCC makes projects D and E unacceptable. If the WACC continued at 9.2% indefinitely, both of these projects would have IRRs equal to or above the cost of capital. Because the MCC breaks as new equity has to come from the sale of common shares, they don't.

> The **investment opportunity schedule** (IOS) is a plot of the IRRs of available projects arranged in descending order.

> The *MCC and IOS plotted together* show which projects should be undertaken.

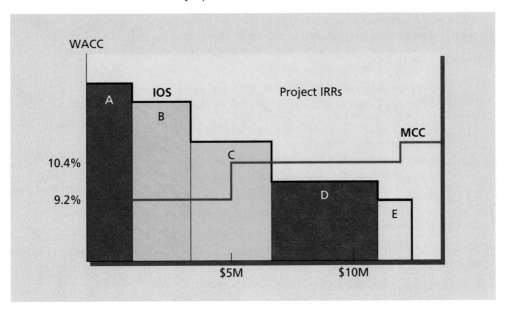

FIGURE 15.2
Marginal Cost of Capital (MCC) Schedule and Investment Opportunity Schedule (IOS)

---

6 Occasionally the cost of debt or preferred increases *before* the shift from retained earnings to outside equity. Then that point isn't the *first* break in the MCC as we've described.

Interpreting the MCC

The portrayal in Figure 15.2 seems to imply that Brighton should evaluate the first $5 million of capital projects with a WACC of 9.2% and projects using the next $5 million with a WACC of 10.4%. However, this approach is cumbersome in that it requires keeping track of more than one WACC. The same effect is achieved by taking a marginal approach and defining the WACC as the rate at which the IOS and the MCC intersect, 10.4% in the illustration.

This is an important point. A firm's WACC for a planning period (usually a year) is determined by the availability of financial resources *and* the pattern of investment opportunities projected during that period.

THE COST OF CAPITAL—A COMPREHENSIVE EXAMPLE

In this section we'll work through a comprehensive example of the calculations necessary to develop a firm's WACC and MCC curve. We'll also comment on *practice* as we go along.

Example 15.8

Baxter Metalworks Inc. has the following elements of capital.

Debt: Baxter issued $1,000, 30-year bonds 10 years ago at a coupon rate of 9%. The 5,000 bonds were sold at par. Similar bonds are now selling to yield 12%.

Preferred shares: 20,000 preferred shares were sold five years ago at their $100 par value to yield 10%. Similar securities now yield 13%.

Common equity: The company was originally financed with the sale of 1 million common shares at $10 a share. Accumulated retained earnings are currently $3 million. The shares are now selling at $12.50.

Target capital structure: We won't get into the reasoning behind the idea that one mix of capital components might be better than another until Chapter 16. For now, assume that Baxter has chosen the following target capital structure.

Debt	20%
Preferred shares	10%
Common equity	70%

This means that management attempts to keep the market values of the capital components reasonably close to these proportions over time as money is raised.

Other information:

- Baxter's marginal income tax rate is 40%.
- Flotation costs average 10% on the sale of common and preferred shares.
- Short-term Treasury bills currently yield 7%.
- An average share currently yields a return of 13.5%.
- Baxter's beta is 1.4.
- The firm is expected to grow at 6.5% indefinitely.
- The annual dividend paid last year was $1.10 per share.
- Next year's business plan includes earnings of $2 million, of which $1.4 million will be retained.

Calculate Baxter's capital component weights and its WACC before and after the retained earnings break. Sketch the firm's MCC.

■ **Solution:** We'll solve this problem and illustrate some important points along the way with the following steps.

1. Find book values and weights (for reference only).
2. Find market values and weights.
3. Compare target, book, and market weights, and comment on practice.
4. Find capital component costs.
5. Compute WACCs.
6. Sketch MCC.

1. Book Values and Weights of Baxter's Capital Components

First, we'll re-create the capital section of Baxter's balance sheet.

Debt (5,000 bonds @ $1,000)		$ 5,000,000
Preferred shares (20,000 shares @ $100)		2,000,000
Common equity		
Common shares (1 million shares @ $10))	$ 10,000,000	
Retained earnings	3,000,000	13,000,000
Total capital		$ 20,000,000

Now calculate the book weights by stating debt, preferred equity, and common equity as percentages of total capital. This calculation is made for reference only, because we don't use book values to calculate WACC.

Capital Component	Value	Weight
Debt	$ 5,000,000	25%
Preferred	2,000,000	10
Common equity	13,000,000	65
	$ 20,000,000	100%

2. Market Values and Weights

To calculate capital component weights based on market values, we have to find the current market value of the securities underlying each component.

Debt: The market value of Baxter's debt is based on the current price of its outstanding bonds. That price is different from face value, because the market interest rate is no longer equal to the bond's coupon rate. The calculation is made by using the bond formula. In this case, $k = 6\%$, $n = 40$, PMT = $45, and FV = $1,000.

$$P_b = PMT[PVFA_{k,n}] + FV[PVF_{k,n}]$$
$$= \$45[PVFA_{6,40}] + \$1,000[PVF_{6,40}]$$
$$= \$45(15.0463) + \$1,000(0.0972)$$
$$= \$774.28$$

Because 5,000 bonds are outstanding, the market value of the debt is

$$\$774.28 \times 5,000 = \$3,871,400$$

Preferred shares: The preferred shares were issued to yield 10% at a $100 par value. Therefore the preferred dividend is $10. The market yield is now 13%, so each preferred share is valued as follows.

$$P_p = \frac{D_p}{k} = \frac{\$10}{0.13} = \$76.92$$

For the 20,000 preferred shares outstanding, their total market value is

$$\$76.92 \times 20,000 = \$1,538,400$$

Common equity: The market value of Baxter's common shares is easy to calculate. The shares are selling at $12.50 and there are 1 million outstanding, so their value is

$$\$12.50 \times 1,000,000 = \$12,500,000$$

Market value–based weights: Next we summarize and compute the capital component weights based on market values.

Capital Component	Value	Weight
Debt	$ 3,871,400	21.6%
Preferred shares	1,538,400	8.6
Common	12,500,000	69.8
	$ 17,909,800	100.0%

Calculator Solution

Key	Input
n	40
I/Y	6
FV	1,000
PMT	45

Answer

PV	774.31

Use Excel® Function PV

As you can see, calculating market value weights is somewhat tedious. This is especially true if a number of different classifications of shares and bonds are all outstanding at the same time.

3. Book, Market, and Target Capital Structures

At this point it's appropriate to stop and compare the alternative capital structures we've talked about. These are the target structure and structures based on book and market values. The results are summarized as follows.

	Book	Market	Target
Debt	25%	21.6%	20%
Preferred shares	10	8.6	10
Common	65	69.8	70
	100%	100.0%	100%

Notice that, in this example, the weights aren't very different from one another. Of course, that's not always the case, but it does happen quite a bit. It's especially true that the market value–based weights and the target structure are quite similar.

In the rest of this example we'll use the market value weights, noticing that they're very close to the target structure.

4. Capital Component Costs

Next, we'll calculate the cost of each capital component using the rules developed earlier.

Debt: The cost of debt is given by Equation 15.1. It's equal to the return being received by debt investors adjusted for taxes.

$$\text{Cost of debt} = k_d(1 - T)$$
$$= 0.12(1 - 0.40)$$
$$= 7.2\%$$

Preferred shares: Equation 15.4 gives us the cost of preferred either through consideration of the preferred dividend relative to its market price or by directly adjusting the market yield for flotation costs. Because we're given a market yield of 13% in this case, we'll do the latter.

$$\text{Cost of preferred shares} = \frac{k_p}{(1 - f)} = \frac{13\%}{(1 - 0.10)} = 14.4\%$$

Common equity: We'll deal with the cost of common equity in two steps. First we'll estimate the cost of retained earnings, and then we'll find the cost of new common shares.

Retained earnings: We'll approach the cost of retained earnings in the two ways we've considered, and then reconcile the results.

CAPM: Equation 15.5 gives the return required on Baxter's shares by a typical investor in terms of the risk-free rate, the market return, and Baxter's beta.

$$\text{Cost of RE} = k_B = k_{RF} + (k_M - k_{RF})\beta_B$$
$$= 7.0\% + (13.5\% - 7.0\%)1.4$$
$$= 16.1\%$$

Dividend growth: Equation 15.7 gives the expected return on Baxter's shares given its current price, recent dividend history, and anticipated growth rate.

$$\text{Cost of RE} = k_e = \frac{D_0(1 + g)}{P_0} + g$$
$$= \frac{\$1.10(1.065)}{\$12.50} + 0.065$$
$$= 0.094 + 0.065$$
$$= 15.9\%$$

Reconciliation: In this case the two approaches give similar results, which are summarized as follows.

CAPM	16.1%
Dividend growth	15.9%

Hence, using 16.0% for the cost of retained earnings seems reasonable.

New common shares: The return on equity raised through the sale of new common shares is estimated by using the dividend growth model adjusted for flotation costs. Equation 15.8 yields

Cost of new common shares = k_e

$$= \frac{D_0(1 + g)}{(1 - f)P_0} + g$$

$$= \frac{\$ 1.10(1.065)}{(0.90)\$ 12.50} + 0.065$$

$$= 0.104 + 0.065$$

$$= 16.9\%$$

Notice that the cost of new common shares is 0.9% higher than the cost of retained earnings.

A note on accuracy: As we've said before, it's important to realize that return/cost calculations with respect to common equity are not as accurate as our tenth of a percent figures seem to imply. An estimate that's good to about a half percent is generally the best we can hope for.

Some *judgment* is required in *reconciling* the results of the different approaches to the *cost of common equity.*

5. Computing the WACC

Deriving the WACC is now a straightforward weighted average calculation. We'll use weights based on market values. The calculation has to be done twice because of the two different costs of common equity, for retained earnings and new shares. The results will be the WACCs before and after the retained earnings breakpoint.

The computation is laid out in the table below. The entries in the weight column are the decimal equivalents of the percentages of each component in the capital structure based on market values. Treat the pre-break and after-break pairs of columns separately. Multiply the cost of each component by the number in the weight column to get the factor column. Then add the factors for the WACC. We use results rounded to the nearest tenth of a percent in applications.

Capital Component	Weight	Pre Break Cost	Pre Break Factor	After Break Cost	After Break Factor
Debt	0.216	7.2%	1.56	7.2%	1.56
Preferred shares	0.086	14.4	1.24	14.4	1.24
Common	0.698	16.0	11.17	16.9	11.80
			WACC = 13.97%		WACC = 14.60%
		Use rounded values: 14.0%			14.6%

6. The MCC

The MCC schedule shows the WACC before and after the retained earnings breakpoint. To plot it we have to know how much capital will have been raised when the break occurs.

Baxter expects to generate $1.4 million in retained earnings next year, and every dollar raised is assumed to be 69.8% common equity—either retained earnings or new common shares. To locate the breakpoint we have to answer the following question: $1.4 million is 69.8% of what total capital amount? To get the answer, simply divide $1.4 million by 0.698, the fractional component of common equity in the capital structure.

The calculation is

$$\frac{\$1,400,00}{0.698} = \$2,005,731$$

For practical purposes we'll round this result and assume that the retained earnings breakpoint is $2 million. The plot of Baxter's MCC can then be drawn as follows.

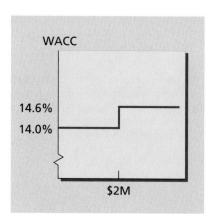

At some point to the right the MCC would step upward again as Baxter approaches the limits of its money-raising capability, and the various capital components become more expensive. However, we can't predict exactly where those steps will be in the same way that we can forecast the break-point due to running out of retained earnings.

A POTENTIAL MISTAKE—HANDLING SEPARATELY FUNDED PROJECTS

http

Visit the Cost of Capital Resources, Ibbotson Associates at http://corporate. morningstar.com/ ib/html/home.htm to see what analysis is available on the cost of capital.

Sometimes a project is proposed that is to be funded entirely by a single source of capital. This situation can create some confusion about the application of the WACC in practice.

For example, a firm might float a bond issue and use the proceeds entirely to fund just one project. It's logical to ask whether the cost of capital used to evaluate the project should be the cost of the bond issue and not the firm's WACC. Because debt tends to be the cheapest form of capital, such an approach would make the project more likely to be accepted.

Although it seems that a close matching of a source of funds with its use would be appropriate whenever possible, it's a mistake in capital budgeting, which has to be conducted within the context of the firm's overall capital-raising capability. Firms cannot continue to raise low-cost debt indefinitely without from time to time raising higher-cost common equity. In other words, firms have a limited debt capacity that can be used up until a further infusion of common equity is made.

Let's consider an illustration in which the firm is borrowing exclusively to fund a project to see what can happen if we base the accept/reject decision on the cost of debt alone. For simplicity we'll assume that the firm has no preferred shares. Imagine that its cost of debt and cost of equity are 8% and 12%, respectively, and that the capital structure is half debt and half equity so the WACC is 10%. Suppose the project proposed has an IRR of 9%, is evaluated against the 8% cost of debt, and is therefore accepted. Notice that it would have been rejected if evaluated against the WACC of 10%.

Revisiting EVA®

Recall that at the end of our study of ratio analysis in Chapter 3 (page 89) we introduced two new performance measurement concepts: *market value added (MVA)* and *economic value added (EVA)*. We're now in a better position to appreciate EVA.

EVA is important because of a shortcoming in the concept of net income, the traditional measure of financial performance. Net income begins with revenue and sub-

tracts costs and expenses *including interest* to arrive at the so-called "bottom line." Hence, the traditional income statement charges operations with the cost of debt, but *ignores the cost of preferred and common equity*. That means net income implicitly treats shareholders' equity as a free resource, which, of course, it isn't. EVA corrects that problem by charging for the use of all capital instead of just debt. The charge is calculated by multiplying total capital by the *cost of capital* as developed in this chapter. The EVA calculation is expressed as follows.

EVA = EBIT (1 − T) − (Debt + Equity) × (Cost of capital %)

EBIT (1 − T) is operating income *after tax,* which is then reduced by the charge for all capital used.

EVA is a very important concept in management today. It's worthwhile to review the broad implications of the idea now that you have a better understanding of the cost of capital.

Now suppose that sometime later another project comes along with an IRR of 11%, and the firm tries to borrow to fund it. However, lenders say the company's debt capacity is exhausted and refuse to advance funds.

Suppose equity money is available to fund the project, but its cost is 12%. Using the same rationale of measuring a project against the cost of the specific capital component funding it, the firm evaluates the second project against the 12% cost of equity and rejects it.

All projects should be evaluated against the *WACC, including* those with *dedicated funding.*

Notice what has happened. The company has accepted a project with an IRR of 9% and rejected one with an IRR of 11%. This obvious error is a result of trying to match funding sources and uses within the constraint of one firm's capital-raising capability. Had the firm evaluated both projects at the WACC of 10%, the correct accept/reject decisions would have been made. The implication is clearly that *all* projects (that are risk-consistent with the firm's operations) should be evaluated at the WACC.

SUMMARY

1 A company's cost of capital is the average rate it pays for the use of its capital funds. That rate provides a benchmark against which to measure investment opportunities in the context of capital budgeting. To be accepted, a project must either have an IRR that exceeds the cost of capital or an NPV that is positive when computed at that rate.

2 The capital components are debt, common equity, and preferred shares. The mix of capital components in use by a company at a point in time is known as its capital structure. A firm's target capital structure is a mix of capital components that management considers optimal and strives to maintain.

3 There are separate component costs of capital for debt, preferred shares, and common equity. Each component cost is related to the return earned by investors owning the security underlying that component. These returns differ because each type of security has different risk characteristics.

4 A firm's weighted cost of capital (WACC) is the average of the costs of its separate

capital components, weighted by the percentages of each component in the firm's capital structure.

5 The value of the capital components can be stated based on either the book or market prices of the underlying securities. Investors' returns and the related component costs of capital can also be stated in either book or market terms. Book values reflect the cost of capital already spent. Market values estimate the cost of capital to be raised in the near future. Market values are appropriate because new projects are generally funded with newly raised money.

6 Calculating the WACC involves three distinct steps.

First, develop a market value–based capital structure. The market value of each capital component is the current market price of the underlying security multiplied by the number of those securities outstanding.

Second, adjust the market returns on the securities underlying the capital components for flotation costs and taxes to reflect the company's effective component costs of capital. The cost of debt is the lender's return adjusted for the tax-deductibility of interest payments. The cost of preferred shares is the investor's return adjusted for flotation costs.

The cost of common equity is the return earned by new buyers of the firm's common shares. It can be estimated using the CAPM or the dividend growth (Gordon) model. The cost of new common shares includes an adjustment for flotation costs.

Finally, put these together to calculate a WACC.

7 A firm's WACC is not independent of the amount of capital raised. In fact, it tends to increase abruptly from time to time as funding requirements are increased. The marginal cost of capital (MCC) is the cost of the next dollar of capital to be raised. The firm should accept projects as long as the internal rate of return (IRR) is above the MCC.

8 A project that is to be funded entirely by a single source of capital should still be evaluated against the WACC. Capital budgeting must be conducted within the context of the firm's overall capital-raising capability.

KEY TERMS

Capital components, p. 531
Capital structure, p. 532
Funds, p. 531
Investment opportunity schedule (IOS), p. 545

Marginal cost of capital (MCC), p. 543
Marginal cost of capital (MCC) schedule, p. 543

Target capital structure, p. 532
Value of capital, p. 534
Weighted average cost of capital (WACC), p. 533

KEY FORMULAS

$$\text{Component cost of capital} = \frac{k}{(1 - f)}$$

(15.1) $$\text{Cost of debt} = k_d(1 - T)$$

(15.2) $$\text{Price of preferred share} = P_p = \frac{D_p}{k_p}$$

(15.3) $$\text{Return on preferred share} = k_p = \frac{D_p}{P_p}$$

(15.4) $$\text{Cost of preferred shares} = \frac{D_p}{(1 - f)P_p} = \frac{k_p}{(1 - f)}$$

(15.5) $$\text{Required return on common share} = k_X = k_{RF} + (k_M - k_{RF})\beta_X$$

(15.6) $$\text{Price of common share} = P_0 = \frac{D_0(1 - g)}{k_e - g}$$

(15.7) $$\text{Cost of retained earnings} = k_e = \frac{D_0(1 + g)}{P_0} + g$$

(15.8) $$\text{Cost of new common shares} = k_e = \frac{D_0(1 + g)}{(1 - f)P_0} + g$$

QUESTIONS

1. Compare the cost of capital concept with the idea of the required return on an equity investment made by an individual. Relate both ideas to the risk of the investment. How would a very risky investment/project be handled in the capital budgeting/cost of capital context?

2. Define the idea of capital structure and capital components. Why is capital structure important to the cost of capital concept? In many capital structure discussions, preferred shares are lumped in with either debt or common equity. With respect to the cost of capital, however, they're treated separately. Why?

3. You are a new financial analyst working for a company that's more than 100 years old. The CFO has asked you and a young member of the accounting staff to work together in reviewing the firm's capital structure for the purpose of recalculating its cost of capital. As you both leave the CFO's office, your accounting colleague says that this job is going to be really easy because he already has the information. In preparing the latest annual report, he worked on the capital section of the balance sheet and has the values of debt, preferred shares, and common equity at his fingertips. He says the two of you can summarize these into a report in five minutes and then go out for a pizza. How do you react and why? Is the fact that the firm is quite old relevant? Why?

4. The investor's return and the company's cost are opposite sides of the same coin— almost, but not quite. Explain.

5. There's an issue of historical versus market value with respect to both the cost of capital components and the amounts of those components used in developing weights. We're willing to accept an approximation for the weights, but not for the cost/returns. Why?

6. A number of investment projects are under consideration at your company. You've calculated the cost of capital based on market values and rates, and analyzed the projects by using IRR and NPV. Several projects are marginally acceptable. While watching the news last night, you learned that most economists predict a rise in interest rates over the next year. Should you modify your analysis in light of this information? Why?

7. Establishing the cost of common equity is the most arbitrary and difficult part of developing a firm's cost of capital. Outline the reasons behind this problem and the approaches available to make the best of it.

8. "Retained earnings are generated by the firm's internal operations and are immediately reinvested to earn more money for the company and its shareholders. Therefore, such funds have zero cost to the company." Is this statement true or false? Explain.

9. Define the marginal cost of capital (MCC) and explain in words why it predictably undergoes a step-function increase (break) as more capital is raised during a budget period.

10. "After the break in the MCC caused by using up retained earnings, the schedule can be expected to remain flat indefinitely." Is that statement right or wrong? If wrong, explain what can be expected to happen to the MCC and why.

11. Why is it appropriate to define the WACC as the highest step on the MCC under the IOS? Is anything lost by using this definition?

Business Analysis

1. You're the newly hired CFO of a small construction company. The privately held firm is capitalized with $2 million in owner's equity and $3 million in variable-rate bank loans. The construction business is quite risky, so returns of 20% to 25% are normally demanded on equity investments. The bank is currently charging 14% on the firm's loans, but interest rates are expected to rise in the near future. Your boss, the owner, started his career as a carpenter and has an excellent grasp of day-to-day operations. However, he knows little about finance. Business has been good lately, and several expansion projects are under consideration. A cash flow projection has been made for each. You're satisfied that these estimates are reasonable.

   The owner has called you in and confessed to being confused about the projects. He instinctively believes that some are financially marginal and may not be beneficial to the company, but he doesn't know how to demonstrate this or how to choose among the projects that are financially viable.

   Assuming the owner understands the concept of return on investment, write a brief memo explaining the ideas of IRR and cost of capital and how they can solve his problem. Don't get into the detailed mechanics of the calculations, but do use the figures given above to make a rough estimate of the company's cost of capital and use the result in your memo.

2. You're the CFO of a small company that is considering a new venture. The president and several other members of management are very excited about the idea for reasons related to engineering and marketing rather than profitability. You've analyzed the proposal by using capital budgeting techniques and found that it fails both IRR and NPV tests with a cost of capital based on market returns. The problem is that interest rates have risen steeply in the last year, so the cost of capital seems unusually high.

   You've presented your results to the management team, who are very disappointed. In fact, they'd like to find a way to discredit your analysis so they can justify going ahead with the project. You've explained your analysis and everything seems well understood except for one point: the group insists that the use of returns currently available to investors as a basis for the cost of capital components doesn't make sense. The vice-president of marketing put his objection as follows. "Two years ago we borrowed $1 million at 10%. We haven't paid it back, and we're still making interest payments of $100,000 every year. Clearly, our cost of debt is 10% and not the 14% you want to use. If you'd use our 'real' cost of debt, as well as of common equity and preferred shares, the project would easily qualify financially." How do you respond?

From the CFO

   (The appropriate response is relatively short. It's worth noting that this kind of thing happens all the time in corporations. Marketing and engineering people often get carried away with "neat" projects that don't make sense financially. The CFO has to watch the bottom line and it's not unusual to be seen as a wet blanket who wants to spoil the others' fun!)

3. The engineering department at Digitech Inc. wants to buy a new state-of-the-art computer. The proposed machine is faster than the one now being used, but whether the extra speed is worth the expense is questionable given the nature of the firm's applications. The chief engineer (who has an MBA and a reasonable understanding of financial principles) has put together an enormously detailed capital budgeting proposal for the acquisition of the new machine, which concludes that it's a great deal. You're a financial analyst for the firm and have been assigned to review the engineering proposal. Your review has highlighted two problems. First, the cost savings projected as a result of using the new machine seem rather optimistic. Second, the analysis uses an unrealistically low cost of capital.

   With respect to the second point, the engineering proposal contains the following exhibit documenting the development of the cost of capital used.

Digitech's capital structure is 60% debt and 40% equity

The computer manufacturer is offering financing at 8% as a sales incentive.

Digitech's tax rate is 40%

Cost of capital = 8% × 0.60 = 4.8%

After tax = 4.8% × (1 − T) = 4.8% × 0.60 = 2.9%

You've checked the market and found that Digitech's bonds are currently selling to yield 14% and the shares are returning about 20%.

How would you proceed? That is, explain the chief engineer's error(s) and indicate the correct calculations.

4. Whitefish Inc. operates a fleet of 15 fishing boats in the North Atlantic Ocean. Fishing has been good in the last few years, as has the market for product, so the firm can sell all the fish it can catch. Angus Bass, the vice-president for operations, has worked up a capital budgeting proposal for the acquisition of new boats. Each boat is viewed as an individual project identical to the others, and shows an IRR of 22%. The firm's cost of capital has been correctly calculated at 14% before the retained earnings break and 15% after that point. Angus argues that the capital budgeting figures show that the firm should acquire as many new boats as it possibly can, financing them with whatever means it finds available. You are Whitefish's CFO. Support or criticize Angus' position. How should the appropriate number of new boats be determined? Does acquiring a large number of new boats present any problems or risks that aren't immediately apparent from the financial figures?

PROBLEMS

1. Blazingame Inc.'s capital components have the following market values.

Debt	$35,180,000
Preferred shares	17,500,000
Common equity	48,350,000

Calculate the firm's capital structure and show the weights that would be used for a weighted average cost of capital (WACC) computation.

2. The Aztec Corporation has the following capital components and costs. Calculate Aztec's WACC.

Component	Value	Cost
Debt	$23,625	12.0%
Preferred shares	4,350	13.5
Common equity	52,275	19.2

3. Willerton Industries Inc. has the following balances in its capital accounts as of 31/12/X3:

Long-term debt	$65,000,000
Preferred shares	15,000,000
Common shares	55,000,000
Retained earnings	37,500,000

Calculate Willerton's capital structure based on book values.

4. Referring to Willerton Industries of the previous problem, the company's long-term debt comprises 20-year $1,000 face value bonds issued seven years ago at an 8% coupon rate. The bonds are now selling to yield 6%. Willerton's preferred is from a single issue of $100 par value, 9% preferred shares that are now selling to yield 8%. Willerton has 4 million common shares outstanding at a current market price of $31. Calculate Willerton's market value–based capital structure.

5. Again referring to Willerton of the two previous problems, assume the firm's cost of common equity is 11% (expected return) based on book values and 15% based upon market values; its marginal tax rate is 40%. Calculate its WACC using its book value–based capital structure ignoring flotation costs. Make the same calculation using the market value–based capital structure. How significant is the difference?

6. A relatively young firm has capital components valued at book and market and market component costs as follows. No new securities have been issued since the firm was originally capitalized.

Component	Value Market	Book	Cost
Debt	$42,830	$40,000	8.5%
Preferred shares	10,650	10,000	10.6
Common equity	65,740	32,000	25.3

 a. Calculate the firm's capital structures and WACCs based on both book and market values, and compare the two.
 b. What appears to have happened to interest rates since the company was started?
 c. Does the firm seem to be successful? Why?
 d. What should be the implication of using a WACC based on book as opposed to market values? In other words, what kinds of mistakes might management make by using the book values?

7. Five years ago Callaghan Inc. issued 6,000 30-year bonds with par values of $1,000 at a coupon rate of 8%. The bonds are now selling to yield 5%. The company also has 15,000 preferred shares outstanding that pay a dividend of $6.50 per share. These are currently selling to yield 4%. Its common shares are selling at $21, and 200,000 shares are outstanding. Calculate Callaghan's market value–based capital structure.

8. The Flooring Company has 142,500 common shares outstanding that are currently selling at $28.63. It has 4,530 bonds outstanding that won't mature for 20 years. They were issued at a par value of $1,000 paying a coupon rate of 6%. Comparable bonds now yield 9%. Flooring's $100 par value preferred shares were issued at 8% and are now yielding 5%; 7,500 shares are outstanding. Develop Flooring's market value–based capital structure.

9. The market price of Brunswick Ltd.'s common shares is $5.50 and 100,000 shares are outstanding. The firm's books show common equity accounts totalling $400,000. There are 5,000 preferred shares outstanding that originally sold for their par value of $50, pay an annual dividend of $3, and are currently selling to yield a 5% return. Also, 200 bonds are outstanding that were issued five years ago at their $1,000 face values for 30-year terms, pay a coupon rate of 7%, and are currently selling to yield 6%. Develop Brunswick's capital structure based on both book and market values.

10. Hecht Corp. issued 30-year bonds 11 years ago with a coupon rate of 9.5%. Those bonds are now selling to yield 7%. The firm also issued some 20-year bonds two years ago with a 6% coupon rate. The two bond issues are rated equally by DBRS and Standard and Poor's Ratings Direct Canada. Hecht's marginal tax rate is 38%.
    a. What is Hecht's after-tax cost of debt?
    b. What is the current selling price of the 20-year bonds?

11. The Loctite Corporation's bonds are currently selling to yield new buyers a 6% return on their investment. Loctite's marginal tax rate is 38%. What is the firm's cost of debt?

12. Jackson Inc.'s preferred shares were issued five years ago to yield 6%. Investors buying those shares on the secondary market today are getting a 4% return. Jackson generally pays flotation costs of 12% on new securities issues. What is Jackson's cost of preferred financing?

13. Fuller, Inc., issued $100, 8% preferred shares five years ago. They are currently selling for $84.50. Assuming Fuller has to pay flotation costs of 10%, what is Fuller's cost of preferred shares?

14. New buyers of Simmonds Inc. common shares expect a return of about 22%. The firm pays flotation costs of 9% when it issues new securities. What is Simmonds' cost of equity:
    a. from retained earnings?
    b. from new shares?

15. Light Inc.'s bonds are selling to yield 5%. The firm plans to sell new bonds to the general public and will therefore incur flotation costs of 6%. The company's marginal tax rate is 40%.
    a. What is Light's cost of debt with respect to the new bonds? (*Hint:* Adjust the cost of debt formula to include flotation costs.)
    b. Suppose Light also borrows directly from a bank at 8%.
        i. What is its cost of debt with respect to such bank loans? (*Hint:* Would bank loans be subject to flotation costs?)
        ii. If total borrowing is 60% through bonds and 40% from the bank, what is Light's overall cost of debt? (*Hint:* Think weighted average.)

16. A few years ago, Hendersen Corp. issued preferred shares paying 8% of their par value of $50. The issue is currently selling for $38. Preferred share flotation costs are 15% of the proceeds of the sale. What is Hendersen's cost of preferred shares?

17. The Pepperpot Company's shares are selling for $52. Its last dividend was $4.50, and the firm is expected to grow at 7% indefinitely. Flotation costs associated with the sale of common shares are 10% of the proceeds raised. Estimate Pepperpot's cost of equity from retained earnings and from the sale of new shares.

18. The Longlife Insurance Company has a beta of 0.8. The average share currently returns 15% and short-term Treasury bills are yielding 4%. Estimate Longlife's cost of retained earnings.

19. The Longlife Insurance Company of Problem 18 has several bonds outstanding that are currently selling to yield 5%. What does this imply about the firm's cost of common equity?

20. Hammell Industries has been using 10% as its cost of retained earnings for a number of years. Management has decided to revisit this decision based on recent changes in financial markets. An average share is currently earning 8%, Treasury bills yield 3.5%, and Hammell's shares are selling for $29.44. The firm just paid a dividend of $1.50, and anticipates growing at 5% for the foreseeable future. Hammell's CFO recently asked an investment dealer about issuing bonds and was told that the market was demanding a 6.5% coupon rate on similar issues. Hammell shares have a beta of 1.4. Recommend a cost of retained earnings for Hammell.

21. Suppose Hammell of the previous problem needs to issue new shares to raise additional equity capital. What is its cost of new equity if flotation costs are 12%?

22. Whitley Motors Inc. has the following capital structure.

Debt: The firm issued 900, 25-year bonds five years ago that were sold at a par value of $1,000. The bonds carry a coupon rate of 7%, but are currently selling to yield new buyers 10%.

Preferred Shares: 3,500 shares of 8% preferred were sold 12 years ago at a par value of $50. They're now priced to yield 11%.

Common Equity: The firm got started with the sale of 10,000 common shares at $100 per share. Since that time earnings of $800,000 have been retained. The shares are now selling for $89. Whitley's business plan for next year projects net income of $300,000, half of which will be retained.

The firm's marginal tax rate is 38%. It pays flotation costs of 8% on all new share issues. Whitely is expected to grow at a rate of 3.5% indefinitely and recently paid an annual common dividend of $4.00.

Develop Whitley's WACC before and after the retained earnings break and indicate how much capital will have been raised when the break occurs.

23. The Longenes Company uses a target capital structure when calculating the cost of capital. The target structure and current component costs based on market conditions follow.

Component	Weight	Cost*
Debt	25%	8%
Preferred shares	10	12
Common equity	65	20

* The costs of debt and preferred shares are already adjusted for taxes and/or flotation costs. The cost of common equity is unadjusted.

The firm expects to earn $20 million next year and plans to invest $18 million in new capital projects. It generally pays dividends equal to 60% of earnings. Flotation costs are 10% for common and preferred shares.

a. What is Longenes' initial WACC?

b. Where is the retained earnings breakpoint in the MCC? (Round to the nearest $0.1 million.)

c. What is the new WACC after the break? (Adjust the entire cost of common equity for flotation costs.)

d. Longenes can borrow up to $4 million at a net cost of 8% as shown. After that the net cost of debt rises to 12%. What is the new WACC after the increase in the cost of debt?

e. Where is the second break in the MCC? That is, how much total capital has been raised when the second increase in WACC occurs?

f. Sketch Longenes' MCC.

24. Taunton Construction Inc.'s capital situation is described as follows.

Debt: The firm issued 10,000 25-year bonds 10 years ago at their par value of $1,000. The bonds carry a coupon rate of 14% and are now selling to yield 10%.

Preferred shares: 30,000 preferred shares were sold six years ago for $50 each. The shares pay a dividend of $6 per year. Similar preferred issues are now yielding 9%.

Common equity: Taunton was initially financed by selling 2 million common shares at $12. Accumulated retained earnings are now $5 million. The shares are currently selling at $13.25.

Taunton's *target capital structure* is as follows.

Debt	30.0%
Preferred shares	5.0
Common equity	65.0
	100.0%

Other information:

- Taunton's marginal tax rate (federal and provincial) is 40%.
- Flotation costs average 12% for common and preferred shares.
- Short-term Treasury bills currently yield 7.5%.
- The market is returning 12.5%.
- Taunton's beta is 1.2.
- The firm is expected to grow at 6% indefinitely.
- The last annual dividend paid on common shares was $1.00 per share.
- Taunton expects to earn $5 million next year.
- The firm can borrow an additional $2 million at rates similar to the market return on its old debt. Beyond that, lenders are expected to demand returns in the neighbourhood of 14%.
- Taunton has the following capital budgeting projects under consideration in the coming year. These represent its investment opportunity schedule (IOS).

Project	IRR	Capital Required	Cumulative Capital Required
A	15.0%	$3 million	$ 3 million
B	14.0	2 million	5 million
C	13.0	2 million	7 million
D	12.0	2 million	9 million
E	11.0	2 million	11 million

a. Calculate the firm's capital structure based on book and market values and compare with the target capital structure. Is the target structure a reasonable approximation of the market value–based structure? Is the book structure very far off?

b. Calculate the cost of debt based on the market return on the company's existing bonds.

c. Calculate the cost of new preferred shares based on their market return.

d. Calculate the cost of retained earnings using two approaches: CAPM and dividend growth. Reconcile the results into a single estimate.

e. Estimate the cost of common equity raised through the sale of new shares using the dividend growth approach.

f. Calculate the WACC based on your component cost estimates and the target capital structure. Use the cost of retained earnings for the common equity component.

g. Where is the first breakpoint in the MCC (the point where retained earnings run out)? Calculate to the nearest $0.1 million.

h. Calculate the WACC after the first breakpoint.

i. Where is the second breakpoint in the MCC (the point at which the cost of debt increases)? Why does this second break exist? Calculate to the nearest $0.1 million.

j. Calculate the WACC after the second break.

k. Plot Taunton's MCC.

l. Plot Taunton's IOS on the same axes as the MCC. Which projects should be accepted and which should be rejected? Do any of those rejected have IRRs above the initial WACC? If so, explain in words why they're being rejected.

m. What is *the* WACC for the planning period?

n. Suppose project E is self-funding in that it comes with a source of its own debt financing. A loan is offered through an equipment manufacturer at 9%. The cost of the loan is

$$9\% \times (1 - T) = 5.4\%$$

Should project E be accepted under such conditions?

25. Newrock Manufacturing Inc. has the following target capital structure:

Debt	25%
Preferred	20
Common equity	55

Investment dealers have advised the CFO that the company could raise up to $5 million in new debt financing by issuing bonds at a 6.0% coupon rate; beyond that amount, new debt would require a 7.0% coupon. Newrock's 8.5% preferred shares, issued at a value of $100 each, currently sell for $112.50. There are 3 million common shares outstanding on which the firm paid an annual dividend of $2.00 recently. The shares currently trade at $36.00. Next year's net income is projected at $14 million and management expects 6% growth in the foreseeable future. Flotation costs are 6% on debt and 11% on common and preferred shares. The marginal tax rate is 40%.

a. Calculate the WACC using the target capital structure and the cost of retained earnings for the common equity component.

b. Plot Newrock's MCC, identifying the levels of funding at which the first two breaks occur, and calculate the WACCs after each break.

c. Newrock has identified the following capital projects for next year:

Project	Investment	IRR
A	$4.0 million	11.0%
B	3.6 million	10.5%
C	8.6 million	13.2%
D	2.0 million	8.7%
E	5.5 million	9.5%
F	5.0 million	7.2%
G	4.1 million	10.5%
H	6.4 million	8.0%

Projects A and B are mutually exclusive, as are Projects C and H. Plot the IOS and the MCC and determine the ideal size of next year's capital program.

Computer Problem

26. (Use an Excel® spreadsheet for this problem. You will find a suggested format at the end of the problem.)

DANIER LEATHER

You are to develop a cash flow forecast and NPV analysis for one of Danier's new power centre stores.

The initial outlay will include $1.5 million for store fixtures, equipment, and leasehold improvements. Incidental store opening costs will be $100,000 (tax-deductible). The initial inventory will cost $450,000 and will be maintained at this level for the first three years. Thereafter, it will increase at the same rate as sales.

Plan for the store to remain open for 10 years and then close down. Closing costs will amount to $200,000 (tax-deductible), but the inventory at that time can be moved to another store. The salvage value of the remaining assets will be zero.

Forecast annual sales at $1.0 million for the first year, $1.5 million for the second year, and $2.0 million for the third year. Thereafter, sales will grow by 3% per year.

Forecast cost of goods sold at 50% of sales and selling, general, and administrative expenses (SG&A) at 20% of sales. The effective tax rate will be 40%.

In year 5, the store will be "remerchandised" (renovated) at a one-time expense of $150,000 (tax-deductible).

The capital cost allowance rate is 20%.

a. Calculate the initial outlay (rows 1–8).

b. Forecast the sales, cost of goods sold, and expenses (excluding CCA) (rows 11–19).

c. Calculate the remerchandising cost in year 5 (rows 25–28).

d. Calculate the closing costs in year 10 (rows 30–33).

e. Forecast the changes to inventory (rows 35–38).

f. Currently, an average share investment returns 12%, and the return on Treasury bills is 4%. Assume that Danier's beta is 0.5. Danier has no debt or preferred shares outstanding. Suggest a cost of capital for Danier (rows 45–46).

g. Calculate NPV for the investment without CCA (rows 50–63).

h. Calculate the NPV of the CCA tax shield and total NPV (rows 70–73).

i. Danier's management treats the forecast in part (b) as the most likely outcome of the investment. To help assess the risk in this investment, construct two additional scenarios:

   i. a best-case scenario where sales after year 3 grow by 5% per year

   ii. a worst-case scenario where there is no sales growth after year 3 and cost of goods sold increases to 60% in year 4 and thereafter. Is the project a good idea then?

Spreadsheet Format

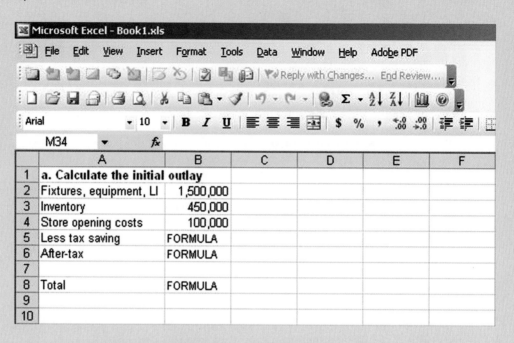

	A	B	C	D	E	F
1	**a. Calculate the initial outlay**					
2	Fixtures, equipment, LI	1,500,000				
3	Inventory	450,000				
4	Store opening costs	100,000				
5	Less tax saving	FORMULA				
6	After-tax	FORMULA				
7						
8	Total	FORMULA				
9						
10						

	A	B	C	D	E	F	G	H	I	J	K
11	**b. Forecast the sales, cost of goods sold and expenses (excluding CCA)**										
12		Year 1	Year 2	Year 3	Year 4	Year 5	Year 6	Year 7	Year 8	Year 9	Year 10
13	Sales	1,000,000	1,500,000	2,000,000	FORMULA	FORMULA	FORMULA	FORMULA	FORMULA	FORMULA	FORMULA
14	COGS	FORMULA	FORMULA	FORMULA	FORMULA	FORMULA	FORMULA	FORMULA	FORMULA	FORMULA	FORMULA
15	Gross profit	FORMULA	FORMULA	FORMULA	FORMULA	FORMULA	FORMULA	FORMULA	FORMULA	FORMULA	FORMULA
16	SG&A	FORMULA	FORMULA	FORMULA	FORMULA	FORMULA	FORMULA	FORMULA	FORMULA	FORMULA	FORMULA
17	EBT	FORMULA	FORMULA	FORMULA	FORMULA	FORMULA	FORMULA	FORMULA	FORMULA	FORMULA	FORMULA
18	Tax	FORMULA	FORMULA	FORMULA	FORMULA	FORMULA	FORMULA	FORMULA	FORMULA	FORMULA	FORMULA
19	Operating cash flows	FORMULA	FORMULA	FORMULA	FORMULA	FORMULA	FORMULA	FORMULA	FORMULA	FORMULA	FORMULA
20											
21											
22											
23											
24											
25	**c. Calculate the remerchandising cost in year 5**										
26	Cost					150,000					
27	Less tax saving					FORMULA					
28	After-tax					FORMULA					
29											
30	**d. Calculate the closing costs in year 10**										
31	Store closing costs										200,000
32	Less tax saving										FORMULA
33	After-tax										FORMULA
34											
35	**e. Forecast the changes to inventory**										
36		Year 1	Year 2	Year 3	Year 4	Year 5	Year 6	Year 7	Year 8	Year 9	Year 10
37	Ending inventory	450,000	450,000	450,000	FORMULA	FORMULA	FORMULA	FORMULA	FORMULA	FORMULA	FORMULA
38	Change	–	–	–	FORMULA	FORMULA	FORMULA	FORMULA	FORMULA	FORMULA	FORMULA
39											
40											
41											
42											
43											
44											
45	**f. Calculate the cost of capital**										
46	Cost of capital =	FORMULA									
47											

Microsoft Excel - Book1.xls

File   Edit   View   Insert   Format   Tools   Data   Window   Help   Adobe PDF

M80   ▼   *fx*

	A	B	C	D	E	F
48						
49						
50	g. Calculate NPV					
51		Total	Operating CF	Inventory Change	Remer-chandising	Closing
52	CF0	FORMULA				
53	CF1	FORMULA	FORMULA			
54	CF2	FORMULA	FORMULA			
55	CF3	FORMULA	FORMULA			
56	CF4	FORMULA	FORMULA	FORMULA		
57	CF5	FORMULA	FORMULA	FORMULA	FORMULA	
58	CF6	FORMULA	FORMULA	FORMULA		
59	CF7	FORMULA	FORMULA	FORMULA		
60	CF8	FORMULA	FORMULA	FORMULA		
61	CF9	FORMULA	FORMULA	FORMULA		
62	CF10	FORMULA	FORMULA	FORMULA		FORMULA
63	Net Present Value	FUNCTION				
64						
65						
66						
67						
68						
69						
70	h. Calculate the NPV of the CCA tax shield and total NPV					
71	Net Present Value of CCA Tax Shield =	FORMULA				
72	Net Present Value of Cash Flows	FORMULA				
73	Total Net Present Value	FORMULA				
74						

Chapter 16

Capital Structure and Leverage

Learning Objectives

1 Explain the differences between operating and financial leverage.

2 Calculate and explain what is meant by breakeven.

3 Calculate the effects that operating leverage and financial leverage have on EPS.

4 Calculate an indifference EBIT.

5 Describe how financial leverage affects the cost of capital, the value of the firm, and the value of a share.

6 Discuss the Modigliani and Miller (MM) theory of capital structure in perfect and imperfect markets.

7 Explain whether or not there is an optimal capital structure.

How much debt should a company have? That is a question that both managers and scholars alike have been trying to answer for a long time. Managers know intuitively that taking on debt is beneficial, especially if they can earn more on the investment than the cost of debt. They also know that the government allows interest payments on debt to be deducted for tax purposes, so that the investment hurdle rate is even lower. But the question remains, how much debt is too much?

We introduced the idea of capital structure in Chapter 15 as a necessary underpinning to the cost of capital concept. In this chapter we'll discover there's a great deal more to capital structure than calculating the WACC. In fact, its management is one of the most important things financial executives do.

Used properly, capital structure management can be an effective approach to improving financial performance. It can turn good results into better ones, and can even raise the price of a company's shares.

However, the technique has to be used with caution because its benefits come at a price. The cost of improving performance with capital structure can be increased risk. And risk, as we've already learned, can be a serious problem. In this chapter, we'll learn all about the benefits and the costs of managing results through capital structure.

BACKGROUND

In Chapter 15, we said that capital structure describes the mix of debt, preferred shares, and common equity a firm employs. In this chapter, we'll simplify that definition by assuming that preferred shares are essentially a form of debt.[1] Hence, from here on, when we refer to capital structure we'll mean the mix of just two components: debt and (common) equity, within capital.

"Leverage" is a general term that refers to an ability to multiply the effect of some effort. The term comes from physics where a lever is used to multiply force. *Financial leverage* refers to using borrowed money to multiply the effectiveness of the equity invested in a business enterprise.

Financial leverage refers to debt in the capital structure. It multiplies the effectiveness of equity but adds risk.

The borrowed money with which financial leverage is concerned is the debt in a company's capital structure. Hence the terms "financial leverage" and "capital structure" are somewhat synonymous. To be unleveraged means to operate with only equity capital.

The idea is quantified by the percentage of debt within total capital (Debt + Equity). Thus, 10% financial leverage implies a capital structure that's 10% debt and 90% equity.

The debt management ratios, introduced in Chapter 3, page 81, address the use of debt financing.

The Central Issue

The study of capital structure revolves around a central question: Can the use of debt (leverage) increase the value of a firm's equity? Stated slightly differently: Can it increase share price?

In our study of the Du Pont equations in Chapter 3, we saw how debt financing can magnify return on equity (page 83).

We need to be sure we understand exactly what this question means. To illustrate, think about a firm with $1 million in equity capital and no debt. Then suppose it borrows $0.25 million, buys up a quarter of its own shares, and retires them. In effect it's traded a quarter of its equity for debt. The procedure is called a capital restructuring.

Capital restructuring involves changing leverage by shifting the mix of debt and equity.

Intuitively, the process shouldn't affect the price of the shares still outstanding. Three-quarters of the original shares now represent three-quarters of the former equity, so nothing should have changed on a per-share basis.

But in fact, adding financial leverage in the manner we've just described often increases the price of the remaining shares and the value of the firm. However, the effect isn't consistent, and there are circumstances under which adding leverage decreases share price and a firm's value.

In other words, there's a relationship between capital structure and share price, but it's neither precise nor totally understood. Studies in the field attempt to explain the nature of the

Under certain conditions, changing leverage increases share price. An optimal capital structure maximizes share price.

---

1 This assumption is based on the fact that preferred share dividends are fixed in amount, and in that respect are more like interest payments than like common share dividends.

You can think of debt and preferred shares as offering investors returns that are more or less constant regardless of how the company is doing financially. Equity or common shares, on the other hand, offer a return that tends to vary with the business's performance.

relationship better and predict when additional financial leverage will increase or decrease price and value.

In particular, we want to discover whether there's an optimal capital structure that maximizes share price, all other things held constant.

After covering a little more background, we'll look at an example to see just how leverage works.

Risk in the Context of Leverage

In Chapter 11, we learned that risk and return are related and have a great deal to do with determining share prices. Here again, we'll find that risk plays an important role in setting values. In fact, leverage influences share price because it alters the risk/return relationship in an equity investment. We'll understand that better as we go along.

Measures of Performance

Operating income (EBIT) is unaffected by financial leverage.

We'll often refer to EBIT, ROE, and EPS in this chapter, so it's worthwhile to review their meaning.

EBIT, earnings before interest and taxes, is also called operating income. It's the lowest line on the income statement that's independent of financing. In other words, because EBIT is above interest expense, it is unaffected by whether or not the firm is leveraged.

ROE and EPS are return on equity and earnings per share, respectively. They're defined as follows.

$$\text{ROE} = \frac{\text{NI}}{\text{Equity}} \text{ and EPS} = \frac{\text{NI}}{\text{Number of shares}}$$

where NI is earnings after tax or net income, the bottom line of the income statement.

Investors regard EPS as an important indicator of future profitability.

ROE and EPS are overall measures of business performance in that they include both the results of operations and the effects of financing. Both measures are important to investors when they consider buying a company's shares, but EPS is especially significant. It is usually taken as an indication of the future earning power of the firm and is therefore a major determinant of the share's market price.

EBIT, ROE, and EPS were addressed in Chapters 2 and 3 (pages 24 and 75). It's not a bad idea to review those sections now.

Redefining Risk for Leverage-Related Issues

Leverage-related risk is variation in ROE and EPS.

We're used to thinking of risk in finance as variation in the return on an investment. In this chapter we'll narrow our focus and think of risk as variation in financial performance measured by ROE and EPS. This notion is separable into two pieces: business risk and financial risk.

Business risk is the variation in EBIT.

BUSINESS RISK Business risk is variation in a firm's operating performance measured by EBIT. It arises from variations in revenues, costs, and expenses. Hence, business risk is defined as variation in EBIT itself.[2]

FINANCIAL RISK In an unleveraged firm (one with no debt), the variation in ROE and EPS is identical to the variation in EBIT. In a leveraged firm, the variation in ROE and EPS is always greater than the variation in EBIT. Further, the more leverage the firm uses, the larger is the incremental variation.

---

2 Be careful not to confuse the business risk we're talking about here with the broader concept of business-specific risk from Chapter 11. Business-specific risk includes variation in EBIT as well as other things tied to a specific company or industry. For example, concern over the possibility of additional regulation of an industry could depress share prices even though financial results are unchanged. Such regulation or the threat of it would then be an element of business-specific risk, but not business risk as we're defining it here.

This leads to the definition of financial risk as the additional variation in ROE and EPS that arises as a result of using financial leverage (debt). The idea is illustrated in Figure 16.1. The left column shows that business operations produce EBIT to which we add financing to produce ROE and EPS. In other words, EBIT measures operations, but ROE and EPS measure overall performance, which is a combination of operations and financing.

Financial risk is the *additional* variation in ROE and EPS brought about by *financial leverage.*

The second and third columns show the sources of variation in the measures and how that variation is defined as risk. It's important to notice that business risk flows down into ROE and EPS by itself. Financial risk is added only if there is debt financing.

Leverage and Risk—Two Kinds of Each

From what we said in the last section, it's clear that financial leverage is associated with, and indeed causes, financial risk. We've also defined business risk as the variation in EBIT. It turns out there's another type of leverage, which has an influence on business risk that's similar to the influence financial leverage has on financial risk. This concept is called *operating leverage.*

Operating leverage is related to a company's cost structure rather than to its capital structure. Cost structure describes the relative amounts of fixed and variable cost in productive and administrative processes.

Operating leverage is the use of fixed as opposed to variable cost in a firm's cost structure. Cost structure is the mix of fixed and variable cost used by a firm.

When the term "leverage" is used by itself, it generally refers to *financial leverage*, which is the more important concept. We'll discuss operating leverage, and relate it to financial leverage later in this chapter.

Our Approach to Leverage

In the remainder of this chapter we'll take an in-depth look at leverage. We'll begin by examining how financial leverage works in practical, real-world terms. Then we'll have an equally pragmatic look at operating leverage. After examining both, we'll make a comparison between them and look at how they interact.

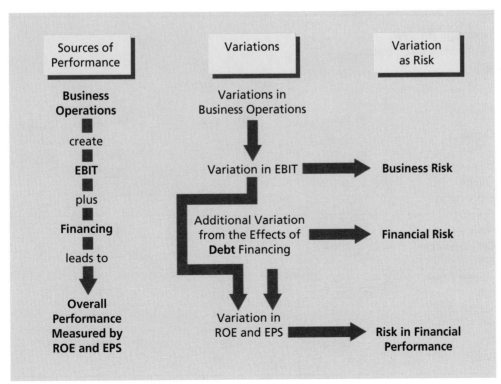

FIGURE 16.1
Business and Financial Risk

Then we'll spend some time studying capital structure theory. We'll do that without much mathematics, but when we're done we'll have a good grasp of the approach taken by finance scholars. We'll also see that the theoretical results are essentially the same as those we arrived at intuitively, but for somewhat different reasons.

FINANCIAL LEVERAGE

Now that we've developed the appropriate background, we can begin an investigation into just why leverage does what it does. We'll begin with an intuitive explanation.

The Effect of Financial Leverage

The underlying reason that leverage may increase share prices is that under certain conditions it improves financial performance measured in terms of ROE and EPS. However, it sometimes makes performance worse and always increases risk. Hence, it's not immediately clear when leverage will be a benefit and when it won't.

To understand how leverage works, we'll examine the financial results of a rising young company, the Alberta Balloon Corporation, or ABC for short. We'll look at how ABC performs under three assumptions about its use of leverage. We'll examine a case with no debt, one with 50% debt, and a highly leveraged situation with 80% debt.

Each scenario is represented by a column in Table 16.1. The capital structures are shown at the top of each column along with the number of shares outstanding. Moving from left to right, the share numbers are calculated by assuming borrowed money is used to retire shares that can be bought at their book value of $10 per share.

The issue we want to explore is what happens to financial performance as we vary leverage while holding the level of operating income (EBIT) constant. In other words, given some level of EBIT, are we better off with more or less leverage?

TABLE 16.1

Effect of Increasing Financial Leverage When the Return on Capital Employed Exceeds the Cost of Debt

Leverage Analysis
Alberta Balloon Corporation
($000)

	Leverage Scenarios		
	1 **0% Debt**	**2** **50% Debt**	**3** **80% Debt**
Capital			
Debt	$ —	$ 500	$ 800
Equity	$ 1,000	500	200
Total	$ 1,000	$ 1,000	$ 1,000
Shares @ $10	100,000	50,000	20,000
Revenue	$ 1,000	$ 1,000	$ 1,000
Cost/expenses	800	800	800
EBIT	$ 200	$ 200	$ 200
Interest (10%)	—	50	80
EBT	$ 200	$ 150	$ 120
Tax (40%)	80	60	48
NI	$ 120	$ 90	$ 72
ROE	12%	18%	36%
EPS	$ 1.20	$ 1.80	$ 3.60

To answer that question, we'll assume EBIT of $200,000, as displayed toward the middle of each column. The next four lines complete the income statement. Interest is 10% of debt, and taxes are figured at a 40% rate.

Return on equity (ROE) and earnings per share (EPS) are displayed next. These are the performance measures in which we're most interested.

The Good News about Financial Leverage

The important thing to observe in the table is the progression of ROE and EPS as we move to the right. As leverage increases, both measures go up dramatically.

Notice why this happens in terms of computations. ROE and EPS are calculated by dividing NI by equity and the number of shares, respectively.

As debt is added, NI declines because of increasing interest charges. However, equity and the number of shares outstanding shrink as debt replaces equity in the capital structure and shares are retired. In this case, equity and shares are shrinking proportionately faster than earnings, so the ratios increase.

This is the good news about leverage. If basic profitability is good, a dollar-for-dollar replacement of equity with debt improves financial performance as measured by ROE and EPS.[3] Then if investors react positively to the increases they may bid up the price of ABC's shares.

> When *profitability* is good, *EPS* and *ROE* increase as leverage increases.

The Return on Capital versus the Cost of Debt

The benefit of leverage illustrated in Table 16.1 makes sense because ABC's operating income (EBIT) represents an after-tax return on capital that exceeds its cost of debt. In other words, the company makes more with borrowed money than it pays for the privilege of borrowing.

The after-tax return on capital can be measured by a ratio called the *return on capital employed (ROCE)*. The ROCE looks at the profitability of operations without regard to how the firm is financed, but does so after tax. This amounts to calculating what the after-tax earnings on EBIT would be if there were no deductible interest, and then dividing by total capital.

The resulting number can be compared to the return on assets, the return on equity, or the after-tax cost of debt. The computation is given by Equation 16.1.

> The *ROCE* measures the profitability of *operations* before financing charges on a basis *comparable to ROE.*

(16.1)
$$ROCE = \frac{EBIT\,(1 - T)}{Debt + Equity}$$

Calculating Equation 16.1 for any of the columns in Table 16.1 yields 12%. This says that ABC is able to earn 12% after tax on any capital it uses.

If you're a little confused by the ROCE concept, just concentrate on the first column. In that case, because there's no debt and no interest, the ROCE is simply the ROE, which is 12%.

$$ROCE = \frac{\$200(1 - 0.40)}{\$1,000}$$

$$= 12\%$$

Now notice that ABC's after-tax cost of debt (assuming there are no preferred shares) is

$$k_d(1 - T) = 10\%(1 - 0.4) = 6\%$$

where k_d is the interest rate the company pays and T is the tax rate. This is only half of what the business earns on its capital, so it makes sense to use someone else's (borrowed) money.

---

3 A moderating effect that's not included in the illustration is that interest rates generally go up at high levels of debt. That means the interest cost might really be somewhat higher in the third column than the amount shown. However, the effect is unlikely to reverse the trend of increasing ROE and EPS shown.

When the *ROCE* *exceeds* the after-tax cost of debt, more leverage *improves* *ROE and EPS.*

Whenever a firm can earn an ROCE that exceeds its after-tax borrowing rate, it seems to make sense to use as much borrowed money as possible. In this case, every dollar borrowed frees up a dollar of equity and earns ABC's owners the 6% difference.

We'll learn shortly that other things affect the advisability of borrowing, but it's a basic truth that recorded financial results improve as equity is traded evenly for debt if the ROCE exceeds the after-tax cost of debt.

The Other Side of the Coin—The Bad News about Leverage

Unfortunately, leverage works in two directions. When a company is earning an ROCE that's less than the after-tax cost of debt, leverage makes results worse! To see that, we'll reconstruct Table 16.1 assuming bad weather causes a downturn in ABC's balloon business. The result is displayed in Table 16.2.

Assume revenues and earnings fall off to the point where the ROCE is just 4.8% (see the ROE in the first column of Table 16.2). That's less than the 6% cost of debt.

Now look at the progression from column to column as the firm moves from equity into debt. ROE and EPS decrease with increasing leverage. That's because the firm is earning less on capital (4.8%) than it's paying for the use of borrowed funds (6%).

When *ROCE is less* *than* the after-tax cost of debt, more leverage makes *ROE and EPS worse.*

This is another basic truth about leverage. Results are worse when ROCE is less than the after-tax cost of debt. This can cause investors to bid the price of the firm's shares down. Clearly it doesn't make much sense to increase leverage intentionally in this situation, and financial managers don't do it unless something else makes borrowing unavoidable.

Managing through Leverage

The foregoing suggests that under certain conditions management may be able to manipulate financial results and share price by changing the firm's capital structure. This is indeed true, but it has to be done with some caution.

TABLE 16.2

Effect of Increasing Financial Leverage When the Cost of Debt Exceeds the Return on Capital Employed

Leverage Analysis
Alberta Balloon Corporation
($000)

	Leverage Scenarios		
	1 0% Debt	2 50% Debt	3 80% Debt
Capital			
Debt	$ —	$ 500	$ 800
Equity	$ 1,000	500	200
Total	$ 1,000	$ 1,000	$ 1,000
Shares @ $10	100,000	50,000	20,000
Revenue	$ 800	$ 800	$ 800
Cost/expenses	720	720	720
EBIT	$ 80	$ 80	$ 80
Interest (10%)	—	50	80
EBT	$ 80	$ 30	$ —
Tax (40%)	32	12	—
NI	$ 48	$ 18	$ —
ROE	4.8%	1.8%	0%
EPS	$ 0.48	$ 0.36	$ 0.00

> *It takes time to change capital structure, but operating results can turn around overnight. That means a firm can expand leverage during good times and then be caught by an unexpected business downturn. When that happens, there may be a precipitous drop in ROE and EPS as well as in share price.*

The following example illustrates the management of EPS.

Example 16.1

Selected financial information for the Scanterbury Corporation follows.

Scanterbury Corporation at $10M Debt
($000 except per-share amounts)

EBIT	$ 23,700	Debt	$ 10,000
Interest (@ 12%)	1,200	Equity	90,000
EBT	$ 22,500	Capital	$ 100,000
Tax (@ 40%)	9,000	Number of shares =	9,000,000
NI	$ 13,500		

Share price = $10

$$ROE = \frac{NI}{Equity} = \frac{\$13,500}{\$90,000} = 15\%$$

$$EPS = \frac{NI}{Number\ of\ shares} = \frac{\$13,500,000}{9,000,000} = \$1.50$$

Notice that Scanterbury's total capital is $100 million. It pays 12% interest on debt of $10 million and its combined provincial and federal tax rate is 40%. The company's shares are selling at their book value of $10 per share. The treasurer believes that debt can be traded for equity without immediately affecting the price of the shares or the rate at which the firm can borrow.

Management believes that it is in the best interest of the company and its shareholders to move the firm's EPS from its current level up to $2.00 per share. However, no opportunities are available to increase operating profit (EBIT) above the current level of $23.7 million.

Will borrowing more money and retiring shares raise Scanterbury's EPS, and if so, what capital structure will achieve an EPS of $2.00?

■ **Solution:** EPS will increase if the ROCE exceeds the after-tax cost of debt. Calculate ROCE by writing Equation 16.1 and substituting from the problem.

$$ROCE = \frac{EBIT\ (1 - T)}{Debt\ +\ Equity}$$

$$= \frac{\$23.7M(1 - 0.4)}{\$100.0M}$$

$$= \frac{\$14.2M}{\$100.0M}$$

$$= 14.2\%$$

The after-tax cost of debt is the interest rate paid times (1 minus the tax rate).

$$k_d(1 - T) = 12\%(1 - 0.4) = 7.2\%$$

which is obviously less than 14.2%. Hence, trading equity for debt will improve EPS.

The second part of the question asks us to find the capital structure that results in an EPS of $2.00. Conceptually the easiest way to do that is through trial and error. Simply choose a series of debt levels and recompute the financial results until a value is found that yields EPS = $2.00.

An even easier way is to use Excel® and Goal Seek. We've left the equations exposed so that you can see that the Capital is set to $100,000 and for every $10 borrowed the firm will retire one share and reduce equity by the same $10.

	A	B	C	D	E
1	EBIT	23700		Debt	30000
2	Interest @ 12%	=0.12*E1		Equity	=E3-E1
3	EBT	=B1-B2		Capital	100000
4	Tax @ 40%	=0.4*B3		Number of Shares	=E2/10
5	NI	=B3-B4			
6				EPS	=B5/E4
7					
8					
9					
10					
11					
12					
13					
14					
15					
16					

Goal Seek [X]

Set cell: E6

To value: 2.00

By changing cell: E1

[OK] [Cancel]

Scanterbury Corporation

We've told Goal Seek that we want the EPS to be $2.00 and that we'd like the debt level to be adjusted. As an exercise, show that the answer is $45.15 million.

An Alternative Approach (optional)

An algebraic approach is available that is computationally more efficient even though it's mathematically a bit complex. The idea is to write ratios and/or parts of financial statements as equations that can be used to solve for unknown financial quantities. Those who are not mathematically inclined can skip to the next section without loss of continuity.

In this case, we'll use the definition of some ratios, the income statement from EBIT to NI, the relationship between debt and interest, and the definition of capital to construct an equation that will lead us to the exact level of debt we need.

We'll begin by noticing that there's a simple relationship between EPS, ROE, and book value per share.

$$\text{EPS} = \text{ROE} \times \text{Book value per share}$$

Convince yourself that this is true by substituting the definitions of these ratios found on page 566.

Since Scanterbury's shares are selling at their book value of $10.00, retiring shares won't change that value, so we can write

$$\text{EPS} = \text{ROE}(\$10) = \frac{\text{NI}}{\text{Equity}}$$

where Equity = Number of shares × $10.

Next consider the bottom part of Scanterbury's income statement. NI can be written as

$$\text{NI} = (\text{EBIT} - I)(1 - T)$$

where I is interest and T is the tax rate. (EBIT − I) is earnings before tax (EBT), which is adjusted to earnings after tax by multiplying by $(1 - T)$.

Interest is debt times the interest rate, k_d, so we can write

$$I = k_d(\text{Debt})$$

Substituting this into the expression for NI yields

$$\text{NI} = [\text{EBIT} - (k_d)(\text{Debt})](1 - T)$$

Further, total capital is debt plus equity, so

$$\text{Equity} = \text{Total capital} - \text{Debt}$$

Substituting these expressions for NI and equity into the previous equation yields

$$\text{EPS} = \frac{[\text{EBIT} - (k_d)(\text{Debt})](1 - T)}{\text{Total capital} - \text{Debt}} \times \$10.00$$

Everything in this equation except debt is available in the problem. If we treat debt as the unknown and set EPS equal to $2.00, we have a single equation in a single unknown, the solution to which is the value of debt at which EPS is exactly $2.00. Substituting we have

$$\$2.00 = \frac{[\$23,700,000 - (0.12)(\text{Debt})](1 - 0.4)}{0.1[\$100,000,000 - \text{Debt}]}$$

from which

$$\text{Debt} = \$45,156,250$$

Hence, the capital structure that produces a $2.00 EPS is roughly 45% debt and 55% equity.

Financial Leverage and Financial Risk

Tables 16.1 (page 568) and 16.2 (page 570) show that financial leverage is a two-edged sword. It multiplies good results into great results, but it also multiplies bad results into terrible results. This means that when business conditions change, performance measured by ROE or EPS makes wider swings for more leveraged organizations than for those with relatively less debt. The incremental variation in results is what we've called *financial* risk.

We can illustrate the idea with the Alberta Balloon Corporation using Tables 16.1 and 16.2. The first table represents relatively good times, while the second reflects harder times and lower earnings. Within each table there's a no-leverage situation in the first column and a high-leverage case in the third column.

To see the effect of financial leverage on risk, we'll compare the changes in ROE in the first and third columns, respectively, between the two tables. The analysis is shown in Table 16.3.

Because there's no financial leverage in column 1 of Tables 16.1 and 16.2, the difference in those ROEs represents the variability of the basic business's results. In other words, that change is due to business risk.[4]

The difference in the column 3 ROEs represents the sum of the variabilities arising from operations and from financing. The incremental variability, the difference between the two differences, is a result of financial risk. This difference is shown on the fourth line.

In ABC's case, business risk accounts for a swing of 7.2% in ROE. The financial risk associated with 80% leverage, however, accounts for a swing of (36.0% − 7.2% =) 28.8% in ROE. In other words, financial risk is four times as large as business risk in bad times (28.8%/7.2% = 4). The result makes sense, because 80% debt represents a high degree of leverage.

To check your understanding, show that the financial risk associated with 50% debt (column 2) is 1.25 times the level of business risk.

A good way to think of these ideas is to say that leverage magnifies changes in operating income (EBIT) into larger changes in ROE and EPS. Further, the more leverage there is, the larger is the magnification.

Financial risk is the increased variability in financial results that comes from *additional leverage.*

	ROE	
	Column 1 **No Debt**	**Column 2** **80% Debt**
Good times (Table 16.1)	12.0%	36.0%
Bad times (Table 16.2)	4.8	0.0
Difference	7.2%	36.0%
Incremental difference in ROE due to financial leverage = 36.0% − 7.2% = 28.8%		

TABLE 16.3
Financial Leverage and Risk

4 We generally measure business risk at EBIT, but when there's no financial leverage the result is the same at ROE. To see this, notice that in column 1 the ratio of EBIT in Table 16.1 to EBIT in Table 16.2 is the same as the ratio of ROE in Table 16.1 to ROE in Table 16.2.

Putting the Ideas Together—The Effect on Share Price

Our study of the Alberta Balloon Corporation has demonstrated two important effects of leverage:

1. During periods of reasonably good performance, leverage enhances results in terms of ROE and EPS.
2. Leverage adds variability to financial performance when operating results change. This means that performance is riskier with more leverage.

Both phenomena become more pronounced as the level of leverage increases.

Leverage enhances performance while it adds risk, pushing share prices in opposite directions.

These effects drive share prices in opposite directions. The first, enhanced performance under likely conditions, makes the expected return on a share investment higher. That makes the shares more desirable to investors, which causes them to bid up their price.

In ABC's case, for example, suppose everyone expects prosperity consistent with Table 16.1 (page 568) next year, believing the chances of a recession are very remote. Then ABC's expected EPS with no leverage is $1.20 from the first column. That expectation can be increased to $1.80 by moving to the leverage position in column 2. If no one is too worried about poor economic conditions, the higher expected performance is just accepted at its face value.

The second effect makes a share investment riskier, and we know from the principle of risk aversion (Chapter 11, page 390 and 398) that investors don't like that. Hence, the second effect tends to drive investors away, lowering the price.

The key question is which effect dominates and when?

Real Investor Behaviour and the Optimal Capital Structure

It turns out that at low to moderate levels of debt, investors value the positive effects of leverage a great deal and virtually ignore concerns about increased risk. This is especially true if the economic outlook is good. Hence, increases in leverage tend to raise share prices when leverage is low or moderate.

When leverage is low, a little more has a positive effect on investors, but at high debt levels concerns about risk dominate, and the effect of more is negative.

As leverage increases, however, concerns about risk and poor performance begin to overwhelm the benefits of enhanced return in people's minds. Thus, at higher levels, further increases in leverage have a negative effect on share price.

In other words, as leverage increases from nothing to very high levels (all other things held constant), share price increases, reaches a maximum, and then decreases. The idea is shown graphically in Figure 16.2. The maximum point on the graph is conceptually important. It corresponds to the optimal capital structure. By definition this is the capital structure (percentage of debt, level of leverage) that maximizes share price.

Finding the Optimum—A Practical Problem

No one doubts that the response pattern of share price to leverage is generally as pictured in Figure 16.2 or that there is indeed some optimal level of debt that produces a maximum price. The problem is that no one has a way to determine exactly where the maximum is for a particular company at a particular time.

As leverage increases, its effect goes from positive to negative. The most positive effect defines the optimal capital structure.

The appropriate level of leverage tends to vary with the nature of a company's business as well as with the economic climate. A firm whose basic business is relatively volatile would be expected to use less leverage than a company in a stable business. That's because a high level of business risk compounded by a high level of leverage produces an extremely risky company.

With respect to economic climate, investors are more sensitive to risk when the outlook is poor than when it's good. The optimal level of leverage therefore should be lower in bad times because investors are repelled by increasing risk sooner.

Unfortunately, these ideas aren't particularly quantifiable, so we aren't able to locate the optimum along the horizontal axis of Figure 16.2 with any accuracy.

That doesn't mean that capital structure thinking is useless. However, it is more of a general guide than a precise set of instructions for managing a company. The accepted wisdom is more or less as follows.

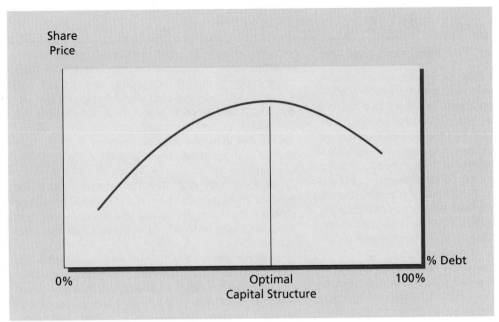

FIGURE 16.2
The Effect of
Leverage on
Share Price

As a practical matter the optimal capital structure *cannot be precisely located.*

From the CFO

1. *A firm with good profit prospects and little or no debt is probably missing an opportunity by not using borrowed money if interest rates are reasonable.*
2. *For most businesses, the optimal capital structure is somewhere between 30% and 50% debt.*
3. *Debt levels above 60% create excessive risk and should be avoided unless cash flows are very stable (for example, those of a public utility).*

Keep in mind that these are rough guidelines with lots of exceptions, and are not hard rules.

The Target Capital Structure

We referred to a *target capital structure* during our discussion of the cost of capital in Chapter 15. We said the target structure is one that management prefers over any other and attempts to maintain as it raises money. We're now in a position to better appreciate that idea.

A firm's *target capital structure* is management's estimate of the optimal capital structure.

The target capital structure is just an approximation of the optimal capital structure. It is management's best guess at a level of leverage that maximizes the firm's share price.

You may recall that in Chapter 15 we weren't concerned about stating target and actual capital structures with a great deal of precision. The reason should be apparent now. We can't find the optimal structure with a high degree of accuracy, so it doesn't make much sense to get too detailed about a guess at it.

The Effect of Leverage When Shares Aren't Trading at Book Value

There's an important detail that shouldn't be missed in what we've been doing. We've presented illustrations of changes in leverage in which equity is replaced by debt. They have all involved changes in the number of shares outstanding that are proportionate to the changes in equity.

That proportionality is ensured by assuming that the shares can be purchased for retirement at a market price equal to their book value. When that isn't the case, things can be somewhat more complex. The relationship between ROE and EPS can be shown to be

$$EPS = ROE \times Book\ value\ per\ share$$

When shares are purchased for retirement at book value, the book value per share of the remaining shares stays the same and the transaction has essentially the same effect on EPS that

Insights REAL APPLICATIONS

AOL Time Warner: The Perils of Leverage

In 2000, America Online (AOL), the famous Internet provider, and Time Warner, a media giant with interests in publishing and the film industry, merged in what was billed as a marriage of "old media" and "new media." Unfortunately, the "media marriage" has so far produced little but red ink. Within months, America Online's business went into a steep slump, and the shares of the combined company, AOL Time Warner (since named Time Warner Inc.), plummeted, wiping out more than $100 billion in market value. To make matters worse, Time Warner's print publishing business suffered a significant decline in advertising revenue after the September 11, 2001, terror attack on the World Trade Center.

A big part of the reason that the company suffered as badly in the stock market as it did may have been due to excessive leverage. The combined company reported long-term debt as of September 30, 2002, of $28.2 billion. At first glance, that doesn't seem excessive relative to the company's reported assets of $161 billion at that time. Indeed, few analysts would argue that debt of about ($28/$161 =) 17% of assets is too much.

But a closer look at the balance sheet may have led investors to a different conclusion. The problem is likely to have been that more than half of the assets reported represented intangibles, the future values of which are difficult to ascertain. Over half of the total assets figure, about $82 billion, was goodwill, an intangible representing the excess of purchase prices paid to acquire companies in the past over the fair market value of the assets actually brought on board. Other intangibles accounted for approximately $45 billion more of the balance sheet's asserted value. If cautious investors refused to value these assets in their thinking, they were left with only about $34 billion in "hard" assets like cash, receivables, equipment, and property. Under those assumptions, the $28 billion in debt represents 82% of assets, a very big number in most industries, implying that AOL Time Warner is a highly leveraged and therefore very risky company.

In early 2003, AOL Time Warner took most of the goodwill off its balance sheet, reporting a $99 billion loss on the transaction. The move was mandated by new accounting rules and made the company's debt load more obvious.

The company's CEO, Richard Parsons, vowed to pay down debt and turn the business around. In a conference with Wall Street analysts he characterized 2003 as a "reset" year from which AOL Time Warner would re-emerge with new "momentum." Observers thought that was doable because the firm's underlying businesses were profitable.

Progress toward that goal has been significant but slow. By 2005 the company had succeeded in reducing its long-term debt obligations by more than 20%. In 2006, that figure had risen by nearly 75% (to just under $35 billion) as the firm expanded its cable business through the acquisition of Adelphia Communications Corporation and an aggressive share repurchase plan.

Sources: WSJ.com, "AOL Posts a $98.7 Billion Loss on New Goodwill Write-Down," January 30, 2003; Time Warner Inc. *2006 Annual Report.*

---

it does on ROE. However, when shares are purchased for retirement at a price different from their book value, the book value of the remaining shares changes. Therefore the transaction can have different effects on ROE and EPS. Our results generally hold for ROE, but may not for EPS.

This phenomenon adds to the general imprecision of the ideas with which we've been working. The important point is the general direction in which leverage drives share price, not the exact amount of the effect.

The Degree of Financial Leverage (DFL)—A Measurement

Financial leverage magnifies changes in EBIT into larger changes in ROE and EPS. It is of interest to know just how large that magnification is at any particular level of leverage.

For example, suppose that a firm anticipates a 20% drop in EBIT. If the company has no debt, ROE and EPS will also drop by 20%. But what drop should be expected if the firm's capital is 30% or 40% debt? Clearly the question is important if management is interested in the effect changes in ROE and EPS may have on investors.

It's possible to answer the question by using a concept called the *degree of financial leverage*, abbreviated DFL. The DFL lets us quantify the effectiveness of leverage by relating *relative* changes in EPS and EBIT at any level of leverage.[5]

The idea is expressed as follows.

(16.2)
$$DFL = \frac{\%\Delta EPS}{\%\Delta EBIT}$$

where %ΔEPS and %ΔEBIT mean the relative changes in EPS and EBIT, respectively.

The best way to visualize the meaning of the DFL is to rewrite Equation 16.2 by multiplying through by %ΔEBIT.

(16.2a)
$$\%\Delta EPS = DFL \times \%\Delta EBIT$$

This expression says that relative changes in EBIT are multiplied by the DFL to arrive at relative changes in EPS. That is, DFL tells you the percentage change in EPS resulting from a 1% change in EBIT. For example, if a firm's DFL is 1.5 and EBIT changes by 20%, EPS will change by (1.5 × 20% =) 30%.

If financial statements are available, the DFL can be calculated by assuming a small change in EBIT, working through to the resulting change in EPS, and substituting the relative changes into Equation 16.2. However, that approach is rather tedious. An easier method is available by using the following formula.

(16.3)
$$DFL = \frac{EBIT}{EBIT - I} \text{ or } \frac{EBIT}{EBT}$$

where *I* is interest.[6]

The derivation of Equation 16.3 is a little involved, so we'll leave it to the more mathematically inclined and just accept the result.

> The *DFL* relates relative *changes in EBIT* to relative *changes in EPS.*

Example 16.2

Selected income statement and capital information for the Mallaig Manufacturing Company follows ($000).

		Capital	
Revenue	$5,580	Debt	$1,000
Cost/expense	4,200	Equity	7,000
EBIT	$1,380	Total	$8,000

Currently, 700,000 common shares are outstanding. The firm pays 15% interest on its debt and anticipates that it can borrow as much as it reasonably needs at that rate. The income tax rate is 40%.

Mallaig is interested in boosting its share price. To do that, management is considering restructuring capital to 50% debt in the hope that the increased EPS will have a positive effect on price.

---

5 A relative change is a percentage change. For example, a 5% change in the number 20 is a change of 1 unit, because 1 is 5% of 20. An increase to 21 is a positive 5% change. A decrease to 19 is a negative 5% change. In general, a relative change in a number is the change divided by the number itself, expressed as a percentage. If we represent the change in the number N by ΔN, the relative change in N is expressed as

$$\%\Delta N = \frac{\Delta N}{N} \times 100$$

If N is 20 and ΔN is 1, we have

$$\%\Delta N = \frac{1}{20} \times 100 = 5\%$$

6 From a common shareholders' viewpoint, preferred shares are just as bad as debt. That is, any preferred dividend must be paid before the common shareholders get anything. If the company must pay preferred dividends, there will be an impact on ROE and EPS as well. That means *I* should be the *total* of interest and preferred dividends.

In reality, for most companies the preferred dividend is insignificant as compared to their interest bill and as a result many analysts consider financial leverage simply as the effect that fixed interest charges have on shareholder returns. Our discussion makes this simplifying assumption.

However, the economic outlook is shaky, and the company's CFO thinks there's a good chance that deterioration in business conditions will reduce EBIT next year. At the moment Mallaig's shares sell for their book value of $10 per share.

Estimate the effect of the proposed restructuring on EPS. Then use the degree of financial leverage to assess the increase in risk that will come along with it.

■ **Solution:** First, we'll calculate the proposed capital structure and display it alongside the current structure. Because equity can be traded at its book value, the restructuring is a straightforward exchange of equity for debt with a proportionate reduction in the number of shares outstanding.

	Current	Proposed
Capital		
Debt	$ 1,000	$ 4,000
Equity	7,000	4,000
Total	$ 8,000	$ 8,000
Shares outstanding	700,000	400,000

Next, calculate projected NI and EPS at the current level of business for both capital structures.

	Current	Proposed
EBIT	$ 1,380	$ 1,380
Interest (15% of debt)	150	600
EBT	$ 1,230	$ 780
Tax (@ 40%)	492	312
NI	$ 738	$ 468
EPS	$ 1,054	$ 1,170

It's easy to see that if business conditions remain unchanged, the proposed structure will yield a higher EPS.

Next, use Equation 16.3 to calculate the DFL under each structure.

$$DFL_{cur} = \frac{EBIT}{EBIT - I} = \frac{\$1,380}{\$1,380 - \$150} = 1.12$$

$$DFL_{prop} = \frac{EBIT}{EBIT - I} = \frac{\$1,380}{\$1,380 - \$600} = 1.77$$

Now we can see why the CFO is concerned. EPS will be much more volatile under the proposed structure than it is currently. To illustrate, suppose business deteriorates and EBIT declines by 30%; that's not unusual. We can use Equation 16.2a to see what will happen under both the current and proposed structures.

Under the current structure, EPS will decline by a percentage calculated as follows.

$$\%\Delta EPS_{cur} = DFL_{cur} \times \%\Delta EBIT$$
$$= 1.12 \times 30\%$$
$$= 33.6\%$$

But under the proposed structure, the percentage decline will be

$$\%\Delta EPS_{prop} = DFL_{prop} \times \%\Delta EBIT$$
$$= 1.77 \times 30\%$$
$$= 53.1\%$$

Now apply these percentage declines to the projected EPS figures to see what they'll become under both structures if the business deterioration does occur.

Current: $1.054(1 − 0.336) = $0.70
Proposed: $1.170(1 − 0.531) = $0.55

The implication is that if the proposed capital structure is adopted *and* a substantial downturn occurs, the resulting EPS will be lower than the EPS under the old structure. Clearly, adopting the proposal adds substantial risk.

The impact of the proposed restructuring on share prices is arguable. We can't say with certainty whether or not the positive effect of the EPS increase will overcome the negative effect of increased risk. It all depends on the current perceptions of investors.

The uncertainty can be expressed in terms of the graph in Figure 16.2. The question revolves around just where the company currently is on the graph and whether the restructuring will carry it past the peak. We can't say for sure. However, using the DFL to analyze the risk increase gives management a much better feel for the trade-offs involved than it would get if only the EPS impact were considered.

It's unfortunate that the DFL concept isn't used a great deal in practice. In the Mallaig problem, many analysts would have stopped after calculating the two EPS values under good conditions. They'd have understood that risk was increased, but wouldn't have tried to quantify the increase for the benefit of the decision maker. We're certain our current readers will rectify that situation in a few years.

EBIT–EPS ANALYSIS

We've learned that financial leverage can enhance results at normal levels of operating profit, but makes those results more volatile at the same time. If that knowledge is to do any good, managers need to be able to use it to make intelligent choices about the amount of leverage their companies should employ given a set of expectations about future business.

This means that managers need a way of quantifying and analyzing the trade-off between results and risk implied by moving from one level of leverage to another. EBIT–EPS analysis provides a graphic portrayal of the trade-off that makes the choice relatively straightforward.

To illustrate, let's go back to the Alberta Balloon Corporation and assume that management expects the relatively good year reflected in Table 16.1 (page 568). To keep the illustration simple, we'll assume that the choice is between the leverage scenarios of columns 1 and 2 only, although any other combination of debt and equity could be analyzed.

The EBIT–EPS technique involves graphing EPS as a function of EBIT for each leverage level, as shown in Figure 16.3. We'll begin with the all-equity case in column 1 of Table 16.1. The table gives us an EPS of $1.20 at an EBIT of $200,000. That's a point on the EBIT–EPS

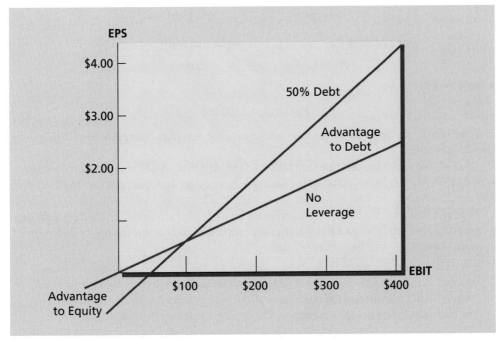

FIGURE 16.3
EBIT–EPS
Analysis for
Alberta Balloon
Corporation from
Table 16.1,
Columns 1 and 2

graph for zero leverage. EPS is a linear function of EBIT, so we need only one other point to draw the graph. We'll choose EBIT of $400,000 and calculate EPS.

EBIT	$ 400,000
Interest (10%)	—
EBT	$ 400,000
Tax (40%)	160,000
NI	$ 240,000
Number of shares	100,000
EPS	$ 2.40

These points determine the line labelled "No Leverage" in Figure 16.3.

For the 50% debt scenario, column 2 of Table 16.1 shows an EPS of $1.80 at an EBIT of $200,000. A calculation like the one we've just done (using $50,000 in interest and 500,000 shares) gives a second point at which EPS is $4.20 when EBIT is $400,000. These points determine the line labelled "50% Debt" in the diagram.

The two lines represent EPS at various levels of operating profit under their respective assumptions about leverage. Notice that they cross one another, making different choices of leverage superior on either side of the intersection. We prefer the higher EPS of the upper line anywhere other than at the intersection, where we're indifferent between the two choices.

It's important to be able to find the indifference point. In general, the formula of an EPS−EBIT line is the financial computation of EPS from EBIT stated in algebraic form.

$$\text{EPS} = \frac{(\text{EBIT} - I)(1 - T)}{\text{Number of shares}}$$

where

$$I = \text{interest}$$
$$T = \text{tax rate}$$

Compare the equation to the steps in the partial income statement above. In the numerator, $(\text{EBIT} - I)$ is earnings before tax (EBT), which is adjusted to earnings after tax by multiplying by $(1 - T)$. That, divided by the number of shares outstanding, is EPS.

We can find the indifference point by equating the EPS for the no-leverage line with that for the 50% leverage line.

No Leverage	**50% Debt**
$\dfrac{(\text{EBIT} - \$0)(1 - 0.4)}{100,000}$	$= \dfrac{(\text{EBIT} - \$50,000)(1 - 0.4)}{50,000}$

Solving for EBIT yields

$$\text{EBIT}_{\text{indif}} = \$100,000$$

In other words, the lines cross, and our preference for leverage changes when EBIT passes through $100,000.

Notice how useful the diagram is. It tells management that if EBIT is expected to stay above $100,000, the firm is better off with the higher leverage option. It also gives an indication of how much better off the firm will be for any level of EBIT.

The risk that comes with leverage is reflected by what happens to EPS in the 50% debt case if operating profits fall below $100,000. In that range, ABC will be on the upper line without leverage, but on the lower line with 50% debt.

From the CFO

The analysis doesn't make the leverage decision for ABC's management. But, combined with an idea of the likely variability of EBIT, it gives them all they need to make an informed choice. If EBIT is unlikely to fall much below $100,000, higher leverage is appropriate. On the other hand, if big swings are common, little or no leverage may be the wiser decision.

OPERATING LEVERAGE

We mentioned operating leverage briefly at the beginning of the chapter. The concept deals with the fixed costs rather than capital, but the functions and effects are similar to those of financial leverage. Operating leverage also has the ability to combine with financial leverage to produce alarmingly volatile results. For this reason, we need to be familiar with the workings of operating leverage even though it's not exactly a capital structure issue. We'll begin our study with some background.

Terminology and Definitions

The term "operations" refers to a firm's business activities exclusive of debt financing. In terms of the income statement, those activities involve the items from sales down to operating income (EBIT).

Risk in Operations—Business Risk

A firm's EBIT varies over time for a variety of reasons including fluctuating sales, changes in cost conditions, and the effectiveness of management. Recall that we've already defined variation in EBIT as *business risk* (page 566).

Variation in EBIT is defined as *business risk.*

It's important to realize that every business has some variation in its operating results, but some have more than others. The amount depends to a great extent on the nature of the business. Some industries have stable conditions of demand and cost, while in others things go up and down like roller coasters. Generally, most of the variation in EBIT comes about as a result of changes in the level of sales.

Fixed and Variable Costs and Cost Structure

A business's costs can generally be separated into two categories, *fixed* and *variable.* A fixed cost doesn't change when the level of sales changes, but a variable cost does.

Cost structure is the mix of *fixed and variable* costs in a firm's operations.

Fixed costs (or overhead) are things like rent, amortization, utilities, and management salaries. Variable costs include direct labour, direct materials, and other items that go up and down with volume, like sales commissions. Costs that don't fit neatly into either category can usually be separated into fixed and variable components for purposes of analysis. Segregating costs and expenses into fixed and variable categories is not always straightforward; however, even a rough estimate can provide some valuable insight to a manager.

A firm's *cost structure* is the mix of fixed and variable costs used in its operating processes. The idea is analogous to the concept of capital structure describing the mix of debt and equity within capital.

Operating Leverage Defined

Given the similar concepts of cost structure and capital structure, operating leverage is defined with respect to cost just as financial leverage is defined with respect to capital. Operating leverage refers to the amount of fixed cost in the cost structure. Thus, if a firm's costs are largely fixed, it has a great deal of operating leverage.

Operating leverage increases as the proportion of *fixed cost* increases.

A good way to get a feel for cost structure and operating leverage is to imagine a factory that can be run in one of two ways: either with a lot of people and a few machines, or with a lot of machines and a few people. We tend to describe the first organization as labour intensive or utilizing manual processes and the second as capital intensive or automated.

People represent variable cost because they can be let go when sales and production decline. Machines, on the other hand, represent fixed cost because they can't be laid off during a downturn. Hence, the automated plant has more operating leverage than the labour-intensive plant.

Breakeven analysis shows the mix of *fixed and variable* cost and the volume required for *zero profit/loss* or *EBIT = 0.*

Breakeven Analysis

Breakeven analysis is widely used to determine the level of activity a firm must achieve to stay in business in the long run. The technique explicitly lays out the effect of sales volume on a firm's use of fixed and variable costs. In doing that it provides an excellent insight into the nature and effect of operating leverage. We'll develop the breakeven model and then use it to illustrate operating leverage.

Overview of Breakeven

The term "breakeven" means zero profit or loss, generally measured at EBIT (operating income). At breakeven, revenue exactly equals costs and expenses, and the firm just survives. Breakeven analysis is a way of looking at operations to determine the volume, in either units or dollars, a company must sell to achieve this zero-profit, zero-loss situation.

In what follows we'll use the term "cost" broadly to include items generally referred to as expense. Both costs and expenses can be fixed or variable.

Breakeven Diagrams

Fixed and variable costs are represented graphically in the first two panels of Figure 16.4. Cost is plotted along the vertical axis and unit sales (Q for quantity) along the horizontal axis. Fixed cost is constant as sales increase, while variable cost increases proportionately with sales.

The two diagrams are generally combined by plotting variable cost on top of fixed cost. The result is shown in the third panel where the diagonal line represents total cost, the sum of fixed and variable costs.

Breakeven is at the intersection of revenue and total cost.

The *breakeven diagram* is depicted in Figure 16.5. It's formed by overlaying a line representing revenue on the total cost diagram. At any level of sales, revenue is just PQ, price multiplied by quantity. A revenue line is shown in Figure 16.5 starting from the origin and extending upward to the right.

Breakeven is the level of sales at which revenue equals cost. On the diagram it's the point where the total cost line and the revenue line intersect. The breakeven volume is directly below that point on the horizontal axis, indicated by $Q_{B/E}$ on the diagram.

At any sales volume, the firm's profit or loss is the difference between revenue and total cost. This can be measured by the difference in the heights of those lines above the axis. The shaded area between the two lines to the right of their intersection represents profitable operations and the shaded area to the left represents losses.

For more on breakeven analysis go to http://www.dinkytown.net/java/BreakEven.html.

The Contribution Margin

Every sale makes a contribution of the difference between price and variable cost.

Every time a unit is sold, one unit's worth of variable cost is incurred. The amount by which price exceeds that unit variable cost is called the contribution made by the sale. Expressed as an equation,

(16.4)
$$C_t = P - V$$

where

C_t is the contribution,
P is price, and
V is variable cost per unit.

The term implies a contribution to profit and fixed cost. Notice that the unit contribution is the same anywhere on the breakeven diagram, that is, at any level of sales.

FIGURE 16.4
Fixed, Variable, and Total Cost

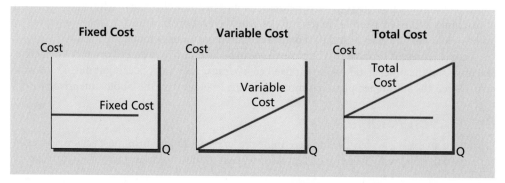

FIGURE 16.5
The Breakeven
Diagram

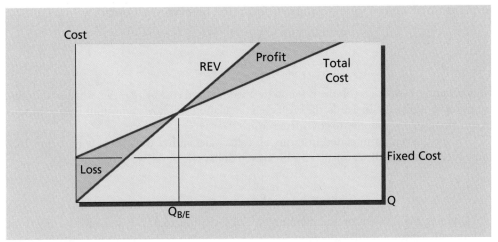

Contribution can be expressed as a percentage of revenue by dividing by the price, P. It's then called the **contribution margin**, which we'll write as C_M. Dividing Equation 16.4 by P, we have

(**16.5**)
$$C_M = \frac{P - V}{P}$$

Contribution is the
difference between
price and variable cost
per unit that is "con-
tributed" toward
profit and fixed costs.
The **contribution
margin** is the contri-
bution expressed as
a percent of price.

Example 16.3

Suppose a company can make a unit of product for $7 in variable labour and materials, and sell it for $10. What are the contribution and contribution margin?

■ **Solution:** The contribution comes directly from Equation 16.4.

$$C_t = P - V$$
$$= \$10 - \$7$$
$$= \$3$$

The contribution margin comes from Equation 16.5.

$$C_M = \frac{P - V}{P} = \frac{\$3}{\$10} = 0.3 = 30\%$$

Calculating the Breakeven Sales Level

EBIT is revenue minus cost, which can be expressed in terms of price and quantity as cost, which can be expressed in terms of price and quantity as

(**16.6**)
$$EBIT = PQ - VQ - F_C$$

where
$$P = \text{Price per unit}$$
$$V = \text{Variable cost per unit}$$
$$Q = \text{Quantity sold}$$
$$F_C = \text{Total fixed cost}$$

Notice in this equation that P and V are multiplied by Q to represent revenue (PQ) and total variable cost (VQ), but fixed cost is represented by a single variable, F_C. EBIT is revenue minus both cost components, variable and fixed.

Breakeven occurs where revenue (PQ) equals total cost (VQ + F_C); hence EBIT = 0. To find that point, rewrite Equation 16.6 with EBIT = 0.

$$0 = PQ - VQ - F_C$$

Then factor out Q, rearrange terms, and solve for the breakeven value of Q, which we've called $Q_{B/E}$.

$$Q(P - V) - F_C = 0$$

(16.7)
$$Q_{B/E} = \frac{F_C}{P - V}$$

Breakeven volume is fixed cost divided by contribution.

Notice that the breakeven volume is found by dividing fixed cost by $(P - V)$, which is the contribution per unit sold. In words, the breakeven calculation tells how many units have to be sold to contribute enough money to cover fixed costs.

The breakeven point stated in terms of dollar sales rather than units is Equation 16.7 multiplied by price, P. If we call $S_{B/E}$ the breakeven dollar sales level, we have

(16.8)
$$S_{B/E} = \frac{P(F_C)}{P - V}$$

Dividing the numerator and denominator of Equation 16.8 by P and substituting from Equation 16.5 gives a useful expression.

(16.9)
$$S_{B/E} = \frac{F_C}{\frac{(P - V)}{P}} = \frac{F_C}{C_M}$$

Equation 16.9 says that the breakeven sales level is just fixed cost, F_C, divided by the *contribution margin*, C_M (stated in decimal form).

Example 16.4

What is the breakeven sales level in units and dollars for the company in Example 16.3 if the firm has fixed costs of $1,800 per month?

■ **Solution:** For the breakeven point in units, write Equation 16.7 and substitute.

$$Q_{B/E} = \frac{F_C}{P - V} = \frac{\$1,800}{\$3} = 600 \text{ units}$$

As each unit sells for $10, the breakeven sales level in dollar terms, from Equation 16.8, is just

$$\$10 \times 600 = \$6,000$$

Alternatively, the last result is available from Equation 16.9 by dividing fixed cost by the contribution margin expressed in decimal form.

$$S_{B/E} = \frac{F_C}{\frac{(P - V)}{P}} = \frac{F_C}{C_M} = \frac{\$1,800}{0.3} = \$6,000$$

This calculation essentially tells us how many sales dollars, each of which contributes 30 cents to fixed costs and profit, it takes to cover $1,800 in fixed costs.

Notice that breakeven volumes in either units or dollars are stated per period of time. In Example 16.4 the period is a month because fixed costs were given on a monthly basis.

The Effect of Operating Leverage

Breakeven analysis gives us an excellent approach to understanding exactly how operating leverage works. We'll begin by examining the breakeven diagrams for two firms that use different amounts of operating leverage. This is equivalent to saying that they differ with respect to their cost structures, with one having relatively more fixed cost than the other. The diagrams are shown in Figure 16.6.

For convenience we'll assume that both firms have the same breakeven volume shown at sales level A in the diagrams. Recall that the diagrams reflect profit or loss in terms of EBIT in

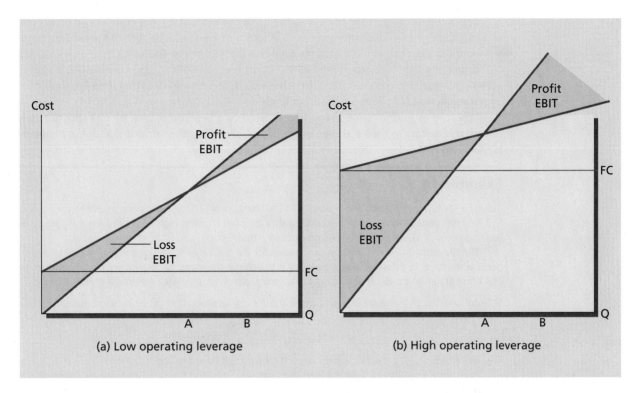

(a) Low operating leverage   (b) High operating leverage

the shaded areas on either side of the breakeven points. As output expands, profit grows as we move further to the right of breakeven. On the other hand, if volume falls below the breakeven level, losses grow as we move further to the left.

The Risk Effect

Notice the relative speed with which profit or loss grows as we move away from volume level A in the two diagrams. The high operating leverage firm on the right expands profits much faster than the low leverage firm on the left. However, it also expands losses much faster if output falls below the breakeven at A.

This is the essence of operating leverage. Any movement away from point A produces some change in EBIT in the low leverage company. The same movement away from A will produce a *larger* change in EBIT in the higher leverage firm. In other words, the increased leverage *magnifies* the change in EBIT that results from a given change in sales volume.

Thus, operating leverage can be said to increase the variation in EBIT as a result of variations in sales. Because variation in EBIT is defined as business risk, it follows that *increased operating leverage increases business risk.*

The effect can be appreciated from the geometry of the diagrams. The high leverage firm has a smaller variable cost, which makes its total cost line flatter than that of the low leverage firm. That means it diverges from the revenue line faster.

Stated another way, the high leverage firm gets a larger contribution from each sale, so it accumulates profits or losses faster as it moves away from the breakeven. Of course, this is true for movement between any two sales levels along the horizontal axis. The trade-off is that the high leverage firm has more fixed cost to cover before it makes a profit than the low leverage firm.

The Effect on Expected EBIT

More operating leverage implies higher operating profit at any output above the breakeven. To see this, consider point B in both diagrams of Figure 16.6. The geometry of the diagrams shows that at the same distance above the breakeven output, the higher fixed cost firm will always make more EBIT.

FIGURE 16.6
Breakeven Diagrams at High and Low Operating Leverage

As volume moves away from breakeven, profit or loss *increases faster* with more *operating leverage.*

Variation in EBIT (business risk) is *larger* with *more operating leverage.*

In general, the higher the fixed cost, the higher profit is at a given point above breakeven. Imagine the F_C line sliding upward in the diagram of Figure 16.6b with the breakeven point staying the same. That would flatten the total cost line and widen the profit triangle.

Hence, if a firm is relatively sure of its output level, a public utility, for example, it's better off to trade variable costs for fixed. In other words, increasing operating leverage multiplies operating income (EBIT) at likely output levels.

What we've said assumes that a higher fixed cost is accompanied by a proportionately lower variable cost so the breakeven point stays more or less the same. If that doesn't happen, higher fixed cost doesn't necessarily mean anything.

Example 16.5

Suppose the low leverage firm in Figure 16.6a has fixed costs of $1,000 per period, sells its product for $10, and has variable costs of $8 per unit. Further suppose that the high leverage firm in Figure 16.6b has fixed cost of $1,500 and also sells product for $10 a unit.

The diagram shows the breakeven volumes for the two firms to be the same. What variable cost per unit must the high leverage firm have if it is to achieve the same breakeven point as the low leverage firm? State the trade-off at the breakeven point. Which structure is preferred if there's a choice?

■ **Solution:** Compute the breakeven volume for the low leverage firm (a) by writing Equation 16.7.

$$Q_{B/E-a} = \frac{F_C}{P - V} = \frac{\$1,000}{\$10 - \$8} = 500 \text{ units}$$

This will also be $Q_{B/E-a}$, the breakeven volume for the high leverage firm.

Now write Equation 16.7 for the high leverage firm, showing the variable cost per unit as an unknown, V_b. Then substitute the given price and fixed cost and the calculated breakeven volume.

$$Q_{B/E-b} = \frac{F_C}{P - V_b}$$

$$500 \text{ units} = \frac{\$1,500}{\$10 - V_b}$$

Solving for V_b yields

$$V_b = \$7$$

and

$$C_t = \$10 - \$7 = \$3$$

Summarizing, we have the following.

	Low Leverage	High Leverage
Contribution	$ 2	$ 3
Fixed cost	$ 1,000	$ 1,500

Thus, at breakeven, a $1 differential in contributions makes up for a $500 difference in fixed cost.

For an expected level of sales somewhat above breakeven, the preferable structure depends on volatility. If expectations are for relatively stable business, the high fixed cost model gives better operating results. However, if sales are likely to vary, especially below the breakeven point, the low fixed cost structure might be better in the long run.

The Degree of Operating Leverage (DOL)— A Measurement

The DOL relates relative changes in volume (Q) to relative changes in EBIT.

Operating leverage amplifies changes in sales volume into larger changes in EBIT. It can be quantified and measured with an idea called the *degree of operating leverage*, abbreviated DOL. The concept is similar to the DFL we discussed earlier.

The DOL is the ratio of the relative change in EBIT to a relative change in sales. We can write this as

$$(16.10) \qquad\qquad DOL = \frac{\%\Delta EBIT}{\%\Delta Q}$$

We'll forego the derivation here, but it can be shown that the DOL can be expressed as follows.

$$(16.11) \qquad\qquad DOL = \frac{Q(P - V)}{Q(P - V) - F_C} \ \text{ or } \ \frac{CM}{EBIT}$$

where the variables have the meanings we've been using.

Example 16.6

The Cowichan Corp. sells its products at an average price of $10. Variable costs are $7 per unit and fixed costs are $600 per month. Evaluate the degree of operating leverage when sales are 5% and then 50% above the breakeven level.

■ **Solution:** First, compute the breakeven volume using Equation 16.7.

$$Q_{B/E} = \frac{F_C}{P - V} = \frac{\$600}{\$10 - \$7} = 200 \text{ units}$$

Breakeven plus 5% and 50% implies sales of 210 and 300 units, respectively. Use Equation 16.11 to calculate the DOL at 210 units per month and at 300 units. At 210 units we have

$$\begin{aligned} DOL_{Q=210} &= \frac{Q(P - V)}{Q(P - V) - F_C} \\[2mm] &= \frac{210(\$10 - \$7)}{210(\$10 - \$7) - \$600} \\[2mm] &= 21 \end{aligned}$$

At 300 units, we have

$$\begin{aligned} DOL_{Q=300} &= \frac{300(\$10 - \$7)}{300(\$10 - \$7) - \$600} \\[2mm] &= 3 \end{aligned}$$

As with DFL, the DOL indicates a relative change. We multiply the DOL by the percentage change in sales to arrive at the relative change in EBIT. For this example, if sales increased by 5%, we would expect EBIT to change by (5% × 3 =) 15%. Notice that the DOL *decreases* as the output level increases above breakeven.

Comparing Operating and Financial Leverage

Operating leverage connects sales with EBIT in much the same way that financial leverage connects EBIT with ROE and EPS.

Recall that financial leverage can improve performance in ROE and EPS, and that it amplifies changes in EBIT into larger relative changes in those ratios. Similarly, operating leverage can enhance EBIT at a given sales level, and expand variations in sales into larger relative variations in EBIT. The idea is illustrated in Figure 16.7.

Another similarity has to do with the nature of operating and financial costs. Financial leverage involves substituting debt for equity in the firm's capital structure, while operating leverage involves substituting fixed cost for variable cost in its cost structure.

Notice, however, that debt is a fixed cost method of financing in that it pays a fixed amount of interest to investors regardless of how well the company does. Equity, on the other hand, is a variable cost form of financing, because the dividends paid to shareholders can be varied or eliminated if the firm isn't doing well. Hence, both forms of leverage involve substituting fixed cash outflows for variable cash outflows.

Financial and operating leverage are similar in that both can enhance results while increasing variation.

FIGURE 16.7
The Similar
Functions of
Operating and
Financial Leverage

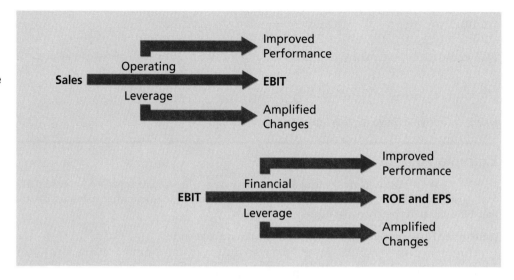

Finally, there's a similarity but not an exact match between the two kinds of leverage with respect to the two kinds of risk we've defined. Financial risk is the additional variation in ROE and EPS caused by financial leverage, while business risk is variation in EBIT that's enhanced by operating leverage. Both kinds of leverage make their respective risks larger as the levels of leverage increase. However, financial leverage is the sole cause of financial risk, while some business risk would exist even if there were no operating leverage. These last ideas are summarized in Figure 16.8.

Two final points of comparison are worth noting. First, virtually all productive processes involve the use of some equipment that generates fixed cost. Therefore, all firms have some operating leverage. On the other hand, many firms use no debt and therefore have no financial leverage.

Second, financial leverage is more controllable than operating leverage. For example, technology dictates the minimum and maximum amounts of machinery needed to make most products, so management's choice of an operating leverage level may be relatively limited. On the other hand, management can generally choose the amount of debt a firm uses within very broad limits.

The Compounding Effect of Operating and Financial Leverage

The effects of *financial and operating* leverage *compound* one another.

An important result of the existence of two kinds of leverage is that they compound one another. Changes in sales are amplified by operating leverage into larger relative changes in EBIT, which in turn are amplified into still larger relative changes in ROE and EPS by financial

FIGURE 16.8
Risk and Cost
Relationships
between Operating
and Financial
Leverage

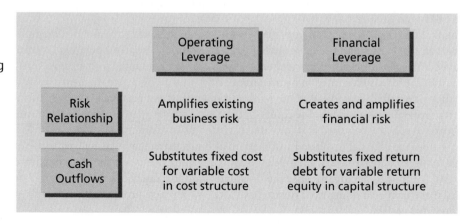

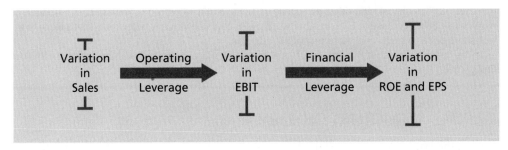

FIGURE 16.9
The Compounding
Effect of Operating
and Financial
Leverage

leverage. The net effect can be quite large because the combined effect of the two kinds of leverage is multiplicative rather than additive.

This means that fairly modest changes in the level of sales can lead to dramatic swings in ROE and EPS in companies that use both operating and financial leverage. The idea is illustrated in Figure 16.9.

The compound effect of operating and financial leverage can be measured by a concept called the *degree of total leverage*, abbreviated DTL. The DTL is simply the product of DOL and DFL.

> The *DTL* reflects the combined effect of both kinds of leverage.

$$(16.12) \qquad \text{DTL} = \text{DOL} \times \text{DFL}$$

If you did not calculate DOL and DFL using the same expected sales levels, simply multiply Equations 16.11 and 16.3 and simplify to get:

$$\text{DTL} = \frac{\text{CM}}{\text{EBIT}} \times \frac{\text{EBIT}}{\text{EBIT} - I}$$

Simplifying further we get

$$(16.13) \qquad \text{DTL} = \frac{\text{CM}}{\text{EBIT} - I} \text{ or } \frac{\text{CM}}{\text{EBT}}$$

Example 16.7

The Carragana Company is considering replacing a manual production machine. The money to buy the machine will be borrowed. The replacement of people with a machine will alter the firm's cost structure in favour of fixed cost, while the loan will move the capital structure in the direction of more debt. The firm's leverage positions at expected output levels with and without the project are summarized as follows.

	DOL	DFL
Current	2.0	1.5
Proposed	3.5	2.5

The economic outlook is uncertain and some managers fear a decline in sales of as much as 10% in the coming year. Evaluate the effect of the proposed project on risk in financial performance.

■ **Solution:** Currently, the degree of total leverage is

$$\text{DTL} = \text{DOL} \times \text{DFL}$$
$$= 2(1.5)$$
$$= 3$$

This means that a 10% decline in sales could result in a 30% decline in EPS. Stated another way, the relative volatility of EPS is three times that of sales.

Under the proposed conditions, the DTL would be much larger.

$$\text{DTL} = \text{DOL} \times \text{DFL}$$
$$= 3.5(2.5)$$
$$= 8.75$$

Here, EPS is almost nine times as volatile as sales, and a 10% drop in volume could produce as much as an 88% decrease in EPS. In other words, EPS could be virtually wiped out. That's likely to affect share prices a great deal more than a 30% decline.

The conclusion is that the proposal has a great deal more inherent risk than one might think at first glance.[7]

CAPITAL STRUCTURE THEORY

During the last 50 years, financial scholars have devoted a great deal of thinking to capital structure. They've essentially been addressing the same question we posed at the beginning of this chapter: Does capital structure affect share price and the market value of the firm, and if so, is there an optimal structure that maximizes either or both? The scholarly approach is more mathematical than the work we've been doing, but the results are essentially the same. Structure does affect price and value, and there is an optimum, but there's no way to find it with any precision.

Capital structure theory is one of the more important elements of modern financial thought, and has yielded some valuable insights into real-world problems. Hence, it's important that professionals be familiar with the theoretical approach and understand the nature of the results. Fortunately, we can do that without mastering a great deal of mathematics.

Background—The Value of the Firm

The theory approaches capital structure by focusing on the market value of the firm and its cost of capital. The assumption is that if market value can be increased by manipulating capital structure, an increase in share price must follow.

We'll need to become familiar with the terminology and principles used before getting into the theory itself.

Notation

First, let's define the notation (symbols) we'll be using. The market value of the firm is the total market value of all of its debt and equity securities represented as follows.

$$V_d = \text{market value of the firm's debt}$$
$$V_e = \text{market value of the firm's shares (equity)}$$
$$V_f = \text{market value of the firm in total}$$

(16.14)
$$V_f = V_d + V_e$$

> Theory begins by assuming a world *without taxes or transaction costs*, so investors' returns are exactly component capital costs.

Investors' returns on the firm's securities will be

k_d = return on an investment in debt (bonds) and

k_e = return on an investment in equity (shares)

In our study of the cost of capital (Chapter 15), we said that the firm's costs of debt and equity were the investors' returns adjusted for flotation costs and taxes. Theory operates in an abstract world. It assumes away flotation costs and begins by assuming there are no taxes.

---

7 The degree of leverage concepts are both a little tricky. The volatility implied by both ratios increases with the addition of debt or fixed cost, but it's even more sensitive to the proximity of breakeven points. Examine equation 16.3 for the DFL and equation 16.11 for the DOL. Notice that both denominators are zero at breakeven points. In the case of the DOL, the denominator is EBIT, which is zero at the breakeven we've been talking about in this section. For the DFL, the denominator is EBT, which is zero when interest equals operating income.

In the neighbourhood of those points, the denominators are very small so the fractions are very large. Hence, we get large relative changes in EPS or EBIT, but those changes may not be very large in absolute terms because we're operating EPS or EBIT levels near zero.

Leverage and Business Strategy

Business strategy involves understanding the factors that define industrial competition. An important issue in strategy is predicting how companies will react to troubled times or competitive challenges. Leverage plays a big part in those predictions.

The more heavily a firm is leveraged, either financially or operationally, the more quickly it loses money when volume decreases. The effect is compounded when both forms of leverage are present. This means that leveraged companies react aggressively when something threatens their volume. They cut prices, increase advertising, and offer special promotions at the drop of a hat to keep volume up. That tends to make the industries in which they operate chaotic and less attractive for everyone. Japanese firms provide a great example of the phenomenon. They're known for their competitiveness, some of which can be traced to exceptional leverage.

Although leverage ratios have been declining, Japanese companies tend to carry more debt than Canadian and American firms. In other words, they're highly leveraged financially. Firms are also focused on low unit cost, which they achieve with large automated plants. That implies high fixed cost and commensurately high operating leverage.

Therefore, the costs of debt and equity are exactly k_d and k_e, respectively. The cost of capital is then a weighted average of these, which we'll write as

$$k_a = \text{Average cost of capital}$$

Value Is Based on Cash Flow, Which Comes from Income

In Chapters 9 and 10, we saw that the value of any security is the present value of the cash flows that come from owning it, and all cash flows paid to investors come from earnings. Hence, earnings ultimately determine value.

We'll focus on operating income (EBIT), which is by definition the earnings stream available to either debt or equity investors. To avoid some notational confusion later, we'll refer to operating income as OI rather than EBIT in this section.

Assume OI is completely divided between interest and dividend payments, so we can write

(16.15) $$OI = I + D$$

where

$$I = \text{Total annual interest payment to bondholders}$$
$$D = \text{Total annual dividend payment to shareholders}$$

Debt is assumed to be perpetual.[8] Whenever principal is paid off, a new amount of equal size is immediately borrowed; hence, I is constant year after year. Because no income is retained, the company doesn't grow, and OI remains constant as well. Then Equation 16.15 implies that dividend payments are also constant. In other words, each stream of annual payments, I and D, is a perpetuity.

The values of the firm's debt and equity are then the present values of these perpetuities, and we can write

Dividend and interest payments are both assumed to be perpetuities, and the firm's market value is the sum of their present values.

(16.16) $$V_d = \frac{I}{k_d}$$

and

(16.17) $$V_e = \frac{D}{k_e}$$

where k_d and k_e are the costs of debt and equity. Using Equation 16.14, we can also write

(16.18) $$V_f = \frac{I}{k_d} + \frac{D}{k_e}$$

---

8 We discussed perpetuities briefly in Chapter 8. Preferred shares also have features comparable to perpetual debt.

The nature of the weighted average return is such that the following expression is essentially equivalent to Equation 16.16.

$$(16.19) \qquad\qquad V_f = \frac{OI}{k_a}$$

In words, these equations say that the value of the firm is determined by the costs of its debt and equity, and that we can look at them together through the average cost of capital, k_a. Keep in mind that lower rates mean higher values.

Returns drive value in an inverse relationship.

This is an important way of looking at things. It means that we can think of returns as driving value. For example, if something causes investors to require a higher return on an investment in a company's shares, Equation 16.17 says that this will drive the value of the firm's equity down. If the return on debt remains the same, the cost of capital, k_a, will also rise and overall value will drop.

Graphic Portrayals

The foregoing means that we can look at value by tracking the behaviour of the three returns, k_d, k_e, and k_a, as capital structure changes. We're particularly concerned with the behaviour of k_a, the average cost of capital, because of its relation to overall value.

Earlier we talked about share price and value increasing to a maximum as leverage increases. Equation 16.19 tells us that this is equivalent to k_a decreasing to a minimum. The idea is illustrated in Figure 16.10, where value and share price, V_f and P_s, achieve a maximum while k_a reaches a minimum at the same capital structure.

In what follows, we'll find it useful to include k_e and k_d in the bottom graph of portrayals like Figure 16.10 to analyze how changes in the two component costs of capital influence the average cost.

The Early Theory by Modigliani and Miller

The theoretical ball got rolling in 1958 when two well-known scholars named Franco Modigliani and Merton Miller published a paper on the effect of capital structure on value.[9] Modigliani and Miller are cited often, and it's become common to refer to them as MM.

Restrictive Assumptions in the Original Model

MM's work was a sophisticated mathematical model of the financial world. It included a number of restrictive assumptions about the behaviour of firms and individuals that made it less than realistic. Nevertheless, it provided important insights into the effects of capital structure on value. Later work relaxed some of the restrictions and led to the state of the theory as it is today.

Perfect capital markets have no income taxes and no transaction costs, and borrowing and lending rates are the same.

For our purposes the most important restrictions[10] were the following.

1. There are no income taxes.
2. Securities trade in perfectly efficient capital markets in which there are no transaction costs.
3. Investors and companies can borrow as much as they want at the same rate. That is,
   a. rates don't go up as one borrows more money, and
   b. the rate is the same for investors and companies.

MM initially assumed there were no costs to bankruptcy.

The second assumption contains an important subtlety. Among other things, it says that there are no costs associated with bankruptcy. This idea sounds like a contradiction to many students and needs to be explained.

---

9 See Franco Modigliani and Merton H. Miller, "The Cost of Capital, Corporation Finance, and the Theory of Investment," *American Economic Review*, 48 (June 1958), pp. 261–297.
10 These are called *perfect capital market* assumptions.

FIGURE 16.10
Variation in Value
and Average
Return with Capital
Structure

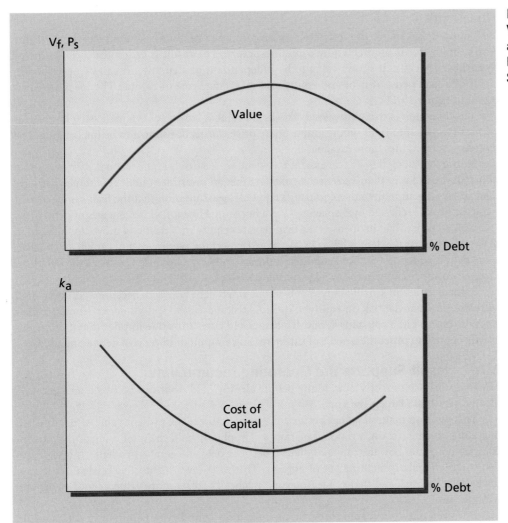

A bankrupt company goes through two processes. First it loses value because of deteriorating business conditions; then it goes into bankruptcy proceedings, which involve either a restructuring of debt or a liquidation of assets.

The assumption of zero bankruptcy cost implies that no legal or administrative fees are incurred in restructuring or liquidating, and if liquidation is required assets are sold for a value close to what they were worth to the company.

In other words, bankruptcy costs are fees and losses on the sale of used assets. The term does not refer to the loss in value that put the business into a bankruptcy situation in the first place.

The Assumptions and Reality

Clearly, the assumptions of the original MM model were unrealistic. First, and most obvious, there are income taxes.

Second, the legal and administrative expenses of bankruptcy are quite large, and assets sold under duress usually bring only a fraction of their original value. In fact, these costs often eat up most of what's left in a bankrupt company.

Third, individuals usually pay higher interest rates than firms, and anyone's rates generally go up as more money is borrowed.

In spite of these problems, the MM model made an insightful contribution to thinking on the subject of capital structure and provided a starting point for a great deal more effort.

The Result

In capital structure theory, the **independence hypothesis** is the original restrictive model by Modigliani and Miller that shows share price to be independent of capital structure. Under MM's initial set of restrictions, *value is independent* of capital structure.

MM showed that under the restrictive assumptions we've discussed and several others, the firm's total value is unaffected by capital structure. The result is called the independence hypothesis, because it shows value to be independent of structure. It can be described in terms of a firm's cost of debt and equity and its average cost of capital. The ideas are illustrated in Figure 16.11.

The top graph is straightforward. The firm's value is constant with increasing leverage as we move from left to right on the graph. Share price can also be shown to be unchanging. The bottom graph requires more explanation.

Notice that along the vertical axis, at zero debt, we have only equity capital, so $k_e = k_a$. Also notice that k_d is lower than k_e, reflecting the fact that an investment in debt is somewhat safer than an investment in the same company's equity. The assumption that the firm can borrow at a constant rate is reflected by displaying k_d as a horizontal line for all percentages of debt.

As *cheaper debt* is added, the *cost of equity increases* because of increased risk such that the weighted average *cost of capital remains constant.*

Now consider what happens as the firm replaces equity with debt and moves to the right in the graph. Because the debt is lower in cost, you'd expect the average cost of capital, k_a, to fall as more debt is added to the financing mix. It doesn't, however, because k_e rises as the debt load increases, compensating in the average for the lower-cost debt.

Some increase in k_e will always come about when debt is added, because additional debt increases the financial risk on equityholders. As risk increases, equityholders demand higher rates of return. But a constant k_a and the associated constant value implies that k_e increases exactly enough to offset the benefit of the increasing amount of lower cost debt being used.

MM's Result Supports the Operating Income View

MM's result wasn't exactly new. Many people already held what can be called an operating income view that's largely the same.

This position maintains that because the firm's value is the present value of its expected operating income stream, a rational market will implicitly hold the total value of that stream constant no matter how the capital is divided between debt and equity. In a sense, this view says that you can't make something out of nothing. The firm's investment value is whatever it is on the basis of income, and that's that. You can't magically create more value by fooling around with the mix.

However, until MM came along, no one had a very good explanation of how this would happen in the marketplace. That is, no one could satisfactorily explain a *process* that would hold investment value constant as leverage is added or subtracted.

The Arbitrage Concept

MM propose that *arbitrage* between leveraged and unleveraged firms will hold *value constant* as debt increases.

MM proposed that a process of arbitrage[11] driven by equity investors seeking to *maximize their returns* would hold the value of a firm constant through changes in leverage. The argument is quite complex, but essentially says that if the value of a firm were to go up due to adding leverage, shareholders could get a better return by selling its shares, borrowing some money on their own, and investing in a similar but unleveraged company (the arbitrage is between the leveraged and unleveraged companies). MM's assumption of uniform interest rates comes into play as investors borrow money on their own.

The sell-off would drive the price of the leveraged firm down while the buying would put upward pressure on the price of the unleveraged firm, driving the two values together. The entire process then holds the value of any firm constant as leverage is increased. (Don't try to figure out why this should work from what we've said here. We haven't gone into

---

11 Arbitrage essentially means making a profit by buying and selling the same thing at the same time in two different markets. For example, suppose you noticed that gold was selling for $640 in London and $650 in Tokyo. You could make a profit by simultaneously placing a buy order in London and a sell order in Tokyo.

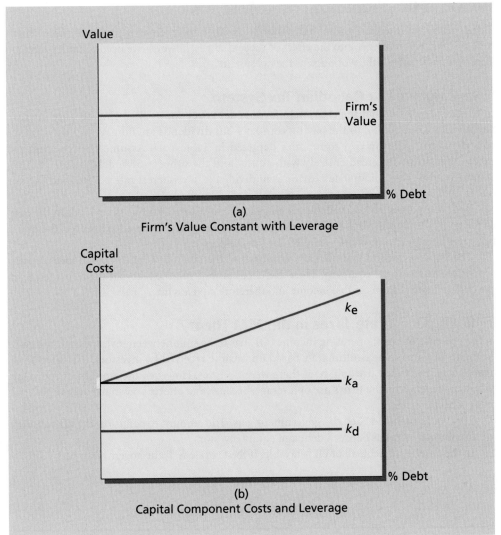

FIGURE 16.11
The Independence
Hypothesis

enough detail to do that. It's enough that you get a rough appreciation of the conceptual approach.)

MM were said to have provided behavioural support for the operating income argument. In other words, they showed how the behaviour of investors in financial markets might hold the total value of a firm constant through changes in capital structure. Keep in mind, however, that to do this they had to assume the absence of taxes, no transaction costs for investing (like brokers' commissions), and that everyone could borrow as much as they wanted at the same rate.

Interpreting the Result

It's important to understand what this early result implies about the real world. It doesn't say that a firm's value and its share price are unaffected by leverage. We know that this isn't true. What it does imply is that the reason leverage affects value stems from market imperfections, like taxes and transaction costs, and not from the basic interaction of investors and companies. That's an important insight into why things are the way they are.

The MM result implies that leverage affects value because of *market imperfections*.

Relaxing the Assumptions—More Insights

Things really got interesting when the assumptions that excluded taxes and bankruptcy costs were relaxed. Before we get into the effect of those changes, however, we need to understand an important point about the workings of the tax system.

Financing and the Canadian Tax System

The tax system *favours debt financing* because *interest is tax-deductible* while dividends are not.

In Chapter 2, we saw that the tax system favours debt over equity financing because interest payments are deductible to the paying company but dividends are not. We'll illustrate this concept again with the two companies depicted in Table 16.4. Assume they're identical except that one is financed entirely with equity and the other is 50% debt financed. Also assume both pay out all after-tax earnings in dividends, the interest rate is 10%, and the tax rate is 40%.

Both companies pay all available earnings to the investors who furnish capital. In the case of the equity-financed company, that means all NI goes to shareholders. However, the other firm pays interest to bondholders and NI to shareholders.

The important point is shown at the bottom of the table. *Total* payments to investors are *higher* for the leveraged company. The difference comes from the fact that the leveraged firm can deduct interest from taxable income and therefore *pays less tax.*

Including Corporate Taxes in the MM Theory

In the presence of taxes, operating income (OI) has to be split between investors and the government. Because value is ultimately based on income received by investors, this lowers the firm's value from what it would be if there were no taxes. However, the amount of the value reduction depends on the firm's use of leverage, because that affects how much tax the government collects.

Let's focus on how much the government gets. The amount depends on the tax rate and the distribution of funds between debt and equity investors.

In the absence of debt, all of OI is taxable. If the tax rate is T, the government gets

$$(a) \qquad\qquad T(OI)$$

TABLE 16.4
The Tax System Favours Debt Financing

	All Equity	50% Debt 50% Equity
EBIT	$ 100	$ 100
Interest (10% of debt)		50
EBT	$ 100	$ 50
Tax (40% of EBT)	40	20
Net income (NI)	$ 60	$ 30
Dividend	60	30
Net retained	$ 0	$ 0
Capital		
Debt	$ 0	$ 500
Equity	1,000	500
Total capital	$ 1,000	$ 1,000
Payments to Investors		
Interest	$ 0	$ 50
Dividends	60	30
Total	$ 60	$ 80

However, interest is tax-deductible, so if there's debt and an amount of interest, I, the government gets only

(b)
$$T(OI - I) = T(OI) - TI$$

The difference in what the government gets with and without debt is the difference between (a) and (b), which is TI. Thus, when a firm uses debt financing, the government's take is reduced by TI every year.

In the MM model with taxes, *interest* provides a *tax shield* that reduces government's share of the firm's earnings.

Stated conversely, debt results in a yearly perpetuity of TI dollars to be divided among investors that wouldn't be available if debt weren't used. The amount TI is called the *tax shield* associated with debt financing.

The impact of the tax shield on value is simply the present value of the perpetuity TI capitalized at discount rate k_d.

(16.20)
$$\text{PV of tax shield} = \frac{TI}{k_d}$$

This can be written more conveniently by recognizing that interest is just debt times the interest rate.

(16.21)
$$I = Bk_d$$
$$\text{where } B = \text{Debt (think of bonds)}$$

Substituting into Equation 16.20 yields

(16.22)
$$\text{PV of tax shield} = \frac{TI}{k_d} = \frac{TBk_d}{k_d} = TB$$

Value is increased by the *PV* of the *tax shield*. The benefit of *debt* is the *tax rate* times the *debt amount.*

TB is also referred to as the benefit of debt. In words, Equation 16.21 says that having debt in the capital structure increases a firm's value by the magnitude of that debt times the tax rate.

For example, suppose an all-equity firm that has a tax rate of 40% and a market value of $2 million restructures by trading $1 million in shares for the same amount in bonds. The implication of the MM theory with taxes is that the firm's market value will increase by

$$0.4 \times \$1 \text{ million} = \$400,000$$

to $2.4 million.

The benefit of debt accrues *entirely to shareholders* because bond returns are fixed.

Further, the *increment in value will all accrue to the shareholders* because the value of the bonds is fixed by the terms of the bond contract and current interest rates.

This is a very significant conclusion. It says that a firm can increase its value and the wealth of shareholders at a constant rate by trading equity for debt until it is financed virtually 100% with debt (we say virtually because there has to be some equity). The result is represented in Figure 16.12.

In the MM model with taxes, *value increases* steadily as *leverage is added.*

The top graph shows the market value of the firm increasing from its all-equity value as the addition of debt increases the present value of the tax shield along with leverage. The lower graph shows the behaviour of the component and weighted average costs of capital. Notice that with the inclusion of taxes the cost of debt is $k_d(1 - T)$ rather than just k_d.

In this representation, the average cost of capital falls with the inclusion of more low-cost debt. The cost of equity increases at the same time, but not fast enough to overcome the effect of the low-cost debt.

Including Bankruptcy Costs in the MM Theory

Bankruptcy costs eventually make investors *raise required rates*, which *lowers value.*

The probability of business failure increases as a firm takes on more debt. As explained earlier, bankruptcy costs are *additional* losses that accrue primarily to shareholders when companies fail. As leverage increases past some point, investors become conscious enough of bankruptcy costs to begin raising their required rates of return. In other words, investors begin to worry that they

FIGURE 16.12
MM Theory
of Taxes

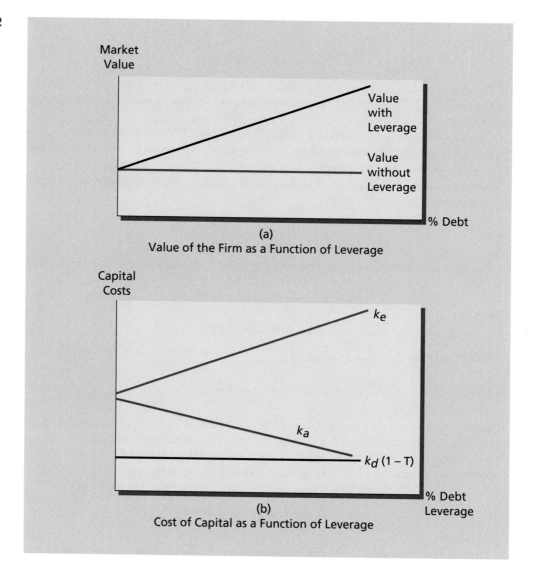

(a)
Value of the Firm as a Function of Leverage

(b)
Cost of Capital as a Function of Leverage

will incur losses due to bankruptcy cost if the firm fails. This happens first to equity investors and later to bondholders. As investor required rates go up, so do the firm's capital costs.

The effect is shown in Figure 16.13b. As we move to the right, critical points are passed after which k_e and then k_d begin to climb. It's important to notice that the average cost of capital, k_a, does not begin to increase as soon as k_e starts upward. That's because it is still being driven downward by the mix change coming from the replacement of high-cost equity with low-cost debt. The minimum value of k_a is reached only after k_e has gone up quite a bit, perhaps reinforced by an increase in k_d.

Now consider the top diagram that shows the firm's value. According to Equations 16.16 through 16.19, increasing required returns have a depressing effect on value as we continue to the right after one or both of the returns begin to rise. However, the growing tax shield continues to add value at the same time.

At first the rate effect isn't strong enough to overcome the tax effect and the net result of more leverage is still an increase in value. Before long, however, the growing spectre of failure overwhelms the tax effect, and value begins to decline with additional leverage. The peak in value coincides with the minimum in k_a.

The *MM model* with taxes and bankruptcy costs concludes that an *optimal capital structure exists.*

Summarizing the Results

In short, the MM model with taxes and bankruptcy costs says that additional leverage increases the value of a firm when total leverage is relatively low. However, a maximum is eventually reached, after which further increases reduce value. Unfortunately, the theory does not provide a method for finding the maximum.

Notice that this result is essentially the same as the one we developed by using an intuitive approach early in the chapter. A little leverage helps, a lot hurts, and it's hard to find the perfect amount.

However, the reasons for the conclusion are different. The MM model attributes the benefit of leverage solely to taxes, while the intuitive approach relies on the impact of improved performance on investors' attitudes and perceptions. Both attribute leverage's negative effects to risk.

Learn more about how companies raise capital at http://strategis.ic. gc.ca/epic/site/ sofsdf.nsf/en/Home.

FIGURE 16.13
MM Theory with Taxes and Bankruptcy Costs

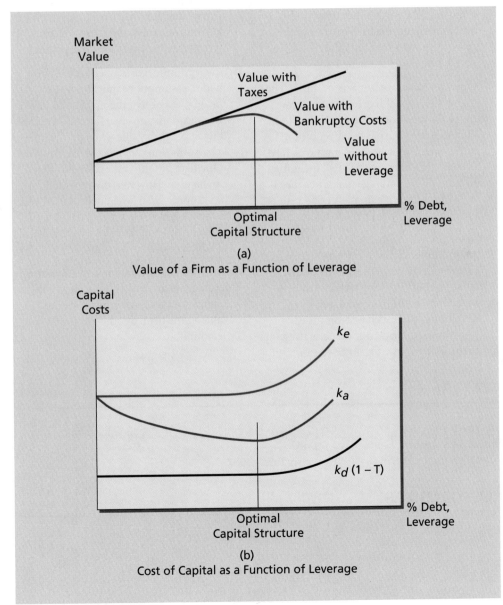

(a)
Value of a Firm as a Function of Leverage

(b)
Cost of Capital as a Function of Leverage

SUMMARY

1 Leverage means either using fixed costs to replace variable costs (operating leverage) or assuming debt (financial leverage) in order to magnify returns to shareholders. Both types of leverage produce high returns when business conditions are good, and the opposite when conditions are poor.

2 The level of sales needed to just cover operating costs, that is to get EBIT = 0, is called breakeven. Breakeven analysis is a way of looking at operations to determine the volume, in either units or dollars, a company must sell to achieve this zero-profit, zero-loss situation. Breakeven does not include financing costs.

3 Operating leverage impacts on EBIT. The higher the level of fixed operating costs, the more variation there will be in EBIT. Financial leverage has no effect on EBIT but it magnifies shareholder returns. The presence of either one of these magnifies EPS and ROE. Leverage magnifies the effects of changes; it can make good results look great and poor or marginal results look disastrous.

4 An indifference EBIT can be calculated to assist decision makers in deciding what level of financial leverage to use. Indifference EBIT is calculated by developing the EPS equation for each financing scenario and then equating them. With a little algebra, we can then solve for the level of EBIT that would make those two equations equal. Armed with this information, the decision maker then forecasts the most likely EBIT and begins adjusting financing accordingly.

5 At moderate levels of debt, financial leverage enhances ROE and EPS. This makes the shares more desirable and the share price increases. As the amount of debt increases, the cost of capital decreases. In theory, this increases the firm's value; however, such high levels of debt increases risk and these concerns have a negative effect on share price.

6 The MM model using perfect capital market assumptions quickly shows that the debt to equity ratio appears to have no effect on firm value. Capital structure does affect firm value when perfect market assumptions are relaxed, particularly if the firm has interest tax shields that can be used. However, the potential for bankruptcy exists when debt is used and lenders begin to charge higher rates on the debt and add restrictive covenants, all of which cost the firm money.

7 With the positive and negative aspects of leverage we are left with the idea that capital structure may impact on the value of the firm, but the extent may be very limited.

KEY TERMS

Breakeven analysis, p. 581
Business risk, p. 566
Capital restructuring, p. 565

Contribution margin, p. 583
Cost structure, p. 567

Independence hypothesis, p. 594
Operating leverage, p. 567

KEY FORMULAS

(16.1)
$$\text{ROCE} = \frac{\text{EBIT}\,(1 - T)}{\text{Debt} + \text{Equity}}$$

(16.3)
$$\text{DFL} = \frac{\text{EBIT}}{\text{EBIT} - I} \text{ or } \frac{\text{EBIT}}{\text{EBT}}$$

(16.5)
$$C_M = \frac{P - V}{P}$$

(16.7)
$$Q_{B/E} = \frac{F_C}{P - V}$$

(16.9)
$$S_{B/E} = \frac{F_C}{\frac{(P - V)}{P}} = \frac{F_C}{C_M}$$

(16.11)
$$DOL = \frac{Q(P - V)}{Q(P - V) - F_C} \text{ or } \frac{CM}{EBIT}$$

(16.13)
$$DTL = \frac{CM}{EBIT - I} \text{ or } \frac{CM}{EBT}$$

(16.16)
$$V_d = \frac{I}{k_d}$$

(16.17)
$$V_e = \frac{D}{k_e}$$

(16.18)
$$V_f = \frac{I}{k_d} + \frac{D}{k_e}$$

(16.19)
$$V_f = \frac{OI}{k_a}$$

(16.22)
$$\text{PV of tax shield} = \frac{TI}{k_d} = \frac{TBk_d}{k_d} = TB$$

QUESTIONS

1. The user of leverage might be thought of as taking advantage of the provider. Between shareholders and bondholders, who is the user and who is the provider? Give an explanation using words or illustrations that might support this view. What does the provider get in return?

2. Relate business and financial risk as defined in this chapter to the risks described in Chapter 11.

3. Why are ROE and EPS such important measures of performance to investors?

4. "Both business risk and financial risk would exist with or without either type of leverage. Leverage just makes them more significant." Are those statements true or false? Explain.

5. Briefly explain the pros and cons of financial leverage.

6. Explain in words the ROCE test for the advisability of adding leverage. That is, what is the test really telling us? When will it indicate a company is doing the wrong thing?

7. Explain the difference between a fixed and a variable cost. How do these concepts change as the time horizon lengthens? In other words, are the same things fixed over a five-year

planning period that are fixed in a typical one-year period? What about a 10-year period? What's the relevant period when we're talking about operating leverage?

8. Why do labour-intensive processes involve less operating leverage than automated processes? What fixed costs are associated with automation? Why can't those costs be eliminated by just selling the machinery?

9. Explain the idea of breakeven analysis in a brief paragraph.

10. Describe the concept of the breakeven point in words by using the concept of contribution and fixed costs. (Give a short answer.)

11. Summarize the effect of operating leverage on EBIT.

12. "The risk added by financing is small and insignificant in relation to the inherent risk in most businesses." Is that statement true or false? Discuss.

13. Describe generally how leverage affects share prices. What forces are at work, driven by what effects?

14. The central issue underlying the study of leverage is whether or not it influences share price and whether there's an optimal structure. But the whole idea seems kind of fuzzy and uncertain. Why are people so interested? (*Hint:* Think of management's goals and of the world of mergers.)

15. The Braithwaite Tool Co. is considering a major modernization and automation of its plant using borrowed funds. Fully discuss a serious financial negative that could result from the project.

16. Show that the DOL is infinite (not defined) in Equation 16.11 at the breakeven point.

17. Explain the idea of bankruptcy costs. Why are they important to investors? When do investors start to worry about them?

18. Briefly describe the result of MM's original restrictive model. Why was it important in spite of its serious restrictions?

19. Briefly summarize the operating income argument that was supported by the original MM result.

20. Outline the arbitrage process proposed by MM that supports the operating income argument. What is the arbitrage between?

21. Explain in words how the tax system favours debt financing.

22. In a short paragraph, describe the result of adding taxes to the MM model.

23. In another short paragraph, describe the effect of adding bankruptcy costs to the MM model with taxes.

24. Compare the implications of the MM model with taxes and bankruptcy costs to the things we discovered by studying the Alberta Balloon Corporation.

Business Analysis

1. The Armageddon Corp. is in big trouble. Sales are down and profits are off. On top of that, the firm's credit rating has been reduced so it's facing very high interest rates on anything it borrows in the future. Current long-term borrowing represents 60% of capital but at fixed interest rates, so it won't be affected.

   The firm's major shareholder, the Apocalypse Group, has scheduled a conference with management to discuss the company's problems. Everyone is very nervous about this conference, and the executive team is meeting to decide what to tell Apocalypse.

   Charlie Gladhand, the director of marketing, came into the meeting wearing a wide grin. He explained that he'd read an article about leverage that contained the solution to the company's problem. The article told of several successful firms that had, to the delight of their owners, become more successful by borrowing money. Charlie suggests that Armageddon dazzle the Apocalypse Group by borrowing heavily in the next few days before the conference.

   Critique Charlie's idea.

2. You're interested in investing in the Peters Company, which has shown a remarkable increase in EPS during the last three years. Investigating, you find that the company's debt to equity ratio has increased dramatically over the same period and is now 4:1. How does this information affect your feelings about Peters as an investment?

3. You're the CFO of Axelrod Trucking, a privately held firm whose owner, Joe Axelrod, is interested in selling the company and retiring. He therefore wants to pump up its value by any means possible. Joe read an article about leverage in a business magazine the other day, and has sent you a memo directing that you restructure the firm's capital to the "optimum" in order to maximize the company's value. Prepare a brief response to Joe's memo.

4. The Beulah Company currently has good earnings and a capital structure that's 20% debt. Its EPS is in the top 25% of firms in its industry. Top management's compensation is in large part based on the year-end price of the company's shares. It's now October and the president, Harry Upscale, is looking for ways to pump that price before December 31. Harry invests in shares himself and pays a great deal of attention to EPS when buying and selling. He also understands that leverage can magnify EPS. However, he knows little more than that about finance. Harry has strongly suggested to the treasurer that Beulah restructure its capital to 65% debt to enhance EPS and increase share price.

   You're an analyst in the firm's treasury department. The treasurer has asked you to prepare an analysis of Harry's proposal to help him talk the boss out of the idea. You've calculated the company's current DFL at 2.2, and projected that it would be 5.8 at the proposed leverage level. Draft a memo from the treasurer to Harry tactfully explaining why his idea may not work and might actually have a result opposite to what he wants to achieve.

5. The Plunkett Company is a large manufacturer of capital goods. (The demand for capital goods typically swings up and down a great deal between good and bad economic times.) Business has been good lately and is expected to remain so in the foreseeable future. The firm is currently relatively labour intensive in its processes. The chief engineer, Sarah Quickwrench, has suggested a major project to modernize and automate the plant. At the output level planned for next year, the project will reduce total cost by 10%. Sarah has presented the idea to the management team in a totally positive light. The other executives are caught up in Sarah's enthusiasm and are ready to proceed. You're Plunkett's CFO, and feel that all sides of an issue should be discussed before it is approved. What concerns

do you have? How would you present them in a way that keeps you from appearing to be overly negative?

6. The Wycombe Company is doing well and is interested in diversifying, so it's been looking around for an acquisition target. The Albe Company has been found with the help of an investment dealer. Albe is quite profitable and is about half the size of Wycombe. This size relationship is reflected in their market values. Both firms are financed entirely by shareholders' equity. The investment dealer has advised that it will be necessary to pay a premium of about 30% over market price to acquire Albe. Wycombe's president is having a hard time with this news and has asked you for advice. Construct and explain an approach to the acquisition that might make the premium easier to rationalize. Would it affect your argument if neither Albe nor Wycombe was particularly profitable? If so, how?

PROBLEMS

1. The Watson Waterbed Works Inc. has an EBIT of $2.75 million, can borrow at 15% interest, and pays combined provincial and federal income taxes of 40%. It currently has no debt and is capitalized by shareholders' equity of $12 million. The firm has 1.5 million common shares outstanding that trade at book value.
   a. Calculate Watson's NI, ROE, and EPS currently and at capital structures that have 20%, 40%, 60%, and 80% debt.
   b. Compare the EPS at the different leverage levels, and the amount of change between levels as leverage increases. What happens to the effect of more debt as leverage increases from a little to a lot?

2. The Galiano Computer Company has the following selected financial results.

	10% Debt	40% Debt	75% Debt
Debt	$ 10,000		
Shareholders' equity	90,000		
Total capital	$ 100,000		
Shares @ $5	18,000		
EBIT	$ 18,000		
Interest (15%)	1,500		
EBT	$ 16,500		
Tax (40%)	6,600		
NI	$ 9,900		
ROE			
EPS			

The company is considering a capital restructuring to increase leverage from its present level of 10% of capital.
   a. Calculate Galiano's ROE and EPS under its current capital structure.
   b. Restate the financial statement line items shown, the number of shares outstanding, ROE, and EPS if Galiano borrows money and uses it to retire shares until its capital structure is 40% debt assuming EBIT remains unchanged and the shares continue to sell at their book value. (Develop the second column of the chart shown.)

c. Recalculate the same figures assuming Galiano continues to restructure until its capital structure is 75% debt. (Develop the third column of the chart.)

d. How is increasing leverage affecting financial performance? What overall effect might the changes have on the market price of Galiano's shares? Why? (Use words only. *Hint:* Consider the move from 10% to 40% and that from 40% to 75% separately.)

3. Reconsider the Galiano Computer Company of the previous problem assuming the firm has experienced some difficulties and its EBIT has fallen to $8,000.

   a. Reconstruct the three column chart assuming Galiano's EBIT remains at $8,000.

   b. Interpret the result in terms of share price and the advisability of restructuring capital under these conditions.

   c. Could these results have been predicted more easily? Use the ROCE concept to come to the same conclusion.

4. Assume Galiano Computer Company of the last two problems is earning an EBIT of $15,000. Once again, calculate the chart showing the implication of adding more leverage. Verbally rationalize the result.

5. The Canterbury Coach Corporation has EBIT of $3.62 million and total capital of $20 million, which is 15% debt. The 425,000 shares outstanding sell at book value. The firm pays 12% interest on its debt and is subject to a combined provincial and federal tax rate of 40%. Canterbury is contemplating a capital restructuring to either 30%, 45%, 60%, or 75% debt.

   a. At the current level of profitability, will more debt enhance results? Why?

   b. Calculate the NI, ROE, EPS, and the DFL at the current and proposed structures, and display your results in a systematic table.

   c. In a short paragraph referring to your table, discuss the trade-off between performance and increased risk (reflected in the DFL) as leverage increases. Do some levels seem to make more sense than others? What business characteristics would make the higher leverage levels less of a problem?

6. The Tanenbaum Tea Company wants to show the stock market an EPS of $3 per share, but doesn't expect to be able to improve profitability over what is reflected in the financial plan for next year. The plan is partially reproduced below.

Tanenbaum Tea Company
Financial Projection 20X1
($000)

EBIT	$ 18,750	Debt	$ 13,000
Interest (@ 12%)	1,560	Shareholders' equity	97,000
EBT	$ 17,190	Capital	$ 110,000
Tax (@ 40%)	6,876		
NI	$ 10,314	Number of shares =	3,700,000

Tanenbaum's shares sell at book value. Will trading equity for debt help the firm achieve its EPS goal, and if so, what debt level will produce the desired EPS?

7. Baldor Corp. has the following operating results and capital structure ($000).

Revenue	$ 6,000	Debt	$ 1,200
Cost/expenses	4,500	Shareholders' equity	8,800
EBIT	$ 1,500	Total	$10,000

The firm is contemplating a capital restructuring to 60% debt. Its shares are currently selling for book value at $25 per share. The interest rate is 9% and combined provincial and federal taxes are 42%.

a. Calculate EPS under the current and proposed capital structures.

b. Calculate the DFL under both structures.

c. Use the DFL values to forecast the resulting EPS under each structure if operating profit falls off by 5%, 10%, or 25%.

d. Comment on the desirability of the proposed structure versus the current one as a function of the volatility of the business.

e. Is share price likely to be increased by a change to the proposed capital structure? Discuss briefly.

8. You're a financial analyst at Pinkerton E-Commerce Graphic Systems (PEGS), a successful entrant in a new and rapidly growing field. As in most new fields, however, rapid growth is anything but assured, and PEGS' future performance is uncertain.

The firm expects to earn operating profits of $4 million next year, up from $1 million last year. To support this enormous growth, the firm plans to raise $15 million in new capital. It already has capital of $5 million, which is 40% debt.

PEGS can raise the new money in any proportion of debt and equity management chooses. The CFO is considering three possibilities: all equity, $8 million debt and $7 million equity, and all debt.

Interest on the current debt as well as on new borrowing is expected to be 10%, and the company pays provincial and federal income taxes at a combined rate of 40%. Equity will be raised by selling shares at the current market price of $10, which is equal to their book value.

The CFO has asked you to prepare an analysis to aid management in making the debt/equity decision. You are also to provide a recommendation of your own.

a. Prepare an EBIT–EPS analysis of the situation showing a line for the capital structure that results from each of the three options. (Calculate EPS under each new capital structure at EBIT levels of $1 million, $2 million, and $4 million. Then graph EBIT versus EPS for each option. Refer to Figure 16.3 on page 579. Show last year's EPS on the graph.)

b. Discuss the effect the options might have on share price.

c. Make a subjective recommendation under each of the following assumptions about the $4 million operating profit forecast. Support your position with words and references to your EBIT–EPS analysis.

   i. The $4 million operating profit projection is a best-case scenario. Anything from $2 million to $4 million has an equal probability of occurring.

   ii. The $4 million is a fair estimate with about a 60% probability. However, performance better than $4 million is unlikely. Results could range anywhere from zero to $4 million.

   iii. The $4 million is an easy target. There's an even chance of anything between $4 million and $8 million.

9. Cranberry Wood Products Inc. spends an average of $9.50 in labour and $12.40 in materials on every unit it sells. Sales commissions and shipping amount to another $3.10. All other costs are fixed and add up to $140,000 per month. The average unit sells for $32.00.

a. What are Cranberry's contribution and contribution margin?
b. What is the firm's breakeven point in units?
c. Calculate the dollar breakeven point in two ways.
d. Sketch the breakeven diagram.
e. Calculate the DOL when sales are 20%, 30%, and 40% above breakeven.

10. Refer to the Cranberry company of the previous problem:
    a. Suppose automated equipment is added that increases fixed costs by $20,000 per month. How much will total variable cost have to decrease to keep the breakeven point the same?
    b. Calculate the DOL at the same output levels used in part (e) of the previous problem.
    c. Comment on the differences in DOL with and without the additional equipment.

Questions 11–14 refer to Burl Wood Projects (BWP) a manufacturer of high-quality furniture.

11. BWP projects sales of 100,000 units next year at an average price of $50 per unit. Variable costs are estimated at 40% of revenue, and fixed costs will be $2.4 million. BWP has $1 million in bonds outstanding on which it pays 8%, and its marginal tax rate is 40%. There are 100,000 shares outstanding, which trade at their book value of $30. Compute BWP's contribution, contribution margin, NI, DOL, and EPS.

12. BWP intends to purchase a machine that will result in a major improvement in product quality along with a small increase in manufacturing efficiency. The machine will cost $1 million, which will be borrowed at 9%. The quality improvement is expected to have a significant impact on BWP's competitive position. Indeed, management expects sales to increase by 5% in spite of a planned 10% price increase. The efficiency improvement combined with the price increase will result in variable costs of 36% of revenue. Fixed cost, however, will rise by 19%.
    a. Compute BWP's new contribution, contribution margin, NI, DOL, and EPS if it purchases the new machine.
    b. If all of BWP's projections come to pass, how will share price be influenced? What factors should be considered in estimating a share price change?

13. Calculate BWP's DFL and DTL before and after the acquisition of the new machine.

14. Use the information from the previous two problems. Calculate BWP's breakeven point in units and dollars, with and without the purchase of the new machine.

15. The Spitfire Model Airplane Company has the following modified income statement ($000) at 100,000 units of production.

Revenue	$ 10,000
Variable cost	6,500
Fixed cost	2,200
EBIT	$ 1,300
Interest (@ 10%)	500
EBT	$ 800
Tax (@ 40%)	320
NI	$ 480
Number of shares	20,000

    a. What are Spitfire's contribution margin and dollar breakeven point?

    b. Calculate Spitfire's current DFL, DOL, and DTL.

    c. Calculate the current EPS and estimate what it would become if sales declined by 25%. Use the DTL first and then recalculate the modified income statement. (Assume a negative EBT generates a negative tax.)

16. The Carmacks Metal Stamping Company is planning to buy a new computer-controlled stamping machine for $10 million. The purchase will be financed entirely with borrowed money, which will change Carmacks' capital structure substantially. It will also change operations by adding $1.5 million in fixed cost and eliminating $2 million in variable cost at the current level of sales. The firm's current financial position is reflected in the following statement ($000).

Revenue	$18,000		
Variable cost	10,000	Debt	$ 5,000
Fixed cost	5,000	Shareholder's Equity	15,000
EBIT	$ 3,000	Total	$ 20,000
Interest (@ 10%)	500		
EBT	$ 2,500	Number of shares	750,000
Tax (@ 40%)	1,000	EPS	$ 2.00
NI	$ 1,500		

    a. Restate the financial statements with the new machine, and calculate the dollar breakeven points with and without it.

    b. Calculate the DFL with and without the new machine.

    c. Calculate the DOL with and without the new machine. (*Hint:* You don't need Q to use Equation 16.11, because PQ is revenue and VQ is total variable cost.)

    d. Calculate the DTL with and without the new machine.

    e. Comment on the variability of EPS with sales and the source of that variability.

    f. Is it a good idea to buy the new machine if sales are expected to remain near current levels? Give two reasons why or why not. What has to be anticipated for the project to make sense?

17. Schoen Industries pays interest of $3 million each year on bonds with an average coupon rate of 7.5%. The firm has 4.5 million shares outstanding and pays out 100% of earnings in dividends. Earnings per share (EPS) is $3.50. Schoen's cost of equity is 12%. Calculate the firm's total value (the value of its debt plus that of its equity) under the assumptions of Modigliani and Miller's simplest model (i.e., that there are no taxes and no transactions costs in financial markets).

18. Assume Schoen Industries of the last problem is subject to income tax at a rate of 40%.

    a. Recalculate the value of the firm assuming there is no tax shield associated with debt and compare it to the value calculated in the last problem. That is, assume interest is subtracted in calculating earnings, but is not deductible in calculating taxes. How much value has theoretically been lost to investors as a result of taxes? Which investors suffer the loss, shareholders or bondholders?

    b. What is the value of the tax shield associated with the firm's debt? What is the benefit of debt? Calculate the theoretical value of the firm including the benefit of debt and compare it with the value calculated in the last problem. Who gets the incremental value resulting from the tax shield?

c. Under what conditions, assuming bankruptcy costs are introduced, are investors likely to receive the full benefit of debt calculated in part b? Use words only.

19. Algebraically derive

$$EPS = ROE \times Book\ value\ per\ share$$

(*Hint:* Write the definitions of ROE, EPS, and book value, then start substituting.)

Chapter 17

Dividends, Stock Splits, and Share Repurchases

Learning Objectives

1 Explain that investors buy shares because they expect an acceptable return from dividends and/or receipts when the shares are sold.

2 Explain that the dividend decision for a company is whether to pay cash dividends now or retain earnings for future growth, both of which benefit shareholders.

3 Explain the dividend irrelevance theory.

4 Discuss dividends foregone as an alternate source of financing.

5 Explain some of the arguments regarding investors' preferences for and against current dividends.

6 Explain the impact of corporate development on dividend policy.

7 Note some of the legal and contractual limitations on dividend policy.

8 Explain dividend policy and discuss some common examples.

9 Explain the process of declaring and paying dividends.

10 Discuss dividend reinvestment plans.

11 Explain the nature, purposes and procedures of stock splits, stock dividends, share repurchases and reverse stock splits.

Many investors buy shares for the dividends they expect to receive. They might be surprised to learn that some financial theory suggests that they should be indifferent as to whether or not they actually receive dividends currently!

In this chapter we'll concern ourselves with common share dividends, the payments made by companies to equity investors.[1] Dividends present an interesting puzzle in modern finance. People are basically divided on their importance to investors and as to whether or not their payment has an influence on share prices. Practitioners tend to think dividends are important to share prices, while scholars feel that in theory they shouldn't make much difference. The debate is significant because of the central role dividends occupy in the fabric of finance. To understand the issues, we'll need to review a little background.

BACKGROUND

Dividends as a Basis for Value

Dividends are a critical piece of the financial system because of their role in determining the value of shares. Recall that in Chapter 10 we came to the conclusion that share prices depended *entirely* on expected future dividends. We need to review those ideas and revise our focus slightly for the present discussion.

Dividends are the *basis of value* for shares.

The relationship between dividends and value can be viewed from the perspective of an individual investor or from that of the market as a whole.

The Individual Perspective

An individual buys shares because he or she expects an acceptable return from dividends and from the receipts when the shares eventually are sold. Today's price is the present value of those future cash flows discounted at the appropriate rate for an equity investment in the company. If an investor plans to hold a share for *n* years, these ideas can be written as follows.

For information on dividend rates and yields for shares listed on the Toronto Stock Exchange, go to the Stingy Investor at http://www.ndir.com/SI/strategy/dogs.shtml and click on the *High Dividend Yield* links.

$$(17.1) \qquad P_0 = \frac{D_1}{(1 + k)} + \frac{D_2}{(1 + k)^2} + \ldots + \frac{D_n}{(1 + k)^n} + \frac{P_n}{(1 + k)^n}$$

where P_0 = Today's share price

D_i = The dividend in the *i*th year ($i = 1, 2, \ldots, n$)

P_n = The selling price of the share in the *n*th year

k = The expected return on equity

This idea was developed in more detail in Chapter 10 in Equation 10.5, page 360.

The Whole Market View

In Chapter 10 we went on to develop the whole market focus by replacing P_n with the present value of the remaining dividends stretching infinitely into the future. We argued that the buyer in year *n* would have a model in mind similar to Equation 17.1, and replacing P_n with that model would conceptually push the selling price farther into the future. We could apply this mental process as many times as we liked to get the eventual selling price infinitely distant in time, at which point its present value would be zero. Hence, we could work with a model that had an infinite dividend stream rather than a finite stream followed by a price.

Valuation can be based on a series of dividends and on *eventual selling price.*

Our Current Focus

Both the finite and infinite stream models are valid expressions for valuation. In Chapter 10 we focused on the infinite stream. Here we'll make use of the individual model with a finite time horizon.

---

1 Although payments made to preferred shareholders are also called "dividends," we will focus on common share dividends.

Understanding the Dividend Decision

The dividend decision is simple on the surface. It relates to how much of its earnings a firm should pay out in dividends, with the options ranging from nothing to everything. However, it's important that we understand all of the implications involved in the choice, because some aren't entirely obvious.

The Discretionary Nature of Dividends

We need to keep in mind the fact that dividends are legally *discretionary*. A company's board of directors has the authority to determine the amount of every dividend, including whether anything is paid at all.

This is a very significant point. In spite of the importance of dividends in the valuation process, they are never assured. The purchase of a share includes no guarantee of future dividends, regardless of what has been paid in the past.

The Dividend Decision

A firm's earnings belong to its shareholders. The **dividend decision** is a choice made by management on behalf of those shareholders about what to do with their earnings. Theoretically, there are only two alternatives: earnings can be paid out as dividends now, or retained for reinvestment in the business. Both options benefit shareholders, but in different ways.

The dividend option gives shareholders an immediate cash payment that they can spend or reinvest as they please. Retaining earnings, on the other hand, involves investing the money in business projects that are expected to enhance profitability. Those higher profits cause the share price to increase, which means share owners hold more valuable financial assets. It's important to focus on the different characteristics of the benefits created by the two mechanisms.

A dividend gives shareholders *current income* they can spend immediately. Current income is important to some investors because they need it to live on. To others it's less significant because they don't need it immediately and would just reinvest it.

Share price appreciation, on the other hand, can't be spent without selling the shares, which many people don't want to do right away. Hence, retaining earnings produces *deferred income*.

The dividend decision is the choice between paying more or less in *near-term* dividends. That implies trading off between the two shareholder benefits. It is not a question of whether the shareholder gets a dividend or gets nothing.

THE DIVIDEND CONTROVERSY

The central issue about dividends is whether paying them or paying larger rather than smaller dividends has a positive, negative, or neutral effect on a firm's share price. The question can also be stated in terms of shareholder preferences. Do shareholders prefer current or deferred income as just described? Presumably, doing what they prefer will make shares more desirable, and their price will be bid up to some extent. In other words, we'd like to know whether or not it's generally possible for management to partially accomplish the goal of maximizing shareholder wealth by manipulating the firm's dividend-paying policy.

There are three major arguments regarding investors' preferences for or against dividends and several lesser but related theories that tend to tie things together. None of them is entirely right or wrong.

Dividend Irrelevance

The position endorsed by most theorists is that dividends should matter very little to share price if they matter at all. The reasoning behind this idea can be seen from Equation 17.1. In that equation, suppose early dividends such as D_1 and D_2 are reduced or eliminated, thereby increasing retained earnings. The additional income retained may cause the company to become more profitable and/or grow faster. That, in turn, will make the eventual selling price of the share, P_n, higher, and may also make later dividends like D_n larger.

The **dividend irrelevance theory** hypothesizes that the negative impact on P_0 of reducing or eliminating early dividends is offset by the positive effect of an increased selling price in period n as well as larger later dividends. Hence, the current price of the share, represented by P_0, is independent of changes in the early dividends.

Tailoring the Cash Flow Stream

The irrelevance argument clearly makes sense if investors don't have a preference for current income. If they do, we have to reason a little harder.

A preference for current income means that people care about the pattern of cash flows from an investment as well as about the present value of the entire stream of payments (the security's price). For example, retirees who need a certain amount of current income from investments to live comfortably will be upset if a share they hold reduces its dividends, regardless of the fact that the present value of the whole stream doesn't change.

Does this imply that if management reduces or eliminates dividends in the near term, investors who need current income have to get out of their investment? In theory the answer is no, because an investor in need of cash can always sell some of his or her shares for cash. The portion of the holding that isn't sold appreciates because of the retention of additional earnings, so the value of the original investment can be maintained in spite of the sell-off, even though the number of shares owned decreases.

Dividend irrelevance theory is a logical argument that shareholders should be indifferent to the payment of dividends, because the value of eliminated dividends is *offset by growth-created value* in the future.

Investors can *tailor* their income stream by selling off shares of a growing company that doesn't pay dividends.

Example 17.1

Peter and Rita Mann are retirees who have most of their savings invested in 10,000 shares of Ajax Corporation. Ajax sells for $10 per share and pays a yearly dividend of $0.50 per share. The firm hasn't grown for some time. The Manns depend on their Ajax dividends to supplement their retirement income.

This year Ajax discontinued the dividend, but began to grow at 5% per year because of the additional retained earnings. How can the Manns maintain their income and their position in Ajax? Assume there are no costs to buying and selling securities, and that income taxes can be ignored.

■ **Solution:** At $10 each, the Manns' 10,000 Ajax shares were originally worth a total of (10,000 × $10 =) $100,000. That's the principal amount of their investment that they want to maintain. At the same time, they have to generate a yearly income stream of (10,000 × $0.50 =) $5,000 to replace the dividend that's no longer being paid.

After a year of growth at 5%, Ajax's shares are worth $10.50 each. The Manns can raise $5,000 in cash by selling

$$\frac{\$5,000}{\$10.50} = 476 \text{ Shares}$$

At the appreciated price, the remaining (10,000 – 476 =) 9,524 shares are worth

$$\$10.50 \times 9,524 = \$100,002$$

Hence, the gross amount of the Manns' investment is maintained. (The numbers aren't quite exact because we have to deal in whole shares.) As an exercise, calculate the required sell-off in the second year.

It's easy to imagine the reverse situation in which a firm's dividend provides *more* cash than an investor currently needs. In such a case, some of the cash received can be used to buy more shares in the same company. That effectively reduces the dividend and expands the investor's stake in the firm.

Summarizing, it's theoretically possible to *tailor* one's current income from an equity investment in a growing company to any level by buying or selling shares.

Transaction Costs

All of this works fine as long as trading in and out of the shares doesn't cost anything. Much of formal economic theory operates in a hypothetical world where this is the case. Capital markets are assumed to be *perfect,* which among other things implies that securities can be traded without incurring costs. In such a world people would truly be indifferent to the payment of dividends.

In reality, however, financial markets are burdened with imperfections, including transaction costs such as brokerage commissions. Consider the Manns from Example 17.1. If they have to pay commissions to sell shares, the process of tailoring a current income stream will have a cost. That may make it impossible for them to stay in the Ajax investment.

As a practical matter, if the commissions are low, selling shares to generate current income can remain a reasonable thing to do. But if the commissions are significant, selling off shares can become a prohibitively costly process. Then the discontinuation of the dividend would probably drive the Manns and others like them away from Ajax. If most of the firm's shareholders were affected that way, Ajax's market price would drop.

Clearly, the more significant the transaction costs, the less valid the irrelevance theory becomes.

> Transaction costs are the costs of trading securities, including brokerage commissions. They tend to make tailoring an income stream impractical.

Income Taxes

In Chapter 2 we saw how the income tax system treats various types of investment income. It's worth noting that the tax system plays a subtle part in the indifference theory. Notice that the idea depends on trading short-run dividend income for price appreciation in the longer run. We've described that trade-off in pretax terms in Example 17.1 (page 613); however, the tax system can add a complication.

Capital gains may be taxed at lower rates than dividend income. Therefore, the difference in the tax rates on those types of income should be included in the offsetting idea. This is conceptually easy to do. To the extent capital gains are taxed at lower rates than dividend income, it takes a proportionately smaller increase in P_n to offset the value of a near-term dividend reduction than it would if the rates were the same. We will return to the effect of income taxes when discussing dividend aversion on page 615.

The View From Within the Company

From the perspective of the firm, dividends represent an outflow of cash that could be used for other things. Specifically, paying dividends reduces retained earnings, which are a source of funds for capital budgeting projects.

> Firms *prefer not to pay dividends* if they can avoid selling new shares, because *retained earnings cost less* than new shares.

Recall that in Chapter 15 (page 543) we dealt with what happens when the firm runs out of retained earnings before it runs out of projects. We concluded that if more equity is needed after retained earnings are exhausted, the company raises it by selling additional shares. This means that a dividend paid may result in the need to sell new shares, because it reduces retained earnings.

This doesn't create a problem if the new shares are sold in a perfectly efficient market without incurring *flotation costs.*[2] In that case, the firm would be internally indifferent between paying and not paying dividends. The cash used for dividends would simply be replaced by selling shares as needed.

From the CFO

> However, if there are flotation costs, an expense is associated with selling new shares. Then paying dividends leads to incurring extra cost, and management has a definite preference for not paying dividends. This preference is shared by the shareholders because more cost ultimately means less earnings.

Needless to say, flotation costs do exist in the real world, and they're quite significant.

---

2 Recall that flotation costs are the transaction costs associated with issuing new securities.

Dividend Preference

The **dividend preference theory** maintains that generally shareholders prefer receiving dividends to not receiving them. The argument is based on the uncertainty of the future. It asserts that shareholders prefer current dividends to future capital gains, because something paid today is more certain to be received than something expected in the future. The idea can be put in somewhat cynical terms by saying that shareholders don't trust management to use the cash on hand today to grow the firm into something larger and more valuable later on.

Under **dividend preference** investors prefer immediate cash to *uncertain* future benefits.

Notice that this is not a time value of money argument. It doesn't say that people prefer the dividend today because it's worth more. It says they'd rather have it now to be sure of getting it. The argument is often called the *bird in the hand theory* from the old cliché, "A bird in the hand is worth two in the bush" (because you may not catch either of those in the bush).

The reasoning has one rather substantial flaw. If shareholders are concerned about reinvesting dividend money in a firm because they're afraid it will be lost, why have they invested in that firm in the first place?

Dividend Aversion

The **dividend aversion theory** asserts that investors generally prefer that companies not pay dividends in order to enhance share prices later on. The argument is based on the taxation of capital gains so its persuasiveness depends on current tax law.[3]

Under **dividend aversion theory** investors may prefer future capital gains to current dividends because of lower *tax rates on capital gains.*

The assumption underlying the idea is that dividends are often taxed at higher rates than capital gains. Notice that in Equation 17.1 the dividend decision involves trading early dividends for a higher selling price in period n. The current dividend is investment income, but the appreciated price represents a capital gain when the share is sold. Hence the trade-off between a dividend today and a higher price later has to be modified to reflect the fact that, after taxes, investors may get to keep more of the capital gain than the dividends. The tax treatment of capital gains is not only more favourable, but also is deferred until the share is sold. That clearly makes the deferred gain more desirable.

The Canadian governments and their tax departments regularly make changes to the tax treatment of capital gains. It's important to realize that governments are capable of reversing themselves and reducing or eliminating capital gains tax benefits in the future. The issue is politically sensitive because capital gains largely accrue to the wealthy, so favourable rates are a break for the rich. As of 2007, capital gains often enjoy a substantial tax advantage over dividend income, particularly for taxpayers in the higher *tax brackets.*[4]

If a company has a large percentage of wealthy shareholders who are in a high tax bracket, it may pay out lower dividends to allow these shareholders to defer their personal taxes. Low-income shareholders, such as retirees who need dividend income, will prefer higher dividends.

From the CFO

Other Theories and Ideas

After all this we're still not sure whether there ought to be a general preference for or against dividends. There are a few other ideas that can help us understand the overall picture.

The Clientele Effect

The clientele argument is that individual investors do have definite dividend preferences because of their need for more or less current income. These preferences arise because transaction costs make tailoring a cash flow stream by buying and selling shares very expensive.

3 See our discussion of personal income taxes on investment income in Chapter 2 page 41.
4 When investments are held within a *tax shelter*, such as a registered retirement savings plan, neither dividends nor capital gains are taxable until receipts are withdrawn from the shelter. At that time, withdrawals are taxed at the taxpayer's full marginal tax rate, whatever the source of the income.

It's easy to visualize the kinds of people who have various preferences. Retirees living on fixed incomes, for example, are likely to need dividend income to supplement pensions and other incomes. Young professionals with plenty of disposable income, on the other hand, may be willing to bet on capital gains in the longer run if the expected return is higher. People tend to gravitate toward the type of company that meets their needs. The retirees are likely to prefer companies like public utilities that are stable and tend to pay regular dividends. The young professionals may like "small capital growth companies" that don't pay dividends at all but may offer huge price appreciation.

The clientele effect is especially important to public utilities, such as water and electric companies. Utilities are often regulated monopolies, meaning they have no competitors, but the prices they can charge are limited by the government. As a result their performance is very stable, and they typically pay out most of their earning in dividends. Utilities attract investors like retirees who value stability and depend on receiving regular dividend income.

Corporate investors have an incentive to buy high-dividend payout shares. A corporate shareholder is exempt from tax on dividends, but not on capital gains.

A public company's dividend payment record is sometimes a criterion as to whether or not shares are eligible for purchase by certain pension or mutual funds. If the dividend payments are interrupted, then the shares become an ineligible investment for the fund, which reduces the clientele for the shares.

Each company develops a *clientele* of investors whose needs match its dividend-paying characteristics, hence the term clientele effect. The most significant implication of the effect is that once a clientele is established, it's unwise to change dividend practices. Such a change would be almost guaranteed to alienate shareholders who invested in the firm at least partially because they liked its dividend policy. It would cause them to migrate away from its shares, creating a general downward pressure on its share price.

The Residual Dividend Theory

The residual dividend theory focuses on the firm's internal need for capital. Earlier we mentioned that dividends reduce retained earnings, and therefore can force the sale of additional shares when a company needs equity capital for projects. Further, we noted that equity from new shares is more expensive than retained earnings because of flotation costs.

Under the residual dividend theory, companies recognize the cost effectiveness of retained earnings, and fund the equity portion of all viable projects with earnings before paying any dividends. Anything left over is paid out as a dividend. The term "residual" comes from this *leftover* status of the dividend.

The residual theory has an intuitive appeal, but it isn't the way most companies work. Most managers see a value in dividends and set them aside first rather than last. Further, most companies can come up with a virtually unlimited number of capital projects that look good on paper. As a result, a firm that truly adhered to the residual theory might never pay a dividend.

The Signalling Effect of Dividends

Rightly or wrongly, financial markets have come to read a great deal of information into the payment or nonpayment of a dividend. Indeed, the dividend is viewed as a way for management to send a message to its shareholders. People seem to have more faith in the message carried by dollars and cents than by spoken words. The phenomenon is called the *information* or signalling effect of dividends, and is especially significant when earnings change.

If earnings turn down, the continuation of a regular dividend is viewed as a statement by management that the business is fundamentally sound and that the downturn is temporary. As a result, firms generally continue paying their normal dividends in the face of temporary decreases in earnings. The message to shareholders is, "EPS is off a little, but don't worry about it. Things will be fine. In the long run we expect to have plenty of money, so here's your regular dividend."

From the CFO

The **clientele effect** maintains that investors choose shares *for dividend policy*, so any *change* in payments is disruptive.

According to the **residual dividend theory**, dividends are paid from earnings only *after all viable projects are funded.*

From the CFO

The **signalling effect** means that cash dividends signal *management's confidence* in the future.

In the same vein, an increase in the dividend is a stronger statement of management's confidence in the future. A dividend increase accompanying rising earnings is a statement that the earnings improvement is expected to be permanent, and signifies a generally bright future. An increase in the face of a downturn is a clear attempt to allay shareholders' fears.

On the other hand, a decrease in dividends is taken as terrible news. It generally comes after a sustained reduction in earnings, and tells the market that management doesn't expect the company to have the cash it had in the past. Investors usually react negatively and tend to sell off the shares, depressing their price. A decrease without an associated decline in earnings is a more mysterious but nevertheless dark message that isn't well received either.

As a result of all this, companies sometimes maintain or even raise dividends in an attempt to forestall negative investor reactions to serious problems. This practice is clearly inappropriate.

The signalling effect is very real and makes it difficult to tell what investor preferences for cash dividends really are. For example, suppose a firm has steady earnings but reduces its regular dividend, explaining to shareholders that it needs more money for capital projects. In spite of the explanation, the share's price drops. Is the drop due to the fact that investors prefer a higher dividend, or is it because they don't quite believe management's explanation and suspect operating problems are coming? That's very difficult to determine.

Insights PRACTICAL FINANCE

The Painful Decision to Cut Dividends

Companies are reluctant to reduce dividends because of the signalling and clientele effects. They do it only when forced to by poor earnings or fundamental changes in their businesses. The example of Bombardier Inc. is worth noting.

In 2007, Bombardier Inc (Bombardier) was a U.S.$4 billion manufacturer of passenger and business aircraft and mass transit systems with customers and manufacturing facilities around the world. In May 2007, investors sent Bombardier share prices soaring to their highest level in three years when the company announced its latest results. Net income for the first quarter had more than tripled from the same period in 2006. Revenue had increased 12%, driven mostly by increased aircraft deliveries. On May 30, Bombardier B Class shares closed up 12% to $5.36.

In contrast to the euphoria, some shareholders grilled Chief Executive Officer Laurent Beaudoin about high levels of executive compensation while the company hadn't paid dividends in two years. The common dividend had been cut from 18 cents per share to 9 cents per share in 2003, and was suspended in 2005.

The dividend cut in 2003 was part of a massive restructuring necessitated by falling profits and a heavy debt load. Profit for the preceding fiscal year had dropped precipitously as airlines delayed or cancelled deliveries of new aircraft after 9/11. In addition, Bombardier carried a heavy debt load of U.S.$ 18 billion, some 80% of its capital, giving the company a credit rating just one notch above junk bond status. The restructuring substantially reduced the debt by issuing new shares, selling off Bombardier's recreational (Seadoo and Skidoo) operations, and halving the dividend.

On March 31, 2005 Bombardier posted another U.S. $85 million full-year loss, primarily due to the marketing of

its new C-Series passenger jet. At the urging of the DBRS bond rating service, subsequent dividends were suspended indefinitely, saving $160 million per year. Bombardier shares promptly fell 5% to $2.70 on the TSX, but later recovered to rise 17% on the year. The accompanying chart reflects the movement in the price of Bombardier's Class B shares in the context of its earnings and dividend history.

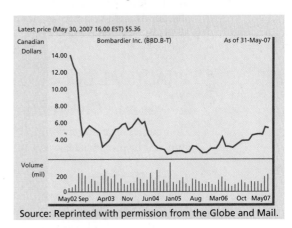

Source: Reprinted with permission from the Globe and Mail.

In response to the shareholders' comments on dividends above, Mr. Beaudoin said: "I cannot give an exact date, but I can say that if the current situation continues to improve, we could be able to restore dividends to the shareholders in the near future".

Sources: Sean Silcoff, "Bombardier Stock Flies High," *National Post*, May 30, 2007; "Bombardier Axes Dividend; CEO Tells Shareholders to 'Be Patient,'" CBC News, www.cbc.ca, March 31, 2005; Robert Barker, "Bombardier May Be Going Places," *Newsweek*, June 16, 2003.

The Expectations Theory

The **expectations theory** is a refinement of the signalling effect. It says that investors form expectations of what a company's next dividend will be and can become alarmed if those expectations aren't met, even if the dividend actually paid is steady or increasing.

For example, suppose a company whose dividend has been $2.00 per share achieves a substantial improvement in business, and people form the expectation that the next dividend should be $2.20. Then suppose the firm pays $2.10, an increase, but a smaller one than expected. The expectations theory says that investor reaction is likely to be negative because expectations weren't met, and that the shares' price may very well fall.

Conclusion

The conclusion is that we don't really have a conclusion. No one knows with certainty whether paying more or less in dividends generally increases or decreases share prices. Most practising financial professionals believe that dividends have a positive effect on prices. Scholars tend to say that notion can't really be proven.

As a practical matter, many large companies do pay dividends. Cash dividends from Canadian corporations tend to be much more stable than corporate earnings. When earnings declined drastically in 2001 and 2002, dividends were greater than earnings.

The Corporate Life Cycle and Dividend Policy

A firm's dividend policy is often influenced by its stage of corporate development. A small firm attempting to establish itself in its market may decide to pay no dividends because it needs all of its retained earnings for reinvestment in the business and has little or no access to capital markets.

As growth continues, the firm may want to defer dividends while it raises additional capital externally. As the firm matures, its ability to generate cash flows from its operations increases and its need for expansion funds may decline. In this situation, it may pay out significant cash dividends and, in fact, may face intense pressure to do so from the financial markets and its shareholders. For a case in point, see "The Maturing Giant?" on page 629.

PRACTICAL CONSIDERATIONS

Legal and Contractual Restrictions on Dividends

Companies aren't always entirely free to pay whatever dividends they want. Restrictions are imposed by provincial law and contractual agreements.

Legal Restrictions

The laws governing corporate dividend practices differ among the various regulatory agencies but two generalizations are possible.

First, dividends can't be paid out of capital; they must come from retained earnings. Second, a firm can't pay dividends if it is insolvent (meaning that its liabilities exceed its assets) or if the payment of dividends would make the company insolvent. These rules are designed to protect creditors. Otherwise an insolvent company facing bankruptcy proceedings could sell its assets and pay a dividend to shareholders with the cash received. This would eliminate access to the assets by the creditors at the last minute and leave the creditors with a loss that should be the shareholders'.

Contractual Restrictions

DEBT CONTRACTS Business loans and bond issues usually come with restrictions on the behaviour of the borrowing company that are designed to ensure repayment. Such contractual agreements are called *indentures* (for bonds) and *covenants* (for loans). The restrictions are generally aimed at conserving cash and maintaining prudent, conservative business practices. (See Chapter 9, page 331.)

It isn't uncommon for indentures and covenants to restrict or prohibit the payment of dividends on common shares under certain conditions. For example, a lender might stipulate that if EBIT falls below two times debt service (the sum of interest and principal payments) in any period, no cash dividends can be paid. This restriction would protect the interests of creditors by preventing cash from being siphoned off to shareholders when it looks like financial troubles might be approaching.

Loan indentures and covenants may limit dividend payments to protect creditors' interests.

PREFERRED SHARES Another common restriction on the payment of dividends on common shares is the cumulative feature of dividends on preferred shares. Recall that preferred shares pay a fixed dividend into the indefinite future, but that the payment isn't quite guaranteed. The *cumulative feature* generally specifies that if one or more preferred dividends are passed, no common share dividends can be paid until they're caught up cumulatively. (See Chapter 10, page 374.)

The cumulative feature of preferred shares limits dividend payments on common shares.

Dividend Policy

Dividend policy refers to the rationale under which a firm determines what it will pay in dividends. The term encompasses both the amount paid and the pattern under which changes in the amount occur over time.

Dividend policy is how a firm determines what to pay in dividends.

Before getting into different policies, we need two definitions. The **dividend payout ratio** is the ratio of the dividends paid to earnings. It can be thought of in total or in per-share terms.

*The **dividend payout ratio** states dividends as a fraction of earnings.*

$$(17.2) \qquad \text{Dividend payout ratio} = \frac{\text{Dividend}}{\text{Earnings}} = \frac{\text{Dividend per share}}{\text{EPS}}$$

For example, a payout ratio of 40% would mean that the firm pays a cash dividend of 40 cents out of every dollar it earns. The concept contains a subtlety that's worth pointing out. The dividend is paid in cash, but the earnings figure doesn't represent cash availability. That's because net income (earnings) includes accrual accounting entries for both income and cost. Hence, in any particular year, more or less cash may be available to pay dividends than is implied by earnings. More significantly, a firm with even a modest payout ratio may have trouble paying the appropriate dividend if it has other substantial cash needs. These might include capital expenditures and debt repayment.

Stability refers to the constancy of dividends over time. A **stable dividend** is constant in amount from period to period but is usually increased occasionally. A dividend with a *stable growth rate* increases by a more or less constant percentage over time.

*A **stable dividend** is nondecreasing.*

Recall that a decrease in dividends generally carries a bad signalling effect. Managements therefore try to keep dividends from ever going down. As a result, the term "stable" tends to imply a dividend that can go up or flatten out, but that doesn't decline.

Alternative Policies
Three dividend policies are common.

TARGET PAYOUT RATIO A firm following this policy selects a long-run payout ratio with which it's comfortable. However, it doesn't apply that ratio blindly each year. To do so would result in dividends that fluctuate up and down with earnings. From what we've learned about signalling, that would have a negative effect on the share's market price. The actual payout ratio is generally somewhat below the target to allow for variations in earnings without forcing a decrease in dividends.

Typical policies include a target payout ratio, a stable dividend, and year-end extras.

STABLE DIVIDEND PER SHARE A constant dividend is paid regardless of earnings unless business conditions deteriorate so badly that the firm's ability to continue paying comes into doubt. If things go well and the company grows, the dividend is raised from time to time. A stable dividend per share is by far the most common practice.

Insights **REAL APPLICATIONS**

Earnings and Dividends of Selected Canadian Corporations

The following table provides earnings and dividend per share information for selected Canadian corporations. Data have been adjusted for stock splits where applicable.

	2006	2005	2004	2003	2002	2001
Bank of Montreal						
Earnings per share	$ 5.25	$ 4.73	$ 4.53	$ 3.51	$ 2.73	$ 2.72
Dividends per share	$ 2.26	$ 1.85	$ 1.59	$ 1.34	$ 1.20	$ 1.12
Dividend payout ratio	43%	39%	35%	38%	44%	41%
BCE Inc						
Earnings per share	$ 2.25	$ 2.04	$ 1.65	$ 1.90	$ 2.66	$ 0.56
Dividends per share	$ 1.32	$ 1.32	$ 1.20	$ 1.20	$ 1.20	$ 1.20
Dividend payout ratio	59%	65%	73%	63%	45%	214%
Canadian Tire						
Earnings per share	$ 4.35	$ 4.04	$ 3.60	$ 3.06	$ 2.56	$ 2.25
Dividends per share	$ 0.66	$ 0.58	$ 0.50	$ 0.40	$ 0.40	$ 0.40
Dividend payout ratio	15%	14%	14%	13%	16%	18%
Danier Leather Inc.						
Earnings per share	−$ 0.84	−$ 0.03	−$ 1.03	$ 0.78	$ 1.57	$ 1.75
Dividends per share	$ 0.24	$ 0.24	$ 0.00	$ 0.00	$ 0.00	$ 0.00
Dividend payout ratio	N/A	N/A	0%	0%	0%	0%
Enbridge						
Earnings per share	$ 1.81	$ 1.65	$ 1.93	$ 2.02	$ 1.80	$ 1.46
Dividends per share	$ 1.15	$ 1.04	$ 0.92	$ 0.86	$ 0.76	$ 0.70
Dividend payout ratio	64%	63%	48%	43%	42%	48%
Magna International						
Earnings per share (US$)	$ 4.86	$ 5.99	$ 6.99	$ 5.23	$ 5.83	$ 6.55
Dividends per share (US$)	$ 1.52	$ 1.52	$ 1.48	$ 1.36	$ 1.36	$ 1.36
Dividend payout ratio	31%	25%	21%	26%	23%	21%
Manulife Financial						
Earnings per share	$ 2.53	$ 2.05	$ 1.83	$ 1.66	$ 1.45	$ 1.20
Dividends per share	$ 0.73	$ 0.58	$ 0.50	$ 0.39	$ 0.30	$ 0.25
Dividend payout ratio	29%	28%	27%	23%	21%	21%
Petro-Canada						
Earnings per share	$ 3.45	$ 3.45	$ 3.32	$ 3.15	$ 1.86	$ 1.60
Dividends per share	$ 0.40	$ 0.40	$ 0.30	$ 0.20	$ 0.20	$ 0.20
Dividend payout ratio	12%	12%	9%	6%	11%	13%
WestJet Airlines						
Earnings per share	$ 0.88	$ 0.19	−$ 0.14	$ 0.79	$ 0.70	$ 0.53
Dividends per share	$ 0.00	$ 0.00	$ 0.00	$ 0.00	$ 0.00	$ 0.00
Dividend payout ratio	0%	0%	0%	0%	0%	0%

The Bank of Montreal has maintained an uninterrupted dividend since 1829. It has stated that its dividend policy is to pay out 35–45% of earnings over time. *Canadian Tire* maintained a constant dividend of $0.40 per share for more than a decade, despite increased earnings. However, it increased its dividends beginning in 2004. Similarly *BCE* paid out a constant dividend of $1.20 per share for the four years ending in 2004, and increased it by 10% in 2005. BCE had not previously increased its dividend since 1995 due to heavy capital expenditures for new technology; in fact BCE reduced its dividend to $1.20 per share after it spun off Nortel in 2000. *Danier Leather* did not pay dividends until 2005, preferring to invest operating cash flows in expansion. In 2005 and 2006, it paid $0.24 per share, although it incurred losses. Dividends were suspended in 2007.

Enbridge's high payout ratio is comparable to that of a public utility. *Magna* has increased dividends per share even as earnings per share have declined, undoubtedly reflecting the personal preferences of its founder and controlling shareholder, Frank Stronach. *Manulife*'s dividend and payout ratio have increased with the growth in its earnings per share. *Petro-Canada*'s payout averaged 10.5% over the period. *WestJet* paid no dividends due to heavy capital commitments for aircraft and poor operating results in 2004 and 2005.

Sources: Yahoo! Finance Canada at http://ca.finance.yahoo.com; Globe Investor at http://www.globeinvestor.com.

SMALL REGULAR DIVIDEND WITH A YEAR-END EXTRA IF EARNINGS PERMIT With this policy, management more or less assures shareholders of the regular dividend, but maintains the ability to either pay or forego the year-end extra. In theory this gives the firm the ability to lower its dividend level without a negative informational effect. In other words, the firm attempts to defeat the signalling effect of a reduction by keeping shareholders from counting on the extra payment. Unfortunately, people get used to the extra payment very quickly.

Insights PRACTICAL FINANCE

A Compromise Dividend Policy

A recent survey of U.S. financial executives indicated that many firms appear to follow a compromise dividend policy based upon a few main goals:

1. Avoid reducing dividends per share.

2. Maintain a stable dividend or a target dividend payout ratio.

3. But take advantage of good investment opportunities, particularly in "growth" companies.

Less important factors included the personal taxes paid by shareholders and the flotation costs of issuing new shares as a financing alternative.

Source: A. Brav, J.R. Graham, C.R. Harvey, and R. Michaely, "Payout Policy in the 21st Century," *Journal of Financial Economics*, Vol. 77, Iss. 3, September 2005.

The Mechanics of Dividend Payments

In the work we've done so far, we've treated dividends as annual cash flows. In practice, however, virtually all companies make dividend payments quarterly.[5]

Key Dates

Every quarterly dividend has four key *dates* associated with it.

THE DECLARATION DATE The amount of each quarterly dividend is authorized by the firm's board of directors. A separate authorization occurs every quarter even if the firm's policy is to pay the same amount repeatedly. The date on which the board authorizes the dividend is called the declaration date.

THE DATE OF RECORD Shares are *registered securities*, meaning that a list is kept indicating the name of the *owner of record* of every share. When a share is sold, ownership is transferred on the record from the seller to the buyer.[6] When the board authorizes a dividend, it stipulates a date of record. The dividend is payable to owners of record as of the date of record.

THE PAYMENT DATE The board also stipulates the date on which the dividend cheque is to be mailed. This is the payment date.

For recent dividend declarations, go to the Canada Newswire website at http://www.newswire.ca. Select *Other Search Options, Search By:* and *News Releases—By Keyword.* In the Keyword box, type "declares dividend."

Dividends are authorized on the **declaration date** for owners as of the **date of record** and are sent on the **payment date**.

---

5 The annual figures people work with are generally the latest quarterly figure times four.
6 Most large companies use specialized firms called *transfer agents* to do this recordkeeping chore. See Chapter 9, page 327.

THE EX-DIVIDEND DATE When shares are sold, it can take a few days to update the ownership records, so a sale made shortly before the date of record might not be recognized for payment purposes. To allow for a paperwork lag, brokerage firms stop *reporting* share trading *for dividend purposes* two business days prior to the date of record. This cutoff is called the ex-dividend date.

The **ex-dividend date** is the date on which a share trades without a declared dividend that has yet to be paid. An investor who buys shares on or after this date does *not* receive the pending dividend.

Figure 17.1 is a graphic representation and some sample dates. The ex-dividend date is significant with respect to stock market activity. An investor who purchases the shares prior to the ex-dividend date receives the next dividend; one who purchases on or after that date does not. In the example, the shares trade without the dividend starting on the morning of May 10.

As ex-dividend dates pass, shares generally drop in price, reflecting the loss of the dividends to new purchasers. Interestingly, the drop tends to be 20% to 30% less than the full amount of the dividend. The difference is believed to be due to the fact that investors value the dividend *after taxes* rather than before.

Dividend Reinvestment Plans

Large companies offer automatic **dividend reinvestment plans (DRIPs)** to shareholders. The company keeps the dividends of participating shareholders and gives them additional shares instead.

Many large companies offer shareholders an optional dividend reinvestment plan (DRIP) under which the company keeps the dividends of participating shareholders and gives them additional shares instead.

For example, if a firm paid a $0.50 dividend and someone owned 100 shares, his or her dividend cheque would be for $50. In a DRIP, if the share was selling for $25 at the time, that person would receive two additional shares instead of the money.

Dividend reinvestment plan shares can come from either of two sources, depending on the nature of the plan. In one approach the undistributed dividends are pooled and used to buy existing shares on the open market. The shares are then distributed back to the participating shareholders. This kind of plan is just a service provided to shareholders and doesn't significantly benefit the company.

Go to the Stingy Investor at http://www.ndir.com/SI/DRPs/DRPs.shtml for a list of companies on the TSX offering DRIPs.

In the second kind of plan, the company issues new shares at a price that may be slightly below market. This approach has two benefits. Shareholders avoid the brokerage fees associated with buying outstanding shares, and it provides the company with a source of new equity capital that's free of flotation costs. Over 100 companies on the Toronto Stock exchange offer DRIPs, including the Bank of Montreal, BCE Inc, Enbridge, Imperial Oil, Magna International, and Thomson Corp.[7]

FIGURE 17.1
The Dividend Declaration and Payment Process

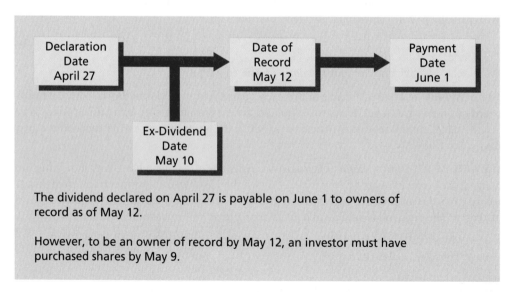

The dividend declared on April 27 is payable on June 1 to owners of record as of May 12.

However, to be an owner of record by May 12, an investor must have purchased shares by May 9.

---

7 Many companies that offer DRIPs also offer *share purchase plans (SPPs)* that allow shareholders to buy additional common shares for cash through the company.

TAX TREATMENT It's important to understand the tax treatment of reinvested dividends. In the reinvestment process, shareholders *effectively* receive cash and use it to buy more shares. The company just administers the transaction on their behalf. For this reason, the Canada Revenue Agency (CRA) treats the reinvested dividend as taxable income even though the shareholder never had the cash in hand.

Stock Splits and Stock Dividends

Companies sometimes revise the number of shares they have outstanding through stock splits and stock dividends. These transactions increase the count of shares in the hands of shareholders with no other real effect.

Stock Splits

A **stock split** issues new shares in numbers proportionate to those already outstanding. We'll illustrate the idea with a two-for-one split.

A firm with 100,000 shares outstanding executes a two-for-one split by issuing an additional share to all current shareholders for every share they already own. After the split there are 200,000 shares outstanding and all shareholders hold twice as many shares as they held before.

It's important to realize that, after a split, every shareholder has the same proportion of outstanding shares he or she had previously. Therefore, the split doesn't result in any change in ownership or control.

Because there are twice as many shares after the split representing ownership of the same company, each share is worth half as much as it was before. But because each shareholder owns twice as many shares, there's no change in anyone's wealth. In effect, a split doesn't do anything but change the arithmetic involved in keeping track of shares.

A split doesn't have to be two-for-one; it can be made in any proportion. For example, a 1.5-for-one split implies that shareholders get one new share for every two they already own. A 1.25-for-one split would give one new share for every four owned. In any case, the effect is the same: the proportionate ownership of the company is unchanged, as is the wealth of shareholders.

For a real-world example of stock splits, see "Stock Splits at Microsoft Corporation," on page 625.

Stock Dividends

A **stock dividend** is the payment to common shareholders of a dividend in the form of common shares. In the case of a 10% stock dividend, a shareholder with 100 shares would receive 10 additional shares. In the case of a 100% stock dividend, a shareholder with 100 shares would receive 100 additional shares.

For example, in 2004 the Bank of Nova Scotia declared a 100% stock dividend, with each outstanding common share being entitled to one additional common share. This action doubled the number of the bank's outstanding common shares (and effectively achieved a two-for-one split).[8]

Accounting Treatment of Stock Splits and Stock Dividends

A stock dividend is in reality just a small split. The two transactions are the same conceptually, and neither creates any real economic value. However, their respective accounting treatments differ substantially. Accounting for splits is very simple, while handling stock dividends is more complicated. We'll illustrate with an example after reviewing the standard shareholders' equity accounts.

Recall that the shareholders' equity section of the balance sheet is divided into the following two accounts.[9]

Stock splits and stock dividends issue new shares to *existing shareholders* in proportion to the number already held.

For recently announced stock splits go to the Canada Newswire site at http://www.newswire.ca. Select *Other Search Options, Search By* and *News Releases—By Keyword.* In the Keyword box, type "stock splits."

A **stock split** is a change in the number of shares outstanding by issuing new shares in proportion to those already owned.

Stock splits and stock dividends *don't change ownership* or control and have *no real value* to shareholders.

For recently announced stock dividends go to the Canada Newswire site at http://www.newswire.ca. Select *Other Search Options, Search By* and *News Releases—By Keyword.* In the Keyword box, type "stock dividends."

A **stock dividend** is essentially a stock split. It is the payment to common shareholders of a dividend in the form of common shares.

---

8 See http://www.scotiabank.com. Search for "stock splits."
9 For this purpose, we assume that there are no preferred shares outstanding.

- *Common shares* carries the value received for all outstanding shares.
- *Retained earnings* represent the sum of all past earnings that haven't been paid out in dividends.

The shareholders' equity of Eagle Inc. is presented in Table 17.1. The firm sold 2 million common shares at $4, and later earned $4 million, which was not distributed as dividends, but *retained* in the company.

TABLE 17.1
Eagle Inc. Shareholders' Equity

Common shares (2 million shares outstanding)	$ 8,000,000
Retained earnings	4,000,000
Total common equity	$ 12,000,000
Book value per share	$ 6.00

ACCOUNTING FOR A SPLIT The impact of a split on the shareholders' equity accounts is very simple. The number of shares is increased and the book value per share is reduced proportionately. If Eagle were to split two-for-one, the number of shares would double and book value per share would halve.[10] The result is illustrated in Table 17.2.

TABLE 17.2
Eagle Inc. Shareholders' Equity after a Two-for-One Stock Split

Common shares (4 million shares outstanding)	$ 8,000,000
Retained earnings	4,000,000
Total common equity	$ 12,000,000
Book value per share	$ 3.00

Notice that the dollar amounts in the three accounts are unchanged. The changes appear in the number of shares outstanding and the book value per share. Also notice that no reference needs to be made to the current market price of the share to account for a split.

A stock *split* simply changes *book value* and the *number of shares*. The capital accounts are unaffected.

ACCOUNTING FOR A STOCK DIVIDEND The common shares account has to be increased for the market value of the newly issued shares as though the new shares had been sold at a price equal to the market value of the shares just before the stock dividend. The balancing entry reduces retained earnings by the amount added to the common shares account.

We'll illustrate with a 10% stock dividend for Eagle Inc. that results in 200,000 new shares. Assume the shares are selling for $10 before the dividend.

The common shares account is increased by the market value of the new shares,

$$200,000 \times \$10 = \$2,000,000$$

At the same time, retained earnings are reduced by $2,000,000.

Because the addition to the common shares account is offset by the reduction to retained earnings, total shareholders' equity doesn't change. Book value per share does change, however, because of the additional shares. The result is shown in Table 17.3.

In a *stock dividend*, equity is moved from retained earnings into the common shares account to give the *appearance of a sale* at market price.

The entry recording a stock dividend is said to *capitalize* the market value of the new shares into the common shares account. It seems to be an attempt to reflect the creation of new market

TABLE 17.3
Eagle Inc. Shareholders' Equity after a 10% Stock Dividend

Common shares (2.2 million shares outstanding)	$10,000,000
Retained earnings	2,000,000
Total common equity	$12,000,000
Book value per share	$5.45

10 Earnings per share would also be reduced proportionately. If Eagle were to split two-for-one, earnings per share would halve.

value even though total shareholders' equity doesn't change. This is misleading, because no new economic value is created by a stock dividend.

Rationale for Stock Splits and Stock Dividends

Because stock splits and dividends don't seem to have any real economic meaning, it's fair to ask why companies do them. The reasons make some sense.

THE TRADING RANGE ARGUMENT FOR SPLITS Many financial professionals feel that a share loses its appeal to small investors if the price of a single share gets too high. For example, suppose a share of IBM sold for $20,000. Then no one could invest in the company unless they had at least that much money. Most small investors would be out of the market for IBM shares.

To keep the markets for their equity as broad as possible, companies split their shares from time to time to keep prices in a **trading range**. Most people feel this is somewhere between $10 and $50.

It can be argued that keeping the market for a share broad in this manner puts an upward pressure on price, because it maximizes the number of potential buyers. Whether or not that's true is debatable. Nevertheless, virtually all companies use splits to keep prices in trading ranges. Check the listings in *The Globe and Mail's Report on Business;* you'll find very few issues trading at prices over $100.

Splits keep share prices in a **trading range**, which is a price range in which shares are thought to appeal to the widest variety of investors.

Insights REAL APPLICATIONS

Stock Splits at Microsoft Corporation

Several statistical studies indicate that there is no free lunch, and that share prices do drop somewhat proportionately with stock splits and stock dividends. Let's look at the history of stock splits at Microsoft Corporation (Microsoft).

On February 18, 2003, Microsoft common shares closed at $24.63 (all financial data in US$) per share.

On March 13, 1986, you might have bought 100 common shares of Microsoft at a market price of $29.00 per share. Your cost then would have been $2,900 plus broker's commissions.

Microsoft shares split nine times from 1987 to 2003 (see the table below). A major motivation for Microsoft to split its shares would be to keep board lots[11] of its shares "affordable" for investors.

Your original 100 shares would have become 28,800 shares, worth $709,344! (Keep in mind that the share price increases were due primarily to huge revenue and earnings growth during the technology sector boom before 2000, and that the share splits were the result, not the cause of these price increases.)

Of course, you would have had to hold on to those shares through some periods of severe "volatility" in the share price, particularly after the technology bubble burst in 2000, but your patience would still have been handsomely rewarded with a 38% average annual gain in the value of your shares! (For an update on changes in Microsoft's share structure and price, see "The Maturing Giant?" on page 629)

Date of Stock Split	Amount	Number of Shares	Share Price Before Split	Share Price After Split	Value After Split
18/2/03	2 for 1	28,800	$ 48.30	$ 24.63	$ 709,344
29/3/99	2 for 1	14,400	178.13	92.69	1,334,736
23/2/98	2 for 1	7,200	155.13	84.75	610,200
9/12/96	2 for 1	3,600	152.88	80.00	288,000
23/5/94	2 for 1	1,800	97.75	52.38	94,284
15/6/92	3 for 2	900	112.50	73.50	66,150
27/6/91	3 for 2	600	102.25	68.12	40,872
16/4/90	2 for 1	400	120.75	59.25	23,700
21/9/87	2 for 1	200	115.00	62.00	12,400
13/3/86	Purchase	100	29.00		2,900

Source: Yahoo! Finance Canada at http://ca.finance.yahoo.com.

11 A *board lot* is a standard number of shares used when trading. The size of the board lot (100, 500, or 1,000) depends on the price of the shares.

Stock dividends are an attempt at signalling.

For historical information on the effect of stock splits on share prices for other companies, go to Yahoo! Finance at http://ca.finance. yahoo.com/l. Input the corporate name and click *Historical Prices*.

For recently announced share repurchases go to the Canada Newswire site at http://www. newswire.ca. Select *Other Search Options, Search By* and *News Releases—By Keyword.* In the Keyword box, type "repurchases."

Repurchasing shares is an alternative to paying a dividend.

GIVING SOMETHING THAT DOESN'T COST ANYTHING Stock dividends tend to be used as signalling devices. They're often employed when companies want to send a positive message, but for some reason can't give as large a cash dividend as they'd like.

For example, a firm might give a stock dividend in addition to its regular cash dividend if things are going exceptionally well but it needs to conserve cash for investment in projects. Conversely, a stock dividend might be offered if things are going poorly, and no money is available for cash dividends, but management wants to make a positive statement by giving shareholders something. The value of such practices is clearly questionable.

The Effect on Price and Value

Splits and stock dividends increase shares outstanding without changing the economic value of the underlying company. It's generally accepted by scholars and most professionals that the transactions result in proportionate drops in market price, so shareholders see no real financial gain.

However, there's an underlying sentiment among some investors that something is gained with a split or a stock dividend. This probably comes from the fact that the transactions, especially splits, usually come along when prices are rising. Hence the split or dividend takes on a positive information effect through a general association with rising prices.

A Potential Point of Confusion

It's important not to confuse a stock dividend with the dividend reinvestment plans we talked about in the last section. In a dividend reinvestment, shareholders are actually purchasing additional shares and, because everyone doesn't participate, the proportional ownership of the company changes.

SHARE REPURCHASES

From time to time companies buy up their own shares. There are several reasons for doing this, but the most important is that it's an effective substitute for a dividend.

Repurchase as an Alternative to a Dividend

A firm with the cash in hand to pay a dividend can use the money to buy back and retire some of its own shares instead. Doing that reduces the number of shares outstanding, thereby increasing the EPS of the remaining shares. If the market attaches the same price/earnings (P/E) ratio to the shares after the repurchase that it did before, the remaining shares will go up in price. As a result, the remaining shareholders will see an appreciation in the value of their shares in lieu of a cash dividend. A numerical illustration will make the idea clear.

Suppose the Johnson Company has after-tax earnings of $5 million and 2,500,000 common shares outstanding. Also suppose the shares trade at a P/E ratio of 10. Then EPS and market price are as follows.

$$EPS = \frac{NI}{Number\ of\ shares} = \frac{\$5,000,000}{2,500,000} = \$2.00\ per\ share$$

$$Market\ price = EPS \times P/E = \$2.00 \times 10 = \$20$$

Now suppose Johnson has $1 million that it can distribute in dividends. If it does so, the dividend per share will be

$$Dividend = \frac{\$1,000,000}{2,500,000} = \$0.40\ per\ share$$

However, suppose the company uses the $1 million to buy its own shares instead of paying a dividend. Then it can purchase and retire

$$\frac{\$1,000,000}{\$20} = 50,000 \text{ shares}$$

After the repurchase, there will be

$$2,500,000 - 50,000 = 2,450,000 \text{ shares left outstanding}$$

If earnings don't change, EPS will then be

$$\text{EPS} = \frac{\$5,000,000}{2,450,000} = \$2.04 \text{ per share}$$

Finally, if the P/E ratio remains the same, the market price of the remaining shares will be

$$\text{Market price} = \text{EPS} \times \text{P/E} = \$2.04 \times 10 = \$20.40$$

Under these assumptions, buying back the shares results in a price appreciation in the remaining shares just equal to the dividend. The company has spent the available cash and shareholders have received value, but no dividend was paid.

Notice that the repurchase substitutes a potential capital gain for current cash income. Therefore, to spend the value they've received, shareholders would have to sell some of their shares.

Methods of Repurchasing Shares

Shares can be repurchased in three ways. The first and simplest method is to buy the shares on the open market.[12] However, this can be difficult to do quickly and without affecting the market price if a large number of shares are to be acquired.

The second method is to make a **tender offer** to buy shares at a set price from any shareholders interested in selling.[13] In this approach, shareholders are invited to "tender" their shares for purchase at the proposed price, which is generally somewhat above the current market price. If too many shares are tendered, the firm buys a pro rata portion of all those offered.

In the third method, the firm makes a negotiated deal with a large investor that holds a big block of shares. Such investors are frequently institutions such as mutual funds, pension funds, or insurance companies. This approach can involve some risk, because the price negotiated with a large and powerful investor will generally be above the shares' market price. In essence the firm is buying one shareholder's shares at a *premium* with money belonging to all shareholders. It's easy to interpret this as unfair to those who aren't being bought out. Remaining shareholders have been known to sue management over the issue.

> A **tender offer** is an offer to shareholders to purchase shares at a specified price, usually for the purpose of acquiring a company.

Other Repurchase Issues

The Opportunistic Repurchase

If a company's shares are undervalued,[14] repurchasing shares can be beneficial to the remaining shareholders. This can happen if the market takes a sudden downturn that's expected to be temporary. Let's consider an example.

Suppose Catatonic Inc. has 100,000 shares outstanding that sell at their book value of $10. This means that the market sees the firm as worth $1 million, the book value of its equity. Also suppose the firm has $100,000 in available cash. Then imagine that the stock market loses 30% of its value, and Catatonic shares fall to $7.00.

Assume management believes that the market will recover within a reasonable period and the firm's shares will again sell at book value. The company therefore uses its cash of $100,000 to repurchase shares. At $7 per share it acquires

> Repurchases are appropriate when a share is *temporarily undervalued* or the firm has *excess cash*.

---

12 In Canada, these are called *normal course issuer bids.*
13 This is called a *substantial issuer bid.*
14 A security is said to be undervalued if it is selling in a financial market for less than its true worth. Clearly, this reflects a difference of opinion about that true worth.

$$\frac{\$100,000}{\$7.00} = 14{,}286 \text{ shares}$$

This leaves $(100{,}000 - 14{,}286\ 5)\ 85{,}714$ shares outstanding.

Later, the market recovers and again values the firm at book equity, which is now $900,000 because $100,000 was spent on repurchasing shares. Each share will then have a market value of

$$\frac{\$900,000}{\$85,714} = \$10.50$$

This amount is $0.50 more than the value of a share before the market downturn. Management earned the extra value for the remaining shareholders by taking advantage of the temporary drop in market price. Of course, it was earned at the expense of shareholders who sold at $7.

The situation described in the illustration is exactly what happened during the stock market decline of 2002. The market lost approximately 30% of its value in a few weeks, and then stabilized. Many corporations recognized the situation as a buying opportunity and rushed to repurchase shares. That turned out to be the right thing to do at the time, because the market subsequently recovered. Unfortunately, it's not easy to determine when a share is temporarily undervalued.[15]

Repurchases to Dispose of Excess Cash

A period of high earnings that isn't expected to be repeated can leave the company with a one-time sum of money. If there aren't sufficient capital investment opportunities available to use up the funds, they should be distributed to shareholders.

Excess cash can be distributed by paying a one-time dividend. However, such a payment can create problems because of the signalling effect. As we have seen earlier in this chapter (page 617), managers are reluctant to increase and then decrease dividends, because they anticipate a negative information impact from the decrease that more than offsets the positive effect of the extra money paid.

A share repurchase can be a solution to the dilemma. It effectively distributes the money to the shareholders, but tends not to generate expectations of future distributions the way a dividend might.

Repurchases to Restructure Capital

It should be clear from our work in Chapter 16 that restructuring capital in the direction of debt involves repurchasing equity. Indeed, capital restructuring is a major reason for repurchases. In a transaction to restructure toward debt, the firm simply borrows money and uses the proceeds of the loan to buy back its shares.

Other Motives for Repurchases

Stock options are an important part of the compensation package of corporate management. When managers exercise their stock options, earnings and ownership are diluted. Companies may repurchase shares to offset the exercise of the options.

Repurchases may be used as a defense against unfriendly takeovers, by reducing the number of publicly traded shares on the market and increasing the control of senior management and major shareholders.

Taxes

Corporations may decide to distribute cash to their shareholders through a share repurchase rather than a dividend to secure tax advantages for the shareholders. A dividend is taxable to the

---

15 This example is presented just to illustrate the effect of buying undervalued shares. The market doesn't price companies on the basis of their book values.

individual shareholders on receipt, and they have no choice about whether or not to receive the dividend. In a share repurchase, there is no tax effect on the shareholders until they sell their shares. For those who do sell, the *gain* on the sale and not the sale proceeds is taxed as a capital gain.

Insights REAL APPLICATIONS

The Maturing Giant?

On July 20, 2006, Microsoft Corporation (Microsoft) announced that it planned to spend up to $40 billion (all financial data in US$) to repurchase its shares, a sum that would pay for 17% of its outstanding shares at the then current share price ($22.85). The repurchase plan involved two initiatives; a tender offer for up to $20 billion worth of shares, expiring in one month, and a five-year share repurchase program expiring in 2011.

The company could well afford the buyback, producing $35 million in operating cash flow every *day*, (90% from its Windows® and Office® software) and sitting on almost $35 billion of cash at that time. In addition, its balance sheet was debt-free.

For years, Microsoft had been under mounting pressure to put its cash to work on new products and acquisitions, or to return the cash to its shareholders. Many Wall Street money managers, as well as institutional investors such as pension funds and mutual funds, had called for a major share buyback as "financial engineering" to increase earnings per share and dividends.

They had unhappily watched the share price stagnate for some five years, as the growth rates in revenue and earnings slowed. The price hit a four-year low of $21.46 in June 2006, following the company's announcement that its consumer launch of Vista®, its first upgrade to Windows® since 2000, would be delayed once again to early 2007.

In fact the company had already returned $87 billion to its shareholders between 2001 and 2006 through dividends and a previous buyback of $30 billion in 2004.

Microsoft Chief Executive Steve Ballmer had initially resisted another buyback, wanting to retain the cash in order to expand the company's product line, make further acquisitions, and overhaul its online unit to better compete with Google, Yahoo, and other Internet-based competitors.

At the heart of the buyback debate were two questions:

1. Was Microsoft still a growth company that needed ready cash for expansion?

2. Or, were its growth days in the past, (see "Stock Splits at Microsoft Corporation," page 625), and was Microsoft now a utility that should be paying out as much cash from its operations as possible?

Increasingly, the financial markets were of this latter view. Microsoft decided to appease its investors and buy back its shares, rather than focus primarily on expansion. On May 29, 2007, Microsoft common shares closed at $30.79 per share.

Sources: Carmen Fleetwood, "Microsoft Rally Likely to Last," *National Post*, November 3, 2006, p. FP9; Simon Avery, "Microsoft Unveils Major Share Buyback," *The Globe and Mail Report on Business*, July 21, 2006, p. B9; Jason Kirby, "Awakening Microsoft," *National Post*, June 19, 2006, p. FP1; Yahoo! Finance Canada at http://ca.finance.yahoo.com.

REVERSE STOCK SPLITS

Another method used to reduce the number of shares outstanding is the **reverse stock split**, in which a company issues one new share for a certain number of old shares. Once the process is complete, the share price is higher and the number of shares in issue is lower. A company might, for example, call in all of its shares and reissue one new share for every two owned. This would halve the number of shares outstanding and generally double the price.

A **reverse stock split** is a method used to reduce the number of shares outstanding. A company issues one new share for a certain number of old shares.

For example, assume a shareholder has 100 shares of ABC at $10 a share. After a 2:1 reverse split, the shareholder would have 50 shares at $20 a share. There is no change in the equity amount for either the corporation or its shareholders.

Reverse stock splits are usually due to a significant decline in the share's price. To avoid the embarrassment of a once proud share becoming a "penny" stock, and the perception that the business is failing, the reverse split provides an inexpensive means for the company to increase the share price by decreasing the number of shares outstanding. A share *repurchase* or "buyback," on the other hand, would require substantial cash expenditure by the company.

Additional pressures to raise share prices involve the eligibility requirements for inclusion in stock market indices, or for purchase by pension and mutual funds. Eligibility in many

http

For recently an-
nounced reverse
stock splits, go to the
Canada Newswire
site at http://www.
newswire.ca.
Select *Other Search
Options, Search By:*
and *News Releases—
By Keyword*. In the
Keyword box, type
"reverse stock splits."

From the CFO

indexes, such as the S&P/TSX Composite Index, requires that a company's share price be above a certain level. Mutual funds often use the constituents of a particular index as the pool from which they select investments. A share that drops out of the index, therefore, drops out of sight of such institutional investors. As well, some pension funds and mutual funds adhere to guidelines that do not permit them to invest in shares that trade below a certain floor level, perhaps $1, $5, or even $10. When company share prices drop dramatically, they risk being dropped from indices and automatically overlooked by mutual funds. Finally, most stock exchanges have minimum share price requirements to maintain a listing on their exchange.

Some analysts and institutional investors have a negative view of reverse stock splits, considering them a last-ditch attempt to boost a share's price. Such an action suggests to them that the company management does not believe that they can boost the share price through growth. Many reverse splits have not worked, in the sense that the share price did not rise proportionately.

Insights REAL APPLICATIONS

A Reverse Stock Split for Nortel Networks Corporation

On December 1, 2006, Nortel Networks Corporation (Nortel) implemented a reverse stock split in a consolidation ratio of 1-for-10. Upon completion of the consolidation, Nortel closed at $24.21.

Closing at $2.44 on the previous day, Nortel shares were down a staggering 98% from their 2000 peak of $124.50. In the U.S., Nortel had been dropped from the S&P 500 Index, and its listing on the New York Stock Exchange was threatened.

Nortel had stated that it was taking this action for three reasons:

1. to return the company's share price to a level that is typical of other major widely owned public companies

2. to better position the company to comply with the New York Stock Exchange's minimum stock price conditions in order that the common shares of the company would not be delisted from that exchange

3. to meet investing guidelines for certain institutional investors and investment funds that were then prevented under their investing guidelines from investing in the company's common shares at the then depressed price level

Subsequently, Nortel shares closed at a high of $37.24 in February 2007, but were selling below $16.00 in December of that year.

Sources: http://www.nortelnetworks.com. Click *Investor Relations*; Yahoo! Finance Canada at http://ca.finance.yahoo.com.

SUMMARY

1 An individual buys shares because he or she expects an acceptable return from dividends and from the receipts when the shares eventually are sold. Today's price is the present value of those future cash flows discounted at the appropriate rate for an equity investment in the company.

2 The dividend decision for a company is whether to pay cash dividends now or retain earnings for growth, both of which

benefit shareholders. Retaining earnings involves investing the money in business projects that are expected to enhance profitability. Those higher profits cause the share price to increase.

3 The dividend irrelevance theory argues that shareholders should be indifferent to the payment of dividends in any period, because dividends eliminated currently will be offset by additional dividends and/or capital gains in the future. If investors prefer current income, they can sell some of their shares. The portion of the holding that isn't sold appreciates because of the retention of additional earnings. However, transaction costs and differing tax treatments make tailoring an income stream impractical.

4 Paying dividends reduces retained earnings, which are a source of funds for capital budgeting projects. Firms prefer not to pay dividends to avoid the flotation costs of selling new shares.

5 Under dividend preference theory, investors prefer immediate cash to uncertain future benefits. The dividend aversion theory asserts that investors generally prefer that companies not pay dividends in order to enhance share prices later on. Investors prefer future capital gains to current dividends because of lower taxes on capital gains.

According to the clientele argument, individual investors have definite dividend preferences because of their need for more or less current income, so any change in payments is to be avoided. Dividends may be viewed as a way for management to send a message to shareholders about its confidence in the future. According to expectations theory, dividends that fail to fulfill shareholders' expectations send a negative message even if the payment is good.

6 A firm's dividend policy is often influenced by its stage of corporate development. A young, small firm may decide to pay no dividends because it needs all of its retained earnings for reinvestment in the business and has little or no access to capital markets. As the firm matures it may pay out significant cash dividends and, in fact, may face intense pressure to do so from the financial markets and its shareholders.

7 Dividends can't be paid by an insolvent firm and must come from current or prior earnings. Loan indentures and covenants may limit dividend payments to protect creditors' interests. The cumulative feature of preferred shares limits dividend payments on common shares.

8 Dividend policy refers to how a firm determines what it will pay in dividends, including both the amount paid and the changes over time. Typical policies include a target payout ratio, a stable dividend, and year-end extras if earnings permit.

9 Dividends are authorized on the declaration date for owners as of the date of record and are sent on the payment date. Companies make dividend payments quarterly.

10 In a dividend reinvestment plan, the company keeps the dividends of participating shareholders and gives them additional shares instead.

11 A stock split is a change in the number of shares outstanding by issuing new shares in proportion to those already owned. A stock dividend is the payment to common shareholders of a dividend in the form of common shares. Neither change ownership or control nor have no real value to shareholders.

Stock splits keep share prices in a trading range to appeal to the widest variety of investors. Stock dividends are used as signalling devices to send a positive message, without paying a cash dividend.

Instead of paying a cash dividend, companies may repurchase and cancel their own shares. The effect is to increase the EPS and market price of the remaining shares. This may also be done when the company has excess cash, when it wants to restructure its capital for more debt and less equity, as a defense against unfriendly takeovers, or to secure tax advantages for its shareholders.

In a reverse stock split, a company issues one new share for a certain number of old shares. Once the process is complete, the share price is higher and the number of shares in issue is lower. No cash payments are required.

KEY TERMS

Clientele effect, p. 616
Date of record, p. 621
Declaration date, p. 621
Dividend aversion theory, p. 615
Dividend decision, p. 612
Dividend irrelevance theory, p. 613
Dividend payout ratio, p. 619

Dividend policy, p. 619
Dividend preference theory, p. 615
Dividend reinvestment plan (DRIP), p. 622
Ex-dividend date, p. 622
Expectations theory, p. 618
Payment date, p. 621
Residual dividend theory, p. 616

Reverse stock split, p. 629
Signalling effect, p. 616
Stable dividend, p. 619
Stock dividend, p. 623
Stock split, p. 623
Tender offer, p. 627
Trading range, p. 625
Transaction costs, p. 614

KEY FORMULAS

(17.1) $\text{Price of a share} = P_0 = \dfrac{D_1}{(1+k)} + \dfrac{D_2}{(1+k)^2} + \dots + \dfrac{D_n}{(1+k)^n} + \dfrac{P_n}{(1+k)^n}$

(17.2) $\text{Dividend payout ratio} = \dfrac{\text{Dividend}}{\text{Earnings}} = \dfrac{\text{Dividend per share}}{\text{EPS}}$

QUESTIONS

1. Dividends are said to be the basis for the value of shares. If that's true, how do we explain the fact that companies (such as Bombardier, Inc.) that pay no dividends often have substantial market value? (Such companies are usually relatively young and in high-growth fields.) First explain the phenomenon in terms of the individual valuation model (a stream of dividends followed by a selling price, Equation 17.1). Then reconcile the idea with the whole market model (an infinite stream of dividends). Can you explain cases in which managements claim that their companies will never pay dividends? (*Hint:* Does such a claim make sense?)

2. Given the importance of dividends to the well-being of equity investors, why do they put up with the fact that dividends are discretionary?

3. Fully explain the choices implied by the dividend decision. Are the results of the choices known or uncertain?

4. There is said to be a controversy over dividends. What is it and why is it important?

5. Canadian Tire paid the same annual dividend ($0.40 per share) from 1992 until 2003. Its earnings per share increased from $0.96 in 1992 to $3.06 in 2003. Comment on the possible reasons for this pattern.

6. You're a financial analyst for a large mutual fund. You're doing an analysis of the Truebright Apparel Company, which makes stylish cotton clothes for teenagers. The company has recently been under attack by foreign competition and seems to have lost its edge in the fashion market. EPS fell from $2.00 to $1.80 to $1.20 over the past three years. Dividends were held steady at $1.00 per share in spite of the declining earnings for two

years. Last year the dividend was raised to $1.50. Why do you think the dividend was maintained and then raised? How would this affect your recommendation?

Business Analysis

1. You're the treasurer of SuperTech Inc., a high-technology firm in the fast-growing computer business. The management team has recently been trying to decide on a long-term dividend policy. Earnings are good, but the firm has far more investment opportunities than income.

   There's no doubt that the company will need to sell more equity in the near future to fund its growth. Therefore management wants to do everything possible to maximize share price, including making the right dividend decision.

   This morning the chief engineer, Susan Stein, came into the meeting and professed to have the answer to the firm's problems. She said she's been taking a finance course at night, and that her instructor assured her that dividends don't matter to share price. According to Susan, that's because investors are perfectly capable of tailoring their own income stream from any investment. Therefore, she suggests not paying any dividends and using the money for projects.

   How would you respond to Susan's suggestion? Do you think she's missed part of her instructor's message? Is it possible that her suggestion is right, but for the wrong reason? What would you recommend that SuperTech do?

2. The Tanglefern Corporation has traditionally paid out 60% of its earnings in dividends. Recently some marvellous growth opportunities have arisen that involve only a little risk but require a lot of cash. Most of the executive team thinks the firm should do two things to raise the cash needed to take advantage of the opportunities. They want to (1) sell more shares and (2) suspend dividend payments for two to three years. The dividend suspension would be accompanied by an explanation to shareholders of what was going on. You're the company's CFO. Prepare a response to the others' suggestion. Do the two proposed actions taken together create a particular problem?

3. You're a bank officer considering making a loan to a small family-owned company. The firm's principal owner is a hard-working, conservative woman who has built up the company over a number of years. However, two of her grown children are now active in the company's management. They're both bright and hard working, but have a reputation for taking business risks as well as for extravagant living. You'd like to make the loan, but are concerned about a potential change in the character of the company. How might you make the loan and still protect your bank's investment?

4. Your pal, Fred Blinder, came into class this morning grinning from ear to ear. It seems a share in which he advised his parents to invest is doing fabulously well. Fred said the firm usually pays a dividend of $2.00 a share, which is about 4% of its recent $50 market price. Yesterday, however, his folks got a letter that said the cash dividend was being passed, but instead the firm was issuing a stock dividend of one share for every 10 owned. Fred calculates that's worth the equivalent of $5 a share, two and a half times the normal cash dividend! Fred has told you all this knowing you're taking finance. He's asked you what you think, obviously expecting praise and approval. What would you say to Fred?

5. Blazingame Mill Works recently sold a tract of land it had owned for 30 years. All expenses and taxes have been paid, and the company has $10 million sitting in the bank as a result of the sale. As there aren't any pressing investment opportunities available, the board would like to distribute the money to shareholders. Most of the board members are high-income individuals and major shareholders themselves. Discuss the company's options for disposing of the money.

PROBLEMS

1. Richard Inouye just bought 1,000 shares of Sisson Electronics at $40 per share. He plans to hold the shares for one year before selling. Sisson is in the process of selecting a new dividend policy. The firm will either pay out all of its earnings in dividends or retain and reinvest them all. Analysts expect the shares to be worth $45 in one year's time if no dividends are paid and $40 if dividends of $5 per share are distributed. How much difference will Sisson's decision make in Richard's after-tax income assuming that he is in the third tax bracket? (See the discussion of tax on investment income, page 41.)

2. The Argo Pamphlet Company's dividend payout ratio is 35%. It is currently paying an annual dividend of $1.30.
   a. What is Argo's EPS?
   b. What is the market price of Argo's shares if its P/E ratio is 14?
   c. How much current income per share will shareholders lose if Argo cuts its payout ratio to 20% and nothing else changes?
   d. If the change in payout ratio does not affect the share price, approximately how many shares would a shareholder who owns 1,000 shares have to sell to make up her loss in current income? Ignore tax effects and transaction costs.

3. Randal Flapjack is a retired short-order cook living on a fixed income in the country of Utopia where all financial markets are perfectly efficient. Randal has 20,000 shares of the Suzette Corp., which pays an annualized dividend of $1.00 per share. Suzette sells at a P/E of 10, has maintained a payout ratio of 50% for many years, and has not grown in some time. Management has recently announced that it will reduce Suzette's payout ratio to 25% but expects earnings to grow at 5% from now on.
   a. What is Suzette's current share price?
   b. How much current income is Randal losing as a result of management's action?
   c. If Randal keeps his money in Suzette shares but needs to maintain his current income, how many shares will he have to sell in the first year?
   d. What will be the value of his remaining shares at the end of a year if the P/E remains the same? Is his investment still growing? Why?

4. Biltmore Industries has grown at an average of 6% per year over its long history. Its share price is currently $40.00, and its most recent dividend was $2.50. Biltmore just announced that it plans to discontinue dividends for several years to take advantage of some growth opportunities. Analysts expect the share price to increase by 10% per year for at least the next two years because of this growth.

   Aldo Bartolo owns 4,000 shares of Biltmore and has counted on his dividend payments to supplement his retirement income. Now it appears that he will have to start selling off his Biltmore shares to replace this lost income. How many shares will Aldo have to sell in each of the next two years to replace his lost dividend income? Ignore taxes and transaction costs.

5. The Holderall Rope and Yarn Co. has 2 million common shares outstanding. Its capital structure is two-thirds equity. The firm expects earnings of $10 million next year and anticipates capital spending of $12 million on projects. Assume that the projects will be funded with money raised in the debt/equity proportions of the existing capital structure. If the firm adheres to a residual dividend policy, how much will the dividend per share be next year?

6. The Montreal Company has a dividend reinvestment plan in which shareholders owning 25% of its common shares participate. Last year the firm's EPS was $4.20, and its payout ratio was 50%. There are 2 million common shares outstanding. How much new capital did Montreal raise through the reinvestment program?

7. Segwick Petroleum Ltd. has a dividend reinvestment plan in which new shares are issued to participating investors. Segwick's payout ratio is 40%, and 30% of the shareholders participate in the plan. The firm's return on equity is 10%. What percentage increase in equity capital does the plan provide?

8. Harrison Hardware anticipates $2 million in net income next year and a 20% participation in the firm's dividend reinvestment plan. Management expects to spend $2.375 million on new capital projects, and maintain the current capital structure (which is 64% equity) without issuing new shares. What dividend payout ratio has Harrison included in its plan for next year?

9. You own 1,000 shares of Jennings Corp., which are currently selling for $88. Calculate the number of shares you would own and the market price of the shares after each of the following stock splits.
   a. A two-for-one stock split
   b. A three-for-one stock split
   c. A three-for-two stock split
   d. A three-for-four reverse stock split
   e. A five-for-three stock split

10. The Addington Book Company has the following equity position. The shares are currently selling for $3.

Common shares (8 million shares outstanding)	$ 20,000,000
Retained earnings	12,000,000
Total common equity	$ 32,000,000
Book value per share	$ 4.00

   a. What was the average price at which the company originally sold its shares?
   b. Reconstruct the shareholders' equity statement above to reflect a four-for-one stock split.
   c. Reconstruct the statement to reflect a 12.5% stock dividend.

11. Seinway Corp. just declared a 10% stock dividend. Before the dividend the shares sold for $34 and the shareholders' equity section of the firm's balance sheet was as follows:

Common shares (10,000,000 shares)	$ 61,000,000
Retained earnings	87,500,000
Total	$ 148,500,000

   Restate the shareholders' equity accounts and estimate the share price after the dividend.

12. Wysoski Enterprises is considering a stock dividend. The firm's capital includes 3 million shares issued at an average price of $8. Retained earnings total $20 million. State the

shareholders' equity accounts now and after each of the following possible stock dividends.

    a. Wysoski declared a 5% stock dividend, and the current price per share is $15.

    b. Wysoski declared a 10% stock dividend, and the current price per share is $20.

    c. Wysoski declared a 15% stock dividend, and the current price per share is $23.

13. The Alligator Lock Company is planning a two-for-one stock split. You own 5,000 common shares of Alligator, which are currently selling for $120 a share.

    a. What is the total value of your Alligator investment now, and what will it be after the split?

    b. Alligator's CFO says that the value of the shares will decline less than proportionately with the split because the stock is now out of its trading range. If the decline is 45%, how much will the split make you?

14. The Featherstone Corp. has $8 million in cash for its next dividend but is considering a share repurchase instead. Featherstone has 10 million shares outstanding, currently selling at $40 per share. The P/E is 20 on EPS of $2.

    a. If the dividend is paid, how large will it be per share?

    b. If shares are repurchased, how many shares will remain outstanding and what will the new EPS be?

    c. If the P/E holds at 20, what will the new share price be and how much per share will continuing shareholders have gained? How does that compare with the dividend that could have been paid?

    d. Are there other considerations? (Explain in words only.)

15. Parnell Bolts Inc. has 20 million common shares outstanding and net income of $30 million. The shares sell at a P/E of 15. The company has $5 million available to pay the next quarterly dividend, but is considering a share repurchase instead.

    a. If Parnell pays the cash dividend, what will be its dividend yield on an annualized basis?

    b. How many shares are redeemed if the repurchase option is chosen and the shares are acquired at market value?

    c. What will be the EPS after the repurchase if earnings remain unchanged?

    d. What will be the new share price if the P/E remains unchanged?

16. Tydek Inc. just lost a major lawsuit and its share price dropped by 40% to $6. There are 3.5 million shares outstanding with a book value per share of $10. The company has $5 million in cash readily available. The CFO feels that the decline in price is temporary and the firm's shares are an excellent investment at this time. If Tydek spends the entire $5 million repurchasing its own shares and the market to book value ratio returns to its former level, how much more will each remaining share be worth than it was before the temporary price decline?

17. The stock market is generally depressed, and the price of Westin Metals Inc.'s common shares has been below its historic average value for some time. The shares are trading at $35 which represents a P/E of 19 on earnings of $7,000,000. Before the current slump, Westin generally maintained a P/E of at least 24. Despite the general downturn, the firm is doing well, and the CFO is considering a share repurchase to enhance the position of shareholders who retain their shares when the market recovers. She has identified a piece of real estate the company owns but isn't using, which was purchased 20 years ago for $2,000,000 and can be sold for $9,000,000 today. Using the proceeds of such a sale would

make it possible to do the repurchase without impacting dividends or the capital budget. The CFO has asked you to quantify the effect of her plan on share price, and make a recommendation as to whether she should present it to the Board of Directors. Assume it takes two years for the market to recover and that Westin's P/E returns to 24 at that time. Also assume earnings grow at 5% per year until then and the company's marginal tax rate is 37%. Round number of shares calculations to the nearest whole share. Round earnings per share calculations to the nearest cent.

PART 6

Current Topics

NEL

Chapter 18

Derivative Securities

Learning Objectives

1 Describe what an option is and why it is called a derivative security.

2 Describe the basic features of call and put options.

3 Discuss why an investor might want to buy or sell options.

4 Calculate the intrinsic value of put and call options.

5 Explain how and where options are traded.

6 Discuss the differences between investor-created options and company-created options.

7 Explain how warrants and convertibles are related to options.

In Chapter 14, we introduced the concept of real options, that is, the ability or right to take a certain course or action. Although we discuss the use of options in managing financial resources, many individuals use options on a daily basis. For example, charities often sell books of coupons. If you purchase one of these books, you own a number of options. These coupons or options can be used at your discretion. When will you use them? You'll use these coupons if you want the good or service that the coupon offers and using the coupon will save you money. You make a choice, you have an option.

Options are securities that make it possible to invest in shares without actually holding shares. We'll discuss options in some detail and then briefly describe warrants, which are similar but less common.

An **option** is a contract that gives one party a *temporary* right to buy or sell an asset from or to the other at a fixed price. It's a good idea to understand a little about the general concept before we get into financial options.

> Options and warrants make it possible to *invest* in shares *without holding shares.*

> An **option** grants a *temporary right to buy or sell* an asset at a fixed price.

OPTIONS IN GENERAL

Options are used in business all the time. An option to buy real estate, which we introduced in Chapter 14 (page 524), will familiarize us with the way they work, and lead us into options on shares. Suppose a company is interested in building a new factory, and has identified a desirable site, but will need six months to make a final decision on the project. How can it hold onto the right to buy the land without making a commitment now?

The solution can be an option contract granting the firm the right to buy the site within six months at a stipulated price. That locks in the land's availability and price, but leaves management free not to make the purchase. Of course the company has to pay the landowner for that privilege, but the price (of the option) is a small fraction of the value of the real estate. The option is a purchase contract that's suspended at the discretion of the buyer for a limited time, after which it expires. Now consider the following possibility that will help us move into financial options.

Suppose after almost six months, the firm decides it's not going to build the factory but notices that the price of real estate has gone up 30%. What should it do?

Clearly, it should exercise the option and sell the land for a profit,[1] which will be made without owning the land while it appreciated.[2] This is possible with any asset on which options are sold. The big advantage of options is that they cost far less than the underlying assets. That advantage is what financial options are all about.

> *Although the idea may seem a little foreign, you likely have used options at some time. The option we just described is acting like a coupon. That is, the owner of the coupon has the right, but not the obligation, to use the coupon should she decide to. When will the holder use the coupon? When it is in her best interest to do so. That is, by using the coupon she pays less than the current prevailing price. Can the coupon owner lose? Absolutely, if the coupon owner paid to buy the right and she does not use it, the coupon owner will lose the cost of the coupon.*

> Optionholders can speculate on asset price changes without holding the assets.

> *From the CFO*

Investor-Created Options on Shares

Options to buy shares are conceptually similar to real estate options, but people don't buy them because they want to acquire shares. They're generally purchased solely to speculate on price movements. However, some investors might use them to limit potential losses on their portfolio (hedging).

Unlike options on real estate, options on shares are themselves securities, and can be traded in financial markets. An option to *buy* a share is known as a **call option** or just a **call**. Options to sell real estate and other assets are unusual, but options to sell shares are common. They're known as **put options** or simply **puts**. We'll discuss calls and puts separately in the sections that follow.

Options are the most important example of a class of financial assets known as **derivative securities**. A derivative is so named because it derives its value from the price of another, *underlying* security. Since an option gives its owner the right to buy or sell a particular share, its value is derived from the price of that underlying share.

Investors are interested in share options because they provide speculative leverage. As discussed in Chapter 16, *leverage* refers to any technique that amplifies the return on an investment. Option leverage comes from the fact that the return on an investment in options can be

> **Calls** are options to *buy*. **Puts** are options to *sell*.

> The value of a **derivative security** is based on that of another, *underlying* security.

> Leverage amplifies the return on an investment.

---

1 When the company does that the landowner loses this gain on the appreciation of his property. The possibility of this happening is another reason the landowner is paid for the option.
2 Speculating essentially means betting on an asset's short-term price movements. Sophisticated speculators generally have knowledge of the market for the asset that reduces their risk.

many times larger than the return on an investment in the underlying shares. We'll describe how that works shortly.

Call Options

Imagine that a share is selling for $55 and someone offers you a contract under which she agrees to sell you that share for $60 anytime during the next three months. This is a basic *call option*. It grants its owner the right to *buy* a share at a fixed price for a specified period, typically three, six, or nine months. At the end of that time the option expires and can no longer be *exercised*.

The price of the contract is the *option price* or *premium*, which we'll call P_{Op}. It's always a great deal less than the share's price. An option on a share worth $55 might sell for $2 or $3.

The idea is portrayed graphically in Figure 18.1. The share's current price is called just that, but the $60 is known as the option's **strike price**, *striking price*, or **exercise price**.

Ask yourself the following questions. Would you pay anything for this option contract? Why? And if you would pay for the deal, what factors would make you pay more or less? Think about these questions before reading on.

An investor might be willing to pay for the option, because there's a chance that the share's price will exceed $60 in the next three months. If that happens, an option owner can buy at $60 and immediately sell for the higher market price. For example, suppose you paid $1 for the option and the share price went to $63. You'd exercise at $60, and immediately sell for $63, making the $3 difference less the $1 paid for the option contract.

Notice that the $2 profit is a 200% return on the $1 investment in the option. But also notice that if the share price doesn't pass $60 in three months, the option expires and the $1 is lost. That's a 100% loss on the investment.

Let's look more closely at the profit potential on a call option and on the share itself. For simplicity we will assume the investor could have bought a share for $60 or the call option for $1 on the same day three months ago.

Market Price Three Months Later	Profit/Loss on Call Option		Profit/Loss on Owning the Share	
$59	−$1	−100%	−$1	−1.67%
$60	−$1	−100%	$0	0%
$61	$0	0%	+1	+1.67%
$62	+$1	+100%	+2	+3.33%
$63	+$2	+200%	+3	+5.00%

What we can quickly see is that for a very small price change, the call option can make either a tremendous positive or a tremendous negative return on the original investment (the premium) while the percentage returns on the share itself are far less spectacular. Why is there

An option to *buy* a share at a **strike price** sells for the *option price or premium*.

FIGURE 18.1
Basic Call Option Concepts

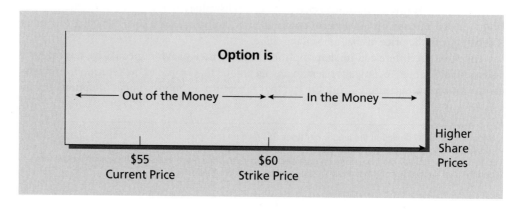

such a difference? Because of the price being "bet" by the investor. If the share price drops below the original purchase price, the owner of the share is not compelled to sell at a loss. Assuming that he does not have to use the money from this investment to live, he can keep the share and hope to make a gain on it down the road.

Based on our discussion so far, we have reasoned out two factors that make options more or less appealing. First, an option on a volatile share is worth more than one on a stable issue, because the share price is more likely to go above the strike price in the allotted time. Second, investors are willing to pay more for options with more time until expiration, because that gives the share price more time to move past the strike price.

The Call Option Writer

There are two parties to an option contract: a buyer and a seller. Don't confuse buying and selling the option contract with buying and selling the optioned share. Until now we've focused on option buyers who have the right to buy shares at the strike price.

Option *originators* are said to *write* options.

Terminology with respect to option sellers can be a little tricky. The first person to sell an option contract is the person who creates it by agreeing to sell the share at the strike price. She is said to *write* the option. Once it's written, the option contract becomes a security and the writer sells it to the first buyer, who may sell it to someone else later on. No matter how many times the option is sold, the writer remains bound by the contract to sell the underlying share to the current owner at the strike price if he exercises the option.

A call option writer hopes the underlying share price will remain stable (or drop). If it does, she will have a gain from the receipt of the option premium. We'll talk about writing options in more detail later. The writer is obliged to honour her part of the contract. That means the writer must deliver a share to the call buyer at the exercise price, if the buyer decides to exercise.

Intrinsic Value

If the share's current price is below the strike price as we've shown in Figure 18.1, we say the call option is *out of the money*. If the share price is above the strike price, we say the call option is *in the money* (if the share price is far above the strike price, we say the call option is *deep in the money*).

When an option is in the money, it has an immediate minimum value that doesn't depend on the underlying share price moving higher. We call that the option's *intrinsic value*. For example, suppose that the share underlying the option in Figure 18.1 is selling for $65. Then the option to buy at $60 must be worth at least $5, because an option owner can exercise at $60 and immediately sell at $65 for a $5 gain (less the option premium).[3]

In general, an option's *intrinsic value* is the difference between the current price of the underlying share and the option's strike price. The relationship is reflected in Equation 18.1.

An option's *intrinsic value* is the *difference* between the *current price* of the share and the *strike price*.

(**18.1**)
$$V_{IC} = P_S - P_{Strk}$$

where V_{IC} = Intrinsic value of a call option

P_S = Current price of the underlying share

P_{Strk} = The option's strike price.

V_{IC} is simply zero when the share price is less than the strike price (i.e., when the option is out of the money and $P_S < P_{Strk}$).

---

3 The gain is also less any brokerage costs, of course. For simplicity, we will ignore transaction costs on the buying and selling of call and put options.

It's apparent from Equation 18.1 that the intrinsic value of an option is a linear function of the price of the underlying share, P_S. A graph of the value of a call option with a $60 strike price, called *an option at $60*, is shown in Figure 18.2. Notice that the intrinsic value is horizontal at zero to the left of the strike price and slopes upward to the right of the strike price. The intrinsic value of an option at any other strike price would simply be a parallel upward sloping line emerging from the horizontal axis at that price.

Figure 18.2 also shows the actual market price of the option, P_{Op}, the curved line lying above the intrinsic value. It's important to notice that the option always sells for a price that's at or above its intrinsic value. The difference between the intrinsic value and the option premium is called the option's **time premium**, shown as the space between the two dark lines in Figure 18.2.

> **Time premium** is the difference between intrinsic value and the option price.

Investors are willing to pay premiums over intrinsic value for call options, because of the chance that they will profit if the underlying share price goes higher. The exact shape of the graph of a particular option's premium depends on the share's volatility, the time until expiration, and the attitude of the market about the underlying company. The general shape is shown in Figure 18.2. The premium is generally largest when a share's price is near but a little below the option's strike price and diminishes as the share price rises.

This characteristic shape is a result of the way the leverage offered by the option varies with the price of the underlying share. It's important to understand why that shape takes the form it does.

Options and Leverage

As discussed earlier, financial leverage is a term used to describe any technique that amplifies return on investment (ROI). For example, suppose a traditional investment in a share results in a 10% return. Then a leveraged investment in the same share might result in a 40% or 50% return over the same period. Unfortunately leverage works on losses too, so if the share's return turned out to be –10%, the leveraged investment would have produced –40% or –50%.

Options are one of a number of leveraging techniques. We'll refer to Figure 18.2 to see how they work. In the diagram, imagine that the underlying share is trading at $58 and that the time premium on a call option is $2.[4] (The option premium is also $2 because its intrinsic value is

FIGURE 18.2
The Value of a Call Option

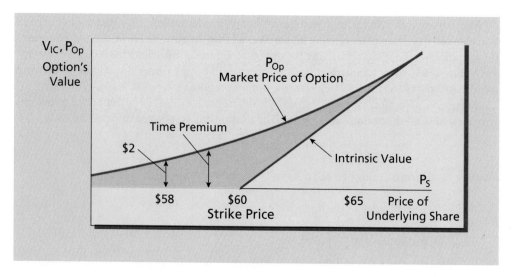

4 We're just assuming this premium for illustrative purposes. The actual premium would depend on factors such as the underlying share's volatility and the time until expiration as well as the demand for options at the time; $2 is a reasonable value.

zero.) Now imagine that the share price increases to $65, the option is exercised, and the optioned share is sold. We'll ignore brokerage commissions for simplicity.

First, let's look at an investment in the share over the same period. It would have been purchased at $58 and sold at $65 for a $7 profit and a return on investment (ROI) of

$$\text{ROI} = \frac{\$7}{\$58} = 12.1\%$$

Now consider investing in the option. The buyer initially paid $2 for the option. Then he exercised, buying the underlying share at $60 and immediately selling at $65 for a $5 gain, which was reduced by the $2 option premium. Hence the option buyer's net gain is $3. *But* he had only the $2 option premium tied up in the transaction. Hence his ROI is

$$\text{ROI} = \frac{\$3}{\$2} = 150\%$$

Notice the tremendous leveraging power of the option to multiply the investor's return. The option's ROI is (150/12.1=) 12 times that of a straight investment in shares. The potential of this kind of return contributes a great deal to the option's value when the share price is just below the strike price.

The call option isn't quite as good a deal when the share is trading above the strike price. There are two reasons for that. First, the share price has to rise higher to make a given profit. That's generally less likely to happen than the same gain from a lower starting price. Second, the buyer has to pay an intrinsic value in addition to the time premium for the option. That makes his investment larger, which decreases the leverage effect. These factors contribute to the diminishing value of the time premium as the share price increases over the strike price. Hence the option's price in Figure 18.2 approaches the intrinsic value line as we move to the right. A numerical example is provided in footnote 5.[5]

The time premium is smaller further to the left of the strike price simply because it becomes less likely that the share will ever move into the money.

Options offer a great deal of *leverage*.

Options That Expire

It's important to keep in mind that options are exercisable only over limited periods at the end of which they expire and become worthless. That makes option investing very risky. For example,

Options become *worthless* when they expire.

5 Suppose the premium is $1 when the share price is $65. This means that an option buyer pays the intrinsic value of ($65 − $60 =) $5 plus the $1 premium or $6 for the option. Then suppose the share price goes up by another $7 to $72.

First consider the return on an investment in the share. It would be purchased at $65 and sold at $72 for a $7 profit and a return on investment (ROI) of:

$$\text{ROI} = \frac{\$7}{\$65} = 10.8\%$$

Now consider the return on the option. The buyer exercises at $60 and sells his share at $72 for a $12 gain. But the option cost $6, so his profit on the whole transaction is ($12 - $6 =) $6, and his ROI is

$$\text{ROI} = \frac{\$6}{\$6} = 100\%$$

if a call option is purchased out of the money, and the underlying share value never exceeds the strike price, the option expires and the buyer loses the price paid for it. It's important to realize that's a 100% loss.

If a call option is purchased at a price that includes a positive intrinsic value (to the right of $60 in Figure 18.2), and the underlying share goes down in value, the option buyer's loss at expiration is the time premium paid plus the decrease in intrinsic value. That will be a 100% loss only if the share price declines all the way to the strike price.

As its expiration date approaches, any option's time premium shrinks to virtually zero. Notice that anyone owning an option with a positive intrinsic value just before expiration must act quickly to avoid losing that value.

Trading in Options

The *largest options exchange* is the *Chicago Board Options Exchange (CBOE)*. In Canada, options are sold primarily through the *Montreal Exchange (ME)*.

Option *prices move very rapidly*.

Up until now we've spoken as if buyers always hold options until they are either exercised or expire. In fact, that's not the case. Options can be bought and sold between investors at any time up to their expiry date. Options on selected shares are traded on a number of exchanges. The largest, oldest, and best-known options exchange is the Chicago Board Options Exchange (CBOE). In Canada, options are traded primarily on the Montreal Exchange (ME).

Price Volatility in the Options Market

Option prices move up and down with the prices of the underlying securities, but the relative movement is much greater for options. For example, in Figure 18.2 we said the call option might sell for $2 when the underlying share price was $58. Now suppose that the share price goes up to $65 while there's still some time until expiration. Observe from the graph that the option sells for a price that includes its intrinsic value of ($65 − $60 =) $5, and a smaller time premium. Assume that premium is $1 (not shown), so the option's price is $6.

The share's $7 price movement from $58 to $65 is a 12.1% increase, but it's driven the option's price to triple in value from $2 to $6 (a 200% increase). As a result of this phenomenon, prices in options markets are extremely volatile and fast moving.

Options Are Rarely Exercised before Expiration

In the situation just described, suppose the option owner feels further increases in the underlying share price are unlikely and wants to close out his investment even though there's a good deal of time left until expiration. In that case, virtually all traders would sell the option to another investor rather than exercise it. That's because exercising brings only ($65 − $60 =) $5, which is less than the $6 option premium.

- Options are rarely exercised before expiration.
- American options may be exercised any time up to and including the expiry date, while European options may be exercised only on their expiry date.

Exercising requires throwing away whatever value is in the time premium, in this case $1. As a result, options are rarely exercised before expiration, when the time premium shrinks to zero.

Options actively traded in the market (exchange traded) are *American* options. American options may be exercised anytime up to and including the expiry date. Another type of option, a *European* option, may be exercised only on its expiry date. Most European options have been customized between the buyer and the seller and are done for portfolio management purposes. These customized contracts are rarely resold (if they are, there is no organized secondary market; they are sold in the over-the-counter market). The terms *European* and *American* have no bearing on where the options are sold.

The Downside and Risk

It's important to think about the upside and downside of option trading at the same time. There's a chance of a very high return through leverage, but there's also a good chance of a total loss. That's another way of saying leverage works both ways, amplifying losses as well as gains. It's a big mistake to get so caught up in the potential gains that you lose sight of the losses that are possible.

Speculating in options involves a good chance of total loss.

Writing Options

As we mentioned earlier, investors can issue or *write* option contracts, which are bought by other investors. People write options for the premium income they receive when they're sold. But option writers lose whatever their buyers make. Option writers and buyers essentially take opposite sides of bets on which way underlying share prices will move. This is often termed a *zero sum game.* In zero sum games, no wealth is created between investors—the wealth is simply "rearranged," from one investor's pocket to another investor's pocket!

Options are written either covered or naked. In a *covered* call option, the writer owns the underlying share at the time the option is written. If the share price goes up and a call option buyer exercises, the writer must sell the option owner his share at the strike price. The option writer isn't out any additional cash, but he missed out on the price appreciation he would have had if he hadn't written the option. When we say the writer covered, we typically are saying that the writer bought the share in the market.

A call option is written covered when the writer owns the optioned share.

For example, suppose an investor has a share purchased some time ago for $40 (so he covered at $40), that's currently selling for $55, and writes a call option on it at a strike price of $60. Then suppose the share price goes to $70 and the buyer exercises. The investor must sell the share for $60 even though it's now worth $70. In a sense he's had an "opportunity loss" of $10 by not being able to sell at $70. In reality he realizes a gain of $20 plus the option premium over his original $40 cost.

Someone who writes a *naked* call option doesn't own the underlying share at the time she writes the option. She therefore faces more risk. In the situation described in the last paragraph, if the option had been written naked, the writer would have had to buy a share at $70 and sell it to the option buyer when he exercised at $60. Hence she'd have lost $10 on the contract, made up somewhat by the option premium received earlier.

A call option is written naked when the writer does not own the optioned share.

Example 18.1

The following information refers to a three-month call option on shares of Oxbow Inc.

Price of underlying share	$30
Strike price of three-month call	$25
Market price of the option	$8

a.   What is the intrinsic value of the option?
b.   What is the option's time premium at this price?
c.   Is the call in or out of the money?
d.   If an investor writes and sells a covered call option, acquiring the covering share now, how much has he invested?
e.   What is the most the buyer of the call can lose?
f.   What is the most the writer of the naked call can lose?

Just before the option's expiration Oxbow is selling for $32.

g.   What is the profit or loss from buying the call?
h.   What is the profit or loss from writing the naked call?
i.   What is the profit or loss from writing the covered call if the covering share was acquired at the time the call was written?

■ **Solution:**

a. Write Equation 18.1 and substitute

$$V_{IC} = P_S - P_{Strk} = \$30 - \$25 = \$5$$

b. The time premium is the difference between the option's price or premium and its intrinsic value

$$\text{Time premium} = P_{Op} - V_{IC}$$
$$= \$8 - \$5$$
$$= \$3$$

c. The call option is in the money because it has a positive intrinsic value.

d. To establish a covered call, the investor buys the share at its market price and sells an option immediately. The option's price therefore offsets the investment in the share.

$$\text{Investment} = \text{Price of share} - \text{Price of call option}$$
$$= P_S - P_{Op}$$
$$= \$30 - \$8$$
$$= \$22$$

It is unlikely that a writer would think about writing this call as the exercise price is below the share price. Why? The call option is already in the money.

e. The most any option buyer can lose is the option premium, $8 in this case.

f. A writer of a naked call has to buy the share on the open market if her buyer exercises the option. In theory the share can rise to any price, so the naked call writer can lose an infinite amount. In practice a prudent investor would limit her losses by purchasing the share when it started to move up. As in part (d), a naked call writer would think twice about writing an already in the money call option.

g. The call owner exercises the option paying the strike price, and simultaneously sells the share at market price. Any resulting gain (loss) is reduced (made worse) by the price paid for the call.

Market price of share at time of exercise		$32
Less: Strike price	$(25)	
Price of option	(8)	(33)
Loss		$(1)

h. An investor who wrote a naked call buys the share at market price when the option is exercised and sells at the strike price. The result is improved by the price received for the option.

Market price of share at time of exercise		$(32)
Plus: Strike price	$25	
Price of option	8	33
Gain		$ 1

i. An investor who wrote a covered call bought the share at market price when the option was written and sells it at the strike price. The result is improved by the price received for the option.

Market price of share at time of exercise		$(30)
Plus: Strike price	$25	
Price of option	8	33
Gain		$ 3

Put Options

A put is an option to sell.

A *put option*, or just a *put*, is an option to sell at a specified price over a designated period. Investors buy puts if they think that the price of the underlying security is going to fall.

A put buyer profits if the optioned share's price falls.

For example, suppose a share is currently selling for $55 and a put option is available to sell at a strike price of $50. The option buyer makes money if the share price drops to $45 by buying a share at that price and selling it to the option writer at $50.

Put options are in the money when the share is selling below the strike price, $50 in this case. The idea is shown graphically in Figure 18.3.

The intrinsic value of a put is the difference between the strike price and the current price of the share when that difference is a positive number, otherwise it is zero. The relationship is expressed in Equation 18.2.

(18.2)
$$V_{IP} = P_{Strk} - P_S$$

where V_{IP} = Intrinsic value of a put option

P_S = Current price of the underlying share

P_{Strk} = The option's strike price

When the share is trading above the strike price, the intrinsic value is just zero (i.e., when the option is in the money and $P_S > P_{Strk}$). As with call options, puts sell for a time premium over their intrinsic values. This idea is shown in Figure 18.4.

In essence, owning a put option guarantees the minimum price that the share could be sold for.

As with call options, the put buyer has the right, not the obligation, to exercise the put (that is, sell the share at a certain price). The put writer has the obligation to buy the share at the exercise price, should the put buyer decide to exercise the put.

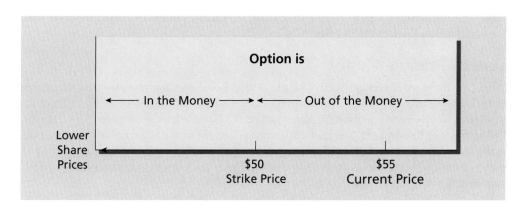

FIGURE 18.3
Basic Put Options Concepts

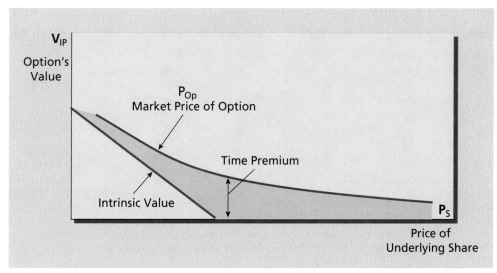

FIGURE 18.4
The Value of a Put Option

Reading Option Prices

In general, to create options an investor contacts a broker and asks to write a call or a put. The broker then expresses this interest on the floor of the option exchange and, if another investor is willing to buy the option, the option is created. The option buyer is charged a premium.

Option exchanges have many regulations and allow options to be created on shares that have met certain minimum quality standards and are widely held. Options are issued in series and they expire on the third Friday of the expiry month.

An option contract is typically sold for 100 shares of the underlying security, although the price is quoted for one option for one share.

In Table 18.1, the listing for Ballard Power on Monday June 11, 2007, there were eight different options available for purchase. On the far right side of the first row, we are given the closing price of Ballard Power shares that day: $4.44.

The first column of the table indicates the strike price on the option, the second column indicates the month of expiry. We can see in the third column that there were three put options available, the rest were call options. On June 11, 20 July 5 call options and 140 July 5 put contracts were traded.

The bid and ask columns indicate that the most a buyer was willing to pay for the option, the ask, is the minimum price a seller was willing to accept for the option. The last column, open interest, is the total number of contracts outstanding (for the previous day). At the bottom of the chart, you see total option volume; this is the number of contracts traded that day. The total open interest is the number of contracts outstanding on Ballard Power (both puts and calls). If a particular option was popular that day, its trading volume can easily be larger than the open interest (look at the Oct 6 call).

The Chicago Board Options Exchange offers a self-paced tutorial in option trading and pricing. http://www.cboe.com/LearnCenter/Tutorials.aspx.

Option Pricing Models

When we discussed shares earlier in Chapter 10 and bonds in Chapter 9, we studied pricing models that allowed us to predict the prices those securities should command in financial markets. (See the bond equation on page 314 and the Gordon model on page 363.) Options, like shares and bonds, are traded securities, so it's logical to ask if a similar pricing model exists for them. The modelling problem is more difficult for options than for shares and bonds, because it's hard to express an option's value as the present value of a stream of future cash flows.

TABLE 18.1
Typical Quotes Prices for Monday, June 11, 2007

Ballard Power (BLD) 4.44

Strike	Expiry	Put/Call	Volume	Bid	Ask	Open Int
5	July	C	20	0.08	0.15	545
5	July	P	140	0.60	0.70	188
6	July	C	20	0.01	0.07	625
5	Oct	C	103	0.30	0.40	65
5	Oct	P	30	0.75	0.90	151
6	Oct	C	200	0.15	0.20	232
7	Oct	C	48	0.10	0.15	571
5	Jan	P	10	0.85	1.00	10

Total option vol. 571   Total open int. 5,737
Total option vol. 638   Total open int. 4,755

Source: National Post http://www.canada.com/nationalpost/financialpost/fpmarketdata/options_stock.html, retrieved June 11, 2007. Reprinted with permission from Ballard Power Systems, www.ballard.com.

A viable option pricing model was developed some years ago by two well-known financial scholars, Fischer Black and Myron Scholes.[6] The **Black–Scholes option pricing model** has achieved significant popularity despite the fact that it is extremely complex mathematically. This is possible because calculators and spreadsheets have been programmed to carry out the complex math after being given a few straightforward inputs. As a result, real-world practitioners use the model frequently. The model was designed for pricing European options; however, it is often applied to American options as most options are not exercised until prior to maturity.

> Option prices can be estimated using the **Black–Scholes option pricing model**.

The Black–Scholes model determines option prices as a function of the following variables:

- the current price of the underlying share
- the option's strike price
- the time remaining until the option's expiration
- the volatility of the market price of the underlying share
- the risk-free interest rate

A brief description of how these factors affect the price of a call option is summarized in Table 18.2 on page 652.[7]

At this point in your study, you should just be aware that the Black–Scholes model exists and that it gives reasonable but not precisely accurate results similar to those of share pricing models. For those interested in the model, we've included a brief appendix at the end of this chapter that gives you the basics.

Company-Created Options on Shares

It's important to notice that the options we've been discussing up until now are strictly secondary-market instruments (see Chapter 7, page 234, and page 642). That is, they're traded *between investors*, and the companies that issue the underlying shares are not involved. These "investor-created" options are simply "bets" between investors with differing points of view; the companies that are being bet on don't get any money when options on their shares are written or exercised.

> Options are *secondary-market* activities. The underlying *companies* are *not involved*.

In some cases, companies issue options on their own shares. This is done for a variety of reasons including rewarding employees, reducing the cost of borrowing, and raising new equity capital.

Employee Stock Options

For many years, companies have given certain employees stock options as part of their compensation. Employee options are actually more like warrants (to be discussed next) than traded options because they don't expire for several years and strike prices are always set well above current share prices. Employees who receive options generally get less in salary than they otherwise would.

> *Stock options* are often used *in lieu of* a portion of *salary*.

Workers like being paid with options if the firm has a bright future, because even a few options can be worth more than the salary foregone. For example, many ordinary employees at high-tech firms like Microsoft became millionaires during the 1980s and 1990s because of employee stock options. See "The Maturing Giant?" in Chapter 17, page 629.

> Employee stock options *don't* require any cash outlay when issued.

---

6 "The Pricing of Options and Corporate Liabilities," *Journal of Political Economy* 81 (May–June 1973): pp. 637–654.

7 These factors also affect the value of put options. With the exception of time remaining to maturity and volatility, when any of the other factors increase, the effect on the value of put options is opposite to that of call options (i.e., when the current share price increases, the value of a put option decreases).

TABLE 18.2
Effects on Call
Price if Factor
Increases

Individual Factor	Effect on the Price of a Call Option if the Factor Increases	Rationale
Current share price	Increases	If the price of the share increases, the option buyer will make more money. If she decides not to exercise the option and there is still time until the option matures, she will still be able to reap the benefit of the higher share price.
Strike price	Decreases	If the exercise price were to increase, the price of the underlying asset must go up even further before the option will be worth anything. In that case, the person buying the option would not be willing to pay as much as he would for an option that had a lower exercise price.
Time remaining to maturity	Increases	The longer the time period, the better chance that the option will expire in the money (or even better—deep in the money!). Therefore, given the choice between two time periods, a short period versus a long period, an investor would be willing to pay slightly more for the longer-term option.
Volatility of share price	Increases	Increased volatility means that the option owner could make lots of money if the share price increases. By the same token, if the price moves downward, she could lose her investment.
Risk-free rate of return	Increases	As discussed on page 646, option buyers rarely exercise the option; rather, they will sell the option (or they will settle in cash with the seller at maturity). Why? If the option buyer decides to actually buy the shares, he needs to come up with the money to do so, and often that means borrowing. If all the investor wanted was the upside return (dollars or percentages) he wouldn't bother with exercising, and, therefore, the options are slightly more valuable to him.

Companies favour paying people with options because there is no cash outlay when the options are issued. Beyond that, supporters argue that the practice has an important role in keeping North American companies leaders in innovation. They maintain that the chance of getting rich through options attracts the best and brightest people to new companies with innovative ideas. Without options, struggling new firms couldn't afford that kind of talent and would not prosper.

Senior executives are the biggest recipients of employee stock options.

Employee options have a dilutive effect on the interests of other shareholders, but until recently, most investors were willing to accept that.

Insights **REAL APPLICATIONS**

DANIER LEATHER

Employee Stock Options at Danier Leather Inc.

(For the financial statements and other financial information about Danier Leather Inc., refer to Appendix 3A, page 92.)

Danier has a stock option plan where options to purchase Subordinate Voting Shares are issued to directors, officers, and employees.

A summary of the status of the stock option plan at June 24, 2006, and changes during the year is presented below:

Stock Options	Shares	Weighted-Average Exercise Price
Outstanding at beginning of year	645,400	$ 11.13
Granted	–	–
Exercised	(7,100)	6.85
Forfeited	(20,000)	11.93
Outstanding at end of year	618,300	11.15
Options exercisable at end of year	577,800	11.03

Stock options with set *exercise prices* and *vesting periods* were awarded to employees and directors. *Exercisable* options were those for which the vesting period had lapsed. The options had a maximum term of 10 years. There were no options granted during Fiscal 2006.

Under CICA rules prior to Fiscal 2004, Danier was not required to include the options granted in Fiscal 2003 as an expense. Had Danier determined and expensed the related compensation cost at the *grant date* of the stock options, its net earnings and earnings per share for the year ended June 24, 2006 would have been reduced as indicated in the following table:

	As Reported	Pro Forma
Net loss (000)	($5,503)	($5,745)
Basic loss per share	($0.84)	($0.88)
Diluted loss per share	($0.84)	($0.88)

The net loss would have increased by $242,000, and the basic and diluted loss per share would have increased by $0.04.

Source: Danier Leather Annual Report, 2006.

Example 18.2

Bing Xi is the president and CEO of Wellbridge Communications Corp., a high-tech firm with excellent growth potential. Bing's compensation package includes a salary and cash bonuses totalling $4.0 million per year if the board of directors decides he's done a good job. Exactly what constitutes a "good job" has never been defined.

Three years ago the board granted Bing an option on 200,000 Wellbridge shares at $20 per share. The shares were selling for $19 at the time. The board was happy to do this because it didn't cost the company anything and gave Bing an incentive to stay with the company and work hard to help make it successful.

The option period begins two years from the date of issue, which is at the end of June of this year. The option expires after three more years. It is now June 15 and Wellbridge shares currently sell for $48.65. Assuming the board of directors is still pleased with Bing and he exercises his stock option as soon as he can, how much will he make this year?

■ **Solution:** Bing will receive cash compensation as follows:

Salary and bonus	$ 4,000,000

Exercising his stock options and selling at the current market price will lead to the following gain:

Proceeds of sale (200,000 × $48.65=)	$ 9,730,000
Less option payment (200,000 × $20.00=)	(4,000,000)
Gain on option	$ 5,730,000

Hence Bing's income for the year will be

Cash payments from company	$ 4,000,000
Stock option	5,730,000
Total	$ 9,730,000

Although not unusual for senior executives, Bing will make more on stock options than he's paid in cash. But Bing's option gain isn't exactly free to the company. The 200,000 new shares could have been sold to investors at or near the $48.65 market price. So Bing's gain is in a sense the company's cost.[8]

The executive stock option system sets up a conflict of interest that may lead to dishonest reporting.

From the CFO

The Executive Stock Option Problem

The biggest recipients of employee stock options are senior executives. In larger companies, pay packages of top people typically include salary in the millions of dollars and options that can generate income in the tens of millions of dollars.

In recent years, a great deal of criticism has been levelled at option-rich packages for top management. It is argued that such pay structures give executives too much incentive to maximize short-term share prices. In other words, since the personal wealth of CEOs and CFOs is directly tied to share price through options, they may be tempted to take extreme measures to keep prices up at the expense of other goals.

We discussed this situation in Chapter 3 but we'll recap these ideas here. It is important to recognize that financial results drive share prices and that top executives may be tempted to manipulate financial results. The situation is a classic conflict of interest; someone in control of a system that determines his own pay has an incentive to manipulate the system to the detriment of other goals.

As we have seen, there are a number of unethical ways to make financial results seem better than they are and the decision to engage in such practices rests with senior executives. If the methods are used, overstated financial results can be interpreted favourably by investors who bid share prices up while the executives make fortunes by exercising their stock options.

Option-based compensation isn't the only problem, but many feel the system sets up a climate that encourages management to focus on short-term financial results, and inevitably leads to less than honest reporting.

The accounting and share price manipulation scandals of recent years led to a major review of financial reporting and auditing procedures as well as legislation aimed at punishing knowing deception by senior executives. A major issue within the overhaul continues to be a requirement that companies recognize employee stock options as expenses at the time they're issued. Although reform is ongoing, many issues remain unresolved.

The Moral Hazard of Stock-Based Compensation and Wealth

A moral hazard[9] is a situation that tempts people to act in immoral or unethical ways. Unfortunately, stock-based compensation plans like the one illustrated in Example 18.2 create a moral hazard that can have dire consequences. In the example, notice that CEO Bing's compensation is directly tied to Wellbridge's short-run share price, since there's a limited period during which it can be exercised.

He is therefore motivated to take actions that will hold the share price up as the end of June approaches. For example, suppose management knows something that if released to investors would cause a $10 decrease in share price. That would personally cost Bing $2 million if it happened before he could exercise his options. As a result Bing may be tempted to suppress the information until he's exercised his options or to fabricate information that makes the company's future look brighter than it is.

---

8 Remember, opportunity costs involve forgoing an opportunity rather than paying out money. They don't appear in accounting records, but are nevertheless real.

9 Moral hazard exists when a person can make money easily by acting in an unethical or immoral way. For example, if it were possible to insure a $200,000 house for $400,000, the owner would be tempted to burn it down for a profit. That's why you can't insure property for more than it's worth. It's nice to believe that people will act ethically, but it's safer not to tempt them.

WARRANTS

Warrants are similar to call options, but are issued by the underlying companies themselves. When a warrant is exercised, the company issues new shares in return for the exercise price. Warrants are therefore primary market (see Chapter 7, page 234) instruments.

Warrants are like call options in that they give their owners the right to buy shares at a designated price over a specified period. They differ in that the time period over which warrants can be exercised is generally much longer than that of options. Most options are good for nine months or less, with a few lasting as long as two years. Warrants, on the other hand, typically run for several years, and may occasionally be extended beyond their initial term.

Warrants are usually issued in conjunction with other financing instruments as "sweeteners" to make the primary security more attractive. For example, suppose Jones Inc. wants to borrow, but isn't in good financial condition, so lenders (bond buyers) have rejected its bonds. Assume Jones has excellent long-term prospects if it survives its current difficulties, and that its shares are selling for $40.

Under these conditions, lenders may be enticed to take Jones's bonds if the firm *attaches* one or more warrants to each bond giving the owner the right to buy a share at $50 within the next five years. The warrants provide an incentive to buy the bonds if people think that the share is likely to go over $50 before five years have passed.

Warrants can generally be *detached* and sold independently at a market value of their own. That effectively reduces the price of the bonds and increases their yield to the investor. Alternatively bondholders can keep the warrants and exercise them for a quick gain if the share's price rises above $50.

Notice that if the warrants are exercised, the company receives an equity infusion based on a price of $50 rather than the higher market price. That is, it receives cash and its equity position on the balance sheet increases. As the company is uncertain as to when (if ever) the warrants will be exercised, they are considered a form of *delayed equity financing*. Note that the bonds that were originally issued with warrants attached are unaffected by the exercise of the warrants.

> **Warrants** are like options but are *issued by companies*, which receive *equity* at exercise.

> **Warrants** are *sweeteners attached* to other securities.

> **Warrants** are generally *detachable* and traded independently.

> Haemacure Corporation announced a warrant issue January 17, 2007. Read the press release at http://www.newswire.ca/en/releases/archive/January2007/17/c6801.html.

CONVERTIBLE BONDS

A convertible bond is exchangeable for a fixed number of shares from the issuing company at the bondholder's discretion.[10] The number of shares exchanged for the bond is determined by a **conversion ratio** that's set at the time the bond is issued. For example, a $1,000 par value *convertible* with a 50:1 conversion ratio would exchange for 50 shares. Notice that stating the conversion ratio along with the bond's par value implies a **conversion price**. In this case the bond converts at a share price of

$$\frac{\$1,000}{50} = \$20$$

In general,

(18.3) $$\text{Conversion ratio} = \frac{\text{Bond's par value}}{\text{Conversion price}} = \text{Shares exchanged}$$

> *Convertible bonds* are exchangeable for shares at a **conversion price**. The conversion price states the **conversion ratio** along with the bond's par value.

> Convertibles let bondholders participate in share price appreciation.

Ordinary bonds are generally safer investments than shares in the same company, but don't offer the share's potential for price appreciation. A *convertible feature* allows bondholders to enjoy some of that price appreciation if the firm is successful.

Conversion prices are usually set 15% to 30% *above* the share's market price at the time the convertible is issued. Then if share price rises above the conversion price, convertible owners make money by converting and selling their shares at the appreciated market price.

---

10 Convertibles are always debentures, unsecured bonds.

In exchange for this potential, investors are generally willing to accept lower yields on convertibles than on ordinary bonds. That means they can be issued at lower coupon rates and cost borrowers less in interest expense.

Example 18.3

Dean Neri purchased one of Algo Corp's 9%, 25-year convertible bonds at its $1,000 par value a year ago when the company's common shares were selling for $20. Similar bonds without a conversion feature returned 12% at the time. The bond is convertible into shares at a price of $25. The shares are now selling for $29. Algo pays no dividends. (We will ignore brokerage costs.)

   a. Dean *exercised* the conversion feature today and immediately sold the shares he received. Calculate the total return on his investment.

   b. What would Dean's return have been if he had invested $1,000 in Algo's shares instead of the bond?

   c. Comment on the difference between the returns in parts (a) and (b) and from investing in a nonconvertible bond.

   d. Would the convertible have been a good investment if the share price had fallen?

■ **Solution:**

   a. Use Equation 18.3 to calculate the number of shares exchanged for the bond.

$$\text{Shares exchanged} = \frac{\text{Par value}}{\text{Conversion price}}$$

$$= \frac{\$1,000}{\$25}$$

$$= 40 \text{ shares}$$

The proceeds of selling those shares at the current market price were

$$40 \times \$29 = \$1,160$$

In addition the bond paid interest during the year of

$$\$1,000 \times 0.09 = \$90$$

So total receipts from the bond investment were

$$\$1,160 + \$90 = \$1,250$$

The bond cost Dean $1,000, so his gain is

$$\$1,250 - \$1,000 = \$250$$

for a return on the invested cost of

$$\frac{\$250}{\$1,000} = 25\%$$

   b. If Dean had invested $1,000 in Algo's shares, he would have purchased

$$\frac{\$1,000}{\$20} = 50 \text{ shares}$$

each of which would have increased in value by

$$\$29 - \$20 = \$9$$

for a total gain of

$$50 \times \$9 = \$450$$

His return would have been

$$\frac{\$450}{\$1,000} = 45\%$$

c. Investing in Algo's ordinary debt would have returned 12%. Investing in its shares returned 45%. The convertible, at 25%, allowed bond investors to participate in some, but not all, of the unusually high return enjoyed by share investors this year.

d. Convertibles limit risk relative to investing in shares. Had Algo's share price fallen, an investment in them would have generated a negative return. But Dean's return would have been the convertible's 9% coupon rate unaffected by the shares' poor performance. That's less than the 12% offered by ordinary debt, but substantially better than a loss.

Convertibles are less risky than shares.

The Effect of Conversion on the Financial Statements and Cash Flow

When conversion occurs, an accounting entry is made that takes the par value of converted bonds out of long-term debt, and places it in the shareholders' equity accounts as if new shares had been sold at the conversion price. (See Chapter 2, page 33 for shareholders' equity accounting.)

It's important to notice that there is no *immediate* cash flow impact from a conversion; the transaction is strictly on the company's books. However, conversion has important ongoing cash flow implications. The original debt is gone, so interest payments stop immediately, but the newly created shares may be entitled to dividends. Since many companies that issue convertibles don't pay dividends, conversion usually implies a decrease in cash outflow.

Conversion also strengthens the balance sheet by removing debt and adding shareholders' equity, which improves all debt management ratios (Chapter 3, page 81). As with warrants, convertibles are often considered a form of deferred equity financing and, because the company is uncertain as to when the bonds will be converted, it often includes various features to entice or force conversion.

Convertibles as Deferred Share Purchases

Notice that it's possible to look at an investment in a convertible as a deferred purchase of equity (shares). If a substantial increase in share price is very likely, eventual conversion is virtually assured. That means the bond and associated interest payments can be viewed as temporary, and the long-term effect of the transaction is a sale of shares.

Conversion has no immediate cash flow impact, but affects ongoing cash flow.

Advantages of Convertible Bonds

Several advantages can make convertibles attractive to issuing companies and investors.

Convertibles can be deferred share purchases.

Advantages to Issuing Companies

1. Convertible debt tends to be offered by risky companies that have problems with conventional borrowing. Risky businesses pay higher interest rates than more stable firms and sometimes are completely unable to borrow. For these firms, convertible features are *sweeteners* that can entice lenders to accept lower rates or lend where they ordinarily would not.
2. A convertible can be viewed as a way to sell shares at a price above market. In Example 18.3, if Algo's management was sure that the firm's shares were undervalued when the convertible was issued, and that it would eventually be converted, they were essentially selling shares at the conversion price of $25 when the market price was $20.
3. Recall from our discussion in Chapter 9 that lenders generally insist on reducing their risk with bond indentures that limit the activities of borrowers while debt is outstanding. When debt is convertible, lenders view themselves as purchasing equity, so they're less concerned about restrictions. As a result convertible bonds usually have mild indentures or none at all.

Convertibles:
- Offer *lower* interest rates
- May sell shares at *above market* prices
- Have *fewer* restrictions

Advantages to Buyers

Convertible bond buyers may enjoy the following advantages:

1. Convertibles offer buyers the chance to participate in the share price appreciation offered by risky equity investments.
2. At the same time, convertibles offer a way to limit the risk associated with equity investments that can result in big losses as well as big gains.

Forced Conversion

Conversion can be *forced* by a *call feature.*

Reconsider Example 18.3 on page 656 and imagine that after Algo's shares have risen to $29, Dean decides to indefinitely delay exercising his bond's conversion feature. He might do that because he expects the share price to remain at or above $29 and can collect interest on his investment until he's ready to close out his position in Algo altogether. This is better than converting and holding the shares, because Algo doesn't pay dividends.

Algo's management wants its bond converted for two reasons. They'd not only like to avoid paying further interest, but also want to exchange debt for equity to strengthen the balance sheet. For these reasons convertibles are almost always issued with call features that can be used to *force* conversion. Typically convertible call features have call premiums of one year's coupon interest. (See Chapter 9, page 321 for call features.)

For example, suppose in our continuation of Example 18.3, Algo calls the bond to force conversion. Dean is then faced with a choice. He can either accept the call price of $1,090,[11] or convert and sell his shares for a total of $1,160 as calculated in the example. Clearly a rational investor will convert.

Issuers generally call convertibles when share prices have risen to levels that are 10% to 15% above conversion prices.

Overhanging Issues

When *share prices don't rise*, convertibles become *overhanging issues.*

Recall that the purpose of issuing convertibles may not be to borrow money, but may be to sell equity at a price above market. In those cases, convertibles become problems if share prices don't increase enough to make the bonds' conversion values more than their call prices (i.e., calls won't force conversion).

For example, suppose in Example 18.3 that Algo's share price rises to $27 and stops. Conversion at that price yields

$$40 \times \$27 = \$1,080$$

which is less than the call price of $1,090, so investors will accept a call rather than converting. Essentially, an overhanging issue means Algo is stuck with debt it doesn't want.[12]

Valuation (Pricing) Convertibles

Valuing a convertible is somewhat complicated because the security's value (price) can depend on *either* its value as a traditional bond *or* the market value of the shares into which it can be converted. Let's look at a diagram to illustrate this idea before examining a numerical example. Figure 18.5 graphs the value (price) of a convertible against the underlying share's price.

We'll assume market interest rates are such that an otherwise identical bond without a conversion feature would sell for its par value of $1,000. *This is the convertible's value as a bond.* On the diagram, it is the horizontal line that intersects the vertical price axis at $1,000. We'll assume that market interest rates don't change so this figure remains constant throughout the illustration. It's important to realize that the convertible's value as a bond doesn't have to be

---

11 $1,000 plus one year's interest at 9%.
12 It would rather have equity to avoid paying interest and make its balance sheet stronger.

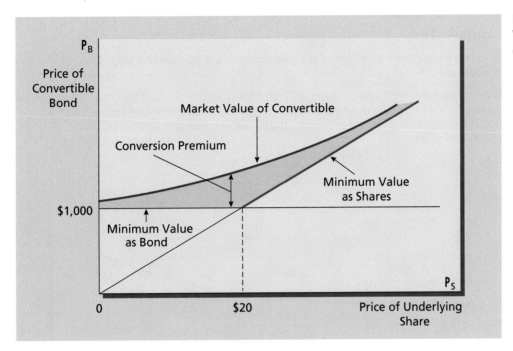

FIGURE 18.5
Value of a
Convertible Bond

par. It depends on the market interest rate and can be any figure calculated using the bond equation (see page 314). We'll demonstrate this in an example shortly.

The diagonal line from the origin represents the convertible's value as shares. It is simply the number of shares exchanged (the conversion ratio) multiplied by the current share price. Let's assume that this particular bond is convertible into 50 shares, so the equation of the diagonal line is

$$P_B = 50\,P_S$$

where P_B and P_S are the prices of the bond and the share, respectively.

Notice that at low share prices the convertible's value as a bond is higher than its value as shares. At higher prices, it's worth more as shares.

At any share price, the convertible is worth *at least the larger* of its value as a bond or as shares. That means the higher of the share and bond value lines represent minimum values of the convertible as a function of share price. In the figure, this minimum value path is represented by the boldfaced line running along the horizontal from $1,000 and breaking upward along the minimum value as shares line.

The market value of a convertible lies above the minimum value line, because there's always a possibility that the share price will go up and improve the return of the bond's owner still further. That possibility gives the convertible a little extra value. In the diagram, the market value of the convertible is shown as a curved line above the bent minimum value line. The difference between market value and the appropriate minimum is the *conversion premium*.

The minimum values as shares and as a bond are equal at the intersection of the two minimum value lines. That point can be found by substituting the value as a bond into the equation of the diagonal value as shares line. In this illustration we have

$$P_B = 50\,P_S$$
$$\$1,000 = 50\,P_S$$
$$P_S = \frac{\$1,000}{50}$$
$$= \$20$$

A convertible is worth at *least* the *larger* of its value *as shares* or *as a bond.*

The *conversion premium* is the *excess* of a convertible's *market value* over its *value as shares or a bond.*

Some websites have convertible bond calculators, such as the one at CFO.com. http://tools.cfo.com/calc/CBond/input.jsp.

Example 18.4

What was the conversion premium of the Algo convertible in Example 18.3 (page 656) at the time it was issued?

■ **Solution:** A diagram for this problem is shown below. Find the results of the following calculations on it as we move through the solution. Summarizing from Example 18.3, Algo's convertible bond was issued for 25 years at a coupon rate of 9%. The market rate was 12%, and the bond was exchangeable into 40 shares.

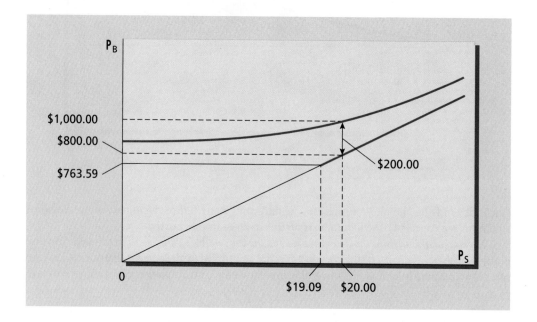

To solve this problem we have to find the breakpoint on the minimum value line and decide whether the share price was to the right or left of it when the convertible was issued. That will tell us which minimum value formulation to use in calculating the conversion premium.

First calculate the minimum value of the convertible as a bond by writing Equation 9.4 (page 314), and substituting the following from the problem:

$$PMT = \frac{\$1,000(0.09)}{2} = \$45$$

$$k = \frac{12}{2} = 6$$

$$FV = \$1,000$$

$$n = 25 \times 2 = 50$$

$$P_B = PMT[PVFA_{k,n}] + FV[PVF_{k,n}]$$

$$= \$45[PVFA_{6,50}] + \$1,000[PVF_{6,50}]$$

$$= \$45(15.7619) + \$1,000(0.0543)$$

$$= \$709.29 + \$54.30$$

$$= \$763.59$$

Next note that the conversion ratio is ($1,000/$25 =) 40, so the equation of the value as shares line is

$$P_B = 40\ P_S$$

Find the share price at the break in the minimum value line by substituting P_B = $763.59 into the equation of the minimum value as shares line and solving for P_S.

$$P_B = 40\ P_S$$
$$\$763.59 = 40\ P_S$$
$$P_S = \$19.09$$

When the convertible was issued, the market price of the share was $20, which is to the right of the breakpoint in the diagram. That means the convertible's value as shares is the appropriate minimum. Calculate the bond's minimum value as shares at a share price of $20 by substituting into the equation for the minimum value as shares line.

$$\begin{aligned} P_B &= 40\ P_S \\ &= 40 \times \$20 \\ &= \$800 \end{aligned}$$

Dean bought the convertible for a market price of $1,000, so our solution is:

$$\begin{aligned} \text{Conversion premium} &= \text{Market price} - \text{Minimum} \\ &= \$1,000 - \$800 \\ &= \$200 \end{aligned}$$

Calculator Solution

Key	Input
n	50
I/Y	6
FV	1,000
PMT	45

Answer

PV	763.59

Use Excel® Function PV

Effect on Earnings Per Share—Diluted EPS

Earnings per share (EPS) is net income (earnings after tax), less preferred dividends, divided by the number of common shares outstanding. Essentially, EPS is a firm's money-making power stated on a per share basis. We mentioned the idea briefly in Chapter 3 (page 61), and we studied it again in Chapter 10.

EPS is a key factor in pricing shares.

> In everyday finance EPS is a key factor in determining the value of common shares. Investors decide how much they're willing to pay for shares based in large part on the issuing company's EPS. A growing EPS is a positive sign, while one that's stagnant or declining can lead to a depressed share price. Indeed, EPS is so important that it and the related price earnings ratio (P/E ratio, see page 75) are often the first things investors look at when studying potential investments.

From the CFO

Convertible securities have an important impact on EPS, but before we can appreciate it we have to understand the idea of dilution.

Dilution

Suppose a company with 1,000 shares outstanding has a total value of $100,000, so each share is worth $100. Now suppose the company sells 100 new shares to new investors at $100 each for a total of $10,000. Would the old shareholders object to the sale?

The answer is no because the additional equity contributed by the new investors would increase the value of the company just enough to keep the value of the old shares constant. After the purchase there would be 1,100 shares, but the firm would be worth an extra $10,000 and each share would still be worth ($110,000/1,100=) $100.

But suppose the new shares were priced at only $50 for a total of $5,000. The equity contribution would increase the firm's value to only $105,000, but there would still be 1,100 shares outstanding. So the value of each share, new and old, would be ($105,000/1,100 =) $95.45.

Notice that the new shareholders get a big gain because their investment of $50 per share is suddenly worth $95.45. But that gain is at the expense of the old shareholders who see a drop of

($100 − $95.45 =) $4.55 in their per share value. In a situation like this, we would say that dilution took place: the old shareholders' interests were *diluted* by the sale of new shares at a price below that of the old ones.

Earnings dilution is an easy extension of the same idea. Suppose the firm earns 10% on the value figures above. Then, before the sale of the shares EPS is

$$\text{EPS} = \frac{\text{Earnings}}{\text{Number of shares}} = \frac{\$100,000 \times 0.10}{\$1,000} = \$10$$

Selling new shares at $100 per share results in

$$\text{EPS} = \frac{\text{Earnings}}{\text{Number of shares}} = \frac{\$110,000 \times 0.10}{\$1,100} = \$10$$

But the sale at $50 per share yields

$$\text{EPS} = \frac{\text{Earnings}}{\text{Number of shares}} = \frac{\$105,000 \times 0.10}{\$1,100} = \$9.45$$

Here, we'd say that the existing shareholders had suffered an earnings dilution in that their EPS diminished. Since a drop in EPS generally leads to a drop in share price, shareholders are very concerned about dilution or potential dilution in earnings.

Convertibles and Dilution

Convertible securities cause dilution. Consider the Algo convertible in Example 18.3 (page 656). Recall that the bond was convertible into shares at a price of $25, and was exercised when the market price of the shares was $29. That means Dean, the convertible owner, got $29 per share when he sold his converted shares, but Algo got an equity injection of only $25 per share in the form of a shift of debt into equity. This has the same dilutive effect as a sale of new shares at $25 when their market value is $29.

In other words, dilution just about always happens when a company's share price rises after a convertible is issued. Because of this phenomenon, the existence of unexercised convertibles always represents a *potential* dilution in a firm's EPS.

Disclosure of the Dilutive Potential of Convertibles

Investors use EPS to help determine the price they're willing to pay for shares. But if there are unexercised convertibles, future EPS may be smaller than expected simply because of their dilutive effect. That's a problem because it could result in investors' being misled into paying too much for the shares.

In response to the problem, the accounting profession, acting through the Canadian Institute of Chartered Accountants (CICA), created rules requiring that companies report potential dilution from convertible and certain other securities in their financial statements. The rules have been modified several times since they first appeared; nevertheless, the latest version requires that companies report two EPS figures: *basic EPS* and *diluted EPS*.

Basic EPS is what you would expect: earnings after tax divided by the number of shares outstanding during the year. If the number of shares isn't constant during the year, an average is used.

Diluted EPS is calculated assuming all existing convertibles are exercised, creating new shares as of the beginning of the year. Essentially, it shows the worst-case scenario for dilution.[13]

EPS calculations sound simple but can be complicated because of midyear changes in the number of shares outstanding and the effects of the assumed conversions on income. Here's an example illustrating the latter complication.

---

13 Review the reporting of basic and diluted earnings per share for Danier Leather on page 653. Potential dilution in this case arose from outstanding employee stock options.

Example 18.5

Montgomery Inc. issued 2,000 convertible bonds in 2003 at a coupon rate of 8% and a par value of $1,000. Each bond is convertible into Montgomery's common shares at $40 per share.

Management expected the share price to rise rapidly after the convertible was issued and led to a quick conversion of the bond debt into equity. However, a recessionary climate has prevented that from happening, and the bonds are still outstanding.

In 2007 Montgomery had net income of $3 million. One million shares were outstanding for the entire year, and Montgomery's marginal tax rate was 40%. Calculate Montgomery's basic and diluted EPS.

■ **Solution:**
Basic EPS

The basic EPS calculation is very simple because the number of shares outstanding was constant for the entire year.

$$\text{Basic EPS} = \frac{\text{Net income}}{\text{Shares outstanding}} = \frac{\$3,000,000}{1,000,000} = \$3.00$$

Diluted EPS

Diluted EPS assumes all convertibles are exercised at the beginning of the year. Two adjustments have to be made to the EPS calculation above. The first adds newly converted shares to the denominator, while the second adjusts net income in the numerator for the after-tax effect of the interest saved when the bond debt is eliminated.

Use Equation 18.3 to calculate the number of new shares issued for each bond converted.

Calculating diluted EPS requires adjusting the number of shares and net income to reflect less after-tax interest expense.

$$\text{Shares exchanged} = \frac{\text{Bond's par value}}{\text{Conversion price}} = \frac{\$1,000}{\$40} = 25$$

Then multiply by 2,000 bonds for the total number of new shares issued, and add that to the original number of shares outstanding

$$\text{Shares from conversion} = 2,000 \times 25 = 50,000$$
$$\text{New shares outstanding} = 1,000,000 + 50,000 = 1,050,000$$

The 2,000 bonds pay interest at 8% on a $1,000 par value. Hence the interest saved by their conversion into equity is

$$\text{Interest saved} = 0.08 \times \$1,000 \times 2,000 = \$160,000$$

But since interest is tax-deductible at 40%, paying it saved taxes of

$$\$160,000 \times 0.40 = \$64,000$$

so the improvement in net income from eliminating the interest is

$$\$160,000 - \$64,000 = \$96,000$$

And net income for calculating diluted EPS is

$$\$3,000,000 + \$96,000 = \$3,096,000$$

Then

$$\text{Diluted EPS} = \frac{\$3,096,000}{1,050,000} = \$2.95$$

Other Convertible Securities

Convertible features can be associated with certain other securities. The most common is preferred shares. We introduced preferred shares briefly in Example 8.14 (page 289) and studied them in detail in Chapter 10. Convertible preferred shares are similar to convertible bonds in that both are potentially dilutive. They're treated similarly in the calculation of diluted EPS.

Certain securities that are not convertibles can also result in issuing new shares at prices below market. Until exercised they too represent potential dilution, and the calculation of diluted EPS must be adjusted for them. The most common example is a *warrant*, which we discussed earlier in this chapter.

SUMMARY

1 A derivative security derives its value from the price of another, underlying security. Call and put options give their owner the right to buy or sell a particular share; therefore, their value is derived from the price of that underlying share.

2 Call options, like coupons, allow the holder to buy shares at a certain price, for a certain period. A put option allows its owner to sell the underlying share at a certain price for a certain period.

3 Investors with different views on what is going to happen to the underlying share price enter into an agreement to buy or sell the underlying share at a certain price. If the investor is optimistic, he might buy a call option. If he is correct, he'll be setting the maximum price he'd be willing to pay for that share (within the specified time period). Put options are often used as insurance policies to protect (*hedge*) the shareholder against a future fall in the price of shares.

4 A call option becomes valuable when the market price of the underlying security rises above the exercise price in the option. The benefit to the call option owner is the difference between the market price of the share and the strike price. With a put, the option becomes valuable when the market price of the underlying security falls below the exercise price on the option. The put option owner will receive the difference between the strike price and the current market price.

5 Calls and puts are traded between investors in the secondary market. In-the-money options are often settled for cash.

6 Call and put options are normally referred to as investor-created options. They don't necessarily have a position in the underlying share. Company-created options are similar although now the company offering the option allows the option holder the right to buy a share of the company. Such options often accompany debt issues by the company.

7 Companies offering warrants provide the warrant owner with the opportunity to buy a stated number of shares from the company at a specified price over an extended period of time. Warrants are often used as sweeteners for bond issues. Warrants can be detached and traded separately. Convertible bonds and convertible preferred shares provide the investor with the opportunity to convert the securities to common shares before a future date. Convertibles have value as a debt instrument and as equity.

KEY TERMS

Basic EPS, p. 662
Black–Scholes option pricing model, p. 651
Call (option), p. 641
Conversion price, p. 655

Conversion ratio, p. 655
Derivative security, p. 641
Diluted EPS, p. 662
Earnings dilution, p. 662
Exercise price, p. 642

Option, p. 640
Put (option), p. 641
Strike price, p. 642
Time premium, p. 644
Warrant, p. 655

KEY FORMULAS

(18.1) $$V_{IC} = P_S - P_{Strk}$$

(18.2) $$V_{IP} = P_{Strk} - P_S$$

(18.3) $$\text{Conversion ratio} = \frac{\text{Bond's par value}}{\text{Conversion price}} = \text{Shares exchanged}$$

QUESTIONS

1. "Options are more exciting than investing in the underlying shares because they offer leverage." Explain this statement.

2. Is investing in options really investing or is it more like gambling?

3. What is the most you would be willing to pay for a call option, ignoring transaction costs? Why?

4. As an investor, which type of option would be of more use to you—an American option or a European option? Why? Would you be willing to pay extra for this type of an option? Why?

5. Why do put options, warrants, and call options all trade above their minimum value? What factors would make these options trade at even higher prices?

6. Ignoring transaction costs, what would be the most that you would be willing to pay for a put option? Why?

7. Some investors describe shares as simply being call options on the company's assets. Explain what they mean. Does a company have to have debt in order for this to be true?

8. Delores has been following a particular company and is quite uncertain about the company's prospects. She has decided to buy both a put and a call option contract on its shares. Both options have the same exercise price. Would Delores ever be able to profit from her decision to buy these options? If so, when? Why would an investor ever consider holding both types of options in her portfolio?

9. You have recently been hired as an analyst of the Mayo Corporation. The company has just finished a dismal year in which its financial performance was clearly below expectations. The company isn't in danger of failing, but it's clear that earnings and growth could be much better. The market price of Mayo's shares reflects this lukewarm performance. They are currently selling for $32, down substantially from their peak of $48 a little over two years ago.

     The company would like to raise additional equity but the managers are concerned that with the low share price, issuing additional shares will be too devastating to the existing shareholders. The CEO has asked you to prepare a brief to present to the board of directors discussing the possibility of a convertible bond issue and a bond issue with warrants. The board will be interested in knowing whether either of these options will assist both the company and its existing shareholders.

10. Assume in the previous problem that the company decides on issuing a convertible debenture. Is there any way for the company to ensure that the debenture is converted should the share price rise above the conversion price? How?

Business Analysis

1. Paliflex Corp. needs new capital, but is having difficulty raising it. The firm's share price is at a 10-year low, so selling new equity means giving up an interest in the company for a very low price. The debt market is tight and interest rates are unusually high, making borrowing difficult and expensive. In fact, Paliflex isn't certain that anyone will lend to it because it's a fairly risky company.

   On the other hand, the firm's long-term prospects are good, and management feels that the share price will recover within a year or two. Ideally, management would like to expand the company's equity base, so it can borrow more later on, but at the moment the share price is just too low.

   Suggest a capital strategy that addresses both the short and the long run, explaining why it is likely to work.

2. Bernard Industries is considering building new capacity for its plant, but the managers are uncertain of the timing. A neighbouring business has offered to sell Bernard its building at a cost of $500,000 today. Bernard knows this is a good deal, but the building would require substantial refurbishing to bring it up to code for Bernard's manufacturing process. The cost to refurbish would likely be in the range of $150,000 and would take a minimum of six months to complete. Once complete, Bernard estimates that this increased capacity would be sufficient for about 10–12 years.

   Bernard has also been investigating purchasing a new plant altogether. The cost would be slightly over $1.8 million and would take roughly 1.5 years to complete. Bernard would need to commit to the new plant within the next few weeks and the cost to secure the site and begin the development plans is $300,000, nonrefundable. Bernard figures that this new plant would meet the company's needs for 20 years after completion.

   Sales over the past number of years have exceeded projections and, although Bernard is conservative in projections for the upcoming year, all indications are that next year will be even better than anticipated.

   Discuss these projects in terms of call or put options. Are these options valuable to Bernard? Which one do you think has the most value? Why?

PROBLEMS

The solutions in Appendix B are based on using either a financial calculator or Excel®. Slight rounding differences will occur if using financial tables.

1. Put and call options are bought on a per contract basis. A contract is typically on 100 shares, so a $2 premium would result in a $200 contract. For each of the following options, calculate the profit or loss to the investor (option buyer) *per option contract*. Ignore transaction fees.

	Type	Premium	Strike Price	Market Price of Common Share at Options Maturity
a.	Call	$0.50	$32.00	$38.50
b.	Call	$0.75	$32.50	$36.25
c.	Call	$1.00	$35.00	$35.50
d.	Call	$0.50	$29.75	$29.75
e.	Put	$0.50	$32.00	$29.75
f.	Put	$0.75	$32.50	$35.50
g.	Put	$1.00	$35.00	$36.25
h.	Put	$0.50	$29.75	$28.50

2. Calculate the breakeven price for each of the puts and calls listed in the previous problem. Remember that breakeven simply means there is no profit or loss so the breakeven price is the price that the underlying share must be at so that the investor will neither gain nor lose by exercising the option (that is, he will have a profit of zero). Ignore transaction fees.

3. Looking at your answers to the previous problem, develop a formula for calculating the breakeven price for call options and one for calculating the breakeven price on put options.

4. Frank holds shares of Yuduno Inc. and is worried about possible price fluctuations from its present level of $26. A friend was explaining what options were to Frank and suggested that he consider buying puts to protect the value of his portfolio. Frank thought this was a good idea but, since he was a little short of cash, he decided that he would also write some call options so that he could afford to buy the puts. Frank's option transactions were as follows:

Action	Option Type	Strike	Maturity	Premium
Buy	Put	$24.00	9 months	$1.40
Sell	Call	$28.00	9 months	$1.50

   Calculate what Frank's profit or loss would be on his "strategy" if the market price for Yuduno shares were (remember to calculate the profit or loss per contract):
   a. $20
   b. $22
   c. $24
   d. $26
   e. $28
   f. $30
   g. Given your answers to parts (a) through (f) above, roughly graph the payoff diagram for Frank. What can you tell Frank about his first investment in option contracts?

5. Donald bought 100 shares of Minton Mountain Mints one year ago for $65 per share. The price of the shares has remained fairly constant over the past year; however, Donald is concerned that the share price might fall in the near future due to an overabundance of mint. Donald heard that investors can "hedge" their portfolios by purchasing options. Describe what Donald might be able to accomplish if he were able to purchase put options on the share with an exercise price of $62 if the share price is
   a. above $62
   b. below $62
   Has Donald accomplished anything by purchasing put options on his shares?

6. Seth Harris is an avid investor who likes to speculate on share price changes. Lately he's become bored with the slow movement of most share prices and thinks options might be more exciting. He has been following Opal Club Inc., a women's apparel manufacturer.

Opal's share price has been stable for more than a year, but Seth is convinced it will increase in the near future but probably not rapidly.

Amanda Johnson owns 1,000 shares of Opal Club purchased a year ago at $37. She thinks the share's price will continue in the upper $30s indefinitely and may even fall a little. Her broker has recommended writing options as a source of income on stagnant shares.

Opal is selling for $38, and six-month call options at a $36 strike price sell for $4.

This morning, Amanda wrote call options on her 1,000 shares, which Seth bought through the Montreal Exchange. At the time of that transaction

a. What was the intrinsic value of the option?

b. What was the option's time premium?

c. Was the call in or out of the money?

d. How much has Amanda invested?

e. What is the most Seth can make or lose?

f. What is the most Amanda can make or lose?

It is almost six months later, Opal is selling for $44, Amanda's options are about to expire, and Seth exercises.

g. What is Seth's profit or loss?

h. What's Amanda's profit or loss?

i. Does Amanda incur an "opportunity loss"? If so, how much is it?

j. What would Amanda's profit or loss have been if her call had been written naked?

7. Yahk Inc. currently has common shares selling at $55. The company also has a convertible bond issue with the following terms:

Coupon rate:	6% per annum, paid semiannually
Face value:	$1,000
Conversion ratio:	20
Time to maturity:	8 years
Yield on identical straight debt:	8% per annum, paid semiannually.

a. What is the conversion price?

b. What is the bond value?

c. What is the conversion value of this debenture?

d. What is the minimum price this bond should sell for?

e. What is the conversion value premium if the bond is currently selling for $1,170?

f. What is the bond value premium if the bond is currently selling for $1,170?

8. A convertible preferred share is currently selling for $100. This share may be converted to five common shares, and the current price of a common share is $15.

a. What is the conversion value?

b. What is the conversion value premium?

c. Why might an investor be interested in this type of preferred share?

9. A company just sold a new 10-year debenture that had detachable warrants. Each $1,000 bond had 40 warrants attached and the combined package (debenture plus warrants) sold for $1,000. The coupon rate on the debenture was 7% per annum, paid semiannually. Each warrant allowed the owner to purchase two common shares of the company at a price of $20 per share. Recently, debentures of similar quality and maturity were issued and are now priced to yield 8%. Calculate the value of the warrants.

10. Recalculate the value of the warrants in the previous question assuming the market rate on similar quality and maturity bonds dropped to 4% per annum.

11. Pacheco Inc. issued convertible bonds 10 years ago. Each bond had an initial term of 30 years, had a face value of $1,000, paid a coupon rate of 11%, and was convertible into 20 Pacheco shares, which were selling for $30 per share at the time. Since then the price of a Pacheco share has risen to $65, and the interest rate has dropped to 8%. What are the bonds worth today? Comment on the function of the bond valuation procedure for convertibles.

12. The Maritime Engineering Corp. sold 1,500 convertible bonds two years ago at their $1,000 par value. The 20-year bonds carried a coupon rate of 8% and were convertible into shares at $20 per share. At the time, the firm's shares were selling for $15, and similar bonds without a conversion feature were yielding 10%. Maritime's shares are now selling for $25. The firm does not pay dividends.
    a. Calculate the return on investment from buying the bond when it was issued, exercising the conversion today, and immediately selling the shares received.
    b. What would the return on an investment in Maritime's shares have been?
    c. What was the conversion premium of the bond at the time it was issued?
    d. Last year Maritime had net income (NI) of $4.5 million and 3 million shares outstanding. The company's marginal tax rate was 34%. Compute Maritime's basic and diluted EPS.

13. Lindstrom Corp. reported earnings after tax (NI) of $2,160,000 last year along with basic EPS of $3. All of Lindstrom's bonds are convertible and, if converted, would increase the number of outstanding shares by 15%. Lindstrom is subject to a total effective tax rate of 40% and has a TIE of 10. Compute Lindstrom's diluted earnings per share.

14. Bob Merribucks has recently heard that investing in warrants can be much more profitable than investing in shares. Bob has found a company that recently issued warrants and is trying to decide whether to buy 100 shares of the company or 100 warrants. The shares currently sell for $40 while the warrants sell for $2. The warrants allow for the purchase of two common shares at a price of $40. Assume Bob will hold the shares or warrants for one year and then sell them. Ignore transaction fees and taxes.
    a. If, at the end of the year, the shares are now worth $55, what dollar and percentage return would Bob have on his
       i. common share investment?
       ii. warrant investment, assuming he exchanges the warrants for shares and then sells the shares?

b. Describe what benefits would accrue to Bob (if any) by investing in the warrants.

c. If, at the end of the year, the shares were worth only $39, what dollar and percentage return would Bob have on his
   i. common share investment?
   ii. warrant investment?

d. Describe to Bob what some of the hazards of investing in warrants might be, as compared to investing in shares.

APPENDIX 18A

The Black-Scholes Option Pricing Model

Recall that earlier in this chapter (see page 651 and Table 18.2 on page 652) we discussed five factors that affected the value of call options, namely,

- the current price of the underlying share
- the option's strike price
- the time remaining until the option's expiration
- the volatility of the market price of the underlying share
- the risk-free interest rate

The Black–Scholes model[14] uses all of these factors to derive the value of a call option. The model makes a number of assumptions. To keep our explanation straightforward, we'll discuss only a few of the more relevant ones. The model is applied to the valuation of European options; however, it is useful in valuing American options as well, since many American options are not exercised until close to maturity (see the discussion on page 646). We'll also assume that the share will not be paying dividends nor will its variance change over the life of the option. Lastly, we'll assume that the investor can borrow (or lend) at the risk-free rate of return. Although these seem quite restrictive (and perhaps unattainable) they are not too unreasonable, given the relatively short life span of a typical call option.

THE MODEL AND ITS APPLICATION

The Black-Scholes model inputs all the five factors to derive the theoretical value of a call option on that share. Many studies have shown that this derived value is very close to the actual price the option trades.

(18.A1)
$$C = SN(d_1) - Xe^{-rt}N(d_2)$$

where C = the value of the call option

S = current share price

X = exercise or strike price of the call option

r = the risk-free interest rate, usually annualized as a continuously compounded rate

t = time, in years, until the option matures

N(d) = the probability standardized, normally distributed random variable is less than or equal to d.

---

14 Fisher Black and Myron Scholes, "The Pricing of Options and Corporate Liabilities," *Journal of Political Economy* 81 (May–June 1973), p. 637–654.

$$d_1 = \frac{\ln\left(\dfrac{S}{X}\right) + [r + .5(\sigma^2)]^t}{\sigma\sqrt{t}}$$

$$d_2 = d_1 - \sigma\sqrt{t}$$

e = 2.71828, the base of the natural log function

ln = natural logarithm

σ = standard deviation per year of the continuously compounded rate of return on the share

Once you have the data, applying this formula is quite straightforward. For example, calculate the value of a three-month call option that will allow you to purchase one share of Clearwater Company for $45. The shares currently sell for $50 and will pay no dividends this year. You estimate the standard deviation of the share's returns as 32% per year, and the risk-free rate is 4% per year.

First, calculate d_1 and d_2:

(18.A2)
$$d_1 = \frac{\ln\left(\dfrac{50}{45}\right) + (0.04 + 0.5(0.32)^2)0.25}{0.32\sqrt{0.25}}$$

$$= \frac{0.1054 + 0.0228}{0.160}$$

$$= 0.8013$$

and

(18.A3)
$$d_2 = d_1 - \sigma\sqrt{t}$$

$$= 0.8013 - 0.160$$

$$= 0.6413$$

Next, we need to determine the probability that a value from a standard normal distribution will be less than a specific value, say d_1 or d_2. To do this, we can use a table such as Table 18A.1, which gives us the cumulative normal distribution. Looking down the (z) column until we reach 0.80 we get a corresponding probability of 0.7881. This is our $N(d_1)$. Following the same process for the second variable, (except down to 0.60 and then across to .04) we find a corresponding probability of 0.7389. Armed with these two numbers, we are now ready to finish filling in the variables on the model.

TABLE 18A.1 Standard Normal Cumulative Distribution Function

z	0.00	0.01	0.02	0.03	0.04	0.05	0.06	0.07	0.08	0.09
−3.4	0.0003	0.0003	0.0003	0.0003	0.0003	0.0003	0.0003	0.0003	0.0003	0.0002
−3.3	0.0005	0.0005	0.0005	0.0004	0.0004	0.0004	0.0004	0.0004	0.0004	0.0003
−3.2	0.0007	0.0007	0.0006	0.0006	0.0006	0.0006	0.0006	0.0005	0.0005	0.0005
−3.1	0.0010	0.0009	0.0009	0.0009	0.0008	0.0008	0.0008	0.0008	0.0007	0.0007
−3.0	0.0013	0.0013	0.0013	0.0012	0.0012	0.0011	0.0011	0.0011	0.0010	0.0010
−2.9	0.0019	0.0018	0.0018	0.0017	0.0016	0.0016	0.0015	0.0015	0.0014	0.0014
−2.8	0.0026	0.0025	0.0024	0.0023	0.0023	0.0022	0.0021	0.0021	0.0020	0.0019
−2.7	0.0035	0.0034	0.0033	0.0032	0.0031	0.0030	0.0029	0.0028	0.0027	0.0026

z	0.00	0.01	0.02	0.03	0.04	0.05	0.06	0.07	0.08	0.09
−2.6	0.0047	0.0045	0.0044	0.0043	0.0041	0.0040	0.0039	0.0038	0.0037	0.0036
−2.5	0.0062	0.0060	0.0059	0.0057	0.0055	0.0054	0.0052	0.0051	0.0049	0.0048
−2.4	0.0082	0.0080	0.0078	0.0075	0.0073	0.0071	0.0069	0.0068	0.0066	0.0064
−2.3	0.0107	0.0104	0.0102	0.0099	0.0096	0.0094	0.0091	0.0089	0.0087	0.0084
−2.2	0.0139	0.0136	0.0132	0.0129	0.0125	0.0122	0.0119	0.0116	0.0113	0.0110
−2.1	0.0179	0.0174	0.0170	0.0166	0.0162	0.0158	0.0154	0.0150	0.0146	0.0143
−2.0	0.0228	0.0222	0.0217	0.0212	0.0207	0.0202	0.0197	0.0192	0.0188	0.0183
−1.9	0.0287	0.0281	0.0274	0.0268	0.0262	0.0256	0.0250	0.0244	0.0239	0.0233
−1.8	0.0359	0.0351	0.0344	0.0336	0.0329	0.0322	0.0314	0.0307	0.0301	0.0294
−1.7	0.0446	0.0436	0.0427	0.0418	0.0409	0.0401	0.0392	0.0384	0.0375	0.0367
−1.6	0.0548	0.0537	0.0526	0.0516	0.0505	0.0495	0.0485	0.0475	0.0465	0.0455
−1.5	0.0668	0.0655	0.0643	0.0630	0.0618	0.0606	0.0594	0.0582	0.0571	0.0559
−1.4	0.0808	0.0793	0.0778	0.0764	0.0749	0.0735	0.0721	0.0708	0.0694	0.0681
−1.3	0.0968	0.0951	0.0934	0.0918	0.0901	0.0885	0.0869	0.0853	0.0838	0.0823
−1.2	0.1151	0.1131	0.1112	0.1093	0.1075	0.1056	0.1038	0.1020	0.1003	0.0985
−1.1	0.1357	0.1335	0.1314	0.1292	0.1271	0.1251	0.1230	0.1210	0.1190	0.1170
−1.0	0.1587	0.1562	0.1539	0.1515	0.1492	0.1469	0.1446	0.1423	0.1401	0.1379
−0.9	0.1841	0.1814	0.1788	0.1762	0.1736	0.1711	0.1685	0.1660	0.1635	0.1611
−0.8	0.2119	0.2090	0.2061	0.2033	0.2005	0.1977	0.1949	0.1922	0.1894	0.1867
−0.7	0.2420	0.2389	0.2358	0.2327	0.2296	0.2266	0.2236	0.2206	0.2177	0.2148
−0.6	0.2743	0.2709	0.2676	0.2643	0.2611	0.2578	0.2546	0.2514	0.2483	0.2451
−0.5	0.3085	0.3050	0.3015	0.2981	0.2946	0.2912	0.2877	0.2843	0.2810	0.2776
−0.4	0.3446	0.3409	0.3372	0.3336	0.3300	0.3264	0.3228	0.3192	0.3156	0.3121
−0.3	0.3821	0.3783	0.3745	0.3707	0.3669	0.3632	0.3594	0.3557	0.3520	0.3483
−0.2	0.4207	0.4168	0.4129	0.4090	0.4052	0.4013	0.3974	0.3936	0.3897	0.3859
−0.1	0.4602	0.4562	0.4522	0.4483	0.4443	0.4404	0.4364	0.4325	0.4286	0.4247
0.0	0.5000	0.4960	0.4920	0.4880	0.4840	0.4801	0.4761	0.4721	0.4681	0.4641
0.0	0.5000	0.5040	0.5080	0.5120	0.5160	0.5199	0.5239	0.5279	0.5319	0.5359
0.1	0.5398	0.5438	0.5478	0.5517	0.5557	0.5596	0.5636	0.5675	0.5714	0.5753
0.2	0.5793	0.5832	0.5871	0.5910	0.5948	0.5987	0.6026	0.6064	0.6103	0.6141
0.3	0.6179	0.6217	0.6255	0.6293	0.6331	0.6368	0.6406	0.6443	0.6480	0.6517
0.4	0.6554	0.6591	0.6628	0.6664	0.6700	0.6736	0.6772	0.6808	0.6844	0.6879
0.5	0.6915	0.6950	0.6985	0.7019	0.7054	0.7088	0.7123	0.7157	0.7190	0.7224
0.6	0.7257	0.7291	0.7324	0.7357	0.7389	0.7422	0.7454	0.7486	0.7517	0.7549
0.7	0.7580	0.7611	0.7642	0.7673	0.7704	0.7734	0.7764	0.7794	0.7823	0.7852
0.8	0.7881	0.7910	0.7939	0.7967	0.7995	0.8023	0.8051	0.8078	0.8106	0.8133
0.9	0.8159	0.8186	0.8212	0.8238	0.8264	0.8289	0.8315	0.8340	0.8365	0.8389
1.0	0.8413	0.8438	0.8461	0.8485	0.8508	0.8531	0.8554	0.8577	0.8599	0.8621
1.1	0.8643	0.8665	0.8686	0.8708	0.8729	0.8749	0.8770	0.8790	0.8810	0.8830
1.2	0.8849	0.8869	0.8888	0.8907	0.8925	0.8944	0.8962	0.8980	0.8997	0.9015
1.3	0.9032	0.9049	0.9066	0.9082	0.9099	0.9115	0.9131	0.9147	0.9162	0.9177
1.4	0.9192	0.9207	0.9222	0.9236	0.9251	0.9265	0.9279	0.9292	0.9306	0.9319
1.5	0.9332	0.9345	0.9357	0.9370	0.9382	0.9394	0.9406	0.9418	0.9429	0.9441
1.6	0.9452	0.9463	0.9474	0.9484	0.9495	0.9505	0.9515	0.9525	0.9535	0.9545
1.7	0.9554	0.9564	0.9573	0.9582	0.9591	0.9599	0.9608	0.9616	0.9625	0.9633
1.8	0.9641	0.9649	0.9656	0.9664	0.9671	0.9678	0.9686	0.9693	0.9699	0.9706
1.9	0.9713	0.9719	0.9726	0.9732	0.9738	0.9744	0.9750	0.9756	0.9761	0.9767
2.0	0.9772	0.9778	0.9783	0.9788	0.9793	0.9798	0.9803	0.9808	0.9812	0.9817
2.1	0.9821	0.9826	0.9830	0.9834	0.9838	0.9842	0.9846	0.9850	0.9854	0.9857
2.2	0.9861	0.9864	0.9868	0.9871	0.9875	0.9878	0.9881	0.9884	0.9887	0.9890

2.3	0.9893	0.9896	0.9898	0.9901	0.9904	0.9906	0.9909	0.9911	0.9913	0.9916
2.4	0.9918	0.9920	0.9922	0.9925	0.9927	0.9929	0.9931	0.9932	0.9934	0.9936
2.5	0.9938	0.9940	0.9941	0.9943	0.9945	0.9946	0.9948	0.9949	0.9951	0.9952
2.6	0.9953	0.9955	0.9956	0.9957	0.9959	0.9960	0.9961	0.9962	0.9963	0.9964
2.7	0.9965	0.9966	0.9967	0.9968	0.9969	0.9970	0.9971	0.9972	0.9973	0.9974
2.8	0.9974	0.9975	0.9976	0.9977	0.9977	0.9978	0.9979	0.9979	0.9980	0.9981
2.9	0.9981	0.9982	0.9982	0.9983	0.9984	0.9984	0.9985	0.9985	0.9986	0.9986
3.0	0.9987	0.9987	0.9987	0.9988	0.9988	0.9989	0.9989	0.9989	0.9990	0.9990
3.1	0.9990	0.9991	0.9991	0.9991	0.9992	0.9992	0.9992	0.9992	0.9993	0.9993
3.2	0.9993	0.9993	0.9994	0.9994	0.9994	0.9994	0.9994	0.9995	0.9995	0.9995
3.3	0.9995	0.9995	0.9995	0.9996	0.9996	0.9996	0.9996	0.9996	0.9996	0.9997
3.4	0.9997	0.9997	0.9997	0.9997	0.9997	0.9997	0.9997	0.9997	0.9997	0.9998

Thus, the value of the call options is $C = 50(0.7881) - (45e^{-0.04 \times 0.25} \times 0.7389)$

$$= 39.41 - 32.92$$

$$= \$6.49$$

We'll leave our discussion of the Black-Scholes model here and encourage you to work through a few of the online tutorials offered by the Montreal Exchange and the Chicago Board Options Exchange (see the http sidebar for the web addresses). They are easy to follow and provide a wealth of information.

Check out the free option pricing calculators at http://www.mx.ca/accueil_en.php (under *Trading Tools* click on *Options Calculator*) and http://www.cboe.com/default.aspx (under Learning Centre choose *Free Tools* then click on *Options Calculator*).

PROBLEMS

1. Calculate the value of the call option using the Black-Scholes Model for the following:

	Share Price	Strike Price	Annualized σ	Risk-free Rate of Return (Continuously Compounded)	Time to Maturity (Years)
a.	$32	$30	50%	5.4%	0.40
b.	$38	$40	42%	6.0%	0.50
c.	$42	$43	68%	8.2%	0.25
d.	$57	$55	37%	7.4%	0.50
e.	$83	$83	15%	6.2%	0.10
f.	$48	$47	24%	4.8%	0.75
g.	$62	$65	33%	5.6%	1.00

2. Redo your calculation for question (1a) assuming the price of the share has increased by $1.

3. Redo your calculation for question (1a) assuming that the annualized volatility has increased to 55%.

4. Redo your calculation for question (1a) assuming that the annualized risk-free rate has increased to 6.4%.

5. Redo your calculation for question (1a) assuming that the time to maturity is now 0.2 years.

6. Redo your calculation for question (1a) assuming that the exercise price is $31.

7. If the call option for question (1a) was actually selling for $5.50, what would you do? Write them or buy them?

A final note: Just to prove to yourself that the model works, compare your answers for questions 2 though 6 with factors and effects listed in Table 18.2 on page 652.

Chapter 19

Corporate Restructuring

Learning Objectives

1 Discuss why companies may wish to restructure through merger or divestiture.

2 Explain what defensive tactics are, who might use them, and what shareholders might think of such tactics.

3 Describe what happens to a firm that becomes insolvent and discuss the options that may be available to it.

Corporate mergers seem to be announced almost on a daily basis these days. For example, why did Domtar Corporation acquire the fine-paper unit of Weyerhaeuser Company and why did Weyerhaeuser divest itself of that unit? Why did Sapporo Breweries Limited acquire Sleeman Breweries Ltd. and why did Anadarko sell off its relatively newly acquired Canadian assets to Canadian Natural Resources? In this chapter we will explore some of the reasons given by these companies in this chapter.

Corporate restructuring is a broad term that describes a number of the ways in which firms are reorganized. It refers to changes in capital structure (Chapter 16), changes in ownership, merging companies together or breaking them apart (divestitures), modification of asset structures, and certain changes in methods of doing business. In addition, business failure and bankruptcy usually result in some kind of restructuring.

In recent years, corporate mergers have been the most publicized restructuring activities. They occur when two or more firms combine under one ownership.

In this chapter, we'll examine several of the ways in which companies restructure, beginning with a fairly detailed look at mergers.

> **Corporate restructuring** describes a number of ways in which companies are reorganized.

MERGERS AND ACQUISITIONS

Mergers are an important force in modern business. They've reshaped Canadian industry several times in the last century, and continue to have a significant effect on companies and financial markets.

Basic Definitions, Terminology, and Procedure

A **merger** is loosely defined as any *combination* of two or more businesses under *one ownership*. In a merger, all but one legal entity cease to exist; in a **consolidation**, all dissolve to form a new entity.

The terms "merger," "acquisition," and "consolidation" all mean the combination of two (or more) business units under a single controlling ownership. In day-to-day practice, the word "merger" is loosely used to mean any business combination, but technically each term refers to a particular type of transaction.

A **merger** is a combination of two or more businesses in which all but one legally cease to exist, and the combined organization continues under the original name of the one surviving firm. A **consolidation** occurs when all of the combining legal entities dissolve, and a new one with a new name is formed to continue into the future. These ideas are illustrated in Figure 19.1 for combinations involving two firms. The left side illustrates a merger of company B into company A, while the right side shows A and B consolidating into C.

In an **acquisition** or **takeover**, one firm acquires the shares of another, called the **target**.

The merger situation is also called an **acquisition**, because the shares of the firm that goes out of existence are usually acquired by the continuing firm. In the left diagram, A is the *acquiring firm* and B is the **target** of the acquisition. The combination is also sometimes described as a **takeover**, because most of the time company A literally takes over company B. That term tends to have a hostile meaning, implying that A takes over B against the wishes of B's management.[1]

An important subtlety in all of this is that the size of combining companies doesn't determine the nature of the combination. As a general rule, A would be larger than B in the merger/acquisition shown on the left in Figure 19.1 and the two would be about the same size in the consolidation shown on the right. However, that isn't a requirement or always the case. There are many examples of smaller firms taking over larger ones.

Relationships

It's important to understand the relationships that come about when firms join together regardless of what the combination is called legally. In one situation, firms combine willingly, more or less as equals, even if there's a difference in their sizes. This is the general situation implied by a consolidation.

In the other situation, one firm dominates the resulting relationship because it acquires the other's shares. That's the usual case in an acquisition or merger. The management of the acquired firm generally works for the management of the acquiring firm after the merger. It's important to note that a merger can be accomplished with the friendly approval of the acquired firm's management or against its wishes.

Shareholders

Any merger or consolidation represents a change in ownership. In the merger shown on the left of Figure 19.1, company B goes out of existence. That means its shareholders give up their

FIGURE 19.1
Basic Business Combinations

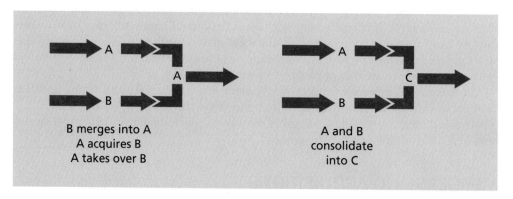

B merges into A
A acquires B
A takes over B

A and B
consolidate
into C

---

1 "Takeover" is a fairly general term, simply implying that one group takes control from another. This can occur outside a merger if one group of shareholders takes over control from another within a single company.

shares (in B) for something else, usually either cash or shares in A. In the consolidation shown on the right, the shareholders of both A and B give up their shares for shares in C.

No one can force the shareholders of a corporation as a group into a business combination. They have to be willing to give up their shares for the price offered in the deal. In the context of an acquisition, this means that a majority of the shareholders of the target (acquired) company must approve the price offered for their shares. (If a majority approves, dissenters may be forced to go along.)

> A *majority* of the *target's shareholders* must accept the price offered by the acquiring company.

The major issue in the analysis of mergers is the value given for the shares of the companies that go out of existence. For example, consider a merger (Figure 19.1, left-hand diagram) in which A's shares were selling for $10 a share and B's for $5 just before merger talks began. Negotiations would have to start with an offer of at least $10 or one share of A for every two shares of B. Anything less wouldn't interest B's shareholders.

The Friendly Merger Procedure

In what follows we'll be primarily concerned with the merger (acquisition) situation shown on the left in Figure 19.1. The merger process generally begins with the would-be acquirer's management contacting the target's management and proposing the deal.

A *friendly merger* takes place when the management (and board of directors) of the target company agrees that the combination would be a good idea and cooperates with the acquirer. In such a case, negotiations between the two management groups on the price to be paid for the target's shares and other issues proceed until an agreement is reached. After that, the proposal is submitted to the shareholders for a vote, with a recommendation by the target's board for approval. The percentage required for approval depends on the corporate charter and the relevant federal or provincial regulations.

> In a *friendly* merger, the target's management approves of the deal and *cooperates* with the acquiring company.

If the shareholders approve the merger, each firm files the appropriate papers with the jurisdiction in which it's incorporated, cash or new share certificates are issued to the shareholders of the acquired company, and the deal is consummated.

The Unfriendly Procedure

When a target firm's management and board are opposed to a merger, they refuse to take it to their shareholders. If the acquiring firm doesn't accept the refusal, it can approach the target's shareholders directly. The merger then becomes hostile or unfriendly. Sometimes the acquiring firm doesn't even try to deal with the target's management, but approaches its shareholders directly in an effort to take the company's management by surprise.

> In an *unfriendly merger*, the target's management resists and may use *defensive* tactics to stop the deal.

In an unfriendly merger, the acquiring firm makes a tender offer to the target's shareholders. This is a special kind of a proposal made to buy shares. It offers to pay shareholders a fixed price for shares (usually in the form of cash, securities, or some combination), but contains a provision stating that if the price isn't accepted on enough shares to gain control of the company, the deal is off. If the tender price is right, enough shares to gain control are offered and the acquiring firm takes over by purchasing them.

> An acquiring firm can bypass a target's management by making a *tender offer* directly to shareholders.

While all this is going on, the target company's management is likely to be contesting the proposal with what are known as defensive tactics. Once an acquisition attempt is under way, these tactics usually consist of efforts to convince shareholders not to sell to the acquirer. They generally have a limited effect if the price offered is fairly high. The target's management can also seek a preemptive merger with another acquirer that it feels is more desirable. We'll talk more about these tactics later, along with defensive measures that managements can take before an acquirer comes along.

It's important to realize that the hostility in an unfriendly merger is between the managements or boards of directors of the two companies, not the shareholders. To most shareholders, the target company is just an investment. If someone offers a high enough price for their shares, they'll sell without a second thought.

Why Unfriendly Mergers Are Unfriendly

Mergers usually come up when an acquiring company shows an interest in a target. They can be congenial affairs or outright battles between the managements of the two companies.

To understand the difference, recall that most companies are run by professional managers, theoretically for the sole benefit of shareholders. In fact, however, managers run companies for their own benefit as well as for the good of shareholders. (Recall the agency problems discussed in Chapter 1, page 10 and Chapter 3, page 63.)

There are two basic reasons a target's management might resist a merger. One is that the deal offered by the acquiring firm doesn't give the target's shareholders enough value. The argument is that the market price of the company's shares is temporarily depressed, and the offer, which is always above the market price, doesn't represent what the shares are really worth. This reason is generally given publicly.

The other reason is more self-serving. After mergers, it's common for the management team of acquired companies to lose a good deal of power and influence. In fact, key executives of target companies often lose their jobs within a short time. This phenomenon is a great incentive to resist being acquired, especially by a company with a history of treating its acquisitions ruthlessly or if the managers know that they have been doing a poor job and are sure to be replaced. In some cases, mergers are about the only way to get rid of entrenched but ineffective management.

A target's management may resist a merger in its own self-interest or because the price offered is too low.

From the CFO

Economic Classification of Business Combinations

A common method of classifying mergers[2] describes the relationship between the businesses of the merging firms. This relationship is important because it helps to define the economic impact of the transaction.

Merger relationships:
- **vertical**—suppliers and customers
- **horizontal**—competitors
- **conglomerate**—unrelated

VERTICAL MERGER When a firm acquires one of its suppliers or one of its customers, the merger is said to be a vertical merger. The idea is that the companies are at different stages along a vertical production process from raw materials to end product. An automobile manufacturer acquiring a steel mill, or a cereal maker acquiring a grocery distributor, would be examples of a vertical merger.

HORIZONTAL MERGER A horizontal merger occurs if the merging firms are in the same kind of business, usually as competitors. This kind of merger has the effect of reducing competition in the industry. For example, if one maker of personal computers acquired another, the merger would be horizontal.

CONGLOMERATE MERGER A conglomerate merger occurs when the lines of business of the merging companies have nothing to do with one another. If an electronics company acquires a potato chip maker, the merger is conglomerate. A company that comprises a collection of unrelated businesses is known as a conglomerate. Onex Corporation recently acquired a large proportion of Tube City IMS Corporation, a U.S. steelmaking company in an industry completely unrelated to Onex's other holdings.

The Role of Investment Dealers

Recall that investment dealers are organizations that help companies issue securities (Chapter 7, page 234). They function between investors and companies issuing securities by undertaking the sale of the securities to the investing public.

Investment dealers are also instrumental in mergers and acquisitions, typically acting as advisors to acquiring companies. They generally assist in establishing a value for the target company and help the acquiring firm raise the money to pay for the target's shares when that's necessary.

Investment dealers also advise reluctant targets on defensive measures.

2 In the rest of this chapter, we'll use the term "merger" loosely to mean either a merger or a consolidation.

Competition and Mergers

Canada is committed to the maintenance of a competitive economy in which most industries (for example, airlines, banks, and oil and gas companies) consist of at least a few competing firms.

A competitive economy is characterized by opportunity and fair dealing. Opportunity exists because anyone with the right resources can enter any industry and compete with established firms. Fair dealing comes from the notion that consumers are assured of reasonable treatment because no single firm can raise its prices too high without losing business to rivals. These ideas have been endorsed by the government to a much greater extent in Canada and the United States than in other industrialized nations.

Competition legislation was enacted in Canada in 1889 and has been amended from time to time since then. Its objective is to prohibit certain activities that can reduce the competitive character of the economy.

The *Competition Act* and Mergers

When the number of firms in an industry shrinks, the remaining firms become more powerful and competition is reduced. When that happens, we say that the industry becomes more concentrated. Because mergers combine two or more firms into a single unit, they clearly have the potential to increase concentration and reduce competition. As a result, they come under the purview of the *Competition Act*.[3]

It's fairly obvious that horizontal mergers combining two or more competitors have an anticompetitive effect, but vertical mergers can also be anticompetitive. They can act indirectly, doing things like locking an acquiring firm's competitors out of sources of supply.[4] Conglomerate mergers don't generally have significant anticompetitive effects.

The *Competition Act* limits the freedom of companies to merge. Proposed mergers over a certain size must be reviewed by the federal government's Competition Bureau which evaluates whether or not they constitute an excessive reduction in competition. Those requiring further investigation go before the Competition Tribunal. If it is decided that a merger's effect is too detrimental, the merger will be blocked by the government. A total block by the government is rare, though; most often the merger is approved subject to some of the merged company's assets being sold to a third party.

> The *Competition Act* laws prohibit mergers that significantly *reduce competition.*

> The *Competition Act* is a body of legislation aimed at maintaining the competitive nature of the economy.

The Reasons Behind Mergers

Most mergers don't turn out to be as successful as expected when they're undertaken. That poor record makes it important to take a hard, critical look at why people put companies together in the first place.

Synergies

The most persuasive reason for a merger is that for some reason the merged organization will perform better than the sum of the performances of the unmerged businesses. This means that some extra value is available in the combination that can be shared by the owners of the two (or more) merging companies. This phenomenon is called synergy. It means that the whole is more than the sum of its parts. Here's an example.

> A **synergy** exists when performance together is better than the sum of separate performance.

---

3 This is federal legislation administered by the Competition Bureau.
4 Suppose two competing firms buy a critical input from a low-cost supplier. Then one firm acquires the supplier and refuses to sell the cheap input to the other. The second firm has to use a more expensive substitute and is forced to raise prices to cover the increased cost. This gives the first firm a price advantage that could drive the second out of business.

Suppose one company makes lawnmowers and another makes snowblowers.[5] The lawnmower factory produces in the winter (for sale in the summer) and is idle in the summer. The snowblower plant produces in the summer (to be ready for the winter) and is idle in the winter. If these companies merge, their similarly manufactured products can be produced in one factory that operates year-round, thus saving the cost of the second factory. This saving is a synergy available by combining the two businesses.

Synergies are usually cost-saving opportunities like the one we've just described. Less frequently, they take the form of an enhancement of some kind. For example, suppose that a breakfast cereal manufacturer with a recognized brand name acquires the maker of an unknown pancake mix. Marketing the acquired product under the cereal company's name might accelerate its success dramatically because of the recognition and acceptance accorded to the brand name.

From the CFO

Synergies sound good, but in practice have proven difficult to find and harder to implement.

Growth

Companies can grow either internally or externally. Internal growth occurs when firms get larger by selling more in current businesses or starting new ventures. External growth refers to getting larger by acquiring other companies.

External growth through acquisition is usually much faster than *internal* growth.

External growth is much faster than internal growth. A firm can become large in its own industry by acquiring a rival much more quickly than by taking market share from others in competitive battles. Similarly, a company can get into a new industry much more quickly by acquiring a firm already in that business than by starting its own entry from scratch. The quest for rapid growth is therefore a major reason for undertaking acquisitions.

Diversification to Reduce Risk

A firm with *diversified* operations is *more stable* than a company that does a single thing.

A company that acquires other firms that aren't in exactly the same business is said to diversify itself. It becomes a collection of diverse businesses merged together under one control. Such a firm is generally less risky than a company in just one business when risk is defined as variation in financial performance.

The reasoning behind this phenomenon is identical to the logic that leads us to diversify a portfolio of shares (see Chapter 11). Each business unit's performance moves up and down over time, but they don't move entirely together. Variations tend to be offset, and the organization's combined performance remains fairly steady.

This kind of stability is sometimes given as a reason to justify mergers. However, it isn't obvious that the logic is appropriate in that context. In fact, a strong counterargument can be summarized as follows.

When a company acquires another firm, it effectively diversifies the portfolios of its shareholders. The acquiring company becomes a combination of what it was before and the newly acquired business, so its shareholders have an interest in both firms and are exposed to the risks and returns associated with both.

But shareholders don't need or want the firms in which they've invested to do that. Suppose A is thinking about acquiring B. If A's shareholders want to invest in B, they can just sell some shares of A and buy B. In other words, shareholders can diversify their own portfolios. They don't need or want the companies in which they've invested to do it for them. This logic leads to the conclusion that managements diversify through acquisition to stabilize their own positions rather than in their shareholders' interests.

Economies of Scale

Horizontal mergers can lead to a larger company that produces at a lower cost than any of the merging organizations do individually. Scale economies are a variation on the synergy idea.

---

5 The parts and processes used to manufacture snowblowers are similar to those used to make lawnmowers.

Guaranteed Sources and Markets

Vertical mergers can lock in a firm's sources of critical supplies or create captive markets for its product. However, many companies are now finding it to be more profitable to actually outsource many of their activities.

Acquiring Assets Cheaply

A firm in need of certain assets can sometimes get them by buying a company that already owns them. This can occasionally be cheaper than purchasing the assets alone, either new or used. It usually occurs when the target firm isn't doing well and its shares are selling below book value.

Tax Losses

A firm that's making a profit pays taxes on its earnings, but a firm that's losing money doesn't get a credit for its losses. In such a case merging the companies might save on total taxes paid. For example, consider the following possible combination of Rich Inc. and Poor Inc.

Acquiring a firm with a tax loss can *shelter* the acquirer's *earnings.*

	Rich Inc.	**Poor Inc.**	**Merged**
EBT	$2,000	$(1,000)	$1,000
Tax (35%)	700	0	350
NI	$1,300	$(1,000)	$ 650

Operating independently, Rich pays tax of $700 and Poor pays nothing, for a total of $700. Merged, however, Poor's loss can offset Rich's profit before the tax calculation is made, so the combined company pays only $350 in tax.

However, CRA won't allow the offset if the primary reason for the merger is tax avoidance. There have to be other demonstrable business reasons behind the combination for the favourable treatment to be allowed.

Ego and Empire

Although it's impossible to prove, powerful people at the top of large organizations sometimes seem to make acquisitions for the sake of making their empires larger. Part of the reason may be that executive pay tends to be more a function of the size of the organization managed than of its success. It is argued that the ego/empire phenomenon has led to a number of acquisitions in which the prices paid for target companies were inflated far above what the firms were reasonably worth.[6] This phenomenon is a windfall for the shareholders of the target at the expense of the acquirer's owners.

Critics maintain that *empire building* is behind many mergers that don't seem to make sense otherwise.

Holding Companies

Holding company is a general term for a corporation that owns other corporations known as subsidiaries. The holding company is also called the parent of the subsidiaries, which are legally separate companies. When one firm is acquired by another, it can be integrated into the acquirer's operations or be held as a subsidiary.

Parent or **holding companies** own *subsidiaries* as legally separate entities.

The holding company/subsidiary form of organization can be advantageous if it makes sense to keep two or more business operations separate and distinct. For example, it's generally possible to keep the liabilities of different subsidiaries separate, so the failure of one doesn't financially affect the parent or the other subsidiaries.

6 Richard Roll, "The Hubris Hypothesis of Corporate Takeovers," *Journal of Business*, 59, No. 2 (April 1986): pp. 197–216.

The holding company organization has another advantage in that it can control a subsidiary without owning all of its equity. An interest as small as 10% can sometimes effectively control a widely held company in which no other single shareholder owns more than 1% or 2%. As a general rule, 25% ownership virtually guarantees control. This means that an "acquiring" company can in some ways control a target without expending the resources necessary to acquire it entirely.

On the other hand, holding companies don't make sense if the benefits of a merger depend on realizing synergies from combined operations.

Businesses acquired in conglomerate mergers are typically held as subsidiaries of a holding company.

The History of Merger Activity in Canada and the United States

There have been four periods of intense merger activity in Canada and the United States in the last hundred years or so. They're often referred to as merger waves.

Wave 1: The Turn of the Century, 1897–1904

At the turn of the twentieth century a wave of horizontal mergers transformed the U.S. into a nation of industrial giants.

The mergers at the turn of the century were largely horizontal and occurred in primary industries, such as mining, metals production, food products, transportation, and energy.

The mergers of the first wave were characterized by large companies absorbing small ones, sometimes by means of unfair and even violent tactics. Large firms often used their power and wealth to force smaller rivals out of business, and then bought the ruined companies at a fraction of their original worth.

Wave 2: The Roaring Twenties, 1916–1929

The second merger wave began during the First World War and ended with the stock market crash of 1929. It was fuelled by postwar prosperity and the general boom climate of the 1920s. Mergers in this period also tended to be horizontal and resulted in the concentration of several industries into oligopolies.[7]

Wave 3: The Swinging Sixties, 1965–1969

The late 1960s were the era of the conglomerate merger. Companies like ITT, Litton Industries, and CP Rail acquired firms in totally diverse fields that had absolutely nothing to do with one another. In contrast to the first two merger waves, this period's mergers resulted in relatively little change in concentration within industries. That is, the number of firms competing in particular industries didn't change much as a result of mergers.

Many of the conglomerate mergers of the 1960s were stock market phenomena without economic substance.

The conglomerate mergers of the 1960s were financial phenomena rather than actions driven by operating business considerations. When a large company with a high P/E ratio (see Chapter 3, page 75) acquires a smaller firm with a lower P/E ratio by paying for the target with its own shares, the result can be an increase in the earnings per share (EPS) of the merged company. If the stock market attaches the same P/E to the acquiring firm after the acquisition that it did before, its share price will rise even though there's no expectation of improved performance by either company. A large number of business combinations in the 1960s were motivated by stock market games rather than by sound economic reasoning.

Because so much of this period's merger activity was conglomerate in nature, there was relatively little increase in concentration within industries. That is, the number of firms competing in particular industries didn't change much as a result of mergers. This was a contrast with the first two merger waves in which concentration increased substantially.

---

7 An oligopoly is an industry dominated by a few powerful firms (as opposed to a monopoly, an industry in which there's only one seller). The automobile industry is an oligopoly.

An Important Development during the 1970s

Prior to the 1970s, hostile takeovers were viewed as somewhat unethical, and large, reputable companies did not undertake them. If a large firm's merger overture was rejected by a target's board of directors, the effort was generally dropped. Further, reputable investment dealers didn't participate in financing hostile takeovers.

All of that began to change in 1974 with the acquisition of ESB, the world's largest maker of batteries, by the Toronto-based International Nickel Company (INCO) assisted by Morgan Stanley, perhaps the most prestigious name in investment banking at the time.

That transaction and a few others established the hostile takeover as an acceptable financial manoeuvre.[8]

The hostile takeover become an acceptable financial manoeuvre during the 1970s.

Wave 4: Bigger and Bigger, 1981–?

Merger activity slacked off during the 1970s but resumed in the early 1980s and has been relatively intense ever since. It's important to notice that this latest period of heavy activity has lasted more than 25 years, far longer than any of the previous waves. And it isn't expected to end any time soon.

There were three "ups and downs" during the more than 25-year period, prompting some analysts to define waves of shorter duration. The first of these took place during the late 1980s; the second occurred in the late 1990s. The third started in 2004, and continued to grow well into 2006. Despite these variations, we'll consider the entire period a single wave since activity during the recent low periods generally exceeds the peaks of the earlier three waves.

Recent merger activity has several distinguishing characteristics.

SIZE Very large mergers have become more common, often involving the leading firms in their respective industries.

GLOBAL IN NATURE Major mergers increasingly involve large corporations from different countries. Such combinations create incredibly powerful companies with global influence. The 1998 acquisition of Chrysler, the number-three U.S. automaker, by Germany's Daimler-Benz, manufacturer of Mercedes-Benz, to form DaimlerChrysler AG is a familiar example.

HORIZONTAL MERGERS AND THE *COMPETITION ACT* Recall that the best reason for a merger is generally a cost-saving synergy, which is usually accomplished by combining firms that do the same or similar things and eliminating redundant overhead. That kind of saving usually comes from horizontal mergers, which are generally between competitors, and tend to reduce competition in the industry in question.

Traditionally, in enforcing the *Competition Act*, the Competition Bureau and its counterpart authorities in other countries scrutinized horizontal mergers carefully and disallowed those that had anticompetitive effects. That made it difficult to find an economically successful merger. Recently, however, the government has taken a much more relaxed attitude toward enforcing the competition rules, and has allowed mergers that almost certainly would have been struck down a few years ago.

EASY FINANCING A major contributing factor to the current blizzard of mergers is the fact that interest rates have remained at historically very low levels for a long time. That makes debt-financed acquisitions not only feasible but also profitable. Further, financial institutions are awash with cash and aren't too worried about risk. That makes them willing to lend enough money to would-be acquirers to make the deals happen.

HOSTILITY The proportion of hostile actions is still small but has increased, especially at the large end of the spectrum. More important, the threat of hostile takeover now pervades corporate life. Few decisions are made at the tops of today's large corporations that don't include consideration of the risk of being taken over.

---

8 For a detailed treatment of the important developments of the 1970s, see Patrick A. Gaughan, 1991. *Mergers and Acquisitions.* New York: Harper Collins.

RAIDERS The corporate raider emerged as a new kind of player in high finance. A raider is a financier who makes his or her living (a very good one!) by mounting hostile takeovers. Raiders can make money whether the takeover is successful or not.

DEFENSES Defensive measures have emerged as a new field because of the prevalence of hostile takeover activity. They are actions the target of a hostile takeover can take to avoid losing control. We'll discuss them in some detail later.

ADVISORS Investment dealers and lawyers have aggressively expanded their roles as merger advisors, earning very substantial fees in the process. Indeed, they're probably responsible for instigating much of the current merger activity. They advise acquiring companies, as well as advising reluctant targets on defensive measures.

Social, Economic, and Political Effects

It's important to realize that the players in these mergers represent some of the largest firms in their respective industries and that their activities touch the daily lives of virtually every Canadian. Notice that these major mergers represent both economic concentration within industries (e.g., energy) and a concentration of power and control among related industries (entertainment and communications, for example). There are few examples of conglomerate mergers lately.

The long-term economic and political implications of today's megamergers are as yet unclear. On the one hand, it can be argued that the large and powerful companies being created are more efficient than the sum of the unmerged organizations would ever be, and therefore are better able to compete in an increasingly global marketplace. On the other hand, the massive accumulation of economic power currently taking place can be seen as having the potential to change the open and competitive nature of the economy for the worse. We won't know the bottom line for quite some time.

Merger Analysis and the Price Premium

The question of price comes up immediately in any acquisition. In other words, what should an acquiring company be willing to pay for a particular target? The question is answered by a merger analysis that attempts to pin down what an acquisition is worth to an acquiring company.

In theory, merger analysis is a straightforward capital budgeting exercise. The acquiring firm makes a projection of the cash flows the target is expected to generate over the indefinite future, and does a standard capital budgeting analysis to determine whether the acquisition viewed as a project has a positive NPV (see Chapter 12). The price paid for the target's shares is the project's initial outlay.

As in any capital budgeting analysis, two estimating issues are involved. First, the project's cash flows have to be forecast. Second, an appropriate discount rate has to be chosen.

Estimating Merger Cash Flows

Estimating the cash flows associated with a proposed merger should be a straightforward financial planning exercise with respect to the target company, with two exceptions. The first exception involves making a provision in the analysis for any synergies that are expected as a result of the acquisition. The second requires that the cash flows recognized by the acquiring company be stated net of funds that will need to be reinvested in the business to provide for whatever growth is expected. We'll demonstrate these ideas in an example shortly.

In practice, however, estimating cash flows in a merger context is especially difficult. Remember all the things we said in earlier chapters about the accuracy of financial plans (Chapter 6) and cash flow estimates (Chapter 13). Our conclusion was that it's hard to project financial statements because of the inherent uncertainty of the future and because of the biases of the people making the estimates.

Recent merger activity has been characterized by *very large* combinations frequently involving *industry leaders*.

http

McCarthy Tétrault is a law firm active in mergers and acquisitions in various industries. Review recent notable transactions at http://www.mccarthy.ca/en/transactions/mergers.asp.

These problems are especially acute in a merger. The acquiring company has to do the analysis, but it generally doesn't have easy access to detailed information about either the target's future prospects or its past history. In a friendly merger, the target's management tends to be interested in pumping up the price, so information shared with the potential acquirer is biased optimistically. In an unfriendly merger, management won't share any internal data at all.

It's not unusual for these conditions to lead to terribly inaccurate cash flow estimates. The tendency is to overstate the value of the target. That mistake can turn an acquisition into a financial disaster for the acquiring company, because it pays too much for the acquired firm. Of course, the same transaction is a financial windfall for the shareholders of the target, who get an unrealistically high price for their shares.

Merger pricing is a *capital budgeting* exercise, but cash flows are *hard to estimate*, and there's a tendency to *overpay*.

The Appropriate Discount Rate

Because the acquisition is an equity transaction, it should be evaluated using a discount rate that reflects the cost of equity funds. Further, the target's equity rate should be used, not the acquiring firm's. That's because the risk in the project viewed from the perspective of the acquiring firm is inherently that of the target company.

The Value to the Acquirer and the Per-Share Price

The acquiring firm's analysis yields a value (an NPV) for the target company. That value divided by the number of shares the target has outstanding is an indication of the amount the acquiring company should be willing to pay, per share, to make the acquisition. Anything less indicates a bargain for the acquirer and its shareholders; anything more represents an irrational transfer of wealth from the shareholders of the acquirer to those of the target.

The Price Premium

It's important to realize that whether a merger is friendly or hostile, the price offered to the target's shareholders is generally higher than the shares' market price. To understand this point, consider that any firm's shareholders always have the option of selling their shares at the market price, but at any particular time only a few actually do sell. Most shareholders don't sell on any given day because the market price is less than the value of the shares to them at that time.

In an acquisition, the acquiring firm has to offer a price that will cause the owners of a majority of the shares outstanding to sell at once. That price obviously has to be above the current market price. The amount by which the price offered exceeds the target's market price before word of the acquisition gets out is called the *premium*. A major issue in acquisitions is choosing a price that's just high enough to attract a majority of shares but no higher. Anything above that level represents a waste of the acquirer's money.

It should be clear from this that, for a merger to make financial sense, the value of the target to the acquiring firm must exceed the company's market value at that time.

THE EFFECT ON MARKET PRICE The fact that a premium over market price is virtually always paid for the shares of an acquired firm creates a speculative opportunity. If an investor buys the shares of a company that is acquired shortly afterward, he or she is virtually assured of a quick profit because of the premium that will be associated with the acquisition. This practice is an example of speculation.

This opportunity causes the market price of a company's shares to increase rapidly as soon as the fact that the firm is an acquisition target becomes known. Such a firm is said to be **in play**. The phenomenon clearly makes it advisable for the acquiring firm to keep merger negotiations secret.

Two other facts are important. First, it is illegal *insider trading* for people in any way associated with merger negotiations to make a short-term profit on price increases that come about as a result of the merger. This includes executives of the firms involved as well as peripheral players like the investment dealers and lawyers who advise on the transactions.

A company is **in play** when it is the object of an acquisition attempt. Most acquisitions are made at *price premiums*, which leads to **speculation** on *in-play* shares, which drives prices up.

It is *illegal* for *insiders* to make short-term profits on *price movements* from the *acquisition* process.

Second, an investment strategy has emerged in which people buy the shares of firms that are likely acquisition targets, without knowledge of specific merger initiatives. Investors using this strategy are hoping that some of the firms whose shares they buy will be placed in play in the near future.

THE POINT OF NEGOTIATIONS If a target company is indeed worth more than its market value to an acquiring company, a gain is available to the extent of the difference between the two values. Merger negotiations involve determining how that gain is to be distributed between the shareholders of the acquiring firm and those of the target.

The target's shareholders get their portion immediately in the form of the price premium paid for their shares. The remainder of the gain becomes incorporated into the value of the acquiring firm, and thereby accrues to its shareholders.

This means that, in a friendly merger, the negotiations basically represent the dividing up of the gain between the two shareholder groups. In a hostile merger, the acquiring firm estimates the gain and offers a share of it to the target's shareholders in its tender offer price.

From the CFO

> *Keep in mind through all this that the gain is very difficult to estimate and particularly easy to overstate.*

Calculating a Price and the Problem of Terminal Values

From the acquirer's perspective, merger analysis is a capital budgeting exercise using the NPV technique, which we studied in Chapter 12. Recall Equation 12.1, the definition of NPV, which we'll repeat here for convenience.

$$(12.1) \qquad \text{NPV} = -C_0 + \frac{C_1}{(1 + k)} + \frac{C_2}{(1 + k)^2} + \dots + \frac{C_n}{(1 + k)^n}$$

A project's NPV is simply the sum of the present values of all the associated cash flows represented by $C_0, C_1, C_2 \dots, C_n$. Recall that C_0 is the initial cash outlay required to get the project started. As an outflow, it is represented as a negative number. The subsequent C-values are generally positive and represent the project's cash inflows over the next n years. (Division by the $(1 + k)^i$ factors just takes the present value of each C.)

In a merger analysis, C_0 is the total amount that the acquirer will pay for the target's shares. The subsequent C-values are the sums of the yearly cash flows expected to be generated by the target plus any synergies management thinks will come from the combination of the companies.

Any project is worth doing only if it has a positive NPV. In a merger context, that means C_0 must be less than the sum of the present values of the other C-values. Hence that sum is the *most* an acquiring company should be willing to pay for the target's shares. Dividing by the number of shares the target has outstanding gives the maximum per-share price the acquirer should be willing to pay to make the acquisition.

Example 19.1

Alpha Corp. is analyzing whether or not it should acquire Beta Corp. Alpha has determined that the appropriate interest rate for the analysis is 12%. Beta has 12,000 shares outstanding, and its cash flows including synergies over the next three years are estimated to be as follows ($000):

	Year		
	1	**2**	**3**
Cash flow	$200	$220	$250

Alpha's management is fairly conservative and feels that the acquisition should be justified by cash flows projected over no more than three years. Management believes projections beyond that are too risky to be considered reliable. What is the maximum Alpha should pay for a share of Beta?

■ **Solution:** The present value of Beta's positive cash flows is calculated as follows:

Year	Cash Flow	$PVF_{12,n}$	Present Value
1	$ 200,000	0.8929	$ 178,580
2	220,000	0.7972	175,384
3	250,000	0.7118	177,950
			$ 531,914

Hence, the maximum Alpha should pay for all of Beta's shares is $531,914. This is the initial outlay (C_0) in the NPV equation and would result in a zero NPV. At that price, Alpha would be indifferent to the acquisition.

Dividing by the number of shares outstanding gives the maximum per share price Alpha should be willing to pay.

$$\text{Maximum acquisition price} = \frac{\$531,914}{12,000} = \$44.33$$

Notice that, in Example 19.1, the acquirer's management was financially conservative, and based the target's value on only three years of forecast cash flows. Unfortunately, acquirers are often not financially conservative, and are willing to value targets based on long-term forecasts. This creates what can be called the *terminal value problem*.[9]

As a merger analysis proceeds, detailed cash flow projections are generally made for a finite number of years, usually three to five. But most acquisitions are envisioned to last forever, and there's a tendency to project a stream of cash flows that goes on indefinitely after the three- to five-year detailed forecast, and to include it in the analysis. This tends to produce results that strongly favour doing the acquisition. The question is, how real are those results? A more realistic (and therefore more complex) example will make these ideas clear.

Example 19.2

The Aldebron Motor Company is considering acquiring Arcturus Gear Works Inc. and has made a three-year projection of the firm's financial statements, including the following revenue and earnings estimate. Period 0 is the current year and not part of the forecast. Figures are in millions of dollars.

	Year			
	0	**1**	**2**	**3**
Revenue	$1,500	$1,650	$1,815	$2,000
NI	95	106	117	130

Aldebron expects that synergies will net $10 million after tax per year. It also expects that cash equal to amortization will have to be reinvested to keep Arcturus's plant operating efficiently, and that 60% of the remaining cash generated by operations will need to be invested in growth opportunities. Otherwise the balance sheet will remain relatively unchanged.

Results beyond three years become increasingly difficult to forecast in any detail, so Aldebron's plan simply assumes a 6% annual growth in all of the target's figures after the third year.

Currently 90-day Treasury bills are yielding 5.75% and the S&P/TSX Composite Index returns 12%. Arcturus's beta is 1.8 and the firm has 20 million shares outstanding, which closed at $19 a share yesterday. The firm has no debt.

How much should Aldebron be willing to pay for Arcturus's shares? Discuss the quality of the estimate.

■ **Solution:** First we'll compute the appropriate discount rate for the present value calculations using the capital asset pricing model (CAPM) approach (see Chapter 11, page 411). Recall that the target's firm's cost of capital is the appropriate discount rate to apply (page 685). If the firm has no

9 See Chapter 13, page 477 for more discussion of terminal values.

debt, we can easily calculate the cost of capital by determining the return demanded by the target firm's equityholders. The SML yields the following.

$$k_x = k_{RF} + (k_M - k_{RF})\beta_x$$
$$= 5.75\% + (12\% - 5.75\%)1.8$$
$$= 17\%$$

Next, we complete the rough cash flow estimate for the target for the first three years, using the information given.

Arcturus Gear Works, Inc. Estimated Cash Flows ($ millions)

	Year			
	0	**1**	**2**	**3**
Revenue	$1,500	$1,650	$1,815	$2,000
NI (unmerged)	95	106	117	130
Synergies	10	10	10	10
NI/cash flow (merged)*	105	116	127	140
Reinvested (60%)	63	70	76	84
Cash flow to Aldebron	$ 42	$ 46	$ 51	$ 56

* We haven't added back amortization because of our assumption that cash equal to that amount must be reinvested to maintain the plant.

Cash flows after the periods planned in detail are generally summarized in a single *terminal value* assumption. In this case, Aldebron is assuming that the last year's flow, $56 million, will grow at 6% per year indefinitely. The value of a known payment that will grow at a known rate can be calculated by using the constant growth share valuation model (Gordon model) we studied in Chapter 10 (page 363). Recall Equation 10.10.

$$\textbf{(10.10)} \qquad P_0 = \frac{D_0(1 + g)}{k - g}$$

In this application, we'll rewrite the equation, replacing P_0 with the terminal value (TV) we're looking for while D_0 becomes the year 3 cash flow, which we'll call C_3. We've already calculated the discount rate, k, and g is the growth rate assumed after year 3.

$$TV_3 = \frac{C_3(1 + g)}{k - g} = \frac{\$56M(1.06)}{0.17 - 0.06} = \$540 \text{ million}$$

Hence, the cash flow stream in our capital budgeting calculation is as follows ($ million).

	Year		
	1	**2**	**3**
Operating cash flow	$46	$51	$ 56
Terminal value			540
Total	$46	$51	$596

Notice how large the terminal value is compared to the three annual cash flows. This is not unusual. Next we'll take the present value of the entire stream at the discount rate we calculated earlier. To make a point later on, we'll keep the three-year forecast and the terminal value calculation separate.

$$PV = \frac{\$46M}{1.17} + \frac{\$51M}{(1.17)^2} + \frac{\$56M}{(1.17)^3} + \frac{\$540M}{(1.17)^3}$$
$$= \$112M + \$337 \text{ million}$$
$$= \$449 \text{ million}$$

This procedure indicates that Arcturus is worth about $449 million to Aldebron. Notice that approximately three-quarters of this figure comes from the terminal value assumption.

In other words, the absolute maximum that Aldebron should consider paying for Arcturus is $449 million, which, if there are 20 million shares outstanding, is $22.45 per share.

If the current share price is $19.00, this represents an 18.2% premium over its market price calculated as follows.

$$\frac{\$22.45 - \$19.00}{\$19.00} = 18.2\%$$

The Quality of the Estimate

From the CFO

It's important to understand how arbitrary the valuation process we've just illustrated can be, especially the terminal value calculation. Even though it represents the period about which we know the least (the distant future), the terminal value accounts for fully three-quarters of the final valuation. That means our results are highly sensitive to the assumptions made about the long-term future. In other words, modest changes in those assumptions can make huge differences in total value.

For example, suppose a more optimistic person did the forecast and decided that a 9% long-term growth rate was more appropriate for Arcturus. Under that assumption the terminal value is $763 million and has a present value of $476 million. The total value of the firm is then

$$PV = \$112 \text{ million} + \$476 \text{ million} = \$588 \text{ million}$$

Notice that, under this more aggressive but still reasonable assumption, the terminal value represents 81% of the target's final calculated value. The maximum acquisition price is then ($588 million/20 million =) $29.40, which implies a premium of [($29.40 – $19.00)/$19.00 =] 54.7%.

This means that an enormous range of values can be calculated for the offering price in an acquisition like this one. Good judgment is called for to avoid basing a multimillion-dollar deal on too high a price.

Although premiums this big have been paid in some large and sophisticated acquisitions in recent years, it's hard to believe a company can be worth so much more than its market value. The implication is that something else must be motivating the deal. Many observers have attributed such actions to sheer ego on the part of the executives in charge of the acquiring firms.

Paying for the Acquisition—The Junk Bond Market

Acquiring a company involves giving its shareholders something of value in return for their shares. That something is generally one or a combination of three things: cash, shares in the acquiring firm, or debt of the acquiring firm.

For example, suppose the firms in Example 19.2 (page 687) agreed to a price of $25 for Arcturus's shares. At the same time, suppose Aldebron's shares were selling for $10 a share. The following are a few of the combinations that might be offered for 100 shares of Arcturus.

Cash	Aldebron Shares	Bond
$2,500	–	–
–	250 shares	–
1,000	50 shares	$1,000
1,500	100 shares	–

To the extent that cash is offered, the acquiring firm must either have it or be able to raise it. Investment dealers have played an important role in the most recent merger wave by helping companies raise money to pay for acquisitions. In particular, the *junk bond market* was a product of the 1980s that helped acquirers borrow money to pay for acquisitions.

Recall from Chapter 9 (page 328) that *junk bonds* are low-quality bonds that pay high yields because the firms that issue them are risky. Prior to the 1980s, it was virtually impossible for any small, risky company to borrow regardless of the interest rate it offered on its bonds.

Junk bonds are issued by *financially weak* firms and pay high interest rates. They are frequently used to *fund high-risk acquisitions.*

How a Trendy Soft Drink Gave Cereal Giant Quaker Oats a $1.4 Billion Case of Indigestion

On March 28, 1997, *The Wall Street Journal* carried the modest headline "Quaker Oats to Sell Its Snapple Business." The article announced the end of a story that may be the most flagrant example ever of overpaying for an acquisition.

Only two and a half years earlier, Quaker had paid US$1.7 billion for Snapple, a leader in "new age" soft drinks. The *WSJ* article reported that the business was being sold for a mere US$300 million, a loss of US$1.4 billion.

The loss amounted to US$8.40 per share of Quaker stock. To indicate its magnitude the newspaper noted that in the same quarter a year earlier Quaker's earnings were about US$0.23 per share. This might suggest that the Snapple disaster wiped out about ($8.40/$0.23 =) 36 quarters or nine years of earnings!

Snapple caught on in the early 1990s with sales growing from US$95 million in 1991 to US$516 million in 1993. This blistering growth caught Quaker's eye, and probably fuelled the acquisition price of 20 times earnings, which was twice the P/E ratio of other beverage companies. Further, Quaker already marketed Gatorade, and probably expected big synergies with Snapple.

But there was trouble from the very beginning that Quaker should have anticipated. First, the long-term growth rate of the beverage industry was only about 3%. That meant Snapple's supernormal growth couldn't last forever. Second, other firms including Coke and Pepsi had aggressively entered the new age market. By the time of the acquisition, Snapple's growth had stalled and its earnings estimates were dropping sharply.

It's hard to imagine how Quaker could have made so great an error. Snapple's 1993 earnings were about US$68M. Quaker could have used the techniques of Example 19.1 to derive the kind of growth rate assumptions that would have been necessary to support an acquisition price of US$1.7 billion. For example, if Quaker's required rate of return on the deal was only 15%, Snapple had to have been forecast to grow at about 11% forever to justify the price. That was incredibly optimistic when the overall beverage market was growing at just 3% and the competition included market-savvy giants like Coke and Pepsi!

So why was Quaker willing to pay so much for Snapple? It's hard to say. A *BusinessWeek* article published about six months earlier observed that some investors felt it may have had something to do with the "excitement of a splashy deal."

Sources: Wall Street Journal (March 28, 1997); *BusinessWeek* (September 23, 1996); Arthur J. Thompson and A. J. Strickland, 1996. *Strategic Management: Concepts and Cases*, 9th ed. Chicago: Richard D. Irwin.

During that period, however, investment dealers started pooling risky bonds into funds, claiming that the failure rate of risky companies was only a little higher than that of more reputable firms. Then it was argued that if the failure rate of risky companies is only 1% or 2% higher than that of stable companies, but the pool of their bonds pays 5% or 6% more interest, an investor is better off with a share of the risky pool than with a stable firm's bond.

Investors bought the idea, and suddenly high-risk ventures could borrow substantial sums of money. A prime use of that money was paying for the shares of target companies in risky acquisitions. In other words, the acquiring company would issue junk bonds and use the borrowed money to make acquisitions.

It turned out that the basic premise on which the junk bond market was founded wasn't true. Risky firms failed only slightly more often than higher-rated firms *in good economic times*. In bad times, however, they failed a lot more often. A recession came along in the late 1980s, and the junk bond market collapsed.

The junk bond market was pioneered by an individual named Michael Milken who worked for the firm of Drexel Burnham Lambert. The firm later failed, and Milken spent some time in jail for his activities during the period. In the 1990s and early 2000s, high-yield debt has reemerged as a source of financing.[10]

---

10 At the time of writing (July 2007), Thomson Learning was selling high-yield debt (or junk bonds) to pay for its buyout from its parent company Thomson Corporation by Apax Partners and OMERS Capital Partners. Part of the original deal had to be scrapped as the high-yield markets began to soften.

The Capital Structure Argument to Justify High Premiums

Recall that in Chapter 16 (page 574) we came to the conclusion that capital structure can affect the market price of shares. In particular, we said that replacing equity with debt where there was little or no debt to begin with can sometimes cause the company's share price to rise.

When the money used to buy out a target's shareholders is raised by borrowing, the result is frequently a more leveraged firm with new owners. If this results in a market value increment, the increment is argued to be a justification for paying a high premium for the acquisition's shares.

Even when this happens, it's hard for a reasonable person to justify premiums in the neighbourhood of 50% over market value.

The Effect of Paying Too Much

An acquiring company that pays too much for an acquisition with either its shares or cash on hand transfers wealth from its own shareholders to those of the target. This represents a violation of the acquiring management's responsibility to act in the best interest of its shareholders, but isn't likely to cause problems beyond that.

On the other hand, paying too much with borrowed money results in a company that's heavily burdened with debt and the associated interest payments. That can cause the combined firm to perform poorly or fail in the future.

In the context of Example 19.2, if Aldebron borrows as much as $588 million to buy Arcturus, and Arcturus's cash flows turn out to be less than expected, there won't be enough money available to service the debt. That can mean bankruptcy.

Defensive Tactics

Defensive tactics are things management can do to prevent a company from being acquired. They can be divided into two categories: things that can be done after a takeover attempt is under way, and things that can be done in anticipation of such an attempt.

> A reluctant target's management can use **defensive tactics** to *avoid* being acquired.

Tactics after a Takeover Is Under Way

After an acquiring firm has announced its intentions, a target's management can take the following actions.

CHALLENGE THE PRICE By this tactic, management attempts to convince the shareholders that the acquirer's price is too low. This usually amounts to arguing that the market has temporarily undervalued the shares, and that the shareholders will do a lot better by holding on until the price rises above the amount offered.

CLAIM A VIOLATION OF THE *COMPETITION ACT* Management can approach the Competition Bureau and claim the merger is anticompetitive, hoping that the government will intervene.

ISSUE DEBT AND REPURCHASE SHARES This tends to drive up the share price, making the price offered by the acquirer less attractive. It also increases the firm's leverage, making the company less desirable from a capital structure point of view.

SEEK A WHITE KNIGHT Some acquirers are particularly unattractive because they have a history of treating the management and employees of acquired companies poorly. A target's management will sometimes try to find an alternative acquirer with a better reputation. Such an alternative suitor is known as a white knight.

> A **white knight** is an alternative acquirer with a *better reputation* for its treatment of acquired firms.

GREENMAIL Mergers are sometimes initiated when a powerful group acquires a substantial but minority interest in a company. This can signal its intention to acquire a controlling interest later. Managements have eliminated such threats by buying the group's shares at a price in excess of the shares' market value. Essentially management buys off the attacker with the company's money in a process known as paying greenmail. Other shareholders have been known to become upset over this practice and sue the board of directors.

> **Greenmail** is an above-market payment made by a firm to buy shares owned by a potential acquirer.

Tactics in Anticipation of a Takeover

Several things can be written into a corporation's charter and bylaws that make it difficult to acquire without the cooperation of management.

STAGGERED ELECTION OF DIRECTORS Companies are run by boards of directors, which are normally elected annually by shareholders. The annual election of directors implies that if an outside party gains a controlling interest in the firm's shares, it can elect a new board and begin running the firm relatively promptly. However, if the elections of board members are staggered so that only, say, one-third are elected each year, it will take some time for a new controlling interest to take over the board and thereby control the company. That makes the acquisition less attractive. This tactic is popular in the U.S. but has become an issue for shareholder-rights activists. Staggered elections are less useful in Canada as shareholders can call a special meeting and have directors removed.

APPROVAL BY A SUPERMAJORITY Mergers have to be approved by shareholders owning a majority of the firm's shares. However, the definition of the majority required is written into the corporation's bylaws. Requiring approval by a supermajority, say 80%, of shareholders makes taking control of the company more difficult. In Canada most mergers require a two-thirds majority.

> A **poison pill** is a clause in a firm's bylaws that makes it prohibitively expensive for an acquiring firm to take control.

POISON PILLS Poison pills are legal devices embedded in corporate bylaws that are designed to make it prohibitively expensive for outsiders to take control without the support of management. Conceptually, the acquirer commits financial suicide by swallowing the target along with its poison pill.

There are any number of poison pill arrangements, but there's also some uncertainty surrounding them. Some ideas can prove to be illegal and therefore aren't binding. Other arrangements can be discriminatory against certain groups of shareholders or can be shown to be an irresponsible squandering of the firm's resources. In such cases, the directors who approve the arrangements can be exposed to personal lawsuits by unhappy shareholders. The following are a few of the more common poison pill arrangements.

> *Golden parachutes* are exorbitant severance packages for a target's management.

Golden Parachutes Golden parachutes are contracts between a company and its senior managers that guarantee exorbitant severance packages if those managers are fired after a take-over. In addition to making the managers rich, the cash drain can debilitate the company.

Accelerated Debt A firm can include a provision in its debt contracts that requires the principal amounts to become due immediately if the firm is taken over. Most firms don't have the cash available to make such a payment, so a takeover would put them into default. If that happens, the acquirer is forced to come up with enough cash to pay off all of the acquired firm's debt immediately after the acquisition. This is generally distasteful to acquiring firms.

Share Rights Plans (SRPs) A share rights plan is a complicated arrangement in which current shareholders are given rights, which are securities that enable them to buy shares in the merged company typically at a drastically reduced price after a takeover. That means an acquiring company has to be willing not only to buy the shares of a target, but also to turn over a number of its own shares to the target's shareholders at, say, half price. This doesn't prevent an acquisition, but can make it very expensive.

OTHER KINDS OF TAKEOVERS—LBOS AND PROXY FIGHTS

So far we've associated takeovers with acquisitions of one firm by another. However, changes in ownership and control can occur outside of business combinations.

Leveraged Buyouts (LBOs)

> In a **leveraged buyout** **(LBO)** investors *take a company private* by buying its shares with borrowed money. The *result* of a *leveraged buyout* is usually a *risky, debt-laden company*.

A **leveraged buyout (LBO)** is a transaction in which a publicly held company's shares are purchased by a group of investors. The company is then no longer publicly traded, but becomes a *private or closely held* firm owned by the group of investors, who may be the firm's management.

The investor group gets the money to buy the shares by contributing a relatively small amount of its own equity and borrowing the rest. The amount borrowed can turn out to be more than 95% of capital, hence the term *"leveraged" buyout*. The borrowed funds usually come through asset-based financing, meaning the loans are secured by the firm's own assets.

For example, imagine a firm that has no debt and $100 million in shareholders' equity. Now suppose the management team purchases the shares by contributing $5 million of its own money and borrowing the rest. The firm's capital structure before and after the LBO is as follows ($ millions).

	Before LBO	**After LBO**
Debt	$ 0	$ 95
Shareholders' equity	100	5
Total capital	$100	$100

It's important to understand that nothing has changed with respect to the operating ability of the company to generate money. However, the post-LBO firm has to pay interest on debt of $95 million, making it a very risky company.

Notice that the LBO is a takeover but not a merger. The company has been taken over by a group of investors, but it hasn't been merged with anything.

Specialized LBO companies help put together LBOs and assist in borrowing the necessary money. The best known of these is Kohlberg, Kravis, & Roberts (KKR), which is famous for its 1988 LBO of RJR Nabisco, a combined tobacco and food products company. Prior to the LBO, the firm's shares were trading at about $55 per share. The deal was finally done at $106 per share for a total of more than $25 billion. In Canada, Onex Corporation (page 678), created in 1984, is the undisputed leader in buyouts. It currently holds stakes in several companies with combined sales of nearly $19 billion.

After an LBO is completed, the object is to reduce the debt load as quickly as possible. This can sometimes be accomplished by selling off divisions or assets and using the proceeds to pay down the debt.

LBOs have been criticized as profit-driven financial manipulations that can destroy sound companies. Our numerical illustration gives an indication of what is meant by this accusation. Before the LBO, the company was a conservatively financed firm, presumably with good operating prospects (otherwise the acquiring group wouldn't have been interested). After the LBO, the same firm was in serious danger of collapse under the weight of its debt.

Proxy Fights

A *proxy* is a legal document that gives one person the right to act for another on a certain issue. When corporations elect boards of directors, management usually solicits shareholders for their proxies to use in voting for directors. In other words, management asks shareholders for their proxies to vote for the board members it has proposed. There's generally no opposition, and the proxies are willingly granted by most of the shareholders.

However, sometimes a group of shareholders becomes dissatisfied with management and seeks to gain control of the board. Such a dissident group can also solicit the proxies of the other shareholders for the election of board members. If the dissidents win, they can elect their representatives to the board and take control of the firm.

A **proxy fight** occurs when more than one group simultaneously solicits shareholders' proxies for the election of directors. A takeover is said to occur if the dissident group wins.

In a **proxy fight**, opposing groups solicit shareholders' *proxies* for the election of directors.

Notice that no change in ownership is associated with a proxy fight. The same shareholders own the firm before and after the battle, but the controlling interest on the board changes.

Typically these fights are lost by the dissidents as they use their own cash to launch the fight while the managers have the luxury of using the company's funds to launch their defence!

DIVESTITURES

A **divestiture** means getting rid of a business unit.

A **divestiture** is the opposite of an acquisition. A company decides that for some reason it would be better off without a particular business operation and gets rid of it.

The Reasons for Divestitures

Companies *divest* operations to *raise money*, or because of poor *performance* or lack of *strategic fit*.

There are several reasons for divestitures.

CASH The straightforward reason to sell anything is a need for cash. A firm can simply sell off a noncritical piece of itself because it needs the money for something else.

After LBOs, firms tend to have huge debt burdens that can sometimes be partially paid down by selling assets or noncritical operations for cash.

Acquisition targets sometimes have operations that acquirers don't want but which can't be separated from the things they do want before the merger. It's relatively common to divest unwanted divisions shortly after the acquisition and use the money received to reduce the expense of the original takeover.

STRATEGIC FIT Sometimes companies have divisions or subsidiaries that don't fit into their long-term plans. This can be especially true if there's been a change in the firm's strategic thinking.

POOR PERFORMANCE Certain operations just never become acceptably profitable. Eventually even the most patient of managements will want to get rid of them.

Methods of Divesting Operations

There are basically three ways to divest a business unit: sale, spinoff, and liquidation.

SALE FOR CASH AND/OR SECURITIES An operation can be sold to another company or to an investor group. The first situation is a friendly acquisition of the operation by the other company. The second is an LBO.

SPINOFF A spinoff occurs when two parts of a firm are recognized to be strategically incompatible, but there's no desire to get rid of either. In other words, management believes that it's in the shareholders' best interest to keep both pieces, but it's operationally better to separate them completely. A **spinoff** is accomplished by setting up the operation to be divested as a separate corporation and giving shareholders of the original company a share of the new firm for every share of the old firm they own.

A **spinoff** involves setting up an operation as a separate company and giving its shares to shareholders in proportion to their holdings of the original firm.

After the spinoff, the two companies are owned by exactly the same shareholders, who are then free to trade the shares separately. After a relatively short time, the ownership is usually no longer identical.

Here's an example. Suppose a stable company begins to acquire and develop a few riskier business divisions. After a few years the firm has two distinct sides, one conservative and one risky. However, many of the original shareholders invested in the company because it was stable, so they're not comfortable with its new risky side. It makes sense to spin off the risky section and let the unhappy shareholders sell their shares in it while maintaining or increasing their holdings in the conservative business. As an example, Nortel Networks Corporation was a spinoff from BCE in 2000.

Insights REAL APPLICATIONS

Canadian Pacific Limited

Prior to its breakup, Canadian Pacific Limited was a conglomerate with five operating businesses: PanCanadian Petroleum Limited, Fording Coal, CP Rail, CP Hotels & Resorts, and CP Ships. In 2001 the company split along these lines into five operating companies; the stated rationale for the move by the Canadian Pacific Limited management team was to "unlock shareholder value." Those investors who held Canadian Pacific Limited shares prior to announcement of the breakup (February 2001) and agreed to the arrangement where they received shares in the five operating businesses found the value of their holding increase from about $40 to roughly $60 (October 2001).

LIQUIDATION In a liquidation, the divested business is simply closed down and its assets are sold off piecemeal. Liquidation is generally a last resort to dispose of businesses that have failed badly.

BANKRUPTCY AND THE REORGANIZATION OF FAILED BUSINESSES

Failure is an unpleasant but real fact of business life. Roughly 8,000 businesses fail each year, including some very substantial firms. We'll begin our discussion of the subject by defining exactly what is meant by failure.

Failure and Insolvency

Business failure can be defined economically in a long-run sense or in more immediate commercial terms. We're primarily concerned with the commercial concept and its implications, but it's important to understand the economic idea and appreciate the distinction between the two.

A business fails economically if it is unable to provide an adequate return to its owners. For example, suppose a company consistently pays its bills and earns a profit, but never makes more than a 1% or 2% return on the equity invested by its shareholders. After a while, investors will seek to get their capital out of such a company, and it will be closed as a failure.

The economic failure we've just described is an issue between a business and its owners. Commercial failure, on the other hand, is an issue between a business and its *creditors*. A business fails commercially when it can't pay its debts; this condition is known as insolvency. A firm is said to be *technically insolvent* when it can't meet its short-term obligations as they come due. It is *legally insolvent* if its liabilities exceed its assets.

A commercial failure is generally also an economic failure, but a business can be an economic failure without ever failing in the legal or commercial sense.

> A firm is **insolvent** and a *commercial failure* if it can't pay its near-term debts.

Potential Actions by Creditors Against an Insolvent Company

Imagine that an insolvent company owes money to a number of creditors. Then suppose one secured creditor takes possession of the firm's producing assets to satisfy its debt.

This would be good for the one creditor, but would be very bad for everyone else involved. If the insolvent firm loses its production equipment, it probably goes out of business immediately. In most cases that means all the employees lose their jobs and the firm's shareholders lose their entire investments. Further, because the company no longer has the ability to earn money, none of the other creditors is likely to be paid anything.

In most cases it would be better for the firm to continue in business and use its earnings to pay off its debts slowly. This implies that it has to stop doing whatever made it insolvent in the first place, if that's possible. The problem is that each creditor is looking out for itself and wants to have its debts satisfied out of the firm's assets before they're paid out to someone else.

Bankruptcy—Concept and Objectives

Bankruptcy is a legal proceeding designed to preclude the situation we've just described. When an insolvent firm goes into bankruptcy, the court may protect it from its creditors and at the same time determine whether it should be kept running or closed down.

A firm can be insolvent because its business has gone bad to the point of failure or it has too much debt in an otherwise survivable situation. In the first case, it's better to shut the company down before it loses any more money and salvage as many of its assets as possible to pay off its debts. In the second case, the firm may be able to make good on all of its debts if it's given enough time, so it may be appropriate to keep it running if whatever made it insolvent in the first place can be changed. Of course, some situations are a combination of both conditions, which makes the judgment a tough call.

> A **bankruptcy** proceeding protects a failing firm from creditors until a resolution is reached to close or continue it.

If an insolvent company appears to be worth more as a going concern than the value of its assets, it goes through a reorganization under the supervision and protection of the court. This involves a restructuring of its debt and a plan to pay everyone off as fairly as possible.

If the court decides that the company is a lost cause, worth more dead than alive, it orders a *liquidation*. In a liquidation, the firm's assets are sold under the court's supervision and the proceeds are used to pay creditors in accordance with a schedule of priorities included in the bankruptcy laws.

In summary, bankruptcy is a federal legal procedure designed to prevent as much pain and loss as possible when firms fail. A firm isn't *bankrupt* or *in bankruptcy* until the action is filed in court. Until that time it's just insolvent. A bankrupt firm *emerges from or comes out of* bankruptcy after a reorganization in which its creditors agree to some settlement of their claims. In Canada there are two statutes dealing with bankruptcy and reorganization: the *Bankruptcy and Insolvency Act (BIA)* and the *Companies' Creditors Arrangement Act (CCAA)*. Our discussion below is based on the *Bankruptcy and Insolvency Act (1992)*.

Bankruptcy Procedures—Reorganization, Restructuring, Liquidation

A *petition* can be initiated by either the insolvent company itself or by its creditors. When the debtor firm itself files the petition, the bankruptcy is said to be *voluntary*. When creditors do the filing the action is *involuntary*. Once either petition is filed in federal court, the firm is protected from creditors' further legal actions related to its debts until the bankruptcy is resolved.

Normally, a firm in bankruptcy is permitted to continue in business. To prevent it from doing so would usually cause the kinds of losses described in the last section. However, there may be a concern that the company's management will cause a further deterioration in its financial position during the proceedings. There's also a concern that assets will be removed during this period, leaving an empty shell to satisfy creditors. To guard against these dangers, the court may appoint a **trustee** to oversee the company's operation while it's in bankruptcy.

> A **trustee** in bankruptcy oversees the operation of a firm in bankruptcy to *protect* the interests of *creditors*.

Reorganization

A **reorganization** is a business plan under which the firm can continue to operate and pay off its debts. Management and the company's shareholders invariably favour reorganization over liquidation, because there's generally little or nothing left for shareholders after a liquidation. Once the petition is filed, management has 30 days to come up with an acceptable reorganization plan.[11]

> A **reorganization** is a plan under which an insolvent firm *continues to operate* while attempting to pay off its debts.

Reorganization plans are judged on two general criteria: *fairness* and *feasibility*. Fairness implies that claims are satisfied in accordance with an order of priorities that's part of the bankruptcy laws. We'll talk about those priorities later. Feasibility refers to the likelihood that the plan will actually come to pass. It's important to realize that a reorganization plan is a business/financial plan just like those we discussed in Chapter 6. As such, it's based on a set of assumptions that may or may not be realistic. A court is unlikely to approve a plan that's based on unrealistic assumptions.

To be accepted, a reorganization plan has to be approved by the firm's creditors and then accepted by the court. Once a reorganization plan is accepted, the firm can emerge from bankruptcy. Then it's generally the responsibility of the court-appointed trustee to oversee the plan's implementation.

Debt Restructuring

> **Debt restructuring** involves concessions that *lower* an insolvent firm's *payments* so it can continue in business.

The heart of most reorganization plans is a **restructuring** of the firm's debt. Keep in mind that insolvent firms are bankrupt because they couldn't pay their debts. Therefore they aren't likely to be able to work themselves out of their troubles under the debt payment schedules that

---

11 The firm may apply for extensions up to five months after the initial 30 days.

existed before the bankruptcy petition was filed. What's generally necessary is some kind of a reduction in payments. Restructuring the firm's debt makes such a reduction possible.

Debt restructuring can be accomplished in two ways. The simplest is an *extension* whereby creditors agree to give the firm a longer time to repay its obligations. A temporary deferral of principal and sometimes interest payments is quite common. The second approach is a *composition* in which creditors agree to settle for less than the full amount owed them.

It's important to understand the position of creditors in a bankruptcy case. If they demand immediate payment of the full amounts of their debts, the bankrupt firm will fail and they'll receive only a small fraction of what they're owed. On the other hand, if they accept less in terms of either the amount paid or its timing, they may stand to get a great deal more money in the long run. Therefore they have an incentive to compromise and make concessions.

A common method of accomplishing a debt restructuring is the conversion of debt into equity. Creditors give up their debt claims (loans, bonds, accounts receivable) in return for shares in the bankrupt company. This immediately reduces the debt service burden on the company in trouble and eases its cash flow problems (assuming it doesn't pay dividends on the new equity).

After such a conversion, creditors have equity positions in the troubled company. These aren't worth much initially, but if the firm survives and perhaps prospers, they can be worth more in the long run than the debt given up. Notice that in a conversion the original shareholders receive a benefit in terms of the forgiveness of some of their company's debt. In return their ownership is diluted.

Extensions, compositions, and debt to equity conversions are common approaches to restructuring.

Example 19.3

The Adcock Company has 50,000 common shares outstanding at a book value of $40, pays 10% interest on its debt, and is in the following financial situation.

Adcock Company Selected Financial Information ($000)

Income and Cash Flow		Capital	
EBIT	$ 200	Debt	$6,000
Interest	(600)	Equity	2,000
EBT	(400)	Total capital	$8,000
Tax	—		
NI	(400)		
Amortization	200		
Principal repayment	(100)		
Cash flow	$ (300)		

Notice that although the company has a positive EBIT, it doesn't earn enough to pay its interest, let alone repay principal on schedule. Without help of some kind, it will fail shortly. Devise a composition involving a debt for equity conversion that will keep the firm afloat.

■ **Solution:** Suppose the creditors (perhaps a number of bondholders) are willing to convert $3 million in debt to equity at the $40 book value of the existing shares. This would require the firm to issue 75,000 new shares, resulting in the following financial situation.

Adcock Company Selected Financial Information
After Debt to Equity Conversion ($000)

Income and Cash Flow		Capital	
EBIT	$ 200	Debt	$3,000
Interest	(300)	Equity	5,000
EBT	$ (100)	Total capital	$8,000
Tax	—		
NI	$ (100)		
Amortization	200		
Principal repayment	(50)		
Cash flow	$ 50		

Notice that the company now has a slightly positive cash flow and can at least theoretically continue in business indefinitely. However, the creditors now own a controlling interest in the firm.

Liquidation

Liquidation involves closing a troubled firm and selling its assets.

When the court decides that a bankrupt business isn't worth continuing it orders a liquidation, which involves selling off the firm's assets and using the proceeds to pay off as many of the firm's debts as possible. The process is conceptually simple but can be administratively involved.

Unauthorized *transfers out* of a bankrupt firm can be *recovered* by the trustee.

The liquidation is accomplished by a court-appointed trustee who first looks for and attempts to recover any unauthorized transfers out of the firm around the time of the bankruptcy filing. This is an important step. When business owners anticipate bankruptcy, they frequently try to remove assets from the company. Doing that is illegal because those assets should rightly be used to satisfy creditors' claims. It's the trustee's job to find and recover such articles and payments.

Next, the trustee supervises the sale of the business's assets, gathering the proceeds into a pool of funds that can be used to satisfy creditors' claims. Finally, the trustee distributes the available funds to the various claimants.

It's important to realize that claimants aren't just lenders in the traditional sense. They include vendors who sold to the company on credit, employees who are owed wages, customers who may have put down deposits on merchandise, the government (which may be owed taxes), and the people and organizations that are part of the bankruptcy proceeding. This last group includes lawyers and the court itself, which are owed fees for their services. In addition, the company's shareholders are claimants to the extent of whatever is left over after everyone else is satisfied.

Distribution Priorities

The *Bankruptcy and Insolvency Act* contains *priorities* for the *distribution* of assets among claimants.

The distribution of funds in bankruptcy follows an order of priority laid down by the *Bankruptcy and Invsolvency Act*. This order is used to determine the sequence of payment in liquidation and as the basis for the fairness judgment in evaluating reorganization plans. Basically the priority rule says that all claimants are not equal in the eyes of the law.

It's important to understand the implications of this rule. The funds available from liquidation usually amount to a fraction of the value of the claims against the company. For example, a firm with total claims of $1 million might end up with a pool of funds from liquidation of $300,000. The priority rule says that the claimants do not all get 30 cents on the dollar for their debt. Some get more and some get less.

Secured debt is backed by specific assets (the security or collateral) that become the property of the lender in the event of default.

SECURED DEBT The first distinction made among claimants is between *secured* and *unsecured creditors*. A secured creditor's debt, known as secured debt, is guaranteed by a specific asset. For example, when money is borrowed to buy a car, the loan is generally secured by the automobile itself. That means if the loan isn't paid, the car is sold and the money from the sale must be used to satisfy that debt before any other. Unsecured debts aren't tied to particular assets and just rely on the general creditworthiness of the borrower.

Secured creditors are paid out of the proceeds of the sale of *pledged assets*.

Secured obligations are each paid out of the proceeds of the sale of the related assets before the liquidation pool is established. To the extent that any individual secured debt is more or less than the value of its securing asset, the difference becomes unsecured debt or an addition to the pool, depending on whether the debt or the value of the asset is larger.

PRIORITIES FOR PAYMENT OF CLAIMS After all secured debts are paid, unsecured claims are paid out of the remaining pool of funds in the following order:

1. Administrative expenses of the bankruptcy proceedings
2. Salaries, wages, and commissions up to $2,000 per employee
3. Municipal taxes owed within two years preceding bankruptcy
4. Rent for preceding three-month period
5. Certain unpaid contributions to employee benefit plans

6. Other unpaid taxes
7. Unsecured creditors
8. Preferred shareholders
9. Common shareholders

Common shareholders receive only the bankrupt firm's residual value after all other obligations have been paid. That's often nothing at all.

Insights ETHICS

Is Bankruptcy Too Easy?—What about Ethics?

Is bankruptcy unethical, unfair, or just too easy? That question has been around as long as bankruptcy laws have existed. Here's a quote from the work of the famous French author Balzac written 170 years ago:

"What is a bankrupt, father?" asked Eugenie.

"A bankrupt," replied her father, "is guilty of the most dishonourable action that can dishonour a man. ... A bankrupt ... is a thief whom the law unfortunately takes under its protection. ... A bankrupt is worse than a highwayman. ..."

—Honoré de Balzac, *Eugenie Grandet*, p. 108 (1833)

Many creditors feel the same way today. They think it's unfair to let debtors off the hook for fair debts that they might be able to pay if more pressure was put on them over a longer period. They decry bankruptcies of convenience and popular guidebooks on how to use court procedures to escape debts. In other words, they think bankruptcy is legalized theft from those who have extended credit in good faith.

There's undoubtedly an ethical issue in bankruptcy. Is it right to allow people or companies to completely escape the repayment of substantial debts and start over with a clean slate? Creditors believe that it isn't and have been lobbying Parliament for years to toughen bankruptcy laws.

In November 2005, the government made changes to the *Bankruptcy and Insolvency Act* and the *Companies' Creditors Arrangement Act* and introduced Bill C-55. Although Bill C-55 has yet to be implemented, it essentially will make the solutions harder, not easier.

Some groups oppose the new bill, claiming that its biggest supporters are lenders that lose money when overextended borrowers escape into bankruptcy. Their point is that many lenders create their own problems by lending to individuals and companies without doing adequate credit checks. Such a practice is alleged to tempt consumers to make purchases using easy credit that they cannot afford to repay.

So which argument is right and which is wrong? Was bankruptcy too easy; or is it now too hard? Or have unethical or greedy lenders made us credit junkies, sadly over our heads in debt? And did those lenders deserve to get stuck from time to time? And ... is our government doing the right or the wrong thing by making it tougher to get a "fresh start" through bankruptcy?

Sources: Morgan D. King, "Bankruptcy Reform in a Nutshell." http:www.bankruptcyfinder.com/nutshellking.html; and Almar Latour and Rebecca Blumenstein, "Verizon to MCI: Drop Dead," *The Wall Street Journal* (May 15, 2003): pp. B1–B16. The Standing Senate Committee on Banking, Trade, and Commerce, May 8, 2003.

SUMMARY

1 Some firms believe that by merging they will see increased value by taking advantage of synergies and economies of scale; others hope for increased growth potential, and still others see it as a good way to diversify the risk of being in one specific industry. There are disadvantages too; shareholders often believe that the merger occurred at their expense, that is, the management of the company decided to undertake the merger so that managers could build an empire.

Some companies do the opposite—that is, they divest themselves of certain divisions. They may use some of the same reasons put forward for mergers but use a different approach. For example, they may say that the division no longer fits within the firm's strategic plans or that they believe that, although the firm enjoys synergies, shareholders do not fully appreciate them and therefore various divisions should be sold off.

2 Defensive tactics are various activities or policies that management might use to discourage a takeover attempt. This can include activities such as increasing the debt load, arguing that the acquirer's price is too low or introducing poison pills and the like. Some of the tactics clearly are to the advantage of the management teams at the shareholders' expense.

3 Another type of corporate restructuring that isn't as pleasant is bankruptcy and reorganization. When a company can no longer pay its creditors, it is insolvent. Creditors will be anxious to recover some of their investment and will look to the courts for assistance. The troubled company may then be allowed time to restructure itself or be liquidated.

KEY TERMS

Acquisition, p. 676
Bankruptcy, p. 695
Competition Act, p. 679
Conglomerate merger, p. 678
Consolidation, p. 676
Corporate restructuring, p. 675
Debt Restructuring, p. 696
Defensive tactics, p. 691
Divestiture, p. 694
Greenmail, p. 691

Holding company, p. 681
Horizontal merger, p. 678
In play, p. 685
Insolvency, p. 695
Leveraged buyout (LBO), p. 692
Liquidation, p. 698
Merger, p. 676
Poison pill, p. 692
Proxy fight, p. 693

Reorganization, p. 696
Secured debt, p. 698
Speculation, p. 685
Spinoff, p. 694
Synergy, p. 679
Takeover, p. 676
Target, p. 676
Trustee, p. 696
Vertical merger, p. 678
White knight, p. 691

KEY FORMULAS

(12.1)
$$NPV = -C_0 + \frac{C_1}{(1 + k)} + \frac{C_2}{(1 + k)^2} + \dots + \frac{C_n}{(1 + k)^n}$$

QUESTIONS

1. Define vertical, horizontal, and conglomerate mergers and describe the economic effects of each.

2. "Hostile acquisitions create animosities between the shareholders of the acquired and acquiring companies." Comment on the truth of this statement.

3. The Highland Instrument Company has revenues of about $300 million per year. Its management is interested in expanding into a new type of product manufactured primarily by Lowland Gauge Inc., a firm with sales of about $200 million annually. Both firms are publicly held with a broad base of shareholders. That is, no single interest holds a large percentage of the shares of either firm. Describe the types of business combination that might be available for the two firms. Include ideas like merger, consolidation, acquisition, friendly, and hostile. How would Highland's management get started? Do the relative sizes of the two firms have any implications for the kinds of combination that are possible or likely?

4. Industry A is dominated by 10 large firms, each with sales of approximately $500 million per year. A proposal to merge two of these firms was approved by the Competition Bureau as not violating the *Competition Act*. Industry B is locally defined and much smaller. It is dominated by three small firms, each selling about $50 million per year. A merger between two of these companies was prohibited under the *Competition Act*. Explain the logic under which the merger of two $500 million giants can be allowed while the relatively insignificant merger of two small companies is disallowed.

5. Suppose an industry is dominated by three firms, one of which is twice as large as the others, which are about equal in size. Could a merger of the two smaller firms actually increase competition in the industry?

6. Clarington Corp. has a division that's been performing well but doesn't fit into the company's current long-term strategic plans. Describe the methods through which it can divest itself of the operation.

7. The Blivitt Company has been losing money and experiencing serious cash flow problems lately. The main problem is a large debt to the First National Bank that was incurred to purchase a computer that's now obsolete. Bill Blivitt, the firm's owner, has stated his intention to declare bankruptcy to rid the company of the loan. He expects to go in and out of bankruptcy protection in a few weeks and emerge essentially as before but without the loan. Write a note to Bill explaining bankruptcy procedures and why this is probably an unrealistic approach on his part.

Business Analysis

1. The Cranston Company would like to acquire the Lamont Company, but overtures made to management have been emphatically rebuffed. Forty-five percent of Lamont's shares are owned by five investors who were involved in the company's founding and continue to be active in its management. Charlie Hardnose, Cranston's director of corporate development, has suggested a hostile takeover that would bypass Lamont's management. Could this work and does it seem to be a very good idea in this situation?

2. You're a seasoned financial executive who's recently been hired as the CFO of the Pilaster Corporation. The firm has just finished two years in which its financial performance has been clearly below par. The company isn't in danger of failing, but it's clear that earnings and growth could be much better. The market price of Pilaster's shares reflects this luke-warm performance. It is currently selling for $32, down substantially from its peak of $48 a little over two years ago. (The market has been generally flat in the last two years.)

   Several observers have blamed the lacklustre performance on the firm's CEO, Gerald Beanweather, and his top assistants. This team installed some new technological and managerial methods several years ago that haven't worked out well. Recently, they've been talking about returning to the old, time-tested methods, which most of the team now feels will bring the firm back to its usual performance levels. In fact, your hiring was part of the turnaround effort.

   It's currently 7:00 a.m. on a cold, bleak Monday morning in February. On the previous evening the CEO's secretary phoned the entire executive team to tell them an emergency meeting was set for this morning. The group is now assembled, waiting to hear what's going on.

   At 7:01 a.m. Gerry walks into the room, obviously upset. He says that yesterday after-noon he received a call from Harvey Highroller, the CEO of Marble Inc., the leading firm in the industry. Marble is interested in acquiring Pilaster and is willing to offer $37 per share, a premium of more than 15%. Marble has a history of making both friendly and unfriendly acquisitions.

    a. What kind of combination is Marble currently proposing?

    b. What is likely to happen if Pilaster's management rejects Marble's offer?

    c. Is Marble likely to be successful over management's objections?

    d. Why is Gerry so personally upset?

    e. Should you be personally upset?

    f. Is Marble's offer a good deal for Pilaster's shareholders?

    g. What should Pilaster's management do to avoid acquisition by Marble?

    h. Do you think Marble is likely to be successful in an unfriendly merger attempt over Pilaster's defences?

    i. If Marble is not successful, what can the Beanweather team do to reduce the chances of a similar attack in the future?

3. The Blue Tag Company and the Pink Label Corporation both make packaging and labelling equipment. The following facts are relevant.
   - Both firms use similar production and sales methods.
   - Pink Label has been losing money for years, while Blue Tag has been and is expected to continue to be profitable.
   - There is a great deal of overhead in label making.
   - The industry is dominated by the much larger Yellow Marker Co., which is difficult to compete with because of its size advantage.

   The managements of the two companies are considering a merger. What arguments can be made in favour of such a combination?

4. The Phlanders Flange Company has been doing quite well lately and would like to accelerate its growth within the flange industry. Harry Flatiron, the firm's CEO, has become interested in growth through acquisition because of some exciting articles in the business press. In particular he's interested in a friendly acquisition of the Framingham Flange Factory, whose general manager, Jack Daniels (a major shareholder in Framingham), he's known for some time.

   Harry is prone to quick action based on brief analyses that he does himself. In the past his instincts have been pretty good, and this style has not as yet caused any major mistakes. Harry has taken Framingham's own estimate of its future cash flows and long-term growth rate along with synergies he and Jack have estimated to come up with a projected value for the company. All this has led to a proposal to offer Framingham's shareholders a 60% premium on the price of their shares.

   You're Phlanders's CFO, but Harry has done all this on his own. He's about ready to make a verbal offer to Framingham's management, and has asked you to check over his figures. His arithmetic is correct, but you're very concerned about the validity of his assumptions.

   Prepare a short memo to Harry outlining the risks associated with value estimates in mergers and the consequences of a mistake. Include advice on how to proceed.

5. You're the CFO of the Littleton Lighting Company. Joan Brightway, the president, has approached you and the firm's other senior executives with a proposal to take the company private through an LBO. She says that this is a good time to do it because the economic outlook is shaky and the firm's share price is depressed; therefore, it will take less money to acquire control. You agree that the weak outlook has depressed the share

price, but this might argue against an LBO at this time. You also suspect that some fundamental weakness is developing in the demand for the firm's product.

Certain successful LBOs have received a lot of favourable press lately, and you're concerned that Joan and the other nonfinancial executives may not appreciate the risks involved in the procedure. Prepare a memo outlining what's involved in an LBO and why the manoeuvre is risky, especially with respect to the business's performance in the immediate future. Make a recommendation on the analyses that should be undertaken prior to going forward.

PROBLEMS

The solutions in Appendix B are based on using either a financial calculator or Excel®. Slight rounding differences will occur if using financial tables.

1. The target of an acquisition generates cash flows of $8 million per year with a risk level consistent with a return on equity of 16%.
    a. How much should an acquirer be willing to pay if it won't consider more than five years of future earnings in setting a price?
    b. What is the per-share price if the target has 300,000 common shares outstanding?
    c. Assume the acquirer intends to pay for the acquisition with its own shares, which are currently selling for $36 per share. How many shares must be offered for each of the target's shares?

2. Montreal Materials Inc. is considering acquiring Noble Products, which produces a number of products that would enhance Montreal's product line. Last year, Noble reported a $30 million loss. Montreal has estimated that Noble will break even in the fourth year after acquisition. The improvement in performance will come in four equal steps. Assuming Montreal can demonstrate that the acquisition is not simply for tax purposes, calculate the present value of the tax savings that will result during the four-year period at a 12% discount rate. Assume Montreal has EBT far exceeding $30 million and is subject to a 40% marginal tax rate.

3. Harrison Ltd. is considering acquiring Pugs International Inc. Pugs had cash flows of $15 million last year and has 2.5 million shares outstanding, which are currently selling at $29 per share. The discount rate for analysis has been correctly estimated at 14%.
    a. How much should Harrison be willing to pay for Pugs in total and per share if the firm is not expected to grow significantly and management insists that acquisitions be justified by no more than ten years of projected cash flows?
    b. Make the same calculations assuming management will consider an indefinite stream of cash flows.
    c. Make the calculations once again assuming management is very aggressive and is willing to assume Pugs' income will go on forever growing at a rate of 3% per year.
    d. Comment on the results of parts a, b, and c.

4. The Johnson Machine Tool Company is thinking of acquiring Lethbridge Gear Works Inc. Lethbridge is a stable company that produces cash flows of $525,000 per year. That figure isn't expected to change in the near future, and no synergies are expected from the acquisition. Johnson's management has estimated that the appropriate risk-adjusted discount rate for pricing calculations is 15%. Lethbridge has 200,000 common shares outstanding.
    a. What is the most Johnson should be willing to pay for Lethbridge if management is financially conservative and insists that an acquisition must justify itself within 10 years? State the price in total and per share.
    b. How much should Johnson be willing to pay, in total and per share, if management takes a more aggressive position and will consider Lethbridge's income as continuing forever? (*Hint:* Estimate Lethbridge's value as a perpetuity starting immediately.)

   c. What total and per-share prices are implied if Johnson's executives are financially very aggressive and assume that their management will transform Lethbridge into a better company that will grow at 3% per year indefinitely?

   d. Comment briefly on the differences in your answers to parts (a), (b), and (c).

5. Grandma's Cookies Inc. is considering acquiring Mother's Baked Goods Inc. After consideration of all benefits, synergies, and tax effects, Grandma (originally a finance major) has estimated that the incremental cash flows from the acquisition will be about $150,000 per year for 15 years. (Grandma is financially conservative and reluctant to base decisions on benefits projected farther into the future.) She has also estimated the project's discount rate, appropriately adjusted for risk, at 12%.

   Mother's is a privately owned firm with 20,000 shares outstanding. Grandma is confident that the owners will sell for $50 a share, but not for less. Should Grandma acquire Mother's?

6. Sourdough Mills has considered acquiring Mrs. Baird's Bakery as an expansion strategy. Mrs. Baird's Bakery generated positive cash flows of $5.3 million last year, and cash flows are expected to increase by 4% per year in the foreseeable future. Mrs. Baird's has 1.3 million shares outstanding, and the appropriate discount rate is 11%.

   a. If Sourdough assumes this level of cash flow will continue forever, what is the most that it should pay for each share of Mrs. Baird's Bakery?

   b. If Sourdough wants the investment justifiable considering only five years of cash flow, what is the most it should pay for the shares?

   c. What if it will consider a 10-year planning period?

   d. If Mrs. Baird's Bakery shares are currently selling for $35 per share, what would you do if you were Sourdough Mills?

7. Hay River Motors is considering making a takeover bid for the chain of Richard's Auto Superstores. Richard's has 800,000 shares outstanding, which are trading at $18 per share. Richard's generated $2.5 million in cash last year, and cash flows are expected to increase by 6% per year for at least 10 years. Assume the appropriate discount rate is 12%. What percent premium can Hay River afford to offer for Richard's shares if management wants to justify the investment over ten years? nine years? eight years?

8. Frozen North Outfitters Inc. makes thermal clothing for winter sports and outdoor work. It is considering acquiring Downhill Fashions Corp., which manufactures and sells ski clothing. Downhill is about one-quarter of Frozen's size and manufactures its entire product line in a small rented factory on a high hilltop in Saskatchewan. It costs about $1 million a year in overhead to operate in that factory. Frozen produces its output in a less romantic but more practical southern location. Its factory has at least 50% excess capacity. Frozen's plan is to acquire Downhill and combine production operations in its southern factory, but otherwise run the companies separately.

   Downhill's beta is 2.0, Treasury bills currently yield 5%, and the S&P/TSX Composite Index is yielding 9%. The marginal combined federal and provincial income tax rate for both firms is 40%. Because Downhill will no longer be maintaining its own production facilities, only a minimal amount of cash will have to be reinvested to keep its equipment current and for future growth. This amount is estimated at $100,000 per year. Selected financial information for Downhill follows.

Revenue	$ 12,500,000
NI	$ 1,300,000
Amortization	$ 600,000

   a. Calculate the appropriate discount rate for evaluating the Downhill acquisition.

   b. Determine the annual cash flow (net of amortization) expected by Frozen from Downhill if the acquisition is made (don't forget to include the synergy).

   c. Calculate the value of the acquisition to Frozen assuming the benefits last for (i) five years, (ii) 10 years, and (iii) 15 years.

   d. Downhill has 250,000 shares outstanding. Calculate the maximum price Frozen should be willing to pay per share to acquire the firm under the three assumptions in part (c).

   e. If Frozen is willing to assume that the benefits of the Downhill acquisition will last indefinitely but will not grow, what should it be willing to pay per share?

9. In the previous problem, assume that the cash flow from the Downhill acquisition grows at 10% from its initial value for one year and then grows at 5% indefinitely (starting in the third year). Calculate the value of the firm and the implied share price under these conditions. Use a terminal value at the beginning of the period of 5% growth. What price premium is implied, in dollars and as a percentage, if Downhill's shares are currently selling at $62? Comment on the range of values in the results of this and the last problem.

10. Benson's Markets is a five-store regional supermarket chain that has done very well by using modern management and distribution techniques. Benson competes with Foodland Inc., a larger chain with 10 stores. However, Foodland has not kept pace with technological and merchandising developments, and has been losing money lately. Foodland's owners are interested in retiring and have approached Benson's with a proposal to sell the chain for $50 million.

     Within each chain, individual stores perform uniformly. Typical results for an average store in each company are as follows.

Typical Single-Store Results for Benson's and Foodland Supermarkets ($000)

	Benson's	Foodland
Revenue	$ 45,000	$ 38,000
Cost of product	38,500	33,500
Store overhead: Amortization	400	300
Other	4,600	4,700
EBT	$ 1,500	$ (500)
Tax	600	—
NI	$ 900	$ (500)

     If Benson were to make the acquisition, it would immediately close three of Foodland's stores that are located close to its own markets and sell the buildings for about $1 million each. The remaining stores would operate at their current loss levels for about two years, during which time they would be upgraded to Benson's operating standards. The upgrades would cost $3 million per store, spread over the first two years. After that, the acquired stores would have about the same operating performance as Benson's other stores. Benson's CFO believes that a discount rate of 12% is appropriate for the risk associated with the proposition. Benson's marginal tax rate is 40%.

   a. Calculate the value of the acquisition to Benson's, assuming there is no impact on any of Benson's five original stores. Assume that the incremental cash flow from the acquired stores goes on forever but does not grow. Should Benson pay Foodland's price? If not, does the deal look good enough to negotiate for a better price? What is the most Benson should be willing to pay?

b. (No calculations are needed here—just ideas.) Are there reasons beyond the calculations in part (a) that argue in favour of the acquisition? (*Hint:* Think along two lines about the competitive situation. First, what will happen if Benson doesn't buy Foodland? Second, what effect will the acquisition have on Benson's existing stores?)

c. Could the ideas in part (b) be quantified into adjustments to the results in part (a)? Make your own estimate of the impact of such ideas on the price Benson should be willing to pay.

11. Lattig Corp. had a $2.0 million cash flow last year and projects that figure to increase by $200,000 per year for the next five years (to $3.0 million). After that, Lattig expects an annual growth rate of 6% forever. Assume the discount rate is 12%.

a. What percentage of the total present value of Lattig's projected cash flows comes from its terminal value assumption for cash flows after the first five years?

b. Recalculate the result in part (a) if Lattig raises its terminal value growth rate forecast to 7% and then to 8%.

c. What other terminal value-related issues should be considered by anyone thinking about acquiring Lattig? (Use words only.)

12. Integrity Group, an association of venture capitalists, is considering using a leveraged buyout to purchase Schrag Co., a well-established high-tech firm. Schrag has long-term debt with a book value of $15 million and a debt to equity ratio of 1:10. The firm's shares are currently selling at 120% of book value. Integrity Group has $25 million to contribute to the buyout and feels that it will have to offer a 25% premium over the shares' current market price in order to make the deal work. Estimate Schrag's capital structure after the leveraged buyout.

13. Lee & Long, a clothing manufacturer, is considering filing for bankruptcy. The firm has EBIT of $1.4 million and long-term debt of $40 million on which it pays interest at an average rate of 8.5%. It also has capital assets (gross) totalling $60 million. Amortization expense averages 5% of gross capital assets per year, and the long-term debt matures evenly over the next 20 years.

a. Calculate Lee & Long's current cash flow.

b. Assume that Lee & Long's management can convince its creditors to convert 25% of its debt into equity by exchanging their bonds for newly issued shares at book value. Calculate Lee & Long's cash flow after the debt restructuring.

14. Garwood Industries has filed for bankruptcy and will probably be liquidated. The firm's balance sheet ($millions) is shown below:

Current assets	$ 6.5	Current liabilities	$ 8.5
Capital assets (net)	30.8	Long-term debt	16.5
Total assets	$ 37.3	Shareholders' equity	12.3
		Total liabilities and shareholders' equity	$ 37.3

The administrative costs of bankruptcy total $1.6 million. Current assets can be sold for 60% of book value and capital assets for 25% of book value. Twenty percent of the long-term debt is secured. All of the remaining debt is unsecured. Assume there are no additional costs. How many cents on the dollar will unsecured creditors (including trade creditors) receive on the money owed them?

15. The Hamilton Corp. has 35,000 common shares outstanding with a book value of $20 per share. It owes creditors $1.5 million at an interest rate of 12%. Selected financial results are as follows.

Income and Cash Flow		Capital	
EBIT	$ 80,000	Debt	$1,500,000
Interest	180,000	Shareholders' equity	700,000
EBT	$(100,000)		$2,200,000
Tax	0		
NI	$(100,000)		
Amortization	50,000		
Principal repayment	(75,000)		
Cash flow	$(125,000)		

Restructure the financial line items shown assuming a composition in which creditors agree to convert two-thirds of their debt into equity at book value. Assume Hamilton will pay tax at a rate of 25% on income after the restructuring, and that principal repayments are reduced proportionately with debt. Who will control the company, and by how big a margin after the restructuring?

Chapter 20

International Financial Management

Learning Objectives

1 Describe the various forms of international business.

2 Discuss the effect of exchange rate changes on the firm's profitability and cash flow.

3 Compute foreign exchange conversions.

4 Define spot and forward exchange rates.

5 Evaluate techniques to hedge foreign exchange risk.

6 Outline the factors affecting exchange rates.

7 Discuss techniques for managing international working capital.

8 Discuss the features of international bond and stock markets.

9 Consider the unique features of planning for foreign direct investment.

10 Discuss the nature of political risk.

11 Discuss the nature of economic risk.

12 Demonstrate the nature of translation risk.

International business is now pervasive throughout the Canadian economy. In the past, a relatively small number of Canadian firms imported manufactured goods or exported commodities, primarily to the United States; now, most companies export and import as a matter of course. Many have set up manufacturing facilities or entered licensing agreements overseas. With the growth of Internet commerce, many individuals routinely buy and sell articles and services over the World Wide Web. This chapter is designed to introduce you to some of the major issues in international financial management.

> The volume of *international business* is steadily *increasing* worldwide.

GROWTH IN INTERNATIONAL BUSINESS

In the last 50 years, business has become increasingly international.[1] The change has occurred in three distinct ways.

First, we do more business with other countries than ever before. In 2006, exports accounted for 36% of Canadian gross domestic product (GDP). This was several times as much as the U.S. or Japan, in terms of the percentage of GDP. In terms of U.S. dollars, Canada was in the top 10 worldwide in both exports and imports.

> International business has expanded from import/export to include *operating full-scale businesses* in other countries.

The Canada–U.S. trading relationship was the largest in the world. In 2006, 79% of Canada's exports went to the U.S., and 66% of our imports came from the U.S. Both exports and imports have grown significantly under the North American Free Trade Agreement (NAFTA). Exports from and imports to the U.S. averaged some $1.7 billion per day. Other important Canadian trading partners include China, Japan, the United Kingdom, Germany, and France.

Second, the nature of international business has changed: 50 years ago, doing business with a foreign country generally meant importing and exporting goods. Now, Canadian businesses often choose from several other methods of operating outside Canada.

> Building or buying a business in another country is a **foreign direct investment**, while buying foreign securities is a **portfolio investment**. A **multinational corporation** (MNC) is a company with wholly or partially owned affiliates in foreign countries.

- They may *license* their product or *franchise* their service to foreign operators.
- In conjunction with one or more partner companies, they may set up a foreign corporation to conduct foreign operations (*joint venture*).
- They may set up or buy a foreign *affiliate*, a foreign corporation in which they own 100% of the equity (a *wholly owned subsidiary*) or less, but that they control.

Both foreign joint ventures and foreign affiliates are examples of **foreign direct investment (FDI)**. A corporation with FDI is called a **multinational corporation (MNC)**.

By 2006, Canadian corporations had invested $523 billion in direct investments in foreign enterprises, up 14% in 2006. Forty-three percent of Canadian FDI was in the U.S. In fact, Canada was the fifth largest investor in the U.S.

FDI in Canada amounted to $449 billion, up 10% in 2006. The U.S. dominated FDI in Canada with 61% of the total. In 2006 and 2007, many Canadian multinationals, particularly those in resource sectors, were acquired by foreign purchasers. (See Table 20.1)

Third, financial markets are also increasingly international: 50 years ago it was somewhat unusual for an investor to buy the shares of a foreign company. Today, people make **portfolio investments** in foreign shares and bonds all the time.

> For detailed statistics and trends on Canada's international trade and foreign investments go to the Department of Foreign Affairs and International Trade at http://www.dfait-maeci.gc.ca/eet/menu-en.asp#trade.

Virtually all companies of any size have some international dealings. It's clearly important, therefore, that we understand the basic financial principles of doing business with companies from other countries. Such business has all of the problems and challenges of operating domestically but includes several additional complications and risks.

Differences in political systems, economic systems, legal systems, language, culture, economic development, and local practices must all be addressed. Foreign governments intervene in international business. Foreign exchange fluctuations are a major risk. We'll begin by examining exchange rates in some detail.

---

1 The term "global" is often used to describe business's current international character. It implies that less-developed countries are now included in the trading community along with the developed nations.

710 Part 6: Current Topics

TABLE 20.1
Some Prominent
Canadian Firms
Acquired by
Foreign Purchasers
Since 2000

Company	Industry	Purchaser	Country	Price (US$)	Year
BCE Inc.	Telecommunication	2 private equity groups (41%)	U.S.	$35 billion	2007
Alcan Ltd.	Aluminum	Rio Tinto PLC	U.K.	$38.1 billion	2007
Domtar	Paper maker	Weyerhauser Co.	U.S.	$3.3 billion	2007
ATI Technologies Inc.	Graphic chip maker	Advanced Micro Devices Inc.	U.S.	$5.3 billion	2006
Fairmont Hotels & Resorts Inc.	Hotelier	Saudi and U.S. interests		$3.3 billion	2006
Sleeman Breweries Ltd.	Brewery	Sapporo Breweries Ltd.	Japan	$272 million	2006
Falconbridge Ltd.	Nickel producer	Xstrata PLC	Switzerland	$20.2 billion	2006
Inco Ltd.	Nickel producer	Companhia Vale do Rio Doce	Brazil	$18.7 billion	2006
Intrawest Corp.	Travel and resort operator	Fortress Investment Group LLC	U.S.	$1.8 billion	2006
Hudson's Bay Co.	Department store retailer	Jerry Zucker	U.S.	$1 billion	2006
Four Seasons Hotels Inc.	Hotelier	Saudi and U.S. interests		$3.7 billion	2006
Dofasco Inc.	Steel maker	Arcelor SA	France	$5.2 billion	2006
CP Ships Ltd.	Shipping	TUI AG	Germany	$2.3 billion	2005
Molson Inc.	Brewery	Adolph Coors Co.	U.S.	$7.1 billion	2005
Westcoast Energy	Pipeline	Duke Energy Corp.	U.S.	$8.4 billion	2001
Gulf Canada Resources Ltd.	Resources	Conoco Inc.	U.S.	$6.3 billion	2001
Newbridge Networks Corp	Telecom maker	Alcatel SA	France	$7.1 billion	2000
Seagram Co. Ltd.	Distillery	Vivendi SA	France	$31.2 billion	2000

Source: David Olive, "A Nation in Industrial Retreat," *Toronto Star*, May 13, 2007, p. A1. Reprinted with permission—Torstar Syndication Serivces.

CURRENCY EXCHANGE

Companies operate and expect to be paid in the currency of the countries in which they're located. That means anyone wanting to buy from a firm in another country has to acquire some of that country's currency first.

For example, if the Canadian Wing Foot Shoe Company wants to buy expensive running shoes from an American supplier, it has to pay the bill in U.S. dollars, not Canadian dollars. But, if the Canadian importer has only Canadian dollars, it has to exchange some Canadian dollars for U.S. dollars to make the purchase. We say that the importer buys U.S. dollars with Canadian dollars.

A **foreign exchange market** is a financial market in which the currencies of different countries are traded. **Foreign exchange** is a general term for the currency of foreign countries.

The Foreign Exchange Market

The purchase is accomplished in the **foreign exchange market**, which is organized for the purpose of exchanging currencies (a general term for the currencies of foreign countries is **foreign** exchange). The foreign exchange market operates much like other financial markets, but isn't located in a specific place like a stock exchange. Rather, it's a network of brokers and banks based in financial centres around the world. The Canadian banks participate in the market and provide exchange services to their clients.

Exchange Rates

Currencies are traded at an exchange rate, which is, in effect, the price of each currency in terms of the other. In our illustration, Wing Foot needs to know how many U.S. dollars can be purchased for a Canadian dollar. That lets it calculate how many Canadian dollars it will need to pay the American firm's price in U.S. dollars.

The essence of the foreign exchange market is a table of exchange rates like Table 20.2. The table shows two reciprocal rates for each currency. For the moment, ignore the *forward* rates in some currencies; we'll get to those shortly. Rates in the first column are called the *direct quote* and show the number of Canadian dollars required to buy one unit of the foreign currency. Rates in the second column are known as *indirect quotes* and represent the inverse relationship, how many units of the foreign currency it takes to buy one Canadian dollar. The direct and indirect quotes are reciprocals of one another.[2]

Suppose Wing Foot wants to import 500 pairs of shoes that cost a total of US$35,000. The exchange rate table indicates that US$1 is worth CDN$1.0469, so that it will have to exchange US$35,000 × CDN$1.0469 = CDN$36,642 (to the nearest dollar) to pay for the shoes. In other words, the cost of the purchase is expected to be CDN$36,642.

Alternatively, the US$35,000 could be divided by 0.9552 (the ratio of the value of the U.S. dollar to the Canadian dollar) to reach the same result.

The Unique Status of the U.S. Dollar

Since the Second World War, the U.S. dollar has been the world's leading currency. In a sense it functions as international money. The U.S dollar has this unique role because people have more confidence in its continuing value than they have in the value of any other currency. This confidence no doubt stems from America's unique status as a superpower in both military and economic terms.[3]

Many transactions, such as commodities contracts, are priced in U.S. dollars. In addition, several countries use the U.S. dollar as their official currency, or *peg* their currency to the U.S. dollar.

Most international businesspeople are usually willing to take U.S. dollars in trade because they're confident that American money can be exchanged for their own currencies at any time and that its value isn't likely to fall suddenly. (The exchange rate is still needed to determine how many U.S. dollars something priced in another currency is worth.) In fact, a U.S. dollar may be preferable to their own currency, which may not be as stable.

The Euro—A Common European Currency

By January 1, 2008, 15 European countries will have adopted a common currency, the euro. A single currency is supposed to help solidify Western Europe into an economic force better able to compete with the United States and Japan. It should also stabilize trade among the countries sharing the currency because the flows of goods between them will no longer be influenced by exchange rates.

The participating nations include Germany, France, Belgium, Italy, and Spain. Interestingly, Great Britain has stayed with the pound sterling, at least for the time being.

An **exchange rate** states the price of one currency in terms of another.

For daily exchange rates on over 200 currencies, historical rates for over 60 currencies, and a facility to forecast future rate trends, go to the University of British Columbia site: http://fx.sauder.ubc.ca.

The *U.S. dollar* is the world's leading currency and in some ways serves as "international money."

The **euro** is a common European currency adopted by 15 of the members of the European Union (EU).

2 Notice the wide range of values carried by the currency units of different countries. The Japanese yen, for example, was worth less than 1 cent in mid-2007. People sometimes associate such a low value with a weak or failing economy. The association comes from the fact that economies in crisis often undergo hyperinflation (an extremely high inflation rate) during which the value of their currencies drops very rapidly. However, a low unit value by itself, if stable, is just a convention and has no economic significance. It may be a little unnerving, however, to go shopping in Tokyo and see a $100 item priced at 11,700 yen!
3 Having said that, in recent years, U.S. trade and budget deficits have contributed to a significant depreciation of the U.S. dollar against other major currencies. (See page 716.)

TABLE 20.2
Exchange Rates,
July 12, 2007

	Direct Quote ($ Per Unit of Foreign Currency)	Indirect Quote (Foreign Currency Units Per $)
Argentina (Peso)	0.3380	2.9586
Australia (Dollar)	0.9043	1.1058
Brazil (Real)	0.5583	1.7912
Chile (Peso)	0.002028	493.0966
China (Renminbi) (Yuan)	0.1384	7.2254
Czech Republic (Koruna)	0.0511	19.5695
Europe (Euro)	1.4422	0.6934
1-month forward	1.4427	0.6931
3-months forward	1.4436	0.6927
6-months forward	1.4448	0.6921
Hong Kong (Dollar)	0.1339	7.4666
India (Rupee)	0.0260	38.4615
Indonesia (Rupiah)	0.000116	8,620.6897
Japan (Yen)	0.008544	117.0412
1-month forward	0.008573	116.6453
3-months forward	0.008628	115.9017
6-months forward	0.008712	114.7842
Mexico (New Peso)	0.0972	10.2881
Philippines (Peso)	0.0228	43.8596
Russia (Ruble)	0.0411	24.3309
South Africa (Rand)	0.1507	6.6357
South Korea (Won)	0.00114	877.1930
Switzerland (Franc)	0.8702	1.1492
Taiwan (Dollar)	0.0319	31.3480
Thailand (Baht)	0.0339	29.4985
United Kingdom (Pound)	2.1240	0.4708
1-month forward	2.1217	0.4713
3-months forward	2.1170	0.4724
6-months forward	2.1100	0.4739
United States (Dollar)	1.0469	0.9552
1-month forward	1.0462	0.9558
3-months forward	1.0449	0.9574
6-months forward	1.0435	0.9583

Source: *BMO Capital Markets*, at http://bmonesbittburns.com/economics/fxrates. Noon rates for July 12, 2007. Reprinted courtesy of BMO Capital Markets.

The Effect of Exchange Rates on Prices and Quantities

It's important to notice that the exchange rate is part of the cost of product to a firm importing foreign goods. To illustrate, let's continue the running shoes example we began in the last section. The expected cost per pair at the time of ordering is

$$\frac{CDN\$36,642}{500} = CDN\$73.28$$

The exchange rate is part of the cost of product paid by an importing firm.

plus shipping and handling. Hence, a reasonable retail price might be CDN$147 (assuming roughly a 100% retail markup).

But what would happen if the exchange rate were less favourable? Suppose, for example, that the direct quote is 1.10. Then the expected cost of the shipment would be

$$US\$35,000 \times \frac{CDN\$1.10}{US\$1} = CDN\$38,500$$

A single pair would cost

$$\frac{CDN\$38,500}{500} = CDN\$77$$

and a reasonable retail price might be CDN$154.

In other words, the exchange rate has an influence on the domestic prices of imported goods. The more a foreign currency costs, the more expensive that nation's products are when offered to Canadian buyers, regardless of their cost in the country of origin.

It's an economic fundamental that when a product is more expensive, people buy less of it. For foreign goods, that means that higher prices due to less favourable exchange rates lead to decreased imports. In our illustration, the 1.10 rate implies a CDN$7 higher retail price for a pair of shoes. Wing Foot, the Canadian importer, might well feel that the product won't sell at such a price and may order fewer than 500 or forego the order entirely. Conversely, a more favourable exchange rate makes foreign products cheaper in Canada, causing larger quantities to be demanded, leading to more imports. We'll come back to this important concept later.

> Exchange rates affect the *quantity of foreign product demanded* in an importing country.

Cross Rates

Given the information in Table 20.2, it's possible to develop an exchange rate between any two currencies without going through dollars. These are called **cross rates**.

For example the exchange rate between U.S. dollars and British pounds can be calculated from the indirect quote column of Table 20.2 as follows:

$$\frac{0.4708\pounds \text{ per CDN\$}}{US\$0.9552 \text{ per CDN\$}} = US\$0.4929 \text{ per } \pounds$$

> In foreign exchange markets, a **cross rate** is an exchange rate between any two currencies developed without going through dollars.

Changing Exchange Rates and Exchange Rate Risk

Exchange rates are constantly changing, sometimes quite rapidly and by significant amounts. We'll get into why they change in a little while, but first it's important to understand the implications of the fact that they do change.

Insights | REAL APPLICATIONS

Is Your Team Winning? Credit the Canadian Dollar!

Professional sports franchises in Canada, such as Toronto Blue Jays, Toronto Raptors, and the six National Hockey League (NHL) teams must pay their player salaries in U.S. dollars. They were much healthier competitively or financially in 2007 than in 2002 because of the significant increase in the Canadian dollar.

The dollar has risen from just under 62 cents in 2002 to about 95 cents in July 2007. This allowed small-market NHL clubs such as the Calgary Flames to increase their payrolls in U.S. dollars without a corresponding increase in the Canadian dollar costs. In the 2001–2002 NHL season, the Flames' payroll was US$26.92 million, which cost the team about $43.42 million in Canadian funds based on a 62-cent dollar. In the 2006–2007 season, the Flames payroll had ballooned to US$43.60 million, but with the dollar at 95 cents, the club's cost in Canadian funds amounted to $45.89 million, an increase of less than 6% from 2001–2002.

Over the same timeframe, the payroll of the Toronto Maple Leafs fell from US$51.57 million to $45.38 million, largely due to the league salary cap instituted in 2005. The combination of the reduced payroll and the higher dollar improved club profits in Canadian dollars by almost $32 million!

Source: Adapted from David Naylor, "Small Markets, Big Spending," *The Globe and Mail*, February 20, 2007, p. S1.

Exchange rate risk is the chance of gain or loss from exchange rate movement that occurs *during* a transaction.

Moving exchange rates give rise to exchange rate risk, a very important facet of international business. Exchange rate risk means that a firm can make or lose money on an international transaction because of rate movements aside from the business deal itself.

For example, imagine that Wing Foot ordered its 500 shoes on July 12, 2007, when the Canadian/American exchange rate was 1.0469. At that time it expected to pay the CDN$36,642 we calculated earlier for the shipment. Also suppose the purchase contract called for payment three months after the order is placed.

When the Canadian importer returns to the foreign exchange market three months after ordering, the U.S. dollar rate is unlikely to be the same. For the sake of illustration, suppose the direct quote had risen to 1.10. That meant paying the bill for US$35,000 cost Wing Foot (US$35,000 × 1.10=) CDN$38,500.

That's CDN$1,858 more than was expected at the time the order was placed. The implication is that the profit made on the Canadian sale of the shoes would be reduced by CDN$1,858 just due to the fluctuation in the exchange rate.

Of course, the rate could have gone the other way. In that case, more profit than expected would have been made. The point is that exchange rate variation throws an element of risk into Wing Foot's business that wouldn't be there if the shoes were purchased domestically.

Transactions subject to exchange rate risk, and the companies that undertake such transactions, are said to have *exchange rate exposure.*

Spot and Forward Rates

Forward rates quote prices for *future delivery* of currencies.

The exchange rates we've described so far are spot rates, meaning that they're good for immediate, "on the spot" transactions.[4] Notice that the major currencies also have quotes on forward rates for one, three, and six months. These rates are quotes for delivery of the currency the indicated number of months in the future. Notice that they're somewhat different from the spot rates. The difference reflects the movement that banks expect in the future relationship between the two currencies.

For example, Table 20.2 shows that on July 12, 2007, the U.S. dollar was expected to become slightly less valuable in terms of the Canadian dollar during the next six months. To see this, notice the decrease in the direct quote from 1.0469 to 1.0435; this says that it would take a little less Canadian money to buy a U.S. dollar in the future. The indirect quote showed the same thing, looking from the Canadian dollar to the U.S. dollar; a Canadian dollar was expected to buy slightly more U.S. money in the future, because the indirect quote rose from 0.9552 to 0.9583.

When a foreign currency is expected to become less valuable in the future, as in this case, the forward currency is said to be selling at a *discount* over the spot currency. In the reverse situation, when a future dollar will buy less of the foreign currency than a present dollar, the forward currency is said to be selling at a *premium.*

The Terminology of Exchange Rate Movements

When a currency becomes or is expected to become less valuable in terms of Canadian dollars, we say that it is becoming weaker or it is falling against the dollar. The same idea can also be expressed by saying that the dollar is becoming stronger or rising against the foreign currency. On July 12, 2007, the U.S. dollar was expected to weaken against the Canadian dollar, which was expected to strengthen against the U.S. dollar.

Hedging with Forward Exchange Rates

As we've said many times, people usually avoid risk whenever they can, and exchange rate risk is no exception. Most companies prefer to operate without it and are willing to pay a premium to do so.

---

4 Delivery on spot transactions is made within two days.

The forward market provides a way to eliminate foreign exchange risk from international transactions with a process called hedging.[5] A firm that knows it will need foreign currency at some time in the future can *lock* in an exchange rate by contracting with a bank for future delivery at the appropriate forward rate.

In our illustration, Wing Foot could negotiate with its Canadian bank a three-month *forward contract* for *buying* U.S. dollars at the time that it placed the shoe order. The three-month forward rate was 1.0449, which was a little less expensive than the current spot rate (this isn't always the case; as often as not the forward rate is higher), so the shipment would cost

$$US\$35,000 \times 1.0449 = CDN\$36,572$$

Once the forward contract was written, exchange rate risk was eliminated from the transaction, as US$35,000 would be delivered by the bank in three months in exchange for CDN$36,572 from Wing Foot. Wing Foot would then remit the U.S. funds to its supplier. The firm is said to have *covered* its obligation with a *forward market hedge*. It avoided the resulting exchange loss if the spot rate for the U.S. dollar three months later was above CDN$1.0449. For example, if the U.S. dollar unexpectedly rose to CDN$1.10, the firm would have avoided a foreign exchange loss of $US\$35,000 \times (1.10 - 1.0449) = CDN\$1,929$. Of course, it also forfeited the foreign exchange *gain* if the spot rate for the U.S. dollar in three months' time was below $1.0449!

Forward contracts can be written between any two currencies, for any amount, and for any length of time, at the discretion of the bank. There is a cost, however, because banks incorporate a charge for the service in their rate quotations.

Foreign exchange *futures* and foreign exchange *options* may provide alternative methods to hedge foreign exchange risk. However, these tools are available only in relatively few "hard" currencies, and are in set denominations and contract periods.

The forward market enables companies to transfer foreign exchange risk, for a price, to professionals who are in the business of bearing such risks.

Supply and Demand—The Source of Exchange Rate Movement

Simply stated, an exchange rate is the price of a unit of foreign currency. For example, Table 20.2 tells us that on July 12, 2007, US$1 cost CDN$1.0469.

We can think of the U.S. dollar as a commodity offered for sale in a free market. Its price, like that of any commodity, is determined by the interaction of supply and demand.

The supply and demand factors that establish and change foreign exchange rates stem from *foreign currency flows* between nations. In turn, these flows result from international transactions in trade goods and services, as well as the flow of investment capital between countries.

Trade and investment flows are sensitive to both *economic* factors and *political* factors.

Examples of economic factors include world demand for our principal resources and our level of interest rates relative to those of other advanced economies. Examples of political factors include Canadian government policies, direct government intervention, and political turmoil.

We will address these political factors further in the next section.

> *The strength or weakness of the Canadian dollar is normally viewed in terms of the U.S. dollar. Any factor that drives up the value of the U.S. dollar will normally cause a decline in the Canadian dollar/U.S. dollar exchange rate, and vice versa. For a better understanding of what's happening at the time, we must investigate how the Canadian dollar is trending against other major currencies, such as the euro, pound sterling, and yen.*

From the CFO

In today's world, the factors that cause exchange rate movement change all the time. Hence the supply and demand curves for foreign exchange are constantly shifting, as is their

---

5 *Hedge* is a general term applied to an arrangement that reduces or avoids risk.

The Growing Strength of the Canadian Dollar

The table beside compares the relative value of the Canadian dollar (direct quotes*) against the currencies of Canada's major trading partners over the five-year period 2002 to 2006 inclusive. Note that the dollar has strengthened against all the currencies, not just against the U.S. dollar! The primary reason is the world-wide commodities boom and demand for our natural resources. A strong dollar reduces costs for Canadian firms that import from, travel to, or acquire new FDI in foreign countries, but reduces revenue for exporters, travel and hospitality services, and recipients of foreign investment income.

Currency	2002	2006	% Change
US$	1.5704	1.1341	27.8
U.K. £	2.3582	2.0886	11.4
Japan ¥	0.012554	0.009753	22.3
Europe Euro	1.4832	1.4237	4.0
South Korea Won	0.001262	0.001188	5.9
Mexico Peso	0.1630	0.1041	36.1
China Renminbi/ Yuan	0.1897	0.1422	25.0

*Source: Average calendar year exchange rates from Canada Revenue Agency at http://www.cra-arc.gc.ca.

intersection, the exchange rate. Since fluctuations in currency values result in foreign exchange risk, the financial manager must understand what factors might cause a particular exchange rate to change significantly.

Governments and the International Monetary System

Recall that earlier we said exchange rates influence the domestic prices of imported goods. Let's pursue that idea a little further.

Suppose a nation's currency suddenly *strengthens* relative to the currencies of other countries. We'll use the Canadian dollar to illustrate, but the results are true for any currency. As a result of a strengthening dollar, two things happen, one good and the other bad. First, imported goods become cheaper, because a dollar buys more foreign exchange and hence more foreign product. That's generally good for consumers, and people like it.

At the same time, however, Canadian exports become more expensive in other countries. That means fewer are sold and the demand for exported product diminishes. The result is a reduction in Canadian production and eventually a loss of jobs, which of course is bad.

Conversely, if the dollar *weakens*, foreign products become more expensive here, which leads to a general lowering of our standard of living. However, our exports increase because they're cheaper in other nations, and the increased business creates jobs here.

Summarizing, we can say that exchange rates affect the domestic economy through two opposing forces: the cost of imported goods, and the employment and income generated by producing goods for export.

A strong dollar makes imports cheaper, but has a negative effect on employment because it reduces exports.

Government Influence on Exchange Rates

It's important to recognize that these opposing forces need to be kept in balance. In other words, it isn't good for an economy if the exchange rate goes too far in either direction. Cheap imports aren't worth excessive unemployment, and low unemployment isn't worth a substantially higher cost of living. For that reason, there is occasional government intervention in foreign exchange markets to keep rates within what they feel are reasonable ranges.

For example, the Canadian government, may, through the Bank of Canada, buy or sell Canadian dollars in the foreign exchange market to slow the advance or decline of the exchange rate for the dollar against other major currencies. Such intervention most often occurs during periods of rampant speculation. The Bank of Canada will usually conduct these activities in concert with the U.S. Federal Reserve and other G8 central banks.

Sometimes governments intervene in foreign exchange markets to keep exchange rates within desirable limits.

Buying Canadian dollars adds to other demands for dollars and thus raises the exchange rate for dollars in terms of the other currencies.

A government's ability to *support* a weakening currency in this way is limited because it has to pay for its purchases of its own money with either gold or foreign exchange already in its possession. Both of these are clearly of limited availability.

Conversely, if a currency is too strong, the government may sell its own currency. This action has the effect of increasing supply and lowering its cost in terms of other currencies.

In recent years, the Bank of Canada has more often changed Canadian interest rates to affect the value of the dollar and to keep it in a desirable trading range. For instance, the bank raises interest rates to attract foreign short-term investments to Canada. This inflow of foreign funds increases demand for Canadian dollars. The higher rate can also serve to lower inflation.

The International Monetary System

The international monetary system is the set of rules by which countries collectively administer the exchange of currencies. The system in place at the present time, which we've been describing, is known as a floating exchange rate system. That means exchange rates are determined essentially by free market forces. Some government intervention does occur, but not much and it's usually the result of an agreement among several nations to maintain economic stability.

The floating rate system has been in effect since the early 1970s. Since then, the *major ("hard") currencies* of the world have fluctuated constantly based on demand and supply factors. Among the major currencies are the British pound sterling, the European euro, the Japanese yen, the Canadian dollar, and of course, the U.S. dollar.

Some of the *non-major* currencies of the world are on a fixed or pegged exchange rate *system,* whereby they try to maintain a *fixed* (or *semi-fixed*) relationship with respect to the U.S. dollar, one of the other major currencies, a combination of major currencies, or some type of international foreign exchange standard. China provides an example of a "pegged" exchange rate; in 2005, China raised the value of its currency, the *yuan,* by two percent to 8.11 per U.S. dollar, and started linking it to a basket of currencies. China intervenes in the foreign exchange markets, limiting gains or losses in the yuan to 0.3% per day.

These rates are set by the countries' central banks in consultation with the International Monetary Fund, a United Nations organization whose mandate is to further stability in global exchange rates.

Under the pegged rate system, market forces tend to pressure the set rate, but each country under the system has the responsibility of holding its exchange rate nearly constant. These countries maintain the value of their currencies by buying and selling in the foreign exchange market as we described in the last section.

It sometimes is impossible to keep certain exchange rates constant. When that happens, a nation might go through a *revaluation* to officially raise the value of its currency relative to the U.S. dollar or, more likely, a devaluation to lower its value. Financial and monetary crises have resulted in major devaluations recently, in Mexico (1995), Russia (1995), several countries in Southeast Asia (1997–1998), Argentina (2001–2002), and Venezuela (2002–2003).

Convertibility

Not all currencies are convertible. An inconvertible currency can't be exchanged in the way we've described in this chapter. To have a convertible currency, a nation must allow it to be traded on foreign exchange markets and be willing to accept the resulting value. The currencies of Russia and China have traditionally not been fully convertible. In fact, there were some 85 countries in July 2007 that imposed some restrictions on converting their currencies.

Inconvertibility doesn't mean that there isn't an exchange rate. If you want to buy a Russian product, the Russian government will be glad to sell you the *rubles* you need at its official exchange rate (see Table 20.2 on page 712). However, the system works only one way. If you have rubles, there is generally no one willing to buy them for dollars or any other major currency at the exchange rate set by the Russian government.

In a **floating exchange rate** system, *market forces* set rates with little *intervention* from governments.

In a **pegged exchange rate** system, governments set the rates and attempt to maintain them against market pressures.

In foreign exchange markets, **devaluation** is a significant decrease in the value of a currency compared to major currencies, such as the U.S. dollar.

A **convertible currency** can be exchanged for other currencies on foreign exchange markets. A currency that is **inconvertible** cannot be exchanged for other currencies at *market-determined* rates.

Inconvertibility is a significant impediment to international business. Suppose a Canadian company establishes a branch in Russia and makes a profit doing business there. The profit is in rubles, and because the currency isn't convertible it's very difficult to repatriate it back into the company's home country. To get value out of the country, it's generally necessary to buy something made in Russia with the ruble profit (like vodka), export it to the home country, and sell it there. Unfortunately, nations with nonconvertible money don't tend to have a great many things that people in other countries want to buy.

MANAGING INTERNATIONAL WORKING CAPITAL

The financial manager in a purely Canadian business is responsible for raising the funds necessary to run the business, giving appropriate consideration to the cost of the funds and the financial risks involved.

Short-term funds are raised from sources such as trade credit and bank operating loans.

Funds are invested for the short term in cash, receivables, and inventory. The financial manager is concerned that these assets are maintained at reasonable levels, given the needs of the company, and that they earn the required return.

The financial manager in an *international* business will use these techniques for domestic Canadian operations, but the techniques applied to international business must be extended to recognize a different sphere of opportunities and challenges.

In this section, we will consider some of the unique practices available internationally to obtain short-term financing, including international trade credit and foreign-sourced bank loans. We will then review some techniques for managing short-term assets located outside Canada, including cash, trade receivables, and inventory.

International Trade Credit

Payments in international transactions are often made in a foreign currency, particularly in U.S. dollars. A Canadian importer with accounts payable denominated in a foreign currency is exposed to exchange rate risk. The risk is that the Canadian dollar will depreciate against the foreign currency. This risk can often be hedged by buying the currency in the forward market, but doing so may be costly. Where possible, the importer should buy from countries with "soft" (weak) currencies.

To reduce its credit risk, and to expedite payment, the foreign supplier may ask the Canadian importer for a *letter of credit* from the importer's bank, guaranteeing payment of the supplier's invoice. The letter of credit is a specialized banking technique for financing international trade. In this case, the letter of credit is written by the bank of the (Canadian) importer to the foreign supplier, stating that the Canadian bank guarantees payment of the supplier's invoice if all of the underlying agreements are met.

Payment terms are negotiated, and range from payment on shipment to payment 180 days after delivery. For large orders by major Canadian corporations with long maturity dates, the underlying documents, including the bank guarantee, may form the basis of a *banker's acceptance* (see Chapter 5).

Letters of credit are usually not used for imports from the U.S., from affiliated companies, or from foreign suppliers who are well acquainted with the Canadian exporter. In these cases, some form of "open account" arrangement (for example, net 30 days) is common.

Foreign Bank Loans

In some ways, arranging short-term financing for international trade is no different from financing operations in Canada. In both cases, companies must finance purchases of inventory, and then continue to finance accounts receivable before collecting any cash payments from sales. However, typical trade transactions are relatively large in size, and export sales may have long maturity dates. Therefore, trading companies may have to finance larger dollar amounts for longer periods than companies that operate only in Canada. Some banks are

The **letter of credit** provides a bank guarantee that the exporter will be paid according to the contract of sale.

http

For a "crash course" on trade finance, go to the Toronto Dominion Bank at http://www.tdcommercialbanking.com/tradefinance/crash/crash.jsp.

reluctant to lend to Canadian exporters or importers, particularly small firms, because of the foreign risk involved.

MNCs that operate *affiliates* in foreign countries often finance their operations, at least in part, in those foreign financial markets. For example, a Canadian company operating a subsidiary in the United Kingdom may borrow pounds sterling at a British bank to acquire inventory in the U.K. This technique minimizes exchange risk and improves the company's business ties to the local community.

As an alternative, MNCs regularly finance their international operations through **eurocurrency loans**—large short-term or medium-term loans denominated in one or more major foreign currencies, often the U.S. dollar (**eurodollar** loans) or the euro. If the British subsidiary above borrowed U.S. dollars in the United Kingdom, this would constitute a eurodollar loan.

Eurocurrency loans are usually obtained from foreign banks, although Canadian banks have participated in eurocurrency lending. Eurocurrency loans are usually unsecured, made in multiples of $1 million, and for terms of one year or less.

They allow large Canadian companies to access capital markets outside Canada when interest rates in Canada are elevated. Borrowers are able to arrange large loans quickly, confidentially, and at attractive interest rates. Interest rates tend to be cheaper than domestic rates in either Canada or the U.S. The interest rate is usually based on a premium over the London Interbank Offer Rate (LIBOR).[6]

The MNC may borrow the foreign currency either directly or through a foreign subsidiary, as in our example. The company uses the foreign currency in its foreign operations or converts it to Canadian dollars for use at home. There is foreign exchange risk associated with such loans.

Eurocurrency loans are also available in *Canadian* dollars. Foreign exchange risk is avoided while allowing Canadian firms to access foreign capital markets.

> **Eurocurrency loans** are large short-term or medium-term loans denominated in one or more major foreign currencies and available from foreign banks. **Eurodollars** are U.S. dollars deposited in banks in other countries and available for eurodollar (eurocurrency) loans.

Short-Term Asset Management

In managing foreign-sourced current assets—such as cash, money market instruments, trade receivables, or inventory—the financial manager needs to be aware of the specialized techniques and the types of additional risks involved.

Global Cash Management

Assume that we are financial managers in a MNC headquartered in Winnipeg. Our global communications system indicates that our affiliate in Tokyo has just received a large remittance in yen from one of its major customers. Once the foreign affiliate's needs have been addressed, the local manager in the subsidiary may be told to invest the excess funds in the Japanese money market, or to remit them back to the parent in Canada. Mechanisms to repatriate the funds might include dividends, management fees, royalties, and repayment of loans and interest. Whatever the form the repatriation takes, *electronic funds transfer* (EFT) is available worldwide to execute the international inflow of cash.

If we decide to leave the yen in Japan, we may hedge our net exposure in yen to exchange risk through forward contracts or other mechanisms.

Global cash management in a MNC can be quite complicated because of factors such as

- foreign government restrictions on the outflow of funds; for example, exchange controls
- high rates of inflation and volatile exchange rates in the foreign countries. In these circumstances, the parent presumably will want to move cash back to Canada, or to another low inflation, stable currency location
- foreign government tax systems

---

6 LIBOR is the interest rate charged between international banks for overnight money (short-term loans).

We will examine these factors more closely in our section on Foreign Direct Investment, starting on page 723.

International Money Market Investments

Eurocurrency deposits are large sums of $1 million or more, converted to a foreign currency and held on deposit in Canadian or foreign banks.

In Chapter 4, we saw that a financial manager has a variety of Canadian money market securities from which to choose to invest surplus funds. These securities include Treasury bills, commercial paper, and term deposits.

The money market is *an international* market, so the financial manager in a MNC is not limited in choice to just Canadian dollar investments. Those companies with excess cash can make short-term and safe foreign currency deposits at attractive interest rates.

Large companies may make eurocurrency deposits—large sums of $1 million or more, possibly converted to a foreign currency (often the U.S. dollar) and held on deposit in Canadian or other non–U.S. banks. For example, if a Canadian company deposited U.S. dollars in a U.K. bank, this would create a eurodollar deposit. A euroCanadian deposit is a Canadian dollar deposit outside Canada. Terms can range from a single day to five years.

Bank swapped deposits are also foreign currency deposits. To protect against a rise in the Canadian dollar, the deposits are hedged using forward or future contracts.

Bank *swapped deposits* are foreign currency deposits in Canadian or foreign banks, placed there to earn a better return than might be available on similar Canadian dollar deposits. To protect against a rise in the Canadian dollar, the deposits are *hedged* using forward or future contracts.

Foreign Receivables

Managing foreign receivables is often significantly different from managing Canadian receivables.

Longer trade terms, of 90 days or more, are common on overseas sales. In addition, international sales may be larger in size. Exporters then have to finance larger amounts for longer time periods than companies that operate only in Canada.

Payments are often received in a foreign currency, particularly in U.S. dollars. A Canadian exporter that has receivables denominated in a foreign currency faces the risk that the Canadian dollar will *appreciate* in value relative to the foreign currency. To reduce the foreign exchange risk, the Canadian exporter may *hedge* the receivables by selling the currency in the *forward market*, but doing so may be costly and is not possible for all currencies, particularly those of developing countries. The exporter should avoid billing sales in "soft" (weak) currencies.

The foreign customer may be less well known than customers based in Canada, and therefore, poses a greater credit risk. To reduce the credit risk, the Canadian exporter may ask the foreign customer for a *letter of credit* from the customer's bank, guaranteeing payment of the exporter's invoice. The Canadian exporter may accelerate receipt of cash by discounting the guaranteed receivable at its own bank, or with a *factor*.

Letters of credit are normally not used for exports to the U.S., to affiliated companies, or to foreign customers who are well known to the exporter. For sales not guaranteed by letter of credit, the exporter may check the potential customer's credit with international credit agencies, such as D&B Canada (see Chapter 4).

Credit insurance for non-payment of receivables due to credit problems is available (at a price) from the Export Development Corporation of Canada (EDC), a Crown corporation. EDC also has programs in place to provide financing to foreign customers that wish to purchase equipment and other capital goods from Canadian companies.

International Inventory Management

Inventory management becomes even more complicated for Canadian importers as they set up foreign sources of supply, whether they are independent or joint ventures. Lower costs for imports must be balanced against the additional risks of sourcing internationally and of managing the logistics of more complex supply chains.

A Canadian importer close to the Canadian–U.S. border may be able to rely on cross-border just-in-time techniques to minimize inventory investments. The automobile plants in Southern

Ontario provide an example. Otherwise importers of parts and merchandise are most interested in a reliable source of supply.

MNCs must consider a number of factors in managing their inventories in other countries. In addition to maintaining the appropriate level of inventory in various locations around the world, a multinational must deal with exchange rate fluctuations, tariff and non-tariff barriers, and other foreign country rules and regulations. Politically, the inventories could be subject to wars, expropriation, blockages, and other forms of government intervention.

Insights **REAL APPLICATIONS**

DANIER LEATHER

Danier Leather International

(For the financial statements and other financial information about Danier Leather Inc., refer to Appendix 3A, page 92.)

Foreign Exchange Risk

Danier sources a majority of its garments (finished goods) from independent foreign contract manufacturers located primarily in the Far East. About 75% of Danier's products are imported (from China) and 25% are sourced in Canada. At June 24, 2006, Danier had outstanding *letters of credit* of approximately $7.3 million for imports of finished goods inventories to be received. A significant portion of Danier's raw material of skins is also purchased from foreign vendors.

Payment terms for imports are usually in U.S. dollars. In particular, a significant portion of Danier's imported finished goods purchases are sourced in China. The Chinese currency (the Renminbi ("RMB") or Yuan is being allowed to float against a basket of foreign currencies. Fluctuations of the Renminbi could result in higher U.S. dollar costs to Danier.

Accordingly, Danier's foreign currency exposure is mainly related to potential declines in the Canadian dollar versus the U.S. dollar. During the fiscal years 2006 and 2005, Danier purchased its foreign exchange requirements on the *spot market* and did not enter into any *forward*

contracts. However, from time-to-time the Company utilizes derivative financial instruments in the management of its foreign currency exposure.

Other Risks of Foreign Sourcing

Other risks associated with foreign sourcing include economic and political instability, transportation delays and interruptions, inability to meet Danier's quality standards, production delays, disruption of imports due to financial difficulties of a supplier, trade and foreign tax laws, restrictions on the transfer of funds, tariffs and quotas, and boycotts or other actions in North America prompted by domestic concerns regarding foreign labour practices.

International Expansion

Danier began its international expansion with two mall stores in Long Island, New York, and, in 2003, a mall store in Paramus, New Jersey. However, because of continuing poor operating performance, Danier closed these stores in Fiscal 2005.

The company foresaw significant longer-term opportunities in the European, Asian, and South American markets, with their healthy demand for leather garments and goods. Danier planned to explore foreign *licensing* opportunities in 2007 and beyond.

Sources: Danier Leather Annual Report, 2006; Danier Inc. Annual Information Form, September 11, 2006, available at http://www.sedar.com. Reprinted with permission of Danier Leather Inc.

INTERNATIONAL CAPITAL MARKETS

Today, it is common for individuals and businesses to make investments in countries other than their own. Examples include a direct investment in facilities in another country and a portfolio investment in the securities of a corporation based in another country. These activities require the flow of capital funds among nations, and several institutional practices have arisen to finance those flows.

Qualisteam provides links to worldwide capital markets at http://www.qualisteam.com.

An **international bond** is sold outside the home country of the borrower.

A bond issued by a foreign company but denominated in *local* currency is a **foreign bond**.

A **eurobond** is denominated in a currency other than that of the country in which it is sold and issued by a foreign borrower.

The International Bond Market

In earlier chapters, we talked about bonds issued by Canadian corporations sold in Canada. (Keep in mind that selling a bond means the issuing company is borrowing money from the bond's buyer.) It is possible, however, for companies to borrow internationally by selling bonds outside their own countries. Any bond sold outside the home country of the borrower is called an **international bond**.

International bonds provide creditworthy borrowers the opportunity to obtain large amounts of debt financing quickly in their choice of currency. The bond can be *denominated* in the currency of the issuing company's home country (for example, Canada), or in the currency of the country in which it is sold, or in some third currency. An international bond is usually denominated in one of the "hard" currencies such as the U.S. dollar, the euro, the British pound, or the Japanese yen.

A bond denominated in the currency of the country in which it is sold, but issued by a foreign borrower, is called a **foreign bond**. For example, a Japanese auto manufacturer like Honda or Toyota might want to open an assembly plant in Canada financed in some part by borrowing. It could do so by issuing Canadian dollar-denominated bonds in Toronto, registering them with the Ontario Securities Commission, and selling them through the Canadian bond market. To Canadian buyers, the bonds would be just like those of Canadian companies except for the headquarters location of the issuing company. Importantly, they would be subject to all of the registration and disclosure requirements of Canadian securities law, which tend to be more stringent than the requirements of some other nations. Most foreign bonds issued by Canadian companies are issued in U.S. dollars in the United States.

A bond denominated in a currency other than that of the country in which it is sold is called a **eurobond**. Eurobonds are issued in multiple countries, but denominated in a single currency, usually the foreign issuer's home currency. They are called eurobonds because historically the securities were first developed in Europe. However, they don't have to be sold in Europe or denominated in euros, or issued by a European company. For example, Honda could sell bonds denominated in Japanese yen to Canadians in Canada or to people in any other country, and a Canadian multinational could sell a U.S. dollar–denominated eurobond in international financial centres, such as Tokyo or Singapore.

The U.S. dollar and the euro are the most frequently used currencies for eurobonds. Some are denominated in Canadian dollars. Only large, internationally known companies have issued eurobonds. Canadian examples include Petro-Canada and Bombardier.

Eurobonds have several distinguishing features. First, securities regulations in most countries require a much lower level of disclosure for eurobonds than for domestic or foreign bonds. This significantly lowers the flotation costs of issuing them in comparison with the cost of issuing foreign or domestic bonds. Second, eurobonds are usually issued in *bearer* form, so the owner is not identified. Third, most governments don't withhold income tax on eurobond interest payments. The second and third features make eurobonds attractive to some investors, perhaps those who are interested in privacy and/or avoiding their own countries' taxes.

In recent years, many large Canadian multinationals have been using both types of international bonds to raise financing. These issues allow Canadian corporations to access foreign capital markets, providing greater availability of long-term funds and lower costs of financing. They also entail greater exchange risk when the bonds are denominated in a foreign currency. MNCs often use *hedging* strategies to manage their risks of fluctuation in interest and foreign exchange rates. An issue in Canadian dollars would not be subject to exchange rate fluctuations.

The International Stock Market

In this section we look at how Canadian multinationals can raise equity capital abroad. They may do so for many different reasons:

- to take advantage of greater availability of capital and/or lower flotation costs in world markets (Canada's equity markets represent a very small percentage of the world's equity markets by capitalized value)
- to comply with foreign government regulations on minimum levels of local ownership
- to increase the loyalty of foreign employees toward the firm
- to improve the global image of the corporation
- To take advantage of the growing desire on the part of investors to diversify their investment portfolios internationally

Major centres for international share issues include the London, New York, Tokyo, Zurich, and Frankfurt stock markets. Many large Canadian MNCs have listed their shares on *multiple* stock exchanges, including those above. BCE, for example, is listed on the New York, London, and Swiss exchanges.

Correspondingly, many international firms are listed on the TSX or TSX Venture exchanges in Canada. For example, Sony and DaimlerChrysler are listed on the TSX.

FOREIGN DIRECT INVESTMENT

Foreign direct investment (FDI) is really a special case of capital budgeting (see Chapters 12 to 15). The major motivation for FDI is that the rate of return is often higher than the return on domestic investments. Foreign investments may offer lower labour or other costs of production, lower tax rates, or special foreign government incentives.

Canadian multinationals have also invested in foreign countries for *strategic* reasons. The U.S. has received the largest portion of our FDI (43% by 2006). One of the major driving forces has been to locate production facilities close to the large regional U.S. markets. Political stability, access to advanced technology, and continued economic growth in the U.S. have also been important factors. Many companies have set up operations in Europe to avoid EU import tariffs on Canadian goods.

MNCs can also reduce many of their risks by diversifying internationally. We have seen in portfolio theory (Chapter 11) that portfolio risk may be reduced by combining investments whose returns are not positively correlated.

At times, multinationals make such strategic decisions, even though the project may not have a positive net present value. For instance, a corporation such as PepsiCo may follow its chief competitor (Coca-Cola) into new markets to prevent being shut out in the future.

When analyzing a proposed FDI in an overseas subsidiary or joint venture, Canadian corporations will consider the costs of the initial investment, the expected cash flows from the investment, and the possible risks. Several factors that are unique to international business need to be examined when making long-term foreign investment decisions.

Future Cash Flows

Measuring cash flow to be received can be complicated. For instance, many countries offer significant incentives to MNCs to locate operations in their countries. These incentives may include outright government grants, subsidized facility costs, low-interest or no-interest loans, and tax holidays. For example, both the Canadian and American governments offered extensive incentives to the Japanese automobile companies to set up assembly plants in our respective countries. Obviously, such incentives must be recognized in estimating operating cash flows.

In addition, the MNC must consider both *foreign taxes* and *Canadian taxes* on profit earned in foreign countries. These taxes will reduce cash flows from the investment. As well, the foreign government may partially or totally block cash flows back to the parent in Canada.

Finally, all future after-tax cash flows must be converted from the foreign currency involved to Canadian dollars using exchange rate forecasts for the life of the project.

Taxes on International Business

International taxation is a very complex issue for some Canadian MNCs. A Canadian company can export into another country without paying income taxes in that country, providing it does not set up an office or place of business in that country (a permanent establishment).

But a multinational based in Canada with a *foreign affiliate* may be liable for tax on the same income in both Canada and in the country where the foreign affiliate is located. When the same income is taxed twice, it is called *double taxation*.

Double taxation occurs when the same income is taxed in two different countries. Tax treaties and foreign tax credits may reduce or eliminate double taxation.

The foreign country will usually tax the net business income of the affiliate. In addition to taxing business income, the other country may impose *withholding taxes* on certain types of payments out of the country. Payments subject to withholding taxes include dividends, interest, royalties, and management fees. Then, when this income arrives in Canada, it is subject to Canadian tax! Fortunately, the impact of double taxation in this situation is reduced or eliminated by *tax treaties* exempting such income from tax in Canada or by Canadian *tax credits* for foreign taxes paid.

Canadian and foreign income tax rules are key variables in deciding where to locate foreign operations, how to finance them, and how to repatriate their earnings back to Canada.

Risks in Foreign Direct Investment

There is also the issue of the unique risks attached to international cash flows. These include political risks and foreign exchange risks. The presence of these types of risk will influence the discount rate to be used when calculating net present value. The discount rate should be increased to reflect the additional risks stemming from the exchange rate and political situation. The MNC can reduce these risks by diversifying its operations internationally, that is, by setting up affiliates in various parts of the world.

Political Risk

When capital is invested in another country, especially through direct investment, it becomes subject to the authority of the government of that country. **Political risk** refers to the probability that the value of a firm's investment in a foreign country will be reduced by political actions taken primarily by the country's government.

Political risk is the chance that a foreign government will **expropriate** (seize) property or will impose rules and regulations that will *impair operations*.

In the worst case, foreign governments can **expropriate** (or seize) property located within its borders without compensating the owner. Expropriation is relatively rare, but it has happened in a number of countries, including Chile, Bolivia, Cuba, Libya, Iraq, and Iran.

Although not as drastic as expropriation, certain other actions can reduce the value of a foreign operation substantially. They take the form of arbitrarily imposed rules and regulations on operations and ownership. For example, a host country government can implement the following:

- raise taxes of all kinds on the business
- limit the amount of profit that can be taken out of the country, either directly or through controls on currency conversion
- require that key inputs be purchased from local suppliers at arbitrary prices
- limit the prices charged for product sold within the country
- require part-ownership by citizens of the host country, forcing sale of an interest in the business at an unrealistically low price

Political risk also includes potential losses due to the actions of politically motivated terrorist groups. In the past these have included sabotage and bombing of property, as well as the murder and kidnapping for ransom of key executives.

Political risk is quite small in industrialized nations where Canada has invested most heavily, such as the U.S., Western European countries, Japan, Taiwan, and Australia. It can be substantial, however, in some areas of the Middle East, Africa, Asia, and South America, and in places where the political climate is unstable or free enterprise capitalism is new to the population and the government, like the former Soviet Union and the Eastern Bloc countries. If the host country government is unstable, the exchange rate may also be subject to depreciation.

Before investing in a country, the MNC must investigate its political stability, and its government's rules, regulations, and incentives regulating incoming FDI. To guard against adverse changes in the future, the multinational may establish a *joint venture* with local interests[7] or with other foreign companies. In addition, it may obtain political risk insurance from the Export Development Corporation (EDC).

Foreign Exchange Risks in the MNC

Earlier we defined exchange rate risk as the potential gain or loss that arises from changes in the exchange rate between the time an international transaction is contracted and the time it's completed. This idea is also called transaction risk because it arises from transactions as they occur. Transaction gains and losses have real profit and cash flow impacts because they're realized in cash as they happen. For this reason, they're taxable events. As we have seen, an international business can suffer real transaction losses on foreign exchange whether or not it has foreign subsidiaries or joint ventures.

Economic Risk

Economic risk refers to the potential long-run impact of exchange rate fluctuations on the value of a foreign affiliate. In particular, if the local exchange rate declines steadily over time, the affiliate (and its parent) may suffer real financial loss. In capital budgeting terms, the dollar value of future cash inflows can be dramatically reduced if the local currency depreciates against the dollar.

> **Economic risk** refers to the potential long-run losses to the affiliate (and its parent) from a steady decline in the local exchange rate.

For example, assume that a U.S. subsidiary of a Canadian multinational generated cash flows after tax (CFAT) of US$10.0 million per year over the five-year period 2002–2006 inclusive. If the exchange rate had stayed constant over the period at the average rate for 2002 (US$1 = CDN$1.57), the annual CFAT in U.S. dollars would be converted to CDN$15.7 million each year. But the U.S. dollar depreciated against the Canadian dollar over the period. As shown in the following table, the CFAT in Canadian dollars would decrease to CDN$11.3 million by 2006.

CFAT (US$)	Year	FX Rate*	CFAT (CDN$)
$10.0	2002	1.57	$15.7
$10.0	2003	1.40	$14.0
$10.0	2004	1.30	$13.0
$10.0	2005	1.21	$12.1
$10.0	2006	1.13	$11.3

Source: Canada Revenue Agency at http://www.cra-arc.gc.ca.

In the short term, specific cash flows can perhaps be hedged by using forward contracts. Long-term exchange risk can best be minimized by financing the project in the local currency, sourcing its material and labour locally, or moving operations to "hard" currency countries. However, exchange rates also generate the risk of another type of gain or loss.

Translation Risk

Translation risk refers to the potential gain or loss that arises from translating the financial statements (especially the balance sheet) of a foreign subsidiary from the local currency into Canadian dollars for consolidation with the parent company's financial statements.

> **Translation** gains/ losses arise when assets and liabilities held in a foreign country are translated into dollars.

---

7 *Before* operating in many foreign countries, it is often necessary to enter into a joint venture agreement with local corporations or government agencies. Joint ventures are common in most *developing* nations. Many require that the local interests own more than 50% of the shares in the joint venture corporation.

If the local currency has weakened recently against the dollar, translating it at the new rate gives a lower dollar value for the net assets of the foreign subsidiary. This difference implies that the foreign subsidiary has lost value in terms of dollars. That loss has to be recognized in the consolidation procedure. This is a *translation loss*.

Of course, if the foreign currency had *strengthened* against the dollar, the firm would have had a *translation gain*.

The Relevance of Translation Gains and Losses

Translation losses can occur on the consolidated financial statements of Canadian MNCs if the Canadian dollar is strong on the day that assets and liabilities in foreign currencies are translated into Canadian dollars. Thus, translation losses are unrealized and reflect the exchange rate on that date only. As long as the foreign subsidiary is not sold and the proceeds repatriated to Canada, the loss isn't realized in cash; it's only on paper and is something of an abstraction.

Recognizing this, the accounting rules for consolidating international "self-sustaining" subsidiaries specify that translation gains and losses are not to be included in consolidated income statements. Rather they're shown cumulatively in an account that adds to or offsets shareholders' equity. And because they're not realized, they're not taxable.

Insights **REAL APPLICATIONS**

Wal-Mart International

Wal-Mart, with 2006 revenue of US$345 billion, is the world's largest private enterprise. Outside the U.S. it operated in 13 countries, including Mexico, Canada, China, and Japan. Its international operations generated US$77.1 billion of its total revenue. In 2007 Wal-Mart planned to increase its international space about 10% (300 stores).

Mexico

Wal-Mart saw the January 1, 1994, implementation of the North American Free Trade Agreement as a chance to expand its operations to Canada and Mexico. In Mexico, the company realized that it had a lot to learn about the local market, so it set up a 50–50 joint venture with a local Mexican retailer and opened up 14 stores in 1994, establishing a practice of buying minority stakes in foreign retailers, then increasing its holdings to a majority over time.

Wal-Mart planned for 24 more stores in 1995. However, expansion plans were put on hold when Mexican government inspectors made a surprise visit to Wal-Mart's new superstore in Mexico City. The inspectors charged that some 15% of the store's products were improperly labelled or lacked instructions in Spanish, and ordered the store closed for 72 hours until the oversights were corrected. Wal-Mart saw this bureaucratic red tape as a deliberate attempt by government officials to delay its expansion plan, pointing out that some 40% of the products involved were purchased from a Mexican distributor.

To make matters worse, Mexico underwent a financial crisis in 1994. With a major depreciation in the Mexican peso, Wal-Mart saw the translated dollar value of its Mexican assets and earnings fall by more than 35%. At the same time, the sharp drop in confidence among Mexican businesses and consumers led to a decline in sales at the Mexican stores.

Subsequently the fortunes of Wal-Mart in Mexico and of Mexico itself have revived, so at the end of 2006, Wal-Mart was the country's largest retailer and employer, with 919 stores, all operated as majority-owned subsidiaries and profitable as a group.

Canada

Given Canada's similarities of income, culture, and government policies with the U.S., Wal-Mart entered Canada in 1993 through a straight acquisition of Woolco Canada. Wal-Mart's arrival hastened the departure of many Canadian competitors, including Kmart Canada and the T. Eaton Company. At the end of 2006, Wal-Mart had 290 stores in Canada, with plans to open 28 to 30 new stores in 2007, both conventional stores and supercentres, carrying a full array of groceries.

Japan

Because of the significant linguistic, cultural, and geographic distance between the U.S. and Japan, Wal-Mart entered the Japanese market in the early 1990s via a strategic alliance with a Japanese retailer. In 2002 it purchased a 6% interest in one of Japan's largest supermarket groups, and by 2004 held a controlling share. At the end of 2006, Wal-Mart had 392 stores in Japan.

What is Wal-Mart's biggest difficulty in Japan? It is how to satisfy finicky Japanese consumers without sacrificing its efficient cost structure. In order to succeed in Japan, Wal-Mart must localize its merchandise without impairing its massive economies of scale. Another challenge is Japan's complicated network of suppliers, wholesalers, and other middlemen. In the U.S. and other countries, Wal-Mart buys directly from the manufacturer, bypassing the middlemen.

China

Foreign retailers are looking to tap China's fast-growing economy, large population, and expanding middle class. Penetrating the Chinese market is challenging because it is highly fragmented with dominant local companies, and getting government approvals to open new stores can be a slow process. In 2006 Wal-Mart operated 84 stores in China, mostly "hypermarkets" (supercentres), with plans to add 18 to 20 more. In addition, it agreed to acquire a competing hypermarket chain of 100 stores over 3 years, giving it the largest food and department store network in China.

India

India's booming economy includes a retail sector growing 30% per year and dominated by more than 12 million small "mom and pop" stores. In 2006 Wal-Mart announced a joint venture with a large Indian company to open hundreds of stores under a franchise agreement in that market. The joint venture would allow Wal-Mart to skirt government regulations that bar most foreign retailers from investing directly in multi-product retail chains in India.

Missteps

In 2006, Wal-Mart decided to withdraw from South Korea and Germany after years of large losses. In Germany it sold its 85 stores to a competitor, absorbing a US$1 billion loss in the process. Wal-Mart had suffered for eight years from stiff competition from cut-rate retailers, strong unions, and labour restrictions. Its big-box stores in power centres were not popular with German consumers. Other cultural differences played a role in Wal-Mart's demise. Reportedly, male shoppers often interpreted the permanent smiles of sales staff as flirting.

Sources: Rajesh Mahapatra, "Wal-Mart Juggernaut Gets Set to Roll into India," *Toronto Star*, November 28, 2006, p. D3; Kate Linebaugh, "Wal-Mart Buys Retail Chain in China," *The Globe and Mail*, October 17, 2006, p. B14; Simon Beck, "Teutonic Army Stops the Wal-Mart Invasion," *The Globe and Mail*, August 5, 2006, p. B2; *Wal-Mart 2006 Annual Report.*

SUMMARY

1 A Canadian firm can operate in a foreign country in various modes: as an exporter/importer, a licensor/franchisor, a joint venture partner, or a Canadian parent of an operating subsidiary.

2 International transactions, including trade and international investments, are denominated in foreign currencies. Exchange rates for major currencies fluctuate rather freely, based on the demand and supply factors generating foreign currency flows among countries. Changes in exchange rates expose international business to foreign exchange risk.

3 Balances and cash flows in Canadian dollars often must be converted to foreign currencies to settle transactions with or to produce reports for foreign parties. Balances and cash flows in foreign currencies often must be converted to Canadian dollars to settle transactions with or to produce reports for Canadian parties.

4 A spot exchange rate is used for the immediate delivery of a foreign currency. A forward exchange rate is the rate fixed today by contract for delivery of the foreign currency at a fixed date in the future.

5 The international firm can reduce its foreign exchange risk by hedging in the exchange forward market. A firm expecting to pay foreign currency in the future may buy foreign exchange forward. A firm expecting to receive foreign currency in the future may sell foreign exchange forward. A firm may also hedge some currency risks in the futures and options markets.

6 Floating foreign exchange rates are set by forces of supply and demand, generated by cash flows among countries. Other exchange rates are determined by some form of government intervention in foreign exchange markets.

7 The international firm requires specialized techniques for managing its working capital and has access to additional sources of short-term financing. Letters of credit are available to provide guarantee of payment to vendors. Foreign currency loans may provide effective financing.

8 Large MNCs may raise long-term financing on international capital markets through the issue of foreign bonds, eurobonds, and shares.

9 FDI requires consideration and planning for exchange rate fluctuations, multiple levels of government regulation and taxes, and political risk.

10 Political risk entails the possibility of unexpected foreign government policy, local opposition, or terrorist activity that significantly damages the value of a firm's FDI.

11 Economic risk entails the potential decline in value of a FDI due to long-run depreciation in the value of the local currency.

12 Translation risk entails the potential loss on foreign exchange resulting from translating a foreign subsidiary's financial statements into the home currency of the parent company.

KEY TERMS

Convertible currency, p. 717
Cross rate, p. 713
Devaluation, p. 717
Economic risk, p. 725
Euro, p. 711
Eurobond, p. 722
Eurocurrency loans, p. 719
Eurodollars, p. 719
Exchange rate, p. 711
Exchange rate risk, p. 714
Expropriate, p. 724

Floating exchange rate, p. 717
Foreign bond, p. 722
Foreign direct investment (FDI), p. 709
Foreign exchange, p. 710
Foreign exchange market, p. 710
Government intervention, p. 716
Hedging, p. 715
Inconvertible currency, p. 717

International bond, p. 722
Letter of credit, p. 718
Multinational corporation (MNC), p. 709
Pegged (fixed) exchange rate, p. 717
Political risk, p. 724
Portfolio investment, p. 709
Translation risk, p. 725

QUESTIONS

1. Describe the ways in which the forms of international business have changed during the last 50 years. Include the concepts of a MNC and the different types of foreign operations.

2. You are determined to have your company enter a new foreign market in Southeast Asia. You must decide whether to establish a subsidiary there. What return and risk factors beyond the normal domestic financial analysis go into an FDI study?

3. Differentiate between a spot exchange rate and a forward exchange rate.

4. Forward contracts are always more expensive than spot transactions. Comment on this statement in reference to the current 90-day forward rate for the U.S. dollar.

5. Explain how the Export Development Corporation can help Canadian firms to conduct international business.

6. What generates the supply of and the demand for foreign exchange? What makes the exchange rate for the Canadian dollar move around?

7. Why might the government be interested in influencing exchange rates from time to time? How would it go about moving the exchange rate?

8. Describe the difference between a floating and a pegged exchange rate system.

9. How and why is the U.S. dollar unique among the world's currencies?

10. What is a letter of credit? Outline the main steps in establishing a letter of credit for a Canadian exporter.

11. What are eurocurrency loans? What are the advantages and disadvantages of raising money in this way?

12. What is meant by an inconvertible currency?

13. Differentiate between a foreign bond and a eurobond. Provide theoretical examples of both, from the point of view of a Canadian MNC raising money in capital markets.

14. Why do major corporations list their shares on foreign stock exchanges?

15. Differentiate between transaction exposure and economic exposure in terms of foreign exchange risk.

Business Analysis

1. You're the treasurer of Warm Wear Inc., which imports wool shoes from around the world. Kreploc, a company in the country of Slobodia, has a product that your marketing department would like to carry and doesn't require payment until 90 days after delivery.

   Unfortunately the Slobodian blivit tends to vary in value by as much as 30% over periods as short as three months. This makes you reluctant to do business with Kreploc because of exchange rate risk. The marketing department can't understand why you have any concerns at all. Prepare a brief explanation including an illustration of why you're concerned.

2. You're the CFO of the Overseas Sprocket Company, which imports a great deal of product from Europe and the Far East and is continually faced with exchange rate exposure on unfilled contracts. Harry Byrite, the head of purchasing, has a plan to avoid exchange rate losses. He suggests that the firm borrow enough money from the bank to buy a six-month supply of foreign exchange, which would be kept in a safety deposit box until used. "We'd never have another unexpected exchange rate loss again," says Harry. Prepare a polite response to Harry's idea. Explain why you do or don't like it, and suggest an alternative if you feel that one is appropriate.

3. You're the CFO of the Kraknee Roller Skate Company, which sells roller skates worldwide and also builds and operates roller rinks. Some time ago Archie Speedo, the head of international marketing, proposed selling skates in Russia. Everyone thought he was crazy, but

the idea turned out to be very successful. Archie lined up a talented Russian importer who managed to sell more skates than anyone imagined possible. Now Archie has proposed a new Russian venture. He wants to open and operate a roller rink in Moscow. He says that since the breakup of the Soviet Union, Russians are interested in Western pastimes, and a roller rink in the capital city would make a fortune. Based on his earlier success in Russia, the rest of the executive team is in favour of the idea. You, however, have some concerns. Write a memo explaining how the roller rink proposal differs from exporting skates to Russia, and what problem is likely even if the venture is as commercially successful as the skates. What other risk is involved?

DANIER LEATHER

4. (Refer to the Insight box "Danier Leather International" on page 721.)
At some time in the future, Danier may establish an operation (FDI) in South America. Assume that it plans to establish a wholly owned subsidiary in Argentina, a major skins producer. Explain briefly the potential risks for Danier in such an investment.

PROBLEMS

Use the exchange rates in Table 20.2 on page 712 for Problems 1 and 2.

1. A Canadian importer owes vendors the following sums:
   a. 140,560 U.S. dollars
   b. 392,000 Australian dollars
   c. 1,362,000 Mexican pesos
   d. 680,540 British pounds
   e. 14,673 euros
   State each debt to the nearest Canadian dollar.

2. The Cline family made a trip to Europe in 2007. They paid the following amounts in local currency for hotel, entertainment, and transportation.

England	855 pounds
France	1,462 euros
Czech Republic	10,000 koruna
Airfares	2,500 U.S. dollars

   How much did the trip cost in Canadian dollars? Round to the nearest dollar.

3. Bob and Chris received a grant through their university to travel to Germany to do research. The grant awarded them $2,000 for room and board during their stay. It was paid to them in dollars on May 31 at which time the euro was worth $0.70980. They bought and spent the euros in Germany during July when the euro was worth $0.71597.
   a. In euro terms, how much were they awarded in May?
   b. Did the change in the euro work to their advantage or disadvantage?

4. The following direct quote exchange rates are found on the spot market today.
   a. Euro: 1.50
   b. U.S. dollar: 1.10
   c. British pound: 2.15
   d. Japanese yen: 0.010

Calculate the price of a Canadian dollar in terms of each currency, (the indirect quote). Round to two decimal places.

5. Franco Harris, CFO of Alston Concrete Products, is currently evaluating the purchase of an innovative machine that tests the strength of concrete. The machine is sold only in England, and Alston has a price quote at £52,500 from the manufacturer that's good for 60 days. Franco has read that the British pound is expected to strengthen against the dollar by 15% during the next two months. Currently the pound is worth $2.15. If Franco believes the currency forecast is accurate, should Alston buy the machine now or wait until just before the price quote expires? How much difference might the decision make in dollars?

6. Suppose a car manufactured in Japan in the mid-1980s, when there were 200 yen to the dollar, cost 2.5 million yen to produce and was marked up 25% for sale in Canada. Assume the car's cost in yen and markup are the same today, but the exchange rate is 120 yen to the dollar.
   a. What did the car sell for in Canadian dollars in the mid-1980s?
   b. What does it sell for now?

7. In 2007, the Ballard Motor Company ordered six German-built engines at 15,000 euros each, when the direct exchange rate was 1.45, and elected not to cover the obligation with a forward contract. When the bill was due three months later the rate was 1.35. Ballard's marginal tax rate is 40%.
   a. How much was the exchange rate gain or loss on the deal?
   b. What kind of exchange rate gain or loss was it?
   c. What was the tax impact?

8. The Latimore Company invested $8.5 million in a new plant in Italy when the exchange rate was 1.45 dollars to the euro. At the end of the year, the rate was 1.65 dollars to the euro.
   a. Did Latimore make or lose money on the exchange rate movement? If so, how much?
   b. What kind of exchange rate gain or loss was it?
   c. What was the tax impact?

9. One year ago, a Canadian investor bought 1,000 shares of General Motors (GM) at US$30. The exchange rate at that time was CDN$1.13 = US$1.
   a. Assume that GM's shares declined by US$3 over the past year, but the U.S. dollar strengthened by 10% against the Canadian dollar. What is the total percentage return to the Canadian investor?
   b. Now assume that GM's shares increased by US$2 while the U.S. dollar weakened by 5%. What is the total percentage return to the Canadian investor?

10. Using Table 20.2 (page 712), input the spot and forward rates for the British pound ($/£) as of July 12, 2007:
    • Spot
    • 30-day forward
    • 90-day forward
    • 180-day forward

     a. Was the pound selling at a discount or premium in the forward market?

     b. What was the 30-day forward premium (or discount)?

     c. What was the 90-day forward premium (or discount)?

     d. Suppose you executed a 30-day forward contract to exchange £50,000 into Canadian dollars. How many dollars would you get 30 days later?

     e. Assume a British importer entered into a 180-day forward contract with TD Canada Trust to buy CDN$500,000. How many pounds will the British company deliver in six months to get the Canadian dollars?

11. A Japanese importer owes a Canadian exporter CDN$450,520. Using the exchange rates in Table 20.2, answer the following questions.

     a. What is her bill in yen if she pays immediately?

     b. What would the bill be if the importer wanted to lock in an exchange rate today but pay in three months?

     c. Why is one rate different than the other?

12. Hampshire Motors Ltd., a British manufacturing company, wants to buy a production machine that isn't available in England. Comparable products are made by a Canadian company and a French firm. The Canadians have quoted Hampshire a price of CDN$175,000, while the French want 192,000 euros. How much is each price in British pounds? Calculate a cross rate to state the French quote in pounds. Use the exchange rates in Table 20.2.

13. Canada Corporation is considering an FDI in England. The initial cash outlay will be $50 million. The current foreign exchange rate is $1.00 = £0.50, so the investment in foreign currency will be £25 million. The investment will have a useful life of five years, after which it will be worth nothing.

    Sales are expected to be £25 million pounds yearly. Annual costs and cash expenses will be £12.5 million. The British income tax rate is 25%. Straight-line amortization is used for British taxes.

    The English subsidiary will remit all of its after-tax profits to the Canadian parent as a dividend. Assume there are no further British taxes on the remittance, or Canadian taxes on the dividend received. The risk-adjusted cost of capital is 15%.

     a. What is the net present value of the project, in Canadian dollars, assuming that the exchange rate remains unchanged during the life of the project?

     b. What is the net present value of the project, in Canadian dollars, if the exchange rate forecast is

$$Year\ 0: \$1 = £0.50$$
$$Year\ 1: \$1 = £0.55$$
$$Year\ 2: \$1 = £0.60$$
$$Year\ 3: \$1 = £0.65$$
$$Year\ 4: \$1 = £0.70$$
$$Year\ 5: \$1 = £0.75$$

14. Hanover Inc. spent £11.5 million building a factory in Germany early in 2002 when the euro cost $1.40. The plant operation was set up as a self-sustaining (independent) German subsidiary to manufacture product for sale and distribution in Europe and the

United Kingdom. Hanover closed its consolidated books for the 2007 *fiscal* year on
July 12, 2007. Hanover is subject to a 40% tax rate in Canada and a 45% rate
in Germany.

- a. How much did Hanover make or lose on the value of its German factory due to exchange rate movements in the five years since it was built? Use Table 20.2.
- b. Explain the tax impact of the gain or loss?
- c. Where does the gain or loss show up in Hanover's financial statements?

Appendix A

Financial Tables

	TABLE A-1			**Future Value of $1**		$FVF_{k,n} = (1 + k)^n$							
						INTEREST RATES							
Periods	0.50%	0.67%	0.75%	1%	1.50%	2%	2.50%	3%	3.50%	4%	4.50%	5%	6%	7%
1	1.0050	1.0067	1.0075	1.0100	1.0150	1.0200	1.0250	1.0300	1.0350	1.0400	1.0450	1.0500	1.0600	1.0700
2	1.0100	1.0134	1.0151	1.0201	1.0302	1.0404	1.0506	1.0609	1.0712	1.0816	1.0920	1.1025	1.1236	1.1449
3	1.0151	1.0201	1.0227	1.0303	1.0457	1.0612	1.0769	1.0927	1.1087	1.1249	1.1412	1.1576	1.1910	1.2250
4	1.0202	1.0269	1.0303	1.0406	1.0614	1.0824	1.1038	1.1255	1.1475	1.1699	1.1925	1.2155	1.2625	1.3108
5	1.0253	1.0338	1.0381	1.0510	1.0773	1.1041	1.1314	1.1593	1.1877	1.2167	1.2462	1.2763	1.3382	1.4026
6	1.0304	1.0407	1.0459	1.0615	1.0934	1.1262	1.1597	1.1941	1.2293	1.2653	1.3023	1.3401	1.4185	1.5007
7	1.0355	1.0476	1.0537	1.0721	1.1098	1.1487	1.1887	1.2299	1.2723	1.3159	1.3609	1.4071	1.5036	1.6058
8	1.0407	1.0546	1.0616	1.0829	1.1265	1.1717	1.2184	1.2668	1.3168	1.3686	1.4221	1.4775	1.5938	1.7182
9	1.0459	1.0616	1.0696	1.0937	1.1434	1.1951	1.2489	1.3048	1.3629	1.4233	1.4861	1.5513	1.6895	1.8385
10	1.0511	1.0687	1.0776	1.1046	1.1605	1.2190	1.2801	1.3439	1.4106	1.4802	1.5530	1.6289	1.7908	1.9672
11	1.0564	1.0758	1.0857	1.1157	1.1779	1.2434	1.3121	1.3842	1.4600	1.5395	1.6229	1.7103	1.8983	2.1049
12	1.0617	1.0830	1.0938	1.1268	1.1956	1.2682	1.3449	1.4258	1.5111	1.6010	1.6959	1.7959	2.0122	2.2522
13	1.0670	1.0902	1.1020	1.1381	1.2136	1.2936	1.3785	1.4685	1.5640	1.6651	1.7722	1.8856	2.1329	2.4098
14	1.0723	1.0975	1.1103	1.1495	1.2318	1.3195	1.4130	1.5126	1.6187	1.7317	1.8519	1.9799	2.2609	2.5785
15	1.0777	1.1048	1.1186	1.1610	1.2502	1.3459	1.4483	1.5580	1.6753	1.8009	1.9353	2.0789	2.3966	2.7590
16	1.0831	1.1122	1.1270	1.1726	1.2690	1.3728	1.4845	1.6047	1.7340	1.8730	2.0224	2.1829	2.5404	2.9522
17	1.0885	1.1196	1.1354	1.1843	1.2880	1.4002	1.5216	1.6528	1.7947	1.9479	2.1134	2.2920	2.6928	3.1588
18	1.0939	1.1270	1.1440	1.1961	1.3073	1.4282	1.5597	1.7024	1.8575	2.0258	2.2085	2.4066	2.8543	3.3799
19	1.0994	1.1346	1.1525	1.2081	1.3270	1.4568	1.5987	1.7535	1.9225	2.1068	2.3079	2.5270	3.0256	3.6165
20	1.1049	1.1421	1.1612	1.2202	1.3469	1.4859	1.6386	1.8061	1.9898	2.1911	2.4117	2.6533	3.2071	3.8697
21	1.1104	1.1497	1.1699	1.2324	1.3671	1.5157	1.6796	1.8603	2.0594	2.2788	2.5202	2.7860	3.3996	4.1406
22	1.1160	1.1574	1.1787	1.2447	1.3876	1.5460	1.7216	1.9161	2.1315	2.3699	2.6337	2.9253	3.6035	4.4304
23	1.1216	1.1651	1.1875	1.2572	1.4084	1.5769	1.7646	1.9736	2.2061	2.4647	2.7522	3.0715	3.8197	4.7405
24	1.1272	1.1729	1.1964	1.2697	1.4295	1.6084	1.8087	2.0328	2.2833	2.5633	2.8760	3.2251	4.0489	5.0724
25	1.1328	1.1807	1.2054	1.2824	1.4509	1.6406	1.8539	2.0938	2.3632	2.6658	3.0054	3.3864	4.2919	5.4274
26	1.1385	1.1886	1.2144	1.2953	1.4727	1.6734	1.9003	2.1566	2.4460	2.7725	3.1407	3.5557	4.5494	5.8074
27	1.1442	1.1965	1.2235	1.3082	1.4948	1.7069	1.9478	2.2213	2.5316	2.8834	3.2820	3.7335	4.8223	6.2139
28	1.1499	1.2045	1.2327	1.3213	1.5172	1.7410	1.9965	2.2879	2.6202	2.9987	3.4297	3.9201	5.1117	6.6488
29	1.1556	1.2125	1.2420	1.3345	1.5400	1.7758	2.0464	2.3566	2.7119	3.1187	3.5840	4.1161	5.4184	7.1143
30	1.1614	1.2206	1.2513	1.3478	1.5631	1.8114	2.0976	2.4273	2.8068	3.2434	3.7453	4.3219	5.7435	7.6123
32	1.1730	1.2369	1.2701	1.3749	1.6103	1.8845	2.2038	2.5751	3.0067	3.5081	4.0900	4.7649	6.4534	8.7153
34	1.1848	1.2535	1.2892	1.4026	1.6590	1.9607	2.3153	2.7319	3.2209	3.7943	4.4664	5.2533	7.2510	9.9781
36	1.1967	1.2702	1.3086	1.4308	1.7091	2.0399	2.4325	2.8983	3.4503	4.1039	4.8774	5.7918	8.1473	11.4239
38	1.2087	1.2872	1.3283	1.4595	1.7608	2.1223	2.5557	3.0748	3.6960	4.4388	5.3262	6.3855	9.1543	13.0793
40	1.2208	1.3045	1.3483	1.4889	1.8140	2.2080	2.6851	3.2620	3.9593	4.8010	5.8164	7.0400	10.2857	14.9745
48	1.2705	1.3757	1.4314	1.6122	2.0435	2.5871	3.2715	4.1323	5.2136	6.5705	8.2715	10.4013	16.3939	25.7289
50	1.2832	1.3941	1.4530	1.6446	2.1052	2.6916	3.4371	4.3839	5.5849	7.1067	9.0326	11.4674	18.4202	29.4570
60	1.3489	1.4898	1.5657	1.8167	2.4432	3.2810	4.3998	5.8916	7.8781	10.5196	14.0274	18.6792	32.9877	57.9464
120	1.8194	2.2196	2.4514	3.3004	5.9693	10.7652	19.3581	34.7110	62.0643	110.663	196.768	348.912	1088.19	3357.79
180	2.4541	3.3069	3.8380	5.9958	14.5844	35.3208	85.1718	204.5034	488.9483	1164.13	2760.15	6517.39	35896.8	*
240	3.3102	4.9268	6.0092	10.8926	35.6328	115.889	374.738	1204.85	3851.98	12246.2	38717.7	*	*	*
300	4.4650	7.3402	9.4084	19.7885	87.0588	380.235	1648.77	7098.51	30346.2	*	*	*	*	*
360	6.0226	10.9357	14.7306	35.9496	212.704	1247.56	7254.23	41821.6	*	*	*	*	*	*

Periods	8%	9%	10%	11%	12%	13%	14%	15%	16%	18%	20%	24%	30%	36%
1	1.0800	1.0900	1.1000	1.1100	1.1200	1.1300	1.1400	1.1500	1.1600	1.1800	1.2000	1.2400	1.3000	1.3600
2	1.1664	1.1881	1.2100	1.2321	1.2544	1.2769	1.2996	1.3225	1.3456	1.3924	1.4400	1.5376	1.6900	1.8496
3	1.2597	1.2950	1.3310	1.3676	1.4049	1.4429	1.4815	1.5209	1.5609	1.6430	1.7280	1.9066	2.1970	2.5155
4	1.3605	1.4116	1.4641	1.5181	1.5735	1.6305	1.6890	1.7490	1.8106	1.9388	2.0736	2.3642	2.8561	3.4210
5	1.4693	1.5386	1.6105	1.6851	1.7623	1.8424	1.9254	2.0114	2.1003	2.2878	2.4883	2.9316	3.7129	4.6526
6	1.5869	1.6771	1.7716	1.8704	1.9738	2.0820	2.1950	2.3131	2.4364	2.6996	2.9860	3.6352	4.8268	6.3275
7	1.7138	1.8280	1.9487	2.0762	2.2107	2.3526	2.5023	2.6600	2.8262	3.1855	3.5832	4.5077	6.2749	8.6054
8	1.8509	1.9926	2.1436	2.3045	2.4760	2.6584	2.8526	3.0590	3.2784	3.7589	4.2998	5.5895	8.1573	11.7034
9	1.9990	2.1719	2.3579	2.5580	2.7731	3.0040	3.2519	3.5179	3.8030	4.4355	5.1598	6.9310	10.6045	15.9166
10	2.1589	2.3674	2.5937	2.8394	3.1058	3.3946	3.7072	4.0456	4.4114	5.2338	6.1917	8.5944	13.7858	21.6466
11	2.3316	2.5804	2.8531	3.1518	3.4785	3.8359	4.2262	4.6524	5.1173	6.1759	7.4301	10.6571	17.9216	29.4393
12	2.5182	2.8127	3.1384	3.4985	3.8960	4.3345	4.8179	5.3503	5.9360	7.2876	8.9161	13.2148	23.2981	40.0375
13	2.7196	3.0658	3.4523	3.8833	4.3635	4.8980	5.4924	6.1528	6.8858	8.5994	10.6993	16.3863	30.2875	54.4510
14	2.9372	3.3417	3.7975	4.3104	4.8871	5.5348	6.2613	7.0757	7.9875	10.1472	12.8392	20.3191	39.3738	74.0534
15	3.1722	3.6425	4.1772	4.7846	5.4736	6.2543	7.1379	8.1371	9.2655	11.9737	15.4070	25.1956	51.1859	100.713
16	3.4259	3.9703	4.5950	5.3109	6.1304	7.0673	8.1372	9.3576	10.7480	14.1290	18.4884	31.2426	66.5417	136.969
17	3.7000	4.3276	5.0545	5.8951	6.8660	7.9861	9.2765	10.7613	12.4677	16.6722	22.1861	38.7408	86.5042	186.278
18	3.9960	4.7171	5.5599	6.5436	7.6900	9.0243	10.5752	12.3755	14.4625	19.6733	26.6233	48.0386	112.455	253.338
19	4.3157	5.1417	6.1159	7.2633	8.6128	10.1974	12.0557	14.2318	16.7765	23.2144	31.9480	59.5679	146.192	344.540
20	4.6610	5.6044	6.7275	8.0623	9.6463	11.5231	13.7435	16.3665	19.4608	27.3930	38.3376	73.8641	190.050	468.574
21	5.0338	6.1088	7.4002	8.9492	10.8038	13.0211	15.6676	18.8215	22.5745	32.3238	46.0051	91.5915	247.065	637.261
22	5.4365	6.6586	8.1403	9.9336	12.1003	14.7138	17.8610	21.6447	26.1864	38.1421	55.2061	113.574	321.184	866.674
23	5.8715	7.2579	8.9543	11.0263	13.5523	16.6266	20.3616	24.8915	30.3762	45.0076	66.2474	140.831	417.539	1178.68
24	6.3412	7.9111	9.8497	12.2392	15.1786	18.7881	23.2122	28.6252	35.2364	53.1090	79.4968	174.631	542.801	1603.00
25	6.8485	8.6231	10.8347	13.5855	17.0001	21.2305	26.4619	32.9190	40.8742	62.6686	95.3962	216.542	705.641	2180.08
26	7.3964	9.3992	11.9182	15.0799	19.0401	23.9905	30.1666	37.8568	47.4141	73.9490	114.475	268.512	917.333	2964.91
27	7.9881	10.2451	13.1100	16.7386	21.3249	27.1093	34.3899	43.5353	55.0004	87.2598	137.371	332.955	1192.53	4032.28
28	8.6271	11.1671	14.4210	18.5799	23.8839	30.6335	39.2045	50.0656	63.8004	102.967	164.845	412.864	1550.29	5483.90
29	9.3173	12.1722	15.8631	20.6237	26.7499	34.6158	44.6931	57.5755	74.0085	121.501	197.814	511.952	2015.38	7458.10
30	10.0627	13.2677	17.4494	22.8923	29.9599	39.1159	50.9502	66.2118	85.8499	143.371	237.376	634.820	2620.00	10143.0
32	11.7371	15.7633	21.1138	28.2056	37.5817	49.9471	66.2148	87.5651	115.520	199.629	341.822	976.099	4427.79	18760.5
34	13.6901	18.7284	25.5477	34.7521	47.1425	63.7774	86.0528	115.805	155.443	277.964	492.224	1500.85	7482.97	34699.5
36	15.9682	22.2512	30.9127	42.8181	59.1356	81.4374	111.834	153.152	209.164	387.037	708.802	2307.71	12646.2	64180.1
38	18.6253	26.4367	37.4043	52.7562	74.1797	103.987	145.340	202.543	281.452	538.910	1020.67	3548.33	21372.1	*
40	21.7245	31.4094	45.2593	65.0009	93.0510	132.782	188.884	267.864	378.721	750.378	1469.77	5455.91	36118.9	*
48	40.2106	62.5852	97.0172	149.797	230.391	352.992	538.807	819.401	1241.61	2820.57	6319.75	30495.9	*	*
50	46.9016	74.3575	117.391	184.565	289.002	450.736	700.233	1083.66	1670.70	3927.36	9100.44	46890.4	*	*
60	101.257	176.031	304.482	524.057	897.597	1530.05	2595.92	4384.00	7370.20	20555.1	56347.5	*	*	*
120	10253.0	30987.0	92709.1	*	*	*	*	*	*	*	*	*	*	*
180	*	*	*	*	*	*	*	*	*	*	*	*	*	*
240	*	*	*	*	*	*	*	*	*	*	*	*	*	*
300	*	*	*	*	*	*	*	*	*	*	*	*	*	*
360	*	*	*	*	*	*	*	*	*	*	*	*	*	*

TABLE A-2			Present Value of $1			$\text{PVF}_{k,n} = (1 + k)^{-n}$							

INTEREST RATES

Periods	0.50%	0.67%	0.75%	1%	1.50%	2%	2.50%	3%	3.50%	4%	4.50%	5%	6%	7%
1	0.9950	0.9934	0.9926	0.9901	0.9852	0.9804	0.9756	0.9709	0.9662	0.9615	0.9569	0.9524	0.9434	0.9346
2	0.9901	0.9868	0.9852	0.9803	0.9707	0.9612	0.9518	0.9426	0.9335	0.9246	0.9157	0.9070	0.8900	0.8734
3	0.9851	0.9803	0.9778	0.9706	0.9563	0.9423	0.9286	0.9151	0.9019	0.8890	0.8763	0.8638	0.8396	0.8163
4	0.9802	0.9738	0.9706	0.9610	0.9422	0.9238	0.9060	0.8885	0.8714	0.8548	0.8386	0.8227	0.7921	0.7629
5	0.9754	0.9673	0.9633	0.9515	0.9283	0.9057	0.8839	0.8626	0.8420	0.8219	0.8025	0.7835	0.7473	0.7130
6	0.9705	0.9609	0.9562	0.9420	0.9145	0.8880	0.8623	0.8375	0.8135	0.7903	0.7679	0.7462	0.7050	0.6663
7	0.9657	0.9546	0.9490	0.9327	0.9010	0.8706	0.8413	0.8131	0.7860	0.7599	0.7348	0.7107	0.6651	0.6227
8	0.9609	0.9482	0.9420	0.9235	0.8877	0.8535	0.8207	0.7894	0.7594	0.7307	0.7032	0.6768	0.6274	0.5820
9	0.9561	0.9420	0.9350	0.9143	0.8746	0.8368	0.8007	0.7664	0.7337	0.7026	0.6729	0.6446	0.5919	0.5439
10	0.9513	0.9357	0.9280	0.9053	0.8617	0.8203	0.7812	0.7441	0.7089	0.6756	0.6439	0.6139	0.5584	0.5083
11	0.9466	0.9295	0.9211	0.8963	0.8489	0.8043	0.7621	0.7224	0.6849	0.6496	0.6162	0.5847	0.5268	0.4751
12	0.9419	0.9234	0.9142	0.8874	0.8364	0.7885	0.7436	0.7014	0.6618	0.6246	0.5897	0.5568	0.4970	0.4440
13	0.9372	0.9172	0.9074	0.8787	0.8240	0.7730	0.7254	0.6810	0.6394	0.6006	0.5643	0.5303	0.4688	0.4150
14	0.9326	0.9112	0.9007	0.8700	0.8118	0.7579	0.7077	0.6611	0.6178	0.5775	0.5400	0.5051	0.4423	0.3878
15	0.9279	0.9051	0.8940	0.8613	0.7999	0.7430	0.6905	0.6419	0.5969	0.5553	0.5167	0.4810	0.4173	0.3624
16	0.9233	0.8991	0.8873	0.8528	0.7880	0.7284	0.6736	0.6232	0.5767	0.5339	0.4945	0.4581	0.3936	0.3387
17	0.9187	0.8932	0.8807	0.8444	0.7764	0.7142	0.6572	0.6050	0.5572	0.5134	0.4732	0.4363	0.3714	0.3166
18	0.9141	0.8873	0.8742	0.8360	0.7649	0.7002	0.6412	0.5874	0.5384	0.4936	0.4528	0.4155	0.3503	0.2959
19	0.9096	0.8814	0.8676	0.8277	0.7536	0.6864	0.6255	0.5703	0.5202	0.4746	0.4333	0.3957	0.3305	0.2765
20	0.9051	0.8756	0.8612	0.8195	0.7425	0.6730	0.6103	0.5537	0.5026	0.4564	0.4146	0.3769	0.3118	0.2584
21	0.9006	0.8698	0.8548	0.8114	0.7315	0.6598	0.5954	0.5375	0.4856	0.4388	0.3968	0.3589	0.2942	0.2415
22	0.8961	0.8640	0.8484	0.8034	0.7207	0.6468	0.5809	0.5219	0.4692	0.4220	0.3797	0.3418	0.2775	0.2257
23	0.8916	0.8583	0.8421	0.7954	0.7100	0.6342	0.5667	0.5067	0.4533	0.4057	0.3634	0.3256	0.2618	0.2109
24	0.8872	0.8526	0.8358	0.7876	0.6995	0.6217	0.5529	0.4919	0.4380	0.3901	0.3477	0.3101	0.2470	0.1971
25	0.8828	0.8470	0.8296	0.7798	0.6892	0.6095	0.5394	0.4776	0.4231	0.3751	0.3327	0.2953	0.2330	0.1842
26	0.8784	0.8413	0.8234	0.7720	0.6790	0.5976	0.5262	0.4637	0.4088	0.3607	0.3184	0.2812	0.2198	0.1722
27	0.8740	0.8358	0.8173	0.7644	0.6690	0.5859	0.5134	0.4502	0.3950	0.3468	0.3047	0.2678	0.2074	0.1609
28	0.8697	0.8302	0.8112	0.7568	0.6591	0.5744	0.5009	0.4371	0.3817	0.3335	0.2916	0.2551	0.1956	0.1504
29	0.8653	0.8247	0.8052	0.7493	0.6494	0.5631	0.4887	0.4243	0.3687	0.3207	0.2790	0.2429	0.1846	0.1406
30	0.8610	0.8193	0.7992	0.7419	0.6398	0.5521	0.4767	0.4120	0.3563	0.3083	0.2670	0.2314	0.1741	0.1314
32	0.8525	0.8085	0.7873	0.7273	0.6210	0.5306	0.4538	0.3883	0.3326	0.2851	0.2445	0.2099	0.1550	0.1147
34	0.8440	0.7978	0.7757	0.7130	0.6028	0.5100	0.4319	0.3660	0.3105	0.2636	0.2239	0.1904	0.1379	0.1002
36	0.8356	0.7873	0.7641	0.6989	0.5851	0.4902	0.4111	0.3450	0.2898	0.2437	0.2050	0.1727	0.1227	0.0875
38	0.8274	0.7769	0.7528	0.6852	0.5679	0.4712	0.3913	0.3252	0.2706	0.2253	0.1878	0.1566	0.1092	0.0765
40	0.8191	0.7666	0.7416	0.6717	0.5513	0.4529	0.3724	0.3066	0.2526	0.2083	0.1719	0.1420	0.0972	0.0668
48	0.7871	0.7269	0.6986	0.6203	0.4894	0.3865	0.3057	0.2420	0.1918	0.1522	0.1209	0.0961	0.0610	0.0389
50	0.7793	0.7173	0.6883	0.6080	0.4750	0.3715	0.2909	0.2281	0.1791	0.1407	0.1107	0.0872	0.0543	0.0339
60	0.7414	0.6712	0.6387	0.5504	0.4093	0.3048	0.2273	0.1697	0.1269	0.0951	0.0713	0.0535	0.0303	0.0173
120	0.5496	0.4505	0.4079	0.3030	0.1675	0.0929	0.0517	0.0288	0.0161	0.0090	0.0051	0.0029	0.0009	0.0003
180	0.4075	0.3024	0.2605	0.1668	0.0686	0.0283	0.0117	0.0049	0.0020	0.0009	0.0004	0.0002	0.0000	0.0000
240	0.3021	0.2030	0.1664	0.0918	0.0281	0.0086	0.0027	0.0008	0.0003	0.0001	0.0000	0.0000	0.0000	0.0000
300	0.2240	0.1362	0.1063	0.0505	0.0115	0.0026	0.0006	0.0001	0.0000	0.0000	0.0000	0.0000	0.0000	0.0000
360	0.1660	0.0914	0.0679	0.0278	0.0047	0.0008	0.0001	0.0000	0.0000	0.0000	0.0000	0.0000	0.0000	0.0000

Periods	8%	9%	10%	11%	12%	13%	14%	15%	16%	18%	20%	24%	30%	36%
1	0.9259	0.9174	0.9091	0.9009	0.8929	0.8850	0.8772	0.8696	0.8621	0.8475	0.8333	0.8065	0.7692	0.7353
2	0.8573	0.8417	0.8264	0.8116	0.7972	0.7831	0.7695	0.7561	0.7432	0.7182	0.6944	0.6504	0.5917	0.5407
3	0.7938	0.7722	0.7513	0.7312	0.7118	0.6931	0.6750	0.6575	0.6407	0.6086	0.5787	0.5245	0.4552	0.3975
4	0.7350	0.7084	0.6830	0.6587	0.6355	0.6133	0.5921	0.5718	0.5523	0.5158	0.4823	0.4230	0.3501	0.2923
5	0.6806	0.6499	0.6209	0.5935	0.5674	0.5428	0.5194	0.4972	0.4761	0.4371	0.4019	0.3411	0.2693	0.2149
6	0.6302	0.5963	0.5645	0.5346	0.5066	0.4803	0.4556	0.4323	0.4104	0.3704	0.3349	0.2751	0.2072	0.1580
7	0.5835	0.5470	0.5132	0.4817	0.4523	0.4251	0.3996	0.3759	0.3538	0.3139	0.2791	0.2218	0.1594	0.1162
8	0.5403	0.5019	0.4665	0.4339	0.4039	0.3762	0.3506	0.3269	0.3050	0.2660	0.2326	0.1789	0.1226	0.0854
9	0.5002	0.4604	0.4241	0.3909	0.3606	0.3329	0.3075	0.2843	0.2630	0.2255	0.1938	0.1443	0.0943	0.0628
10	0.4632	0.4224	0.3855	0.3522	0.3220	0.2946	0.2697	0.2472	0.2267	0.1911	0.1615	0.1164	0.0725	0.0462
11	0.4289	0.3875	0.3505	0.3173	0.2875	0.2607	0.2366	0.2149	0.1954	0.1619	0.1346	0.0938	0.0558	0.0340
12	0.3971	0.3555	0.3186	0.2858	0.2567	0.2307	0.2076	0.1869	0.1685	0.1372	0.1122	0.0757	0.0429	0.0250
13	0.3677	0.3262	0.2897	0.2575	0.2292	0.2042	0.1821	0.1625	0.1452	0.1163	0.0935	0.0610	0.0330	0.0184
14	0.3405	0.2992	0.2633	0.2320	0.2046	0.1807	0.1597	0.1413	0.1252	0.0985	0.0779	0.0492	0.0254	0.0135
15	0.3152	0.2745	0.2394	0.2090	0.1827	0.1599	0.1401	0.1229	0.1079	0.0835	0.0649	0.0397	0.0195	0.0099
16	0.2919	0.2519	0.2176	0.1883	0.1631	0.1415	0.1229	0.1069	0.0930	0.0708	0.0541	0.0320	0.0150	0.0073
17	0.2703	0.2311	0.1978	0.1696	0.1456	0.1252	0.1078	0.0929	0.0802	0.0600	0.0451	0.0258	0.0116	0.0054
18	0.2502	0.2120	0.1799	0.1528	0.1300	0.1108	0.0946	0.0808	0.0691	0.0508	0.0376	0.0208	0.0089	0.0039
19	0.2317	0.1945	0.1635	0.1377	0.1161	0.0981	0.0829	0.0703	0.0596	0.0431	0.0313	0.0168	0.0068	0.0029
20	0.2145	0.1784	0.1486	0.1240	0.1037	0.0868	0.0728	0.0611	0.0514	0.0365	0.0261	0.0135	0.0053	0.0021
21	0.1987	0.1637	0.1351	0.1117	0.0926	0.0768	0.0638	0.0531	0.0443	0.0309	0.0217	0.0109	0.0040	0.0016
22	0.1839	0.1502	0.1228	0.1007	0.0826	0.0680	0.0560	0.0462	0.0382	0.0262	0.0181	0.0088	0.0031	0.0012
23	0.1703	0.1378	0.1117	0.0907	0.0738	0.0601	0.0491	0.0402	0.0329	0.0222	0.0151	0.0071	0.0024	0.0008
24	0.1577	0.1264	0.1015	0.0817	0.0659	0.0532	0.0431	0.0349	0.0284	0.0188	0.0126	0.0057	0.0018	0.0006
25	0.1460	0.1160	0.0923	0.0736	0.0588	0.0471	0.0378	0.0304	0.0245	0.0160	0.0105	0.0046	0.0014	0.0005
26	0.1352	0.1064	0.0839	0.0663	0.0525	0.0417	0.0331	0.0264	0.0211	0.0135	0.0087	0.0037	0.0011	0.0003
27	0.1252	0.0976	0.0763	0.0597	0.0469	0.0369	0.0291	0.0230	0.0182	0.0115	0.0073	0.0030	0.0008	0.0002
28	0.1159	0.0895	0.0693	0.0538	0.0419	0.0326	0.0255	0.0200	0.0157	0.0097	0.0061	0.0024	0.0006	0.0002
29	0.1073	0.0822	0.0630	0.0485	0.0374	0.0289	0.0224	0.0174	0.0135	0.0082	0.0051	0.0020	0.0005	0.0001
30	0.0994	0.0754	0.0573	0.0437	0.0334	0.0256	0.0196	0.0151	0.0116	0.0070	0.0042	0.0016	0.0004	0.0001
32	0.0852	0.0634	0.0474	0.0355	0.0266	0.0200	0.0151	0.0114	0.0087	0.0050	0.0029	0.0010	0.0002	0.0001
34	0.0730	0.0534	0.0391	0.0288	0.0212	0.0157	0.0116	0.0086	0.0064	0.0036	0.0020	0.0007	0.0001	0.0000
36	0.0626	0.0449	0.0323	0.0234	0.0169	0.0123	0.0089	0.0065	0.0048	0.0026	0.0014	0.0004	0.0001	0.0000
38	0.0537	0.0378	0.0267	0.0190	0.0135	0.0096	0.0069	0.0049	0.0036	0.0019	0.0010	0.0003	0.0000	0.0000
40	0.0460	0.0318	0.0221	0.0154	0.0107	0.0075	0.0053	0.0037	0.0026	0.0013	0.0007	0.0002	0.0000	0.0000
48	0.0249	0.0160	0.0103	0.0067	0.0043	0.0028	0.0019	0.0012	0.0008	0.0004	0.0002	0.0000	0.0000	0.0000
50	0.0213	0.0134	0.0085	0.0054	0.0035	0.0022	0.0014	0.0009	0.0006	0.0003	0.0001	0.0000	0.0000	0.0000
60	0.0099	0.0057	0.0033	0.0019	0.0011	0.0007	0.0004	0.0002	0.0001	0.0000	0.0000	0.0000	0.0000	0.0000
120	0.0001	0.0000	0.0000	0.0000	0.0000	0.0000	0.0000	0.0000	0.0000	0.0000	0.0000	0.0000	0.0000	0.0000
180	0.0000	0.0000	0.0000	0.0000	0.0000	0.0000	0.0000	0.0000	0.0000	0.0000	0.0000	0.0000	0.0000	0.0000
240	0.0000	0.0000	0.0000	0.0000	0.0000	0.0000	0.0000	0.0000	0.0000	0.0000	0.0000	0.0000	0.0000	0.0000
300	0.0000	0.0000	0.0000	0.0000	0.0000	0.0000	0.0000	0.0000	0.0000	0.0000	0.0000	0.0000	0.0000	0.0000
360	0.0000	0.0000	0.0000	0.0000	0.0000	0.0000	0.0000	0.0000	0.0000	0.0000	0.0000	0.0000	0.0000	0.0000

| TABLE A-3 | | | Future Value of an Annuity of $1 | | | $FVFA_{k,n} = \sum_{i=1}^{n} (1+k)^{n-i}$ | | | | | | | |

INTEREST RATES

Payments	0.50%	0.67%	0.75%	1%	1.50%	2%	2.50%	3%	3.50%	4%	4.50%	5%	6%	7%
1	1.0000	1.0000	1.0000	1.0000	1.0000	1.0000	1.0000	1.0000	1.0000	1.0000	1.0000	1.0000	1.0000	1.0000
2	2.0050	2.0067	2.0075	2.0100	2.0150	2.0200	2.0250	2.0300	2.0350	2.0400	2.0450	2.0500	2.0600	2.0700
3	3.0150	3.0200	3.0226	3.0301	3.0452	3.0604	3.0756	3.0909	3.1062	3.1216	3.1370	3.1525	3.1836	3.2149
4	4.0301	4.0402	4.0452	4.0604	4.0909	4.1216	4.1525	4.1836	4.2149	4.2465	4.2782	4.3101	4.3746	4.4399
5	5.0503	5.0671	5.0756	5.1010	5.1523	5.2040	5.2563	5.3091	5.3625	5.4163	5.4707	5.5256	5.6371	5.7507
6	6.0755	6.1009	6.1136	6.1520	6.2296	6.3081	6.3877	6.4684	6.5502	6.6330	6.7169	6.8019	6.9753	7.1533
7	7.1059	7.1416	7.1595	7.2135	7.3230	7.4343	7.5474	7.6625	7.7794	7.8983	8.0192	8.1420	8.3938	8.6540
8	8.1414	8.1892	8.2132	8.2857	8.4328	8.5830	8.7361	8.8923	9.0517	9.2142	9.3800	9.5491	9.8975	10.2598
9	9.1821	9.2438	9.2748	9.3685	9.5593	9.7546	9.9545	10.1591	10.3685	10.5828	10.8021	11.0266	11.4913	11.9780
10	10.2280	10.3054	10.3443	10.4622	10.7027	10.9497	11.2034	11.4639	11.7314	12.0061	12.2882	12.5779	13.1808	13.8164
11	11.2792	11.3741	11.4219	11.5668	11.8633	12.1687	12.4835	12.8078	13.1420	13.4864	13.8412	14.2068	14.9716	15.7836
12	12.3356	12.4499	12.5076	12.6825	13.0412	13.4121	13.7956	14.1920	14.6020	15.0258	15.4640	15.9171	16.8699	17.8885
13	13.3972	13.5329	13.6014	13.8093	14.2368	14.6803	15.1404	15.6178	16.1130	16.6268	17.1599	17.7130	18.8821	20.1406
14	14.4642	14.6231	14.7034	14.9474	15.4504	15.9739	16.5190	17.0863	17.6770	18.2919	18.9321	19.5986	21.0151	22.5505
15	15.5365	15.7206	15.8137	16.0969	16.6821	17.2934	17.9319	18.5989	19.2957	20.0236	20.7841	21.5786	23.2760	25.1290
16	16.6142	16.8254	16.9323	17.2579	17.9324	18.6393	19.3802	20.1569	20.9710	21.8245	22.7193	23.6575	25.6725	27.8881
17	17.6973	17.9376	18.0593	18.4304	19.2014	20.0121	20.8647	21.7616	22.7050	23.6975	24.7417	25.8404	28.2129	30.8402
18	18.7858	19.0572	19.1947	19.6147	20.4894	21.4123	22.3863	23.4144	24.4997	25.6454	26.8551	28.1324	30.9057	33.9990
19	19.8797	20.1842	20.3387	20.8109	21.7967	22.8406	23.9460	25.1169	26.3572	27.6712	29.0636	30.5390	33.7600	37.3790
20	20.9791	21.3188	21.4912	22.0190	23.1237	24.2974	25.5447	26.8704	28.2797	29.7781	31.3714	33.0660	36.7856	40.9955
21	22.0840	22.4609	22.6524	23.2392	24.4705	25.7833	27.1833	28.6765	30.2695	31.9692	33.7831	35.7193	39.9927	44.8652
22	23.1944	23.6107	23.8223	24.4716	25.8376	27.2990	28.8629	30.5368	32.3289	34.2480	36.3034	38.5052	43.3923	49.0057
23	24.3104	24.7681	25.0010	25.7163	27.2251	28.8450	30.5844	32.4529	34.4604	36.6179	38.9370	41.4305	46.9958	53.4361
24	25.4320	25.9332	26.1885	26.9735	28.6335	30.4219	32.3490	34.4265	36.6665	39.0826	41.6892	44.5020	50.8156	58.1767
25	26.5591	27.1061	27.3849	28.2432	30.0630	32.0303	34.1578	36.4593	38.9499	41.6459	44.5652	47.7271	54.8645	63.2490
26	27.6919	28.2868	28.5903	29.5256	31.5140	33.6709	36.0117	38.5530	41.3131	44.3117	47.5706	51.1135	59.1564	68.6765
27	28.8304	29.4754	29.8047	30.8209	32.9867	35.3443	37.9120	40.7096	43.7591	47.0842	50.7113	54.6691	63.7058	74.4838
28	29.9745	30.6719	31.0282	32.1291	34.4815	37.0512	39.8598	42.9309	46.2906	49.9676	53.9933	58.4026	68.5281	80.6977
29	31.1244	31.8763	32.2609	33.4504	35.9987	38.7922	41.8563	45.2189	48.9108	52.9663	57.4230	62.3227	73.6398	87.3465
30	32.2800	33.0889	33.5029	34.7849	37.5387	40.5681	43.9027	47.5754	51.6227	56.0849	61.0071	66.4388	79.0582	94.4608
32	34.6086	35.5382	36.0148	37.4941	40.6883	44.2270	48.1503	52.5028	57.3345	62.7015	68.6662	75.2988	90.8898	110.218
34	36.9606	38.0203	38.5646	40.2577	43.9331	48.0338	52.6129	57.7302	63.4532	69.8579	77.0303	85.0670	104.184	128.259
36	39.3361	40.5356	41.1527	43.0769	47.2760	51.9944	57.3014	63.2759	70.0076	77.5983	86.1640	95.8363	119.121	148.913
38	41.7354	43.0845	43.7798	45.9527	50.7199	56.1149	62.2273	69.1594	77.0289	85.9703	96.1382	107.710	135.904	172.561
40	44.1588	45.6675	46.4465	48.8864	54.2679	60.4020	67.4026	75.4013	84.5503	95.0255	107.030	120.800	154.762	199.635
48	54.0978	56.3499	57.5207	61.2226	69.5652	79.3535	90.8596	104.408	120.388	139.263	161.588	188.025	256.565	353.270
50	56.6452	59.1104	60.3943	64.4632	73.6828	84.5794	97.4843	112.797	130.998	152.667	178.503	209.348	290.336	406.529
60	69.7700	73.4768	75.4241	81.6697	96.2147	114.052	135.992	163.053	196.517	237.991	289.498	353.584	533.128	813.520
120	163.879	182.946	193.514	230.039	331.288	488.258	734.33	1123.70	1744.69	2741.56	4350.40	6958.24	18119.8	47954.1
180	290.819	346.038	378.406	499.580	905.625	1716.04	3366.87	6783.45	13941.4	29078.2	61314.4	*	*	*
240	462.041	589.020	667.887	989.255	2308.85	5744.44	14949.5	40128.4	*	*	*	*	*	*
300	692.994	951.025	1121.12	1878.85	5737.25	18961.7	65910.7	*	*	*	*	*	*	*
360	1004.52	1490.36	1830.74	3494.96	14113.6	62328.1	*	*	*	*	*	*	*	*

Payments	8%	9%	10%	11%	12%	13%	14%	15%	16%	18%	20%	24%	30%	36%
1	1.0000	1.0000	1.0000	1.0000	1.0000	1.0000	1.0000	1.0000	1.0000	1.0000	1.0000	1.0000	1.0000	1.0000
2	2.0800	2.0900	2.1000	2.1100	2.1200	2.1300	2.1400	2.1500	2.1600	2.1800	2.2000	2.2400	2.3000	2.3600
3	3.2464	3.2781	3.3100	3.3421	3.3744	3.4069	3.4396	3.4725	3.5056	3.5724	3.6400	3.7776	3.9900	4.2096
4	4.5061	4.5731	4.6410	4.7097	4.7793	4.8498	4.9211	4.9934	5.0665	5.2154	5.3680	5.6842	6.1870	6.7251
5	5.8666	5.9847	6.1051	6.2278	6.3528	6.4803	6.6101	6.7424	6.8771	7.1542	7.4416	8.0484	9.0431	10.1461
6	7.3359	7.5233	7.7156	7.9129	8.1152	8.3227	8.5355	8.7537	8.9775	9.4420	9.9299	10.9801	12.7560	14.7987
7	8.9228	9.2004	9.4872	9.7833	10.0890	10.4047	10.7305	11.0668	11.4139	12.1415	12.9159	14.6153	17.5828	21.1262
8	10.6366	11.0285	11.4359	11.8594	12.2997	12.7573	13.2328	13.7268	14.2401	15.3270	16.4991	19.1229	23.8577	29.7316
9	12.4876	13.0210	13.5795	14.1640	14.7757	15.4157	16.0853	16.7858	17.5185	19.0859	20.7989	24.7125	32.0150	41.4350
10	14.4866	15.1929	15.9374	16.7220	17.5487	18.4197	19.3373	20.3037	21.3215	23.5213	25.9587	31.6434	42.6195	57.3516
11	16.6455	17.5603	18.5312	19.5614	20.6546	21.8143	23.0445	24.3493	25.7329	28.7551	32.1504	40.2379	56.4053	78.9982
12	18.9771	20.1407	21.3843	22.7132	24.1331	25.6502	27.2707	29.0017	30.8502	34.9311	39.5805	50.8950	74.3270	108.437
13	21.4953	22.9534	24.5227	26.2116	28.0291	29.9847	32.0887	34.3519	36.7862	42.2187	48.4966	64.1097	97.6250	148.475
14	24.2149	26.0192	27.9750	30.0949	32.3926	34.8827	37.5811	40.5047	43.6720	50.8180	59.1959	80.4961	127.913	202.926
15	27.1521	29.3609	31.7725	34.4054	37.2797	40.4175	43.8424	47.5804	51.6595	60.9653	72.0351	100.815	167.286	276.979
16	30.3243	33.0034	35.9497	39.1899	42.7533	46.6717	50.9804	55.7175	60.9250	72.9390	87.4421	126.011	218.472	377.692
17	33.7502	36.9737	40.5447	44.5008	48.8837	53.7391	59.1176	65.0751	71.6730	87.0680	105.931	157.253	285.014	514.661
18	37.4502	41.3013	45.5992	50.3959	55.7497	61.7251	68.3941	75.8364	84.1407	103.740	128.117	195.994	371.518	700.939
19	41.4463	46.0185	51.1591	56.9395	63.4397	70.7494	78.9692	88.2118	98.6032	123.414	154.740	244.033	483.973	954.277
20	45.7620	51.1601	57.2750	64.2028	72.0524	80.9468	91.0249	102.4436	115.380	146.628	186.688	303.601	630.165	1298.82
21	50.4229	56.7645	64.0025	72.2651	81.6987	92.4699	104.7684	118.8101	134.841	174.021	225.026	377.465	820.215	1767.39
22	55.4568	62.8733	71.4027	81.2143	92.5026	105.4910	120.4360	137.6316	157.415	206.345	271.031	469.056	1067.28	2404.65
23	60.8933	69.5319	79.5430	91.1479	104.6029	120.2048	138.2970	159.2764	183.601	244.487	326.237	582.630	1388.46	3271.33
24	66.7648	76.7898	88.4973	102.1742	118.1552	136.8315	158.6586	184.1678	213.978	289.494	392.484	723.461	1806.00	4450.00
25	73.1059	84.7009	98.3471	114.4133	133.3339	155.6196	181.8708	212.7930	249.214	342.603	471.981	898.092	2348.80	6053.00
26	79.9544	93.3240	109.1818	127.9988	150.3339	176.8501	208.3327	245.7120	290.088	405.272	567.377	1114.63	3054.44	8233.09
27	87.3508	102.7231	121.0999	143.0786	169.3740	200.8406	238.4993	283.5688	337.502	479.221	681.853	1383.15	3971.78	11198.0
28	95.3388	112.9682	134.2099	159.8173	190.6989	227.9499	272.8892	327.1041	392.503	566.481	819.223	1716.10	5164.31	15230.3
29	103.966	124.1354	148.6309	178.3972	214.5828	258.5834	312.0937	377.1697	456.303	669.447	984.068	2128.96	6714.60	20714.2
30	113.283	136.3075	164.4940	199.0209	241.3327	293.1992	356.7868	434.7451	530.312	790.948	1181.88	2640.92	8729.99	28172.3
32	134.214	164.037	201.138	247.324	304.848	376.516	465.820	577.100	715.747	1103.50	1704.11	4062.91	14756.0	52109.8
34	158.627	196.982	245.477	306.837	384.521	482.903	607.520	765.365	965.270	1538.69	2456.12	6249.38	24939.9	96384.6
36	187.102	236.125	299.127	380.164	484.463	618.749	791.673	1014.35	1301.03	2144.65	3539.01	9611.28	42150.7	*
38	220.316	282.630	364.043	470.511	609.831	792.211	1031.00	1343.62	1752.82	2988.39	5098.37	14780.5	71237.0	*
40	259.057	337.882	442.593	581.826	767.091	1013.70	1342.03	1779.09	2360.76	4163.21	7343.86	22728.8	*	*
48	490.132	684.280	960.172	1352.70	1911.59	2707.63	3841.48	5456.00	7753.78	15664.3	31593.7	*	*	*
50	573.770	815.084	1163.909	1668.77	2400.02	3459.51	4994.52	7217.72	10435.6	21813.1	45497.2	*	*	*
60	1253.21	1944.79	3034.82	4755.07	7471.64	11761.9	18535.1	29220.0	46057.5	*	*	*	*	*
120	*	*	*	*	*	*	*	*	*	*	*	*	*	*
180	*	*	*	*	*	*	*	*	*	*	*	*	*	*
240	*	*	*	*	*	*	*	*	*	*	*	*	*	*
300	*	*	*	*	*	*	*	*	*	*	*	*	*	*
360	*	*	*	*	*	*	*	*	*	*	*	*	*	*

TABLE A-4	Present Value of an Annuity of $1	$PVFA_{k,n} = \sum_{i=1}^{n} (1+k)^{-i}$

INTEREST RATES

Payments	0.5%	0.67%	0.75%	1%	1.5%	2.0%	2.5%	3.0%	3.5%	4%	4.5%	5%	6%	7%
1	0.9950	0.9934	0.9926	0.9901	0.9852	0.9804	0.9756	0.9709	0.9662	0.9615	0.9569	0.9524	0.9434	0.9346
2	1.9851	1.9802	1.9777	1.9704	1.9559	1.9416	1.9274	1.9135	1.8997	1.8861	1.8727	1.8594	1.8334	1.8080
3	2.9702	2.9604	2.9556	2.9410	2.9122	2.8839	2.8560	2.8286	2.8016	2.7751	2.7490	2.7232	2.6730	2.6243
4	3.9505	3.9342	3.9261	3.9020	3.8544	3.8077	3.7620	3.7171	3.6731	3.6299	3.5875	3.5460	3.4651	3.3872
5	4.9259	4.9015	4.8894	4.8534	4.7826	4.7135	4.6458	4.5797	4.5151	4.4518	4.3900	4.3295	4.2124	4.1002
6	5.8964	5.8625	5.8456	5.7955	5.6972	5.6014	5.5081	5.4172	5.3286	5.2421	5.1579	5.0757	4.9173	4.7665
7	6.8621	6.8170	6.7946	6.7282	6.5982	6.4720	6.3494	6.2303	6.1145	6.0021	5.8927	5.7864	5.5824	5.3893
8	7.8230	7.7652	7.7366	7.6517	7.4859	7.3255	7.1701	7.0197	6.8740	6.7327	6.5959	6.4632	6.2098	5.9713
9	8.7791	8.7072	8.6716	8.5660	8.3605	8.1622	7.9709	7.7861	7.6077	7.4353	7.2688	7.1078	6.8017	6.5152
10	9.7304	9.6429	9.5996	9.4713	9.2222	8.9826	8.7521	8.5302	8.3166	8.1109	7.9127	7.7217	7.3601	7.0236
11	10.6770	10.5724	10.5207	10.3676	10.0711	9.7868	9.5142	9.2526	9.0016	8.7605	8.5289	8.3064	7.8869	7.4987
12	11.6189	11.4958	11.4349	11.2551	10.9075	10.5753	10.2578	9.9540	9.6633	9.3851	9.1186	8.8633	8.3838	7.9427
13	12.5562	12.4130	12.3423	12.1337	11.7315	11.3484	10.9832	10.6350	10.3027	9.9856	9.6829	9.3936	8.8527	8.3577
14	13.4887	13.3242	13.2430	13.0037	12.5434	12.1062	11.6909	11.2961	10.9205	10.5631	10.2228	9.8986	9.2950	8.7455
15	14.4166	14.2293	14.1370	13.8651	13.3432	12.8493	12.3814	11.9379	11.5174	11.1184	10.7395	10.3797	9.7122	9.1079
16	15.3399	15.1285	15.0243	14.7179	14.1313	13.5777	13.0550	12.5611	12.0941	11.6523	11.2340	10.8378	10.1059	9.4466
17	16.2586	16.0217	15.9050	15.5623	14.9076	14.2919	13.7122	13.1661	12.6513	12.1657	11.7072	11.2741	10.4773	9.7632
18	17.1728	16.9089	16.7792	16.3983	15.6726	14.9920	14.3534	13.7535	13.1897	12.6593	12.1600	11.6896	10.8276	10.0591
19	18.0824	17.7903	17.6468	17.2260	16.4262	15.6785	14.9789	14.3238	13.7098	13.1339	12.5933	12.0853	11.1581	10.3356
20	18.9874	18.6659	18.5080	18.0456	17.1686	16.3514	15.5892	14.8775	14.2124	13.5903	13.0079	12.4622	11.4699	10.5940
21	19.8880	19.5357	19.3628	18.8570	17.9001	17.0112	16.1845	15.4150	14.6980	14.0292	13.4047	12.8212	11.7641	10.8355
22	20.7841	20.3997	20.2112	19.6604	18.6208	17.6580	16.7654	15.9369	15.1671	14.4511	13.7844	13.1630	12.0416	11.0612
23	21.6757	21.2579	21.0533	20.4558	19.3309	18.2922	17.3321	16.4436	15.6204	14.8568	14.1478	13.4886	12.3034	11.2722
24	22.5629	22.1105	21.8891	21.2434	20.0304	18.9139	17.8850	16.9355	16.0584	15.2470	14.4955	13.7986	12.5504	11.4693
25	23.4456	22.9575	22.7188	22.0232	20.7196	19.5235	18.4244	17.4131	16.4815	15.6221	14.8282	14.0939	12.7834	11.6536
26	24.3240	23.7988	23.5422	22.7952	21.3986	20.1210	18.9506	17.8768	16.8904	15.9828	15.1466	14.3752	13.0032	11.8258
27	25.1980	24.6346	24.3595	23.5596	22.0676	20.7069	19.4640	18.3270	17.2854	16.3296	15.4513	14.6430	13.2105	11.9867
28	26.0677	25.4648	25.1707	24.3164	22.7267	21.2813	19.9649	18.7641	17.6670	16.6631	15.7429	14.8981	13.4062	12.1371
29	26.9330	26.2896	25.9759	25.0658	23.3761	21.8444	20.4535	19.1885	18.0358	16.9837	16.0219	15.1411	13.5907	12.2777
30	27.7941	27.1088	26.7751	25.8077	24.0158	22.3965	20.9303	19.6004	18.3920	17.2920	16.2889	15.3725	13.7648	12.4090
32	29.5033	28.7312	28.3557	27.2696	25.2671	23.4683	21.8492	20.3888	19.0689	17.8736	16.7889	15.8027	14.0840	12.6466
34	31.1955	30.3320	29.9128	28.7027	26.4817	24.4986	22.7238	21.1318	19.7007	18.4112	17.2468	16.1929	14.3681	12.8540
36	32.8710	31.9118	31.4468	30.1075	27.6607	25.4888	23.5563	21.8323	20.2905	18.9083	17.6660	16.5469	14.6210	13.0352
38	34.5299	33.4707	32.9581	31.4847	28.8051	26.4406	24.3486	22.4925	20.8411	19.3679	18.0500	16.8679	14.8460	13.1935
40	36.1722	35.0090	34.4469	32.8347	29.9158	27.3555	25.1028	23.1148	21.3551	19.7928	18.4016	17.1591	15.0463	13.3317
48	42.5803	40.9619	40.1848	37.9740	34.0426	30.6731	27.7732	25.2667	23.0912	21.1951	19.5356	18.0772	15.6500	13.7305
50	44.1428	42.4013	41.5664	39.1961	34.9997	31.4236	28.3623	25.7298	23.4556	21.4822	19.7620	18.2559	15.7619	13.8007
60	51.7256	49.3184	48.1734	44.9550	39.3803	34.7609	30.9087	27.6756	24.9447	22.6235	20.6380	18.9293	16.1614	14.0392
120	90.0734	82.4214	78.9416	69.7005	55.4985	45.3554	37.9337	32.3730	28.1111	24.7741	22.1093	19.9427	16.6514	14.2815
150	105.3499	94.6346	89.8642	77.5201	59.5217	47.4358	39.0149	32.9377	28.4074	24.9303	22.1921	19.9867	16.6640	14.2852
180	118.5035	104.6405	98.5934	83.3217	62.0956	48.5844	39.5304	33.1703	28.5130	24.9785	22.2142	19.9969	16.6662	14.2856
240	139.5807	119.5542	111.1449	90.8194	64.7957	49.5686	39.8933	33.3057	28.5640	24.9980	22.2216	19.9998	16.6667	14.2857
300	155.2068	129.5645	119.1616	94.9466	65.9009	49.8685	39.9757	33.3286	28.5705	24.9998	22.2222	20.0000	16.6667	14.2857
360	166.7916	136.2834	124.2818	97.21833	66.3532	49.9599	39.9944	33.3325	28.5713	25.0000	22.2222	20.0000	16.6666	14.2857

Payments	8%	9%	10%	11%	12%	13%	14%	15%	16%	18%	20%	24%	30%	36%
1	0.9259	0.9174	0.9091	0.9009	0.8929	0.8850	0.8772	0.8696	0.8621	0.8475	0.8333	0.8065	0.7692	0.7353
2	1.7833	1.7591	1.7355	1.7125	1.6901	1.6681	1.6467	1.6257	1.6052	1.5656	1.5278	1.4568	1.3609	1.2760
3	2.5771	2.5313	2.4869	2.4437	2.4018	2.3612	2.3216	2.2832	2.2459	2.1743	2.1065	1.9813	1.8161	1.6735
4	3.3121	3.2397	3.1699	3.1024	3.0373	2.9745	2.9137	2.8550	2.7982	2.6901	2.5887	2.4043	2.1662	1.9658
5	3.9927	3.8897	3.7908	3.6959	3.6048	3.5172	3.4331	3.3522	3.2743	3.1272	2.9906	2.7454	2.4356	2.1807
6	4.6229	4.4859	4.3553	4.2305	4.1114	3.9975	3.8887	3.7845	3.6847	3.4976	3.3255	3.0205	2.6427	2.3388
7	5.2064	5.0330	4.8684	4.7122	4.5638	4.4226	4.2883	4.1604	4.0386	3.8115	3.6046	3.2423	2.8021	2.4550
8	5.7466	5.5348	5.3349	5.1461	4.9676	4.7988	4.6389	4.4873	4.3436	4.0776	3.8372	3.4212	2.9247	2.5404
9	6.2469	5.9952	5.7590	5.5370	5.3282	5.1317	4.9464	4.7716	4.6065	4.3030	4.0310	3.5655	3.0190	2.6033
10	6.7101	6.4177	6.1446	5.8892	5.6502	5.4262	5.2161	5.0188	4.8332	4.4941	4.1925	3.6819	3.0915	2.6495
11	7.1390	6.8052	6.4951	6.2065	5.9377	5.6869	5.4527	5.2337	5.0286	4.6560	4.3271	3.7757	3.1473	2.6834
12	7.5361	7.1607	6.8137	6.4924	6.1944	5.9176	5.6603	5.4206	5.1971	4.7932	4.4392	3.8514	3.1903	2.7084
13	7.9038	7.4869	7.1034	6.7499	6.4235	6.1218	5.8424	5.5831	5.3423	4.9095	4.5327	3.9124	3.2233	2.7268
14	8.2442	7.7862	7.3667	6.9819	6.6282	6.3025	6.0021	5.7245	5.4675	5.0081	4.6106	3.9616	3.2487	2.7403
15	8.5595	8.0607	7.6061	7.1909	6.8109	6.4624	6.1422	5.8474	5.5755	5.0916	4.6755	4.0013	3.2682	2.7502
16	8.8514	8.3126	7.8237	7.3792	6.9740	6.6039	6.2651	5.9542	5.6685	5.1624	4.7296	4.0333	3.2832	2.7575
17	9.1216	8.5436	8.0216	7.5488	7.1196	6.7291	6.3729	6.0472	5.7487	5.2223	4.7746	4.0591	3.2948	2.7629
18	9.3719	8.7556	8.2014	7.7016	7.2497	6.8399	6.4674	6.1280	5.8178	5.2732	4.8122	4.0799	3.3037	2.7668
19	9.6036	8.9501	8.3649	7.8393	7.3658	6.9380	6.5504	6.1982	5.8775	5.3162	4.8435	4.0967	3.3105	2.7697
20	9.8181	9.1285	8.5136	7.9633	7.4694	7.0248	6.6231	6.2593	5.9288	5.3527	4.8696	4.1103	3.3158	2.7718
21	10.0168	9.2922	8.6487	8.0751	7.5620	7.1016	6.6870	6.3125	5.9731	5.3837	4.8913	4.1212	3.3198	2.7734
22	10.2007	9.4424	8.7715	8.1757	7.6446	7.1695	6.7429	6.3587	6.0113	5.4099	4.9094	4.1300	3.3230	2.7746
23	10.3711	9.5802	8.8832	8.2664	7.7184	7.2297	6.7921	6.3988	6.0442	5.4321	4.9245	4.1371	3.3254	2.7754
24	10.5288	9.7066	8.9847	8.3481	7.7843	7.2829	6.8351	6.4338	6.0726	5.4509	4.9371	4.1428	3.3272	2.7760
25	10.6748	9.8226	9.0770	8.4217	7.8431	7.3300	6.8729	6.4641	6.0971	5.4669	4.9476	4.1474	3.3286	2.7765
26	10.8100	9.9290	9.1609	8.4881	7.8957	7.3717	6.9061	6.4906	6.1182	5.4804	4.9563	4.1511	3.3297	2.7768
27	10.9352	10.0266	9.2372	8.5478	7.9426	7.4086	6.9352	6.5135	6.1364	5.4919	4.9636	4.1542	3.3305	2.7771
28	11.0511	10.1161	9.3066	8.6016	7.9844	7.4412	6.9607	6.5335	6.1520	5.5016	4.9697	4.1566	3.3312	2.7773
29	11.1584	10.1983	9.3696	8.6501	8.0218	7.4701	6.9830	6.5509	6.1656	5.5098	4.9747	4.1585	3.3317	2.7774
30	11.2578	10.2737	9.4269	8.6938	8.0552	7.4957	7.0027	6.5660	6.1772	5.5168	4.9789	4.1601	3.3321	2.7775
32	11.4350	10.4062	9.5264	8.7686	8.1116	7.5383	7.0350	6.5905	6.1959	5.5277	4.9854	4.1624	3.3326	2.7776
34	11.5869	10.5178	9.6086	8.8293	8.1566	7.5717	7.0599	6.6091	6.2098	5.5356	4.9898	4.1639	3.3329	2.7777
36	11.7172	10.6118	9.6765	8.8786	8.1924	7.5979	7.0790	6.6231	6.2201	5.5412	4.9929	4.1649	3.3331	2.7777
38	11.8289	10.6908	9.7327	8.9186	8.2210	7.6183	7.0937	6.6338	6.2278	5.5452	4.9951	4.1655	3.3332	2.7778
40	11.9246	10.7574	9.7791	8.9511	8.2438	7.6344	7.1050	6.6418	6.2335	5.5482	4.9966	4.1659	3.3332	2.7778
48	12.1891	10.9336	9.8969	9.0302	8.2972	7.6705	7.1296	6.6585	6.2450	5.5536	4.9992	4.1665	3.3333	2.7778
50	12.2335	10.9617	9.9148	9.0417	8.3045	7.6752	7.1327	6.6605	6.2463	5.5541	4.9995	4.1666	3.3333	2.7778
60	12.3766	11.0480	9.9672	9.0736	8.3240	7.6873	7.1401	6.6651	6.2492	5.5553	4.9999	4.1667	3.3333	2.7778
120	12.4988	11.1108	9.9999	9.0909	8.3333	7.6923	7.1429	6.6667	6.2500	5.5556	5.0000	4.1667	3.3333	2.7778
150	12.4999	11.1111	10.0000	9.0909	8.3333	7.6923	7.1429	6.6667	6.2500	5.5556	5.0000	4.1667	3.3333	2.7778
180	12.5000	11.1111	10.0000	9.0909	8.3333	7.6923	7.1429	6.6667	6.2500	5.5556	5.0000	4.1667	3.3333	2.7778
240	12.5000	11.1111	10.0000	9.0909	8.3333	7.6923	7.1429	6.6667	6.2500	5.5556	5.0000	4.1667	3.3333	2.7778
300	12.5000	11.1111	10.0000	9.0909	8.3333	7.6923	7.1429	6.6667	6.2500	5.5556	5.0000	4.1667	3.3333	2.7778
360	12.5000	11.1111	10.0000	9.0909	8.3333	7.6923	7.1428	6.6666	6.2500	5.5555	5.0000	4.1666	3.3333	2.7778

Appendix B

Answers to Selected Problems

CHAPTER 1

1. a. $50,000 outflow
   b. i. $5,000
      ii. $2,000
      iii. $30,000

CHAPTER 2

2. $19,000
4. a. $11,400
   b. $(17,500)
6. Net income $2,951,600
8. $35,753,425
10. Increase of $110,000
12. Borrow. Tax savings $11,000
14. Total shareholders' equity $9,425,000
16. a. Total cash from operating activities ($2,572)
18. a. Total assets $6,200
    b. Net income $200
    c. Ending cash $1,200
20. Total cash from financing activities $6,385,000
22. b. Ending cash balance $1,071
24. a. $54,000
    b. 31%
26. a. $8,930
    b. $89,280
    c. $124,300
    d. $615,060
    e. $109,080
28. a. $1,874,300, $424,748, 22.7%
    b. $1,874,300, $674,748, 36%
    c. $1,874,300, $638,748, 34.1%

CHAPTER 3

2. a. Net income $765 12.8%, $9,170 14.3%
4. a. $4,315,068
   b. $616,439
6. $875,000
8. 80%
10. Accts receivable = $197,260; Inventory = $125,000; Current assets = $572,260; Current liabilities = $248,809; LT debt = $462,321; Shareholders' equity = $711,130; ROA = 11.2%; ROE = 22.5%
12. NI = $840,000; Total assets = $4,600,000; Book value/ share = $7.59; Market to book value = 2.42

14. a.

	Thomas	Jerold
Current ratio	2.1	4.2
Quick ratio	0.8	3.5
Inventory turnover	2.9	14.2
Average collection period	22 days	36 days

Jerold

b.

	Thomas	Jerold
Debt Ratio	47.7%	41.7%
Times Interest Earned	3.1	2.4

Both

c.

	Thomas	Jerold
Return on sales	3.9%	2.1%
Return on assets	5.5%	3.4%
Return on equity	10.5%	5.8%

Thomas

16. a. Ending cash $2,875
    b. Gross profit margin = 45%
       Return on sales = 8.6%
       Return on assets = 13.7%
       Return on equity = 21.3%
       Price earnings ratio (P/E) = 11.7
       Market to book value = 2.5
       Current ratio = 5.5
       Quick ratio = 4.0
       Average collection period (ACP) = 56 days (rounded)
       Inventory turnover
       COGS/inventory = 6.2×
       Sales/inventory = 11.3×
       Capital asset turnover 3.3×
       Total asset turnover 1.6×
       Debt ratio 35.7%
       Debt to equity ratio 0.41:1
       Times interest earned (TIE) 7.6×
       Cash coverage 9.3
       Fixed charge coverage 1.6×

CHAPTER 4

2. 115 days; 85 days
4. No; cost exceeds the savings by $1,541
6. $2.45
8. a. Yes; Increase in EBT $2,901,370
10. a. Yes. EBT is $2,048,000 higher
    b. No.
12. a.

Credit score	20X3	20X2	20X1
	26.4	27.8	55.0

14. a. 40
    b. 50
    c. $2000; $2000
    d. $25,160
    e. No. Net loss $11,160
16. b. 280 units
18. a. 160 units
    b. $250
    c. 120 units
    d. $240
    e. 44%, 20%
20. a. Breakeven number of failures = $27,500 / $9,000 = 3.1

CHAPTER 5

2. a. 37.2%
   b. 36.9%
   c. 9.2%
   d. 62.4%
   e. 24.6%
4. (1) a. 24.8%
       b. 32.2%
       c. 7.4%
       d. 8.8%
6. $50,523.25
8. $586,500
10. 10%
12. The bank company loan is cheaper by $1,016
14. 32.5%
16. $558,000; 31%
18. a. 16.0%
    b. 15.3%; (b)
20. a. 9.3%
    b. 24.8%
    c. 24.3%
    d. 18.1%; (a)

CHAPTER 6

2. a.

YEAR	1	2	3	4	5
a. COGS	$33,925	$38,280	$43,320	$49,000	$55,000
b. A/R	$11,027	$10,849	$10,411	$10,788	$10,959
c. Inventory	$8,481	$7,656	$7,220	$7,538	$7,857

4. a. $7,200,000
   b. $48,442
   c. $17.4M
6. 13%
8. $437,667
10. a. 4.8% b. 37.5%
12. Interest $8,476; NI $27,483
    Debt $63,087; Total assets $339,482
14. Revenue $83,417; EBIT $12,215; Interest $2,715
    Long term debt $22,625; Total assets $73,535
    CF from Op activity $7,611; Net CF ($894)
16.

	Dec	Jan	Feb	Mar
Cuml cash flow (loan)	−528	−140	−182	−293

   b. Ending AR = 640; INV = 275; AP = 275

CHAPTER 7

2. 1-year 3.0%; 5-year 3.50%; 10-year 3.35%
4. 13.5%
6. 3%
8. 2%
10. 3%, 3%
12. a.

Term	k
1	6.1%
5	9.8%
10	12.8%
20	13.5%

CHAPTER 8

2. a. $8,273.07
   b. $8,081.35
   c. $6,686.76
   d. $14,851.74
4. a. 4 years
   b. 4 years
   c. 3 years
   d. 12.68%; 10.38%

6. a. 15%
   b. 7.9 years
   c. 6.6 years
8. a. $159.67
   b. $4,740.83
10. a. 5%
    b. 7.4%
12. a. $7,994.80
    b. $6,913.81
    c. $6,433.35
14. 12%
16. $27,597.28
18. 18%; 19.56%
20. $6,783.89
22. Payment $1,547.85; Ending bal $149,483.36
24. a. 13.5 years; $1,353.96
26. a. $1,058.79
    b. $879.08
    c. $203,164.40
    d. $159,347.46
    e. $112,065.75
28. $20,132.41
30. $23,862.01
32. a. $18,179.69
    b. $2,118.11
34. $301.40
36. a. $13,484.19
    b. 21.23%
38. $513.35

CHAPTER 9

2. a. 12%
   b. 6%
   c. 8%
4. a. 10.4%
   b. 8.6%
   c. 6.5%
   d. 9.2%
   e. 5.8%
6. a. $849.54
   b. $1,197.93
   d. $1,000
8. 27
10. a. Old $824.41; new $654.98
12. a. $1,000
    c. Old $852.48; new $515.16
14. $28,424,000
16. With call $1,347.52; without call $1,718.41
18. $106.78
20. Market rate 10%: $1,019; $1,077; $1,124; $1,183

APPENDIX 9A

2. PVA = $46,676, must be capitalized
4. a. $17,824
   b. 12.384%
6. Purchase ($304.67)M; lease with purchase ($338.32)M

CHAPTER 10

2. $63.64
4. $25; $50; $100
6. $53.00
8. a. $405.00
10. a. $124.33, $93.25, $74.60
    d. (1) $92.95; $73.80; $61.50; (2) $73.20; $61.00; $52.29
12. $69.92
14. $60.06
16. 47.4%
18. $87.58
20. $10.09; avoid the investment
22. 6 years: $70; $77; $85; $93

CHAPTER 11

2. No. $k = 20\%$
4. b. 5; 1.58; 0.316
6. 10%; 2.12%; 0.21
8. 36.98%
10. 9.4%
12. 0.956; 1.026
14. 1.1
16. a. 7.84%; 10.44%
18. a. 11.2%
    b. lower
20. 10.6%; $26.47
22. a. $34.46
24. a. 8.2%
    b. 7.0%
    c. $39.62
26. $17.42 to $38.93
28. Current $19.96, new $18.52
30. a. Beta 2, k 13%: $36; $51; $86; $263
    b. Beta 2, k 17%: $23; $28; $37; $53

CHAPTER 12

2. a. 2 years
   b. $52
   c. 1.07

4. a. Yes; payback approximately 2.5 years
   b. Yes; NPV = $628
   c. Yes; PI = 1.08
6. a. 2.6 years; yes
   b. $3,803; yes
   c. 16% (approx); yes
   d. 1.15; yes
8. a. 3.6 years
   b. 12%; acceptable
   c. $3,871; acceptable
10. a. H: 5.4 years; L: 5.0 years; low
    b. H: 7%; L: 9%; low
    d. H: NPV = $34,038; PI = 1.04
       L: NPV = $84,690; PI = 1.11
       Low is selected by NPV and PI
12. a. 7%
    b. 4%

14.   NPV   IRR
   a. $(196.40)   10%
   b. $(377.30)   8%
   c. $(15.10)   12%
16. a. A: 1.7 years   B: 3.5 years;   A
    b. A: $10,407   B: $12,385;   B
    c. A: 35%   B: 25%;   A
    d. A: $4,333   B: $2,324;   A
18. a. $73,125
    b. $72,039.42
20. 22.11%; 21.19%; 4.01%; 9.93%; 12.78%
22. a. A = 15.24%; B = 10.86%
24. 6.44 yrs; 10.75%; $57,954, 1.15
26. D, C, and B

CHAPTER 13

2. $(90,000) $37,000 $37,000 $28,000 $42,000
4. $138,000
6. ($50,000) $11,300 $11,300 $11,300 $29,300
8. CF_0 (10,000)
   CF_1 900
   CF_2 1,395
   CF_3 767
   CF_4 422
   CF_5 1,232
10. a. **Year   NCF**
       0   ($500,000)
       1   100,000
       2–5   139,000
       6–8   104,000
    b. 3.9 years, $108,000, 1.22
    c. Accept
    d. Revised NPV = $11

12. Year   Cash Flow
    0       $(200,000)
    1–4 $48,400
    5       $148,400
14. $6,033,900
16. a.

C_0	C_1-C_5	C_6
$(150,000)	$38,450	$27,950

    b. 3.9 years, $11,534, accept
18. a. NCF ($270) $12 $45 $61 $86 $106 $115
    b. 4.6 years
    c. −$7; no
    e. $91
    f. $478
20. a. CF_0 ($1,410,000)
       CF_1 330,000
       CF_2 330,000
       CF_3 330,000
       CF_4 330,000
       CF_5 565,000
    b. $426,022
    c. Accept
22. NPV = ($41,516); no
24. b. NCF: (2,288,000)
            (73,000)
            363,000
            632,000
            972,000
            1,057,000
            2,758,000
    c. 4.4 years, $1,309,000, 1.57, accept
    d. (3) 14%

CHAPTER 14

2. ($35,980)
4. $122,434.60
6. Best: $360,995; .01080
   Worst: $94,517; .00788
   Most likely: $211,995
8. ($000)
   a.

Path	NPV	Prob.
1	$2,895.3	0.18
2	$1,356.3	0.42
3	$(1,937.1)	0.32
4	$(2,398.8)	0.08

   b. $279.0

10. ($000)
    a.

Path	NPV	Prob.
1	−61.19	0.24
2	−185.15	0.36
3	657.79	0.16
4	409.87	0.24
		1.00

Expected NPV 122.58

12. b. $(M)

Path	NPV	Prob.
1	$21.0	0.42
2	$7.5	0.18
3	$(0.6)	0.28
4	$(6.0)	0.12
		1.00

   c. $9.28
14. a. Expected NPV: $15.49 M
    b. ($0.29); no
16. NPV = 149,644 at 9.3%; NPV = (67,308) at 20.52%; no

CHAPTER 15

2. 16.8%
4. Debt: $76,620,050 | 35.2
   Preferred shares: 16,875,000 | 7.8
   Common equity: 124,000,000 | 57.0
   $217,495,050 | 100.0
6. a. WACC – Market: 17.9%; WACC – Book: 15.3%
8. Debt $3,279,494 | 38.3%
   Preferred shares 1,200,000 | 14.0%
   Common equity 4,079,775 | 47.7%
   $8,559,269 | 100.0%
10. a. 4.34%
    b. $898.55
12. 4.55%
14. a. 22%
    b. 24.18%
16. 12.39%
18. 12.8%
20. CAPM: 9.8%
    Gordon Model: 10.3%
22. 7.7%, 7.9%, $284,091

24. a.

	Book		Market	
	Value	Weights	Value	Weights
Debt	$10,000,000	24.7%	$13,074,800	31.4%
Preferred	$1,500,000	3.7%	$2,000,000	4.8%
Common equity	$29,000,000	71.6%	$26,500,000	63.8%
	$40,500,000	100.0%	$41,574,800	100.0%

   b. 6%
   c. 10.2%
   d. CAPM = 13.5%, dividend growth = 14%, reconciliation: 14%
   e. 15.1%
   f. 11.4%
   g. $4,200,000
   h. 12.1%
   i. $6,700,000
   j. 12.9%
   l. Accept A, B, and C. Reject D, E. D
   m. 12.9%
   n. No
26. a. 2,010,000
    b.

	Year 1	Year 2	Year 3	Year 4	Year 5
Cash flows	180,000	270,000	360,000	370,800	381,924

	Year 6	Year 7	Year 8	Year 9	Year 10
Cash flows	393,382	405,183	417,338	429,859	442,754

   c. 90,000
   d. 120,000
   e.

	Year 1	Year 2	Year 3	Year 4	Year 5
Ending	$450,000	$450,000	$450,000	$463,500	$477,405
Change	–	–	–	13,500	13,905

	Year 6	Year 7	Year 8	Year 9	Year 10
Ending	$491,727	$506,479	$521,673	$537,324	$553,443
Change	14,322	14,752	15,194	15,650	16,119
Recovery					(553,443)

   f. 8%
   g. 415,290
   h. 412,698, 827,988
   i. (1) NPV = 946,641, yes; (2) NPV = 170,143, yes

CHAPTER 16

2. a. 11.0%; $0.55
   b. 12.0%; $0.60
   c. 16.2%; $0.81
4. At EBIT = $15,000, ROCE and after tax cost of debt are both 9%
6. $31.52M debt
8. a. EPS under each option

options	1	2	3
EBIT $4,000	$1.27	$1.80	$4.60
$2,000	$0.60	$0.60	$0.60
$1,000	$0.27	$0.00	($1.40)

10. a. $1 per unit or $20,000 b. 6.0; 4.3; 3.5
12. a. $35.20; 64%; $402,000; 4.4; $4.02
14.

	Without	**With**
Units	80,000	81,137
$	$4,000,000	$4,462,535

16.

	Current	**With**
a.	$11,251	$11,701
b.	1.20	1.75
c.	2.67	2.86
d.	3.2	5.0

18. a. $62.50M
    b. $1.2M; $16M; $124.75M

CHAPTER 17

2. a. $3.71
   b. $51.94
   c. $0.56
   d. 11 shares
4. Year 1 = 241 shares
   Year 2 = 233 shares
6. $1.05 million
8. 30%
10. a. $2.50

12. a. Common shares (3,150,000 shares) $26,250,000
       Retained earnings   17,750,000
                                           $44,000,000

    b. Common shares (3,300,000 shares)   30,000,000
       Retained earnings   14,000,000
                                           $44,000,000

    c. Common shares (3,450,000 shares) $34,350,000
       Retained earnings   9,650,000
                                           $44,000,000

14. a. $0.80
    b. 9.8 million; $2.04
    c. $40.80, $.80
16. $1.25

CHAPTER 18

2. a. $32.50
   b. $33.25
   c. $36
   d. $30.25
   e. $31.50
   f. $31.75
   g. $34
   h. $29.25
4. a. $410
   b. $210
   c. $10
   d. $10
   e. $10
   f. $(190)
6. a. $2
   b. $2
   c. in
   d. 33,000
   e. $4,000
   f. make $4,000
   g. $4,000
   h. $3,000
   i. $4,000
   j. $(4,000)
8. a. $75
   b. $25
10. $0
12. a. 41%
    b. 66.7%
    c. $171.59
    d. Basic: $1.50 Diluted: $1.49

14. a i. $15; 37.50%
    ii. $28; 1,400%
   c. i. −$1; −2.50%
      ii. Lose his investment of $2; −100%

APPENDIX 18A–USING TABLE

2. $6.19
4. $5.30
6. $4.85

CHAPTER 19

2. $14,954,000
4. a. $2,634,854; $13.17
   b. $3,500,000; $17.50
   c. $4,375,000; $21.88
6. a. $60.57;
   b. $16.84
   c. $28.99
8. a. 13%
   b. $2,400,000
   c. $8,441,000; $13,023,000; $15,510,000

d. $33.76; $52.09; $62.04
e. $73.85
10. a. $45,708,000
12. Debt: $215M; equity: $25M
14. $0.31

CHAPTER 20

2. $7,052
4. a. 0.67 euros
   b. 0.91 U.S. dollars
   c. 0.47 British pounds
   g. 100.00 Japanese yen
6. a. $15,625
   b. $26,041
8. a. $971,429
10. a. Discount
    b. $0.0023
    c. $0.0070
    d. $106,085
    e. £236,967
12. £82,390, 0.6790£ / €; £130,368
14. $485,300

Appendix C
Summary of Key Formulas

Chapter 2

The balance sheet equation: Assets = Liabilities + Shareholder's equity

Net working capital = Current assets − Current liabilities

Beginning common shares + New shares = Ending common shares

(2.1) Total income − Tax deductions = Taxable income

Taxable income × Tax rates = Total tax

Total tax − Tax credits = Net tax payable

(2.2) $\text{Average tax rate} = \dfrac{\text{Tax liability}}{\text{Taxable income}}$

Chapter 3

$\text{Growth in sales} = \dfrac{\text{Current year sales} - \text{Prior year sales}}{\text{Prior year sales}}$

$\text{Growth in net income} = \dfrac{\text{Current year net income} - \text{Prior year net income}}{\text{Prior year net income}}$

$\text{GPM} = \dfrac{\text{Gross margin}}{\text{Sales}}$

$\text{OM} = \dfrac{\text{EBIT}}{\text{Sales}}$

$\text{ROS} = \dfrac{\text{Net income}}{\text{Sales}}$

$\text{ROA} = \dfrac{\text{Net income}}{\text{Total assets}}$

$\text{ROE} = \dfrac{\text{Net income}}{\text{Shareholders' equity}}$

$\text{P/E ratio} = \dfrac{\text{Share price}}{\text{EPS}}$

$\text{Market to book value ratio} = \dfrac{\text{Share price}}{\text{Book value per share}}$

$\text{Current ratio} = \dfrac{\text{Current assets}}{\text{Current liabilities}}$

$\text{Quick ratio} = \dfrac{\text{Current assets} - \text{Inventory}}{\text{Current liabilities}}$

$\text{ACP} = \dfrac{\text{Accounts receivable}}{\text{Sales}} \times 365$

$\text{Inventory turnover} = \dfrac{\text{Cost of goods sold}}{\text{Inventory}}$

$$\text{Average holding period (days)} = \frac{365}{\text{Inventory turnover}}$$

$$\text{Inventory turnover (sales basis) } (\times) = \frac{\text{Sales}}{\text{Inventory}}$$

$$\text{Capital asset turnover} = \frac{\text{Sales}}{\text{Capital assests}}$$

$$\text{Total asset turnover} = \frac{\text{Sales}}{\text{Total assests}}$$

$$\text{Debt ratio} = \frac{\text{Long-term debt + Current liabilities}}{\text{Total assests}}$$

$$\text{Debt to equity ratio} = \frac{\text{Long-term debt}}{\text{Shareholders' equity}}$$

$$\text{TIE} = \frac{\text{EBIT}}{\text{Interest}}$$

$$\text{Cash coverage} = \frac{\text{EBIT + Amortization}}{\text{Interest}}$$

$$\text{Fixed charge coverage} = \frac{\text{EBIT + Lease payments}}{\text{Interest + Lease payments}}$$

$$\text{ROA} = \frac{\text{Net income}}{\text{Sales}} \times \frac{\text{Sales}}{\text{Total assets}}$$

$$\text{Equity multiplier} = \frac{\text{Total assets}}{\text{Equity}}$$

$$\text{ROE} = \frac{\text{Net income}}{\text{Sales}} \times \frac{\text{Sales}}{\text{Total assests}} \times \frac{\text{Total assets}}{\text{Shareholders' equity}}$$

$$\text{EVA} = \text{EBIT}\,(1 - T) - (\text{Debt + Shareholders' equity})\,(\text{Cost of capital \%})$$

CHAPTER 4

$$\text{Payable payment period} = \text{Accounts payable} \times \frac{365}{\text{Cost of goods sold}}$$

$$\text{Accounts receivable} = \text{Sales} \times \frac{\text{Average collection period}}{365}$$

(4.1) $\quad r = \dfrac{100 - P}{P} \times \dfrac{365}{d}$

(4.2) $\quad \text{Carrying cost} = C\left(\dfrac{Q}{2}\right)$

(4.3) $\quad N = \dfrac{D}{Q}$

(4.4) $\quad FN = F\left(\dfrac{D}{Q}\right)$

(4.5) $\quad TC = C\left(\dfrac{Q}{2}\right) + F\left(\dfrac{D}{Q}\right)$

(4.6) $\quad EOQ = \left(\dfrac{2FD}{C}\right)^{\frac{1}{2}}$

CHAPTER 5

(5.1) Cost of missing discount $= \dfrac{\text{Discount percentage}}{100\% - \text{Discount percentage}} \times \dfrac{365}{\text{Final payment date} - \text{Last discount date}}$

(5.2) $\text{APR} = \dfrac{I}{P} \times \dfrac{365}{d}$

(5.3) $\text{APR} = \dfrac{(M - P)}{P} \times \dfrac{365}{d}$

CHAPTER 6

(6.2) Forecast total assets $-$ Forecast current liabilities $-$ Last year's shareholders' equity $+$ Forecast dividends $=$ Forecast debt $+ (1 - T) [\text{EBIT} - \text{Int}\%(0.5)(\text{Last year's debt} + \text{Forecast debt})]$

(6.3) Growth in assets $-$ Growth in current liabilities $-$ Earnings retained $=$ External funding requirement

(6.6) $\text{NI}_{\text{next year}} = \text{ROS} \times (1 + g) \text{ Sales}_{\text{this year}}$

(6.7) Earnings retained $= (1 - d)\text{ROS} \times (1 + g) \text{ Sales}_{\text{this year}}$

(6.8) $\text{EFR} = g[\text{Assets}_{\text{this year}} - \text{Current liabilities}_{\text{this year}} - \text{NI}(1 - d)] - \text{NI}(1 - d)$

(6.9a) $g_s = \dfrac{\text{NI}(1 - d)}{\text{Shareholders' equity}}$

(6.9b) $g_s = \text{ROE}(1 - d)$

(6.10) $g_s = (1 - d) \times \dfrac{\text{NI}}{\text{Sales}} \times \dfrac{\text{Sales}}{\text{Assets}} \times \dfrac{\text{Assets}}{\text{Equity}}$

CHAPTER 7

(7.1) $k = \text{Base rate} + \text{Risk premium}$

(7.2) $\text{Base rate} = k_{\text{PR}} + \text{INFL}$

(7.3) $k = k_{\text{PR}} + \text{INFL} + \text{DR} + \text{LR} + \text{MR}$

CHAPTER 8

(8.3) $\text{FV}_n = \text{PV}(1 + k)^n$

(8.5) $\text{PV} = \text{FV}_n \times \dfrac{1}{(1 + k)^n}$

(8.13) $\text{FVA}_n = \dfrac{\text{PMT}(1 + k)^n - 1}{k}$

(8.15) $\text{EAR} = \left(1 + \dfrac{k_{nom}}{m}\right)^m - 1$

(8.16) $k^\star = \left(1 + \dfrac{k_{nom}}{m}\right)^{\frac{m}{n}} - 1$

(8.22b) $\text{PVA} = \dfrac{\text{PMT}}{k}\left(1 - \dfrac{1}{(1 + k)^n}\right)$

(8.25) $\text{FVAd}_n = \text{PMT}[\text{FVFA}_{k,n}](1 + k)$

(8.26) $PVAd = PMT[PVFA_{k,n}](1 + k)$

(8.27) $PV_p = \dfrac{PMT}{k}$

CHAPTER 9

(9.4) $P_B = PMT[PVFA_{k,n}] + FV[PVF_{k,n}]$

(9.5) $P_B\,(Call) = PMT\,[PVFA_{k,m}] + CP[PVF_{k,m}]$

After-tax cost of debt $= k(1 - T)$

CHAPTER 10

(10.1) $k = \dfrac{D_1 + (P_1 - P_0)}{P_0}$

(10.5) $P_0 = \dfrac{D_1}{(1 + k)} + \dfrac{D_2}{(1 + k)^2} + \dots + \dfrac{D_n}{(1 + k)^n} + \dfrac{P_n}{(1 + k)^n}$

(10.7) $D_n = D_0(1 + g)^n$

(10.10) $P_0 = \dfrac{D_0(1 + g)}{k - g} = \dfrac{D_1}{k - g}$

(10.11) $P_0 = \dfrac{D}{k}$

(10.12) $k_e = \dfrac{D_1}{P_0} + g$

(10.13) $P_p = \dfrac{D_p}{k_p}$

CHAPTER 11

(11.1) $k = \dfrac{\text{Interest paid}}{\text{Loan amount}}$

(11.2) $k = \dfrac{D_1 + (P_1 - P_0)}{P_0}$

(11.3) $Slope = \dfrac{Rise}{Run} + \dfrac{\Delta k_x}{\Delta k_M} = \beta_x = Beta$

(11.4) $k_X = k_{RF} + (k_M - k_{RF})\beta_X$

CHAPTER 12

(12.1) $NPV = -C_0 + \dfrac{C_1}{(1 + k)} + \dfrac{C_2}{(1 + k)^2} + \dots + \dfrac{C_n}{(1 + k)^n}$

(12.2) $0 = -C_0 + \dfrac{C_1}{(1 + IRR)} + \dfrac{C_2}{(1 + IRR)^2} + \dots + \dfrac{C_n}{(1 + IRR)^n}$

(12.3) $\text{NPV} = -C_0 + C[\text{PVFA}_{k,n}]$

(12.4) $0 = -C_0 + C[\text{PVFA}_{\text{IRR},n}]$

(12.5) $\text{PI} = \dfrac{\dfrac{C_1}{(1+k)} + \dfrac{C_2}{(1+k)^2} + \ldots + \dfrac{C_n}{(1+k)^n}}{C_0}$

$\text{PVA} = \text{PMT}[\text{PVFA}_{k,n}]$

CHAPTER 13

(13.1) $\text{PV} = (C - S_{\text{pv}})\left(\dfrac{dT}{k+d}\right)\left(\dfrac{1+0.5k}{1+k}\right)$

(13.2) $\text{PV} = C\left(\dfrac{dT}{k+d}\right)\left(\dfrac{1+0.5k}{1+k}\right) - S_{\text{pv}}\left(\dfrac{dI}{k+d}\right)$

CHAPTER 15

$\text{Component cost of capital} = \dfrac{\text{Investor's return}}{(1-f)} = \dfrac{k}{(1-f)}$

(15.1) $\text{Cost of debt} = k_{\text{d}}(1-T)$

(15.2) $P_{\text{p}} = \dfrac{D_{\text{p}}}{k_{\text{p}}}$

(15.3) $k_{\text{p}} = \dfrac{D_{\text{p}}}{P_{\text{p}}}$

(15.4) $\text{Cost of preferred shares} = \dfrac{D_{\text{p}}}{(1-f)P_{\text{p}}} = \dfrac{k_{\text{p}}}{(1-f)}$

(15.5) $k_{\text{X}} = k_{\text{RF}} + (k_{\text{M}} - k_{\text{RF}})\beta_{\text{X}}$

(15.6) $P_0 = \dfrac{D_0(1-g)}{k_{\text{e}} - g}$

(15.7) $k_{\text{e}} = \dfrac{D_0(1+g)}{P_0} + g$

(15.8) $k_{\text{e}} = \dfrac{D_0(1+g)}{(1-f)P_0} + g$

CHAPTER 16

(16.1) $\text{ROCE} = \dfrac{\text{EBIT}(1-T)}{\text{Debt} + \text{Equity}}$

(16.3) $\text{DFL} = \dfrac{\text{EBIT}}{\text{EBIT} - I} \text{ or } \dfrac{\text{EBIT}}{\text{EBT}}$

(16.5) $C_{\text{M}} = \dfrac{(P-V)}{P}$

(16.7) $Q_{\text{B/E}} = \dfrac{F_{\text{C}}}{(P-V)}$

(16.9) $S_{B/E} = \dfrac{\dfrac{F_C}{(P - V)}}{P} = \dfrac{F_C}{C_M}$

(16.11) $DOL = \dfrac{Q(P - V)}{Q(P - V) - F_C}$ or $\dfrac{CM}{EBIT}$

(16.13) $DTL = \dfrac{CM}{(EBIT - I)}$ or $\dfrac{CM}{EBT}$

(16.16) $V_d = \dfrac{I}{k_d}$

(16.17) $V_e = \dfrac{D}{k_e}$

(16.18) $V_f = \dfrac{I}{k_d} + \dfrac{D}{k_e}$

(16.19) $V_f = \dfrac{OI}{k_a}$

(16.22) PV of tax shield $= \dfrac{TI}{k_d} = \dfrac{TBk_d}{k_d} = TB$

CHAPTER 17

(17.2) Dividend payout ratio $= \dfrac{\text{Dividend}}{\text{Earnings}} = \dfrac{\text{Dividend per share}}{\text{EPS}}$

CHAPTER 18

(18.1) $V_{IC} = P_S - P_{Strk}$

(18.2) $V_{IP} = P_{Strk} - P_S$

(18.3) Conversion ratio $= \dfrac{\text{Bond's par value}}{\text{Conversion price}} = \text{Shares exchanged}$

(18.A1) $C = SN(d_1) - Xe^{-rt}N(d_2)$

(18.A2) $d_1 = \dfrac{\ln\left(\dfrac{S}{X}\right) + [r + .5(\sigma^2)]t}{\sigma\sqrt{t}}$

(18.A3) $d_2 = d_1 - \sigma\sqrt{t}$

Glossary

(Numbers in parentheses refer to the chapter(s) containing the main discussion of the term.)

A

ABC system
A system of controlling inventory that recognizes the differing cost and importance of various items. *A* parts are expensive and/or important and are controlled carefully. *C* parts are cheap and plentiful, so little effort is expended to monitor them. *B* parts are between *A*s and *C*s. (4)

Accelerated amortization
See *amortization*. (2)

Accounting period
In business, time is divided into accounting periods—usually months, quarters, and years—during which the accounting system accumulates transactions and produces financial reports. Also see *financial statements*. (2)

Accounting system
Generates the data on costs, earnings, and financial position required for making financial decisions. (2)

Accrual
An accrual is an accounting entry used to recognize expenses and liabilities associated with transactions that are not entirely complete; for example, a payroll accrual for unpaid wages. (2)

Accrual method
The standard accounting method for reporting revenues and costs, assets and liabilities in the financial statements. (2)

Accumulated amortization
The sum of all amortization written off to date. Carried as an offset to the value of a capital asset, so at any time the net book value of the asset is the difference between its original cost and its accumulated amortization. Also see *amortization*. (2)

Acquisition
A merger in which one company acquires the shares of another. May be friendly or hostile (unfriendly). See *merger*. (19)

Agency
A relationship between two parties in which one (the principal) employs the other (the agent) in a decision-making capacity. (1)

Agency problem
In corporations, managers are the agents of shareholders and are often able to take advantage of the relationship by diverting corporate resources to their own use. Excessive pay is the primary example. The general situation is described as the agency problem. Costs associated with controlling the agency problem are agency costs. (1)

Aging schedule
An accounts receivable analysis that classifies and totals accounts by age category. The older the account, the greater the risk that it will prove to be uncollectible, and the more attention it will receive. (4)

Amortization
The accounting entry allocating the cost of a capital asset against income over the asset's life. Amortization methods include straightline and accelerated amortization. Straightline amortization is evenly prorated. Accelerated amortization is any method that shifts amortization forward in an asset's life. Accelerated methods increase early charges and reduce those that come later, keeping total amortization constant. Capital cost allowance, used for tax purposes, is a type of accelerated amortization. Amortization is a noncash charge, so net income is generally less than true cash flow by at least the amount of amortization. Also see *accumulated amortization, capital cost allowance*. (2)

Amortized debt
A debt in which the principal is repaid over the life of the loan rather than in a lump sum at the end. (8)

Annual percentage interest rate (APR)
Calculated on the loan amount, the dollar amount of interest paid, the length of the loan, and the timing of repayment. See *nominal interest rate*. (5, 8)

Annual report
A yearly report on a company's performance prepared by management. An annual report includes financial statements and generally contains verbal discussions of the firm's operations and prospects. Also see *financial statements*. (3)

Annuity
A finite series of equal payments at equal intervals of time. In an ordinary annuity, the payments occur at the end of the time periods. In an annuity due, they occur at the beginning. (8)

Annuity due
See *annuity*. (8)

Arbitrage
Making a profit by buying and selling the same thing at the same time in two different markets. (16)

Ask
The minimum price a seller is willing to accept for a security. (18)

Asset management (turnover) ratios
Financial ratios that measure the firm's ability to generate revenue using its assets. Examples include inventory turnover, capital asset turnover, and total asset turnover. Also see *ratio analysis*. (3)

Average collection period (ACP)
A financial ratio that measures how long it takes to collect on credit sales. Also called days sales outstanding (DSO). ACP is an indicator of the collectibility of the receivables and the efficiency of the credit and collection system. The closer the ACP to the firm's credit terms, the better. (3)

Average tax rate
See *tax rates*. (2)

B

Balance sheet
Financial statement as of a moment in time. It says that, at the end of the accounting period, the company owns a particular list of assets and owes a particular list of creditors, the difference representing the book value of the shareholders' equity. (2)

Bankers' acceptance (BA)
A promissory note or draft of a corporate borrower with a guarantee of payment by a chartered bank. Often sold in the money market. Also see *money market*. (5)

Bankruptcy
A federal court procedure to protect a failing firm from its creditors until the best solution to its problems can be found. Also see *insolvency*. (19)

Base rate
The rate at which people lend money when there's no risk involved in the loan. It has two components: the pure interest rate (also known as the earning power of money), and the expected rate of inflation over the life of the loan. (7)

Basic EPS
Earnings after tax divided by the weighted average number of shares outstanding during the year. (18)

Bearer bond
An unregistered bond, owned by the "bearer," the person in possession. Contrast with *registered bond (security)* (9)

Benchmarking
A type of analysis in which a company compares its ratio values with those of a key competitor or group of competitors, primarily to identify areas for improvement. (3)

Beta
The measure of market risk in portfolio theory. The degree to which a share's return moves with the market's return. (11)

Bid

The most a buyer is willing to pay for a security. (18)

Black–Scholes option pricing model

A viable option pricing model, developed by financial scholars Fisher Black and Myron Scholes, that gives results similar to those of stock pricing models. (18)

Blanket inventory lien

In finance, gives the lender in an inventory loan a lien against all inventories held by the borrower. The borrower remains in complete physical control of the inventory, but commits to use the proceeds on sale to pay off the loan. Compare with *trust receipt*. (5)

Board of directors

The governing body of a corporation, elected by common shareholders. (10)

Bond

A security reflecting a relatively long-term debt relationship between the issuer (borrower) and the buyer (investor/lender). (1)

Bond indentures

Contractual agreements associated with bonds that limit the activities of borrowing companies. (9)

Bond rating

A measure of the likelihood of default on payment of interest or principal. Ratings are prepared by rating agencies. Dominion Bond Rating Service (DBRS) and Standard and Poor's Ratings Direct Canada are two Canadian bond rating agencies. (9)

Book value

For a company, the value of equity, equal to total assets minus total liabilities. Book value can be stated in total or per share. For an asset, book value is the net of original cost minus accumulated amortization, and is generally referred to as net book value. (3)

Bottom-up planning

Business planning based on inputs from lower-level management. The process tends to understate achievable performance because people set easily achievable goals for themselves. Also see *business plan*. Contrast with *top-down planning*. (6)

Breakeven analysis

A technique for finding the volume at which a firm breaks even financially—that is, earns zero profit. (16)

Broker

See *stockbroker*. (1)

Brokerage firm (house)

A company of stockbrokers generally having the right to trade on an exchange. (7)

Budget

A short-term, financially detailed business plan, usually covering about a calendar quarter. (6)

Business plan

A document projecting a firm's physical and financial performance into the future. Business plans can be short or long range. Long-range plans are "strategic" and tend to be more verbal than financial. Shorter-term plans are described as "operational," and detail the more routine running of the business. (6)

Business risk

Variation in a company's financial performance caused by changes in business conditions. (16)

Business-specific risk

Variation in the return on a share investment caused by things that affect specific businesses or industries. Also called *unsystematic risk*. Contrast with *market risk*. (11)

C

Call (option)

The right to purchase a share at a specified price over a designated period of time. See *option*. Compare with *put (option)*. (18)

Call provision (feature)

A provision in a bond contract that allows the borrowing organization to "call" in the bond and pay it off early. Calls are generally exercised when interest rates have dropped substantially since the bond's issue. An additional payment known as the call premium must usually be made to the investor if the call is exercised. Most call features cannot be exercised during an initial call-protected period. (9)

Canadian controlled private corporation (CCPC)

In the *Tax Act*, a relatively small, closely held private corporation with fewer than 100 employees and a small market share. It is allowed relatively low rates of tax. (2)

Capital

Long-term assets or the money used to support long-term assets and projects. Long-term debt and equity on the balance sheet. Also see *capital asset*. (2)

Capital asset

A real or tangible asset that is acquired for long-term use in the business. Capital assets include property, plant, and equipment. (2)

Capital asset pricing model (CAPM)

A statistical model of the investment world aimed at explaining how required returns are determined in financial markets and thereby how share prices are set. Also see *security market line*. (11)

Capital asset turnover

A financial ratio measuring the relationship of the firm's capital assets to the year's sales. Defined as Sales ÷ Capital assets. (3)

Capital budgeting

Analysis techniques concerned with justifying money spent on long-term assets and projects. Projects may be expansions, replacements, or new ventures. (12)

Capital component

One of three sources of capital: long-term debt, preferred shares, or equity. (15)

Capital cost allowance (CCA)

The system of amortization prescribed for tax computations, usually on a declining balance (accelerated) basis. Classes and maximum amortization rates are set for various types of capital assets. For example, computer equipment is Class 45, and the maximum CCA rate is 45% per year, applied to the balance remaining (undepreciated capital cost) in the class. Provides a tax-deductible expense. The higher amortization in the early years of the asset's life results in lower tax in those years, because taxable income is lower. Also called *tax amortization*. Also see *undepreciated capital cost*. (2, 13)

Capital gain

The difference between the proceeds on sale and book value of an investment or capital asset held over a period of time. The portion of the capital gain (currently 50%) that is subject to income tax is the *taxable capital gain*. (2)

Capital gain yield

The capital gain on a share divided by the price at which it was purchased. (10)

Capital lease

A lease in which the lessee effectively acquires ownership of the leased asset. Also called a financing lease. Accounted for by showing the leased asset on the balance sheet offset by a liability representing the obligation to make future lease payments. Compare with *operating lease*. (9)

Capital market

A financial market in which long-term (at least one year) debt and shares are traded. (7)

Capital rationing

In capital budgeting, the process of allocating available capital among projects to maximize total NPV. (12)

Capital restructuring

Changing a firm's capital structure intentionally by buying and selling shareholders' equity and bonds simultaneously. (16)

Capital structure

The mix of the three capital components (debt, preferred shares, and equity) used by a firm. The optimal capital structure is the structure at which share price is maximized, all other things held equal. Also see *target capital structure*. (15)

Cash conversion cycle

The time from the disbursement of cash to pay for inventory to the receipt of cash for product sold. The cash conversion cycle is shorter than the operating cycle by the period during which the firm holds a payable for the inventory. Compare with *operating cycle*. (4)

Cash forecast (budget)
A forecast of cash flows based on expected receipts and disbursements rather than on projections of income statement and balance sheet accounts. (6)

CCA tax shield
The tax savings that the firm will experience from being able to claim CCA on its capital assets. (13)

Chief financial officer (CFO)
The executive in charge of the financial function. (1)

Clean-up requirement
The requirement that borrowers pay off all short-term debt for some period each year. Prevents funding long-term projects with short-term debt. (5)

Clientele effect
The theory that firms attract equity investors at least in part because of their dividend-paying policies. The firm has a "clientele" of shareholders whose need for current or deferred income matches the firm's dividend practices. The impli-cation is that it isn't a good idea to change dividend policies because such a change is bound to displease most shareholders. (17)

Closing price
The price of a security in the last trade of a business day. (7)

Collateral
An asset backing a loan. In the event of default the collateral becomes the property of the lender to satisfy the obligation. Also called security for the loan. Also see *blanket inventory lien, trust receipt, pledging receivables*. (1)

Collection agency
A firm that specializes in collecting debts, especially overdue receivables, for a percentage of the amount collected. (4)

Collections policy
The manner and aggressiveness with which a firm pursues payment from delinquent customers. (4)

Commercial paper
Very short-term debt issued by major companies and financial intermediaries. Sold at a discount. (5)

Commitment fee
Also called a standby fee, this is a fee charged by a bank for guaranteeing to have loanable funds available. The fee is charged on unborrowed amounts up to the maximum of the guarantee. See *revolving credit agreement*. (5)

Common share or common stock
The security representing ownership of a corporation. Portion of shareholders' equity. (10)

Common size statement
A firm's income statement with every line stated as a percentage of revenue. A balance sheet with every line stated as a percent of total assets. Used to compare companies of different sizes or to identify performance trends in a single company over time. (3)

Competition Act
A body of legislation aimed at maintaining the competitive nature of the economy. The Act can prohibit certain mergers on the basis that they reduce competition. (19)

Compounding period
The period of time after which interest is credited to the depositor's account for purposes of computing subsequent interest. (8)

Compound interest
The concept of earning interest on previously earned interest. A sum earning compound interest grows exponentially over time. (8)

Concentration banking
Employing one centralized bank account to manage the balances in remote accounts. Balances are generally transferred electronically into the concentration bank daily. (4)

Conglomerate merger
A merger between companies in unrelated businesses. (19)

Consolidation
A combination of two or more businesses in which all of the old legal entities dissolve and a new one with a new name is formed to continue into the future. (19)

Contribution (margin)
In breakeven analysis, contribution is the difference between price and variable cost that is "contributed" toward profit and fixed costs. The contribution margin is the contribution expressed as a percentage of price. (16)

Controller
The executive in charge of the accounting function in most companies. The controller generally reports to the CFO in large companies. (1)

Covenants
See *restrictive covenants* (5).

Covered
Refers to whether an option writer has a position in the underlying security. For a covered call writer, the writer owns the underlying share. (18)

Conversion price
Stating the conversion ratio along with the bond's par value. Also see *conversion ratio*. (18)

Conversion ratio
A ratio set at the time bonds are issued; determines the number of shares that can be exchanged for a bond. (18)

Convertible bond
A bond that can be converted into a specified number of shares at the owner's discretion. (9)

Convertible currency
A currency that can be exchanged for other currencies on foreign exchange markets. Contrast with *inconvertible currency*. (20)

Corporate restructuring
A broad term describing a number of ways in which companies are reorganized. Includes capital restructure, mergers, and reorganizations in bankruptcy as well as changes in certain methods of doing business. (19)

Corporation
A form of business organization in which the business is a separate legal entity subject to a corporate tax on whatever it earns. (1)

Corporation tax
A tax levied by the federal and provincial governments on a corporation, which is a taxpayer separate from its shareholders. (2)

Cost of capital
The average rate a firm pays its investors for the use of their funds, adjusted for taxes and administrative costs. Also called the WACC (weighted average cost of capital). Developed from the costs of individual capital components which are the rates, adjusted for taxes and flotation costs, that are paid on debt, preferred shares, and common equity. The component costs are (weighted) averaged to get the WACC. (12, 15)

Cost of goods sold
Spending closely associated with production or purchase of the products for sale. Contrast with *expense*. (2)

Cost structure
The mix of fixed and variable cost used by a firm. (16)

Coupon rate, coupon payment
The interest rate paid by a bond on its face value. The dollar amount of the interest payment, which is usually made semiannually. (9)

Credit agency (bureau)
An organization that maintains records of the bill-paying histories of most companies and assigns credit ratings to firms that indicate how well they've paid their bills in the past. The agency's subscribers can receive credit reports on companies with which they're considering doing business. (4)

Creditor
Anyone owed money by a business, including lenders, vendors, employees, or the government. (1)

Credit policy
A business's guidelines for identifying the customers to whom it is willing to sell on credit, and the level of credit to be allowed. It is a statement of the minimum customer quality the business will accept for credit sales. (4)

Credit scoring

The process of calculating a numerical credit rating for a customer based on financial information collected, and granting or refusing credit as a result. (4)

Crossover rate

The discount rate that makes the net present values of two mutually exclusive projects equal. At the crossover rate, the investor is indifferent between the two projects. (12)

Cross rate

In foreign exchange markets, an exchange rate between any two currencies developed without going through dollars. (20)

Cumulative feature of preferred shares

A provision to enhance the safety of preferred shares. If preferred dividends are passed, no common dividends can be paid until preferred dividends are caught up cumulatively. (10)

Cumulative voting

A method of electing boards of directors in which shareholders can cast all of their votes for a single seat. Enables minority interests to get at least some representation on the board. (10)

Current assets

Assets expected to become cash in less than one year. Current assets are largely cash, receivables, and inventories. (2)

Current liabilities

Obligations expected to require cash in less than one year; usually payables and accruals. (2)

Current yield

A bond's annual interest payment divided by its market price. (9)

D

Date of record

When a dividend is declared, it is paid to owners of record on the transfer agent's books as of the date of record. Also see *declaration date*. (17)

Debenture

An unsecured bond. (9)

Debt management ratios

Financial ratios that measure the financial risk the firm has assumed by borrowing. Examples include debt ratio, debt to equity ratio, times interest earned, cash coverage, and fixed charge coverage. Also see *ratio analysis*. (3)

Decision tree

A timeline representation used in planning projects subject to multiple outcomes. Wherever an event has several outcomes, the timeline branches into as many paths, each with a probability. The result is a proliferation of possible paths to completion, each representing an outcome, its financial implication, and its probability. Hence, the decision tree

specifies a probability distribution for the project's overall financial outcome. (14)

Declaration date

The date on which a firm's board of directors declares a dividend. (17)

Declining balance amortization

A method of accelerated amortization where the cost of the asset is amortized over its service life, but annual amortization expense (using a higher amortization rate than for straight-line) is based on the net book value rather than the cost of the asset. See *amortization, capital cost allowance*. (12)

Default risk

The risk of loss to a lender from the borrower's failure to pay the full amount due including interest and principal. (7)

Defensive tactics

Actions taken by the management of a company to resist or avoid being acquired. (19)

Degree of financial leverage

The ratio of the relative change in EPS or NI relative to a change in EBIT. (16)

Degree of operating leverage

The ratio of the relative change in EBIT to a relative change in sales. (16)

Degree of total leverage

The ratio of the relative change in EPS or NI relative to a change in sales. (16)

Derivative security

A security whose price is derived from the price of another security. The most common example is an option to buy or sell shares. The value of the option is related to the price of the shares being bought or sold. See *option*. (18)

Devaluation

In foreign exchange markets, a significant decrease in the value of a currency compared to major currencies, such as the U.S. dollar. A financial or monetary crisis is often the incentive for a government to officially lower the value of its currency relative to the U.S. dollar. (20)

Diluted EPS

Earnings per share reflecting the hypothetical conversion or exercise of all convertibles, warrants, and options outstanding. (18)

Dilution

The reduction in earnings per share (EPS) and book value per share that results from the conversion of convertible securities or the exercise of warrants or employee stock options. Diluted values for earnings per share and book value per share reflect the hypothetical conversion or exercise of all convertibles, warrants, and options outstanding. Also see *book value*. (18)

Discount

Generally a reduction in price or value. In finance, a reduction in the present value of a future sum due to effect of compound interest. Also see *discounted cash flow*. (8)

Discounted cash flow

Calculations involving the present and future values of money under the action of compound interest. Also called the time value of money. (8)

Diversification

In finance, selecting a portfolio of different (diverse) investments to limit the overall risk borne by the investor. (11)

Divestiture

Getting rid of a business unit. The reverse of an acquisition. (19)

Dividend

The payment made by a corporation to an equity investor (shareholder). (10)

Dividend aversion theory

A logical argument that shareholders should be averse to the payment of dividends. (17)

Dividend decision

The decision by management regarding the portion of earnings paid to shareholders as dividends. The alternative is to retain the money, investing it in the company for future growth. (17)

Dividend irrelevance theory

A logical argument that shareholders should be indifferent to the payment of dividends. (17)

Dividend payout ratio

Dividend per share over earnings per share. A firm may select a target payout ratio to satisfy shareholders while retaining funds for business needs. (17)

Dividend policy

The rationale under which a firm determines what it will pay in dividends, both in amount paid and the pattern under which changes in the amount occur over time. Also see *dividend decision*. (17)

Dividend preference theory

A logical argument that shareholders should prefer the payment of dividends. (17)

Dividend tax credit

The tax credit allowed to shareholders to compensate for the corporation tax already paid. The dividend tax credit reduces the effective amount of personal tax on the dividend. (2)

Dividend yield

A share's annual dividend divided by its current price. (7)

Double taxation of corporate earnings

The primary financial disadvantage of the corporate form. A corporation's earnings are subject to corporate tax when earned and personal tax when paid to shareholders as dividends. The dividend tax credit serves to compensate the shareholder for the fact that their dividend has been reduced because of corporate tax paid. Also see *dividend tax credit*. In foreign direct investment, double taxation is a situation where the income of the foreign affiliate is taxed in the foreign country and in Canada. Tax treaties and foreign tax credits may reduce or eliminate this form of double taxation. (1, 20)

Dunning

Pursuing a customer for payment of an overdue receivable. (4)

Du Pont equations

A series of relationships between financial ratios that illustrates the inner workings of businesses and how performance in one area influences performance in others, and ultimately ROE (return on equity). (3)

E

Earnings after tax (EAT)

A measure of a firm's profitability. Also called net income or "the bottom line." (2)

Earnings before interest and taxes (EBIT)

A measure of a firm's performance without regard to how it is financed. Also called *operating income* or *operating profit*. (2)

Earnings dilution

A drop in EPS caused by a sale of shares at a below-market price. (18)

Economic order quantity (EOQ) model

A technique for minimizing the sum of inventory ordering and carrying costs. Also see *inventory ordering costs* and *inventory carrying costs*. (4)

Economic risk

In foreign direct investment, refers to the potential long-run impact of exchange rate fluctuations on the value of a foreign affiliate. In particular, if the local exchange rate declines steadily over time, the affiliate (and its parent) may suffer financial loss. (20)

Economic value added (EVA)

A measure of income that recognizes the cost of equity as well as debt. A positive EVA represents a contribution to shareholder wealth over that required by an equity investor, and is viewed as an increment to market value added (MVA). EVA is after-tax EBIT less the product of capital and the cost of capital. Also see *market value added*. (3)

Effective annual rate (EAR)

The annually compounded rate that pays the same interest as a lower rate compounded more frequently. (8)

Efficient market hypothesis

The assertion that information travels around the financial system so quickly that share prices virtually always reflect all available information. The concept implies that technical analysis is useless. (10)

Electronic Data Interchange (EDI)

The direct, electronic information exchange and direct computer-to-computer transactions between businesses. (4)

Embedded annuity

A series of regular payments within an uneven stream of payments (8)

Equity

An ownership interest. See also *shareholders' equity*. (1)

Equity multiplier

Total assets divided by equity. A financial ratio in the Du Pont equations measuring the effect on return on equity from the use of debt. Also see *Du Pont equations*. (3)

Equivalent annual annuity (EAA) method

In capital budgeting, a method for dealing with projects with unequal lives. The EAA method converts the net present value of each project into an equivalent annual amount (in NPV terms). This amount can then be used to select the better project. Also see *net present value*. (12)

Euro

A common European currency adopted by 15 of the members of the European Union. (20)

Eurobond

A bond denominated in a currency other than that of the country in which it is sold and issued by a foreign borrower. Contrast with *foreign bond*. (20)

Eurocurrency loans

Large short-term or medium-term loans denominated in foreign currencies and available from foreign banks. Eurocurrency loans allow large Canadian companies to access capital markets outside Canada when interest rates in Canada are elevated. (20)

Eurodollars

U.S. dollars deposited in banks in other countries and available for eurodollar (eurocurrency) loans. Also see *eurocurrency loans*. (20)

Exchange

In capital markets, a company that provides a physical or electronic marketplace and the administrative capability of transferring shares from one owner to another. (7)

Exchange rate

In international business, the rate at which one currency can be traded for another. Spot rates are available for current trades. Forward rates are available for currency to be delivered in a specified period of time. (20)

Exchange rate risk (exposure)

The risk that international trade dealings will earn more or less than expected because of movement in exchange rates before the transaction is completed. Also called transaction risk. (20)

Ex-dividend date

The date on which a share trades without a declared dividend that has yet to be paid. Two days prior to the date of record.

Also see *date of record, declaration date, payment date*. (17)

Exercise price

See *strike price*. (18)

Expectations theory (with respect to dividends)

A dividend that's lower than expected will be taken as a negative by investors even if it is larger than previous dividends. A variation on the signalling effect of dividends. (17)

Expectations theory (with respect to interest rates)

A theory explaining the shape of the interest yield curve. The curve slopes upward or downward depending on whether expectations about future interest and inflation rates are increasing or decreasing. (7)

Expected return

The return an investor believes is most likely on an investment—that is, the investor understands that the actual return may be somewhat different in certain investments like shares. The mean of the probability distribution of returns. (11)

Expense

An item of expenditure not closely related to production. Also called *operating expense*. Compare to *cost of goods sold*. (2)

Expropriate

In foreign direct investments, the seizure of assets held in a foreign country by the government of that country. Also see *political risk*. (20)

External funding requirement

Defined as (Growth in assets) – (Growth in current liabilities) – (Earnings retained). Provides an estimate of funding needs assuming all financial items vary directly with sales. (6)

F

Face value

The amount of principal to be repaid by the borrower. Also called *par value*. (9)

Factoring receivables

Selling receivables to a financing source for an amount less than their face value. (5)

Finance

(noun) The art and science of handling money. (1)

Finance

(verb) To raise money to acquire an asset to do some project. (1)

Financial analyst

A person who studies the financial results of businesses and makes recommendations on their values as investments. (1, 3)

Financial assets

Shares and bonds. More generally a document giving its owner a claim to certain future cash flows. Shares base that claim on ownership (equity), while bonds base it on debt. Also called a *security*. (1)

Financial books

The regular statements of the company, not to satisfy the tax rules. They differ from the tax books primarily in the area of amortization. Contrast with *tax books*. (2)

Financial economics

A somewhat archaic term for financial theory emphasizing the field's roots in economics. (1)

Financial information

The results of business operations stated in money terms; the material in financial statements, but not entirely limited to those documents. (3)

Financial instrument

See *financial assets*.

Financial intermediary

An institution that sells shares in itself and invests the funds collected on behalf of its investors. Mutual funds are the primary example. (7)

Financial leverage

The use of borrowed money to multiply financial performance in terms of ROE and EPS. (2)

Financial markets

Markets in which financial assets are traded; for example, the stock market. (1, 7)

Financial plan

A projection of a company's financial statements into the future based on a series of assumptions about what the business and the environment will do. Part of a business plan. Also see *business plan*. (6)

Financial statements

Reports created from accounting records that summrize a firm's performance and position in money terms. The three principal statements are the income statement, balance sheet and statement of cash flows. Also see *financial books*. (2)

Financing activities

Deal with the capital accounts: long-term debt and equity. (2)

Financing lease

See *capital lease*. (9)

Fixed financial charge

An expense item that must be paid regardless of how the firm is performing. Essentially, interest and lease payments. (3)

Float

Money tied up in the cheque-clearing process. (4)

Floating exchange rate

In foreign exchange markets, a rate determined essentially by global supply and demand for the currency, with little intervention by governments. (20)

Floor broker

A broker who buys and sells on the trading floor of a stock exchange; for example, the New York Stock Exchange. (7)

Flotation costs

The administrative cost of issuing new securities. Consists largely of commissions and marketing fees, but printing and engraving costs can also be significant. (9)

Forecast

A short-term projection of a company's financial results; for example, most firms do regular cash forecasts to predict their immediate funding needs. Also see *cash forecast (budget)*. (6)

Foreign bond

A bond denominated in the currency of the country in which it is sold, but issued by a foreign borrower. Compare with *eurobond*. (20)

Foreign direct investment (FDI)

In international business, building or buying facilities in another country. (20)

Foreign exchange

A general term for the currency of foreign countries. (20)

Foreign exchange market

A financial market in which the currencies of different countries are traded. (20)

Free cash flow

Cash generated by a business above that needed for asset replacement and growth. (2)

Fundamental analysis

A systematic process in which a security is valued by estimating the performance of the underlying company and the future cash flows associated with owning the security. These are discounted to arrive at an intrinsic value for the security. Contrast with *technical analysis*. (10)

Funds

Generally another term for cash. (15)

Future value

The amount a present sum will grow into at a specified interest rate over a specified period of time. (8)

G

GAAP

See *generally accepted accounting principles*.

Generally accepted accounting principles (GAAP)

The general rules by which financial records are kept and financial statements are presented. (3)

Going concern value

The value of a firm as a profit-earning business as opposed to as a collection of assets. (3)

Golden parachute

A contract between a company and its senior management that provides for

lucrative payouts to these managers should the company be taken over and the managers subsequently be fired. (19)

Gordon model

A mathematical model for valuing shares based on an assumed constant growth rate of dividends into the indefinite future. (10)

Government intervention

In foreign exchange markets, governments may intervene to keep exchange rates within desirable limits. (20)

Greenmail

To avoid an unfriendly acquisition, a firm may buy shares owned by a potential acquirer at a price above the market price of the shares. The above-market payment is greenmail. (19)

Gross margin

Revenue less cost of goods sold where cost is spending closely associated with production. (2)

H

Hedging

A manoeuvre or contract that eliminates risk from a transaction. In international trade, eliminating exchange rate risk by purchasing a forward contract for delivery of foreign exchange at a specified rate at a specified time. (20)

Holding company

A company that owns other companies. A parent company. (19)

Horizontal merger

A merger between companies in the same line of business, usually as competitors. (19)

I

Income statement

Financial statement showing *revenue* earned and *costs and expenses* incurred over the accounting period. Also see *financial statements*. (2)

Income tax

A percentage of net income paid by a taxpayer (whether an individual or a corporation) to the taxing authority. The tax is levied on a base of taxable income, which is income subject to tax, less certain tax deductions. Also see *tax deductions*. (2)

Income trust

A form of business where investors provide money to the trust to purchase stable, income producing assets. Funds from operating the assets are then distributed to the investors rather than be reinvested in the business. (10)

Inconvertible currency

In foreign exchange markets, a currency that cannot be exchanged for other currencies at market-determined rates. The foreign government involved will sell its currency at its official exchange rate. However, if you have the foreign currency, there is generally no one willing to buy it for dollars or any other major currency at the exchange rate set by the foreign government. Also called *nonconvertible currency*. (20)

Incremental cash flows
The change in cash flows, after tax, that results from making a business decision, such as a capital investment. (13)

Indentures
Contractual agreements associated with bonds that limit the activities of the issuing companies. The limitations are designed to reduce the risk that the firm won't be able to pay the bond's interest and principal. (9)

Independence hypothesis
In capital structure theory, the original restrictive model by Modigliani and Miller that shows share price to be independent of capital structure. (16)

Indirect agency costs
Hard-to-quantify costs of management not acting in the best interests of shareholders. (1)

Initial public offering (IPO)
Shares in a new company offered to the public for the first time. Such shares tend to make a volatile, high-risk investment. Also see *primary market*. (7)

In play
A company is in play when it is the object of an acquisition attempt. (19)

Insider information
Information about companies that can influence share price that is available to insiders but not to the general public. It is illegal to make short-term profits using insider information. (7)

Insolvency
A firm is technically insolvent when it can't pay its short-term debts. Legal insolvency implies that the firm's liabilities exceed its assets. Also see *bankruptcy*. (19)

Institutional investor
A business organization that buys and sells securities. Generally a fund of some kind, such as a mutual fund or a pension fund that invests the pooled money of its clients. Also see *financial intermediary*. (7)

Interest
The return on a debt investment. (7)

Interest rate model
An abstract portrayal of how interest rates work. (7)

Interest rate risk
The risk of loss to an investor from changes in the price of a bond that arise from changes in the market interest rate. Also called *price risk* and *maturity risk*. (7)

Internal rate of return (IRR)
A capital budgeting technique that rates projects according to their expected return on invested funds. The higher the return, the better. (12)

International bond
A bond sold outside the home country of the issuing organization (borrower). May be a foreign bond or a eurobond. (20)

Intrinsic value
An underlying or fundamental value. In securities analysis, the price of a security (usually a share) derived from extensive analysis of the issuing company and its industry. (10) In financial options, the difference between the market price of the underlying share and the price at which an option on that share can be exercised (the strike price) if that difference is positive, zero if it is not. (18)

Inventory carrying costs
Costs associated with holding inventory, including financing charges, storage and security, insurance, taxes on assets, shrinkage, damage, and obsolescence. Compare with *inventory ordering costs*. Also see *economic order quantity model*. (4)

Inventory ordering costs
The expenses of placing orders with suppliers, receiving shipments, and processing materials into inventory. Compare with *inventory carrying costs*. Also see *economic order quantity model*. (4)

Inventory turnover ratio
Cost of goods sold (or sales) divided by inventory. A financial ratio that indicates whether or not a firm has excess funds tied up in inventory. (3)

Invest (investing, investment)
Using a resource (usually money) to improve the future rather than for current consumption. Investment by companies generally means buying assets to be used in their businesses. Investment by individuals usually means buying financial assets (shares, bonds, savings accounts) that earn a return. (1)

Investing activities
Occur when the firm buys (invests in) or sells things such as equipment that enable it to do business; also include purchases and sales of long-term financial assets. (2)

Investment-grade bonds
Bonds above a certain quality rating. DBRS: BBB; S&P: BBB. (9)

Investment opportunity schedule (IOS)
A schedule of capital budgeting projects arranged in decreasing order of IRR. (15)

Iterative technique
A procedure that finds a solution to a problem through a repetitive series of calculations. Also known as a numerical method. (6)

J

Junk bonds
Risky bonds issued by heavily leveraged or risky companies that pay high rates of interest. Also called high-yield bonds. (9)

Just in time (JIT) inventory system
In theory, manufacturing parts arrive "just in time" to be used in production, minimizing the need for inventories. (4)

L

Lead time
In inventory management, the estimated time in advance of need when a restocking order has to be placed. (4)

Leaning on the trade
See *stretching payables*. (2)

Lease
An agreement for the use of an asset in return for payments over a specified period. In recent years, long-term leases have often been used to acquire assets rather than purchasing them with debt or equity capital. Lease payments then become fixed financial obligations similar to interest. (9)

Letter of credit
In international trade, a letter of credit provides a bank guarantee that the exporter will be paid according to the contract of sale if all of the underlying agreements are met. To reduce its credit risk, the exporter asks the foreign importer (customer) for a letter of credit from the importer's bank, guaranteeing payment of the exporter's invoice, provided that the exporter delivers the goods and trade documents in good order. (20)

Leveraged buyout (LBO)
A process in which an investor group buys up a company's shares using a small amount of equity and borrowing the rest of the money required. The debt is often secured by the firm's assets. The investor group is often the firm's management, and the company goes from being publicly held to being privately held. (19)

Leveraged lease
A three-party leasing arrangement in which a lender extends credit to a lessor to acquire equipment which is then leased to a user. The loan is usually secured by the leased equipment. Sophisticated tax advantages are associated with the technique. (9)

Limited liability
An advantage of the corporate form. Shareholder liability for the actions of a company is limited to amount invested. That is, a claim against the corporation cannot be made against a shareholder simply because the shareholder is an owner. (1)

Line of credit

A relatively informal, nonbinding agreement with a bank as to the maximum amount a firm can borrow during a period of time. (5)

Liquidation

Ending a firm's life by selling off its assets. (19)

Liquidity

With respect to a company, the ability to pay its bills in the short run. With respect to an asset, the readiness with which it can be converted to cash. (2)

Liquidity preference theory

A theory of the shape of the yield curve. The curve slopes upward because, all other things equal, investors prefer shorter, more liquid investments. They must therefore be induced to lend longer with higher rates. (7)

Liquidity ratios

Financial ratios that measure the firm's ability to pay its upcoming liabilities when due. Examples include the current ratio and the quick ratio. Also see *ratio analysis*. (3)

Liquidity risk

The risk of loss to an investor from the inability to sell a security to another investor at a price close to its true value. (7)

Listed company

A firm that is traded on an organized exchange is "listed" on that exchange. Unlisted companies are traded not on an exchange but on the over-the-counter market in Canada. Also see *exchange*. (7)

Lock box system

A service provided by banks to accelerate the collection of cash once a cheque has been mailed to a payee. Its purpose is to shorten float. Also see *float*. (4)

Long-term debt

Usually consists of bonds and long-term loans. (2)

Loss carryovers

The tax system allows corporations with a business loss or net capital loss in a year to apply these losses to prior years or future years to recover or reduce taxes. (2)

M

Marginal cost of capital (MCC)

The cost of the next dollar of capital to be raised. (15)

Marginal cost of capital (MCC) schedule

A plot of the WACC (weighted average cost of capital) against the total amount of capital to be raised in a planning period. The MCC rises as more capital is raised and the costs of individual components experience step function increases. (15)

Marginal tax rate

The rate at which the next dollar of income will be taxed. Generally the taxpayer's bracket rate. Also see *tax rates, tax bracket*. (2)

Marketable securities

Highly liquid short-term debt investments held by companies instead of cash. Marketable securities provide nearly the liquidity of cash but earn a modest return. Also referred to as *near cash* or *cash equivalents*. (2)

Market to book value ratio

A financial ratio that is a broad indicator of what the market thinks about a particular share. Defined as Share price ÷ Book value per share. (3)

Market risk

Variation on the return on a share investment caused by things that tend to affect all shares. Also called *systematic risk*. Contrast with *business-specific risk*. (11)

Market segmentation theory

A theory of the shape of the interest yield curve. The debt market is segmented by term, and each segment is independent of the others. Hence, the curve slopes upward or downward depending on supply and demand conditions in the various market segments. (7)

Market value added (MVA)

The excess of market value measured by the product of share price and the number of shares outstanding over the book value of equity. An indication of the effectiveness of management in contributing to shareholder wealth. Also see *economic value added*. (3)

Market value ratios

Financial ratios that compare certain financial statement figures to the value the stock market places on the firm. Examples include the price/earnings ratio and the market to book value ratio. Also see *ratio analysis*. (3)

Matching principle

Concept that recognition of an asset's cost should match its service life, and that recognition of revenue should occur in the period when it is earned. Also see *amortization*. (2)

Materials requirement planning (MRP) system

A computerized process for ordering and/or scheduling production of the inventories that a manufacturer requires to satisfy customer demand. (4)

Maturity matching principle

The idea that the maturity of financing should match the duration of the asset being financed. (4)

Maturity risk

The risk of loss to an investor from changes in the price of a bond that arise from changes in the market interest rate.

Also called *price risk* and *interest rate risk*. The term "maturity risk" emphasizes the fact that interest-induced price changes are larger with longer maturities. (7)

Merger

The combination of two or more businesses under one ownership in which all but one legal entity cease to exist, and the combined organization continues under the name of the surviving firm. When the surviving firm acquires the shares of the other(s), the transaction can be called an acquisition. A merger is friendly if it has the approval and support of the acquired (target) firm's management. It is unfriendly if the target's management resists. The term "merger" tends to be used loosely to refer to any business combination. (19)

Money market

A financial market in which short-term (less than one year) debt securities are traded. (7)

Monte Carlo simulation

A capital budgeting technique for incorporating risk into capital budgeting. The approach involves the use of numbers drawn randomly from probability distributions for each future cash flow in a capital budgeting project, in order to provide a good approximation of the probability distribution of the project's NPV. (14)

Mortgage bond

A bond secured by real estate. (9)

Mortgage loan

A loan secured by real estate. Commonly referred to simply as a mortgage. (8)

Multinational corporation (MNC)

A company with wholly or partially owned affiliates in foreign countries. See also *foreign direct investment*. (20)

Mutual fund

An investment vehicle in which investors contribute to a fund that uses their pooled money to invest in shares, bonds, and other financial assets. The fund owns the assets, while the investors own shares or units of the fund. (1)

Mutually exclusive projects

In capital budgeting, projects that automatically exclude one another. Projects are mutually exclusive either because they're different approaches to doing the same thing or because limited resources preclude doing more than one. Contrast with *stand-alone project*. (12)

N

Naked

Refers to an option writer who does not have a position in the underlying security. For a call writer, this means that the writer does not own the underlying share. (18)

NASDAQ

A segment of the U.S. stock market that deals in publicly traded stocks that are not listed on an organized exchange. NASDAQ is an acronym for the National Association of Securities Dealers Automated Quotation system over which shares are traded. (7)

Net present value (NPV)

A capital budgeting technique that rates projects according to the total present value of all their associated cash flows, both positive and negative. The higher the total or net present value, the better. (12)

Net present value profile

A project's NPV profile is a graph of its NPV versus the cost of capital. It crosses the horizontal axis at the IRR. (12)

Net working capital

See *working capital*. (2)

Nominal interest rate

The named or quoted rate usually stated on an annually compounded basis. May be different from the effective rate due to non-annual compounding. (8)

Normal growth

In share pricing models, dividend growth at a rate less than the expected rate of return. Growth rates in excess of the rate of return are super normal. (10)

Note

A security reflecting an intermediate-term debt relationship between the issuer and the holder. (8)

O

Operating activities

The things that a company does on a day-to-day basis to conduct its business; they involve the income statement and current balance sheet accounts. (2)

Operating cycle

The time from the acquisition of inventory until cash is collected from product sales. Compare with *cash conversion cycle*. (4)

Operating lease

A lease in which the lessee does not effectively acquire ownership of the leased asset. Accounted for as a stream of expense payments on the income statement. No entry is made on the balance sheet to reflect the acquisition of the asset. Compare with *capital lease*. (9)

Operating leverage

The use of fixed as opposed to variable cost in a firm's cost structure. (16)

Operating loan

Provides financing for working capital and expenses. (5)

Operating plan

A short- to intermediate-term business plan addressing a firm's methods and goals over the period covered. Most companies have an annual operating plan. Also see *business plan*. (6)

Option

The contracted right to buy or sell a security at a fixed price within a predetermined period of time, usually three to nine months. Options give speculators the chance to profit on movements in securities' prices without actually owning those securities. For example, the owner of an option to buy will profit if the underlying security's market price rises substantially above the price specified in the option during the option period. (18)

Option price

The price an option holder pays for a contract. Also known as the option premium in financial options. (14)

Over-the-counter (OTC) market

A network of securities dealers who trade unlisted (on an exchange) shares for clients. (7)

P

Partnership

A form of business organization in which two or more people agree to share in the business. The two common types of partnerships are general (all partners share in the management and liabilities) and limited (limited partners provide cash for the partnership to operate, but the general partners make the decisions). (1)

Par value

See *face value*. (10)

Payback period

A capital budgeting technique that rates projects according to the speed with which they return invested money. (12)

Payment date

The date on which a dividend cheque is mailed. (17)

Pegged (fixed) exchange rate

An exchange rate set by the government of a country, which attempts to maintain the rate against exchange market pressures. The rate normally is set at a fixed (or semi-fixed) relationship with respect to the U.S. dollar, another major currency, or a group ("basket") of currencies. (20)

Percentage of sales method

A simple, approximate approach to forecasting financial statements for an existing business involving estimating the company's sales growth rate, and assuming that all income statement and balance sheet line items grow at the same rate (vary directly with revenue). Implicitly assumes that the firm's efficiency and all of its operating ratios stay the same through the growth period. (6)

Permanent working capital

The minimum levels of current assets required to operate a business. See also *working capital*. (4)

Perpetual bonds

Bonds with no maturity date. Also see *bond*. (9)

Perpetuity

An infinite series of equal payments at equal intervals of time. (8)

Perquisites

Privileges and luxuries provided to executives. (1)

Personal guarantee

Generally, a guarantee made by the owner of a small business corporation when a loan is made to the business. The owner pledges his or her personal assets in addition to that of the company. Personal guarantees circumvent the limited liability feature of the corporate form in the context of lending to small businesses. Also see *limited liability*. (1)

Planning assumption

An assumption about the future on which a business plan is based. The assumption must be reflected in the firm's financial projections by calculating the specific financial statement figures it implies. Also see *business plan*. (6)

Planning horizon

The time a business plan covers. Typically between a few months and five years. (6)

Pledging receivables

Borrowing money using receivables as collateral. (5)

Poison pill

A corporate tactic to avoid being acquired. A poison pill is a clause written into a firm's bylaws that makes it prohibitively expensive for an acquiring firm to take control. (19)

Political risk

In international business, the chance that the value of a firm's investment in a foreign country will be reduced by political actions of either the foreign government or terrorists. Also see *expropriate*. (20)

Portfolio

In finance, a collection of investments. (1)

Portfolio investment

In international finance, investment in the securities of a foreign company or government. (20)

Portfolio theory

A body of thought aimed at forming investment portfolios that minimize risk for a given return. (11)

Precautionary demand

The cash in the bank that firms need for emergency needs. Compare with *transactions demand* and *speculative demand*. (4)

Preemptive rights

A shareholder's right to maintain her proportionate ownership in a corporation. The shareholder has the right to buy a share of any newly issued shares that are proportionate to her fractional ownership of the company before the new issue. The right is not a matter of law but must be written into the corporation's bylaws. (10)

Preferred share or preferred stock

A security that pays a constant dividend "forever." A hybrid between a bond and a common share. (10)

Present value

The value today of a sum promised at a specified time in the future given a rate of interest. The amount that would have to be deposited today at the specified interest rate to grow into the promised sum on the specified date. Also called *discounted cash flow*. Also see *net present value, time value of money*. (8)

Price/earnings (P/E) ratio

The ratio of a firm's share price to its earnings per share (EPS). A measure of the value the stock market places on the company and its future prospects. (3)

Primary market

A subdivision of financial markets in which securities are sold for the first time. The sale is by the issuing company to investors. Also see *initial public offering*. Compare with *secondary market*. (7)

Prime rate

The bank's lending rate for its largest and most creditworthy customers. (5)

Privately held company

A company that is not registered with a securities commission, whose securities therefore may not be sold to the general public. Also called a closely held company. (7)

Profitability index (PI)

A capital budgeting technique that rates projects according to the ratio of the present value of cash inflows to the present value of cash outflows. Essentially a variation on the NPV technique. The higher the PI the better. Also see *net present value*. (12)

Profitability ratios

Financial ratios measuring the profit performance of a firm. They include return on sales (ROS), return on assets (ROA), and return on equity (ROE). Also see *ratio analysis*. (3)

Progressive tax system

An income tax structure in which higher incomes are taxed at higher rates. (2)

Proprietorship

A form of business organization in which the business is indistinguishable from the owner; business profit is taxed as personal income to the business owner. Contrast with *corporation*. (1)

Prospectus

A document disclosing the details of a security and the underlying business to prospective investors. Also see *primary market*. (7)

Proxy

The right to act for another on a specific issue. In finance, the right to cast another's vote in the election of corporate directors. Incumbent directors routinely solicit shareholders' proxies for reelection. (10)

Proxy fight

A fight for control of a corporation when two or more interests compete for the proxies of shareholders in the election of directors. (19)

Publicly traded company

A company that is registered with a securities commission and whose securities therefore may be sold to the general public. Contrast with *privately held company*. (7)

Pure interest rate

The earning power of money. An interest rate without an inflation component or premiums for risk. (7)

Pure play company

A firm in a single line of business, as opposed to a firm with divisions in several businesses. (14)

Put (option)

The right to sell a stock to another at a specified price over a designated period of time. See *option*. Compare with *call (option)*. (18)

R

Ratio analysis

A technique of analyzing the strength of a company by forming (financial) ratios out of sets of numbers from the financial statements. (3)

Real asset

A tangible object with value derived from the service it provides, such as a house or a car. Distinguish from a financial asset, which is a piece of paper giving its owner a claim to future cash flows. (1)

Real interest rate

The interest rate that currently exists less the inflation adjustment. (7)

Real option

The ability to take a course of action that under certain circumstances leads to a benefit. The circumstances that make the action desirable are uncertain, and maintaining the ability to take it requires expenditures before that uncertainty is resolved. Hence, bearing the preliminary cost gives one the option of taking an action in the future that may or may not turn out to be desirable. Real options may increase the estimated NPV of a project and reduce its risk.

Common examples include abandonment options, expansion options, investment timing options, and flexibility options. (14)

Recourse

Under a loan agreement, if accounts receivable are pledged with recourse, uncollectible accounts remain the responsibility of the borrower, and the lender may recover the value of the defaulted accounts from the borrower. Also see *pledging receivables*. (5)

Red herring

A prospectus for the sale of a security not yet approved by a securities commission. Stamped with the word "PRELIMINARY" in red letters. (7)

Registered bond

Bond for which the issuer or a transfer agent keeps a list of the names of owners. Interest payments are made to owners of record as of specified dates. Contrast with *bearer bond*. (9)

Reinvestment assumption

In capital budgeting, the rate of compound interest at which future cash flows are assumed to be reinvested. In NPV analysis, this rate is the cost of capital used. In IRR analysis, this rate is the internal rate of return. (12)

Reorder point

The inventory level at which an order is placed with a supplier. Calculated so that the expected usage during the ordering lead time will bring the stock to its lowest planned level just as the new supply is delivered. (4)

Reorganization

In bankruptcy, a plan to restructure the failing company so that it may continue in business. Also see *bankruptcy*. (19)

Required return

The minimum return that keeps an investor owning a particular share. Generally a function of the risk perceived in the investment. (11)

Residual claim

Shareholders' claim to income and assets is the residual after all other claims are satisfied. (10)

Residual dividend theory

The idea that corporations pay dividends with whatever money is left over out of earnings after all projects with a positive NPV are undertaken. (17)

Residual value

The value of a leased asset at the termination of the lease. (9)

Restrictive covenants

Contractual agreements associated with loans that limit the activities of borrowing companies. The limitations are designed to reduce the risk that the firm won't be able to pay the loan's interest and principal. (9)

Restructuring

A change in a bankrupt firm's debt obligations aimed at allowing it to continue in business. In an extension, creditors agree to give the firm longer to pay. In a composition, creditors agree to settle for less than the full amount owed. (19)

Retained earnings

Net income of a corporation that has not been distributed to shareholders as dividends. Together with common and preferred shares outstanding, retained earnings form a portion of shareholders' equity. (2)

Return

The payment to an investor for the use of funds. Usually expressed as a percentage of the investment. (7)

Return on assets (ROA)

Net income divided by total assets. A financial ratio measuring performance concentrating on profitability and asset utilization. (3)

Return on capital employed

After tax earnings before interest divided by total capital. A ratio that measures the profitability of operations before financing costs. (16)

Return on equity (ROE)

Net income divided by equity. A financial ratio measuring performance concentrating on profitability, asset utilization, and the use of borrowed money. (3)

Return on sales (ROS)

Net income divided by sales revenue. A financial ratio measuring performance, concentrating on profitability. (3)

Reverse stock split

A method used to reduce the number of shares outstanding. A company issues one new share for a certain number of old shares. Once the process is complete the share price is higher and the number of shares in issue is lower. Reverse stock splits are usually due to a significant decline in the share's price. (17)

Revolving credit agreement

A formal, binding agreement with a bank as to the maximum amount a firm can borrow during a period of time, provided that the borrower meets the terms and conditions of the agreement. Interest is paid on the amount borrowed and a commitment or standby fee is paid on the unused balance. Compare with *line of credit*. (5)

Risk

In finance, the probability that the return on an investment will be more or less than expected. The variability of the return on a particular investment. The variance of the probability distribution of return. (7)

Risk-adjusted rate

In capital budgeting, a higher rate used in place of the cost of capital to reflect especially risky projects. (14)

Risk aversion

The premise that most people prefer lower-risk investments when expected returns are about equal. (11)

Risk-free rate

The interest rate excluding all risk premiums. The risk-free rate consists of the pure rate and an inflation adjustment. It is approximated by the three-month Treasury bill rate. Written as k_{RF}. Also see *pure interest rate*. (7)

Risk premium

A component of a rate of interest or return that compensates the investor for bearing some kind of risk. (7)

ROA

See *return on assets*. (3)

ROCE

See *return of capital employed*. (16)

ROE

See *return on equity*. (3)

ROS

See *return on sales*. (3)

S

Safety stock

Extra inventory carried to prevent stockouts in the event of heavy demand or delayed delivery. Also see *stockout*. (4)

Salvage value

The estimated proceeds on disposal, if any, of an asset at the end of its useful life. (12)

Scenario analysis

A business planning technique in which the implications of variations in planning assumptions are explored. Also known as "*what if*"-ing. Also see *business plan, planning assumption*. (6)

Seasoned issue

An older bond. (9)

Secondary market

Sales of existing securities between investors. Compare with *primary market*. (7)

Secured debt

Debt backed by specific assets (the security or collateral) that become the property of the lender in the event of default. Also see *collateral*. (19)

Securities analysis

A systematic approach to valuing securities, especially shares, by studying an issuing firm's business and industry. The securities analyst plays an important role in the financial industry. Also see *technical analysis, fundamental analysis*. (10)

Securitization of receivables

Financing technique that involves the sale of receivables by large firms to securities dealers or other financial intermediaries. The issuing firm thus receives immediate cash for future cash flows. (5)

Security market line (SML)

The central element of the capital asset pricing model (CAPM). The SML purports to explain how the market sets the required return on a share investment. Also see *capital asset pricing model*. (11)

Self-liquidating debt

Debt that is paid off when the item financed becomes cash in the borrower's hands. Also see *maturity matching principle*. (4)

Senior debt

The debt having priority over a subordinated debenture. (9)

Share

A financial asset representing a share of ownership of a corporation. Entitles the owner to dividends if any are paid. Also called stock. Shares may be preferred or common. Also see *common share*. (1)

Shareholders' equity

An ownership interest in a corporation. The portion of a firm's capital representing funds belonging to its shareholders. An equity investment is an investment in shares. See *equity*. (1)

Signalling effect

The idea that dividends send a message about management's confidence in the future of the firm—that is, paying a regular or increased dividend signals that the firm is fundamentally sound even if it appears to be having problems. The signalling idea leads to the practice of holding dividends constant or raising them in the face of poor financial performance. Also known as the *information effect* of dividends. (17)

Sinking fund

A series of payments made into an account dedicated to paying off a bond's principal at maturity; an arrangement to guarantee that funds are available to pay off the principal at maturity. (8)

Specialist

An official in a stock exchange. The specialist is assigned the shares of specific companies and is responsible for conducting an orderly market in those securities. (7)

Speculation

The assumption of measured risks in the hope of financial gain, usually with substantial knowledge of the processes that generate gains and losses. (19)

Speculative demand

The cash that firms keep in the bank to take advantage of unexpected opportunities. Compare with *precautionary demand* and *transactions demand*. (4)

Spinoff

A method of divesting a business unit by setting it up as a separate company and giving its shares to shareholders in proportion to their holdings of the original firm. After the spinoff, shareholders can trade the two shares separately. (19)

Spontaneous financing

Financing provided by current liabilities that arises automatically as a result of doing business. Examples are trade credit and accruals. (4)

Stable dividend

A dividend that may remain constant or increase over time but that does not decrease. (17)

Stand-alone project

In capital budgeting, a project with no competition either for the task it is to accomplish or for resources. Contrast with *mutually exclusive projects*. (12)

Stand-alone risk

The risk associated with investing in a share that's held by itself, outside a portfolio. Stand-alone risk depends on the volatility of a share's own return rather than on the effect its inclusion has on the volatility of the return of a portfolio. (11)

Standby fee

See *commitment fee*. (5)

Statement of cash flows

One of a firm's financial statements. Constructed from the income statement and balance sheet, it details the movement of cash in and out of the company due to operating activities, investing activities, and financing activities. Operating activities have to do with running the business on a day-to-day basis. Investing activities occur when the firm buys (invests in) or sells things such as equipment that enable it to do business. Financing activities have to do with raising money and servicing the obligations that come along with it. (2)

Stockbroker

A person licensed to assist investors in buying and selling securities for a commission. (1)

Stock dividend

Essentially a stock split. A stock dividend is the payment to common shareholders of a dividend in the form of common shares. In the case of a 10% stock dividend, a shareholder with 100 shares would receive 10 additional shares. See *stock split*. (17)

Stock market

The network of exchanges, brokers, and investors that trade in shares. (1)

Stockout

An inventory shortage. (4)

Stock split

A change in the number of shares outstanding by issuing new shares in proportion to those already owned. All shareholders' proportionate ownership is

maintained, and no economic value is created. Used to keep share prices within a desirable trading range. Also see *trading range*. (17)

Strategic plan

A long-term business plan addressing broad issues of what a company's management wants it to become and how it is to do business. (6)

Stretching payables

Paying invoices after they're due according to the terms of sale. Also called *leaning on the trade*. (2, 5)

Strike price

The price at which an optioned share can be bought or sold. Also called the exercise price or striking price. Also see *business plan, option*. (18)

Subordinated debt

Debt with a lower priority for the payment of interest and principal than other (senior) debt. Contrast with *senior debt*. (9)

Sunk cost

In capital budgeting, a cost associated with a project expended prior to making the decision to undertake that project (for example, the cost of research into the idea). Since sunk funds are already spent, they cannot alter future costs or benefits, and should not be included in the analysis leading to a decision. (13)

Sustainable growth rate

The rate at which a firm can grow if none of its financial ratios changes and it doesn't raise any new equity by selling shares. The growth in equity created by additional retained earnings. (6)

Synergy

A situation in which two companies operating together under one ownership perform better than the sum of their separate performances. A popular reason claimed for mergers. (19)

Systematic risk

See *market risk*. (11)

T

Takeover

The transfer of control over a company from one group to another. The term generally has a hostile implication. (19)

Target

The company that is the object of a corporate acquisition or merger. See *merger*. (19)

Target capital structure

The capital structure that management strives to maintain as new capital is raised. An estimate of the structure that maximizes share price. Also see *capital structure*. (15)

Tax amortization

An incentive to business provided by the Canadian government and the Canada

Revenue Agency that involves capital cost allowance (CCA), which provides a tax-deductible expense for accelerated amortization (depreciation). Higher amortization in a given year results in lower tax in that year, because taxable income is lower. (2)

Tax books

Financial records and statements generated by using the tax rules. They differ from the financial books primarily in the area of amortization. Also see *financial books*. (2)

Tax bracket

A range of income over which the tax rate is constant. The tax rate is higher, the higher the tax bracket. The bracket rate is usually the marginal tax rate for taxpayers in that bracket. Normally taxpayers will pay that rate on their last dollar of income. Also see *marginal tax rate, progressive tax system*. (2)

Tax deductions

Costs and expenses that can be deducted from income to reduce taxable income. Also see *income tax*. (2)

Tax rates

Combined rates levied by the federal and provincial governments on taxable income to determine tax payable. The average tax rate is a composite of the various bracket rates to which the taxpayer's income is subject. It is the percentage of taxable income paid in income taxes. Equals a taxpayer's total tax bill divided by taxable income. Also see *tax bracket, marginal tax rate*. (2)

Technical analysis

An approach to valuing securities by examining past patterns of price and volume. The technique is based on the idea that such patterns repeat themselves. Contrast with *fundamental analysis*. Also see *ratio analysis, securities analysis*. (10)

Temporary working capital

The additional levels of current assets required to support seasonal peaks in the business. Compare with *permanent working capital*. (4)

Tender offer

A general offer to shareholders to purchase shares at a specified price, usually for the purpose of acquiring a company. (17)

Term

The time until a debt security's principal is due to be repaid. Also called the debt's maturity or time until maturity. (7)

Terminal value

In capital budgeting, the present value of repetitive future cash flows beyond the finite planning period.

Terms of sale

The conditions under which a sale is made primarily with respect to payment. Terms include a date on which payment is due and often specify a prompt payment discount that may be taken if payment is made within a specified time. (2)

Time premium

In an option, the difference between intrinsic value and the option price. Also see *intrinsic value, option price*. (18)

Time value of money

Calculations involving the present and future values of money under the action of compound interest. Also called discounted cash flow. Also see *future value, present value*. (8)

Top-down planning

Business planning based on a set of goals forced on the organization by senior management. Top-down planning has a tendency to lead to excessively optimistic plans. Also see *business plan*. Contrast with *bottom-up planning*. (6)

Trade credit

Credit granted in the normal course of business between companies. That is, vendors don't usually demand immediate payment for their products. Also called *accounts payable, vendor financing*. (2)

Trading range

A price range in which shares are thought to appeal to the widest variety of investors. Typically between $10 and $50. Stock splits function to keep prices within a trading range when the share is appreciating. (17)

Transaction costs

The costs of trading securities, including brokerage commissions. (17)

Transactions demand

The cash in the bank that firms need to pay bills for the goods and services they use. Compare with *precautionary demand* and *speculative demand*. (4)

Transfer agent

An organization that keeps records of the owners of a company's securities. When a security is sold by one investor to another, ownership is transferred on the record by the transfer agent. Transfer agents are often trust companies. (9)

Translation risk

In foreign direct investments, refers to the unrealized gain or loss that arises from translating the financial statements of a foreign subsidiary from the local currency into Canadian dollars for consolidation with the parent company's financial statements. If the Canadian dollar is weak on the day that accounts in foreign currencies are translated into Canadian dollars, the exchange rate may give a lower dollar value for the net income and net assets of the foreign subsidiary. This difference implies that the foreign subsidiary has lost value in terms of dollars. Thus, translation losses are unrealized and reflect the exchange rate on that date only. Compare with *economic risk*. (20)

Treasurer

The executive in charge of external financing in most large companies. The treasurer generally reports to the CFO. (1)

Treasury bill

A short-term obligation of the federal or provincial governments with maturities up to one year. Sold in the money market at a discount. (7)

Trust receipt

Also known as a *chattel mortgage agreement*, this is an inventory loan arrangement in which the financed inventory is identified by serial number and cannot be sold legally without the lender's permission. When the items are sold, the proceeds must be used to repay the lender. Under a warehousing arrangement, the financed inventory is placed in a warehouse and the borrower's access to it is controlled by a third party. Compare with *blanket inventory lien, warehousing*. (5)

Trustee

With respect to bonds, an organization that ensures compliance with the conditions set forth in the indenture. (9) With respect to bankruptcy, a person who administers the bankrupt organization to ensure funds are properly handled. (19)

U

Undepreciated capital cost

The undepreciated value of assets remaining in an asset class that is the basis for the amount of CCA claimed. UCC for tax purposes is comparable to net book value for accounting purposes, although differences often exist. Also see *capital cost allowance*. (13)

Unsystematic risk

See *business-specific risk*. (11)

V

Valuation

A systematic process to determine the price at which a security should sell in financial markets. (9)

Value of capital

In cost of capital, the value of capital can be stated based on the book or market prices of the underlying securities. Book values reflect the prices at which the securities were originally sold and the cost of capital already spent. Market values reflect the current market prices of those same securities and estimate the cost of capital to be raised in the near future. For calculating the weighted average cost of capital (WACC), market values are appropriate because new projects are generally funded with newly raised money. See also *cost of capital*. (15)

Vertical merger

A merger between companies when one is a supplier or a customer of the other. See also *merger*. (19)

W

Warehousing

In finance, a method of securing the lender's interest when borrowing is secured by inventories. The inventory is placed in a warehouse operated by a third party. When it is drawn out of the warehouse by the borrower, a pro rata share of payment on the loan is due. Compare with *trust receipt*. (5)

Warrant

A security that grants its owner the right to purchase one or more shares at a designated price over a limited period. Similar to a call option except that a warrant is issued by the company that issued the underlying shares while a call is issued (written) by another investor. Also different in that warrants tend to be exercisable over much longer periods than calls. (18)

Weighted average cost of capital (WACC)

See *cost of capital*. (15)

"What if"-ing

See *scenario analysis*. (6)

White knight

When a firm is an acquisition target by an unattractive suitor, a more desirable acquirer is known as a white knight. (The original suitor may be known for particularly ruthless treatment of acquired companies.) (19)

Widely held company

A corporation whose ownership is distributed over a large number of people with no single individual or group having a significant proportion. (1)

Working capital

The balance sheet accounts associated with day-to-day operating activities. Gross working capital is generally defined as current assets and net working capital as current assets minus current liabilities. Permanent working capital is the minimum levels of current assets required to operate a business. Temporary working capital is the additional levels of current assets required to support seasonal peaks in the business. (2)

Y

Yield curve

The relationship between interest rates and the term of debt, generally expressed graphically. A normal yield curve is upward-sloping, reflecting rates that increase with increasing term. An inverted curve is downward-sloping. Also see *expectations theory (with respect to interest rates).* (7)

Yield to call (YTC)
Bond pricing calculations assuming the bond will be called at the end of the protected period. Also see *bond, call.* (9)

Yield to maturity (YTM)
The average annual rate of return required by investors over the remaining term of a bond; affected by market interest rates, the time remaining to maturity, and the bond's rating. Also see *bond.* (9)

Z

Zero balance account
An empty disbursement account established at the firm's concentration bank for its various divisions. Divisions write cheques on their ZBAs that are automatically funded out of a master account at the concentration bank as they're presented for payment. Also see *concentration banking.* (4)

Zero coupon bond
A bond that pays no interest during its life. A "zero" sells for the present value of the principal repayment. However, Canada Revenue Agency imputes interest during the bond's life on which the bondholder must pay tax. Also see *bond.* (9)

Index

Appendix C

Summary of Key Formulas

Chapter 2

The balance sheet equation: Assets = Liabilities + Shareholder's equity

Net working capital = Current assets − Current liabilities

Beginning common shares + New shares = Ending common shares

(2.1)   Total income − Tax deductions = Taxable income

Taxable income × Tax rates = Total tax

Total tax − Tax credits = Net tax payable

(2.2) $\text{Average tax rate} = \dfrac{\text{Tax liability}}{\text{Taxable income}}$

Chapter 3

$$\text{Growth in sales} = \frac{\text{Current year sales} - \text{Prior year sales}}{\text{Prior year sales}}$$

$$\text{Growth in net income} = \frac{\text{Current year net income} - \text{Prior year net income}}{\text{Prior year net income}}$$

$$\text{GPM} = \frac{\text{Gross margin}}{\text{Sales}}$$

$$\text{OM} = \frac{\text{EBIT}}{\text{Sales}}$$

$$\text{ROS} = \frac{\text{Net income}}{\text{Sales}}$$

$$\text{ROA} = \frac{\text{Net income}}{\text{Total assets}}$$

$$\text{ROE} = \frac{\text{Net income}}{\text{Shareholders' equity}}$$

$$\text{P/E ratio} = \frac{\text{Share price}}{\text{EPS}}$$

$$\text{Market to book value ratio} = \frac{\text{Share price}}{\text{Book value per share}}$$

$$\text{Current ratio} = \frac{\text{Current assets}}{\text{Current liabilities}}$$

$$\text{Quick ratio} = \frac{\text{Current assets} - \text{Inventory}}{\text{Current liabilities}}$$

$$\text{ACP} = \frac{\text{Accounts receivable}}{\text{Sales}} \times 365$$

$$\text{Inventory turnover} = \frac{\text{Cost of goods sold}}{\text{Inventory}}$$

$$\text{Average holding period (days)} = \frac{365}{\text{Inventory turnover}}$$

$$\text{Inventory turnover (sales basis) } (\times) = \frac{\text{Sales}}{\text{Inventory}}$$

$$\text{Capital asset turnover} = \frac{\text{Sales}}{\text{Capital assests}}$$

$$\text{Total asset turnover} = \frac{\text{Sales}}{\text{Total assests}}$$

$$\text{Debt ratio} = \frac{\text{Long-term debt + Current liabilities}}{\text{Total assests}}$$

$$\text{Debt to equity ratio} = \frac{\text{Long-term debt}}{\text{Shareholders' equity}}$$

$$\text{TIE} = \frac{\text{EBIT}}{\text{Interest}}$$

$$\text{Cash coverage} = \frac{\text{EBIT + Amortization}}{\text{Interest}}$$

$$\text{Fixed charge coverage} = \frac{\text{EBIT + Lease payments}}{\text{Interest + Lease payments}}$$

$$\text{ROA} = \frac{\text{Net income}}{\text{Sales}} \times \frac{\text{Sales}}{\text{Total assets}}$$

$$\text{Equity multiplier} = \frac{\text{Total assets}}{\text{Equity}}$$

$$\text{ROE} = \frac{\text{Net income}}{\text{Sales}} \times \frac{\text{Sales}}{\text{Total assests}} \times \frac{\text{Total assets}}{\text{Shareholders' equity}}$$

$$\text{EVA} = \text{EBIT}\,(1 - T) - (\text{Debt + Shareholders' equity})(\text{Cost of capital \%})$$

CHAPTER 4

$$\text{Payable payment period} = \text{Accounts payable} \times \frac{365}{\text{Cost of goods sold}}$$

$$\text{Accounts receivable} = \text{Sales} \times \frac{\text{Average collection period}}{365}$$

(4.1) $\quad r = \dfrac{100 - P}{P} \times \dfrac{365}{d}$

(4.2) $\quad \text{Carrying cost} = C\left(\dfrac{Q}{2}\right)$

(4.3) $\quad N = \dfrac{D}{Q}$

(4.4) $\quad FN = F\left(\dfrac{D}{Q}\right)$

(4.5) $\quad TC = C\left(\dfrac{Q}{2}\right) + F\left(\dfrac{D}{Q}\right)$

(4.6) $\quad EOQ = \left(\dfrac{2FD}{C}\right)^{\frac{1}{2}}$

CHAPTER 5

(5.1) Cost of missing discount $= \dfrac{\text{Discount percentage}}{100\% - \text{Discount percentage}} \times \dfrac{365}{\text{Final payment date} - \text{Last discount date}}$

(5.2) $\text{APR} = \dfrac{I}{P} \times \dfrac{365}{d}$

(5.3) $\text{APR} = \dfrac{(M - P)}{P} \times \dfrac{365}{d}$

CHAPTER 6

(6.2) Forecast total assets $-$ Forecast current liabilities $-$ Last year's shareholders' equity $+$ Forecast dividends = Forecast debt $+ (1 - T) [\text{EBIT} - \text{Int}\%(0.5)(\text{Last year's debt} + \text{Forecast debt})]$

(6.3) Growth in assets $-$ Growth in current liabilities $-$ Earnings retained $=$ External funding requirement

(6.6) $\text{NI}_{\text{next year}} = \text{ROS} \times (1 + g)\, \text{Sales}_{\text{this year}}$

(6.7) Earnings retained $= (1 - d)\text{ROS} \times (1 + g)\, \text{Sales}_{\text{this year}}$

(6.8) $\text{EFR} = g[\text{Assets}_{\text{this year}} - \text{Current liabilities}_{\text{this year}} - \text{NI}(1 - d)] - \text{NI}(1 - d)$

(6.9a) $g_s = \dfrac{\text{NI}(1 - d)}{\text{Shareholders' equity}}$

(6.9b) $g_s = \text{ROE}(1 - d)$

(6.10) $g_s = (1 - d) \times \dfrac{\text{NI}}{\text{Sales}} \times \dfrac{\text{Sales}}{\text{Assets}} \times \dfrac{\text{Assets}}{\text{Equity}}$

CHAPTER 7

(7.1) $k = \text{Base rate} + \text{Risk premium}$

(7.2) $\text{Base rate} = k_{\text{PR}} + \text{INFL}$

(7.3) $k = k_{\text{PR}} + \text{INFL} + \text{DR} + \text{LR} + \text{MR}$

CHAPTER 8

(8.3) $\text{FV}_n = \text{PV}(1 + k)^n$

(8.5) $\text{PV} = \text{FV}_n \times \dfrac{1}{(1 + k)^n}$

(8.13) $\text{FVA}_n = \dfrac{\text{PMT}(1 + k)^n - 1}{k}$

(8.15) $\text{EAR} = \left(1 + \dfrac{k_{nom}}{m}\right)^m - 1$

(8.16) $k^* = \left(1 + \dfrac{k_{nom}}{m}\right)^{\frac{m}{n}} - 1$

(8.22b) $\text{PVA} = \dfrac{\text{PMT}}{k}\left(1 - \dfrac{1}{(1 + k)^n}\right)$

(8.25) $\text{FVAd}_n = \text{PMT}[\text{FVFA}_{k,n}](1 + k)$

(8.26) $\text{PVAd} = \text{PMT}[\text{PVFA}_{k,n}](1 + k)$

(8.27) $\text{PV}_\text{p} = \dfrac{\text{PMT}}{k}$

CHAPTER 9

(9.4) $\text{P}_\text{B} = \text{PMT}[\text{PVFA}_{k,n}] + \text{FV}[\text{PVF}_{k,n}]$

(9.5) $\text{P}_\text{B}\,(\text{Call}) = \text{PMT}\,[\text{PVFA}_{k,m}] + \text{CP}[\text{PVF}_{k,m}]$

After-tax cost of debt $= k(1 - T)$

CHAPTER 10

(10.1) $k = \dfrac{\text{D}_1 + (\text{P}_1 - \text{P}_0)}{\text{P}_0}$

(10.5) $\text{P}_0 = \dfrac{\text{D}_1}{(1 + k)} + \dfrac{\text{D}_2}{(1 + k)^2} + \ldots + \dfrac{\text{D}_n}{(1 + k)^n} + \dfrac{\text{P}_n}{(1 + k)^n}$

(10.7) $\text{D}_n = \text{D}_0(1 + g)^n$

(10.10) $\text{P}_0 = \dfrac{\text{D}_0(1 + g)}{k - g} = \dfrac{\text{D}_1}{k - g}$

(10.11) $\text{P}_0 = \dfrac{\text{D}}{k}$

(10.12) $k_e = \dfrac{\text{D}_1}{\text{P}_0} + g$

(10.13) $\text{P}_\text{p} = \dfrac{\text{D}_\text{p}}{k_\text{p}}$

CHAPTER 11

(11.1) $k = \dfrac{\text{Interest paid}}{\text{Loan amount}}$

(11.2) $k = \dfrac{\text{D}_1 + (\text{P}_1 - \text{P}_0)}{\text{P}_0}$

(11.3) $\text{Slope} = \dfrac{\text{Rise}}{\text{Run}} + \dfrac{\Delta k_\text{x}}{\Delta k_\text{M}} = \beta_\text{x} = \text{Beta}$

(11.4) $k_\text{X} = k_{\text{RF}} + (k_\text{M} - k_{\text{RF}})\beta_\text{X}$

CHAPTER 12

(12.1) $\text{NPV} = -\text{C}_0 + \dfrac{\text{C}_1}{(1 + k)} + \dfrac{\text{C}_2}{(1 + k)^2} + \ldots + \dfrac{\text{C}_n}{(1 + k)^n}$

(12.2) $0 = -\text{C}_0 + \dfrac{\text{C}_1}{(1 + \text{IRR})} + \dfrac{\text{C}_2}{(1 + \text{IRR})^2} + \ldots + \dfrac{\text{C}_n}{(1 + \text{IRR})^n}$

(12.3) $\text{NPV} = -C_0 + C[\text{PVFA}_{k,n}]$

(12.4) $0 = -C_0 + C[\text{PVFA}_{\text{IRR},n}]$

(12.5) $\text{PI} = \dfrac{\dfrac{C_1}{(1+k)} + \dfrac{C_2}{(1+k)^2} + \cdots + \dfrac{C_n}{(1+k)^n}}{C_0}$

$\text{PVA} = \text{PMT}[\text{PVFA}_{k,n}]$

CHAPTER 13

(13.1) $\text{PV} = (C - S_{\text{pv}})\left(\dfrac{dT}{k+d}\right)\left(\dfrac{1+0.5k}{1+k}\right)$

(13.2) $\text{PV} = C\left(\dfrac{dT}{k+d}\right)\left(\dfrac{1+0.5k}{1+k}\right) - S_{\text{pv}}\left(\dfrac{dI}{k+d}\right)$

CHAPTER 15

$\text{Component cost of capital} = \dfrac{\text{Investor's return}}{(1-f)} = \dfrac{k}{(1-f)}$

(15.1) $\text{Cost of debt} = k_d(1-T)$

(15.2) $P_p = \dfrac{D_p}{k_p}$

(15.3) $k_p = \dfrac{D_p}{P_p}$

(15.4) $\text{Cost of preferred shares} = \dfrac{D_p}{(1-f)P_p} = \dfrac{k_p}{(1-f)}$

(15.5) $k_X = k_{RF} + (k_M - k_{RF})\beta_X$

(15.6) $P_0 = \dfrac{D_0(1-g)}{k_e - g}$

(15.7) $k_e = \dfrac{D_0(1+g)}{P_0} + g$

(15.8) $k_e = \dfrac{D_0(1+g)}{(1-f)P_0} + g$

CHAPTER 16

(16.1) $\text{ROCE} = \dfrac{\text{EBIT}(1-T)}{\text{Debt} + \text{Equity}}$

(16.3) $\text{DFL} = \dfrac{\text{EBIT}}{\text{EBIT} - I} \text{ or } \dfrac{\text{EBIT}}{\text{EBT}}$

(16.5) $C_M = \dfrac{(P-V)}{P}$

(16.7) $Q_{B/E} = \dfrac{F_C}{(P-V)}$

(16.9) $S_{B/E} = \dfrac{\dfrac{F_C}{(P - V)}}{P} = \dfrac{F_C}{C_M}$

(16.11) $DOL = \dfrac{Q(P - V)}{Q(P - V) - F_C}$ or $\dfrac{CM}{EBIT}$

(16.13) $DTL = \dfrac{CM}{(EBIT - I)}$ or $\dfrac{CM}{EBT}$

(16.16) $V_d = \dfrac{I}{k_d}$

(16.17) $V_e = \dfrac{D}{k_e}$

(16.18) $V_f = \dfrac{I}{k_d} + \dfrac{D}{k_e}$

(16.19) $V_f = \dfrac{OI}{k_a}$

(16.22) $PV \text{ of tax shield} = \dfrac{TI}{k_d} = \dfrac{TBk_d}{k_d} = TB$

CHAPTER 17

(17.2) $\text{Dividend payout ratio} = \dfrac{\text{Dividend}}{\text{Earnings}} = \dfrac{\text{Dividend per share}}{\text{EPS}}$

CHAPTER 18

(18.1) $V_{IC} = P_S - P_{Strk}$

(18.2) $V_{IP} = P_{Strk} - P_S$

(18.3) $\text{Conversion ratio} = \dfrac{\text{Bond's par value}}{\text{Conversion price}} = \text{Shares exchanged}$

(18.A1) $C = SN(d_1) - Xe^{-rt}N(d_2)$

(18.A2) $d_1 = \dfrac{\ln\left(\dfrac{S}{X}\right) + [r + .5(\sigma^2)]t}{\sigma\sqrt{t}}$

(18.A3) $d_2 = d_1 - \sigma\sqrt{t}$

Just What You Need to Know and Do NOW!

CengageNOW is an online teaching and learning resource that provides you more control in less time and delivers better student outcomes—NOW!

What instructors are saying...

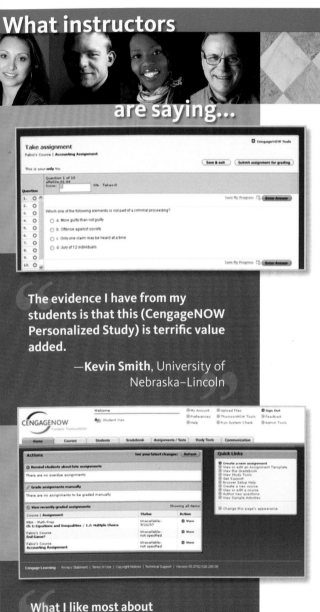

> The evidence I have from my students is that this (CengageNOW Personalized Study) is terrific value added.
>
> —**Kevin Smith**, University of Nebraska–Lincoln

> What I like most about CengageNOW is the simplicity of using it...
>
> —**Mina Yavari**, Hancock College

CENGAGENOW IS AN ONLINE TEACHING AND LEARNING RESOURCE.

CengageNOW offers all of your teaching and learning resources in one intuitive program organized around the essential activities you perform for class - lecturing, creating assignments, grading, quizzing, and tracking student progress and performance. CengageNOW's intuitive "tabbed" design allows you to navigate to all key functions with a single click and a unique homepage tell you just what needs to be done and when. CengageNOW, in most cases, provides students access to an integrated eBook, interactive tutorials, videos, animations, games, and other multimedia tools to help them get the most out of your course.

CENGAGENOW PROVIDES MORE CONTROL IN LESS TIME

CengageNOW's flexible assignment and grade book options provides you more control while saving you valuable time in planning and managing your course assignments. With CengageNOW, you can automatically grade all assignments, weigh grades, choose points or percentages and set the number of attempts and due dates per problem to best suit your overall course plan.

CENGAGENOW DELIVERS BETTER STUDENT OUTCOMES

CengageNOW Personalized Study; a diagnostic tool (featuring a chapter specific Pre-test, Study Plan, and Post-test) empowers students to master concepts, prepare for exams, and be more involved in class. It's easy to assign and if you want, results will automatically post to your grade book. Results to Personalize Study provide immediate and ongoing feedback regarding what students are mastering and why they're not - to both you and the student. In most cases, Personalized Study links to an integrated eBook so students can easily review topics.

academic.cengage.com/now

CengageNOW MAKES IT EASIER TO DO WHAT YOU ALREADY DO.

Designed by instructors for instructors, CengageNOW mirrors your natural workflow and provides time-saving, performance-enhancing tools for you and your students—all in one program!

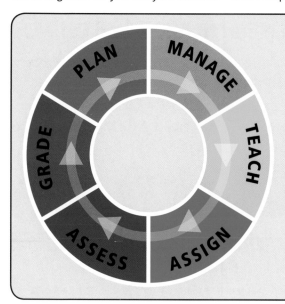

YOU CAN USE CENGAGENOW TO...

- ▶ **Plan** your curriculum;
- ▶ **Manage** your course and communicate with students;
- ▶ **Teach** with more freedom;
- ▶ **Assign** practice or homework to reinforce key concepts;
- ▶ **Assess** student performance outcomes;
- ▶ **Grade** with efficiency and control to get the results you want.

STUDENTS CAN USE CENGAGENOW TO...

- ▶ **Manage** their time;
- ▶ **Prepare** for class;
- ▶ **Practice & Reinforce** key concepts learned in class;
- ▶ **Study** for exams more effectively;
- ▶ **Get the Grade** they want.

The flexibility of CengageNOW allows you to use a single aspect of the program, or for maximum power and effectiveness, to use all of the teaching and learning resources to create and customize your own material to match your course objectives.

CENGAGENOW SEAMLESSLY INTEGRATES WITH POPULAR COURSE MANAGEMENT PROGRAMS

  eCollege™

CengageNOW on Blackboard, WebCT, and eCollege provides students with seamless single sign-on access to CengageNOW through the school's course management system (CMS). After entering a simple access code just once at the beginning of the term, students get seamless access to both their CMS and CengageNOW textbook specific assignments and activities, with results flowing to your Blackboard, WebCT, or eCollege gradebook. Rich content, seamless integration with CengageNOW functionality, and only one gradebook to manage.

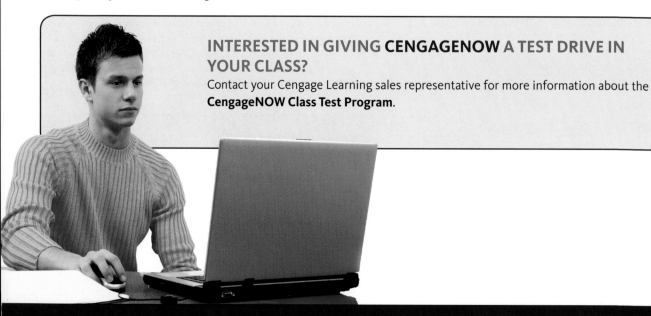

INTERESTED IN GIVING CENGAGENOW A TEST DRIVE IN YOUR CLASS?

Contact your Cengage Learning sales representative for more information about the **CengageNOW Class Test Program**.

academic.cengage.com/now